D0713093

Encyclopedia of Rhythm & Blues and Doo-Wop Vocal Groups

Mitch Rosalsky

The Scarecrow Press, Inc.
Lanham, Maryland, and London
2000

SCARECROW PRESS, INC.

Published in the United States of America
by Scarecrow Press, Inc.
4720 Boston Way
Lanham, Maryland 20706
http://www.scarecrowpress.com

4 Pleydell Gardens, Folkestone
Kent CT20 2DN, England

British Library Cataloguing in Publication Information Available

Library of Congress Cataloging-in-Publication Data

Rosalsky, Mitch, 1943–
    Encyclopedia of rhythm & blues and doo-wop vocal groups / Mitch
Rosalsky.
        p.   cm.
    Includes discographies.
    ISBN 0-8108-3663-7   (cl. : alk. paper)
    1. Popular music—United States Dictionaries.   2. Musical groups—
United States Dictionaries.   I. Title: Encyclopedia of rhythm & blues and
doo-wop vocal groups.
    ML102.P66R67   2000   99-32194
    781.643′08—dc21   CIP

♾™ The paper used in this publication meets the minimum requirements of American
National Standard for Information Sciences—Permanence of
Paper for Printed Library Materials, ANSI/NISO Z39.48–1992.
Manufactured in the United States of America.

Maintaining the theme of this work, this book is
"Dedicated to the One I Love," my wife, Marilyn, whose support and strength
have always been with me during the years she spent alone allowing me this
"labor of love." Thanks, Marilyn!

Contents

Foreword

by Dennis Ostrom

Rhythm and blues is the end product of gospel, minstrel singing, live trios, and the blues, with a touch of barbershop quartet singing thrown in for harmony. The earliest recordings (on cylinders) were by black artists who transferred the vocalizings of plantation workers. They often sang during their long, tedious days in the fields, perhaps to keep their minds occupied and shorten the workday. Gospel music was as important to their religion as their beliefs, and it made up the most important root of R&B vocal groups. Jive combos such as the Cats and the Fiddle, the Lewis Bronzeville Five, the Four Riff Brothers (later to become the Ink Spots), and others added the rhythm. Barbershop quartet harmony was much too regimented and disciplined. It was a predominantly white endeavor that influenced pop and big band vocal groups more than R&B.

Fundamentally, the groups vocalizing for black and white audiences in the 1930s and 1940s were the Mills Brothers, the Ink Spots, the Charioteers, the Delta Rhythm Boys, the Deep River Boys, and several others. These were the ensembles whose style was ultimately copied by the two vocal groups credited with fathering R&B groups as we know them—the Ravens and Sonny Til and the Orioles. An overwhelming majority of the groups that followed were, in some way, influenced by these groups.

When the infectious beat of rock 'n' roll emerged, black vocal groups had an important element to add to their already bluesy jump tunes and ballad staples. This is where the definitive split originated. The beat changed its course to white America in the form of rock 'n' roll, concentrating in the 1950s on single artists, bands (instrumental or those fronted with a vocalist), and a few scattered vocal groups consisting of three or four members. They would cover black R&B tunes or offer big band or original pop stylings.

Rhythm and blues groups almost always had four or five vocal members. The lead, bass, and first tenor were the most easily recognized vocal parts and were critical in making or breaking a song. As the 1950s ended and the 1960s began, R&B groups began to stray from the mold slightly. Up-tempo tunes began taking on more varied styles, lending themselves to new dances and rhythms. Vocal ballads began to acquire a new sound that became known as "soul." Groups that retained four members usually managed to sustain a closer resemblance to their 1950s roots. In the 1960s, however, many groups began surfacing with only three members, offering chord structures that usually did not allow for a bass or even a baritone. A sweet tenor falsetto lead was the attraction. Groups such as the Stylistics, the Delfonics, and the Van Dykes carried the vocal group into the mid-1970s and on to disco.

From the pop–rock 'n' roll form, as it cruised alongside the R&B–soul transformation, another style emerged. This offshoot of pop vocal styling, discussed earlier, is now known as doo-wop. This vocal group styling was begun by whites of predominantly Italian-American heritage who admired and emulated the R&B groups of the 1950s. Doo-wop tunes were sometimes played on R&B stations, depending on the material being presented and whether it was more strongly R&B than doo-wop. This form of doo-wop, largely credited to the late Gus Gossert, was the result of these white groups trying to copy what they heard and learned from R&B groups. Backgrounds would become more patterned and standard, perhaps with a strong bass, adding a counterpart of intertwining harmony of staccato tones. The tenor was also a critical voice but was not usually as pleasant sounding as an R&B tenor. Like black R&B groups, doo-wop groups did not need instruments to originate or rehearse their material, thus the perpetuation of "street corner" groups.

These street corner groups were prevalent commercially until the mid-1960s and then basically disappeared, leaving one of their derivative styles, a cappella, to continue as a subculture in a few regions of the country. It is as active today as it was then but is quite splintered and varied in style.

To define doo-wop groups is virtually impossible. Rhythm and blues was, and still is, a serious art form influenced and styled by African-Americans. It reflected that heritage and God-given talent. Doo-wop is "fun singing" primarily by white, Italian-American males. Of course, others—including Anglo-Americans, Hispanic Americans, and Afro-Americans—also contributed. It was more of a pastime, a way to attract girls, or, if you were lucky, earn a few bucks at the tavern or the school dance. Most distinctive is the fact that the majority of doo-wop groups had to "learn" to sing that style. It did not come to them naturally.

Foreword

by George Tompkins

Rhythm and blues vocal group harmony music can trace its roots back to blues, gospel, and jazz in the mid-1940s. This style of music began to solidify with many of the pop–blues groups of the day such as the Ink Spots and the Delta Rhythm Boys. Using a base of pop–blues, many groups began to improvise and experiment with various new vocal techniques such as bass leads and the now famous floating tenor.

In 1949, a young songwriter named Deborah Chessler wrote a beautiful ballad called "It's Too Soon to Know." She brought this song to a newly formed Baltimore group called the Orioles, and with their unique vocal styling they charted what many record collectors still consider to be the first rhythm and blues vocal group harmony recording.

During the next two decades, literally thousands of vocal groups emerged from various towns and cities across the United States. Some of these groups vanished from the recording scene almost as quickly as they appeared, and little or nothing is known about their personnel. A good number of these vocal groups, however, were lucky enough to achieve moderate fame. Much is known about the personnel makeup and changes within these groups.

In the early to middle 1960s, a resurgence of interest in vocal group harmony music, spurred by Irving "Slim" Rose's Times Square Record Shop and the legendary *Time Capsule Show,* began to gain strength in the New York metropolitan area. Suddenly, vocal group harmony records became the focus of a new breed of record collectors with a thirst not only for the records themselves but for more knowledge about the various groups that recorded these priceless treasures. Along with this thirst for knowledge came the birth of some famous and now defunct magazines such as *Bim Bam Boom, Record Exchanger, Yesterday's Memories,* and *Time Barrier Express,* to name a few. Thanks to knowledgeable record collectors like Sal Mondrone, Marcia Vance, Lou Silvani, Bob Pruter, Marv Goldberg, and Pete Grendysa, among countless others, every record collector who could afford to buy original records could now, with some spare change left, afford to learn exactly who the members of vocal groups like the Spaniels, Five Keys, Five Sharps, and Wrens really were.

Much as Ferdie Gonzalez's *Disco-File* and Jeff Kreiter's *Group Collector's Record Guide* have served as veritable bibles of vocal group harmony discographical information, this book will achieve a similar goal, especially to those of us whose memories have gone to the same place as our hair, eyesight, teeth, and good looks. This endeavor, written by my friend, long-time record collector and student of vocal group harmony music, Mitch Rosalsky, is the definitive answer to *Who's Who* in vocal group harmony music. Assisted in his research by some of the authors of those famous biographies in those never-to-be-forgotten magazines, this book is a testimony of the need to give immortality to the individuals whose beautiful voices have thrilled us for years. Every effort has been made to document the most correct information available and known to date with respect to the members of these great vocal groups. At last it's all here in alphabetical order, so that in case you're an aging former disk jockey, like myself, who suddenly draws a blank when trying to name the exact members of the Five Keys group that recorded "I Took Your Love for a Toy" on King, all you have to do is turn to the Five Keys, and you're a genius once again. If you are anything like me, you will be thanking Mitch over and over again for this long overdue treasure.

Introduction

I have been interested in popular music as far back as I can remember. When I was a youngster, I would anxiously listen each Sunday morning to Martin Block's *Make Believe Ballroom* to learn what the Top 40 records were for that week. Block would always preface his show with the top five tunes in country and western and do the same for rhythm and blues. This is when my interest began. Rosemary Clooney, Theresa Brewer, Eddie Fisher, Guy Mitchell, and many others were my first heroes. Vocal groups eventually took their place after the Crew Cuts had their unique hit called "Sh Boom," and I was "hooked." (It wasn't until years later I learned that the Chords, a black group from the Morrisania section of the borough I grew up in—the Bronx—wrote and first recorded "Sh Boom.")

What is now referred to as "vocal group rhythm and blues" soon became my hobby and fascination. I was one of the many visitors each Sunday to Times Square Records, where I would purchase the vocal group recordings I remembered hearing back in the mid-1950s. These weekly excursions to Times Square took place in the very early 1960s. I encountered many nameless but interesting characters and came to realize that there were others who were also interested in mid-1950s black vocal group music.

Then in 1963 Tom Luciani and Joe Marchesani began broadcasting the *Time-Capsule Show* over WFUV-FM from Fordham University. This program provided me with several mind-blowing revelations, for example, the Penguins, who recorded "Earth Angel," had many other discs to their credit. "In the Still of the Night" wasn't the only recording by the Five Satins other than "To the Aisle," and the Five Keys also recorded many other extraordinary discs for Aladdin besides what they had done for Capitol.

Vocal group harmony, specifically black vocal group harmony, began before the Civil War with the unrehearsed, impromptu singing that the slaves did while performing their arduous tasks in the plantation fields of the South. Today, with the widespread availability of compact discs, recorded but previously unreleased tunes have surfaced, allowing us to hear the brilliance of the Dinwiddie Colored Quartet, the Four Harmony Kings, and many others too numerous to mention here. Vocal group gospel music and barbershop quartets are historically important but are not included in this encyclopedia. It should nevertheless be noted that gospel group harmonies are equally intricate and are quite close to R&B.

Gospel and barbershop groups achieved a modicum of local success during the first two decades of the twentieth century. Then in the 1930s came the Ink Spots and the Mills Brothers. Their unique stylings and haunting renditions of popular tunes, coupled with their incredible vocal similarities to the musical instruments used on their recordings, made them enormously popular. Many groups tried to emulate the sound of these two ensembles, but it wasn't until the mid-1940s that the Delta Rhythm Boys, the Cats and the Fiddle, the Deep River Boys, and others began capitalizing on the new popular sound—race music—first presented by the Ink Spots and the Mills Brothers. This music came to be called "rhythm and blues." In the late 1940s came the Ravens and the Orioles. The recordings of these two groups, in my view, marked the beginnings of R&B vocal group harmony. A song recorded by Elvis Presley had been done, decades before, by the Ink Spots. The Beatles, who became hugely popular in the mid-1960s, performed songs previously recorded by both Chuck Berry and Little Richard. A tune entitled "Take Me As I Am" by the Duprees on Coed Records was released in 1962. According to the label, the Duprees wrote the tune in addition to recording it, but that was a critical error. The Demens recorded and wrote the tune in 1957 for the Teenage label.

In contrast to the music of the late 1960s, the music of the 1950s rarely alluded to social issues of the day. Nevertheless, it played an important role in the lives of those of us who listened to it, and it continues to evoke memories of the events of that era. Death, birth, hairstyles, clothing, military service, and cars were some of the subjects of songs that were popular at that time.

Using This Book

My purpose in assembling the material for this volume was to gather historical data addressing rhythm and blues and doo-wop vocal groups from every resource available. Let me state here that I dislike the term "doo-wop." I feel that it is a demeaning and pejorative term for the music I have loved most of my adult life. Nevertheless, the term refers the reader or listener to a certain type of music. I do not use this term myself, and it is only mentioned occasionally in this book. Doo-wop has no exact definition. If ten collectors of vocal group harmony music were asked for their definition, ten different definitions would be given. *Webster's Collegiate Dictionary* defines doo-wop as "a vocal style of rock and roll characterized by the a cappella singing of nonsense syllables in rhythmical support of the melody." But this definition is not accurate. Doo-wop is singing with, or without, musical accompaniment. It may include sensible syllables as well as "nonsense syllables." The dictionary dates the term to the year 1969. This is almost correct. To my recollection, the term was first used in the 1960s to describe four- and five-part vocal group harmonies. A New York disc jockey playing 1950s and 1960s white and black vocal group harmony tunes was the first to use the word to refer to a type of music. If I were asked to define doo-wop, I would reply "music recorded and performed in the latter 1950s to the mid-1960s usually by white quartets and quintets."

During my many years collecting, researching, and loving this music, I have found no authoritative source—no absolute place, publication, or individual to call upon to answer my questions definitively. It is my hope that this endeavor will begin to fill a part of that void and start placing the "missing pieces" in the puzzle we have all been working on, so that someday it might be complete.

Additionally, the frustration I encounter whenever reading new accounts addressing a vocal group, written by an individual whose work I have always trusted implicitly, is interesting! I always compare new material with what I have previously documented on the same group. Sometimes I spot inconsistencies and discrepancies. Two conflicting reports discussing the same group may have been written by equally knowledgeable collectors, both interviewing former members of the group in question. Names may vary or may be spelled differently. Sometimes the group's place of origin differs. Once a photograph that was part of an LP or CD's liner notes showed a group I was familiar with and the name shown below the photo was totally wrong! New collectors are the most negatively affected by such blunders because they do not know what the group they are listening to or reading about looks like. Once I telephoned the guilty magazine and, after I apprised it of its errant ways, a staff member confessed knowledge of the mistake but stated that it was learned too late for corrective inclusion. I was told that the misinformation had been provided to them by the current publishers of the group's total recorded output! Further to this point, a history of a group recently passed my way that discussed a group previously written about some fifteen to twenty years ago by the very same writer. When I compared this new article with the one written long ago, I found factual data to be different! This is a very well-known R&B historian whose work I've always trusted. That trust is no longer assumed. A number of books that were written some time ago contain incorrect information. This, of course, was not done intentionally. It simply reflected the writer's knowledge at the time. These accounts are then quoted and used as a resource by many other writers. Where no other references were available, I had to use these accounts myself. In addition, I interviewed several past performers who also gave me incorrect information. Errors are unfortunately common among written histories of rhythm and blues vocal groups. I am certain that this is equally true of my work, and I would like to ask readers who find a fact or statistic with which they disagree, or who have knowledge of a group I may have omitted, to make me aware of this. Be prepared to substantiate your correcting data. Remember, we are relying on the memories of performers and collectors attempting to retrieve information from thirty to forty-five years ago! You may reach me at Mitch Rosalsky, P.O. Box 517, Parsippany, New Jersey 07054.

Purpose of This Book

This book's main purpose is to provide R&B vocal group collectors, collectors of music reference material, disc jockeys, and other music enthusiasts with information concerning the performers in R&B vocal groups, including other groups with which they sang. Second, this book also presents, in one volume, the group's place of origin, brief biography, and in most cases their discography (when available).

Criteria for Inclusion

Besides the lead singer, only one other group member needed to be known for the group to be included. The group's place of origin, history, and discography were not criteria for inclusion. The book's primary goal is to provide the names of vocal group artists and all the groups they ever sang with. Popular groups like the Crew Cuts, Four Freshmen, Four Coins, or the white Four Aces are not included.

Girl groups were the exception rather than the rule until the late 1950s. Groups such as the Bobbettes, the Chantels, and the Shirelles emerged with noticeable impact. Their popularity increased into the 1960s, but their body of work has never been highly regarded by collectors, perhaps because this style of music has always been of primarily male interest. Although I show the names of the Supremes in the index of performers, I do not discuss them at length in the first section of the book because they are a Motown/soul/pop trio. With a few exceptions, trios are not included in this book, since a trio is not considered a "full" vocal group. Soul trios and groups, male and female, will be covered in a book written by experts in that field. (Beckman, Hunt, and Kline, *Soul Harmony Singles, 1960–1990* [Three-On-Three Publishing, 1998].) Addressing the years the book covers, I start where information has been made available to R&B vocal group music collectors, beginning very early in the twentieth century. I chose 1965 as the cutoff year, but in some items critical post-1965 data is reflected. This is also true for groups that began recording before 1965 and continued past that year. Simply put, this is a selective and subjective work discussing groups both important and critical to the collector and R&B historian.

Resources Used

In assembling the material for this book, I extracted information from all the resources available to me. I used factual and statistical data from magazines, CD and LP liner notes, newspaper articles, books, interviews with individuals who belonged to these groups, and data retrieved from Internet discussions.

Personnel

The personnel listed at the head of each group's entry represent the first group of singers to record as that specific group, for example, the Moonglows. Despite Alexander "Pete" Graves's prominence with the Moonglows, his name is not included with the initial listing of group personnel because he was added to the group when it began recording for the Chance label. He was not with the Moonglows on the Champagne label the year before. Other personnel changes (if any) affecting each of the groups are shown below the main headings along with other important data.

Discographies

Unlike many other reference works dealing with this subject, in this volume I have attempted to assemble the discographies chronologically. There are several groups whose discography, because of its length, is not shown. Wherever this occurs, it is so noted in the discography section for that group with the following notation: (too extensive; exists elsewhere). Although the discographies primarily include the originally released 78 rpm and 45 rpm recordings, second pressings or unreleased pressings are shown when critically important.

Acknowledgment

I have tried my best to credit the resource I used for each group's profile. Any omissions that may exist are strictly inadvertent. If I have omitted a source of information used for this book, please let me know and I will correct it in a future edition.

Spelling

The spelling of performers' names may not always be accurate. The individuals interviewed for this information were not always certain of the spelling of their former colleagues' names. Additionally, the compilers of this information sometimes had to rely on their own ability to properly spell performers' names when the names were supplied verbally by persons being interviewed. In several places I have used [sic], meaning, "this is the way I found it in the resource I used."

Current Information

Recently uncovered information is included when historically important. An example of this is the data shown addressing the relatively new ensemble the Morrisania Revue, a group made up of past R&B group members from the Morrisania section of the Bronx who are still performing in the 1990s! The same may be said of the Five Keys material on Groove, recently released on an RCA compact disc. How can this important material be ignored today? (Or, for that matter, why was it never released in the past?)

Appendix: Index of Performers and Corresponding Groups

The names appearing in the appendix do not always come from material found in the first section of the book, which may show the specific group's profile. If I learned a performer's name and group, I included it in this appendix, whether or not the performer's group is discussed at length or even appears in the encyclopedia.

Deceased Performers

The notation (d) next to a name indicates that this person is deceased.

Acknowledgments

I would like to thank Marv Goldberg for his assistance with a great deal of the factual editing of the book. Additionally, his contributions to the information used herein are certainly appreciated. Marv has been writing on this subject for more than twenty-five years and continues today. Thanks, Marv!

I would like to thank George Tompkins, Dennis Ostrom, Neil Hirsch, and Jerry Skokandich for their contributions as well as their ears, listening to me and advising me on many nebulous and vague issues.

I would also like to thank the following individuals: Dave Antrell, Todd Baptista, Freddie Barksdale, Dean Barlow, Mike Bauer, Bob Bosco, Lucille "Vicky" Burgess, Waldo Champen, Herbie Cox, Arthur Crier, Jim Dawson, Jim Dunn, Ed Engel, Barbara English, Bob Ferlingere, Donn Fileti, Galen Gart, Ferdie Gonzalez, Pete Grendysa, Eddie Gries, Phil Groia, Nikki Gustafson, Dave Hinckley, Bob Hyde, Ronnie Italiano, Jimmy Keyes, Rich Kriz, Jeff Kreiter, George Lavatelli, Lillian Leach, Milton Love, William Luisi, Bobby Mansfield, Trudy McCartney, Don Mennie, Jimmy Merchant, Tony Middleton, Sal Mondrone, George Moonoogian, Joe Morea, Jerry Osborne, Sal Passantino, Steve Propes, Robert Pruter, Lou Rallo, Mike Redmond, Jack Saperstein, Louie Silvani, Gordon Skadberg, Billy Dawn Smith, Mike Sweeney, Bobby Thomas, Eugene Tompkins, Marcia Vance, Jay Warner, Lenny Welch, and Drew Williamson.

Finally, thanks go to the following publications: *American Singing Groups, Big Town Review, Bim Bam Boom, Doowop . . . The Chicago Scene, Disco-File, DISCoveries, Echoes of the Past, Goldmine, Group Collector's Record Guide, Harmony Tymes, Money Records, Paul's Record Magazine, Record Collector's Monthly, Record Exchanger, Rockin' Records, Time Barrier Express, White and Still Alright,* and *Yesterday's Memories.*

The
Encyclopedia

Academics (New Haven, Conn.)

Personnel Dave Fisher (lead), Bill Greenburg (tenor), Marty Cantor (2d tenor), Ronnie Marone (baritone), and Richie Greenburg (bass)

Notes

The Academics went to school with the Ember Starlarks and participated in battles of the groups. The Academics became very good friends with the Starlarks, who later introduced them to Joel Alderman. He liked the Academics' sound and later recorded them on a new label he started—Anchor.

Because another organization in New Jersey had its own "Anchor" label prior to Alderman's Anchor, the Anchor records were pulled and the label was either changed to "Ancho" or, as some stories have it, the Ancho discs were attributed to a printing error.

Charlie Luth replaced Richie Greenburg in 1958 (Elmont) and in 1965, he joined the Frontiers (Philips).

The Academics stopped recording and performing in 1961 due to a lack of interest.

After the group broke up, Dave Fisher formed the Highwaymen in college and they later recorded "Michael."

In the notes accompanying the Relic CD *Lighter Shade of Doo Wop,* Donn Fileti shows the second tenor as Marty "Carter."

Discography

Ancho 101 Too Good to Be True/Heavenly Love (1957)
Ancho 103 Darla, My Darling/At My Front Door (1957)
Elmont 1001 Drive-in Movie (1958)
Elmont 1002 Something Cool/Drive-in Movie (1958)
Source: Joel Alderman in *Rhythm & News* 1.

Accents (Hollywood, Calif.)

Personnel James Jackson (lead), Israel Goudeau (tenor), Robert Draper (tenor), Bobby Armstrong (baritone), Billy Hood (bass)

Notes

Arvid Garrett was a later member.

Discography

Blue Mill 111 Baby Blue/Don't Expect a Miracle (1955)
Accent 1025 Don't Go/Cool-A-Roo (1956)
Accent 1031 Yes, Yes/Forever Yours (1956)
Accent 1036 Voice of the Bayous/Where Will You Be? (1957)
Brunswick 55100 Dreamin' and Schemin'/Wiggle, Wiggle (1958)
Brunswick 55123 Ching A Ling/I Give My Heart to You (1959)
Brunswick 59254 Tell Me/Better Watch Out Boy (1959)
Coral 62151 Autumn Leaves/Anything You Want Me to Be (1959)

VeeJay 484 A Hundred Wailin' Cats/Our Wonderful Love (1962)
Mercury 72154 Enchanted Garden/Tell Me Now (1963)
Challenge 59254 Tell Me/Better Watch Out Boy (1964)
Source: Bob Ferlingere, *Discography of R&B and R&R Vocal Groups.*

Accents (Brooklyn, N.Y.)

Personnel Mike Lasman (lead), Shelly Weiss (1st tenor), Allan Senzan (2d tenor), Ian Kaye (baritone)

Notes

Lasman had previously recorded as Mike for Mike and the Utopians, who did "Erline" on Cee Jay.
   This group first recorded on Guaranteed as the Dreamers.
   This is the Accents Scott English used on his "High on a Hill" disc.
   Bob Kutner from the Boptones also sang with this Accents group.

Discography

Sultan 5500 Where Can I Go?/Rags to Riches (1961)
Sources: Lou Silvani, *Collecting Rare Records*; Jay Warner, *American Singing Groups.*

Ad Libs (Newark, N.J.)

Personnel Hugh Harris (lead), Norman Donnegan (tenor), Danny Austin (?), Mary Ann Thomas (lead), Dave Watt (bass)

Notes

This group evolved from the Creators on Diamond and T-Kay, which included Harris and later Ad Libs member John Alan.
   The group brought "Boy from New York City" to Red Bird Records chiefs Jerry Lieber and Mike Stoller in 1964, who recorded the Ad Libs and were successful with the song. Blue Cat was the production unit assigned to produce "Boy from New York City" and George Goldner (Rama, Gee). The Ad Libs' recording sessions were directed by Goldner.
   In his article in *Record Collector's Monthly* Joe Sicurella spells Donnegan's name with one *n* (Donegan).

Discography

Blue Cat 102 Kicked Around/The Boy from New York City (1964)
Blue Cat 114 He Ain't No Angel/Ask Anyboy (1965)
Blue Cat 119 On the Corner/Oo-We Oh Me Oh Me Oh My (1965)
Blue Cat 123 Johnny My Boy/I'm Just a Down Home Girl (1965)
A.G.P. 100 Human/New York in the Dark (1966)
Karen 1527 Every Boy and Girl/Thinking of Me (1966)
Phillips 40461 Don't Ever Leave Me/You're in Love (1967)

Share 104 Giving Up/Appreciation (1969)
Share 106 The Boy from New York City/Nothing Worse Than Being Alone (1969)
Capitol 2944 Love Me/Know Well about You (1970)
Passion 1 Spring and Summer/I Don't Need a Fortune Teller (1984)
Johnny Boy JBR 4A Santa's on His Way/I Stayed Home (1989)
Johnny Boy 1988 2B The Tide Has Turned/The Tide Has Turned (1988)
Johnny Boy 1988 3B Close to Me/Close to Me (1988)
Source: Joe Sicurella in *Record Collector's Monthly* 18.

Admirals (Omaha, Neb.)

Personnel Willie Barnes (lead), Wesley DeVereaux (1st tenor), Gene McDaniels (2d tenor), James Farmer (baritone), Richard Beasley (bass)

Notes

The Admirals formerly were the Sultans on Duke.
   Second tenor Gene McDaniels later went on to record "100 Pounds of Clay."
Wesley DeVereaux is the son of Wynonie Harris.
   Despite the fact that they were under contract with King Records at the time and
King was in Cincinnati, all three Admirals' discs were recorded in New York City
in January and February 1955.

Discography

King 4772 Oh Yes/Left with a Broken Heart (1955)
King 4782 Close Your Eyes/Give Me Your Love (1955)
King 4792 It's a Sad, Sad Feeling/Ow (1955)
Source: Galen Gart, *Duke/Peacock Records.*

Admirations (Brooklyn, N.Y.)

Personnel Joe "Cookie" Lorello (lead), Fred Mastanduno (1st tenor), John Mahlan (2d tenor), Ralph Minichino (baritone), Lou Moschella (bass)

Notes

This group adopted its name from Admiration cigars. It was formed in 1958. After
they had been heard by several Mercury executives, the Admirations were contacted
by Mercury in 1959 and asked to record soon after.
   Mercury provided the Admirations' recording no promotion effort.
   As a result, the songs received little airplay and the group, no royalties.
   In 1961, the group disbanded and Mahlan joined the army.
   The group re-formed later in 1961 with Lorello's wife replacing Mahlan and Joe
Mertens in for the departed Minichino.
   The reformed Admirations went back to Mercury and recorded four more songs.
Two of these were later released by Mercury, but they are not often seen.
   Personnel changes on the second recording session had Mertens at 2d tenor and
Dianne Salemme (Lorello's wife) executing the falsetto parts.

Discography

Mercury 71521 The Bells of Rosa Rita/Little Bo-Peep (1959)
Mercury 71833 To the Aisle/Hey Señorita (1961)
Mercury (UNR) It Happened All So Fast/Remember the Day
Source: Bob Galgano in *Bim Bam Boom* 13.

Aladdins (San Diego, Calif.)

Personnel Edward Williams (lead), Ted Harper (2d tenor), Alfred Harper (baritone), Gaylord Green (bass)

Notes

Members of the Aladdins grew up on the same street in San Diego.

The group toured as the Capris with Johnny Otis for a year in 1953. Otis had discovered the group at a local show in San Diego and then introduced them to Eddie Mesner of Aladdin Records, who thought highly of the group, signed them, and changed their name to the Aladdins, after his label.

The Aladdins cut four records for the Aladdin label. None of these discs ever lived up to the expectations that the label management had for them.

In 1955, Al Harper and Eddie Williams joined the Colts and Ted Harper joined the Penguins and later the Coasters, staying with that group for ten years.

When the Aladdins disbanded, their manager, Buck Ram, built a new group around Williams—the Fortunes on Antler.

Discography

Aladdin 3275 Remember (EW)/Cry Baby Cry (TH) (1955)
Aladdin 3298 I Had a Dream Last Night (EW)/Get Off My Feet (TH & EW) (1955)
Aladdin 3314 All of My Life (EW)/So Long, Farewell, Bye-Bye (EW & TH) (1955)
Aladdin 3358 Help Me (EW)/Lord Show Me (EW) (1956)
Source: Marv Goldberg and Mike Redmond with Teddy Harper in *Record Exchanger* 14.

Alley Cats (Los Angeles)

Personnel Bobby Sheen (1st tenor), Sheridan "Rip" Spencer (baritone), Brice Coefield and Gary Pipkin (tenor), James Barker (bass)

Notes

Chester Pipkin also sang with the Alley Cats. Bobby Sheen is better known as "Bob B. Soxx" of Bob B. Soxx and the Blue Jeans.

Sheen was specifically at this session for his high tenor vocal ability.

Discography

Philles 108 Puddin' 'n' Tain/Feel So Good (1962)
Epic 9778 Lily of the West/I Should Have Stayed Home Tonight (1965)
Source: Marv Goldberg in *DISCoveries,* February 1995, article on the Valiants; Travis Klein, liner notes with the *Itzy II* CD.

Altairs (Pittsburgh, Pa.)

Personnel George Benson (lead), William Herndon (1st tenor), Nathaniel Benson (2d tenor), Richard Harris (baritone), Ralph Terry (bass)

Notes

Lead George Benson is the same George Benson who had a successful solo career later on.

Late in the Altairs' career, following many failures, Dinah Washington became their mentor. Washington put together a new supergroup in 1962, known as D's Gentlemen, with the Altairs as its nucleus. They were William Herndon (1st tenor), Johnny Carter (from the Dells), Nat Benson (2d tenor), Cornel Gunter, Richard Harris (baritone), and Chuck Barksdale (bass from the Dells).

When Washington died in 1963, the group naturally disbanded.

Richard Harris and Richard Herndon were also with the Marcels.

Discography

Amy 803 If You Love Me/Groovie Time (1960)
Sources: Jay Warner, *American Singing Groups*; Carl Janusek and Nancy Janusek in *Echoes of the Past* 8.

Ambassadors (Newark, N.J.)

Personnel David Watson, Louis Van Dyke

Notes

The two names above are the writers credited for "Darling I'm Sorry" on the Timely label, and it is assumed that they are members of the group.

Discography

Timely 1001 Darling I'm Sorry/Willa Bea (1954)
Timely (UNR) Calling for Love/Moanin' (1954)
Source: Donn Fileti, liner notes with Relic's *Timely* CD.

Ambers (California)

Personnel Ralph Mathis (lead), Herman "Sonny" Chaney (1st tenor), Valerio "Val" Poliuto (2d tenor), Manuel "Manny" Chavez (baritone), Charles "Jasper" Middleton (bass)

Notes

Ralph Mathis (rumored to be Johnny Mathis's younger brother) was in the Ebb studios to record for Lenora Rupe's label. A backup vocal group was needed to be the "Ambers" (there never was an Ambers group); the Jaguars happened to be there that same day and became the Ambers for the session.

Since Ralph's brother Johnny was very popular at the time of these recordings, it's surprising that no one thought of capitalizing on this.

Discography

Ebb 142 Never Let You Go/I'll Make a Bet (1958)
Greezie 501 Listen to Your Heart/Loving Tree (1958)
Todd 1042 All of My Darling/So Glad (1959)
Source: Jim Dawson, liner notes with the Ace *Ebb* CD.

Angels (Philadelphia)

Personnel Sonny Gordon (lead), Charles Wright (bass)

Notes

Gordon sang for the Philadelphia Hearts (after Lee Andrews) on Chancellor and for a later group, the Turbans.

Discography

Grand 115 Wedding Bells Are Ringing in My Ears/Times Have Changed (1954)
Grand 121 Lovely Way to Spend an Evening/You're Still My Baby (1955)
Irma 105 Leaving You Baby/Sha-Wa-Wa (1956)
Source: Donn Fileti, liner notes with the Relic CD *Golden Era of Doo Wops—The Groups of Grand Records.*

Angels (Orange, N.J.)

Personnel Peggy Sanciglia (lead), Barbara Allbut, Phyllis "Jiggs" Allbut

Notes

Prior to forming the Angels, Barbara and sister "Jiggs" sang with the Starlets, who recorded "P.S. I Love You" in 1960 for the Astro label. The record did nothing and the girls walked away from the Starlets.

In 1961 they formed the Angels, working hard to perfect their talent.

They wound up at Caprice Records, where they recorded "Til." It did quite well, as did many of their follow-up recordings.

Due to the changing times and the changing music (Beatles), coupled with the Vietnam War, the Angels, because of their successes with their hits, toured extensively, making many live appearances. Eventually they broke up.

Discography

Caprice 107 Til/A Moment Ago (1961)
Caprice 112 Cry Baby Cry/That's All I Ask of You (1962)
Caprice 116 Everybody Loves a Lover/Blow Joe (1962)
Caprice 118 You Should Have Told Me/I'd Be Good For You (1962)
Smash 1834 My Girlfriends' Back/ (Love Me) Now (1963)
Smash 1854 I Adore Him/Thank You and Goodnight (1963)
Smash 1870 Wow Wow Wee/Snowflakes and Teardrops (1963)
Smash 1885 Little Beatle Boy/Java (1964)
Smash 1915 Jamaica Joe/Dream Boy (1964)

RCA 9129 I Had a Dream I Lost You/What to Do (1967)
RCA 9246 Go Out and Play/You'll Never Get to Heaven (1967)
RCA 9404 With Love/You're the Cause of It (1967)
RCA 9541 The Modley/If I Didn't Love You (1968)
RCA 9612 The Boy with the Green Eyes/But for Love (1968)
RCA 9681 Marry-Go-Round/So Nice (1968)
Polydor 14222 Poppa's Side of the Bed/You're All I Need to Get By (1968)
Source: Curt Krafft in *Story Untold* 4.

Antones (Mingo Junction, Ohio)

Personnel Joey Pizzoferrato (lead), George Regan, Peter Graceffa, Anthony "Chatta" Johnson (d)

Notes

"Chatta" Johnson was a beautician and the shop he owned was called "Antones." They practiced there and named their group for it—the Antones.

In 1956 they met manager Athena Dallas, who knew Sid Nathan of King Records and Ahmet Ertegun of Atlantic. The Antones recorded masters for Nathan and Ertegun but nothing ever came of them.

In October 1956 they traveled to Wheeling, West Virginia, to record for Black Crest Records. They recorded their first two sides for Black Crest, "Jenette" and "You Are the One." In November, they returned to Black Crest for two more sides.

Pizzoferrato changed his name to "Ferra" when they began recording for Black Crest Records in Wheeling in 1956. He changed it to "Farr" in later years.

Their first release for Black Crest did well locally. But there was trouble between the group and label management, and the Antones asked for their release and for their unreleased masters.

Finally, in January 1957, they were granted the release as they had requested.

In early 1957, "Chatta" Johnson was eased out of the group due to a personality conflict with the other members. He was replaced by Sam Ciafardone. This occurred just prior to their second Black Crest recording.

In 1957, because of internal disputes, the Antones broke up.

Discography

Black Crest 106 You Are the One/Jenette (1956)
Black Crest 107 Time for Love/All of My Life (1957)
Sources: Carl Janusek and Nancy Janusek in *Echoes of the Past* 28; Carl Janusek and Nancy Janusek in *Story Untold* 10.

Appeggios (California)

Personnel Melvin Alexander, Frank Alexander

Notes

The Alexander brothers had also been together in the Arrows and the Convincers.

Discography

Aries 001 Mary/I'll Be Singing (1963)
Source: Donn Fileti, liner notes with the Relic LP *Best of Flash Records.*

Aquatones (Queens, N.Y.)

Personnel Larry Vannata, Barbara Lee, Vic Kastel, Mike Roma

Notes

The group first assembled in 1957. While appearing at a local talent contest, they were "discovered" and signed to a recording contract with Fargo Records.

Their drummer, Russ Nagy, came from the "I've Had It" Bellnotes.

They recorded many 45s and an LP for Fargo.

After much touring and all their recordings, they split up in 1960 with each going their separate way.

Discography

Fargo 1001 You/She's the One for Me (1958)
Fargo 1002 Say You'll Be Mine/So Fine (1958)
Fargo 1003 Our First Kiss/The Drive-in (1958)
Fargo 1005 My Treasure/My One Desire (1959)
Fargo 1015 Every Time/There's a Long, Long Trail (1959)
Fargo 1111 My Darling/For You, for You (1960)
Fargo 1016 Crazy for You/Wanted (1961)
Fargo 1022 Say You'll Be Mine/My Treasure (1962)
Sources: Donn Fileti, liner notes with the Relic CD *Best of Fargo Records;* Larry Vannata in *Big Town Review 3.*

Arrogants

Personnel Frank Ayala, Sal Giarraffa, Augie Miuzzo, Ray Morrow

Discography

Big A 12184 Make Up Your Mind/Tomboy (1960)
Lute 6226 Canadian Sunset/Mirror Mirror (1962)
Vanessa 200 Take Life Easy/Stone Broke (1962)
Candlelight 425 Canadian Sunset/Mirror, Mirror (1963)
Sources: Jerry Osborne, *Rockin' Records*; unsigned liner notes with the *Starlight Serenade* CD; Steve Propes, conversation with author.

Arrows (California)

Personnel Melvin Alexander, Frank Alexander, Leroy Bishop, Franklin Dixon, Lee Perkins

Notes

This group joined the Flash label in 1958.

The Alexander brothers later moved on and formed the Appeggios on Aries; they were also with the Convincers on Movin'.

Discography

Flash 132 Annie Mae/Indian Bop Hop (1958)
Hugo 11171 I'm Checking on you Baby (1964)
Hugo 11172 No Other Arms (1964)
Sources: Donn Fileti, liner notes with the Relic LP *Best of Flash Records;* Ferdie Gonzalez, *Disco-File.*

Avalons (Newport News, Va.)

Personnel James Dozier (lead), Rafael Ingram (1st tenor), George Cox (2d tenor), Charles Crowley (baritone), Bernard Purdie (bass)

Notes

Before the Avalons recorded, Maryland Pierce was their 2d tenor. But he joined the Five Keys and remained with that group throughout his performing and recording career. When he left to join the Five Keys, Ingram joined the Avalons.

Ray Ingram and James Dozier sang lead on "Chains around My Heart" and "It's Funny, but it's True." Ingram is the brother of Ripley Ingram of the Five Keys and had been a member of the Sentimental Four, the original name of the Five Keys before they began recording.

The Avalons made many appearances locally and throughout Canada, where they toured for several months. During this time, their manager got them a recording contract with Groove. This is also the Unart Avalons group.

Discography

Groove 0141 Chains around My Heart (RI/JD)/Ooh She Flew (1956)
Groove 0174 It's Funny, But It's True (RI/JD)/Sugar, Sugar (1956)
Unart 2007 Heart's Desire/Ebbtide (1958)
Casino 108 You Do Something to Me (RI)/You Can Count on Me (1959)
Sources: Jason Amal in *Big Town Review* 1; Bjorn Jentoft in *Rhythm & News* 1.

Avons (Englewood, N.J.)

Personnel Bob Lea (lead), Irvin "Flea" Watson (1st tenor) (d), Wendell Lea (2d tenor), Bill Lea (baritone), Curtis Norris (bass)

Notes

While Bill Lea was doing homework, he noticed the name Avon, which is a river in England. He and the guys loved it and chose it for their name.

In 1956, Ed Prindle, an Englewood resident, took the group to Hull records on Broadway in New York for an audition with Blanche "Bea" Kaslon, who liked them.

Bass Curtis Norris joined the service and was replaced by Franklin Cole after their first recording, Cole went into the service after Hull 726 and was replaced by George "Jitters" Coleman, who went into the service after Hull 731 and was never replaced.

The group's last two recordings were made with four men: Bob Lea (lead), Wendell Lea (2d tenor), Bill Lea (baritone), and Irvin Watson (1st tenor).

Bill Lea went into the service and was replaced by Sonny Harley on their last record (Hull 754). In 1962 they broke up.

Discography

Hull 717 Our Love Will Never End/I'm Sending S.O.S. (1956)
Hull 722 Baby/Bonnie (1957)
Hull 726 You Are So Close to Me/Gonna Catch You Nappin' (1957)
Hull 728 What Will I Do?/Please Come Back to Me (1959)
Hull 731 What Love Can Do/On the Island (1959)
Hull 744 Whisper (Softly)/If I Just (Had My Way) (1961)
Hull 754 Grass Is Greener on the Other Side/Girl to Call My Own (1962)
Source: G. Lavatelli in *Bim Bam Boom* 1.

Aztecs, José & (Cincinnati, Ohio)

Personnel Jose Williams (lead), Roy Johnson (1st tenor), Gordon Hunt (baritone), Stokes Anderson (bass)

Notes

Influenced by the Diablos, the Aztecs organized in 1955 in Cincinnati, Ohio.

The material listed below remained unreleased until Roadhouse LP 5001 *Candy Bar Boogie* was issued.

Williams also sang with the Incas.

The group had one release in 1956, Tonight/Rose on the defunct Echo label.

Discography

Echo Tonight/Rose (1956)
Roadhouse LP 5001 My Aching Heart (1956)
Roadhouse LP 5001 Wait a Minute Baby (1956)
Roadhouse LP 5001 Does She Know? (1956)
Roadhouse LP 5001 Why Did You Leave Me? (1956)
Roadhouse LP 5001 Baby-Baby (1956)
Source: Les Moss, liner notes with *Candy Bar Boogie* LP/CD on Roadhouse.

Bachelors (Washington, D.C.)

Personnel Waverly "Buck" Mason (lead), James "Toy" Walton (1st tenor), Walter Taylor (2d tenor), Herbert Fisher (baritone), John Bowie (bass)

Notes

The group formed in 1947 as the Caverliers and shortly thereafter became the Jets. For two years they appeared locally, and in 1953 they turned professional.

Charles Booker helped them arrange material and they used his house to practice. He later became a semipermanent sixth member.

In 1952 Earthaline Lee managed the group, still known as the Jets. She arranged for their first recording session with Eddie Heller's Rainbow Records in New York. Walter Taylor was scheduled to sing lead on "Drag It Home Baby" at that first session but became hoarse that day and Charles Booker filled in.

In 1953, Amos Milburn saw the Jets perform and set up a recording session with his label, Aladdin, in New York. Because Mesner of Aladdin was aware of another group called the Jets, they were renamed the Bachelors and recorded as the Bachelors for Aladdin.

The Aladdin recording didn't do well and the Bachelors then auditioned for Atlantic, Apollo, and Teddy Reig and Jack Hook's Royal Roost label in early 1956. Royal Roost accepted them and the Bachelors recorded four sides for Royal Roost, two of which were released on that label.

James "Toy" Walton also recorded with the L'Cap-Tans on Anna, the Jets, the Links, and the Clovers. He also sang with the Knickerbockers, who were together for several years but never recorded. Lead "Buck" Mason was drafted into the army and Robert Russell took his place.

Walter Taylor left after the Royal Roost session and Charles Booker replaced him. Taylor had left briefly before and was replaced by Don Covay for a short period.

Herb Fisher also left and was replaced by James Taylor.

In 1957, Clovers' manager Lou Krefetz started the Poplar label and invited the group to record for him. The group now consisted of Robert Russell, James Taylor, James Walton, and John Bowie. They recorded one disc at Poplar and broke up in 1958.

Discography

Aladdin 3210 Can't Help Lovin' You (BR)/Pretty Baby (WT) (1953)
Royal Roost 620 You've Lied (RR)/I Found Love (CB) (1956)
Royal Roost UNR Baby (RR)/Raining in My Heart (JB) (1956)
Poplar 101 After (JT)/You Know, You Know (I Love you) (RR) (1957)
Source: Marv Goldberg in *Yesterday's Memories* 2, 4.

Bachelors (Bronx, N.Y.)

Personnel Grover "Dean" Barlow (lead), Waldo Champen (1st tenor), William Lindsay (2d tenor), Billy Baines (d) (baritone), Joe "Ditto" Dias (bass)

Notes

This group evolved from the third "coming" of Dean Barlow & the Crickets. They executed the final two Crickets' Jay-Dee sessions for that label.

They then moved to Earl records, where they became the Bachelors, cut two records which went nowhere, and broke up soon after.

Sammy Lowe and Tommy Smalls (Dr. Jive) owned the Earl label located on 9th Avenue in New York City in 1956. Lindsay was also a member of the Crickets, Dean Barlow and the Montereys, Cadillacs, Starlings, and Twilighters on MGM.

Waldo "Champ" Champen also sang with the Five Delights, Moodmakers, Supremes (Old Town), Cadillacs, Dean Barlow and the Montereys, Five Chimes, and the Morrisania Revue.

Allen Scott, a 1st tenor, was a later member and Dias sang with the Chords.

Discography

Earl 101 I Want to Know about Love (CB)/Delores (WC) (1956)
Earl 102 Baby (DB)/Tell Me Now (BL) (1956)
Sources: Dean Barlow, interview by author, April 23, 1994; Waldo Champen, interview by author, July 15, 1994.

Bachelors (Philadelphia)

Personnel Joe Van Loan (lead), Elijah Harvey (2d tenor), Jim Miller (baritone), Allen Scott (bass)

Notes

Other than the Mercury recording, the other recordings were the property of Van Loan and were first released on a Songmaster LP produced by collectors Jack Sbarbori and Jim Hunt. The group was also known as the Canaanites and recorded spiritual songs for Gotham.

In 1948, the Canaanites decided to record secular tunes. At that time they changed their name to the Bachelors.

They got a recording contract with Mercury and released "Hereafter" in 1949. They produced their own session at Mercury. "Trust in Me" was recorded during this same time period but was not released until 1954 as by the Joe Van Loan Quartet.

In 1949, Van Loan went with a new group, the Songmasters.

Discography

Mercury 8159 Yesterday's Roses/Hereafter (1949)
Songmaster LP 800 That's My Desire
Songmaster LP 800 Little Coquette
Source: Jim Hunt and Jack Sbarbori, liner notes with the Songmaster LP *The Early Songs of Joe Van Loan.*

Balladiers (New York)

Personnel Joel Turner (lead), Thomas Herman (1st tenor), Joe Burgess (2d tenor), James Stevens (baritone)

Notes

It is not known whether the Balladeers on RCA or Billy Mathews and the Balladeers are the same group discussed here.

Discography

Aladdin 3008 Keep Me with You/Please Don't Deceive My Heart (1949)
Aladdin 3123 Forget Me Not/What Will I Tell My Heart (1952)
Source: Michel Ruppli, *Aladdin Discography* (Greenwood Press).

Ballads (Durham, N.C.)

Personnel Willie Logan (lead), Murrie Eskridge (1st tenor), O. C. Perkins (2d tenor), O. C. Logan (bass)

Notes

Eskridge and Perkins also sang with the Palms and the Sheppards.
   The Logans became Willie Logan and the Plaids on Jerry-O.

Discography

Venture 615 God Bless Our Love/My Baby Knows How to Love Her Man
Source: Bob Pruter, *Doowop . . . The Chicago Scene.*

Ballads (West Haven, Conn.)

Personnel Dick Arnold, Jack McCoy, Sonny Manzo, Phil Babin, Jack Knect

Discography

Franwill 5028 Before You Fall in Love/Broke (1956)
Ron-Cris 1003 Somehow/Knee-Bop (1960)
Source: Donn Fileti, liner notes with the Relic CD *Golden Era of Doo Wops—The Groups of Standord Records.*

Barons (New York)

Personnel Larry Harrison (lead) (d), Luther Dixon (2d tenor), Roger Wainwright (baritone), Danny Hicks (bass)

Notes

Larry Harrison had previously been with the Four Buddies. Luther Dixon does lead on "A Year and a Day."
   The group became the Buddies on Decca.
   Hicks also sang with the Four Buddies and the Orioles.

Discography

Decca 48323 A Year and a Day/My Baby's Gone (1954)
Decca 29293 Exactly Like You/Forget about Me (1954)
Source: Bob Ferlingere, *A Discography of R&B and R&R Vocal Groups.*

Barons (New Orleans)

Personnel Billy Gold (lead), Andrew Fisher (2d tenor), Danny (baritone), George Bonney (bass)

Notes

The EMI *Lost Dreams* LP credits this group as the probable backup for Bernie Williams's "Why Fool Yourself."

The group moved to the West Coast and finished their Imperial sides there. Fisher and Bonney left the Barons to form the West Coast Marquis.

Discography

Imperial 5343 Boom, Boom/Eternally Yours (1955)
Imperial 5359 My Dream, My Love/I Know I Was Wrong (1955)
Imperial 5370 Searching for Love/Cold Kisses (1955)
Imperial 5383 Cryin' for You Baby/So Long, My Darling (1956)
Imperial 5397 Don't Walk Out/Once in a Lifetime (1956)
Source: Jim Dawson and Steve Propes, liner notes with the EMI LP *Lost Dreams.*

Barons, Richard Lewis & (Los Angeles)

Personnel Richard Lewis (lead), Marvin Phillips, Jesse Belvin

Notes

This was a California ensemble that included some of the most musically talented individuals on the West Coast. It was formed in 1950.

Discography

Modern 818 Forever (MP)/Believe in Me (1951)
Source: Billy Vera, liner notes with the Specialty CD *Jesse Belvin–The Blues Balladeer.*

Barries (New Haven, Conn.)

Personnel Guy Villano, Al Battista, Nickie Delano, Joe Marturiello, Jimmie O'Connor

Notes

Andy Smith joined the Barries after Delano and Maturiello left.

Nicky Delano was "Nicky" of Nicky and the Nobles.

Discography

Ember 1101 Mary-Ann/Tonight-Tonight (1964)
Source: Donn Fileti, liner notes with the Relic LP *Ember.*

Basin Street Boys (Los Angeles)

Personnel Ormande Wilson (lead), Reuben Saunders, Artie Waters (a.k.a. Arthur Rainwater, Gene Price)

Notes

The name of this group has nothing to do with a street in New Orleans. The name had belonged to a 1930s group led by Steve Gibson of the Red Caps from Lynchburg, Virginia.

Ormande Wilson was a friend of the 1930s group and learned much from them. Prior to his association with the Basin Street Boys, Wilson was with the Plantation Boys. When the Plantation Boys broke up, Wilson took several members and formed an early Dreamers group in Los Angeles. The lead for this Dreamers group was Carl Jones, later of the Delta Rhythm Boys. Ormande Wilson was Steve Gibson's stepbrother.

Ray Funk's liner notes with the Official LP refer to the Basin Street Boys as a Los Angeles group, whereas Benway's notes with the *Night Train* CD call it a Philadelphia group.

On Exclusive 215 and 220 they backed vocalist Judy Carroll.

Sam Hutchersoon and George Thompson were later members.

Discography

Exclusive 215 I Want to Be Loved/Changes (w/Judy Carol) (1945)
Exclusive 220 Jumping At the Jubilee/Nothing Ever Happens to Me (1945)
Exclusive 225 Vootnay On the Votnay/I Sold My Heart to the Junkman (1946)
Exclusive 229 I Need a Knife, Fork, and Spoon/This Is the End of a Dream (1946)
Exclusive 239 I'm Gonna Write a Letter to My Baby/Josephine (1947)
Exclusive 245 For You/Ain't Got No Loot (1947)
Exclusive 247 I'll Get Along Somehow/Exactly You (1947)
Exclusive 19X Summertime Gal/Satchelmouth Baby (1947)
Exclusive 21X You're Mine/Near to You (1947)
Exclusive 39X I Sold My Heart to the Junkman/Voot Nay on the Vot Nay (1948)
Cash 1052 I Sold My Heart to the Junkman/Lost in the Night
Flame 1002 I Sold My Heart to the Junkman/Exactly Like You
Mercury 8106 If I Can't Have You/Come to Me (1948)
Mercury 8120 Please Give My Heart a Break/To Make a Mistake Is Human (1948)
Sources: Ray Funk, liner notes with the Official LP *Basin Street Boys;* Richie Benway, notes to the Night Train CD *Satchelmouth Baby.*

Bay Bops (Brooklyn, N.Y.)

Personnel Danny Zipfel (lead), Barney Zarzana (baritone/bass), George Taylor Jr. (1st tenor), Bobby Serrao (2d tenor)

Notes

The group began in Brooklyn in 1954 calling themselves the Starlighters. As they matured, they would practice and make many local appearances at school and church functions, but unlike the other group members, Zipfel aspired to bigger things.

The Bay Bops formed as a result of the breakup of two groups that were simultaneously performing at a dance in Brooklyn in 1957.

Later in 1957 they each chipped in $15 for a demo. Upon leaving the studio they met Frank Military, who agreed to represent them. He took them to Coral who signed the Bay Bops to a six month contract and during March 1958 the group recorded "Joanie" and "Follow the Rock." Neil Sedaka, a Brooklyn local, helped with the vocal arrangement of "Joanie." "Follow the Rock" was written by Billy Dawn Smith. Following the success of "Joannie," the Bay Bops split into two factions—Zipfel versus the other three. Later that year, Zarzana and his three brothers, Vinnie, Sal, and Michael, attempted to record again for Decca. Difficulties here too prevented this from happening. Zarzana later sang with the Parakeets on Atlas.

Discography

Coral 61975 Joannie/Follow the Rock (1958)
Coral 62004 My Darling, My Sweet/To the Party (1958)
Source: Bob Diskin in *Record Collector's Monthly* 33.

Beale Street Boys (Memphis, Tenn.)

Personnel William Barnes (1st tenor), Bob Davis (2d tenor), James Pugh (baritone), David Pugh (bass)

Notes

The Pughs were twin brothers from Memphis, Tennessee. Barnes was from Rolling Fork, Mississippi, and Davis from Charleston, Mississippi. They all met while attending LeMoyne College in Memphis.

They started their career on WREC radio in Memphis. Morton Downey Sr. discovered them and brought them to New York City, where they were signed by CBS radio. They were regular guests on Downey's show and appeared on several other radio shows, including *Harlem Serenade* and *Voice of Columbia.*

The Beale Street Boys first appeared in 1947. This was a mature quartet with a smooth sound. Interestingly, in 1934 and again in 1937, in the files of Columbia Records, six tunes recorded by a group called the Beale Street Boys can be found. It cannot be confirmed as the same group, as these were never released. They were signed to record with the newly formed MGM Records in 1948. They recorded eight sides for MGM and then just disappeared. Their sound has been compared to that of the Mills Brothers, the Delta Rhythm Boys, and the Ravens. I list the OBA sides in the discography below, as the labels state, "The Beale Street Boys." However, these were recorded more than ten years after the MGM discs. It is possible that this is the same group. The sound on OBA is older than that of 1960.

Source: Writer credits on at least one side of each disc show the name Bob Davis.

Discography

MGM 10141 Why Does It Have to Rain Sunday/Teach Me Baby (1948)
MGM 10197 Wedding Bells/Baby Don't Be Mad at Me (1948)
MGM 10273 Home/Wait'll I Get You in My Dreams Tonight (1948)

MGM 10505 Wish I Had a Dime/I've Kept Everything the Same for You (1949)
OBA 101/102 Next Christmas/There's Nothing Greater Than a Prayer (1960)
OBA 109 As High as My Heart/My Last Rainy Day (1960)
Sources: George Moonoogian in *Record Collector's Monthly* 18; George Moonoogian in *Echoes of the Past* 36, 38; Pete Grendysa in *Record Finder;* Ferdie Gonzalez, *Disco-File.*

Beavers (New York)

Personnel Freddie Hamilton (lead), Dick Palmer (1st tenor), Ray Johnson (2d tenor), John Wilson (baritone)

Notes

This group formed February 1949. Dick Palmer was a Palmer Brothers' sibling. He also appeared with the Blenders as well as the Palmer Brothers.

The group's music teacher, Joe Thomas, also did work for the Delta Rhythm Boys and knew their manager, Paul Kapp. Paul's brother was Dave Kapp, an influential person at Coral, who got the Beavers a recording contract there. (Dave Kapp went on to form Kapp Records.)

In 1950, one of the songs recorded by the Beavers, "Rag Mop," was initially released by the Ames Brothers. It was subsequently "covered" by many other artists, including Lionel Hampton and the Hamptones, who were none other than the Beavers!

Also in 1950 they recorded several sides for RCA. None of these, however, were ever released.

Ray Johnson and Dick Palmer left to join the Blenders, replacing James DeLoach and Tommy Adams respectively.

Johnson left the Blenders in 1951 and joined Maithe Marshall of the Ravens, baritone Willis Saunders, and Phil Shaw to form the Marshall Brothers.

A few months after the Marshall Brothers broke up, Johnson joined the Dominoes, replacing Bill Brown who left to form the Checkers.

Discography

Sittin' In With 524 That Lucky Old Sun/If My Dream Would Come True (Herb Lance backed by the Beavers) (1949)
Coral 65018 If You See Tears in My Eyes (JW)/I Gotta Do It (FH) (1949)
Coral 65026 I'd Rather Be Wrong Than Blue (JW)/Big Mouth Mama (FH) (1950)
Decca 24855 Rag Mop (as the Hamptones) 1950
Sources: Marv Goldberg in *Yesterday's Memories* 1–2; Marv Goldberg in *DISCoveries,* December 1989.

Bel-Aires (Hartford, Conn.)

Personnel Larry Lee Harper (lead), John Hall (1st tenor), James Jenkins (2d tenor), Elijah "Prez" McKinney (baritone), Louis Clayton (bass)

Notes

This group was formed in 1955 in Hartford, Connecticut, while living in the same housing projects. After much practice, they appeared at a talent show at New York's Radio City Music Hall and made many other live appearances in their home state of Connecticut.

In Paul Bezanker's column, he states the group formed in 1957 and that the original group included Henry Hall.

The group backed up Larry Lee in 1959 on the M.Z. recording of Can I Be in Love/Stolen Love. Henry Hall, their regular lead, was in the service at that time and they had to recruit Larry Lee Harper for the recording.

The group's name changed several times, from the Bellaires to the Five Bellaires to the Bel Aires, and so on. They had many auditions and many records were pressed with numerous labels, but none of them were ever released. In 1959 they had an audition at Old Town that went very well, but the Fiestas' recording of "So Fine" was taking off and Hy Weiss had to devote time to that pursuit, which seriously delayed the Bel Aires from recording. They returned to Hartford discouraged.

Discography

M.Z. 006 Stolen Love/Can I Be in Love? (1959)
Sources: Bill Derick in *Record Collector's Monthly* 45; Paul Bezanker in *Paul's Record Magazine,* January 1976.

Bel-Aires (Los Angeles)

Personnel Donald Woods (tenor), Andrew Blue (tenor), Randolph Bryant (baritone), Ira Foley (bass)

Notes

On their first two recordings they were known as the Bel-Aires and after Death of an Angel, they became the Vel-Aires.

According to the liner notes with *Best of Flip-1* CD, they also became the Medallions on Dootone backing Vernon Green.

Discography

Flip 303 This Paradise/Let's Party Awhile (1954)
Flip 304 White Port & Lemon Juice/This Is Goodbye (1954)
Source: Liner notes with *Best of Flip-1* CD.

Bel Aires (Chicago)

Personnel Millard Edwards (lead), Ezell Williams (1st tenor), Frank Taylor (2d tenor), James Dennis Isaac (bass)

Notes

The Bel Aires first got together in 1957 calling themselves the Del Ricos and eventually joined producer Bill Shepard. He had been recording Chicago vocal groups since 1953 and found them two fine tunes and an excellent arrangement. He also secured the facilities of Decca, a major label, for the group whose name he had changed. The record initially did well but never really took off.

Isaac and Edwards previously sang with the Sheppards on United and Theron.

Allen and Edwards were brothers. Edwards formerly dabbled in harmony in high school singing with the Five Stars who went on to be called the El Dorados.

The Chicago-based Ballads were disbanding just as Taylor and Williams received their draft notices. Members from both groups teamed to form the Apex and Vee Jay Sheppards (Edwards, Allen, Isaac, and O. C. Perkins as well as Murrie Eskridge, who had been with the Palms on United). Larry Lee was also in this group.

Discography

Decca 30631 My Yearbook/Rockin' an' Strollin' (1958)
Sources: Bob Pruter in *Record Collector's Monthly* 34; Bob Pruter, *Doowop . . . The Chicago Scene.*

Bellnotes (Long Island, N.Y.)

Personnel Russ Nagy, Carl Bonura, Ray Caroni, Lenny Giambalvo, John Casey

Notes

Russ Nagy joined forces with Larry Vannatta of the Aquatones in the 1970s to start a new Aquatones group.

Discography

Time 1004 I've Had It/Be Mine (1958)
Time 1010 Old Spanish Town/She Went That-a-Way* (1959)
Time 1013 Betty Dear/That's Right (1959)
Time 1015 Don't Ask Me Why/You're a Big Girl Now (1959)
Time 1017 No Dice/White Buckskin Sneakers & Checkerboard Socks (1959)
Madison 136 Shortnin' Bread/To Each His Own (1960)
Source: Donn Fileti, liner notes with the Relic CD *Best of Fargo Records.*

Bells (New York)

Personnel Joe Van Loan (lead), Willis Saunders (a.k.a. Sanders) (tenor), Willie Ray (baritone), Bob Kornegay (bass)

Notes

There is an unusual relationship between the Rama Bells and the Du Droppers (Red Robin, Groove) and the Ravens on Argo.

Discography

Rama 166 What Can I Tell Her Now?/Let Me Love, Love You (1955)
Source: Marv Goldberg in *DISCoveries.*

Belltones (Yonkers, N.Y.)

Personnel Ronnie Baker (lead), Al Brandon, Billy Lee, Joe Raguso, Paul Fernandez

Notes

This group originally recorded "I Love You" on Scatt and then recorded for J&S as the Belltones.
 Richie Pettagano joined the group later.

Discography

Scatt 1609/1610 The Merengue/I Love You (1958)
J&S 1609 The Merengue/I Love You (1958)
Source: Bob Ferlingere, *A Discography of R&B and R&R Vocal Groups.*

Belltones (Philadelphia)

Personnel Freddie Walker (lead), Estelle Powell (alternate lead), Irv Natson Jr. (1st tenor), Donald Burnett (2d tenor), Harry Paschall Jr. (baritone), Hardy Hall Jr. (bass)

Notes

Burnett and Paschall later sang with Farris Hill and the Madison Brothers and later with the Royal Demons and Little Joe and the Thrillers.
 Piano accompaniment came from Natson, who played by ear.
 Natson and Walker had a romantic interest in Estelle Powell. As a result, "Estelle" was written by those two, with Fred and Estelle sharing lead duties on the song. Natson and Walker collaborated on the lyrics, another manifestation of their feelings, to impress the young songstress.
 Ultimately, Natson and Powell were married and were living in Philadelphia in the 1980s.
 In an interview the Natsons confirmed that their Belltones had nothing to do with any other Belltones group.
 "Estelle" was their only recording.
 All Belltones' sides (released and unreleased) were recorded at the same session.
 In Donn Fileti's liner notes accompanying Relic's *Golden Era of Doo Wops—Grand Records,* he states that the flip of the legendary "Carol" was "Tell Me Dear." Despite the fact that "Carol" never materialized through 1995, there are still reports that this disc was seen in the early 1960s by a reputable collector.

Discography

Grand 102 Estelle/Promise Love (1954)
Sources: Charlie Horner and Don Leins.

Belmonts, Dion & (Bronx, N.Y.)

Personnel Dion DiMucci (lead), Angel D'Aleo (1st tenor), Fred Milano (2d tenor), Carlo Mastrangelo (bass)

Notes

This group originated in the Bronx in 1957. They attended Roosevelt High School on Fordham Road near Fordham University and were named after Belmont Avenue, a street in the neighborhood in which they lived.

Dion's first recording was in 1957: "The Chosen Few" by Dion and the Timberlanes on Mohawk 105. It is interesting that Dion never met the members of the Timberlanes. Their voice parts were merged electronically to produce their record.

Coincidentally, the Belmonts also recorded for Mohawk (106) performing "Teen-age Clementine" at the same time. This was before Dion and they joined forces. When the combining actually took place, their first record was "We Went Away" on Mohawk 107.

In 1958 they signed with the new Laurie label and recorded "I Wonder Why," which hit big.

Because of their black sound, they were one of the first white groups to play the Apollo Theater in New York's Harlem.

In January 1959 they were on the fateful tour in which Buddy Holly, Richie Valens, and the Big Bopper died in a plane crash. Because of the horrible weather, the Belmonts chose to stay on the bus and not fly with the others.

Dion went solo in the middle of 1960 and later joined another Bronx group, the Tremonts. The Belmonts reassembled in 1966 for two recordings that turned out to be unsuccessful.

Discography

Mohawk 107 We Went Away/Tag Along (1957)
Laurie 3013 I Wonder Why/Teen Angel (1958)
Laurie 3015 No One Knows/I Can't Go On (Rosalie) (1958)
Laurie 3021 Don't Pity Me/Just You (1958)
Laurie 3027 A Teenager in Love/I've Cried Before (1959)
Laurie 3035 Every Little Thing I Do/A Lover's Prayer (1959)
Laurie 3044 Where or When/That's My Desire (1959)
Laurie 3052 Wonderful Girl/When You Wish upon a Star (1960)
Laurie 3059 In the Still of the Night/A Funny Feeling (1960)
ABC 10868 Berimbau/My Girl the Month of May (1966)
ABC 10896 For Bobbie/Movin' Man (1967)
Source: Jay Warner, American Singing Groups.

Belmonts (Bronx, N.Y.)

Personnel   Carlo Mastrangelo (lead), Angel D'Aleo (1st tenor), Fred Milano (2d tenor)

Notes

Following Dion's departure from the Belmonts to perform as a solo act, the group carried on with recording and appearances.

In 1962 Mastrangelo was replaced by Frank Lyndon. Lyndon was replaced in 1972 by Warren Gradus and in 1976 Gradus was replaced by Freddie Cannon.

Discography

Mohawk 106 Santa Margherita/Teenage Clementine (1957)
Laurie 3080 We Belong Together/Such a Long Way (1961)
Surprise 1000 Smoke from Your Cigarette/Tell Me Why (1961)
Sabrina 500 Smoke from Your Cigarette/Tell Me Why (1961)
Sabrina 501 Don't Get Around Much Anymore/Searching for a New Love (1961)
Sabrina 502 I Need Someone/That American Dance (1961)
Sabrina 503 I Confess/Hombre (1962)
Sabrina 505 Come On Little Angel/How about Me? (1962)
Sabrina 507 Diddle-De-Dum/Farewell (1962)
Sabrina 509 Ann-Marie/Ac-Cent-Tchu-Uate the Positive (1963)
Sabrina 517 Let's Call It a Day/More Important Things to Do (1964)
Sabrina 519 Why/C'Mon Everybody (1964)
United Art 809 I Don't Know Why, I Just Do/Wintertime (1964)
United Art 904 Then I Walked Away/Today My Love Has Gone Away (1965)
United Art 966 I Got a Feeling/To Be with You (1965)
United Art 50007 Come with Me/You're a Mystery (1966)
Source: Jay Warner, *American Singing Groups.*

Beltones (New York)

Personnel David Banks, Herb Rooney, Clayton "Dickie" Williams, Andrew Pope

Notes

Rooney also sang with the Exciters.

Discography

Hull 721I Talk to My Echo/Oof Goof (1957)
Sources: Jay Warner, *American Singing Groups*; M. Goldberg article on the Internet, June 6, 1999.

Belvederes (Chicago)

Personnel Eddie Sullivan (lead), Jerome Brown (tenor), Kenneth Brown, Willie Crowley, John Staples

Notes

In 1958, Sullivan and Staples left the Four Gents to join Crowley and the Brown brothers to form this group.

Jerome Brown also sang with the Five Bells.

Tenor Robert Higgenbotham later sang with the Belvederes. He had also been with the Dusters.

Discography

Dot 15852 Hey Honey/Hey Suzanne (1958)
Trend 009 Let's Get Married/Wow Wow Mary Mary (1958)
Source: Bob Pruter, *Doowop . . . The Chicago Scene.*

Ben Smith Quartet

Personnel Ben Smith, Ed Sneed, Lannie Scott, Artie Long

Discography
Coleman 110 By the Candleglow/Slippery Smith (1949)
Abbey 3012 You Are Closer to My Heart/Blue Got Me Walking (1950)
Columbia 30208 Where Did She Go/Leave That Dog Alone (1950)
Columbia 30214 She Knows How the Drops Will Fall/Got Me Crying (1950)
Source: George Moonoogian in *Record Collector's Monthly.*

Big Three Trio (Chicago)

Personnel Leonard Caston (lead), Bernardo Saunders, Willie Dixon

Notes
Named after the Big Three of World War II—Churchill, Stalin, and Roosevelt—this group formed in 1945. In 1946 they went to Memphis to cut four sides for Jim Bulleit's Bullet Records label.

Saunders left after those sessions and Caston recruited Ollie Crawford. Crawford and Willie Dixon had been in the Five Breezes together (1940).

Dixon had been in the Four Jumps of Jive (Dixon, Gene Gilmour, Bernardo Dennis, and Ellis Hunter) and recorded four sides for Mercury. Crawford filled in periodically with the Four Jumps of Jive just prior to forming the Big Three Trio.

Leonard Caston was also in the Five Breezes and the Four Jumps of Jive and was the father of Leonard Caston (Radiants). Between 1947 and 1949 the Big Three Trio cut thirty sides for Columbia.

In 1948, Dixon met the Chess brothers, who had a nightclub in Chicago and wanted to start their own label. As the Big Three Trio was winding down at this time, the Chess brothers drew on Dixon's experience in the recording business, and he joined them in their front office.

Discography
Bullet 274 Get Up Those Stairs, Mademoiselle/Lonely Roamin' (1946)
Bullet 275 Signifying Monkey/You Sure Look Good to Me (1946)
Columbia 30019 Signifying Monkey/If the Sea Was Whiskey (1947)
Columbia 37358 Signifying Monkey/If the Sea Was Whiskey (1947)
Columbia 30053 Ebony Rhapsody/When I Been Drinking (1947) (with R. Howard)
Columbia 30055 Money Tree Blues/Lonely Roamin' (1947)
Columbia 37584 Money Tree Blues/Lonely Roamin' (1947)
Columbia 30103 After a While/Baby, I Can Go on without You (1947)
Columbia 37983 After a While/Baby, I Can Go on without You (1947)
Columbia 30105 Help Me Baby/Too Many Drivers (with R. Howard) (1947)
Columbia 37573 Ebony Rhapsody/When I Been Drinking (with R. Howard) (1947)
Columbia 38029 Too Many Drivers/Help Me Baby (with R. Howard) (1947)
Columbia 38145 Where Shall I Go?/It's Hard to Go through Life Alone (Howard) (1948)

Columbia 30108 It Can't Be Done/No More Sweet Potatoes (1948)
Columbia 38064 It Can't Be Done/No More Sweet Potatoes (1948)
Columbia 30110 '88 Boogie/You Sure Look Good to Me (1948)
Columbia 38093 '88 Boogie/You Sure Look Good to Me (1948)
Columbia 30113 Where Shall I Go?/It's Hard to Go through Life Alone (Howard) (1948)
Columbia 30125 Big Three Boogie/Evening (1948)
Columbia 30127 I Keep on Worrying/Why Be So Blue? (1948) (with R. Howard)
Columbia 30142 Reno Blues/I'll Be Right Someday (1948)
Columbia 30144 Just Can't Let Her Be/Since My Baby Been Gone (1948)
Columbia 30156 I Feel Like Steppin' Out/Hard Notch Boogie Beat (1949)
Columbia 30166 Big 3 Stomp/Ain't Gonna Be Your Monkey Man no More (1949)
Columbia 30174 Get Her off My Mind/No One to Love Me (1949)
Delta 202 Don't Let That Music Die/Till the Day I Die (1949)
Delta 208 Appetite Blues/Cigarettes, Whiskey and Wild Women (1949)
Columbia 30190 Don't Let That Music Die/Practicing the Art of Love (1950)
Columbia 30222 Till the Day I Die/Goodbye Mr. Blues (Bullet) (1950)
Columbia 30228 There's Something on My Mind/Why Do You Do Me Like You Do? (1950)
Columbia 30239 Blip Blip/Appetite Blues (1951)
Dot 1124 Signifying Monkey/You Sure Look Good to Me (1951)
Okeh 6807 Lonesome/Violent Love (1951)
Okeh 6842 It's All Over Now/Tell That Woman (1951)
Okeh 6863 Blue Because of You/Got You on My Mind (1952)
Okeh 6901 You Don't Love Me No More/My Love Will Never Die (1952)
Okeh 6944 Come Here Baby/Be a Sweetheart (1953)
Columbia 40494 Ebony Rhapsody/You Made Me Love You (1955)
Sources: Bruce Eder in *Goldmine;* CD notes, *Willie Dixon and the Big Three Trio— Roots of the Blues;* Dr. Horse, CD liner notes, *Big Three Trio.*

Blenders (New York)

Personnel Ollie Jones (lead/2d tenor) Abel DeCosta (1st tenor) (d), Tommy Adams (baritone), James DeLoach (bass)

Notes

In 1946, when the Ravens were just forming, Jimmy Ricks needed a 1st tenor. Ollie Jones, who had been a 2d tenor, filled the part and became the original 1st tenor with the Ravens on their Hub recordings. Apparently Ricks considered Jones the temporary 1st tenor until he could find a tenor whose voice matched the other Ravens. When Ricks found Maithe Marshall, Ollie Jones left and joined the Four Notes, a touring group.

The Four Notes played carnivals, which were very popular at the time. In 1948, Jones decided to form his own group. He first met bass James DeLoach. Then Jones took Tommy Adams from the Four Notes and found 1st tenor Abel DeCosta.

The group was called the Blenders and went to Jimmy Ricks for advice. He took them to National Records for an audition, ultimately leading to their recording for National. Ricks also greatly assisted them with bookings.

Lee Magid of National became their manager. When Magid left National for Decca, he took the Blenders with him. After being with Decca a few months, Tommy Adams fell ill and left the group.

Adams was replaced by Dick Palmer of the Palmer Brothers.

DeLoach too fell ill and was temporarily replaced by Ray Johnson.

In 1951, DeLoach returned and Ray Johnson moved to baritone. Soon thereafter, Johnson and Palmer left the group. Palmer was replaced by Napoleon "Snaggs" Allen in 1953 and performed on the Decca recordings.

Their eight recordings for Decca were not particularly successful and the label dropped them. They then joined MGM, which was just building up its black R&B lineup.

At MGM they met the creative Joe Davis. When Davis left MGM in 1953, he took the Blenders with him to his Jay Dee Records.

They had their biggest seller at Jay Dee, "Don't Play Around with Love." On one of the takes, Davis asked the group to sing "Don't Fuck Around with Love." Davis had interesting promotional intentions for this version.

One of the sides recorded for Davis was "Somebody's Lying," which was released several years later as by the Millionaires.

Jones and DeCosta later joined the Cues.

Lord Westbrook later spent time with the Blenders.

This Blenders group disbanded in 1954. Jones formed the Cues for Atlantic Records along with DeCosta. Both DeCosta and Ray Johnson have passed away.

Discography

National 9092 I Can Dream, Can't I? (TA)/Come Back Baby Blues (JDL) (1949)
Decca 48156 Gone (OJ)/Honeysuckle Rose (OJ) (1950)
Decca 48158 Count Every Star/Would I Still Be the One in Your Heart (1950)
Decca 48183 I'm So Crazy for Love (OJ)/What about Tonight (OJ) (1950)
Decca 27403 The Masquerade Is Over (OJ/RJ)/Little Small Town Girl (OJ) (1951)
Decca 27587 All I Gotta Do Is Think of You (OJ)/Busiest Corner in My Hometown (OJ/RJ) (1951)
Decca 48244 My Heart Will Never Forget/You Do the Dreamin' (1951)
Decca 28092 I'd Be a Fool Again (OJ)/Just a Little Walk with Me (JDL) (1952)
Decca 28241 Never in a Million Years (JDL)/Memories of You (JDL) (1952)
MGM 11488 I Don't Miss You Anymore (OJ)/If That's the Way You Want It Baby (OJ) (1953)
MGM 11531 Please Take Me Back (OJ)/Isn't It a Shame? (1953)
Jay-Dee 780 You'll Never Be Mine Again (OJ)/Don't Play Around with Love (OJ/JDL) (1953)
Decca 31284 Tell Me What's on Your Mind/When I'm Walkin' with My Baby (OJ) (1961)
Sources: Marv Goldberg and Mike Redmond in *Yesterday's Memories* 1–2; Marv Goldberg and Mike Redmond in *DISCoveries.*

Blenders (Chicago)

Personnel Gail Mapp (lead), Harold Jones, Albert Hunter, Goldie Coates, Delores Johnson

Notes

Jones and Hunter had been members of an ad hoc group, the Maples on Blue Lake. Jones had also been with the Five Chances and Hunter with the Clouds.

Although one of the labels reads "Goldie Coates and the Blenders," it is understood that Gail Mapp always sang lead (as contrasted in Pruter's *Doowop . . . The Chicago Scene,* which cites several cuts on which Coates did lead).

This group also recorded as the Candles on the Nike label.

Discography

Cortlandt 103 Everybody's Got a Right/What Have You Got? (1962)
Witch 114 Everybody's Got a Right/Daughter (1962)
Witch 117 Boys Think/Squat and Squirm (1963)
Mar-V-Lous 6010 Love Is a Good Thing Going/Your Love Has Got Me Down (1966)
Source: Bob Pruter, *Doo-wop . . . The Chicago Scene.*

Blossoms (Los Angeles)

Personnel Fanita Wright Barrett (1st tenor), Annette Williams (1st tenor), Nanette Williams Jackson (2d tenor), Gloria Jones (baritone)

Notes

This group got its start at the famous Fremont High School in Los Angeles in the summer of 1953. They sang at school talent shows and became associated with deejay Johnny Otis.

They began as the Dreamers on Flip with Richard Berry. They also did backup work for stars such as Etta James, Jesse Belvin, and Ed Townsend.

Vocal coach Eddie Beale brought them to Capitol, where Tom Fransend renamed them the Blossoms.

In 1961 the Williams twins left. Darlene Wright became lead, and the group became a trio.

Because the Crystals (Philles) were reluctant to fly to the West Coast and because Phil Spector believed their "He's a Rebel" would do well, the Blossoms were used for this recording with the Crystals' name on the label.

In December 1967 Jeannie King replaced Gloria Jones. Whether Darleen Wright is also Darlene Franklin, I do not know, but Franklin joined the Blossoms coming from the Combo Echos group. Franklin later became the well-known Darlene Love.

Discography

Capitol 3822 He Promised Me/Move On (1957)
Capitol 3878 Little Louie/Have Faith in Me (1958)
Capitol 4072 Baby Daddy-O/No Other Love (1958)
Challenge 9109 Son-in-Law/I'll Wait (1961)

Challenge 9122 Hard to Get/Write Me a Letter (1961)
Challenge 9138 Big Talking Jim/The Search Is Over (1962)
Okeh 7162 I'm in Love/What Makes Love? (1962)
Reprise 0436 Good, Good Lovin'/That's When the Tears Start (1966)
Reprise 0477 My Love, Come Home/Lover Boy (1966)
Reprise 0522 Deep into My Heart/Let Your Love Shine on Me (1966)
Reprise 0639 Good, Good Lovin'/Deep into My Heart (1967)
Ode 101 Stoney End/Wonderful (1967)
Ode 106 Wonderful/Cry Like a Baby (1967)
MGM 13964 Tweedle Dee Dee/You Got My Number (1968)
Ode 125 Stoney End/Wonderful (1969)
Bell 780 You've Lost That Loving Feeling/Something So Wrong (1969)
Bell 797 Soul and Inspiration/Stand By (1969)
Bell 857 I Ain't Got to Love Nobody Else (1970)
Bell 937 One Step Away/Break Your Promise (1970)
Lion 108 It's All Up to You/Touchdown (1972)
Lion 125 Cherish What Is Dear to You/Shockwave (1972)
Source: Paul Bezanker in *Paul's Record Magazine,* October 1975.

Blue Jays (Los Angeles)

Personnel Chester Pipkin (lead), Lee Goudeau (tenor), Dewey Terry (1st tenor), Don (Bowman) Harris (2d tenor), Bobby Armstrong (baritone), Leon Washington (bass)

Notes

Most of this group's material was recorded on three Dig EPs as the Kicks, Mambos, and Vita Squires moonlighting for extra funds.
    Harris and Terry were later known as Don and Dewey.

Discography

Bluejay 102 I Really Love You/Write a Letter (1961)
DIG EP Pledging My Love (1955)
Source: Bob Ferlingere, *A Discography of R&B and R&R Vocal Groups.*

Blue Jays (Venice, Calif.)

Personnel Leon Peels (lead), Van Earl Richardson (1st tenor), Alexander Manigo (2d tenor), Keith Rush (baritone), Leonard Davidson (bass)

Notes

This group disbanded less than a year after recording "Lover's Island."
    Milestone label had eighteen cuts and folded in less than two years.
    Peels also sang with the Hi Tensions.

Discography

Milestone 2008 Lover's Island/You're Gonna Cry (1961)
Milestone 2009 Tears Are Falling/Tree Tall Len (1961)

Milestone 2010 Let's Make Love/Rock, Rock, Rock (1961)
Milestone 2012 The Right to Love/Rock, Rock, Rock (1962)
Milestone 2014 Tall Len/Venus, My Love (1962)
Source: Donn Fileti, liner notes with the Relic CD *Lovers Island.*

Bluejays (Washington, D.C.)

Personnel Waymond Mooney (lead), Andy Magruder (1st tenor), Robert Stroud (2d tenor), Moise Vaughn (baritone)

Notes

In 1950, Andy Magruder was a seventh-grade student whose desire it was to form a vocal group. Magruder did just that and formed a group he initially called the Bluejays. This group consisted of the four individuals shown above. Late in 1952, the Bluejays won a citywide contest and their recording career began to snowball. They went to a studio that charged only $1.25 to record each song. Two of the many songs recorded that day are those below. Many years later, Les Moss of Roadhouse Records found this tape. He apparently used the name scribbled on the box in which it was found.

The record shown below came from those very tapes of the Bluejays' recordings found by Moss. Because of his desire to press the tunes on his Roadhouse label, he used the name they had used back in 1952.

Discography

Roadhouse 1004 Sweet Pauline/Could I Adore You (1952)
Source: Marv Goldberg and Mike Redmond in *Yesterday's Memories* 4.

Blue Notes (Philadelphia)

Personnel John Atkins (lead), Lawrence Brown, Harold Melvin, Bernard Williams

Notes

Harold Melvin founded the Philadelphia street corner Blue Notes in the mid-1950s. It is said that Melvin never sang lead, but his name later appeared on Blue Notes' record labels as a result of his critical role and importance in their beginning.

Although the few existing accounts that discuss the Blue Notes do not include the recordings of a Blue Notes group on George Goldner's Rama or Tico labels, I have interviewed several reliable R&B historians who believe this was the same group.

Teddy Pendergrass, Billy Paul, Todd Randall (sang lead Josie 814), and Reggie Barnes (d) all appeared with the Blue Notes at one time or another. Charlie Horner's liner notes with Collectables *Blue Notes* LP refer to a Bernard Williams. Several other accounts I've read refer to Bernard Wilson.

The Red Top/Val-Ue group consisted of Harold Melvin, Bernard Williams, Jesse Gillis, Franklin Peaker (lead), Roosevelt Brodie, and Sharon Paige.

In Sequel's *Jubilee/Josie–4* CD liner notes, George Povall and Gordon Skadberg refer to Franklin Peaker as Franklin Parker.

In those same liner notes Povall and Skadberg state that "the Bluenotes have remained active since 1956" (this would then preclude the Rama and Tico discs in the following discography).

Franklin Peaker and Bernie Wilson began their own Blue Notes group in the mid-1960s. They were also doing backup work for the Harthon label. The Harthon group consisted of Peaker, Wilson, Weldon McDougal, and Vivian McDougal, his wife. Also with this group was Jesse Gillis Jr. and Roosevelt Brodie.

In *Collecting Rare Records,* Lou Silvani states that the Josie group and the Val-Ue group are the same.

Discography

Rama 25 If You'll Be Mine/Too Hot to Handle (1953)
Tico 1083 Charlotte Amalie/Make a Box (1954)
Josie 800 If You Love Me/There's Something in Your Eyes, Eloise (1956)
Josie 814 With This Pen/Letters (1957)
Josie 823 The Retribution Blues/Wagon Wheels (1957)
Value 213 My Hero/A Good Woman (1960)
Value 215 O Holy Night/Winter Wonderland (1960)
Gamut 100 Shrimp Boats Are Coming/My Heart Cries for You (1961)
Port 70021 If You Love Me/There's Something in Your Eyes, Eloise (1961)
20th Century 1213 Blue Star/Pucker Your Lips (1961)
Lost 105 Letter/She Is Mine (1961)
3 Sons 103 W-P-L-J/While I'm Away (1962)
Landa 703 You May Not Love Me/Get Out (1963)
Arctic 135 Go Away/What Can a Man Do (1963)
Red Top 135 My Hero/A Good Woman (1963)
Harthon 136 It's Needless to Say/Focused on You [sic] (1964)
UNI 55132 Never Gonna Leave You/Hot Chills and Cold Thrills (1969)
Sources: Jay Warner, *American Singing Groups;* Charlie Horner, liner notes with the Collectables LP *Bluenotes*; Gordon Skadberg and George Povall, liner notes with the *Jubilee/Josie R&B Vocal Groups* CDs.

Blue Sky Boys (Orangeburg, N.Y.)

Personnel Dennis Ostrom (lead and all voice parts)

Notes

Recording for Sal Passantino's Blue Sky label, Ostrom overdubbed himself four times, well before the sophisticated equipment phenomenon later in existence.

Ostrom also sang with the Bon Aires, the Citadels, and the Relic Vibraharps.

Discography

Blue Sky 100 You Came to Me/Call on Me (1971)
Blue Sky 101 Cherie/I'm Just Another One in Love with You (1972)

Blue Sky 107 Wedding Bell Are Ringing in My Ears (1973)
Blue Sky 108 This Silver Ring (1974)
Blue Sky 109 My Vow to You/Darlene (1974)
Source: Dennis Ostrom, interview by author, March 1994.

Bobbettes (Manhattan, N.Y.)

Personnel Emma Pought (lead tenor), Reather Dixon (lead baritone), Laura Webb (tenor), Helen Gathers (tenor), Jannie Pought (tenor)

Notes

An appearance on Herb Sheldon's TV show brought this group to the attention of Atlantic records and their first recording contract.

Following appearances on TV, radio, and various clubs they were seen by James Dailey, who was then managing the Desires, the Demens, and the Ospreys. Dailey had them change their name from the Harlem Queens to the Bobbettes and brought them to Atlantic.

Originally, "Mr. Lee" contained derogatory lyrics about a fifth-grade teacher of theirs. Atlantic made them change the lyrics before releasing the record.

After "Mr. Lee," they stayed with Atlantic for two years with little success.

They did backup work for Clyde McPhatter and Ivory Joe Hunter.

They recorded for Triple-X and then George Goldner's End, Gone, and Galliant Records.

Gathers left in 1961 and the group has remained a quartet ever since.

They recorded for King and later for Jubilee and in 1966 they cut one disc for RCA and in 1967 one for Diamond.

In 1977, the Bobbettes recorded as the Sophisticated Ladies for the Mayhew label.

Discography

Atlantic 1144 Mr. Lee/Look at the Stars (1957)
Atlantic 1159 Speedy/Come-A Come-A (1957)
Atlantic 1181 Zoomy/Rock and Ree-Ah-Zole (1958)
Atlantic 1194 The Dream/Um Bow Wow (1958)
Atlantic (UNR) Sonny (1958)
Atlantic (UNR) Woop Woop (1958)
Atlantic (UNR) Blessed Love (1958)
Atlantic (UNR) Zoomy, Zoomy (1958)
Atlantic (UNR) Skippy Doo Dah (1958)
Atlantic 2027 Don't Say Goodnight/You Are My Sweetheart (1959)
Atlantic 2069 I Shot Mr. Lee/Untrue Love (1960)
Triple-X 104 I Shot Mr. Lee/Billy (1960)
Triple-X 106 Dance with Me Georgie/Have Mercy Baby (1960)
End 1093 Teach Me Tonight/Mr. Johnny Q (1961)
End 1095 I Don't Like It Like That–Pt 1/Pt. 2 (1961)
Gone 5112 I Don't Like It Like That/Mr. Johnny Q (1961)
Galliant 1006 I Cried/Oh My Papa (1961)

King 5490 Oh Mein Papa/Dance with Me, Georgie (1961)
King 5551 Looking for a Lover/Are You Satisfied (with Your Love) (1961)
King 5623 My Dearest/I'm Stepping Out Tonight (1962)
Jubilee 5427 Over There (Stands My Baby)/Loneliness (1962)
Jubilee (UNR) Moon of Love (1962)
Jubilee (UNR) Yeah (1962)
Diamond 133 Teddy/Row, Row, Row (1962)
Jubilee 5442 Broken Heart/Mama Papa (1963)
Diamond 142 Close Your Eyes/Somebody Bad Stole De Wedding Bell (1963)
Diamond 156 My Mama Said/Sandman (1964)
Diamond 166 In Paradise/I'm a Climbing a Mountain (1964)
Diamond 181 You Ain't Seen Nothin' Yet/I'm Climbing a Mountain (1965)
Diamond 189 Teddy/Love Is Blind (1965)
RCA 47-8832 Having Fun/I've Gotta Face the World (1966)
RCA 47-8983 It's All Over/Happy Go Lucky, Me (1966)
RCA (UNR) Soldier Boy (1966)
RCA (UNR) Walk by Me (1966)
RCA (UNR) Funny Feeling (1966)
Mayhew 712297 That's a Bad Thing to Know (1971)
Mayhew 712298 All in Your Mind (1971)
Mayhew 37 Tighten Up Your Own/Looking for a New Love (1972)
Mayhew 861 It Won't Work Out (1974)
Mayhew 862 Good Man (1974)
QIT Love Rhythm/I'll Keep Coming Back (1981)
Sources: Marv Goldberg in Y*esterday's Memories* 2, no. 30; Pete Grendysa in *Goldmine;* Dennis Garvey in *Goldmine,* February 21, 1992.

Bon-Aires/Bonaires/Bonairs (New Jersey)

Personnel George Lavatelli (lead), Mike Paladino (tenor), Dennis Diamond (tenor), Scotty MacLerie (baritone)

Notes

On Catamount, Dennis Diamond left and Ken Fleming and Richie Burns were added. On Flamingo, Dennis Diamond left and Blue Sky Boys' Dennis Ostrom joined. On UGHA, Mike Paladino left and Tom Vitale joined.

Discography

Rust 5077 My Love, My Love (SM)/Bye Bye (GL) (1964)
Rust 5097 Shrine of St. Cecilia (SM)/Jeannie Baby (GL) (1965)
Rust TR3 Blue Beat (MP/GL)/Driving Alone (GL/DD) (1965)
Catamount 130 My Heart's Desire (GL/KF)/New Me (GL) (1976)
Flamingo 1000 Cherry (GL)/At Night (RB) (1976)
Flamingo 1001 Out of Sight, Out of Mind (RB)/Love You (GL) (1976)
Flamingo 1002 What Did She Use? (DO)/ The Angels Sang (RB) (1977)
Source: George Lavatelli and Dennis Ostrom, interview by author, March 1994.

Bop Chords (Manhattan, N.Y.)

Personnel Ernest Harriston (lead), William Dailey (1st tenor), Ken "Butch" Hamilton (2d tenor), Morris "Mickey" Smarr (baritone), Leon Ivey (bass)

Notes

This group formed as a result of neighborhood groups' popularity with the girls (Channels, Willows, Ladders, etc.).

They were introduced to the Robinson Brothers and Danny Robinson liked them immediately. He signed them to record their own tune Castle in the Sky/My Darling to You.

The success of this endeavor had them record their second Holiday disc, When I Woke Up This Morning/I Really Love Her So.

Personal conflicts, disillusionment, and disgust lead to the first Bop Chords' breakup. The second group was made up of Harriston, Hamilton, and newcomers Peggy Jones and baritone "Skip" Boyd with Smarr, Dailey, and Ivey leaving. The re-formed Bop Chords then recorded their third and last Holiday disc, So Why/Baby.

The third group broke up in 1957 and Harriston occasionally recorded as a fill-in with Shep and the Limelites and the Lovenotes. As Ernie Johnson, he cut You Need Love/Tell Her for Me on Asnes in 1962.

Second tenor Ken "Butch" Hamilton also sang with the Five Wings on King in 1955 in tributes to Johnny Ace ("Johnny's Still Singing" and "Johnny Has Gone").

Discography

Holiday 2601 Castle in the Sky/My Darling to You (1956)
Holiday 2603 When I Woke Up This Morning/I Really Love Her So (1956)
Holiday 2608 Baby/So Why (1957)
Sources: Michael Klink in *Time Barrier Express* 1, no. 8; Lynn McCutcheon in *Record Exchanger* 9.

Boptones (Brooklyn, N.Y.)

Personnel Nick Lampariello (lead), Bob Kutner (1st tenor), John Ench (2d tenor), Dave Antebi (bass)

Notes

Kutner later joined the Vocal-Airs on Herald who did "Dance, Dance." He also joined the Quotations and the Accents on Sultan.

Discography

Ember 1043 Be My Pussycat/I Had a Love (1958)
Sources: Donn Fileti, liner notes with Relic's LP *Ember;* Bob Diskin in *Record Collector's Monthly.*

Bowties, Cirino & (Brooklyn, N.Y.)

Personnel Cirino Colocrai (lead) (real name Del Serino), Jimmy Piro, John Granada, Vince Sepaldo

Notes

In their repertoire when touring, the Three Chuckles, who knew Del Serino, sang "Runaround."

"Runaround" became a huge hit and was eventually purchased by RCA from Serino.

RCA then signed Serino as a staff writer for their Regent label; here he wrote "Foolishly."

Because Serino sang and performed his demos so well, he was asked to form his own group to sing some of his tunes.

The group was eventually heard by Jack Hook and Teddy Reig of Royal Roost Records, who signed them and changed Serino's name to "Cirino" and had him record "Rosemarie."

The Bowties had some success, appearing with Alan Freed, Ed Sullivan, and Jack Paar. They broke up soon after their sudden success.

Discography

Royal Roost 614 My Rosemarie/My Baby's in Love with Me (1955)
Royal Roost 619 This Must Be the Place/Again (1955)
Royal Roost 622 Snap Jack/After Love (1956)
Royal Roost 624 Ever Since I Can Remember/Rock, Pretty Baby (1956)
Source: Marcia Vance and Ed Engel in *Paul's Record Magazine,* February 1976.

Boyfriends, Wini Brown & (New York)

Personnel Wini Brown (lead), Harriet Calendar, Percy Green, Fred Francis, Warren Suttles (baritone)

Notes

This is one of the many times when Warren Suttles left the Ravens to seek success on his own. The following discography shows that his attempt was not very successful.

Joe Van Loan replaced Calendar on "Heaven Knows Why."

Discography

Mercury 5870 Here in My Heart/Your Happiness Is Mine (1952)
Mercury 8270 Heaven Knows Why/Be Anything—Be Mine (1952)
Source: Marv Goldberg, "Ravens," *DISCoveries.*

Brochures (Canton, Ohio)

Personnel Ed McIlwain (lead) (d), Lucius Hood (1st tenor), Robert Hood (2d tenor), Butch Hogan (baritone), Charles Bazen (bass)

Notes

In Relic's *Apollo* LP liner notes, the name of the late lead of the Brochures differs from the name in their CD liner notes, where it is shown as "McLwain."

Discography

Apollo 757 They Lied/My In-Laws Are Outlaws (1961)
Source: Donn Fileti, liner notes with Relic's *Apollo-4.*

Bronzeville Five, Lewis (Chicago)

Personnel   Royal Brent (lead), Arthur Butler (1st tenor), Benny Holman (2d tenor), Alfred Elkins (baritone), Clyde Townes (bass)

Notes

Clyde Townes started in the late 1920s with several gospel groups and jazz bands. Townes met Holman during this period. Holman too was performing in a jazz ensemble. When their bands split up, they got together with other vocalists and "barnstormed" the area (this was 1935–1936). They called themselves the Five Aces of Rhythm. This quintet generally consisted of Arthur Butler, Benny Holman, Alfred Elkins, Townes, and at lead Royal Brent.

Like the many other groups of their era, the Lewis Bronzeville Five were self-contained. They each played instruments and vocally harmonized as well. They were close friends, practicing incessantly. When not on the road touring or performing, they were home practicing. They had a huge repertoire containing around eighty songs.

It was in April–May 1940 that the Lewis Bronzeville Five cut eight sides for the RCA subsidiary, Bluebird Records. They would soon be leased out to Montgomery Ward for repressing.

Mabel Sanford Lewis became their manager and arranged for a thirteen-week slot over WHIP radio in Chicago. Their recording of "Oh Mabel Oh" was dedicated to Mabel Lewis. It was Lewis who suggested the change in the group's name. However, it turned out that Lewis was a crook! The group received not a penny for their thirteen weeks at WHIP. The payment went to Mabel Lewis.

When Lewis's dishonesty became known, the group took the issue to the union and she was put out of the business.

But this bad experience took its toll, and the group broke up between 1940 and 1941.

Discography

Bluebird 8433 Cotton Blossom Blues/Laughing at Life (1940)
Bluebird 8445 Mississippi Fire Blues/Natchez Mississippi Blues (1940)
Bluebird 8460 Low-Down Gal Blues/Linda Brown (1940)
Bluebird 8480 It Can Happen to You/Oh! Mabel, Oh! (1940)
(Note: These four Bluebird recordings were also released on the Montgomery Ward label, song for song. Second tenor Benny Holman's name is quoted from various articles. It has been seen elsewhere as Benny Helman. At this writing, the correct form is not known.)
Sources: Record Collector's Monthly, May 6, 1991; Ray Funk and Doug Seroff, liner notes with the *Human Orchestra* LP; Rick Whitesell in *Goldmine,* November 1980.

Brown Dots (New York)

Personnel Ivory "Deek" Watson (lead), Jimmy Nabbie (1st tenor), Pat Best (tenor), Jimmy Gordon (baritone)

Notes

Resulting from a personality clash, Deek Watson left the Ink Spots to form his own "Ink Spots" group. They appeared for several months but when they were about to record, the original Ink Spots started litigation to stop them from using the name.

Watson changed the name to a similar-sounding one—the Brown Dots.

Personal problems between Watson and the three other members led the other members to secretly form the Sentimentalists using Danny Owens, who had been with the Colemanaires, as lead. This occurred in 1948. Because bandleader Tommy Dorsey owned the name Sentimentalists, the group changed its name to coincide with the number of songs in their repertoire that they hadn't as yet recorded—Four Tunes.

For the last four records the Brown Dots cut, Watson formed a new group (Four Tunes) that began on Manor 1166.

Pat Best sang with the Four Tunes as baritone and Jimmie Nabbie as tenor.

Watson also sang with the Ink Spots, Riff Brothers, and King Jack and the Jesters.

Discography

Manor 1005 Let's Give Love Another Chance (PB)/31 Miles for a Nickel (DW) (1945)

Manor 1009 For Sentimental Reasons (JN)/You're Heaven Sent (JN) (1945)

Manor 1015 Just in Case You Change Your Mind (PB&DW)/You're a 1945 Heartache to Me

Manor 1016 That's What She Gets/Escuchame (1945)

Manor 1017 Is It Right? (PB)/Patience & Fortitude (DW&PB) (1945)

Manor 1026 Surrender (JN)/Satchelmouth Baby (PB&DW) (1945)

Manor 1027 If I Can't Have You/I'm Loving You for You (PB) (1946)

Manor 1032 Please Give a Broken Heart a Break (JN)/Well Natch (DW) (1946)

Manor 1040 Rumors Are Flying (PB)/You Took All My Love (1946)

Manor 1041 It's a Pity to Say Goodnight (all)/For Sentimental Reasons (1946)

Manor 1044 How Can You Say I Don't Care (JN)/Long-Legged Lizzie (DW) (1946)

Manor 1057 I Don't Know from Nothing, Baby (PB)/Shout Brother Shout (DW) (1947)

Manor 1075 That's What She Gets (1947)

Majestic 1244 I've Got the Situation Well in Hand/Pray for the Lights to Go Out (1948)

Manor 1163 Just in Case You Change Your Mind (PB&DW)/Let's Give Love Another Chance (PB) (1949)

Manor 1166 As Tho' You Don't Know/Darktown Strutters' Ball (1949)

Manor 1170 At Our Fireplace/Bow-Wow-Wow (1949)

Manor 1171 If I Could Be with You (w/Gwen Bell)/After Awhile (1949)

Manor 1179 You Better Think Twice/My Bonnie Lies over the Ocean (1949)

Source: Marv Goldberg and Mike Redmond in *Yesterday's Memories* 1.

Buccaneers (Philadelphia)

Personnel Ernest "Sonny" Smith (lead), Julius Robinson (1st tenor), Richard Gregory (2d tenor), Donald Marshall (bass)

Notes

This group was discovered by two undergraduate Temple University students in a Philadelphia nightclub in 1952.

For some unknown reason, Rama 24 was released before Rama 21.

Sam Johnson was also a member.

Discography

Southern 101 Dear Ruth/Fine Brown Frame (1953)
Rainbow 211 Dear Ruth/Fine Brown Frame (1953)
Rama 24 In the Mission of St. Augustine/You Did Me Wrong (1953)
Rama 21 The Stars Will Remember/Come Back My Love (1953)
Source: Donn Fileti, Marv Goldberg, and Mike Redmond in *Bim Bam Boom* 10.

Buckeyes (Steubenville, Ohio)

Personnel Howard Allsbrooks (lead), Leroy Swearingen (1st tenor), Bruce Robinson (tenor), Ray Manson (bass), Ronnie Collins (bass)

Notes

After hearing the Buckeyes perform, their manager, Athena Dallas, brought them to the attention of King records in Cincinnati.

It is curious that despite all this activity taking place in Ohio, the group was sent to New York to record.

After recording four sides for DeLuxe in 1956 (which were all released in 1957), the Ohio recording giant, realizing no success, released the Buckeyes in 1959. They then changed their name to the Stereos, replaced members who had left, and were soon recording under their new billing.

Ester Thompson was also a member.

Discography

DeLuxe 6110 Since I Fell for You (HA)/By Only You (HA) (1957)
DeLuxe 6126 Dottie Baby (HA)/Begging You Please (HA) (1957)
Source: Jeff Kreiter in *Story Untold* 5.

Buddies (Baltimore, Md.)

Personnel Leon Harrison (lead) (d), Luther Dixon (2d tenor), Roger Wainwright (baritone), Danny Ferguson (bass)

Notes

This group became the Barons on Decca and evolved from the Four Buddies on Savoy.

Discography

Glory 230 I Stole Your Heart/I Waited (1954)
Source: Donn Fileti, liner notes with Relic's *Glory* CD.

Butlers (Philadelphia)

Personnel Frankie Beverly (lead), John Fitch (1st tenor), Sonny Nicholson (2d tenor), T. Conway (baritone), Joe Collins (bass)

Notes

Members of this group all attended Germantown High School and began vocalizing together in 1960.

When they saw an ad placed by Jamie/Guyden in their local paper, they took the subway to the recording company's facilities, auditioned for the Philadelphia label, and soon signed a contract.

Within two months their record was on Philadelphia's airwaves.

Their initial release did not do too well and they left the Jamie/Guyden organization.

Discography

Guyden 2081 When I Grow Older/Loveable Girl (1963)
Source: Jamie Guyden, liner notes with the Bear Family CD *Doop Doo Wah.*

Byrds, Bobby Byrd & (Los Angeles)

Personnel David Ford (lead), Gaynell Hodge (2d tenor), Clyde Tillis (baritone), Bobby Byrd (bass)

Notes

Group also recorded as the Hollywood Flames and Satellites, among others.

Byrd was also known as Bobby Day.

Discography

Cash 1031 Let's Live Together As One/The Truth Hurts (1956)
Source: Jim Dawson, liner notes with the Earth Angel LP *The Hollywood Flames.*

Cabaliers, Cab Calloway & (New York)

Personnel Cab Calloway (lead), Dick Palmer (1st tenor), Ernest Palmer (2d tenor), Clarence Palmer (baritone)

Notes

Clarence, Dick, and Ernest had performed as the Palmer Brothers in the late 1930s. Clarence went on to be the lead voice for the Jive Bombers' "Bad Boy" on Savoy.

Dick Palmer was 1st tenor for the Beavers on Coral and baritone for the Blenders on Decca.

This group had performed as the Sparrows with the Al Sears band.

Discography

Okeh 6616 I Want to Rock/T'aint No Good (1942)
Okeh 6634 Minnie the Moocher/One O'Clock Jump (Count Basie) (1942)
Columbia 36611 I'll Be Around/Virginia, Georgia and Caroline (1942)
Brunswick 80015 Minnie the Moocher/Kickin' the Gong Around (1943)
Okeh 6717 I'll Be Around/Virginia, Georgia, and Caroline (1944)
Sources: Bjorn Jentoft in *Rhythm and News* 1; Pete Grendysa in *Story Untold.*

Cabin Boys

Personnel Delores Jackson (lead), Tyre Swanger, Raymond Nelson, Harold Waugh

Notes

This self-contained instrumental/vocal group was formed in 1934.

The group had a repertoire of more than 1,000 tunes—vocal and instrumental. It was a very popular nightclub attraction but recorded very few discs.

Discography

Decca 7396 Cloudy/Carelessly (both w/Delores Jackson) (1938)
Source: George Moonoogian in *Record Collector's Monthly* 46.

Cabineers (New York)

Personnel Maggie Forman (lead), Bill Westbrook (1st tenor), Walter Springer (2d tenor), Herb Kenney (bass)

Notes

There were two Cabineers groups, one from New York and the other from Cleveland. The Cleveland group originated in the 1930s and the New York group in the 1940s.

The Cabineers who recorded for Decca was another group with the same name. According to Lou Silvani in his *Collecting Rare Records,* the Cabineers on Prestige, Decca, and Abbey were the same group.

Bill Kenny and Adriel McDonald sang with the Cabineers but never recorded with the group.

According to liner notes for the Sequel *Jubilee/Josie-2* CD, the Cues started as the Cabineers. This cannot be confirmed, and which Cabineers group is being referred to remains uncertain.

In Billy Vera's liner notes with Specialty's *Coast to Coast* CD, he refers to the Cabineers as a quartet. A photograph included with these liner notes shows the Cabineers as a quintet. However, the man shown with a guitar may have been an instrumental contributor. These same liner notes state that the group had two recording sessions for Prestige: one on July 2, 1951, and the other in December 1951.

Discography

Abbey 72 Whirlpool/You're Just a Great Big Heartache (1949)
Abbey 3001 Tell Me Now/How Can I Help It? (1949)
Abbey 3003 Whirlpool/You're Just a Great Big Heartache (1949)
Prestige 902 My, My, My/Baby, Where'd You Go? (1951)
Prestige 904 Each Time/Lost (1951)
Prestige 917 Baby Mine/What's the Matter with You? (1952)
Sources: Lou Silvani, *Collecting Rare Records*; Billy Vera, liner notes with the Specialty CD *Coast to Coast*; Doug Seroff and Ray Funk, liner notes with the *Human Orchestra* LP.

Caddys, Jesse Powell & (New York)

Personnel Jesse Powell (lead), James Bailey (tenor), Waldo Champen (lead), Bill Lindsay (bass)

Notes

This group appears to be another offshoot of the Cadillacs. But in the summer of 1995, Champen related to the author that he was never a part of this group.

Discography

Josie 834 Ain't You Gonna (instrumental) (1958)
Source: Waldo Champen, interview by author, August 1995.

Cadets (Los Angeles)

Personnel Aaron Collins (lead/2d tenor), Will "Dub" Jones (lead/bass), Willie Davis (1st tenor), Ted Taylor (d) (1st tenor), Lloyd McCraw (d) (baritone)

Notes

This group recorded simultaneously as the Cadets and the Jacks. In 1955 Modern Records had the group record as the Cadets, covering other discs that were selling well. They were also Modern's backup group for single vocalists. Willie Davis did the majority of the lead chores for the Jacks while Aaron Collins and Will "Dub" Jones did the same for the Cadets.

Aaron Collins's sisters, Rosie and Betty, were the Teen Queens. Lloyd McCraw left to be replaced by Thomas "Pete" Fox from the Flairs. Prentice Moreland (d) was temporarily replacing Ted Taylor on the "Stranded in the Jungle" session. He came up to the microphone and in his high tenor voice sang, "Great kooga mooga, let me outta here." This had not been rehearsed.

Moreland sang with the Cadets only in the studio.

Aaron Collins and another house group (white) did "Pretty Evey" and "Rum, Jamaica, Rum." The disc, however, was shown as being by the Cadets. On the day of the session, the Cadets were nowhere to be found and the other house group had to fill in.

In 1958, "Dub" Jones left the Cadets to become the Coasters' bass. He was replacing Bobby Nunn and stayed with the Coasters for about ten years. The new Cadets were then Thomas Miller (baritone) and George Hollis (bass). The two had joined from the Flairs on ABC. Lloyd McCraw was also gone.

Randy Jones briefly replaced Hollis in 1961 and the group was now the Peppers on the Ensign label.

In 1962 Willie Davis and Lloyd McCraw reunited to record as the Thor-A-Bles on Titanic.

On October 22, 1988, Ted Taylor and his wife were killed in a car crash.

Discography

Modern 956 I Cry/Don't Be Angry (1955)
Modern 960 Rollin' Stone/Fine Lookin' Baby (1955)
Modern 963 I Cry/Don't Be Angry (1955)
Modern 969 So Will I/Annie Met Henry (1955)
Modern 971 If It Is Wrong/Do You Wanna Rock? (1955)
Modern 985 Church Bells May Ring/Heartbreak Hotel (1956)
Modern 994 Stranded in the Jungle/I Want You (1956)
Modern 1000 Dancin' Dan/I Got Loaded (1956)
Modern 1006 Fools Rush In/I'll Be Spinning (1956)
Modern 1012 Heaven Help Me/Love Bandit (1956)
Modern 1017 You Belong to Me/Wiggie Waggie Woo (1957)
Modern 1019 Pretty Evey/Rum, Jamaica Rum (1957)
Modern 1024 Hands across the Table/Love Can Do Most Anything (1957)
Modern 1026 Ring Chimes/Baby Ya Know (1957)
Jan-Lar 102 Car Crash/Don't (1960)
Source: Jim Dawson in *Goldmine,* April 26, 1996.

Cadillacs (New York)

Personnel Earl Carroll (lead), LaVerne Drake (tenor), James "Poppa" Clark (tenor), Johnny "Gus" Willingham (baritone), Bobby Phillips (bass)

Notes

The personnel listed recorded together only on the Cadillacs' first session, which produced their first two releases.

After "Wishing Well," Earl Wade of the Crystals and Charles "Buddy" Brooks joined the Cadillacs, replacing Clark and Willingham.

J. R. Bailey joined in May 1956, replacing LaVerne Drake, who had a drinking problem and has been reported dead (as has Brooks).

In the spring of 1957, the Cadillacs split and two new groups evolved, the first including J. R. Bailey, Bobby Spencer, Bill Lindsay, and Waldo Champen. The second group consisted of Earl Carrol, Earl Wade, Bobby Phillips, and Charlie Brooks. After several failures by both groups, and under the guidance of Esther Navarro, the Cadillacs re-formed with Carroll, Wade, Phillips, Bailey, and new member, "Caddy" Spencer.

In October 1957 Brooks left and was replaced by Bobby Spencer from the other Cadillacs.

Earl Carroll left to join Howard Guyton and the Pearls due to less activity as lead with the Cadillacs. In June 1960 Carroll left the Pearls to form another Cadillacs. They were Carroll, Roland Martinez of the Vocaltones and Solitaires, Kirk Davis, and bass Ronnie Bright from the Valentines.

The 1960s Cadillacs group was on Mercury and was made up of Earl Carroll, Bobby Spencer, Roland Martinez, Milton Love (Solitaires), and Reggie Barnes of the FiTones. In the 1960s there was yet another group: Carroll, Martinez, Curtis Williams, and Ray Brewster (both of the Penguins and the Hollywood Flames), Irving Lee Gail from the Fury Miracles and Apollo Vocaltones.

"Speedoo" joined the Coasters in 1964, when Ray Brewster, Alvin "Bobby" Baylor, Freddie Barksdale, and Milton Love were together to record "Fool."

The last of the recording Cadillacs got together in the 1970s. This group contained Bailey, Phillips, Spencer, and LeRoy Binns of the Charts.

All the recording and performing Cadillacs add up to eighteen known configurations.

Discography

Josie 765 Gloria/I Wonder Why (1954)
Josie 769 Wishing Well/I Want to Know about Love (1954)
Josie 773 Sympathy/No Chance (1955)
Josie 778 Down the Road/Window Lady (1955)
Josie 785 Speedoo/Let Me Explain (1955)
Josie 792 Zoom/You Are (1956)
Josie 798 Betty My Love/Woe Is Me (1956)
Josie 805 The Girl I Love/ (That's All) I Need (1956)
Josie 807 Shock-a-Doo/Rudolph the Red-Nosed Reindeer (1956)
Josie 812 Sugar Sugar/About That Gal Named Lou (1957)
Josie 820 My Girl Friend (JRB)/Broken Heart (BS) (1957)
Josie 836 Speedoo Is Back/A-Look Here (1958)
Josie 842 I Want to Know/Holy Smoke Baby (1958)
Josie 846 Peek-a-Boo/Oh Oh Lolita (1958)
Josie 857 Jay Walker/Copy Cat (1959)
Josie 861 Please, Mr. Johnson/Cool It Fool (1959)
Josie 866 Romeo/Always My Darling (1959)
Josie 870 Bad Dan McGoon/Dumbell (1959)
Josie 876 It's Love/Tell Me Today (Speedo w/Ray Brewster) (1960)
Josie 883 That's Why/The Boogie Man (1960)
Mercury 71738 Thrill Me So/I'm Willing (1960)
Smash 1712 You Are to Blame/What You Bet? (1961)
Capitol 4935 La Bomba/I Saw You (Bobby Ray &) (1963)
Arctic 101 Fool/The Right Kind of Lovin' (w/Ray Brewster) (1964)

Source: Sal Mondrone, Tom Luciani, Steve Flam, and Ralph Newman in *Bim Bam Boom* 1, 5.

Caldwells

Personnel Alex Caldwell (baritone lead), Helen Stewart (tenor lead), Oleatha Grangel (tenor), John Dennis (baritone)

Notes

This group recorded for RCA and for Rainbow from 1947 to 1950 and was split evenly between men and women. They joined Rainbow in 1949. They also recorded for Philadelphia's Algene label.

Discography

Algene 1920 Strange It May Seem/There Is No Greater Love (1947)
RCA 20-2613 I Don't Worry Any More/I Gotta Move (1947)
RCA 20-2906 I Wanna Do What I Wanna Do (When I Wanna Do It)/Man Friday (1948)
RCA 20-3179 It's Like Taking Candy from a Baby/Within Your Heart (1948)
Rainbow 10094 I Just Found Out/Bring It On Down to My House (1949)
Rainbow 10097 I Still Feel the Same about You/Exactly Like You (1949)
Rainbow 80025 After My Laughter Came Tears/Loving Up a Solid Breeze (1949)
Rainbow 127 I Don't Worry Any More (1951)
Sources: George Moonoogian in *Record Collector's Monthly* 35; 47; Neil Hirsch, interview by author.

Californians (Los Angeles)

Personnel Jesse Belvin (d)

Notes

It is stated in the liner notes accompanying the Jesse Belvin Specialty CD that Belvin overdubbed himself and was the only member of the "group." This has not been confirmed or denied. However, listening to the disc demonstrates that Belvin's voice is heard briefly and the other voices are clearly not his.

Discography

Federal 12231 My Angel/Heavenly Baby (1955)
Source: Billy Vera, liner notes with the Specialty CD *Jesse Belvin—The Blues Balladeer.*

Calvaes (Chicago)

Personnel James "Zeke" Brown (lead), James Bailey, Paul Morgan, Donald "Duck" Coles, Donald Handley

Notes

The Calvaes formed in a public housing project in Chicago in 1953. The group was apparently an outstanding live act but, because of poor promotion, went nowhere.

Oscar Boyd was also a member of the Calvaes and led the group on the Checker side. Brown sang lead on the Cobra discs.

Discography

Cobra 5003 Fine Girl/Mambo Fiesta (1956)
Cobra 5014 Born with Rhythm/Lonely, Lonely Village (1957)
Checker 928 Anna Macora/So Bad (1959)
Sources: Pete Grendysa, liner notes with the Chess CD boxed set *Chess Rhythm & Roll*; Bob Pruter, *Doowop . . . The Chicago Scene.*

Calvanes (Los Angeles)

Personnel Herman Pruitt, Lorenzo Robert Adams (1st tenor), Joe Hampton (2d tenor), Stewart Crunk (d) (baritone), Jack Harris (bass)

Notes

This group assembled in 1954 in Los Angeles Manual Trades High School. Cornel Gunter coordinated their efforts, listening and suggesting improvements, and eventually got them an audition with Dootsie Williams at Dootone at his home/studio. They soon recorded "Don't Take Your Love from Me," which was a local hit. Their next session, "Florabelle," did not do so well.

But Dootone and the late Dootsie Williams took little interest in the Calvanes in light of the success of the Penguins, Medallions, and Meadowlarks. Pruitt left the group six months after recording "Florabelle" and joined the Youngsters on Empire as lead tenor. The Calvanes stayed together and in 1958 produced two releases for Deck.

in 1961, Pruitt, Adams, Crunk, and new bass, Sidney Dunbar, recorded for RCA as a new Nuggets group (not the Capitol group).

Resulting from the successes of the many years of revivals, Dootsie Williams released the Calvanes' "Fleeoowee" on an LP in 1972.

Discography

Dootone 371 Don't Take Your Love from Me/Crazy over You (1955)
Dootone 380 Florabelle/One More Kiss (1956)
Dootone EP They Call Me Fool (1956)
Dootone (UNR) Fleeoowee
Deck 579 Dreamworld/Five, Seven, or Nine (1958)
Deck 580 My Love Song/Horror Pictures (1958)
Source: Marv Goldberg and Dave Hinckley in *Yesterday's Memories* 11.

Camelots (Brooklyn, N.Y.)

Personnel David Nichols, Joe Mercede (d) (1st tenor), Milton Pratt (d) (2d tenor), Elijah Summers (baritone), Julius Williams (bass)

Notes

By the time the Camelots reached Ember Records in 1964, the Beatles had already come to the United States and the British invasion was about to begin. Ember was "on its last financial leg" and about to close shop. Therefore, it could not provide adequate promotion for the group, and their record went nowhere.

Williams later became the bass for the Tremaines on Old Town.

In 1963 Eddie Fishman and Sal Russo were added to the group, which signed a contract with Ember records and recorded as the Harps.

When Brenda, the Cupids' lead singer, died, the Camelots filled in on dates to which the Cupids were legally obligated.

In 1981, a new Camelots came on the music scene that featured Milton Pratt (lead), Michael Regan (2d tenor), Joe Pitts (baritone), Ernest Burnside (1st tenor), and Julius Williams (bass).

Discography

Aanko 1001 Your Way/Don't Leave Me Baby (1963)
Aanko 1004 Sunday Kind of Love/My Imagination (1963)
Ember 1108 Pocahontas/Searchin' for My Baby (1964)
Cameo 334 Don't Leave Me Baby (1964)
Times Square 32 Dance Girl (1964)
Relic 530 Chain of Broken Hearts/Rat Race (1965)
Dream 1001 I Wonder/Your Way (1967)
Sources: Ed Engel, liner notes with Ace and Sparkletone *Laurie* CD; Mal Freedman in *'50s Revisited* 1–2. Camelots article.

Cameos (Orange, N.J.)

Personnel Patricia Coleman, Patrick Coleman (1st tenor), William Coleman (2d tenor), Walter Jones (baritone), John "Buster" Sayles (bass)

Notes

Patrick Coleman was later with the Ocapellos, who recorded "The Stars."

Discography

Dean 504 Lost Lover/Wait Up (1960)
Johnson 108 Lost Lover/Wait Up (1960)
Source: Donn Fileti, liner notes with the Relic LP *Best of Johnson Records.*

Cameos (Philadelphia)

Personnel Earl Worsham (lead), John Christian (1st tenor), Tony Lewis (2d tenor), Reggie Price (baritone), James Williams (bass)

Notes

Rufus Hunter, who joined later, had been with the Magnificents, Five Bells, and the Five Chimes.

Discography

Cameo 123 Merry Christmas/New Years Eve (1957)
Source: Earl Worsham, interview by Marv Goldberg, *DISCoveries,* October 1995.

Cameos (Los Angeles)

Personnel Vernon Green (lead), Kenneth Williams (tenor), Frank Marshall (tenor)

Notes

According to Jim Dawson's liner notes accompanying the Ace Medallions CD entitled *Speedin',* the Dootone Cameos was a trio fronted by Green. No label credit acknowledged his presence.

Discography

Dootone 365 Craving/Only for You (1955)
Sources: Jim Dawson, liner notes with the Ace Medallions CD *Speedin'*; Marv Goldberg in *Record Collector's Monthly* 42.

Cameos (Pittsburgh, Pa.)

Personnel Donald Carter (lead), Dorland Nelson (1st tenor), Fred Wynn (2d tenor), Bernard Spencer (baritone), Alex Spencer (bass)

Notes

Songwriter/arranger Bob Vogelsberger assembled this Cameos group from the groups coming to him to audition.
　The Spencers were brothers.

Discography

Matador 1808 I Remember When/We'll Still Be Together (1960)
Matador 1813 Never Before/Canadian Sunset (1960)
Source: Ed Salamon, liner notes with Alanna CD Pittsburgh *R 'n' B and Rock and Roll.*

Camerons (New York)

Personnel Robert Browne, Pat Gaines, William Raabe

Notes

This first of two Camerons groups that recorded for the Cousins label in the Bronx sometimes included Diane Umhauer, but not the session that produced the disc shown below.
　The group began in a neighborhood home for the blind and were probably vision impaired. This Camerons group produced only one recording.

Discography

Cousins 1/2 Cheryl/Boom Chic-A-Boom (1960)

Source: Ed Engel and Lou Cicchetti, liner notes with West Side CD *Group Harmony—Out of the Bronx.*

Camerons

Personnel Bob Falcone, Al Crisci, Mike DeMartino

Notes

In spite of the same name, label, and time period, this Camerons group and the group described in the preceding entry are not the same.

Apparently Lou Cicchetti of Cousins owned the name and, after realizing that the other group was no longer making use of it, gave the name Camerons to this group, which was once known as the Idols.

Once this disc was recorded and released by Cousins, it was purchased and rereleased by Felsted Records.

This Camerons group would later go on to record as the Demilles on Laurie.

Discography

Cousins 1003 Guardian Angel/The Girl That I Marry (1961)
Source: Ed Engel and Lou Cicchetti, liner notes with the West Side CD *Group Harmony—Out of the Bronx.*

Canaanites (Philadelphia)

Personnel Joe Van Loan (lead), Elijah Harvey (2d tenor), James Miller (baritone), Alan Scott (bass)

Notes

When Joe Van Loan was discharged from the service in 1946, he formed a vocal group called the Canaanites. The Canaanites appeared on the Philadelphia TV show *Take Ten,* which was hosted by Gene Crane.

They eventually landed a contract with Philadelphia's Gotham Records and recorded many gospel and spiritual tunes. They also performed many secular tunes and in 1948 changed their name and style. They began calling themselves the Bachelors.

The Canaanites' only recordings are contained on a Songmaster LP 800 produced by Jim Hunt and Jack Sbarbori (discography).

Discography

Merry Christmas
Today
When I Get Home
September Song
Peg of My Heart
Sources: Jim Hunt and Jack Sbarbori, liner notes with Songmaster LP *Joe Van Loan;* Marv Goldberg in *DISCoveries,* Ravens article.

Candles, Rochell & (Los Angeles)

Personnel Rochell Henderson (lead), Johnny Wyatt (d) (lead/1st tenor), Mel Sasso (baritone), T. C. Henderson (bass)

Notes

The Swingin' label was owned by California deejays Hunter Hancock and Roger Davenport.

Rochell Henderson came to Los Angeles in 1958 and did some gospel singing. He was not related to T. C. Henderson. He quickly learned that secular tunes provided more financial rewards and formed the Candles. They performed in the Los Angeles area and soon felt ready to record. They cut "Once upon a Time" in 1960, which was released early in 1961 and was a good seller. The group spent the next year touring on the success of their hit tune "Once upon a Time."

Although their follow-ups sold well, none could compare with the sales of "Once upon a Time." By 1964, Swingin' began to have financial and other difficulties, and the Candles moved to Challenge. Not much happened there either.

After leaving the Candles, Wyatt recorded "Something I Want to Tell You" in 1966 for Josie records (946) as Johnny and the Expressions.

Wyatt died in 1983, long after the group stopped recording.

Discography

Swingin' 623 Once upon a Time/When My Baby Is Gone (1960)
Swingin' 634 So Far Away/Hey, Pretty Baby (1961)
Swingin' 640 Beg of My Heart/Squat with Me Baby (1961)
Challenge 9158 Each Night/Turn Her Down (1962)
Challenge 9191 Annie's Not an Orphan Anymore/Let's Run Away and Get Married (1963)
Swingin' 652 Big Boy Pete/A Long Time Ago (1964)
Bingo You Are the Future/The Girl Is Alright
Source: Donn Fileti, liner notes with Relic's *Best of Swingin'* LP/CD.

Cane Cutters, Sugar Boy & (New Orleans)

Personnel James "Sugarboy" Crawford (lead), Edgar Myles (tenor), Warren Myles, Irving Bannister (baritone)

Notes

Edgar Myles also sang with the Sugar Lumps and the Sha Weez.

Discography

Checker 783 I Don't Know What I'll Do/Overboard (1953)
Checker 787 Jock-O-Mo/You, You, You (1954)
Checker 795 I Bowed on My Knees/No More Heartaches (1954)
Source: Marv Goldberg and Dave Hinckley in *Yesterday's Memories* 11, article on the Sha Wees.

Capitols (Pittsburgh, Pa.)

Personnel Mickey Toliver (male lead), Doris Goens (female lead), Arthur Dixon (1st tenor), Ricky Toliver (baritone), Ike Weems (bass)

Notes

Under the guidance of Pittsburgh deejay Jay Michael, who had them audition for George Goldner when he was in town on a visit, the Capitols recorded "Rose Marie" and "Millie" for Goldner's Cindy Records.

Despite good sales of "Rose Marie" and "Millie," Cindy released only two of their masters.

When the contract with Goldner's company expired after five years, the original group went to Pittsburgh's Gateway Records, where they stayed for a year and had one release: Day By Day/Little Things.

Fred McCray was the alternate baritone for the Capitols.

Their recordings always kept them busy with appearances. In spite of this, they eventually called it quits.

Discography

Cindy 3002 Rosemarie/Millie (Mickey Toliver and) (1957)
Gateway 721 Day By Day/Little Things (1964)
Sources: Travis Klein, liner notes with the Itzy II CD *Pittsburgh's Greatest Hits*; Ken Berger in *Story Untold* 8; Carl Janusek and Nancy Janusek in *Story Untold* 8.

Capitols (Brooklyn, N.Y.)

Personnel Nathaniel "Lil John" Epps (lead), Billy Hall (1st tenor), Eddie Jacobs (2d tenor), Clarence Collins (baritone), Kurtis Scott (a.k.a. Kurt Harris) (bass)

Notes

Clarence Collins eventually joined Little Anthony's Chesters. Kurtis Scott also spent some time with the Capitols group without recording. Butch and Kurtis rehearsed with the Chips and both did fill-in work with the Revalons (Pet), the Doom Lang Tokens, and the Five Discs. Eddie Jacobs sang with the Pearls. These were all friends from the Fort Greene section of Brooklyn.

Buddy Bailey also did fill-in work with the Capitols, as did Richard Mitchell.

Discography

Pet 807 Angel of Love (NE)/'Cause I Love You (NE) (1958)
Source: Dave Hinckley and Marv Goldberg in *Goldmine,* April 1979.

Capris (Philadelphia)

Personnel Rena Hinton (lead), Ruben Wright, Eddie Warner, Harrison Scott, Bobby Smart

Notes

The Capris stayed together only briefly, as several members joined the air force following their third Gotham single in 1956.

They got together in 1960 to record "My Weakness" for 20th Century (a Gotham subsidiary). Fred Hale replaced Harrison Scott on this disc. (In Charlie Horner's liner notes with the Collectables LP, he states that this was 1958.)

Ruben Wright's lead voice is heard on "How Long."

Herb Johnson also sang with the Capris.

Discography

Gotham 304 God Only Knows/That's What You're Doing to Me (1954)
Gotham 306 It Was Moonglow/Too Poor to Love (1955)
Gotham 308 It's a Miracle/Let's Linger Awhile (1956)
20th Century 1201 My Weakness/Yes, My Baby, Please (1960)
Lifetime 1001 Oh, My Darling/ (1961)
Lifetime 1002 Rock, Pretty Baby (1961)
Sources: Charlie Horner, liner notes with Collectables LP *Gotham Recording Stars, The Capris*; George Moonoogian, liner notes with the Flyright CD *Capris*.

Capris (Queens, N.Y.)

Personnel Nick Santamaria (lead), Mike Mincelli (1st tenor), Vinny Narcardo (2d tenor), Frank Reina (baritone), John Apostol (bass)

Notes

"There's a Moon Out Tonight" was released in 1958 on Planet, but the group disbanded shortly thereafter as a result of poor sales. Mike got married, Nick enlisted in the service, and the Capris were gone. In 1960 collector interest in the tune forced rerelease on Jerry Green's Lost Night label. In 1961, success brought Old Town's interest and it issued the song.

Discography

Planet 1010/1011 There's a Moon Out Tonight/Indian Girl (1958)
Lost Nite 101 There's a Moon Out Tonight/Indian Girl (1960)
Old Town 1094 There's a Moon Out Tonight/Indian Girl (1960)
Trommers 101 There's a Moon Out Tonight/Indian Girl (1961)
Old Town 1099 Where I Fell in Love/Some People Think (1961)
Old Town 1103 Why Do I Cry?/Tears in My Eyes (1961)
Old Town 1107 Girl in My Dreams/My Island in the Sun (1961)
Mr. Peeke 118 Limbo/From the Vine Came the Grape (1962)
Sources: Pete Grendysa in *Goldmine*; Art Turco and Bob Galgano in *Record Exchanger.*

Capris (San Diego, Calif.)

Personnel Teddy Harper, Alfred Harper, Edward Williams, Gaylord Green

Notes

The Capris formed in San Diego, California, in 1953. Various people would hang out at the Harper home to sing. A dozen of them eventually went on to form vocal groups.

The group would practice on the front lawn and neighbors would come out to listen and enjoy the harmonies.

Harper provided the names of other performers associated with the Capris. They were Ronald Richie, Clifford Hearst, and Edward Duncan (no relation to Cleve Duncan of the Penguins).

The group appeared at local events and clubs. While at San Diego's Victory Theater, they were discovered by Johnny Otis. He brought them to Los Angeles, changed their name to the Aladdins, and got them a recording contract with Aladdin Records. They made no recordings as the Capris.

Source: Marv Goldberg and Mike Redmond in *Yesterday's Memories* 6.

Cap-Tans (Washington, D.C.)

Personnel Sherman Buckner (lead), Floyd Bennett (1st tenor), Alfred "Buddy" Slaughter (2d tenor), Harmon Bethea (tenor), Lester Fountain (baritone)

Notes

In 1950, Lillian Claiborne managed a group called the Buddies and another group called the Progressive Four. She convinced Progressive Four member Harmon Bethea to leave that group and join up with the Buddies, who were going through some personnel changes. He did and the new group was the Cap-Tans.

Claiborne became the Cap-Tans' manager. She recorded their material and sold the tunes to different labels. In July 1950, the Cap-Tans began recording secular music for Claiborne's DC label.

In 1951, Cap-Tans baritone Lester Fountain was drafted and Raymond Reader replaced him. The 1951 tunes on Coral contained Reader.

When Fountain returned, the Cap-Tans regrouped. The new lineup was Fountain, Slaughter, Bradford Fenwick, Elmo "Chico" Anderson, and Lorenzo Miller. This group did not return to Claiborne. They had major troubles creating new material and soon parted company.

Bethea returned to spiritual music with his new group, the Progressiveaires consisting of Bethea, Moses Oliver, Paul Davis, James Baker, and Ezra Davis. When Davis left, they became the Octaves. Both groups had one release for Claiborne's DC Records.

In the late 1950s, they became the L'Cap-Tans performing secular music. The Hollywood Records group consisted of Lester Britton (lead), Richard Stewart (first tenor), Elmo "Chico" Anderson (2d tenor), and Bethea. These four, plus Jim Belt, recorded for Savoy, Loop, and Hawkeye.

The Sabu group was Bethea, Johnny Hood, George Nicholson, Robert Osborn, and Paul Earl.

The Cap-Tans that recorded for Anna was composed of Roosevelt "Tippie" Hubbard (Clovermen), James Toy Walton (Bachelors), Bethea, and Belt.

In 1963, when the group stabilized, it was Bethea, Johnny Hood, Richard Stewart, and Eddie Young.

In order to have "something different" when the British invasion began, they initially became Maskman and the Cap-Tans. In 1968, Stewart and Young left and were replaced by Paul Williams and Tyrone Gray, and they then became Maskman and the Agents.

Discography

DC 8054 You'll Always Be My Sweetheart/Coo-Coo Jug-Jug (featuring Paul Chapman) (1950)
DC 8064 Goodnight Mother/Let's Put Our Cards on the Table (featuring Paul Chapman) (1950)
Dot 1009 I'm So Crazy for Love (SB)/Crazy 'Bout My Honey Dip (HB) (1950)
Dot 1018 With All My Love (SB)/Chief Turn the Hose on Me (HB/AS) (1950)
Gotham 233 My My Ain't She Pretty (HB/AS)/Never Be Lonely (FB) (1951)
Gotham 268 Yes (SB/HB)/Waiting at the Station (HB) (1951)
Coral 65071 Asking (SB)/Who Can I Turn To? (SB) (1951)
Dot 15114 With All My Love/I'm So Crazy for Love (1953)
Anna 1122 I'm Afraid (TH)/Tight Skirts (HB) (1960)
Loop 100 Revenue Man (BJ)/Crazy about a Woman (1962)
DC 0433 A Big Bite of the Blues/Ain't No Big Thing (1962)
Hawkeye 0430 Annie Penguin (BJ)/Rockin' in the Jungle (LC)
Sabu 103 Whenever I Look at You (HB)/Round the Rocket (HB) (1963)
Sabu 501 You Better Mind (HB)/I Wanna Make Love (HB) (1963)
Source: Dave Hinckley and Marv Goldberg in *Yesterday's Memories* 8.

Cardinals (Baltimore, Md.)

Personnel Ernie Lee Warren (lead), Meredith Brothers (d) (1st tenor), Jack Sam Aydelotte (2d tenor), Donald Jack Johnson (baritone), Leon "Tree Top" Hardy (bass)

Notes

This group started in 1946 as the Mellotones from east Baltimore with Meredith Brothers, Ernie Lee Warren, Leon Hardy, and Jack Johnson. They soon met fifth member Sam Aydelotte at a Baltimore amateur show.

Donald Johnson worked in a record shop and the proprietor was often visited by Ahmet Ertegun and Herb Abramson of Atlantic Records. The Mellotones were there on a visit and auditioned for the two. Following their performance, they were signed with Atlantic.

Atlantic changed their name to the Cardinals, as there already was a Mellotones. The current craze at the time was to name groups after birds. Their singing style changed from pop to R&B.

Lead Ernie Lee Warren was drafted in 1952 and missed one of the Cardinals' sessions. Replacing Warren for that session was Leander Lance Tarver, who is heard on "The Bump," "She Rocks," and "Please Baby." Warren was home on leave when "You Are My Only Love" was recorded and thus six voices are heard on this gem.

After Warren satisfied his military obligation in 1954, he rejoined the group. Tarver simultaneously left and tenor Johnny Douglas took his place. Douglas is heard performing lead chores on "Offshore."

Aydelotte was on the "Miserlou" session instead of Johnny Douglas and from that time on (except on "Offshore"), the original group was intact.

In 1958, Warren re-formed the Cardinals. They were Warren, Johnson Brothers, Johnny Douglas, and Jim Boone. This group was together only briefly, and the Cardinals then became an integrated group in favor of white members, four to one. Jerry Passion, Jerry Donahue, Lee Cornell, and Jimmy Harrison were the white members who would later become the Trend-Els on Tilt.

James "Little Caesar" Brown and Luther MacArthur were early members who only performed with the group and never did any recording.

Meredith Brothers passed away many years ago.

Discography

Atlantic 938 Shouldn't I Know/Please Don't Leave Me (1951)
Atlantic 952 I'll Always Love You/Pretty Baby Blues (1951)
Atlantic 958 Wheel of Fortune/Kiss Me Baby (1952)
Atlantic 972 The Bump/She Rocks (1952)
Atlantic 995 You Are My Only Love/Lovey Darling (1953)
Atlantic 1025 Under a Blanket of Blue/Please Baby (1954)
Atlantic 1054 The Door Is Still Open/Miserlou (1955)
Atlantic 1067 Come Back My Love/Two Things I Love (1955)
Atlantic 1079 Here Goes My Heart to You/Lovely Girl (1955)
Atlantic 1090 Off Shore/Choo Choo (1956)
Atlantic 1103 The End of the Story/I Won't Make You Cry Anymore (1956)
Atlantic 1126 One Love/Near You (1957)
Source: Phil Chaney and Ronnie Italiano, liner notes with the Plaza CD *Come Back My Love.*

Carnations (Bridgeport, Conn.)

Personnel Matthew Morales (lead), Harvey Arrington, Edward Kennedy, Carl Hatton, Tommy Blackwell (bass)

Notes

The Carnations on Lescay backed up Bo Diddley on "I'm Sorry" and "Crackin' Up" on Checker (from an article in *Bim Bam Boom* by Will Anderson in which he interviews Carl Hatton in prison). Don Fileti discussed this same subject in his liner notes with Relic's *Beltone* LP.

Morales and Arrington sang with the Startones on Ember and Tommy Blackwell was the brother of Arthur Blackwell of the Startones.

Discography

*No Time for Tears/Betty
Lescay 3002 Long Tall Girl/Is There Such a World? (1961)
*When he was interviewed by Donn Fileti, Carl Hatton could not recall the small Connecticut label on which these sides were recorded.
Source: Will Anderson in *Time Barrier Express* 8.

Carollons, Lonnie & (Brooklyn, N.Y.)

Personnel Irving Brodsky (lead as "Lonnie"), Richard Jackson (1st tenor), Eric Nathanson (2d tenor), Jimmy Laffey (baritone), Artie Levi (bass)

Notes

This was an interracial group. Jackson was black and the others were white.

The liner notes accompanying Relic's *Mohawk* CD show the lead singer's name as Irving Brosky.

Discography

Mohawk 108 Chapel of Tears/My Heart (1958)
Mohawk 111 Trudy/Hold Me Close (1958)
Mohawk 112 Backyard Rock/You Say (1958)
Street Corner 101 My Heart/Chapel of Tears (1973)
Source: Donn Fileti, liner notes with Relic's *Mohawk* LP/CD.

Carols (Detroit)

Personnel Tommy Evans (lead/bass), Richard Coleman (1st tenor), William Davis (2d tenor), Wilbert Tindle (baritone)

Notes

Tommy Evans is the same individual who went on to sing with the Ravens and the Drifters. In the 1960s he joined the Drapers and the Floaters.

In 1952, Richard Coleman married and Kenneth Duncan became the new first tenor.

In 1954, with the Ravens having difficulties with Jimmy Ricks, road manager Nat Margo, who had seen Tommy Evans perform, sent for him to join the Ravens and replace Jimmy Ricks. This was the end of the Carols, however. Ricks, who owned a piece of the Ravens, came back several times, preventing Evans from ever recording with them. When the Drifters released Bill Pinkney, Evans was recruited to replace him and stayed with the group several years.

Discography

Columbia 30210 Please Believe in Me/Drink Gin (1950)
Columbia 30217 If I Could Steal You from Somebody Else/I Should Have Thought (1950)
Savoy 896 Fifty Million Women/I've Got a Feeling (1953)
Savoy (UNR) Call for Me/Mighty Lak a Rose
Source: Marv Goldberg and Mike Redmond in *Bim Bam Boom* 13.

Carpets (Kansas City, Mo.)

Personnel James Gadson (lead), Tom Gadson, Elmer Powell, John King, Charlie Tillman

Notes

Group members ranged in age from sixteen to nineteen. All members attended the same high school. James and Tom Godson were brothers.

This group's sound was far more mature than their ages at the time of recording would suggest. It's no wonder, then, that when auditioning for Federal A&R chief Ralph Bass, they were immediately given a recording session. The product from this date was two Federal releases, neither of which did anything. Consequently, nothing else was recorded.

Discography

Federal 12257 Why Do I?/Let Her Go (1956)
Federal 12269 Lonely Me/Chicken Backs (1956)
Sources: D. Romanello, G. Povall, and C. Bucola, liner notes with King-Federal-DeLuxe CD *Great Googa Mooga*; Marv Goldberg, interview by author.

Carter Rays (Philadelphia)

Personnel Eddie Carter (lead), Harold Cade

Notes

Cade also sang with the Ed Carter Quartet.

Discography

Grand 107 Take Everything but You/Cool Wailin' Papa (1954)
Jubilee 5142 Goodnight Sweetheart/Love Me Boy (1954)
Sound 105 Ooh Baby/These Are the Thing That Matter (1956)
Lyric 2001 My Secret Love/Ding Dong Daddy (1956)
Gone 5005 My Secret Love/Ding Dong Daddy (1957)
Mala 433 Bless You/Keep Listening to Your Heart (1961)
Source: Charlie Horner, liner notes with the Collectables LP *Grand Records.*

Casanovas (Highpoint, N.C.)

Personnel Chester Mayfield (lead), Willie McWilliams (1st tenor), Mike Stowe (2d tenor), William Samuels (baritone), Frank McWilliams (d) (bass)

Notes

"Hush-A-Mecca," led by Samuels, relates his experiences in Korea.

William Samuels was the brother-in-law of Lowman Pauling from the Five Royales.

The unreleased "My Love for You" was lead by Mike Stowe, as was "My Baby's Love," "For You and You Alone," and "You Are My Queen." D. Mayfield filled in for the Casanovas. The Mayfields were nephews of the McWilliams.

Frank McWilliams passed away in the early 1960s.

Discography

Apollo 471 That's All (CM)/Are You for Real? (WS) (1955)
Apollo 474 Hush-A-Mecca (WS)/It's Been a Long Time (CM) (1955)
Apollo 477 I Don't Want You to Go (CM)/Please Be My Love (CM) (1955)
Apollo 483 My Baby's Love/Sleepy Head Mama (CM) (1955)
Apollo 519 Please Be Mine (CM)/For You and You Alone (MS) (1957)
Apollo 523 Good Lookin' Baby/You Are My Queen (MS) (1957)
Source: Don Fileti, liner notes with the Relic LP *Best of the Casanovas.*

Casanovas, Little Romeo & (Queens, N.Y.)

Personnel Sam Cantos (lead), Gary Willett (1st tenor), Ron Buchter (2d tenor), Greg Malmeth (baritone/bass)

Notes

This group was also the Ovations on Josie.

Discography

Ascot 2192 Remember Lori/That's How Girls Get Boys (1965)
Source: Gordon Skadberg, liner notes with Sequel's *Jubilee/Josie R&B Vocal Groups.*

Cascades (Chicago)

Personnel Joe Brackenridge (lead), Stacy Steele Jr. (1st tenor), Willie C. Robinson (2d tenor), Henry Brackenridge (baritone), Charles Johnson (bass)

Notes

Robinson also sang with the Von Gayles and the Pace Setters.

The above group minus Henry Brackenridge had been the Von Gayles. The McCormick release shown below may be the only release on the label.

Discography

McCormick 105 Pains in My Heart/Only One I Can Spare (1964)
Renee 105 Pains in My Heart/Only One I Can Spare (1964)
Source: Bob Pruter, *Doowop . . . The Chicago Scene.*

Cashmeres (Philadelphia)

Personnel Grover Mitchell, Henry Boyd, Romeo Schuler, Ralph Riley, Mark Alan

Notes

Lee Sampson was a later replacement.

There has always been some doubt concerning the Cashmeres. The group by that name on Herald and Mercury was the same group.

Donn Fileti in his liner notes with the Herald CD names the group's personnel. He states parenthetically, "Mark Allen (there was a DJ Mark Allen on WNJR Newark; he may have been the group's manager)." I cannot confirm this.

Discography

Mercury 70501 Yes, Yes, Yes/My Sentimental Heart (1954)
Mercury 70617 Boom Mag-A-Zeeno-Vip Vay/Don't Let It Happen Again (1954)
Mercury 70679 There's a Rumor/Second-Hand Heart (1955)
Herald 474 Little Dream Girl/Do I Upset You? (1956)
Source: Donn Fileti, liner notes with Relic's *Herald* CD.

Cashmeres (Brooklyn, N.Y.)

Personnel Windsor King (1st tenor), William Cutty Jordan, Arnita Neta Arnold, Bobby Bowers, Jean Reeves

Notes

King had also been with the Royal Sons (later the Five Royales) and after his time with the Cashmeres, he joined three girls and the group became King and the Sharpettes. The other group he was with was the Cosytones. They recorded two discs, one on Melba and the other on Willow.

After the Cosytones, King met an unnamed group near his home in Brooklyn. He was tending bar, and after he heard the group, he offered to be their lead singer. The group readily accepted his offer. Soon King met the owners of Lake Records, who liked his voice. When he told them of his group, they asked that he bring them around when they were ready for an audition.

He rehearsed them incessantly and finally brought them to Lake, where they recorded their first disc.

This did nothing. Their second Lake disc, "Satisfied," did so well that it had to be leased out for better distribution. The Cashmeres were eventually brought to Laurie by Lake management. This turned out to be a poor decision, as none of their Laurie discs did anything. They were next brought to Josie. Again nothing doing.

Lake management took them all over but realized no success anywhere. They next went to Decca and had their name changed. In the interview, King could not remember the new name.

Discography

Lake 703 Four Lonely Nights/Everything's Gonna Be Alright (1960)
Lake 705 Satisfied–Pt. 1/Satisfied–Pt. 2 (1960)
Laurie 3078 A Very Special Birthday/I Believe in St. Nick (1960)
Laurie 3088 I Gotta Go/Singing Waters (1961)
Laurie 3105 Baby Come on Home/Poppa Said (1961)
Josie 894 Life-Line/Where Have You Been? (1961)
ACA 1216/1217 Stairsteps to Heaven/Nag Nag (1962)
Source: Ken Berger and Larry Cedilnik in *Record Exchanger* 17.

Cashmeres, Eddie Jones & (New York)

Personnel Eddie Jones, Barbara Joyner, Lorraine Joyner, Annette Swinson, Valerie Swinson

Notes

This group recorded "Daddy Can I Go to the Hop" in 1959, according to Gordon Skadberg's liner notes with the Sequel CD *Herb Abramson's Festival of Hits.*
This Eddie Jones is probably the same performer who sang lead for the Demens.

Discography

Daddy Can I Go to the Hop (1959)
Source: Gordon Skadberg, liner notes with the Sequel CD *Herb Abramson's Festival of Hits.*

Casinos (Philadelphia)

Personnel Milton Harlan, James Frazier, Eddie Carter

Notes

John Ward, James White, and Ben Miller were later additions to the group.

Discography

Maske 803 I'm Falling/Speedy (1959)
Source: Lou Silvani, *Collecting Rare Records.*

Caslons (Brooklyn, N.Y.)

Personnel Sal Mondeuri (lead), Richie Smith (1st tenor), Lou Smith (2d tenor), Joe Carvelli (baritone), Bernie Belkin (bass)

Notes

The Caslons initially got together in 1960 in the Flatbush section of Brooklyn as students at Madison High School. They made many local appearances and rehearsed a great deal. It was their manager/promoter Lou Stallman who wrote "Anniversary of Love." The Caslons recorded demo tapes and Stallman took them around to record companies for their review. Shortly after recording "Anniversary of Love" in spring 1961, Bernie Belkin joined the army, leaving the Caslons. Since most performances at the time were lip-synched, the group decided to remain a quartet.
Late in 1961, Amy Records released "For All We Know." Nothing happened with this release and Lou Smith decided to join the army. The Caslons' magic was gone and the group split.

Discography

Seeco 6078 Anniversary of Love/The Quiet One (1961)
Amy 836 For All We Know/Settle Me Down (1961)
Source: Bob Diskin in *Record Collector's Monthly* 53.

Castelles (Philadelphia)

Personnel George Grant (lead), Octavius Anthony (1st tenor), Frank Vance (2d tenor), William Taylor (baritone), Ronald Everett (bass)

Notes

The Castelles personified the Philadelphia Sound so often discussed in vocal group collectors' conversations. When the Castelles started their harmonizing in 1949, their average age was eleven! They were neighborhood friends who started singing at school dances.

Vance was the songwriter who wrote the group's signature song "My Girl Awaits Me," which the group recorded at a penny arcade. On their way home, they stopped at a small appliance and record shop made famous by the photograph on the Collectables LP *Treegoob's* to listen to the recording. Treegoob's owner, Herb Slotkin, liked what he heard and asked the group if they had a manager representing them. When the group said no, Slotkin spoke with associate, Jerry Ragovoy, about the group. The two agreed to represent the Castelles. As the two wanted to avoid the hassles involved with recording companies, they decided to form their own label. This was Grand Records.

"My Girl Awaits Me," the label's first release, was issued in November 1953. It did well in the East Coast's major cities.

One great R&B tune after another was released, which, decades later, became R&B classics.

Walt Miller, an occasional stand-in, wrote Marcella and assumed Taylor's place as baritone on both sides of this disc. Miller was also lead on "I'm a Fool to Care."

Following "Heavenly Father" and "My Wedding Day," Vance and Everett left. Clarence Scott, a friend from Philadelphia, joined the group, now a quartet. They moved to the Atlantic subsidiary Atco, taken there by Slotkin to record one disc.

Billy Taylor did some work with the Spaniels, the Dominoes, the Orioles' Charlie Parker and Lana recordings, and the Modern Red Caps.

George Grant joined his old friend from the Dreams, George Tindley with the Modern Red Caps. He later went on to sing with an Ink Spots group. In the early 1990s, Grant recorded for Classic Artists Records. He showed us that he still had it.

Discography

Grand 101 My Girl Awaits Me (GG)/Sweetness (OA) (1953)
Grand 103 This Silver Ring (GG)/Wonder Why (BT) (1954)
Grand 105 Do You Remember? (GG)/If You Were the Only Girl (GG) (1954)
Grand 109 Over a Cup of Coffee (GG)/Baby Can't You See? (OA) (1954)
Grand 114 Marcella (GG)/I'm a Fool to Care (WM) (1954)
Grand 122 Heavenly Father (GG)/My Wedding Day (GG) (1955)
Atco 6069 Happy and Gay (CS)/Hey Baby Baby (GG) (1956)
Sources: Charlie Horner, liner notes with Collectables LP *Sweet Sound of the Castelles*; Donn Fileti, liner notes with Relic CD *Sweetness*; Wayne Stierle in *Bim Bam Boom*; Marv Goldberg in *DISCoveries*.

Casual Crescendos (Berkeley, Calif.)

Personnel Anna Lois Jones (lead), Ernie ——— (tenor), George Banks (baritone), Odell Alford (bass)

Notes

This was the Music City group the Crescendos, after Wanda Burt left due to illness and Cynthia Badie left to go to college.

They recorded for the MRC label.

Discography

MRC 12001 Wish That You Were Here/Uncle Ben's Concentrated Blueberry Jam (1963)
Source: Jim Dawson, liner notes with the Titanic CD *Music City–1.*

Casuals (Dallas)

Personnel Fred Gary Mears (lead), Paul Kearney (d) (tenor), Jay Joe Adams (baritone)

Notes

Another Casuals group, a quintet on Dot, emerged when "So Tough" began to do well. Backbeat Records owner Don Robey was then forced to rename his Casuals the Original Casuals. He sent them on a tour to promote their record, which was the first chart hit Robey had with a white trio!

In 1960 Paul Kearney accidentally shot and killed himself.

Discography

Casuals/Original Casuals
Backbeat 503 So Tough/I Love My Darling (1957)
Backbeat 510 Ju-Judy/Don't Pass Me By (1958)
Backbeat 514 Three Kisses Past Midnight/It's Been a Long Time Girl (1958)
Source: Galen Gart and Roy Ames in *Duke/Peacock Records.*

Catalinas (Brooklyn, N.Y.)

Personnel Hank Ferrara (lead), Sam Infantino (1st tenor), Richie Brooks (2d tenor), Jerry Ascher (baritone), Mike Harris (bass)

Notes

In 1959, because Glory records was doing nothing with the Catalinas and because they were still under contract with Glory, the Catalinas recorded for Up Records as the Inventions.

Discography

Glory 285 Marlene/With Your Girl (1958)
Source: Ed Engel in *Harmony Tymes* 3.

Cats and Jammer Three (Chicago)

Personnel Bill Samuels (lead), Sylvester Hickman, Adam Lambert

Notes

This group was formed through an evolution of jazz bands and personnel (Miles Davis was once a part of one of these configurations). It was a self-contained group since members both sang and played musical instruments. Samuels met Hickman when he heard him in a Chicago band with his brother-in-law. In another band (Sonny Thompson Band) Hickman met Adam Lambert.

In spring 1945, the three sat separately in a lounge listening to another band. Somehow they met one another and later that night agreed to combine forces. They opened at the same club as the Cats and Jammer Trio the next week!

Their first Mercury recording, "I Cover the Waterfront," featured more group harmony than their later recordings.

After leaving Mercury in 1949, they became the Bill Samuels Trio and recorded for Miracle.

Samuels moved to Minneapolis and became a solo act. He died in the early 1970s.

Adam Lambert sang with the Four Shades of Rhythm in 1951–1952.

Discography

Mercury 2003 Jockey Blues/I Cover the Waterfront (1945)
Mercury 2021 100 Hundred Years from Today/I'm Comin' Home to Stay (1946)
Mercury 2051 That Chick's Too Young to Fry/Candy Store Jump (1946)
Mercury 8006 I'm Falling for You/That Chick's Too Young to Fry (1946)
Mercury 8012 Port Wine/Ghost of a Chance (1946)
Mercury 8021 My Bicycle Tillie/I Surrender Dear (1946)
Mercury 8029 Open Up That Door, Richard/Candy Store Jump (1947)
Mercury 8033 For You/My Baby Didn't Even Say Goodbye (1947)
Mercury 8037 I Know What You're Puttin' Down/Lilacs in the Rain (1947)
Mercury 8042 When I Close My Eyes/Where's My Baby? (1947)
Mercury 8064 If I Had Another Chance/One for the Money (1947)
Mercury 8086 Stompin' Those Blues Away/Moonglow (1948)
Mercury 8116 It's Love Time/That Someone Is You (1949)
Miracle 143 Let Me Off Uptown/Say It Isn't So (1949)
Miracle 152 New Jockey Blues/I've Got the Blues (1950)
Mercury 70205 I Cover the Waterfront/Don't Worry 'bout Me (1953)
Source: Pete Grendysa in *Record Collector's Monthly* 8.

Cats and the Fiddle (Chicago)

Personnel Austin Powell (lead), Jimmy Henderson (d) (1st tenor), Ernie Price (2d tenor), Chuck Barksdale (d) (bass)

Notes

Like other groups of their time, the Cats and the Fiddle were a self-contained vocal/instrumental group.

Early on, they performed at weddings, proms, and graduations. It was at one of these functions that an RCA Records agent offered to record them. They soon recorded for Bluebird Records, a Victor subsidiary.

Because of the 1930s and 1940s heritage of race music, public acceptance was slow. If they had lasted into the 1950s, perhaps they would have been accepted sooner. At this time, they appeared in many motion pictures.

Henderson left the group when he came down with meningitis and was temporarily replaced by Herbie Miles (Bluebird 8519; 8585). Henderson passed away within a year and was replaced by Lloyd "Tiny" Grimes at 1st tenor. He stayed with the group for two years. Wanting to further his musical career as well as improve his financial condition, Grimes left the group in California and was replaced by Mifflin "Pee Wee" Branford.

Barksdale died in 1941 and was replaced by George Stainback.

When Powell was drafted in 1941, Hank Haslett replaced him. The next year, Herbie Miles replaced Haslett. Powell returned in 1945. The group recorded nothing new during the war due to shortages of recording material.

When they began recording for Manor records in 1945 they recut "I Miss You So" with Ernie Price singing lead. Stanley Gaines filled in at bass for the group and Emmitt Slay filled in at tenor.

Emmitt Slay replaced Branford briefly in 1947. Johnny Davis replaced him permanently and in 1948 a fifth member was added: Shirley Moore! Moore was with the group on two Manor cuts and two Gotham cuts and was later replaced by Doris Knighton.

The 1949 group was Powell, Branford, Price, and Stainback. Although he never recorded with the group, Napoleon Snaggs Allen, later a member of the Blenders, was used as a utility replacement.

In mid-1950, the group fell apart and Powell reorganized them as follows: Johnny Davis (tenor), Stanley Gaines (bass), Dottie Smith, and Beryl Booker. The group's name was later changed to the Austin Powell Quintet.

Discography

Bluebird 8216 Nuts to You/Killin' Jive (1939)
Bluebird 8248 Gang Busters/Please Don't Leave Me Now (1939)
Bluebird 10484 Thursday Evening Swing/Killer Diller Man from the South (1939)
Bluebird 10547 We Cats Will Swing for You/Till the Day I Die (1939)
Bluebird 8402 Chant of the Rain/I'd Rather Drink Muddy Water (1940)
Bluebird 8429 I Miss You So/Public Jitterbug No. 1 (1940)
Bluebird 8443 When I Grow Too Old to Dream/Left with the Thought of You (1940)
Bluebird 8465 Gone/Mr. Rhythm Man (1940)
Bluebird 8489 That's on, Jack, That's on/Just a Roamer (1940)
Bluebird 8519 Hep Cats Holiday/In the Midst of a Dream (1940)
Bluebird 8535 Nothing/That's All I Mean to You (1940)
Bluebird 8560 Pigs Idea/You're So Fine (1940)
Bluebird 8585 Hush-a-Bye/Swing the Scales (1940)
Bluebird 8639 I'll Always Love You Just the Same/One Is Never Too Old to Swing (1941)
Bluebird 8665 If I Dream of You/I'm Gonna Pull My Hair (1941)
Bluebird 8685 I'm Singing/My Darling (1941)
Bluebird 8705 Crawlin' Blues/Until I Met You (1941)
Bluebird 8847 I Don't Want to Set the World on Fire/Blue Skies (1941)

Bluebird 8870 Lawdy-Clawdy/Sighing and Crying (1941)
Bluebird 8902 Another Day/Stomp Stomp (1942)
Bluebird 8932 Life's Too Short/Part of Me (1942)
Manor 1023 Romance without Finance/Life's Too Short (1945)
Manor 1037 Please Don't Leave Me Now/Shorty's Got to Go (1946)
Manor 1045 I'd Rather Drink Muddy Water/Walkie Talkie (1946)
Manor 1064 That's My Desire/When Elephants Roost in Bamboo Trees (1947)
Manor 1067 They Don't Understand/I'm Stuck with You (1947)
Manor 1078 Where Are You?/I'm Gonna Pull My Hair (1947)
Manor 1086 You're So Fine/Darling Can't We Make a Date? (1947)
Manor 1112 Honey, Honey, Honey/I'm Afraid of You (1948)
Manor 1140 The New Look Blues/That's What I Thought You Said (1948)
Manor 6000 I Miss You So/My Sugar's Sweet to Me (1948)
Gotham 197 I'll Never Never Let You Go/Start Talking Baby (1949)
Gotham 239 Do You Love Me?/Movin' Out Today (1950)
Decca 48151 Wine Drinker/Lover Boy (1950)
Source: Lawrence Cohn, liner notes with the Bluebird LP *Cats and the Fiddle.*

Cavaliers (Chicago)

Personnel John Pruitt (lead), James Dennis "Brother" Isaac (1st tenor), Oscar Boyd (2d tenor), George "Sonny" Parker (baritone), Nathaniel Tucker (bass)

Notes

This group originated in 1953 as the Cavaliers, organized by Andre Williams of "Bacon Fat" fame. They would later become the United and Theron Sheppards. Williams specifically geared them to be like the Chance Flamingos, who had just come off their beauty, "Golden Teardrops." Williams was the Cavaliers' first baritone. He left the group before recording and was replaced by Oscar Robinson from the Five Thrills who recorded for Parrot.

The Cavaliers would later evolve into the Sheppards, who executed "Mozelle" on Theron.

Source: Bob Pruter, *Doowop . . . The Chicago Scene.*

Caverliers Quartet (Brooklyn, N.Y.)

Personnel Lester Gardner (lead), Marlowe Lowe Murray (1st tenor), Cecil Holmes (baritone), Ron Anderson (bass)

Notes

Members of this group all hailed from the same Fort Greene section of Brooklyn in 1952 and later that year signed with the Atlas/Angletone organization. In 1953, their only release, You Thrill Me So/Dynaflow, was issued.

Murray, Holmes, and Anderson were later members of the FiTones.

When this group disbanded, an interim group, which never recorded, was formed. One member of this interim group was Monte Owens, later of the Solitaires. Ron Mosely and Leroy Randolph were the others.

Discography

Atlas 1031 You Thrill Me So/Dynaflow (1953)
Sources: Arthur Crier, interview by author, April 23, 1994; liner notes with Relic LP/CD *Fi-Tones*; Phil Groia in *Bim Bam Boom.*

Cellos (New York)

Personnel Alton Campbell (lead), Billy Montgomery (1st tenor), Cliff Williams (2d tenor), Bobby Thomas (baritone), Alvin Williams (bass)

Notes

This group first got together in the Manhattan neighborhood of Charles Evan Hughes High School as the Marcals. Realizing there was no benefit in naming themselves after toilet tissue, they changed their name to the Cellos. Their high school specialized in textile trades, which drew students from all over the city. Thus members of the group came from various sections of New York.

After forming, they practiced a great deal and finally cut a demo. The engineer for that session was James Merenstein, the nephew of Charles Merenstein, who was running Apollo Records at the time. James liked them and brought them to Apollo for an audition. Apollo management had them sign a contract and scheduled their first recording session.

They recorded four songs at that first session. "Rang Tang Ding Dong" was released late in 1957. James Merenstein became their manager. "Rang Tang Ding Dong" did very well in sales and another session was held. None of their future releases did anything despite the quality of the ballads. Group members ultimately drifted apart.

Discography

Apollo 510 You Took My Love/Rang Tang Ding Dong (AC/BM) (1957)
Apollo 515 Under Your Spell/The Juicy Crocodile (AW) (1957)
Apollo 516 The Be-Bop Mouse/Girlie That I Love (AW) (1957)
Apollo 524 I Beg for Your Love (AC)/What's the Matter for You? (AW) (1958)
Source: Donn Fileti, liner notes with the Relic LP *Cellos.*

Centuries (New Haven, Conn.)

Personnel Milton White, Clarence Thomas

Discography

Times Square 5 Crying for You/Oh Darling (1963)
Times Square 15 Betty/Ride Away (1963)
Source: Liner notes with Relic LP/CD *Times Square.*

Centurys (Pittsburgh, Pa.)

Personnel Bernard Dupree (lead), Melvin Cornelius (baritone)

Discography

Fortune 533 Oh Joe Joe/Take My Hand (1959)
Sources: Devora Brown, liner notes with Fortune's *Treasure Chest of Musty Dusties*;
Carl Janusek in *Echoes of the Past* 32.

Chances (New York)

Personnel Milton Love (lead), Bobby Baylor (2d tenor), Reggie Barnes (2d tenor),
Monte Owens (tenor), Freddie Donovan (bass)

Notes

This group was an offshoot of the Solitaires mixed with members from other New
York groups (FiTones, Vocaltones, Willows, Mello-Moods). It also included Winston "Buzzy" Willis and Freddie Barksdale.

Cecil Holmes sang with the Chances and was also with the Caverliers, FiTones,
and Solitaires. Roland Martinez also sang with this group.

Discography

Roulette 4549 Through a Long and Sleepless Night/What Would You Say (1964)
Source: Milton Love, interview by author, April 1995.

Chandeliers (Kansas City, Mo.)

Personnel Luther Rice (lead), William Watson (1st tenor), Reginald Johnson
(tenor), George Chambers (2d tenor), Jesse Watson (bass)

Notes

The Chandeliers came together in 1954 as students at Lincoln High School (except
for Jesse Watson, who attended another high school). They practiced three to four
times each week.

Their manager was Sol Davis, who was a friend of one of their neighbors. He
learned that a talent scout was coming to their area in 1957. The scout turned out
to be Tommy Robinson, the owner of Atlas/Angletone. After hearing them at one
of their practice sessions, he was impressed enough to sign them to a three-year
contract.

"Blueberry Sweet" was released in January 1958 and was the label's biggest hit.
Donn Fileti's liner notes with Relic's *Best of Atlas/Angletone* LP report Robinson's
claim that this disc was selling at the rate of 3,000 copies a day for several weeks.
But this was hard to follow and the record following their "Blueberry Sweet" did
absolutely nothing.

The local success of "Blueberry Sweet," however, generated a demand for live
appearances by the Chandeliers. But their follow-ups to "Blueberry Sweet" lacked
its unique quality and did nothing.

They tried to find another label to record for, but their three-year contracts with
their manager, Davis and Atlas Records' Robinson, prohibited this from ever happening.

Unlike most groups, the Chandeliers did get some royalties. But they learned in the spring of 1959 that most of these funds went to Sol Davis. Within several weeks they simply stopped singing.

In June and July 1959, William, Jesse, and Luther joined the navy. Except for the singing they did at boot camp, the Chandeliers never performed again.

Discography

Angletone 521 Blueberry Sweet/One More Step (1958)
Angletone 529 Dolly/Dancin' in the Congo (1958)
Sources: Members of the group, interview by Marv Goldberg in *DISCoveries,* April 1998; Donn Fileti, liner notes with the Relic LP *Best of Atlas/Angletone.*

Channels (New York)

Personnel Earl Lewis (lead), Larry Hampden (1st tenor), Billy Morris (2d tenor), Edward Dolphin (baritone), Clifton Wright (bass)

Notes

Sometime late in 1955, Larry Hampden, Billy Morris, and Edward Dolphin, and two others formed a quintet they called the Channels. They were from the 115th Street area of Harlem in New York City. The bass and lead left the group and the three remaining members (shown above) found Earl Lewis and Clifton Wright singing with a group called the Lotharios at a talent show. The two were convinced to join the Channels. They won the next talent show at which they appeared.

They somehow met Bobby Robinson, signed a two-year contract with his new Whirlin' Disc Records, and recorded their "Closer You Are," written by the fifteen-year-old Earl Lewis. Its unique styling has made it an R&B classic. Their second disc, "The Gleam in Your Eyes," was also written by Lewis—when he was ten years old.

Other Whirlin' Disc records followed and were great sides, but none did as well as "The Closer You Are." Label support diminished and they soon auditioned for George Goldner's Gone Records. It was on Gone that the beautiful standard "That's My Desire" was recorded. The disc was arranged by former Valentines lead, Richard Barrett. The Gone tune revived the Channels' popularity, but Clifton Wright left after that recording.

In 1959, the Channels went back to Bobby Robinson and his new Fury label. The group's first effort for Fury, "My Love Will Never Die," backed with "Bye Bye Baby," did quite well in New York, Chicago, and Los Angeles. Despite what other accounts say about the group backing Earl Lewis on the two Fury sides, it turned out to be Jackie and the Starlites. Earl Lewis's regular group was late for the session that day and Robinson, paying for the session time, substituted the Starlites, who were also recording that day, enabling Robinson to avoid the exorbitant session fees. (This story was told to the writer by Earl Lewis himself in August 1984.)

Following Edward Dolphin's departure from the group after "My Love Will Never Die" and "Bye Bye Baby," Billy Montgomery and Alton Campbell from the Cellos joined and are first heard on "The Girl Next Door" and "My Heart Is Sad" on Fire Records.

Discography

Whirlin' Disc 100 The Closer You Are/Now You Know I (1956)
Whirlin' Disc 102 The Gleam in Your Eyes/Stars in the Sky (1956)
Whirlin' Disc 107 I Really You/What Do You Do? (1956)
Whirlin' Disc 109 Flames in My Heart/My Lovin' Baby (1957)
Gone 5012 That's My Desire/Stay As You Are (1957)
Gone 5019 Altar of Love/All Alone (1958)
Fire 1001 My Heart Is Sad/The Girl Next Door (1959)
Groove UNR You Changed My Life Around (1964)
Groove 58-0046 Anything You Do/I've Got My Eyes on You (1964)
Groove 58-0061 Old Chinatown/You Can Count on Me (1965)
Rare Bird 5017 She Blew My Mind/Breaking Up Is Hard to Do (1971)
Channel 1000 Gloria/You Said You Loved Me (1971)
Channel 1001 We Belong Together/Hey Girl, I'm in Love with You (1972)
Channel 1003 Close Your Eyes/Work with Me Annie (1973)
Channel 1004 Over Again/In My Arms to Stay (1973)
Channel 1006 Thousand Miles Away/Don't Let the Green Grass Fool Ya (1974)
Sources: Charlie Horner, liner notes with the Lost Nite LP *Earl Lewis and the Channels*; Jay Warner, *American Singing Groups.*

Channels (Chester, Pa.)

Personnel Charlie Toole, Charlie Reynolds, Gene DiGienerio, James Liott, Gene Williams (2d tenor)

Notes

This was a white group attempting to capitalize on the name.

Discography

Mercury Jungle Lights/Earth Quake (1959)
Mercury Lonely (1959)
Source: Bob Ferlingere, *A Discography of R&B and R&R Vocal Groups.*

Chanteclaires (New York)

Personnel Randolph Stewart (lead), David Sheffield, Roy Evans

Notes

The Chanteclaires got together in 1958 and recorded "Snatchin' Peaches" and "Down at Ling Ting Laundry" in 1959.

The lead singer, Randy Stewart, was soon to be one of the Fiestas on Old Town. He was originally an office employee for Hy Weiss's Old Town label and was added to the group in 1960.

The two songs mentioned above were never released as singles and were never heard prior to 1985, when the LP *R&B Laff Blast from the Past* was issued. Consequently, this entry includes no discography.

Source: Gordon Skadberg, liner notes with Sequel CD *Herb Abramson's Festival of Hits.*

Chantels (Bronx, N.Y.)

Personnel Arlene Smith (lead), Sonia Goring, Rene Minus, Jackie Landry, Lois Harris

Notes

The girls had been schoolmates since the second grade in a religious school in the Bronx. They went to a community center at P.S. 124, where they practiced with the Sequins of Red Robin fame.

Aware of the hit by Frankie Lymon and the Teenagers on Gee, the girls went to see George Goldner. He was not in that day and they chose to audition for the Valentines, who were performing at an Alan Freed show at the time. When Richard Barrett heard them, he was thrilled with their vocal excellence.

Barrett saw Arlene Smith's talent and rehearsed the group endlessly until he felt that they were ready for live appearances. He got them their first engagement at a Jocko stage show.

Because they received no royalties and little other remuneration, the Chantels split.

On End 1103 the group had already parted and George Goldner used a totally different group, the Veneers, to record as the Chantels. The Princeton cuts were the same two songs cut by the Veneers for End.

The lead for the Veneers hooked up with the Chantels minus Arlene Smith for the Carlton material ("Look in My Eyes," etc.).

Three of the original Chantels were in the group backing Richard Barrett on "Come Softly to Me" and "Summer's Love."

Helen Powell of the Click-Ettes joined a later Chantels.

Arlene and Her Girlfriends on Old Town were not Arlene Smith and the Chantels but imitators.

Discography

End 1001 He's Gone/The Plea (1957)
End 1005 Maybe/Come My Little Baby (1957)
End 1015 Every Night/Whoever You Are (1958)
End 1020 I Love You So/How Could You Call It Off? (1958)
End 1026 Sure of Love/Prayee (1958)
End 1030 If You Try/Congratulations (1958)
End 1037 I Can't Take It/Never Let Go (1958)
End 1048 Goodbye to Love/I'm Confessin' (1959)
Gone 5056 Walking through Dreamland/Come Softly to Me (w/Barrett) (1959)
Gone 5060 Summer's Love/All Is Forgiven (1959)
End 1069 Whoever You Are/How Could You Call It Off? (1960)
End 1103 Believe Me/I (Veneers as Chantels) (1961)
End 1105 I'm the Girl/There's Our Song Again (1961)
Carlton 555 Look in My Eyes/Glad to Be Back (1961)
Carlton 564 Well, I Told You/Still (1961)

Carlton 569 Here It Comes Again/Summertime (1961)
Big Top 3073 Love, Love, Love/He Knows I Love Him Too Much (1961)
Ludix 101 Eternally/Swamp Water (1963)
Ludix 106 That's Why You're Happy/Some Tears Fall Dry (1963)
TCF 123 There's No Forgetting You/Take Me As I Am (1965)
Verve 10387 Soul of a Soldier/You're Welcome to My Heart (1966)
Verve 10435 Indian River/It's Just Me (1966)
Princeton 102 Believe Me (My Angel)/I (Veneers as Chantels) (1969)
RCA 74-0347 I'm Gonna Win Him Back/Love Makes All the Difference (1970)
Spectorious 150 Everything/Good Girls (1970)
Source: Phil Groia in *Bim Bam Boom* 9.

Chanters (Queens, N.Y.)

Personnel Larry Pendergrass (lead), Fred Paige (tenor), Bud Johnson Jr. (tenor), Elliot Green (baritone), Bobby Thompson (bass)

Notes

The Chanters formed in 1957 from a group of Queens, New York, friends. Bud Johnson Sr., the band leader, got them their first audition with King. It is Johnson's name that is referred to on labels reading Bud Johnson and the Chanters. The younger Johnson never sang lead for the Chanters.

Because their parents felt they were too young to tour and perform at stage shows, the Chanters were relatively unknown in the 1950s. It wasn't until collecting began that the group became more familiar to R&B collectors.

They added a voice and did backup work as the Voices Six. This added voice was Stevie Garner.

Fred Paige went into the service and was replaced by Freddy Johnson, Bud's cousin. He can be heard on "For Sentimental Reasons." For this cut, the group was known as the Voices Five.

In 1966 Fred Paige sang with the Del-Vons on Wells 1001.

Discography

DeLuxe 6162 My My Darling (LP)/I Need Your Tenderness (LP) (1958)
DeLuxe 6166 Row Your Boat (LP)/Stars in the Skies (LP) (1958)
DeLuxe 6172 Five Little Kisses (LP)/Angel Darling (FP) (1958)
DeLuxe 6177 No, No, No (LP)/Over the Rainbow (LP) (1958)
DeLuxe 6191 I Make This Pledge (LP)/No, No, No (LP) (1961)
DeLuxe 6194 At My Door (LP)/My My Darling (LP) (1961)
DeLuxe 6200 Row Your Boat (LP)/No, No, No (LP) (1963)
Source: Marv Goldberg in *Goldmine.*

Chanters, Billy Butler & (Chicago)

Personnel Billy Butler (lead), Errol Bates (1st tenor), John Jordan (2d tenor), Jesse Tillman (baritone), Alton Howell (bass)

Notes

Billy Butler was Jerry Butler's younger brother. Errol Bates was tenor Jerry Bates's brother. He also sang with the Chanters.

After recording their first single, which turned out to be a disappointment, Alton and John left; the group became Billy Butler and the Enchanters (a trio).

After they learned of Garnet Mimms and the Enchanters, they reverted to Billy Butler and the Chanters.

Discography

Okeh 7201 Can't Live without Her/My Heart Is Hurtin' (1964)
Okeh 7207 Nevertheless/My Sweet Woman (1964)
Okeh 7221 Tomorrow Is Another Day/I Can't Work No Longer (1965)
Okeh 7227 You Ain't Ready/You're Gonna Be Sorry (1965)
Source: Bob Pruter, *Doowop . . . The Chicago Scene.*

Chanters, Gene Ford & (Santa Monica, Calif.)

Personnel Gene Ford (lead), Alan Boyd, Billy Boyd, Ethyl Brown

Notes

Billy Boyd sang with the Cats on Federal. He was Alan Boyd's brother.

After their discs with RPM and Kem in 1954, they moved to Combo in 1955.

Discography

RPM 415 Tell Me, Thrill Me/She Wants to Mambo (1954)
Kem 2740 Lonesome Me/Golden Apple (1955)
Combo 92I Love You/Hoy Mamma (1955)
Sources: Ted Carroll, liner notes with the Ace CD *Fifties*; Jeff Kreiter, *Group Collector's Record Guide.*

Chanteurs (Chicago)

Personnel Sollie McElroy (lead), Eugene Gino Record (1st tenor), Robert Squirrel Lester (2d tenor), Clarence Johnson (baritone), ——— Reid (bass)

Notes

Johnson, Lester, and Record joined with Marshall Thompson and Creadel Jones of the Desideros to form the Chi-Lites.

In his interview by Lou Rallo appearing in the November 1997 issue of *DISCoveries,* McElroy refers to the Chanteurs as the Chi-Lites. He states that he "recorded six sides with the Chi-Lites [Chanteurs] and only one was ever released."

Discography

Vee Jay 519 You've Got a Great Love/The Grizzly Bear (1963)
Sources: Bob Pruter, *Doowop . . . The Chicago Scene*; Solly McElroy, interview by Lou Rallo in *DISCoveries,* November 1997.

Chapelaires (Pittsburgh, Pa.)

Personnel Bill Schmidt (1st tenor), Tony Rausch (2d tenor), Ross Melodia (baritone), Bob Bubarth (bass)

Notes

This group was formed in 1955 while they were attending junior high school singing in a church choir. They initially called themselves the Chapel Boys but did not really become enthusiastic about their vocal ability until 1958.

Following several personnel changes, they became the Chapelaires. As they attained a following, appearances escalated. In 1960 they recorded their first disc for the HAC label. HAC consisted of the letters of the first names of the label's owners—Hal, Al, and Chuck. The disc was released in 1961 but did not do anything. At the end of 1961 the group returned to the studio to cut three more sides.

Although their second release realized some sales, they did not receive a penny. They were making some dollars doing nightclub dates. In 1962, Schmidt was drafted.

They eventually added two other members. The change in both size and membership led to a new name, the Softwinds. In 1964 the Softwinds were asked by a Pennsylvania record producer to record for him at Gateway as the Chapelaires. They agreed and the result is summarized in the discography below.

The Gateway recording, despite its quality, never made any noise and the Chapelaires were not heard from again.

Discography

HAC 101 Not Good Enough/I'm Still in Love with You (1961)
HAC 102 Gloria/Under Hawaiian Skies (1961)
Gateway 746 It's Impossible/Vacation Time (1964)
Source: Carl Janusek in *Echoes of the Past* 39.

Chaperones (Long Island, N.Y.)

Personnel Tony Amato (lead), Roy Marchesano (1st tenor), Tommy Ronka (2d tenor), Nick Salvato (baritone), Richard Messina (bass)

Notes

The Chaperones all came from Long Island, New York. It was a tremendous thrill and quite meaningful to be able to record for Josie, one of the labels responsible for some of the music they adored during their teenage years.

Lou Jordan sang lead on the Chaperones' third release, "Paradise for Two." In the Sequel CD liner notes, it is stated that the bass for the Chaperones was Dave Kelly.

The Chaperones backed up Lee Adrian on "Barbara, Let's Go Steady" and "I'm So Lonely."

Discography

Josie 880 Cruise to the Moon/Dance with Me (1960)
Josie 885 Shining Star/My Shadow and Me (1961)

Josie 888 Paradise for Two/Close Your Eyes (1961)
Josie 891 Blueberry Sweet/Man from the Moon (1962)
Sources: Liner notes with the Sequel CD *Whiter Shade of Doo Wop*; Kenny Cohen in *Harmony Tymes* 3; George Povall and Gordon Skadberg, liner notes with the Jubilee/Josie CD *R&B Vocal Groups-4*.

Chaps (Pittsburgh, Pa.)

Personnel Ron Fulton (lead), Joe Cesario (1st tenor), George Esposito (2d tenor), Sonny (baritone), Bob Savastano (bass)

Notes

The Chaps were selected to be the on-screen group for the TV show *Shindig*. When a group member decided to return to Pittsburgh from California, where *Shindig* was produced, they unfortunately missed appearing on the show and gaining national exposure.

Discography

Brent 7016 One Lovely Yesterday/Perfect Night for Love (1960)
Matador 1814 They'll Never Be/Heaven Must Have Run Out of Angels (1961)
Source: Travis Klein, liner notes with the Itzy II CD *Pittsburgh's Greatest Hits.*

Charades (Los Angeles)

Personnel Syl Grigsby (lead), Raymond Baradat (tenor), Johnny T. Johnson (baritone)

Notes

The Charades was formed in 1957 and performed mainly at school functions and community affairs. After several years of many personnel changes and no recordings, the group finally had their first release on Northridge Records; others followed (see below).

Interestingly, Ava Records was owned by Fred Astaire and distribution was by MGM.

Discography

Northridge 1002 For You/Sofia (1962)
Ava 154 Turn Him Down/Please Be My Love Tonight (1963)
Original Sound 47 Take a Chance/Close to Me (1964)
Source: Ian Clark article on the Charades.

Chargers (Los Angeles)

Personnel Benny Louis Easley (lead), Dunbar John White (1st tenor), Jimmy Norman Scott (2d tenor), Johnny "Junior" White (baritone), Mitchell Alexander (bass)

Notes

The White brothers were neighbors of Joann and Jesse Belvin, who took the Chargers under their wing and brought them to RCA (where Belvin was under contract). The Belvins wrote most of the Chargers' songs and rehearsed them daily. Jesse sang in the background on each of their songs. In addition, according to the session logs and other documentation, Jesse Belvin was a paid performer of the Chargers (Billy Vera's liner notes with the RCA CD).

Jimmy Norman teamed up with H. B. Barnum and Ty Terrell (Robins). This group was the Dyna-Sores and they recorded on Rendezvous 120. Norman also recorded with the Viceroys on Little Star 107 I'm So Happy/Uncle Sam Needs You and on Smash 1716. And again with the Viceroys on Original Sound 15 Ball 'n' Chain/ Dreamy Eyes. In 1963, Jimmy Norman was backed by the O'Jays on Little Star 126 on Love Is Wonderful/What's the Word? Do the Bird. Norman had an active solo career in the 1970s and beyond.

Mitchell Alexander had been in the Feathers.

Discography

RCA 47-7301 Old MacDonald (BE)/Dandilyon (BE) (1958)
RCA 47-7417 The Counterfeiter (BE)/Here in My Heart (JN) (1959)
Sources: Drew Williamson in *Record Collector's Monthly*; Marv Goldberg in *Goldmine,* July 1987; Billy Vera, liner notes with RCA CD *Rock 'n' Roll Party-2.*

Charioteers (Wilberforce, Ohio)

Personnel Wilfred Billy Williams (lead), Eddie Jackson (2d tenor), Ira Williams (baritone), Howard Daniel (bass)

Notes

The Charioteers began as the Harmony Four at Wilberforce College, under the direction of their music teacher (and the group's bass), Howard Daniel.

Following their first few releases for Decca in 1935, and Vocalion and Brunswick, the group performed backing vocal accompaniment for Mildred Bailey.

Arthur Lee Simpkins replaced Billy Williams during Williams's brief stay in the service. When Williams formed his own quartet, Herbert Dickerson replaced him.

Robert Bowers became 1st tenor, replacing Jackson. John Harewood also joined, as did Peter Lubers.

The Charioteers spent many years with Bing Crosby as backup and vocal group performers.

Henry King replaced Eddie Jackson.

The Charioteers signed and recorded for Jerry Blaine's Josie Records in 1955.

Discography

Decca 420 Along Tobacco Road/Ridin' Around in the Rain (1935)
Decca 421 Little David Play on Your Harp/Snowball (1935)
Brunswick 8237 Let's Have Harmony/The Man Who Cares (1938)
Brunswick 8459 Steal Away to Jesus/Water Boy (1938)

Brunswick 8468 Swing Low, Sweet Chariot/All God's Chillun Got Shoes (1938)
Vocalion 4015 Song of the Volga Boatman/Dark Eyes (1938)
Vocalion 4068 Speak to Me of Love/A Brown Bird Singing (1938)
Vocalion 4125 Laughing Boy Blues/Sing You Sinners (1938)
Vocalion 5025 Forget If You Can/My Gal Sal (1938)
Vocalion 5209 Don't Dally with the Devil/I Feel Like a Motherless Child (1939)
Columbia 35229 I'm Gettin' Sentimental over You/Why Should I Complain (1939)
Columbia 35424 So Long/The Gaucho Serenade (1940)
Columbia 35693 Water Boy/Swing Low, Sweet Chariot (1940)
Columbia 35718 Go Down Moses/Were You There? (1940)
Columbia 35736 Darling Je Vous Aime Beaucoup/Calling Romance (1940)
Columbia 35741 I'm in His Care/All God's Chillun Got Shoes (1940)
Columbia 35749 Love's Old Sweet Song/Silver Threads among the Gold (1940)
Columbia 35765 I Don't Want to Cry Anymore/Only Forever (1940)
Columbia 35779 Calliope Jane/I Should Have Known You Years Ago (1940)
Columbia 35787 Steal Away to Jesus/Jesus Is a Rock in a Weary Land (1940)
Columbia 35811 The Call of the Canyon/We'll Meet Again (1940)
Columbia 35851 Goodnight, Mother/My Heart's on Ice (1940)
Columbia 35887 Old Folks at Home/Carry Me Back to Old Virginny (1941)
Columbia 35942 May I Never Love Again/Why Is a Good Gal Hard to Find? (1941)
Columbia 35981 Between Friends/I'll Forget (1941)
Columbia 36027 Braggin'/You Walk By (1941)
Columbia 36094 I Understand/A Dream for Sale (1941)
Okeh 6220 All Alone and Lonely/Careless Love (1941)
Okeh 6247 Daddy/Down, Down, Down (1941)
Okeh 6292 Wrap Up Your Troubles in Dreams/I Heard of a City Called Heaven (1941)
Okeh 6310 The Cowboy Serenade/Yes Indeed (1941)
Okeh 6332 I Don't Want to Set the World on Fire/One Two Three O'Lairy (1941)
Okeh 6390 Elmer's Tune/Hawaiian Sunset (1941)
Okeh 6424 Nothin'/Call It Anything, It's Love (1941)
Okeh 6509 I Got It Bad and That Ain't Good/Cancel the Flowers (1941)
Okeh 6589 Tica-Tee Tica-Ta/The Train Song (1942)
Columbia 36730 Sylvia/This Side of Heaven (1944)
Columbia 36792 Don't You Notice Anything New/It Doesn't Cost You Anything to Dream (1945)
Columbia 36854 Lily Belle/Don't Forget Tonight, Tomorrow (w/F. Sinatra) (1945)
Columbia 36903 No Soup/One More Dream (1946)
Columbia 37074 On the Boardwalk/You Make Me Feel So Young (1946)
Columbia 37195 Bagels and Lox/Rogue River Valley (1946)
Columbia 37240 Open the Door, Richard/You Can't See the Sun When You're Crying (1947)
Columbia 37384 Say No More/Chi Baba, Chi Baba (1947)
Columbia 37399 So Long/Ride Red Ride (1947)
Columbia 37518 Sylvia/I'm Gettin' Sentimental over You (1947)
Columbia 37519 The Gaucho Serenade/We'll Meet Again (1947)
Columbia 37546 I Miss You So/You're Breaking in a Brand New Heart (1947)

Columbia 37853 I've Got a Home in That Rock/Jesus Is a Rock in a Weary Land (w/F. Sinatra) (1947)
Columbia 37912 I'm in the Mood for Love/Sweet Lorraine (1947)
Columbia 37913 Sleepy Time Gal/My Fate Is in Your Hands (1947)
Columbia 37914 If I Could Be with You/On the Sunny Side of the Street (1947)
Columbia 37915 I Can't Get Started/Sweet Marie (1947)
Columbia 38065 What Did He Say/Ooh Looka There, Ain't She Pretty (1948)
Columbia 38115 Now Is the Hour/Peculiar (w/Buddy Clark) (1948)
Columbia 38187 When I Grow Too Old to Dream/The Last Thing I Want Is Your Pity (1948)
Columbia 38261 Run, Run, Run/The Tourist Trade (1948)
Columbia 38329 It's Too Soon to Know/Until (1948)
Columbia 38438 A Kiss and a Rose/A Cottage in Old Donnegal (1949)
Columbia 38602 This Side of Heaven/Hawaiian Sunset (1949)
Harmony 1059 Who/Don't Ever Leave Me (1949)
Keystone 1416 S'posin'/I'm the World's Biggest Fool (1952)
Josie 787 I've Got My Heart on My Sleeve/Don't Play No Mambo (1955)
Josie UNR One Fried Egg (1955)
RCA 47-6098 Easy Does It/Tremble, Tremble, Tremble (1955)
Tuxedo 891 Thanks for Yesterday/I'm a Stranger (1955)
Tuxedo 892 Forget If You Can/Sleepy River Moon (1955)
MGM 12569 The Candles/I Didn't Mean to Be Mean to You (1957)
Sources: Pete Grendysa and Rick Whitesell in *Goldmine*; Pete Grendysa and George Moonoogian in *Record Exchanger*; George Povall, liner notes with the Sequel CD *Jubilee/Josie R&B Vocal Groups.*

Charm (Jersey City, N.J.)

Personnel Kevin Lucas (lead/1st tenor), Kenneth Gene Day (1st tenor), Robert Lee Michael Shaw (2d tenor) (baritone), Michael Alexander (bass)

Notes

This was a group discovered by Ronnie Italiano and presented at his UGHA meeting/show as a relatively young a cappella group.

The majority of Charm's output is contained on their Clifton LP 1005 and therefore is not shown here.

Discography

Clifton 98 Morse Code of Love/It's So Hard to Say Goodbye to Yesterday (1992)
Source: Ronnie Italiano, liner notes with the Clifton CD *It's So Hard to Say Goodbye to Yesterday.*

Charmers (New York)

Personnel Lucille "Vicky" Burgess (lead/tenor), Eugene Sonny Cooke (lead/baritone), Alfred Todman (1st tenor), James Cooke (2d tenor), George Daniels (bass)

Notes

Lucille "Vicky" Burgess sings lead on the Central sides and Sonny Cooke performs lead vocals on the Timely label recordings.

This group became the Chorals on Decca. The lead for the Chorals was Irwin Williams. Burgess was gone after Central and would later join the Rama Joytones.

Discography

Central 1002 The Beating of My Heart/Why Does It Have to Be Me? (1954)
Central 1006 Tony My Darling/In the Rain (1954)
Timely 1009 I Was Wrong/The Mambo (1954)
Timely 1011 The Church on the Hill/Battle Axe (1954)
Sources: Donn Fileti, liner notes with the Relic CD *Golden Era of Doo Wops*; Vicky Burgess, interview by author in *Timely,* April 23, 1994.

Charms, Otis Williams & (Cincinnati, Ohio)

Personnel Otis Williams (lead), Donald Peak (1st tenor), Roland Bradley (2d tenor), Joseph Penn (baritone), Richard Parker (bass)

Notes

In 1955, after three releases, all but Williams left with Rockin' label owner Henry Stone, who was forming the Chart label. There were now two Charms groups: the group led by Otis Williams on DeLuxe (now a quartet) and the original DeLuxe quartet still on that label.

"Hearts of Stone" was written by Rudy Jackson, 2d tenor for the Jewels.

The three new members with Williams were Chuck Barksdale (from the Dells, who returned to that group after the Williams group recorded "Ivory Tower"), Rollie Willis, and Larry Graves. Their first release was DeLuxe 6090 and showed "Otis Williams and His New Group" on the label.

In January 1956 Barksdale and Graves left. Joining Rollie Willis were Lonnie Carter, Matt Williams, and Winfred Gerald, making the group a quintet again. DeLuxe 6095 was their first release.

In 1960, Lonnie Carter joined with original Charms Donald Peak, Richard Parker, Joe Penn, and Roland Bradley to form the Esco's [sic] on Federal and Esta.

The remaining members stayed with Williams; this group recorded for King. Williams would later record for Okeh with a mixed gender group.

Much later Williams became the country artist he always dreamed of being.

Discography

Charms

Rockin' 516 Loving Baby/Heaven Only Knows (1952)
DeLuxe 6000 Loving Baby/Heaven Only Knows (1953)
DeLuxe 6014 What Do You Know about That?/Happy Are We (1953)
DeLuxe 6034 Please Believe in Me/Bye Bye Baby (1954)
DeLuxe 6050 Quiet Please/Fifty-five Seconds (1954)
DeLuxe 6056 My Baby Dearest Darling/Come to Me Baby . . . (1954)

DeLuxe 6062 Who Knows?/Hearts of Stone (1954)
DeLuxe 6065 Two Hearts, Two Kisses/The First Time We Met (1955)
DeLuxe 6072 Mambo Sh-Mambo/Crazy Crazy Love (1955)
DeLuxe 6076 Ling Ting Tong/Bazoom (Need Your Lovin') (1955)
DeLuxe 6080 Whadaya Want/Ko Ko Mo (1955)
DeLuxe 6082 Whadaya Want (Alt)/Ko Ko Mo (Alt) (1955)
DeLuxe 6087 Let the Happenings Happen/When We Get Together (1955)
DeLuxe 6089 It's You You You/One Fine Day (1955)

Otis Williams And His New Group

DeLuxe 6088 Miss the Love/Tell Me Now (1955)
DeLuxe 6090 Gum Drop/Save Me, Save Me (1955)
DeLuxe 6091 That's Your Mistake/Too Late I Learned (1955)
DeLuxe 6092 Do Be You/Rolling Home (1956)

Otis Williams & The Charms

DeLuxe 6093 In Paradise/Ivory Tower (1956)
DeLuxe 6095 It's All Over/One Night Only (1956)
DeLuxe 6097 Whirlwind/I'd Like to Thank You Mr. DJ (1956)
DeLuxe 6098 Gypsy Lady/I'll Remember You (1956)
DeLuxe 6105 Pardon Me/Blues Stay Away from Me (1957)
DeLuxe 6115 Walking after Midnight/I'm Waiting Just for You (1957)
DeLuxe 6130 Nowhere on Earth/No Got De Woman (1957)
DeLuxe 6137 One Kind Word from You/Talking to Myself (1957)
DeLuxe 6138 United/Don't Deny Me (1957)
DeLuxe 6149 Well Oh Well/Dynamite Darling (1957)
DeLuxe 6158 Oh Julie/Could This Be Magic? (1958)
DeLuxe 6160 Baby-O/Let Some Love in Your Heart (1958)
DeLuxe 6165 Burning Lips/Red Hot Love (1958)
DeLuxe 6174 Don't Wake Up the Kids/You'll Remain Forever (1958)
DeLuxe 6178 My Friends/The Secret (1958)
DeLuxe 6181 Pretty Little Things/Welcome Home (1959)
DeLuxe 6183 Watch Dog/My Prayer Tonight (1959)
DeLuxe 6185 I Knew It All the Time/Tears of Happiness (1959)
DeLuxe 6186 In Paradise/Who Knows? (1959)
DeLuxe 6187 Blues Stay Away from Me/Funny What True Love Can Do (1959)
King 5323 Chief Um (Take it Easy)/It's a Treat (1960)
King 5332 Silver Star/Rickety Rickshaw Man (1960)
King 5372 Image of a Girl/Wait a Minute, Baby (1960)
King 5389 So Be It/The First Sign of Love (1960)
King 5421 Wait/And Take My Love (1960)
King 5455 Little Turtle Dove/So Can I (1960)
King 5497 You Knew How Much I Care/Just Forget about Me (1961)
King 5527 Pardon Me/Panic (1961)
King 5558 Two Hearts [diff. version]/The Secret (1961)
King 5682 Only Young Once/When We Get Together [diff. Version] (1962)
King 5816 It'll Never Happen Again/It Just Ain't Right (1963)
King 5880 Friends Call Me a Fool/Unchain My Heart (1963)

Okeh 7225 Baby You Turn Me On/Love Don't Grow on Trees (1965)
Okeh 7235 I Fall to Pieces/Gotta Get Myself Together (1965)
Okeh 7248 Welcome Home/I Got Loving (1966)
Okeh 7261 Ain't Gonna Walk Your Dog No More/Your Sweet Love (1966)

Tiny Tops and the Charms
Federal 12309 Ring around My Finger/Come Oh, Come Oh, Come Oh (1957)

Charms
Chart 608 Love, Love Stick Stov [sic]/Love's Our Inspiration (1955)
Chart 613 Heart of a Rose/I Offer You (1956)
Chart 623 I'll Be There/Boom Diddy Boom Boom (1956)
Source: Ronnie Italiano and Pete Grendysa in *Goldmine.*

Charts (New York)

Personnel Joe Grier (lead), Steven Brown (d) (1st tenor), Glenmore Jackson (2d tenor), Leroy Binns (baritone), Ross Buford (bass)

Notes

The Charts began in 1956 on 115th Street in Harlem as an octet, the Thrilltones, reducing themselves to five members later that year. They practiced on Harlem street corners and building hallways until they were ready for the Apollo's Amateur Night.

Their unique style yielded a hostile crowd at the Apollo, who booed them off-stage. Les Cooper of the Whirlers and the Empires on Whirlin' Disc, as well as the Prestos on Mercury, were there that evening. Seeing something different, Apollo management asked the teenaged group to be taken to their manager. The group was immediately taken to Danny Robinson (Bobby Robinson's brother) of Holiday and Everlast Records to record.

"Deserie" was released in 1957 and received tremendous airplay. Since then, it has become an R&B classic on the East Coast. The song's writer, lead Joe Grier, sold off the royalties to "Deserie" to famous vocal group photographer James Kreigsman. "Deserie's" flip, the up-tempo "Zoop," also began to add to the disc's sales.

While each one of their follow-ups matched "Deserie" and "Zoop" in their unique styling, none of them did as well as their first recording. After their last Everlast disc, "My Diane," showed nothing at the cash registers, Grier joined the service late in 1958 and the Charts disbanded.

In 1966, a re-formed Charts attempted to rejuvenate "Deserie" on the Wand label. Binns and Brown were now joined by Frankie Harris and Tony Pierce.

Binns and Brown later became bass and 1st tenor for the Cadillacs. Binns sang with Cornel Gunter's Coasters and the Dell Vikings. Brown sang with Cleveland Still's Dubs.

Raymond Binns, Leroy's brother, joined later as tenor, as did John Bruce.

Discography

Everlast 5001 Deserie/Zoop (1957)
Everlast 5002 Dance Girl/Why Do You Cry? (1957)

Everlast 5006 You're the Reason/I've Been Wondering (1957)
Everlast 5008 All Because of Love/I Told You So (1957)
Everlast 5010 My Diane/Baby Be Mine (1957)
Guyden 2021 For the Birds/Ooba Gooba (1959)
Wand 1112 Desiree/Fell in Love with You Baby (1966)
Wand 1124 Living the Night Life/Nobody Made You Love Me (1966)
Sources: Marv Goldberg in *Record Collector's Monthly* 52; Marcia Vance in *Bim Bam Boom* 3.

Chateaus (Newport News, Va.)

Personnel Edwin Hall (lead), George Winfield (1st tenor), Oliver Sidney (2d tenor), Leroy Jones (falsetto), Theodore Jones (bass)

Notes

Formed in 1952 when the members were in their late teens, the Chateaus played local theaters and club dates in the same area in which the Five Keys originated.

After coming to New York in 1956, the Chateaus met Leroy Kirkland, who was individually responsible for their recording sessions at both Epic and Warner Bros.

After their first recording, "Darling Je Vous Aime Beaucoup," they did not record again for three years, when they finally recorded for Warner Bros. This experience too met with little success.

Hall sang lead on all Warner Bros. recordings, replacing Sidney on Epic.

After ten years together, they drifted apart.

Rudy West, in his attempt to re-form the Five Keys in 1973, called on the Chateaus-less Leroy Jones to be the new Five Keys.

George Winfield was Willie Winfield's cousin.

Discography

Epic 9193 Darling Je Vous Aime Beaucoup (OS)/Let Me Tell You Baby (LJ) (1956)
Warner Bros 5023 Satisfied/Brown Eyes (1958)
Warner Bros 5043 The Masquerade Is Over (EH)/If I Didn't Care (EH) (1959)
Warner Bros 5071 Ladder of Love (EH)/You'll Reap What You Sow (EH) (1959)
Source: Marv Goldberg and Mike Redmond in *Yesterday's Memories* 8.

Chavelles (Los Angeles)

Personnel Billy Spicer (Billy Storm) (1st tenor), Sheridan Rip Spencer (2d tenor), Brice Coefield (baritone), Walter Carter (bass)

Notes

Coefield also appeared with Storm in the Valiants, Untouchables, and Alley Cats. The Chavelles are, man for man, the Cal-West Sabers. Gary Pipkin and Chester Pipkin were also members of the Chavelles.

Discography

Vita 127 Valley of Love/Red Tape (1956)
Source: Marv Goldberg in *DISCoveries.* Article on the Valiants.

Checkers (New York)

Personnel John Carnegie (d) (lead), Charlie White (d) (lead), Joe ——— (baritone), Bill Brown (d) (bass)

Notes

Bill Brown formed the Checkers in 1951 after leaving the Dominoes. Another original member was Charlie White, later of the Clovers. It has recently been learned that tenor John Carnegie and one other performer, known simply as Joe, made up the balance of the original group.

According to Michel Ruppli's King-Federal-DeLuxe label logs, the Checkers' first two sessions only show Charlie White and Bill Brown. It wasn't until the September 26, 1953 session in New York that David Baughan's name is shown. At that session, four songs were recorded: "A Friend in Need" (never issued), "You Never Had It So Good" (King 4673), "White Cliffs of Dover" (King 4675), and "I Promise You" (King 4673).

Perry Hayward, of the Sparrows on Jay Dee and the Performers on Tip Top, recorded with the Checkers on King 4626 (Ghost of My Baby/I Wanna Know). Hayward was filling in for Carnegie, who had been drafted. This was Hayward's only session with the Checkers. David Martin, also of the Sparrows, filled in on King 4751 Mama's Daughter/I Wasn't Thinking, I Was Drinking and on King 4764 Can't Find My Sadie/Trying to Hold My Girl.

"Little" David Baughan came to the group just after Hayward's one recording. He joined the group on King 4673. He was also a member of the Harps. He sang lead for the Drifters on one session. He also sang with the Harmony Grits and the Original Drifters.

Later members included lead Eddie Harris (later of the DeLuxe Blue Dots) and James Williams. Harris replaced David Baughan.

Discography

King 4558 Flame in My Heart/Oh, Oh, Oh Baby (1952)
King 4581 Night's Curtains/Let Me Come Back (1952)
King 4596 Love Wasn't There/My Prayer Tonight (1953)
King 4626 Ghost of My Baby/I Wanna Know (1953)
King 4673 You Never Had It So Good/I Promise You (1954)
King 4675 Without a Song/White Cliffs of Dover (1954)
King 4710 House with No Windows/Don't Stop Dan (1954)
King 4719 You've Been Fooling Around/Over the Rainbow (1954)
King 4751 Mama's Daughter/Wasn't Thinking, Was Drinking (EH/BB) (1954)
King 4764 Can't Find My Sadie (EH)/Trying to Hold My Girl (EH/BB) (1955)
King 5156 Heaven Only Knows/Nine More Miles (1958)
Federal 12375 White Cliffs of Dover/Let Me Come Back (1959)
Sources: Perry Hayward, interview by Marv Goldberg in *DISCoveries,* August 1997; Ron James, interview by Marv Goldberg, 1996; Michel Ruppli, *The King Labels.*

Cherokees (Philadelphia)

Personnel Russell Carter (lead), Melvin Story, Karl English (1st tenor), George Pounds (bass)

Notes

The Cherokees got together in 1949–1950. They were trained vocalists who were also able to dance, read music, and perform comedy. They did not do the corner singing that most other groups did—their parents would not permit it.

They made several chaperoned appearances at local Philadelphia nightspots in 1949 through 1952.

In 1954 they won a Philadelphia talent contest over every other amateur group in town. They won with what is now known as "Please Tell Her So." The prize was a recording contract with Grand Records. And record they did!

Tenor Thomas Lee joined the Cherokees on Grand 109.

Following Story's draft notification and their second release on Grand, the remaining four Cherokees enlisted in the army in 1954. In 1964 Billy Taylor was recording for Swan Records in Philadelphia. Needing a backup group, he found English, Story, Thomas Lee, and Pete Kevin, a bass. They recorded "La La" for Swan as the Cobras.

Discography

Grand 106 Rainbow of Love (RC)/I Had a Thrill (1954)
Grand 109 Please Tell Me So/Remember When (1954)
Lost Nite 321 Rainbow of Love/I Had a Thrill (1961)
Lost Nite 325 Please Tell Me So/Remember When (1961)
Lost Nite 379 Brenda/By the Candlelight (1963)
Sources: Liner notes with Relic *Grand Records* CD; Bob Bosco in *Echoes of the Past* 32.

Cherokees (New Haven, Conn.)

Personnel Fred Parris, Marshall Lassiter, Bobby Bowden, Count Hopkins, Dickie Arnold

Notes

Fred Parris of the Five Satins produced these recordings and sang in the background on them as well. This is not the "Rainbow of Love" Cherokees group who recorded for Grand.

Discography

United Artists 367 My Heavenly Angel/Bed Bug (1961)
Source: Bob Galgano, Tom Luciani, Marcia Vance, and Steve Flam in *Bim Bam Boom* 1, 3.

Chessmen (Washington, D.C.)

Personnel Alan Johnson (lead), Willie Hardman (1st tenor), Robert Brown (2d tenor), Cecil Gentry (bass)

Notes

This group was formed in 1960. The PAC (Potomac Arts Corporation) label released its only record, I Believe/Lola.

When one group member's obligations to his family made him unable to travel, the group split.

Discography

PAC 100 I Believe/Lola (1960)
Source: Alan Lee in *Yesterday's Memories* 8.

Chesters (Brooklyn, N.Y.)

Personnel Anthony Gourdine (lead), Tracy Lord (1st tenor), Ernest Wright Jr. (2d tenor), Clarence Collins (baritone), Glouster Nat Rogers (bass)

Notes

Following the failure of the Duponts vocal group on Winley and Royal Roost, lead singer Gourdine began looking for another group to sing with. He met the Chesters, and it was a perfect fit.

At a party in Jamaica, Queens, the group was introduced to a member of the Cellos, who had "Rang Tang Ding Dong" on the charts at the time. He got them an audition with Charles Mehrenstein at Apollo. At the audition they sang several of Anthony's original tunes, which were eventually recorded. They officially became the Chesters at this time. Before going to Apollo, the group tried to hook up with Richard Barrett at End Records (the label Anthony would eventually sing for), but Barrett was terribly busy with the Chantels, Isley Brothers, and Frankie Lymon and the Teenagers.

The Chesters recorded for Apollo, but poor promotion and financial difficulties did not allow their disc to succeed, and they called it quits.

Baritone Keith Williams, Collins's predecessor, also recorded with the Highway QCs, as did Collins. Williams left as rehearsals and so on were interfering with his schoolwork.

The liner notes accompanying Relic's *Apollo-4* CD state that Keith Williams was the baritone for the group and omit Clarence Collins.

Discography

Apollo 521 The Fires Burn No More/Lift Up Your Head (1957)
Sources: S. Flam, R. Newman, and J. Apugliese in *Bim Bam Boom* 9; Steve Kolanjian, liner notes with Rhino CD *Best of Little Anthony & the Imperials.*

Chestnuts (New Haven, Conn.)

Personnel Ruby Whittaker (d) (lead), Lyman Hopkins Jr. (1st tenor), Lyman Hopkins Sr. (2d tenor), Frank Hopkins (baritone), Reuben White, Jimmy Curtis (bass)

Notes

The Chestnuts, under contract with Joe Davis's Davis label, were told by Davis that the group needed something unique to set them apart from other vocal groups. Reuben White, who knew Ruby Whittaker, contacted her and she ultimately became their lead singer.

Whittaker, following a modicum of recording and performing success, was driven to alcohol and died in the late 1960s of a heart attack at the age of twenty-nine.

Jimmy Curtis also sang with Connecticut's Five Satins and the Four Haven Knights. Lymon and Frank Hopkins were brothers. On the Chestnuts' recording session log Jimmy Curtis does not appear. Lymon Hopkins Sr. does.

After Curtis and Whittaker departed from the group, a third Hopkins brother, Arthur, was added, as was Bill Baker (d. 1994).

On the Elgin recordings as the Five Chestnuts, Bill Baker sang lead and Sonny Washburn performed tenor duties.

Discography

Davis 447 Love Is True/It's You I Love (1956)
Davis 452 Forever I Vow/Brother Ben (1956)
Standord 100 Who Knows Better Than I?/Mary, Hear Those Love Bells? (1957)
Eldorado 511 I Feel So Blue/Who Knows Better Than I? (1957)
Elgin 007/008 Won't You Tell My Heart?/Tell Me Little Darling (1959)
Elgin 013/014 Wonderful Girl/Chit Chat (1959)
Source: Bob Galgano and Tom Luciani in *Bim Bam Boom* 2.

Chi-Lites (Chicago)

Personnel Marshall Thompson, Eugene Gino Record (1st tenor), Robert "Squirrel" Lester (2d tenor), Clarence Johnson (baritone), Creadel Jones (bass)

Notes

The Chi-Lites formed in 1960, with Johnson and Lester coming from the Chanteurs.

The Chi-Lites originally called themselves the Hi-Lites and cut one record for Mercury in 1963. But another group was already calling themselves the Hi-Lites, so they simply added a C to Hi-Lites and changed their name to Chi-Lites.

The group signed with Blue Rock Records in 1965, but none of their output for the label did anything. Their big move was with Revue and then to Brunswick in 1969; from there on, they had a series of pop hits lasting well into the 1970s.

In Lou Rallo's article in *DISCoveries,* November 1997, he documents an interview he had with Sollie McElroy before his passing during which McElroy referred to the Chanteurs as the Chi-Lites. After releasing one record with the Chanteurs, they left McElroy to form the Chi-Lites.

Discography

Blue Rock 4007 I'm So Jealous/The Mix Mix Song (1965)
Blue Rock 4020 Ain't You Glad/The Monkey (1965)
Blue Rock 4037 Never No More/Beach Party (1965)
Revue 11005 Love Is Gone/Love Me (1967)
Revue 11018 My Baby Loves Me/That's My Baby for You (1968)
Brunswick 55398 Give It Away/What Do I Wish For (1969)
Brunswick 55414 Let Me Be the Man My Daddy Was/The Twelfth of Never (1969)
Brunswick 55422 To Change My Love/I'm Gonna Make You Love Me (1969)
Brunswick 55426 Twenty-four Hours of Sadness/You're No Longer Part of My Heart (1970)
Brunswick 55438 I Like Your Lovin'/You're No Longer Part of My Heart (1970)
Brunswick 55442 Are You My Woman?/Trouble's A-Comin' (1970)
O'Retta 888 I Won't Care about You/You Did That to Me (1970)
Brunswick 55450 Trouble's A-Comin'/Give More Power to the People (1971)
Brunswick 55455 We Are Neighbors/What Do I Wish For (1971)
Brunswick 55458 I Want to Pay You Back/Love Uprising (1971)
Brunswick 55462 Have You Seen Her/Yes I'm Ready (1971)
Brunswick 55471 Oh Girl/Being in Love (1972)
Brunswick 55478 The Coldest Days of My Life, Part 1; Part 2 (1972)
Brunswick 55483 A Lonely Man/The Man and the Woman (1972)
Brunswick 55489 We Need Order/Living in the Footsteps of Another Man (1972)
Brunswick 55491 A Letter to Myself/Sally (1973)
Brunswick 55496 My Heart Keeps on Breakin'/Just Two Teenage Kids (1973)
Brunswick 55500 Stoned Out of My Mind/Someone Else's Arms (1973)
Brunswick 55503 I Found Sunshine/Marriage License (1973)
Brunswick 55505 Homely Girl/I Never Had it So Good (1973)
Brunswick 55512 There Will Never Be Any Peace/Too Good to Be Forgotten (1974)
Brunswick 55514 You Got to Be the One/Happiness Is Your Middle Name (1974)
Brunswick 55515 Toby/That's How Long (1974)
Brunswick 55520 It's Time for Love/Here I Am (1975)
Brunswick 55525 The Devil Is Doing His Work/I'm Not a Gambler (1975)
Brunswick 55528 You Don't Have to Go (instrumental) (1976)
Mercury 73844 Happy Being Lonely (1976)
Mercury 73886 Vanishing Love/I Turn Away (1976)
Sources: Jay Warner, *American Singing Groups*; Lou Rallo in *DISCoveries,* November 1997.

Chimes (Los Angeles)

Personnel Cornelius Gunter (lead), Beverly Thompson (1st tenor), Thomas Pete Fox (2d tenor), Obediah Young Jessie (baritone), Richard Berry (bass)

Notes

The Chimes also performed as the Five Hearts, Five Hollywood Bluejays, Flairs, Hollywood Bluejays, Rams, and Whips. For the record, Beverly Thompson was a man.

Discography

Flair 1051 Love Me, Love Me, Love Me/My Heart's Crying for You (1956)
Sources: Marv Goldberg and Mike Redmond in *Record Exchanger* 13; Lynn McCutcheon in *Bim Bam Boom*; Marv Goldberg and R. Whitesell in *Yesterday's Memories*; Jim Dawson, liner notes with the Ace LP *Flair Label.*

Chimes (Los Angeles)

Personnel Horace "Pookie" Wooten (tenor), David Cobb (2d tenor), Charles Jackson (tenor), Booker Jones, Barbara McNeill (bass)

Notes

Second tenor Charles Patterson joined the group later. He also sang with the Shields, as did Wooten.
   Bill "Smokey" Robinson sang with the Chimes.

Discography

Specialty 555 Zindy Lou/Tears on My Pillow (1955)
Specialty 570 Especially/Check Yourself (w/Tony Allen) (1956)
Specialty 574 Chop Chop/Pretty Little Girl (1956)
Source: Ray Topping, liner notes with the *Dig Legendary Masters* CD.

Chimes (Knoxville, Tenn.)

Personnel Benjamin Washington (lead), James Myers (1st tenor), Herbert Myers (2d tenor), Charles Holloway (bass)

Notes

The members of this group were joined by James's brother John Myers and formed the Five Pennies.
   Earlier they were the Four Jokers.

Discography

Arrow 724 Please Call/The Letter Came This Morning (1958)
Arrow 726 Lovin' Baby/A Faded Memory (1958)
Sources: Lynn McCutcheon in *Bim Bam Boom* 3; Marv Goldberg in *Yesterday's Memories.*

Chimes (Brooklyn, N.Y.)

Personnel Lenny Coco (lead), Pat DePrisco (1st tenor), Richard Mercardo (2d tenor), Joe Croce (baritone), Pat McGuire (d) (bass)

Notes

The Chimes started singing together in 1957 on Brooklyn street corners and subway stations.

They went to a recording studio to record some demos. The recording engineer liked their work and called a Tag Records executive, and soon they were signed up with Tag.

Pat McGuire was killed in an automobile accident in 1962. Because the group members had been so close, McGuire was never replaced.

In 1963, the Chimes went to Metro Records and then to Vee Jay.

But Vee Jay was concentrating on the Beatles at that time and did not promote the Chimes. In 1965 the group broke up.

Discography

Tag 444 Once in a While/Summer Night (1960)
Tag 445 I'm in the Mood for Love/Only Love (1961)
Tag 447 Let's Fall in Love/Dream Girl (1961)
Tag 450 Paradise/My Love (1962)
Metro 1 Who's Heart Are You Breaking/Baby's Coming Home (1963)
Vee Jay 605 Two Times Two/Only Forever (1964)
Source: Drew Williamson in *Record Collector's Monthly* 40.

Chips (Brooklyn, N.Y.)

Personnel Charles "Kinrod" Johnson (lead), Theodore Black (lead), Nathaniel "Lil John" Epps (2d tenor), Shedwick Bubbie Lincoln (1st tenor), Paul Fulton (bass)

Notes

The members of this group met at the Warwick (N.Y.) State School for Boys in Goshen, New York.

Sammy Strain joined the second configuration of the Chips, replacing Black. For two years Strain was a member of the RCA Fantastics and the RCA Blue Chips ("Puddle of Tears"). In the 1960s he became a regular in Little Anthony's Imperials.

In the latter 1970s he was in California as a member of the O'Jays.

Paul Fulton joined the Poets ("She Blew a Good Thing Sue"). He also sang with the Invitations, Blue Chips, and the Velours (Cub). Kinrod had a brief stint as bass with the Platters.

Lil John sang lead with the Capitols on "Angel of Love."

Lincoln also sang with the Invitations.

Dave Eason later sang 1st tenor for the Chips.

Discography

Josie 803 Rubber Biscuit/Oh My Darling (1956)
Source: Ralph Newman and Freddie Toscano in *Yesterday's Memories* 27.

Chirps, Marvin & (New York)

Personnel Marvin Williams (lead), Ellis Johnson (bass)

Notes

Despite the fact that the Tip Top label was located in Richmond, Virginia, this group was from New York.

Discography

Tip Top 202 Sixteen Tons (EJ)/I'll Miss You This Christmas (MW) (1958)
Source: Bob Ferlingere, *A Discography of R&B and R&R Vocal Groups.*

Chorals (New York)

Personnel Irwin Williams (lead), Alfred Toddman (1st tenor), Eugene Cooke (tenor), Robert Cassidy, George Daniels

Notes

Cooke and Toddman had previously been with the Charmers on Timely.

Discography

Decca 29914 In My Dream/Rock 'n' Roll Baby (1956)
Source: Phil Groia, *They All Sang on the Corner.*

Chord-A-Roys, Bobby Roy & (Brooklyn, N.Y.)

Personnel Mike Regal (lead), Robert Walden

Notes

Robert Walden was the same Robert Walden who went on to play Rossi on the *Lou Grant* TV show.

Discography

JDS 5001 Little Girl Lost/Girls Were Made for Boys (1959)

Chords (Bronx, N.Y.)

Personnel Carl Feaster (d) (lead), Jimmy Keyes (d) (1st tenor), Floyd Buddy McRae (2d tenor), Claude Feaster (baritone), William "Ricky" Edwards (bass)

Notes

The three Morris High School groups, the Tunetoppers, included the Feaster brothers, Buddy McRae's Keynotes and Jimmy Keyes' Four Notes. They all joined Ricky Edwards, who came from a group called the Chords. These groups were all performing "Sh Boom." The four groups merged, first as the Keynotes and then as the Chords. This was 1951.

They were eventually brought to Bobby Robinson's Red Robin Records for an audition, but Robinson turned them away. They then went to Atlantic who liked them and had them record for their Cat subsidiary in 1954.

Because of the "In the Woods" Chords on Gem, the Cat group was forced to change their name first to the Chord Cats and then to the Sh Booms. Ultimately they recorded "More, More, More" by Lionel Thorpe on Roulette.

When the group left the Atlantic conglomerate, McRae was replaced by Arthur Dix (Popular 5) and Ricky by Joe Ditto Dias (who was an on-and-off member). Dias had already been a member of the Crickets with Dean Barlow and the Bachelors.

Keyes, in 1963, formed the Popular Five on Rae Cox, along with Arthur Dix. Keyes was also involved with the Five Chimes.

Bobby Spencer recorded with one of the Chords groups when Claude Feaster went into the army.

Discography

Cat 104 Sh Boom (CF)/Cross over the Bridge (CF) (1954)
Cat 104 Sh Boom (CF)/Little Maiden (CF) [Re-pressed June 1954] 1954
Cat 109 Zippity Zum (CF)/Bless You (CF) (1954)
Cat 112 A Girl to Love (CF)/Hold Me Baby (CF) [Chordcats] (1955)
Cat 117 Could It Be? (CF)/Pretty Wild (CF) [Sh Booms] (1955)
Vik 0295 Lulu (CF)/I Don't Want to Set the World . . . (JD) [Sh-Booms] (1957)
Roulette 4144 More, More, More/Lover, Lover, Lover (1960)
Atlantic 2074 Blue Moon (CF)/Short Skirts (CF/WE) [Sh Booms] (1961)
Atco 6213 Sh Boom (CF)/Little Maiden (CF) [Reissue] (1961)
Sources: Jimmy Keyes, interview by the author, April 23, 1994; Sal Mondrone, interview, July 6, 1996; Marv Goldberg and Mike Redmond in *Yesterday's Memories* 7.

Chryslers, Little Nate & (Brooklyn, N.Y.)

Personnel Nate Bouknight (lead), Kirk Harris, Jay McKnight

Notes

Nate Bouknight had formerly been the lead singer for the Shells on Johnson. The disc below was produced after the Shells had parted and Bouknight and Harris joined McKnight and one other singer to record as Little Nate and the Chryslers. Harris sang with the Dubs, replacing Cleveland Stills.

Discography

Johnson 318 Cry Baby Cry/Someone Up There (1959)
Source: Donn Fileti, liner notes with the Relic CD *Best of Johnson Records.*

Claremonts (Bronx, N.Y.)

Personnel Diana Sanchez (lead), Sylvia Sanchez, Josephine Josie Allen

Notes

When Apollo chief Charles Merenstein (Bess Berman's legatee) formed the Doe label, he brought the Claremonts with him and renamed them the Tonettes. The girls' adopted cousin was Vince Castro, who did "Bong Bong," on which they backed up Castro.

On "Oh What a Baby," as the Tonettes, Josephine sang lead.

Discography

Apollo 517 Why Keep Me Dreaming/Angel of Romance (1957)

Apollo 751 Why Keep Me Dreaming/Angel of Romance (1963)
Source: Donn Fileti, liner notes with Relic CD/LP *Apollo.*

Classics (Los Angeles)

Personnel W. Stevenson, J. Marls, E. Gabrie

Notes

Dale Fitzimmons and Mitchell Tableporter joined the group on Crest.

At Class Records, little is remembered about this group, whose Class disc was released during the winter of 1958.

Discography

Class 219 If Only the Sky Was a Mirror/Gosh But This Is Love (1957)
Crest 1063 Let Me Dream/You're the Prettiest One (1959)
Source: Donn Fileti, liner notes with the Class LP *Best of Class Records.*

Classics (Brooklyn, N.Y.)

Personnel Emil Stuccio (lead), Tony Victor (1st tenor), John Gambale (2d tenor), Jamie Troy (bass)

Notes

The members of this group grew up as friends and lived on the same Brooklyn street. They started singing in 1958, beginning as the Perrenials. The harmony sounded good to them, and a group logically formed.

While playing at a Brooklyn nightspot, they were introduced by the emcee as the Perrenials. The emcee played with the name, suggesting that their name be changed to something he could pronounce, hence the Classics.

They were good friends of the Passions, who, with their manager, helped them get an audition; the Classics got the session. Their "Cinderella" did well locally but was not a national hit. "Till Then" sold fairly well, but their follow-ups didn't do anything. British music was invading the music scene, and this basically marked the end for the group. They never recorded again but remained together for appearances.

Discography

Dart 1015 So in Love/Cinderella (1960)
Dart 1032 Angel Angela/Eenie, Meenie, Meinee, and Mo (1961)
Dart 1038 Life Is But a Dream/That's the Way (1961)
Mercury 71829 Life Is But a Dream Sweetheart/That's the Way (1961)
Musicnote 118 P.S. I Love You/Wrap Your Troubles in Dreams (1962)
Musicnote 1116 Till Then/Enie, Minie, Mo (1963)
Streamline 1028 Life's But a Dream/Nuttin' in the Noggin (1964)
Bed-Stuy 222 Again/The Way You Look Tonight (1964)
Source: Steve Flam in *Bim Bam Boom* 6.

Cleartones (Raleigh, N.C.)

Personnel Thermon Ruth, Allen Bunn, Jimmy Gorman, Melvin Coldten, Junius Parker

Notes

The personnel listed above originally recorded gospel songs as the Selah Jubilee Singers. Upon realizing there was little money to be made singing religious music, Ruth and Bunn left the Selahs and went to New York City, having formed another vocal group, and began looking for a record company interested in their ability to record secular music. This new group consisted of Bunn, Ruth, and some of Bunn's North Carolina friends, David McNeil, Haddie Rowe Jr., and Raymond "Pee Wee Barnes." Ruth's friend Eugene Mumford, recently released from prison, also joined this group of singers.

The singers eventually formed the Apollo Larks. Before recording as the Larks, however, they cut gospel and secular tunes as the Southern Harmonaires, the Cleartones, the Sons of Zion, the Four Sons and the Four Barons to earn some quick cash. Four of these miscellaneous recordings were done on the same day!

Discography

Signature 15242 Am I Asking Too Much (1949)
Source: Jeff Beckman, *Big Town Review* 3.

Clefftones (Queens, N.Y.)

Personnel Cas Bridges (lead), Robert Adams, Al Jackson, Cliff Driver (pianist), Herschel Guerrant (pianist)

Notes

Bridges came from the Four Fellows on Triboro and the Victorians on Saxony. He supposedly dropped out of the Four Fellows for personal reasons. He had been with them for about eighteen months.

Pianist Herschel Guerrant was blind.

This group had nothing to do with the Cleftones on Gee.

Discography

Old Town 1011 My Dearest Darling/The Masquerade Is Over (1955)
Sources: Liner notes with *Old Town Doo Wop-2* CD; Sal Mondrone, "Rare Sounds," *Bim Bam Boom.*

Clefs (Arlington, Va.)

Personnel Scotty Mansfield (lead), Pavel Bess (1st tenor), Frankie Newman (2d tenor), Fred Council (baritone), Leroy Flack (bass)

Notes

The Clefs was formed in 1951 by high school students emulating the popular groups of the day. They made appearances locally for about a year.

In 1952 they recorded demos and got them to Lillian Claiborne, who wound up managing the group and got them to Chess Records in Chicago. In a 1972 interview, Mansfield does not think well of Claiborne and feels that she managed them poorly.

Although "We Three" by the Clefs was never a hit, it got them bookings for two years.

In the same interview referred to above, Mansfield insisted that they recorded another tune for Chess entitled "Sorry," but it was never released. Claiborne told the group that Chess wasn't interested. Several years after Claiborne made this statement, Phil Chess claimed he never received anything else from or by the Clefs!

James Sheppard (not from the Heartbeats or Shep & the Limelights) was a utility member at baritone and 2d tenor. Gerald Bullock was a bass who filled in later.

After moving to Peacock Records from Chess and finding little success, the group decided it was time for a name change. They became Scotty Mann and the Masters.

At Peacock the group recorded under two different names but found little success. Finally they decided to call it quits.

Discography

Chess 1521 We Three (SM)/Ride On (SM) (1952)
Peacock 1643 I'll Be Waiting (SM)/Please Don't Leave Me (PB) (1955)
Peacock 1665 The Mystery Man (PB)/Just a Little Bit Of Loving (FC) (1955; as Scotty Mann & the Masters)
Source: Marv Goldberg in *Yesterday's Memories* 4.

Cleftones (Queens, N.Y.)

Personnel Herbie Cox (lead), Charlie James (1st tenor), Berman Patterson (2d tenor), William "Buzzy" McLain (baritone), Warren Corbin (d) (bass)

Notes

Cox moved to New York from Cincinnati in 1947. In 1952 he was in Queens in the eighth grade where he met Warren Corbin and became good friends. The two shared the same dream of forming a vocal group. This took a while to come to fruition, as they were particular about the sound they were trying to reach. When they finally got the right foursome in place, they began to practice, calling themselves the Clefs. They were in the eleventh grade in Jamaica High School in Queens.

Herb Cox, Warren Corbin, Charlie James, and Buzzy McClain continued with their harmonizing, next calling themselves the Silvertones. McClain got his friend Berman Patterson to become the fifth member.

When they began their senior year at Jamaica High School, they became the Cleftones. At this time they became more serious about their singing.

When they felt ready, the group began seeking out a label that would give them a chance to record. They first visited Bobby Robinson, who told them to come back when they had more material. Next they went to Hull, Old Town, Baton, and Apollo. These auditions also went nowhere. Finally they went to George Goldner's Rama/ Tico offices on the west side of Manhattan.

The audition with Goldner was better received. Goldner liked them and their tunes and gave them a contract for them and their parents to sign. He also asked them to return the following week to record! In an interview, Cox stated that the recording session was the picture of disorganization. Vocal groups would line up outside the studio waiting for their turn to record. On any given evening, there might have been four to five groups waiting for their time inside. However, Cox also went on to say that Goldner was very helpful and encouraging to the Cleftones at the start.

The first lineup of singers (above) recorded all their tunes from 1955 until 1959. In 1959, Gene Pearson, formerly with another Queens group, the Rivileers, replaced departing McClain. Pearson remained with the Cleftones through 1963. Another addition was Pearson's friend Patricia Spann. Pat became the first and only female member of the Cleftones.

Over the years, Cox's cousin Tony Gaines and Cox's friend Nick Saunders were other additions.

The Clefftones on Old Town was a different group.

Discography
Gee 1000 You Baby You/I Was Dreaming (1955)
Gee 1011 Little Girl of Mine/You're Driving Me Mad (1956)
Gee 1016 Can't We Be Sweethearts?/Neki-Hokey (1956)
Gee 1025 String Around My Heart/Happy Memories (1956)
Gee 1031 Why You Do Me Like You Do/I Like Your Style of Making Love (1957)
Gee 1038 See You Next Year/Ten Pairs of Shoes (1957)
Gee 1041 Hey Babe/What Did I Do That Was Wrong? (1957)
Gee 1048 Lover Boy/Beginners at Love (1957)
Roulette 4094 Trudy/She's So Fine (1958)
Roulette 4161 Mish Mash Baby/Cuzin' Casanova (1959)
Roulette 4302 Shadows on the Very Last Row/She's Gone (1960)
Gee 1064 Heart and Soul/How Do You Feel? (1961)
Gee 1067 For Sentimental Reasons/Deed I Do (1961)
Gee 1074 Blues in the Night/Earth Angel (1961)
Gee 1077 Again/Do You (1962)
Gee 1079 There She Goes/Lover Come Back to Me (1962)
Gee 1080 Some Kind of Blue/How Deep Is the Ocean? (1962)
Ware 6001 He's Forgotten You/Right from the Git Go (1964)
Sources: Herbie Cox, interview by S. West in *Goldmine*, February 1992; interview, Herbie Cox, interview by author, April 23, 1994; liner notes with the Rhino CD *Best of the Cleftones.*

Clickettes/Click-Ettes/Clicketts (New York)

Personnel Barbara English (lead), Trudy McCartney, Charlotte McCartney, Sylvia Hammond

Notes

The Dice label, located on Tiffany Street in east Bronx, was owned by Johnnie Richardson and her mom, Zell Sanders, and was affiliated with the J&S and Scatt labels. Galen Gart reports that Dice 96 was released in 1959 and the group itself began in 1958.

The Teen Clefs on Dice included one singer (Shirley) who periodically filled in for the Click-Ettes and is shown in the photograph of that group. The Click-Ettes therefore was a quartet.

The personnel on Guyden included Barbara English, Jean Bolden, Sylvia Hammond, and Barbara Saunders. Other later members included Helen Powell Leibowitz, who later sang with the Chantels.

During an interview by the author, Barbara English and Trudy McCartney (on June 29, 1996) listened to the Click-Ettes' tune on Checker and stated that this was the Hearts. They also relate that the Avalons on Dice were most of the Click-Ettes and an unremembered guy.

Group members also related that the Rinky Dinks, who performed backup for Bobby Darin at Atco, were the Click-Ettes!

Discography

Dice 83/84 A Teenager's First Love/Jive-Time Turkey (1958)
Dice 92/93 To Be a Part of You/Because of My Best Friend (1958)
Dice 94/95 Why Oh Why/Warm, Soft and Lovely (1959)
Dice 96/97 Lover's Prayer/Grateful (1959)
Dice 100 But Not for Me/I Love You I Swear (1960)
Guyden 2043 Where Is He?/The Lone Lover (1960)
Sources: Barbara English and Trudy McCartney, interview by author, June 29, 1996; John Clemente, liner notes with the Jamie/Guyden CD *Doop Doo Wah.*

Clientelles (Upper Darby, Pa.)

Personnel Jimmy Dilks (lead), Tommy Pyne (1st tenor), Chuck Frederico (2d tenor), Jack Shingle (baritone), Mike Orlando (bass)

Notes

The Clientelles formed in Upper Darby, Pennsylvania, in 1960. Group members changed frequently. Once they were in place, the members shown above became dedicated and practiced religiously for three years at the home of their manager, who eventually took them to a club in North Philadelphia where they were quite successful. The club, however, had different intentions.

Without their manager present, group members and their parents met with one of the owners of this club who asked that each member contribute $100 to help launch their musical career. The group's manager was never aware of this and soon brought them to a studio to cut some demos. He paid $500 for their time and an additional $500 to a record pressing plant for the discs. The only thing he received was some 500 to 1,000 records pressed on the mysterious M.B.S. Records label. Although several other records are known to exist on the M.B.S. label, the situation with the Clientelles remains cloudy.

The Clientelles did many local shows to support their disc, but nothing positive was ever realized; there was no promotion, support, or airplay. By 1962, the Clientelles' entertainment career was finished.

Discography

M.B.S. 107 Church Bells May Ring/My Love (1960)
Source: Bob Bosco in *Record Collector's Monthly* 51.

Climbers (New York)

Personnel Joe Rivers (lead), Melvin Lewis (baritone)

Notes

Lewis was also a later member of the Jesters.
    Joe Rivers was the Joe of Johnny and Joe who recorded for Chess.

Discography

J&S 1652 My Darling Dear/Angels in Heaven Know I Love You (1957)
J&S 1658 I Love You/Trains, Cars & Boats (1957)
Source: Donn Fileti, liner notes with the Relic CD *Winley.*

Clippers, Johnny Blake & (New York)

Personnel Johnny Blake (lead), Leon Briggs, Donald Razor (2d tenor)

Notes

Briggs also sang with the Velvets and Carl Hogan and the Miracles on Fury. Razor recorded with the Valentines and the Velvets.

Discography

Gee 1027 Bella Marie/I'm Yours (1957)
Source: Phil Groia, *They All Sang on the Corner.*

Clips (Nashville, Tenn.)

Personnel Bill Hall (lead), Byron Smith, Curtis Smith, Denver Larkin

Notes

Bill Hall's brother was Ed Hall, the Nashville disc jockey who is considered by many to be a pioneer of black radio in Nashville.
    Bill Hall went on to sing and record with the Sonics on Chess.

Discography

Republic 7102 Wish I Didn't Love You So/Your Lovin' Moves Me (1954)
Calvert 105 Let Me Get Close to You, Baby/Kiss Away (1956)
Source: Daniel Cooper, liner notes with the Ace CD *Across the Tracks-2.*

Cliques (Los Angeles)

Personnel Jesse Belvin (lead) (d), Eugene Church (lead) (d)

Notes

It was originally rumored that Belvin alone was the Cliques, but it has since been learned that Eugene Church joined Belvin to form the Cliques on Modern Records.

Discography

Modern 987 The Girl in My Dreams/I Wanna Know Why (1956)
Modern 995 I'm in Love with a Girl/My Desire (1956)
Source: Ted Carroll, Ray Topping, and Jim Dawson, liner notes with the Ace CD *The Fifties.*

Clouds (Chicago)

Personnel Sherrard Jones (lead), Al Butler, William English, Bobby Walker, Albert Hunter (Parrot only)

Notes

Hunter went to the Maples from the Clouds.

In 1979 a bootleg LP, *Parrot Doo Wop,* contained, for the first time anywhere, their "Say You Love Me." Later this song was included on a Relic LP.

In 1956, the Clouds cut a record with Cobra: Rock and Roll Boogie/I Do.

Discography

Cobra 5001 I Do/Rock and Roll Boogie (1956)
Source: Bob Pruter, *Doowop . . . The Chicago Scene.*

Clovers (Washington, D.C.)

Personnel John Buddy Bailey (d) (lead), Matthew McQuater (2d tenor), Harold Lucas (d) (baritone), Harold Winley (bass)

Notes

The Clovers formed in 1946 as a trio in a Washington, D.C., high school. In 1948, baritone Harold Lucas and neighborhood friend Matthew McQuater joined Buddy Bailey, the only remaining member of the original trio. They soon met bass Harold Lucas at an amateur show in the D.C. area and the Clovers were born!

They initially sang pop tunes at area clubs and in 1950 were discovered by their eventual manager, Lou Krefetz, who got the group an audition with Rainbow Records in New York. This resulted in their first recording, Yes Sir, That's My Baby/When You Come Back to Me. Because Rainbow showed little support and or promotion for their disc, they left Rainbow for Atlantic three months later.

In 1952, Buddy Bailey was drafted and was initially replaced by John Philip, who didn't fit in and only lasted until the beginning of 1953, when he was replaced by

Charlie White (d) of the Dominoes and Checkers. White began recording with the Clovers on March 4, 1953, and is first heard on the group's "Good Lovin'." Due to personal problems at home (which the Clovers would not tolerate), White had to leave in November 1953. In 1955 he formed the Playboys, who were the Cues who recorded for the Atlantic subsidiary label CAT. Charlie White was replaced by Billy Mitchell, whose first record with the Clovers "Your Cash Ain't Nothin' but Trash." When Bailey was discharged from the service, Mitchell stayed on and the two alternated at lead for the first-time quintet!

The Clovers enjoyed much success with their beautiful Atlantic ballads and their catchy up-tempo tunes. But in 1956, after "Love, Love, Love," they hit a dry spell. In 1957, manager Lou Krefetz started his own Poplar label and in May 1958 the Clovers joined him at Poplar, whose catalog was purchased by United Artists.

Krefetz arranged to be made UA's national sales manager, but the Clovers' popularity continued to fade and they ultimately returned to Atlantic for one session in 1961. The disc released from this session did not do well and the group began to splinter into other factions—one led by Bailey and the other by Lucas. McQuater left the entertainment business and became a Dallas businessman. Bailey and Winley got day jobs and the two groups recorded simultaneously into the 1970s but with no regularity. The Bailey group consisted of Bailey, Mitchell, James "Toy" Walton, and Robert Russell. This group had several releases on Winley in 1962. It was also that year that Mitchell left the Clovers and was replaced by Roosevelt "Tippie" Hubbard, who had been with the Knickerbockers and the L'Cap-Tans.

Clovers discs were released on Porwin, Port, Tiger, Brunswick, and Josie. On the Stenton label, the group was called Tippie and the Cloverman.

The Clovers group on Porwin consisted of Nate Bouknight (from the Shells), Peggy Winley Mills (Harold and Paul's sister), and Amy Winley (Paul's wife).

Later in 1963, Bailey, Lucas, and Winley reunited to form a new Clovers trio and remained together for about a year.

At the start of 1965, Harold Winley decided to call it quits and Bailey and Lucas went back to Atlantic with James Taylor and Robert Russell. The tunes they cut for Atlantic were eventually sold to Port.

In 1968, Winley came back to the Clovers with Bobby Adams at lead, Johnny Taylor, and Ray Loper of the Five Keys. This was the Josie group.

Russell died in 1969 and was replaced by John Bowie. Lucas and Bailey died in 1994. Pianist Bill Harris died of cancer in 1988.

Discography

Rainbow 11-122 Yes Sir That's My Baby/When You Come Back to Me (1950)
Atlantic 934 Don't You Know I Love You So/Skylark (1951)
Atlantic 944 Fool, Fool, Fool/Needless (1951)
Atlantic 963 One Mint Julep/Middle of the Night (1952)
Atlantic 969 Ting-A-Ling/Wonder Where My Baby's Gone? (1952)
Atlantic 977 I Played the Fool/Hey Miss Fannie (1952)
Atlantic 989 Yes It's You/Crawlin' (1953)
Atlantic 1000 Here Goes a Fool/Good Lovin' (1953)
Atlantic 1010 Comin' on/The Feeling Is So Good (1953)
Atlantic 1022 Lovey Dovey/Little Mama (CW) (1954)

Atlantic 1035 I've Got My Eyes on You/Your Cash Ain't Nothin' but Trash (1954)
Atlantic 1046 I Confess/All Rightie Oh Sweetie (1954)
Atlantic 1052 Blue Velvet/If You Love Me (1954)
Atlantic 1060 Love Bug/In the Morning Time (1955)
Atlantic 1073 Nip Sip/If I Could Be Loved by You (1955)
Atlantic 1083 Devil or Angel/Hey Doll Baby (1955)
Atlantic 1094 Love, Love, Love/Your Tender Lips (1956)
Atlantic 1107 From the Bottom of My Heart/Bring Me Love (1956)
Atlantic 1118 Baby Baby Oh My Darling/A Lonely Fool (1956)
Atlantic 1129 Here Comes Romance/You Good-Looking Woman (1957)
Atlantic 1139 I, I, Love You/So Young (1957)
Atlantic 1152 Down in the Alley/There's No Tomorrow (1957)
Atlantic 1175 Wishing for Your Love/All about You (1958)
Poplar 110 The Gossip Wheel/Please Come on to Me (1958)
Poplar 111 The Good Old Summertime/Idaho (1958)
Poplar 139 The Good Old Summertime/Idaho (1958)
United Artists 174 Old Black Magic/Rock and Roll Tango (1959)
United Artists 180 Love Potion 9/Stay Awhile (1959)
United Artists 209 One Mint Julep/Lovey (1960)
United Artists 227 Easy Lovin'/I'm Confessin' That I Love You (1960)
United Artists 263 Yes It's You/Burning Fire (1960)
United Artists 307 Have Gun/The Honeydripper (1961)
Atlantic 2129 The Bootie Green/Drive It Home (1961)
Winley 255 Wrapped Up in a Dream/Let Me Hold You (1961)
Winley 265 Be My Baby/They're Rockin' Down the Street (1961)
Porwin 1001 Stop Pretending/One More Time (1963)
Porwin 1004 It's All in the Game/That's What I Will Be (1963)
Brunswick 55249 Love, Love, Love/The Kickapoo (1963)
Tiger 201 Bossa Nova Baby/The Bossa Nova (1963)
Josie 992 Too Long without Some Loving/for Days (1968)
Josie 997 Try My Lovin' on You/Sweet Side of a Soulful Woman (1968)
Sources: Seamus McGarvey in *Juke Blues* 13; Marv Goldberg and Mike Redmond in *Record Exchanger* 15; Pete Grendysa in *Record Collector's Monthly* 35; Marv Goldberg in *DISCoveries,* October 1997.

Clowns, Huey Smith & (New Orleans)

Personnel Huey Smith (lead), Edward Ross, "Scarface" John Williams

Notes

Smith also sang with the Pitter Pats and the Hueys following his successful career in the late 1950s on Ace. His style is referred to as an example of New Orleans rhythm and blues.

Discography

Ace 530 Rockin' Pneumonia and the Boogie Woogie Flu—Pt. 1/Pt. 2 (1957)
Ace 538 Just a Lonely Clown/Free, Single, and Disengaged (1958)

Ace 545 Don't You Just Know It?/High Blood Pressure (1958)
Ace 553 Don't You Know, Yockomo/Well I'll Be John Brown (1958)
Ace 562 Genevieve/Would You Believe It? (1959)
Ace 584 Beatnick Blues/for Cryin' Out Loud (1960)
Vin 1024 I Didn't Do It/They Kept On (1960)
Imperial 5721 The Little Moron/Someone to Love (1961)
Imperial 5747 Behind the Wheel—Pt. 1/Pt. 2 (1961)
Imperial 5772 More Girls/Sassy Sara (1961)
Imperial 5789 Snag-A-Tooth Jeannie/Don't Knock It (1961)
Ace 649 Pop-Eye/Scald-Dog (1962)
Ace 8002 Talk to Me Baby/If It Ain't One Thing, It's Another (1962)
Constellation 102 He's Back Again/Quiet as It's Kept (1963)
Source: Jeff Hannusch, liner notes with the Bandy LP *Huey Piano Man Smith.*

Clusters (Brooklyn, N.Y.)

Personnel Charlie Scardina (lead), Tom Mordente (1st tenor), Donnie Milo (2d tenor), Henry Rico Ferro (baritone), Joe Gugliaro (bass)

Notes

The Clusters were formed in the Bushwick section of Brooklyn in 1957. Members were between fifteen and seventeen years of age. They were initially four background singers looking for a lead. They approached neighbor Tony Passalacqua, who said that he had just put his own group together (the Fascinators) and told them of his friend Charlie Scardina. The Clusters heard and liked him, and he became their new lead voice.

They recorded some demos and began soliciting the popular R&B record companies in New York City for an audition. They made an appointment with Bobby Robinson of Fury Records in Harlem. Robinson was shocked to see a white group and politely told them he didn't have room for them on his roster.

The group next solicited the Ivy label, who liked them and recorded them. The next thing they knew, the two sides had come out on Tee Gee, to which Ivy management leased the sides. Tee Gee was a subsidiary of Gone—a George Goldner label!

"Darling Can't You Tell" and "Pardon My Heart" had Arlene Smith in the background. The fact that the Tee Gee people (Gone) dubbed in Arlene Smith's voice was, and still is, a total mystery to the group. This disc was released during the summer of 1958 and its success meant many live appearances for the Clusters.

In 1959 Ivy brought the Clusters back to record, and those tunes were leased out to Epic. This was "Forecast of Our Love."

Following this recording, Scardina was the first to leave. The rest of the Clusters soon split up, as Ivy management did not want the group without lead Scardina.

Discography

Tee Gee 102 Darling Can't You Tell/Pardon My Heart (1958)
Epic 9330 Long-Legged Maggie/Forecast of Our Love (1959)
End 1115 Darling Can't You Tell/Pardon My Heart (1962)
Source: Bob Diskin, *Record Collector's Monthly* 47 (August-September 1990).

Coasters (Los Angeles)

Personnel Carl Gardner, Leon Hughes (tenor), Billy Guy (baritone), Bobby Nunn (bass)

Notes

In 1955, the Robins were sold to Atlantic by Lieber and Stoller. Some members chose to stay with Lieber and Stoller and some chose to leave. Lead singer Carl Gardner and bass Bobby Nunn stayed with Lieber and Stoller and added Billy Guy and Leon Hughes. They became the Coasters, named after their native West Coast.

Leon Hughes had been with the Hollywood Flames and the Lamplighters.

Richard Berry is heard on "Riot in Cell Block 11," and Will "Dub" Jones is on "Shopping for Clothes."

Other Coasters members include Obie "Young" Jessie (baritone), Leroy Binns (baritone), Cornell Gunter (tenor), Earl Carroll (tenor), Ronnie Bright (bass), Teddy Harper (tenor), Jimmy Norman Scott (tenor), Bobby Sheen (Bobb B Soxx), Bobby Steger (Cornel Gunter's group), and Nathaniel Wilson (bass).

Discography

Atco 6064 Down in Mexico/Turtle Dovin' (1956)
Atco 6073 Brazil/One Kiss Led to Another (1956)
Atco 6087 Searchin'/Young Blood (1957)
Atco 6098 Idol with the Golden Head/My Baby Comes to Me (1957)
Atco 6104 What Is the Secret of Your Success?/Sweet Georgia Brown (1957)
Atco 6111 Gee, Golly/Dance (1958)
Atco 6116 Yakkety Yak/Zing Went the Strings of My Heart (1958)
Atco 6126 The Shadow Knows/Sorry but I'm Gonna Have to Pass (1958)
Atco 6132 Charley Brown/Three Cool Cats (1959)
Atco 6141 Along Came Jones/That Is Rock & Roll (1959)
Atco 6146 Poison Ivy/I'm a Hog for You (1959)
Atco 6153 What about Us?/Run, Red, Run (1959)
Atco 6163 Besame Mucho—Pt. 1/Pt. 2 (1960)
Atco 6168 Wake Me, Shake Me/Stewball (1960)
Atco 6176 The Snake and the Book Worm/Shoppin' for Clothes (1960)
Atco 6186 Wait a Minute/Thumbin' a Ride (1961)
Atco 6192 Little Egypt/Keep on Rolling (1961)
Atco 6204 Girls, Girls, Girls—Pt. 1/Pt. 2 (1961)
Atco 6210 Just Like Me/Bad Blood (1961)
Atco 6219 Ridin' Hood/Teach Me How to Shimmy (1962)
Atco 6234 The Climb/The Climb (instrumental) (1962)
Atco 6251 The P.T.A./The Bull Tick Waltz (1963)
Atco 6287 Speedo's Back in Town/'Tain't Nothin' to Me (1964)
Atco 6300 Lovey Dovey/Bad Detective (1964)
Atco 6321 Wild One/I Must Be Dreaming (1964)
Atco 6341 Lady Like/Hungry (1965)
Atco 6356 Money Honey/Let's Go Get Stoned (1965)
Atco 6379 Crazy Baby/Bell-Bottom Slacks and a Chinese Kimono (1965)

Atco 6407 She's a Yum Yum/Saturday Night Fish Fry (1966)
Date 1552 Soul Pad/Down Home Girl (1967)
Date 1607 She Can/Everybody's Woman (1968)
Date 1617 Everybody's Woman/D. W. Washburn (1968)
Turntable 504 Act Right/The World Is Changing (1969)
King 6385 Love Potion 9/D. W. Washburn (1971)
King 6389 Cool Jerk/Talkin' 'Bout a Woman (1972)
King 6404 Soul Pad/D. W. Washburn (1973)
Sal Wa 1001 Take It Easy Greasy/You Move Me (1975)
Sources: Liner notes with the Rhino CD *Atlantic*; Phil Silverman in *Record Collector's Monthly* 25.

Cobras (Philadelphia)

Personnel Billy Taylor (lead), Karl English, Thomas Lee, Melvin Story, Pete Kevin (bass)

Notes

Delton "Satan" McCall of the Dreams on Savoy and the Orioles also sang with the Cobras.

Ricky Cordo was another member of the Cobras, and Taylor was originally with the Castelles on Grand. English, Lee, and Story were members of the original Cherokees on Grand.

Discography

Monogram 519 Thumpin'/Don't Even Know Your Name (1964)
Swan 4176 La La/Goodbye Molly (1964)
Casino 1309 La La/Goodbye Molly (1965)
Source: Bob Bosco in *Echoes of the Past.*

Cobras (Columbus, Ohio)

Personnel Otis Lee, Nate Lee, Jimmy Randell

Notes

The Dukes, who recorded for Specialty, had come to California from Columbus, Ohio, looking for fame and stardom.

When stardom never came, they all went their separate ways. Otis Lee joined the service and returned home to Ohio when his boot camp obligation was finished and joined friend Jimmy Randell and brother Nate to reactivate the Cobras group they had all been involved with.

"Sindy" by the Squires was popular at the time and Otis Lee, who had already gone to Modern Records with his new group, the Cobras, auditioned for Modern management, who asked them to cover "Sindy." It's interesting that Modern was indecisive about the spelling of the name and it was released as "Sindy" and "Cindy" on the label.

Shortly after their session with Modern, Otis Lee was permanently assigned to Bremerton, Washington, and this meant the end of the Modern Cobras.

Discography

Modern 964 Sindy (OL)/I Will Return (OL) (1955)
Source: Marv Goldberg in *DISCoveries,* July 1998.

Coleman Brothers (Montclair, N.J.)

Personnel Danny Owens (lead), Russell Coleman (1st tenor), Lander Coleman (2d tenor), Wallace Coleman (baritone), Mervin Coleman (bass)

Notes

Everett Coleman was another participating brother.

J. Eldridge replaced Mervin Coleman in the mid-1940s to run the group's business interests. Mervin passed away in 1959.

Clarence Paul, who joined later, was also with the Five Royales precursor, the Royal Sons, in the late 1940s.

Discography

Decca 8662 Low Down the Chariot/His Eye Is on the Sparrow (1944)
Manor 100 It's My Desire/The End of My Journey (1945)
Manor 101 He'll Understand/Milky White Way (1945)
Manor 102 Plenty of Room in the Kingdom/I Can See Everybody's Mother (1945)
Manor 1003 Plenty of Room in the Kingdom/I Can See Everybody's Mother (1945)
Coleman 5961 One Day/Lonesome Valley (1945)
Coleman 5964 You May Run On/My Prayer (1945)
Coleman 5985 Brother/Packing Up (1946)
Coleman 6003 Sleep on, Mother/Never Turn Back (1946)
Coleman 6004 Yes, We All Shall Meet in Heaven/Forgive Me Lord (1946)
Coleman 6018 Walls of Jericho/Dry Bones (1946)
Decca 8673 Get Away Mr. Satan, Get Away/Raise a Rukus Tonight (1946)
Decca 48041 Sending Up My Timber/Where Shall I Be? (1946)
Decca 48051 Seek/We're Living Humble (1947)
Manor 1055 Now What a Time/When the Saints Go Marching In (1947)
Manor 1065 Noah/My Eye Is on the Sparrow (1947)
Coral 65003 Low Down the Chariot/His Eye Is on the Sparrow (1949)
Arco 1208 Plenty of Room in the Kingdom/I Can See Everybody's Mother (1949)
Regal 3281 Goodnight Irene/Ooh La La (1950)
Source: Pete Grendysa in *Goldmine* 36.

Collegians (New York)

Personnel Harlan Jackson, William Tarkenton, Henry Brown, Tim Holley, James "Charlie" McKay

Notes

This group formed in the mid-1950s in the Sugar Hill section of Harlem. It is believed that the group identified above is the Winley configuration. Members of the X-Tra group were Harlan Jackson, Roger Hayes, William Tarkenton, Henry Brown, and Vernon Riley.

In 1957, Roger Hayes and James "Charlie" McKay joined the X-Tra Collegians from the Okeh Schoolboys.

Interestingly, in Paul Winley's liner notes with the Winley LP *Sing Along with the Collegians,* where he names the group members, Winley states that the Collegians are Tim Holley, Henry Brown, and William Tarkenton. Surely the Collegians were not a trio, as Winley only names the three. On Relic's Winley LP, the photograph shows four men.

Discography

Winley 224 Zoom, Zoom, Zoom/On Your Merry Way (1957)
X-Tra 108 Let's Go for a Ride/That Heavenly Night (1957)
Winley 261 Oh I Need Your Love/Tonite, Oh Tonite (1961)
Winley 263 Right Around the Corner/Teenie Weenie Little Bit (1962)
Sources: Paul Winley, liner notes with Winley LP *The Collegians*; Donn Fileti, liner notes with the Relic LP *Best of Winley Records.*

Colognes (Los Angeles)

Personnel Kenneth Sinclair, Al McDonald

Notes

The two names above are known thanks to Lummie Fowler. Fowler also believes that Sinclair sang with the Elgins and was with the Six Teens on their "A Casual Look."

This was the second Lummtone 45 rpm to be released.

Discography

Lummtone 102 A River Flows/A Bird and a Bee (1959)
Source: Donn Fileti, liner notes with the Relic LP *Best of Lummtone Records.*

Colonairs (New York)

Personnel David Francis, Henry Williamson, Kenneth Dames

Notes

Williamson had been the lead for the Sunbeams on Herald 455.

Part of the Colonairs group would later become the Orients on Laurie ("Shouldn't I").

Discography

Ember 1017 Can't Stand to Lose You/Sandy (1957)

Tru-Lite 127 Do-Pop-Si /Little Miss Muffet (1964)
Source: Marv Goldberg in *DISCoveries*, article on the Sunbeams.

Colts (Bakersfield, Calif.)

Personnel Joe Grundy, Reuben Grundy, Carl Moland, Leroy Smith

Notes

The Colts were one of Buck Ram's vocal groups from the West Coast. Joe, Reuben, and Carl grew up together and sang in the same church choir.

Leroy Smith was from New Jersey and met the others at Los Angeles City College. Smith was once a contender for the 1953 Golden Gloves championship.

In May 1956 two of the original members left and were replaced by Eddie Williams from the disbanded Aladdins and Don Wyatt of the Fortunes and the Hollywood Flames.

Baritone Ray Brewster joined later, as did Al Harper from the Aladdins and Prentice Moreland.

Discography

Mambo 112 Adorable/Lips Red as Wine (1955)
Vita 112 Adorable/Lips Red as Wine (1955)
Vita 121 Honey Bun/Sweet Sixteen (1956)
Vita 130 Never No More/Hey You, Shoobeebooboo (1956)
Antler 4003 Sheik of Araby/Never No More (1959)
Antler 4003/4007 Sheik of Araby/Guiding Angel (1959)
Delco 4002 I Never Knew/Oh When You Touched Me (1959)
Plaza 505 Sweet Sixteen/Hey Pretty Baby (1962)
Sources: Bob Ostrowski in *Bim Bam Boom* 3; Donn Fileti, liner notes with the Relic CD *Groups of Vita Records.*

Columbus Pharaohs (Columbus, Ohio)

Personnel Morris Wade (lead), Robert Taylor (1st tenor), Ronald Wilson (baritone), Bernard Wilson (bass)

Notes

This group had connections to the Four Pharaohs and the Egyptian Kings.

First Tenor Robert Taylor was Bobby of Bobby Taylor and the Vancouvers.

Lead Morris Wade later rerecorded "Give Me Your Love" with the Egyptian Kings on the Nanc label.

Discography

Esta 290 China Girl/Give Me Your Love (1957)
Source: Bob Hyde, liner notes with the CD *Old Town Doo Wop-3.*

Concords (New York)

Personnel Milton Love (lead), Joe Willis (1st tenor), Bob Thompson (2d tenor), Jim Hunter (bass)

Notes

Milton Love was with this group before he joined the Solitaires.

Members all lived in Manhattan and attended Seward Park High School. They began singing in 1952 and retained Morty Shad as their manager.

Shad arranged for the Concords to record for Harlem Records. At the time of the Concords' recording, Harlem was also about to record Pearl Reeves and label management thought it good business sense to record Reeves backed by the Concords!

After Love auditioned for and was accepted by the Solitaires, he left the Concords to join the Old Town group. In an interview, Solitaires bass, Pat Gaston, related that after hearing Love, they asked the other applicants to return home.

Discography

Harlem 2328 Monticello/Candlelight (1954)
Harlem 2332 You Can't Stay Here/I'm Not Ashamed (w/Pearl Reeves) (1955)
Source: Marv Goldberg and Mike Redmond in *Record Exchanger* 16.

Concords (Brooklyn, N.Y.)

Personnel Mike Lewis (lead), Murray Moshe, Charles Presti, Steve Seider

Notes

This group formed in the late 1950s and began performing and recording in the early 1960s.

The group shown above recorded for Rust. On Herald, Mike Lasman sang lead. He was the same Mike of Mike and the Utopians.

Other members were Dickie Goldman, Teddy Grable (Epic Lead), Sal Tepedino, and Bobby Ganz.

Discography

RCA 47-7911 Again/The Boy Most Likely (1961)
Gramercy 304 Cross My Heart/Our Last Goodbye (1961)
Gramercy 305 My Dreams/Scarlet Ribbons (1962)
Rust 5048 Away/One Step from Heaven (1962)
Herald 576 Marlene/Our Love Wasn't Meant to Be (1962)
Herald 578 Cold and Frosty Morning/Don't Go Now (1963)
Epic 9697 It's Our Wedding Day/Should I Cry? (1964)
Sources: Ed Engel, liner notes with Ace and Sparkletone *Laurie* CDs; Ed Engel, liner notes with the RCA CD *Rock 'n' Roll Party-2*.

Consorts (Bronx, N.Y.)

Personnel Bruce Laurent, Sal Donnarumma, Billy Abbate, Eddie Jacobucci

Notes

This group took its name from a social club in the Bronx, New York.

The master from this recording was immediately acquired from Lou Cicchetti of Cousins Records in the Bronx by ABC Records subsidiary Apt Records.

Discography

Cousins 1004 Please Be Mine/Time after Time (1962)
Apt 25066 Please Be Mine/Time after Time (1962)
Source: Ed Engel and Lou Cicchetti, liner notes with the West Side CD *Group Harmony-Out of the Bronx.*

Continentals (Brooklyn, N.Y.)

Personnel Daniel Hicks (lead), Herman Montgomery (1st tenor), Buddy Payne (baritone), John Pearson (bass)

Notes

Phil Groia's *They All Sang on the Corner* and the Relic liner notes accompanying the *Rumble* CD state that the Continentals became the Quinns on Cyclone. When I spoke with Leon McClain of the Quinns, he responded, "No way!"

Cooper Payne replaced John Pearson. Joe Carillo was also a bass with the group.

Discography

Whirlin' Disc 101 Fine, Fine Frame/Dear Lord (1956)
Whirlin' Disc 105 Picture of Love/Soft and Sweet (1956)
Sources: Liner notes with the Relic CD *Rumble*; Phil Groia, *They All Sang on the Corner.*

Continentals (New York)

Personnel James Gooden (lead), Sidney Gray (tenor) Bill Davis (tenor), Tommy ——— (baritone), Demetrius Cleare (bass)

Notes

When the Crows split up, Bill Davis joined the Rama Continentals on their only record, "You're An Angel."

The younger Gooden had been Davis's sister's friend from childhood.

Because the Rama record did poorly, the Continentals moved to 20th Century Fox and recorded "The Fly," which was never released.

In 1963, Davis joined the Honeycoles, who recorded for Columbia, but the recording was never released.

Discography

Rama 190 You're an Angel/Giddy Up and Ding Dong (1956)
Source: Marv Goldberg, liner notes with the Murray Hill LP *Gee It's the Crows.*

Contours (Detroit)

Personnel Sylvester Potts, Joe Billingsley, Dennis Edwards, Billy Gordon, Billy Hoggs

Notes

Gordon, Hoggs, Billingsley, and Sylvester originally formed the Contours in 1959. When Hubert Johnson joined the group, he became the contact with Motown Records as he communicated with distant cousin Jackie Wilson to audition them. Wilson then spoke with his friend Berry Gordy at Motown on their behalf.

This ultimately led to a contract with Motown, and their first release on the label came in 1962. This went nowhere but then Gordy gave them a song he had written specifically for them, "Do You Love Me?"

Joe Stubbs of the Falcons, Levi Stubbs's brother, later sang with the Contours, as did Breeze Hatcher.

Discography

Motown 1008 Whole Lotta Woman/Come On and Be Mine (1961)
Motown 1012 Funny/The Stretch (1961)
Gordy 7005 Do You Love Me?/Move Mr. Man (1962)
Gordy 7012 Shake Sherry/You Better Get in Line (1962)
Gordy 7016 Don't Let Her Be Your Baby/It Must Be Love (1963)
Gordy 7019 You Get Ugly/Pa, I Need a Car (1963)
Gordy 7029 Can You Do It/I'll Stand by You (1964)
Gordy 7037 The Day When She Needed Me/Can You Jerk Like Me (1964)
Gordy 7044 Searching for a Girl/First I Look at the Purse (1965)
Gordy 7052 Determination/Just a Little Misunderstanding (1966)
Gordy 7059 It's So Hard Being a Loser/Your Love Grows More Precious (1967)
Source: Norm N. Nite, *Rock On.*

Contrasts, Billy Vera & (Westchester, N.Y.)

Personnel Billy Vera (lead), Ronnie Hinds, Bob Powers, Al Esposito

Notes
The group later changed its name to Blue-Eyed Soul.

Discography
Rust 5051 All My Love/My Heart Cries (1962)
Source: Ed Engel, liner notes with the Ace CD *Laurie Vocal Groups.*

Convincers (Los Angeles)

Personnel Melvin Alexander, Frank Alexander

Notes

The two Alexander brothers also sang with the Appegios.

Discography

Movin 100 Rejected Love/Go Back Baby (1962)
Source: Donn Fileti, liner notes with the Relic LP *Best of Flash.*

Cookies (New York)

Personnel Margie Hendricks (lead), Ethel McCrae, Dorothy Jones

Notes

The Cookies trio filled in for Ray Charles as the Raelets. They also did a great deal of female background work for Atlantic with Joe Turner, Chuck Willis, Varetta Dillard, Carole King, Neil Sedaka, and so on.

The liner notes with Sequel's *Jubilee/Josie R&B Vocal Groups-3* CD refer to the lead as Margie Hendrix and to McCrae as Ethyl.

Pat Lyles was a later replacement.

Discography

Lamp 8008 Don't Let Go/All Night Mambo (1954)
Atlantic 1061 Precious Love/Later, Later (1955)
Atlantic 1084 In Paradise/Passion Time (1956)
Atlantic 1110 Down by the River/My Lover (1956)
Josie 822 Hippy-Dippy-Daddy/King of Hearts (1957)
RCA 47-7144 The Rules of Love/Star of Fortune (w/V. Dillard) 1958
Atlantic 1176 Substitute/Learning to Love (w/L. Baker) (1958)
Atlantic 1180 Yes Indeed/I Had a Dream (w/R. Charles) (1958)
Atlantic 2079 In Paradise/Passing Time (1960)
Source: Norm N. Nite, *Rock On*; Gordon Skadberg, liner notes with the Sequel CD *Jubilee/Josie R&B Vocal Groups-3.*

Coolbreezers (Washington, D.C.)

Personnel Joe Reuth (lead), Richard Stewart (1st tenor), Bob Armstrong, William Primrose, Earl J. Williams, Sonny Williams (bass)

Notes

The Coolbreezers began singing as a gospel group. Bea Williams, sister of Earl and Sonny Williams, assumed the role of manager and had them record some rhythm and blues demos that she sent to New York for evaluation.

As a result, ABC Paramount had them record one record that went nowhere and then Bea started her own label—BALE. The group released two discs on the Bale label.

Earl Williams also sang bass for the Twilighters on Marshall.

Discography

ABC 9865 You Know I Go for You/My Brother (1957)
Bale 100/101 Eda Weda Bug/The Greatest Love of All (1958)
Bale 102/103 Let Christmas Ring/Hello, Mr. New Year (1958)
Source: Alan Lee, *Yesterday's Memories 8.*

Copesetics (New York)

Personnel Rosetta Brown, Betty Ann Williams

Notes

Little is known about the Copesetics. The release listed below is their only try for performance excellence. They came from East 135th Street in the Harlem section of Manhattan.

Discography

Premium 409 Collegian/Believe in Me (1956)
Source: Donn Fileti, liner notes with Relic's *Premium.*

Cordovans (New York)

Personnel Irvin Cox, Alvin Grant, Alvin Hassell

Notes

According to Donn Fileti's liner notes with the Relic LP *Best of Johnson Records,* Irvin Cox was a member of this group; Grant and Hassell, who wrote the songs, were probably in the group.

Discography

Johnson 731 Come On Baby/My Heart (1960)
Source: Donn Fileti, liner notes with the Relic LP *Best of Johnson Records.*

Coronets (Cleveland, Ohio)

Personnel Charles Carruthers (lead), Lester Russaw (1st tenor), Sam Griggs (2d tenor), George Lewis (baritone), Bill Griggs (bass)

Notes

After graduating from high school, Sam Griggs got married and money became a concern. He rounded up brother Bill, Lester Russaw, and George Lewis. They then began looking for a lead singer and found Charles Carruthers.

During a rehearsal for a show with the Orioles, the Coronets were practicing a song entitled "Don't You Think I Ought to Know?" This tune had previously been done by Hadda Brooks, and the Coronets adapted it to their style. The Orioles heard them practicing the tune and took it back with them. Within a month they released it on the flip side of "Crying in the Chapel." Nothing did well.

Discouraged by these failures, they next went to a recording studio and recorded a dub of "Nadine" and "I'm All Alone," which they took to Alan Freed's office in Cleveland. Freed never saw the group at the time, but apparently he sent the dub to the Chess facility and in June 1953, they had their first session at Chess.

Carruthers (in 1953) and Russaw (in 1954) were drafted and Charles Brown took over lead for the last two sides, "Corbella" and "Beggin' and Pleadin' " (which were not released at that time).

In 1955, Bobby Ward became the new lead with "Don't Deprive Me" on Stirling. Stirling management sold the remaining masters to RCA, which they released on their Groove subsidiary.

Willie Brooks became the new first tenor and Lucky Jordan was now the bass. The group next recorded on the Job label with "Footsteps." After this, nothing positive was happening and in 1960 the group disbanded.

The rumor that *Mission Impossible* star Greg Morris was in this group is absolutely true. Greg was a part-time member who filled in when needed.

Discography

Chess 1549 I'm All Alone/Nadine (1953)
Chess 1553 It Would Be Heavenly/Baby's Coming Home (1953)
Stirling 903 The Little Boy/Don't Deprive Me (1955)
Groove 0114 I Love You More/Crime Doesn't Pay (1955)
Groove 0116 Hush/The Bible Tells Me So (1955)
Job 100 Footsteps/Long John Silver (1960)
Source: Marv Goldberg, *Record Collector's Monthly* 45; Pete Grendysa, liner notes with the Chess CD boxed set *Chess Rhythm & Roll.*

Corsairs (LaGrange, N.C.)

Personnel Jay Uzzell (lead), James Uzzell, Moses Uzzell, George Wootten

Notes

This group was composed of three brothers and a cousin and was formed in North Carolina in 1958.

They worked locally for a while and soon moved to Newark, New Jersey, looking for a recording deal. This would come to pass in New Jersey when they met the owner of the Tuff label, who habitually gave his early hits to Chess to distribute.

Landy McNeil joined in 1965 and led the group on its last recording before their demise.

Their "Smokey Places" did well for Tuff, but the follow-ups did not do as well and the Corsairs simply disappeared later in 1965.

Discography

Smash 1715 It Won't Be a Sin/Time Waits (1961)
Tuff 1808 Smokey Places/Thinkin' (1962)
Tuff 1818 I'll Take You Home/Sittin' on Your Doorstep (1962)
Tuff 1830 Dancing Shadows/While (1962)

Tuff 1840 At the Stroke of Midnight/Listen to My Little Heart (1962)
Tuff 1847 Stormy/It's Almost Sunday Morning (1963)
Tuff 375 Save a Little Monkey/Save a Little Monkey (1964)
Tuff 402 On the Spanish Side/The Change in You (1965)
Sources: Pete Grendysa, liner notes with the Chess CD boxed set *Chess Rhythm &
Roll*; Jay Warner, *American Singing Groups.*

Corvairs (New York)

Personnel Nelson Shields (lead), Joe Shepard (1st tenor), Prince McKnight (tenor),
Ronald Judge (baritone), Billy Faison (bass)

Notes

Shields and Judge, from Newport News, Virginia, also sang for the Leaders on Glory.
They had just left the disbanded Leaders and while in New York, they met the other
three. Floyd Buddy McRae, formerly of the Chords, became their manager and early
in 1962, he got them a recording contract with Comet Records. (The Corvairs on
Cub, Clock and Crown were different groups.)

    After leaving Comet with no success, they went to the Beltone/Lescay/Leopard
facility and in April, 1963, recorded four sides for Leopard. Still unknown at this
writing is why one release from this session called the group the Westsiders.

    The other two sides were released as Leopard 5005, only on those discs the group
was called the Corvairs.

Discography

Comet 2145 True True Love (all)/Hey, Sally Mae (NS) (1962)
Leopard 5005 I Don't Wanna Be without You/The Girl with the Wind in Her Hair
(1963)
Source: Marv Goldberg in *DISCoveries,* March 1996, article on Leaders.

Corvets (Bronx, N.Y.)

Personnel Joe Lento (lead), Vince Zeccola (tenor), George DeAlfonso (2d tenor),
Richie Howell (baritone), Vince Hallup, Hank Shuh (bass)

Notes

This group was organized in the mid-1950s in the Bronx, New York. Prior to cutting their first record for Way Out, they called themselves Freddie and the Stead-
ies. When they were scheduled to record, they changed their name to the Corvets.

    The Way Out label was one that Zeccola founded, produced for, and distributed.
His reason for doing this was that no other recording company wanted the Corvets
on their label.

    They next cut a demo and took it to Broadway's Brill Building, where they tried
again to impress a recording company.

    Executives at Laurie apparently liked what they heard and had them record the
Laurel disc. Following the recording, Jules Hahn replaced Richie Howell.

If you've ever wondered about similarities in the sound of the Bob Knight Four's "Good Goodbye" disc and the Corvets' disc "So Long," there's good reason. Their unscrupulous manager had lifted Hallup's voice track from the Corvets recording and put it on the Bob Knight Four record. Needless to say, a new manager was found. Despite their persistence and a new label (20th Century Fox), success was not in the cards for the Corvets.

Discography

Way Out 101 Lenora/My Darling (1958)
Laurel 1012 Alligator in the Elevator/So Long (1960)
20th Century Fox 223 Only Last Night/Shark in the Park (1960)
Source: Vinnie Zeccola in *Record Exchanger* 31.

Counts (Indianapolis, Ind.)

Personnel Chester Brown (lead), Bobby Penick (1st tenor), Robert Wesley (2d tenor), Bobby Young (baritone), James Lee (bass)

Notes

This group formed in 1953 in an Indianapolis high school choir. They appeared at the usual school talent contests and vaudeville-type shows, calling themselves the Five Diamonds.

While they were appearing at one of these local shows, someone saw them and arranged for them to see Dot label management in Gallatin, Tennessee.

Dot immediately changed their name to the Counts, and Darling Dear/I Need You Always was released in January 1954. These two songs were recorded in someone's living room!

Many recordings followed.

Their "Let Me Go Lover" was a huge national hit, but not the Counts' recording of it. The Joan Weber cover was the big national seller.

Success avoided them.

In 1958, with no hits for two years, Dot decided not to renew their contract, ending the group's recording career.

This five-member group began in Gary, Indiana, in 1953, did a lot of touring, and is still performing today with the same five singers.

Discography

Dot 1188 Darling Dear (CB)/I Need You Always (CB) (1953)
Dot 1199 Hot Tamales (CB)/Baby Don't You Know? (CB) (1954)
Dot 1210 My Dear, My Darling (CB)/She Won't Say Yes (CB) (1954)
Dot 1226 Waitin' Around for You (CB)/Baby I Want You (CB) (1954)
Dot 1235 Let Me Go Lover (CB)/Wailin' Little Mama (BY) (1954)
Dot 1243 From This Day on (CB)/Love and Understanding (BY) (1955)
Dot 1265 Sally Walker (BY)/ I Need You Tonight (CB) (1955)
Dot 1275 Heartbreaker (CB)/To Our Love (CB) (1956)
Dot 244 Darling Dear (CB)/I Need You Always (CB) (1960)
Dot 16105 Darling Dear (CB)/I Need You Always (CB) (1960)

Source: Marv Goldberg in *DISCoveries,* December 1995; special thanks to George Lavatelli.

Craftys (New York)

Personnel Phil Johnson (lead), Harold Johnson (2d tenor), Al Cleveland (baritone), Arthur Crier (bass)

Notes

Obviously named after record entrepreneur Morty Craft, with whom the Craftys were associated.
  This group is also known as the Halos.

Discography

7 Arts 708 L-O-V-E/Heartbreaking World (1961)
Elmor 310 Zoom, Zoom, Zoom/I Went to a Party (1962)
Sources: Marcia Vance and Marv Goldberg in *Yesterday's Memories* 12; liner notes with the Collectables Halos CD *Nag*; Arthur Crier, interview by author.

Creators (Hudson County, N.J.)

Personnel Hugh Harris (lead), James Wright, John Angel Allen, Danny Austin, Chris Coles (bass)

Notes

The Creators recorded for Brooklyn's T-Kay label owned by Diamond Records. Sales of the disc were poor overall, but it was a minor hit in the Midwest.
  With a few personnel changes, the Creators later became the Ad Libs.

Discography

T-Kay 110 I'll Never Do It Again/He's Got It (1962)
Source: Joe Sicurella in *Record Collector's Monthly* 18.

Creators (Los Angeles?)

Personnel Charles Perry (lead), Gentry Bradley, Don Neal, Gerald Middleton, Thomas Harris

Notes

Charles Perry, following his one disc for Dootsie Williams's Dootone label, recorded as a solo artist on deejay Hunter Hancock's Magnum label.
  Over the years many groups have called themselves the Creators, but this group has no connection to any of them.

Discography

Dootone 463 I've Had You/Drafted, Volunteered, Enlisted (1961)
Source: Jim Dawson, liner notes with the Ace CD *Dootone Doo Wop-3.*

Crenshaws (Los Angeles)

Personnel Carl White (lead), John Sonny Harris (tenor), Medero White (tenor), Al Frazier (baritone), Turner "Rocky" Wilson (bass)

Notes

This group was the product of many other Los Angeles vocal groups, with Frazier being the common denominator. They began as the West Coast Mello-Moods in 1948 or 1949. They next became the Emanons, the Lamplighters, Tenderoots, Sharps, Four After Fives, and ultimately the Crenshaws before finally becoming the Rivingtons.

Harris had been with Johnny Staton and the Feathers. Mathew Nelson and Joe Green were also members of the Crenshaws.

When Frazier was looking for a moniker for the group, he was living close to a street bearing that name, which he chose for the group.

Discography

Warner Brothers 5254 Moonlight in Vermont/He's Got the Whole World (1962)
Warner Brothers 5505 Offshore/Wishing Star (1965)
Sources: Jack Sbarbori in *Record Exchanger* 16; Art Turco in *Record Exchanger* 28.

Crescendos (Berkeley, Calif.)

Personnel Wanda Burt (lead), Cynthia Badie (tenor), Ernie ——— (tenor), George Banks (baritone), Odell Alford (bass)

Notes

The Crescendos came together when the singers were in junior high school. They signed with Music City in 1960.

Initial successes on Music City led to George Goldner's leasing the group's first record for his Gone label.

Wanda Burt's severe emotional problems forced her into hospital care. Anna Lois Jones took her place with the Crescendos, and eventually the group changed its name to the Casual Crescendos and recorded for the MRC label.

Cynthia Badie left the group to attend college. In the late 1980s she became the manager of the New Edition.

In Wayne Stierle's *West Coast Doo Wop Collection–1,* Luther McDaniel is listed as a member of this group. (McDaniel was also a member of the Four Deuces, who did W-P-L-J on the Music City.)

The band leader on the Crescendos cuts was Larry Graham, who went on to form Graham Central Station.

Discography

Music City 831 My Heart's Desire/Take My Heart (1960)
Music City 839 Teenage Prayer/I Don't Mind (1961)
Gone 5100 My Heart's Desire/Take My Heart (1961)
Source: Jim Dawson, liner notes with the two Earth Angel *Music City* LPs.

Crescendos (Los Angeles)

Personnel Bobby Relf (lead), Prentice Moreland (tenor), Bobby Byrd (tenor), Will "Dub" Jones (bass)

Notes

Moreland and Jones sang with the Cadets and Jacks. Moreland sang with the DuDroppers, Colts, Fortunes, and Hollywood Flames. Relf also sang for the Laurels, Phantoms, and Lovers. Bobby Byrd sang with the Hollywood Flames and many other West Coast vocal groups.

Discography

Atlantic 1109 Finders Keepers (BR)/Sweet Dreams (WJ) (1956)
Atlantic 2014 Sweet Dreams (WJ)/I'll Be Seeing You (RR) (1959)
Source: Alan Lee, *Yesterday's Memories* 8.

Crescents, Billy Wells & (Cleveland, Ohio)

Personnel William Burwell (lead), Albert Banks (tenor), Leroy McQueen (baritone), Garfield "Buddy" Jackson (bass)

Notes

William Burwell was also known as Billy Wells. Truancy difficulties with his high school forced him to leave the group and it disbanded briefly. When they reunited, Lawyer (Henry) Curtis replaced Burwell at lead and they continued to make personal appearances.

Buddy Jackson eventually left the group and was replaced by James Arnold Porter, who became the Crescents' new bass.

In the early 1960s, Curtis was drafted and Art Blakey replaced him at lead.

In 1964 the group changed their name and their sound. They became the Wigs and made one recording for the Golden Crest label.

Discography

Reserve 105 Julie/I Love Only You (1956)
Source: Leroy McQueen, interview by Galen Gart.

Crescents, Pat Cordel & (Staten Island, N.Y.)

Personnel Vito Picone, Ronnie Jones, Carman Romano, Pat Croccitto (Cordel)

Notes

This group was really a precursor to the Elegants, who did "Little Star." They began in 1955–1956 on Staten Island in New York. Like many groups, they started singing for the fun of it, did church functions and dances, and were heard by someone who took them to their friend at Club Records.

They were signed by the Club organization and recorded soon after. The disc had some success leading to tours and appearances. Because Pat Croccitto was only fifteen years old, traveling was virtually impossible, which led to many difficulties and ultimately caused their breakup.

After the group disbanded, Croccitto became a June Taylor dancer. Picone and Romano formed the nucleus of the Elegants, adding Arthur Venosa, James Moschella, and Frank Tardogno for the balance of the group.

Discography

Club 1011 Darling Come Back/My Tears (1956)
Michelle 502 Darling Come Back/My Tears (1959)
Victory 1001 Please Come Back/My Tears (1963)
Source: Ed Engel in *Time Barrier Express* 21.

Crests (New York)

Personnel Johnny Mastroangelo (Maestro) (lead), Talmadge Gough (1st tenor), Patricia Van Dross (2d tenor), Harold Torres (baritone), J. T. Carter (baritone/bass)

Notes

In 1955, some junior high school students decided to form a vocal group and sang at schools, hospitals, and other local functions. This without the services of Johnny Mastroangelo.

After about a year, Johnny joined the group, which in 1956 adopted the name "Crests."

Al Browne's wife gave them his phone number when she heard them singing in the subway, and just weeks later, they were signed to record for Joyce, with which Browne was affiliated. In 1957, Sweetest One/My Juanita was released. These sides did fairly well in the New York area, but when the legendary Slim Rose of Times Square Records released this disc in 1962, it did really well. This was also true of their second record, No One to Love/Wish She Was Mine.

In 1958, Patricia dropped out as a result of the travel involved with promoting disc. At this time, the Crests were about to sign with Coed Records and the travel was going to be more frequent. Pat was Luther Van Dross's sister.

Billy Dawn Smith was responsible for bringing the Crests to Coed Records' George Paxton, who signed them in 1958.

On Coed the group became a quartet: Johnny at lead, Talmadge at 1st tenor, Harold at 2nd tenor, and J.T. at baritone/bass. They did quite well for Coed.

It was Coed's ultimate scheme or plan to separate Maestro from the rest of the Crests. Racial problems were always discussed as well as other similar reasons for their breakup, like J.T.'s insatiable desire for promotion with tee shirts, pictures, books, and so on. Apparently the novelty of the interracial group had worn off and Coed felt it was time for something new!

After the group split in two, James Ancrum sang lead. Kenneth Head briefly filled in for Ancrum on their Trans-Atlas release.

Discography

Joyce 103 My Juanita/Sweetest One (1957)
Joyce 105 No One to Love/Wish She Was Mine (1957)
Coed 501 Pretty Little Angel/I Thank the Moon (1958)
Coed 506 Sixteen Candles/Beside You (1958)
Coed 509 Six Nights a Week/I Do (1959)
Coed 511 Flower of Love/Molly Mae (1959)
Coed 515 The Angels Listened In/I Thank the Moon (1959)
Coed 521 A Year Ago Tonight/Paper Crown (1959)
Coed 525 Step By Step/Gee (1960)
Coed 531 Trouble in Paradise/Always You (1960)
Coed 535 Journey of Love/If My Heart Could Write a Letter (1960)
Coed 537 Isn't it Amazing/Molly Mae (1960)
Coed 543 Good Golly Miss Molly/I Remember (1960)
Coed 561 Little Miracles/Baby I Gotta Know (1961)
Times Square 2 No One to Love/Wish She Was Mine (1962)
Times Square 6 Baby/I Love You So (1962)
Trans-Atlas 696 The Actor/Three Tears in a Bucket (1962)
Selma 311 Guilty/Number 1 With Me (1962)
Selma 4000 Did I Remember/Tears Will Fall (1963)
Coral 62403 A Love to Last a Lifetime/You Blew Out the Candles (1964)
Parkway 987 Heartburn/Try Me (1966)
Parkway 999 Come See Me/I Care about You (1966)
Parkway 118 My Time/Is It You (1967)
Source: Harvey Mandell and Ronnie Italiano in *Harmony Tymes* 1–2.

Crickets, Dean Barlow & (Bronx, N.Y.)

Personnel Grover "Dean" Barlow (lead), Harold Johnson (d) (1st tenor), Eugene Stapleton (2d tenor), Leon Carter (baritone), Rodney Jackson (bass)

Notes

The Crickets, from the Morrisania section of the Bronx, got together in 1951, singing at parties and practicing for three years.

They met Joe Davis from MGM who signed them to do two sessions at the label. When Davis left MGM, he took both the Crickets and the Blenders with him to his own Jay Dee label. The Crickets recorded seven songs at their first Jay Dee session.

A second group evolved, with Barlow at lead, J. R. Bailey at tenor, Bobby Spencer at baritone, and Freddy Barksdale at bass.

A third group, made up of Barlow, Robert Bynum at 1st tenor, William Lindsay at 2d tenor, and Joe Ditto Dias at bass was structured. With one personnel change (Bynum), this group later became the Bachelors on Earl.

Still another configuration had Barlow, Waldo Champen, Lindsay, Billy Baines, and Dias. (Donn Fileti's liner notes on Relic's *Crickets* LP does not acknowledge this group.)

Barlow later sang with the Montereys and the Bachelors and also established a solo performing and recording act. This was the reason for their split.

Discography

MGM 11428 You're Mine/Milk and Gin (1953)
MGM 11507 For You I Have Eyes/I'll Cry No More (1953)
Jay-Dee 777 Dream and Wishes (1953)
Jay-Dee 781 I'm Not the One You Love/Fine As Wine (1953)
Jay-Dee 785 Changing Partners/Your Love (1954)
Jay-Dee 786 Just You/My Little Baby' Shoes (1954)
Jay-Dee 789 Never Give Up Hope/Are You Looking for a Sweetheart? (1954)
Jay-Dee 795 Man from the Moon/I'm Going to Live My Life Alone (1954)
Beacon 104 Be Faithful/I'm Not the One You Love (1954)
Davis 459 Man from the Moon/I'm Going to Live My Life Alone (1958)
Beacon 555 Be Faithful/I'm Not the One You Love (1963)
Source: Marv Goldberg, *Yesterday's Memories* 2; liner notes with the Relic LP/CD *The Crickets.*

Criterions (Belmar, N.J.)

Personnel John Mangi (lead), Tommy Picardo (tenor), Tim Hauser (1st tenor), Jimmy Ruff (2d tenor), Steve Casagrande (baritone), Joe Ernst (bass)

Notes

This group began in early 1958, when Hauser and Picardo were classmates in high school. Tim Hauser is the same Tim Hauser who sang with the Manhattan Transfer.

The group met Al Browne in New York City and auditioned for him on several occasions. But they did not succeed until Mangi replaced Hauser at lead and Hauser changed to 1st tenor and the group became a sextet.

Hauser's father was a friend of Alan Freed's engineer and the owner of a new label—Cecelia. The group changed its name to the Kents and then the Criterions and recorded "I Remain Truly Yours," which did well in New York. It was picked up and later released by Laurie.

Tommy West, a later member of the Criterions, went on to future success, joining Hauser with Manhattan Transfer.

Discography

Cecelia 1010 Don't Say Goodbye/Crying the Blues over Me (1959)
Cecelia 1208 I Remain Truly Yours/You Just You (1959)
Laurie 33056 I Remain Truly Yours/You Just You (1965)
Sources: Liner notes with the Ace CD *Laurie Vocal Groups*; Ed Engel, liner notes with the CD *Brooklyn's Doo Wop Sound.*

Crowns, Arthur Lee Maye & (Los Angeles)

Personnel Arthur Lee Maye (lead), Johnny Morris (1st tenor), Johnny Coleman (2d tenor), Richard Berry (baritone), Charles Holm (d) (bass)

Notes

When Arthur Maye was a sixteen-year-old student at Jefferson High School in Los Angeles (1955), he heard that Modern/RPM records was looking for new voices. He went down to their facility and within weeks recorded for them. After releasing eight sides for the music complex and having little to show for it, Maye decided that he was ready for a change. Coincidentally, Maye heard from Art Rupe of Specialty Records, also in Los Angeles, suggesting that he come and record for his label. This is when Maye and the Crowns joined Specialty and recorded the Berry/Maye tune "Gloria."

When asked about the financial aspects of vocal group recording in the 1950s, Maye related that groups were usually given $50–75 for a session but they never received royalties. He would look at *Cashbox* and see that the Crowns' record was doing okay. But when he asked for additional rewards, he was always told that he had already gotten them.

Berry was singing with the Flairs, Crowns, and Dreamers at the same time. Maye stated that he sometimes sang with the Flairs.

Maye's brother Eugene did some fill-in work with the Crowns.

He also was with the Millionaires on Specialty, doing "Ain't No Achievement."

Because he believed that doo-wop music was fading in the latter 1950s, Maye allowed Henry Strogin to borrow the Crowns for some recordings.

Lou Silvani's *Collecting Rare Records* shows the Crowns' lineup as Maye, Berry, Charles Colbert, Joe Moore, and Johnny Coleman. Maye eventually went on to become a professional baseball player.

When he came up to the major leagues, he dropped the Arthur and was known to his baseball fans as Lee Maye.

Discography

Modern 944 Set My Heart Free (ALM)/I Wanna Love (ALM) (1955)
RPM 424 Truly (ALM)/Oochie Pachie (ALM) (1955)
RPM 429 Love Me Always (ALM)/Loop De Loop De Loop (ALM) (1955)
RPM 438 Please Don't Leave Me (ALM)/Do the Bop (ALM) (1955)
Specialty 944 Gloria (ALM)/Oh Rooba Lee (ALM) (1956)
Dig 124 This Is the Night for Love/Honey Honey (1956)
Dig 133 Whispering Wind/A Fool's Prayer (1956)
Sources: Liner notes with Titanic's *The Best of Flip-1* CD; Rip Lay in *Big Town Review 1*.

Crowns, Henry Strogin & (Los Angeles)

Personnel Henry Strogin (lead), Eugene Maye (1st tenor), Charles Colbert (2d tenor), Joe Moore (baritone), Johnny Coleman (bass)

Notes

This group was formed when lead singer Lee Maye became a major league baseball player known as Lee Maye. Apparently, Strogin approached Maye and asked his permission to borrow the Crowns to record with. Feeling that the popularity of vocal group music was diminishing, Maye sanctioned Strogin's using the Crowns.

Discography

Dynamic 1002 Why Did You Go Away/My Achin' Feet (1960)
Amazon 1001 I'll Tag Along/I Love L.A. (1960)
Ball 1015 I'll Tag Along/Why Did You Go Away? (1961)
Source: Marv Goldberg in *Whiskey, Women, and . . .* 17.

Crowns (New York)

Personnel Ben E. Nelson (King) (lead), Ellsbeary Hobbs (d. 1996), James "Poppa" Clark, Dock Green, Charlie Thomas

Notes

The Five Crowns evolution resulted in the Crowns on the R&B label and while appearing at an Apollo concert, they impressed Drifters manager, George Treadwell. Following the show, Treadwell asked to see them at Atlantic Records where he then offered them the opportunity to become the new Drifters. They accepted and the group became the latter-day Drifters. The reason behind his walking away from the old Drifters was the lack of record sales and an incipient drinking problem facing the entire group.

Discography

R&B 6901 I'll Forget about You/Kiss and Make Up (1958)
Source: Jay Warner, *American Singing Groups.*

Crows (New York)

Personnel Daniel "Sonny" Norton (d) (lead), Harold Major (tenor), Mark Jackson (tenor), Bill Davis (baritone), Gerald Hamilton (d) (bass)

Notes

The members of this group got together at a Manhattan high school. They sang at school, on street corners, and in hallways and subways. Jerry Wittick was with them at this time.

They went on to perform at the Apollo amateur night and were spotted by one of George Goldner's talent agents.

The Apollo appearance brought them some uncredited backup work for Jerry Blaine at Jubilee. The Four Notes on Jubilee 5085, backing Frank "Fat Man" Humphries's I Can't Get Started/Lu Lu Belle Blues was the group's start. On Jubilee 5095 "Paint a Sky for Me," Viola Watkins's name is all that appears on the label. Watkins was a distant relative of Bill Davis, and the Crows was the group backing Watkins.

Before they started to record, original member Jerry Wittick left to join the service. He was replaced by guitarist/tenor Mark Jackson. This new personnel lineup (as above) did not change during their recording career. Every one of the records giving the Crows credit on the label included the above members.

Rama's George Goldner first heard the group at the home of Viola Watkins one evening and was so impressed by both that he had the Crows back Watkins on "Seven Lonely Days." Watkins backed the Crows on "No Help Wanted."

"Gee" and "I Love You So," written by Davis, were recorded next, and their success took the group on tour all over the country.

Their subsequent recordings were failures, however, due to poor promotion, and following "Sweet Sue" they drifted apart.

When the group split up, Davis went to sing with the Rama Continentals on their only record, "You're An Angel," in December 1955.

On the label of West Coast pressings of "Call a Doctor," the artist, for some unknown reason, is listed as the Jewels.

Discography

Rama 3 Seven Lonely Days (SN)/No Help Wanted (SN) (1953)
Rama 5 Gee (SN)/I Love You So (SN) (1953)
Rama 10 Call a Doctor (SN)/Heartbreaker (SN) (1953)
Rama 29 Baby (SN)/Untrue (SN) (1954)
Rama 30 Miss You (SN)/I Really, Really, Love You (SN) (1954)
Tico 1082 Mambo Shevitz (SN)/Mambo No. 5 (instrumental) (1954)
Rama 50 Baby Doll (SN)/Sweet Sue (BD) (1954)
Sources: Phil Groia, *They All Sang on the Corner*; Jeff Beckman and Hank Feigenbaum in *Big Town Review* 2; Steve Propes in *Goldmine*; Galen Gart in *Goldmine*.

Cruisers (Washington, D.C.)

Personnel Eugene Williams (lead), Paul Long, McKinley Anthony (2d tenor), Randy Hamilton

Notes

These four singers were neighborhood friends who met in the mid-1950s.

While Paul Long was in the service, he was stationed on a navy cruiser, which suggested the group's name.

By 1960, after practicing and performing locally, they felt ready to record. Because facilities in the D.C. area were limited, they headed for Philadelphia.

They got local club work in Philly and were heard by a man who went on to be their manager and who took them to V-Tone Records. They recorded the great If I Knew/Crying over You, which was fairly successful in the East.

Their other tunes showed no promise and the group returned to Washington. Gene Williams remained in Philadelphia and later formed the Strollers (no relation to the States' group). They recorded "There's No One but You" for Carlton in 1961. Although the Cruisers and the Strollers had a similar sound, it was only Gene Williams who sang for both.

In the mid-1960s Williams was asked to re-form the Cruisers and subsequently two records were released on Gamble Records.

Discography

V-Tone 207 If I Knew/Miss Fine (1960)

V-Tone 213 Cryin' over You/Don't Tease Me (1960)
Guyden 2069 Cryin' over You/Don't Tease Me (1962)
Gamble 207 I Need You So/Take a Chance (1967)
Gamble 4000 Picture Us/Mink and Sable Mable (1970)
Sources: Alan Lee in *Yesterday's Memories* 8; Donn Fileti, liner notes with the Relic
LP *V-Tone.*

Crystals (New York)

Personnel Earl Wade (lead), Johnny Hopson (tenor), Martin Brown (tenor), Teddy
Williams (bass)

Notes

The group was from Manhattan's 142d street vicinity. Like all groups at the time,
they sang on neighborhood street corners until they were discovered by Luna Records
owner, Charles Lopez.

They recorded the Luna classic "Come to Me Darling" on May 13. In August they
changed their name to the Opals and moved to Apollo Records. Their first release
for Apollo, "My Heart's Desire," backed by "Oh But She Did," was released later
in 1954, although it was recorded at the same May 13, 1954 session as "Come to
Me Darling."

Earl Wade, of course, following the demise of the Opals/Crystals went on to join
his neighborhood friends, the Cadillacs.

Discography

Luna 101 Squeeze Me Baby/Come to Me Darling (1954)
Luna 5001 Squeeze Me Baby/Come to Me Darling (1954)
Source: Donn Fileti, liner notes with Relic LP/CD *Timely.*

Crystals (New Orleans)

Personnel Cleveland Jackson (lead), Marcel Scott, Douglas Landry, General Jackson, Emery Johnson

Notes

The members of this group were all eighteen years of age when they recorded the
disc shown below, their only one for Specialty.

Discography

Specialty 657 In the Deep/Love You So (1958)
Source: Donn Fileti, liner notes with the *Golden Groups* Specialty CD.

Crystals, Sam Hawkins & (New York)

Personnel Sam Hawkins (lead), James Bailey (tenor), Ronnie Bright (baritone),
Fred Barksdale (bass)

Notes

Bob Ferlingere's book shows that Robert (Bobby) Spencer and Waldo "Champ" Champen were members of this group. We dealt directly with Fred Barksdale who told us that neither Spencer nor Champen were members. (The above personnel listing and everything else discussed herein has been taken from our discussion with Freddie. This was confirmed in a pursuant conversation with Champen.)

Sam Hawkins was scheduled to record for George Goldner's Gone Records one specific day in 1958 and Goldner wanted to have backing vocal accompaniment. Bailey, Bright, and Barksdale were at these facilities that same day and Goldner asked them to listen to Hawkins' song and create an interesting background.

The rest, as they say, is history!

Discography

Gone 5042 King of Fools (SH)/The Watchamacallit (SH) (1958)
Gone 5054 When Nobody Loves You/She Didn't Notice Me (1959)
Sources: Bob Ferlingere, *A Discography of R&B and R&R Vocal Groups*; Mitch Rosalsky in *DISCoveries,* March 1996.

Crystals (Bronx, N.Y.)

Personnel Joe Garcia (lead), Donnie Cruz (1st tenor), Joe Patriarca (2d tenor), John Angelo (baritone), Joe Carillo (bass)

Notes

Started in 1957 in a Bronx high school.

Carillo came from Brooklyn from the Whirlin Disc Continentals, and they soon changed their name to Metros.

This group first recorded as the Metros who recorded All of My Life/Lookin' on the Just label.

They were later taken to MGM, where they took their old name Crystals back and recorded for the MGM subsidiary Cub—this was 1959.

Discography

Cub 9064 Watching You/Oh My Love (1959)
Source: Ed Engel in *Echoes of the Past* 10.

Crystals (Brooklyn, N.Y.)

Personnel Barbara Alston (lead), Pat Wright (tenor), Delores "Dee Dee" Kennibrew (tenor), Merna Girard (2d tenor), Mary Thomas (baritone)

Notes

In 1960, Benny Wells, a former big band musician and manager, rehearsed his acts at P.S. 73 on MacDougal Street. He made use of the school's music facilities for these activities. In the fall of 1960 Wells decided to structure a female vocal group. He got seventeen-year-old Barbara Alston, his niece, from the Bedford-Stuyvesant section of Brooklyn; fifteen-year-old Delores "Dee Dee" Kennibrew from the Crown Heights section; seventeen-year-old Mary Thomas of Williamsburg (recommended by Alston); and seventeen-year-old Merna Girard. Seventeen-year-old Pat Wright completed the quintet.

Their only live appearance prior to recording took place in 1961, when Wells brought them to the Celebrity Club in Freeport, Long Island, to get the feeling of the stage and of performing live.

They were rehearsing "There's No Other" in its original up-tempo style on a March evening in Manhattan, when they were overheard by Phil Spector. He took the tune and slowed it down, giving it the sound people grew to love.

They continued to practice until the night of the prom for three of the members. This was also the night they were scheduled to record. The three, Barbara, Mary, and Merna showed up at 10 P.M. to record "There's No Other" and "Oh Yeah, Maybe Baby." These were released in September 1961 on the Philles label, started by Spector and Lester Sill. Their first major live appearance was at the Apollo in Harlem.

Phil Spector's influence on the group's singing style is first heard on "Uptown," released in March 1962. Six voices are heard, as Delores "Lala" Brooks was brought in to replace the pregnant Merna Girard, who had enough energy to perform on "Uptown" before leaving.

Their next big disc was "He's a Rebel," previously turned down by the Shirelles. Darlene Love and the Blossoms actually did vocals on the tune instead of the Crystals. Spector knew that the Crystals were reluctant to fly to the West Coast from New York and apparently the Blossoms were asked by Spector to fill in for them. The label on the disc shows the artist as the Crystals. This side was a huge hit.

Mary Thomas left to marry after "He's a Rebel" and the group chose to remain a quartet. Soon after this the Crystals recorded the original version of "On Broadway." But this tune was a hit for the Drifters, and it was relegated to the Crystals' album *He's a Rebel* popular at the time. Darlene Love and the Blossoms were once again the actual artists on "He's Sure the Boy I Love," the Crystals' next single.

In March 1963, the Crystals' manager finally decided to make better use of Lala Brooks and used her in place of Darlene Love in a California studio to cut "Da Doo Run Run." This was released in April 1963 under the name of the Crystals but was actually Lala and the Blossoms. The tune was another big seller, but the Crystals' frustration was beginning to show.

Their seventh released disc was totally the Crystals. "Then He Kissed Me" became their biggest international seller and other discs followed. In January 1964, Pat left to marry and was replaced by Frances Collins, who had toured with the Crystals in February 1964.

Releases in 1964 did not fare as well and in 1965 the Crystals signed with United Artists. They had two releases for UA and then Barbara married and the group split up around 1967. Dee Dee also married but in 1971 made an attempt to re-form the group with Lala, Barbara, and Mary for a Richard Nader revival show from 1971 to 1972. Husbands and babies, however, took precedence.

Discography

Philles 100 There's No Other/Oh Yeah Maybe Baby (1961)
Philles 102 Uptown/What a Nice Way to Turn Seventeen (1962)

Philles 105 He Hit Me/No One Ever Tells You (1962)
Philles 106 He's a Rebel/I Love you Eddie (1962)
Philles 109 He's Sure the Boy I Love/Walkin' Along (1962)
Philles 111 The Screw—Pt. 1/Pt. 2 (UNR) (1963)
Philles 112 Da Doo Run Run/Git It (1963)
Philles 115 Then He Kissed Me/Brother Julius (1963)
Philles 119 Little Boy/Harry and Milt (1964)
Philles 122 All Grown Up/Irving (1964)
UA 927 My Place/You Can't Tie a Good Girl Down (1965)
UA 994 I Got a Man/Are You Trying to Get Rid of Me Baby? (1966)
Michelle 4113 Ring-A-Ting-A-Ling/Should I Keep on Waiting? (1967)
Sources: Jay Warner, *American Singing Groups*; Wayne Jones in *Goldmine,* December 1980.

Cubans (Los Angeles)

Personnel David Johnson (lead), Johnny Simmons (tenor), Curtis ——— (baritone), Leroy Sanders (bass)

Notes

When David Johnson was discharged from the air force in 1958, his flight took him to Los Angeles. After some moving around, he settled in southern California. In Los Angeles, he met Leroy Sanders (bass), Johnny O'Simmons (1st tenor), Early Harris (2d tenor), and Curtis ——— (tenor). They started calling themselves the Cubans.

The Cubans' recordings were all cut for Flash in Hollywood on January 13, 1959. Four sides were recorded that day and the one disc reflected below was released. Due to relentless work by Donn Fileti of Relic Records, we know of the other two songs: "Don't Go Baby" and "Oh Miss Dolly" released on Relic's Flash LP 5049. Interestingly, this same Relic LP refers to a James Bedford as one of the members of the Cubans. In an interview conducted by Gagnon and Guerre for their Little Caesar and the Romans article, in which they interviewed Sanders and Johnson, neither remembers a James Bedford. They named all the members in a photograph, but Bedford was not among them.

Sanders and Simmons had also been members of the Cuff Links on Dooto in 1959; Johnson somehow met Lummie Fowler, who had recently started the Lummtone label. He asked Johnson to assemble a group and join him at Lummtone. They were now the Upfronts. Several years later they became Little Caesar and the Romans.

Discography

Flash 133 Tell Me (EH)/You've Gone So Long (DJ) 1958
Sources: Donn Fileti, liner notes with the Relic LP *Best of Flash*; Rick Gagnon and Dave Guerre article discussing Little Caesar and the Romans in *Goldmine.*

Cubans, Joe Alexander & (St. Louis, Mo.)

Personnel Joe Alexander (lead), Charles Berryn, Faith Douglass, Freddie Golden

Notes

Faith Douglass was the daughter of Oscar Washington, owner of Ballad Records.
  Charles Berryn is Chuck Berry; this Ballad disc was his first recording.

Discography

Ballad 1008 Oh Maria/I Wish You Well (JA)
Source: Goldmine 76 (September 1982); Charlie Horner, *Vocal Group Guide to St. Louis.*

Cubs (New York)

Personnel Lee Witherspoon, David Makonnen, Beni Israel, Tafari Makonnen

Notes

In his liner notes accompanying Savoy's *Doo Wop Delights* LP, Steve Propes states that the lead might possibly be a female.
  The personnel listed above suggest that anything is possible.

Discography

Savoy 1502 I Hear Wedding Bells/Why Did You Make Me Cry? (1956)
Source: Steve Propes, liner notes with the Savoy LP *Doo Wop Delights—The Roots of Rock.*

Cues (New York)

Personnel Ollie Jones (d) (lead), Dave ——— (1st tenor), Robey Kirkland (baritone), Frank ——— (bass)

Notes

This group was primarily assembled to do background work for Atlantic's existing artists. Ollie Jones from the Blenders was contacted, Robie Kirk, Abel DeCosta, Jimmy Breedlove, and Eddie Barnes. Although they were nameless at the time, they backed Ruth Brown as the Rhythmaires, LaVerne Baker as the Gliders, Joe Turner as the Blues Kings, Ivory Joe Hunter as the Ivorytones, and so on.
  Under the pseudonym Winfield Scott, Robey Kirkland wrote many R&B tunes for many major artists and groups (Five Keys, LaVern Baker, et al.).
  Ollie Jones of course sang with the Ravens and the Blenders.
  Abel DeCosta also came from the Blenders and later performed with the Ink Spots. Eddie Barnes and Jimmy Breedlove joined later.
  The Cues were also known as Carmen Taylor's Boleros.
  Jimmy Stewart of the Ravens, as well as Greg Carroll and Larry Harrison of the Four Buddies, all sang with the Cues, substituting for an absent or ill member as needed.

The Cues backed up Lenny Welch on "Since I Fell for You" (Cadence).

The Cues and Charlie White were the Playboys on Cat (Atlantic). The Cues recorded for Capitol from 1955 to 1957 but were not very successful. By 1959 the need for backing vocals disappeared, as did the Cues.

According to Sequel's *Jubilee/Josie* CD, "The Cues began as the Cabineers backing Bing Crosby" (this cannot be confirmed).

Discography

Lamp 8007 Scoochie, Scoochie/Forty Leven Dozen Ways (1954)
Jubilee 5201 Only You/I Fell for Your Loving (1955)
Capitol 3245 Burn That Candle (JB)/Oh My Darling (OJ) (1955)
Capitol 3310 Charlie Brown (OJ)/You're on My Mind (1956)
Capitol 3400 Destination 2100+65 (OJ)/Don't Make Believe (JB) (1956)
Capitol 3483 Girl I Love (ADC)/Crackerjack (JB) (1956)
Capitol 3582 Why? (JB)/Prince or Pauper (OJ) (1956)
Prep 104 I Pretend/Crazy, Crazy Party (1957)
Sources: Pete Grendysa, liner notes with the *Cues* CD; liner notes with Sequel's *Jubilee/Josie* CD; Bear Family's *Why?* CD; Marv Goldberg and Mike Redmond in *Yesterday's Memories* 3.

Cuff-Links/Cufflinx (Sacramento, Calif.)

Personnel Robert Truesdale (lead), John Anderson (1st tenor), Marshall Lamb (2d tenor), Everett Tyson (baritone), Alfred Gaitwood (bass)

Notes

The original Cufflinx got together in 1956 while in the air force stationed at Fort McClellan near San Francisco. This group shown above is the one that recorded the group's first release "Guided Missiles," which did fairly well in big cities on both coasts.

Their follow-ups were good tunes but did not fare as well.

Interestingly, this group was composed of several sets of singers, probably because of their air force obligation. Dootone would simply reuse the name each time a song was recorded by a group with no name. For some reason, Dootsie Williams chose to credit the group as the Cufflinx.

The Cufflinx name appears on the labels of eight Dootone and Dooto recordings. The second Cufflinx, which began in 1958, appear on 422, 433, 434, and 438. This group consisted of Johnny Simmons, Moses Walker, Elroy Coleman, Raymond Durden, and Henry Houston.

Gaitwood in the first group was from Brooklyn, New York, but the rest of the members were from the West Coast. Gaitwood also sang with the Smoothtones who recorded for Jem while he was stationed with the air force in Pittsburgh.

Interestingly, in 1958, Gene Autry started a new label, Challenge, and had a vocal group called the Kuf Linx.

Williams, sensing an opportunity, formed a second group of Cuff Links in order to capitalize on the popularity of this new group's success with their Challenge recording.

Tyson performed lead on "Guided Missiles," and it remains unclear as to which group recorded on each Cufflinx release.

Coleman went to the Raindrops, and he and Durden went to the Sunrisers. Simmons also sang with the Romans.

Discography

Dootone 409 Guided Missiles/My Heart (1956)
Dooto 413 How You Lied/The Winner (1957)
Dooto 414 Twinkle/Off Day Blues (1957)
Dooto 422 It's Too Late Now/Saxaphone Rag [sic] (1957)
Dooto 433 So Tough/My Love Is with You (1958)
Dooto 434 A Fool's Fortune/Trick Knees (1958)
Dooto 438 Lawful Wedding/Zoom (1958)
Dooto 474 Changing My Love/I Don't Want Nobody (1963)
Source: Jim Dawson, liner notes with the Ace CD *Dootone Doo Wop-1, 3.*

Cupids (Los Angeles)

Personnel Tony Allen (lead), Horace Pookie Wooten, Charles Jackson, David Cobb, Booker Washington, Barbara McNeill

Notes

This group was also the Chimes on Dig, the Lions, and the Wonders on Jamie.

Discography

Aladdin 3404 Now You Tell Me/Lillie Mae (1958)
Source: Ray Topping, liner notes with the *Dig Legendary Masters* CD.

Cyclones (Los Angeles)

Personnel Godoy Colbert (lead), Stanley Richardson, Robert Harris (2d tenor), Noel Collins (baritone)

Notes

Harris and Richardson were also in the Pharaohs with Richard Berry.

It is rumored that Berry sang for this group, but this cannot be confirmed. Neither discographies of Berry's recordings nor a personal interview show Berry with the Cyclones on Flip.

The only mention of Berry is in the writer's credits, as he wrote "My Dear."

Discography

Flip 324 My Dear/Do You Love Me? (1957)
Sources: K. Efron on WFUV's *R&B Group Harmony Revue*; S. Propes liner notes with Donna CD *One Teardrop Too Late.*

Daffodils (Chicago)

Personnel Clyde Williams (tenor), Johnny "Chubby" Jones

Notes

The Daffodils, managed by Levi McKay (who also managed the Five Chances, the Fasinoles, and the Fortunes), was a training ground that McKay used in switching singers from one group to another.

Johnny Jones's real name was Hilliard Jones. He and Williams eventually moved up to the Five Chances.

Discography

CJ 100 Wine/These Kissable Lips (1956)
Source: Bob Pruter, *Doowop . . . The Chicago Scene.*

Danderliers (Chicago)

Personnel James Campbell (lead, ballads), Dallas Taylor (d) (lead, fast sides), Bernard Dixon (1st tenor), Walter Stephenson (baritone), Richard Thomas (bass)

Notes

These were neighborhood friends who attended two different Chicago high schools.

After graduation, they began singing in earnest. A United Records executive heard them singing in a local park and asked if they were interested in recording! This was 1954, and they auditioned several times for the United/States complex. In March 1955, they had their first recording session.

Dallas Taylor stated in an interview that the group's name was taken from the dandelion flower.

The Danderliers stayed together for four years. After they left States Records, they recorded four sides for Mercury that were never released.

Walter Stephenson attended the same high school as the Moroccos, El Dorados, and the Dukays.

Louis Johnson replaced Richard Thomas at bass on the third release. Thomas was unhappy about the group's financial situation. He had a good job and a family that made traveling with the group very difficult.

After "My Love" the Danderliers drifted apart.

In 1967 Taylor got the group together again and recorded Walk On with Your Nose Up/All the Way on Midas. Only Dixon was not on this recording, as he was in the army at the time.

Dallas Taylor joined a later Dells group and recorded "Swingin' Teens" on Vee Jay with Chuck Barksdale and Verne Allison. He died in 1986.

Discography

States 147 Chop Chop Boom/My Autumn Love (1955)
States 150 Shu-Wop/My Loving Partner (1955)
States 152 May God Be with You/Little Man (1956)

States 160 My Love/She's Mine (1956)
B&F 150 Shu-Wop/My Loving Partner (1960)
B&F 160 My Love/She's Mine (1960)
B&F 1344 Chop Chop Boom/My Autumn Love (1960)
Midas 9004 All the Way/Walk On with Your Nose Up (1967)
Sources: Bob Pruter in *Record Collector's Monthly* 47; liner notes with the Chess *Rare Windy City* LP; Ralph Surley in *Bim Bam Boom.*

Danleers (Brooklyn, N.Y.)

Personnel Jimmy Weston (lead), Johnny Lee (1st tenor), Willie Ephraim (2d tenor), Nat McCune (baritone), Roosevelt Mays (bass)

Notes

The Danleers formed while the members were still teenagers in Brooklyn in 1958. They retained the services of manager/songwriter/mentor Danny Webb. Weston and Lee worked with each other and decided to form a singing group. They spoke with three other colleagues at work and formed the vocal group they were dreaming of. When Danny Webb felt they were ready to record, they signed up with the Mercury-distributed Amp-3 Records. When Mercury saw "One Summer Night" begin to take off, the masters were purchased by the bigger label—Mercury.

The group's first release on Amp-3 Records was initially issued with the group billed as the Dandleers. When it was eventually released on Mercury, the name was corrected to Danleers.

After the Mercury group broke up (which was quite soon after the hit), the remaining members of the Danleers and what was left of Danny Webb's other group, the Webtones (MGM), formed a new Danleers group and recorded for Epic.

The Epic group consisted of Jimmy Weston (lead), Louis Williams (1st tenor), Douglas Ebron (2d tenor), Terry Wilson (baritone) and Frankie Clemens (bass). *(Note:* On the Mercury *Danleers* CD [1996], the bass is referred to as Clemons. The five members above, recorded all the Epic sides.)

Bill Carey joined later as baritone/bass. Carey had been with the Four Fellows on Tri-Boro and the Victorians on Saxony.

Discography

Amp-3 1005 One Summer Night/Wheelin' and Dealin' (1958)
Mercury 71322 One Summer Night/Wheelin' and Dealin' (1958)
Mercury 71356 I Really Love You/My Flaming Heart (1958)
Mercury 71401 A Picture of You/Prelude to Love (1958)
Mercury 71441 I Can't Sleep/Your Love (1959)
Epic 9367 If You Don't Care/Half a Block from an Angel (1959)
Epic 9421 I'll Always Be in Love with You/Little Lover (1960)
Everest 19412 Foolish/Just Lookin' Around (1961)
Smash 1872 If/Were You There? (1964)
Smash 1895 Where Is the Love/The Angels Sent You (1964)
LeMans 004 The Truth Hurts/Baby You've Got It (1964)
Sources: R. Weize, liner notes with the Bear Family CD *Danleers*; Marv Goldberg in *Record Exchanger* 24; Jay Warner, *American Singing Groups.*

Dappers (Boston)

Personnel George "Dapper" Cromwell (lead), Roland Clements (tenor)

Notes

This is the Peacock group.

Clements also performed with the Sophomores on Dawn and was the brother of Donald Clements, who was with that group.

Cromwell later recorded as George "Dapper" Cromwell and the Uniques for the Dapper label, doing the standard "My Mother's Eyes."

Discography

Peacock 1651 Come Back to Me/Mambo Oongh (1955)
Source: Galen Gart and Roy Ames in *Duke/Peacock Records.*

Dappers (New York)

Personnel Larry Harrison (lead), Greg Carroll (tenor), Leonard Puzey (baritone), Jerome Robinson (bass)

Notes

Larry Harrison was with the Four Buddies, the Buddies, and the Barons. Greg Carroll also sang with the Four Buddies, as well as with the Orioles. Leonard Puzey sang with the Ravens.

Before ever making any appearances supporting the recording for Groove, the Dappers disbanded. Carroll and friend Al Showell joined forces with the female duo the Sweethearts—Pat Wilson and Joy Wright. Puzey was still the baritone. These five were the second Dappers group, which recorded for Rainbow. This group disbanded because Joy left to start her family.

Greg Carroll had been with the Four Buddies on Savoy and the Orioles.

Discography

First Group
Groove 0156 Unwanted Love (LH)/That's All, That's All, That's All (LH) (1956)

Second Group
Rainbow 373 Bop Bop Bu (GC)/How I Need You Baby (GC/JW) (1957)
Source: Marv Goldberg and Mike Redmond in *Yesterday's Memories* 12.

Darchaes, Ray & (Asbury Park, N.J.)

Personnel Ray Dahrouge (lead), Tony Juliano (falsetto), Louie Scalpati (1st tenor), Sal Capalungo (2d tenor), Denny Testa (baritone), Sam Siciliano (bass)

Notes

These were high school chums from Asbury Park. Nicky Addeo would often sing with them and in 1963 he replaced Dahrouge.

In *Story Untold-1* in the "Nicky Addeo Story" Ronnie Italiano writes that despite the fact that there were sometimes six to eight members of this group, they used four or five for recordings.

In 1962 the group consisted of Siciliano, Addeo, Rufus Edwards, Louie, and Pat Siciliano.

Discography

Aljon 1249/1250 Carol/Little Girl So Fine (1962)
Sources: Ronnie Italiano in *Story Untold*; liner notes with the Aljon CD *Brooklyn's DooWop Sound* from 1996.

Dates, Lincoln Fig & (Brooklyn, N.Y.)

Personnel Ivan Lincoln "Fig" Figueroa (d) (lead), Steve Aspromonti (1st tenor), Manuel Banuchi (2d tenor), John Giglioni (baritone), Edward Cruz (bass)

Notes

This group formed in Brooklyn in 1956, originally calling themselves the Shadows. At the time of their first recording session, their manager changed their name to Lincoln Fig and the Dates. Their one release on Worthy was not very successful.

Discography

Worthy 1006 Way Up (LF)/Kiss Me Tender (LF) (1958)
Source: Bill Schwartz in *Time Barrier Express* 3, no. 2.

Dawns (Philadelphia)

Personnel Bill Horton (lead), Joe Moody, Robert Byrd, George Willis

Notes

Horton had been with the Silhouettes. The Dawns formed when the Silhouettes' popularity began to fade. They cut one tune for Philadelphia's Lawn records, as Bill Harton and the Dawns [sic].

Discography

Lawn 241 Like to See You in That Mood/Shadow (1964)
Source: Charlie Horner and Don Leins in *Harmony Tymes* 2, article about the Silhouettes.

Billy Dawn Quartet (Brooklyn, N.Y.)

Personnel Billy Dawn Smith (lead), Donny Myles (Donny Schested) (tenor), Tommy Smith (baritone), Sonny Benton (bass)

Notes

This group formed in the late 1940s in the Crown Heights section of Brooklyn. They released four discs all under four names: Billy Dawn Quartet, Mighty Dukes, Four Dukes, and the Heralds.

Al Browne, their accompanist, sometimes filled in at baritone for Tommy Smith, Billy Dawn Smith's brother. (*Note:* In the *Yesterday's Memories* story about this group, baritone Tommie Smith's name is spelled both Tommie and Tommy.)

Looking for assistance, the group teamed up with Mello-Moods manager Joel Turnero, who brought them to Duke Records. Their first release was as the Mighty Dukes. They then became the Four Dukes ("Crying in the Chapel").

When they went to Al Silver's Herald label, their name changed to the Heralds.

After the Heralds split up in 1955, Smith, Bea Caslon (a Herald secretary), and William Henry Miller (father of the Miller Sisters) pooled their resources and began the Hull label.

Donny Myles later went on to sing with the Victorians. According to the Relic CD liner notes and the same *Yesterday's Memories* story, his family name was Sehested.

Discography

Decatur 3001 This Is the Real Thing Now (BDS)/Crying for My Baby (BDS) (1952)
Sources: Marv Goldberg and Rick Whitesell in *Yesterday's Memories* 12; Donn Fileti, liner notes with the Relic CD *Herald.*

Daylighters (Chicago)

Personnel Dorsey Wood (lead), Tony Gideon, Eddie Thomas, George Wood

Notes

In 1961 Gideon was drafted and Gerald Sims took over lead chores.

Charles Colbert joined the Daylighters from the Trinidads.

Because the group was considered to be inactive in 1963, another Daylighters group, consisting of Ronnie Strong, Donald Jenkins, Walter Granger (Fortunes), and two other former members from the old group, joined to form this new Daylighters group.

It is understood that because of legal issues, management changed this new group's name to the Delighters. Then Gideon's army hitch was over and he returned home. He re-formed the Daylighters to include himself, Eddie Thomas, Charles Colbert, baritone Curtis Burrell, and tenor Ulysses McDonald.

By 1963, Burrell had left the group.

Discography

Bea and Baby 103 Mad House Jump/You're Breaking My Heart (1959)
C.J. 611 Why Did You Have to Go/Please Come Back (1960)
C.J. 614 Tough Love/Sweet Rocking Mama (1960)
Nike 1011 This Heart of Mine/Bear Mash Stomp (1961)
Astra 1001 This Heart of Mine/Bear Mash Stomp (1961)
Tip Top 2002 Baby I Love You/Cool Breeze (1962)
Checker 1051 No One's Gonna Help You/War Hoss Mash (1963)
Tolie 9028 Here Alone/Whisper of the Wind (1964)
Tip Top 2008 Hard-Headed Girl/Oh Mom (1964)
Tip Top 2009 I Can't Stop Crying/Magic Touch (1964)

Tip Top 2010 for My Baby/Sweeter (1965)
Source: Bob Pruter, *Doowop . . . The Chicago Scene.*

Deans

Personnel Ralph Maffei (lead), Joe Macaluso (tenor), Tom Cori (baritone), Fred Khoury (bass)

Notes

Originally the Four Playboys, the group changed its name out of admiration for Dean Martin, calling itself first the Dinos and finally the Deans.

Discography

Mohawk 114 I'll Love You Forever/My Heart Is Low (1960)
Mohawk 119 Humpty Dumpty/La Chaim (1961)
Mohawk 126 It's You/I Don't Want to Wait (1961)
Laurie 3114 I Don't Want to Wait/Little White Gardenia (1961)
Sources: Liner notes with the Sparkletone CD *Laurie*; Donn Fileti, liner notes with the Relic CD *Golden Groups/Mohawk Records.*

Debonaires (Long Island, N.Y.)

Personnel Robert Adino, Mike DiBenedetto, Edwin Lamboy, Frank Reina, Ed Johnson (bass)

Notes

This group began with several personnel combinations in 1957. Eventually, Adino and DiBenedetto were introduced to Lamboy and Reina. Although one of these groups, Lucille Val and the Echos, recorded a disc that seems to have been released, we do not know the label. The group members all attended Boys High School. Between the school and their neighborhood came the Mystics, the Passions, Little Anthony and the Imperials, the Velours, and so on.

They played at local clubs, fairs, and various nightspots and were soon spotted by Bert Keyes of Gee Records.

For quite some time it was rumored that this group, due to their sound, was black. However, this is simply not correct.

They cut a second release, but the payola scandal was in high gear at that time and probably prevented its release.

When everything pending fell through, the members became disenchanted and broke up.

Discography

Gee 1008 Won't You Tell Me/I'm Gone (1956)
Gee 1054 We'll Wait/Make Believe Lover (1959)
Source: Ed Engel in *Harmony Tymes* 1.

Debonaires (Atlanta)

Personnel Arthur Simon, Emory Cloud, Milton Boykin

Notes

Sometimes referred to as the Five Debonaires, this was the Herald group. According to Donn Fileti's liner notes, their Herald disc was written and published by Milton Lowery from Atlanta, Georgia. It is therefore possible that the Debonaires/ Five Debonaires were from that locale as well.

Discography

Herald 509 Darling/Whispering Blues (1957)
Source: Donn Fileti, liner notes with the Relic LP *Best of Herald.*

De'Bonairs (Chicago)

Personnel Ralph Johnson (lead), Virgil Talbert (1st tenor), William Sonny Nelson (2d tenor), Earl Vanorsby (baritone), Edward Johnson (bass)

Notes

Their Ping record, "Mother's Son," was recorded at the Chess facilities in Chicago. This tune did so well at the start that Vee Jay had one of its own groups, the Delegates, cover it.

In 1958 Homer Talbert joined the group adding, both his vocal ability and his expert piano playing skills. He replaced bass Edward Johnson. Richard James replaced baritone Vanorsby.

The group gradually began to break up and by 1964 no longer existed.

Discography

Ping 1000 Lanky Linda/Mother's Son (1956)
Ping 1001 Say a Prayer for Me/Cracker-Jack Daddy (1956)
B&F 1353 Fool's Love/Ah-La-La (1958)
Source: Bob Pruter, *Doowop . . . The Chicago Scene.*

Deckers (Philadelphia)

Personnel Sam Connors (lead), John Williams (1st tenor), Larry Williams (baritone), Ben Hart (bass)

Notes

The Deckers began in Philadelphia in 1954.

That same year, Larry Williams entered the service and was replaced by Curtis Barnes. Williams returned home in 1957 and rejoined the group, which encountered an opportunity to record for NAR. The group at that time was Sam Conners, Curtis Barnes, John and Larry Williams, and Ben Hart.

Just after this first recording, Barnes left to join a spiritual group. At that time they met Jack Green, who had formed the Yeadon label, and they recorded Yeadon's first release, "Sincerely with All My Heart." Because of Green's unfamiliarity with record promotion, nothing was done and the disc did poorly.

In the 1960s the group changed their name to the Buddies (Red Top, Val-Ue, Swan) and the Tiffanies (Swan).

The group later became Teddy and the Twilights.

Discography

NAR 225 Oh, Where Did You Go?/Why Did I Go? (1957)
Yeadon 101 Sincerely with All My Heart/Come Back Baby (1958)
Yeadon 1041 Sincerely with All My Heart/The Thing (1958)
Source: Charlie Horner and Steve Applebaum in *Yesterday's Memories* 9.

Decoys, Connie & (Bronx, N.Y.)

Personnel Connie Strachan-Questell (lead), Herbert Joseph (1st tenor), Isaac Gordon (d) (2d tenor), Malcolm Quick (baritone), Marian Green (bass)

Notes

The Decoys came from the Melrose section of the Bronx in New York. They are proud to say that their "It's Going to Be Alright" on the Times Square label was one of Irving "Slim" Rose's best-selling discs. Al Browne produced the disc specifically for Rose and his down-in-the-subway record phenomenon.

Discography

Aanko 1005 I Want Only You/Tomorrow (1963)
Times Square 8 It's Going to Be Alright/Oh Baby (1963)
Times Square 9 I Want Only You/Tomorrow (1964)
Velvet 1001 Listen to Me/Always Be Good (1964)
Sources: Donn Fileti, liner notes with the Relic LP *Best of Times Square Records;* Malcolm Quick, interview by author, April 23, 1994.

Deep River Boys (Hampton, Va.)

Personnel Harry Douglas (lead), Vernon Gardner (1st tenor), George Lawson (2d tenor), Edward Ware (d) (bass)

Notes

The Deep River Boys met at the Hampton Institute in Virginia. When all four realized they had similar intentions to sing, they left school and set off for New York. They were quite successful, performing many songs at many dates.

They were named after their theme song, "Deep River," quite early in their career.

Their first recording was for Bluebird Records in 1940. They sang on many radio shows, spent a brief time on Broadway, and did quite well for themselves.

Like other groups of their time (e.g., Delta Rhythm Boys, Golden Gate Quartet), the Deep River Boys went to Europe after the war seeking success, since changing music styles were becoming popular with the young set in the United States. They were very popular in England, playing the Paladium five consecutive years.

Lawson decided to retire from singing in 1950. James Lundy and then Carter Wilson replaced him (April 1952).

Edward Ware retired in 1956 due to a recurring illness. He died later that year. He was replaced by Al Bishop. Vernon Gardner also retired in 1956 and the group became a trio.

Ray Beatty was a 2d tenor replacement for the group. Hugh Bryant was a baritone replacement, as was Rhett Butler.

Discography

RCA 26533 Nothing but You/Every Sunday Afternoon (1940)
Bluebird 10676 I Was a Fool to Let You Go/Bullfrog and the Toad (1940)
Bluebird 10847 A Bird in the Hand/You Don't Know Nothin' (1940)
Bluebird 11178 My Heart at Thy Sweet Voice/Cherokee (1941)
Bluebird 11217 Utt Da Zay/I Wish I Had Died in My Cradle (1941)
RCA 27579 God Bless the Child/Motherless Child (w/B. Wain) (1941)
Bluebird 11569 By the Light of the Silvery Moon (no group) (1942)
Majestic 1017 My Guy's Come Back (no group) (1945)
Majestic 1023 Just-A-Sittin' and a Rockin' (no group) (1946)
Pilotone 5147/48 Git On Board Little Children/We Are Walking in the Light (1946)
Pilotone 5149/50 Swing Low, Sweet Chariot/Go Down Moses (1946)
Pilotone 5151/52 On Freedom/Honey, Honey, Honey (1946)
Pilotone 5153/54 My Castle On the Nile/I'm Trampin' (1946)
RCA 20-1863 Story of Ee-Bobba-Lee-Bob/That Chick's Too Young to Fry (1946)
RCA 20-1990 Foolishly Yours/William Didn't Tell (1946)
RCA 20-2157 Charge It to Daddy/Jealous (1947)
RCA 20-2265 Live Humble/Seen Four and Twenty Elders (1947)
RCA 20-2305 Dream Street/Get Up Those Stairs Mademoiselle (1947)
RCA 20-2397 Bloop-Bleep/I Left Myself Wide Open (1947)
RCA 20-2448 By the Light of the Silvery Moon (w/F. Waller) (no group) (1947)
RCA 20-2517 Heads You Win, Tails I Lose/It Had to Be You (1947)
RCA 20-2610 I'm Sorry I Didn't Say I'm Sorry/What Did He Say? (1947)
RCA 20-2622 Purgatory/Swing Low, Sweet Clarinet (1948)
RCA 20-2808 I Wanna Sleep/Two Blocks Down, Turn to the Left (1948)
RCA 20-2998 Ain't Misbehavin'/That's What You Need to Succeed (1948)
RCA 20-3203 It's Too Soon to Know/Recess in Heaven (1948)
RCA 22-0003 Wrapped Up in a Dream/Don't Ask Me Why (1949)
RCA 22-0013 No One, No Sweeter Than You/Cry and You Cry Alone (1949)
RCA 22-0078 Free Grace/If You Love God—Serve Him (1950)
RCA 50-0078 Free Grace/If You Love God—Serve Him (1950)
RCA 47-3235 Solid as a Rock/Mine Too (w/Count Basie) (1950)
RCA 45-0013 Necessity/Old Devil Moon (1951)
Beacon 9143 Truthfully/Doesn't Make Sense to Me (1952)
Beacon 9146 All I Need Is You/Sleepy Little Cowboy (1952)
RCA 47-5268 Oo-Shoo-Be-Doo Bee/The Biggest Fool (1953)
Jay Dee 788 No One Else Will Do/Truthfully (1954)
Vik 0205 Whole Wide World/All My Love Belongs to You (1956)

Vik 0224 You're Not Too Ol'/How Dear Can It Be? (1956)
Gallant 101/102 Nola/Kissin' (1959)
Gallant 2001 I Don't Know Why/Timbers Gotta Roll (1959)
Seeco 6046 I Don't Know Why/Timbers Gotta Roll (1960)
Wand 117 Are You Certain/The Vanishing American (1961)
Michelle 1001 More 'n' More Amour/The Clouds before the Storm (1965)
Sources: Pete Grendysa in *Goldmine* 38; Donn Fileti, liner notes with the Relic CD
Jay Dee.

Deeptones (New Jersey)

Personnel George Vereen (1st tenor), Fletcher Smith (tenor), Furman (Thurman?)
Hayes (2d tenor), Calvin Williams (baritone), Carroll Dean (bass)

Notes

Prior to recording as the "Four Deeptones" for Coral in 1951, the group was on
record labels as the "Deeptones."

Vereen and Williams also sang for the Four Knights (and Vereen for the Stereos).
Ivy Floyd replaced Fletcher Smith.

After the Four Deeptones, they changed their name to the HiLiters and recorded
for the HiCo label.

Discography

Muzicon 736 My Prayer/Shadrack (1946)
Source: Pete Grendysa in *Goldmine,* May 8, 1987.

Delacardos

Personnel Harold Ford, Vernon Hill, Robert Gates, Christopher Harris

Discography

Elgey 1001 Letter to a Schoolgirl/I'll Never Let You Down (1960)
United Artists 276 I Got It/Thing-A-Ma-Jig (1960)
United Artists 310 Hold Back the Tears/Mr. Dillon (1961)
Shell 308 Dream Girl/I Just Want to Know (1961)
Shell 311 Love Is the Greatest Thing/Girl, Girl (1962)
Imperial 5992 On the Beach/Everybody's Rockin' (1963)
Source: Bob Ferlingere, *A Discography of R&B and R&R Vocal Groups.*

Delcos (South Bend, Ind.)

Personnel Peter Woodard (lead), Glen Madison (1st tenor), Richard Green (2d
tenor), Ralph Woods (baritone), Otis Smith (bass)

Notes

All group members attended South Bend Central High. After a great deal of practice,
they finally recorded Arabia/These Three Little Words in 1962 for the Ebony label.

None of the Delcos' follow-ups to Arabia/Three Little Words did anything and the group decided to disband.

In 1972 Glen Madison was singing with the Penguins.

Discography

Ebony 01/02 Arabia/These Three Little Words (1962)
Showcase 2501 Arabia/Three Little Words (1962)
Sound Stage 7 2501 Those Three Little Words/Arabia (1963)
Sound Stage 7 2515 Still Miss You So/Just Ask (1964)
Source: Marv Goldberg in *Record Exchanger* 11.

Delegates (Chicago)

Personnel Delecta "Dee" Clark (lead), Doug Brown (2d tenor), Teddy Long (baritone), John Carter (bass)

Notes

The Delegates were also known as the Kool Gents.

Long had been a member of the El Dorados.

First tenor John McCall was a later member of the Delegates.

The second coming of the Delegates found a different group behind Clark, which included Vee Jay A&R chief Calvin Carter and songwriter Oscar Brown Jr.

Discography

Vee Jay 212 The Convention/Jay's Rock (Big Jay McNeely) (1956)
Vee Jay 243 Mother's Son/I'm Gonna Be Glad (1957)
Source: Billy Vera, liner notes with the Vee Jay CD *A Taste of Doo Wop.*

Dells (Harvey, Ill.)

Personnel Johnny Funches (d) (lead), Marvin Junior (1st tenor), Vern Allison (2d tenor), Lucius McGill (baritone), Chuck Barksdale (bass)

Notes

The Dells began as the El Rays on Checker with their recording of "Darling I Know" and "Christine."

As a result of the failure of their El Rays effort and no success with "Tell the World" or "Dreams of Contentment" as the Dells, when they recorded "Oh What a Night," Chuck Barksdale abandoned the group and joined Otis Williams and the Charms. His bass part on "Oh What a Night" was taken by Calvin Carter. Lucius McGill left for a job in the post office. His brother Mickey assumed his place.

The success of "Oh What a Night" brought Barksdale back to the group.

In an interview, Marvin Junior candidly relates that it was the Moonglows who really taught the Dells their harmony and stage presence. The Moonglows showed a keen interest in the potential of the Dells.

A car wreck in 1958 broke Mickey's leg and put him in the hospital. Barksdale went through the windshield, but the four remaining members appeared at the show in Philadelphia despite the tragedy. As a result of the mishap, the Dells did not perform for two years.

Funches's wife was against his continuing with the group due to their run of failures and, in 1958, Johnny Carter of the Flamingos was brought in. (An article by Robert Pruter in *Record Collector's Monthly* [November–December 1991] says that this was 1960.)

During the next year (1959) they learned modern harmony, and Dinah Washington had the Dells join her on the road and in the recording studio.

In 1961, most of the Dells returned to Vee Jay to record "Swinging Teens," with Danderliers' lead Dallas Taylor fronting the group.

Due to financial difficulties, the Dells disbanded again, with Carter and Barksdale remaining with Dinah and her group (D's Gentlemen), which now consisted of Cornel Gunter and three members of the Altairs. This ended when Washington died in 1963.

Following a long list of failures, the group became a significant soul entity as well as a backup group for many single artists.

Discography

Vee Jay 134 Tell the World (1955)
Vee Jay 166 Dreams of Contentment/Zing, Zing, Zing (1955)
Vee Jay 204 Oh What a Nite/Jo Jo (1956)
Vee Jay 230 I Wanna Go Home/Movin' On (1956)
Vee Jay 236 Why Do You Have to Go?/Dance, Dance, Dance (1957)
Vee Jay 251 A Distant Love/O-Bop She-Bop (1957)
Vee Jay 258 Pain in My Heart/Time Makes You Change (1957)
Vee Jay 274 The Springer/What You Say Baby (1958)
Vee Jay 292 I'm Calling/Jeepers Creepers (1958)
Vee Jay 300 My Best Girl/Wedding Day (1958)
Vee Jay 324 Dry Your Eyes/Baby Open Up Your Heart (1958)
Vee Jay 338 Oh What a Nite/I Wanna Go Home (1958)
Vee Jay 376 Swingin' Teens/Hold On to What You've Got (1961)
Argo 5415 God Bless the Child/I'm Going Home (1962)
Argo 5428 Eternally/The (Bossa Nova) Bird (1962)
Argo 5442 If It Ain't One Thing It's Another/Hi Diddley Dee Dum Dum (1962)
Argo 5456 After You/Goodbye Mary Ann (1963)
Vee Jay 595 Shy Girl/What Do We Prove? (1964)
Vee Jay 615 Oh What a Good Nite/Wait till Tomorrow (1964)
Vee Jay 674 Stay in My Corner/It's Not Unusual (1964)
Vee Jay 712 Hey Sugar (Don't Get Serious)/Poor Little Boy I (1965)
Cadet 5538 Thinkin' About You/The Change We Go Thru (for Love) (1966)
Cadet 5551 Run for Cover/Over Again (1966)
Cadet 5563 You Belong to Someone Else/Inspiration (1967)
Cadet 5574 There Is/I I Love You (1967)
Cadet 5590 There Is/Show Me (1968)
Cadet 5599 Wear It on Our Face/Please Don't Change Me Now (1968)
Cadet 5612 Stay in My Corner/Love is So Simple (1968)
Cadet 5621 I Want My Momma/Always Together (1968)

Cadet 5631 Make Sure (You Have Someone to Love You)/Does Anybody Know I'm Here? (1968)
Cadet 5636 I Can't Do Enough/Hallways of My Mind (1969)
Cadet 5641 Hallelujah Baby/Medley: Can Sing a Rainbow/Love Is Blue (1969)
Cadet 5649 Oh What a Night/Believe Me (1969)
Cadet 5658 On the Dock of the Bay/When I'm in Your Arms (1969)
Cadet 5663 Oh What a Day/The Change We Go Thru for Love (1969)
Cadet 5667 Open Up My Heart/Nadine (1970)
Cadet 5672 Long Lonely Nights/A Little Understanding (1970)
Cadet 5679 The Glory of Love/A Whiter Shade of Pale (1971)
Cadet 5683 Freedom Means/The Love We Had (Stays on My Mind) (1971)
Cadet 5689 Oh My Dear/It's All Up to You (1972)
Cadet 5691 Walk on By/This Guy's in Love with You (1972)
Cadet 5694 I'd Rather Be with You/Just as Long as We're in Love (1972)
Cadet 5696 Closer/Give Your Baby a Standing Ovation (1973)
Cadet 5698 My Pretending Days Are Over/Let's Make It Last (1973)
Cadet 5700 I Miss You/Don't Make Me a Storyteller (1973)
Cadet 5702 Two Together Is Better Than One/I Wish It Was Me You Loved (1974)
Cadet 5703 Bring Back the Love of Yesterday/Learning to Love You Was Easy (1974)
Cadet 5703 Sweeter As the Days Go By/Learning to Love You Was Easy (1974)
Cadet 5707 You're the Greatest/The Glory of Love (1975)
Cadet 5710 Love is Missing From Our Lives/I'm in Love (1975)
Sources: Bob Pruter in *Record Collector's Monthly* 50; Jack Sbarbori in *Record Exchanger* 22.

Delltones (Long Island, N.Y.)

Personnel Della Simpson (a.k.a. Della Griffin) (lead), Sherry Gary, Frances Kelley, Gloria Alleyne (a.k.a. Gloria Lynne and Gloria Lynn)

Notes

The Delltones started as the Enchanters in 1952, recording for Jubilee. When they eventually split up, Frances Kelly, Della Simpson, and Gloria Lynne formed the Delltones.

Through Della's husband, who was managing them at this time, they got a contract to record for Coral Records' Brunswick subsidiary.

In June 1953 they had their first session for Brunswick. The first disc from this session was released in July. At this time they were playing local nightspots.

The Dell Tones moved to Rainbow Records in 1954 when little happened at Brunswick. Their only Rainbow disc was released in April. It should also be noted at this point that their name went from Dell Tones to Delltones and finally DellTones.

Sometime during the summer of 1954, Gloria left to go solo. Shirley Bunny Foy replaced her in the DellTones. Soon after this, Sherry Gary left and was replaced by Renee Stewart. The DellTones now consisted of Della Simpson, Frances Kelley, Bunny Foy, and Renee Stewart. Sometime in 1955, Frances Kelley left and was replaced by Algie Willie.

In 1955, they switched to Sol Rabinowitz's Baton Records. They had one session at Baton that yielded four sides, all of which were released. Their live appearance schedule continued. Baton released their second disc in March 1956. In May 1956 Gloria Bell was added. Late in 1956, Renee left and the DellTones soon became history.

Discography

Brunswick 85015 My Heart's on Fire (GA/DS)/Yours Alone (GA) 1953
Rainbow 244 I'm Not in Love With You (DS)/Little Short Daddy (DS) (1954)
Baton 212 Don't Be Long (DS)/Baby Say You Love Me (DS) (1955)
Baton 223 My Special Love (DS)/Believe It (DS) (1956)
Sources: Dave Penny and Gordon Skadberg, liner notes with the two *Jubilee Jezebels* CDs; Marv Goldberg's article on the Enchanters and Delltones in January 1998 issue of *DISCoveries.*

Del Rios

Personnel William Bell, James Taylor, Lewis Williams, Norman West

Discography

Meteor 5038 Alone on a Rainy Nite/Lizzie (1956)
Stax 125 Just across the Street/There's a Love (1962)
Rust 5066 Valerie/Mystery (1963)
Source: Ferdie Gonzalez, *Disco-File.*

Delroys (Queens, N.Y.)

Personnel Reggie Walker (bass/lead), John Blount (1st tenor), Ronald Coleman (2d tenor), Robert Coleman (baritone)

Notes

The members got together in 1956 in the Long Island City, New York, projects. They were around fourteen or fifteen years old at the time.

After "Bermuda Shorts," Robert Taylor replaced John Blount, who was discouraged. Taylor, Walker, and the Coleman brothers recorded "Wise Old Owl" for the Sparkell label, featuring Taylor on lead.

In 1961 following "Wise Old Owl," the group disbanded due to military obligations. Ron Coleman joined up with lead Ray Pain, 2d tenor Norman Baquie, and baritone Cliff Davis to record Love Me Tenderly/Pleasing You on the Carol label.

In 1964 Ron once again joined up with Reggie Walker and Walter Pope and recorded one tune, "Alimony," for Al Browne's Moon label.

In 1982, brothers Ron and Robert Coleman rejoined Reggie Walker to re-form the Delroys for revival appearances.

In the Relic CD liner notes, the 1st tenor's name is given as John Blunt. In addition, the label for the last recording is shown as Sparkdell.

Discography

Apollo 514 Bermuda Shorts (RW)/Time (backing Milton Sparks) (1957)
Sparkell 102 Wise Old Owl (BT)/Strange Land (BT) (1959)
Carol 4113 Love Me Tenderly (RP)/Pleasing You (RP) (1961)
Sources: Marv Goldberg in *Record Collector's Monthly* 44; Bob Pruter in *Record Exchanger* 30.

Del Satins (New York)

Personnel Stan Sommers (lead), Les Cauchi (1st tenor), Richie Greene (d) (2d tenor), Freddie Ferrara (baritone), Tommy Ferrara (bass)

Notes

The five members of this group were together for ten years, singing on street corners, buses, and subways.

Little success followed their initial recordings, but "Teardrops Follow Me" was a regional hit.

In the liner notes accompanying the Sequel CD *A Whiter Shade of Doo Wop* members are listed as Stan Ziska, Les Cauchi, Bobby Field, Fred Ferrara, and Tom Ferrara.

This group did all the background work for Dion from 1962 to 1964, and this association led them to great successes.

Time passed and their thoughts and philosophies began differing—a split was not too far away.

Following Stan Sommers's departure to do a solo act, Carl Parker joined as lead but simply could not fill Sommers's place in the group.

Richie Greene passed away, and Les and Freddie joined the Brooklyn Bridge.

Discography

End 1096 I'll Pray for You/I Remember the Night (as the Dell Satins) (1961)
Win 102 Counting Teardrops/Remember (1962)
Laurie 3132 Teardrops Follow Me/Best Wishes, Good Luck, Goodbye (1962)
Laurie 3149 Ballad of a Dee Jay/Does My Love Stand a Chance? (1962)
Columbia 42802 Feelin' No Pain/Who Cares? (1963)
Mala 475 Believe in Me/Two Broken Hearts (1964)
B.T. Puppy 506 Hang Around/My Candy Apple 'Vette (1965)
B.T. Puppy 509 Sweets for My Sweet/A Girl Named Arline (1965)
B.T. Puppy 514 Relief/The Throwaway Song (1965)
Diamond 216 A Little Rain Must Fall/Love, Hate, Revenge (1967)
B.T. Puppy 563 A Girl Named Arline/I'll Do My Crying Tomorrow (1969)
Sources: Arlene Kramer in *Bim Bam Boom* 3; Ace and Sparkletone Laurie CD liner notes.

Deltairs (Queens, N.Y.)

Personnel Barbara Thompson (lead), Barbara Lee, Carol Stansbury, Thelma Stansbury, Shirley Taylor

Notes

This was a group from the Jamaica section of Queens in New York City, the same area in which the Heartbeats, Cleftones, Rivileers, and the Five Sharps had originated.

The Deltairs had some gospel training in their background. Carol and Thelma Stansbury were sisters.

Discography

Ivy 101 Lullaby of the Bells/It's Only You Dear (1957)
Ivy 105 I Might Like It/Standing At the Altar (1958)
Felsted 106 Who Would Have Thought It/You Won't Be Satisfied (1958)
Sources: Bob Ferlingere, conversation with author; John Clemente, conversation with author; N. Gustafson and J. Dunn on the Internet. Available at: www.members.aol.com/wawawaooh/main.htm.

Delta Rhythm Boys
(Langston, Okla./New Orleans)

Personnel Elmaurice Miller (1st tenor), Traverse Crawford (d) (2d tenor), Essie Atkins (baritone), Otha Lee Gaines (d) (bass)

Notes

This group originated in 1935 at Langston Univerity in Oklahoma. They all transferred to Dillard University in New Orleans because they learned of a new music program starting there. They were awarded full scholarships at Dillard but never fully used those awards, leaving college to perform on radio shows, recordings, live performances, and even Broadway!

Through their manager, Paul Kapp, the younger brother of Jack and Dave Kapp, the Delta Rhythm Boys got their first recording date in 1940.

They were becoming very successful, but like all groups they found their traveling, both in the United States and South America, becoming too burdensome. The normal evolutionary changes would soon begin.

Clint Holland, later of the Four Knights, became 1st tenor and Kelsey Pharr (d) was baritone. Holland was replaced by Carl Jones at lead shortly after. This took place during the very early 1940s.

Kelsey Pharr died in Hawaii in 1942 and it was 1949 when their annual trips to Sweden began. Pharr was replaced by Hugh Bryant (d). According to Jay Warner's *American Singing Groups*, Pharr died in 1960.

It was also in 1942 that Jones decided to spend more time at home. Paul Kapp found them 1st tenor Herb Coleman.

They signed with RCA in December 1947, when they had many great releases. In 1949, they recorded for Atlantic as the Four Sharps, and it was also in 1949 that the group made their initial trip to Stockholm and London.

Walter Trammell became their new first tenor, and Ray Beatty the second tenor. Coleman was shot to death and Barry Johnson joined as tenor. Baritone Harry Lewis was also a member.

Lee Gaines died late in 1987 and group member Hugh Bryant sang a eulogy to Gaines at his funeral but died in the middle of this performance. This was basically the end of the Delta Rhythm Boys.

Discography

Decca 8514 Gimme Some Skin/Chilly 'n' Cold (1940)
Decca 8522 Dry Bones/Joshua Fit the Battle of Jericho (1940)
Decca 8530 Star Dust/Would It Be Asking Too Much? (1940)
Decca 8542 My Imaginary Love/My Blue Heaven (1940)
Decca 3661 When That Man Is Dead and Gone (Bailey)/Jenny (Bailey) (1941)
Decca 3691 Georgia on My Mind (Bailey)/I'm Afraid of Myself (Bailey) (1941)
Decca 8554 I Do, Do You (Believe in Love)/The Things I Love (1941)
Decca 8561 She Believed a Gypsy/Do You Care? (1941)
Decca 3755 Rockin' Chair (Bailey)/Sometimes I'm Happy (Bailey) (1941)
Decca 3888 Everything Depends on You (Bailey) (no group) (1941)
Decca 3953 It's So Peaceful in the Country (Bailey) (no group) (1941)
Decca 8578 Take the A Train/Let Me Off Uptown (1941)
Decca 8584 Playing the Game/Down on the Delta Shore (1941)
Decca 18187 Since I Kissed My Baby Goodbye (F. Astaire) (no group) (1941)
Decca 18188 Wedding Cake Walk (F. Astaire) (no group) (1941)
Decca 4128 When I'm Gone, You'll Soon Forget/When You're Gone I Won't Forget (1941)
Decca 11083 Georgia on My Mind (MB)/Rockin' Chair (MB) (1941)
Decca 4266 Mad about Her, Sad about Her, How Can I Be Glad without Her Blues/ Keep Smilin', Keep Laughin', Be Happy (1942)
Decca 4406 Dry Bones/Praise the Lord and Pass the Ammunition (1942)
Decca 4440 Do Nothin' till You Hear from Me/Travelin' Light (1944)
Decca 18650 Gee, Ain't I Good to You?/Is There Somebody Else? (1945)
Decca 23425 It's Only a Paper Moon (EF)/Cry You Out of My Heart (EF) (1945)
Decca 23451 Baby Are You Kiddin'/Honeydripper (1945)
Decca 18739 Just A-Sittin' and A-Rockin'/Don't Knock It (1945)
Decca 23541 Just A-Sittin' and A-Rockin'/No Pad to Be Had (1946)
Decca 18911 But She's My Buddy's Chick/Walk It Off (1946)
Decca 23670 For Sentimental Reasons (EF)/It's a Pity to Say Goodnight (EF) (1946)
Decca 11083 Georgia on My Mind (MB)/Rockin' Chair (MB) (1946)
Decca 25019 Georgia on My Mind (MB)/Rockin' Chair (MB) (1946)
Decca 23771 Hello, Goodbye, Forget It/Just Squeeze Me (Don't Tease Me) (1946)
Decca 24193 A One-Sided Affair (L. Paul)/What Would It Take? (L. Paul) (1946)
Victor 20-2183 Bye-Bye Alibi Baby/Jenny Kissed Me (1947)
Victor 20-2271 Hey John (Put Your Glasses On)/I'm Awfully Strong for You (1947)
Victor 20-2365 Every So Often/Come In Out of the Rain (1947)
Victor 20-2436 My Future Just Passed/I'm in Love with a Gal (1947)
Victor 20-2460 Dry Bones/September Song (1947)
Victor 20-2461 Take the A Train/East of the Sun (1947)
Victor 20-2462 St. Louis Blues/Every Time We Say Goodbye (1947)
Victor 20-2463 One O'Clock Jump/If You Are but a Dream (1947)
Victor 20-2588 Little Small Town Girl/Ain't Gonna Worry about a Soul (1947)

Victor 20-2855 Never Underestimate the Power of a Woman/You're Mine, You (1948)
Victor 20-3007 I Can't Tell a Lie to Myself/My Blue Heaven (1948)
Musicraft 597 Don't Ask Me Why/Fantastic (1949)
Atlantic 889 Sweetheart of Mine/The Laugh's on Me (1949)
Atlantic 899 I'll Come Back (Someday) (R. Brown)/Why? (R. Brown) (1950)
Decca 48138 You Go to Your Church I'll Go to Mine/Beyond the Sunset-Should You Go to First (1951)
Atlantic 900 Nobody Knows/If You See Tears in My Eyes (1951)
Atlantic 905 Sentimental Journey (no group) (1952)
Mercury 1408 On the Sunny Side of the Street/They Didn't Believe Me (1952)
Mercury 1409 Lover Come Back to Me/All the Things You Are (1952)
Victor 47-5094 I'll Never Get Out of This World Alive/I'm Used to You (1952)
Victor 47-5217 Dancing with Someone/Long Gone Baby (1953)
Atlantic 1023 It's All in Your Mind (R. Brown)/Sentimental Journey (RB) (1954)
Decca 29136 It's Only a Paper Moon (EF)/For Sentimental Reasons (EF) (1954)
Decca 29273 Have a Hope, Have a Wish, Have a Prayer/Mood Indigo (1954)
Decca 29329 Shoes/Kiss Crazy Baby (1954)
Decca 29528 Headin' for the Bottom/Babylon (1955)
Decca 29582 Don't Ever Change a Picture on the Wall/That's Just the Way I Feel (1955)
Decca 30466 Dry Bones/Joshua Fit the Battle of Jericho (1957)
Philips 40023 Work Song/My Own True Love (1962)
Sources: Pete Grendysa in *Goldmine* 34; Pete Grendysa in *Record Collector's Monthly* 39.

Deltars (Brooklyn, N.Y.)

Personnel Pearl McKinnon (lead), Carl Williams (1st tenor), James Straite (2d tenor), Luther Morton (baritone), Aaron "Bootsie" Broadnick (bass)

Notes

The Deltars started as the Mints then became the Young Lads. When McKinnon finally joined, they became the Deltars.

They had one disc released on Fury, but it failed. They claimed that Bobby Robinson of Fury Records was preoccupied with Gladys Knight and the Pips at the time and did not devote adequate time to them and their record.

Apparently they had heard of gigs at which they were supposedly appearing but had never been told about them. This happened several times.

After four masters, one record, and no appearances, they broke up.

Discography

Fury 1048 Teenager's Dream/Dance, Dance, Dance (1961)
Source: James Straite in *Yesterday's Memories* 4.

Del Vikings (Pittsburgh, Pa.)

Personnel Norman Wright (lead), Corinthian "Kripps" Johnson (d) (1st tenor), Don Jackson (2d tenor), David Lerchey (baritone), Clarence Quick (d) (bass)

Notes

The group that originally formed was all black. They met in 1955 at an air force base in Pittsburgh and won various air force talent contests. The demands that the service put on them were the reason for the group's dynamics and ever-changing personnel.

Pittsburgh deejay Barry Kaye thought he could record them and had them rehearse in the basement of his home. The resulting tapes are the tunes on the Luniverse LP, to which music was added several years after the original recording. These recordings were done after two members of the original group were shipped off to Germany. This is when the group became integrated.

The Dot follow-up to "Come Go with Me" was led by country singer Joey Briscoe. Next came "What Made Maggie Run" and "Little Billy Boy," which failed to chart.

The Del Vikings split into two groups because members of the group that signed with Fee Bee were all underage. Fee Bee was left with Kripps Johnson and Don Jackson. These two were the only members who had signed with Fee Bee who were of age. Clarence Quick remained at Mercury with Norman Wright (who named the group), David Lerchey, and newcomer William Blakely, who was Clarence Quick's cousin.

Mercury wound up as the exclusive owners of the Del Vikings. Kripps now sang with Chuck Jackson, Don Jackson, Arthur Budd, and Ed Everett as the Versatiles. By 1957, Kripps was in the Mercury group and Ritzy Lee replaced Gus Backus in 1958. Clarence Quick's group included Wright, Lerchey, Backus, and William Blakely.

Mercury and Dot records were released simultaneously as Mercury used Del Vikings and Dot used Dell Vikings. Also in 1957, the army shipped Gus Backus to Germany. Later that year, Kripps joined the Mercury group and finally there was one Del Vikings.

For the next thirty years these two groups appeared all over, sometimes with Quick and Kripps Johnson appearing together! The Mercury group with Joe Lopes in for David Lerchey appeared in *The Big Beat* motion picture in 1957.

After Mercury, they recorded for the Columbia subsidiary Alpine. They recorded "The Sun" for Alpine Records lead by Billy Woodruff.

Soon after, they signed with ABC. The group on ABC included Kripps Johnson, Clarence Quick, Ritzy Lee, Billy Woodruff, Willy Green, and Doug White.

Kripps's last group included Johnson, Norman Wright, Ritzy Lee, John Byas, and David Lerchey.

Discography

Fee Bee 205 Come Go With Me/How Can I Find True Love? (1956)
Dot 15538 How Can I Find True Love/Come Go With Me (1957)
Luniverse 106 Somewhere Over the Rainbow/Hey Señorita (1957)

Luniverse 110 Yours/Heaven and Paradise (1957)
Luniverse 113 In the Still of the Night/White Cliffs of Dover (1957)
Dot 15571 What Made Maggie Run?/Little Billy Boy (1957)
Dot 15592 Don't Be a Fool/Whisperine Fool (1957)
Mercury 71132 Cool Shake/Jitterbug Mary (1957)
Fee Bee 206 Down in Bermuda/Maggie (1957)
Fee Bee 210 What Made Maggie Run/Down By the Stream (1957)
Fee Bee 210 What Made Maggie Run/Uh Uh Baby (1957)
Dot 15636 I'm Spinning/When I Come Home (1957)
Fee Bee 214 Whispering Bells/Don't Be a Fool (1957)
Mercury 71198 I'm Spinning/When I Come Home (1957)
Fee Bee 218 I'm Spinning/You Say You Love Me (1957)
Dot 15673 Woke Up This Morning/Willette (1957)
Fee Bee 221 I Want to Marry You/Willette (1957)
Fee Bee 221 I Woke Up This Morning/Willette (1957)
Mercury 71180 Come Along With Us/What'cha Gotta Lose? (1957)
Fee Bee 227 Finger Poppin' Woman/Tell Me (1957)
Fee Bee 902 Baby, Let Me Be/True Love (1957)
Mercury 71241 Your Book of Life/Snowbound (1957)
Mercury 71266 The Voodoo Man/Can't Wait (1958)
Mercury 71345 Pretty Little Things Called Girls/You Cheated (1958)
Mercury 71390 Flat Tyre/How Could You? (1958)
Checker 886 Half Moon/Speedillac (1958)
Dot 16092 Come Go with Me/How Can I Find True Love (1960)
Alpine 66 Pistol Packin' Mama/The Sun (1960)
Ship 214 Sunday Kind of Love/Over the Rainbow (1961)
ABC 10208 I'll Never Stop Crying/Bring Back Your Heart (1961)
ABC 10248 I Hear Bells/Don't Get Slick on Me (1961)
ABC 10278 Kiss Me/Face the Music (1962)
ABC 10304 One More River to Cross/The Big Silence (1962)
ABC 10341 Confession of Love/Kiliminjaro (1962)
ABC 10385 Angel Up in Heaven/The Fishing Chant (1963)
ABC 10425 Sorcerer's Apprentice/Too Many Miles (1963)
Mercury 30112 Come Along With Me/A Sunday Kind of Love (1963)
Gateway 743 I've Got to Know/We Three (1964)
Luniverse 114 Girl, Girl/There I Go (1970)
Scepter 12367 Come Go With Me/When You're Asleep (1972)
Bim Bam Boom 111 Cold Feet/I Want to Marry You (1972)
Bim Bam Boom 113 Watching the Moon/You Say You Love Me (1972)
Bim Bam Boom 115 I'm Spinning/Girl, Girl (1972)
Blue Sky 104 Over the Rainbow/Hey Senorita (1972)
Broadcast 1123 You Are Invited/Heaven on Earth (1973)
Fee Bee 173 Hollywood and Wine/Welfare Blues (1977)
Sources: Pete Grendysa in *Goldmine*; John Broven, liner notes with the Flyright CD *Come Go with Me*; Wayne Stierle in *DISCoveries*; Stefan Pingel's biography of the Del Vikings entitled *Del Vikings Discography*. Independently published.

Delvons (Brooklyn, N.Y.)

Personnel Vito Balsamo (lead), Eddie Parducci (1st tenor)

Notes

Balsamo of course went on to form Vito and the Salutations while Parducci followed later.

Discography

J.D.F. 760 Please Stay/Stay Clear of Love (1967)

Del-Vons (New York)

Personnel Ben Monroe (lead), Earl Price (1st tenor), Mickey Paige (2d tenor), Ray Jackson (baritone), Fred Paige (bass)

Notes

Fred Paige was formerly with the Chanters.

Discography

Wells 1001 Gone Forever (BM)/All I Did Was Cry (FP) (1966)
Source: Marv Goldberg, "Yesterday's Memories," *Goldmine*, article on the Chanters.

Demens (New York)

Personnel Eddie Jones (lead), Jimmy Caines (1st tenor), Thomas Cook (2d tenor), Frankie Cook (baritone), Tommy Outlaw (bass)

Notes

After arriving in New York (from California), Eddie Jones started as a member of the Solitaires. But the army intervened just before recording. Bobby Baylor took his place with the Solitaires and the rest of the story is well-known.

His new group, the Demens, formed on 61st Street and Columbus Avenue in Manhattan.

When the Demens were ready to record, they searched for a recording company and were successful on their first try—at Teenage Records on Eighth Avenue.

They had one session during which they recorded four songs, all of which were released. There was very little promotion and little evidence of the record company doing anything to assist their output. The label management and the label disappeared and the Demens had to go elsewhere.

Finding themselves in this strange position, the Demens continued to make stage appearances. Finally they signed with Jerry Winston, owner of the Newport label. He made them change their name to the Emersons (because of the missing Teenage management who were needed to obtain a release and avoid litigation).

Discography

Teenage 1006 Take Me As I Am/You Broke My Heart (1956)
Teenage 1008 Hey Young Girl/The Greatest of Them All (1956)
Source: Dave Hinckley and Marv Goldberg in *Yesterday's Memories* 9.

Demolyrs (Brooklyn, N.Y.)

Personnel Robert Vignaplano (lead), Ralph Marsella (1st tenor), Robert Ciapetta
(2d tenor), Alex Narducci (baritone), Michael Manno (bass)

Notes

The Demolyrs performed a great deal of backup vocals as well as instrumental backgrounds for various artists on various labels.

They recorded the disc below at New York's CBS studios, and it was released on
UWR. They made some club and other social functions after the recording, but the
British invasion was taking hold, and this marked the end of the Demolyrs.

They broke up in the mid-1960s because some of the members were drafted.

Discography

UWR 900 Hey Little Rosie/Rain (1964)
Source: Bob Diskin in *Record Collector's Monthly* 46.

Desideros (Chicago)

Personnel Marshall Thompson (lead), Eddie Sullivan (tenor), Del Brown (tenor),
Joe Manual (baritone), Creadel Jones (bass)

Notes

People who remember them say that this was an outstanding live act.

It is understood that on "Flat-Foot Charlie" Robert Goley was in the group.

Discography

Renee 1040 I Pledge My Love/Flat-Foot Charlie (1963)
Source: Bob Pruter, *Doowop . . . The Chicago Scene.*

Desires (New York)

Personnel Robert "Bootsie" White (lead), Charles Hurston (1st tenor), James
Whittier (2d tenor), Jerome "Smitty" Smith (baritone), Charles Powell (bass)

Notes

When the Apt group the Jivetones split apart, they all returned to their homes in
Rochester, New York. One member of the group, Jim Whittier, came back to Harlem,
where he met up with the other members of the Desires.

They started practicing quite often and Eddie Jones, formerly of the Demens and
the Newports, became their vocal coach; James Dailey became their manager. Dailey

got the group a contract with Bea Kaslon's Hull Records. Let It Please Be You/Hey Lena were released by Hull in 1959.

This first release had an excellent reception in the East, providing the Desires with many live appearances. The second release, Rendezvous with You/Set Me Free, was released in 1960 and live dates mounted.

The Desires recorded a third single, but Hull's financial position was poor and it was never released. In spite of this, they did a lot of touring on the East Coast. Hull owner Bea Kaslon (Casalin) died suddenly, which acted as a catalyst in Hull's rapid decline. Due to the group's one year of inactivity, they began drifting apart. The year 1961 marked the end of the Desires.

Bill Schwartz's article in *Time Barrier Express* 21 refers to baritone Smith as Jerome. In Joe Sicurella's article in the same periodical, he refers to Smith as George.

The Desires' recording on Smash was by a different group!

Discography

Hull 730 Let It Please Be You/Hey Lena (1959)
Hull 733 Set Me Free/Rendezvous with You (1959)
Sources: Bill Schwartz in *Time Barrier Express* 21; Joe Sicurella in *Bim Bam Boom* 11.

Devotions (Queens, N.Y.)

Personnel Ray Sanchez, Bob Weisbrod, Bob Hovorka, Joe Pardo, Frank Pardo

Notes

After first organizing in 1960 and organizing the group as efficiently as they could, they rehearsed and practiced seven nights a week, four hours each night until they felt ready to record.

They first approached Delta Records with their versions of older songs. Delta management told them to come back with original material. They later returned with "Rip Van Winkle." Following its release, poor promotion resulted in poor sales and the owner of Delta sold the master to Roulette.

Roulette let it lay dormant for several years and then included it in an oldies LP. A deejay in Pittsburgh played "Rip Van Winkle" incessantly on his show and the response was good enough for Roulette to rerelease it in 1964.

By this time the group had fallen apart and its members were widely scattered. Joe Pardo had already left and was replaced by Louis DeCarlo. In 1963, Weisbrod and Sanchez were drafted. Roulette called and asked to get the group back together. The Sanchez brothers were no problem, Hovorka lived nearby, and DeCarlo was easily found. A bass was needed and Larry Frank filled the bill.

Roulette had them record several more tunes that failed upon release. Because of this failure and Roulette's lack of support, they disbanded in 1965.

Discography

Delta 1001 Rip Van Winkle/For Sentimental Reasons (1961)
Roulette 4406 Rip Van Winkle/For Sentimental Reasons (1962)
Roulette 4541 Rip Van Winkle/For Sentimental Reasons (1964)
Roulette 4556 Sunday Kind of Love/Tears from a Broken Heart (1964)

Roulette 4580 Snow White/Zindy Lou (1964)
Source: Jeff Beckman in *Bim Bam Boom* 2.

Diablos (Detroit)

Personnel Nolan Strong (d) (lead), Juan Gutierrez (tenor), Willie Hunter (baritone), Quentin Ewbanks (d) (bass)

Notes

The Diablos got together in high school in 1950. After four years of practicing and making local appearances, they felt ready for a piece of the pie that so many groups were enjoying.

According to Phil Groia in his *They All Sang on the Corner* Nolan Strong was a student of Billy Ward's (Dominoes). This book also states that Nolan Strong and Barrett Strong (Money) were cousins.

When they went to Fortune Records in Detroit for an audition, they sang for co-owner Devora Brown. After hearing them, she signed them on the spot.

After "The Wind" was released, bass Quentin Ewbanks and tenor Juan Gutierrez left the group and Ewbanks was replaced by George Scott. Nolan's brother Jim (d) replaced Gutierrez.

Nolan was drafted in 1956 and Jimmy took his place until he was discharged in 1958. During this time only Oh Harriet/Come Home Little Girl was released with Jimmy doing lead chores.

In 1960 J. W. Johnson replaced George Scott at bass. In 1963 the Diablos' lineup consisted of Nolan Strong, Willie Hunter, J. W. Johnson, Bob Calhoun, and Cy Iverson.

Bob Chico Edwards joined one of the later Diablos groups.

Nolan Strong died in 1977 at the age of 43.

The Regency CD liner notes spell the bass's name Eubanks.

Discography

Fortune 509/510 Adios My Desert Love/An Old-Fashioned Girl (1954)
Fortune 511 The Wind/Baby Be Mine (1954)
Fortune 514 Route 16/Hold Me until Eternity (1955)
Fortune 516 Daddy Rockin' Strong/Do You Remember What You Did? (1955)
Fortune 518 The Way You Dog Me Around/Jump, Shake, and Move (1955)
Fortune 519 You Are/You're the Only Girl, Delores (1956)
Fortune 522 Try Me One More Time/A Teardrop from Heaven (1956)
Fortune 525 Can't We Talk This Over?/The Mambo of Love (1957)
Fortune 529 My Heart Will Always Belong to You/For Old Time Sake (1958)
Fortune 531 Goodbye Matilda/I Am with You (1959)
Fortune 532 If I Could Be with You/I Wanna Know (1959)
Fortune 536 Since You're Gone/Are You Gonna Do? (1960)
Fortune 544 Blue Moon/I Don't Care (1962)
Fortune 532 If I/I Wanna Know [reissue] (1963)
Fortune 553 I Really Love You/You're My Love (1963)
Fortune 563 Village of Love/Real True Love (1964)
Fortune 564 Are You Making a Fool Out of Me?/You're My Happiness (1964)

Sources: Pete Grendysa in *Goldmine,* January 1986; liner notes with the Regency CD *Diablos.*

Diadems (Pittsburgh, Pa.)

Personnel Cleveland "Butch" Martin (lead), Earl Thompson (1st tenor), Robert Thompson (2d tenor), Jerry Hill (baritone), Jimmy Mitchell (bass)

Notes

The Diadems began in the early 1950s when Martin (who was blind) and Earl Thompson formed a self-contained group of ten who were all eleven to twelve years old.

The group was then known as the El Moroccos. In 1956, they reduced their members to six: Martin, Earl Thompson, Jerry Hill, Alvin Allsberry, Gerald Johnson, and Arlene Gore. In the next few years, Allsberry and Gerald Johnson left, and in 1958 they were replaced by Jimmy Mitchell and Robert Thompson (Earl's brother).

Arlene left in 1959 and the group began calling itself the Countdowns.

In 1960, because they wanted to record, they traveled to New York, where they met Teacho Wiltshire, who had a song for them, "Shake It Up Baby." They executed this quite well and Wiltshire wanted them to hang around New York, but several of them had plans to marry and they returned "home" to Pittsburgh. At that time they began calling themselves the Diadems.

They signed to record with Lavere (LaVerve in *Echoes of the Past*) and had their first release. Wiltshire called them to record "Shake It Up Baby," which was now "Twist and Shout," but because of their contract they remained in Pittsburgh.

In 1962, they moved to Fee Bee subsidiary Star Records. Soon after, they were with Goodie Records and Goldie Records, which were also affiliated with Fee Bee.

After "I'll Do Anything" was released, Jimmy Mitchell became ill and the group became inactive.

In 1965 they resurfaced as the Torches and in 1967 they cut a disc on Sonic as the Rhythm Rascals ("Why Do You Have to Go"). They carried that name into the 1970s.

Discography

Lavere 187 What More Is There to Say/Ala Vevo (1961)
Star 514 Why Don't You Believe Me?/Yes, I Love You Baby (1963)
Goodie 207 Dancing on Moonbeams/My Little Darling (1964)
Goldie 715 I'll Do Anything/Goodnight Irene (1964)
Source: Carl Janusek and Nancy Janusek in *Echoes of the Past* 10.

Dials (Yonkers, N.Y.)

Personnel Sal Corrente (a.k.a. Sal Anthony) (lead), Dario Bianchini, Joe Raguso, Frank Rangone, Joe Rasulo

Notes

The five singers making up Philips' Dials met in the Park Hill Athletic Club in Yonkers, New York, in 1961. They began singing at the club just for the fun of it. Soon a crowd of other athletic club members gathered and encouraged them to pursue a professional vocal career. The five singers all came from Yonkers and had grown up and attended school together.

They continued to appear at club functions and at one of these functions were discovered by Lou DeLucia who immediately signed them to a contract to manage them. Following this, he christened them the Dials.

This group is not the Dials who cut sides for Hilltop.

Discography

Philips 40040 At the Start of a New Romance/These Foolish Things (1962)
Source: Ed Engel and Lou Cicchetti, liner notes with the Dee Jay Jamboree CD *Group Harmony out of the Bronx.*

Diamonds (New York)

Personnel Harold "Sonny" Wright (d) (lead), Myles Hardy (1st tenor), Ernest Ward (2d tenor), Daniel Stevens (bass)

Notes

The Diamonds started in 1948 as a trio; Ernest Ward was later added to form a quartet. They soon told the Apollo's Bobby Schiffman of their intentions and he became their manager. Atlantic Records learned of Schiffman's acceptance of the group and signed them to Atlantic in 1952.

As the Diamonds, they toured Canada's Quebec province, changing their repertoire for the French-speaking audience. They began recording for Atlantic in December 1952.

Because of the payola scandal, the Diamonds broke up in 1955. Wright formed the Regals, with whom he had been moonlighting. Four of the Regals later joined Sonny Til as his new Orioles without Wright. In 1957, Wright started a new group, the Metronomes, and recorded several great sides for Cadence and then faded into history.

The lack of success that plagued these groups made Wright quit group singing and go it alone, which he did for years. In 1997 he passed on.

Discography

Atlantic 981 A Beggar for Your Kisses/Call Baby, Call (1952)
Atlantic 1003 Two Love Have I/I'll Live Again (1953)
Atlantic 1017 Romance in the Dark/Cherry (1953)
Sources: S. Mondrone and T. Denehey in *Bim Bam Boom* 4; Jay Warner, *American Singing Groups*; Dave Hinckley in the *New York Daily News.*

Dimples, Eddie Cooley &

Personnel Eddie Cooley (lead), Beverly Coates, Carolyn Coates, Barbara Sanders

Discography

Royal Roost 621 Priscilla/Got a Little Woman (1956)

Royal Roost 626 Driftwood/A Spark Met a Flame (1957)
Royal Roost 628 Hey You/Pull Mon Pull (1957)
Triumph 609 Leona/Be My Steady (1959)
Sources: Jeff Kreiter, *Group Collectors Record Guide*; R. Ferlingere's, *A Discography of R&B and R&R Vocal Groups*; Norman Nite's Rockon.

Dinwiddie Colored Quartet (Philadelphia)

Personnel Sterling Rex (1st tenor), Clarence Meredith (2d tenor), Harry B. Cruder (bass), James Mantell Thomas (bass)

Notes

This group was named for Dinwiddie County, Virginia, forty miles south of Richmond, although they were originally from Philadelphia. George Moonoogian wrote this in his "Wax Fax" article in issue 49 of *Record Collector's Monthly*.

The quartet recorded six songs, each a one-sided 78, in October 1902 for the Monarch label, a subsidiary of Victor. When these songs were rereleased by Victor's Bluebird label, the credit read Dinwiddie Colored Quartet to ensure that consumers knew what they were purchasing.

Discography

Monarch/Victor 1714 Down on the Old Campground (1902)
Monarch/Victor 1715 Poor Mourner (1902)
Monarch/Victor 1716 Steal Away (1902)
Monarch/Victor 1724 My Way Is Cloudy (1902)
Monarch/Victor 1725 Gabriel's Trumpet (1902)
Monarch/Victor 1726 We'll Anchor Bye and Bye (1902)
Sources: Liner notes with the Document CD *Earliest Negro Vocal Quartets*; George Moonoogian in *Record Collector's Monthly* 49.

Diplomats, Dino & (New York)

Personnel Rafael Cedano (lead), Richard Morgan (1st tenor), Jackie Jones (2d tenor), Woody Carter (baritone), Charles Humber (bass)

Notes

This group began in 1957 when the members were in school with Frankie Lymon. They called themselves the Lionels and then the Universals.

The Diplomats cut their first Laurie disc in 1961 as a quintet, and the next year they became a quartet. They remained a quartet for all their future recordings.

Discography

Laurie 3103 My Dream/I Can't Believe (1961)
Vida 0100/0101 Homework/Hush-A-Bye My Love (1961)
Vida 0102/0103 Soft Wind/Such a Fool for You (1962)
Source: Ed Engel, liner notes with the Ace CD *Laurie*.

Dixieaires (New York)

Personnel Clyde Reddick (lead), Arlandus Wilson, Conrad Frederick, Henry Owens, J. C. Ginyard (d)

Notes

J. C. Ginyard left the Jubalaires in 1948 (or 1946 according to Mark Marymount in Collectables *DuDroppers* CD liner notes) to sing and manage the Dixieaires, then considered a jubilee/pop group.

That first Dixieaires group lasted until 1950. Some of the members had wives and children and the group's financial reward for their recordings and appearances was insufficient to maintain their families.

Later in 1950 (Sittin' In With 553) the second Dixieaires group was formed.

Bob Kornegay sang bass for the Dixieaires. Willie Ray and Joe Van Loan were also members.

According to Pete Grendysa, Tom Moran and Johnny Hines joined up with Ginyard to form his Dixieaires group.

Discography

Gotham 163 Go Long/Long, Lean and Lanky (1948)
Gotham 167 Keep Me with You/Things Got Tough Again (1948)
Lenox 506 Precious Memories/Way Down in Egypt (1948)
Coleman 102 Soon Now/The Sun Will Shine (1948)
Melojazz 7008 Wade in the Water/Swing Down Chariot (1948)
Exclusive 37X Just a Closer Walk with Thee/Handwriting on the Wall (1948)
Exclusive 38X Loose the Man/Hide Me in Thy Bosom (1948)
Lenox 514 Joshua/My Time Ain't Long (1949)
Lenox 518 You Can't Cure the Blues/Until You Say You're Mine (1949)
Lenox 530 Doomed/Gamblin' Man (1949)
Lenox 531 My Dungeon Shook/You Better Get Ready (1949)
Exclusive 50X Elijah/My Trouble Is Hard (1949)
Exclusive 66X Poor and Needy/Will the Circle Be Unbroken (1949)
Exclusive 82X Movin' Up the King's Highway/When the Moon Goes Down (1949)
Exclusive 87X Time's Winding Up/He Is Coming Again So Soon (1949)
Exclusive 98X A Home in That Rock/Friends Let Me Tell about Jesus (1949)
Exclusive 116X Playing with Fire/Casey Jones (1949)
Exclusive 117X Christ ABCs/I Can See My Saviour Standing There (1949)
Spiritials 5000 Buckle My Shoe/He Never Said a Mumblin' Word (1949)
Sources: Mark Marymount, liner notes with the Collectable CD *DuDroppers*; J. C. Ginyard, interview by Pete Grendysa.

Dixieaires (New York)

Personnel J. C. Ginyard, Joe Floyd, Johnny Hines, Jimmy Smith

Notes

Ginyard was also with the Jubalaires, Golden Gate Quartet, Du Droppers, and other groups.

Ginyard, along with Willie Ray, Bob Kornegay, and Joe Van Loan, recorded the second Dixieaires' disc on Harlem, the only record cut as the Dixieaires by that foursome.

Discography
Sunrise 319 You Better Run/My God Call Me This Morning (1948)
Sunrise 2117 Wade in the Water/Swing Down Chariot (1948)
Sunrise 2118 Little Wooden Church/Run On for a Long Time (1948)
Sittin In With 553 Pray/Don't Let That Worry You (1950)
Sittin In With 2003 The Coming of the King/Rock in the Harbor (1950)
Sittin In With 2012 Joe Louis Is a Fightin' Man/Shoulder Up My Cross (1950)
Sittin In With 2013 Just Getting Ready/When That Great Ship Went Down (1950)
Sittin In With 2017 God Is the Greatest Creator/Send Me Jesus (1951)
Sittin In With 2019 Christ ABC/Loose the Man (1951)
Sittin In With 2020 Just a Closer Walk with Thee/Feed Me, Jesus (1951)
Prestige 2001 Thee Governor/Bloodstained Banner (1952)
Harlem 1012 Well Done/Gabriel, Sound Your Trumpet (1954)
Harlem 2326 Travelin' All Alone/I'm Not Like I Used to Be (1955)
Source: J. C. Ginyard, interview by Pete Grendysa.

Dodgers (Brooklyn, N.Y.)

Personnel Thomas Fox, Harold Winley [?]

Notes
According to the unsigned liner notes accompanying the Aladdin/Imperial CD *R&B Vocal Group Magic,* Paul Winley, later founder of Winley Records and brother of Paul Winley of the Clovers, was a member of the Dodgers. *(Note:* The author seriously doubts the accuracy of this statement.)

Discography
Aladdin 3259 You Make Me Happy/Let's Make a Whole Lot of Love (1954)
Aladdin 3271 Cat Hop/Drip Drop (1955)
Source: Unsigned liner notes with the Aladdin/Imperial CD *R&B Vocal Groups.*

Dominoes, Billy Ward & (New York)

Personnel Clyde McPhatter (lead), Charlie White (2d tenor), William Joseph LaMont (baritone), Bill Brown (bass)

Notes
Billy Ward came out of the service (where he had a musical position) and came to New York to attend the Juliard School of Music. His mentor and employer, Rose Marks, advised him to form a vocal group, which was becoming an important factor in the world of rhythm and blues music. After several false starts, first with an integrated group, which failed, and then an all-black ensemble, which did not do well either, he assembled another all-black group, the Dominoes, named by Ward.

As a result of their appearance on Arthur Godfrey's *Talent Scouts* TV program in 1950, King-Federal management signed them to a contract.

In November 1950, the Dominoes had their first recording session with King's new subsidiary, Federal Records.

In March 1951, "Sixty Minute Man" was released and was a huge success.

In late 1951, White left to join the Checkers with Bill Brown. Later that year he left the Checkers to join the Clovers. David McNeil took Brown's spot with the Dominoes, and James Van Loan assumed White's 2d tenor position.

In 1953, Jackie Wilson replaced McPhatter. Milton Grayson joined the Dominoes on the later Federal sides and was also with them later on Decca. In June 1953 McNeill entered the service and his bass part was taken by Cliff Givens. The baritone voice was then assumed by Milton Merle.

In 1954 the group consisted of Wilson, James Van Loan, Milton Merle, and Cliff Givens.

Van Loan left in 1954. He was temporarily replaced by brother Joe and Prentice Moreland, who lasted with the Dominoes until they went with Jubilee Records and then Decca (1956), where their style changed considerably. Later in 1956, they signed with Liberty.

In 1957 Jackie Wilson left to go solo with Brunswick, which eventually led to a very successful single act.

It was on Liberty that Eugene Mumford joined the Dominoes. After several recordings, Mumford left to perform as a solo act. A few years later he joined the Golden Gate Quartet.

In 1960 the group consisted of Monroe Powell (1st tenor), Robbie Robinson (2d tenor), Milton Merle (baritone), and Cliff Givens (bass). Later in the 1960s, Bruce Cloud sang tenor for the group. In 1975 Wilson collapsed on stage and remained in a coma until he died in 1984. McPhatter, who went solo after the Drifters, died in June 1972.

Discography

Federal 12001 Chicken Blues/Do Something for Me (1951)
Federal 12010 Harbor Lights/No Says My Heart (1951)
Federal 12016 Other Lips, Other Arms/The Deacon Moves In (Little Esther) (1951)
Federal 12022 Sixty Minute Man/I Can't Escape from You (1951)
Federal 12036 Heart to Heart/Lookin' for a Man (Little Esther) (1951)
Federal 12039 Weeping Willow Blues/I Am with You (1951)
Federal 12059 When the Swallows Come Back to Capistrano/That's What You're Doing to Me (1952)
Federal 12068 Deep Sea Blues/Have Mercy Baby (1952)
Federal 12072 That's What You're Doing to Me/Love, Love, Love (1952)
Federal 12105 No Room/I'd Be Satisfied (1952)
Federal 12106 Yours Forever/I'm Lonely (1952)
Federal 12114 The Bells/Pedal Pushin' Papa (1952)
Federal 12129 These Foolish Things/Don't Leave Me This Way (1953)
Federal 12139 Where Now Little Heart/You Can't Keep a Good Man Down (1953)
King 1280 Rags to Riches/Don't Thank Me (1953)
King 1281 Christmas in Heaven/Ringing in a Brand-New Year (1953)
Federal 12162 My Baby's 3-D/Until the Real Thing Comes Along (1954)

Federal 12178 I'm Gonna Move to the Outskirts of Town/Tootsie Roll (1954)
Federal 12193 Above Jacob's Ladder/Little Black Train (1954)
King 1342 Tenderly/A Little Lie (1954)
King 1364 Three Coins in the Fountain/Lonesome Road (1954)
King 1368 Little Things Mean a Lot/I Really Don't Want to Know (1954)
Jubilee 5163 Come to Me Baby/Gimme, Gimme, Gimme (1954)
Jubilee 5213 Sweethearts in Paradise/Take Me Back to Heaven (1954)
Federal 12209 If I Never Get to Heaven/Can't Do 60 No More (1955)
Federal 12218 Cave Man/Love Me Now or Let Me Go (1955)
King 1492 Learning the Blues/May I Never Love Again (1955)
King 1502 Give Me You/Over the Rainbow (1955)
Federal 12263 Bobby Sox Baby/How Long, How Long Blues (1956)
Decca 29933 St. Therese of the Roses/Home Is Where You Hang Your Heart (1956)
Decca 30043 Will You Remember/C'Mon Snake Let's Crawl (1956)
Decca 30149 Evermore/Half a Love (1956)
Federal 12301 St. Louis Blues/One Moment with You (1957)
Decca 30199 Till Kingdom Come/Rock Plymouth, Rock (1957)
Decca 30420 To Each His Own/Ghost of a Chance (1957)
Decca 30514 September Song/When the Saints Go Marching In (1957)
Liberty 55071 Star Dust/Lucinda (1957)
Liberty 55099 Deep Purple/Do It Again (1957)
Liberty 55111 My Proudest Possession/Someone Greater Than I (1957)
Liberty 55126 Sweeter As the Years Go By/Solitude (1958)
Liberty 55136 Jennie Lee/Music, Maestro Please (1958)
Liberty 55181 Please Don't Say No/Behave Hula Girl (1959)
King 5322 Have Mercy Baby/Sixty Minute Man (1960)
ABC 10128 The World is Waiting for the Sunrise/You're Mine (1960)
ABC 10156 The Gypsy/You (1960)
Ro-Zan 10001 Man in the Stained-Glass Window/My Fair Weather Friend (1961)
King 5463 Lay it on the Line/That's How You Know When You're Growing Old (1961)
King 6002 I'm Walking behind You/This Love of Mine (1965)
King 6016 O Holy Night/What Are You Doing New Year's Eve? (1965)
Sources: Jeff Beckman in *Big Town Review* 1; Marv Goldberg in *DISCoveries.*

Don Juans (Detroit)

Personnel Andre Williams (lead), Eddie Hurt (tenor), Lonnie Heard (2d tenor), James Drayton (baritone), Charles Evans (bass)

Notes

The Don Juans and the Five Dollars were the same group, with the exception of lead Joe Simmons of the Five Dollars, who recorded for Fortune Records in Detroit. There were times when both groups recorded simultaneously!

Discography

Fortune 824 Pulling Time/Going Down to Tia Juana (w/A. Williams) (1955)

Fortune 825 Baby I Love You So/It Must Be Love (w/Joe Weaver) (1956)
Fortune 520 Ooh Ooh Those Eyes/Cha-Cha of Love (w/Don Lake) (1956)
Fortune 828 It's All Over/Bobby Jean (w/A. Williams) (1956)
Fortune 836 This is a Miracle/Calypso Beat (w/Little Eddie) (1956)
Fortune 839 Come on Baby/The Greasy Chicken (w/A. Williams) (1956)
Fortune 842 My Last Dance With You/Hey! Country Girl (w/A. Williams) (1958)
Hi-Q 5017 It's Nice/Cha-Lypso of Love (1960)
Source: Susan Winson and Rich Adcock, liner notes with the Fortune LP *Treasure Chest of Musty Dusties–2.*

Dootones (Los Angeles)

Personnel Charles Gardner (tenor), Ronald Barrett (tenor), H. B. Barnum (baritone), Marvin Wilkins (bass)

Notes

H. B. Barnum and his drummer friend Ronald Barrett played in a jazz band while they were still in their teens. They found Gardner and Wilkins and formed a vocal group in 1954. They rehearsed night after night at Barnum's house until they came to the attention of Dootsie Williams.

After meeting with Williams and backing other Dootone groups, Williams put together the group listed above. Their first disc, "Teller of Fortune," was released in April 1955. The group toured all over the West Coast. They joined Vernon Green, who was groupless at the time, and became the live show Medallions. But these performances did not generate a living wage, and the group members, who were hungry, split apart soon thereafter.

Ronald Barrett also recorded with the Meadowlarks and was Fanita Barrett's (Richard Berry & the Dreamers) brother.

H. B. Barnum joined the Robins on Whippet and later became owner of the R&B label Munrab (Barnum spelled and pronounced backward).

In 1961 several of the Dootones got back together as the Marathons on Arvee. During the 1960 doo-wop resurgence, Dootsie Williams found an unreleased Dootones song, "Down the Road." In order to release it, he paired it with "Soldier Boy" by an unknown group. On Dooto 470, Strange Love Affair/The Day You Say Goodbye, Williams released this disc as by the Dootones. Nobody knows who this group was (also true of 471).

Discography

Dootone 366 Teller of Fortune (CG)/Ay Si Si (MW) (1955)
Dooto 470 Strange Love Affair/The Day You Said Goodbye (1962)
Dooto 471 Sailor Boy/Down the Road (1962)
Source: Marv Goldberg and Rick Whitesell in *Yesterday's Memories* 11.

Do Re Mi Trio (Los Angeles)

Personnel Al "Stomp" Russell (tenor), Joel Cowan (tenor), William Joseph (a.k.a. Doc Basso) (bass)

Notes

The first Do Re Mi Trio group recorded for Leon Rene's Excelsior Records in 1947. This was followed by Queen, DeLuxe, and Ivin [sic] Ballen's 20th Century label. Joe Davis replaced bass William Joseph in 1946, and the Russell-Cowan-Davis group only recorded for the Decca subsidiary Commodore.

Davis lasted six months after recording and left during the American Federation of Musicians strike in 1947. He was replaced by Curtis Wilder, who sang tenor. The trio became an all-tenor vocal group.

Cowan left in 1950 to join Camille Howard and the trio disbanded. A year later Russell met Alton Buddy Hawkins, who had sung with the progressive group the Keynotes, in Philadelphia. Al Moore joined them in 1951 and the Do Re Me Trio was reborn.

The last known roster consisted of Al Russell, Buddy Hawkins, and Al Moore. After being together for several months, they recorded some sides for the Columbia subsidiary Okeh. They went on to record for many other labels and remained together for many more years.

Discography

Commodore 7504 There's a Man at the Door (JC/AR)/Teresa (AR) (1947)
Commodore 7505 Wrapped Up in a Dream (AR)/The Wise Old Man (AR) (1947)
Commodore 7549 How Can I Smile (AR)/You Can't Love Two (AR) (1948)
Commodore 7550 Cabaret (AR)/Darling You Make It So (AR) (1948)
Ivory 750 Tell Me You Love Me (CW)/Only One Dream (AR) (1949)
Ivory 752 I Done No Wrong/I'll Get You When the Bridge Is Down (1949)
Ivory 754 Rhumba Blues (AR)/I Couldn't Help It (AR) (1949)
Columbia 39385 No More Dreams (BH)/I Want to Be with You Always (1951)
Okeh 6806 May That Day Never Come (AR)/How Can You Say You Love Me (AR) (1951)
Okeh 6831 I Couldn't Help It (AR)/I'll Be Waiting (AR) (1951)
Okeh 6845 I Love Each Move You Make (AR)/I Don't Want to Be Alone for Christmas (AR) (1951)
Rainbow 181 I'm Used to You (BH/AM)/She Would Not Yield (AR) (1952)
Brunswick 80218 I'll Never Stop Being Yours (AR)/I'm Only Human (BH) (1952)
Variety 1001 Holding Hands (BH)/Tell Me You Love Me (BH) (1953)
Variety 1002 Oo-Wee (all)/I'm Used to You (BH/AM) (1953)
Coral 61184 I'll Never Fail You (BH)/I Don't Want to Set the World on Fire (1954)
Reet 101 Holding Hands/I D Double Dare You (1955)
Carlton 460 That's the Way Life Goes (BH)/How I Love My Baby (BH) (1956)
Stere-O-Craft 112 On a Slow Boat to China/Saturday Night Fish Fry (1959)
Source: Marv Goldberg and Rick Whitesell in *Yesterday's Memories* 12.

Dots (Hollywood)

Personnel Jeanette Baker (lead), Johnny Flamingo (a.k.a. Melvin Broxton) (tenor)

Notes

The Caddy label was a California music organization owned by deejay Dick "Huggy Boy" Hugg.

Discography

Caddy 101 I Confess/I Wish I Could Meet You (1957)
Caddy 107 I Lost You/Johnny (1957)
Caddy 111 Good Luck to You/Heartsick and Lonely (1957)
Source: Galen Gart, *American Record Label Directory,* 1940; 1959.

Dovers (New York)

Personnel Miriam Grate (lead), Bobby Johnson (lead), Eddie Quinones (tenor), Wyndham Porter (baritone), James Sneed (bass)

Notes

Johnson, Quinones, and Porter later joined Roland Martinez and Tommy Grate to form the Apollo Vocaltones.

Frank Edwards (1959) and "Keno" (possibly Charles Stapleton) replaced Johnson and Quinones to form the second Dovers group.

James Sneed later married Miriam Grate.

Discography

Apollo 472 My Angel (MG) /Please Squeeze (BJ) (1955)
Apollo (UNR) My Love
Apollo (UNR) Only Heaven Knows
Apollo (UNR) Your Love
Davis 465 Sweet as a Flower/Boy in My Life (1959)
New Horizon 501 Devil You May Be/The Sentence (1961)
Source: Donn Fileti, liner notes with the Relic CDs *Jay Dee* and *Apollo-2.*

Dozier Boys (Chicago)

Personnel Eugene Teague (d), Benny Cotton, Cornell Wiley, Frank "Red" Bell

Notes

The Dozier Boys was a self-contained vocal/instrumental combo from Chicago that played at the best local clubs in the Midwest. They had a long run at one of Chicago's Grand Hotels. Regardless of the town in which they were appearing, they always appeared at the best spots in smaller towns and the second-best spots in the big cities.

Joe Boyce, the member I interviewed, was a nonsinging vibes player with the group in the mid-1950s. Interestingly, in his discussion in *Echoes of the Past* magazine article addressing the Dozier Boys, R&B historian George Moonoogian theorizes that the name came from a unique conjugation of the verb to doze or to nap. Moonoogian continues that the individual who does the dozing is a dozier. The Random House dictionary confirms this theory but spells the word "dozer."

Where did the name Dozier Boys come from? Boyce explained that Cornel Wiley's mother and father divorced and his mother married a pharmacist. This pharmacist was quite generous with the group. He bought their uniforms and instruments, and helped with traveling expenses, and so on. His last name was Dozier, and Wiley felt that since Dozier was so generous to members of the group, they should give themselves a name in his honor, hence, Dozier Boys!

Joe Boyce, who joined the group several years after it formed, now lives and works in the New York metropolitan area. He is employed in New York's financial district. In 1994 he played the vibes on the *Morrisania Review* CD. He was asked to join the Doziers late in 1956 and remained with them until February 1958. Joe explained to this writer in March 1998 that he never sang for the group, but when you were a Dozier Boy, regardless of your function, you were listed as a Dozier Boy and included in their photos.

Boyce also related that he and Herbie Hancock attended the same high school. When Hancock had his first gig, Boyce played with him! Joe also related that the Dozier Boys competed on Arthur Godfrey's *Talent Scouts* show but a scoring error caused the Doziers to lose the contest. On their way home they learned that they had won the show and returned to accept their prize!

During our conversation, Boyce referred to Frank Bell as "the albino."

Discography

Aristocrat 1105 The Holidays Are Over/In a Travelin' Mood (1948)
Aristocrat 1106 He's Got Her and Gone/In Every Man's Life (1948)
Aristocrat 3001 St. Louis Blues/She Only Fools with Me (1949)
Aristocrat 3002 Big Time Baby/Music Goes Round and Round (1949)
Aristocrat 409 All I Need Is You/She's Gone (1950)
Chess 1436 You Got to Get It/Pretty Eyes (1950)
United 143 I Keep Thinking of You/Linger Awhile (1953)
United 163 Early Morning Blues/Cold, Cold Rain (1953)
Fraternity 767 Early Morning Blues/Special Kind of Lovin' (1957)
Janie 457 Special Kind of Lovin'/Wandering Lover (1957)
Apt 25014 I Am So/My Heart Is Yours (1958)
Sources: Uncredited writer-historian, United CD *Rare Windy City R&B Vocal Groups-1;* George Moonoogian in *Echoes of the Past* 33; Joe Boyce, conversation with Mitch Rosalsky, March 25, 1998; Robert Pruter and Robert L. Campbell in their Internet piece, April 1998, available at www.hubcap.clemson.edu/~camber/index.html.

Drapers (New York)

Personnel Wilbur "Yonkie" Paul (lead), Jesse Facing (tenor), Richard Lewis (tenor), Dock Green (baritone), Leroy Brown (bass)

Notes

While the group was still at Gee, a second (Gee) Drapers group formed and consisted of Johnny Moore, Ike Mason, Charlie Hughes, Dock Green, and Tommy Evans.

Evans also sang with the Carols, Ravens, Drifters, and Floaters; Hughes sang for the DuDroppers and the Drifters.

Mason sang also for the Duvals.

Johnny Moore was the lead for the United/States Hornets and for the Drifters. Curiously, in an interview with Marv Goldberg, Moore related that he was *not* the lead for the Hornets but apparently told another researcher that he was. Human nature tells us to place more credence in a statement that tells you what someone did not do.

Discography

Vest 831 Best Love/One More Time (1960)
Gee 1081 You Got to Look Up/Your Love Has Gone Away (1963)
Source: Jeff Kreiter, *Group Collector's Record Price Guide.*

Dreamers (Philadelphia)

Personnel Mitchell Stevens, Harry Palters, Leroy Sproul, Kent Peeler, Robert Mott, Buddy Nolan

Notes

Consistent with Donn Fileti's statement in his liner notes accompanying Relic's *Grand* CD, these were probably the same Dreamers who sang Melba/No Man Is an Island for Rollin'.

In Lou Silvani's *Yesterday's Memories* article, he expresses the opinion that these two recordings are by the same Philadelphia Dreamers and were probably cut at the same time in 1954, but the Rollin' song was never released. A black Philadelphia record shop owner apparently found the tapes and released them on his own Rollin' label in the 1960s. Jared Weinstein and Eddie Gries wound up with the stampers and pressed 200 authentic-looking reissues in 1963. After all this time, we still do not know why it was never released by Grand.

Discography

Grand 131 535/Tears in My Eyes (1955)
Rollin' 1001 Melba/No Man Is an Island (1959)
Sources: Donn Fileti, liner notes with the Relic CD *Grand Records*; Louie Silvani in *Yesterday's Memories.*

Dreamers (Yonkers, N.Y.)

Personnel Frank Cammarata (lead), Bob Malara (1st tenor), Luke Berardis (2d tenor), John "Bud" Trancynger (baritone), Dom Canzano (bass)

Notes

This group had their beginnings in Yonkers, New York, in 1958. They were spotted in a regional talent contest by George Goldner, which led to a contract for them with his Goldisc Records.

Their first song, "Teenage Vows of Love," was a hit in the East as well as many cities in the Midwest.

In 1962, because of poor sales with their Goldisc effort, they moved to Cousins Records and recorded the Tony Bennett song, "Because of You." It was also in 1962 that Canzano and Berardis dropped out of the group and were replaced by Frank Digilio and Frank Nicholas. This occurred before the Cousins recording. Another member was Dario Bianchini from the Dials.

Cousins owner, Lou Cicchetti, placed the "Because of You" master with Columbia, which owned the publishing rights to the tune. He hoped that if Columbia had it on its label, it would give it an extra push. Columbia relegated the disc to their May Records subsidiary, where it realized a quick death.

They apparently recorded four more tunes, which have never been released, and made several live appearances before breaking up in 1965.

(Note: Although this Dreamers group recorded in the early 1960s, they are not the Dreamers who recorded for APT or Guaranteed.)

Discography

Goldisc 3015 Teenage Vows of Love/Natalie (1961)
Cousins 1005 Because of You/Little Girl (1962)
May 133 Because of You/Little Girl (1962)
Source: Bob Belniak in *Echoes of the Past* 5; Ed Engel and Lou Cicchetti, liner notes with the Dee Jay Jamboree CD *Group Harmony out of the Bronx.*

Dreamers (New York)

Personnel Mike Lasman (lead), Shelly Weiss (1st tenor), Allan Senzan (2d tenor), Ian Kaye (baritone)

Notes

This group also recorded as the Accents on Sultan and the Concords on Herald.

Lasman was the Mike of Mike and the Utopians who recorded "Erline" for Cee Jay.

Discography

Guaranteed 219 Canadian Sunset/Mary, Mary (1961)
Source: Donn Fileti, liner notes with the Relic CD *Everlast.*

Dreamers (New York)

Personnel Harriet Calender (lead), Percy Green, Warren Suttles (baritone), Freddie Francis

Notes

This group recorded only one disc for Jubilee before moving to Mercury. Warren Suttles came from the Ravens, probably during one of his several departures from the group.

It has also been learned that Joe Van Loan spent some time with this group.

Discography

Jubilee 5053 These Things I Miss/Can't Get Started with You (1951)
Mercury 5843 Ain't Gonna Worry No More/I'm Gonna Hate Myself in the Morning (1951)

Mercury 70019 Walkin' My Blues Away/Please Don't Leave Me (1952)
Source: George Povall, liner notes with the Sequel CD *Jubilee/Josie R&B Vocal Groups.*

Dreamers, Richard Berry & (Los Angeles)

Personnel Richard Berry (lead), Gloria Jones (tenor), Nanette Williams (tenor), Annette Williams (2d tenor), Fanita Barrett

Notes

The Dreamers later evolved into the Phil Spector Blossoms.
   The Williams girls were twins.
   Berry sang with the Flairs, Jayos, Hollywood Blue Jays, Crowns, Five Hearts, Pharaohs, and the Jaguars.
   Baritone/bass Johnny Coleman also appeared with the Dreamers.
   Gloria Jones also sang for the Blossoms and did some sessions with the Pharaohs.
   Fanita Barrett was Ronald Barrett's sister. Barrett had been with the Dootones.
   Jennell Hawkins of Ricky and Jennell was reported to be the lead singer of the Dreamers in the liner notes accompanying *The Best of Flip-2* CD.

Discography

Flair 1052 Bye Bye/At Last (1955)
Flair 1058 Daddy Daddy/Baby Darling (1955)
Flair 1075 Together/Jelly Roll (1955)
Source: Liner notes with the Titanic CD *Best of Flip.*

Dreamlovers (Philadelphia)

Personnel Conrad "Clifton" Dunn (lead), Tommy Ricks (1st tenor), Cleveland Hammock (2d tenor), James Ray Dunn (bass)

Notes

The Dreamlovers began singing on Philadelphia street corners, in school gyms, and in local appearances in 1956 as the Romances. Their original lead, William Johnson, was shot to death by a jealous guy over a young woman, and he never recorded with the group. Out of respect for Johnson, the group changed its name to Dreamlovers.
   It was the Dreamlovers backing Chubby Checker on "The Twist." They also backed up Dee Dee Sharpe on "Mashed Potato Time" and many other artists.
   Morris Gardner joined as full-time lead in 1959.
   Tenor Donald Hogan, the group's guitarist, sang lead on "Annabelle Lee." They soon joined the Heritage label, where they did their biggie, "When We Get Married."
   They next joined End Records, where they did "If I Should Lose You." Their next moves were to Cameo, Mercury, Columbia, Warner Bros., and Swan. The heyday for R&B ballads had passed and soul music was gaining popularity as black music.
   Morris Gardner left the Dreamlovers in 1963, and the group split up in 1973.

Discography

V-Tone 211 Home Is Where the Heart Is/Annabelle Lee (1960)
V-Tone 229 Time/May I Kiss the Bride (1961)
Heritage 102 When We Get Married/Just Because (1961)
Heritage 104 Welcome Home/Let Them Love (1961)
Heritage 107 Zoom Zoom Zoom/While We Were Dancing (1962)
End 1114 If I Should Lose You/I Miss You (1962)
Columbia 42698 Sad Sad Boy/If I Were a Magician (1963)
Columbia 42752 Black Bottom/Sad Sad Boy (1963)
Columbia 42842 Pretty Little Girl/I'm Through with You (1963)
Cameo 326 Oh Baby Mine/These Will Be the Good Old Days (1964)
Warner Bros. 5619 You Gave Me Somebody to Love/Doin' Things Together (1965)
Casino 1308 Together/Amazons and Coyotes (1965)
Mercury 72595 The Bad Times Make the Good Times/Bless Your Soul (1966)
Mercury 72630 Calling Jo-ann/You Gave Me Somebody to Love (1966)
Sources: Donn Fileti, liner notes with the Relic CD *Dreamlovers;* Donn Fileti, liner notes with the Relic LP *V-Tone*; Wayne Jancik in *Goldmine,* December 1990.

Dreams (Philadelphia)

Personnel George Tindley (d) (lead), Bernard Harris (1st tenor), Bobby Henderson (2d tenor), Wesley Hayes (baritone), Stephen Presbury (bass)

Notes

The Dreams began in 1953 in Philadelphia as the Royal Flames. This name was soon changed to the Dreams. Lead George Tindley got the group their appearance at the Apollo's amateur night and they took second place.

Soon after the Apollo appearance, they were contacted by someone from the Newark-based Savoy Records who apparently was in the audience at the Apollo. They went to Savoy and had their first session in April 1954, during which they recorded Darlene/A Letter to My Girl. The record did well locally.

The Dreams' next session took place in October 1954, when they recorded I'm Losing My Mind/Under the Willow. Their last session with Savoy was in March 1955. In this session they recorded I'll Be Faithful/My Little Honeybun.

Nothing ever happened with their discs, but they made many live appearances and tours on the East Coast. Since Harris was still in school, their touring was limited.

In June 1956 Herald Records announced that they had signed the Dreams. Henderson could not be found for the first session with Herald, and Billy Taylor of the Castelles filled in. Before this disc was released, Tindley felt that he wanted his name on the disc. Herald agreed, but Tindley chose Kenny Esquire and changed the group's name to the Starlites. The record was "They Call Me a Dreamer."

Discography

Savoy 1130 Darlene/A Letter to My Girl (1954)
Savoy 1140 I'm Losing My Mind/Under the Willow (1954)
Savoy 1157 I'll Be Faithful/My Little Honeybun (1955)
Sources: Marv Goldberg, liner notes with the Savoy LP *Vocal Group Albums*; Steve

Propes, liner notes with the Savoy LP *Doo Wop Delights: The Roots of Rock*; Marv Goldberg in *DISCoveries,* December 1997.

Dreams, Darnell & (New York)

Personnel Darnell Jessamay (lead), Alvin Brandon Jr., James Roberts, Robert DeBerry, Garfield Dorsey

Notes

This group was originally called the Essentials and was referred to Lou Cicchetti of Cousins Records. Cicchetti's name was given to Al Brandon. The group came to Cicchetti with two original songs that were eventually recorded on Cicchetti's West Side label.

Jessamay became famous as a result of her affiliation with the Vestelles, who recorded for Decca.

Discography

West Side 1020 The Day before Yesterday/I Had a Love (1964)
Source: Ed Engel and Lou Cicchetti, liner notes with the Dee Jay Jamboree CD *Group Harmony Out of the Bronx.*

Dreamtones (Springfield, Mass.)

Personnel Major Branch (lead), Drew Thompson (1st tenor), Clarence Thomas (2d tenor), Milton White (baritone), George "Val" Poitier (bass)

Notes

The individual members met at a local club and began to harmonize. They all came from Springfield, Massachusetts.

Poitier had been with the Mint Juleps who did "Bells of Love" on Herald before joining the Dreamtones. In their article on this group in *Paul's Record Magazine,* Nay Nassar and Ken Wickman show the bass's last name as Portier. However, they go on to say that he was the first cousin of actor Sidney Poitier. Therefore, the bass was George Val Poitier.

Milton's mother had a rooming house where many of the touring R&B groups of the day would stay while passing through Springfield.

In 1957, the group went to New Haven and signed and recorded with Marty Kugell's Klik label.

This group backed up the Mitlo Sisters on their Klik recording of "Oh Lonely Sea."

Discography

Klik 8505 Stand Beside Me/Love in the Afternoon (1957)
Express 501 Praying for a Miracle/Jelly Bean (1959)
Astra 551 A Lover's Answer/Mean Man (1959)
Source: Nay Nassar and Ken Wickman in *Paul's Record Magazine* 17–18.

Drifters (New York, 1953–1957)

Personnel Clyde McPhatter (d) (lead), David Baughan (d) (1st tenor), William "Chick" Anderson (2d tenor), David Baldwin (baritone), James Johnson (bass)

Notes

Lead singer Clyde McPhatter was unhappy with his treatment, handling, and lack of financial rewards with Billy Ward and the Dominoes. He let his dissatisfaction be known in the industry, and it remains uncertain whether he left or was fired. In any case, he thought of assembling his own group. Atlantic head Ahmet Ertegu, had seen McPhatter perform earlier and signed him up with Atlantic in May 1953. Ertegun then told Clyde to begin assembling a group.

The first order of business was to name the group, and "Drifters" filled the bill. The Drifters group shown above is not the classic Drifters group, but in order to maintain the integrity of the philosophy of this book, the group shown is the first to record as the Atlantic Drifters. Shortly thereafter the members changed to include McPhatter, Andrew, and Gerhart Thrasher, Bill Pinkney, William Ferbie, and Walter Adams. Although the group formed in New York City, the members were all originally from the Carolinas. This second group recorded the Drifter's first Atlantic release, "Money Honey."

Their audiences were quite receptive to their recordings. The group enjoyed great success and did a great deal of touring and live appearances.

William Ferbie and Walter Adams left and Jimmy Oliver replaced Adams. Pinkney would later sing with the Flyers, Harmony Grits, and the Original Drifters.

In July 1954, McPhatter announced his departure from the Drifters. Little David Baughan was an interim replacement for McPhatter, recording "Honey Bee," which was not released until 1961! Baughan, then sixteen, came from the Checkers on a temporary basis. He later sang with the Harps on Savoy and eventually succumbed to alcohol addiction. Johnny Moore took his place.

Johnny Moore came from the Hornets on States Records and also recorded with the Drapers later. Bill Pinkney brought him into the group. By September 1955, the label released five new sides by the Drifters, most of which were led by Moore. These received a great reaction from the fans.

In February 1956 "Your Promise to Be Mine," a rare lead by Gerhart Thrasher, was a tremendous hit.

Bill Pinkney was fired because of a salary dispute and he joined the Flyers. The Drifters now consisted of Bobby Hendricks at lead, replacing Johnny Moore (who had been drafted), Dee Ernie Bailey, and Billy Kennedy. Pinkney was replaced by Tommy Evans, formerly of the Carols. Charlie Hughes joined several days after, replacing Andrew Thrasher, who left with Pinkney. Eventually Hughes was drafted and was replaced by Jimmy Milner.

Discography

Atlantic 1006 Money Honey/The Way I Feel (1953)
Atlantic 1019 Lucille/Such a Night (1954)
Atlantic 1029 Honey Love/Warm Your Heart (1954)
Atlantic 1043 Bip Bam/Someday You'll Want Me to Want You (1954)

Atlantic 1048 White Christmas/Bells of St. Mary's (1954)
Atlantic 1055 Whatcha Gonna Do?/Gone (1955)
Atlantic 1078 Adorable/Steamboat (1955)
Atlantic 1089 Ruby Baby/Your Promise to Be Mine (1956)
Atlantic 1101 Soldier of Fortune/I Got to Get Myself a Woman (1956)
Atlantic 1123 Fools Fall in Love/It was a Tear (1957)
Atlantic 1141 Drifting Away from You/Hypnotized (1957)
Atlantic 1161 Yodee Yakee/I Know (1957)
Atlantic 1187 Drip Drop/Moonlight Bay (1958)
Sources: Pete Grendysa, Marv Goldberg, and Mike Redmond in *Record Exchanger* 18; Jay Warner, *American Singing Groups.*

Drifters (New York, 1958–1965)

Personnel Ben E. Nelson (King) (lead), Charlie Thomas, Dock Green (baritone), Elsbeary Hobbs (d) (bass)

Notes

While the Drifters were appearing at New York's Apollo Theater for a 1958 show, their manager, George Treadwell, was impressed with another group appearing at the same bill. The Crowns, who had cut a record for the R'n'B label, was that group. Treadwell, aware of an incipient drinking problem with the members of the current Drifters, signed the Crowns up to be the new Drifters ensemble.

Their first release was "There Goes My Baby," which was totally different from anything the Drifters had ever done before. Between the instrumentation and Nelson's great lead, this record reached sales never before attained by the first group. This was followed by "Dance with Me" and "True Love, True Love." Their sound was now becoming less R&B and more pop, but success was there. By May 1960 the group shown above recorded their last Atlantic sides.

The group that recorded Atlantic 2098–2117 consisted of Rudy Lewis (lead), Charlie Thomas (1st Tenor), Dock Green (baritone), and Tommy Evans (bass). Dock Green left in November 1962. Gene Pearson, just having left the Cleftones, replaced him. Tommy Evans would soon leave as well. During the next several years Drifters recordings were released that did not do as well as in the past.

In 1964, Rudy Lewis died suddenly. His last song was "Vaya Con Dios" (Spanish for "farewell"). Johnny Moore returned and took over the lead spot till the end of the year. Now the Drifters were Johnny Moore, Charlie Thomas, Eugene Pearson, and Tommy Evans.

Interestingly, a short time after Lewis died, Drifters' former manager Lover Patterson decided to form another Drifters group. This one was made up of Charlie Hughes, Dock Green, and Tommy Evans (who had recently left the second group). Bill Pinkney, Drifters' former bass, set up the Original Drifters with David Baughan, the Thrasher brothers, and Pinkney.

The next several years saw a plethora of personnel changes.

Discography

Atlantic 2025 There Goes My Baby/Oh My Love (1959)

Atlantic 2040 Dance with Me/True Love, True Love (1959)
Atlantic 2050 This Magic Moment/Baltimore (1960)
Atlantic 2062 Lonely Winds/Hey Señorita (1960)
Atlantic 2071 Save the Last Dance for Me/Nobody but Me (1960)
Atlantic 2087 I Count the Tears/Suddenly There's a Valley (1960)
Atlantic 2096 Some Kind of Wonderful/Honey Bee (1961)
Atlantic 2105 Please Stay/No Sweet Lovin' (1961)
Atlantic 2117 Sweets for My Sweet/Loneliness or Happiness (1961)
Atlantic 2127 Room Full of Tears/Somebody New Dancin' with You (1961)
Atlantic 2134 When My Little Girl Is Smiling/Mexican Divorce (1962)
Atlantic 2143 What to Do/Stranger on the Shore (1962)
Atlantic 2151 Jackpot/Sometimes I Wonder (1962)
Atlantic 2162 Up on the Roof/Another Night with the Boys (1962)
Atlantic 2182 On Broadway/Let the Music Play (1963)
Atlantic 2191 Rat Race/If You Don't Come Back (1963)
Atlantic 2201 I'll Take You Home/I Feel Good All Over (1963)
Atlantic 2216 In the Land of Make-Believe/Vaya Con Dios (1963)
Atlantic 2225 One-Way Love/Didn't It? (1964)
Atlantic 2237 Under the Boardwalk/Don't Want to Go On without You (1964)
Atlantic 2253 I've Got Sand in My Shoes/He's Just a Playboy (1964)
Atlantic 2260 Saturday Night at the Movies/Spanish Lace (1964)
Atlantic 2261 The Christmas Song/I Remember Christmas (1964)
Atlantic 2268 At the Club/Answer the Phone (1965)
Atlantic 2285 Come On Over to My Place/Chains of Love (1965)
Atlantic 2292 Follow Me/The Outside World (1965)
Atlantic 2298 Far from the Maddening Crowd/I'll Take You Where the Music's Playing (1965)
Sources: Pete Grendysa, Marv Goldberg, and Mike Redmond in *Record Exchanger* 18; Jay Warner in *American Singing Groups.*

Drivers (Cincinnati)

Personnel Willie Price (tenor), Charlie Harris, Leroy Harmshaw, Carl Rogers, Leroy Smith

Notes

The members of this group were purportedly truck drivers, which accounts for the group's name.

Paul McCoy was a later member of the Drivers, as were James Pate and Edison Thompson. McCoy sang on the RCA disc.

Discography

DeLuxe 6094 Smooth, Slow, and Easy/Women (1956)
DeLuxe 6104 My Lonely Prayer/Midnight Hours (1957)
DeLuxe 6117 Dangerous Lips/Oh Miss Nellie (1957)
RCA 7023 Blue Moon/I Get Weak (1957)
Lin 1002 A Man's Glory/Teeter Totter (1958)

172 • The Encyclopedia

Source: Dan Romanello, George Povall, and Chris Bucola, liner notes to the Sequel CD *Great Googa Mooga.*

Dubs (New York)

Personnel Richard Blandon (d) (lead), Cleveland Still (1st tenor), Billy Carlisle (d) (2d tenor), James "Jake" Milton (baritone), Tommy Gardner (bass)

Notes

As a result of Richard Blandon's attending a Scale-Tones rehearsal session, two of the Five Wings (Blandon and Carlisle) and the Scale-Tones (Still, Miller, and Gardner) merged to form the Dubs.

Previously they were known as the Marvels. After calling themselves the Dubs, they recorded "Don't Ask Me" for manager Hiram Johnson's Johnson label. The demand for the disc became so great that Johnson went to George Goldner and struck a deal by which the tune was guaranteed national distribution on Goldner's Gone Records. At this time Tommy Gardner left the group and was replaced by Tommy Grate.

Following their initial successes with Gone, they realized little or no profit and decided to disband. In 1958, they re-formed for ABC and a new tenor, Cordell Brown, replaced Cleveland Still. It was at this time that Kirk Harris joined the Dubs. Cleveland Still returned for the group's 1961 session.

The Josie group, which took shape in 1963, included Richard Blandon, Cordell Brown, Jake Miller, and Tommy Gardner.

Blandon died in 1992 and there had been many changes prior to that tragedy. In 1980, Still surfaced once again with Steven Brown from the Charts, John Truesdale, Bernard Jones, and lead Leslie Anderson.

Discography

Johnson 102 Don't Ask Me to Be Lonely/Darling (1957)
Gone 5002 Don't Ask Me/Darling (1957)
Gone 5011 Could This Be Magic/Such Lovin' (1957)
Gone 5020 Beside My Love/Gonna Make a Change (1958)
Gone 5034 Be Sure (My Love)/Song in My Heart (1958)
Gone 5046 Chapel of Dreams/Is There a Love for Me? (1958)
Gone 5069 Chapel of Dreams/Is There a Love for Me? (1959)
ABC 10056 No One/Early in the Evening (1959)
Mark-X 8008 Be Sure My Love/Song in My Heart (1960)
ABC 10100 Don't Laugh At Me/You'll Never Belong to Me (1960)
ABC 10150 For the First Time/Ain' That So (1960)
ABC 10198 If I Only Had Magic/Joogie Boogie (1961)
ABC 10269 Down, Down, Down I Go/Lullaby (1961)
End 1108 This to Me Is Love/Now That We Broke Up (1962)
Gone 5138 You're Free to Go/Is There a Love for Me? (1962)
Josie 911 Wisdom of a Fool/This I Swear (1963)
Wilshire 201 Your Very First Love/Just You (1963)
Johnson 097 Connie/Home under My Hat (1973)

Johnson 098 Somebody Goofed/I Won't Have You Breaking My Heart (1973)
Clifton 2 Where Do We Go from Here?/I Only Have Eyes for You (1973)
Clifton 5 Heartaches/You're Welcome (1975)
Sources: Wayne Stierle in *Bim Bam Boom* 1; Todd Baptista in *Echoes of the Past* 20; Gordon Skadberg and George Povall, liner notes with the Sequel CD *Jubilee/ Josie R&B Vocal Groups–5.*

Ducanes (Bergenfield, N.J.)

Personnel Louis Biscardi (lead), Jeff Breny (1st tenor), Rick Scrofani (2d tenor), Eddie Brian (baritone), Dennis Buckley (bass)

Notes

Members of the Ducanes met while they were still in high school in New Jersey (Bergen Catholic and Bergenfield High School) and decided to start a vocal group. They practiced a great deal and soon felt they were ready to audition and make a recording.

In 1961 they arranged for an appointment with Hill and Range Publishers in New York, who thought their song was terrible. Upon leaving, they met Phil Spector, who was in the outer office. He asked them to perform for him and then signed them to an independent contract with his organization.

After rehearsing the Ducanes extensively, Spector got them a contract with George Goldner and his Goldisc label. The disc shown below is the only disc the Ducanes ever released. The group disbanded in 1963.

The Eddie Brian discussed above was still active in 1997 and appeared at various UGHA events in New Jersey.

Discography

Goldisc 3024 I'm So Happy/Little Did I Know (1961)
Sources: Don Mennie in *Record Collector's Monthly* 39; Frank Aita in *Record Exchanger* 23.

Du Droppers (New York)

Personnel J. C. Ginyard (d) (lead), Willie Ray (tenor), Harvey Ray (baritone), Eddie Hashaw (bass)

Notes

In 1952, after leaving the Dixieaires, Ginyard met the Ray brothers, and they decided to form their own group. These three had a background in gospel.

After the group's first session, bass Eddie Hashaw left and was replaced by bass Bob Kornegay on Red Robin 116. (Curiously, in the liner notes accompanying Charly's *Fire and Fury Story* CD, it is stated that Kornegay joined when they began recording for Groove.)

At the end of 1952, they signed with RCA. Red Robin, having two sides remaining in their files, released these at the same time as the first RCA disc.

Prentice Moreland auditioned for the group in early 1954 and joined for just one session. In August 1954, another fifth member was added—Joe Van Loan. Harvey Ray left and the group was a quartet again.

Robert Bowers, tenor, replaced Willie Ray and Charlie Hughes, who was with the Drapers and the Drifters, was added in 1955.

In June 1955 they had their last recording session. Following that, Ginyard left for the Golden Gate Quartet, where he remained until 1971. He died in Switzerland in 1978. He had also been with the Jubalaires and the Dixieaires.

Kornegay, Van Loan, and Orville Brooks later formed a new group—the Valiants—who had several recordings.

Discography

Red Robin 108 Can't Do Sixty No More/Chain Me Baby (1952)
Red Robin 116 Come On and Love Me Baby/Go Back (1953)
RCA 47-5229 I Wanna Know/Laughing Blues (1953)
RCA 47-5321 I Found Out/Little Girl, Little Girl (1953)
RCA 47-5425 Whatever You're Doin'/Somebody Work on My Baby's Mind (1953)
RCA 47-5504 Don't Pass Me By/Get Lost (1953)
RCA 47-5543 The Note in the Bottle/Mama's Gone, Goodbye (1953)
Groove 0001 Speed King/Dead Broke (1954)
Groove 0013 Just Whisper/How Much Longer (1954)
Groove 0036 Boot 'Em Up/Let Nature Take It's Course (1954)
Groove 0104 Give Me Some Consideration/Talk That Talk (1955)
Groove 0120 You're Mine Already/I Wanna Love You (1955)
Sources: Liner notes with the Dr. Horse CD *Can't Do Sixty No More*; Brian Stilwell in *Echoes of the Past* 7; Marv Goldberg and Mike Redmond in *Bim Bam Boom* 13; Donn Fileti, liner notes with the Relic CD *Red Robin Golden Doowops*; Adam Komorowski, liner notes with the Charly CD *Fire and Fury.*

Dukays (Chicago)

Personnel Gene Chandler (born Eugene Dixon) (lead), Shirley Johnson (1st tenor), Ben Broyles (2d tenor), Earl Edwards (baritone), James Lowe (bass)

Notes

This group formed in 1957 in Chicago's south side Englewood neighborhood and started neighborhood singing. Dixon (Chandler) left for the army in 1957 and returned in 1960. The group stayed together during his absence and when he returned, he rejoined them.

Although it is not shown on the label, the Dukays backed Gene Chandler on his "Duke of Earl" hit. Apparently their distributor and their labels were torn between "Duke of Earl" and "Nite Owl." Because the two were released simultaneously, Gene Chandler's name appeared on the label without the group.

Shirley Johnson was Chandler's cousin.

Before going to Vee Jay, Shirley Johnson left and was replaced by Margaret Cookie Stone.

When the "Duke of Earl" hit, Chandler had already decided to go solo. Then Charles Davis joined the Dukays (1962), replacing Chandler. He had also been with the Trinidads. "Please Help" was the first song led by Davis. He later went on to become a member of the Artistics.

Jerry Murray, who was with One-Der-Ful, gave the Dukays an opportunity to record again on his own Jerry-O label in 1964. Their first release did fine, but their second did not and they then were only used for backups.

Ben Broyles was first to drift away. Following his departure, Claude McCrae, who had been with the Pastels on United, came on as lead and Richard Dixon replaced Broyles.

A little later Donald Rudolph replaced McCrae. The group grew despondent, however, and finally parted.

Discography

Nat 4001 The Big Lie/The Girl's a Devil (1961)
Nat 4002 Nite Owl/Festival of Love (1961)
Vee Jay 430 Nite Owl/Festival of Love (1962)
Vee Jay 442 I'm Gonna Love You So/Please Help (1962)
Vee Jay 460 I Feel Good All Over/I Never Knew (1962)
Vee Jay 491 Every Step/Combination (1962)
Jerry-O 105 The Jerk/Mo Jerk (1964)
Jerry-O 106 Mellow-Feznecky/Sho Nuf M.F. (1964)
Source: Bob Pruter in *Record Exchanger* 27.

Dukes (Oklahoma)

Personnel D. Nero, W. Armistead, E. Edwards, W. Moon, R. Williams

Notes

The Imperial Dukes are not the same group as the one that recorded for Specialty. This other group was from New Orleans and recorded sessions in 1956.

Discography

Imperial 5401 Teardrop Eyes/Shimmies and Shakes (1956)
Imperial 5415 Wini Brown/Cotton-Pickin' Hands (1956)
Source: Dave Antrell, liner notes with the *Lost Dreams* LP.

Dukes (Pasadena, Calif.)

Personnel Otis Lee, James McCarey, Philip Murph, James Cousar

Notes

This Dukes group had nothing to do with the "Teardrop Eyes" group. They originally formed in Columbus, Ohio, in 1952. Cousar, Murph, and McCarey were neighborhood friends. Along with another singer named Talbert, they played local clubs and functions.

In June 1954 they went to Los Angeles to better their performance and finances. In Pasadena they met Otis Lee, who had been with a Cobras group in California. After much practice, Lee contacted Art Rupe of Specialty Records and arranged for an audition in September 1954. Rupe liked them and arranged for a recording session.

They recorded four songs at the session and Rupe had the group provide some backup tracks for some older Lloyd Price recordings. Rupe apparently felt that since vocal groups were the rage, it made sense to add vocal group harmonies to several of Price's previously recorded songs—especially since he was currently in the service. Otis Lee joined the service as well.

Late in October 1954, Cousar, who remained in California and enrolled in school, recalls that the others had returned to Ohio after they had been in California for five months, cut perhaps six tunes plus the two Lloyd Price overdubs, and never made one live appearance!

The first Specialty releases were the two Lloyd Price cuts. In January 1955 Specialty released the first Dukes disc, Ooh Bop She Bop/Oh Kay. Neither side did well and this was the end for the Dukes.

In June 1955 Otis Lee returned to Ohio, having finished his boot camp obligation, and joined up with brother Nate Lee and Jimmy Randell to reactiviate their old group, the Cobras. Modern Records used them to cover "Sindy," which had been recorded by another Pasadena group, the Squires.

Discography

Specialty 543 Ooh Bop She Bop/Oh-Kay (1954)
Source: Marv Goldberg in *DISCoveries,* July 1998. Article on the Dukes.

Duponts (Brooklyn, N.Y.)

Personnel Anthony Gourdine (lead), William Doc Dockery (tenor), William Bracey (baritone), William Delk (baritone)

Notes

This group was formed in 1954 while the members were at Boys Vocational High School in Brooklyn. They wanted to form a vocal group, which was the thing to do at that time. After they had practiced a great deal, Dockery's father, who knew Paul Winley, got the group an audition. This was a very opportune time, as Winley had a desire to start a new label.

"You," written by Winley, was the first tune to be recorded on the Winley label. Winley, however, did not have the funds to properly promote the Duponts new recording and it died soon after release. Interestingly, because of Gourdine's later success with the Imperials, Savoy purchased the masters from Winley in 1958 and released it again—this time on Savoy! This time too it failed.

Alan Freed's manager, Jack Hook, then took them to Royal Roost, a jazz label, which he and Teddy Reig owned. At Royal Roost they recorded "Prove It Tonight," another failure on a new label. Discouraged by their failure, they disbanded and reformed in 1958 to record for Roulette (sans Gourdine), "Screamin' Ball at Dracula Hall," without success.

Discography

Winley 212 You/Must Be Falling in Love (1956)

Royal Roost 627 Prove It Tonight/Somebody (1956)
Savoy 1552 You/Must Be Falling in Love (1958)
Roulette 4060 Screamin' Ball at Dracula Hall/Half Past Nothing (without Anthony)
(1958)
Sources: J. Apugliese, S. Flam, and R. Newman in *Bim Bam Boom* 9; Art Turco in
Record Exchanger 14; Steve Kolanjian, liner notes with the Rhino's *Best of Little
Anthony and the Imperials.*

Duprees (Jersey City, N.J.)

Personnel Joey Vann (Canzano) (d) (lead), Joe Santollo (d) (1st tenor), John
Salvato (2d tenor), Mike Arnone (d) (baritone), Tom Bialaglow (d) (bass)

Notes

Before recording and before calling themselves the Duprees, the group went through
several personnel adjustments. They had their beginnings in Jersey City in 1956 as
the Utopians and later the Parisiennes. Originally there were black members in the
group. By 1959, the group recorded a demo tape and sent it to Coed Records. Coed
liked their "product" and signed them to the label. Coed management changed their
name to the Duprees.

"You Belong to Me" was their initial single and it did well with its big band sound.
This was followed with other early 1950s tunes, which fared better until 1963, when
they had their last top twenty single. When Tom Bialaglow left the group in November 1963, it became a quartet.

Joey Vann left the group in 1964 and Mike Kelly assumed his lead chores.

Interestingly, the Duprees recorded the Demens' "Take Me As I Am" and credited themselves as writers when they (and we) knew that it was Demens lead Eddie
Jones who wrote the song.

In 1965 the Duprees went to Columbia Records and recorded four more singles
through early 1967 but none did well. In 1968 they signed up with Heritage but did
nothing with that label either.

In today's group, Mike Arnone is the only original member. John Salvato is out
of the business and the remaining original members, according to Rhino's notes, have
passed on under mysterious circumstances.

Discography

Coed 569 You Belong to Me/Take Me As I Am (1962)
Coed 571 My Own True Love/Ginny (1962)
Coed 574 I'd Rather Be Here in Your Arms/I Wish I Could Believe You (1962)
Coed 576 Gone with the Wind/Let's Make Love Again (1963)
Coed 580 Take Me As I Am/I Gotta Tell Her Now (1963)
Coed 584 Why Don't You Believe Me?/The Things I Love (1963)
Coed 585 Have You Heard?/Love Eyes (1963)
Coed 587 It's No Sin/The Sand and the Sea (1963)
Coed 591 Where Are You?/Please Let Her Know (1964)
Coed 593 So Many Have Told Me/Unbelievable (1964)
Coed 595 It Isn't Fair/So Little Time (1964)
Coed 596 I'm Yours/Wishing Ring (1965)

Columbia 43464 Norma Jean/She Waits for Him (1965)
Columbia 43577 Let Them Talk/The Exodus Song (1966)
Columbia 43802 It's Not Time Now/Didn't Want to Have to Do It (1966)
Columbia 44078 I Understand/Be My Love (1967)
Heritage 804 My Special Angel/Ring of Love (1968)
Heritage 805 Goodnight My Love/Ring of Love (1968)
Heritage 808 My Love, My Love/The Sky's the Limit (1968)
Heritage 811 Two Different Worlds/Hope (1969)
Heritage 826 Have You Heard?/Have You Heard? (1969)
RCA 10407 Delicious/The Sky's the Limit (1975)
Source: Jay Warner, *American Singing Groups.*

Durhams (Upper Darby, Pa.)

Personnel Walt Taylor (lead), Phil Corey (1st tenor), Tony Julian (2d tenor), Lou Ferri (baritone), Jimmy Salzman (bass)

Notes

The Durhams emerged in 1960 after joining forces with the Baroques, another Upper Darby vocal group. After practicing and rehearsing for several months, they met with Eddie Gries of Relic Records in New Jersey. Gries liked them and placed their material on one of Relic's a cappella LPs.

Because of an army obligation, regular baritone Artie Wolf could not attend the Relic recording session and Lou Ferri took his place. The Relic LPs were in stores by the summer of 1963!

Salzman and Wolf were drafted, leaving the remaining three members. This essentially marked the end of the Durhams.

Discography

Relic 1018 Sincerely/Seconds of Soul (1963)
Source: Bob Bosco in *Record Collector's Monthly* 48.

Duvals (New York)

Personnel Wilbur "Yonkie" Paul (lead), Richard Lewis (1st tenor), Jesse Facing (tenor), Dock Green (baritone), Bill Bailey (bass)

Notes

This is actually the Five Crowns of Rainbow and Old Town fame simultaneously recording (or moonlighting as it is now known) under another name for Rainbow and another label.

Discography

Rainbow 335 You Came to Me/Ooh Wee Baby (1956)
Source: Donn Fileti, liner notes with the Relic CD *Rainbow Records.*

Duvals (Evanston, Ill.)

Personnel Charles Perry (lead), Charles Woodridge (2d tenor), Arthur Cox (baritone), Andrew Thomas (bass)

Notes

The Duvals formed in 1961 when Perry came home from the service.

Tenor Carlton Black was added in 1962 and became lead singer and primary songwriter. He did not replace Perry, who remained, and the group then became a quintet.

Discography

Boss 2117 What Am I?/Cotton (1963)
Red Rocket 471 What Am I?/Cotton (1963)
Source: Bob Pruter, *Doowop . . . The Chicago Scene.*

Dynamics (Pittsburgh, Pa.)

Personnel George Winesburgh (lead), Jimmy Shoup (1st tenor), Earl Viney (2d tenor), Dock Johns (baritone), Donny Fuchs (bass)

Notes

After many false starts, the above ensemble got together in 1956 and soon got serious about their singing.

They entered and won a talent contest promoted by Pittsburgh deejay Jay Michael, which won them a recording contract with New York's Cindy Records. This led to their release on Cindy, Gone Is My Love/Saints Go Marching In.

Problems with their manager and with Cindy management caused them to record their next disc on their own Impala label.

Viney later had problems with his voice changing and was replaced by John Korman. Before they could even record with Korman, however, he left the group.

Disenchanted, Winesburgh left and the remaining three first got Dick Knauss of the then unknown Marcels, who would later hit with "Blue Moon." Knauss, however, returned to the Marcels and then Jimmy Shoup left.

Johns and Fuchs then added Ron Barnett and Dick Spracier. The group had two releases on their Dynamic label.

Realizing no success, the group disbanded in 1963–1964.

Discography

Cindy 3005 Gone Is My Love/Saints Go Marching In (1957)
Dynamic 109 Don't Be Late/Eenie Meenie (1957)
Impala 501 Moonlight/Someone (1958)
Seeco 6008 Moonlight/Someone (1959)
La Vere 186 Wrap Up Your Troubles in Dreams/I Can't Give You Anything but Love (1961)
Dynamic (N/A) Darling/Don't Leave Me (1962)

Dynamic (N/A) Wasted/Don't Leave Me (1962)
Dynamic 579 Christmas Plea/Dream Girl (1962)
Dynamic 1002 Delsinia/So Fine (1963)
Source: Carl Janusek and Nancy Janusek in *Story Untold* 9.

Earls (Bronx, N.Y.)

Personnel Larry Chance (Larry Figueroa) (lead), Robert Del Din (1st tenor), Eddie Harder (2d tenor), Jack Wray (bass)

Notes

Larry Chance (as Larry Figueroa) came to the Bronx from Philadelphia in 1957. Because he went to school with Chubby Checker, Frankie Avalon, and Danny Rapp (Danny and the Juniors), he assembled his new friends from New York and formed the Earls.

They signed with Rome Records and their first release, "Looking for My Baby," was issued in 1961.

In 1962, producer/arranger Stan Vincent reworked the song "Remember When," calling it "Remember Then," and got Old Town's Hy Weiss to record it. This became a huge hit for the Earls.

When group member Larry Palumbo was killed in a parachuting accident in 1959, the song "I Believe" was recorded in his honor. To this day the Earls sing it at performances, dedicating it to Palumbo. "I Believe" was released as the demo originally brought to Old Town for audition.

Sometime after 1964, Wray and Del Din left and were replaced by Bob Moricco and Ronnie Calabrese.

In 1967 the Earls moved to ABC. Clarence Collins and Kenny Seymour of the Imperials joined them on their only ABC release.

Discography

Rome 101 Life Is but a Dream/Lost Love (1961)
Rome 101 Life Is but a Dream/Without You (1961)
Rome 102 Lookin' for My Baby/Cross My Heart (1961)
Rome 5117 I'll Never Cry/My Heart's Desire (1962)
Old Town 1130 Remember Then/Let's Waddle (1962)
Old Town 1133 Never/I Keep A-Tellin You (19630
Old Town 1141 Eyes/Look My Way (19630
Old Town 1145 Cry, Cry, Cry/Kissin' (1963)
Old Town 1149 I Believe/Don't Forget (1963)
Old Town 1169 Oh, What a Time/Ask Anybody (1964)
Old Town 1182 Remember Me Baby/Amor (1965)
Mr. G 801 If I Could Do It Over Again/Papa (1967)
ABC 11109 It's Been a Long Time Coming/My Lonely Room (1968)
Source: Jay Warner, *American Singing Groups.*

Ebbtides, Nino & (Bronx, N.Y.)

Personnel Antonio Aiello (lead), Tony Delesio (2d tenor), Vinnie Drago (baritone), Rudy ——— (bass)

Notes

Nino and the Ebbtides started as the Ebbtides in the Bronx in 1956. Aiello and Drago found Delesio and someone remembered as Rudy. After practicing, they met Murray Jacobs, who had the group cut the two Acme sides in 1957.

Group members interviewed could not recall Rudy's last name. The *Story Untold* account states that Rudy came from the Pearls. None of the Pearls groups included a Rudy. Perhaps the Rudy referred to was in a similar-sounding group, the Ebbtides.

By the time they recorded their second single, "Puppy Love," Jacobs had them do it for his newly formed label, Recorte, in 1958.

Ralph Bracco replaced Rudy and Tony Imbimbo assumed Tony Delesio's position. Eventually, in 1960, Tony DiBari replaced Ralph Bracco.

The Ebbtides also backed up the Rockin' Chairs on "Memories of Love" and "Girl of Mine." In an interview with Ed Engel, Nino Aiello states that he sang in the background with the Rockin' Chairs on their Recorte disc, "A Kiss Is a Kiss."

In 1960 the group moved to the Marco label for one unsuccessful disc. Next was Madison for two more records. Madison had financial problems and soon went out of business.

By the end of 1961, they were with Mr. Peacock Records. They recorded one of their best discs for Mr. Peacock, "Happy Guy." But Mr. Peacock failed to promote the tune properly and nothing happened. By 1965, the Ebbtides decided to call it quits.

Discography

Acme 720 Franny, Franny/Darling, I'll Love Only You (1958)
Recorte 405 Puppy Love/You Make Me Wanna Rock 'n' Roll (1958)
Recorte 408 The Real Meaning of X-Mas/Two Purple Shadows in the Snow (1958)
Recorte 409 I'm Confessin'/Tell the World I Do (1959)
Recorte 413 Don't Look Around/I Love Girls (1959)
Marco 105 Someday/Little Miss Blue (1961)
Madison 162 Those Oldies but Goodies/Don't Run Away (1961)
Madison 166 Juke Box Saturday Night/I'll Fall in Love (1961)
Mr. Peacock 102 Happy Guy/Wished I Was Home (1961)
Mr. Peacock 117 Lovin' Time/Stamps Baby, Stamps (1962)
Mr. Peeke 123 Nursery Rhymes/Tonight (1963)
Mala 480 Automatic Reaction/Linda Lou Garrett (1964)
Source: Mike Piazza in *Bim Bam Boom* 7.

Ebbtones (Watts, Calif.)

Personnel Danny Kristian (lead), Fred Romain (lead), George Hollis, Kenneth Byle

Notes

The record by the Ebbtones was Lee Rupe's first release on Ebb Records—a label she started after her divorce from the owner of Specialty Records. The Ebbtones' disc was released in April 1957.

Each side of this disc was led by different artists, the A side by Danny Kristian and the B side by Freddie Romain. Romain and Kristian started with the Native Boys on the Combo label. Both sang lead for that group. Hollis and Byle sang with Cornel Gunter's Flairs and Ermines. In his liner notes accompanying Ace's *Ebb Story-2,* Jim Dawson states, "This is probably the same Ebbtones who recorded three singles for Crest in 1956–1957." As a result of Marv Goldberg's article in the September 1996 issue of *DISCoveries,* we've learned that Dawson's supposition appears to be incorrect.

Discography

Ebb 100 I've Got a Feeling/Danny's Blues (1957)
Sources: Jim Dawson, liner notes with the Ace CD *Ebb Story, 1–2*; Marv Goldberg in *DISCoveries,* September 1996.

Ebb-Tones (Los Angeles)

Personnel Al Frazier, Carl White (tenor), John "Sonny" Harris, Turner "Rocky" Wilson

Notes

This foursome was also the Four After Fives, Rebels, Rivingtons, Sharps, Tenderfoots, and the Twisters.

Discography

Crest 1016 I Want You Only/That's All (1956)
Crest 1024 Baby/What Makes a Man Fool Around? (1956)
Crest 1032 Hum/Dust Off the Bible (1956)
Source: Marv Goldberg and Mike Redmond in *Record Exchanger* 13, article about the Flairs.

Ebonaires (Los Angeles)

Personnel Richard Brown (tenor), Eddie Jones (tenor), James Bradley, John Dix, Lewis E. Young

Notes

Little is known about this quintet other than the personnel listed above, but it's interesting to note the possibility that Eddie Jones (above) might be the same person who performed lead for the Demens [sic]. Jones's background starts in California prior to coming east at about this same time. After relocating to New York, he was initially part of the prerecording Solitaires. When he was inducted into the army before the Solitaires began recording, he was replaced.

Discography

MGM 10361 Bye, Bye, Bye, Bye/Come In, Mr. Blues (1949)
Modern 656 Song of the Wanderer/Sleepy Time Gal (1949)
Aladdin 3211 Three O'Clock in the Morning/Baby, You're the One (1953)
Aladdin 3212 You're Nobody till Somebody Loves You/Lawd, Lawd, Lawd (1954)
Money 220 The Very Best Luck in the World/Hey Baby Stop (1956)
Colonial 117 We're in Love/Thinkin' and Thinkin' (1959)
Source: Billy Vera, liner notes with the CD *Doo Wop from Dolphin's of Hollywood.*

Echos (Los Angeles)

Personnel Marzetta Freeman (lead), Elmo Jones (1st tenor), Miles Grayson (2d tenor), Edward DeVold (baritone), Darlene Franklin (bass)

Notes

Marzetta Freeman and Darlene Franklin were added following original lead Mosby Carter's entrance into the service. The two girls are featured on the Echos' only Combo single, 128 (Aye Señorita/My Little Honey).

John Christman, Benjamin Washington, and Cliff Curry (Five Pennies) joined later, as did 2d tenor Harold Grayson.

The above group backed Little Clydie on Specialty.

When DeVold and Jones began their college education, the Echos broke up.

Discography

Combo 128 My Little Honey/Aye Señorita (1956)
Source: Donn Fileti, liner notes with the Relic LP *Combo–3.*

Edsels (Campbell, Ohio)

Personnel George Jones Jr. (lead), Larry Green (1st tenor), James Reynolds (2d tenor), Harry Green (baritone), Marshall Sewell (bass)

Notes

After returning home from the air force, Jones and Reynolds decided to form a vocal group. They located other friends in the area and began practicing. It was also at this time that they started calling themselves the Edsels.

The group soon began doing variety shows and appearing at local nightspots. They sang "Rama Lama Ding Dong" at these appearances, which Jones had written while in the service.

A friend enabled them to record several demos that were eventually taken to Little Rock's Dub Records; "Rama Lama Ding Dong" was recorded in the summer of 1958 for Dub.

The Dub recording did not do well on its first try, and the Edsels began looking for another label. They wound up at Roulette, but their one recording for Roulette did not do well either. They next recorded "What Brought Us Together" for Tammy Records in 1960. This disc did very well.

Because of the success of the Marcels' "Blue Moon," a New York disc jockey began playing "Rama Lama Ding Dong" and it was reborn. An Old Town subsidiary, Twin Records, then rereleased it.

As a result of this success, the owner of Dub, who had several unreleased tunes in the can by the Edsels, sold the masters to Dot. Edsels records were now being released by many labels. It was at this time that the group signed with Capitol.

They lasted into the 1960s, but finally the lack of financial rewards led the group to disband.

Discography

Dub 2843 Rama Lama Ding Dong/Bells (1958)
Roulette 4151 Do You Love Me?/Rink-A-Din-Ki-Do (1959)
Tammy 1010 What Brought Us Together?/Don't Know What to Do (1960)
Twin 700 Rama Lama Ding Dong/Bells (1961)
Tammy 1014 Three Precious Words/Let's Go (1961)
Ember 1078 Three Precious Words/Let's Go (1961)
Capitol 4588 My Jealous One/Bone Shaker Joe (1961)
Dot 16311 Could It Be?/My Whispering Heart (1962)
Capitol 4675 Shake, Shake Sherry/If Your Pillow Could Talk (1962)
Capitol 4836 Shaddy Daddy Dip Dip/Don't You Feel? (1962)
Sources: Jeff Kreiter in *Story Untold* 6; Jeff Kreiter in *Record Exchanger* 31.

Egyptians, King Pharaoh & (Columbus, Ohio)

Personnel Morris Wade (tenor), Robert Taylor (1st tenor), Bob Lowery (baritone), Ronnie Wilson (bass)

Notes

This group was an offshoot of the Four Pharaohs.

Discography

Federal 12413 By the Candlelite/Shimmy Sham (1961)
Source: Dave Ardit in *Bim Bam Boom* 13.

Egyptian Kings (Columbus, Ohio)

Personnel Morris Wade (lead), Paul Moore, Pete Oden, Leo Blakely (bass)

Notes

This group was another splintering of the Four Pharaohs and had also been King Pharaoh and the Egyptians.

While on tour in Los Angeles in 1963, they met up with former manager Howard Ransom, whose friend owned the local Nanc record label. The group once again changed its name to the Egyptian Kings and recorded Give Me Your Love/Baby I Need Love for Nanc. In an interview, Leo Blakely claimed that the group recorded another disc, School Days/The Move Around, but it was never released.

In 1964 Pete Oden departed and Paul Moore's cousin William Suber replaced him. In 1968 the group disbanded.

Discography

Nanc 1120 Give Me Your Love/Baby I Need Your Love (1963)
Nanc (UNR) School Days/The Move Around
Source: Dave Ardit in *Bim Bam Boom* 13.

El Capris (Pittsburgh, Pa.)

Personnel Eddie Jackson (lead), James Scott (1st tenor) Theodore McCrary (2d tenor), Leon Gray (baritone), William Germany (baritone), Larry Hill (bass), James Ward (bass)

Notes

The El Capris formed in 1954 in Pittsburgh by neighborhood friends. Initially they called themselves the Bluebirds; believing that bluebird in Spanish was Capri, they changed their name to El Capris.

As a result of winning a school talent contest, they were awarded an audition with Bullseye Records in New York. Label management liked them and a recording session was set up. Their first record was released in March 1956. It did nothing.

Staying local, the group want to Pittsburgh's Fee Bee records and cut at least four sides. The first was Fee Bee 216 "Your Star." As shown below, this came out with two different flip sides. Their next release was on Fee Bee subsidiary Ringo Records.

(Note: In an interview with Bill Germany, he states that the flip of the Ring-O disc "Quit Pulling My Woman" was not the El Capris!)

By 1958, Jackson, Scott, Hill, and Ward called it quits and were replaced by 1st tenor Percy Wharton and bass Sam Askew. This new group of El Capris recorded for the Paris label Ivy League Clean/They're Always Laughing at Me.

Discography

Bullseye 102 (Shimmy Shimmy) Ko Ko Wop (EJ)/Oh but She Did (EJ) (1956)
Fee Bee 216 Your Star (EJ)/All Night (LG) (1957)
Fee Bee 216 Your Star (EJ)/To Live Again (EJ) (1957)
Ring-O 308 Safari (TMC)/Quit Pulling My Woman (not the El Capris) (1957)
Paris 525 Ivy League Clean (LG)/They're Always Laughing at Me (LG) (1958)
Source: Marv Goldberg in *DISCoveries,* August 1995.

Elchords (New York)

Personnel Butchie Saunders (lead), Ron Talbert (1st tenor), Elliot Johnson (2d tenor), Raphael ———— (baritone), David Ballott (bass)

Notes

While Jimmy Jones and the Pretenders were at a session recording "Tonight" for Holiday Records, Jones produced another session that same day, "Peppermint Stick" by Butchie Saunders and the Elchords. This information is contained in an article written by Joe Sicurella for *Harmony Tymes* 2.

Sicurella goes on to report Jones's statement that the members of this group were from his upper Manhattan neighborhood. He also said that the lyrics to the song were not suggestive. Dave "Baby" Cortez played piano for the session. Jones provided names of the Elchords: Cookie at bass, Lefty, Elliot, and Bernard Johnson. At lead, Little Butchie Saunders. It was on the Good label because Jones felt it was a "Good" record. It was published by Don Music, where Jimmy worked. Jones wrote "Peppermint Stick" with his friend Bobby Moore.

Saunders's real name was John L. Brown. He also sang for the Vells. Jones planned other recordings for the Elchords, but he lost $7,000 on the first disc because of a dispute with George Goldner's distributors, Tico-Roulette.

Discography

Good 544 Peppermint Stick/Gee I'm in Love (1957)
Source: Joe Sicurella in *Harmony Tymes* 2.

Eldaros (Syracuse, N.Y.)

Personnel Jimmy Singleton (lead), Raymond Green (1st tenor), James Crawford (2d tenor), Kenneth Tucker (baritone), Levi Hall (bass)

Notes

The Eldaros got together in 1957. They recorded several demos that received Syracuse airplay. This exposure got the group many performances in the area.

It was also in 1957 that the Eldaros recorded "Please Surrender" for Vesta.

Discography

Vesta 101/102 Rock A Bock/Please Surrender (1958)
Source: Robert Green in *Story Untold* 5.

El Dorados (Chicago)

Personnel Pirkle Lee Moses (lead), Arthur Bassett (tenor), Jewel Jones (1st tenor), Louis Bradley (2d tenor), James Maddox (baritone), Richard Nickens (bass)

Notes

Originally called the Five Stars, Pirkle Lee Moses and the original bass, Robert Glasper, joined the air force together. Moses came home in ninety days and Glasper decided to remain. When Moses rejoined the Five Stars, they then became six and changed their name to the El Dorados.

Arthur Bassett sang lead on "Baby I Need You" while Moses led the flip, "My Lovin' Baby." Hazel McCollum sang lead on "Annie's Answer." Bassett went into the air force and Pirkle Lee Moses then performed lead chores for most of the remaining songs. Bassett left after the One More Time/Little Miss Love session. Moses also sang with the Major-Minors.

"I'll Be Forever Loving You" was originally recorded by another Vee Jay group, the Five Knights of Rhythm, but it was never released. Vee Jay thought it was ideal for the El Dorados.

Bass Richard Nickens left after "I Began to Realize" to enter the army. The group then became a quartet.

In 1957, group members felt they were not being treated fairly and left for Oakland, California. Moses, not feeling the same, remained. It was reported in Dave Antrell's liner notes with the Rhythm LP that the group was doing a little moonlighting as the Tempos and recorded "Promise Me" and "Never Too Late" for Rhythm.

The last recording by the original group was "A Rose for My Darling."

Robert Bitts is heard on "I Began to Realize" and "There in the Night."

As a result of the Delegates parting with their lead, Dee Clark, the remaining members joined forces with Pirkle Lee Moses. The new El Dorados were Moses, Johnny Carter, Teddy Long, John McCall, and Douglas Brown. This new group recorded two songs for Vee Jay, The Lights Are Low/Three Reasons Why.

These last two recordings (1958) didn't hit and the El Dorados finally packed it in 1959.

The remaining members of the El Dorados, calling themselves These Four El Dorados, included Jewell Jones, James Maddox, Louis Bradley, and new lead, Marvin Smith. They recorded for Academy Records.

In the 1960s baritone George Kemp (a.k.a. George Prayer) and Melvin Morrow from the Moroccos and the Major-Minors were added.

Discography

Vee Jay 115 My Loving Baby/Baby I Need You (1954)
Vee Jay 118 Annie's Answer/Living with Vivian (1954)
Vee Jay 127 One More Chance/Little Miss Love (1954)
Vee Jay 147 At My Front Door/What's Buggin' You Baby? (1955)
Vee Jay 165 I'll Be Forever Loving You/I Began to Realize (1955)
Vee Jay 180 Now That You've Gone/Rock and Roll's for Me (1956)
Vee Jay 197 A Fallen Tear/Chop Ling Soon (1956)
Vee Jay 211 There in the Night/Bim Bam Boom (1956)
Vee Jay 250 Tears on My Pillow/A Rose for My Darling (1957)
Vee Jay 263 Three Reasons Why/Boom Diddie Boom (1958)
Vee Jay 302 Lights Are Low/Oh What a Girl (1958)
Source: Bob Pruter in *Record Collector's Monthly* 48; Bob Pruter, *Doowop . . . The Chicago Scene*; Dave Hinckley in *Goldmine*.

Elegants (Staten Island, N.Y.)

Personnel Vito Picone (lead), Arthur Venosa (1st tenor), Frank Tardogna (2d tenor), Carmen Romano (baritone), James Moschello (bass)

Notes

The Elegants began as Pat Cordell (Croccitto) and the Crescents. This group's first recording was written by Vito Picone (*see* Crescents, Pat Cordell &). The young woman's dad was quite hesitant about his fifteen-year-old daughter traveling all over the United States with four adolescent young men, and his concern ended the Crescents.

Picone and Romano started again, joining forces with three other local Staten Island friends and calling themselves the Elegants. They practiced a great deal and made many local appearances.

Vito and Arthur wrote "Little Star" and performed it at all their live appearances. The Secrets, another Staten Island group, heard it and were rumored to have been trying to record it. As a result, the Elegants worked feverishly to record it first.

Because they liked the Heartbeats, they went to Hull. Owner Bea Caslon loved the song and had the Elegants record it. Caslon knew Hull could not support the disc. She licensed it, and the group, to ABC. It was never released on Hull. In June 1958 "Little Star" was released on ABC subsidiary APT. It was a tremendous success.

Tardogno did lead on "True Love Affair."

Follow-ups continued but did not do well. In early 1959 the Elegants were severed from ABC and APT. Hull, still involved with the group, released "Little Boy Blue," but this didn't do well either.

They went to United Artists and then back to ABC and several others. When Picone had an automobile accident, he and the group parted. This was really the beginning of the end.

Picone re-formed the group to record for Laurie in 1965. In addition to Picone, the group consisted of Freddie Redmond, Nino Amato, Bruce Cop, and the original bass, Jimmy Moschella.

Discography

Apt 25005 Little Star/Getting Dizzy (1958)
Apt 25017 Please Believe Me/Goodnight (1958)
Apt 25029 True Love Affair/Pay Day (1959)
Hull 732 Little Boy Blue/Get Well Soon (1960)
United Artists 230 Speak Low/Let My Prayers Be with You (1960)
United Artists 295 Happiness/Spiral (1960)
ABC 10219 Tiny Cloud/I've Seen Everything (1961)
Photo 2662 A Dream Come True/Dressin' Up (1963)
Laurie 3283 A Letter from Viet Nam/Barbara Beware (1965)
Laurie 3324 Belinda/Lazy Love (1965)
Bim Bam Boom 121 Lonesome Weekend/It's Just a Matter of Time (1974)
Sources: Sparkletone *Laurie* CD liner notes; Ed Engel in *Time Barrier Express* 3, no. 1.

Elements (Southern California)

Personnel Jimmy Smith (lead), Kenny Sinclair, Carl Lewis, William DeVase, Darryl Lewis

Notes

Darryl Lewis, Kenny Sinclair, and William DeVase were three of the original members of the Six Teens who recorded "A Casual Look" on Flip Records.

After their time as the Six Teens, Darryl Lewis and his brother, Carl, along with Kenny Sinclair, William DeVase, and lead Jimmy Smith, formed the Elements, who recorded "Lonely Hearts Club" as the Elements on Titan.

Carl would soon leave to pursue his acting career. Oscar McDonald replaced him and that ensemble was the Elgins who recorded for Flip, Lummtone, Titan, and Valiant.

Discography

Titan 1708 Lonely Heart's Club/Bad Man (1960)
Sources: Nikki Gustafson's Internet piece on the Elgins, available at: www.members.aol.com/wawawaooh/main.htm.

Elgins (Bronx, N.Y.)

Personnel Michael Jacks (lead), Henry Volpato, Kenny Hettinger, Russell Dell

Notes

As a result of their hanging out at Cousins' Record Shop on Fordham Road in the Bronx, this Elgins group was given the opportunity by shop and label owner, Lou Cicchetti, to record. Eventually Cicchetti leased their recording to Dot Records.

Discography

Dot 16563 Cheryl/Tell Gina (1963)
Source: Unsigned liner notes with the Dee Jay Jamboree CD *Out of the Bronx.*

Elgins (Southern California)

Personnel Jimmy Smith (lead), Kenny Sinclair, William DeVase, Darryl Lewis, Oscar McDonald

Notes

This West Coast Elgins quintet formed in Los Angeles in 1959. Smith and McDonald had attended high school together in Beaumont, Texas. Lewis, Sinclair, and DeVase were high school mates in southern California. Lewis and Sinclair had originally been members of the Six Teens, who recorded "A Casual Look" on the Flip label. Following their recordings for Flip, Kenny Sinclair and Darryl Lewis reunited with William DeVase and got Carl Sinclair, Kenny's brother, and Jimmy Smith to form the Elements, who recorded "Lonely Hearts Club Band" on Titan Records.

After the Titan release, Carl Williams left the Elements and Smith brought McDonald in as a replacement ultimately forming the Elgins. Smith also cut Flip 347 as by Jimmy Smith and the Lockettes.

Discography

Flip 353 Casey/Uncle Sam's Man (1960)
Titan 1724 Extra, Extra/My Illness (1961)
Lummtone 112 Finally/I Lost My Love in the Big City (1963)

Lummtone 113 Your Lovely Ways/Finding a Sweetheart (1964)
Valiant 712 Street Scene/You Found Yourself Another Fool (1965)
Sources: Ferdie Gonzalez, *Disco-File*; N. Gustafson's Internet piece, available at: www.members.aol.com/wawawaooh/main.htm.; Donn Fileti, liner notes with the Relic LP *Best of Lummtone.*

El Pollos (Cleveland, Ohio)

Personnel Robert Chalmers (lead), Tommy Hobbs (1st tenor), Philip Dorroh (2d tenor), George Scott (baritone), Robert Manley (bass)

Notes

The group started in Cleveland in 1956, calling themselves the Capitols.

They were neighborhood friends who sang on street corners, at amateur shows, and at house parties. When they learned of another group called the Capitols, they became the El Pollos.

There was a record shop in their neighborhood whose owner liked the guys. He bought them uniforms and an older car. In 1958, they met Shelly Haims, who owned Studio Records. Haims auditioned the group and as a result signed them to a contract and arranged a recording session. The two sides they recorded were released in 1958.

Before they first recorded, Walter Jones was in the group at 2d tenor. When they first recorded, Jones had left and their guitarist, Philip Dorroh, replaced him.

They next met a salesman from Neptune Records in Chicago selling "The Time" by Baby Washington. After hearing the El Pollos, he brought them to New York to record for Neptune.

The El Pollos on Neptune and Studio, therefore, were the same group!

Realizing no success, they disbanded in 1959.

Discography

Neptune 1001 Why Treat Me This Way?/School Girl (1958)
Studio 999 These Four Letters/High School Dance (1958)
Source: Marv Goldberg in *DISCoveries,* June 1997.

El Rays (Harvey, Ill.)

Personnel Johnny Funches (lead), Marvin Junior (1st tenor), Verne Allison (2d tenor), Mickey McGill (baritone), Chuck Barksdale (bass), Lucius McGill (bass)

Notes

The El Rays came together at Thornton High School in Harvey, Illinois, in 1952. Judging from their name selection, they were obviously not proficient in Spanish. They wanted to call themselves The Kings in Spanish, which is Los Reyes. Instead they called themselves the El Rays, which means The Rays.

While performing in Chicago, the El Rays were taught harmony and vocalizing by the Moonglows. As the El Rays, they did local gigs and nightspots and other local functions.

Four members of the El Rays finished high school in 1954, and Lucius McGill dropped out to take a job at the post office. By 1955, the group sounded so good that they signed with Vee Jay. They were down to five members and were now known as the Dells.

"Oh What a Night" really hit big and established the Dells as a big-time vocal group *(see* Dells).

Discography
Checker 794 Darling I Know/Christine (1954)
Sources: Bob Pruter in *Record Collector's Monthly* 50; Pete Grendysa, liner notes with the Chess CD boxed set *Chess Rhythm & Roll.*

El Torros (St. Louis, Mo.)

Personnel Lloyd Lockett (lead), George Davis (1st tenor), Fred Green (2d tenor), Johnny Stemach (baritone), Odis Hearon (bass)

Notes

The El Torros originally began in 1951, using several different names and appearing at local clubs and events. After much practice, they continued the local appearances. Following the live shows, many personnel changes and several years, they signed with the King-Federal-DeLuxe organization in 1956. However, because nothing was happening for them with King, they asked for and got their release from the Cincinnati conglomerate.

They next added tenor Fred Green, who had previously been with the Mellards, another St. Louis group that had recorded for Ballad.

They soon auditioned for the *Ted Mack Amateur Hour.* Interestingly, although they never appeared on the show, during the audition, Mack accidentally introduced them as the El Torros. They liked the name and kept it.

They continued to do live performances and in 1957 were spotted by Bobby Bland and Junior Parker. Bland and Parker were impressed enough to recommend them to Don Robey, owner of the label both were with at the time—Duke/Peacock.

A session was scheduled for them in Chicago on April 1957. Don Robey attended and Yellow Hand/Dance with Me were recorded, along with two other tunes. The former two tunes were released on Duke in June 1957 and met with little success.

A second session took place in St. Louis in April 1958. Duke 194 was released in June and did not fare well. Because of its poor sales, it ultimately became the harder disc for collectors to find when the collecting hobby began.

In 1959, Fred Green departed. He was replaced by Billy Davis, who later recorded with the Fifth Dimension. Davis appeared with the El Torros but never recorded with them. On their final session for Don Robey's Duke label, Davis had been drafted and a replacement remembered only as Calvin replaced him.

In 1960, because of the Drifters' success with a tune of the same name, Robey rereleased the El Torros' "Dance with Me."

The El Torros backed Dinah Washington, Dakota Staton, and Roy Hamilton on their St. Louis appearances. They recorded their final Duke release (353) in 1962. Because of no sales of this last Duke recording, Davis left soon, followed by Lockett.

As a result of the poor sales, in 1964 they changed their name to the Mustangs and made another recording for Robey, who released it on one of his other labels—Sure-Shot.

According to Charlie Horner, in his *Vocal Group Guide to St. Louis,* the lead singer of the El Torros is referred to as Lloyd Luckett. This El Torros group had nothing to do with the other misspelled El Torros on Fraternity.

Discography

Duke 175 Yellow Hand (LL)/Dance with Me (LL) (1957)
Duke 194 You Look Good to Me (LL)/Barbara Jean (all) (1958)
Duke 321 Dance with Me (LL)/What's the Matter? (FG) (1960)
Duke 333 Two Lips (all)/You May Say Yes (LL) (1961)
Duke 353 Doop Doop a Walla Walla (CC)/ Mama's Cookin (LL) (1962)
Sources: Charlie Horner, *Vocal Group Guide to St. Louis*; Marv Goldberg in *DISCoveries,* June 1998.

El Venos (Pittsburgh, Pa.)

Personnel Leon Daniels (lead), Anna Mae Jackson (female lead), Daniel Jackson (1st tenor), Leon Taylor (2d tenor), Joey Daniels (baritone), Bernard Palmer (bass)

Notes

The group formed in 1955 when the members were all sixteen years old. Like many other groups, they began with street corner a cappella.

Dee Jay Porky Chedwick helped the El Venos secure an audition with the RCA organization.

Geraldine/Now We're Together were recorded at the group's first session with RCA in 1956. Five songs were recorded at that session, but only those mentioned above were released.

Following a little local success in New York and New England, they decided to go to New York to audition for Calico Records. They recorded several tunes for Calico that were never released.

Leon Daniels and Joey Daniels were brothers, and Anna Mae Jackson and Daniel Jackson were brother and sister. (According to Billy Vera's liner notes with the RCA CD *Rock 'n' Roll Party-2,* the Daniels men were uncle and nephew.)

Joey Briscoe, who later sang with the Del Vikings, sang lead on some sides recorded for the Amp-3 label that were never released.

Anna Mae Jackson later changed her name to Anne Kieth and recorded under that name on Memo.

Joey Daniels left after the Vik recordings and was replaced by Jimmy Wright.

Leon Taylor left and was replaced by Eddie Hicks, who had been with Mickey Toliver and the Capitols.

Discography

Groove 0170 Geraldine/Now We're Together (1956)
Vik 0305 My Heart Beats Faster/You Must Be True (1957)

Sources: Billy Vera, liner notes with the RCA CD *Rock 'n' Roll Party–2*; Carl Janusek and Nancy Janusek in *Echoes of the Past* 20.

Emanons (New York)

Personnel Robert Coleman (lead), Carl White (1st tenor), Ralph Steeley (2d tenor), James Dukes (baritone), James Hill (bass)

Notes

Little is known about this Emanons group. According to Gordon Skadberg's liner notes for the *Jubilee/Josie R&B Vocal Groups* CD, this Emanons group had nothing to do with the ABC Paramount or Winley groups of the same name.

Discography

Gee 1005 Hindu Baby/Change of Time (1956)
Josie 801 Blue Moon/Wish I Had My Baby (1956)
Sources: Phil Groia, *They All Sang on the Corner*; Gordon Skadberg, liner notes with the Sequel CD *Jubilee /Josie R&B Vocal Groups.*

Emanons (Brooklyn, N.Y.)

Personnel Jim Danella (lead), Joe Buono (tenor), Phil DeVito (baritone), Mike Buono (bass)

Notes

All members came from the Bensonhurst section of Brooklyn and formed the group in 1957. Sometime in 1958 they approached Paul Winley of Winley Records. After hearing them, he signed them to a recording contract.

Immediately after cutting their Winley record, Phil DeVito left and was replaced by Tom Sfraga. We Teenagers/Dear One began to do well and ABC bought the rights to it and released it. The original writer materialized, and claiming that the Emanons had stolen it from him. Soon afterward ABC decided to "kill," the record and the Emanons' career was over!

This article refers to the white Emanons. "Wish I had My Baby" was executed by the black group.

Discography

Winley 226 We Teenagers (Know What We Want)/Dear One (1958)
ABC 9913 We Teenagers (Know What We Want)/Dear One (1958)
Source: Ken Berger in *Record Exchanger* 16.

Emblems (U.S. Marines)

Personnel William Johnson, Harvey Hardy, Anderson Gilchrist, Silvester Kinney, T. Stauch

Notes

The group's publicity shot shows them as an integrated vocal group that met in the U.S. Marines.

Discography

Bayfront 107 Poor Humpty Dumpty/Would You Still Be Mine? (1962)
Bayfront 108 Too Young/Bang Bang Shoot 'Em Daddy (1962)
Sources: Liner notes with the Relic CD *Tip Top*; liner notes with the Finbarr CD *$10,000 Worth of Doo Wop.*

Emeralds (St. Louis, Mo.)

Personnel Billy Davis, Tommy Moore, Joe Humphrey, Clive ———

Notes

This group started singing gospel music in 1956 but did not record until 1959.

They played local clubs and nightspots in St. Louis.

In 1959, the Emeralds cut four sides for the Bobbin label.

Davis later went on to sing with the Fifth Dimension and married Marilyn McCoo of that group. Following his stint with the Emeralds and before joining the army, Davis sang with the El Torros (no recordings).

Discography

Bobbin 107 That's the Way It's Gotta Be/Maria's Cha Cha (1959)
Bobbin 127 Lover's Cry/Rumblin' Tumblin' Baby (1960)
Source: Charlie Horner, *Vocal Group Guide to St. Louis.*

Emeralds (Pittsburgh, Pa.)

Personnel Bill Pazman (lead), Don Munhall (baritone), Dom Slebrich (tenor), George Grimes (bass)

Notes

Group first got together in 1956 doing record hops and other local events.

Pittsburgh disk jockey Jay Michael liked them and called on them frequently to appear at dances and other shows he was doing. He hooked them up with Dickie Goodman's Eldorado Records, where they recorded several masters. But the group felt that they had performed poorly on the masters and decided not to sign any contract with Goodman or Eldorado.

Munhall brought the group's demo tape to New York and landed a contract with ABC Paramount Records. At their session, they did two ballads and three up-tempo tunes. In January 1958 their ABC Paramount disc was released. Their second was released in August 1958.

They made many appearances for Jay Michael at record hops. Because he liked them so much, he was trying to live the rest of their lives. This did not sit well with them and early in 1959 they chose to split up.

Discography

ABC-Paramount 9889 You Belong to My Heart/The One I Adore (1958)
ABC-Paramount 9948 I'm Dreaming/Confess (1958)
Source: Carl Janusek and Nancy Janusek in *Story Untold* 10.

Emersons (New York)

Personnel Eddie Jones (lead), Jimmy Caines (1st tenor), Thomas Cook (2d tenor),
Frankie Cook (baritone)

Notes

This group started as the Demens on Teenage. When that label's management disappeared, they were signed by Jerry Winston's company of record labels. He had them change their name to the Emersons (Teenage management could not be found to release them).

They recorded for several labels after becoming the Emersons. Realizing no success, they disbanded in 1962.

Discography

Newport 7004 Hungry/Joannie, Joannie (1957)
Cub 9027 Dr. Jekyll and Mr. Hyde/The Hokey Pokey (1959)
United Artists 379 Down in the Valley/Loneliness (1962)
Source: Dave Hinckley and Marv Goldberg in *Yesterday's Memories* 9.

Emotions (Brooklyn, N.Y.)

Personnel Joe Favale (lead), Tony Maltese (1st tenor), Larry Cusamano (2d tenor),
Joe Nigro (baritone), Dom Collura (bass)

Notes

The Emotions began in 1959.

The group recorded originally as the Runarounds on PIO. Because another group called themselves the Runarounds, the boys changed their name to the Emotions. The PIO release was a bomb but they kept working on their vocals.

After changing their name, they cut several demos. They took these demos to many record labels, and Kapp Records ultimately signed them.

Their first release as the Emotions on Kapp was the favorite, "Echo." Unfortunately, Kapp was preoccupied at the time with Ruby and the Romantics and gave little attention or promotion to the Emotions.

The success of "Echo" generated many appearances in the New York Tri-State area for the Emotions, including many local events.

Because there was little favorable reaction to their Kapp discs, the group decided to move over to Laurie Records. At this time Maltese left and was replaced by Sal Covais from the Shy-Tones on Fonsca.

Frank Cox sang with the group on Kapp.

When the Laurie disc did not do well, the group moved to 20th Century Fox Records. They had four records released on 20th Century, all of which did nothing. Many other labels followed that also did nothing.

As a result of both the British invasion and the popularity of soul music, they wisely decided to call it quits.

Discography

Kapp 490 Echo/Come Dance Baby (1962)
Kapp 513 A Million Reasons/L-O-V-E (1963)
Laurie 3167 Starlit Night/Fool's Paradise (1963)
20th Fox 430 A Story Untold/One Life, One Love, One You (1963)
20th Fox 452 Rainbow/Little Miss Blue (1963)
20th Fox 478 Boomerang/I Love You Madly (1963)
20th Fox 623 Heartstrings/Everything (1964)
Karate 506 Hey Baby/I Wonder (1965)
Calla 122 Baby, I Need Your Loving/She's My Baby (1966)
Sources: Liner notes with the Ace *Laurie* and Sparkletone *Laurie* CD; Joe Sicurella in *Story Untold* 10; Ed Engel in *Record Exchanger* 22.

Empires (New York)

Personnel John Barnes (from Virginia) (lead), Les Cooper (tenor), Bobby Dunn (baritone), William Goodman (bass)

Notes

Group members came to New York City from Virginia in 1952. They first sang at church functions, parties, clubs and schools prior to recording for the Harlem label in 1954. They auditioned for many labels before Morty Shad's Harlem signed them.

On Harlem 2333 the words "featuring Johnny Ace Jr." appear beneath the group's name. This was simply a sales ploy by label management. On 2334 the Empires were backing Lightning Junior (a.k.a. Champion Jack Dupree). The label simply says "The Empires."

They moved to Wing in 1955 and cut three discs for Wing and Mercury. Buck Ram was their manager at Wing, but he spent all his time with the Platters and the Penguins.

They then moved to Whirlin' Disc. Because there was little response to their Whirlin' Disc effort, Bobby Robinson changed their name to the Whirlers (see Whirlers).

When Goodman was drafted, they could not find an adequate bass replacement and decided to break up.

This group was also the Prestos on Mercury.

Cooper was Barnes's uncle.

Discography

Harlem 2325 My Baby, My Baby (LC)/Corn Whiskey (JB) (1954)
Harlem 2333 Magic Mirror (JB)/Make Me or Break Me (JB) (1955)
Harlem 2334 Ragged and Hungry (LJ)/Somebody Changed the Lock (LJ) (1955)
Wing 90023 I Want to Know (JB)/Shirley (BD) (1955)

Mercury 70747 Looking for Love/'Till We Meet Again (1955)
Wing 90050 Tell Me Pretty Baby (BD)/By the Riverside (JB) (1955)
Wing 90080 My First Discovery (JB)/Don't Touch My Gal (JB) (1956)
Whirlin' Disc 104 Whispering Heart (JB)/Linda (JB) (1956)
Amp-3 132 If I'm a Fool/Zippety Zip (1957)
Source: Marv Goldberg and Dave Hinckley in *Yesterday's Memories* 12.

Empires, Eddie Friend & (New York)

Personnel Eddie Friend (lead), Miguel Ayala (1st tenor), Frankie Nieves (2d tenor), Victor Rios (baritone)

Notes

Eddie Friend came to New York from Virginia after his service obligation, looking for a career in something related to music. He felt that Virginia was not the place where his career dream could be fulfilled. New York was the place to be. He lived on West 57th Street, where he met the members of the future Empires. They got together and practiced religiously each evening for many months.

They met writer/producer Phil Medley who heard them, liked them, rehearsed them, and finally told them he would do everything to enable them to record. This was 1959. Medley arranged for an audition with Colpix, who liked the Empires and scheduled a recording session at which Friend could realize his dream.

In the summer of 1959, Colpix released their first recording, which did not do well. A second disc was planned but group members, discouraged about their first disc, split before this second session ever occurred.

Discography

Colpix 112 Tears in My Eyes/Single and Free (1959)
Source: Joe Sicurella in *Record Collector's Monthly* 22.

Enchanters (Detroit)

Personnel Ulysses Hollowell (tenor), George Wade (tenor), Gerald Hollowell (2d tenor), Jack Thomas (bass)

Notes

Alton Hollowell was a later member who had been with the Detroit Falcons. He also sang with the Fabulous Playboys.

Discography

Coral 61756 True Love/Wait a Minute Baby (1956)
Coral 61832 There Goes/Fan Me, Baby (1957)
Coral 61916 Mambo Santa Mambo/Bottle Up and Go (1957)
Coral 62373 True Love Gone/The Day (1963)
Coral 65610 True Love Gone/There Goes a Pretty Girl (1967)
Source: Unsigned liner notes with the Regency CD *Motor City Detroit Doo Wops.*

Enchanters, Garnet Mimms & (Philadephia)

Personnel Garnet Mimms (real name Garrett Mimms) (lead), Sam Bell, Charles Boyer, Zola Pearnell

Notes

Mimms also sang lead for the Gainors, which was basically made up of Enchanters members. Earlier he had been with Little Joe Cook's Evening Star Quartet. It has also been reported that he sang with the Harmonizing Four and other gospel ensembles. Mimms met Sam Bell while with the Evening Star Quartet.

Philadelphia producer Jerry Ragavoy discovered and first recorded Mimms. In the early 1950s, Ragavoy, after hearing the Castelles for the first time, pushed Herb Slotkin and his Grand Records to record "My Girl Awaits Me." Ragavoy was the one who allowed the Enchanters to audition for him in 1963.

Although it cannot be confirmed, Mimms recalls that Dionne Warwick performed backup duties on "Cry Baby."

Discography

United Artists 629 Cry Baby/Don't Change Your Heart (1963)
United Artists 658 Baby Don't You Weep/For Your Precious Love (1963)
United Artists 694 Tell Me Baby/Anytime You Want Me (1963)
United Artists 715 One Girl/A Quiet Place (1964)
United Artists 773 Look Away/One Woman Man (1964)
United Artists 796 A Little Bit of Soap/I'll Make It Up to You (1964)
United Artists 848 It Was Easier to Hurt Her (1965)
United Artists 868 Everytime/Welcome Home (1965)
United Artists 887 Everytime/That Goes to Show You (1965)
Sources: Alan Warner, liner notes with the United Artists LP Motor City to Central Park; liner notes with the Collectables Enchanters CD Cry Baby; Bob Pruter in Goldmine.

Enchanters (Queens, N.Y.)

Personnel Della Simpson (lead), Pearl Bryce (Brice) (2d tenor), Frances Kelley, (bass), Rachel Gist (1st tenor)

Notes

The Enchanters got their start in the Jamaica section of Queens around 1950. Simpson and Kelley worked for the same company and decided to try their hand at a vocal group. Della's friend Pearl Brice was the third member and Rachel Gist, a neighborhood performer, was convinced to join by the others. The girls were around seventeen years of age.

After practicing for a year and playing small clubs, they asked Jerry Blaine to come see them perform at a club in Harlem. They were signed the very next day at Jubilee's facilities in New York and they were recording the following week. In January 1952 their first Jubilee disc was released —Today Is Your Birthday/How Could You? Their second Jubilee disc was released in April.

After their two Jubilee recordings and a December 1952 tour, things began to fall apart. Rachel Gist and Pearl Brice left the other Enchanters to stay home with their families and attend to their marriages. Simpson and Kelley wished to continue with their singing. They then raided another local group, Gloria Alleyne replacing Rachel Gist and Sherry Gary joining to replace Pearl Brice. In addition, a new name, the Delltones (after Della) was chosen.

Discography

Jubilee 5072 Today Is Your Birthday/How Could You (1952)
Jubilee 5080 I've Lost/Housewife Blues (1952)
Sources: Dave Penny, liner notes with the two Sequel CDs *Jubilee Jezebels*; George Povall, liner notes with the Sequel CD *Jubilee/Josie R&B Vocal Groups*; Marv Goldberg in *DISCoveries,* January 1998, article on the Enchanters/Delltones.

Enchanters, Billy Butler & (Chicago)

Personnel Billy Butler (lead), Errol Batts (tenor), Jesse Tillman (baritone)

Notes

In his book *Doowop . . . The Chicago Scene,* Bob Pruter, in his discussion of the near North Side groups of Chicago, refers to Billy Butler and the Enchanters as a group of the soul era. Pruter goes on to say that they had built on the foundation established by area doo-wop groups.

Discography

Okeh 7178 Found True Love/Lady Love (1963)
Okeh 7192 I'm Just a Man/Gotta Get Away (1964)
Source: Bob Pruter, *Doowop . . . The Chicago Scene.*

Enchantments (New York)

Personnel Eugene Sanchez (lead), Victor Velez (1st tenor), Johnny Velez (2d tenor), Angelo Maurino (baritone), Joffrey Green (bass)

Notes

This group got together at Manhattan's Seward Park High School in 1959. They enjoyed making many local live appearances.

They were taken to Bell Sound Studios in New York to record for their manager who wanted to produce their recordings and ultimately sell it to London Records. Their only release came out on Ritz in 1964.

The record did nothing as this was the time the Beatles were getting popular and the Vietnam War was raging. The group, disenchanted, broke up.

Discography

Ritz 17003 I Love My Baby/Pains in My Heart (1964)
Source: Joe Sicurella in *Record Collector's Monthly* 27.

Ermines, Cornel Gunter & (Los Angeles)

Personnel Cornel Gunter (lead), Kenneth Byle (1st tenor), Thomas Miller (baritone), George Hollis (bass)

Notes

Byle, Gunter's cousin, also sang with the Flairs. Gunter sang with the Flairs, Flares, Coasters, Hollywood Bluejays, and D's Gentlemen—a group that toured with Dinah Washington.

Miller also sang with the Flairs and the Flares.

This group (the Ermines) later became the Flairs on ABC Paramount.

Discography

Loma 701 True Love/Peek-Peek-A-Boo (1955)
Loma 703 You Broke My Heart/I'm So Used to You Now (1956)
Loma 704 Keep Me Alive/Muchacha, Muchacha (1956)
Loma 705 I'm Sad/One Thing for Me (1956)
Source: Marv Goldberg and Mike Redmond in *Yesterday's Memories* 10.

Equallos (Chicago)

Personnel Willie Logan (lead), Arthur Ford, Dave Hoskin, O. C. Logan

Notes

The Logan brothers had been with the Ballads on Venture, a group that later became the Sheppards. The brothers formed the Equallos with Ford and Hoskin.

The Equallos' first release was for the MAD label in 1959. This failed to generate any response. Their follow-up release in 1960, although better than their first, did nothing.

In 1962, the Equallos signed with One-Der Ful records and they apparently recorded for One-Der Ful, but nothing was ever released.

In 1963, the Equallos became Willie Logan and the Plaids on Jerry-O, but because music was changing, this recording did nothing.

Discography

Mad 1296 Yodeling/Patty, Patty (1959)
M&M 30 Underneath the Sun/In Between Tears (1960)
Sources: Bob Pruter, *Doowop . . . The Chicago Scene*; Jeff Kreiter, *Group Collector's Record Price Guide.*

Escorts (Roselle, N.J.)

Personnel Marion Saunders (lead), Malcomb Norwood (1st tenor), Robert Hurling (2d tenor), Bobby McLawn (bass)

Notes

The Escorts hailed from Roselle, New Jersey, near Linden. Their only Premium single was released in spring 1956.

They made many local appearances in the Northeast, appearing with the Heartbeats and Lillian Leach and the Mellows in several New Jersey locations.

Discography

Premium 407 Sorry/It's Love to Me (1956)
Source: Donn Fileti, liner notes with the Relic CD *Premium.*

Escorts (Brooklyn, N.Y.)

Personnel Rodney Garrison (lead), Richard Berg, Richard Perry, Richard Rosenberg

Notes

Berg, Perry, and Rosenberg went to high school together in Brooklyn. In addition to their vocal talent, they all played instruments. They started singing in 1960. Through a friend of Berg's at a summer camp, they met with an executive of Coral Records, which ultimately led to a recording session in late 1961.

Their record was not a hit, but it sold well enough for a second pressing, leading to their second release, which was issued early in 1962.

It is felt that their first two recordings did not do well because Coral treated them as a novelty act and not as one performing rock 'n' roll.

On their third release for Coral, Garrison was replaced at lead by Goldie Zelkowitz (later Genya Raven), and she recorded "Somewhere" with the group. Due to a difference of opinion over Goldy's handling of a situation with deejay Murray the K while the others were away at college, Goldy left the group. She was replaced by Bobby Lance. Lance's addition to the group was on their last two discs for Coral.

These final two records were terribly unsuccessful and the Escorts disbanded in 1965.

Discography

Coral 62302 Gloria/Seven Wonders of the World (1962)
Coral 62317 As I Love You/Gaudeamas (1962)
Coral 62336 Somewhere/Submarine Race Watching (1962)
Coral 62349 One Hand, One Heart/I Can't Be Free (1963)
Coral 62372 Something Has Changed Him/Back Home Again (1963)
Coral 62385 My Heart Cries for You/Give Me Tomorrow (1963)
(Note: On Coral 62349 and 62372 the label states "Goldie and the Escorts.")
Source: S. Bennett in *1950s Revisited* 1–2.

Esco's (Cincinnati, Ohio)

Personnel Lonnie Carter (lead), Donald Peak (1st tenor), Roland Bradley (2d tenor), Joseph Penn (baritone), Richard Parker (bass)

Notes

According to Ronnie Italiano's column in issue 18 of *Time Barrier Express,* the Esco's [sic] were formed in 1960 by members of the Charms, without Otis Williams and with Lonnie Carter. They had several releases for Federal.

Discography

Federal 12380 Diamonds and Pearls/We Dance (1960)
Federal 12430 Watcha Bet/Golden Rule of Love (1961)
Federal 12445 Yes, I Need Someone/Thank You Mr. Ballard (1961)
Federal 12493 That's Life/Shame, Shame, Shame (1963)
Source: Ronnie Italiano in *Time Barrier Express* 2, no. 8.

Essentials, Billy & (Philadelphia)

Personnel Billy Carlucci (lead), Mike Lenahan (1st tenor), Johnny Caulfield (2d tenor), Pete Torres (falsetto), Pete D'Antonio (baritone)

Notes

Carlucci attended Philadelphia's Bartram High School, where he met Patti LaBelle and other future vocal stars. He learned a great deal about singing harmony from these performers.

He met other performers in the restroom of a Philadelphia skating rink. After this incident he got a group together and practiced incessantly.

When they felt ready to record, they cut some demos and went to New York City to call on numerous labels. They hit paydirt at Landa Records, a subsidiary of Jamie/ Guyden. When they hooked up with Danny Driscoll, Jamie/Guyden's promotion manager, things clicked, and a record was recorded and released.

While Driscoll was in the midst of doing his best for the group, he was killed by gunfire. The Essentials did two more cuts for the label and then went off to record with several others.

They recorded under many pseudonyms, including the Styles.

Despite the many important people who liked this group, nothing ever came of them and they finally disbanded.

Discography

Landa 691 Steady Girl/The Dance Is Over (1962)
Jamie 1229 Steady Girl/The Dance Is Over (1962)
Jamie 1239 Maybe You'll Be There/Over the Weekend (1962)
Mercury 72127 Lonely Weekend/Young at Heart (1963)
Mercury 72210 Last Dance/Yes Sir, That's My Baby (1963)
Cameo 344 Remember Me Baby/The Actor (1964)
Smash 2045 Babalu's Wedding Day/My Way of Saying (1966)
Smash 2071 Baby Go Away/Don't Cry (1966)
Sources: Bob Hyde and Bob Bosco, liner notes with the Bear Family CD *Jamie/ Guyden*; Ed Engel, liner notes with the Dee Jay Jamboree CD *Philadelphia's Doo Wop Sound.*

Eternals (Bronx, N.Y.)

Personnel Charlie Girona (lead), Fred Hodge (1st tenor), Ernie Sierra (2d tenor), Arnie Torres (baritone), Alex Miranda (d) (bass)

Notes

The group met while the members were in junior high school and continued singing through their high school years.

They were eventually brought to Hollywood Records in 1959. There they were named the Eternals and had their first recording session.

Because the group was very young at the time of recording, they were handled unscrupulously (the usual way), with no royalties or session fees going to the boys.

Ernie Sierra was the lead on "My Girl." His brother Richie became a member at a later session.

After they went to Warwick, litigation began as a result of Hollywood's sense that they were enticed to leave their organization. The lawsuit prevented the group from recording for two years. They became disenchanted and ultimately chose to disband.

George Villanueva was with the group on Warwick. Other members included Hector Garcia, George Santiago, and Jack Damon (Mellokings).

Discography

Hollywood 68/69 Rockin' in the Jungle/Rock 'n' Roll Cha Cha (1959)
Hollywood 70/71 Babalu's Wedding Day/My Girl (1959)
Warwick 611 Blind Date/Today (1960)
Sources: Joe Sicurella in *Big Town Review* 3; Ralph Figueroa, Walt Figueroa, Mickey Castaneda, Joe Miranda, Angel Aglero, and Ernie Sierra in *Time Barrier Express* 2 no. 8.

Excellents (Bronx, N.Y.)

Personnel John Kuse (lead), Denny Kestenbaum, Chuck Epstein, Joe Feldman, Phil Sanchez

Notes

The Excellents hung out together in high school. Four of them attended Columbus High School and one went to Clinton High School.

The Excellents who recorded "I Hear a Rhapsody" on Blast was another group.

Discography

Mermaid 106 Red Robin Rock/Love No One but You (1961)
Blast 205 Coney Island Baby/You Baby You (1962)
Bobby 601 Helene/Sunday Kind of Love (1964)
Source: Phil Silverman in *Record Collector's Monthly* 25.

Excels (New York)

Personnel Fred Orange (lead), Benito Travieso, Raphael Diaz, Harry Hilliard, Joe Robles (bass)

Notes

Travieso, Diaz, and Hilliard formed the Minors on Celeste and made up the core of that group.

Discography

Central 2601 You're Mine Forever/Baby Doll (1957)
Gone 5094 My Foolish Heart/Just You and I Together (1960)
R.S.V.P. 111 Can't Help Lovin' That Girl of Mine/Till You (1961)

Excitements, Elroy & (Pittsburgh, Pa.)

Personnel Leroy Grammer (lead), Ronald Hill (1st tenor), Leon Harvard (2d tenor), Paul Brently (baritone), Wayne Walker (bass)

Notes

This group began as the El Dupreys from Pittsburgh. They were always the opening act for big name groups coming to the area. They split up and later reformed as the Excitements.

Ronald Hill had a medical condition that initially forced him to leave the Excitements. When the group was traveling, Hill stayed home. Therefore on the road the group was a quartet.

When they were about to record for Alanna, they asked Hill to join them for the recording—which he did. Following their audition, they learned that Alanna management loved them and signed them to record. They cut two discs for Alanna, the first of which was released in the fall of 1960.

Following these two recordings, Elroy and the Excitements kept busy with live appearances but did no further recording. Eventually they were released from their contract with Alanna.

After leaving Alanna, they auditioned for Motown but met with no success. They then became Leroy and the Enchantments and recorded for Romac.

Discography

Alanna 188 My Love Will Never Die/No One Knows (1961)
Alanna 565 My Love Will Never Die/No One Knows (1963)
Source: Carl Janusek and Nancy Janusek in *Echoes of the Past* 17.

Exciters (Jamaica, N.Y.)

Personnel Brenda Reid (lead), Carol Johnson (tenor), Lillian Walker, Herb Rooney (bass)

Notes

Rooney sang with the Beltones on Hull in 1957 ("I Talk to My Echo") and the Masters on Bingo with "Lovely Way to Spend an Evening."

When Rooney first met these female singers, they were known as the Masterettes recording on LeSage. Sylvia Wilbur was the fifth member of the Masterettes who did not become one of the Exciters.

The girls came to the attention of Coasters writer/producers Lieber and Stoller. Because they became so involved with them, they called them the Exciters. Rooney joined the Exciters to round out their sound. This is when Sylvia Wilbur left.

They signed up with United Artists in 1962. Their first recording, "Tell Him," sold quite well all over the world. Their second disc, "He's Got the Power," fared well too but not quite as well as "Tell Him."

Rooney and Brenda Reid married in the late 1960s. Lillian and Carol left in the early 1970s and were replaced by Skip McPhee and Ronnie Pace. This new group did a great deal of touring. Rooney and Reid separated in the early 1980s.

Discography

United Artists 544 Hard Way to Go/Tell Him (1962)
United Artists 572 He's Got the Power/Drama of Love (1963)
United Artists 604 Get Him/It's So Exciting (1963)
United Artists 662 Do-Wah-Diddy/If Love Came Your Way (1963)
United Artists 721 Having My Fun/We Were Lovers (1964)
Roulette 4591 Are You Satisfied/Just Not Ready (1964)
Roulette 4614 My Father/Run Mascara (1965)
Roulette 4632 I Knew You Would/There They Go (1965)
Bang 515 A Little Bit of Soap/I'm Gonna Get Him Someday (1965)
Bang 518 Weddings Make Me Cry/You Better Come Home (1966)
Shout 205 You Got Love/Number One (1966)
Shout 214 Soul Motion/You Know It Ain't Right (1967)
RCA 47-9633 If You Want My Love/Take One Step (1968)
RCA 47-9723 Blowing Up My Mind/You Don't Know What You're Missing (1969)
Source: Jay Warner, *American Singing Groups.*

Fabulous Four (Philadelphia)

Personnel Junior Pirollo (lead), James Testa (1st tenor), Bob Finizio (2d tenor), Joe Milaro (baritone)

Notes

This group was originally the Four Js and was renamed the Fabulous Four. Pirollo and Finizio were brothers-in-law.

Discography

Chancellor 1062 In the Chapel in the Moonlight/Mr. Twist (1960)
Chancellor 1068 Let's Try Again/Precious Moments (1960)
Chancellor 1078 Why Do Fools Fall in Love/Sounds of Summer (1961)
Chancellor 1085 Betty Ann/Prisoner of Love (1961)
Chancellor 1090 I'm Coming Home/Everybody Knows (1961)
Chancellor 1098 Everybody Knows/Mr. Twist (1961)
Chancellor 1102 Forever/ (It's No) Sin (1962)
Melic 4114 Welcome Me Home/Oop Shoo Be Doop Bam-A-Lam (1962)
Coral 62479 Got to Get Her Back/Now You Cry (1966)
Sources: Bob Bosco in *Echoes of the Past* 38; Bob Bosco, liner notes for the Bear Family Jamie/Guyden CD *Doop Doo Wah.*

Fabulous Pearls (Tacoma, Wash.)

Personnel Elsie Hall Pierre (lead), Artis Johnson Jr. (d), Ronald Small (a.k.a. Ronald Chance), Reuben Martin

Notes

This group originally got together in 1957 at McCord Air Force Base near Tacoma, Washington, to compete in an air force talent show. They won the contest and consequently appeared on the *Ed Sullivan Show* in August 1958.

In February 1959 the Fabulous Pearls drove from Seattle to Los Angeles to speak to Dootsie Williams. Williams signed them to a one-year contract.

The session was done with Hall pregnant. One of the sides of their first single was entitled "Jungle Bunny." Hall stated that when this was recorded, she and the group were unaware of the racist meaning of the title.

Johnson also sang with the Midnights (Music City) and the Four Pearls with Reuben Martin and Ronald Small (Chance). They also sang as the Four Pearls who recorded for the Dolton label and broke up soon after.

In the liner notes accompanying the 1996 Ace CD *Dootone Doo Wop-1,* Ronald Small is referred to first as Ronald Chance and later in the notes as Ronald Small. Contained in *Dootone Doo Wop-3* is an unreleased tune entitled "Baby Drop Top."

Discography

Dooto 448 My Heart's Desire/Jungle Bunny (1959)
Source: Jim Dawson, liner notes with the Ace CD *Dootone Doo Wop-1.*

Fabulous Playboys (Detroit)

Personnel Carlis "Sonny" Monroe (lead), James Gibson (1st tenor), Chester Flemings (1st tenor), Johnny "Duke" Alvin (2d tenor), Arnet Robinson (baritone), Alton "Bart" Hollowell (bass)

Notes

In 1956 the group was also known as the Playboys.

When Federal contracted with the Fabulous Playboys, their name had to be changed because there was another Playboys group. They became the Ramblers. According to Ferdie Gonzalez in *Disco-File,* this Ramblers and the Jax group were the same.

The group later became the Detroit Falcons, following the breakup of the first group in 1963. Hollowell would later sing with the Enchanters of "There Goes a Pretty Girl" fame as well as with the Fabulous Playboys and the Falcons.

Discography

Contour 101 I Fooled You (CM)/Sweet Peas and Bronc Busters (CM) (1959)
Daco 1001 Nervous (CM)/Forget the Past (CM) (1961)
Apollo 758 Nervous (CM)/Forget the Past (CM) (1961)
Apollo 760 Honky Tonk Woman (CM)/Tears, Tears, Tears (CM) (1961)
Sources: Marv Goldberg, *Whiskey, Women, and . . . ;* Ferdie Gonzalez, *Disco-File.*

Falcons (Detroit)

Personnel Eddie Floyd (lead), Bob Manardo (1st tenor), Joe Stubbs (2d tenor/lead), Mack Rice (baritone), Willie Schofield (bass)

Notes

This Falcons group was formed in 1955 and originally had two white members. In 1957 the group had two lead singers—Floyd and Stubbs.

Lance Finnie replaced Bob Manardo in 1957. Because "You're So Fine" exploded onto the charts in 1959, Chess Records remembered that the Falcons had recorded for them previously. Rather than just release the older cuts, Chess had the Falcons rerecord "This Heart of Mine," which did well in 1959. In 1960 Wilson Pickett was added to replace Joe Stubbs and in 1961 bass Willie Schofield left temporarily and was replaced by Ben (Ken) Knight, formerly of the Imperials on Great Lakes. Joe Stubbs is the brother of the Four Tops' Levi Stubbs. Eddie Floyd was later replaced by Earl Martin. Mack Rice previously sang with the Five Scalders.

After Chess, there was United Artists, LuPine, and Atlantic.

Following the group's last session for Atlantic in 1962, they disbanded in 1963. The classic group then re-formed with Stubbs, Rice, Schofield, Floyd, and Finnie. This lasted for a year, after which this group of Falcons broke up for good.

Falcons' manager Robert West then took one of his other groups, the Fabulous Playboys, renamed them the Falcons, and there was the second group! Johnny Duke Alvin and Carlis Monroe were members. James Gibson was the first tenor.

While scouting for talent in Detroit, Federal's Ralph Bass auditioned the Playboys. He brought them back to Federal in Cincinnati, changed their name to the Ramblers, and recorded them.

Alton Hollowell also was with the group as was Arnet Robinson and Tom Shelton.

Discography

Mercury 70940 Baby That's It (EF)/This Day (AR) (1956)
Silhouette 521 Can This Be Christmas? (EF)/Sent Up (MR) (1957)
Kudo 661 This Heart of Mine (EF)/Romanita (MR) (1958)
Flick 001 You're So Fine (JS)/Goddess of Angels (EF) (1959)
Flick 008 You Must Know I Love You (JS)/That's What I Aim to Do (1959)
Unart 2013 You're So Fine (JS)/Goddess of Angels (1959)
Unart 2022 You're Mine (JS)/Country Shack (JS) (1959)
Chess 1743 This Heart of Mine (EF)/Just for Your Love (JS) (1959)
Anna 1110 This Heart of Mine (EF)/Just for Your Love (JS) (1960)
United Artists 229 The Teacher (JS)/Waiting for You (EF) (1960)
United Artists 255 I Love You (JS)/Wonderful Love (EF) (1960)
United Artists 289 Pow! You're in Love (WP)/Workin' Man's Song (MR) (1960)
United Artists 420 You're So Fine (JS)/Goddess of Angels (EF) (1962)
LuPine 1003 I Found a Love (WP)/Swim (1962)
LuPine 003 You're on My Mind (JS)/Anna (WP) (1962)
Atlantic 2153 La Tee La Tah (MR)/Darling (JS) (1962)
Atlantic 2179 Take This love I've Got (WP)/Let's Kiss and Make Up (WP) (1963)
Atlantic 2207 Oh Baby (CM)/Fine, Fine, Girl (CM) (1963)

LuPine 1020 Lonely Nights (CM)/Has It Happened to You (1964)
Zig Wheel 321/322 I Must Love You (JG)/Love, Love, Love (CM) (1966)
Big Wheel 1967 Standing on Guard (CM)/I Can't Help It (CM) (1966)
Big Wheel 1971 Love Look in Her Eyes (CM)/In Time for the Blues (CM) (1967)
Big Wheel 1972 Good Good Feeling (CM)/Love You Like You Never Never Been Loved (CM) (1967)
Sources: Donn Fileti and Marv Goldberg, liner notes with the Relic CD *Falcons*; Pete Grendysa, liner notes with the Chess CD boxed set *Chess Rhythm & Roll*.

Falcons (New York)

Personnel Goldie Boots Alsup (lead), Vernon Palmer (baritone), Earl Alsup, George Alsup

Notes

After having recorded one session for Savoy, the Falcons left the label. That the name was used by other groups in various areas of the country is indicative of the impact the Savoy Falcons had on record buyers.

Discography

Regent 1041 How Blind Can You Be?/I Can't Tell You Now (1951)
Savoy 893 You're the Beating of My Heart/It's You I Miss (1953)
RCA 47-7076 Stepping Stone/Jigsaw Puzzle (1957)
Sources: Steve Propes, liner notes with the Savoy LP *Doo Wop Delights*; the Alsup family, interview by Marv Goldberg.

Famous Hearts (Philadelphia)

Personnel Sonny Gordon (1st tenor), Thomas Butch Curry (2d tenor), Eddie Custis (baritone), Wendell Calhoun (bass)

Notes

Calhoun and Curry sang with Lee Andrews and the Hearts and the Five Hearts.
  Gordon sang for the Angels on Grand, the Turbans, and the Hearts.

Discography

Guyden 2073 Aisle of Love/Momma (1962)
Source: Marv Goldberg, liner notes with the Collectables CD *Lee Andrews and the Hearts for Collectors Only.*

Fantastics (New York)

Personnel William Forrest (lead), John Cheetom (1st tenor), Donald Haywood (2d tenor), Alfred Pitts (baritone), Larry Lawrence (bass)

Notes

In 1961, the Onyx Velours split apart. Charlie Moffett, Keith Williams, and John Pearson broke away from the others in the group. Jerome Ramos, John Cheetom, and Donald Haywood remained together and added Alfred Pitts to form the Fantastics.

Bill Sutton also sang with the Fantastics.

The liner notes accompanying RCA's *Rock 'n' Roll Party-2* CD state that Sammy Strain of the Imperials was the 1st tenor for the Fantastics and had been with the Chips on Josie, the Blue Chips on RCA, and in the 1970s with the O'Jays. This data appears nowhere else.

Baritone Fred Warner also was a member of the group, as was Kenny Lawrence.

Discography

RCA 47-7572 There Goes My Love/I Wanna Be a Millionaire Hobo (1959)
RCA 47-7664 I Got a Zero/This Is My Wedding Day (1959)
United Artists 309 Dancing Doll/I Told You Once (1961)
Sources: Billy Vera, liner notes with the RCA CD *Rock 'n' Roll Party-1*; Marv Goldberg and Dave Hinckley in *Yesterday's Memories* 7.

Fantasys (Philadelphia)

Personnel Richard Schmidt (lead), Arum Oornazian (tenor), Ben Asero (tenor), Charles Berberian (bass)

Notes

This group got together in west Philadelphia in 1957. They started singing in their spare time.

The Fantasys traveled each day to hang out outside Jamie headquarters, where they met Duane Eddy. In order to stop this group from coming each day, Jamie management agreed to listen to a demo of theirs. Their only disc, (No One But You/ Why Oh Why?), was recorded and it failed. After this recording, they disbanded.

Discography

Guyden 2029 No One But You/Why, Oh Why? (1960)
Source: Bob Bosco, liner notes with the Jamie/Guyden CD *Doop Doo Wah.*

Fascinators (Detroit)

Personnel Clarence Smith (lead), Earl Richardson (tenor) Jerry Potter (2d tenor), Don Blackshear (baritone), Bob Rivers (bass)

Notes

This group began in Detroit around 1949 or 1950.

All members performed lead chores at one time or another. This Fascinators group was the same Fascinators that appeared on the Roadhouse LP.

The Your Copy label was owned by record shop owner Monroe Horn. The group's discs were cut in the rear of a record shop with fair musicians and poor equipment.

The time spent with Parrot owner Al Benson was a whirlwind. He auditioned them on a Saturday, after they had called on Vee Jay and United that morning. That afternoon Benson brought the group to his radio show and that evening he brought them to a club to sing.

Discography

Your Copy 1135 Sweet Baby (DB)/The Bells of My Heart (JP) (1954)
Your Copy 1136 My Beauty, My Own (CS)/Don't Give It Away (DB) (1954)
Blue Lake 112 Don't Give My Love Away (DB)/Can't Stop (ER) (1955)
Roadhouse Aurelia (1956)
Sources: Bob Pruter, *Chicago . . . The Doowop Scene*; Bob Pruter, liner notes with the Relic CD *Parrot*; Les Moss, liner notes with the *Candy Bar Boogie* LP/CD.

Fascinators (Brooklyn, N.Y.)

Personnel Anthony Passalacqua (lead), Nick Trivatto (tenor), Ed Wheeler (tenor), Angelo LaGrecca (baritone), George Cernacek (bass)

Notes

The Fascinators came from the same area of Brooklyn as the Clusters (Tee Gee). Members of the two groups were good friends. The Fascinators were known as the strongest group vocally in the neighborhood.

After earning a solid reputation, the group received offers from various labels. Their manager advised them to sign with Capitol. Their initial session at Capitol produced four sides. The first was released in September 1958. In several local New York areas, Chapel Bells/I Wonder Who was a big seller. It wasn't until six months later that the second two songs, Who Do You Think You Are/Come to Paradise, were finally released by Capitol.

Personal problems haunted one of the members, and Capitol paid little attention to the group. This was compounded by the label's poor promotion of the Fascinators' releases. Despite all this adversity, when Capitol rereleased the group's "Chapel Bells" in 1961, it received a most favorable response. Nevertheless, the group decided it was time to disband.

Passalacqua was the only member to remain in the music business. He would soon record as Tony Richards and the Twilights on Colpix. The Twilights included two of the original Clusters and a member of the Markels.

Because the Twilights first Colpix release was billed as by the Twilights featuring Tony Richards, interior difficulties began to surface and the group eventually broke up.

The next name change was to Tony Mitchell. Despite the association with several labels and big name A&R men, producers were no help.

Although he never made any recordings with the group, Tony sat in with the Soul Survivors.

Discography

Capitol 4053 Chapel Bells/I Wonder Who (1958)
Capitol 4137 Who Do You Think You Are?/Come to Paradise (1959)

Capitol 4247 Oh Rosemarie/Fried Chaicke and Macaroni (1959)
Capitol 4544 Chapel Bells/I Wonder Who (1961)
Source: Ralph Newman in *Bim Bam Boom* 7.

Fascinators (Los Angeles)

Personnel   (?) Albert Jerry Stone, Jewel Akens, Teddy Harper, David Harris

Notes

This group originally called itself Voices of Allah. But when they came to Dootone, Dootsie Williams immediately began calling them the Fascinators. Theirs was truly a cover of the Dukes' Imperial release of the same two sides issued in 1956 on Imperial.

They only recorded one disc for Dootone. Later the same year (1958), they recorded and released a disc on the Freedom label as by Jerry Stone and the Four Dots.

The Jewel Akens shown above is the same singer who, seven years later, recorded "The Birds and the Bees," which became a national top ten hit.

Discography

Dootone 441 Shivers and Shakes/Teardrop Eyes (1958)
Source: Jim Dawson, liner notes with the Ace CD *Dootone Doo Wop-3.*

Fashions (Philadelphia)

Personnel Jacki LaVant, Charles Davis, Herb Williams, Robbie ———, Bobby ———

Notes

Jacki LaVant had just graduated from a vocational high school in north Philadelphia. Her booking agent father initially introduced her to the singers who would eventually sing with her in the Fashions.

The Fashions had only one V-Tone single, I Am Dreaming of You/Lonesome Road, which was released in the winter of 1959. The disc was released twice, each time with a different flip side.

A lack of financial rewards and an abundance of discouragement led the Fashions to disband in 1960.

The last names of Robbie and Bobby have long been forgotten.

Discography

V-Tone 202 I'm Dreaming of You/Lonesome Road (1959)
V-Tone 202 I'm Dreaming of You/I love You So (1959)
Warwick 646 All I Want/Dearest One (1961)
Ember 1084 I Just Got a Letter/Try My Love (1962)
Source: Donn Fileti, liner notes with the Relic LP *Best of V-Tone.*

Feathers (Los Angeles)

Personnel Johnny Staton (d) (lead), Louis Staton (tenor), John Harris (tenor), Don Harris (baritone), Mitchell Alexander (bass)

Notes

In 1953, Johnny Staton was in an air force singing group that was quite successful, winning several amateur talent contests. When Staton was discharged to Los Angeles in 1954, he continued vocal group singing with his three brothers and a sister. Having little luck, most of the siblings abandoned the group singing. Johnny and Louis Staton stayed with it. They eventually teamed up with the rest of the performers who would eventually become the Feathers. They practiced with them until they felt ready for live performances. Ultimately they ran into Johnny Otis, who advised them to look into the Showtime music organization. They followed Otis's advice and signed a contract with Showtime.

They recorded "Johnny Darling" for Showtime. When it began to move, Otis once again intervened, telling the Feathers that Showtime was not properly supporting or promoting their record. He suggested that perhaps they should go to the other big Los Angeles R&B label—Aladdin. Again, the group followed his suggestion.

In 1954, both Aladdin and Showtime claimed the Feathers. A lawsuit followed, as both had released their own version of "Johnny Darling." Eventually Showtime won the suit and the Feathers remained with them.

Alexander also sang with the Chargers, and Johnny Staton sang with the Unforgettables and the Individuals. The Harrises and the Statons were brothers.

The record by Gene Forrest and the Four Feathers on Aladdin who did Dubio/Wiggle had no relation to the Staton/Showtime group (Gene Forrest went on to record with a woman and the two were known as Gene and Eunice).

After the group's breakup, John Harris joined the Lamplighters; then he teamed with Carl White and the Ebbtides and with Carl Ell and his Buddies. Then the Sharps and eventually the Rivingtons.

Jesse Belvin's session, which produced "Dear Heart," "Betty My Darling," and " (This is My) Love Song" was backed up by Johnny, Louis, Isaiah, and James Staton. Johnny Staton told Belvin, "no money, just put our name on the label." This tune was released in the 1970s and for some unknown reason the label read "Jesse Belvin and the Five Keys."

On "Crashing the Party" the group was a family affair—Johnny, Louis, James, and Isaiah Staton with Ray Anderson at bass. For their last recording on Showtime, Anderson was dropped and sister Lenora was added.

In late 1955, with no success or money, the existing group broke up and Johnny Staton formed a new Feathers with Roy Allen (tenor), Renee Beard (second tenor), Carl White (baritone), and Carl's brother, Cleo, at bass. Without Beard, this group recorded as the Unforgettables for Pamela and their recording was done in 1957 and released in 1961.

Discography

Aladdin 3267 Johnny, Darling/Shake 'Em Up (1954)
Show Time 1104 Johnny, Darling/Nona (1954)

Aladdin 3277 I Need a Girl/Standin' Right There (1955)
Show Time 1105 Why Don't You Write Me?/Busy as a Bee (1955)
Show Time 1106 Love Only You/Crashing the Party (1955)
Hollywood 1051 Lonesome Tonight/Dear One (1956)
Source: Johnny Staton, interview by Marv Goldberg in *DISCoveries,* July 1995.

Federals (New York)

Personnel Rudy Anderson (lead), Reggie Barnes (tenor), James Pender (tenor), Kenneth Fox (baritone), Lorenzo Cook (bass)

Notes

The Federals had been the Wheels on Premium who recorded "My Heart's Desire" in 1956.

Reggie Barnes was with the Solitaires and the FiTones.

Discography

Fury 1005 While Our Hearts Are Young/You're the One I Love (1957)
Fury 1009 Dear Lorraine/She's My Girl (1957)
DeLuxe 6112 Come Go with Me/Cold Cash (1957)
Source: Adam Komorowski, liner notes with the Charly CD *Fire/Fury Story.*

Fidelitones (Detroit)

Personnel Freddie Gorman, Sonny Sanders, Brian (Eddie) Holland, Bosco —— (bass)

Notes

Sonny Sanders had been with the Quailtones on Josie. Then the short-lived Fidelitones were formed, and after that Sanders joined the Satintones.

In Steve Towne's *Goldmine* article, he refers to "Eddie" Holland and "Brian" Holland with no explanation other than "Eddie" was a nickname. He seems to say, at times, that they were two separate individuals.

Discography

Marlo 1918 Playboy/Say Hey Pretty Baby (1961)
Source: Steve Towne in *Goldmine,* September 1981; April 1982.

Fiestas (Newark, N.J.)

Personnel Tommy Bullock (lead), Eddie Morris (tenor), Sam Ingalls (baritone), Preston Lane (bass)

Notes

The Fiestas were neighborhood buddies from Newark, New Jersey.

According to one story, they were discovered by Hy Weiss, apparently as a result of their practicing in a restroom adjacent to Weiss's office. At any rate, he heard them and was impressed enough to sign them up with his Old Town label.

Hy Weiss states that it is his feeling that the flip of "So Fine," the beautiful "Last Night I Dreamed," had a lot to do with the sales success of "So Fine." Weiss goes on to say that while "So Fine" was the soul transitional side, "Last Night I Dreamed" was the throwback to 1950s R&B.

Randy Stewart, an Old Town employee, was added to the Fiestas in 1960.

The Fiestas left Old Town and disbanded in 1965 as a result of little further success.

Discography

Old Town 1062 Last Night I Dreamed/So Fine (1959)
Old Town 1069 Our Anniversary/I'm Your Slave (1959)
Old Town 1074 Good News/That Was Me (1959)
Old Town 1080 Dollar Bill/It Don't Make Sense (1960)
Old Town 1090 So Nice/You Could Be My Girl Friend (19600)
Old Town 1104 Mr. Dillon, Mr. Dillon/Look at That Girl (1961)
Old Town 1111 She's Mine/The Hobo's Prayer (1961)
Old Town 1122 The Railroad Song/Broken Heart (1962)
Old Town 1127 I Feel Good All Over/Look at That Girl (1962)
Old Town 1134 The Gypsy Said/Mama Put the Law Down (1963)
Old Town 1140 The Party's Over/Try It One More Time (1963)
Old Town 1148 Foolish Dreamer/Rock a Bye Baby (1963)
Old Town 1166 All That's Good/Rock a Bye Baby (1964)
Old Town 1178 Anna/Think Smart (1965)
Old Town 1189 Ain't She Sweet/I Gotta Have Your Lovin' (1965)
Sources: Dan Nooger and Hy Weiss, liner notes with the Ace CD *Oh So Fine*; Wayne Jancik in *Goldmine*.

Fireflies (New York)

Personnel Lee Reynolds, Richie Adams, Carl Girsoli, Paul Giacolone

Notes

The Fireflies first got together in 1958 as an instrumental ensemble.

Lee Reynolds had been a friend of Gerry Granahan's. The two wrote "Click Clack" for Dickey Doo and the Dont's. This was Granahan's group at that time.

Through his contacts, Granahan got the Fireflies an audition and later a contract with Roulette. There were no hits, but the group played at many local events on the East Coast.

As time passed, the group made their attempt to become a self-contained group, displaying their vocal and instrumental talent.

Granahan then brought them to Ribbon Records, whose management liked them and had them record for Ribbon. Their first record, written by Granahan, was "You Were Mine." This was a tremendous 1959 success.

Many appearances followed and soon Carl left, to be replaced by John Viscelli of Clifton, New Jersey. At the same time, Reynolds began moonlighting with another group, Lee and the Sounds, with Granahan and Vinnie Rodgers.

In mid-1960, the original Fireflies broke up and a new group was assembled. This new group consisted of Reynolds, Richie Spero, Frank Piazza, and Bobby Saranievo. They had one release and were under contract to Taurus Records from 1962 to 1968.

Discography

Roulette 4098 Where the Candlelights Glow /The Crawl (inst) (1958)
Ribbon 6901 You Were Mine/Stella Got a Fella (1959)
Ribbon 6906 My Girl/Because of My Pride (1960)
Canadian American 117 Marianne/Give All Your Love to Me (1960)
Taurus 355 One O'Clock Twist/You Were Mine for a While (1962)
Taurus 366 Good Friends/My Prayer for You (1964)
Taurus 376 Could You Mean More/Runaround (1966)
Taurus 380 Tonight/A Time for Us (1968)
Source: Roy Adams in *Story Untold* 1.

FiTones (Brooklyn, N.Y.)

Personnel Gene Redd (lead), Marlowe Murray (1st tenor), Lloyd Davis (2d tenor), Cecil Holmes (baritone), Ron Anderson (bass)

Notes

The FiTones hailed from the Fort Greene section of Brooklyn, forming their first group, the Caverliers Quartet, in 1952. They recorded for the Atlas/Angletone organization in 1953. Lester Gardner was their lead for this disc.

Holmes, Anderson, and Murray had previously been with the Caverliers Quartet. The fourth member of the Caverliers Quartet was Lester Gardner, as mentioned above. Gene Redd went on to sing lead with the Five Chimes.

Reggie Barnes replaced Lloyd Davis when the FiTones moved to Old Town. Later Barnes was with the latter-day Solitaires.

Gene Redd went on to manage Kool and the Gang, Holmes is the promotion manager for Buddah records, Murray performs with the Harptones, and the others have their own groups.

Discography

Atlas 1050 Foolish Dreams (GR/LD)/Let's Fall in Love (1955)
Atlas 1051 It Wasn't a Lie (LD)/Lots and Lots of Love (1955)
Atlas 1052 I Call to You (GR/LM)/Love You Baby (1956)
Atlas 1055 I Belong to You (LM)/Silly and Sappy (1956)
Atlas 1056 Waiting for Your Call/My Tired Feet (1956)
Old Town 1042 My Faith/My Heart (1957)
Angletone 525 You'll Be the Last/Wake Up (1958)
Angletone 530 What Am I Going to Do/It Wasn't a Lie (1958)
Angletone 536 Deep in My Heart/Minnie (1959)
Sources: Phil Groia in *Bim Bam Boom* 5; Donn Fileti, liner notes with the Relic LP *FiTones.*

Five Bells (Chicago)

Personnel Lester Armstrong, Julius Hawkins, Rufus Hunter, Wardell Staples, Jerome Brown

Notes

This group auditioned repeatedly for Vee Jay but was never accepted. Fortunately, the Five Bells members were so good that they eventually went on to perform and record with other groups.

Hawkins was the brother of Jimmy Hawkins of the Five Buddies on Club 51. Hunter had been with the Magnificents, Cameos, and Five Chimes on Ebony. Jerome Brown had been with Johnny and the Keys.

Discography

Clock 1017 It's You/My Pledge to You (1959)
Source: Bob Pruter, *Doowop . . . The Chicago Scene.*

Five Birds, Willie Headen & (Los Angeles)

Personnel Willie Headen, L. C. Henderson, Willie Morris, Robert Taylor, James Turner

Notes

Willie Headen (pronounced Hayden) had been a gospel singer. While on tour in Los Angeles, he decided to remain there and further his musical career.

In 1956, the popularity of blues music had faded, and Headen and Dootone's Dootsie Williams formed an R&B vocal group that they called the Five Birds.

In the liner notes accompanying Ace's CD *Dootone Doo Wop-3,* written by Jim Dawson, Willie Morris, above, is referred to as Willie Morries.

It's interesting to note that in 1957 Dootsie Williams decided to change his label's name to Dooto for legal reasons, thus avoiding confusion with Duo-Tone, the phonograph needle company.

Discography

Dooto 703 Back Home Again/I Wanna Know (1956)
Authentic 410 Let Me Cry/The Skinny Woman Story (1956)
Source: Jim Dawson, liner notes with the Ace CD *Dootone Story.*

Five Blue Notes (Washington, D.C.)

Personnel Andy Magruder, Fleming Briscoe, Jackie Shedrick (1st tenor), Robert Stroud (2d tenor), Moise Vaughan (baritone/bass)

Notes

This group was founded by Magruder in 1950, when he was in junior high school.

"Could I Adore You" and "Sweet Pauline" were recorded by the Five Blue Notes under their prerecording name, the Bluejays. These songs were eventually released in 1972 by Les Moss of Roadhouse Records. When these unreleased tunes were originally recorded, the group was only a quartet consisting of Magruder, Waymond Mooney, Robert Stroud, and Moise Vaughan.

Jackie Shedrick replaced Mooney, who joined the marines. When lead/tenor Fleming Briscoe was added, the group's name became the Five Blue Notes.

They met William Bosco Boyd, the manager of the Clefs, who suggested that they try to record for a Chicago organization.

They spent a month in Chicago before getting a contract to record. The contract was finally reached with Chance Records, and they recorded four songs that were all released on the Chance subsidiary Sabre.

Magruder, disappointed that he never heard anything about the recordings, left to join the marines. While he was in the service, "My Gal Is Gone" was finally released by Chance/Sabre.

Magruder was discharged in 1958 and found Stroud, Vaughan, Shedrick, and a new tenor, Louis Smalls, performing as the Five Blue Notes. They recorded one record for the Onda label, which went nowhere. They stayed together for a year and broke up for good in 1960.

Magruder then joined the Spaniels as their first tenor. He can be heard on "I Know." Magruder remained with the Spaniels until 1963, when he went on his own as a solo.

Discography
Sabre 103 My Gal Is Gone (AM)/Ooh Baby (FM) (1954)
Sabre 108 The Beat of Our Hearts (FB)/You Gotta Go Baby (MV) (1954)
Onda 108 My Special Prayer/The Thunderbird (1958)
Onda 888 My Special Prayer (RS)/Something Awful (LS) (1959)
Source: Bob Pruter, *Doowop . . . The Chicago Scene.*

Five Bob-O-Links (Hackensack, N.J.)

Personnel Homer Dunn (d), Gerald Fields, Charles Johnson, Charles Perry (baritone), Lenwood Henry (bass)

Notes
Dunn sang lead for the Rivieras. He formed the Five Bob-O-Links in 1952 in Hackensack, New Jersey. Shortly after the Five Bob-O-Links' Okeh recording, the group disbanded.

Dunn, Charles Allen, Ronald Cook, and Andy Jones joined forces as the Four Arts and made appearances throughout Bergen County in New Jersey. Dunn moved to Englewood, New Jersey.

They soon became the El Rivieras and then the Rivieras.

Discography
Okeh Trying/Mailman Blues
Source: Frank Aita and Donn Fileti, liner notes with the Relic CD *The Rivieras—Moonlight Cocktails.*

Five Boroughs (Miami)

Personnel Geno Radicello, Bruce Goldie, Frankie Iovino, Dave Strum, Charles Notabartolo

Notes

This group originated in the New York area but relocated to southern Florida. Frank, Gene, and Bruce share the lead vocals.

In 1986, the Five Boroughs released an LP that featured Tony Passalacqua (Fascinators), Jimmy Gallagher (Passions), and Ernie Southern.

Iovino is from the Bob Knight Four, Notabartolo is from the Casualaires ("At the Dance," 1961), Bruce Goldie is from the Dreamers ("Because of You," 1961), and Dave Strum is from the Excellents ("Coney Island Baby").
Source: Bob Bosco in *Echoes of the Past* 7.

Five Breezes (Chicago)

Personnel Joseph "Cool Breeze" Bell, Gene Gilmour, Leonard Caston, Willie Dixon (bass), Willie Hawthorne

Notes

The Five Breezes were formed in Chicago in 1939.

Dixon and Caston used to sing together and after some success decided to form a quintet called the Five Breezes. They played the circuit in many of Chicago's clubs. In actuality, this was the starting point for Willie Dixon.

In 1940, the Five Breezes were recording for Bluebird Records and cut eight sides.

In 1941, Dixon was arrested on stage for refusing induction into the armed forces. The Five Breezes ceased to exist after Dixon's arrest. Dixon started the Four Jumps of Jive in 1945. Gilmour and Dixon sang together in the Four Jumps of Jive.

Two of the Five Breezes members later became the Big Three Trio.

Discography

Bluebird 6590 Sweet Louise/Minute and Hour Blues (1940)
Bluebird 8614 Return Gal o' Mine/My Buddy Blues (1941)
Bluebird 8679 What's the Matter with Love?/Swingin' the Blues (1941)
Bluebird 8710 Just a Jitterbug/Laundry Man (1941)
Sources: Bruce Eder in *Goldmine,* February 1990; Ray Funk and Doug Seroff, liner notes with the *Human Orchestra* LP.

Five Chances (Chicago)

Personnel Darnell Austell (1st tenor), Reggie Smith (2d tenor), Harold Jones, Howard Pitman (baritone), John Austell (bass)

Notes

This group began singing in junior high school in 1950. In 1954, they won a talent show at which Levi McKay saw and heard them. He became their mentor and guided them with his music business expertise. He ultimately led them to an audition with Chance.

At Chance, Ewart Abner named them the Five Chances. In 1955 they moved to the Parrot subsidiary Blue Lake Records, brought there by manager McKay.

Harold Jones also sang tenor for the Maples on Blue Lake and had been with another Levi McKay group—the Daffodils.

Eddie Stillwell was a part-time lead and Clyde Williams was another addition.

They moved to Blue Lake Records and brought in Johnny "Chubby" Jones to replace John Austell. Jones had also been with the Daffodils. While they were at Blue Lake, members of the group began working with singer Kenneth Childers, who was passionate about getting his voice on record. He paid his way to ensure this! Individuals from other groups joined in and the group, called the Maples, consisted of Childers, Albert Hunter (Clouds), Andrew Smith (Fasinoles), and Harold Jones (Five Chances).

Frank Simms was also a member of the Five Chances.

In 1956, the group moved to States. Harold Jones and Darnell Austell were replaced by Jesse Stafford and Ronald Johnson. The following year, the group moved to the Federal label.

During the latter part of their career, the Five Chances did a great deal of live performances and touring. Their success with concerts was due to their outstanding choreography.

Discography

Chance 1157 I May Be Small/Nagasaki (1954)
Blue Lake 115 All I Want (DA)/Shake-a-Link (1955)
States 156 Gloria (HJ)/Sugar Lips (HJ) (1956)
Federal 12303 My Days Are Blue (HJ)/Tell Me Why (HJ) (1957)
Sources: Bob Pruter, liner notes with the Relic CD *Parrot;* Bob Pruter in *Goldmine;* unsigned liner notes with the Rare *Windy City* CD.

Five Chestnuts (Hamden, Conn.)

Personnel Hayes Baskerville (d), Marvin Baskerville, Norven Baskerville

Notes

Despite the fact that the group's name was the Five Chestnuts, it was the three Baskerville brothers performing. This was also the first release on Clarence Drum's Drum label.

Bill Baker joined the group when Hayes died. The group was then composed of Baker, Lymon, Arthur Hopkins, Reuben White, and Sonny Washburn. At that time they began calling themselves the Chestnuts. This group recorded four sides, all of which were released on Elgin (see Chestnuts).

Discography

Drum 001/002 Chapel in the Moonlight/Chi Chi (1958)
Drum 003/004 Billy/My One and Only Love (1958)
Source: Bjorn Jentoft in *Whiskey, Women, and . . .* 18. Article on Bill Baker.

Five Chimes/Chimes (Bronx, N.Y.)

Personnel Gene Redd (d), John Murray (d) (st), Gary Morrison (d) (baritone), Arthur Crier (bass)

Notes

Gary Morrison, John Murray, and Gene Redd are deceased. Murray died soon after the recordings were done. He was replaced for performances by Waldo Champen. Bobby Spencer and Jimmy Keyes made a bid for the assignment but lost out to Champen. (According to an article by Marv Goldberg and Marcia Vance in *Yesterday's Memories*, Murray was replaced by Bobby Spencer!)

Gary Morrison sang lead on "Never Love Another." Gene Redd was lead on "Dearest Darling," a tune the group didn't much care for at the time.

The group went to Jubilee for a trial but was asked to leave and not come back when Gary Morrison did not show up. The group stayed together for another two years, but it was not the same without Murray. Late in 1955 they split up.

Redd went to the FiTones and Arthur and Gary joined a group called the Hummers, who recorded for Old Town. This was never released at the time by Hy Weiss.

Arthur Crier went on to sing with the Mellows, Halos, Craftys, Little Guy and the Giants, and, in the 1990s, the Morrisania Revue.

Discography

Royal Roost 577 A Fool Was I/Dearest Darling (GR) (1953)
Betta 2011 Rosemarie/Never Love Another (1953)
Source: Arthur Crier, interview by Marcia Vance and Marv Goldberg in *Yesterday's Memories* 12.

Five Crowns (New York)

Personnel Wilbur "Yonkie" Paul, James "Poppa" Clark (lead), Claudie "Nicky" Clark, John "Sonny Boy" Clark, "Dock" Green (baritone)

Notes

In 1952, Dock Green and Wilbur "Yonkie" Paul met the Clark brothers, James "Poppa," John "Sonny Boy," and Claudie "Nicky."

These five grew up in the same neighborhood with the Harptones and were their friends. Nicky Clark later sang with the Harptones. (According to Dock Green, Nicky sang with the Harptones and the Five Crowns at the same time.)

"Yonkie" Paul also sang with the Floaters and the Harptones.

They first recorded for Rainbow in 1952 and made five discs for them. Then they left Rainbow due to a misunderstanding and went over to Old Town Records. After recording there, they returned to Rainbow for three more releases.

In 1953 Nicky left for the Harptones and wasn't replaced immediately. John Clark was next to leave, and the two were replaced by Jesse Facing (tenor) and William "Bugeye" Bailey (bass). In 1954 "Poppa" Clark left to join the Cadillacs and was replaced by Richard Lewis. This new group—Paul, Green, Facing, Bailey, and

Lewis—became known as (and recorded as) the Duvals on Riviera, which was a subsidiary of Rainbow.

Bass Leroy Brown replaced Bugeye.

It should be mentioned that many pictures display Lover Patterson as a singing member of the group. Patterson never sang with the Crowns or Five Crowns.

As a result of poor promotion of their cuts, they decided to break up. In 1955, Dock formed a new Five Crowns group for Gee records with J. D. at lead, Bernard Ward at tenor, Dock Green at baritone, Elsbeary Hobbs at bass, and a tenor remembered as Charlie. They recorded one record for Gee and split!

The last Crowns group dropped the Five because occasionally there were six members. Dock Green, Hobbs, Charlie Thomas (tenor), Ben (E. King) Nelson (tenor), Sy Palmer (tenor). When the Harptones weren't busy, Nicky Clark would show up. On Doc Pomus's R&B Records recording, Clark did not appear and the other five members recorded "Kiss and Make-Up," the only recording on this label.

The Crowns—James Clark (lead), Charlie Thomas (lead), Ben E. King (lead), Dock Green (baritone), and Elsbeary Hobbs (bass)—were performing at the Apollo when George Treadwell approached them and asked them to be the new Drifters. "Poppa" Clark didn't care for this arrangement and left. The group became a quartet and began filling Drifters' dates.

Green left in 1962 and was replaced by Gene Pearson of the Rivileers/Cleftones. Green joined the Drapers, Floaters, and Drifters, and Sy Palmer was a tenor.

Discography

Rainbow 179 A Star/You're My Inspiration (1952)
Rainbow 184 Who Can Be True/$19.50 Bus (1952)
Rainbow 202 Keep It a Secret/Why Don't You Believe Me? (1953)
Rainbow 206 Alone Again/I Don't Have to Hunt No More (1953)
Old Town 790 You Could Be My Love/Good Luck Darlin' (1953)
Old Town 792 Lullaby of the Bells/Later Later Baby (1953)
Riviera 990 You Came to Me/Ooh Wee Baby (1955)
Trans-World 717 I Can't Pretend/Popcorn Willie (1955)
Caravan 15609 I Can't Pretend/Popcorn Willie (1955)
Rainbow 335 You Came to Me/Ooh Wee Baby (1956)
Sources: Liner notes with Relic's *Rainbow* and *Five Crowns*; Marv Goldberg in *Big Town Review* 2.

Five Cs (Gary, Ind.)

Personnel Curtis Nevils, Clarence Anderson, Melvin Carr, Carlos Tolliver

Notes

Coming from the same Indiana town, the Five Cs knew the Spaniels but were from cross-town rival high schools. The fifth C has been unidentified for many years. It may have been an instrumental contributor but is unconfirmed at this writing.

Anderson was a relative of deejay Sam Evans, who brought them to United in 1953. Their first recording session was in December 1953.

The group had another session at United that produced "I Long for You," "There's No Tomorrow," "Going My Way," and "I Want to Be Loved." These were never released until the Japanese P-Vine label issued them on an LP in 1981.

Discography

United 172 Whoo-Ee Baby/Tell Me (1954)
United 180 Goody, Goody/My Heart's Got the Blues (1955)
Sources: Bob Pruter, *Doowop . . . The Chicago Scene;* unsigned liner notes with the Rare CD *Windy City–2.*

Five Debonaires (Atlanta)

Personnel Arthur Simon, Emory Cloud, Milton Boykin

Notes

The group was sometimes referred to as the Debonaires. This Herald release shows Five Debonaires on the label.

Discography

Herald 509 Darlin'/Whispering Blues (1957)
Source: Donn Fileti, liner notes with the Relic Herald CD *Golden Era of Doo Wops.*

Five Delights (Bronx, N.Y.)

Personnel Danny Levy (d), Sonny Jordan, Waldo Champen, Doug Ferrar, George Rosa

Notes

Prior to the Five Delights, Champen and Jordan had been with many other well-known vocal groups (see performers index).

The Newport label was owned and operated by Onyx's Jerry Winston. There was no relationship, however, between his Newport records and the Unart label.

The Five Delights became the Moodmakers on Bambi with two changes: George Rosa was replaced by Ray Figueroa at 2d tenor and Doug Ferrar was replaced at baritone by Eddie Stokes.

In 1994, Waldo Champen joined Lillian Leach, Bobby Mansfield, Dean Barlow, Sammy Fain, Eugene Tompkins, and Arthur Crier to form the Morrisania Review.

Discography

Newport 7002 There'll Be No Goodbyes (EJ)/Okey Dokey Mama (DF) (1958)
Unart 2003 There'll Be No Goodbyes (EJ)/Okey Dokey Mama (DF) (1958)
Abel 228 The Thought of Losing You (EJ)/That Love Affair (WC) (1959)
Source: Waldo Champen, interview by author, July 15, 1994.

Five Discs (Brooklyn, N.Y.)

Personnel Mario DeAndrade (D'Androtti), Paul Albano (1st tenor), Tony Basile (2d tenor), Joe Barselona (baritone), Andrew Jackson (bass)

Notes

The Five Discs had their beginnings in 1954. The Paragons and the Royaltones were two other neighborhood groups who inspired them. The Five Discs practiced at all appropriate vocal group locations.

In the late 1950s, after many personnel changes, the Five Discs, now integrated, came to Manhattan's Brill Building seeking a recording label.

In 1960 Mario and Andrew left the Five Discs and were replaced by Lenny Hutter (from the Chalets) as lead and John Russell on bass.

John Carbone joined as bass lead in 1961. Charlie DiBella replaced John Russell at bass.

New lead Eddie Parducci joined from the Del Vons.

The group moved to Kapp records and recorded as the Boyfriends in 1964.

In 1965, the group became Parducci (lead), Donnie LaRuffa (1st tenor), Frank Arnone (2d tenor), and Barselona (baritone).

In 1968, the group became Dawn on Rust.

Discography

Emge 1004 I Remember/The World Is a Beautiful Place (1958)
Vik 0327 I Remember/The World Is a Beautiful Place (1958)
Dwain 6072 Roses/My Chinese Girl (1959)
Rust 5027 I Remember/The World Is a Beautiful Place (1960)
Calo 202 Adios/My Baby Loves Me (1961)
Yale 243/244 I Don't Know/Come on Baby (1961)
Cheer 1000 Never Let You Go/That Was the Time (1962)
Laurie 3601 Rock and Roll Revival/Gypsy Woman (1972)
Sources: Steve Flam in *Bim Bam Boom* 4; Bob Diskin in *Record Collector's Monthly* 49; Ed Engel, liner notes with the Ace CD *Laurie Vocal Groups.*

Five Dollars (Detroit)

Personnel Joe Simmons, Little Eddie Hurt (d) (tenor), Lonnie Heard (2d tenor), James Drayton (baritone), Andre Williams (bass)

Notes

Andre Williams, who recorded many sides on Fortune, liked the Five Dollars so much that he became their manager. He even sang with them on occasion.

Williams later changed their name to the Don Juans, and they recorded as both groups simultaneously!

Little Eddie Hurt was shot and killed outside a Five Dollars' reunion gala in the early 1990s.

James Drayton later replaced Williams.

Discography

Fortune 821 Harmony of Love/Doctor Baby (1955)
Fortune 826 So Strange/You Know I Can't Refuse (1956)
Fortune 830 I Will Wait/Hard Working Mama (1956)
Fortune 833 You Fool/How Do You Do the Bacon Fat (1957)
Fortune 851 Movin'/Movin' (Diablos) (1960)
Fortune 854 That's the Way It Goes/My Baby-O (1960)
Sources: Liner notes with the Regency CD Detroit Doo Wops: The Five Dollars; Tony Tisovec in *Bim Bam Boom.*

Five Dukes, Bennie Woods & (Providence, R.I.)

Personnel Joe Hill, Joe Simmons (tenor), Sonny Washburn (tenor), Danny Jet (baritone), Therman Blackwell (d) (bass)

Notes

The Five Dukes got together in 1952 as friends in junior high school and remained together through their high school years. They originally called themselves the Four Hearts.

Bennie Woods was the group's manager and made several appearances with them. He never recorded with them. The name Five Dukes came when guitarist Buster Henderson joined.

In 1954, they came to New York City to locate a label that was interested in them and found Tommy Robinson's Atlas Records in Harlem.

In December 1954 "I Cross My Fingers" was released as by Bennie Woods and the Five Dukes. Five years later it was reissued but this time by the Rockin' Townies.

Sonny Washburn, a later member of the Five Dukes, was also a member of the Nutmegs, Rajahs, and Lyres. Washburn joined when Hill was drafted. By the time their record was recorded, Hill was home, but all five vocalists performed at the Atlas session. Hill sang false tenor, Danny Jet sang lead on "I Cross My Fingers," and Simmons performed lead on "Wheel Baby, Wheel."

Discography

Atlas 1040 I Cross My Fingers/Wheel Baby, Wheel (1954)
Source: Marv Goldberg in *DISCoveries.*

Five Du-Tones

Personnel L. Tate, J. Dodd, O. Hayes, V. Rice, ——— Williams

Discography

One-Derful 4814 Come Back Baby/Dry Your Eyes (1963)
One-Derful 4815 Shake a Tasil Feather/Divorce Court (1963)
One-Derful 4818 Monkey See, Monkey Do/The Gouster (1963)
One-Derful 4821 Nobody But/That's How I Love You (1963)

One-Derful 4824 The Cool Bird/The Chicken Astronaut (1964)
One-Derful 4828 Sweet Lips/Let Me Love You (1964)
One-Derful 4831 We Want More/The Woodbine Twine (1964)
One-Derful 4836 Mountain of Love/Outside the Record Hop (1965)
Source: Ferdie Gonzalez, *Disco-File.*

Five Echoes (Chicago)

Personnel Walter Spriggs, Tommy Hunt (2d tenor), Constant "Count" Sims (baritone), Herbert Lewis (baritone), Jimmy Marshall (bass)

Notes

Walter Spriggs from Chance/Sabre sang lead on the first session ("Lonely Mood"). He also acted as the group's agent/manager. Spriggs was never an official member of the group but would often perform and record with them. Additionally, 1st tenor Earl Lewis, a later member, had been with the Flamingos in Chicago and was their lead singer prior to Sollie McElroy.

Tommy Hunt (later of the Flamingos) was drafted after the first session. This was at the group's beginning and he was then known as Charles Hunt. He went AWOL to be at the third session. However this recording (and others made in 1954) was never released as the label closed its doors in 1954. These cuts were eventually released on the Constellation LP in 1964. The FBI eventually caught up to Hunt and had him returned to the army stockade.

Lead Johnny Taylor joined after the first session and had also been with the gospel group the Highway QCs. He also replaced Sam Cooke in the Soul Stirrers.

The group first recorded for Sabre as the Five Echoes and then for Vee Jay as the Five Echos.

Discography

Sabre 102 Baby Come Back to Me (WS)/Lonely Mood (WS) (1953)
Sabre 105 So Lonesome (CS)/Broke (CS) (1954)
Sabre UNR Why Oh Why/That's My Baby
Vee Jay 129 Tell Me Baby/I Really Do (1954)
Vee Jay 156 Fool's Prayer/Tastee Freeze (1955)
Sources: Bob Pruter, liner notes with the Relic CD *Parrot*; Bob Pruter in *Goldmine,* April 1979.

Five Fashions (Stamford, Conn.)

Personnel Bruce Burdock, Robert Waters, Frank Erico, Anthony Matylinsk, Richard Melesk

Notes

When this group added a sixth member they were called A Group Called Us. The sixth member was Richard Bour.

Discography

Catamount 102 Pennies from Heaven/Ten Commandments of Love (1964)
Catamount 103 Solitaire/Over the Rainbow (1965)
Catamount 107 My Girl/Kiss, Kiss, Kiss (1965)
Catamount 116 I'll Be Home for Christmas/ (1966)
Source: Donn Fileti, liner notes with the Relic CD *I Dig Acappella.*

Five Frenchmen (Chicago)

Personnel Reggie Gordon (lead), Harold Foster (1st tenor), Glen Phillips (2d tenor), Henry Currie (baritone), Norman Cummings (bass)

Notes

This group never recorded, but it is still remembered in the late 1990s as an excellent quintet with a strong reputation. The only difficulty was a lack of organization. Apparently Glen Phillips was the group's arranger and vocal coach, giving each singer his part in harmony.

Gordon also sang with the Magnificents and the Rays.
Source: Bob Pruter, *Doowop . . . The Chicago Scene.*

Five Hearts (Los Angeles)

Personnel Arthur Lee Maye (tenor), Johnny Coleman (baritone), Richard Berry (bass)

Notes

The Five Hearts started in 1954, when Arthur Maye, Richard Berry, and Johnny Coleman would sing in the hallways of Los Angeles Jefferson High School. The three performers sang with the Flairs concurrently. Maye was also involved in assembling his own group, which would ultimately be the Crowns.

Flair Records brought the unnamed trio to their studio and recorded them first as the Five Hearts. Their second time in the studio, their recording was released as by the Rams.

(Note: In Marv Goldberg's and Rick Whitesell's story on the Flairs appearing in *Yesterday's Memories* 10 (1977), Marv and Rick interviewed four members of the Flairs, who provided them with the names of five members of the Five Hearts; they did the same for the Rams. Eleven years later, Marv interviewed Lee Maye, who told him that the two groups were trios, composed of the above!)

Discography

Flair 1026 The Fine One/Please Please Baby (1954)
Sources: Marv Goldberg and Rick Whitesell in *Yesterday's Memories* 10; Marv Goldberg in *Whiskey, Women and . . .* 17; Lynn McCutcheon in *Bim Bam Boom* 6.

Five Hearts (Philadelphia)

Personnel Tommy White, Royalston "Roy" Calhoun (1st tenor), Thomas "Butch" Curry (2d tenor), Eddie Custis (baritone), Wendell Calhoun (bass)

Notes

In October 1958, Ted Weems joined the service and Lee Andrews simply left the Hearts. The Hearts stayed together as the Five Hearts. In 1959 they picked up Tommy White as their lead and Eddie Custis as their baritone. Custis had been with the Superiors. Lee Andrews was married to Custis's sister (who had also been with the Superiors).

All the above sang with Lee Andrews and the Hearts at one time or another.

The Arcade record shown below was also released as Casino 107 in 1959. This was the Five Hearts' only recording.

Discography

Arcade 107 Unbelievable/Aunt Jenny (1959)
Source: Marv Goldberg, liner notes with the Collectables CD *Lee Andrews and the Hearts.*

Five Hollywood Bluejays (Hollywood, Calif.)

Personnel Cornelius Gunter, Beverly Thompson (1st tenor), Thomas "Pete" Fox (2d tenor), Obediah "Young" Jesse (baritone), Richard Berry (bass)

Notes

This group got together while the members were students at Jefferson and Fremont High Schools in Los Angeles.

They auditioned for John Dolphin's Dolphin Records on the Hollywood label in 1953, and their "I Had a Love" was released on that label.

They were the Flairs before they changed their name.

Discography

Recorded in Hollywood 162 Put a Nickel in the Jukebox/Safronia Ida B. Brown (1952)
Source: Marv Goldberg and Rick Whitesell in *Yesterday's Memories* 10.

Five Jades (Bronx, N.Y.)

Personnel Ray Goodwin, Joey Figueroa, Spencer Jackson, Bobby Figueroa, Hector Rosado

Notes

Their first record was as the Shadows on the Mellomood label.

Following their first hit, Tony Moreno replaced Ray Goodwin.

After many personnel changes, three of the members joined the army in 1965 and the group disbanded. They met again at a reunion in the 1980s.

Ray Goodwin, Manny Hernandez (d), Dennis Cerrato, and Junior Roman were the second Five Jades recording group.

Discography

Your Choice 907/908 My Reverie/Rosemarie (1965)
Your Choice 909/910 My Girlfriend/How Much I Love You (1965)
Source: Tom Luciani and Joe Marchesani, liner notes with the Relic LP *Velvet Soul.*

Five Jades (Cleveland, Ohio)

Personnel Melvin Smith, James Frierson, Leonard Veal, Leuvenia Eaton, Charles Sonny Turner

Notes

In March 1958, Don Robey, head of the Duke/Peacock Records organization, announced the signing of a group formerly known as the Metrotones who recorded for Reserve Records in Cleveland. The group had changed their name to the Five Jades when their Reserve recording failed.

Robey traveled to Cleveland in April for the Five Jades session. "Without Your Love" and "Rock and Roll Molly" were the two sides recorded and released in May 1958 for Duke Records.

This disc too failed to make any noise. Frierson was soon drafted and replaced by Robert Sheppard. Late in 1958, Sonny Turner left to pursue a solo career and the Five Jades were then made up of Eaton, Veal, Angelo Jones, and Bill Brent from the Hornets on States. In 1959, Leuvenia chose to leave and the group became an all-male ensemble. They changed their name to the Five Gents.

Discography

Duke 118 Without Your Love (LE)/Rock and Roll Molly (ST) (1958)
Source: Marv Goldberg in *DISCoveries*, November 1997.

Five Jets (Detroit)

Personnel Joseph Murphy, Crathman "C. P." Spencer (tenor), Charles Lee (2d tenor), Raymond Dorsey (baritone), Billy Davis (bass)

Notes

The majority of this group had been the Thrillers on the Big Town label who recorded "The Drunkard." According to Marv Goldberg, they were not the Thrillers on the Herald label who released "Lizabeth."

They recorded for Thriller and Big Town as the Thrillers. They were also on DeLuxe and Fortune as the Five Jets, on Mark-X and End as the Five Stars, and on Anna as the Voice Masters.

In Michel Ruppli's *The King Labels: A Discography,* which contains the King-Federal-DeLuxe recording data, the DeLuxe Five Jets is made up of the following: Billy Davis, John Dorsey, Charles Lee, Carl Stewart, and Joseph Murphy.

Goldmine (September 1981) shows the group personnel as follows: C. P. Spencer, Chuck Benson, Walter Gaines, Raymond Dorsey, and Joe Murphy (this according to Jack Sbarbori).

After DeLuxe, Davis quit singing. He was replaced by Billy Lyons, who would later sing with the Royal Jokers.

The Fortune "I'm Wandering" cut was released containing an error made by the Fortune pressing plant personnel. When first released, it contained the Five Dollars tune "You Fool."

Lyons left in late 1956, replacing Thearon Hill in the Royal Jokers. He was replaced in the Five Jets by Walter Gaines. In 1957, Charles Lee was replaced by Henry Jones.

Discography

DeLuxe 6018 I Am in Love/Not a Hand to Shake (1953)
DeLuxe 6053 I'm Stuck/I Want a Woman (1954)
DeLuxe 6058 Tell Me You're Mine/Give In (1954)
DeLuxe 6064 Crazy Chicken/Everybody Do the Chicken (1954)
DeLuxe 6071 Down Slow/Please Love Me Baby (1954)
Fortune 833 I'm Wandering (JM) (1957)
Sources: Donn Fileti, liner notes with Relic's Herald CD; Steve Towne in *Goldmine,* September 1981; Marv Goldberg in *DISCoveries.*

Five Jones Boys (Carbondale, Ill.)

Personnel Jimmy Springs, Charles Hopkins, Louis Wood, Herman Wood, William Hartley

Notes

The members of this group began singing with one another as teenagers when they were all working in a mining camp. In 1937, they settled in Los Angeles after touring the West Coast.

Source: Ray Funk and Doug Seroff, liner notes with the Clanka Lanka *Human Orchestra* LP.

Five Keys (Newport News, Va.)

Personnel Rudy West (d), Ripley Ingram (tenor), Dickie Smith (2d tenor), Maryland Pierce (baritone), Bernie West (bass)

Notes

In 1945, the West brothers and the Ingram brothers joined to form the Sentimental Four. Following Raphael Ingram's induction into the army (1949), Maryland Pierce joined the group. Soon after, James Dickie Smith specifically replaced Ingram. On Ingram's return home, he quickly joined another Newport News, Virginia, group, the Avalons.

Edwin Hall, an original member of the Sentimental Four and the Five Keys left the group because of his imminent marriage. He was replaced by 2d tenor Maryland Pierce. This was 1950.

Dickie Smith sang lead, 2d tenor, and baritone for the Five Keys on Aladdin. He left in 1953 first go solo and then to join the army. He was replaced by Ramon Loper. Smith, by the way, was a cousin of Harptones lead Willie Winfield and grew up with Winfield in Surrey, Virginia.

A group called the Furness Brothers was formerly known as the Four Keys. In 1950 or 1951 they were about to add another brother and their name logically would have been the Five Keys. A lawsuit ensued in fall 1951, which obviously the Furness Brothers lost.

The Five Keys signed with Aladdin in February 1951, and on February 22, 1951, they recorded six sides at New York's WOR Studios. The first Five Keys single was released in April 1951; "Glory of Love" was released in July of that year.

After their time with Aladdin (four years) and before they joined Capitol, they had one session for the RCA subsidiary Groove. Four songs were recorded but never released in the 1950s. Two of these tunes were finally released in the 1990s on the RCA CD *Rock 'n' Roll Party–1*.

The group joined Capitol in 1954 and executed "Ling Ting Tong" with Pierce on lead and with West in the service. Rudy rejoined the group for the second Capitol disc "Close Your Eyes" (written by Chuck Willis), thus replacing Ulysses Hicks, who had filled in for Rudy when he was in the army. Hicks died several months later.

In 1959, the Five Keys had joined King with Dick Threatt performing lead chores. The other Five Keys on King were Bernie West, Maryland Pierce, Dickie Smith, and Ramon Loper.

In 1962 Rudy came out of his quasi-retirement and joined brother Bernie, Ripley Ingram, John Boyd, and Willie Friday. Raymond Haskiss and Daytill Jones were also with the Five Keys.

This group too broke up and the next re-formation came in 1973, when Rudy and the former Chateaus joined forces. West died of a heart attack in May 1998.

Discography

Aladdin 3085 With a Broken Heart/Too Late (1951)
Aladdin 3099 The Glory of Love/Hucklebuck with Jimmy (1951)
Aladdin 3113 It's Christmas Time/Old MacDonald (1951)
Aladdin 3118 Yes Sir, That's My Baby/Old MacDonald (1952)
Aladdin 3127 Red Sails in the Sunset/Be Anything but Be Mine (1952)
Aladdin 3131 Mistakes/How Long? (1952)
Aladdin 3136 I Hadn't Anyone till You/Hold Me (1952)
Aladdin 3158 I Cried for You/Serve Another Round (1952)
Aladdin 3167 Can't Keep from Crying/Come Go My Bail, Louise (1953)
Aladdin 3175 There Ought to Be a Law/Mama (1953)
Aladdin 3190 These Foolish Things/Lonesome Old Story (1953)
Aladdin 3204 Teardrops in Your Eyes/I'm So High (1953)
Aladdin 3214 My Saddest Hour/Oh! Babe (1953)
Aladdin 3228 Someday Sweetheart/Love My Loving (1954)
Aladdin 3245 Deep in My Heart/How Do You Expect Me to Get It (1954)

Groove 0031 I'll Follow You/Lawdy Miss Mary (1954)
Capitol 2945 Ling Ting Tong/I'm Alone (1954)
Aladdin 3263 My Love/Why, Oh Why? (1955)
Capitol 3032 Close Your Eyes/Doggone It, You Did It (1955)
Capitol 3127 The Verdict/Me Make 'Em Pow Wow (1955)
Capitol 3185 I Wish I Never Learned to Read/Don't You Know I Love You (1955)
Capitol 3267 Gee Whittakers/'Cause You're My Lover (1955)
Capitol 3318 What Goes On/You Broke the Rules of Love (1956)
Aladdin 3312 Story of Love/Serve Another Round (1956)
Aladdin (UNR) Ghost of a Chance/Hucklebuck with Jimmy
Aladdin (UNR) Do I Need You?
Aladdin (UNR) If You Only Knew
Aladdin (UNR) White Cliffs of Dover/When You're Gone
Aladdin (UNR) Yearning/Will My Heart Stand a Chance
Capitol 3392 She's the Most/I Dreamt I Dwelt in Heaven (1956)
Capitol 3455 Peace and Love/My Pigeon's Gone (1956)
Capitol 3502 Out of Sight, Out of Mind/That's Right (1956)
Capitol 3597 Wisdom of a Fool/Now Don't That Prove I Love You (1956)
Capitol 3660 Let There Be You/Tiger Lily (1957)
Capitol 3710 Four Walls/It's a Groove (1957)
Capitol 3738 This I Promise/The Blues Don't Care (1957)
Capitol 3786 The Face of an Angel/Boom-Boom (1957)
Capitol 3830 Do Anything/It's a Cryin' Shame (1957)
Capitol T 828 Just for a Thrill/The Gypsy (1957)
Capitol 3861 From Me to You/Whippety Whirl (1957)
Capitol 3948 With All My Love/You're for Me (1958)
Capitol 4009 Emily Please/Handy Andy (1958)
Capitol 4092 One Great Love/Really-O, Truly-O (1958)
King 5251 I Took Your Love for a Toy/Ziggus (1959)
King 5273 Dream On/Dancing Senorita (1959)
King 5302 How Can I Forget You?/I Burned Your Letter (1959)
King 5330 Gonna Be Too Late/Rosetta (1960)
King 5358 I Didn't Know/No Says My Heart (1960)
King 5398 Valley of Love/Bimbo (1960)
King 5646 You Broke the Only Heart/That's What You're Doin' (1961)
King 5496 Stop Your Crying/Do Something for Me (1961)
King 5877 I Can't Escape from You/I'll Never Stop Loving You (1964)
Sources: Steve Kolanjian, liner notes with both EMI's Aladdin CD and the Capitol CD; Marv Goldberg in *DISCoveries*.

Five Lyrics (Cleveland, Ohio)

Personnel Robert Rose, Isaac "Ike" Perry (tenor)

Notes

This was not the group who recorded for Harlem or Vee Jay. Nor were they the Lyrics from San Francisco. They lived in Cleveland, Ohio, sending tapes of their tunes to labels all over the country for the possibility of recording.

Discography

Music City 799 I'm Traving Light/My Honey Sweet Pea (1956)
Source: Jim Dawson, liner notes with the Titanic CD *Music City.*

Five Masks (Dallas)

Personnel Robert Valentine, Al "TNT" Braggs (tenor), Cal Valentine, Jesse Floyd, Billy Fred Thomas

Notes

The Five Masks originally formed in 1955 as the Five Notes who recorded "Park Your Love" and "Show Me the Way" for Chess Records.

This was a Milwaukee-based group that had originally formed in 1955 in Dallas. After a few talent shows in Texas, they moved to Milwaukee, where a deejay took a liking to the group and had them appear on his show. They next moved to Chicago and recorded for Chess. It was after the Chess recordings that they changed their name to the Five Masks.

They moved back to Dallas in 1957 and decided to disband.

Braggs also sang with the Five Stars on Blues Boys Kingdom.

Discography

Jan 101 Forever and a Day/Polly Molly (1958)
Source: Bob Pruter, *Doowop . . . The Chicago Scene.*

Five Notes (Dallas)

Personnel Al "TNT" Braggs, Cal Valentine, Robert Valentine, Jesse Floyd, Billy Fred Thomas

Notes

This was a Milwaukee-based group that had originally formed in Dallas in 1955.

After winning a few talent shows in Dallas, they moved to Milwaukee where a local deejay took a liking to the Five Notes and had them appear at each show he hosted. Next they moved to Chicago and recorded for Chess. After the Chess recordings they changed their name to the Five Masks.

Braggs also sang in the Five Stars (Blues Boys Kingdom).

Discography

Chess 1614 Park Your Love/Show Me the Way (1955)
Source: Bob Pruter, *Doowop . . . The Chicago Scene.*

Five Pennies (Knoxville, Tenn.)

Personnel Benjamin Washington, James Myers (1st tenor), Herbert Myers (2d tenor), John Myers (baritone), Charles Holloway (bass)

Notes

Like many other groups before and after them, the Five Pennies were primarily a backup group. They worked with Donnie Elbert, Nappy Brown, Little Willie John, and so on. They started as the Echos in Knoxville in 1951.

Tenor (and cousin) Benjamin Washington sang lead for this group as well as for the Echos, which they called themselves prior to recording for Savoy in 1955.

James Myers and John Myers were twins.

They met Cliff Curry in 1955 while still in high school in Knoxville. They did a great deal of touring and live performing. For this reason, Curry left the group to continue his education.

They were the group behind Faye Adams on "Shake a Hand" (this was before recording as the Five Pennies on Savoy).

They met Fred Mendelsohn of Savoy Records in 1955 while in New York, under the impression that they were auditioning for Atlantic. Instead, they auditioned for Savoy in Newark, New Jersey, and ultimately signed with them.

At their first session, they backed blues singer Big Miller and also cut "Mr. Moon." It was at this time that Savoy renamed them the Five Pennies. No one knows why.

They learned that their manager back in Knoxville was receiving the royalties from their recordings (despite their name, there were six individuals in the group at that time!)

It's curious that in a Lynn McCutcheon article in *Bim Bam Boom* in which McCutcheon interviewed Thomas Mathews, Mathews discusses his time with the Five Pennies. Marv Goldberg located and interviewed other former members of the Five Pennies for a *Yesterday's Memories* article. These members never heard of Thomas Mathews!

The army drafted Washington, Holloway, and James Myers. Fortunately, they did not leave simultaneously and John and Herbert kept the group going. During this time they strictly did backup work and decided to record for Herald, but their work was never released.

In 1958 Washington, James and Herbert Myers, and Holloway recorded as the Chimes on Arrow 724 and 726.

In the mid-1960s, John Myers formed a new group, the Larks, in Florida. This group was Floyd Lawson (lead), Rudolph Hill (tenor), Lindsey Griffin (1st tenor), John Myers (baritone), and Clemmons Daniels (bass).

In 1967 they re-formed the Five Pennies, including John Myers (baritone), Floyd Lawson (baritone/lead), Lindsay Griffin (1st tenor) and Carl Cuttler (lead), resulting from the Larks from Tampa Florida. By 1967 this group evolved into the Four Pennies (Myers, Griffin, Lawson, and Carl Cuttler).

Discography

Savoy 1181 All Is Well/I'm to Understand (backup to Big Miller) (1956)
Savoy 1182 Mr. Moon (CC)/Let It Rain (BW) (1956)
Savoy 1190 Money (CC)/My Heart Trembles (BW) (1956)
Sources: Lynn McCutcheon in *Bim Bam Boom* 3; Marv Goldberg in *Yesterday's Memories* 6.

Five Rovers (Los Angeles)

Personnel Oliver Stevens, Jay Payton (1st tenor), Henry Swan (baritone), Billy Williams (bass)

Notes

This group, recording as the Rovers, began in 1954. Just after recording their one disc as the Five Rovers for Music City, it was leased out to Capitol Records for greater distribution as sales began to increase.

In an interview with Jim Dawson for his *Music City* LP on Earth Angel, Payton stated that they were never given their royalties because Music City owner, Ray Dobard, always had outstanding debts for studio time, tape, musicians, and so on. When royalties were discussed, Dobard would always show them this list stating that the group still owed him for their expenses.

Discography

Music City 798 Down to the Sea/Change Your Mind (1956)
Source: Jim Dawson, liner notes with the Earth Angel LP *Music City.*

Five Royales (Winston-Salem, N.C.)

Personnel Johnny Tanner, Otto Jefferies (tenor), William Samuels (tenor), Clarence Pauling (baritone), Lowman Pauling (d. 1974) (bass)

Notes

The Five Royales began as a gospel group, the Royal Sons, and changed their musical style to R&B in 1952.

Johnny Tanner's brother Eugene also sang with the Five Royales, replacing Otto Jeffries who was forced to retire. Gene sang lead on approximately a quarter of the group's recordings.

In September 1952 members were Tanner, Jimmy Moore, Obediah Carter, Eugene Tanner, and Lowman Pauling. "You Know I Know" was their first disc.

Not getting their proper cut on record sales forced the group to move to King records in 1954. They played out their contract at King in 1960 and joined Home of the Blues records.

William Samuels later sang with the Casanovas.

Discography

Apollo 434 Too Much of a Little Bit/Give Me One More Chance (1951)
Apollo 441 Courage to Love/You Know I Know (1952)
Apollo 443 Baby Don't Do It/Take All of Me (1952)
Apollo 446 Help Me Somebody/Crazy Crazy Crazy (1953)
Apollo 449 I Want to Thank You/All Righty (1953)
Apollo 452 I Do/Good Things (1954)
Apollo 454 Cry Some More/I Like It Like That (1954)
King 4740 I'm Gonna Run It Down/Behave Yourself (1954)

King 4744 Monkey Hips and Rice/Devil with the Rest (1954)
King 4762 One Mistake/School Girl (1954)
King 4770 Every Dog Has Its Day/You Didn't Learn It at Home (1955)
Apollo 467 With All Your Heart/Six O'Clock in the Morning (1955)
King 4785 Mohawk Squaw/Now I Wonder (1955)
King 4806 When I Get Like This/I Need Your Lovin' Baby (1955)
King 4819 Do unto You/Women about to Make Me Go Crazy (1955)
King 4830 Someone Made You for Me/I Ain't Gettin' Caught (1955)
King 4869 Right around the Corner/When You Walked through the Door (1956)
King 4901 My Wants for Love/I Could Love You (1956)
King 4952 Come On and Save Me/Get Something Out of It (1956)
King 4973 Just as I Am/Mine Forevermore (1956)
King 5032 Tears of Joy/Thirty-Second Lover (1957)
King 5053 Think/I'd Better Make a Move (1957)
King 5082 Messin' Up/Say It (1957)
King 5098 Don't Be Ashamed/Dedicated to the One I Love (1957)
King 5131 The Feeling Is Real/Do the Cha Cha Cherry (1958)
King 5141 Double or Nothing/Tell the Truth (1958)
King 5153 Don't Let It Be in Vain/The Slummer the Slum (1958)
King 5162 The Real Thing/Your Only Love (1959)
King 5191 I Know It's Hard, but It's Fair/Miracle of Love (1959)
King 5237 Wonder Where Your Love Has Gone/Tell Me You Care (1959)
King 5266 It Hurts Inside/My Sugar Sugar (1959)
King 5329 Don't Give No More Than You Can Take/I'm with You (1960)
King 5357 Why/Within My Heart (1960)
Home of the Blues 112 Please Please Please/I Got to Know (1960)
Vee Jay 412 Much in Need/They Don't Know (1961)
King 5453 Dedicated to the One I Love/Miracle of Love (1961)
Home of the Blues 218 If You Don't Need Me/I'm Gonna Tell Them (1961)
Home of the Blues 232 Not Going to Cry/Take Me with You Baby (1961)
Home of the Blues 234 They Don't Know/Much in Need (1961)
Home of the Blues 257 Goof Ball/Catch That Teardrop (1962)
Vee Jay 431 Talk about the Woman/Help Me Somebody (1962)
ABC 10348 Goof Ball/Catch That Teardrop (1962)
ABC 10368 I Want It Like That/What's in the Heart (1962)
Todd 1086 Doin' Everything/I'm Standing in the Shadows (1963)
Todd 1088 Baby Don't Do It/There's Somebody Over There (1963)
Sources: Eddie Hoffman in *Goldmine*; Donn Fileti, liner notes with Relic's *Five Royales* CDs.

Five Satins (New Haven, Conn.)

Personnel Fred Parris, Al Denby (tenor), Ed Martin (baritone), Jim Freeman (bass)

Notes

The Five Satins began as the Scarlets on Red Robin. After many local appearances as the Five Satins, they were discovered by a local label manager who signed them with his organization and had them record and release "In the Still of the Night" on his Standord label. Parris was soon inducted into the service but would return home on leave for recording sessions.

Klik 7905 (She's Gone/The Voice) was recorded on Klik when Parris came home from the service in Japan. This was the only record done by the Satins at that time. Following its release they returned to Ember.

In Bob Belniak's interview with Fred Parris in *Echoes of the Past* 10, Parris states that the group who recorded "In the Still of the Night" was himself, Al Denby, Ed Martin, and Jim Freeman. Parris emphasized that there were only four Satins on "In the Still of the Night." He goes on to say that Denby was sent to Germany after this recording and Peebles then returned to the group.

In addition to the Scarlets and Satins, Parris also sang with the Restless Hearts, Wildwoods, Cherokees, and New Yorkers. With Parris spending much time in the army, a group was re-formed back home with Bill Baker (d), Jim Freeman, Tommy Killebrew, and Ed Martin (Rajahs).

This new group had some hits and many misses. Upon his return in 1958, Parris re-formed his group—Parris, Freeman, Wes Forbes, Lou Peebles, and Sylvester Hopkins.

Forbes sang with the Starlarks, Wildwoods, and New Yorkers.

The group was re-formed again; Dortch and Peebles were out and Al Denby was back in.

The group never again had a record with sales like "In the Still of the Night."

Parris relates that the singers on "Wishing Ring," included himself, Peebles, and three white studio musicians who vocalized with him and Peebles. The three other Satins had not shown up for the session.

Discography

Standord 100 All Mine/Rose Mary (1956)
Standord 200 I Remember/Jones Girl (1956)
Ember 1005 In the Still of the Night/The Jones Girl (1956)
Ember 1005 I Remember/The Jones Girl (1956)
Ember 1008 Wonderful Girl/Weeping Willow (1956)
Ember 1014 Oh Happy Day/Our Love Is Forever (1957)
Ember 1019 To the Aisle/Wish I Had My Baby (1957)
Ember 1025 Our Anniversary/Pretty Girl (1957)
Ember 1028 A Million to One/Love with No Love in Return (1957)
Ember 1056 Shadows/Toni My Love (1959)
First 104 When Your Love Comes Along/Skippity Doo (1959)
Ember 1061 A Night Like This/I'll Be Seeing You (1960)
Ember 1066 Candlelight/The Time (1960)
Ember 1070 Wishing Ring/Tell Me Dear (1961)
United Artists 368 On a Lover's Island/Till the End (1961)
Chancellor 1110 The Masquerade Is Over/Raining in My Heart (1962)
Chancellor 1121 Do You Remember?/Downtown (1962)
Times Square 4 All Mine/Rose Mary (1962)
Times Square 21 Paradise on Earth (1963)
Warner Bros. 5367 Remember Me/Kangaroo (1963)
Sources: Donn Fileti, liner notes with the Relic LP *Five Satins*; Wayne Jones in *Goldmine* 36; Bob Belniak in *Echoes of the Past*.

Five Scalders (Detroit)

Personnel Johnny Mayfield, Sol Tilman (tenor), Gerald Young (tenor), Mack Rice (baritone), James Bryant (bass)

Notes

Mack Rice later sang with the Detroit Falcons. Both groups, the Falcons and the Five Scalders, attended the same high school in Detroit.

Discography

Drummond 3000 If Only You Were Mine (JM)/There Will Come a Time (ST) (1956)
Drummond 3001 Girlfriend (MR)/Willow Blues (ST/JM) (1956)
Sources: Marv Goldberg in *Whiskey, Women and . . .* ; Louie Silvani in *Collecting Rare Records.*

Five Scamps (Kansas City, Mo.)

Personnel Earl Robinson, Terrence Griffin, James Whitcomb (bass)

Notes

The guys met at a Civilian Conservation Corps camp in Kansas City in 1937. Each evening after work they would sit around and harmonize with each other.

In 1947 the group re-formed as a professional vocal/instrumental ensemble.

The two other members making the fourth and fifth Scamps were Rudy Massingill on piano and saxaphone and Wyatt Griffin on guitar. The vocal lineup in 1946 was Earl Robinson (lead), James Whitcomb (bass), and Terrence Griffin (tenor).

The Five Scamps' first recording with five members, for Modern, was released in 1947; the label billed them as the Scamps.

In 1949, they signed a contract with Columbia Records. Their session produced ten tracks, all but one being released in the next two years; now they were listed as the Five Scamps. Evelyn Twine was added to the group in the early 1950s.

Discography

Modern 512 Don't Cry Baby/More Than You Know (1947)
Modern 516 That's My Desire/I Wonder, I Wonder, I Wonder (1947)
Modern 550 Solitude/Chicka Biddie Boogie (1947)
Modern 561 Worry/I'll Never Smile Again (1947)
Modern Music 20-521 I'm Falling for You/Sweet Slumber (1947)
Columbia 30157 Chicken Shack Boogie/Gone Home (1949)
Columbia 30158 Red Hot/With All My Heart (1949)
Columbia 30163 Fine Like Wine/How Nice (1949)
Columbia 30168 The Fishing Song/Good Lover Blues (1949)
Columbia 30177 I Love the Way You Walk/I'm Gonna Cry (1949)
Columbia 30242 Dance Boogie/Gonna Buy Myself a Mule (1949)
Okeh 7049 Red Hot/With All My Heart (1954)
Peacock 1655 Yes My Baby/Waterproof (1955)
Source: Pete Grendysa and Ray Funk in *Record Collector's Monthly* 42.

Five Secrets (Staten Island, N.Y.)

Personnel Dave Concepción, Pat Russo (1st tenor), Vinnie Santorelli (2d tenor), Steve Murphy (baritone), Frank Del Cavo (bass)

Notes

This group had also been the Loungers on Herald. Their recording of "See You Next Year" was of course a white cover of the Cleftones disc.

The Five Secrets formed in 1956 on Staten Island.

Discography

Decca 30350 See You Next Year/Queen Bee (1957)
Source: Donn Fileti, liner notes with the Relic CD *Herald.*

Five Sharps (Queens, N.Y.)

Personnel Ronald Cuffey (d) (lead), Clarence Bassett (1st tenor), Robert Ward (2d tenor), Mickey Owens (bass), Johnny Jackson

Notes

The Five Sharps formed in 1952 in the Jamaica section of Queens in New York City. Like other groups before and after them, they sang at local affairs, school functions, and so on. An independent record producer heard them and consequently brought them to Jubilee to record. Pete Grendysa states in *Goldmine* that it was their manager who arranged for them to record for Jubilee.

Owens and Cuffey were cousins. (Incidentally, it has been shown in many different accounts of the Five Sharps that the lead for the group is either Ronald Cussey or Ronald Cuffey. Ronnie Cuffey appears to be correct.)

Tom Duckett sang and played piano for the Five Sharps as well as many other area groups of the day (e.g., Cleftones, Rivileers, Heartbeats, Harmonaires). Duckett was considered the fifth Sharp.

Bassett and Cuffey later joined Charles Baskerville to sing with the Videos; Bassett joined old friends James Sheppard and Charles Baskerville to sing as Shep and the Limelights.

The Stormy Weather/Sleepy Cowboy release did absolutely nothing; there were no follow-ups and no live appearances. Because of this poor showing, Ward and Duckett were told by their families to leave the Five Sharps.

In 1961, R&B collector Bill Pensebini stumbled upon a 78 rpm copy of "Stormy Weather" in a Brooklyn record shop. At that time, the record was relatively unknown. Pensebini brought the disc to Irving "Slim" Rose, proprietor of the now legendary Times Square Records. Rose had a weekly radio show on WBNX radio and agreed to play the song. Before this could happen, the record broke. Rose offered a reward to anyone with a copy. No one came forward with the copy, despite Rose's offer. This led to the record's reputation and ultimately its value.

In his search for the Jubilee disc, Rose dealt with the record company directly. He learned from Jubilee management that eighty masters had been lost to water damage. One of the lost masters was "Stormy Weather."

Later in 1961, a 78 rpm copy with a hairline crack was found by John Dunn in Brooklyn. Being a knowledgeable collector, Dunn tape-recorded both sides of Jubilee 5104 and put the disc away for safekeeping.

In 1972, the management of *Bim Bam Boom* magazine, an R&B vocal group collectors' magazine, bought the disc for $500. An engineer's services were retained to eliminate the ticking sound made by the nineteen-year-old disc. Following this laborious task, *Bim Bam Boom* released the record on their *Bim Bam Boom* label, selling many copies for $2.50 each!

As soon as the *Bim Bam Boom* reissue appeared, many counterfeits surfaced. These bogus discs were released on various colors of wax. Knowledgeable collectors were aware that the original came out in black only, and not many purchasers were fooled.

In 1977, another copy was found in California.

In a 1998 interview with Clarence Bassett over WFUV at Fordham University, Bassett stated that a Johnny Jackson was also a member, despite all the articles omitting this name.

Discography

Jubilee 5104 Stormy Weather/Sleepy Cowboy (1952)
Sources: Ralph Newman in *Bim Bam Boom* 6; 13; Pete Grendysa in *Goldmine*; Gordon Skadberg and George Povall, liner notes with the Sequel CD *Jubilee/Josie R&B Vocal Groups–4*; Clarence Bassette, inverview by Dan Romanello, July 11, 1998.

Five Sounds, Russ Riley & (New York)

Personnel William "Russ" Riley, Joe Ruff, Leon Carter, Doc Robinson, Charles Blakely

Notes

The Five Sounds were earlier known as the Love Notes, who recorded "Dream Girl" and "Treat Me Right" for Peak/Joyce in 1957.

The liner notes accompanying the *Aljon* Dee Jay Jamboree CD, which was released in 1996, show personnel as Andrew Taylor (lead), Lawrence Campbell (1st tenor), Robert Williamson (2d tenor), Wesley Hazzard (baritone), and Bobby Rivers (bass).

Discography

Aljon 115 Tonight Must Live On/Crazy Feeling (1961)
Source: Liner notes with Dee Jay Jamboree's CD *Brooklyn's Doo Wop Sound.*

Five Stars (Dallas)

Personnel Cal Valentine, Robert Valentine, Al "TNT" Braggs (tenor), Billy Fred Thomas, Jesse Floyd

Notes

This was a Milwaukee-based group that originated in Dallas.

This Five Stars group was also the Five Masks on Jan and the Five Notes on Chess.

Discography

Blues Boys Kingdom 106 So Lonely Baby/Hey Juanita (1957)
Source: Bob Pruter, *Doowop . . . The Chicago Scene.*

Five Stars (Detroit)

Personnel Joseph Murphy, John Raymond Dorsey, Walter Gaines, Crathman "C. P." Spencer, Henry Jones

Notes

This group resulted when the DeLuxe Five Jets broke up and Berry Gordy secured them a recording deal with George Goldner, now at the helm of Mark-X and End. This all took place in 1957.

In mid-1958, the Five Stars became the Voice Masters recording for Anna.

This Five Stars group was not related to the ABC Paramount group or Note, Hunt, Atco, Blues Boys Kingdom, Dot, Kernel, Showtime, or Treat.

Discography

Mark-X 7006 Ooh Shucks (JM)/Dead Wrong (JM) (1957)
End 1028 Blabbermouth (JM/WG)/Baby, Baby (JM) (1958)
Columbia 4-42056 Blabbermouth (JM/WG)/Baby, Baby (JM) (1961)
Source: Marv Goldberg in *DISCoveries,* August 1996.

Five Stars (New York)

Personnel Cleo Perry (lead), William Massey (1st tenor), Clifton Johnson (2d tenor), Barney Fields (baritone), Buster Boyce (bass)

Notes

This group formed in the Bedford-Stuyvesant section of Brooklyn in 1949 while its members were still in high school.

As mentioned in the Inspirators entry, the group began hanging out on Broadway in front of the Brill Building. It was there that they were discovered by Larry Newton, then the general manager for Treat Records.

Their first release, "If Loving You Is Wrong," did not do well and Treat then released "We Danced in the Moonlight" and "Let's Fall in Love." For some reason these two songs were released as by the Five Stars although they were recorded by the Inspirators. According to Bob Hyde's *Old Town Doo Wop-3* CD liner notes, the Five Stars and the Inspirators were the same group. This is also discussed in Marv Goldberg's article in *DISCoveries.* The curious fact here is that no one knows why!

Nothing was happening and in 1958 Newton and Treat struck a deal with Old Town's Hy Weiss and two sides were recorded. Starlight Tonight/Oh What a Feeling was released on Old Town 1053 as by the Inspirators. But nothing happened and the group disintegrated.

Discography

Treat 505 Let's Fall in Love/We Danced in the Moonlight (1955)
Source: Bob Hyde's liner notes with the *Old Town Doo Wop–3* CD.

Five Swans (Berkeley, Calif.)

Personnel Lamont Scott (lead), Delmar Neely (tenor), Phil Shaw (baritone), Curtis Marshall (bass)

Notes

The Five Swans, calling themselves the Swans at their start, made their performing and vocalizing debut while still in junior high school. The fifth member of the Five Swans was George Brown, a nonsinging pianist who accompanied the group.

In an interview, Phil Shaw remarked that both big L.A. R&B 1950s labels, Aladdin and Dootone, approached the group to join them, but Music City's head, Ray Dobard, would not let that take place.

Discography

Music City 795 Lil Girl of My Dreams/Lil Tipa Tina (1956)
Source: Jim Dawson, liner notes with the Earth Angel LP *Music City.*

Five Thrills (Chicago)

Personnel Fred Washington (lead), Gilbert Warren (lead), Obie Washington (2d tenor), Oscar Robinson (baritone), Levi Jenkins (d) (bass)

Notes

This group was formed in 1950, with all of its members coming from the same Chicago neighborhood and elementary school. Fred and Obie Washington were brothers. While in high school and still together, they took some material to various Chicago labels. They recorded material for the United/States organization, nothing was ever released and they moved to Chicago deejay Al Benson's Parrot label, where they finally realized their goal of releasing recordings.

Gilbert Warren, who does lead on "Gloria," later organized and recorded with the Orchids.

Robinson left in early 1954 to join Chicago's Sheppards. He was replaced by Leon Pace.

In producing their CD, the Relic folks found two unreleased sides by the Earls, "LaVerne" and "Darlene (Girl of My Dreams)." Late collector Dave Antrell and another collector, Bob Stallworth, both felt this was the Five Thrills. Stallworth played the two cuts for Levi Jenkins in the 1980s and Jenkins confirmed the fact that this was the Five Thrills, not the Earls.

Before the end of 1954, problems with owner Al Benson caused the dissolution of the group.

Discography

Parrot 796 Feel So Good (FW)/My Baby's Gone (OR) (1953)
Parrot 800 Gloria (GW)/Wee Wee Baby (FW) (1954)
Parrot 803 Girl of My Dreams/LaVerne (recorded as the Earls 1983 in 1954 and released in 1983)
Sources: Donn Fileti, liner notes with the Relic CD *Parrot*; *Record Collector's Monthly,* May 1984; Bob Pruter in *Goldmine.*

Five Tino's (Nashville, Tenn.)

Personnel Luchrie Jordan, Melvin Walker, Marvin Walker, Heywood Hebron, Melvin Jones

Notes

According to reliable sources, the Five Tino's [sic] group is also the Esquires on HiPo and the Teenos on Dub. They met one another at Fisk University.

Discography

Sun 222 Sitting by My Window/Don't Do That! (1955)
Sources: Martin Hawkins, liner notes with the Charly LP *Sun-The Roots of Rock*; Martin Hawkins and Hank Davis, liner notes with the Charly CD *Deep Harmony.*

Five Willows (New York)

Personnel Tony Middleton (lead), Richie Davis (1st tenor), Ralph Martin (2d tenor), Joe Martin (baritone), John Thomas Steele (bass)

Notes

The Five Willows came from 115th Street in Harlem and began singing in 1952. They were on the first Allen record, 1000. It was reviewed in the June 13, 1953, issue of *Billboard.*

The Allen and Pee Dee labels were both owned by Peter Dorain. (According to Pete Grendysa in his September 1988 *Goldmine* article, this is spelled Durain.)

They moved to Herald in 1954. But because Herald paid greater attention to the Nutmegs and Turbans, the Five Willows were not asked back following their two discs.

In 1956, they went with Morty Craft's Melba label and as the Willows recorded "Church Bells May Ring," which was a tremendous success. Interestingly, in his only session with the group, Willows' friend Richie Simon attended the "Church Bells May Ring" session and was the bass on the legendary "Hello, Hello Again, My Friends I Know That We Will Meet Again" lyrics. This had never been rehearsed and Simon never again recorded with the Willows.

Discography

Allen 1000 My Dear Dearest Darling/Rock Little Francis (1953)
Allen 1002 Delores/All Night Long (1953)

Allen 1003 The White Cliffs of Dover/With These Hands (1953)
Pee Dee 290 Love Bells/Please Baby (1954)
Herald 433 Baby, Come a Little Closer/Lay Your Head on My Shoulder (1954)
Herald 442 So Help Me/Look Me in the Eyes (1955)
Source: Tony Middleton, interview by the author, April 1997.

Five Wings (New York)

Personnel Jackie Rue (d) (lead), Billy Carlisle (1st tenor), Frank Edwards (2d tenor), Melvin Flood (baritone), Tommy Grate (bass)

Notes

Jackie Rue (born La Rue) was remembered as something of a mystery man when he was with the Five Wings. The group members were about sixteen or seventeen years old when they started recording as the Five Wings. Rue lived in downtown Manhattan and the others came from the uptown section of the borough.

Tommy Grate and Billy Carlisle later went to the Dubs; Grate also sang with the Vocaltones.

After little success, Rue, Flood, and Edwards left. Edwards was replaced by Kenneth "Butch" Hamilton from the Sonics on Groove and the Bop Chords. On the Five Wings' last session they backed Billy Nelson. Carlisle's cousin, Richard Blandon, was discharged from the service and immediately joined the Five Wings as lead. Little David Baughan took part as well.

The Five Wings split apart at the end of 1955, when Edwards went into the air force and Carlisle and Grate (along with Blandon) were forming the Dubs. Rue went on to form the Starlites.

Discography

King 4778 Johnny Has Gone/Johnny's Still Singing (1955)
King 4781 Rock-a-Locka/Teardrops Are Falling (1955)
Savoy 1183 Walk Along/Pack-Shack-and Stack (w/Billy Nelson) (1956)
King 5199 Rock-a-Locka/Teardrops Are Falling (1959)
Source: Donn Fileti, liner notes with the Relic LP *Jackie and the Starlites.*

Flairs (Los Angeles)

Personnel Cornel Gunter, Beverly Thompson (1st tenor), Thomas "Pete" Fox (2d tenor), Obediah "Young" Jesse (baritone), Richard Berry (bass)

Notes

The Flairs had their beginnings in a Los Angeles High School in 1953 as the Debonaires. Start-up members included Arthur Lee Maye and A. V. Odom, who eventually left and were replaced by Cornel Gunter and Richard Berry.

They auditioned for, and eventually recorded with, John Dolphin's Recorded in Hollywood label. Their first record was released as by the Hollywood Blue Jays. (*Note:* The record "Cloudy and Raining" by the Hollywood Bluejays involves a different group.)

Unhappy with Dolphin, the group moved to Modern Records, where they auditioned for the Bihari brothers. The Biharis liked them and scheduled a first recording session. At that session, they rerecorded "I Had a Love," and their name was now the Flairs—named, of course, after the label.

In one combination or another, the group also recorded under the names of the Hunters, the Whips, Five Hearts, Chimes, Rams, Five Hollywood Blue Jays, and Ermines.

The Flairs were also considered the Flair label's house group.

Richard Berry left in 1953 to pursue a solo act and can be found on the Robins recording of "Riot in Cell Block 11." He later joined forces with three women calling themselves the Dreamers. Thompson left the Flairs shortly after Berry's departure.

In 1956, Cornel Gunter left, forming a new Flairs group (Flares) and joining ABC. They soon departed ABC and went to Loma, where they became the Ermines. Gunter left the Ermines in 1957 to join the Coasters. Vince Weaver, formerly of the Native Boys, joined the Flairs, replacing Gunter. The Flairs at that time were Kenneth Byle (1st tenor and Gunter's cousin), Tommy Miller (baritone), and George Hollis (bass). This was the Flairs group on Buck Ram's Antler label.

Beverly Thompson had departed to form the Five Hearts. Berry's replacement was Randolph Jones (for recording purposes only). Thompson's replacement was Charles Jackson.

In 1956, Berry broke with both groups and got together with Lee Maye and Mel Williams and recorded as the Jayos on Johnny Otis's Dig Records.

Needing cash fast, the Flairs did a session for Tampa records and recorded as the Jac-O-Lacs.

Aaron Collins, 2d tenor of the Jacks/Cadets, sang with the Flairs and Shirley Gunter (Cornel's sister) was with them as well (part-time). Shirley Gunter's presence created dissension among the Flairs and Young Jesse left. Also leaving was Randolph Jones and Pete Fox for the Penguins. Gunter himself left to sing briefly with the Platters.

Berry went on to form the Pharaohs—Berry, Godoy Colbert (1st tenor), Robert Harris (2d tenor), and Noel Collins (baritone).

The group disbanded due to internal conflicts.

Discography

Flair 1012 She Wants to Rock/I Had a Love (1953)
Flair 1019 Tell Me You Love Me/You Should Care for Me (1953)
Flair 1028 Love Me Girl/Gettin' High (1954)
Flair 1041 Baby Wants/You Were Untrue (1954)
Flair 1044 Let's Make with Some Love/I'll Never Let You Go (1955)
Flair 1056 I'll Never Let You Go/Hold Me, Thrill Me, Chill Me (1955)
Flair 1067 She Loves to Dance/My Darling, My Sweet (1955)
Sources: Marv Goldberg and Mike Redmond in *Record Exchanger* 13; Lynn McCutcheon in *Bim Bam Boom* 6; Marv Goldberg and Rick Whitesell in *Yesterday's Memories* 10; Jim Dawson, liner notes with Ace's *Flair Label*.

Flames (Los Angeles)

Personnel David Ford (d), Willie Ray Rockwell (d) (2d tenor), Curley Dinkins (baritone), Robert Byrd (d) (bass)

Notes

This was the original configuration of the Hollywood Flames, who would go on to record under more than ten different names. They originally formed in 1949 at a talent show held in the Largo Theater in Los Angeles and soon were with Johnny Otis. This group recorded for a number of labels (19) under several names: Flames, Four Flames, Hollywood Four Flames, Hollywood Flames, Jets, Ebbtides, and Satellites.

In 1950, the Flames recorded their first single, "Young Girl," with Bobby doing lead. They weren't referred to as the Flames again until they recorded "Strangeland Blues" in 1952 for the Spin label.

When the group went to Aladdin in 1953, Rockwell left and was replaced first by Leon Hughes and then by Gaynel Hodge. Dinkins also left and was replaced by Curtis Williams later of the Penguins.

When Bobby Byrd sang lead, Dinkins moved down to bass.

Patti Ann Mesner joined the group on their Aladdin recordings (*see* Flames, Patti Anne &) and the group was once again called the Flames.

Discography

Selective 113 Please Tell Me Now (BB)/Young Girl (BB) (1950)
Spin 101 Strangeland Blues (WR)/Cryin' for My Baby (BB) (1952)
7–11 2106 Keep On Smiling (DF)/Baby, Baby, Baby (BB) (1953)
7–11 2107 Together (BB)/Pretty Baby (DF) (1953)
Aladdin 3349 So Alone (BB)/Flame Mambo (Patty Anne) (1957)
Sources: Pete Grendysa in *Goldmine*; Bobby Byrd in *Yesterday's Memories* 3; Marv Goldberg in *Yesterday's Memories* 5.

Flames, Patty Anne & (Los Angeles)

Personnel Patty Anne Mesner (lead), David Ford (d) (1st tenor), Leon Hughes (2d tenor), Curley Dinkins (d) (baritone), Robert Byrd (d) (bass)

Notes

Patty Anne was the daughter of Aladdin owner Leo Mesner.

Gaynel Hodge and Clyde Tillis were on Aladdin 3349 replacing Leon Hughes and Curley Dinkins as part of the on-again Flames group.

Discography

Aladdin 3162 My Heart Is Free Again/Midnight (1952)
Aladdin 3198 Sorrowful Heart/Beginning to Miss You (1953)
Aladdin 3280 Shtiggy Boom/Baby, Baby I'm in Love with You (1955)
Aladdin 3349 Flame Mambo (1957)
Sources: Bobby Byrd in *Yesterday's Memories* 3; Marv Goldberg in *Yesterday's Memories* 5.

Flamingos (Chicago)

Personnel Sollie McElroy (d), Johnnny Carter (1st tenor), Zeke Carey (2d tenor), Paul Wilson (baritone), Jake Carey (d) (bass)

Notes

The Carey cousins grew up in Baltimore, down the block from Sonny Til of the Orioles. As youngsters, they played ball with Til, and Zeke's older brother went to high school with him. The cousins moved to Chicago in 1949 or 1950 and in 1952 the Flamingos were born. The 1st tenor, and the Flamingos first lead, was Earl Lewis, who sang with the Flamingos before recording. In an interview with Bob Pruter, Lewis explained his being fired as his own fault—missing rehearsals, spending too much time with girls, religious differences, and so on. Lewis went on to sing with the Five Echoes and was replaced by Sollie McElroy.

Someone who heard the Flamingos singing at a picnic brought them to a night-club, where amateur contests were held. They won these contests and would appear there often.

After high school, the Flamingos went right to their music interest. Jake (the oldest) was just completing college when they were taken to Chicago's United Records for an audition. The members felt they did well, but United management disagreed. About two weeks after their United tryout, they were taken to Chicago's other important R&B label at that time, Chance. About a year after their United rejection the Flamingos cut their first recording for Chance in January 1953: "Someday Someway" and "If I Can't Have You." The rest of their great Chance recordings followed, including the great "Golden Teardrops" (many collectors say that "Golden Teardrops" is sung as a letter written by a junkie to his girlfriend).

According to Jake and Zeke Carey, the Flamingos received no money for any of their Chance recordings! The label was young, operated on a small budget, was understaffed, and kept no records of sales. In addition, funds were not available for promotion—even if they knew how to properly promote a recording. The Careys went on to say that they were in it to impress the girls. They knew nothing about the business and just loved being in front of an audience. During their interview, Jake and Zeke had nothing but nice things to say about Alan Freed.

Art Sheridan's Chance label was not doing well financially. The Flamingos had to be placed with a new label—Al Benson's Parrot Records. They had three great releases for Parrot. On the third Parrot single, Nate Nelson was brought in from Chicago's Velvetones.

Their manager, Ralph Leon, died after working with them for two years. Turmoil set in as group members were forced to learn Leon's various jobs and functions. They learned that he was involved in negotiations with Checker Records when he died.

McElroy later sang with the Moroccos, Nobels, and Chanteurs. He is quoted as saying that he was always uncomfortable with this group as he was the only member who was not Jewish and not related. Johnny Carter went on to sing (and still does) with the Dells. He and Wilson were also cousins. It is interesting that original lead Earl Lewis offers the same religious reasons as his feelings about his leaving, as did McElroy.

"Get with It" on Parrot was led by Nate Nelson, who was now with the Flamingos. Nelson sang lead on this last Parrot disc and later material on Checker. He would eventually become part of the latter-day Platters.

The Flamingos' material on Checker did quite well. "I'll Be Home" sold well despite Pat Boone's cover. "A Kiss from Your Lips" and "Would I Be Crying" also sold well. The group remained intact with Nate Nelson, the Careys, Wilson, and Carter.

When Carter and Zeke Carey were drafted in 1956, members of the Flamingos at that time went their separate ways. In 1957 they regrouped with Nelson, Wilson, Jake Carey, and Tommy Hunt (from the same Five Echoes that Earl Lewis was then with). Hunt had not been with the Five Echoes when he was recruited—he was home in Pittsburgh.

At that time they joined Decca. They recorded ten sides for Decca but were legally obligated to Checker due to Nelson's solo performer contract with Chess/Checker.

In 1958, they signed with George Goldner's End Records in New York. With their success with "I Only Have Eyes for You," Checker, with unissued Flamingos' recordings, released them to capitalize on their End success. None did well.

On End, Tommy Hunt sang lead, replacing Nate Nelson.

Discography

Chance 1133 Someday, Someway/If I Can't Have You (1953)
Chance 1140 That's My Desire/Hurry Home Baby (1953)
Chance 1145 Golden Teardrops/Carried Away (1953)
Chance 1149 Plan for Love/You Ain't Ready (1953)
Chance 1154 Cross Over the Bridge/Listen to My Plea (1954)
Chance 1162 Blues in the Letter/Jump Children (1954)
Parrot 808 Dream of a Lifetime/On My Merry Way (1954)
Parrot 811 I Really Don't Want to Know/Get with It (1954)
Parrot 812 I'm Yours/Ko Ko Mo (1954)
Checker 815 When/That's My Baby (1955)
Checker 821 Please Come Back Home/I Want to Love You (1955)
Checker 830 I'll Be Home/Need Your Love (1956)
Checker 837 A Kiss from Your Lips/Get with It (1956)
Checker 846 The Vow/Shilly Dilly (1956)
Checker 853 Would I Be Crying?/Just for a Kick (1956)
Decca 30335 The Ladder of Love/Let's Make Up (1957)
Decca 30454 Helpless/My Faith in You (1957)
Decca 30687 Where Mary Go/The Rock and Roll March (1958)
End 1035 Lovers Never Say Goodbye/That Love Is You (1958)
Decca 30944 Jerri-Lee/Hey Now! (1959)
End 1040 But Not for Me/I Shed a Tear at Your Wedding (1959)
End 1044 Love Walked In/At the Prom (1959)
End 1046 I Only Have Eyes for You/Goodnight Sweetheart (1959)
End 1046 I Only Have Eyes for You/At the Prom (2d issue) (1959)
End 1055 Yours/Love Walked In (1959)
End 1062 I Was Such a Fool/Heavenly Angel (1959)
End 1065 Mio Amore/You, Me, and the Sea (1960)

End 1068 Nobody Loves Me Like You/You, Me, and the Sea (1960)
End 1070 Besame Mucho/You, Me, and the Sea (1960)
End 1073 Mio Amore/At Night (1960)
End 1079 When I Fall in Love/Beside You (1960)
End 1081 Your Other Love/Lovers Gotta Cry (1960)
End 1085 That's Why I Love You/Kokomo (1961)
End 1092 Time Was/Dream Girl (1961)
End 1099 My Memories of You/I Want to Love You (1961)
End 1111 It Must Be Love/I'm No Fool Anymore (1961)
End 1116 For All We Know/Near You (1962)
End 1121 Flame of Love/I Know Better (1962)
End 1124 True Love/Come on to My Party (1962)
Checker 915 Dream of a Lifetime/Whispering Stars (1959)
Checker 1084 Lover Come Back to Me/Your Little Guy (1964)
Checker 1091 Goodnight Sweetheart/Does It Really Matter? (1964)
End 1046 I Only Have Eyes for You/Love Walked In (3d issue) (1966)
Sources: L. Carl Tancredi, "The Flamingos: The Early Years," *Bim Bam Boom* 4;
Jerry Diez in *R&B Collector*; Bob Pruter in *Goldmine,* May 1979.

Flares (Los Angeles)

Personnel Aaron Collins, Willie Davis (1st tenor), Beverly Harris (2d tenor),
Thomas Miller (baritone), George Hollis (bass)

Notes
This was Buck Ram's Flares group, which formed in 1959.

Hollis had been with the Flairs and the Ermines. Aaron Collins and Willie Davis
had been with the Jacks/Cadets.

Patience Valentine, Betty Williams, Randy Jones, Eddie King, and Robbie
Robinson were other members of the Flares.

Discography
Felsted 8604 Loving You/Hot Cha-Cha Brown (1960)
Felsted 8607 Jump and Bump/What Do You Want If You (1960)
Felsted 8624 Footstompin' (1961)
Press 2800 Rock 'n' Roll Heaven—Pt. 1/Pt. 2 (1962)
Press 2802 Doing the Hully Gully/Truck and Trailer (1962)
Press 2803 Make It Be Me/Mad House (1962)
Press 2807 Do It with Me/Yon He Go (1963)
Press 2808 Shimmy and Stomp/Hand Clapping (1963)
Press 2810 Do It If You Wanna/The Monkey Walk (1963)
Press 2814 I Didn't Lose a Doggone Thing/Write a Song about Me (1964)
Source: Jim Dawson, liner notes with the *Jacks/Cadets* CD on Ace.

Flips, Joey & (Philadelphia)

Personnel Joseph Hall (d), Fred Gerace (1st tenor), James Meagher (d) (2d tenor),
John Smith (baritone), Jeff Leonard (bass), Jimmy Dilks (falsetto)

Notes

This group began in 1959 in Upper Darby, Pennsylvania, harmonizing in the familiar places that made groups sound great—hallways, restrooms, and so on.

Sy Kaplan, who later became their manager, overheard them harmonizing. He was joined by Barry Rich, another collector, and soon after had them record demo tapes. Kaplan felt that original lead Jimmy Dilks was not unique enough and was replaced at lead by diminutive (5 feet) black Joseph Hall.

Rich and Kaplan brought "Bongo Stomp" to Eddie Joy of Joy Records to see if he was satisfied with the Flips song. Joy loved it and soon released it on his label. When the tune began to take off, the Flips began touring up and down the East Coast.

As the story usually goes, Joy and his organization, despite inquiries and litigation, paid the Flips or their management no royalties. Their ensuing releases did poorly. Fortunately, the success of "Bongo Stomp" provided work for the group, including commercials and so on, but personal problems prevailed and after their Cameo disc, they decided to call it quits. Hall, a diabetic, went into insulin shock and died in 1974.

Discography

Joy 262 Bongo Stomp/Lost Love (1962)
Joy 268 Bongo Gully/It Was Like Heaven (1962)
Cameo 327 Fool, Fool, Fool/The Beachcomber (1964)
Source: Bob Bosco in *Record Collector's Monthly* 50.

Flyers (Baltimore, Md.)

Personnel Bobby Hendricks (lead), Dee Ernie Bailey (2d tenor), Billy Kennedy (baritone), Bill Pinkney (bass)

Notes

Following a forced departure from the Drifters in 1956, Bill Pinkney formed the Flyers.

Bobby Hendricks also sang with the Swallows, Drifters, and Original Drifters. Pinkney of course sang with both the Drifters and the Original Drifters. Dee Ernie Bailey spent time with the Swallows on King, Federal, and After Hours. Hendricks went on to later record "Itchy Twitchy Feeling."

They did one recording session for Atco and stayed together for about a year. After this period, they were taken back by the Drifters only to be severed again when Drifters manager George Treadwell put the R&B Five Crowns in place as the new Drifters.

Discography

Atco 6058 My Only Desire/On Bended Knee (1957)
Source: Pete Grendysa, liner notes with the Atlantic CDs *All Night Boogie* and *Don't It Sound Good.*

Fortunes (Chicago)

Personnel Donald Jenkins, Ronnie Strong (tenor), Walter Granger (baritone), William Taylor (bass)

Notes

The Fortunes were an unreleased group who recorded for Parrot. They later cut several sides for Chess (see below) that were not as good as the Parrot cuts but were released. They had won a talent contest in which the prize they were awarded was a recording contract. The Parrot sides, now released, were "Love" and "Bread."

Discography

Parrot (UNR) Love/Bread
Checker 818 My Baby Is Fine/Believe in Me (1955)
Source: Bob Pruter, liner notes with the Relic CD *Best of Parrot.*

Foster Brothers (Evanston, Ill.)

Personnel Laverne Gales (lead), Donald Clay (1st tenor), Lindsay Langston (2d tenor), George Lattimore (bass)

Notes

Clay formed the group in the late 1930s as the gospel quartet the Four Harmonizers.

Gems lead tenor Ray Pettis also sang for the Foster Brothers who recorded for Drexel. He replaced original lead LaVerne Gales. Pettis was the lead singer on four of their records.

They were called the Foster Brothers because they had always called Langston's mother mama. They therefore considered themselves to be foster brothers.

The group was composed of middle-aged men when they made their first recording in 1957. They called it quits in 1961.

Discography

Mercury 71360 If You Want My Heart/Show Me (1958)
Profile 4004 Trust in Me/Why-Yi-Yi (1958)
Hi Mi 3005 I Could Cry/Never Again (1958)
B&F 1333 Revenge/Pretty Fickle Woman (1960)
Dillie 101 Land of Love/Let's Jam (1960)
Source: Bob Stallworth in *Yesterday's Memories* 6.

Four Aces (Fort Worth, Tex.)

Personnel James Ruben Franks, Otha Jackson, Algia Pickett, George Smith

Notes

The members of this group were originally from Fort Worth, Texas, and met in 1944. Before recording, they moved to California, settling in Oakland. Pickett's first name is pronounced Algee, as ascertained in a March 1998 interview by Marv Goldberg.

Like most groups of their time period, they were a self-contained ensemble, playing instruments as well as harmonizing vocally.

Other names associated with the black Four Aces were Orvan "Leroy" Lyles, David McCauley, Robert Parker, and Charles Holmes.

When the white Four Aces became popular, this group began calling themselves the Original Four Aces and recorded for the Big Town label. Because they recorded with another name, the discussion of the Four Aces will stop here.

Discography

Trilon 143 I Wonder, I Wonder, I Wonder/I Wonder, I Wonder, I Wonder (instrumental) (1946)
Trilon 144 Garbage Man (GS)/Put Your Cards on the Table (JF) (1946)
Trilon 145 There's a Rumor Going Around (AP)/St. Louis Boogie (instrumental) (1947)
Trilon 153 Richard Ain't Gonna Open That Door (GS)/Richard's Jam (instrumental) (1947)
Trilon 178 Cherie (JF)/I'll Never Let You Go Again (AP) (1947)
Trilon 179 I'm Crying All the Time (JF)/This Little Chick Went to Market (GS) (1947)
Trilon 180 Ain't It a Cryin' Shame (GS)/Gumbo (GS) (1947)
Four Star 1292 Lazy Navajo (all)/Aces Swing (all) (1949)
Four Star 1324 Too Late (AP)/Jumpin' Out (JF) (1949)
Four Star 1408 Who Is There to Blame? (OJ)/Because I'm in Love with You (1949)
Sources: Bob Ferlingere, *Discography of R&B* and *R&R Vocal Groups*; George Moonoogian, *Echoes of the Past,* August 11, 1997; interview by Marv Goldberg in *DISCoveries,* March 1998.

Four Bars (Washington, D.C.)

Personnel Alfonso Feemster (1st tenor), Melvin Butler (2d tenor), Francis Henry (baritone), Eddie Daye (bass)

Notes

Originally known as the Four Bars of Rhythm, Daye and Butler met in the army. Following their discharge in 1953, they teamed up with friends Alfonso Feemster and Francis Henry. Henry had been with the Rainbows briefly.

Deborah Chessler wanted to manage the Four Bars and bring them to Jubilee, but the Orioles denied her this pursuit. The group's first release however, was on Josie, as were their next two. After these failed, they obtained their release from Josie. Two years later, they began recording for a succession of labels: Cadillac, Len Records, Dayco (Eddie Daye's label), IPS from Detroit, Flying Hawk, and Shelley. Later they were also with Falew and Shrine.

They cut records for many labels over the next ten years. While they were at Cadillac Records, Henry was replaced by Eddie Daye's brother, William. By the time they got to Len, William was replaced by Ellsworth Grimes.

First tenor Otis Grissette replaced Feemster. In the 1960s, Betty Wilson replaced Grissette.

In 1967 Eddie Daye opened a nightclub and gave less time and attention to the group. They disbanded when roadwork became impossible, since Daye's job kept him in the D.C. vicinity.

Discography
Joz 762 Grief by Day, Grief by Night (ED)/Hey Baby (AF) (1954)
Joz 768 If I Give My Heart to You (ED/AF)/Stop It, Quit It (AF) (1954)
Joz 783 Let Me Live (MB)/Why Do You Treat Me This Way? (MB) (1954)
Joz UNR How You Move Me/Grandpa's Inn (1954)
IPS 101 I'm So Helpless/Follow Me (1959)
Time 4 Why Did You Do It?/Phoney Baloney (1959)
Cadillac 2006 Love Me Forever More (MB)/What's on Your Mind? (ED) (1960)
Len 1014 Just Bid Me Farewell (ED)/This Game of Romance (ED) (1960)
Dayco 101 Try Me One More Time (ED)/Comin' On Home (ED) (1962)
Falew 108 I've Got to Move (ED)/Waitin' on the Right Guy (BW) (1965)
Shrine Guess Who Loves You (all)/What Am I Going to Do (ED) (1965)
Dayco Anything to Please My Man (BW)/If I Had to Do It All (1965)
Dayco 2500 Stay On My J.O.B. (ED)/Poor Little Me (all) (1965)
Dayco 4564 Why I've Got to Know/Lean on Me When Heartaches Get . . . (1967)
Dayco 1631 I'm Yours (BW)/All Over Again (BW) (1967)
Sources: Donn Fileti, liner notes with the Relic CD *Len*; Marv Goldberg and Rick Whitesell in *Yesterday's Memories* 11.

Four Bel-Aires (Washington, D.C.)

Personnel Vernon Ricks, Warren Ricks, Albert Robinson, Robert Russell

Notes
The Four Bel-Aires met while working together in a church kitchen. The two Ricks were cousins.

They practiced and eventually recorded a demo, encouraged by deejay Al Jefferson, which was sent to X-Tra Records in New York. X-Tra management was greatly pleased with their demo and a disc was released as X-Tra 111 in 1959, Where Are You/Tell Me Why.

They chose "Where Are You" because they loved the Mello-Moods recording of that tune. This recording was their only release.

Discography
X-Tra 113 Where Are You?/Tell Me Why (1958)
Sources: James Cullinan and Donn Fileti, liner notes with the Finbarr CD *$10,000 Worth of Doo Wop*; Alan Lee in *Yesterday's Memories* 8.

Four Blackbirds (Los Angeles)

Personnel David Patillo, Geraldine Harris (tenor), Leroy Hurte (baritone), Richard Davis (bass)

Notes

All members attended and met at Jefferson High School in Los Angeles and were brought together by Leon René to record in the early 1930s.

Hurte and Patillo both sang with the Jones Boys Sing Band.

Patillo also sang with the Four Toppers and the Red Caps.

Discography

Vocalion Dixie Rhythm (1934)

Source: Doug Seroff and Ray Funk, liner notes with the *Human Orchestra* LP.

Four Blazers (Hollywood, Calif.)

Personnel Ulysses Livingston, George Crawford, LeGrand Mason, Connie Jordan

Notes

This group formed in 1944 as the Hollywood Four Blazes.

They recorded for Melodisc as the Four Blazers and for Lamplighter and Excelsior as the Hollywood Four Blazes.

Discography

Melodisc 1009 Let's Boogie/That's All She Wrote Cause the Pencil Broke
Melodisc 1010 Chicago Boogie/All the Things You Are
Melodisc 1011 Snogqualimie Jo Jo/Jack, You Just Ain't Booted
Source: Pete Grendysa, liner notes with the Country Routes CD *Man That's Groovy.*

Four Blazes (Chicago)

Personnel Ernest Harper, William Shorty Hill, Paul Lindsley Holt, Floyd McDaniel (d)

Notes

Eddie Chamblee, Tommy Braden (lead), and Prentice Butler were later members. The group was also known as the Blazes.

Floyd McDaniel died in 1995 at the age of eighty.

In 1955 they appeared in Cleveland as the Five Blazes with Tommy Braden doing lead.

Discography

United 114 Mood Indigo/Mary Jo (1952)
United 125 Night Train/Rug Cutter (1952)
United 127 Please Send Her Back to Me/Stop Boogie Woogie (1952)
United 146 Not Any More Tears/My Hat's on the Side of My Head (1953)
United 158 Ella Louise/Perfect Women (1953)
United 168 My Great Love Affair/All Night Long (1954)
United 177 Do the Do/Did You Ever See a Monkey Do the Monkey (1954)
She Needs to Be Loved (1955)
Source: Unsigned liner notes with the CD *Rare Windy City Vocal Groups–3.*

Four Bluejackets (Dayton, Ohio)

Personnel Bill Bryant, Doc Bryant, Joe Bryant, Toby Bryant

Notes

The Bryants were all brothers who had enlisted in the navy together. They started to be noticed while they were in the service. They met arranger/pianist Elmer Thomas, who helped them along.

They got great publicity through the navy by appearing around the country in naval hospitals and other service facilities.

They were all honorably discharged in 1946 and signed by the new, independent label—Mercury. They recorded and released four cuts in a year. Following this, they disappeared! Besides their recordings, the only legacy remaining is a rare picture sleeve with their photograph.

Discography

Mercury 8004 Moses Smote the Water/Rock-a-My Soul (1946)
Mercury 8017 Baby, Baby Please Come Home/I Know Who Threw the Whiskey in the Well (1946)
Mercury 8019 Rip, Somebody Done Snagged Their Britches/Little David and I (1946)
Mercury 8031 Jezebel/Weep No More My Children (1947)
Source: George Moonoogian in *Record Collector's Monthly* 45.

Four Blues (Philadelphia)

Personnel Earl Plummer, Arthur Davey, Carroll Jones (bass)

Notes

The Four Blues assembled in Philadelphia and first began recording for Decca. They had two releases for Decca and then switched to the young DeLuxe label in 1945.

The Four Blues recorded both religious and secular music. When recording religious music, they were known as the Golden Echo Quartet.

Plummer was in Steve Gibson's Red Caps and Romaine Brown's Romaines. Arthur Davey also wound up with the Red Caps.

Discography

Decca 8517 Easy Does It/Jitterbug Sadie (1941)
Decca 8637 Bluer Than Bluer Than Blue/Honey Chile (1942)
DeLuxe 1000 Bell-Bottom Trousers/I'm Gone (1945)
DeLuxe 1001 Baby, I Need a Whole Lot of Everything/Chittlins and Pig's Feet (1945)
DeLuxe 1002 Daddy Please Bring That Suitcase In/Things You Want Most (1945)
DeLuxe 1003 I Couldn't Hear Nobody Pray/I Got a Date with Rhythm (1945)
DeLuxe 1004 The Blues Can Jump/When the Old Gang's Back on the Corner (1945)
DeLuxe 1005 Study War No Mo/Noah and the Ark (1945)
DeLuxe 3195 The Blues Can Jump/Am I Asking Too Much? (1948)

Apollo 398 It Takes a Long Tall Brownskinned Girl/Honey Chile (1948)
Apollo 1145 Re-Bo-De-Boom/The Vegetable Song (1950)
Apollo 1160 Missing You/As Long as I Live (1950)
Source: Ray Funk and Marv Goldberg, liner notes with the Relic LP *Goodbye 1940s, Hello 1950s.*

Four Buddies (Baltimore, Md.)

Personnel Leon "Larry" Harrison (d), Greg Carroll (2d tenor), Vernon "Bert" Palmer (d) (baritone), Tommy Smith (bass)

Notes

John Greg Carroll and Larry Harrison were childhood friends in Baltimore. Carroll's older brother, Charlie, had been with the Cats and the Fiddle and the Buds, and music played an important role in their early life. The Orioles, originally the Vibra-Naires, came from the same part of the city and had been friends of Harrison's and Carroll's.

In 1949 they decided to form a vocal group calling themselves the Metronomes with William Duffy and Maurice Hicks. Following a great deal of practice, they were hired by radio station WITH for a fifteen-minute show each Saturday.

In 1950, Johnny Otis came to Baltimore with a show of his. One of the stars of the show was Little Esther. Savoy president Herman Lubinsky learned of her appearance and, as she was on the East Coast, came to Baltimore and had a recording session with her. Lubinsky needed a backing vocal group and the Metronomes were chosen (Savoy 750; the group credited on the label was the Beltones).

Following this episode, Harrison and Carroll voiced an opinion to further their vocal careers. At the same time, Savoy contacted them and invited them to come to New York for a session. Hicks and Duffy chose to remain in Baltimore and were replaced by Vernon "Bert" Palmer and William "Tommy" Carter. After weeks of practice, the four ventured to New York. In October 1950, they recorded "Just to See You Smile Again," "I Will Wait," "Why at a Time Like This" and "Don't Leave Me Now" for Savoy.

The group's name was changed to either the Four Buddies or the Buds. The Four Buddies was chosen but not in time for the release of their first record. Thus "Just to See You Smile Again" has some releases with the Buds and others with the Four Buddies. At this time too the group was temporarily being managed by Brown University football star and producer of the 1955 R&B film *Rockin' the Blues* Fritz Pollard.

In 1951 Vernon Palmer recorded with Savoy's Falcons, hoping that something big might come of the endeavor. Unfortunately for Palmer, nothing positive came out of this attempt at stardom and he rejoined the Four Buddies.

In April 1952 Tommy Carter left and original Metronome Maurice Hicks replaced him. The next month, Palmer left and was replaced by Joseph Walker. This did not work out, and Walker was replaced by Alvin Bowen.

Appearances and recordings diminished and in May 1953, Greg Carroll left to join Sonny Til and the Orioles. Carroll was with the Orioles on "Crying in the Chapel." He was there for a few years before leaving to form the Dappers, who recorded for Groove and Rainbow.

Later Harrison formed his own group, the Buddies on Glory, and recorded some sides with them in 1954. With Maurice Hicks returning, this group would soon record as the Barons on Decca.

Discography

Savoy 769 I Will Wait/Just to See You Smile Again (1950)
Savoy 779 Sweet Slumber/Don't Leave Me Now (1951)
Savoy 789 My Summer's Gone/Why at a Time Like This? (1951)
Savoy 817 Heart and Soul/ (It's No) Sin (1951)
Savoy 823 Simply Say Goodbye/Window Eyes (1951)
Savoy 845 You're Part of Me/Story Blues (1952)
Savoy 866 What's the Matter with Me?/Sweet Tooth for My Baby (1952)
Savoy 888 My Mother's Eyes/Ooh Ow (1953)
Savoy 891 I'd Climb the Highest Mountain (1953)
Savoy unreleased: Moonlight in Your Eyes, I'm Yours, Close to You, Stop Your Hittin' on Me, You Left Me Blue, I Love You, Yes I Do, Got Everything but You, It Could Have Been Me
Sources: Marv Goldberg and Mike Redmond in *Record Exchanger* 12; Marv Goldberg, liner notes with the Savoy CD *Four Buddies . . . Complete on Savoy*; Pete Grendysa, liner notes with the Bear Family CD boxed set *Orioles*.

Four Buddies (Chicago)

Personnel Ularsee Manor, Nathaniel "Sam" Hawkins (tenor), Jimmy Hawkins (tenor), Dickie Umbra (baritone), Willie Bryant (bass)

Notes

This group was formed in 1952, most of the members attending the same two high schools. They rehearsed and practiced for two years and played many local clubs and church functions during that prerecording period.

Jimmy and Sam Hawkins were cousins and despite the name Four Buddies, the group appeared as a quintet. Only when they started to record was the name Four Buddies used more frequently. It is believed that Club 51 did this to capitalize on the name Four Buddies (Savoy). It also explains why their photo shows five members and calls them the Four Buddies.

They had tenor Donald Ventors replacing Sam Hawkins. Soon after this, Ventors was replaced by Irving Hunter.

In 1956, they finally recorded their total output for Club 51; however, most of their work was as backup for single artists Rudy Greene ("You Mean So Much to Me") and Bobby James ("I Need You So").

Lack of success led to disillusionment, disinterest, and eventual breakup.

Discography

Club 51 103 You Mean Everything to Me (Rudy Greene)/Highway No. 1 (Rudy Greene)
Club 51 104 I Need You So/Baby I'm Tired (Bobby James)
Club 51 105 Delores (UM/JH)/Look Out (UM)
Source: Bob Pruter, *Doowop . . . The Chicago Scene.*

Four Dates (Philadelphia)

Personnel Johnny (October) Ottobre, Eddie Gentile, Pat Marioni (baritone), Ernie Spano (bass)

Notes

The Four Dates began in high school in 1956 as the Mel-tones, playing many local nightspots. Ironically, they did a show in nearby New Jersey during which Frankie Avalon backed them on trumpet. Of course, the irony was due to the fact that in a few short years, they would back Avalon as the Four Dates. It was about that time that Johnny Ottobre (October) joined, replacing one of the original members from high school.

Ottobre was buddies with the owners of the new Chancellor label in Philadelphia. One of the owners did not care for their name. Because each member was born in June, the name Four Dates was created and they were off to a New York studio to record "I'm Happy" and "Eloise" in 1957.

Without any label credit, they provided backing vocals for Frankie Avalon on his "Gingerbread." In the meantime, their "I'm Happy" was doing well, and they were asked to appear on Dick Clark's Saturday night ABC show.

Although they received no royalties for any of their three Chancellor recordings, they were treated very well by label management. Wardrobe changes, good hotel accommodations, meals, gas, and so on, were all provided.

Their second Chancellor effort, "Hey Roly Poly" (a tune penned by Jerry Ragavoy) and "I Say Babe," was released in 1958. It was also at this time that they started backing both Avalon and Fabian at live appearances.

The third Chancellor disc for the Four Dates was Teenage Neighbor/I Feel Good, also released in 1958. But Chancellor management was heavily concentrating on Frankie Avalon and Fabian, and thus no promotion dollars were allocated to any Four Dates discs. Following the third release, Ottobre disappeared. He and Spano would later join the Four Js in the early 1960s, who by then were known as the Fabulous Four.

Following the group's breakup, the remaining members backed up Avalon and Fabian in 1958 and 1959.

Discography

Chancellor 1014 I'm Happy/Eloise (1957)
Chancellor 1019 I Say Babe/Hey Roly Poly (1958)
Chancellor 1027 Teenage Neighbor/I Feel Good (1958)
Source: Bob Bosco in *Echoes of the Past* 38.

Four Deeptones (New Jersey)

Personnel Calvin Williams (lead), George Vereen (1st tenor), Furman Hayes (2d tenor), Fletcher Smith (baritone), Carroll Dean (bass)

Notes

The Four Deeptones were previously known, and recorded, as the Deep Tones (for Muzicon) in 1946 and as the Original Kings of Harmony (King Solomon) in 1948.

Although the group most often consisted of five individuals, beginning in 1951 they became known as the Four Deep Tones (for reasons unknown).

Ivy Floyd replaced Fletcher Smith. Following the cool reception to their Coral recordings, they changed their name to the HiLiters and recorded for HiCo.

George Vereen periodically began filling in for Four Knights' lead Gene Alford who was ailing. He filled in for concert dates and some recordings.

In the early 1950s, Williams toured with the Four Knights and an Ink Spots group.

Calvin Williams replaced Clyde Wright in the Golden Gate Quartet in 1971.

Discography

Coral 65061 Castle Rock/Just in Case You Change Your Mind (1950)
Coral 65062 The Night You Said Goodbye/When the Saints Go Marching In (1950)
Source: Pete Grendysa in *Goldmine,* May 8, 1987.

Four Deuces (Salinas, Calif.)

Personnel Luther McDaniel (a.k.a. Lord Luther), Jim Dunbar (1st tenor), Orvis Lee Teamer (baritone), Henry Shufford (bass)

Notes

This group met in 1954, when all but McDaniel were stationed at Fort Ord, California. They had met at a club about ten miles from the army base and this is where they began singing.

A friend advised them to go to Berkeley to Ray Dobard's Music City recording studio and they did. The title "W-P-L-J" comes from the group's favorite drink at that time—white port and lemon juice. "W-P-L-J" turned out to be Music City's biggest hit.

Despite the success of that tune, and the Italian Swiss Colony Wine jingle that came from it, Luther McDaniel stated that he never received a penny in royalties, nothing for writing the song and nothing for the group, even though it was they who did the commercial for Italian Swiss. Not one of the members ever received a thing.

First tenor Walter Simpson was also a member, as was Carl Williams.

Discography

Music City 790 W-P-L-J/Here Lies My Love (1955)
Music City 796 Down It Went/Goose Is Gone (1956)
Source: Jim Dawson, liner notes with the Earth Angel LP *Music City.*

Four Dots (Washington, D.C./Baltimore, Md.)

Personnel George Harris (lead), Rudolph Harris (tenor), Floyd Bennett (baritone), Wilbert Beal

Notes

This group formed in 1950 in the D.C./Baltimore area.

Larry "Lucky" Green, who appeared with the Four Dots, had also been with the Heartbreakers.

Tenor Rudolph Harris also sang with the Four Dots on Dot.
Wilbert Beal joined the Four Dots later.

Discography

Dot 1043 My Dear/You Won't Let Me Go (1951)
Source: Ron Bartolucci, liner notes with the Eagle CD *D.C. Doo Wops.*

Four Dots (Pittsburgh, Pa.)

Personnel Fletcher Williams (lead), Melvin Peters (2d tenor), Kenny Miller (baritone), Marvin Brown (bass)

Notes

The Four Dots began around 1952 as the Mellows and at that time did a great deal of a cappella. In 1955, after practicing relentlessly and sustaining many personnel changes, their manager suggested that they change their name to the Four Dots.

Following their two Bullseye recordings, the group felt the name Four Dots had run its course, and they changed it to the Four Troys. The group recorded one record for the Freedom label as the Four Dots.

Manny Rosemond, who had made appearances with the Four Dots, resurrected the name soon after the first group abandoned it and a second group was born. The lead was Jerry Stone (sometimes Jewel Akens) and 1st tenor was Ike Perry. Rosemond was the 2d tenor and Branch Johnson was the bass. This group too recorded for the Freedom label.

Ike Perry later sang with the Lyrics. Rumors abound that Rosemond and Johnson sang with the Lyrics as well.

In 1965, Jewel Akens recorded "The Birds and the Bees" for the Era label.

Discography

Bullseye 103 Rita/He-Man Looking for a She-Girl (1956)
Bullseye 104 Kiss Me Sugar Plum/Peace of Mind (1956)
Source: Carl Janusek in *Echoes of the Past* 32.

Four Dukes (Brooklyn, N.Y.)

Personnel Billy Dawn Smith, Donny Myles (a.k.a. Donny Schested) (tenor), Tommy Smith (baritone), Sonny Benton (bass)

Notes

This group formed in the late 1940s in the Crown Heights section of Brooklyn, where the members all went to high school. After practicing day after day, a man they knew as Homes [sic], who had a record shop on 124th Street in Harlem, took them there, and across the street from his shop was Decatur Records. He brought them to Decatur, whose management liked the group and had them record a tune they had been holding for the right artist. This turned out to be the Billy Dawn Quartet and the song was "This Is the Real Thing Now."

Their manager, Joel Turnero (who had formerly managed the Mellomoods), was responsible for their next move to Don Robey's Duke Records, where they were billed as the Mighty Dukes and then the Four Dukes. Turnero and the group parted ways in 1954.

The next move was to Herald Records, where their name was changed to the Heralds. While they were with Herald, Billy Dawn Smith was their A&R man. In 1956 the group began to fall apart because Smith became too busy to pay adequate attention to the group.

Smith soon became a co-owner of the Hull label with William Miller and Blanche Bea Caslon, a former secretary at Herald.

Discography

Duke 116 Crying in the Chapel (DS)/I Done Done It (BDS) (1953)
Sources: Marv Goldberg and Rick Whitesell in *Yesterday's Memories* 12; Sal Mondrone, "Rare Sounds," *Bim Bam Boom* 7.

Four El Dorados (Chicago)

Personnel Marvin Smith, Jewel Jones (1st tenor), Louis Bradley (2d tenor), James Maddox (baritone)

Notes

Because they had no hit record in eighteen months and had problems with Vee Jay, the remaining El Dorados broke up late in 1957 following "A Rose for My Darling."

The three remaining El Dorados located a new lead, Marvin Smith (from an existing Chicago gospel group).

With Jewel Jones as their leader-spokesman, they secured a contact with Chicago's Academy Records, and Academy 8138 was released in 1958. Obviously, for legal reasons, they called themselves The Four El Dorados. The Academy record however, did nothing.

Looking for new performing deals, the group went to California later in 1958. Jones had gotten married and he was going to live there. In California, things did not work out and the group, in order to make some money, cut a record for the Rhythm Records people called "A Lonely Boy" as the Tempos. But it did nothing, and they returned to Chicago in 1961. Soon after returning home, the group broke up.

Discography

Academy 8138 A Lonely Boy/Got Little Susie (1958)
Source: Bob Pruter, *Doowop . . . The Chicago Scene.*

Four Epics (Philadelphia)

Personnel Mickey Neil, Jack McKnight, Jimmy Mullin, Rich Lally

Notes

The Four Epics sang for the Laurie organization as well as for Cameo. They also did work at Heritage Records in New York.

At Cameo they were the label's backup group, performing behind Chubby Checker, the Dovells, the Dreamlovers, and so on.

Discography

Heritage 109 I'm On My Way to Love/When the Music Ends (1962)
Laurie 3155 Again/I Love You Diane (1963)
Laurie 3183 How I Wish That I Was Single Again/Dance Joe Anne (1963)
Source: Ed Engel, liner notes with the Ace CD *Laurie Vocal Groups.*

Four-Evers (Philadelphia)

Personnel Jackie Jacobs (lead), Paul Verdi (tenor), Alex Barbadora (2d tenor), Dominick Andrachio (baritone)

Notes

This group initially formed in 1960. After a great deal of practice and patience, the Four-Evers auditioned for the manager of deejay Jerry Blavat, who thought they were great. Fate unfortunately didn't see it that way and they had to wait until March 1963 before a recording of theirs was produced and released on Philadelphia's Jamie label.

Prior to the release, there was no South Street dance in existence and when the disc began to take off, a dance was invented.

The disc did nothing more than good sales in Philadelphia and the group, like others before and after them, disappeared. This Four-Evers have no connection to any other Four-Evers, Four Evers, 4 Evers, or Forevers group.

Discography

Jamie 1247 One More Time/Everybody South Street (1963)
Sources: Bob Hyde and Bob Bosco, liner notes with the Jamie/Guyden CD *Doop Doo Wah*; Jeff Kreiter, *Group Collector's Record Guide*; Bob Bosco in *Echoes of the Past* 40.

Four Fellows (Brooklyn, N.Y.)

Personnel Jimmy McGowan (lead), Milton Bennett (tenor), David Jones (tenor), Larry Banks (baritone)

Notes

The Four Fellows originally got together in the late 1940s in Brooklyn singing gospel songs on local street corners and neighborhood churches. In 1951, they began singing pop. They appeared locally as the Four Toppers at a local benefit appearance in 1952.

While all this was happening, McGowan had been stabbed in 1951 and was hospitalized several times during the next few years. He had originally wanted to be a baseball player, but this was now impossible.

Personnel changes occurred in the group almost every day. Jimmy Beckum of the Majors on Derby, and later the Harptones, was one of the changes, but because he always missed rehearsals, he was replaced. The group was now called the Schemers.

The group's manager, Jimmy Johnson, gave them their name—the Four Fellows. Johnson got them many appearances on local TV as well as their only recording for Derby Records (I Tried/Bend of the River), which went nowhere. As a result, they got a new manager—Teddy Conyers.

Conyers got them a contract with Glory and the Four Fellows was Glory's first artist. While their first cut for Glory was a bomb, "Soldier Boy" came soon and was a hit, the start of a great string of recordings.

Jones also sang for the Rays. Despite the rumors, Harold Miller of the Rays, never recorded or sang with the Four Fellows—he sang with the original formation of the Four Fellows then known as the Four Toppers, in 1953 and only practiced with the Four Fellows.

Jimmy Mobley replaced David Jones in 1956.

Following Mobley and Banks' departure, Gordon Payne (d) replaced Banks at baritone and Alvin Scott took Mobley's place. In addition, Pringle Sims, from the Strangers, sang tenor for the later Four Fellows.

Discography

Derby 862 I Tried (JM)/Bend of the River (DJ) (1954)
Glory 231 I Wish I Didn't Love You So/I Know Love (1955)
Glory 234 Soldier Boy/Take Me Back, Baby (1955)
Glory 236 Angels Say/In the Rain (1955)
Glory 238 Fallen Angel/Hold 'Em Joe (1956)
Glory 241 Petticoat Baby/I'm Past Sixteen (1956)
Glory 242 Darling You/Please Don't Deprive Me of Love (1956)
Glory 244 Please Play My Song/I Sit in My Window (1956)
Glory 248 You Don't Know Me/You Sweet Girl (1956)
Glory 250 Loving You, Darling/Give Me Back My Broken Heart (1957)
Source: Jim McGowan, *Hear Today, Here to Stay.*

Four Fellows (Brooklyn, N.Y.)

Personnel Cas Bridges (lead), Bobby Thompson (tenor), Roy ———, Bill Carey (baritone)

Notes

This was a Brooklyn group that formed in 1953 and recorded their Tri-Boro release, Stop Crying/Break My Bones, the same year.

Bridges left soon after the Tri-Boro disc to join the service. Upon his return, he formed the Clefftones, who recorded "The Masquerade Is Over" for Old Town.

Tenor Donny Myles (Four Dukes, Billy Dawn Quartet, etc.) joined the group when Cas Bridges went into the service.

After leaving the Four Fellows, Carey joined the Danleers when they were recording for Epic Records.

Because of the other Four Fellows group, they called themselves the Victorians when re-forming after Bridges departed. While Bridges was in the service, he wrote "Heartbreaking Moon," which the Victorians cut for Saxony Records.

There is a connection between the last formation of the Four Fellows and the Winners on Rainbow.

Discography

Tri-Boro 101 Stop Crying (CB)/Break My Bones (BC) (1953)
Source: Sal Mondrone, "Rare Sounds," *Bim Bam Boom* 7.

Four Flames (Los Angeles)

Personnel David Ford (lead), Willie Ray Rockwell (d) (2d tenor), Curley Dinkins (baritone), Robert Byrd (bass)

Notes

The group members met one another at a Los Angeles talent show in 1949. They practiced incessantly and soon needed money. They found themselves at Johnny Otis's Barrelhouse performing to fill that need.

Soon they were recording for many labels. Bobby Day Byrd says that each new label meant a new name for the group, but group personnel remained the same.

The group recorded for Specialty and Fidelity as the Four Flames. Fidelity was Specialty's budget label.

Discography

Fidelity 3001 Tabarin (DF)/W-I-N-E (BB) (1951)
Fidelity 3002 The Bounce/The Bounce (instrumental) (1951)
Specialty 423 The Wheel of Fortune (DF)/Later (BB) (1952)
Source: Bobby Byrd in *Yesterday's Memories* 3.

Four Gents (Chicago)

Personnel Eddie Sullivan (born Albert Sullivan), Waymon Bryant, Louis Pritchett, John Staples

Notes

Around 1954, in grade school, Eddie Sullivan met the future members of the Four Gents. Sullivan was with these individuals through high school.

After being together all those years and practicing for so long, they finally recorded the disc shown below.

In 1958, following their only record on the Park label, the group split into two groups. Bryant and Pritchett left to form the Twi-Lites with two others. Sullivan and Staples teamed up with three other vocalists to form the Belvederes.

Discography

Park 113 On Bended Knee (ES)/Linda (ES) (1957)
Source: Bob Pruter, *Doowop . . . The Chicago Scene.*

Four Graduates (Paterson, N.J.)

Personnel Bob Miranda, Tom Gullano (1st tenor), Ralph Devito (baritone), Dave Libert (bass)

Notes

Two years after recording the discs below, the Four Graduates became the Happenings, who recorded for B.T. Puppy Records.

Discography

Rust 5062 Picture of an Angel/Lovely Way to Spend an Evening (1963)
Rust 5084 A Boy in Love/Candy Queen (1964)
Source: Ed Engel, liner notes with the Ace CD *Laurie Vocal Groups.*

Four Haven Knights (New Haven, Conn.)

Personnel Leroy Gomez, Robert Johnson, Thomas Griffin, Everett Johnson, Carl Haley

Notes

The Atlas disc In My Lonely Room/I'm Just a Dreamer was the only recording Atlas Records ever leased. They leased it out to Jimmy Blaine's Cosnat organization for greater distribution. Blaine released it on his Josie label.

  First tenor Jimmy Curtis also sang with the group.

Discography

Atlas 1066 In My Lonely Room/I'm Just a Dreamer (1957)
Josie 824 In My Lonely Room/I'm Just a Dreamer (1957)
Source: Donn Fileti, liner notes with the Relic LP *Best of Angetone.*

Four Jacks (West Coast)

Personnel George Comfort, Bowling Mansfield, Buell Thomas, Ellison White

Notes

This group is known to have backed Lil Greenwood, Little Willie Littlefield, Shirley Haven, and Cora Williams. It is commonly known as having been Federal's studio group in 1952.

  Their records were backed by members of the Johnny Otis band.

  Buell Thomas tried a solo career with Dootsie Williams at Dootone Records (308) before joining up with the Four Jacks.

Discography

Allen 21000 I Challenge Your Kiss/Swing Low, Sweet Chariot (1949)
Allen 21001 Careless Love/Capp's Bop (1949)

Gotham 219 I Cry My Heart Out/Take Me (1950)
Federal 12075 You Met a Fool/Goodbye Baby (1952)
Federal 12067 Last of the Good Rockin' Men/I'll Be Home Again (1952)
Federal 12079 I Ain't Coming Back Anymore/Sure Cure for the Blues (1952)
Sources: George Moonoogian in *Record Collector's Monthly* 46; D. Romanello, G. Povall, and C. Bucola, liner notes with the Sequel King-Federal-DeLuxe CD *Great Googa Mooga.*

Four Jewels (Washington, D.C.)

Personnel Carrie Mingo, Sandra Bears, Margie Clark, Grace Ruffin

Notes

Bears, Clark, and Mingo cut their first record as the Impalas on Checker 999.

They changed their name to avoid being confused with the Cub Impalas and to give themselves more of a female identification.

Ruffin was Billy Stewart's cousin.

After the Chess recordings, Mingo left and they became a trio. When they joined Dimension Records (as the Jewels) in New York, they were joined by Martha Harvin.

Carrie Mingo sang with the Delons until the mid-1970s and the others continued as the Jewels.

Discography

Checker 1039 Loaded with Goodies/Dapper Dan (1963)
Checker 1069 Time for Love/That's What They Put Erasers on Pencils For (1964)
Start 638* Loaded with Goodies (CM)/Fire (SB) (1963)
Start 638* Johnny Jealously (MC)/Someone Special (MC) (1963)
Start 641 All That's Good/I Love Me (1963)
Dimension 1034 Opportunity/Gotta Find a Way (1964)
Dimension 1048 But I Do/Smokey Joe (1964)
Tec 3007 Baby It's You/She's Wrong for You, Baby (1963)
*These two records were released with the same record number.
Sources: Alan Lee in *Yesterday's Memories* 8; Nay Nassar in *Echoes of the Past* 28.

Four Jokers (New York)

Personnel Benjamin Washington (lead), James Myers (1st tenor), Herbert Myers (2d tenor), Charles Holloway (bass)

Notes

Brothers James Myers and Herbert Myers, cousin Ben Washington, and their buddy Charles Holloway recorded as the Four Jokers from 1950 to 1954 for the Apollo and MGM labels.

They later became the Chimes, who recorded two records for the Arrow label.

In 1967, they became the Five Pennies.

Discography

Apollo 1163 The Little Green Man/Catalina Lena (1950)
MGM 11815 Caring/Tell Me Now (1954)
(Note: The information reflected above cannot be confirmed or substantiated and acknowledgment of my resource has not been shown as this is one of the instances where an inadvertent omission was committed.)
Source: Ferdie Gonzalez, *Disco-File.*

Four Js (Philadelphia)

Personnel Joseph "Junior" Pirollo, James Testa (1st tenor), Joseph Paparella (2d tenor), Joe Judge Milaro (baritone)

Notes

Following the Herald recording (see discography), Pirollo and Testa, disillusioned, began recording on a temporary basis for Loma Records in Toronto for about nineteen months. During this period, they were also known as the Four Naturals—a studio group.

After the Four Dates, Fabian's backup group, disbanded, Junior was asked to reform the Four Js to back up Fabian. From mid-1960 through 1962 this new Four Dates (the Four Js) appeared at every Fabian performance and sang backup on all his recordings.

A fifth member, Bob Finizio, was added in 1962.

Discography

United Artists 125 Rock and Roll Age/Be Nice, Don't Fight (1958)
Herald 528 Dreams Are a Dime a Dozen/Kissin' at the Drive-In (1958)
Source: Bob Bosco in *Echoes of the Past* 38.

Four Jumps of Jive (Chicago)

Personnel Leonard Caston, Jimmy Gilmour, Ellis Hunter, Willie Dixon

Notes

This group was the Big Three Trio prior to forming as the Four Jumps of Jive. Ollie Crawford filled in whenever needed.

Discography

Mercury 2001 It's Just the Blues/Satchelmouth Baby (1946)
Mercury 2015 Boo Boo Fine Jelly/Streamlined Woman Blues (1946)
Source: Bruce Eder in *Goldmine.*

Four Kings (Memphis, Tenn.)

Personnel Don Bryant, Jamie Bryant, Lee Jones, Robert "Dusty" Walker

Notes

Lionel Byrd replaced Jamie Bryant sometime after the group was formed.

Discography

Fortune 811 My Head Goes Acting Up/You Don't Mean Me Right (1954)
Fortune 517 Doo-Li-Op/Rose of Tangier (1955)

Four Kittens, Fat Man Mathews & (New Orleans)

Personnel Alan "Fat Man" Mathews, Albert Veal (1st tenor), Dudley Roy (2d tenor), John Morris (baritone), Frank Rushing (bass)

Notes

Mathews and the other four members, previously a gospel quartet, were joined at Imperial by Dave Bartholomew.

This group was previously the Humming Four Quartet, who originally formed in 1932. Interestingly, they were composed of high school running mates.

Buddy Morris, who also performed with the Hawks, sang with the Four Kittens, as did Willie Thrower and Joseph Gaines.

Discography

Imperial 5211 When Boy Meets Girl/Later Baby (1952)
Source: Marv Goldberg and Rick Whitesell in *Yesterday's Memories* 11; Michel Ruppli, *Aladdin/Imperial Labels.*

Four Knights (Charlotte, N.C.)

Personnel Gene Alford (d), Clint Holland (Coral), John Wallace (d) (1st tenor), Clarence Dixon (baritone), Oscar Broadway (bass)

Notes

This group started in 1943 in Charlotte, North Carolina, as the Southland Jubilee Singers trio. The following year, Broadway brought Clarence Dixon to the group and their harmonies caught the attention of the NBC radio station affiliate WSOC in Charlotte, where they received their first broadcast exposure. They were there for a while and then moved to station WBT, Charlotte's big CBS affiliate.

During the group's radio stints in Charlotte, Cy Langois and Ralph Wentworth discovered them. Following the "discovery," the two formed their Langworth label. The first thing they did was rename the group the Four Knights. The Langworth material was next recorded and was only available to radio stations as transcription discs. During this period, the group moved to station WBT.

In 1945, Langois (Langos in the Orbital CD liner notes) took them to New York to appear on Arthur Godfrey's radio show. After this, they signed a recording contract with Decca in 1946 and became fairly well-known. They cut five discs for Decca and in 1949 were moved to the Decca subsidiary, Coral, for three more discs.

They got a chance to appear with Red Skelton on his radio show in 1948. The following year, they began to appear on Skelton's TV show as regulars, and the group then moved to Los Angeles. They lost the Skelton show in 1950 as the pay was felt to be "insufficient" by their management. In 1951, they joined up with Capitol Records and were contracted to record for the music giant. This association brought them great success.

Their soft, sweet harmony brought them many hits in the beginning. Then they began covering R&B songs like the Five Keys' "The Glory of Love," and the Four Aces' "Charmaine and Sin."

In 1953, touring was taking the Four Knights all over the United States and the world from Las Vegas to Rio De Janeiro. They were also appearing on many TV shows, including Perry Como, Ed Sullivan, and, of course, Red Skelton.

At the end of 1953, tenor George Vereen began to temporarily fill in for the ailing Gene Alford, who suffered from epilepsy. Vereen did studio work and live appearances for Alford, who eventually passed away in 1960. Alford was permanently replaced in 1955 by ex-Delta Rhythm Boys member, Clint Holland. Holland performed lead chores on the later Coral discs.

During the mid-1950s Capitol label colleague Nat Cole, who admired the group, asked for the Four Knights to back him on several of his recordings. The first was "A Blossom Fell" and "If I May." A later tune, "That's All There Is to That," charted in the top fifteen of the 1956 pop charts.

Dixon left the group in 1963 and Wallace died in 1978. The group disbanded three years later, in 1981.

Discography

Decca 11003 Just in Case You Change Your Mind/Don't Be Ashamed to . . . (1946)
Decca 24139 So Soon/I'm Falling for You (1947)
Decca 48014 Funny How You Get Along without Me/Walkin' with My Shadow (1946)
Decca 48018 He'll Understand and Say Well Done/Lead Me to That Rock (1947)
Decca 48026 Just in Case You Change Your Mind/Don't Be Ashamed to . . . (1947)
Coral 60046 Wrapped Up in a Dream/Don't Cry, Cry Baby (1949)
Coral 60072 The Crystal Gazer/Fantastic (1949)
Decca 14524 He'll Understand and Say Well Done/Lead Me to That Rock (1950)
Capitol 1587 I Love the Sunshine of Your Smile/Sentimental Fool (1951)
Capitol 1707 Walkin' and Whistlin' Blues/Who Am I? (1951)
Capitol 1787 Got Her off My Hands/I Go Crazy (1951)
Capitol 1806 The Glory of Love/Sin (1951)
Capitol 1840 In the Chapel in the Moonlight/I Want to Say Hello (1951)
Capitol 1875 Cry/Charmaine (1951)
Capitol 1914 Five Foot Two, Eyes of Blue (1951)
Capitol 1930 The Way I Feel/I Wish I Had a Girl (1952)
Capitol 1971 There Are Two Sides to Every Heartache/Walkin' in the Sunshine (1952)
Capitol 1998 Doll with the Sawdust Heart/The More I Go Out With . . . (1952)
Capitol 2087 I'm the World's Biggest Fool/It's a Sin to Tell a Lie (1952)
Capitol 2127 Win or Lose/Doo Wacka Doo (1952)
Capitol 2195 That's the Way It's Gonna Be/Say No More (1952)

Capitol 2234 Lies/One-Way Kisses (1952)
Capitol 2315 Oh, Happy Day/A Million Tears (1952)
Capitol 2403 A Few Kind Words/Anniversary Song (1953)
Capitol 2517 Baby Doll/Tennessee Train (1953)
Capitol 2654 I Couldn't Stay Away from You/I Get So Lonely (1953)
Capitol 2782 I Was Meant for You/They Tell Me (1954)
Capitol 2847 Period/How Wrong Can You Be? (1954)
Capitol 2894 In the Chapel in the Moonlight/Easy Street (1954)
Capitol 2938 Saw Your Eyes/I Don't Wanna See You Crying (1954)
Capitol 3024 Honey Bunch/Write Me Baby (1955)
Capitol 3093 Foolishly Yours/Inside Out (1955)
Capitol 3155 Me/Gratefully Yours (1955)
Capitol 3192 Don't Sit under the Apple Tree/Believing You (1955)
Capitol 3250 Perdido/After (1955)
Capitol 3279 You/Guilty (1955)
Capitol 3339 I Love You Still/Happy Birthday Baby (1956)
Capitol 3386 Bottle Up the Midnight/Mistaken (1956)
Capitol 3494 Don't Depend on Me/You're a Honey (1956)
Capitol 3689 It Doesn't Cost Money/How Can You Not Believe Me? (1957)
Capitol 3730 I Love That Song/Walkin' and Whistlin' Blues (1957)
Coral 61936 When Your Lover Has Gone/Four-Minute Mile (1958)
Sources: Rick Whitesell in *Goldmine*, September 1979; unsigned liner notes with the Orbital CD *Four Knights: Jivin' and Smoothin'*.

Four Naturals (Philadelphia)

Personnel Junior Pirollo, Bob Finizio, Ray Finizio, Mike Travaglia

Notes
Pirollo and Bob Finizio had been with the Four Js. They later re-formed the Four Js to the Fabulous Four to back up Fabian. For a brief period, they were the Four Naturals, sometimes referred to as the Naturals.

Discography
Red Top 11 I Hear a Rhapsody/When I'm Not in Your Arms (1959)
Red Top 123 The Thought of You Darling/Long, Long Ago (1960)
Source: Bob Bosco in *Echoes of the Past* 38.

Four Pearls (Tacoma, Wash.)

Personnel Elsie Pierre, Artis Johnson Jr. (d), Ronald Small, Reuben Martin

Notes
The members of this quartet met while the members were in the service in 1957 near Tacoma, calling themselves the Pearls. They began singing simply to compete in an air force talent contest. In the following year's contest, the Four Pearls won the show.

They soon went to Los Angeles and recorded for Dootsie Williams as the Fabulous Pearls (Dooto 448), but this did nothing.

In 1960, they moved to Dolton Records and recorded Look At Me/It's Almost Tomorrow. This did well in Seattle but poorly elsewhere.

Because of their lackluster showing, they broke up late in 1960.

Johnson also sang with the Midnights on Music City.

Discography

Dolton 26 Look at Me/It's Almost Tomorrow (1960)
Sources: Jim Dawson, liner notes with the Ace CD *Dootone Story*; Jim Dawson, liner notes with the Ace CD *Dootone Doo Wop–3.*

Four Pennies (Tampa, Fla.)

Personnel Carl Cuttler (lead), Lindsey Griffin (1st tenor), John Myers (baritone), Floyd Lawson (bass)

Notes

This group formed in the mid-1960s as an offshoot of the Five Pennies, who did a great deal of backup work for several R&B labels at the end of their career as a vocal group. For a brief time, they were the Larks headquartered in Tampa. In 1967, they became the Four Pennies.

Willie Earl Drummond was a member of, and sang with, the Hollyhocks. Clemmons Daniels was still another member. Herbert Myers sang on several of their sessions.

Tenor Floyd Lawson, in addition to his time with the Four Pennies, was also a member of the Hearts of Stone.

On Brunswick the group consisted of John Myers, Rudolph Hill, James Myers, and Willie Earl Drummond.

Discography

Philips 40202 Juliet/Tell Me, Girl (1964)
Philips 41333 Till Another Day/Until It's Time to Go (1965)
Brunswick 55304 You Have No Time to Lose (FL)/You're a Gas With (1966)
Brunswick 55324 'Tis the Season (HM)/Shake a Hand (HM) (1967)
Source: Marv Goldberg in *Yesterday's Memories* 6.

Four Pharaohs (Columbus, Ohio)

Personnel Morris Wade (lead), Robert Taylor (1st tenor), Ronnie Wilson (baritone), Bernard Wilson (bass)

Notes

This group originally formed in Columbus, Ohio, in 1956 and consisted of the above members. Morris Wade was the only member to make it through several group name changes as well as changes involving personnel. Wade is the one who originally brought the members together.

By 1957, they obtained a manager, who got them a recording contract with a local company, Esta Records. Their first disc, Give Me Your Love/China Girl, was originally released on Esta. Following Esta, the tune was also released on Ransom. Howard Ransom was their manager and the Ransom label was his.

In 1958, the Four Pharaohs did a great deal of national touring, and the Paradise release probably occurred at that time. It is not known for certain why or how this took place, but the group played the Apollo during that time and it is surmised that this was when Old Town released the disc on their Paradise subsidiary label.

Taylor left in 1959 and later joined Bobby Taylor and the Vancouvers. It was also around this time that Bob "Pee Wee" Lowery joined, replacing Bernard Wilson, who had also departed.

While performing in Cincinnati in 1960, they recorded for the Federal label and now called themselves King Pharaoh and the Egyptians. It was just after this recording that Leo Blakely joined. Pee Wee left and Ronnie Wilson did the same. The story behind their name was that their guitarist, Harold Smith, was formerly nicknamed King Pharaoh; hence the name.

In 1961 the group consisted of Leo Blakely, Morris Wade, Paul Moore, and Forest Porter.

While touring in Los Angeles in 1963 they again met Howard Ransom, who owned a label called Nanc with Jimmy Turner. They changed their name again to the Egyptian Kings and rerecorded "Give Me Your Love." On Nanc, the group consisted of Morris Wade, Leo Blakely, Paul Moore, and Pete Oden.

They ultimately disbanded in 1968.

Discography

Ransom 101 Give Me Your Love/China Girl (1957)
Ransom 100 Pray for Me/The Move Around (1957)
Ransom 102 Is It Too Late?/It Was a Night Like This (1957 [?])
Source: Dave Ardit in *Bim Bam Boom* 13.

Four Shades of Rhythm (Cleveland, Ohio)

Personnel Oscar Lindsay, Eddie McAfee, Eddie Myers, Oscar Pennington (d)

Notes

This group originally formed in Cleveland in the late 1930s as neighborhood friends. They began with pop, standard tunes, show tunes, jazz, and so on, establishing their reputation. Soon they were spending a great deal of time in Chicago, where they had become quite popular and were offered a long-term engagement. The move to Illinois brought several personnel changes, and the quintet listed above was put into place.

They did a great deal of touring in early 1948 and did their first recording for Vitacoustic, "One Hundred Years from Today," a song that was recorded by many popular artists of the day. About eighteen months later, they recorded for Old Swingmaster, which was partly owned by Al Benson (later the owner of Parrot Records). One of the tunes from this session was the great "My Blue Walk."

Poor distribution by both Vitacoustic and Old Swingmaster prevented their recordings from achieving widespread popularity. They sold well in Chicago and Cleveland but did not do well elsewhere.

Because of this lack of success, two members left Chicago to return to Cleveland. In 1951, Oscar Pennington was replaced by Adam Lambert (from the Cats and Jammer Three), and Eddie Myers was replaced by Booker Collins.

In 1952 Eddie McAfee, who had just been married, also decided to return to Cleveland. He was replaced by Ernie Harper, who had been with the Five Blazes.

The group of Lindsay, Harper, Lambert, and Collins was the group on Chance. They were also the group who did the 1960 remake of "One Hundred Years from Today." Shortly after the Apex recording, the group broke up.

Discography

Vitacoustic 1005 One Hundred Years from Today (EM)/Howie Sent Me (1947)
Old Swingmaster 13 My Blue Walk (OL)/Baby I'm Gone (OL) (1949)
Old Swingmaster 23 I Can Dream (OL)/Master of Me (OL) (1949)
Chance 1126 Yesterdays/So There (1952)
Mad 1202 Ghost of a Chance (instrumental)/Come Here (OL) (1957)
Apex 967 A Hundred Years from Today/Life with You (1960)
Source: Pete Grendysa in *Record Collector's Monthly* 8; Marv Goldberg in *DISCoveries,* May 1998.

Four Sharps

Personnel Earl Ratliffe (tenor), Clarence Hopkind (baritone), Cliff Givens (bass)

Notes

This group was originally the Melody Masters on Apollo, contrary to liner notes with the Trumpet CD, which state that the group was the Melody Men—this is incorrect! Another error in the Trumpet CD liner notes is the statement that the Four Sharps recorded "My Baby" for Apollo in 1948—wrong! "My Baby" on Apollo was released in 1946. So how could it be recorded in 1948?

The Four Sharps were better known as the Southern Sons who recorded for Bluebird and the Southern Sons Quartet who recorded for Trumpet in the early 1950s.
Source: Marc Ryan, liner notes with the Trumpet CD *Shout Brother Shout.*

Four Tones (Los Angeles)

Personnel Lucius "Dusty" Brooks, Johnny Porter (tenor), Leon Buck, Ira Hardin

Notes

This group, in one form or another, also recorded as Dusty Brooks and the Four Tones, Dusty Brooks and the Tones, and Dusty Brooks and the Four Tones with Raymond Wheaton.

Discography

Bluebird 11408 Goodnight Baby, Goodnight/Someone's Rockin' My Dreamboat (1942)

A-1 1001 I'll Follow You/Do Do Baby (1942)
Ebony 100 Two Hearts to Beat Tonight/What a Fool I Was (1945)
Preview 666/667 Someone Over Here Loves Someone Over There/Hey What You Say (1945)
Preview 668/669 Two Tears Met/Satchelmouth Baby (1945)
Source: Bob Ferlingere, *Discography of R&B and R&R Vocal Groups.*

Four Tones, Dusty Brooks & (Los Angeles)

Personnel Lucius "Dusty" Brooks, Johnny Porter (tenor), Leon Buck, Ira Hardin, Rudolph Hunter

Notes

Other members included Raymond Wheaton, Juanita Brown, Art Maryland, and Joe Alexander.

Discography

Lamarrs Star 101 I'll Follow You/Do Do Baby (1945)
Lamarrs Star 102 Seclusion/Thank You for the Lies (1945)
Lamarrs Star 103 Little Chum/Play Jackpot (1945)
Memo 1002 Uptown Rhythm/Little Chum (1945)
Memo 1003 Please Don't Rush Me/Seclusion (1945)
Memo 1005 Put Your Cards on the Table/Seclusion (1945)
Memo 7001 Please Don't Rush Me/Put Your Cards on the Table (1948)
ABC Eagle 228 Shuffleboard Boogie/I Didn't Cry (1950)
Majestic 123 Ol' Man River/Cream of Wheat (1950)
Majestic 127 Shuffle Board Boogie/I Didn't Cry (1950)
Columbia 30239 Shoo Boogie Mama/Liddy (1950)
Dootone 306 Chili Dogs/You Never Told a Lie (1952)
Sun 182 Heaven or Fire/Tears and Wine (1953)
Source: Bob Ferlingere, *Discography of R&B and R&R Vocal Groups.*

Four Tones, Dusty Brooks & (with Raymond Wheaton) (Los Angeles)

Personnel Ray Wheaton, Lucius "Dusty" Brooks (tenor), Johnny Porter (tenor), Leon Buck, Ira Hardin, Rudolph Hunter

Notes

This group, in one form or another, also recorded as Dusty Brooks and the Four Tones and Dusty Brooks and the Tones.

Discography

Memo 1001 Play Jackpot/Thank You for the Lies (1945)
Source: Bob Ferlingere, *Discography of R&B* and *R&R Vocal Groups.*

Four Toppers (New York)

Personnel Jimmy Springs (d), David Patillo (tenor), Richard Davis (baritone), Steve Gibson (bass)

Notes

The Four Toppers were one of many groups performing on the West Coast in 1938. Steve Gibson had been with the Basin Street Boys (of Virginia, not the Excelsior group). Jimmy Springs had been with the Five Jones Boys and David Patillo and Richard Davis had been members of the Four Blackbirds. Since they all came from top groups, they decided to call themselves the Four Toppers! During the early 1940s, they toured major cities and practiced and perfected their craft.

Since making a living on the West Coast was difficult, they went to New York. At that time Richard Davis and another member from the West Coast (unknown), departed. In New York they met up with Romaine Brown and Emmett Matthews, which made them a quintet. Because of this, they changed their name to the Five Red Caps.

It is believed that no recordings were ever made by the Four Toppers. However, during the 1980s, Savoy released an LP that contained two Savoy tunes and one from their subsidiary label, Regent, by the Four Toppers.

Sources: Marv Goldberg and Pete Grendysa in *Yesterdays' Memories* 4; Jay Warner, *American Singing Groups*.

Four Tops (Detroit)

Personnel Levi Stubbs, Abdul "Duke" Fakir, Renaldo "Obie" Benson, Lawrence Payton

Notes

The members of this group were neighborhood friends in Detroit. At a birthday party in 1954, they got together and gave singing a try. It was excitingly good and the group began practicing the very next day.

They sang at school parties, churches, and other local functions and worked their way into small clubs. After retaining a talent agency, they began performing as backup group for Billy Eckstine, Brook Benton, Della Reese, and others.

In 1962, they met Berry Gordy of Motown Records. Gordy liked them and used them as backup for the Supremes until the right song came along for the Four Tops.

In 1964, Motown's songwriters, Holland, Dozier, and Holland, created "Baby I Need Your Loving." Subsequently the Four Tops had one success after another. They adapted beautifully to the new musical category—soul—and had many hits in this genre.

In 1966 they realized their biggest hit, "Reach Out."

In 1967 Holland, Dozier, and Holland left Motown to start their own label. The Four Tops then began covering other artists' hits.

In 1972, Motown moved to Los Angeles and the Four Tops, wanting to remain in Chicago, signed with Dunhill. At Dunhill they found new songwriters, Dennis Lambert and Brian Potter, who provided material to bring them even more successes!

In 1976, they moved to the Dunhill parent, ABC Records, and had more hits. In the 1990s, the same four were still singing together.

Discography

Chess 1623 Could It Be You/Kiss Me Baby (1956)
Columbia 41755 Ain't That Love/Lonely Summer (1960)
Riverside 4534 Pennies from Heaven/Where You Are (1962)
Motown 1062 Baby I Need Your Loving/Call on Me (1964)
Motown 1069 Without the One You Love/Love Has Gone (1964)
Motown 1073 Ask the Lonely/Where Did You Go (1965)
Motown 1076 I Can't Help Myself/Sad Souvenirs (1965)
Motown 1081 It's the Same Old Song/Your Love Is Amazing (1965)
Motown 1084 Something about You/Darling I Hum Our Song (1965)
Motown 1090 Just as Long as You Need Me/Shake Me, Wake Me (1966)
Motown 1096 Loving You Is Sweeter Than Ever/I Like Everything (1966)
Motown 1102 Reach Out/Until You Love Someone (1966)
Motown 1104 Bernadette/I've Got a Feeling (1967)
Motown 1110 Seven Rooms of Gloom/I'll Turn to Stone (1967)
Motown 1113 You Keep Running Away/If You Don't Want My Love (1967)
Motown 1119 Walk Away Renee/Your Love Is Wonderful (1968)
Motown 1124 If I Were a Carpenter/Wonderful Baby (1968)
Motown 1127 Yesterday's Dreams/For Once in My Life (1968)
Motown 1132 I'm in a Different World/Remember When (1968)
Motown 1147 What Is a Man/Don't Bring Back Memories (1969)
Motown 1159 Don't Let Him Take Your Love from Me/The Key (1969)
Motown 1164 Love/It's All in the Game (1970)
Motown 1170 Still Water (Love)/Still Water (Peace) (1970)
Motown 1175 Just Seven Numbers/I Wish I Were Your Mirror (1970)
Motown 1185 In These Changing Times/Right before My Eyes (1971)
Motown 1189 MacArthur Park–1/MacArthur Park–2 (1971)
Motown 1196 A Simple Game/L.A. (1972)
Motown 1198 Happy/I Can't Quit Your Love (1972)
Motown 1210 Nature Planned It/It'll Never Change (1972)
Dunhill 4330 Keeper of the Castle/Jubilee with Soul (1972)
Dunhill 4334 Guardian De Tu Castillo/Jubilee with Soul (1973)
Dunhill 4339 Ain't No Woman/The Good Lord Knows (1973)
Dunhill 4354 Are You Man Enough/Peace of Mind (1973)
Dunhill 4366 Sweet Understanding Love/Main Street People (1973)
Dunhill 4377 Just Can't Get You Out of My Mind/Brother's Keeper (1973)
Dunhill 4386 One Chain Don't Make No Prison/Turn . . . the Light . . . Love (1974)
Dunhil 15005 Midnight Flower/All of My Love (1974)
ABC 12096 Seven Lonely Nights/ (1975)
ABC 12123 Drive Me Out of My Mind/We All Gotta Stick Together (1975)
ABC 12155 I'm Glad You Walked into My Life/Mama . . . All Right with Me (1975)
ABC 12214 Catfish/ (1976)
ABC 12223 Catfish/Look at My Baby (1976)
ABC 12236 Feel Free/ (1977)
Source: Jay Warner, *American Singing Groups.*

Four Troys (Pittsburgh, Pa.)

Personnel Fletcher Williams (lead), Melvin Williams (2d tenor), Kenny Miller (d) (baritone), Marvin Brown (bass)

Notes

This group became the Four Troys after they and their manager tired of their previous name, the Four Dots (Bullseye). This was 1959.

Kenny Miller left the group in 1959 and was replaced by Kenny Jackson. With Jackson, the Four Troys recorded two sides for the Freedom label.

Discography

Freedom 44013 Suddenly You Want to Dance (KJ) /In the Moonlight (MP) (1959)
Source: Carl Janusek in *Echoes of the Past* 32.

Four Tunes (New York)

Personnel Jimmie Nabbie (lead), Pat Best (baritone), Danny Owens (tenor), Jimmy Gordon (bass)

Notes

Originally an offshoot of, and calling themselves, the Ink Spots. Next they were the Brown Dots. Later they were the Sentimentalists. Finally, because Tommy Dorsey told them he "owned" the name Sentimentalists, they changed again to the Four Tunes. That name was selected because they had only "four tunes" in their repertoire.

Danny Owens had been with the Coleman Brothers.

They had a long and productive career as the backup group with Savannah Churchill (more than two dozen sides). Their first solo single (1946) was released as by the Sentimentalists.

The Four Tunes joined RCA in 1949 and were signed by Jubilee in 1953, following a long hiatus between recordings.

In 1955, the Four Tunes were booked at a hotel in Las Vegas. They remained there for eight years. Also that year, Billy Wells joined them as a fill-in for members on vacation.

They broke up in 1963.

Discography

Manor 1047 I'll Close My Eyes (JN)/Save Me a Dream (JN) (1946)
Manor 1049 I'd Rather Be Safe Than Sorry (PB)/I'll Be Waiting for You (1946)
Manor 1050 Too Many Times/I'll Always Say I Love You (PB) (1946)
Manor 1076 Darling You Make It So (1947)
Manor 1077 Where Is My Love /Sometime Someplace Somehow (1947)
Manor 1083 Wrapped Up in a Dream/I Found Love When I Found You (1947)
Manor 1087 Chillocothe, Ohio/Dreams (1947)
Manor 1093 I Understand/Is It Too Late? (1947)
Manor 1116 Time Out for Tears/All My Dreams (1948)
Manor 1123 Little Jane/Tell Me So (1948)

Manor 1129 I Want to Cry/Someday (1948)
Manor 1131 Confess/Don't Know (1948)
Manor 1141 How Can I Make You Believe In Me?/Don't You Ever Mind? (1948)
Columbia 30145 Where Is My Love?/Take My Lonely Heart (1948)
Columbia 30146 The Best of Friends/The Things You Do to Me (1948)
Manor 8002 Silent Night (PB)/Come All Ye Faithful (PB/JN) (1948)
Manor 8003 Ave Maria (JN)/White Christmas (all) (1948)
Manor 1046 I Want to Be Loved (SC)/Foolishly Yours (SC) (1949)
Manor 1154 My Muchacha/I'm Gonna Ride Tillie Tonight (1949)
Manor 1173 Mister Sun/The Sheik of Araby (1949)
Manor 1195 Someday/Karen Lynn (both sides w/Pat Best) (1949)
RCA 50-0008 You're Heartless/Careless Love (1949)
RCA 50-0016 I'm the Guy/My Last Affair (1949)
RCA 50-0042 I'm Just a Fool in Love/Lonesome Road (1949)
Arco 1202 I'll Never Be Free/Get Yourself Another Guy (S. Churchill) (1949)
Arco 1220 I Want to Cry/My Baby-Kin (1949)
Arco 1222 Daddy, Daddy/Why Was I Born? (1949)
Arco 1229 Don't Try to Explain/Savannah Sings the Blues (1949)
Arco 1236 Don't Cry Darling/Don't Take Your Love from Me (1949)
Arco 1253 I Want to Be Loved/Foolishly Yours (1950)
Arco 1259 The Devil Sat Down and Cried/Can Anyone Explain? (1950)
Arco 1246 You're My Love/Don't Blame My Dreams (1950)
Arco 1257 All My Dreams/Time Out for Tears (1950)
RCA 50-0072 Am I Blue?/There Goes My Heart (1950)
RCA 50-0085 Kentucky Babe/Old-Fashioned Love (1950)
RCA 47-3881 Do I Worry?/Say When (1950)
RCA 47-3967 How Can You Say That I Don't Care/Cool Water (1950)
RCA 50-0131 May That Day Never Come/Carry Me Back to Lone Prairie (1951)
RCA 47-4102 Wishing You Were Here Tonight/The Last Round-Up (1951)
RCA 47-4241 I Married an Angel/The Prisoner Song (1951)
RCA 47-4305 Early in the Morning/My Buddy (1951)
RCA 47-4427 I'll See You in My Dreams/Tell Me Why (1951)
RCA 47-4489 The Greatest Song I Ever Heard/Come What May (1952)
RCA 47-4663 I Wonder/Can I Say Anymore? (1952)
RCA 47-4828 They Don't Understand/Why Did You Do This to Me (1952)
RCA 47-4968 Don't Want to Set the World on . . . /Let's . . . Love Another Chance (1952)
RCA 47-5532 Don't Get Around Much Anymore/Water Boy (1953)
Jubilee 5128 Marie/I Gambled with Love (1954)
Jubilee 5132 Sugar Lump/I Understand (1954)
Jubilee 5135 Do-Do-Do-Do- It Again/My Wild Irish Rose (1954)
Jubilee 5152 The Greatest Feeling in the World/Lonesome (1954)
Jubilee 5165 Don't Cry, Darling/Lamour Toujour Lamour (1954)
Jubilee 5174 Let Me Go Lover/I Sold My Heart to the Junkman (1954)
Jubilee 5183 I Hope/I Close My Eyes (1955)
Jubilee 5200 Tired of Waiting/Time Out for Tears (1955)
Jubilee 5212 Brooklyn Bridge/Three Little Chickens (1955)
Jubilee 5218 You Are My Love/At the Steamboat River Ball (1955)

Jubilee 5232 Rock and Roll Call/Our Love (1956)
Jubilee 5239 I Gotta Go/Hold Me Closer (1956)
Jubilee 5245 Far Away Places/Dancing with Tears in My Eyes (1956)
Jubilee 5255 The Ballad of James Dean/Sayonara (1956)
Jubilee 5276 Cool Water/A Little on the Lonely Side (1957)
Crosby 3 Never Look Down/Don't You Run Away (1958)
Crosby 4 Twinkle Eyes/Starved for Love (1958)
Source: Pete Grendysa in *Goldmine*, 1989.

Four Vagabonds (St. Louis, Mo.)

Personnel John Jordan (lead), Robert O'Neil (1st tenor), Norval Taborn (d) (baritone), Ray Grant (d) (bass)

Notes

This group began their career in high school in St. Louis, Missouri, in 1933. After school days were completed, they did a great deal of radio work, which lasted from the 1940s to the early 1950s. They began recording in 1941, performing war songs for Bluebird.

Next they next went to Mercury, where their discs went nowhere. After Mercury, they went to Apollo. In 1945, Grant's eyesight began failing and he was replaced by bass Bill Sanford (Miracle 141). They ended their recording career in 1947.

Bass Bill Sanford left in 1950 to become the arranger for the Ravens.

Group disbanded in 1952.

Discography

Bluebird 11519 Duke of Dubuque/Slow and Easy (1942)
Bluebird 200810 Rosie the Riveter/I Had the Craziest Dream (1943)
Bluebird 300811 Ten Little Soldiers/Rose Ann of Charing Cross (1943)
Bluebird 300815 Comin' in on a Wing and a Prayer/It Can't Be Wrong (1943)
RCA 20-1677 A G.I. Wish/If I Were You (1945)
Mercury 2050 Taking My Chance With You/When the Old Gang's Back on the Corner (1946)
Atlas 111 Oh, What a Polka/I Can't Make Up My Mind (1946)
Apollo 1030 Kentucky Babe/Hoe Cake, Hominy, and Sassafras Pie (1946)
Apollo 1039 Do You Know What It Means to Miss New Orleans/The Pleasure's All Mine (1947)
Apollo 1055 Dreams Are a Dime a Dozen/Wonder Who's Kissing (1947)
Apollo 1057 The Freckle Song/P.S. I Love You (1947)
Apollo 1060 Ask Anyone Who Knows/Oh My Achin' Heart (1947)
Apollo 1075 Choo-Choo/Lazy Countryside (1947)
Apollo 1076 Gang/Sang Heart of My Heart/That Old Gang of Mine (1947)
Miracle 141 Mighty Hard to Go thru Life Alone/My Heart Cries (1949)
Lloyds 102 P.S. I Love You/Lazy Country Side (1953)
Source: Rick Whitesell, Pete Grendysa, George Moonoogian, and Marv Goldberg in *Yesterday's Memories* 7.

Furys (Los Angeles)

Personnel Tony Allen (tenor), Jimmy Green (tenor), Jerome Evans (baritone)

Notes

Jimmy Green was also a member of the Medallions and was Vernon Green's brother. In 1959 he also recorded with the Shields.

The Mack IV label was owned by actor James McEachin, who appeared in the TV series *Tenafly*.

Discography

Mack IV 112 Zing Went the Strings/Never More (1962)
Source: Marv Goldberg in *Record Collector's Monthly* 42.

Gainors (Philadelphia)

Personnel Garnett Mimms (real name Garrett Mimms) (lead), Sam Bell, Howard Tate, Willie Combo, John Jefferson

Notes

The Gainors were formed when Mimms came out of the service in 1948.

He found his former colleague, Sam Bell, and the two organized a vocal group they called the Gainors. Because the Gainors' first release began to do well, it was leased out to Cameo by the original label, Red Top, for better distribution.

Mimms had earlier been with "Little" Joe Cook's Evening Star Quartet and other gospel groups. He originally met Sam Bell while with the Evening Star Quartet.

Mimms was discovered by Philadelphia producer Jerry Ragavoy, who pushed Herb Slotkin to record the Castelles back in the early 1950s.

In 1961, Mimms and Bell decided to disband the Gainors; this is when they formed the Enchanters.

Discography

Red Top 110 Gonna Rock Tonight/Follow Me (1958)
Cameo 151 Gonna Rock Tonight/The Secret (1958)
Cameo 156 You Must Be an Angel/Follow Me (1958)
Mercury 71466 Message with Flowers/She's My Lollipop (1959)
Mercury 71569 She's Gone/Please Consider (1960)
Mercury 71630 I'm in Love with You/Nothing Means More to Me (1960)
Talley-Ho 102 Where I Want to Be/This Is a Perfect Moment (1961)
Talley-Ho 105 Tell Him/Darlin' (1961)
Sources: Alan Warner, liner notes with the United Artists LP *Motor City to Central Park*; Bob Pruter in *Goldmine,* June 25, 1993.

Gales (Detroit)

Personnel Calvin Fair (lead), Isaiah Jones (tenor)

Notes

This group was the Violinaires on Drummond with a different lead. They were also the Question Marks on Swing Time.

Discography

J-V-B 34 Don't Let the Sun Catch You Cryin'/My Eyes Keep Me in Trouble (1959)
J-V-B 35 Darling Patricia/All Is Well, All Is Well (1960)
Winn 916 Squeeze Me/I Love You (1961)
Source: Unsigned liner notes with the *Best of JVB* LP on the Real Rhythm label.

Gassers (Los Angeles)

Personnel Jesse Belvin (lead), George Parker (1st tenor), Howard Watson (2d tenor), Willie Handerson (baritone), Haydell Mitchell (bass)

Notes

The Gassers' usual lead singer, Tommy "Buster" Williams, in an interview with Billy Vera for the Jesse Belvin Specialty CD liner notes, did not recall why he wasn't at the session that produced the disc shown below, but also stated that this disc might have been Belvin recording by himself!

Discography

Cash 1038 Tell Me/Hum De Dum (1956)
Sources: Billy Vera, liner notes with the Specialty CD *Jesse Belvin—The Blues Balladeer*; Jim Dawson, liner notes with the Earth Angel LP *Hang Your Tears Out to Dry*; Billy Vera, liner notes with the Specialty CD *Doo Wop from Dolphin's of Hollywood*.

Gaylarks (San Francisco)

Personnel Ben Richards (lead), James Moore Jr. (d) (1st tenor), Bobby Davis (d) (2d tenor), Billy Vance (d) (baritone), Carl Lovejoy (bass)

Notes

Richards, Moore, Davis, and Vance started singing in their San Francisco high school. Carl Lovejoy, from nearby Oakland, states that he brought the group to Music City's facilities. It is stated elsewhere that Music City owner Ray Dobard brought the group to his label.

"Ivy League Clothes," although credited to the Gaylarks, was by another Bay area group—the Five Lyrics. The Gaylarks' first recording, "Tell Me Darling," was actually the flip side of the Rovers' "Whole Lot of Love" (1955).

The Gaylarks had a loyal following in the Bay area, but when they went on tour, they failed to receive the same kind of reception.

Discography

Music City 792 Tell Me Darling/Whole Lot of Love (Rovers) (1955)
Music City 793 Li'l Dream Girl/Romantic Memories (1955)

Music City 805 My Greatest Sin/Teenage Mambo (1956)
Music City 812 Somewhere in This World/Just One More Chance (1956)
Music City 819 Ivy League Clothes/Doodle-Doo (1957)
Music City 839 Church on the Hill/Mr. Rock-n-Roll (1957)
Source: Jim Dawson, liner notes with the Earth Angel LP *Music City.*

Gaylords (Detroit)

Personnel Louis Van Dyke (lead), George Copes, Rudy Copes, James Morris, Earl Thomas

Notes

Because there was a pop group at Mercury also called the Gaylords, Savoy changed this group's name to the Imperials. (Since Imperials is hardly an unusual name for an R&B vocal group, the rationale for this move is open to question.)

Louis Van Dyke sang for the Ambassadors on Savoy as well.

Discography

Savoy 852 Get Mad Baby/Go On Baby (1952)
Source: Steve Propes, liner notes with the Savoy LP *Doo Wop Delights—The Roots of Rock.*

Gay Tunes (Brooklyn, N.Y.)

Personnel Earl Kirton (lead), Waymon "Butterball" Carey, Leroy Williams, Harry Pinchback (baritone), Fred Davis

Notes

The Gay Tunes began singing in 1952 in front of two Bedford-Stuyvesant public schools in Brooklyn and continued throughout their high school years. Their release for Timely Records was issued in 1953.

For some unknown reason, four years went by before they were found by tunesmith Al Browne, who recorded them on his Joyce label in 1957.

"I Love You" was written by Kirton for his daughter. It was recorded for Joyce Records in 1957.

According to Lou Silvani in his *Collecting Rare Records,* two of the members are Wayman Corey and Henry Pinchback.

Liner notes accompanying Relic's CD on the Joyce label state that the Gay Tunes may have evolved into the Verdicts, who did "My Life's Desire." The same liner notes show a picture of the Gay Tunes with their first names as Chubby, Leslie, Tony, Charlie, and Freddie.

Discography

Timely 1002 Thrill of Romance/Wh-y-y Leave Me This Wa-Ay-Ay (1953)
Joyce 101 I Love You/You Left Me (1957)
Dome 502 Don't Go/Got You On My Mind (1958)
Source: Donn Fileti, liner notes with the Relic CD *Timely and Joyce.*

Gazelles (Philadelphia)

Personnel Vernon Fusell, Charles Jones, Donald Langston, Donald Lee, Carlton Prater

Notes

We know little about the Gazelles, but we do know that Alethia Prater of Philadelphia, Carlton Prater's mother, undersigned the group's Gotham contract, leading us to surmise that the group members were young.

Discography

Gotham 315 Honest/Pretty Baby, Baby (1956)
Source: George Moonoogian, liner notes with the Flyright CD *I Always Remember.*

G-Clefs (Roxbury, Mass.)

Personnel Ray Gibson (lead), Teddy Scott (tenor), Timmy Scott (tenor), Chris Scott (baritone), Joe Jordan (bass)

Notes

The Scott brothers harmonized in church and school in the early 1950s. Gibson and Jordan were neighbors. The five appeared at local dances and amateur shows, and in 1956 they met a local record producer who had them cut a demo.

Boston's Pilgrim Records soon picked this up and recorded it that same year.

After their second Pilgrim release (720) did not do well, the G-Clefs went to their manager's new label, Paris Records, and cut two discs.

Joe Jordan was drafted in 1957 after the Paris recording of "Symbol of Love." He was replaced by the fourth Scott brother, Arnold. He is first heard on "I Understand" four years later on the Terrace label. Apparently the group stopped singing when Jordan was drafted. However, in 1961 they contacted their old manager and told him of their desire to record again.

The manager, now with the new label, Terrace, had the group record the old Four Tunes song "I Understand." This did quite well but the next four Terrace releases did not.

In 1964, the group went to the Regina label and cut two more singles. By this time they had adjusted themselves to the new soul sound. The Regina discs did not make any noise at the cash registers.

In Donn Fileti's liner notes accompanying Relic's *G-Clefs* CD, lead singer Ray Gibson's name is spelled both as Gipson and Gibson.

Discography

Pilgrim 715 Ka-Ding-Dong (RG)/Darla My Darling (RG/JJ) (1956)
Pilgrim 720 Cause You're Mine (TS)/Please Write While I'm Away (RG) (1956)
Paris 502 Symbol of Love (TS/JJ)/Love Her in the Morning (JJ) (1957)
Paris 506 Zing Zang Zoo (RG)/Is This the Way? (JJ) (1957)
Terrace 7500 I Understand (TS)/Little Girl I Love You (AS) (1961)
Terrace 7503 A Girl Has to Know (RG)/Lad (all) (1962)

Terrace 7507 They'll Call Me Away (TS/AS)/Wake Up Your Mind (all) (1962)
Terrace 7510 Sitting in the Moonlight (RG)/A Lover's Prayer (TS) (1962)
Terrace 7514 All My Trials (AS)/The Big Rain (RG) (1962)
Regina 1314 To the Winner Goes the Prize (AS)/I Believe in All I Feel (AS) (1964)
Regina 1319 Nobody but Betty (AS)/Angel, Listen to Me (AS) (1964)
Veep 1218 I Have (RG)/On the Other Side of Town (TS) (1965)
Veep 1226 This Time (AS)/On the Other Side of Town (AS) (1965)
Loma 2034 Party '66 (all)/Little Lonely Boy (AS) (1966)
Loma 2048 I Can't Stand It (AS/RG)/The Whirlwind (AS/RG) (1966)
G-Clefs Allah (I Shall Sing) (AS) (1969)
Sources: Marv Goldberg in *Whiskey, Women, and . . .* 15; Donn Fileti, liner notes
with the Relic CD *Ka-Ding-Dong.*

Gems (Evanston, Ill.)

Personnel Ray Pettis (lead), Bobby "Pee Wee" Robinson (1st tenor), David
"Moose" Taylor (2d tenor), Wilson Jones (baritone), Rip Reed (bass)

Notes

The group began in 1952 as neighborhood friends who sang locally.

Drexel Records had the Gems on their first four recordings. The Drexel label story
is clouded by many unanswered questions. Members of the Gems never saw the
Drexel offices.

Their first session produced three tunes and their second session, at Drexel, included the Dorothy Logan recording of "Since I Fell for You," with the Gems providing backup vocal harmony.

Sales of all their recordings were poor, although the tunes themselves were great!
The first three discs were only released on red plastic.

Pettis did some solo recording for Drexel and later spent time with the Foster
Brothers at lead. He replaced original lead Lawrence Gales.

In *Doowop . . . The Chicago Scene* Bob Pruter identifies the baritone as Wilson
James.

Discography

Drexel 901 Talk about the Weather/Deed I Do (1954)
Drexel 902 Since I Fell for You (1954)
Drexel 903 I Thought You'd Care/Kitty from New York City (1954)
Drexel 904 Ol' Man River/You're Tired of Love (1954)
Drexel 909 One Woman Man/The Darkest Night (1955)
Drexel 915 Till the Day I Die/Monkey-Face Baby (1957)
Sources: Bob Stallworth in *Yesterday's Memories* 6 (article on the Gems); Bob Pruter,
Doowop . . . The Chicago Scene.

Gems (Chicago)

Personnel Jessica Collins (lead), Theresa Washam, Dorothy Huckleby, Bertha
Walton, Minnie Riperton

Notes

The female Gems were originally teenage classmates from Chicago's West Side. They got together in 1959 and began recording in 1962.

This group was Chess/Checker's studio backup group. They also had one release as by the Lovettes.

According to the liner notes accompanying the *Best of Chess Vocal Groups-2* CD, group members were Jessica Collins, Vandine Harris, Bertha Watts, Dorothy Huckleby, and Theresa Washam. The liner notes with the CD boxed set of Chess recordings entitled *Chess Rhythm & Roll* show the lineup as Jessica Collins, Theresa Washum, Dorothy Hucklebee, Bertha Watts, and Minnie Riperton. This conflicting information comes from the same source, the label they recorded for—the label for which they were the female house group.

In Jeff Kreiter's *Group Collector's Record Price Guide,* Chess 1863 is shown as One More Year/Crush and in Ferdie Gonzalez's legendary *Disco-File,* Chess 1863 is shown as One More Year/Let Your Hair Down.

Discography

Chess 1863 One More Year/Let Your Hair Down (1963)
Chess 1875 A Girl's Impression/If It's the Last Thing I Do (1963)
Chess 1882 A Love of Mine/That's Why They Put Erasers on Pencils (1964)
Chess 1908 I Can't Help Myself/Can't You Take a Hint (1964)
Chess 1917 All of It/Love for Christmas (1964)
Chess 1930 You Make Me Feel So Good/Happy New Love (1965)
Chess 1958 Baby I Want You/That's How It Is (1966)
Chess 2104 Ain't That Loving Me/Girls Can Do It (1971)
Sources: Andy McKaie, liner notes with the Chess CD *Best of Chess Vocal Groups–2*; Pete Grendysa, liner notes with the Chess boxed CD set *Chess Rhythm & Roll.*

Genies (Long Beach, N.Y.)

Personnel Roy Hammond (lead), Bill Jayotis Gaines (Gains) (1st tenor), Claude Johnson, Alexander "Buddy" Faison (baritone), Fred Jones (bass)

Notes

This group originally formed in Long Beach, New York, in 1956 and practiced night after night. In 1958, Bob Shad of Shad Records heard them singing on the boardwalk at Long Beach.

Shad scheduled an audition that led to a recording session and in March 1959 "Who's That Knockin' " was released. The long wait for the release was worthwhile as the record did well, especially on the East Coast.

While the group was on tour, Gaines met a girl and the two left for Canada and were never seen again! For the balance of the tour, they had to alter voice parts but they made it through, regardless.

They next went to Hollywood Records and then to Warwick. None of these efforts proved successful and they eventually parted in 1959.

Claude Johnson soon met Roland Trone and the two painted homes to earn a living. They were overheard singing while on a job and soon became Don and Juan, who did the tremendously successful recording of "What's Your Name?"

(Note: Contrary to popular belief, Trone never sang with the Genies. It was also rumored that Eugene Pitt of the Jive Five was with the Genies as well. This happens to be true. Pitt never recorded with the group, but he did spend some time with them. Contrary to this is the story appearing in Jay Warner's *American Singing Groups* in which Warner states that Pitt never sang with the group.)

Discography

Shad 5002 Who's That Knockin'?/The First Time (1958)
Hollywood 69-1 No More Knockin'/On the Edge of Town (1959)
Warwick 573 There Goes That Train/Crazy Love (1960)
Warwick 607 Just Like the Bluebird/Twistin' Pneumonia (1960)
Warwick 643 Crazy Feeling/Little Young Girl (1960)
Source: Pete Grendysa in *Goldmine,* December 1988; Jay Warner, *American Singing Groups*; Wayne Stierle in *Goldmine,* August 12, 1988.

Gentlemen (Newark, N.J.)

Personnel Ted Larry Bogar (lead), Clifford Dale (1st tenor), Richard Baker (2d tenor), Alonzo "Lonnie" Johnson (baritone), Lucius Harris (d. 1959) (bass)

Notes

This group met in a Newark, New Jersey, barbershop in the early 1950s, playing pinochle. They soon began singing together and after much practice auditioned for Savoy in April 1954. The Newark label passed on the Gentlemen, so they took their demo into New York City and soon signed with Apollo.

After Lucius Harris died in 1959, the group disbanded. Members re-formed in 1962 after a replacement for Harris was found. The replacement is remembered only as Leroy. They then became Ronnie Baker and the Deltones, who recorded for Laurie.

"Story of a Love Gone Cold" by the Gentlemen is the predecessor of "My Story" recorded in 1962 by the Deltones.

Discography

Apollo 464 Tired of You (TB)/Something to Remember You By (CD) (1954)
Apollo 470 Don't Leave Me Baby (TB)/Baby Don't Go (LH) (1955)
Source: Donn Fileti, liner notes with the Relic LP *Apollo–1.*

Gladiolas (Lancaster, S.C.)

Personnel Maurice Williams (lead), William Massey (tenor), Earl Gainey (tenor), Willie Jones (baritone), Norman Wade (bass)

Notes

This group first got together in high school. After a brief time practicing, they found work singing on a radio show on Saturday mornings. This would later help them with their recording career.

Williams contacted Excello Records in Nashville and got an audition. Excello management liked them and gave them their name, Gladiolas. The Gladiolas were a self-contained group, both singing and playing instruments.

Bob Robertson also sang with the Gladiolas. He was an addition to the group on the last two Excello sides. Mack Baskins was still another member.

When the Gladiolas left Excello, they agreed not to use that name again and changed their name to the Zodiacs just prior to joining Herald Records.

Discography

Excello 2101 Little Darlin'/Sweetheart Please Don't Go (1957)
Excello 2110 Run, Run Little Joe/Comin' Home to You (1957)
Excello 2120 I Wanna Know/Hey! Little Girl (1957)
Excello 2136 Shoop, Shoop/Say You'll Be Mine (1958)
Sources: Cub Coda, liner notes with the *Excello Vocal Groups* CD; Gordon Skadberg, liner notes with the Ace CD *Southern Doo Wop.*

Gliders (New York)

Personnel Ollie Jones (lead), Abel DeCosta (1st tenor), Jimmy Breedlove (2d tenor), Robey Kirkland (baritone), Eddie Barnes (bass)

Notes

The Gliders were the universal house group for many single artists as well as vocal groups. They began doing backup for Laverne Baker on Atlantic 1004 How Can You Leave a Man Like This/Soul on Fire in 1953. They continued to execute backup duty until 1959 on Atlantic 2048 Manana/Shake a Hand.

This group also recorded as the Cues, Four Students, Ivorytones, and Rhythmakers and backed many single artists like Baker.

Discography

Atlantic 1047 Tweedlee Dee/Tomorrow Night (1954)
Atlantic 1057 Bop-Ting-a-Ling/That's All I Need (1955)
Atlantic 1075 Play It Fair/Lucky Old Sun (1955)
Atlantic 1087 Get Up Get Up/My Happiness Forever (1956)
Atlantic 1093 Fee Fee Fi Fo Fum/I'll Do the Same for You (1956)
Atlantic 1116 Jim Dandy/Tra La La (1956)
Source: Dennis Garvey in *Goldmine,* July 12, 1991.

Goldenrods (Gary, Ind.)

Personnel Crisby Harris (lead), Hiawatha Burnett (tenor), Cleve Denham (tenor), Jesse Rodgers (baritone), Charles Kolquitt (bass)

Notes

From the same town as the Spaniels, this group, like the Spaniels, got a start by walking in on Vivian Carter at Vee Jay in 1957.

Interestingly Bob Pruter, in *Doo Wop . . . The Chicago Scene,* presents a photograph of the Goldenrods, showing four members and spelling the bass's name Colquitt instead of what's reflected above—Kolquitt. In the text, Bob discusses the group, naming five members (with Denham the addition) and showing the bass's name as Kolquitt.

Discography

Vee Jay 307 Wish I Was Back in School/Color Cartoons (1958)
Source: Bob Pruter, *Chicago . . . The Doowop Scene.*

Goldentones (New York)

Personnel Mildred Harris, Harold Holman, Vernon Harris, Lee McCall, Everett Winder, Melvin Johnson

Notes

This group's only recording was released on Jay Dee and on Beacon. (Interestingly, in Roger Dopson's liner notes with the Charly *Dee Clark* CD, Dopson states that a group composed of Clark, Teddy Long, Cicero Blake, and Johnny Carter, from Chicago, recorded several sides for the tiny Jay Dee label.) In Donn Fileti's liner notes with the Jay Dee LP, totally different names are shown. Fileti goes on to say that the reason we have these statistics is that Joe Davis was such a meticulous businessman and that his files and record keeping were outstanding.

Discography

Jay Dee 806 Run Pretty Baby/The Meaning of Love (1955)
Beacon 560 Run Pretty Baby/The Meaning of Love (1955)
Sources: Donn Fileti, liner notes with the Relic CD *Jay Dee*; Bob Pruter, *Doowop . . . The Chicago Scene.*

Griffins (Washington, D.C.)

Personnel William Ross (lead), Bill Alford (1st tenor), Lewis "Flip" Thompson (2d tenor), Lawrence Tate (baritone), Joshua Bright (bass)

Notes

The Griffins were previously known as the Warblers. The tune shown below as by the Griffins on Mercury, entitled "Scheming," was earlier cut by the Warblers.

Lawrence Tate and William Ross joined the Griffins in 1953 from the RCA Heartbreakers, who had disbanded in 1953.

Discography

Mercury 70558 I Swear by All the Stars Above/Sing to Me (1953)
Mercury 70650 Scheming/Bad Little Girl (1954)
Mercury 70913 My Baby's Gone/Why Must You Go (1954)
Wing 90067 Forever More/Leave It To Me (1954)

Sources: Ron Bartolucci, liner notes with the Eagle CD *D.C. Doo Wops–1*; Billy Vera, liner notes with the RCA CD *Rock and Roll Party–1*.

Guides (Hollywood, Calif.)

Personnel Carlton Beck (lead), Richard Betts

Notes

It was written in the liner notes accompanying the Jamie/Guyden CD *Doop Doo Wah* that there may be some connection between the Guides and the Dandevilles.

Discography

Guyden 2023 How Long Must a Fool Go On/You Must Try (1959)
Source: Bob Bosco, liner notes with the Jamie/Guyden CD *Doop Doo Wah*.

Halos (Bronx, N.Y.)

Personnel J. R. Bailey (lead, some), Phil Johnson (lead, some), Harold Johnson (2d tenor), Al Cleveland (baritone), Arthur Crier (bass)

Notes

Arthur Crier and Carl Spencer were doing background and demo work in the Brill Building in Manhattan and met Al Cleveland in front of that famous building one day. Cleveland was in New York City looking for work using his vocal talent, and thus the three met each other. They were joined by Phil Johnson, Harold Johnson, and J. R. Bailey. Soon, sans Spencer, they formed the Halos.

The group first recorded as the Craftys for Morty Craft. Later the Craftys were renamed the Halos.

The Halos were the background group for Shirley and Lee. According to Mark Marymount's liner notes with Collectables' *Nag—The Halos* CD, the Halos provided this service on their hit "Let the Good Times Roll" as well as others for the New Orleans duo. They also did backup work for Curtis Lee, Barry Mann, Ben E. King, and others.

(Note: I recall listening to "Let the Good Times Roll" on New York radio in 1956. If the Halos assembled in the 1960s, how could they have done backup work in 1956?)

J. R. Bailey (Cadillacs) was with the Halos for recording and was replaced on tours at lead by Phil Johnson of the Duvals on Club and on Kelit, since Bailey did not wish to travel.

Phil Spector used the Halos as background for Curtis Lee's "Pretty Little Angel Eyes" and "Gee, How I Wish You Were Here."

Spector then used them as background for Gene Pitney's "Every Little Breath I Take." They also did backup for Barry Mann ("Who Put the Bomp"), Ben E. King ("Don't Play That Song"), Connie Francis, Dion, Little Eva, and others.

Discography

7 Arts 709 Nag/Copy Cat (1961)
7 Arts 720 Come On/What'd I Say? (1961)
Trans Atlas 690 Village of Love/Mean Old World (1962)
Sources: Mark Marymont, liner notes with the Halos Collectables CD *Nag*; Arthur Crier, interview by author, August 1995.

Hambone Kids (Chicago)

Personnel Delecta "Dee" Clark, Sammy McGrier, Ronny Strong

Notes

The novelty song "Hambone" was released on Okeh in 1952. The three singers shown above were between the ages of eleven and fourteen when the tune became a popular hit.

The three boys were known as the Hambone Kids. The popularity of the disc generated cover versions by Jo Stafford, Frankie Laine, and Tennessee Ernie Ford.

Because their follow-ups to "Hambone" lacked the novelty of their first release, the three decided to disband.

Delecta Clark went on to record as (and become known as) "Dee" Clark and recorded several sides for Vee Jay with the Kool Gents.

Discography

Okeh 6862 Hambone/Boot 'Em Up (instrumental) (1952)
Okeh 6884 Zeke'l Zeke'l/? La Raspa (instrumental) (1952)
Okeh 6914 Piece a Puddin'/Last Night's Party (instrumental) (1952)
Source: Marv Goldberg and Marcia Vance, liner notes with the CBS CD *Okeh Rhythm and Blues.*

Happy Tones (Los Angeles)

Personnel Brice Coefield (lead), Don Trotter (1st tenor), Sheridan "Rip" Spencer (tenor), Chester Pipkin (tenor), Ed Wallace (bass)

Notes

This group was produced as the Valiants evolved. Several personnel changes occurred in the Valiants after Billy Storm left that group, and eventually they began recording as the Untouchables. They recorded for Madison and Liberty Records, among others. Between recording for those two labels, their manager somehow got them a session with Screen Gems Records. When the disc from that session was eventually released, it was issued as by the Happy Tones. No one really knows why this occurred—it could have been a legal issue.

Discography

Colpix 693 Summertime Night/Papa Shame (1963)
Source: Marv Goldberg in *DISCoveries*, article on the Valiants.

Harmonaires (Bronx, N.Y.)

Personnel Clint Holland, Albert George (bass)

Notes

Holland and George were later members of Norman Fox and the Rob Roys.

George was to become the bass for the Bonnevilles on Munich, who coincidentally recorded a different tune entitled "Lorraine."

It is also understood that several of the members of the Harmonaires attended DeWitt Clinton High School in the Bronx.

In order to dispel the rumor that the Harmonaires were from Queens, I offer the following shared explanation/clarification: In his discussion of the Five Sharps in Jay Warner's *American Singing Groups,* Warner refers to "one of the other Jamaica (Queens) vocal groups, the Harmonaires."

It is my belief that Warner is referring to the name originally used by Jamaica's Rivileers. Warner's book states, in the discussion of the second Drifters group, that Dock Green had been with the Harmonaires. I cannot comment on this.

Discography

Holiday 2602 Lorraine/Come Back (1957)
Source: Jay Warner, *American Singing Groups.*

Harmony Grits (New York)

Personnel "Little" David Baughan (lead), Gerhart Thrasher (tenor), Andrew Thrasher (baritone), Bill Pinkney (bass)

Notes

"Little" David Baughan sang with the Drifters, Checkers, Harps, and Original Drifters.

The Thrashers and Pinkney all sang with the Drifters.

Discography

End 1051 Am I to Be the One?/I Could Have Told You (1959)
End 1063 Gee/Santa Claus Is Coming to Town (1959)
Source: Marv Goldberg, liner notes with the Savoy LP *Vocal Group Album.*

Harptones (New York)

Personnel Willie Winfield (lead), Nicky Clark (d) (1st tenor), Bill Dempsey (2d tenor), Bill "Dicey" Galloway (baritone), Bill Brown (d) (bass)

Notes

This group formed early in 1953, when two of Manhattan's street groups, the Harps and the Skylarks, joined forces. Other individuals would join while others would leave. After much practice and several local appearances, they met Leo Rogers of Bruce Records at the Apollo Theater in Harlem. The group was singing in Apollo's amateur night contest, and Rogers liked them enough to invite them to Bruce so that his partners at the recording company, Morty Craft and Monte Bruce, might hear them.

(According to the liner notes accompanying Relic's *Tip Top* recordings, it was Monte Bruce who discovered the Harptones!)

The three loved what they heard, made them aware of another Harps group, and had them change their name to Harptones. That December, Bruce released the classic "Sunday Kind of Love."

Jim Beckum was added in 1954 and first appears on "Life Is But a Dream." This occurred when "Dicey" was drafted. Beckum had been with the Majors on Derby prior to joining the Harptones. In 1955, Leo Rogers purchased the interests in the Bruce label held by Monte Bruce and Morty Craft.

In June 1955 the Harptones left Bruce and signed with Hy Weiss's Old Town Records. They recorded for Weiss on his Paradise subsidiary.

In the early summer of 1956, the group consisted of Winfield, Beckum, Dempsey, and Bobby Spencer. Spencer was from the Cadillacs, Chords, and Crickets. It was this combo that recorded My Memories of You/What Is Your Decision.

Because they felt their records were not being promoted properly, the Harptones moved to George Goldner's Rama Records in the summer of 1956. Jay Warner states in *American Singing Groups* that it was the summer of 1956 that the Harptones appeared in the R&B movie *Rockin' the Blues*. I was personally responsible for acquiring this film from the Library of Congress for Ronnie Italiano's UGHA. This is a 1955 film!

Curtis Cherebin, bass/baritone, was added later. Milton Love from the Solitaires was a fill-in, as was Wilbur "Yonkie" Paul.

Paul had been with the Five Crowns, the Floaters, and the Rainbow Duvals.

Fred Taylor sang with the group when Beckum was ill sometime in 1956.

Harriet Williams was a short-term member of the group subbing for Dempsey when he left to care for his cancer-stricken father. Bass Bill Brown died in 1956, following the group's recording of "The Shrine of St. Cecelia" on Rama. The group could never replace him.

In 1959, they returned to Morty Craft and his new label, Warwick. At this time they were made up of Willie, Dempsey, Harriet Williams, Curtis Cherebin, and Milton Love.

After Warwick, they went to several other labels trying to achieve the magic they once had.

Discography

Bruce 101 A Sunday Kind of Love/I'll Never Tell (1953)
Bruce 102 My Memories of You/It Was Just for Laughs (1954)
Bruce 104 I Depended on You/Mambo Boogie (1954)
Bruce 109 Why Should I Love You?/Forever Mine (1954)
Bruce 113 Since I Fell for You/Oobidee-Oobidee-Oo (1954)
Bruce 128 I Almost Lost My Mind/Ou-Wee-Baby (1955)
Paradise 101 Life Is But a Dream/You Know You're Doing Me Wrong (1955)

Paradise 103 My Success/I've Got a Notion (1955)
Essex 354 I'll Never Tell/Honey Love (1955)
Tip Top 401 My Memories of You/High Flyin' Baby (1956)
Rama 203 Three Wishes/That's the Way It Goes (1956)
Rama 214 On Sunday Afternoon/The Masquerade Is Over (1956)
Rama 221 Shrine of St. Cecelia/Ou-Wee-Baby (1956)
Andrea 100 What Is Your Decision?/Gimme Some (1956)
Gee 1045 Cry Like I Cried/So Good, So Fine (1957)
Warwick 500 Laughing on the Outside/I Remember (1959)
Warwick 512 Love Me Completely/Hep Teenager (1959)
Warwick 551 No Greater Miracle/What Kind of Fool? (1960)
Coed 540 Rain Down Kisses/Answer Me, My Love (1960)
Companion 102 All in Your Mind/The Last Dance (1961)
Companion 103 What Will I Tell My Heart?/Foolish Me (1961)
Cub 9097 Devil in Velvet/Your Love Is a Good Love (1961)
KT 201 I Gotta Have Your Love/Sunset (1962)
Raven 6001 Sunday Kind of Love/Mambo Boogie (1962)
Sources: Liner notes with Relic's Harptones CDs; Phil Groia, *They All Sang on the Corner*; Jay Warner, *American Singing Groups.*

Hawks (New Orleans)

Personnel Allen "Fat Man" Mathews (lead), Joseph Gaines (1st tenor), Albert Veal (2d tenor), John Morris (baritone), Willie Thrower (bass)

Notes

Dave Bartholomew paired Allen "Fat Man" Mathews with a gospel group, the Humming Four, to form Allen "Fat Man" Mathews and the Four Kittens at their start.

In early 1953 they were renamed the Hawks and started to record for Imperial. This lasted until 1955, when they moved to Modern Records.

The Hawks provided vocal backing for Imperial artists such as Dave Collins, with whom they called themselves the Scrubs.

Because the group members were all in their fifties and sixties, they had a limited number of touring engagements and were restricted to the New Orleans vicinity for their bookings.

Following their Modern release in 1956, the Hawks, because of their advanced age, chose to call it quits and retire.

Discography

Imperial 5266 Joe, the Grinder/Candy Girl (1954)
Imperial 5281 She's All Right/Good News (1954)
Imperial 5292 I-Yi/It Ain't That Way (1954)
Imperial 5306 Give It Up/Nobody but You (1954)
Imperial 5317 That's What You Are/All Women Are the Same (1954)
Imperial 5332 It's Too Late Now/Can't See for Lookin' (1955)
Post 2004 Why Oh Why?/These Blues (1955)
Modern 990 It's All Over/Ever Since You Been Gone (1956)

Source: Lynn Abbott, liner notes with the Imperial LP *Dave Bartholemew Presents the Hawks.*

Heartbeats (Queens, N.Y.)

Personnel James Sheppard (d) (lead), Albert "Walter" Crump (1st tenor), Robby Tatum (a.k.a. Robby Brown) (2d tenor), Vernon Seavers (baritone), Wally Roker (bass)

Notes

This group formed in 1953 from the friendship among Crump, Tatum, Seavers, and Roker. They began singing during those years while they attended different high schools. They practiced five hours a day, each day after school, on holidays, and on weekends. Robbie and Vernon were neighbors.

One day at rehearsal, someone told them of a guy who sang each evening at a local park. The four went to hear him sing.

While they were impressed with James Sheppard, he asked to hear them perform. The two factions were so impressed with each other that they decided to join forces.

They appeared at local events, and in the beginning Crump performed the lead chores. At first they called themselves the Hearts. Because the female Hearts got on records first, they came up with Heartbeats Quintet.

The well-known Miller Sisters lived across the street from Seavers, and it was their father, William, who suggested that they visit his friend Ivin Ballen at Gotham Records, a New York label with pressing facilities in Philadelphia. They followed his suggestion and soon came their first disc, "Tormented," recorded for Gotham's subsidiary label, Network Records. This disc sold poorly and William Miller then took the group to Hull Records in New York, where he was a principal owner, along with Billy Dawn Smith and Bea Caslon.

Hull management liked them and had them record "Crazy for You," which did quite well, as did their other Hull recordings through "A Thousand Miles Away." These successes led them to tour with the big names of the day all over the country. Jimmy Sheppard wrote "A Thousand Miles Away" for a girl he loved who had moved to Texas. Sheppard was quite broken up about their separation and consequently wrote the song.

There were never any personnel changes affecting the Heartbeats.

As a result of their successes with Hull, Bea Caslon, who could not properly handle a national hit, sold the Heartbeats and their recording masters to George Goldner of the Rama/Gee/Roulette complex.

Their good fortune continued with the new organization, as well as their personal appearances.

Their financial arrangements were interesting. Their personal manager got 20 percent, their booking agency got 10 percent, their choreographer got 5 percent, and the arranger got 5 percent. Thus 60 percent was left for the quintet to split.

While on tour in Philadelphia, they were performing "A Thousand Miles Away" and Shep fell asleep at the microphone. Crump had to pick up the lead role. Shep eventually woke up during the break of the song. Afterward, backstage the group literally fell apart—this was absolutely the end.

Disenchantment, boredom, and personality conflicts with other members, coupled with an egotistical personality and his own personal difficulties with liquor, caused Shep to contact Charles Baskerville (Videos) and Clarence Bassett (Five Sharps), whom he knew from his old Queens neighborhood, and formed Shep and the Limelites in 1960.

Before forming the Limelites, Shep had a restaurant in the Jamaica section of Queens for two years.

It is reported in Bear Family's *Jamie/Guyden* CD that in 1962, Shep contacted the Roulette organization, which now owned the Rama/Gee complex, concerning retroactive royalties. Shortly after this, James Sheppard was found shot to death along the Long Island Expressway.

It has also been learned (although unconfirmed) that Wally Roker was a member of the soul group the Whispers.

Discography

Network 71200 Tormented/After Everybody's Gone (1955)
Hull 711 Crazy for You/Rock 'n' Roll 'n' Rhythm 'n' Blues (1955)
Hull 713 Darling How Long?/Hurry Home Baby (1956)
Hull 716 People Are Talking/Your Way (1956)
Hull 720 A Thousand Miles Away/Oh Baby Don't (1956)
Rama 216 A Thousand Miles Away/Oh Baby Don't (1956)
Rama 222 Wedding Bells/I Won't Be the Fool Anymore (1957)
Rama 231 Everybody's Somebody's Fool/I Want to Know (1957)
Gee 1043 Hands Off My Baby/When I Found You (1957)
Gee 1047 500 Miles to Go/After New Year's Eve (1957)
Roulette 4054 I Found a Job/Down on My Knees (1958)
Roulette 4091 Sometimes I Wonder/One Day Next Year (1958)
Guyden 2011 One Million Years/Darling I Want to Get Married (1959)
Sources: Phil Groia, liner notes with the Rhino CD *Heartbeats*; Jeff Beckman in *Big Town Review* 3; Wally Roker, interview by Pete Grendysa in *Goldmine*, December 1980.

Heartbeats (Brooklyn, N.Y.)

Personnel Frankie Stropoli (lead), Florence Guida (female lead), Al Rosenberg (1st tenor), Tony Grochowski (2d tenor), Joe Sucamele (bass)

Notes

This group was formed in 1955 while the members were still in high school in Brooklyn. They sang at school dances, church functions, social clubs, and parties.

They somehow met Jerry Blaine of Jubilee who liked them and had them record for that label. Blaine felt that on the flip side of a recording, a girl should do lead and thus sixteen-year-old Florence Guida sang lead on "Boil and Bubble." Interestingly, she did not know anyone in the group and after the recording session never sang with them again.

After meeting the Hull Heartbeats and realizing their popularity, the Jubilee group chose to disband rather than change their name.

Later, Frankie and Tony rejoined with another acquaintance and formed the Three Friends, who recorded "Blanche" for Lido Records.

Discography

Jubilee 5202 Finally/Boil and Bubble (1955)
Source: Ken Berger in *Record Exchanger* 19.

Heartbreakers (Washington, D.C.)

Personnel Robert Evans (lead), James Ross (tenor), Lawrence Tate (baritone), Lawrence Green (baritone), George Davis Jr. (bass)

Notes

In 1948, James Ross and Lawrence Tate formed a singing group. They were later joined by Robert Evans. In 1950, George Davis, who had been lead singer for the Four Dots on Dot came aboard with another former Four Dots member, Larry Green.

(Note: Although this information is not chronologically sound, it is shown as reported in issue 11 of *Bim Bam Boom,* in the Heartbreakers article written by Alan Lee, Donna Hennings, and Les Moskowitz.)

Anyone involved with music in Washington, D.C., at that time had to be associated with Lillian Claiborne. She was the Heartbreakers' manager and obtained a contract for the Heartbreakers to record for RCA Victor. They recorded eight sides during their two sessions with RCA.

They made local appearances in the D.C. area waiting for their records to hit, but it never happened. Each member had personal problems, and bills never stopped piling up. Their managers at their day jobs did not understand their need for days off to make appearances, and so on, and a few of them were let go.

The Heartbreakers disbanded in 1953 due to the above difficulties, coupled with internal conflicts that also began to surface and the lack of positive response to any of their four RCA releases.

Two members, Ross and Tate, became members of the Griffins on Mercury in 1953. Robert Evans formed and sang with the Topps on Red Robin.

Discography

RCA 4327 Heartbreaker (RE)/Wanda (LT) (1951)
RCA 4508 I'm Only Fooling My Heart (JD)/You're So Necessary to Me (RE) (1951)
RCA 4662 Why Don't I? (JD)/Rockin' Daddy-O (RE) (1951)
RCA 4869 There Is Time (RE)/It's OK with Me (JR) (1952)
Roadhouse 1007 Cry Wind Cry (RE)/I Swear by All the Stars Above (JR) (1952)
Roadhouse 1008 Het Baby (RE)/I Only Want to Be Your Guy (LG) (1952)
Roadhouse 1010 Embraceable You/Heartbreaker (live) (1952)
Roadhouse 1012 We're Gonna Have Some Fun/Goodbye Baby (1952)
Roadhouse 1014 Don't Stop Baby (1953)
Sources: Billy Vera, liner notes with the RCA CD *Rock 'n' Roll–1*; Alan Lee, Donna Hennings, and Les Moskowitz in *Bim Bam Boom* 11.

Heartbreakers (Bronx, N.Y.)

Personnel Paul Himmelstein (lead), Henry Jackson (1st tenor), Bobby Higgs (2d tenor), Henry Eli (baritone)

Notes

Paul Himmelstein was discovered as a talented child star in 1952.

By 1954, he joined up with the other members of the Heartbreakers. Himmelstein was thirteen years of age at the time. The others were sixteen and seventeen.

After the group appeared (and won) four weeks in a row at the Apollo's amateur night contest, RCA's Vik Records subsidiary signed the Heartbreakers to a recording contract.

Vik released two discs by the group and then tried to convince Himmelstein to leave them and go solo. Loyalty would not allow him to do this. However, the group broke up soon after anyway.

Discography

Vik 0261 Without a Cause/One, Two, I Love You (1957)
Vik 0299 Love You Till the Day I Die/My Love (1957)
(Note: "Come Back My Love" is featured on the two Vanguard LPs from 1956 and 1960 respectively.)
Sources: Billy Vera, liner notes with the RCA CD *Rock 'n' Roll Party–2*; Rockin' Ray Levy in *Yesterday's Memories* 7.

Hearts (Bronx, N.Y.)

Personnel Joyce West (lead), Hazel Anderson (tenor), Florestine Barnes (tenor), "Ena" Louise Harris Murray (baritone)

Notes

The Hearts began in Harlem in 1954 and were managed by Zell Sanders, Johnnie Richardson's (of Johnnie and Joe) mother. Their first record was their biggest, "Lonely Nights." Sanders also owned the J&S label for which the Hearts would later record.

It was Sanders who initially brought the Hearts to Baton Records.

Baton management made certain that there were always two Hearts groups in place at the same time. Jeannette "Baby" Washington was in the second group.

The name Rex Garvin always appears in the personnel listing for the Hearts. He was the keyboard accompanist for the group. Patricia Ford was a member of the group, as was Pat Williams from the Dappers.

In Pete Grendysa's liner notes in the Bear Family *Cadillacs* box set, he states that Joan Willingham, sister of Cadillacs Gus Willingham, was a member of the Hearts on Baton.

Discography

Baton 208 Lonely Nights/Oo-Wee (1955)

Baton 211 All My Love Belongs to You/Talk about Him, Girlie (1955)
Baton 215 Gone, Gone, Gone/Until the Real Thing Comes Along (1955)
Baton 222 Going Home to Stay/Disappointed Bride (1956)
Baton 228 She Drives Me Crazy/I Had a Guy (1956)
J&S 425/426 My Love Has Gone/You or Me Has Got to Go (1956)
J&S 995 Thousand Years From Today/I Feel So Good (1956)
J&S 1626 Like Later, Baby/ (1957)
J&S 1627 I Want Your Love Tonight/ (1957)
J&S 1657 Dancing in a Dream World/You Wouldn't (1957)
J&S 1660 So Long, Baby/You Say You Love Me (1957)
J&S 10002/10003 If I had Known/There Are So Many Ways (1958)
Tuff 370 Dear Abby/Dear Abby (1963)
Zell's 3377 A Thousand Years from Today/I Feel So Good (1970)
Sources: Liner notes with the *Hearts . . . Lonely Nights* CD; Bill Millar, liner notes
with the Flyright LP *Best of Baton R&B*; Phil Groia, *They All Sang on the Corner.*

Hearts, Lee Andrews & (Philadelphia)

Personnel Lee Andrews (lead), Roy Calhoun (d) (1st tenor), Thomas "Butch"
Curry (2d tenor), Jimmy McCallister (baritone), John Young (bass)

Notes

This group formed in 1952 as a gospel group but soon realized there were greater
financial rewards singing R&B or pop. As a result, in 1954 they began their recording
career in Philadelphia singing secular music.

After auditioning for Philadelphia deejay Kae Williams, the group was taken to
a studio to record. These recordings were ultimately heard by Eddie Heller of Rainbow Records.

Andrews, whose real name was Arthur Lee Andrew Thompson, and the Hearts
recorded six sides for Rainbow. They all failed at the cash register, and the group
left the label in 1954. They didn't reappear for two more years, when they signed
with Ivin [sic] Ballen's Gotham label. The most probable reason for signing with
Gotham is that both Andrews and Calhoun worked for the company. McCallister
joined the navy in 1955 and Ted Weems replaced him. Weems can be heard on the
Gotham material.

Attempting to promote the Gotham tunes, they became friendly with N.Y./Phila-
delphia deejay Jocko Henderson, who eventually recorded "Long Lonely Nights"
on the Mainline label, which he owned with Barry Golder. When the disc's success
became too much to handle, it was given to Chess for more effective distribution.
After three releases with Gotham, they moved to Chess and realized many successes.

Andrews's father, Beechie Thompson, sang with the Dixie Hummingbirds.

Wendell Calhoun replaced bass John Young in 1957.

Ted Weems left for the service in the fall of 1958 and Andrews simply left.

The Hearts became the Five Hearts with Tommy White at lead and Eddie Custis
(formerly of the Superiors) at baritone.

Andrews was married to Custis's sister. The balance of the group was Roy
Calhoun, his brother Wendell Calhoun, and Curry.

After Custis left, Sonny Gordon (Angels) replaced him at lead.

The last reuniting was in 1962, when the Hearts recorded "Together Again." Lee took part in this endeavor.

Andrews also sang with his wife, Jackie, in Congress Alley.

Bobby Bell, Eddie Bell, and Robert Howard joined the group in the 1960s, as did Victoria McAllister and Sandra Mingo.

Discography

Rainbow 252 Maybe You'll Be There/Baby Come Back (1954)
Riviera 965 Maybe You'll Be There/Baby Come Back (1954)
Rainbow 256 White Cliffs of Dover/Much Too Much (1954)
Rainbow 259 The Fairest/Bells of St. Mary's (1954)
Gotham 318 Bluebird of Happiness/Show Me the Merengue (1956)
Gotham 320 Lonely Room/Leona (1956)
Gotham 321 Just Suppose/It's Me (1956)
Mainline 102 Long, Lonely Nights/The Clock (1957)
Chess 1665 Long, Lonely Nights/The Clock (1957)
Argo 1000 Teardrops/The Girl around the Corner (1957)
Chess 1675 Teardrops/The Girl around the Corner (1957)
Casino 452 Try the Impossible/Nobody's Home (1958)
United Artists 123 Try the Impossible/Nobody's Home (1958)
United Artists 136 Why Do I ?/Glad to Be Here (1958)
United Artists 151 All I Ask Is Love/Maybe You'll Be There (1958)
Gowen 1403 Together Again/My Lonely Room (1962)
RCA 8929 You're Taking a Long Time Coming Back/Quiet as It's Kept (1966)
Crimson 1009 Island of Love/Nevertheless (1967)
Crimson 1015 I've Had It/Little Bird (1968)
Lost Nite 1001 Cold Grey Dawn/All You Can Do (1968)
Lost Nite 1004 Oh My Love/Can't Do without You (1968)
Lost Nite 1005 Quiet As It's Kept/Island of Love (1968)
Gotham 323 Sipping a Cup of Coffee/Just Suppose (Alt) (1981)
Gotham 324 Window Eyes/Long Lonely Nights (Alt) (1981)
Gotham 325 I Miss My Baby/Boom (Alt) (1981)
Sources: Marv Goldberg, liner notes with the Collectables double CD *Lee Andrews and the Hearts*; Charlie Horner in *Goldmine.*

Hearts (Philadelphia)

Personnel Tommy White (lead), Roy Calhoun (d) (2d tenor), Eddie Custis (baritone), Wendell Calhoun (bass)

Notes

This group was an evolution of Lee Andrews and the Hearts with residual members, the Calhouns.

Sonny Gordon of the Angels on Grand became the group's new lead when Tommy White left.

Discography

Chancellor 1057 It's Unbelievable/On My Honor (1960)
Source: Charlie Horner in *Goldmine*.

Hearts, Billy Austin & (Brooklyn, N.Y.)

Personnel Billy Austin (lead), Norman Hardy, John Brizant

Notes

Like the Dreamlovers, which made the transition from R&B to soul, Billy Austin and the Hearts made the transition from the easy sound of the 1940s to the great harmony sound of the 1950s.

Discography

Apollo 444 Night Has Come/Angel Baby (1953)
Source: Donn Fileti, liner notes with Relic's LP *Apollo*.

Hearts of Stone (Knoxville, Tenn.)

Personnel Lindsay Griffin (1st tenor), Floyd Lawson (tenor), John Myers (baritone), Carl Cuttler (bass)

Notes

Cuttler, Griffin, Myers, and Lawson also sang with the Four Pennies. Griffin and Myers sang with the Four Pennies' predecessor, the Larks, as did Floyd Lawson.

Discography

V.I.P. 25058 It's a Lonesome Road (CC)/Yesterday's Love Is Over (LG) (1970)
V.I.P. 25064 If I Could Give You the World/You Gotta Sacrifice (1971)
Source: Marv Goldberg in *Yesterday's Memories* 6.

Hepsters (Cleveland, Ohio)

Personnel Raymond Harvin, Art Kirkpatrick, Joe Williams, Willy "Woody" Woodall, Carl Brown

Notes

The Hepsters got together in 1954 as the Five Stars. They were formed by group member Joe Williams.

They practiced endlessly and performed at events such as talent shows and teen benefits. Eventually they auditioned for a local booking agent who liked them and had them change their name to Hepsters.

Little promotion, a lack of the recording industry know-how, and the loss of a great deal of money caused Ronel Records to close its doors early in 1957.

Discography

Ronel 107 I Had to Let You Go/Rockin' and Rollin' with Santa Claus (1955)
Ronel 110 I Gotta Sing the Blues/This-a-Way (1956)
Source: Bob Pruter, *Doo Wop . . . The Chicago Scene.*

Heralds (Brooklyn, N.Y.)

Personnel Billy Dawn Smith (lead), Donny Myles (a.k.a. Donny Schested) (tenor), Tommy Smith (baritone), Sonny Benton (bass)

Notes

This group also recorded as the Billy Dawn Quartet, the Mighty Dukes, and the Four Dukes. When they joined Herald Records in New York, label management changed their name to the Heralds. Al Silver, Herald-Ember owner, must have thought highly of the group, seeing that he named them after the label!

Discography

Herald 435 Eternal Love (BDS)/Gonna Love You Every Day (BDS) (1954)
Sources: Marv Goldberg and Rick Whitesell in *Yesterday's Memories* 12; Sal Mondrone in *Bim Bam Boom* 7.

Hi-Fidelities (Detroit)

Personnel Tony York, Juanita Davis, Sylvester Potts, Huey Davis

Notes

The release by the Hi-Fidelities was the first on the Hi-Q label.
    Several members became the Contours on Gordy.

Discography

Hi-Q 5000 Street of Loneliness/Help, Murder, Police (1957)
Fortune 528 Last Night I Cried/Just Go (1958)
Source: Susan Winson and Rich Adcock, liner notes with the Fortune LP *Treasure Chest of Musty Dusties–2.*

Hi Fi's, Rex Middleton's (St. Louis, Mo.)

Personnel Rex Middleton (lead), Leroy Boyer (tenor), Walter Harper (1st tenor), Tony Locke (tenor), Ernest Washington (baritone)

Notes

This group assembled in 1955. Boyer and Washington were taken from the Swans who recorded for the Ballad label.
    The Hi Fi's toured with Louis Jordan and Dinah Washington, who brought them to the Apollo.

Shirley Kennedy is another performer who recorded with the Hi Fi's.

Discography

CAM 100 I Know This Love Is Real/Wow (1958)
Source: Liner notes with the Verve LP *Rex Middleton's Hi-Fi's.*

Hi-Fives (Garfield, N.J.)

Personnel Dave Brigatti (lead), Pete Grieco (1st tenor), Ronnie Menhardt (2d tenor), Howie Lanza (baritone), Rudy Jezerak (bass)

Notes

This group began in 1956 as the Shal-Vans in Garfield, New Jersey, while the members were attending Garfield High School. They sang at dances and club functions and practiced incessantly.

In 1957, they appeared at New York's Apollo Theater and were received very well. They auditioned for Decca in 1958. Decca did not like their name and began calling them the Hi-Fives. Their first Decca recording was released in February 1958.

Their next Decca disc, Dorothy/Just a Shoulder to Cry On, was issued two months later and sold better than their first release. Despite fair sales, no royalties came their way.

After "Dorothy," Lanza was replaced by Joey Dee who, with Brigatti, later formed Joey Dee and the Starlighters.

Discography

Decca 30576 My Friend/How Can I Win? (1958)
Decca 30657 Dorothy/Just a Shoulder to Cry On (1958)
Decca 30744 Lonely/What's New . . . What's New? (1958)
Source: Ronnie Italiano in *Time Barrier Express* 1, no. 10.

Hi Liters (Newark, N.J.)

Personnel George Vereen (1st tenor), Wiseman Moon (1st tenor), Furman Hayes (2d tenor), Ivy Floyd (baritone), Calvin Williams (baritone)

Notes

The Hi Liters evolved from the Deeptones and the Four Deeptones.

In Pete Grendysa's article in the May 8, 1987, issue of *Goldmine,* Moon's first name is shown as Weisman.

Calvin Williams also sang with the Golden Gate Quartet, a gospel group.

Discography

HiCo 2432 In the Night/Let Me True to You (1958)
HiCo 2435 Over the Rainbow/Baby Please Be True (1958)
Source: Pete Grendysa in *Goldmine,* May 1987.

Hi-Lites, Ronnie & (Jersey City, N.J.)

Personnel Ronnie Goodson (d) (lead), Sonny Caldwell (1st tenor), John Witney (2d tenor), Stanley Brown (baritone), Kenny Overby (bass)

Notes

The group members all attended school together in Jersey City, New Jersey. Ronnie Goodson was the last to join, replacing his predecessor who had been drafted.

Goodson sang in the choirs of several local churches.

Unfortunately a dispute broke out that eventually went into litigation concerning the number of copies sold of "I Wish That We Were Married."

Bill Scruggs replaced Stanley Brown and then Richmond Charles replaced Scruggs.

Goodson and Hi-Lites records began to do poorly as his voice changed. The group's manager became ill at this time as well.

Ronnie died in 1980 at the age of thirty-two.

Discography

Joy 260 I Wish That We Were Married/Twistin' and Kissin' (1962)
Joy 265 Send My Love/Be Kind (1962)
Raven 8000 Valerie/The Fact of the Matter (1962)
Win 250 A Slow Dance/What the Next Day May Bring (1963)
Win 251 The Fact of the Matter/You keep Me Guessing (1963)
Win 252 High School Romance/Uptown-Downtown (1963)
REO A Slow Dance/What the Next Day May Bring (1964)
ABC 10685 Too Young/High School Romance (1965)
Source: Joe Sicurella in *Harmony Tymes* 2.

Hi-Lites (Danbury, Conn.)

Personnel William Tucker (lead), Eugene Hodge (1st tenor), James E. Hodge (2d tenor), Allen Gant (baritone), Sheldon Highsmith (bass)

Notes

This group got together in 1957 and performed at local record hops in Danbury and miscellaneous charity affairs in that locale.

They always pleased their audience with their splendid renditions of classic tunes.

It has been reported in the magazine *Rock 'n' Roll Bulletin* 1 that the Hi-Lites from Connecticut had split up, but their manager had a contract with Julia Records for another disc. Coincidentally, the Tabbys from Hackensack were in the same recording studio as the Hi-Lites' manager and he asked them if they would record "Gloria My Darling" and "I Love You for Sentimental Reasons." The Tabbys agreed, so purportedly the group performing these great tunes was the Tabbys, whereas the name of the group on the record's label is the Hi-Lites. (This group is the Tabbys who had recorded for Time Records and for the Metro label.)

(*Note:* If you own Hi-Lites discs and compare "I Love You for Sentimental Reasons" or "Gloria My Darling" with any of their other material, I doubt you will find much of a difference.)

Discography

Record Fair 500 I'm Falling in Love/Walking My Baby Back Home (1961)
Record Fair 501 For Sentimental Reasons/For Your Precious Love (1962)
Julia 1105 Gloria (My Darling)/Your Precious Love (1962)
Monogram 121 Pretty Face/Maybe You'll Be There (1976)
Sources: Joyce Mariott in the *Bridgeport Sunday Herald*; *Rhythm & News* 1; *Rock and Roll Bulletin* 1.

Hi Tensions (Los Angeles)

Personnel Bobby Parker (lead), David Cook (tenor), Jonathan "Sonny" Allen (tenor), Roy Haggins (baritone), Jack Johnson (bass)

Notes

The Hi Tensions were from south-central Los Angeles. They, like so many of their vocal group predecessors from the Los Angeles area, attended Jefferson High School.

Leon Peels of the Blue Jays also sang with this group. Bobby Parker had also sung lead for the Chanticleers.

Discography

Audio 201 So Far Away/The Clock (1960)
Milestone 2018 Ebbing of the Tide/Got a Good Feeling (1963)
Source: Donn Fileti, liner notes with the Relic LP *Milestone.*

Hi-Tones (Brooklyn, N.Y.)

Personnel Graham L. True, Fred Alvarez, Peter Scavuzzo, Albert Scavuzzo

Notes

Formerly known as the Shy-Tones. As a result of the kidding group members would always take from their 'friends', they decided to change their name to the Hi-Tones.

Discography

King 5414 Fool, Fool, Fool/Let's Have a Good Time (1960)
Candix 307 I've Never Seen a Straight Banana/The Special Day (1960)
Fonsca 201 Lover's Quarrel/Just for You (1960)
Eon 101 That Was the Cause of It All (1961)
Source: Donn Fileti, liner notes with the Relic CD *Tip Top.*

Holidays (Pittsburgh, Pa.)

Personnel Ray Lancianese (lead), Barbara Jo Lippzer (tenor), Charles Corky Hatfield (tenor), Frank Gori (baritone), Frank Grisnick (bass)

Notes

This group began in 1958 as Little Ray and the Valvadears.

They eventually changed their name to Holidays and after much practice went to New York to do some studio recording. They recorded two tunes that were never picked up by any record label and thus were never released.

They returned to Pittsburgh and met the owner of a new label. He took them back to New York to record "Miss You" and "Pretend" for Robbee Records. This release did very well locally, and they returned to Robbee for a second session.

Their second release did not do as well, and they decided it was time to change labels.

They recorded their next disc at Nix Records, One Little Kiss/My Girl. Neither tune did well and they decided to disband.

Discography

Robbee 103 Miss You/Pretend (1960)
Robbee 107 Lonely Summer/Then I'll Be Tired of You (1960)
Nix 537 One Little Kiss/My Girl (1961)
Source: Jeff Kreiter in *Story Untold* 9.

Hollywood Bluejays (Hollywood, Calif.)

Personnel Cornel Gunter (lead), Beverly Thompson (tenor), Thomas "Pete" Fox (2d tenor), Obediah "Young" Jesse (baritone), Richard Berry (bass)

Notes

This group formed out of the Hollywood Flames and ultimately led to the formation of an outstanding West Coast group—the Flairs. The story begins in the halls of Los Angeles's Jefferson High School in 1953. After a great deal of practice, they auditioned for John Dolphin of Recorded in Hollywood Records, who recorded them and released "I Had a Love." However, the group members disliked Dolphin and sought another label.

They soon went to Modern Records, auditioned for the Bihari brothers and a session was set up for the group. "I Had a Love" was recorded again for Flair Records, which changed their name to the Flairs.

In a 1970s interview, Cornel Gunter and other former members of the Flairs stated and confirmed that the group who recorded Cloudy and Raining/So Worried for Recorded in Hollywood in 1952 was a different Hollywood Bluejays.

For the record, Beverly Thompson was a man.

Discography

Recorded in Hollywood 396 I Had a Love/Tell Me You Love Me (1953)
Sources: Marv Goldberg and Mike Redmond in *Record Exchanger* 13; Lynn McCutcheon in *Bim Bam Boom* 6; Marv Goldberg and Rick Whitesell in *Yesterday's Memories* 10.

Hollywood Flames (Watts, Calif.)

Personnel David Ford (d) (lead), Willie Ray Rockwell (d) (2d tenor), Curley Dinkins (baritone), Robert Byrd (d) (bass)

Notes

The Hollywood Flames had their beginnings in 1949, when they met Johnny Otis at his Barrelhouse Club. They performed there and were able to get other singing engagements from people in the audience.

This first group recorded for Selective, Unique, Specialty, Recorded in Hollywood, and Spin.

It has been said that the Hollywood Flames, in one configuration or another, have recorded on eighteen labels and have consisted of David Ford, Gaynel Hodge, Bobby Byrd (d), and Curtis Williams (d).

Curtis left to form the Penguins and was replaced by Clyde "Thinman" Tillis.

Leon Hughes replaced Rockwell, who left the group to join the Lamplighters, with Thurston Harris in 1953. Hughes would later become one of the founding members of the Coasters.

The group on Aladdin, Lucky, Swing Time, Decca, Hollywood, and Money was Ford, Hodge, Byrd, and at the start either Curtis Williams or Curley Dinkins.

Williams left after a year to form the Penguins. When not busy with the Penguins, he would sit in with the Hollywood Flames at their recording sessions.

On Tabarin the recording personnel included Clyde Tillis, David Ford, Robert Byrd, and Curley Dinkins.

At this point Curley Dinkins left the group. Interestingly, he is related to former New York City mayor David Dinkins.

Gaynel Hodge left in 1957 and was replaced by Earl Nelson. It was Googie René who had Bobby Byrd alter his name to Bobby Day.

The basic Ebb group consisted of David Ford, Earl Nelson, Curtis Williams, and Clyde Tillis. This foursome remained constant until 1959, when they moved to New York. Then Eddie Williams and Ray Brewster replaced Williams and Tillis. Curiously, Jim Dawson (liner notes accompanying the Ace CD *Ebb Story–2*) relates this same information and adds that Bobby Day was sometimes with the Ebb ensemble. Dawson's liner notes contain a photograph of the Ebb Hollywood Flames with Cleve Duncan of the Penguins clearly shown, but Dawson says nothing about this.

After the group relocated to New York, John Berry of the Rainbows joined them. This is probably the same time that Tony Middleton and Joe Thompson briefly sang with them.

Discography

Swing Time 345 Let's Talk It Over (DF)/I Know (GH) (1953)
Lucky 001 One Night with a Fool (DF)/Ride Helen, Ride (BB) (1954)
Lucky 006 Peggy (GH)/Ooh La La (DF/BB) (1954)
Lucky 009 Let's Talk It Over (DF)/I Know (GH) (1955)
Decca 29285 Peggy (GH)/Ooh La La (DF/BB) (1954)
Decca 48331 Let's Talk It Over (DF)/I Know (GH) (1954)
Hollywood 104 Peggy (GH)/Ooh La La (DF/BB) (1954)
Money 202 Fare Thee Well (BB)/Clickety Clack I'm Leaving (BB) (1955)
Ebb 119 Buzz, Buzz, Buzz (EN)/Crazy (1957)
Ebb 131 A Little Bird (EN)/Give Me Back My Heart (DF) (1958)
Ebb 144 Frankenstein's Den (CT)/Strollin' on the Beach (all) (1958)
Ebb 149 A Star Fell (EN)/I'll Get By (EN) (1958)
Ebb 153 I'll Be Seeing You (EN)/Just for You (EN) (1958)

Ebb 158 There Is Something on Your Mind (EN)/So Good (EN) (1959)
Ebb 162 Now That You've Gone (EN)/Hawaiian Dream (DF) (1959)
Ebb 163 In the Dark (EN)/Much Too Much (EN) (1959)
Atco 6155 If I Thought You Needed Me (EW)/Every Day, Every Way (EN) (1959)
Atco 6164 Ball and Chain (EN)/I Found a Ball (EN) (1960)
Atco 6171 Devil or Angel (all)/Do You Ever Think of Me? (1960)
Atco 6180 Money Honey (EW)/My Heart's on Fire (CW/DF) (1960)
Chess 1787 Gee (DH)/Yes They Do (DH) (1961)
Coronet 7025 Believe in Me (DH)/I Can't Get a Hit Record (DH) (1962)
Goldie 1101 Believe in Me (DH)/Elizabeth (all) (1962)
Vee Jay 515 Letter to My Love (JB)/Drop Me a Line (TM) (1963)
Symbol 211 Annie Don't Love Me No More (GW)/Dance Senorita (GW) (1965)
Symbol 215 I'm Coming Home (GW)/I'm Gonna Stand by You (JB) (1966)
Sources: Bobby Day Byrd in *Yesterday's Memories* 3; Marv Goldberg in *Yesterday's Memories* 5.

Hollywood Four Flames (Los Angeles)

Personnel David Ford (d) (lead), Willie Ray Rockwell (d) (2d tenor), Curley Dinkins (d) (baritone), Robert Byrd (d) (bass)

Notes

The group used this name, the Hollywood Four Flames, starting with its recordings on the Unique label and the Recorded in Hollywood label.

According to Jim Dawson (*Juke Blues* 13), "While Gaynell [sic] Hodge was the lead singer for the Hollywood Four Flames recording for music entrepreneur John Dolphin, the group recorded 'Emily.' By the time the disc was released, Dolphin credited it to the Turks. Apparently, unusual marketing ploys were habit with Dolphin as he also released a Cash disc featuring the Gassers. In order to insure success, he released it with a song by Jesse Belvin on the A side."

Discography

Unique 003 Dividend Blues (DF)/W-I-N-E (BB) (1951)
Unique 009 Tabarin (DF)/Cryin' for My Baby (BB) (1951)
Unique 015 Please Say I'm Wrong (BB)/Masquerade Is Over (CD) (1951)
Recorded in Hollywood 164 I'll Always Be a Fool (DF)/She's Got Something (BB) (1952)
Recorded in Hollywood 165 Young Girl (BB)/Baby Please (BB) (1952)
Recorded in Hollywood 165 Young Girl (BB)/Glory of Love (DF) (1952)
Sources: Bobby Day Byrd in *Yesterday's Memories* 3; Marv Goldberg in *Yesterday's Memories* 5; Jim Dawson in *Juke Blues* 13.

Hollywood Saxons (Hollywood, Calif.)

Personnel Stan Beverly (lead), Charles Taggart (1st tenor), Maudice Giles (2d tenor), Joe Lewis (baritone), Nathaniel "Buster" Wilson (bass)

Notes

These were friends who routinely played basketball. In the showers that followed, they would sing and eventually liked what they were doing and started a vocal group. They practiced for some time and when they felt ready, they cut their first record on the Our label in 1958. They next recorded for George Matola's Tender label. Next was a session for Capitol Records calling themselves the Portraits.

As the Portraits on Capitol, the Hollywood Saxons recorded twenty sides, but only "Close to You" and "Easy Cash" were released.

Then, as the Tuxedos on Forte, another Matola label, they released "Trouble, Trouble" and "Yes It's True." This was Joe Lewis, Stan Beverley, and Charles Taggart.

After Forte they were renamed the Hollywood Saxons and recorded "Everyday's a Holiday" for Hareco, leased to Swingin' Elf and 20th Century.

The Hollywood Saxons broke up in the mid-1960s and in 1968, Beverley, Giles, Lewis, and Julius Anderson with Carlton Beck at lead, recorded for Swingin'.

Giles also was part of the Squires (Combo), Saxons, Capris, and Portraits. Richard Betts (Senders/Uptones) was a later member.

Discography

Swingin' 631 Everyday's a Holiday/L.A. Lover (1961)
Elf 101 Everyday's a Holiday/L.A. Lover (1962)
Elf 103 It's You (SB)/I'm Your Man (SB) (1962)
Entra 1214 Diamonds (SB)/The Tears Came Rolling Down (SB) (1963)
20th Century Fox 312 Everyday's a Holiday/L.A. Lover (1963)
Swingin' 651 It's You/I'm Your Man (1965)
Swingin' 654 Merry-Go-Round (CB)/Laughing Girl (CT/SB/JL) (1968)
Action Pack 111 Loving You (SB)/Laughing Blues (CT/JL) (1968)
Source: Marv Goldberg and Rick Whitesell in *Yesterday's Memories* 11.

Honey Boys (Baltimore, Md.)

Personnel Calvin "Khaki" Kollette (d) (lead), John "Prince" Billy (1st tenor), Diason "Dixon" Stokes (baritone), Roland "Big Boy" Jackson (bass)

Notes

This group formed in 1954 and performed as amateurs throughout the east Baltimore vicinity.

Through their friend Eddie Rich of the Swallows, they got an audition with Modern Records in their New York facility in 1955.

On their arrival in New York, Modern put them up at a hotel and gave them two songs to familiarize themselves with. They had to learn the songs in ten hours. When they finally got to the studio, Kollette's voice was hoarse and the final take was not his best. This turned out to be their only release for Modern.

In 1956, at their own expense, they cut two sides that were not released until Art Mariano issued them on his Boogie Music label in the 1970s. Eddie Rich does tenor on these sides as Kollette was gone by then.

In 1958, Eddie Rich was replaced by Larry Jones from the Baltimore/Washington Capitols.

Discography

Modern 980 Never Lose Faith in Me (CK)/Vippety Vop (CK) (1955)
Boogie Music Unchained Melody/Honey Love (Recorded in 1956 and released in the 1970s.)
Source: Phil Chaney in *Yesterday's Memories* 8.

Hornets (Cleveland, Ohio)

Personnel James "Sonny" Long (lead), Johnny Moore (tenor), Ben Iverson (baritone), Gus Miller (bass)

Notes

In 1957, a Cleveland skating rink owner heard the Hornets practicing and took them to United Records in Chicago.

During their one and only session at States, they recorded "You Played the Game," "Reelin' and Rockin'," and "Big City Bounce," but they were never released.

Bill Brent replaced Gus Miller at bass after the recording was completed.

Johnny Moore was the mainstay lead singer for the Drifters for the twenty years following Clyde McPhatter and later sang with the Drapers. He was also known as Johnny Darrow.

In 1966, Moore brought Bill Brent into the Drifters for about six months.

In the 1960s Iverson formed another Hornets group and recorded for the Way Out label.

Discography

States 127 Lonesome Baby/I Can't Believe (1953)
Sources: Bob Pruter, *Doowop . . . The Chicago Scene*; liner notes with the Rare *Windy City* CD.

Hummers (Bronx, N.Y.)

Personnel Buddy McCrae, Bobby Spencer, Harold Johnson, Al Springer, Gary Morrison (baritone), Arthur Crier (bass)

Notes

The Hummers recorded for Hy Weiss's Old Town Records. Their song "Gee What a Girl" was recorded for that label but was not released until the *Old Town Doo Wop* CD appeared in 1995.

This song was recorded the same day as "Crazy Love" by the Royaltones.

Crier sang with many other groups including the Halos, the Mellows, the Five Chimes, the Craftys, and in the 1990s the Morrisania Revue.

McCrae sang with Dean Barlow's Crickets and the Chords, who did Sh Boom.

The Hummers broke up in 1956 when Crier, Morrison, and Johnson joined up with Lillian Leach to form the second Mellows group on Celeste and Candlelight.

Sources: Marcia Vance and Marv Goldberg in *Yesterday's Memories* 12; Arthur Crier, interview by author, August 1994.

Hunters (Los Angeles)

Personnel Cornelius Gunter (lead), Beverly Thompson (1st tenor), Thomas Fox (2d tenor), Obediah "Young" Jesse (baritone), Richard Berry (bass)

Notes

This was another name that Flair management used for their house group, the Flairs.

In one form or another, they were also the Hollywood Bluejays, Five Hearts, Whips, Five Hollywood Bluejays, and the Rams.

For the record, Beverly Thompson is a man.

Discography

Flair 1017 Down at Hayden's/Rabbit on the Log (1953)
Sources: Marv Goldberg and Mike Redmond in *Record Exchanger* 13; Lynn McCutcheon in *Bim Bam Boom* 6; Marv Goldberg and Rick Whitesell in *Yesterday's Memories* 10.

Hurricanes (Brooklyn, N.Y.)

Personnel Henry Austin (lead), James Brown (2d tenor), Frederick Williams (baritone), Vernon Britton (bass)

Notes

This group had been the Toppers on Jubilee. After their Hurricanes' stint they became the Memos on Memo.

As the Hurricanes, Jerry Halfhide and Sam Fickling left while James Brown joined as tenor. The name change coincided with the personnel change.

Group manager Jelly Roll got the Hurricanes a contract with King Records. In June 1955 they cut the first of fourteen sides for King. Henry Austin performed most of the leads until 1958, when he left to record as Henry Alston for Skyline Records.

The Hurricanes appeared in the legendary R&B motion picture *Rockin' the Blues* in 1955 with the Harptones, the Wanderers, the Miller Sisters, and others.

They backed up Jerry Dorn on "Wishing Well" and Bubber Johnson on "Come Home" on King Records.

In 1959, Austin rejoined the Hurricanes and recorded their last record, "Priceless." At this time their name was changed to the Memos.

Discography

King 4817 Pistol-Packin' Mama/Poor Little Dancing Girl (1955)
King 4867 Yours/Maybe It's All for the Best (1956)
King 4898 Raining in My Heart/Tell Me Baby (1956)
King 4926 Little Girl of Mine/Your Promise to Me (1956)
King 4947 Dear Mother/You May Not Know (1956)
King 5018 Fallen Angel/I'll Always Be in Love with You (1957)

King 5042 Priceless/Now That I Need You (1959)
Source: Marv Goldberg in *Record Collector's Monthly* 43.

Ideals (Chicago)

Personnel Reggie Jackson (lead), Leonard Mitchell (1st tenor), Robert Tharp (baritone), Sam Stewart (bass)

Notes

This group was formed in 1952, when the members were all freshmen in high school. The group was originally known as the Mel-Tones and started out doing parties, high school functions, weddings, and many local events.

In 1956, Reggie Jackson left to go into the service and his place was taken by Fred Pettis. Pettis had outstanding range, from tenor to baritone, and was with the Ideals until 1958.

This group had outstanding vocal ability and stage presence but lacked original material. They sang the songs of others, whereas label management wanted groups with their own original material.

Wesley Spraggins was a member before recording, as was Major Lance.

Their period of nonrecording came to an end in 1961 following a long time of hanging around Chicago's clubs. A local deejay owned the Paso label and liked the Ideals enough to have them record for Paso.

Eddie Williams joined as the new lead after the first recording. The addition of Williams made the Ideals a five-man group.

In 1963, two former members of the Five Chances, Johnny "Chubby" Jones and Howard Pittman, started a new record label—Cortlandt. This was the Ideals' next stop. But nothing clicked there either and the next move was to St. Lawrence, where they changed their sound to a more melodic one. Just before the move, Williams was drafted and Jackson left temporarily. The group however, remained at three—Mitchell, Tharp, and Stewart.

By the time of the St. Lawrence recording, Jackson was back and Tharp was gone. By 1967, the Ideals were history.

Bob Pruter has stated to the author that there was no relation between the Ideals on Checker who cut Mary's Lamb/Knee Socks and the above ensemble.

Discography

Paso 6401 Together/What's the Matter with You, Sam? (1961)
Paso 6402 Magic/Teens (1961)
Cortland 1001 The Gorilla/L.A. (1963)
Cortland 110 Don Juan/The Gorilla (1963)
Cortland 115 Mo Gorilla/Feeling of a Kiss (1964)
St. Lawrence 1020 I Got Lucky/Tell Her I Apologize (1966)
Sources: Bob Pruter in *Goldmine*; Bob Pruter, *Doowop . . . The Chicago Scene.*

Illusions (Brooklyn, N.Y.)

Personnel Charlie Van Nostrand, Dom Bartolomeo, Sammy Demarco, Ralph Florio, Joseph Dailey Jr.

Notes

In 1958, two vocal groups were competing in a talent contest in a Brooklyn nightspot—Max the Mayors. At the end of the night the two groups combined and formed the Illusions.

The next year, 1960, their first record, "The Letter," was released by Coral.

Discography

Coral 62173 The Letter/Henry and Henrietta (1960)
Axtel 101 Better Late Than Never/Rock and Roll Train (1960)
Ember 1071 Can't We Fall in Love/How High is the Mountain (1961)
North-East 801 Hey Boy/Lonely Soldier (1962)
Mali 104 Hey Boy/Lonely Soldier (1962)
Sheraton 104 Hey Boy/Lonely Soldier (1964)
Relic 512 Hey Boy/Lonely Soldier (1964)
Laurie 3245 In the Beginning/Maybe (1964)
Little Debbie 105 Story of My Life/Walking Boy (1964)
Source: Dom Bartolomeo in *Remember When* 1.

Imaginations (Wantagh, N.Y.)

Personnel Frank Mancuso (lead), Bobby Bloom (d) (1st tenor), Philip Agtuca (2d tenor), Pete Agtuca (baritone), Richie LeCausi (bass).

Notes

The group formed in 1960. Because Mancuso knew the right people, they eventually auditioned and recorded for Music Makers Records. Following this, Goodnight Baby/The Search Is Over was released in 1961.

That first disc did well in the major cities on the East Coast, and Guardian Angel/Hey You was next. This was released on Music Makers as well as Dual Records.

Their next release was recorded for Ballad Records, which ultimately released the record to Laurie, but the disc did not do well.

When Mancuso joined the marines, Bobby Caupin replaced him at lead. Shortly after, the Agtuca brothers and Bloom wanted out, and the group split up.

Discography

Music Makers 103 The Search Is Over/Goodnight Baby (1961)
Music Makers 108 Guardian Angel/Hey You (1961)
Bomarc 301 Guardian Angel/Hey You (1962)
Ballad 500 Mamma's Lttle Baby/Wait a Little Longer Son (1962)
Source: Paul Heller in *Story Untold* 1.

Impacts (New York)

Personnel Kenny Seymour, Harold "Curly" Jenkins, Allen Morton, Renaldo Gamble (bass)

Notes

Gamble also sang with the Schoolboys and the Kodaks. Jenkins sang with the Kodaks as well.

Kenny Seymour spent time with Little Anthony and the Imperials.

Discography

Watts 5599 Soup/Now Is the Time (1958)
RCA 47-7583 Croc-O-Doll/Bobby Sox Squaw (1959)
RCA 47-7609 Canadian Sunset/They Say (1959)
Carlton 548 Darling, Now You're Mine/Help Me Somebody (1961)
Source: Billy Vera, liner notes with the RCA CD *Rock 'n' Roll Party–2.*

Impalas (Brooklyn, N.Y.)

Personnel Joe Frazier (lead), Tony Carlucci (1st tenor), Lenny Randa (2d tenor), Richard Wagner (baritone)

Notes

One of the few white groups with a black lead singer that did not sound white. The second tenor, shown above as Lenny Randa, is discussed in Jay Warner's *American Singing Groups* as Renda.

In the late 1950s they met one another and expressed an interest in forming a vocal group. They began practicing in a neighborhood candy store and on local street corners, where they were heard by Frazier. He offered to assist them with their harmonies and eventually became their lead singer.

Their first release, on Hamilton Records, a local Brooklyn label, made no noise at the cash register, and they found themselves back in the candy store practicing.

In 1959, they were introduced to Alan Freed, which led to an MGM audition. They were signed to the MGM subsidiary Cub. They recorded " (Sorry) I Ran All the Way Home" as their first disc for the label. This disc did very well and provided them with tours and many live appearances. Their next two records for Cub did not fare as well and Cub stopped promoting the Impalas' records.

Discography

Hamilton 50026 First Date/I Was a Fool (1958)
Bunky 7762 I Still Love You/Whip It on Me (1958)
Cub 9022 Sorry/Fool, Fool, Fool (1958)
Cub 9033 Oh What a Fool/Sandy Went Away (1959)
Cub 9053 Peggy Darling/Bye Everybody (1959)
Sundown 115 The Lonely One/Lost Boogie (1959)
Cub 9066 (Speedo &) All Alone/When My Heart Does All the Talking (1960)
Red Boy 113 I Can't See Me without You/When You Dance (1966)
Source: Jay Warner, *American Singing Groups.*

Impalas (Washington, D.C.)

Personnel Sandra Bears (lead), Margie Clark, Carrie Mingo, Grace Ruffin

Notes

This group was originally discovered by Bo Diddley, who was living in the D.C. area at the time. Diddley convinced Chess/Checker management to audition the group, and they recorded as the Impalas on their first Checker release. Their next Checker release was as by the Four Jewels.

Grace Ruffin was the cousin of the late Billy Stewart.

After their Checker cuts went nowhere, they signed up with D.C.'s Start Records and recorded as the Four Jewels. Their work with the new label was popular locally but unheard of elsewhere.

Discography

Checker 999 For the Love of Mike/I Need You So Much (1961)
Source: Alan Lee in *Yesterday's Memories* 8.

Imperials (Detroit)

Personnel Louis Van Dyke (lead), George Copes, Rudy Copes, James Morris, Earl Thomas

Notes

This group was also the Gaylords on Savoy. Because of potential confusion with Mercury's Gaylords, label management had them change their name to the Imperials. *(Note:* Isn't this name heavily used as well?)

Van Dyke also sang for the Ambassadors as well as the Savoy Gaylords.

Discography

Great Lakes 1201 Life of Ease/It Won't Be Very Long (1954)
Great Lakes 1212 You'll Never Walk Alone/Ain't Gonna Tell It Right? (1954)
Derby 858 Why Did You Leave Me?/Hard-Workin' Woman (1954)
Savoy 1104 My Darling/You Should Have Told Me (1954)
Source: Steve Propes, liner notes with the Savoy LP *Doo Wop Delights—The Roots of Rock.*

Imperials, Little Anthony & (Brooklyn, N.Y.)

Personnel Anthony Gourdine (lead), Tracy Lord (1st tenor), Ernest Wright (2d tenor), Clarence Collins (baritone), Gloucester Rogers (bass)

Notes

Anthony's first group was the Duponts on Winley. The performers listed above began as the Chesters on Apollo. Nevertheless, they failed at each undertaking before forming as Little Anthony and the Imperials. Soon the group hooked up with Richard Barrett at George Goldner's End Records and auditioned for him. Goldner was at the audition with Wright at lead. He suggested that Anthony do lead and told Anthony to sing "Tears on My Pillow" in his high tenor voice. Anthony did and the tune was pressed that way.

"Tears on My Pillow" showed the Imperials on the original End label, but it was Alan Freed's introduction that always referred to the group as Little Anthony and the Imperials whenever he played their song. Label management then showed this on all future pressings. The Imperials enjoyed great success, recording twelve discs for End. They enjoyed similar success on other labels.

In 1962 the group split up. Anthony went solo and the group replaced him with George Kerr, who had performed lead for the Serenaders on Chock.

Experiencing little success without Anthony, the group reunited on DCP. With Teddy Randazzo's help, they recorded "I'm on the Outside Looking In" and "Going Out of My Head."

First tenor Sammy Strain performed with the Imperials later on and also performed with the Chips, Fantastics, and O'Jays.

Discography

Liberty 55119 Glory of Love/C'Mon Tiger (1958)
End 1027 Tears on My Pillow/Two People in the World (1958)
End 1036 So Much/Oh Yeah (1958)
End 1038 The Diary/Cha Cha Henry (1959)
End 1047 A Prayer and a Juke Box/River Path (1959)
End 1053 So Near an Yet So Far/I'm Alright (1959)
End 1060 Shimmy Shimmy Ko Ko Bop/I'm Still in Love with You (1959)
End 1067 My Empty Room/Bayou, Bayou, Baby (1960)
End 1074 I'm Taking a Vacation from Love/Only Sympathy (1960)
End 1080 Limbo, Pt. 1/Limbo, Pt. 2 (1960)
End 1083 Formula of Love/Dream (1960)
End 1086 So Near and Yet So Far/Please Say You Want Me (1961)
End 1091 Traveling Stranger/Say Yeah (1961)
End 1104 A Lovely Way to Spend an Evening/Dream (1961)
Roulette 4379 That L'il Ol' Lovemaker Me/It Just Ain't Fair (1961)
Carlton 566 Faithfully Yours/Vut, Vut (1961)
Newtime 503 A Short Prayer/Where Will You Be? (1962)
Newtime 505 The Letter/Go and Get Your Heart Broken (1962)
Roulette 4477 I've Got a Lot to Offer Darling/Lonesome Romeo (1963)
Capitol 4924 I'm Still Dancing/Bermuda Wonderful (1963)
DCP 1104 I'm on the Outside/Please Go (1964)
DCP 1119 Goin' Out of My Head/Make It Easy on Yourself (1964)
DCP 1128 Hurt So Bad/Reputation (1965)
DCP 1136 Take Me Back/Our Song (1965)
DCP 1149 I Miss You So/Get Out of My Life (1965)
DCP 1154 Hurt/Never Again (1965)
Veep 1228 Better Use Your Head/The Wonder of It All (1966)
Veep 1233 You Better Take It Easy Baby/Gonna Fix You Good (1966)
Veep 1239 Tears on My Pillow/Who's Sorry Now? (1966)
Veep 1240 I'm on the Outside Looking In/Please Go (1966)

Veep 1241 Goin' Out of My Head/Make It Easy on Yourself (1966)
Veep 1242 Hurt So Bad/Reputation (1966)
Veep 1243 Our Song/Take Me Back (1966)
Veep 1244 I Miss You So/Get Out of My Life (1966)
Veep 1245 Hurt/Never Again (1966)
Veep 1248 It's Not the Same/Down on Love (1966)
Veep 1255 Don't Tie Me Down/Where There's a Will, There's a Way (1967)
Veep 1262 Hold On to Someone/Lost in Love (1967)
Veep 1269 You Only Live Twice/My Love Is a Rainbow (1967)
Veep 1275 Beautiful People/If I Remember to Forget (1967)
Veep 1278 I'm Hypnotized/Hungry Heart (1967)
Veep 1283 What Greater Love?/In the Back of My Heart (1968)
Veep 1285 Yesterday Has Gone/My Love Is a Rainbow (1968)
Veep 1293 The Gentle Rain/The Flesh Failures (1968)
Veep 1303 Goodbye Good Times/Anthem (1969)
United Artists 50552 Summer's Comin' In/Out of Sight, Out of Mind (1969)
United Artists 50598 Let the Sunshine In/The Ten Commandments of Love (1969)
United Artists 50625 Don't Get Close/It'll Never Be the Same Again (1970)
United Artists 50677 World of Darkness/The Change (1970)
United Artists 50720 If I Love You/Help Me Find a Way (1970)
Janus 160 Father, Father/Each One, Teach One (1971)
Janus 166 Universe/Madeline (1971)
Janus 178 Love Story/There's an Island (1972)
Avco 4635 I'm Falling in Love with You/What Good Am I without You (1974)
Avco 4645/4655 I Don't Have to Worry/I'll Be Loving You Sooner or Later (1974)
Avco 4651 I've Got to Let You Go/Hold On (1975)
Sources: Steve Kolanjian, liner notes with the Rhino CD *Best of Little Anthony & the Imperials*; John Apugliese, Steve Flam, and Ralph Newman in *Bim Bam Boom* 9.

Impossibles (Brooklyn, N.Y.)

Personnel Richard Albanese (lead), Steve Tuttolomondo (1st tenor), Frank Vultaggio (2d tenor), Joe Carrao (baritone), Bob Emerick (bass)

Notes

This group got together in Brooklyn in the late 1950s and spent many evenings in a local park practicing. An independent producer heard them and liked them. He changed their name and became their manager.

This manager had them record at a New York studio and brought the masters to RMP Records, which began to release their discs.

In March 1960 their second RMP record was released. All the while they continued performing at local clubs and parties, making many live appearances.

In 1964, they were spotted while performing at a Clay Cole show by a New York representative for Chess Records of Chicago. He brought them to Chicago for an audition and their name was changed to the Maniacs. But nothing was ever released by the Maniacs and they called it quits in 1965.

Discography

RMP 1030 Well It's Alright/Mr. Maestro (1959)
RMP 500/501 Well It's Alright '66/Everywhere I Go (1960)
RMP 508 I Can't Dance/The Tenant's Blues (1961)
Source: Ken Robertson in *Story Untold* 1.

Impressions (Chicago)

Personnel Jerry Butler (lead), Curtis Mayfield (tenor), Richard Brooks (tenor), Sam Gooden (bass), Arthur Brooks (baritone)

Notes

This group was originally formed in 1957 as a combination of the Brooks Brothers and Sam Gooden from the Roosters with Jerry Butler and Curtis Mayfield of the Northern Jubilee Gospel Singers. The Roosters came from Chattanooga, Tennessee, and the two factions came together in Chicago. They were spotted while performing at a local show and got themselves an audition with Calvin Carter of Vee Jay. The song that made this happen was "For Your Precious Love," which combined the Brooks Brothers' music with Jerry Butler's lyrics.

According to Billy Vera's liner notes with the Vee Jay *Impressions* CD, Butler was formerly a member of a doo-wop group known as the Quails. This is a nonrecording Quails from Chicago who later changed their name to the Serenaders and recorded, without Butler, for Chock.

"For Your Precious Love" was released on Vee Jay in May 1958. For some reason, the song was also on Abner (Ewart Abner) and Falcon. Two more releases followed, and in the fall of 1958 Butler decided to go solo. Three additional Jerry Butler and the Impressions songs were released but went nowhere. One of these had Mayfield doing lead. Mayfield, the group leader, took them to New York and struck a deal with ABC Paramount in 1960.

Fred Cash replaced Jerry Butler when he left the group and Mayfield assumed the lead position. Cash had been with the Roosters prior to joining the Impressions.

The first ABC single was "Gypsy Woman," which did very well.

Several more ABC singles were released, but none did as well as "Gypsy Woman." Then in February 1963, Mayfield, Gooden, and Cash went back to Chicago. The Impressions were now a trio.

The first tune released by this trio was "Sad, Sad Girl and Boy."

Curtis Mayfield began performing various duties in the recording business. He wrote (taking his style closer to gospel), produced, and sang lead. In 1968, when their ABC contract expired, he moved to the Curton label, which he owned. From 1968 to 1976, the trio had nineteen records that hit the charts.

In summer 1970, Mayfield left to go solo and Leroy Hutson replaced him.

Discography

Falcon 1013 For Your Precious Love/Sweet Was the Wine (1958)
Vee Jay 280 For Your Precious Love/Sweet Was the Wine (1958)
Abner 1013 For Your Precious Love/Sweet Was the Wine (1958)
Abner 1017 Come Back My Love/Love Me (1958)

Abner 1023 The Gift of Love/At the County Fair (1958)
Abner 1025 Señorita, I Love You/Lovely One (1958)
Abner 1034 A New Love/Listen (1959)
Bandera 2504 Listen/Shorty's Got to Go (1959)
Vee Jay 424 Say That You Love Me/Señorita I Love You (1961)
ABC 10241 Gypsy Woman/As Long as You Love Me (1961)
Port 70031 Listen/Shorty's Got to Go (1962)
Swirl 107 I Need Your Love/Don't Leave Me (1962)
ABC 10289 Grow Closer Together/Can't You See (1962)
ABC 10328 Little Young Lover/Never Let Me Go (1962)
ABC 10357 Minstrel and Queen/You've Come Home (1962)
ABC 10386 I Need Your Love/I'm the One Who Loves You (1963)
Vee Jay 574 The Gift of Love/At the County Fair (1963)
ABC 10431 Sad, Sad Girl and Boy/Twist and Limbo (1963)
ABC 10487 It's Alright/You'll Want Me Back (1963)
ABC 10511 Talking about My Baby/Never Too Much Love (1963)
ABC 10544 I'm So Proud/I Made a Mistake (1964)
ABC 10554 I Love You/Keep on Pushing (1964)
ABC 10581 See the Real Me/You Must Believe Me (1964)
ABC 10602 Amen/A Long, Long Winter (1964)
ABC 10622 I've Been Trying/People Get Ready (1965)
ABC 10647 Woman's Got Soul/Get Up and Move (1965)
ABC 10670 Meeting over Yonder/I've Found That I've Lost (1965)
ABC 10710 I Need You/Never Could You Be Me (1965)
ABC 10725 Twilight Time/Just One Kiss from You (1965)
ABC 10750 Man Oh Man/You've Been Cheatin' (1965)
ABC 10761 Falling in Love with You/Since I Lost the One I Love (1966)
ABC 10789 Too Slow/No One Else (1966)
ABC 10831 Can't Satisfy/This Must End (1966)
ABC 10869 Love's a Clown/Wade in the Water (1966)
ABC 10900 Little Girl/You Always Hurt Me (1967)
ABC 10932 You've Got Me Runnin'/It's Hard to Believe (1967)
ABC 10964 You Ought to Be in Heaven/I Can't Stay Away from You (1967)
ABC 11022 It's All Over/We're a Winner (1967)
ABC 11071 We're Rolling On–1/We're Rolling On–2 (1968)
ABC 11103 Up Up and Away/I Loved and I Lost (1968)
ABC 11135 Don't Cry My Love/Sometimes I Wonder (1968)
Curtom 1932 Fool for You/I'm Loving Nothing (1968)
Curtom 1934 This Is My Country/My Woman's Love (1968)
ABC 11188 East of Java/Just before Sunrise (1969)
Curtom 1937 My Deceiving Heart/You Want Somebody Else (1969)
Curtom 1940 Seven Years/The Girl I Find (1969)
Curtom 1943 Choice of Colors/Mighty, Mighty (1969)
Curtom 1946 Say You Love Me/You'll Always Be Mine (1969)
Curtom 1948 Amen/Wherever She Leadeth Me (1969)
Curtom 1951 Check Out Your Mind/Can't You See? (1970)
Curtom 1954 Turn On to Me/Soulful Love (1970)
Curtom 1957 Ain't Got Time/I'm So Proud (1971)

Curtom 1959 Love Me/Do You Wanna Win? (1971)
Curtom 1970 This Love's for Real/Times Have Changed (1971)
Curtom 1973 Love Me/I Need to Belong to Someone (1972)
Curtom 1982 Preacher Man/Times Have Changed (1973)
Curtom 1985 I'm Loving You/Thin Line (1973)
Curtom 1994 Times Have Changed/If It's in You to Do Wrong (1973)
Curtom 1997 Finally Got Myself Together/I'll Always Be Here
Curtom 2003 Three the Hard Way/Something's Mighty, Mighty Wrong (1974)
Curtom 0103 Sooner or Later/Miracle Woman (1975)
Curtom 0106 Same Thing It Took/I'm So Glad (1975)
Curtom 0110 First Impressions/Loving Power (1975)
Curtom 0116 I Wish I'd Stayed in Bed/Sunshine (1976)
Cotillion 44210 I'm a Fool for Love/This Time (1976)
Cotillion 44211 I Saw Mommy Kissing Santa Claus/Silent Night (1976)
Sources: Billy Vera, liner notes with the Vee Jay CD *Impressions*; Jay Warner, *American Singing Groups.*

Incas (Washington, D.C.)

Personnel Bob E. Lee (lead), Eddie Belton (1st tenor), José Williams (2d tenor), Maurice Watkins (baritone), Clayton Roberts (bass)

Notes

The group was organized in 1956 and remained together until 1959.
   Watkins and Roberts had been two of the original members of the Ontarios.
   José Williams also sang with the Aztecs.
   No discography is shown because this group had no 45 rpm releases.
   Their total output is showcased on Roadhouse's *Candy Bar Boogie* LP.
   Source: Les Moss, liner notes with the *Candy Bar Boogie* LP/CD.

Individuals (Los Angeles)

Personnel Johnny Staton (lead), Roy Allen (tenor), Joe Cummings (baritone), Art Ward (bass)

Notes

In 1959 Johnny Staton had abandoned the name "Feathers" and formed a group called the Individuals. As incredible as it may seem, they recorded for Showtime, a label with which they had previously been involved in litigation.
   This group also recorded as the Unforgettables on Pamela. Staton, of course, was the lead singer with the Feathers.

Discography

Show Time 595 Met Her at a Dance (JS)/Jungle Superman (all) (1959)
Show Time 598 Dear One (JS)/Jungle Superman (all) (1959)
Source: Marv Goldberg in *DISCoveries,* July 1995, article on the Feathers.

Informers (Philadelphia)

Personnel Roy Walker, Danny Todd, James Marshall, Timothy Jenkins, Henry Smith (bass)

Notes

James Marshall's sisters were in the female Monarchs.

The Informers were also the backup group for the female recording artist A. Debbie, who was married to a member of the band that the Informers used for recording.

In 1967 Marshall and Jenkins were drafted and the group went into a semi-retirement mode. When Marshall came out of the service in 1969, he wanted to start singing again, but there was another group known as the Informers, and they had to change their name to the Fabulous Performers.

Discography

J-Rude 1400 If You Love Me/Hard Way to Go (1965)
Blackjack 1402 A Hard Way to Go/Baby Set Me Free (1965)
Source: Tony Tisovec in *Doo Wop Magazine* 1.

Ink Spots (Indianapolis, Ind.)

Personnel Ivory "Deek" Watson (d) (lead), Jerry Daniels (d) (1st tenor), Charlie Fuqua (d) (2d tenor), Orville "Hoppy" Jones (d) (bass)

Notes

All of the original group members came from other musical ensembles. Orville "Hoppy" Jones came from a trio called the Peanut Boys, while Ivory "Deek" Watson from the Percolating Puppies and the Four Riff Brothers of which "Hoppy" Jones and Watson were members. Charlie Fuqua and Jerry Daniels came from an unnamed band in Indianapolis.

Daniels, Fuqua, and Watson sang with King Jack and the Jesters. About 1931-1932, they landed a fifteen-minute radio gig on WHK in Cleveland and then WLW in Cincinnati. At this time Watson's former partner in the Four Riff Brothers, "Hoppy" Jones, was added as a fourth member. They did a great deal of touring and were beginning to gather a following.

Part of King Jack and the Jesters touring took them to competitive New York, where a problem arose with their name. Orchestra leader Paul Whiteman had a vocal group in his band called the King's Jesters. The new group from Indianapolis lost the ensuing struggle and were then christened the Ink Spots.

While touring, the Ink Spots made many radio performances and live appearances. The group's first recording was for RCA in New York in 1935. They recorded four sides featuring the Ink Spots' unique vocal ability. They left RCA after receiving only a small advance. No royalties!

They then went on a trans-Atlantic tour and returned in December 1935 to New York, where many bookings awaited them.

Bill Kenny joined the group in 1936, replacing Jerry Daniels, who returned to Indianapolis because of ill health and financial problems. Kenny, from Baltimore, sang lead on "If I Didn't Care."

That same year they signed with Decca.

Because Bill Kenny sang lead on the successful "If I Didn't Care," "Deek" Watson's lead duties greatly diminished. In 1936, they signed with Decca. Their lively swing style was gone, partially due to Daniels's departure and Kenny's leads. The Ink Spots' signature ballad style was used on "If I Didn't Care," which was a huge seller. Bill Kenny's haunting ballads had effectively replaced the Deek Watson jump tunes of the past.

Touring continued and their recordings sold well. Another movie, *The Great American Broadcast* (1941), featured the Ink Spots singing "If I Didn't Care." The group was on top in 1942, when U.S. involvement in World War II was increasing and entrenched racial barriers were coming down.

Then a strike by the American Federation of Musicians occurred. Ink Spots recordings released at that time came from older masters stored in inventory, and their income came primarily from their live appearances. When the strike ended, Decca restarted recording and the group was now Bill Kenny, Deek Watson, Charlie Fuqua, and Bernie Mackey. It was now 1943. "Hoppy" Jones became ill during a performance. He returned but Watson soon left. While auditions were being held for a replacement for "Hoppy" Jones, Bill Kenny's brother, Herb, showed up to bid Jones farewell. Herb heard a bass trying out and gave him advice about how to do what the group desired. After this, he was not permitted to leave and ultimately became part of the Ink Spots.

Fuqua was drafted in 1943 and chose his old friend, Bernie Mackey, to replace him. At this time Cliff Givens joined the Ink Spots. When Watson left due to personality conflicts and formed his own Ink Spots group, a court decree forced them to change their name to the Brown Dots. For several dates, the group appeared as a trio and their manager eventually persuaded Billy Bowen to join them.

When Fuqua was due to return from the service, Bernie Mackey and Givens left. In 1944, "Hoppy" Jones passed away.

During the ensuing years in the late 1940s, personality conflicts persisted among members and brought about dissolution. One sore spot was Kenny's freelancing.

Adriel McDonald, their valet, became bass when Herb Kenny chose to leave. McDonald later sang with the Sandmen.

They next joined the King label. Jimmy Holmes was their outstanding lead. The rest of the King Ink Spots consisted of Harold Jackson, Essex Scott, Isaac Royal, and Charlie Fuqua. Leon Antoine joined them on King later. The King Ink Spots was Fuqua's group after the original ensemble splintered in the early 1950s.

(Note: After this, the number of groups and personnel become too prolific and unaccountable.)

Discography

RCA 24851 Swingin' on the Strings/Your Feet's Too Big (1935)
RCA 24876 Don't 'Low No Swingin' in Here/Swing Gate, Swing (1935)
Bluebird 6530 Swingin' On the Strings/Your Feet's Too Big (1936)
Decca 817 'Taint Nobody's Biz-Ness If I Do/Your Feet's Too Big (1936)
Decca 883 Christopher Columbus/Old Joe's Hittin' the Jug (1936)

Decca 1036 Stompin' At the Savoy/Keep Away from My Doorstop (1936)
Decca 1154 Alabama Barbeque/With Plenty of Money and You (1937)
Decca 1236 Swing High, Swing Low/Whoa Babe (1937)
Decca 1251 Let's Call the Whole Thing Off/Slap That Sass (1937)
Decca 1731 Don't Let Old Age Creep Up on You/Yes-Suh (1937)
Decca 1789 Oh Red/That Cat Is High (1938)
Decca 1870 I Wish You the Best of Everything/When the Sun Goes Down (1938)
Decca 2044 Brown Gal/Pork Chops and Gravy (1938)
Decca 2286 If I Didn't Care/Knock-Kneed Sal (1939)
Decca 2507 It's Funny to Everyone but Me/Just for a Thrill (1939)
Decca 2707 You Bring Me Down/Address Unknown (1939)
Decca 2790 Give Her My Love/My Prayer (1939)
Decca 2841 Bless You/I Don't Want Sympathy, I Want Love (1939)
Decca 2966 I'm Through/Memories of You (1939)
Decca 3077 I'm Getting Sentimental over You/Coquette (1939)
Decca 3195 What Can I Do?/When the Swallows Come Back to Capistrano (1940)
Decca 3258 Whispering Grass/Maybe (1940)
Decca 3288 Stop Pretending/You're Breaking My Heart All Over Again (1940)
Decca 3346 I'll Never Smile Again/I Could Make You Care (1940)
Decca 3379 My Greatest Mistake/We Three (1940)
Decca 3432 Do I Worry?/Java Jive (1940)
Decca 3468 I'm Only Human/Puttin' and Takin' (1941)
Decca 3626 Ring, Telephone, Ring/Please Take a Letter Miss Brown (1941)
Decca 3656 We'll Meet Again/You're Looking for Romance (1941)
Decca 3720 That's When Your Heartaches Begin/What Good Would It Do (1941)
Decca 3806 I'm Still without a Sweetheart/So Sorry (1941)
Decca 3958 Keep Cool, Fool/So Sorry (1941)
Decca 3987 Hey, Doc/I Don't Want to Set the World on Fire (1941)
Decca 4045 Nothin'/Someone's Rockin' My Dreamboat (1941)
Decca 4112 Is It a Sin?/It's a Sin to Tell a Lie (1942)
Decca 4194 It Isn't a Dream Anymore/Shout Brother, Shout (1942)
Decca 4303 Don't Leave Now/Foo-Gee (1942)
Decca 18383 Don't Tell a Lie about Me Dear/Who Wouldn't Love You (1942)
Decca 18461 Ev'ry Night about This Time/I'm Not the Same Old Me (1942)
Decca 18466 This Is Worth Fighting For/Just as Though You Were Here (1942)
Decca 18503 Don't Get Around Much Any More/Street of Dreams (1942)
Decca 18528 If I Cared a Little Bit Less/Mine All Mine, My My (1942)
Decca 18542 I Can't Stand Losing You/I'll Never Make the Same Mistake (1943)
Decca 18579 I'll Get By/Someday I'll Meet You Again (1944)
Decca 18583 Don't Believe Everything You Dream/Lovely Way to Spend an Evening (1944)
Decca 18587 Cow-Cow Boogie/When My Sugar Walks Down the Street (1944)
Decca 18657 I Hope to Die If I Told a Lie/Maybe It's All for the Best (1944)
Decca 23356 I'm Making Believe/Into Each Life Some Rain Must Fall (1944)
Decca 18711 I'd Climb the Highest Mountain/Thoughtless (1945)
Decca 23399 I'm Beginning to See the Light/That's the Way It Is (1945)
Decca 18755 I'm Gonna Turn Off the Teardrops/The Sweetest Dream (1946)
Decca 18817 The Gypsy/Everyone Is Saying Hello Again (1946)

Decca 18864 I Cover the Waterfront/Prisoner of Love (1946)
Decca 23615 I Never Had a Dream Come True/To Each His Own (1946)
Decca 23632 If I Didn't Care/Whispering Grass (1946)
Decca 23633 Do I Worry?/Java Jive (1946)
Decca 23634 We Three/Maybe (1946)
Decca 23635 I'll Never Smile Again/Until the Real Thing Comes Along (1946)
Decca 23695 I Get the Blues When It Rains/Either It's Love or It Isn't (1946)
Decca 23757 Bless You/Address Unknown (1946)
Decca 25047 Cow-Cow Boogie/That's the Way It Is (1947)
Decca 23809 That's Where I Came In/You Can't See the Sun When You're Crying (1947)
Decca 23851 I Want to Thank Your Folks/I Wasn't Made for Love (1947)
Decca 23900 Ask Anyone Who Knows/Can You Look Me in the Eyes (1947)
Decca 23936 Everyone Is Saying Hello Again/The Gypsy (1947)
Decca 24111 Information Please/Do You Feel That Way Too (1947)
Decca 24140 Always/White Christmas (1947)
Decca 24173 Just for Me/Just Plain Love (1947)
Decca 24192 Home Is Where the Heart Is/Sincerely Yours (1947)
Decca 24261 I'll Lose a Friend Tomorrow/When You Come to the End of the Day (1947)
Decca 25237 My Reward/You Left Me Everything but You (1947)
Decca 25238 I'll Get By/Just for a Thrill (1947)
Decca 25239 I'd Climb the Highest Mountain/Getting Sentimental over You (1947)
Decca 25240 When the Swallows Come Back to Capistrano/Coquette (1947)
Decca 25344 I'm Gonna Turn Off the Teardrops/Beginning to See the Light (1948)
Decca 25378 Don't Leave Now/Ring, Telephone, Ring (1948)
Decca 24286 I'll Make Up for Everything/It's All Over but the Crying (1948)
Decca 24327 Best Things in Life Are Free/I Woke Up with a Teardrop in My Eye (1948)
Decca 24461 Just for Now/Where Flamingos Fly (1948)
Decca 24496 Aladdin's Lamp/My Baby Didn't Even Say Goodbye (1948)
Decca 24507 Say Something Sweet to Your Sweetheart/You Were Only Fooling (1948)
Decca 24517 Am I Asking Too Much?/Recess in Heaven (1948)
Decca 24566 Bewildered/No Orchids for My Lady (1949)
Decca 24585 It Only Happens Once/As You Desire Me (1949)
Decca 24611 Kiss and a Rose/A Knock on the Door (1949)
Decca 24672 If You Had to Hurt Someone/To Remind Me of You (1949)
Decca 24693 Who Do You Know in Heaven?/You're Breaking My Heart (1949)
Decca 24741 Echoes/Land of Love (1949)
Decca 25431 I Don't Want to Set the World on Fire/Someone's Rockin' My Dreamboat (1949)
Decca 24887 With My Eyes Wide Open I'm Dreaming/Lost in a Dream (1950)
Decca 24933 My Reward/You Left Me Everything but You (1950)
Decca 27102 Sometime/I Was Dancing with Someone (1950)
Decca 27214 Right about Now/The Way It Used to Be (1950)
Decca 27259 Time Out for Tears/Dream Awhile (1950)
Decca 27391 A Friend of Johnny's/If (1951)

Decca 27417 Little Small Town Girl/I Still Feel the Same about You (1951)
Decca 27464 Castles in the Sand/Tell Me You Love Me (1951)
Decca 27493 A Fool Grows Wise/Do Something for Me (1951)
Decca 27494 And Then I Prayed/Somebody Bigger Than You and I (1951)
Decca 27632 What Can You Do?/More of the Same Sweet You (1951)
Decca 27742 Don't Stand Ghost of a Chance/I'm Lucky I Have You (1951)
Decca 25505 That's When Your Heartaches Begin/It's a Sin to Tell a Lie (1952)
Decca 27996 Honest and Truly/All My Life (1952)
Decca 28078 I Must Say Goodbye/I'm Heading Back to Paradise (1952)
Decca 28164 You May Be the Sweetheart of Somebody Else/Under the Honeysuckle Vine (1952)
Decca 28289 Sorry You Said Goodbye/A Bundle from Heaven (1952)
Decca 28412 You Are Happiness/Moonlight Mystery (1952)
Decca 28462 Forgetting You/I Counted on You (1952)
Decca 28738 Don't Mind the Rain/Do You Know What It Means to Be Lonely (1953)
King 1297 Ebbtide/If You Should Say Goodbye (1953)
King 4670 Here in My Lonely Room/Flowers Mr. Florist, Please (1953)
Decca 28982 Don't Put It Off Till Sunday/Just for Today (1954)
Decca 29070 Vows/Rose of Roses (1954)
Decca 29163 What More Can I Do?/Sentimental Baby (1954)
King 1304 Changing Partners/Stranger in Paradise (1954)
King 1336 Melody of Love/Am I Too Late (1954)
King 1378 Planting Rice/Yesterdays (1954)
King 1429 Melody of Love/There Is Something Missing (1954)
Decca 29750 Memories of You/It's Funny to Everyone but Me (1955)
King 1425 Someone's Rockin' My Dreamboat/When You Come to the End of the Day (1955)
King 1512 Don't Laugh at Me/Keep It Movin' (1955)
King 4857 Command Me/I'll Walk a Country Mile (1955)
Grand Award 1001 Do I Worry?/Rock and Roll Rag (1956)
Decca 29957 Every Night about This Time/Driftwood (1956)
Decca 29991 My Prayer/Bewildered (1956)
Decca 30058 The Best Things in Life Are Free/I Don't Stand a Ghost of a Chance with You (1956)
Verve 10071 Darling Don't Cry/You Name It (1957)
Verve 10094 If I'd Only Known You Then/Very Best Luck in the World (1957)
Verve 10198 Secret Love/Little Bird Told Me (1959)
Decca 25533 All My Life/You Were Only Fooling (1961)
Ford 115 Careless Love/Hawaiian Wedding Song (1962)
Sources: Jay Warner, *American Singing Groups*; Pete Grendysa, George Moonoogian, Rick Whitesell, and Marv Goldberg in *Yesterday's Memories* 9.

Inspirations (Philadelphia)

Personnel Carlton Brown, Cedric Wilson, Don Stevens, Jerry Jackson, Willie Wiggins

Notes

This group's place of origin is disputed. It is Philadelphia in Lou Silvani's *Collecting Rare Records* and Hartford, Connecticut, or Springfield, Massachusetts, in Donn Fileti's liner notes with the Relic LP *Best of Apollo Records–3.* I've also seen it stated that they were from San Francisco.

Regarding personnel, with the exception of Willie Wiggins, shown above, who's on everybody's list of Inspirations personnel, Donn Fileti states that it could be assumed that the members might have been the songwriters for their Apollo tunes. In any case, the writers' names are as follows: Joe Warren, Felix Hunt, William Perkins, and Harry Dixon.

Discography

Apollo 494 Raindrops/Maggie (1956)
Lamp 2019 Don't Cry/Indian Jane (1958)
Sources: Donn Fileti, liner notes with the Relic LP *Best of Apollo Records;* Lou Silvani, *Collecting Rare Records.*

Inspirations, Ronnie Vare & (Springfield, Mass.)

Personnel Ronnie Vare (lead), Ed Bently, Harry Gagne, Chuck Bentley, Dave Petronimo

Notes

Bentley, Petronimo, and Gagne began together in 1957. They were soon joined by Ronnie Vare.

Following much practice, they went to a recording studio where they produced several recordings, which they sent to various labels. They had their first disc released on GLO. The label mistakenly read "Ronnie Vare and the Inspirators."

A change of management saw them switch to rockabilly; soon after Chuck Bentley entered the service, and the group soon drifted apart. They broke up in 1960.

Discography

Dell 5203 Love Is Just for Two/Let's Rock Little Girl (1959)
Source: Jungle Jim and Bob Belniak in *Echoes of the Past* 6.

Inspirators (Brooklyn, N.Y.)

Personnel Cleo Perry (d) (lead), William Massey (1st tenor), Clifton Johnson (2d tenor), Barney Fields (baritone), Buster Boyce (bass)

Notes

Formed in high school in 1949. In 1955, following much practice, they began hanging out at the legendary Brill Building in Manhattan, where they met Larry Newton who, at the time, was the general manager for Treat Records.

Two sessions were scheduled in April 1955. The first produced "Let's Fall in Love" and "We Danced in the Moonlight." The second session produced "If Loving You Is Wrong" and "Three Sixty." None of these tunes did anything.

The latter two tunes, "If Loving You Is Wrong" and "Three Sixty," for reasons unknown to Cleo Perry, were released as by the Five Stars. Nothing happened with this disc either.

This was not the Inspirators on GLO nor the Five Stars on Mark-X, End, Columbia, ABC-Paramount, Hunt, Note, ATCO, Dot, or Blues Boy Kingdom.

They recorded several other songs for Treat, but none were ever released. Newton made a deal with Hy Weiss at Old Town, where two songs were recorded, "Starlight Tonight" and "Oh What a Feeling" (June 1958). Nothing happened with these either and the group broke up.

Perry became a soloist for a while but gave up his singing career when his child was born. In 1993 Cleo Perry passed away.

Discography
Treat 502 If Loving You Is Wrong/Three Sixty (1955)
Old Town 1053 Starlight Tonight/Oh What a Feeling (1958)
Source: Marv Goldberg in *DISCoveries,* March 1997.

Intentions (Philadelphia)

Personnel Richard Mignona (lead), John Montmore (1st tenor), John Poloney (2d tenor), Thomas Inzilla (baritone), Bill Lerario (bass)

Notes
The Intentions were a South Philadelphia group.

This was basically a flash-in-the-pan quintet that made one release and then disbanded.

Discography
Jamie 1253 Summertime Angel/Mr. Misery (1963)
Source: Bob Bosco, liner notes with the Jamie/Guyden CD *Doop Doo Wah.*

Interludes (Boston)

Personnel Frankie Anderson (lead), Otha Sonnie (1st tenor) Kenny Loftman (2d tenor), Eddie Adams (baritone), Freddie Jackson (bass)

Notes
This group formed in 1955 as a result of the breakup of several local groups.

They won a national talent hunt sponsored by RCA and cut their only 45 rpm for that label on May 28, 1958.

Several tunes were recorded at this session but only one was released.

The group broke up soon after recording because of discord between members. Certain individuals would not come to practice sessions. If they came at all, they were late. Or they would totally miss performances.

Discography
RCA 47-7283 I Shed a Million Tears/Oo Wee (1958)

King 5633 Darling I'll Be True/Wilted Rose Bud (1962)
Source: Warren Smith in *Record Exchanger* 30 and *Yesterday's Memories* 12.

Intervals (St. Louis, Mo.)

Personnel Paul Grady (lead), Ron Townson, Lamont McLemore, Richard Tru-Love, Fritz Basket (female tenor)

Notes

This group formed in St. Louis in 1961 and obtained a contract to record with Leon and Googie Rene's Class Records. Their only release is the item shown below. There were several unreleased songs, which were done quite well.

Townson and McLemore were later featured in the Fifth Dimension.

Ms. Fritz Basket sang with the Upfronts on Lummtone.

Discography

Class 304 Here's That Rainy Day/Wish I Could Change My Mind (1962)
Source: Donn Fileti, liner notes with the Relic LP *Class.*

Isley Brothers (Cincinnati, Ohio)

Personnel Ronald Isley (lead), O'Kelly Isley (d. 1986), Rudy Isley

Notes

The Isley Brothers began as a quartet but the youngest brother, Vernon, was killed in an auto accident prior to their first recording effort.

The three remaining Isleys left Cincinnati in 1957 for New York. They hooked up with Bill Gordon, former lead of the Colonials on Gee and at that time one of the owners of Teenage Records, along with another music notable, Ben Smith. Teenage recorded the Isley's first record, "The Angels Cried," and a year later they recorded for George Goldner's Cindy Records with "Don't Be Jealous."

Three more Goldner label recordings, two on Gone and one on Mark-X did little. In 1959 they were seen by an RCA representative at a Washington, D.C., performance and in late July of that year recorded "Shout" for RCA. It did quite well and curiously it charted again in 1962. Later that year, they moved to Wand Records and hit again with "Twist and Shout."

They moved to Atlantic in 1961, but their six singles for Atlantic failed. In 1964, they set up their own label, T-Neck. Their first recording on this label, interestingly, featured Jimi Hendrix on guitar. Just before T-Neck, in 1963–1964, they cut several discs for United Artists.

In 1966, they signed with Motown affiliate Tamla. In fall 1969, brother Marvin Isley joined his siblings as a bass to form a quartet.

O'Kelly Isley died of a heart attack in 1986 at the age of forty-eight.

Discography

Teenage 1004 The Cow Jumped Over the Moon/Angels Cried (1957)
Cindy 3009 Don't Be Jealous/This Is the End (1958)

Gone 5022 I Wanna Know/Everybody's Gonna Rock 'n' Roll (1958)
Gone 5048 My Love/The Drag (1958)
RCA 47-7537 Turn to Me/I'm Gonna Knock at Your Door (1959)
Mark-X 8000 The Drag/Rockin' MacDonald (1959)
RCA 47-7588 Shout, Pt. 1/Pt. 2 (1959)
RCA 47-7657 Respectable/Without a Song (1959)
RCA 47-7718 He's Got the Whole World in His Hand/How Deep Is the Ocean? (1960)
RCA 47-7746 Open Up Your Heart/Gypsy Love Song (1960)
RCA 47-7787 Tell Me Who/Say You Love Me Too (1960)
Atlantic 2092 Jeepers Creepers/Teach Me How to Shimmy (1961)
Atlantic 2100 Shine On, Harvest Moon/Standing on the Dance Floor (1961)
Atlantic 2110 Your Old Lady/Write to Me (1961)
Atlantic 2122 A Fool for You/Just One More Time (1961)
Wand 118 Right Now/The Snake (1962)
Wand 124 Twist and Shout/Spanish Twist (1962)
Wand 127 Twistin' with Linda/You Better Come Home (1962)
Wand 131 Nobody but Me/I'm Laughing to Keep from Crying (1963)
Wand 137 Hold On Baby/I Say Love (1963)
United Artists 605 Tango/She's Gone (1963)
United Artists 638 Surf and Shout/Whatcha Gonna Do? (1963)
United Artists 659 Please, Please, Please/You'll Never Leave (1963)
United Artists 714 Who's That Lady?/My Little Girl (1964)
Atlantic 2263 The Last Girl/Looking for a Love (1964)
T Neck 501 Testify, Pt. 1/Pt. 2 (1964)
Atlantic 2277 Wild as a Tiger/Simon Says (1965)
Atlantic 2303 Move Over and Let Me Dance/Have You Ever Been Disappointed? (1965)
Veep 1230 Love Is a Wonderful Thing/Open Up Her Eyes (1966)
Tamla 54128 This Old Heart of Mine/There's No Love Left (1966)
Tamla 54133 Take Some Time Out for Love/Who Could Ever Doubt My (Love?) (1966)
Tamla 54135 I Guess I'll Always Love You/I Hear a Symphony (1966)
Tamla 54146 Got to Have You Back/Just Ain't Enough Love (1967)
Tamla 54154 That's the Way Love Is/One Too Many Heartaches (1967)
Tamla 54164 Take Me in Your Arms/Why When Love Is Gone? (1968)
Tamla 54175 All Because I Love You/Behind a Painted Smile (1968)
Tamla 54182 Just Ain't Enough Love/Take Some Time Out for Love (1969)
T-Neck 901 It's Your Thing/Don't Give It Away (1969)
T-Neck 902 I Turned You On/I Know Who You Been Socking It To (1969)
T-Neck 906 Black Berries, Pt. 1/Pt. 2 (1969)
T-Neck 908 Was It Good To You/I Got to Get Myself Together (1969)
T-Neck 912 Give the Women What They Want/Bless Your Heart (1969)
T-Neck 914 Keep On Doin'/Same Me (1969)
T-Neck 919 If He Can, You Can/Holdin' On (1970)
T-Neck 921 Girls Will Be Girls, Boys Will Be Boys/Get Down Off the Train (1970)
T-Neck 924 Get into Something–1/Get into Something–2 (1970)
T-Neck 927 Freedom/I Need You So (1970)

T-Neck 929 Warpath/I Got to Find Me One (1971)
T-Neck 930 Love the One You're With/He's Got Your Love (1971)
T-Neck 932 Spill the Wine/Take Inventory (1971)
T-Neck 933 Lay Lady Lay/Vacuum Cleaner (1971)
T-Neck 934 Lay Away/Feel Like the World (1972)
T-Neck 935 Pop That Thang/I Got to Find Me One (1972)
T-Neck 936 Work to Do/Beautiful (1972)
T-Neck 937 It's Too Late/ (1973)
T-Neck 2251 That Lady–1/That Lady-2 (1973)
T-Neck 2252 The Highways of My Life/What It Comes Down To (1973)
T-Neck 2253 Summer Breeze-1/Summer Breeze-2 (1974)
T-Neck 2254 Live It Up–1/Live It Up–2 (1974)
T-Neck 2255 Midnight Sky–1/Midnight Sky–2 (1974)
T-Neck 2256 Fight the Power–1/Fight the Power–2 (1975)
T-Neck 2259 For the Love of You/You Walk Your Way (1975)
T-Neck 2260 Who Loves You Better–1/Who Loves You Better–2 (1976)
T-Neck 2261 Harvest for the World/Harvest for the World (instrumental) (1976)
Source: Jay Warner, *American Singing Groups.*

Ivy Leaguers (Los Angeles)

Personnel Louise Williams, Richard Owens (1st tenor), Beverley Picot

Notes

Owens also sang lead for the Jayhawks. He was briefly with the Temptations, Vibrations, Vibes (Allied), and Marathons. He was the first replacement for Eddie Kendricks of the Temptations in 1971.

Owens, Williams, and Picot also sang for the Six Teens on Flip. The two remaining unnamed members were former members of the Dreamers.

Discography

Flip 325 Beware of Love/Deposit Your Love in the Bank of My (Heart) (1957)
Source: Liner notes with the *Best of Flip, 1–2* CD.

Ivy Tones (Philadelphia)

Personnel John Ivey (lead), "Little" Joe Cook (1st tenor), James Green, James Thomas, William Brown (bass)

Notes

The Red Top disc was released in the spring of 1958. As soon as it began to make some noise, it was picked up by Liberty for national distribution.

The group didn't stay together very long. When some of the original members left, Joe Moody and Robert Parks replaced them. They then became the Corvets on Sure Records who recorded "Voodoo Baby."

Apparently two other songs were recorded at the session that produced "Each

Time" and "Ooh Wee Baby." Because the group broke up so fast, these two tunes were never released.

Discography

Red Top 105 Ooh Wee Baby/Each Time (1958)
Source: Donn Fileti, liner notes with the Relic LP *Best of Red Top.*

Jacks (Los Angeles)

Personnel Aaron Collins (lead), Ted Taylor (d. 1988) (1st tenor), Willie Davis (2d tenor), Lloyd McCraw (baritone), Will "Dub" Jones (bass)

Notes

The Jacks/Cadets started as a spiritual group in 1954. They backed Donna Hightower on several of her sides. Contrary to the story, it was not the Jacks behind Paul Anka on "I Confess."

The Bihari brothers owned the legendary Modern, RPM, and Flair Records. One of their other brothers, Lester, owned Meteor Records.

"Dub" Jones also sang with the Coasters, Crescendos, and Tramps. In 1957 Jones left to sing bass for the Coasters, and Davis and Collins formed a new group with Thomas Miller and George Hollis.

Tenor Prentice Moreland sang for the Jacks and was also a member of the DuDroppers, Crescendos, Dominoes, Colts, Fortunes, and the Hollywood Flames. Moreland replaced Ted Taylor. Thomas "Pete" Fox replaced Lloyd McCraw.

Willie Davis was usually the lead for the Jacks' recordings.

Lloyd McCraw worked briefly with the Dixie Hummingbirds gospel group.

The Teen Queens (the Collins sisters) were Aaron Collins's siblings.

George Hollis, a later member of the Jacks, also sang for the Flares and the Peppers with Collins.

In 1958, McCraw, Jones, and Collins started the MJC label. They released "My Reckless Heart" with Willie Davis at lead and billed the group as the Rocketeers (see Rhythm Aces).

In the early 1960s McCraw and Davis were the Thor-Ables on Titanic.

Discography

RPM 428 Why Don't You Write Me? (WD)/Smack Dab in the Middle (DJ) (1955)
RPM 432 Love Me Again (DH)/Dog Gone (DH) (1955)
RPM 433 I'm Confessin' (WD)/Since My Baby' Been Gone (WD) (1955)
RPM 439 Bob-o-Link (DH)/Since You (DH) (1955)
RPM 444 This Empty Heart (WD)/My Clumsy Heart (DJ) (1955)
RPM 454 How Soon? (WD)/So Wrong (WD) (1956)
RPM 458 Why Did I Fall in Love? (WD)/Sugar Baby (DJ) (1956)
RPM 467 Let's Make Up (AC)/Dream a Little Longer (WD) (1956)
RPM 472 I Confess/Blau-Wile Devest Fontaine (1957)
Victory Why Don't You Write Me? (WD)/Sugar Baby (1959)
Kent 344 Why Don't You Write Me? (WD)/This Empty Heart (WD) (1960)
Source: Donn Fileti, liner notes with the Relic LP *The Jacks.*

Jac-O-Lacs (Hollywood, Calif.)

Personnel Cornelius Gunter (lead), Charles Jackson (tenor), Thomas Fox (2d tenor), Obediah "Young" Jesse (baritone), Randolph Jones (bass)

Notes

The Jac-O-Lacs formed in 1956 when members of the Flairs needed some extra cash and they did a session for Tampa Records Tampa, realizing that this was moonlighting as the Flairs were still under contract to Flair, protected the group by changing their name to the Jac-O-Lacs.

This group was still another incarnation of the Flairs as were: the Five Hearts, the Five Hollywood Bluejays, the Hunters, the Whips, and the Rams.

When Gunter's sister, Shirley, joined as the sixth member, internal conflicts occurred and this was the first and last recording for the Jac-O-Lacs.

Discography

Tampa 103 Cindy Lou/Sha-Ba-Da-Ba-Doo (1956)
Source: Marv Goldberg and Rick Whitesell in *Yesterday's Memories* 10.

Jaguars (Los Angeles)

Personnel Herman "Sonny" Chaney (d) (lead), Val Poliuto (tenor), Manny Chavez (baritone), Charles Middleton (bass)

Notes

Like so many other Los Angeles vocal groups, the Jaguars started at Fremont High School. They were then known as the Shadows, an integrated group. Valerio Poliuto was white, Chaney and Middleton were black, and Chavez was Chicano.

They recorded as the Miracles for John Dolphin's Cash label but these tunes were never released.

They changed their name to the Jaguars and early in 1955 auditioned for Aardell, which eventually released three records by the group. One of these was "The Way You Look Tonight." In an interview Chaney stated, "We never saw a dime from that disc."

They did a session for Lee Rupe's Ebb Records and then Charles Middleton joined the air force. The three remaining Jaguars plus Eddie Lewis became the Velvetones (no recordings). One additional contract with Art Laboe's Original Sound Records produced "Thinking of You" in 1959. The personnel on this disc included Manny, Sonny, Val, Tony Allen, and Richard Berry.

(Note: One Reference stated that Allen and Berry simply appeared with the Jaguars and never recorded!)

It's rumored that this group was in the studio the day Ralph Mathis (rumored to be Johnny Mathis's brother) was recording and filled in as the backing group, the Ambers.

Discography

Aardell 0003 I Wanted You/Rock It, Davy, Rock It (1955)

Aardell 0006 Be My Sweetie/Why Don't You Believe Me? (1955)
Aardell 107 Rock It, Davy, Rock It/The Big Bear (1955)
R-Dell 11 The Way You Look Tonight/Moonlight and You (1956)
R-Dell 16 The City Zoo/I Love You, Baby (1957)
Ebb 129 Hold Me Tight/Picadilly (1958)
Original Sound 06 Thinking of You/Look into My Eyes (1959)
R-Dell 117 Don't Go Home/Girl of My Dreams (1960)
Original Sound 20 Thinking of You/Look into My Eyes (1961)
Original Sound 59 The Way You Look Tonight/Baby, Baby, Baby (1965)
Source: Marv Goldberg and Rick Whitesell in *Yesterday's Memories* 10.

Jarmels (Richmond, Va.)

Personnel Nathaniel Ruff (tenor), Earl Christianson (tenor), Ray Smith (baritone), Tommy Eldridge (bass), Paul Burnett

Notes

In the mid-1950s members of the Jarmels attended the same church in Richmond and sang for their school's glee club.

The Jarmels were unique in that the typical Laurie group was a white group from New York. The Jarmels were from Richmond, Virginia, and were black.

It was early in 1961 when manager Jim Gribble brought the Jarmels to Laurie. Their first recording did not do well but their second release, "A Little Bit of Soap," was a huge hit and has remained popular for many years. Their next four releases for Laurie did not fare as well.

The liner notes packaged with the Ace CD *The Mystics Meet the Jarmels* refer to Christianson as Christian.

Discography

Laurie 3085 Little Lonely One/She Loves to Dance (1961)
Laurie 3098 A Little Bit of Soap/The Way You Look Tonight (1961)
Laurie 3116 Gee Oh Gosh/I'll Follow You (1961)
Laurie 3124 Red Sails in the Sunset/Loneliness (1962)
Laurie 3141 Little Bug/One by One (1962)
Laurie 3174 Come On Girl/Keep Your Mind on Me (1963)
Source: John Joosten, liner notes with the Ace CD *The Mystics Meet the Jarmels.*

Jayhawks (Los Angeles)

Personnel James Johnson (lead), Carlton Fisher (2d tenor), David Govan (baritone), Carver Bunkum (bass)

Notes

The Jayhawks were singing at Los Angeles's Fremont High School in 1955 when Charlie "Flash" Reynolds met them. Reynolds was impressed with their vocal talent and soon recorded "Counting My Teardrops" for his Flash label.

In April 1956, they released "Stranded in the Jungle." Although this did well, the cover by the Cadets overshadowed the Jayhawks' release.

After "Love Train" they moved to Aladdin Records and recorded "Everyone Should Know." At this time Carver Bunkum left and Richard Owens took his place. Owens went on to sing with the Ivy Leaguers (Flip), Six Teens, Vibes (Allied), Temptations, and Vibrations.

On Eastman the Jayhawks picked up Don Bradley.

Johnson and Fisher went on to form the Vibrations ("So Blue") in 1960 for the Checker label.

Discography

Flash 105 Counting My Teardrops/The Devil's Cousin (1956)
Flash 109 Stranded in the Jungle/My Only Darling (1956)
Flash 111 Love Train/Don't Mind Dyin' (1956)
Aladdin 3393 Everyone Should Know/The Creature (1957)
Eastman 792 Start the Fire/I Wish the World Owed Me a Living (1959)
Eastman 798 New Love/Better Brown (1959)
Sources: Marv Goldberg in *Bim Bam Boom* 5; Donn Fileti, liner notes with Relic's *Jayhawks* LP.

Jaynetts (Bronx, N.Y.)

Personnel Johnnie Richardson (d), Ethel Davis, Mary Sue Wells, Yvonne Bushnell, Ada Ray

Notes

This group was assembled in the Bronx in 1959 and recorded their huge hit "Sally Go Round the Roses" for the Tuff label in Newark in 1963.

Johnnie Richardson was the Johnnie of the Johnny and Joe who did "Over the Mountain, Across the Sea."

The Jaynetts eventually wound up with J&S Records in the Bronx, a label owned by Johnnie's mom, Zell Sanders. Unfortunately, the Jaynetts never duplicated the success of "Sally Go Round the Roses."

Discography

Tuff 369 Sally Go Round the Roses (instrumental) (1963)
Tuff 371 Keep an Eye on Her (instrumental) (1963)
Tuff 372 Johnny Don't Cry (instrumental) (1963)
Tuff 374 Snowman Snowman, Sweet Potato Nose (instrumental) (1963)
Tuff 377 No Love at All/Tonight You Belong to Me (1963)
J&S 1177 Guy Behind the Daisies/Is It My Imagination (1964)
J&S 1473 Peepin' In and Out the Window/Extra Extra Read All about It (1965)
J&S 1477 Who Stole the Cookie/That's My Boy (1965)
J&S 4418/19 Vangie Don't You Cry/My Guy Is As Sweet As Can Be (1965)
Source: Pete Grendysa, liner notes with the Chess CD boxed set *Chess Rhythm & Roll.*

Jayos (Los Angeles)

Personnel Richard Berry, Harold Lewis (tenor), Arthur Lee Maye (tenor), Mel Williams (baritone), Sonny Moore (bass)

Notes

In a 1971 interview with Rip Lay for *Big Town Review,* Maye stated that the Jayos included himself, Jesse Belvin, Richard Berry, and Mel Williams. This is confirmed in Terry Hansen's piece in *Goldmine* (April 1, 1994). Hansen further states that the Jayos had been put together by Johnny Otis for his Dig label to perform covers of R&B hits.

The total released output of Jayos material was issued on the Dig LP *Johnny Otis Rock 'n' Roll Hit Parade.* Other songs have since been released on the Dig *Legendary Masters* CD. For this reason, and because no singles were ever released, no discography appears below.

Sources: Liner notes with the Ace CD *Legendary Dig Masters–4*; Ray Topping, *The Vocal Groups*; Terry Hansen in *Goldmine,* April 1, 1994.

Jesters (New York)

Personnel Lenny McKay (lead), Adam Jackson (d) (1st tenor), Anthony Jimmy Smith (2d tenor), Leo Vincent (baritone), Noel Grant (bass)

Notes

Group members met and began singing at their junior high school in Harlem. They initially made appearances locally as a quartet. After a year, it was felt that they needed a fifth voice, specifically a tenor. This need was filled by Adam Jackson.

Their first manager was Ann Hayes. Her brother, Roger, sang with both the Schoolboys and the Collegians. Lenny McKay's brother, James, was also with the Collegians.

The Jesters got their break in 1957 at the legendary amateur show at the Apollo theater in New York, They took first place three weeks in a row! After learning of this, Paul Winley offered them a contract (they had previously arranged to record for the Weiss brothers at Old Town Records but backed out at the last minute).

At Winley they hooked up with David "Baby Cortez" Clowney, who did most of their arrangements. They had two releases in 1957, and the original group cut two more in 1958.

Their recording of "I Laughed" was released on Cyclone, a label belonging to Paul Winley's wife. After the Cyclone release, the original group broke up. McKay went to another group, Grant simply left, and Vincent was drafted. Jackson and Smith got Melvin Lewis from the Canaries and the Climbers on J&S. Lewis got his brother, Donald, as the new bass. At this juncture, the group chose to remain a quartet.

In 1959, the Everyone's Laughing Jesters included Adam Jackson, Jimmy Smith, and brothers Don and Melvin Lewis.

They cut several more sides for Winley in 1960 with Jackson at lead. It was at this time that they cut "The Wind."

Interestingly, in 1974, they became a quintet again with Jackson's brother, Ronald, who had also been with the Youngtones on X-Tra.

Discography

Winley 218 So Strange/Love No One but You (1957)
Winley 221 Please Let Me Love You/I'm Falling in Love (1957)
Winley 225 The Plea/Oh Baby (1958)
Cyclone 5011 I Laughed/Now That You're Gone (1958)
Winley 242 The Wind/Sally Green (1960)
Winley 248 That's How It Goes/Tutti Frutti (1960)
Winley 252 Uncle Henry's Basement/Come Let Me Show You (1961)
Source: Dave Hinckley, Marv Goldberg, Marcia Vance, and Phil Groia in *Yesterday's Memories* 6.

Jets (New York)

Personnel Ray Hulbert, Oliver James, Joe Lipscomb, Louis O'Neal

Notes

This group had been the Mello-Tones on Decca, but were not the Mellotones on the Gee label.

Discography

Gee 1020 Heaven above Me/Millie Brown (1956)
Source: Marv Goldberg in *DISCoveries,* January 1, 1995.

Jets (Washington, D.C.)

Personnel Waverly Buck Mason (lead), James "Toy" Walton (1st tenor), Charles Booker (2d tenor), Herbert Fisher (baritone), John Bowie (bass)

Notes

This group began in 1947 in the D.C./Baltimore area and was briefly known as the Caverliers. They were lucky to be seen by Earthaline Lee, who soon became their manager. She set up their first recording session with Rainbow Records in New York late in 1952.

Walter Taylor, regular 2d tenor, was ill for their Rainbow recording session and part-time member, Charles Booker, filled in. Rainbow released their record six months later in 1953.

After having seen the Jets perform, blues singer Amos Milburn got them to move to Aladdin Records. A recording session was soon set up in New York City. Eddie Mesner of Aladdin was aware of another group calling themselves the Jets and changed their name to the Bachelors.

When Mason was drafted, Robert Russell took his spot.

Walton also recorded with the L' Cap-Tans, the Links with Fisher on Teenage, the Clovers, and the Knickerbockers.

Discography

Rainbow 201 The Lovers/Drag It Home Baby (1953)
Source: Marv Goldberg and Mike Redmond in *Record Exchanger* 15.

Jewels (Los Angeles)

Personnel Rudy Jackson (lead), Dee Hawkins (tenor), Johnny Torrence (tenor), Vernon Knight (baritone) James Brown (bass)

Notes

In 1953, this group was known as the Marbles, who recorded for Lucky. The members were formerly gospel performers with the exception of Vernon Knight.

In Marv Goldberg's and the late Rick Whitesell's liner notes accompanying the Jewels *Gold Dust* CD, the tenor's name is spelled Torrance.

In their first session for R&B they recorded "Hearts of Stone." Because there were so many covers of the record, theirs did not do well nationally.

At this time Jackson teamed up with sisters Vera and Hattie Potts and Gladys Jackson and cut a disc for R&B as the Mel-O-Aires.

In 1955, R&B management sold the Jewels' contract to Imperial Records. The Jewels had four releases for Imperial that did not do well. Later in 1956, they split up.

Torrence formed a new Jewels group that had one release for RPM. Following this release, he formed another Jewels that recorded "The Wind" for Buck Ram's Antler Records in 1959.

Torrence also sang for the Pentagons.

Discography

R&B 1301 Hearts of Stone/Runnin' (1954)
R&B 1303 Oh Yes I Know/A Fool in Paradise (1954)
R&B 1306 Rosalie/Living from Day to Day (1955)
RPM 474 She's a Flirt/B-Bomb Baby (1955)
Imperial 5351 Angel in My Life/Hearts Can Be Broken (1955)
Imperial 5362 Natural Natural Ditty/Please Return (1955)
Imperial 5377 How/Rickety Rock (1956)
Imperial 5387 Goin' Goin' Gone/My Baby (1956)
Original Sound 38 Hearts of Stone/Oh Yes I Know (1964)
Sources: Marv Goldberg and Rick Whitesell in *Yesterday's Memories* 10; Marv Goldberg and Rick Whitesell, liner notes with the Gold Dust CD *B-Bomb Baby.*

Jewels (Washington, D.C.)

Personnel Martha Harvin, Sandra Bears, Margie Clark, Grace Ruffin

Notes

This group began as the Four Jewels on Checker and Start. Harvin was not with them at that time.

When Harvin joined them, they began recording for Carole King's Dimension label. In 1968, they backed up James Brown on "I'm Black and I'm Proud."

Discography

Dimension 1034 Opportunity/Gotta Find a Way (1964)
Dimension 1048 But I Do/Smokey Joe (1964)
Source: Nay Nasser in *Echoes of the Past* 28.

Jive Bombers (New York)

Personnel Clarence Palmer (lead), Earl Johnson (tenor), William "Pee Wee" Tinney (baritone), Alan Tinney (bass)

Notes

This group was formed in 1952 by Clarence Palmer. He and brothers Dick and Ernest made up the Palmer Brothers. Earlier, with Cab Calloway, they were the Cabaliers on Okeh.

In 1949, brothers Dick and Ernie retired and Clarence joined up with Sonny Austin's Jive Bombers. They recorded two sides in 1949 for Coral, "125th Street, New York" and "Brown Boy" as Al Sears and the Sparrows.

In 1952, they became Clarence Palmer and the Jive Bombers. Their first three recordings on the Citation label did nothing.

Following some personnel changes, the group included Clarence Palmer, Earl Johnson, and the Tinney brothers—Al and William.

They recorded "Bad Boy" for Herman Lubinsky's Savoy label in Newark, New Jersey, in late 1956. As a result of the success of this disc, the group hung around until the 1960s, when they agreed to call it a career.

Discography

Citation 1160 It's Spring Again/Pork Chop Boogie (1952)
Citation 1161 Brown Boy/Pee Wee's Boogie (1952)
Citation 1162 Saturday Night Fish Fry/Sixty Minute Man (1952)
Savoy 1508 Bad Boy/When Your Hair Has Turned to Silver (1956)
Savoy 1513 If Had a Talking Picture/The Blues Don't Mean a Thing (1957)
Savoy 1515 Cherry/You Took My Love (1957)
Savoy 1535 Is This the End/Just around the Corner (1958)
Savoy 1560 Stardust/You Give Your Love to Me (1959)
Sources: Bjorn Jentoft in *Rhythm and News* 1; Pete Grendysa in *Story Untold* 10.

Jive Five (Brooklyn, N.Y.)

Personnel Eugene Pitt (lead), Jerome Hanna (d) (1st tenor) Richard Harris (2d tenor), Thurmon "Billy" Prophet (baritone), Norman Johnson (d) (bass)

Notes

This group was formed in 1959 by Eugene Pitt in Brooklyn, New York. Through an acquaintance, they were taken to Les Cahan of Beltone Records. Cahan allowed the Jive Five to audition and they sang several previously recorded tunes and one or two originals. Cahan liked "My True Story" very much and signed them to a recording contract. "My True Story" was recorded in December 1960 and released in the spring of 1962.

"My True Story" was a huge hit, reaching third on the pop charts and first on the R&B list. This initial success provided them with many live appearances and a great deal of touring. Many hits were to follow, but none as big as "My True Story."

During the summer of 1962, Jerome Hanna died and was replaced by Andre Coles. Casey Spencer replaced Billy Prophet and Beatrice Best (a man) came on for Richard Harris. Their next tune, "What Time Is It" became a big hit but not as big as "My True Story." Billy Prophet returned, and he and Pitt teamed up with three of the Cadillacs—J. R. Bailey, Bobby Phillips, and Buddy Brooks. This is the group that did "Rain," which was released in March 1963 but did not do very well.

When they recorded for Sketch, Pitt brought Harris, Spencer, and Best back and recorded the Lovenotes' "United." Although this tune fared well in the New York tristate area only, United Artists was interested enough to purchase the master.

The Jive Five released "I'm a Happy Man" for United Artists and this did quite well. Five additional singles were released in the next eighteen months, but none made any noise. They next moved to Musicor. Because they were now four instead of five, they changed their name to the Jyve Fyve.

Discography

Beltone 1006 My True Story/When I Was Single (1961)
Beltone 1014 Never, Never/People from Another World (1961)
Beltone 2019 No Not Again/Hully Gully Calling Time (1962)
Beltone 2024 What Time Is It/Beggin' You Please (1962)
Beltone 2029 Do You Hear Wedding Bells?/These Golden Rings (1962)
Beltone 2030 Lily Marlane/Johnny Never Knew (1963)
Beltone 2034 Rain/She's My Girl (1963)
Sketch 219 United/Prove Every Word You Say (1964)
United Artists 607 United/Prove Every Word You Say (1964)
United Artists 853 I'm a Happy Man/Kiss, Kiss, Kiss (1965)
United Artists 936 A Bench in the Park/Please Baby, Please (1965)
United Artists 50004 Goin' Wild/Main Street (1966)
United Artists 50033 In My Neighborhood/Then Came Heart Break (1966)
United Artists 50069 Ha Ha/You're a Puzzle (1966)
United Artists 50107 You/You Promise Me Great Things (1966)
Musicor 1250 Crying Like a Baby/You'll Fall in Love (1967)
Musicor 1270 No More Tears/You'll Fall in Love (1967)
Musicor 1305 Sugar/Blues in the Ghetto (1968)
Decca 32671 You Showed Me the Light of Love/If You Let Me Make Love (1970)
Decca 32736 I Want You to Be My Baby/If I Had Chance to Love You (1970)
Sources: Liner notes with Relic's *Jive Five* LP/CD; Jay Warner, *American Singing Groups.*

Jive Tones (Rochester, N.Y)

Personnel Jimmy Monroe, John Johnson, John Mays, Bobby Williams, Snooky Williams, Jim Whittier

Notes

The Jive Tones formed while the members were in junior high school in Rochester, New York, in 1954. They started singing just for fun.

The group began by playing local clubs and nightspots. When they felt their vocal and stage acts had been perfected, they went to New York City to look for a recording company. They auditioned for Don Costa at ABC Paramount who thought they were terrific and the Jive Tones were immediately signed to record.

Their first session resulted in four sides. "Ding Dong Ding" and "Geraldine" were released on the ABC subsidiary APT. The disc got some airplay at the start, but it quickly faded. The other two tunes were never released. Due to this failure, the Jive Tones folded.

Following the disintegration, Whittier went back to New York City to try to hook up with another group. At that time, the group he sang with was called the Students. Upon learning of the Checker group from Cincinnati, they changed their name to the Desires.

Discography

Rhythm 5001 Geraldine/Ding Dong Ding (1958)
APT 25020 Geraldine/Ding Dong Ding (1958)
(Note: The Rhythm disc above was released as by the Jiveatones. The cuts on both sides are identical to those on the Apt disc. At this writing, I have not found an explanation. Neither resource shown below addresses this issue, although both of these accounts were written with one of the group's members.)
Sources: Joe Sicurella in *Bim Bam Boom* 11; Bill Schwartz in *Time Barrier Express,* 3, no. 1.

Joe Van Loan Quartet (Philadelphia)

Personnel Joe Van Loan (lead), Elijah Harvey (1st tenor), Walter Taylor (2d tenor), James Miller (baritone), Alan Scott (bass)

Notes

Joe Van Loan also sang with the Bachelors on Mercury, the Bells on Rama, the Dixieaires, DuDroppers, Ravens, Chris Powell's Five Blue Flames, Canaanites, Dreamers (Mercury), Charlie Fuqua's Ink Spots, Valiants (Joy, Cortlandt) and Wini Brown and Her Boyfriends.

Discography

Carver 140 Trust in Me/Until I Fell for You (1953)
Sources: Jack Sbarbori in *Record Exchanger* 18; Marv Goldberg in *DISCoveries.* Ravens article.

833

Jones Boys (New York)

Personnel Jimmy Jones (lead), Bobby Moore (2d tenor), Marvin Walton (baritone), Irving Lee Gail (bass)

Notes

Jimmy Jones had been with the Savoys when he met George Goldner, who purchased the groups' contract from H. Lubinsky of Savoy. Goldner changed their name to the Pretenders and recorded them in two sessions. Then off to another label, Arrow. This was 1956 and their name was now the Jones Boys.

After Whistlin' Man was recorded, Jones never heard from Arrow Records again, except through their lawyers, in regard to the whistling heard in his hit "Handy Man." Apparently Arrow felt "violated" because of the whistling in their release of "Whistlin' Man," which also had some whistling in it, and litigation followed. With Jones's "Handy Man" success, Arrow obviously was trying for a part of it.

Irving Lee Gail sang bass at the Arrow sessions. Gail had been with the Cadillacs, Carl Hogan and the Miracles, Jimmy Jones and the Pretenders, and the Vocaltones.

Discography

Arrow 717 Heaven in Your Eyes/Whistlin' Man (1957)
Source: Marv Goldberg in *Whiskey, Women, and . . .* 16.

Joytones (New York)

Personnel Lucille "Vicky" Burgess (lead), Barbara Brown, Margaret Moore (d)

Notes

The Joytones came from upper Manhattan and the Bronx in New York City. Their Rama sides were recorded and released in 1956. A male quartet known as the Lyrics backed the Joytones on their sides. The Lyrics were part of the Raoul Cita chorus and it was Cita who trained the Joytones.

"My Foolish Heart" was recorded in October 1956. On that recording, Lynn Middleton replaced Barbara Brown. "My Foolish Heart" was released in November 1956.

Burgess came from the Charmers on Timely/Central.

Discography

Rama 191 All My Love Belongs to You/You Just Won't Treat Me Right (1956)
Rama 202 Gee What a Boy/Is This Really the End (1956)
Rama 215 Jimbo Jango/My Foolish Heart (1956)
Sources: Gordon Skadberg, liner notes with the Sequel CD *R&B Heroines: Goldner's Golden Girls.*

Jubalaires/Jubilaires (New Haven, Conn.)

Personnel J. C. Ginyard (tenor), Theodore Brooks, John Jennings, George McFadden, William Johnson (baritone)

Notes

The Jubalaires appeared on Arthur Godfrey's radio show in New York starting in 1941. When they were scheduled to be on the road with a tour, they found three singers and coupled them with one of themselves to become a second Jubalaires group. This second Jubalaires group later became the Shadows on Lee and Decca.

Jasper Edwards (bass), Sam McClure (baritone), and Raymond Reid, along with real Jubalaires' member Orville Brooks, toured as the Jubalaires while the real Jubalaires remained with Godfrey. These three had been with the Melody Kings.

Willie Johnson, who had been with the Golden Gate Quartet, left that group in anger in 1948 and joined the Jubalaires. Johnson toured the country with the Jubalaires for several years and can be heard on several of the group's King recordings and all of their Capitol sides.

They eventually settled in Los Angeles, where they became involved in motion pictures and early television. They appeared on the *Amos and Andy Show* and were in several Elvis Presley movies.

For years they were regulars on the *Phil Harris Show*. In the late 1950s, with the popularity of quartet singing diminishing and needing money to pay bills for his rather large family (a wife and eleven children), Johnson took a job with the Los Angeles Board of Education, from which he retired following twenty-three years of service. Johnson died in 1980.

This Jubalaires group is the King, Capitol, Decca, and Queen ensemble.

Discography

Decca 8666 Before This Time Another Year/All Over but the Shouting (1944)
Decca 18782 I Know/Get Together with the Lord (1946)
Decca 18916 So Lonesome I Could Cry/Don't Know What I'm to Do without You (1946)
Queen 4163 Sunday Kind of Love/Pray (1947)
Queen 4166 Jubes Blues/I've Waited All My Life for You (1947)
Queen 4167 God Almighty Gonna Cut You Down/Go Down Moses (1947)
Queen 4168 My God Called Me This Morning/Ring That Golden Bell (1947)
Queen 4172 Icky Yacky/You're Gonna Have a Wonderful Sweetheart (1947)
Decca 48031 I'm Moving Up the King's Highway/On My Way to Canaan Land (1947)
Decca 48085 Ezekiel Saw the Wheel a-Rollin'/Before This Time (Another Year) (1948)
Decca 48103 Get Right with God/They Put John on the Island (1949)
King 4290 Get Lost/Jean (1949)
King 4303 The Day Is Mine/St. Louis Lou (1949)
King 4325 Let It Rain/I've Waited All My Life for You (1949)
Capitol 70040 St. Louis Blues/It Ain't What You Want You Want That Does . . . (1949)
Capitol 683 Somebody Broke My Dolly/Mene Mene Tekel (1949)
Capitol 784 Home, Home, Home/I Wish I Had a Sweetheart (1949)
King 15040 Chattahoochie Lullaby/Twelve O'Clock and All Is Well (1950)
Capitol 821 Blue Ribbon Gal/The Pal I Loved Stole the Gal That I Loved (1950)
Decca 48186 Get Right with God/Go Down Moses (1950)

Capitol 845 That Old Piano Roll Blues/Dream Is a Wish Your Heart Makes (1950)
Capitol 1054 Pianola/Little Mr. Big (1950)
Capitol 1715 Keep On Doin' What You're Doin'/Rain Is the Teardrops of Angels (1951)
Capitol 1779 Living Is a Lie/As Summer Turns to Fall (1951)
Capitol 1888 David and Goliath/I've Done My Work (1951)
Sources: Marv Goldberg in *DISCoveries* 90; Rick Whitesell, obituary for Willie Johnson in *Goldmine*, October 1980.

Jumping Jacks (Winston-Salem, N.C.)

Personnel Eli Spillman (lead), James Little (tenor) Frank Wilson (d) (tenor/baritone), Daniel McGill (d) (bass)

Notes

This Jumping Jacks group formed in North Carolina in 1942. They practiced for quite some time before making local appearances. More than ten years passed before they made a recording for the Apollo subsidiary label, Lloyds. It should also be noted that they were from the same neighborhood as the Five Royales.

This group called themselves the Jumping Jacks because of their exuberance on stage. This was a very demonstrative and dramatic quartet. They recorded four songs in April 1953 but only the two sides shown below were released.

Unfortunately, neither of the two released songs did well and the group obviously felt that changing their name to the Romeos might change their luck.

This was not the Jumping Jacks who recorded "Embraceable You" on Bruce Records or the New Jersey–based Jumping Jacks featuring Danny Lamego.

Discography

Lloyds 101 Do Let That Dream Come True/Why Oh Why? (1953)
Source: Liner notes with the Relic LP/CD *Best of Apollo-1.*

Juniors, Jimmy Castor & (New York)

Personnel Jimmy Castor (lead), Johnny Williams (1st tenor), Orton Graves (baritone), Al Casey (bass)

Notes

While attending high school at New York's Music and Art High School, the Teenagers approached Castor (who also attended Music and Art) in the lunchroom. They invited him to join the group in place of Frankie Lymon. Castor refused the offer and decided to concentrate on the fundamentals of music, including music theory. He decided to devote himself to his woodwinds.

The group shown above is the ensemble on the Juniors' record on Wing. On Atomic, the lineup was Al Casey, Jimmy Castor, Herbie Greeves, and Howard Kenny Bobo.

Castor would later sing with the Teenagers and the Teenchords.

Discography

Wing 90078 I Promise/I Know the Meaning of Love (1956)
Atomic 100 This Girl of Mine/Somebody Mentioned Your Name (1957)
Source: Phil Groia, *They All Sang on the Corner.*

Kac-Ties (Brooklyn, N.Y.)

Personnel James Smalls, Panama Jennings, Jackie Robinson, David Wolf

Notes

It's rumored by many collectors that the Kac-Ties later became the Relations, who recorded for Kape Records.

Discography

Trans Atlas 695 Smile/Walkin' in the Rain (1962)
Shelly 163 Let Your Love Light Shine/Mr. Were Wolf (1963)
Shelly 165 Let Me in Your Life/Oh What a Night (1963)
Atco 6299 Let Me in Your Life/Oh What a Night (1963)
Kape 502 Walkin' in the Rain/Smile (1963)
Kape 503 Let Your Love Light Shine/Mr. Were Wolf (1963)
Kape 515 Girl in My Heart/Happy Birthday (1964)
Kape 702 Over the Rainbow/Donald Duck (1972)

Kansas City Tomcats

Personnel Walter Spriggs (lead), Lucky Enois (tenor), Jimmy Waters, Brooks Lewis (bass)

Notes

Where this group originated is not known. Earlier Walter Spriggs had been with the Five Echoes from Chicago. Whether or not they were from Kansas City is uncertain. Despite the fact that they recorded for a New York label, theirs is not a New York sound.

As the account goes, the Kansas City Tomcats simply walked into the facilities of Jubilee Records for an audition, which they were granted. Incredibly, they recorded that very same evening in 1955!

This was a self-contained group—they wrote their songs, sang and played their own instruments. After their second release for Josie Records, they were never heard from again.

Discography

Josie 786 Nobody Knows/Meet Me Meet Me Baby (1955)
Josie 797 Blues for Josie/Don't You Know (1956)
Source: Gordon Skadberg, liner notes with the Early Bird CD *Jubilee/Josie R&B Vocal Groups-3.*

Kents (Belmar, N.J.)

Personnel Tim Hauser (lead), Tommy Picardo (1st tenor), Jimmy Ruff (2d tenor), Steve Casagrande (baritone), Joe Ernst (bass)

Notes

This group was established in 1958 by classmates Tommy Picardo and Tim Hauser—the Tim Hauser who later sang with the Manhattan Transfer. They eventually recruited the other three. After practicing, they performed at their first show during summer 1958.

They auditioned for End Records in August 1958 and were rejected. They were soon in the lobby of 1697 Broadway and ran into Al Browne, who liked what he heard and asked them to come to his facility in Brooklyn for an audition. After many demos and little luck, they had Joe Mangi replace Hauser at lead. Hauser moved to 1st tenor and the group then became a sextet.

In 1959 they moved to Cecelia Records, changed their name to the Criterions, and recorded and released "I Remain Truly Yours." The record was a local success and Laurie Records rereleased it in 1964.

In 1969 Hauser was browsing through records in a Greenwich Village music shop when he came upon a disc that contained the first demos they had done for Browne. Apparently the record was released on Relic, an oldies label, and the group's name on the label was the Kents.

Discography

Relic 1013 Don't Say Goodbye/My Juanita (1965)
Source: Donn Fileti, liner notes with the Relic CD *Best of Relic Records.*

Keynotes (New York)

Personnel Floyd Adams (lead), Howard Anderson (1st tenor), Roger Lee (2d tenor), Larry "Spanky" Carter (baritone), Tucker Clark (bass)

Notes

This group began in central Harlem singing alongside numerous neighborhood groups in a bid for the attention of the girls and record company representatives. This was at the end of 1954; the group's dream of recording came true the next year.

Bernard Mathews was a frequent substitute. Floyd Adams was the group's lead on their first two discs and was replaced by Sam Kearney beginning with "In the Evening" and "Now I Know."

It has been said that Apollo owner Bess Berman lost interest in maintaining the R&B vocal groups on Apollo in 1956–1957 due to her preoccupation with retiring to Florida, coupled with the death of her husband, Ike. This may be the reason that the Keynotes' recordings never received adequate promotion. After she finally retired to Florida, nephew Charles Merenstein took over but did an equally poor job.

It's rumored that Floyd Adams was the Inspirations' lead on "Raindrops."

Sam Kearney was indirectly found through Todd Baptista's relationship with Butch Hamilton of the Bop Chords, from the same Harlem area of Manhattan. Until the latter 1990s, not one of the members was ever found. Baptista related that three of the original members are dead and one of the remaining members is physically impaired.

Discography

Apollo 478 Zenda/Suddenly (1955)
Apollo 484 I Don't Know/A Star (1955)
Apollo 493 Really Wish You Were Here/Bye Bye Baby (1956)
Apollo 498 Zup Zup/Now I Know (1956)
Apollo 503 Oh Yeah M-M/In the Evening (1956)
Apollo 513 One Little Kiss/Now I Know (1957)
Index 101 Dum Doodle Dum Dum/Open the Door (1958)
Source: Donn Fileti, liner notes with the Relic CD *Keynotes-In the Evening.*

Keys, Johnny & (Chicago)

Personnel Johnny Keyes, Pirkle Lee Moses, Reggie Gordon, Jerome Browne

Notes

This group was formed in late 1958 or early 1959 with Johnny Keyes and Reggie Gordon (formerly of the touring Magnificents), Jerome Browne (formerly of the Five Bells), and Pirkle Lee Moses (former lead of the El Dorados and other lesser-known groups).

Discography

Mercury Tuscumscari/Lost Teenager (1959)
Source: Bob Pruter in *Doowop . . . The Chicago Scene.*

Keystoners (Philadelphia)

Personnel Norman Smith (d) (lead), Nathaniel "Mitch" Jackson (1st tenor), Al Singleton (baritone), Goliath James (d) (bass)

Notes

This group first got together in 1947 and, like all groups, sang at local functions, at church, on the street, and in school. In 1950, Jackson was drafted and "Sonny" Smith replaced him. Smith performed with this initial group and would later become part of the Buccaneers and still later the Universals.

Many changes in personnel took place. In 1954, Norman, Al, Mitch, and James formed a new vocal group, the Keystoners. At this time they got themselves a manager, Herman Gillespie, who had previously written "Sister Sookey" for Philadelphia's Turbans.

The Keystoners auditioned with a song written by Smith, "The Magic Kiss." Two weeks after the audition, they recorded the tune along with "I'd Write about the Blues." "The Magic Kiss" was released on G&M Records. It soon began to make some noise, and this is when Columbia stepped in and purchased the rights to the tune. They had had the Keystoners redo "Magic Kiss" with "After I Propose" on the flip side. This was released on Columbia's Epic label.

Talmadge Allen performed with the Keystoners. He only recorded on Sleep and Dream/TV Gal. He replaced Mitch Jackson, who had come to realize that income from music left a great deal to be desired and had left.

The Keystoners re-formed in 1982. As the following discography shows, the group has been recording into the 1990s.

Discography

G&M 102 Magic Kiss/I'd Write about the Blues (1956)
Epic 9187 The Magic Kiss/After I Propose (1956)
Riff 202 Sleep and Dream/TV Gal (1957)
Okeh 7210 Magic Kiss/After I Propose (1964)
Starbound 501 I'll Always Remember/Don't Know Why (1984)
Starbound 502 Say Always/That's Why I Dream (1984)
Starbound 509 Hey Girl/Too Soon to Know (1988)
Starbound 514 My Heart Beats Again/You're All I Want for Christmas (1991)
Starbound 515 Gossip/Call My Name (1993)
Starbound 516 Them There Eyes/Sweet Was the Wine (1993)
Source: Bob Bosco, *Echoes of the Past* 28.

King Krooners (Jacksonville, Fla.)

Personnel John Stanberry, Bobby Jones, Cliff Williams, Alfred Corley, Douglas Marshall

Notes

The King Krooners and the King Crooners were the same group.

Interestingly, the King Krooners also recorded "Pretty Little Girl," which went unreleased. This is the same "Pretty Little Girl" performed in 1956 by a New York group, the Monarchs, who had it released on both Neil and Melba.

On the Excello CD *Excello Vocal Groups,* Cub Coda's liner notes imply that the King Krooners were referred to as Little Rico and the King Krooners. Coda asks, "Who the hell is Little Rico?" Coda also discusses the lead as John Standberry.

Discography

Hart 1002 She's Mine All Mine/Lonely Nights (1959)
Excello 2168 Now That She's Gone/Won't You Let Me Know (Crooners) (1959)
Excello 2187 Memories/School Daze (1960)
Sources: Gordon Skadberg, liner notes with the Ace CD *Southern Doo Wop–Shoop Shoop*; Cub Coda, notes with the Excello CD *Excello Vocal Groups.*

Kinglets (Nashville, Tenn.)

Personnel Don "Sonny" Taylor, Ricky Roland, Frank Talley

Notes

Like many groups before and after them, the Kinglets were primarily a backup vocal group for single artists on their labels.

Discography

Calvert 101 Six Days a Week/You Gotta Go (1956)
Bobbin' 104 Pretty Please/My Baby Don't Need Change (1959)
Source: Daniel Cooper, liner notes with the Ace CD *Across the Tracks-2.*

King Odom Four/Quartet (New York)

Personnel David "King" Odom (lead), David "Boots" Bowers (bass), Isaiah Bing,
Cleveland Bing

Notes

This group got together in 1947 and was badly in need of cash. With that in mind,
Isaiah Bing recruited his brother, Cleveland, a baritone, David "Boots" Bowers, a
bass, and David "King" Odom, lead. They all knew each other from their past in
South Carolina and it was decided to call themselves the King Odom Four or sometimes the King Odom Quartet. Sometimes the name was misspelled as Odum.

After assembling, they got themselves a contract with Musicraft in 1949. That
summer they were part of a radio show on NBC called *Swingtime.* Also in 1949,
they went on tour with Savannah Churchill. In 1950, they had moved to Derby and
had four releases for Derby. In 1952, they were with Abbey and then Perspective
Records.

The group broke up in 1952. In 1953, "Boots" and Isaiah Bing joined with Orville
Brooks and Eugene Mumford to record as the Larks on the Apollo subsidiary,
Lloyds. David Odom got some other singers and recorded one disc for Perspective
before calling it a career.

Bowers also sang for the Ravens and the Larks. He was on the Ravens' Argo recording of "A Simple Prayer."

Discography

Musicraft 543 Mary Lou (KO)/Looking Over a Four Leaf Clover (KO) (1948)
Musicraft 554 I'm Living Humble (CB)/They Put John on the Island (CB) (1948)
Musicraft 575 Moonlight Frost (KO)/Who Struck John (KO) (1948)
Musicraft 579 Pickin' a Chicken (KO)/I Found a Twinkle (KO) (1948)
Derby 736 I'm Glad I Made You Cry (KO)/Lover Come Back to Me (1950)
Derby 743 If He Didn't Love Me (KO)/Walkin' with My Shadow (KO) (1950)
Derby 754 What a Wonderful Feeling (KO)/My Heart Cries for You (KO) (1951)
Derby 757 Rain Is the Teardrops of Angels (KO/DB)/All of Me (KO/DB) (1951)
Abbey 15064 Lucky (KO)/Don't Trade Your Love for Gold (KO) (1952)
Perspective 5001 Basin Street Blues/Amazin' Willie Mays (1954)
Source: Marv Goldberg and David Bowers in *Whiskey, Women, and . . .* 18–19.

Kings (Baltimore, Md.)

Personnel Adolphus Holcomb (lead), Robert Hall (1st tenor), Raymond Holcomb
(baritone), Gilbert Wilkes (bass)

Notes

This group assembled in Baltimore in 1950, having been neighborhood friends singing on local streets for years. In 1953, they were spotted at a talent show by the Shad brothers who owned Jax, Harlem, and Sittin' In with Records.

They signed with the Shads and recorded excellent sides for Jax and Harlem. Hall sang lead on the first three and Adolphus Holcomb on the fourth. Their records sold well locally but not as well in the rest of the country. As a result, the Shads had to drop them. Hall left at this time.

James Arthur was a tenor who sang with this group as well as with the Ramblers. Leon Smith also sang with the group. Their next move was to MGM, where they cut the "Vadunt Un Vada Song" (credited to the Ramblers), which did not do well at the cash registers.

Their next move was to Gotham Records. They again did one disc that did that sell well. They then went to New York to George Goldner's Gone Records, which kept them for one release. Next was Jalo for whom they cut nothing, but the time spent and patience shown there ultimately got them a contract to record with RCA. They had two records for RCA in 1958–1959.

Subsequent labels were with Jalo family labels—Jay Wing and Lookie. The Jay Wing release did well and was picked up by Epic.

In 1960, Wilkes and Smith left. Wilkes was replaced by Theodore Estep and vocalist/guitarist Smith, by Rudolph Chew. Thus the new group was the Holcomb brothers, James Arthur, Estep, and Chew. This group recorded for Century as Little Hooks and the Kings. This was 1963.

Discography

Jax 314 Why Oh Why/I Love You Baby (1953)
Jax 316 You Made Me Cry/Baby Be There (1953)
Jax 320 Love No One/Sunday Kind of Love (1954)
Jax 323 You Never Knew/Do You Want to Rock? (1954)
Harlem 2322 Fire in My Heart/You Never Knew (1954)
Gotham 316 God Made You Mine/The Good Book (1956)
Gone 5013 Don't Go/Love Is Something from Within (1957)
Jalo 203 Angel/Come On Little Baby (1958)
RCA 47-7419 Till You/Elephant Walk (1958)
RCA 47-7544 Your Sweet Love/Troubles Don't Last (1959)
Jay-Wing 5806 Surrender/Hold Me (1959)
Lookie 18 Bump-I-Dy-Bump/I Want to Know (1960)
Century 1300 Count Your Blessings/How to Start a Romance (1960)
United Artists 50932 Give the Drummer Some More/I Don't Want to Leave You (1972)
Source: Marv Goldberg and Dave Hinckley in *Yesterday's Memories* 3.

Kings (New York)

Personnel James Van Loan (lead), Paul Van Loan (tenor), Bill Chambers (tenor), Joe Van Loan (baritone), David "Boots" Bowers (bass)

Notes

This Kings group formed in 1956. They were actually the Ravens while recording with the Chess subsidiary, Argo. They recorded "Long Lonely Nights," which Chess had already recorded and released by Lee Andrews and the Hearts and did not wish to cover on one of their other labels. As a result, the Ravens' version was sold to Sol Rabinowitz, owner of Baton Records. He released it on Baton as by the Kings.

Discography

Baton 245 Long Lonely Nights/Let Me Know (1957)
Source: Marv Goldberg in *Whiskey, Women, and . . .* 18–19.

Kings (New Orleans)

Personnel Earl King, Huey Smith, Joseph De Voie, Willie Johnson, Chris Kenner

Notes

The Kings is another vocal group from Louisiana that recorded for a California label.

Huey Smith attained a modicum of success later in his career with national hits like "Rockin' Pneumonia" and "Don't You Just Know It" with the Clowns, recording for the Ace label. Chris Kenner later recorded an equally big tune with "I Like It Like That."

Discography

Specialty 497 What Can I Do/Till I Say Well Done (1954)
Source: Jerry Wexler and Billy Vera, liner notes with the Specialty CD *Creole Kings of New Orleans.*

King Toppers (Dayton, Ohio)

Personnel Grant Kitchings (lead), Welton Young (tenor), Dave Colter (tenor), Don Turner (baritone), Louis Day (bass)

Notes

This group formed in 1954 at Dunbar High School in Dayton, Ohio, initially performing pop, modern harmony, and progressive jazz arrangements. They did many local spots in Ohio for two years and were told by a friend to go to New York City to try to appear at the Apollo's amateur talent show.

They came to New York, retaining the services of many managers along the way, including Aaron Cornelius, who had earlier been with the Regals on Atlantic and the Orioles on Vee Jay. Everyone advised them to abandon their modern harmony, pop, and progressive jazz arrangements because such records did not sell!

They auditioned and recorded for RCA, but the song was never released. Eventually they came to Josie's facilities, where they recorded no. 811 (below) in September 1956. This was released early in 1957, by which time Louis Day had been drafted and Colter had gone and was replaced by their manager Aaron Cornelius.

Their record did not do too well and the group decided to sing whatever they chose—modern sounds or pop. They did just that for a brief period until they decided to split up.

Cornelius went on to sing with the Orioles on Vee Jay. By 1961, Kitchings was with a Keynotes group, which included David Baughan, Bill Brown, and Bill Wells. This quartet was set to record for Capitol when Kitchings was drafted.

Discography

Josie 811 Walkin' and Talkin' the Blues/You Were Waiting for Me (1957)
Source: Marv Goldberg in *Goldmine* 35.

Knickerbockers

Personnel Roosevelt "Tippie" Hubbard (tenor), James "Toy" Walton (tenor), Alonzo Simmons (baritone), Johnny Terry (bass)

Notes

In 1959, James "Toy" Walton formed the Knickerbockers. This followed a one-year and one-recording stint with the Links on Teenage.

Johnny Terry also sang for the Links, as well as the Dominoes and the Drifters. Hubbard sang for the L'Cap-Tans and the Clovers.

Although this ensemble stayed together for four years, they never recorded.
Source: Marv Goldberg in *Yesterday's Memories,* vol. 2, no 4.

Bob Knight Four (Brooklyn, N.Y.)

Personnel Bobby Bovino (lead), Paul Ferrigno (tenor), Ralph Garone (2d tenor), John Ropers (bass)

Notes

John, Ralph, and Bob knew each other from high school. After meeting Paul, they auditioned for the Rifkins, owners of the Dome label. This formation took place in Brooklyn in 1956.

They recorded "Hymn of Love" for Dome, but it was never released.

The original label for "Good Goodbye" was Laurel, contrary to some collectors who believe it was Taurus.

They moved to Josie in 1962 and then to Jubilee in 1963. Their last record for Goal, Willingly/Tomorrow We'll Be Married, included a personnel change. The group on this final recording was John, Ralph, Charlie Licarta, and Frankie Iovino.

In the liner notes accompanying Sequel's *Jubilee/Josie–5* CD, the bass's name is shown as Rogers.

Group members reached the decision to disband because they found no work. This decision was achieved by mutual consent.

Discography

Laurel 1020 Good Good Goodbye/How Old Must I Be? (1961)
Laurel 1023 For Sale/You Gotta Know (1961)

Taurus A-100 So So Long/You Tease Me (1961)
Taurus 356 I'm Selling My Heart/The Lazy Piano (instrumental) (1961)
Josie 899 Memories/Somewhere (1962)
Jubilee 5451 Two Friends/Crazy Love (1963)
Goal 4 Tomorrow We'll Be Married/Willingly (1964)
Sources: Marcia Vance in *Bim Bam Boom* 11; Ed Engel, liner notes with the Ace
CD *Laurie Vocal Groups.*

Knockouts (Northern New Jersey)

Personnel Bob D'Andrea (lead), R. Gallagher, E. Parenti, R. Collada

Notes

The Knockouts, according to Billy Vera's liner notes with the Rhino CD set *Doo
Wop Box 2,* was a New Jersey shore bar band whose main attraction was comedy/
novelty material. They seemed older than the average group, and their appearance
was somewhat seedy.

Discography

Shad 5013 Darling Lorraine/Riot in Cell Block 3-C (1959)
Shad 5018 Rich Boy, Poor Boy/Please Be Mine (1960)
MGM 13010 Fever/You Can Take My Girl (1961)
Tribute 199 Ho Jo Part 1/Ho Jo Part 2 (1964)
Tribute 201 What's On Your Mind?/Tweet-Tweet (1964)
Tribute 1039 Don't Say Goodbye/Ecuador (1965)
Source: Billy Vera, liner notes with the Rhino CD set *Doo Wop Box 2.*

Kodaks/Kodoks (Newark, N.J.)

Personnel Pearl McKinnon (lead), James Patrick (1st tenor), William Franklin (2d
tenor), Larry Davis (baritone), William Miller (bass)

Notes

This Newark-based group started in 1957 with Patrick as lead, Franklin at 2d tenor,
Davis at baritone, and William Miller at bass. Looking for that something differ-
ent, they found Pearl McKinnon. After practicing day after day, they went to Bobby
Robinson's Fury Records on 125th Street in Harlem to audition.

They auditioned for Robinson in his store. He loved them and it was his suggestion to have Pearl sing lead and to call themselves the Kodaks. This was 1957 and
came just after Robinson lost the Teenchords to George Goldner and End Records.

Starting with "Oh Gee, Oh Gosh," their second disc for Fury, their records sold
very well but provided no income for band members.

The lack of royalties caused Davis and Franklin to leave and join the Sonics ("This
Broken Heart"). They were replaced by Harold Jenkins of the Impacts and Richard
Dixon. The two were great dancers but just fair vocalists.

A few months following their third session at Fury, which produced "Kingless

Castle," "Runaround Baby," and "My Baby and Me," James Patrick left and later became part of the Monotones. Miller left to support his burgeoning family, and McKinnon left to marry.

In the fall of 1959, William Miller recruited his wife, Jean, to replace McKinnon. Renaldo Gamble (bass of the Schoolboys/Impacts on RCA), joined at this time. In late 1959, they got together with Harold Jenkins and were with Zell Sanders at J&S Records. "Look Up to the Sky" and "Love Wouldn't Mean a Thing" for Wink Records were great cuts that received a very poor response. Consequently, the group decided to split.

McKinnon's next stop was with Pearl and the Deltars.

(Note: Jeff Beckman's McKinnon interview in *Big Town Review 3* shows a different original group lineup than the one above.)

Discography

Fury 1007 Teenager's Dream/Little Boy and Girl (1957)
Fury 1015 Oh Gee, Oh Gosh/Make Believe World (1957)
Fury 1019 My Baby and Me/Kingless Castle (1958)
Fury 1020 Guardian Angel/Run Around Baby (1958)
J&S 1683/84 Don't Want No Teasing/Look Up to the Sky (1960)
Wink 1004 Twista Twistin'/Let's Rock (1961)
Wink 1006 Mister Magoo/Love Wouldn't Mean a Thing (1961)
Sources: Donn Fileti, liner notes with the Relic CD *The Kodaks;* Jeff Beckman in *Big Town Review* 3; Tony Russo in *Yesterday's Memories* 4.

Kool Gents (Chicago)

Personnel Delecta "Dee" Clark (lead), John McCall (1st tenor), Teddy Long (2d tenor), Doug Brown (2d tenor), Johnny Carter (bass)

Notes

In 1951, this group, initially known as the Goldentones, assembled at Chicago's Marshall High School. Members came and went but by 1953 the new members had settled in. The resulting group basically remained intact for years. At the start, they sang both gospel and secular music.

Delecta Clark was the experienced member of the group. In 1952, along with two friends calling themselves the Hambone Kids, he recorded the novelty tune "Hambone" for Okeh. Hambone sold quite well for the Columbia subsidiary. Clark would hang around the WGS facilities—the Goldentones' neighborhood. There he met deejay Herb Kent, the "Cool Gent."

Because Kent had befriended Clark, he had a keen interest in this group. They asked him if they could use the name Kool Gents as the group's name and Kent, flattered, said yes! He would also get them an audition with Vee Jay's Vivian Carter. Vee Jay management liked the Kool Gents very much and signed them to a contract. They did not record right away but went home to perfect their vocals and stage presence. When they felt ready, they returned to Vee Jay's facilities and recorded. Their "This Is the Night" was released in 1955.

In 1956, the Kool Gents recorded "The Convention." The group's sound on this track differed from their previous recordings. Because of this, coupled with the title of the song, Vee Jay chose to rename them the Delegates.

They made many live appearances in the Chicago vicinity arranged by Vee Jay. In 1956, Vee Jay bought out Ping Records and the Debonairs' release on Ping, "Mother's Son," was given to the Kool Gents to cover. It was a Vee Jay policy to cover a song initially done by a little-known black group with a better-known one. Because this was so unlike the Kool Gents' style, Vee Jay again called them the Delegates.

In 1957, Clark and the remaining members of the group were not getting along very well, and Ewart Abner wanted Clark to go out on his own. Thus it was decided that he would begin a solo career. The group initially was not aware of this change and when they learned of it, they were quite angry. But when informed that Pirkle Lee Moses had left the El Dorados and they would become his group, the anger passed.

The Kool Gents lasted for a short time as the El Dorados and then split up. In 1964, John Carter formed another Kool Gents with the following lineup: Carter, McCall, Danny Edwards, and Eugene "Huffy" Huff. This group performed but never recorded.

Discography

Vee Jay 173 This Is the Night/Do Ya Do (1955)
Vee Jay 207 You Know/I Just Can't Help Myself (1956)
Source: Bob Galgano in *Bim Bam Boom* 2.

Ladders (New York)

Personnel Johnny Jackson (lead), Herb Jennings (1st tenor), Irvin Jones (2d tenor), Ron Clark (baritone), Douglas Jackson (bass)

Notes

Johnny and Douglas Jackson were brothers. The group was managed by Les Cooper of the Empires on Whirlin' Disc, Harlem, Wing, and Amp 3 and the Whirlers on Whirlin' Disc.

The Ladders lived on 115th Street in Manhattan, in the same apartment building as the Bopchords. The Ladders cut only two discs, both for Danny Robinson's labels—Holiday and Vest, the label named after his wife, Vesta.

Discography

Holiday 2611 I Want to Know/Counting the Stars (1958)
Vest 826 My Love Is Gone/Hey Pretty Baby (1959)
Sources: Phil Groia, *They All Sang on the Corner*; Donn Fileti, liner notes with the Relic CD *The Groups of Holiday Records.*

Laddins (New York)

Personnel Sylvester "Sonny" Johnson (lead), Ernest Mickey Goody (1st tenor), Earl Marcus (2d tenor), John Marcus (baritone), Robert Jeffers (Bobby Jay) (bass)

Notes

The Laddins formed as the Pastels in Harlem, New York. After several personnel changes and a great deal of practice, they signed with Central Records. After learning of the Chicago Pastels they changed their name to the Laddins.

They cut their first for Central in 1957. Aside from their vocal ability, they are remembered for their incredible choreography. In a *Goldmine* interview with Bobby Jay, Mr. Jay stated that "Did It" was recorded in a store in Harlem under very crude conditions. Two other tracks were recorded for Central, but both remain unreleased.

They met Jack Hook in one of the "music buildings on Broadway," and he set them up to record for Grey Cliff in 1959. Here too there remain several unreleased tracks. The Isle record was done the year before and released at the same time as the Grey Cliff disc. Again, the additional tracks cut for Isle have never been released.

In 1960, the Laddins met up with Central management again, who wanted them to tour. Instead of a recording contract, the boys asked for, and got, the rights to their Central recording. They sold "Did It" to Slim Rose of Times Square Records and he reissued it. However, this did not provide the guys with one cent! In another venture, they owned a candy store in Harlem with Little Anthony and the Imperials. This failed as well.

Their next label affiliation was with Theater Records, which was distributed by Laurie. The Laddins auditioned for Theater and label management signed them. Regarding their output while with Theater, guess what? Seventeen tracks that have never been issued in the United States.

David Coleman replaced Johnson on lead in 1961. Yvonne Gearing also sang with the Laddins for a brief period, as did Eddie "California" Jones.

Discography

Central 2602 Did It/Now You're Gone (1957)
Grey Cliff 721 Yes, Oh Baby Yes/Light a Candle (1959)
Isle 801 She's the One/Come On (1960)
Theatre 111 Oh How I Hate to Go Home/There Once Was a Time (1961)
Groove 4-5 Try, Try Again/That's What You Do to Me (1962)
Angie 1790 If You Need Me I'll Be There/I'll Kiss Your Teardrops Away (1962)
Angie 1003 Push, Shake, Kick, and Shout (instrumental) (1963)
Bardell 776 Push, Shake, Kick, and Shout (instrumental) (1963)
Butane 779 Dream Baby/Dizzy Jones Birdland (1964)
Sources: Bobby Jay, liner notes with the Relic LP *Laddins Greatest Hits*; Jeff Tamarkin, interview by Bobby Jay in *Goldmine*.

Lamplighters (Los Angeles)

Personnel Thurston Harris (lead), Willie Ray Rockwell (d) (tenor), Al Frazier (baritone), Matthew Nelson (d) (bass)

Notes

In 1952 Willie Ray Rockwell, Matt Nelson, and Leon Hughes were classmates at Jordan High School in Los Angeles. The little money earned by performing created a must situation to keep their day jobs to pay for things like rent. They participated in a talent contest at Johnny Otis's Barrelhouse and lost to a twenty-one-year-old tenor—Thurston Harris. The guys approached Harris and asked him if he would like to be their lead. Harris was most receptive to their proposal.

Harris had come from Indiana, where he had performed with several gospel units. He served his time in the army and was now in Los Angeles looking for work. After meeting each other at the Barrelhouse, they reconvened the following day at that same club and began vocalizing. Soon they were heard by Al Frazier, formerly of the West Coast Mello-Moods, who was in the audience for one of their performances. He went backstage to join the group to advise them about improving their stage presence and immediately became part of the ensemble. It has been learned recently that soon after joining, Frazier, who could not get along with Leon Hughes, asked that he be eliminated from the group, and the group then became a quartet.

Johnny Otis was most instrumental in getting the group a contract with Federal due to his friendship with Federal's Ralph Bass. Additionally, there was always a great deal of internal strife among the group members. Fist fights, drinking, and dope smoking were common. Rockwell had a serious drinking problem that caused him to miss dates. This gradually forced him out of the group and ultimately killed him in a motorcycle accident. Internal conflicts continued, causing Harris to leave the Lamplighters while on tour in Georgia.

Carl White (d. 1980) joined as lead after Thurston Harris went on what he called a sabbatical. Sonny Harris joined as tenor from the Feathers. The Lamplighters simultaneously recorded as the Tenderfoots and reverted to the Lamplighters in 1956.

Becoming too difficult to work with, Thurston Harris was replaced by Turner "Rocky" Wilson in 1957. The group soon became the Sharps with Carl White, Sonny Harris, Al Frazier, and Turner "Rocky" Wilson. This, of course, was the same Sharps who later backed Thurston Harris on "Little Bitty Pretty One."

C. Groom, Harold Lewis, and Pico Grooms were also in the Lamplighters.

Before the Lamplighters broke up, they backed Paul Anka (not the Jacks) on his "Blau Vie DeVeest Fontaine."

In one form or another this group was the Tenderfoots, Sharps (Jamie, Vik, and Aladdin), Four After Fives, Crenshaws, and Rivingtons, in that order.

Discography

Federal 12149 Part of Me/Turn Me Loose (1953)
Federal 12152 Give Me/Be-Bop Wino (1953)
Federal 12156 Sad Life/Move Me Baby (J. Witherspoon) (1953)
Federal 12166 Smootchie/I Can't Stand It (1954)
Federal 12176 I Used to Cry, Mercy, Mercy/Tell Me You Care (1954)
Federal 12182 Salty Dog/Ride Jockey, Ride (1954)
Federal 12192 Five Minutes Longer/You Hear (1954)
Federal 12197 Yum Yum/Goody Good Things (1954)
Federal 12206 I Wanna Know/Believe in Me (1954)
Federal 12212 Roll On/Love, Rock, and Thrill (1955)
Federal 12242 Don't Make It So Good/Hug a Little, Kiss a Little (1955)
Federal 12255 Bo Peep/You Were Sent Down from Heaven (1956)
Federal 12261 It Ain't Right/Everything's All Right (1956)
Decca 29669 After All/Big Joke 1955

Sources: Jim Dawson, liner notes with the Regency CD *Be Bop Wino*; Jay Warner, *American Singing Groups.*

Larados (Dearborn, Mich.)

Personnel Ron Morris (lead), Tom Hust (1st tenor), Bob Broderick (2d tenor), Bernie Turnbull (baritone), Don Davenport (bass)

Notes

The original Larados were high school friends in Detroit in the mid-1950s. The first group sustained many personnel changes. They were friends of the Diablos, coming from the same locale.

When the group visited the Fortune Records facility in Detroit, they met with Jack Brown, who owned Fortune Records with wife Devora. By pointing his finger arbitrarily at a map, he named the group the Larados by pointing at Laredo, Texas. This was early in 1955.

Phil Waddell became their manager. He also managed the Five Scalders on Drummond. Waddell became interested in the Larados because they had such a tight black sound. Previously Waddell had handled only black vocal groups, and the white but black-sounding Larados presented a challenge to Waddell.

Early in 1956 the original group broke up, but one member, Gary Banovetz, met several other singers from another group that had recently split up. These singers teamed up and practiced a great deal. But later in 1956 Banovetz left and was replaced by Don Davenport, bass from the Romeos on Fox.

The Larados were then asked to record for Fox Records. This was 1957 and they recorded four tunes for Fox, but only two were released and met with limited local success.

They then went to New York looking for someone to assist them. They went to the Apollo Theater, but Apollo management would not accept them because they were white! They appeared on Arthur Godfrey's talent scouts show, but neither Godfrey nor his audience cared for them and they returned to Detroit.

They made many live appearances in trade for radio airplay.

Broderick left and Banovetz returned to perform with the group doing backup for a female artist at Fox. The Larados later became the Reflections on Golden World.

Discography

Fox 962/963 Bad Bad Guitar Man/Now the Parting Begins (1957)
Dial 100 Sapphire/You Made Me Blue (1959)
Sources: Jay Repoley in *Story Untold* 6; unsigned liner notes with the Regency CD *Motor City-Detroit Doo Wops.*

La-Rells (Pittsburgh, Pa.)

Personnel Frank Avery (lead), Bob Best (1st tenor), LaFar McCullough (2d tenor), David Parr (baritone), Wilston Anderson (bass)

Notes

The La-Rells got together in the early 1960s, performing at school proms, record hops, variety shows, and club benefits.

After many practice sessions and local appearances, they wound up at Robbee Records, where they had two releases.

Their style was patterned after the Coasters and the Olympics.

After the two releases for Robbee, they recorded one disc for Liberty Records. After their releases met with little success, they chose to disband.

Discography

Robbee 109 Please Be Fair/Everybody Knew (1961)
Robbee 114 I Just Can't Understand/Public Transportation (1961)
Liberty 55430 I Guess I'll Never Stop Loving You/Sneaky Alligator (1962)
Sources: Dick Zinger in *Story Untold* 9; Travis Klein, liner notes with the Itzy II CD, *Pittsburgh's Greatest Hits.*

Larks (Durham, N.C.)

Personnel Eugene Mumford (lead), Raymond "Pee Wee" Barnes (tenor), Thermon Ruth (tenor), Allen Bunn (baritone), David McNeill (bass)

Notes

Thermon Ruth put together a gospel group called the Selah Jubilee Singers. All (except Ruth) were from North Carolina and became very popular there. The members were Junius Parker, Melvin Coldten, Allen Bunn, Ruth, and Jimmy Gorham.

At this time, Eugene Mumford was in prison, falsely accused of various offenses. He remained there for several years until his case was properly investigated by officials. Ruth had known Mumford when the latter was with the Four Internes. He always kept in touch with Mumford. Just before Mumford's release, Bunn and Ruth left the Selahs, eventually joining David McNeill, Haddie Rowe Jr., and Raymond "Pee Wee" Barnes. Mumford teamed up with them and they would soon go to New York to seek their fortune.

They auditioned for Jerry Blaine at Jubilee, Bess Berman at Apollo, Herman Lubinsky at Savoy in Newark, and Regal Records in Linden, New Jersey. Bess Berman at Apollo was a powerhouse in the industry, feared by the others. She convinced the group to choose Apollo. At this time they changed their name to the Larks.

Before recording as the Larks for Apollo, they appeared on Perry Como's show and the Arthur Godfrey program. To earn some quick money, they began recording as the Southern Harmonaires, the Sons of Zion, the Jubilators, the Four Sons, the Four Barons, and the Clear-Tones, recording gospel and secular tunes. This was done in a very short time. Finally, when they began recording for Bess Berman at Apollo in 1950, they were the Larks. Their first disc for the label was released as by the Five Larks.

They cut many successful records and made an equal number of live appearances, but the money, split five ways, was simply not enough. Consequently, the original Larks decided to call it quits in 1952.

Mumford left first for the Golden Gate Quartet, McNeill went to the Dominoes, replacing Bill Brown, Bunn became "Tarheel Slim," "Pee Wee" Barnes became a guitar player with a band, and Ruth returned to North Carolina to become a disc jockey.

In 1954, Mumford organized another Larks group, which recorded for the Apollo subsidiary, Lloyds Records. This group consisted of Mumford, Orville Brooks, David Bowers, and Isaiah Bing. Bowers and Bing had sung with the King Odom Quartet. Brooks had performed with the Golden Gate Quartet. It was this foursome that backed Barbara Gale. This group lasted until late 1955. Mumford then went to the Old Town subsidiary, Whiz Records, with the Serenaders (the same Larks group). Their one recording there didn't do well and Mumford then joined Billy Ward and the Dominoes. In the 1960s, he sang with the Doodlers on RCA.

Discography

Apollo 427 Eyesight to the Blind/I Ain't Fattening Frogs for Snakes (1951)
Apollo 429 Hey Little Girl/Little Side Car (1951)
Apollo 430 Ooh . . . It Feels So Good/I Don't Believe in Tomorrow (1951)
Apollo 435 My Lost Love/How Long Must I Wait for You (1951)
Apollo 1177 Coffee, Cigarettes, and Tears/My Heart Cries for You (1951)
Apollo 1180 Hopefully Yours/When I Leave These Prison Walls (1951)
Apollo 1184 My Reverie/Let's Say a Prayer (1951)
Apollo 1189 Shadrack/Honey in the Rock (1952)
Apollo 1190 Stolen Love/In My Lonely Room (1952)
Apollo 1194 I Live True to You/Hold Me (1952)
Apollo 437 Darlin'/Lucy Brown (1952)
Lloyds 108 Margie/Rockin' in the Rocket Room (1954)
Lloyds 110 If It's a Crime/Tippin' In (1954)
Lloyds 111 When You're Near/Who Walks in When I Walk Out? (1954)
Lloyds 112 No Other Girl/The World Is Waiting for the Sunrise (1954)
Lloyds 114 Os-Ca-Lu-Ski-O/Forget It (1954)
Lloyds 115 Johnny Darlin'/You're Gonna Lose Your Gal (1954)
Apollo 475 Honey from the Bee/No Mama No (1955)
Sources: Jeff Beckman in *Big Town Review* 3; Donn Fileti, liner notes with Relic's *Larks* CDs.

Larks (Los Angeles)

Personnel Don Julian (tenor), Charles Morrison, Ted Walters

Notes

Don Julian came from the Meadowlarks, who recorded for Dootone. After the Meadowlarks disbanded, Julian decided to start another vocal group. He simply called them the Larks. They recorded several items for the Money label. In the fall of 1964, Julian and the group recorded a tune entitled "The Jerk" on the Money label. It became a huge hit and they had many Money releases thereafter.

The Money label in 1964 was being run by the son of John Dolphin. Dolphin, the former head of the important Recorded in Hollywood label.

Discography

Money 106 The Jerk/Forget Me (1964)
Money 110 Mickey's East Coast Jerk/Soul Jerk (1965)
Money 112 Heavenly Father/The Roman (1965)
Money 115 Sad Sad Boy/Can You Do the Duck? (1965)
Money 119 The Answer Came Too Late/Lost My Love Yesterday (1966)
Money 122 Philly Dog/Heaven Only Knows (1966)
Money 127 The Skate/Come Back Baby (1967)
Money 601 I Want You Back/I Love You (1971)
Source: Marv Goldberg and Mike Redmond in *Yesterday's Memories.*

Larks (Philadelphia)

Personnel Jackie Marshall (lead), Calvin Nichols (2d tenor), Earl Oxidine (baritone), Weldon A. McDougal III (bass)

Notes

This group was brought together in the 1960s by Weldon McDougal, who had been hoping to form a vocal group since high school. Following school, he enlisted in the marines, where he formed several R&B groups. He would appear with them in various USO shows. Two years after his discharge from the service, he carefully assembled a group in Philadelphia, seeking out vocalists in that city. Marshall put the Larks together and eventually recorded.

Discography

Sheryl 334 It's Unbelievable/I Can't Believe It (1961)
Sheryl 338 Let's Drink a Toast/There Is a Girl (1961)
Violet 1051 I Want Her to Love Me/Muddy Road (1963)
Guyden 2098 I Want Her to Love Me/Muddy Road (1963)
Guyden 2103 Fabulous Cars and Diamond Rings/Life Is Sweeter Now (1964)
Jett 3001 Love Me True/Love You So (1965)
Source: Weldon McDougal III, liner notes with the Universal Love LP *Unbelievable.*

Laurels (Los Angeles)

Personnel Bobby Relf (lead), Edwin Solomon (tenor), Ted Brown (2d tenor), Donplayelle Duconje, Ronald Brown (bass)

Notes

This group formed in Los Angeles early in 1954.

Bobby Relf was Bob of Bob and Earl. The Laurels were the backing group for Jesse Belvin on Specialty, singing "Gone."

Discography

Combo 66 Fine Fine Baby/T.J. (1955)
X 0143 Truly, Truly/'Tis Right (1955)

Flair 1063 Farewell/Yours Alone (1955)
Source: Ted Carroll and Ray Topping, liner notes with the Ace CD *Fifties.*

L'Cap-Tans (Washington, D.C.)

Personnel Lester Britton (lead), Richard Stewart (1st tenor), Elmo "Chico" Anderson (2d tenor), Harmon Bethea (baritone)

Notes

This group assembled in the late 1950s and recorded for Hollywood. Tenor "Baby" Jim Belt was added, and the resulting quintet did the sides on Savoy Records.

In 1963, the group was made up of Harmon Bethea, Johnny Hood, Richard Stewart, and Eddie Young.

In the late 1960s in order to have something unique, Bethea started wearing a mask. At that time the group was called Maskman and the Cap-Tans. In 1968, Stewart and Young left and were replaced by Paul Williams and Tyrone Gray. To acknowledge the change, the group was renamed the Agents.

"Tippie" Hubbard was also in the group, as was tenor George Nicholson, baritone Robert Osborne, and James "Toy" Walton.

Discography

Hollywood 1092 The Bells Ring Out (LB)/Call the Doctor (HB) (1958)
DC 0416 Homework (BJ)/Say Yes (BJ) (1959)
Savoy 1567 Homework (JB)/Say Yes (JB) (1959)
Source: Dave Hinckley and Marv Goldberg, *Yesterday's Memories* 8.

Leaders (Newport News, Va.)

Personnel Harry Burton (lead), Nelson Shields (1st tenor), Edward Alston (2d tenor), Ronald Judge (d) (baritone), Charles Simpson (bass)

Notes

This group was one of several R&B vocal groups coming from this relatively small town. Newport News, Virginia, was the point of origin for the Five Keys, the Avalons, the Chateaus, and the Leaders (originally known as the Five Swans).

The members of this group came from the same neighborhood and attended the same high school.

Lawyer to be Melvin Nachman heard the group perform and offered to be their manager. They made many local appearances and late in 1954, they won an amateur contest. The prize was a trip to New York to appear at the Apollo Theater's amateur night. They won this contest four weeks in a row.

Someone told Phil Rose, Glory's owner, to see the Five Swans. After he did, he signed them to a one-year contract and changed their name to Leaders. Their first session for Glory was in August 1955. "Stormy Weather" and "A Lover of the Time" were released in September 1955. Since they were all in high school, touring was impossible except for weekends, holidays, and summer vacation.

The Four Knights

Norman Fox and the Rob Roys

Eddie Cooley and the Dimples

The Rivieras

The Five Satins

The Duponts

The Pastels

The Fidelities

The FiTones

The Striders

The Sparrows Quartet

The Demens

The Danleers

The Cruisers

Little Anthony and the Imperials

Little Caesar and the Romans

There were many other Glory recording sessions, but none of the released material ever really did well. Appearances dried up and Glory chose not to renew their contract. Nachman failed to place them elsewhere and this was basically the end of the Leaders.

After they disbanded, Shields and Judge joined three other singers from New York to form the Corvairs, who eventually recorded for Comet.

Discography

Glory 235 Stormy Weather (HB)/Lover of the Time (EA) (1955)
Glory 239 Nobody Loves Me (HB)/Dearest Beloved Darling (EA) (1956)
Glory 243 Can't Help Lovin' That Girl of Mine (HB)/Lovers (EA/HB) (1956)
Source: Marv Goldberg in *DISCoveries.*

Leisure Lads (Philadelphia)

Personnel Bob Aita (lead), Hank Orth (1st tenor), Bobby Maffei (2d tenor), Ralph Fabiano (baritone), Richie Cedrone (bass)

Notes

In 1958, following Danny and the Juniors' huge hit "At the Hop," one of its members, Frank Maffei, learned of his younger brother Bobby's aspiration to similar celebrity status. For that and other ego-satisfying reasons, the Leisure Lads group was formed.

After a great deal of practice, they began public appearances. Pete Lauro, a local musician, brought them to Reco-Arts studio, where they, along with other interested parties, financed a recording and an eventual pressing of five hundred discs on a label named after Delaware County (Delco), where they were all from.

With a record released, their schedule of appearances began to climb. This lasted for some time. When their record began to disappear from radio show playlists, their appearance bookings vanished as well. In 1962 they drifted apart.

Discography

Delco 801 Baby, I'm All Alone/Teenage Memories (1959)
Source: Bob Bosco in *Echoes of the Past 39.*

Limelighters (Bronx, N.Y.)

Personnel Sammy Fain (lead), Eugene Tompkins (1st tenor), William "Dutch" Nadel (2d tenor), Henry Gunter (baritone), Tony Streeter (bass)

Notes

This group was formed in 1954 in the Morrisania section of the Bronx in New York City, patterning themselves after the popular R&B groups of the day. Gunter had been working in a shoe store and one of their styles was called Limelighters; hence, their name.

They got themselves a manager, Buddy Dunk. He was acquainted with someone associated with one of the budget labels and a session was arranged in 1956. The group was given seven songs to familiarize themselves with in one day. They were able to accomplish this. Incredibly, because there was time remaining at the end of the session, two original tunes they wrote, "My Sweet Norma Lee" and "Cabin Hideaway," were recorded. These two songs were ultimately sold to Jubilee's Jerry Blaine. Eventually both were released on the Jubilee subsidary label, Josie.

The other songs recorded that day found their way to budget LPs, EPs, and singles as by the Rockets, Teeners, Four Blades, or Four Angels. This in spite of the fact that the group was a quintet!

Dunk got them to record for several other labels, including Rama, but nothing else was ever released. Murray Hill's LP *Come Dance with Me,* issued in 1976, contained the unreleased Rama cut "Love Conquers All."

Tenor Willie Williams sang for the Limelighters when Streeter went into the service.

Since they were all getting older and nothing ever happened for them professionally, they broke up in 1959. Years later Tompkins and Fain joined with Lillian Leach and the Mellows.

Discography

Josie 795 Cabin Hideaway/My Sweet Norma Lee (1956)
Sources: Nerressa Tompkins, liner notes with the Flyer LP *Limelighters*; Gordon Skadberg, liner notes with the Sequel CD *Jubilee/Josie R&B Vocal Groups.*

Limelites, Shep & (Queens, N.Y.)

Personnel James "Shep" Sheppard (lead), Clarence Bassett (1st tenor), Charles Baskerville (2d tenor)

Notes

Shep and the Limelites were formed in 1961, several years after Sheppard's first group, the Heartbeats, had disbanded. He joined up with Queens neighbors Clarence Bassett, formerly of the Five Sharps on Jubilee and the Videos, and Charles Baskerville, who later went to the Drifters on Atlantic, the Players on Minit, and the Videos.

Bill and Bea Kaslin (Kaslon) were at Hull's forefront in 1955–1956 when the Heartbeats had all their top sellers, "People Are Talking," "Crazy for You," "Darling How Long," and their biggie, "A Thousand Miles Away." The Kaslons had sold publishing rights and masters of the Heartbeats' tunes to Roulette in 1956. When the Kaslons released "Daddy's Home" on Hull in 1961, Roulette sued them, feeling that this new song, with Sheppard's dulcet tones, infringed on the copyright of "A Thousand Miles Away." The ruling was against Hull, which eventually put them out of business.

Bassett went on to sing with the Flamingos and Jimmy Sheppard was mysteriously found dead in 1970, before any of the real R&B revivals.

Ernest Harriston from the Bopchords spent some time with the Limelites.

Discography

APT 25046 I'm So Lonely/One Week from Today (1960)
Hull 740 Daddy's Home/This I Know (1961)

Hull 742 Ready for Your Love/You'll Be Sorry (1961)
Hull 747 Three Steps from the Altar/Oh, What a Feeling (1961)
Hull 748 Our Anniversary/Who Told the Sandman? (1962)
Hull 751 What Did Daddy Do?/Teach Me How to Twist (1962)
Hull 753 Everything Is Going to Be Alright/Gee Baby, What about You (1962)
Hull 756 Remember Baby/The Monkey (1963)
Hull 757 Stick by Me/It's All Over Now (1963)
Hull 759 Steal Away/For You My Love (1963)
Hull 761 Why, Why Won't You Believe Me/Easy to Remember (1963)
Hull 767 I'm All Alone/Why Did You Fall for Me (1964)
Hull 770 Party for Two/You Better Believe (1965)
Hull 772 I'm A-Hurting Inside/In Case I Forget (1965)
Sources: Mike Rascio in *Big Town Review* 2; Donn Fileti, liner notes with the Rhino CD *Best of the Heartbeats.*

Lincolns (New York)

Personnel Harold Anderson (lead), Willie Williams (tenor), John Anderson (baritone), John Miro (bass)

Notes

The Lincolns formed in 1959, following John Miro's stint with the Ospreys and his time backing up the likes of Clyde McPhatter and Ivory Joe Hunter at Atlantic. At that time he joined the others to form the Mercury Lincolns.

The other Lincolns groups (Atlas/Angletone) are not the same.

Discography

Mercury 71553 Baby, Please Let Me Love You (JM)/Can't You Go for Me (HA) (1959)
Source: Marv Goldberg in *Yesterday's Memories* 12.

Links (New York)

Personnel Herbert Fisher (lead), James "Toy" Walton (tenor), Joe Woodley (baritone), Wilbert Hess Dobson (baritone), Johnny Terry (bass)

Notes

This group evolved from the Bachelors, which had recorded earlier for the Royal Roost label.

Fisher and Walton also sang with the Jets on Rainbow. Walton later sang with the Clovers. These two persuaded Wilbert Hess Dobson, Joe Woodley, and Johnny Terry to join forces and become the Links on Teenage.

Terry also sang for the Knickerbockers (no recordings), the Dominoes, and the Drifters.

Discography

Teenage 1009 Baby (HF)/She's the One (HF) (1957)

Sources: Marv Goldberg and Mike Redmond in *Record Exchanger* 15; Marv Goldberg in *Yesterday's Memories* 8.

Lions (Los Angeles)

Personnel Tony Allen (lead), Horace "Pookie" Wooten, David Cobb, Charles Jackson, Booker Washington, Barbara McNeill

Notes

This group had also been the Chimes (Dig), the Wonders, and the Cupids.

Discography

Rendezvous 116 Two-Timing Lover/The Feasts of the Beasts (1960)
Source: Ray Topping, liner notes with the *Dig Legendary Masters* CD.

Loreleis (New York)

Personnel Sylvia Hammond, Gloria Gilbert, Jonasaleise ———

Notes

This group was a trio. Neither Sylvia Hammond nor Gloria Gilbert seems to remember Jonasaleise's last name.
    Hammond sang with the Clickettes as well.

Discography

Brunswick 55271 Why Do I Put Up with You?/Strange Way (1964)
Source: Sylvia Hammond, interview by author, September 1996.

Loungers (Staten Island, N.Y.)

Personnel Dave Concepcion (lead), Pat Russo (1st tenor), Vinnie Santorelli (2d tenor), Steve Murphy (baritone), Frank Del Cavo (bass)

Notes

This group also recorded for Decca as the Five Secrets and the Secrets. After coming over to the Herald/Ember organization in 1957, they were given little or no attention. This was probably due to the label's preoccupation with the Five Satins and the Mellokings. Consequently, there was no promotion or support of any kind, and Herald 534 did not do too well.
    For two years after the Herald release they played local nightspots. Following this, they quietly split up.
    Pat Russo's brother Bernie replaced Murphy, who left before their breakup.

Discography

Herald 534 Remember the Night/Dizzy Spell (1958)
Source: Jay Repoley in *Story Untold,* May–June 1978.

Love Notes (Roxbury, Mass.)

Personnel Bob White (lead), Teddy Santos (tenor), John Davis (2d tenor), Wallace Rose (baritone), Ed Anderson (bass)

Notes

These were neighborhood friends from the Roxbury section of Boston who formed a vocal group in 1952. They got a manager, Cecil Steen, who got the group a contract with Imperial Records early in 1953. This was "Surrender Your Heart," which did well locally. It also provided them with extensive touring promoting the tune. This was difficult, as they all had day jobs and really had to scramble to return to work on a timely basis, following out-of-town one-nighters.

In 1954, Steen got them a contract with Rainbow/Riviera Records. This alliance produced two recordings.

Records on Hub by Jan Strickland and the Shadows were in reality Strickland and the Lovenotes.

This group was the quintet that performed current hits of the day for the Family Library of Recorded Music and Tivoli budget label LPs.

Discography

Imperial 5254 Surrender Your Heart/Get On My Train (1953)
Rainbow 266 Sweet Lulu /I'm Sorry (1954)
Riviera 970 Sweet Lulu/I'm Sorry (1954)
Riviera 975 Since I Fell for You/Don't Be No Fool (1954)
Source: Marv Goldberg in *Whiskey, Women, and . . . .*

Lovenotes (New York)

Personnel Johnny Hicks (lead), Joe Shiloh (1st tenor), Lucy Cedeño (2d tenor), Jimmy Coney (bass)

Notes

This group started their singing career at a talent audition on the lower east side of Manhattan in 1956. Lucy Cedeño was still in junior high school in Williamsburg, Brooklyn, at that time. They auditioned for Holiday's Danny Robinson, Bobby Robinson's younger brother, who signed them to a recording contract.

Lucy Cedeño is Lucy Anderson, wife of Gary "U.S." Bonds.

Two of the male Lovenotes were also in the Ivories on Jaguar and, according to Donn Filetti, probably the Ivories on Mercury as well.

Hicks also sang with the Ivories and the Ivoleers.

In Groia's *They All Sang on the Corner* it is stated that Ernest Harriston of the Bopchords spent some time with the Lovenotes.

Discography

Holiday 2605 United/Tonight (1957)
Holiday 2607 If I Could Make You Mine/Don't Go (1957)

Sources: Donn Fileti, liner notes with the Relic CD *Holiday*; Phil Groia, *They All Sang on the Corner.*

Lucky Charms (Honolulu)

Personnel Ira Johnson (lead), Leroy Richardson (1st tenor), George Richardson (2d tenor), Harold Wells (baritone), Edwin Cyrus (bass)

Notes

This group met in Hawaii while the members were in the service. During rest periods, they would get together and sing harmony. They won several army talent contests and appeared at many army-sponsored shows. This led to their being Hawaii's top R&B act and eventually a contract with International Records.

Since their style was so eclectic, it's obvious they came from all parts of the country. In actuality, they were from Los Angeles, Richmond, Kansas City, Kansas, Pittsburgh, and the little-known town of Babbit, Nevada. This is why there are recordings with the New York sound and others with the typical West Coast sound.

They made appearances on local TV and radio shows, and also appeared with Elvis Presley at an army facility in Honolulu.

The liner notes accompanying their Starfire LP seem to indicate that International Records released no singles, and therefore there is no discography below. The album to which I refer is entitled *Dedicated to You* on Starfire. Richard Lee Ramsey was probably associated with the group vocally. The album's liner notes contain recording dates. These appear to indicate that the recordings on the LP were done in 1956–1958.

Source: Rip Lay and Tony Palmer, liner notes with the Starfire LP *Dedicated to You.*

Lyres (New Haven, Conn.)

Personnel Billy Emery (lead), Walter Singleterry (1st tenor), James "Sonny" Griffin (2d tenor), James "Coco" Tyson (baritone), Leroy Griffin (bass)

Notes

This group was the Nutmegs who began vocalizing in New Haven, Connecticut, as the Lyres in 1953. Billy Emery sang lead for their one recording on J&G. This was before Leroy Griffin's voice matured beautifully and he fronted the Nutmegs.

They went to New York seeking a recording deal and met the DuDroppers, who introduced them to the Rush Music management. Rush executives liked them very much and brought them to Herald Records late in 1955. Al Silver of Herald changed their name to Nutmegs and the rest is history.

In one form or another, this group was later to be called the Rajahs to avoid contractual difficulties with Herald/Ember management with whom they were still under contract.

Discography

J&G 101 Ship of Love/Play Boy (1953)
Source: Donn Fileti, liner notes with the Relic CD *Story Untold.*

Lyrics (San Francisco)

Personnel William Wigfall (lead), James Shellbourne, Woodroe Blake, William Jarvis

Notes

James Landers and Ben Hamilton were also members.

Discography

Rhythm 127 Every Night/Come Back Baby (1959)
Sources: Dave Antrell, liner notes with the Rhythm LP *Rhythm & Blues Classics*;
Dennis Leonis, liner notes with the Rhythm CD *Remembering Rhythm Records.*

Lyrics (San Antonio, Tex.)

Personnel Abel Martinez (lead), Dimas Garza, Carl Henderson, Alex Pato

Notes

The Lyrics got together in 1958 in southern Texas. They are remembered for the many public appearances they made in various southern Texas locales. They did many record hops in conjunction with local San Antonio radio stations.

Only their first release, "Oh Please Love Me," on the Texas Harlem label (101) is remembered. It was picked up by Wildcat Records (0028) and then by Coral (62322). But it did not sell well enough to attract national attention.

This was a racially mixed group. Carl Henderson was black and the others were Hispanic.

Discography

Harlem 101 The Girl I Love/Oh Please Love Me (1959)
Harlem 104 I Want to Know/The Beating of My Heart (1959)
Wildcat 28 The Girl I Love/Oh Please Love Me (1959)
Source: L.R.D., liner notes with the Lyrics Harlem LP *The Lyrics, 1959-1960.*

Madison Brothers, Farris Hill & (Philadelphia)

Personnel Farris Hill (lead), Donald Burnett (1st tenor), Richard Frazier (2d tenor), Harry Paschall (bass)

Notes

This group started in North Philadelphia as the Thrillers who backed Joe Cook on "Peanuts" and "This I Know." Farris Hill sang 2d lead for the Thrillers.

Harry Paschall and Donald Burnett had formerly been with the Belltones on Grand Records who recorded the classic "Estelle."

This group was also the Royal Demons on Pek and on Philadelphia's Rhythm label.

Because they all resembled one another, they became the Madison Brothers on Cedargrove Records.

Discography

APT 25050 Trusting in You/What's the Matter (1960)
Cedargrove 314 Trusting in You/What's the Matter (1960)
Sure 1002 Give Me Your Heart/Baby Don't (1961)
V-Tone 231 Did We Go Steady Too Soon?/The Twirl (1962)
Source: Donn Fileti, liner notes with the Relic LP *V-Tone.*

Madisons (Philadelphia)

Personnel Richard Frazier (2d tenor), Harry Paschall (bass)

Notes

Paschall and Frazier were also members of Little Joe and the Thrillers. Paschall had been with the Belltones on Grand, who recorded the classic "Estelle."

Discography

Cedargrove 314 Trusting in You/What's the Matter (1960)
Lawn 240 Can You Imagine It?/The Wind and the Rain (1964)
MGM 13312 Cheryl Anne/Looking for True Love (1965)
Source: Donn Fileti, liner notes with the Relic LP *V-Tone.*

Mad Lads (Los Angeles)

Personnel John Gary Williams (lead), Julius Green (tenor), William Brown (baritone), James Monroe Warren (bass)

Notes

The group began singing just for the fun of it in high school in 1963, calling themselves the Emeralds. Baritone William Brown worked in Stax's record shop. He persuaded the record shop management to grant the Emeralds an audition. This was granted and the group pleased their audience, who signed them to a contract and immediately changed their name to the Mad Lads. This was 1964.

Their first record, "The Sidewalk Surf," was a terrible failure. Their next attempt, however, "Don't Have to Shop Around," really hit pay dirt, as did their next several releases, one of which stayed on the charts for thirteen weeks!

In 1966, the armed forces conscripted lead singer John Gary Williams and baritone William Brown. Their replacements were Quincy Phillips and Sam Nelson for live appearances; recordings were still done by Brown and Williams while they were on leave.

A change in distributors marked the beginning of the end for Stax and for the group. There were no future recording successes, they continued to make live appearances.

Robert Johnson and Charles Everidge were also members of the Mad Lads, as was James Monroe Warren.

Discography

Capitol 5284 Don't Cry at the Party/I'll Survive (1965)

Volt 127 Don't Have to Shop Around/Tear Maker (1965)
Volt 131 I Want Someone/Nothing Can Break Through (1966)
Volt 135 Sugar, Sugar/Come Closer to Me (1966)
Volt 137 I Want a Girl/What Will Love Tend to Make You Do (1966)
Volt 139 Patch My Heart/You Mean So Much to Me (1966)
Volt 143 For These Simple Reasons/I Don't Want to Lose Your Love (1967)
Volt 150 Mr. Fix-It/My Inspiration (1967)
Volt 162 Whatever Hurts You/No Time Is Better Than Right Now (1968)
Volt 4003 So Nice/Make Room (1968)
Volt 4009 Make This Young Lady Mine/Love Is Here Today and Gone Tomorrow (1969)
Volt 4016 By the Time I Get to Phoenix/No Strings Attached (1969)
Volt 404 Seeing Is Believing/These Old Memories (1970)
Volt 4068 Gone! The Promises of Yesterday/So Glad I Fell in Love with You (1971)
Volt 4080 Let Me Repair Your Heart/Did My Baby Call? (1972)
Volt 4098 I Forgot to Be Your Lover/So Glad I Fell in Love with You (1973)
Sources: Uncredited liner notes with the Collectables LP *Mad Lads Greatest Hits*; Ferdie Gonzalez, *Disco-File*; Bob Ferlingere, *Discography of R&B and R&R Vocal Groups*; Malcolm Baumgart, liner notes with the Stax CD *Rare Stax Vocal Groups*.

Magic Tones (Baltimore, Md.)

Personnel Joseph "Rice" Reed (tenor), Arthur "Boxey" Williams (1st tenor), Gene Hawkins (2d tenor), James Williams (baritone), Willie Ricky Stokes (bass)

Notes

This group was formed in 1951 and after practicing for many weeks felt ready to be recognized. Numerous club appearances led to their being discovered by the manager of the Tilters, who had them brought to New York to record four sides.

Because of Stokes's Jimmy Ricks sound-alike bass, all four sides were bass leads. The group assumed they were recording for Jubilee because of their manager's association with the Marylanders. But when the first disc was released, they were surprised to see it on King! They had signed a contract to do twelve cuts, but this never occurred, nor did they ever see a studio again.

Henry Lewis, bass for the Marylanders, filled in for Stokes at an Apollo show. Stokes had been drafted and this appearance was a commitment they had previously made.

The group disbanded and when Stokes returned, he and Gene Hawkins joined with Robert McGee, Bobby Jackson, and Arthur Williams as the next group of Magic Tones. This group recorded Tears in My Eyes/Spanish Love Song, released in 1957 for Howfum.

Tenors Bobby Jackson and Robert Shue McGee later sang with this group on Howfum, replacing Reed and James Williams. This all took place after Stokes returned from the service.

Discography

King 4665 When I Kneel Down to Pray/Good Googa Mooga (1953)

King 4681 How Can You Treat Me This Way/Cool Cool Baby (1953)
Howfum 101 Tears in My Eyes/Spanish Love Song (1957)
Sources: Phil Chaney in *Yesterday's Memories* 8; D. Romanello, G. Povall, and C.
Bucola, liner notes with the Sequel King-Federal-DeLuxe CD *Great Googa Mooga.*

Magnificents (Chicago)

Personnel Johnny Keyes (lead), Thurman Ray Ramsey (tenor), Fred Rakestraw
(tenor), Willie Myles (bass)

Notes

The members of this group got together in high school in Chicago in 1953. The
group was originally called the Tam-O-Shanters. Just before their graduation, they
sang at a high school show and in the audience was a Chicago deejay known as the
Magnificent Montague. He liked what he saw and heard and decided to try managing the group.

He immediately changed their name to jell with his and the group became the
Magnificents. He then structured an audition at Vee Jay Records, and the
Magnificents recorded their only hit, "Up on the Mountain."

Montague felt a need to add class to the group and brought in Barbara Arrington.
She performed lead chores on "Caddy Bo" and "Hiccup." For these sides, she made
the group a quintet. However, because these discs were poorly received, the group
decided to return to their original four-man format and Arrington was dropped. At
this time, Ramsey left and was replaced by L. C. Cooke, Sam Cooke's brother. James
Scruggs sang with the Magnificents at the same time as Cooke.

In 1956–1957, the group began having difficulties with Vee Jay. Keyes and
Rakestraw formed a touring group of Magnificents with Reggie Gordon, who had
been with the Five Frenchmen and the Rays, and Rufus Hunter, who had been with
the Five Bells, Cameos, and the Universals. Rakestraw and Keyes joined up with
Thurston Harris of the Sharps who did "Little Bitty Pretty One."

In 1958, the Magnificents' manager, Magnificent Montague, assembled another
Magnificents group that began with "Don't Leave Me." Personnel for this group is
unknown. It has been suggested that perhaps this group was the Prodigals.

Discography

Vee Jay 183 Up on the Mountain/Why Did She Go? (1956)
Vee Jay 208 Caddy Bo/Hiccup (1956)
Vee Jay 235 Off the Mountain/Lost Lover (1956)
Vee Jay 281 Ozeta/Don't Leave Me (1958)
Vee Jay 367 Up on the Mountain/Let's Do the Cha Cha (1960)
Sources: Billy Vera, liner notes with *A Taste of Doo Wop-1* CD; Bob Pruter, *Doowop
. . . The Chicago Scene*; Marv Goldberg and Rick Whitesell in *Goldmine,* April 1979.

Majestics (Miami)

Personnel John MacArthur (lead), Sam Moore

Notes

Sam Moore is the Sam from Sam and Dave fame.

Discography

Marlin 802 Nitey Nite/Cave Man Rock (1957)
Source: Bob Ferlingere, *A Discography of R&B and R&R Vocal Groups.*

Majestics (Detroit)

Personnel Johnny Mitchell (d) (lead), C. Autry "Breeze" Hatcher (1st tenor), Alvin English, Cyril Clarke (bass)

Notes

The above group recorded for Contour records. By the time they recorded for Chex, only Johnny Mitchell remained. The new additions were Thomas Mealy (lead), Maurice Fagin (tenor), Pedro Mancha (baritone), and Warren Harris (bass), who replaced Cyril Clark. It is rumored that this second group went on to record as the Monitors on Circus Records.

Discography

Contour 501 Hard Times/Teenage Gossip (1960)
Chex 1000 So I Can Forget/Shoppin' and Hoppin' (1961)
Chex 1004 Treat Me Like You Want to Be Treated/Unhappy and Blue (1962)
Chex 1006 Gwendolyn/Lonely Heart (1962)
Chex 1009 Baby/Teach Me How to Limbo (1963)
Source: Donn Fileti, liner notes with the Relic LP *Best of Chex Records.*

Majestics (Everett, Mass.)

Personnel Tommy Pascarella (lead), Johnny Falzone (tenor), Ed Rogers (tenor), Tommy Guanci (baritone), Steve Catallo (bass)

Notes

The members of this group were all high school friends from Everett, Massachusetts. When they began, they would practice at Catallo's house. This was 1959.

They would make local appearances at various New England dances, church functions, school parties, and some local TV.

Their first release was "The Lone Stranger" for the Sioux label, written in minutes by Falzone. This did so well that Twentieth Century–Fox leased it from Sioux and released it nationally.

Things seemed to be going well until their manager wanted a larger slice of the pie. The group said no, and that basically was the end of this Majestics group.

Discography

Sioux 91459 The Lone Stranger/Sweet One (1959)
20th Century Fox 171 The Lone Stranger/Sweet One (1959)
Source: Charles Lucas in *Record Collector's Monthly* 22.

Majors (Brooklyn, N.Y.)

Personnel Bernard "Jimmy" Beckum (lead), Alvin Scott (1st tenor), Clyde Lee (baritone), William Beebe (bass)

Notes

When he was fourteen, Beckum joined a Pentecostal church and sang with a gospel group, the Harmony Five. Milton Grayson, later of the Dominoes, sang at this church as well. Beckum sang with many gospel groups before moving to R&B. They changed their name to the Majors and were spotted by Phil Rose and Larry Newton of Derby Records.

Eventually, the Majors recorded four records for Derby but none of these sold well. Beckum would later marry the cousin of Willie Winfield's wife, Alice. Through her he met Willie Winfield of the Harptones. When Bill Galloway departed from the Harptones, Beckum was his replacement.

Discography

Derby 763 You Ran Away with My Heart/At Last (1951)
Derby 779 Come On Up to My Room/Laughing on the Outside (1951)
Source: Phil Groia in *Bim Bam Boom* 4, article about the Majors.

Majors (Philadelphia)

Personnel Rick Cordo (lead), Ron Gathers, Gene Glass, Idella Morris, Frank Troutt

Notes

This group met in Philadelphia in 1959. Although they attended different high schools, they hung around together after school and on weekends. This is where and when they started singing. Glass had just returned from the air force.

They met club owner Buddy Caldwell and he persuaded them to record for his Ro-Cal label. They recorded "Lundee Dundee" and "Let Me Whisper in Your Ear" as the Versatiles. "Lundee Dundee" was all they did for Ro-Cal, and two years later, Jerry Ragavoy heard them. Ragavoy liked them enough to get them a recording deal with Imperial. Ragavoy had been in the vocal group business since the early 1950s, when he had the Castelles on Grand performing his work. In the 1960s, Ragavoy became one of the most influential producers of black music.

In 1966, the Majors got another opportunity to shine for ABC Paramount producer Pete De Angelos. They did "Love Is the Answer" as the Performers, which was a terrible failure. Following this, the group disbanded.

Gene Glass and Idella Morris were husband and wife.

Discography

Imperial 5855 A Wonderful Dream/Time Will Tell (1962)
Imperial 5879 She's a Troublemaker/A Little Bit Now (1962)
Imperial 5914 Anything You Can Do/What in the World? (1963)
Imperial 5936 Tra La La/What Have You Been Doin' (1963)
Imperial 5968 Get Up Now/One Happy Ending (1963)

Imperial 5991 Your Life Begins/Which Way Did She Go (1963)
Imperial 66009 Ooh Wee Baby/I'll Be There (1963)
Original 1003 Big Eyes/Go Way (1963)
Source: Wayne Jancik in *Goldmine,* December 28, 1990.

Maples (Chicago)

Personnel Kenneth Childers (lead), Hilliard "Johnny" Jones (1st tenor), Albert Hunter, Andrew Smith, Harold Jones

Notes

It was 1955 and vain Kenneth Childers wanted to hear himself on record. He formed an ad hoc group of singers at Blue Lake Records to accomplish this. The group was made up of Parrot/Blue Lake vocal group personnel.

Harold Jones was with the Five Chances; Hilliard "Johnny" Jones was also known as Johnny "Chubby" Jones when he too was with the Five Chances. Hunter was from the Clouds (only on Parrot), and Andrew Smith came from the Fasinoles.

Opinions about the ballad side of this recording vary from great to horrible. The author sides with those who find it great.

Discography

Blue Lake 111 I Must Forget You/99 Guys (1954)
Source: Bob Pruter, *Doowop . . . The Chicago Scene.*

Marathons (Chicago)

Personnel Jim Johnson (lead), Richard Owens (1st tenor), Carl Fisher (2d tenor), Dave Govan (baritone), Don Bradley (bass)

Notes

In June 1961 the Vibrations (Checker) decided to earn some extra cash by moonlighting. They went to Los Angeles and recorded "Peanut Butter" for the Arvee label as the Marathons. Had the record not done so well, this may have gone unnoticed, but it was a big hit. Chess took Arvee to court and won the case, taking the masters and the profits with them. Soon after, Chess released "Peanut Butter" on its Argo label, which read, "The Vibrations, Named by Others as the Marathons."

Fisher, Owens, Johnson, and Govan also sang with Jayhawks.

Discography

Argo 5389 Peanut Butter/Down in New Orleans (1961)
Chess 1790 Peanut Butter/Down in New Orleans (1961)
Arvee 5027 Peanut Butter/Talkin' Trash (1961)
Arvee 5038 C. Percy Mercy of Scotland Yard/Tight Sweater (1961)
Arvee 5048 Chicken Spaceman/You Bug Me Baby (1962)
Plaza 507 Mashed Potatoes One More Time/Little Pan (1962)
Sources: Bob Pruter, *Doowop . . . The Chicago Scene*; Marv Goldberg and Rick Whitesell in *Yesterday's Memories.*

Marbles (Los Angeles)

Personnel Rudy Jackson (lead), Dee Hawkins (tenor), Johnny Torrence (2d tenor), James Brown (bass)

Notes

This group began in 1953 with Torrence, Hawkins, and Brown all coming from gospel music. That same year they moved to the more financially rewarding rhythm and blues field and found Rudy Jackson (this was the Marbles who had one record released for John Dolphin's Lucky Records).

This group later added a fifth member, Vernon Knight, and they became the Jewels.

Discography

Lucky 002 Golden Girl/Big Wig Walk (1954)
Source: Marv Goldberg and Rick Whitesell in *Yesterday's Memories* 10.

Marcels (Pittsburgh, Pa.)

Personnel Cornelius Harp (lead), Ronald Mundy (1st tenor), Gene Bricker (2d tenor), Dick Knauss (baritone), Fred Johnson (bass)

Notes

The Marcels formed in 1959 as high school friends in Pittsburgh. After practicing for quite some time, they made tapes that were ultimately sent to Colpix, who liked what they heard and had them come to New York to audition. Following this success, they were signed to a contract with Colpix.

Dick Knauss and Gene Bricker were the two white members; in 1961, they were the first to leave. They were replaced by Allen Johnson (Fred's brother) and Walt Maddox (from the Blanders on Smash). The new group consisted of Fred and Allen Johnson, Mundy, Harp, and Maddox.

Mundy left in the fall of 1961 and was not replaced. Harp left in 1962, with Kenny Mitchell replacing him.

Beginning with "Heartaches," the group was all black.

In 1963 they left Colpix and recorded for Chartbound and Kyra. Following these two releases, more were released on 888.

Soon after "How Deep Is the Ocean," Allen Johnson left. Richard Harris and William Herndon were brought in from the Altairs on Amy.

The group of Fred Johnson, Walt Maddox, Richard Harris, and William Herndon remained together for twenty-five years.

Discography

Colpix 186 Blue Moon/Goodbye to Love (1961)
Colpix 196 Summertime/Teeter Totter Love (1961)
Colpix 606 You Are My Sunshine/Find Another Fool (1961)
Colpix 612 Heartaches/My Love for You (1961)
Colpix 617 Don't Cry for Me This Christmas/Merry Twist-Mas (1961)

Colpix 624 My Melancholy Baby/Really Need Your Love (1962)
Colpix 629 Footprints in the Sand/Twistin' Fever (1962)
Colpix 640 Flowerpot/Hold On (1962)
Colpix 651 Loved Her the Whole Week Through/Friendly Loans (1962)
Colpix 665 Alright, Okay, You Win/Lollipop Baby (1962)
Colpix 683 That Old Black Magic/Don't Turn Back on Me (1963)
Colpix 687 Give Me Back Your Love/I Wanna Be the Leader (1963)
Colpix 694 One Last Kiss/Teeter Totter Love (1963)
Chartbound 009 Tell Me/Letter Full of Tears (1963)
Kyra (N/A) Comes Love/Your Red Wagon (1964)
888 101 How Deep Is the Ocean/Lonely Boy (1964)
Queen Bee 47001 In the Still of the Night/High on a Hill (1973)
Sources: Ed Salamon in *Bim Bam Boom* 10; Carl Janusek and Nancy Janusek in *Echoes of the Past* 8.

Marigolds (Lancaster, S.C.)

Personnel Johnny Bragg (lead), Hal Hebb, Henry "Dishrag" Jones, Willie Wilson, Al Brooks

Notes

Bragg previously sang lead for the Prisonaires on Sun. This was a group of inmates at the Tennessee State Penitentiary. Bragg formed the Prisonaires in the early 1950s, receiving much attention in a well-publicized rehabilitation program.

In 1954, Bragg, Hebb, and Jones formed a new group, the Sunbeams, who were eventually renamed the Marigolds. From 1955 to 1956, they had four releases for Excello; they also recorded for Excello as the Solotones.

Discography

Excello 2057 Rollin' Stone/Why Don't You (1955)
Excello 2061 Two Strangers/Love You, Love You (1955)
Excello 2078 Foolish Me/Beyond the Clouds (1956)
Excello 2091 It's You Darling, It's You/Juke Box Rock 'n' Roll (1956)
Source: Gordon Skadberg, liner notes with the Ace CD *Southern Doo Wop.*

Markels (Brooklyn, N.Y.)

Personnel Frank Tesoriere (lead), Joey Corona (1st tenor), Frankie Grillo (2d tenor), Joe Agugliaro (baritone), Tommy Bautz (bass)

Notes

Like the Fascinators and the Clusters, the Markels came from the Bushwick section of Brooklyn. They formed in 1958 when members were all between fifteen and seventeen years of age. They sang in the same venues as those other groups.

Like the Clusters, they solicited Bobby Robinson at Fury Records. Bobby liked them but could do nothing for them. There was R&M Records, in the Bushwick area, that liked the Markels and set up a recording session for them. Late in the summer of 1958, R&M released "Letter of Love" and "Darling I Really Love You." Initially the record did well, especially in Baltimore, but it faded quickly.

Soon after this, bass Tommy Bautz joined the army and the group split up.

In 1960, Tony Passalacqua, Donnie Milo, Joe Gugliaro, and Joe Agugliaro decided to try again and formed Tony and the Twilights. Gugliaro and Agugliaro were cousins.

Discography
R&M 617 The Letter of Love/Darling I Really Love You (1958)
Source: Bob Diskin in *Record Collector's Monthly* 47.

Marquees (Washington, D.C.)

Personnel Reese Palmer (lead), Marvin Gaye (d) (tenor), James Sally Nolan (baritone), Chester Simmons (d) (bass)

Notes
In 1957, James Nolan and Chester Simmons joined the Okeh Marquees. The other members were Reese Palmer and Marvin Gaye.

Tenor Bobby Hawkins and Bobby Hendricks also were members.

In 1958, the Moonglows were making their final appearance in Baltimore. Harvey Fuqua announced from the stage that he was looking for groups to audition to be the new Moonglows. After hearing the Marquees, Fuqua selected them, with bass Chuck Barksdale from the Dells. This is the group that eventually recorded "Twelve Months of the Year."

(Note: In Lynn McCutcheon's *Rhythm & Blues,* Nolan Ellison is listed as a member instead of James Nolan. The two may be the same.)

Discography
Okeh 7096 Wyatt Earp/Hey Little School Girl (1957)
Source: Lynn McCutcheon in *Rhythm & Blues.*

Marquis (New York)

Personnel June Bateman (lead), Charlie ———— (1st tenor), Rocko Mack (2d tenor), Lloyd Lomelino (baritone), Robert "Babe" Stowers (bass)

Notes
Before recording, the Marquis sang on the street corners of Manhattan's upper west side. Lomelino's neighbor became their manager. The Marquis cut a demo for their manager to take with him to record companies on Broadway. Through this endeavor, he got the group a contract with Jerry Winston's Onyx label. Their first record was released in the fall of 1956.

It was unfortunate that Onyx and Winston were paying so much attention to the Pearls and the Velours and virtually none to the label's other groups—particularly the Marquis. Because of this they decided to disband.

The Marquis may have been the first integrated male group with a female lead.

Discography

Onyx 505 Bohemian Daddy (JB)/Hope He's True (JB) (1956)
Source: Donn Fileti, liner notes with the Relic LP *Best of Onyx.*

Marshall Brothers (New York)

Personnel Maithe Marshall (d) (lead), Phil Shaw (1st tenor), Willis Sanders (2d tenor), Raymond Johnson (d) (bass)

Notes

After leaving the Blenders in late 1951, Ray Johnson joined Maithe Marshall, former lead of the Ravens, Phil Shaw, and Willis Sanders. The Ravens had basically split up and Marshall wanted to continue singing. The Marshall Brothers were not together more than three to four months. Sanders went on to sing with the Embers, who had releases for Ember, Herald, Columbia, Dot, Juno, Unart, and Coral.

Dan Nooger's liner notes accompanying the Savoy CD *Mr. Santa's Boogie* state that Marshall later worked with the Bucaneers [sic]. This is not the Rama Buccaneers but a somewhat later group.

In Michel Ruppli's *The Savoy Label—A Discography,* Ruppli addresses the Marshall Brothers' two sessions for Savoy. At both, the vocal lineup consisted of Raymond Johnson, Richie Cannon, Maithe Marshall, and possibly Bob Kornegay. This is for the November 5, 1951, session. For the December 17, 1951, session, the lineup is basically the same.

(Note: Interesting, as Johnson and Kornegay are both basses; I would not place too much faith in this personnel lineup.)

Due to a lack of work, the Marshall Brothers broke up early in 1952.

Discography

Savoy 825 Who'll Be the Fool from Now On? (MM)/Mr. Santa's Boogie (RJ) (1951)
Savoy 828 Just Because (BC)/A Soldier's Prayer (BC) (1952)
Savoy 833 Just a Poor Boy in Love (RJ)/Why Make a Fool Out of Me? (MM) (1952)
Savoy (UNR) It All Comes Back to Me Now (MM)
Savoy (UNR) I Didn't Know (MM)
Savoy (UNR) My Life Is My Life (MM)
Savoy (UNR) I Won't Believe You Anymore
Sources: Dan Nooger, liner notes with the Savoy CD *Mr. Santa's Boogie*; Marv Goldberg, notes to the Savoy LP *Vocal Group Album*; Michel Ruppli, *The Savoy Label—A Discography.*

Marshalls, Bill Cook & (Philadelphia)

Personnel Bill Cook (lead), Maithe Marshall (d) (tenor), Richie Cannon (2d tenor), Willis Sanders (baritone), Ray Johnson (bass)

Notes

The lineup shown above reflects the one shown in Michel Ruppli's Savoy discography. It is doubtful that Richie Cannon was with this group. This is shown here because Ruppli's book is the only resource available.

Apparently Bill Cook was not a singer or a member of this vocal group. He was a disk jockey and the group's manager. He is simply making a recitation on the record.

Discography

Savoy 828 A Soldier's Prayer (BC)/Just Because (BC) (1952)
Sources: Marv Goldberg, liner notes with the Savoy LP *Vocal Group Album*; Michel Ruppli, *Savoy Label—A Discography.*

Marvelettes (Detroit)

Personnel Gladys Horton (lead), Wanda Young, Katherine Anderson, Juanita Cowart, Georgeana Tillman

Notes

The Marvelettes began as a quintet in rural Inkster, Michigan. They all attended Inkster High School, where they entered a high school talent contest. Winning got them an audition with Detroit's Motown Records. Motown management liked them but wanted original material. They then went to a songwriting friend who gave them a song he had written entitled "Please Mr. Postman." Georgia Dobbins, then a member, rewrote the song that night.

After rewriting "Please Mr. Postman," Dobbins left the group to take care of her ill mother. The Marvelettes (then the Marvels), went back to Motown, which liked the song and changed their name to the Marvelettes. In the summer of 1961 Motown released "Please Mr. Postman" on Tamla. In December 1961 it reached the top spot. At this point a rivalry formed between the Supremes and the Marvelettes.

Juanita and Georgianna left the group in 1965 due to ill health, and the group continued as a trio. Gladys departed after she became a mother and was replaced by Anne Brogan. Many hits followed.

Wanda left in 1969; and despite the fact that four more singles were issued, this ended the career of the Marvelettes.

Georgianna married Bruce Gordon of the Contours and passed away in 1980 due to sickle-cell anemia. At this time Wanda married Bobby Rogers of the Miracles.

Discography

Tamla 54046 Please Mr. Postman/So Long Baby (1961)
Tamla 54054 I Want a Guy/Twistin' Postman (1962)
Tamla 54060 All the Love I've Got/Playboy (1962)
Tamla 54065 Beechwood 4-5789/Someday Someway (1962)
Tamla 54072 Strange I Know/Too Strong to Be Strung Along (1962)
Tamla 54077 Locking Up My Heart/Forever (1963)
Tamla 54082 My Daddy Knows Best/Tie a String around Your Finger (1963)
Tamla 54088 As Long As I Know He's Mine/Little Girl Blue (1963)
Tamla 54091 He's a Good Guy/Goddess of Love (1964)
Tamla 54097 You're My Remedy/A Little Bit of Sympathy, A Little Bit of Love (1964)

Tamla 54105 Too Many Fish in the Sea/A Need for Love (1964)
Tamla 54116 I'll Keep Holding On/No Time for Tears (1965)
Tamla 54120 Danger Heartbreak Dead Ahead/Your Cheatin' Ways (1965)
Tamla 54126 Don't Mess with Bill/Anything You Wanna Do (1965)
Tamla 54131 You're the One/Paper Boy (1966)
Tamla 54143 Hunter Get Captured by the Game/I Think I Can Change You (1966)
Tamla 54150 When You're Young and in Love/Take One, Take the Other (1967)
Tamla 54158 My Baby Must Be a Magician/I Need Someone (1967)
Tamla 54166 Here I Am Baby/Keep Off, No Trespassing (1968)
Tamla 54171 Destination: Anywhere/What's Easy for Two Is Hard for One (1968)
Tamla 54177 I'm Gonna Hold On/Don't Make Hurting Me a Habit (1968)
Tamla 54186 That's How Heartaches Are Made/Rainy Mourning (1969)
Tamla 54198 Marionette/After All (1970)
Tamla 54213 A Breath-Taking Guy/You're the One for Me Baby (1971)
Source: Jay Warner, *American Singing Groups.*

Marvelows (Chicago Heights, Ill.)

Personnel Frank Paden (lead), Melvin Mason (tenor), Jesse Smith (1st tenor), Willie Stephenson (tenor), Johnny Paden (bass)

Notes

The Marvelows originated in the Chicago suburb of Chicago Heights with Melvin Mason organizing the group. In 1959 he and Johnny Paden attended Bloom High School in Chicago Heights. Willie Stephenson joined the others and the Marvelows were born!

At first they were Little Satan and the Demons, and then the Mystics playing local clubs in the Chicago area. They eventually named themselves the Marvelows and sang locally for several years. They finally broke up, going their separate ways and singing with other groups.

They reunited in the summer of 1964 as a quintet, with the addition of Jesse Smith at 1st tenor. At this time that they found a manager, who was the cousin of Jesse Smith's wife. He got them a contract with ABC Paramount in October. Their second release for ABC, "I Do," was a substantial hit and generated many live appearances.

In 1966, Jesse Smith was dropped from the Marvelows due to his failure to comply with the group's rules regarding marijuana. The group spent about a year as a four-man ensemble and then brought in Andrew Thomas. To avoid confusion with the West Coast Marvellos, they changed their name to the Mighty Marvelows.

Discography

ABC Paramount 10586 I Deserve to Cry/ (1964)
ABC Paramount 10603 A Friend (MM)/Hey Hey Baby (FP) (1964)
ABC Paramount 10629 My Heart (MM)/I Do (MM) (1965)
ABC Paramount 10708 Your Little Sister/The Sim Sham (1965)
ABC Paramount 10756 Do It (FP)/I've Got My Eye on You (MM) (1966)
ABC Paramount 10802 Fade Away (FP)/You've Been Going with Sally (FP) (1966)

ABC Paramount 10111 In the Morning (MM)/Talking about My Baby (MM) (1968)
ABC Paramount 11073 I'm without a Girlfriend (MM)/I'm So Confused (FP) (1968)
ABC Paramount 11139 Hey Hey Girl (FP)/Wait Be Cool (FP) (1968)
ABC Paramount 11189 You're Breaking My Heart (FP)/Town's Too Much (MM) (1969)
Source: Bob Pruter, *Doowop . . . The Chicago Scene.*

Marvels (Washington, D.C.)

Personnel Sam Gilbert (lead), James "Junior" Isom (2d tenor), Ronald Boyd (baritone), James Mitchell (bass)

Notes

The Marvels were neighborhood friends who began in Washington, D.C., in 1954 appearing at local clubs and talent shows.

In 1957, after three years of playing the neighborhood, they came to New York looking for a recording contract. This they found at Laurie Records. They had one session, which produced the disc below. Isom sang lead on one side and Gilbert on the other. Regardless, neither took off and they returned to their routine, playing clubs in their hometown.

This group became the Senators eight years later in 1964, recording for Winn. Later they became the Satisfactions and recorded for Smash and Lionel.

Discography

Laurie 3016 I Shed So Many Tears/So Young So Sweet (1958)
Source: Dave Hinckley and Marv Goldberg in *Yesterday's Memories* 8.

Marvels (New York)

Personnel Richard Blandon (d) (lead), Cleveland Still (1st tenor), Billy Carlisle (d) (2d tenor), Jake Miller (baritone), Tommy Gardner (bass)

Notes

The ABC Paramount Marvels formed in 1956 as an outgrowth of the Five Wings and the Scale-Tones. They had Hiram Johnson as their manager (inherited from the Five Wings), and got a recording deal with ABC Paramount. They recorded one of the most beautiful ballads on wax, "I Won't Have You Breaking My Heart," for ABC. Because of inadequate support and promotion, the record did poorly.

This group would soon change their name to the Dubs and move to George Goldner's Gone Records.

All but Carlisle came from the Scale-Tones.

Tommy Grate, formerly from the Five Wings, replaced Tommy Gardner at bass.

Discography

ABC 9771 I Won't Have You Breaking My Heart/Jump Rock and Roll (1956)
Source: Marv Goldberg and J. Neilson, liner notes with the Collectables CD *Best of the Dubs.*

Marylanders (Baltimore, Md.)

Personnel Buster Banks (lead), Johnny Paige (2d tenor), David Jones (baritone), Henry Abrams (bass)

Notes

The Marylanders formed in Baltimore in 1946. They began singing in the churches of that city, but in 1947 they switched to secular music, which was more lucrative. The group first called themselves the Marylaneers but when they learned that a gospel group was already using the name, they switched to the Marylanders.

Baltimore deejay Bill Franklin got them a recording contract with Jubilee Records in New York, the home of the Orioles. This was very meaningful to the Marylanders. Although their records did not sell well, being associated with Jubilee netted them many live appearances in the Baltimore area. After the recordings, David Jones left and was replaced by baritone Billy Grey Eyes. Bass Gerard Rossi Carter also sang with the Marylanders.

William George, who later sang with the Marylanders, and Johnny Paige had both spent time with the Stylists.

In 1954, the Marylanders dissolved.

Tenor Freddy Yarbrough and Gerald Carter later sang with the new Marylanders, along with Paige and Banks.

Discography

Jubilee 5079 I'm a Sentimental Fool (BB)/ Sittin' by the River (JP) (1951)
Jubilee 5091 Make Me Thrill Again (BB)/Please Love Me (BB) (1952)
Jubilee 5114 Fried Chicken (JP)/Good Ol' 99 (JP/BB) (1953)
Source: Rick Whitesell and Marv Goldberg in *Yesterday's Memories* 11.

Mascots (Canton, Ohio)

Personnel Eddie Levert (lead), Walter Williams, William Powell, Bobby Massey, Bill Isles

Notes

This group came together in 1957 while attending high school in Canton, Ohio, initially calling themselves the Triumphs. They performed at many local spots in Ohio, including the YMCA and some sock hops. A songwriting friend provided the group with some original material and they were off to New York looking for a recording contract.

They initially had an audition with Decca, but Decca was not pleased with what they heard. King Records was next and Syd Nathan liked them enough to offer them a contract in 1959. He renamed them the Mascots and recorded eight tunes, releasing two discs—the first in 1960 and the second in 1961. It seemed that no one ever purchased either of these two discs.

Cleveland deejay Eddie O'Jay took an interest in the Mascots, renamed them the O'Jays, and did everything he could to foster success.

Discography

King 5377 Do the Wiggle/The Story of My Heart (1960)
King 5435 That's the Way I Feel/Lonely Rain (1960)
Source: Bill Dahl in *Goldmine,* December 28, 1990.

Masquerades (Chicago)

Personnel Howard Scott, Charles Scott, Tommy Scott, Walter Scott, Ike Hickman

Notes

The Masquerades started as the Scott Brothers from Chicago and ended, after their vocal careers were finished in 1963, as the Scott Brothers Band. They began vocalizing in 1957 as the Elpeccios. The Masquerades were discovered by Formal Records management in 1960 in a Chicago nightspot.

The Masquerades recorded nine songs for Formal, four of which eventually appeared on wax.

They went down to St. Louis to record two sides for Ike Turner's Joyce label. Again, nothing happened and in 1963–1964 they decided to call it quits.

Discography

Formal 1012 These Red Roses/Mister Man (1960)
Boyd 1027 The Whip/Fanessa (1961)
Joyce 303 Summer Sunrise/Nature's Beauty (as Five Masqueraders) (1961)
Source: Bob Pruter, *Doowop . . . The Chicago Scene.*

Master Keys (Norfolk, Va.)

Personnel Johnny Moore (tenor), Norman Harris (2d tenor) Melvin Colden (a.k.a. Melvin Coldten) (baritone), J. B. Nelson (bass)

Notes

The Master Keys recorded for one year as the Virginia Four for Decca in 1940. In 1941, Melvin Coldten became the baritone for the Norfolk Jazz Quartet and then was a member of the Selah Jubilee Singers. In 1945, Coldten left the Selahs to join the Master Keys. Nelson also came from the Selahs and was shot to death the next year. The group was forced to disband and Coldten rejoined the Selahs.

The vocal career of the Master Keys lasted about a year. Their recordings were probably all recorded in 1945–1946. It's likely that the 1950 releases were recorded in 1945 but not released until 1950.

Clarence Roberts also sang with the Master Keys; he was eventually replaced by Robert White.

In the LP *Rhythm and Blues in the Night,* there are several cuts by a group billed as the Harlem-Aires—actually the Master Keys. It must also be known that during an interview which George Moonoogian conducted with Thermon Ruth, the Abbey recording was played. After hearing these songs, Ruth stated that neither Nelson, Coldten, nor Johnny Moore's voices can be heard on the recording. Is it then possible that the Abbey record is perhaps by another Master Keys?

Discography

Top 1147 When Will I Know/You're Not the Only Apple (1945)
20th Century 20-17 How Can I Explain/I Got the Blues in the Morning (1946)
20th Century 20-18 You're Not the Only Apple/When Will I Know (1946)
Abbey 3011 Don't Talk Darling/It's Time to Kiss Goodnight (1948)
Abbey 3017 Mr. Blues/Don't Cry Darling (1948)
Jubilee 5004 I Got the Blues in the Morning/You're Not the Only Apple (1949)
Source: George Moonoogian in *Whiskey, Women, and . . .* 9.

Masters, Rick & (Philadelphia)

Personnel Tony Trombetta (lead), Frank Condo (1st tenor), Mikey Silenzio (2d tenor), Richie Finizio (baritone/bass)

Notes

This group was formed in 1962, after the members finished high school. Cameo/Parkway realized that instead of a manager, a youthful twenty-five-year-old was managing their affairs. Cameo/Parkway management took advantage of this situation.

The falsetto on "Let It Please Be You" was provided by Franklin Peaker of Philadelphia's Blue Notes, who happened to be in the studio at the time Rick and the Masters' disc was being recorded. Tommy DiGuillio later replaced Finizio.

Rick and the Masters did a great deal of backup work and made many local appearances. They backed up Lee Andrews on "I'm Sorry Pillow."

Discography

Taba 101 Flame of Love/Here Comes Nancy (1962)
Cameo 226 Flame of Love/Here Comes Nancy (1962)
Cameo 247 Let It Please Be You/I Don't Want Your Love (1963)
Haral 778 A Kissin' Friend/Bewitched, Bothered, and Bewildered (1963)
Source: Bob Bosco in *Record Collector's Monthly* 53.

Meadowlarks, Don Julian & (Los Angeles)

Personnel Don Julian (lead), Ronald Barrett (2d tenor), Earl Jones (baritone), Randolph Jones (bass)

Notes

This group was originally called the Souvenirs at their start in a Los Angeles high school in 1953 (they were not the Meadowlarks on Imperial who recorded "Brother Bill" in 1951).

The original group was a trio made up of Don Julian, Ronald Barrett, and Earl Jones. Cornel Gunter worked with them on harmony and choreography when they were starting.

Bass Randolph Jones was added in 1954 as the fourth member. Jones is primarily remembered for his work with the Penguins. Gunter would soon take them to

RPM Records, where they eventually cut four songs. The Meadowlarks weren't at RPM very long, as they felt RPM management had little interest in them. Sometime before their next recording, Randolph Jones left. Earl Jones moved to bass, and white tenor Glen Reagan, who knew Julian from the school choir, was added. Curiously, the liner notes with the Ace CD *Heaven and Paradise* show Billy Pruett as a member.

Julian took the song he wrote, "Heaven and Paradise," to Dootsie Williams at Dootone Records. Williams liked the tune and scheduled a recording session for it to be recorded for his label. The disc sold well and with its success came a California tour for the Meadowlarks.

Ronald Barrett left after "Always and Always" to join and record with the Dootones. He was replaced by Freeman Bralton. After "This Must Be Paradise," Reagan left for the service and was replaced by Benny Patricks. Both replacements, Bralton and Patricks, came from Julian's school choir. Patricks only appeared with the group. Ronald Barrett would return to record for all future sessions.

Interestingly, the Meadowlarks recorded with Vernon Green as the Medallions on "Push-Button Automobile," "Shedding Tears for You," and "Did You Have Fun?"

After the Meadowlarks' Dootone recordings, Julian went solo. In 1958, he assembled another Meadowlarks group recording for Original Sound Records. This group was composed of Danny Paul, Lloyd Powers, Robert Paul, and Earl Jones. On their second disc for Original Sound the group was Leon Brown, Clydie King, and Earl Jones. When he was scheduled to record for Specialty, Percy Mayfield, who loved the Meadowlarks, had them record the backing vocals. The Maytones name appears on Specialty 537, "My Heart Is Crying." In 1960, the group moved to Dynamite Records. The lineup there consisted of Thomas Turner, Ted Walters, Danny Saunders, and Roosevelt Klein.

Discography

RPM 399 Love Only You/Real Pretty Mama (1954)
RPM 406 Pass the Gin/L.F.M.S.T. Blues (1954)
Dootone 359 Heaven and Paradise/Embarrassing Moments (1955)
Dootone 367 I Got Tore Up/Always and Always (1955)
Dootone 372 This Must Be Paradise/Mine All Mine (1955)
Dootone 394 Oop Boopy Oop/Please Love a Fool (1956)
Dootone 405 Boogie Woogie Teenage/I Am a Believer (1956)
Dooto 424 Blue Moon/Big Mama Wants to Rock (1957)
Original Sound 03 Please/Doin' the Cha Cha Cha (1958)
Original Sound 12 Blue Mood/There's a Girl (1959)
Dynamite 1112 Heaven Only Knows/Popeye (1961)
Magnum 716 The Booglay/Lie (1964)
Jerk 100 Philly Jerk/How Can You Be So Foul?
Sources: Jim Dawson, notes to the Ace CD *Dootone Story*; Marv Goldberg and Mike Redmond in *Yesterday's Memories* 10.

Medallionaires (Chicago)

Personnel Willie Wright (a.k.a. Willie Dial) (lead), Ernest Montgomery (tenor), David Anderson (baritone), Ronald Anderson (bass)

Notes

In 1958, Willie Wright formed the Medallionaires, using personnel from his neighborhood. They included two brothers, David and Ronald Anderson. "Teenage Caravan" received radio airtime in Chicago.

In Bob Pruter's *Doowop . . . The Chicago Scene,* he spells Montgomery's first name Earnest.

Wright had been with the Serenades (Chicago) and the Von Gayles.

Discography

Mercury 71309 Magic Moonlight/Teen-Age Caravan (1958)
Source: Bob Pruter, *Doowop . . . The Chicago Scene.*

Medallions (Los Angeles)

Personnel Vernon Green (lead), Randolph Bryant (1st tenor), Rudolph Brown (2d tenor), Chuck ——— (bass)

Notes

The group shown above, according to Marv Goldberg's interview with Vernon Green and Dootsie Williams, recorded "The Letter" and "Buick 59." Subsequent to that initial session, Rudolph Brown was replaced by Willie Graham. Ira Foley was unable to attend the first session and someone remembered as Chuck filled in for him at that time.

Vernon Green was a victim of polio but still performs. He ran away from home in Denver to live with his grandmother in Los Angeles.

The Medallions formed in Los Angeles in 1954 after Vernon Green was overheard singing by Dootsie Williams, owner of Dootone Records. Williams advised Green to get a vocal group together. Responding to this advice, Green recruited several friends who hung out with him at a local park—Blue, Bryant, and Ira Foley. They practiced for a month and then went to Dootone to record "The Letter" and "Buick 59." Both tunes took off.

Concerning Green's unusual lyrics in "The Letter," "sweet words of pismotality," Green stated in an interview that he enjoyed inventing words and this is one example of his "creative inventing."

Following the recording of "Edna," and long before its release, Donald Woods was added as the group's fifth member. However, difficulties began to surface within the group and all but Green departed. The departed members formed the Bel Aires/Vel Aires, who recorded for Flip. Green was then left alone, which did not last very long. He was initially joined by tenors Frank Marshall and Kenneth Williams to form the Dootone Cameos. They had one release on Dootone, but this did not do well.

Dootsie Williams tried combining Green with the dormant Dootones—Charles Gardner, Ronald Barrett, H. B. Barnum, and Marvin Wilkins. This combination did not last long either.

At the next session, Green had Johnny Morrisette (a.k.a. Johnny Twovoice) sing lead. The label on this disc simply shows the name of Twovoice, but the anonymous Medallions back him up with Jimmy Green (Vernon's brother), Charles Gardner, Albert Johnson, and Otis Scott. On the next two Medallions discs, the group remained the same less Morrisette.

In the discussion above, addressing the Meadowlarks, Don Julian related that it was his group performing backing vocals for Green on "Shedding Tears For You," "Pushbutton Automobile," and "Did You Have Fun." However, in another interview, Green says it's Gardner, Jimmy Green, and Jerome Evans.

But Green's musical endeavors did not yield much in the way of financial rewards, and in 1956 he put the Phantoms together at the request of Specialty Records. After this, Green returned to Dootone (now Dooto) and a new Medallions. The new group consisted of Billy Foster, Jimmy Green, and Joe Williams with lead Vernon Green. It was this ensemble that recorded "For Better or Worse" and "A Lover's Prayer."

In 1962, the group again consisted of Vernon Green, Charles Gardner, Jimmy Green, Albert Johnson, and Otis Scott.

In 1964, Green was in an automobile accident and stopped performing for approximately ten years.

Discography

Dootone 347 Buick 59/The Letter (1954)
Essex 901 I Know/Laki-Lani (1955)
Dootone 357 The Telegram/Coupe DeVille Baby (1955)
Dootone 364 Speedin'/Edna (RB) (1955)
Dootone 379 Dear Darling/Don't Shoot Baby (1955)
Dootone 393 I Want a Love/Dance and Swing (1956)
Dootone 400 Pushbutton Automobile/Shedding Tears For You (1956)
Dootone 407 Did You Have Fun?/My Mary Lou (1956)
Dooto 419 For Better or for Worse/I Wonder, Wonder, Wonder (1957)
Dooto 425 Lover's Prayer/Unseen (1957)
Dooto 446 59 Volvo/Magic Mountain (1959)
Dooto 454 Behind the Door/Rocket Ship (1959)
Dootone 479 Can You Talk?/You Don't Know (1973)
Sources: Marv Goldberg in *Record Collector's Monthly* 42; Wayne Stierle, liner notes with the *West Coast Doo Wop Collection* CD; Jim Dawson, liner notes with the Ace CD *Dootone Story.*

Mello Harps (Brooklyn, N.Y.)

Personnel Arnold "Johnny" Malone (lead), Vernon Staley (1st tenor), Joe Gowder (2d tenor), Daniel Elder (baritone), Ossie Davis (bass)

Notes

These were neighborhood friends who met at a social gathering in the Bedford-Stuyvesant section of Brooklyn in 1955. After securing the falsetto talents of Vernon Staley and Larry Lucy to manage them, they soon recorded for Morty Craft's Do Re Me label.

Ossie Davis left after this first session and was replaced by Bobby Hawkins, who was the brother of basketball star Connie Hawkins. Through a friend, they met band leader Teacho Wiltshire, who sang lead on Tin Pan Alley 159/160.

Staley and Elder left in mid-1956 to be replaced by William Brown and David Forte. Later that same year, they recorded "Our Love Is a Vow."

In 1957, Johnny Malone quit and was replaced by a tenor only remembered as Warren. At one of their practice sessions, they met Doles Dickens who, besides his past career in music, was then managing Casino Records. This is where the Mello Harps moved next. At Casino they did "Gumma Gumma," which was supposed to capitalize on the Chips' "Rubber Biscuit" craze. This same group released sides as by the Levee Songsters.

Joe Gowder left and formed the Leopards on the Leopard label, with David Forte joining him.

Discography

Do-Re-Mi 203 Love Is a Vow (JM/VS)/Valerie (JM) (1955)
Tin Pan Alley 145/146 I Love Only You (VS)/Ain't Got the Money (JG) (1955)
Tin Pan Alley 157/158 What Good Are My Dreams (JM)/Gone (JM) (1956)
Tin Pan Alley 159/160 My Bleeding Heart (TW)/I Couldn't Believe (TW) (1956)
Casino 104 Gumma Gumma (JG)/No Good (WB) (1958)
Sources: Donn Fileti, liner notes with the Relic CD *Relic*; Marv Goldberg in *Record Collector's Monthly* 46.

Mellokings (Mount Vernon, N.Y.)

Personnel Bob Scholl (d) (lead), Jerry Scholl (tenor), Eddie Quinn (2d tenor), Neil Arena (baritone), Larry Esposito (bass)

Notes

The group first got together at Washington High School in Mount Vernon, New York, in 1956. They were originally called the Mellotones and made the rounds of the New York record companies looking for one to put their product on wax. They eventually hooked up with Al Silver at Herald/Ember Records. Within one month, their "Tonite, Tonite" was recorded and released.

The record originally was released as by the Mello Tones, but because of the existence of another Mellotones on Gee, the label was altered to show Mellokings. There were many follow-ups, which failed despite the myriad promotions the label and the group attempted.

Neil Arena and Larry Esposito left in 1958 and were replaced by Louis Janacone and Tony Pinto. The new vocal combination started with "Chip Chip" in January 1959. With the first revival of 1950s music in 1961, "Tonite, Tonite" made another chart appearance that year.

Bob Scholl was drafted in 1959 and passed away in 1975. Eddie Quinn left for a solo career.

Discography

Herald 502 Tonite, Tonite/Do Baby Do (1957)
Herald 507 Chapel on the Hill/Sassafras (1957)
Herald 511 Baby Tell Me Why, Why, Why/The Only Girl (1957)
Herald 514 Valerie/She's Real Cool (1957)
Herald 536 Running to You/Chip, Chip (1959)

Herald 548 Our Love Is Beautiful/Dear Mr. Jock (1960)
Herald 554 Kid Stuff/I Promise (1960)
Herald 561 Penny/Till There Was None (1961)
Herald 567 Love at First Sight/She's Real Cool (1961)
Sources: Pete Grendysa in *Goldmine;* Marv Goldberg and Marcia Vance, liner notes with the Relic LP *Mello-Kings.*

Mello-Moods (New York)

Personnel Ray "Buddy" Wooten (lead), Alvin "Bobby" Baylor (2d tenor), Monte Owens (tenor), Bobby Williams (d) (baritone), Jimmy Bethea Martinez (bass)

Notes

The Mello-Moods began singing in 1950, practicing at Macombs Dam Park in the Bronx. They were the first vocal group to record for Bobby Robinson's Red Robin label in 1951 with "Where Are You." This disc was so popular that Robinson had to give it to Jerry Blaine at Jubilee for national distribution. The group called West 151st Street home. Incredibly, when they initially formed, some members—Bobby Williams, Bobby Baylor, and Monte Owens—were in the eighth grade!

The Mello-Moods had been together about a year when a friend learned of Bobby Robinson's intention to start a label. Since Wooten's mother knew Robinson, they went there for an audition. Robinson knew at the start that this group was unique and signed them to record. Robinson initially called them the Robins after the label but quickly changed their name to the Mello-Moods.

After their first Robin cut, Bobby Baylor dropped out of the group. For a short time he sang and recorded with the Hi Lites on Okeh, followed by the Solitaires. Baylor's departure made the Mello-Moods a quartet. He was not replaced and there were no further personnel changes.

A friend, Jimmy Keyes of the Chords from the Morrisania section of the Bronx, became their manager early on and was later replaced by Joel Turnero.

Bobby Williams died in 1961.

Baylor, Williams, and Owens later became the foundation of the Old Town Solitaires.

Discography

Robin 105 How Could You/Where Are You? (1951)
Red Robin 104 I Couldn't Sleep a Wink Last Night/And You'll Just Have to Go Through Life Alone (1952)
Prestige 799 Call on Me/I Tried, Tried, and Tried (1952)
Prestige 856 I'm Lost/When I Woke Up This Morning (1953)
Source: Marv Goldberg and Mike Redmond in *Record Exchanger* 16.

Mello-Tones (New York)

Personnel Ray Hulbert (lead), Joe Libscomb (2d tenor), Oliver James (baritone), Louis O'Neil (bass)

Notes

These were neighborhood friends who grew up on 132d Street in New York's Harlem. In 1953, responding to the R&B vocal group phenomenon taking place, they got themselves together and decided to form a vocal group. In an inverview Hulbert stated that he ended up singing lead because he was not good at harmony. The members were between fifteen and eighteen years old at their start.

They retained the services of manager Cliff Martinez but got their contract as a result of Hulbert's persistence with Decca management. On April 6, 1954, they had their first session. The record didn't sell particularly well, but the group toured the East Coast on the strength of it.

The group did vocal backup work for Decca before recording at Decca's facilities in their own right.

Lack of success caused O'Neil to leave, and he was replaced by Charlie Carrington. The group scouted around for another recording company and recorded for Hull in 1956, but nothing was ever released.

They later worked with Miriam Grate at Apollo, recording four sides of a cappella tracks for which the group was never given credit. These songs surfaced on a Relic LP of Apollo a cappella material.

After a great deal of research, Marv Goldberg learned that this Mello-Tones group had nothing to do with the Mello-Tones on Gee. Marv listened to the flip side of "I'm Just Another One in Love with You" entitled "I'm Gonna Get What I Came for Last Night" and compared the sound of that up-tempo tune with the up-tempo "Heaven above Me" by the Jets on Gee. He states that that the two groups, the Jets and the Decca Mello-Tones, are the same.

Discography

Decca 48319 I'm Just Another One in Love with You (RH)/I'm Gonna Get (RH) (1954)
Source: Marv Goldberg in *DISCoveries,* January 1, 1995.

Mellow Drops (New Orleans)

Personnel Robert Kidd (lead), Adolph Smith (tenor), Louis Caliste (tenor), Clarence Phoenix (tenor), Billy Tircuit (bass)

Notes

This New Orleans vocal group got together in 1952. They were friends in their early twenties who recorded one disc for the Imperial label. Imperial released their record in 1954.

They later became the Monitors on Aladdin and Specialty and the Señors on Sue. Despite their point of origin (the group was from Louisiana), they recorded for two West Coast labels and later for one from New York.

Discography

Imperial 5324 When I Grow Too Old to Dream (RK)/The Crazy Song (RK) (1954)
Sources: Steve LaVere, liner notes with Imperial's *Rhythm & Blues–1, The End of an Era*; Billy Tircuit, interview by Marv Goldberg.

Mellow Moods (Los Angeles)

Personnel Paul Robi (lead), Lewis Young (tenor), Bob Redd (2d tenor), Al Frazier (baritone), Maurice Hill (bass)

Notes

This group formed on the streets of Los Angeles circa 1948 or 1949 and were the first group calling themselves the Mello Moods. They made many local appearances under that name but never used it to record.

Paul Roby, of course, later joined the Platters. Lewis Young became part of an Ink Spots group and sang with them for about fifteen years.

When Maurice Hill and Bob Redd were married to their respective spouses, the wedding bells signaled the end of the Mellow Moods.

(Note: The Mello Moods on Hollywood are not this group. As discussed above, this group of Mellow Moods never recorded.)

Source: Art Turco in *Record Exchanger* 28.

Mellows, Lillian Leach & (Bronx, N.Y.)

Personnel Lillian Leach (lead), Johnny "Tiny" Wilson (1st tenor), Harold Johnson (d) (2d tenor), Norman Brown (bass)

Notes

One Saturday evening in 1954 Wilson, Johnson, and Brown were harmonizing in the hallway of an apartment house during a party and invited seventeen-year-old Lillian Leach to join them. Johnson had been with Dean Barlow and the Crickets. After the vocalizing, Brown exclaimed, "what a mellow sound they created with Leach" and the name and the group were born!

Johnson soon took the group on an excursion to find a recording company. They wound up at the Crickets' label, Jay Dee Records owned by Joe Davis. Davis liked what he heard and a recording session was immediately scheduled. The beautiful "How Sentimental Can I Be" was the result of this session. Their next single was the classic "Smoke from Your Cigarette."

In spite of the success of "Smoke from Your Cigarette," the Mellows never appeared at an Alan Freed show or at the Apollo (until very recently). Their next singles, despite their quality, did not do well. Norman Brown left the group at this time and was replaced by Gary Morrison. Arthur Crier joined at this time as well, making the group a quintet.

Late in 1955, the group left Davis to join the Brooklyn-based Celeste Records. At Celeste the group was composed of Leach, Arthur Crier, Harold Johnson, John Wilson, and Gary Morrison. They had two discs for Celeste that did not fare well and the next move was to Candlelite Records. Poor sales prevailed and Leach left to wed and raise a family. The Mellows resurfaced with each R&B revival through the 1990s and continued to make many appearances.

While searching through tapes of the Apollo material for reproduction, the Relic Records team found a tape that contained demo tapes of an audition for Lillian Leach and the Mellows. The cuts "So Strange" and "Be Mine" were finally released on a Relic LP featuring Apollo material.

Crier and Johnson went on to form the Halos ("Nag"). He also spent time with the Hummers, Five Chimes, and the Craftys.

Discography

Jay Dee 793 Nothin' to Do/How Sentimental Can I Be? (1954)
Jay Dee 797 Smoke from Your Cigarette/Pretty Baby What's Your Name (1955)
Jay Dee 801 I Was a Fool to Let You Go/I Still Care (1955)
Jay Dee 807 Lovable Lily/Yesterday's Memories (1955)
Celeste 3002 Lucky Guy/My Darling (1956)
Celeste 3004 I'm Yours/Sweet Lorraine (1956)
Candlelight 1011 You've Gone/Moon of Silver (1956)
Sources: Jay Warner, *American Singing Groups*; Donn Fileti, liner notes with Relic's *The Best of Apollo Records-3*.

Mel-O-Aires, Rudy Jackson & (Los Angeles)

Personnel Rudy Jackson (lead), Vera Potts, Gladys Jackson, Hattie Potts

Notes

In 1954, Rudy Jackson, together with three girls he had known from childhood, cut two sides for the R&B label. The record was released as by Rudy Jackson. The Mel-O-Aires were shown on the label as the backing group.

Jackson also sang with the Marbles, a vocal group that became the Jewels.

Discography

R&B 1310 I'm Crying/Enfold Me (1955)
Source: Marv Goldberg and Rick Whitesell in *Yesterday's Memories* 10, article about the Jewels.

Mel-O-Dots (New York)

Personnel Earl "Ricky" Wells (lead), Pat Ross (1st tenor)

Notes

The Mel-O-Dots recorded four sides for Apollo on March 17, 1952. Apparently this was their first and last visit to Apollo's facilities. The other two songs, "Rock My Baby" and "Baby Won't You Please Come Home," were not issued until Relic's Apollo series of LPs released these gems in the 1990s.

Discography

Apollo 1192 One More Time (PR)/Just How Long (ERW) (1952)
Source: Donn Fileti, liner notes with the Relic LP *Best of Apollo Records-1*.

Melody Kings (New Haven, Conn.)

Personnel Orville Brooks (lead), Ray Reid (tenor), Scott King (tenor), Sam McClure (baritone), Jasper Edwards (bass)

Notes

Because radio personality Arthur Godfrey insisted that the Jubalaires not leave his radio show because they were so popular, Edwards, McClure, and Reid went on the road as part of the Jubalaires, along with Orville Brooks, a regular member of the Jubalaires. The balance of the Jubalaires would remain with Godfrey.

Edwards, McClure, and Reid were three members of the Melody Kings. When the Jubalaires' tour ended, so did their performing prospects. At that time they joined up with Scott King.

After practicing and appearing as the Melody Kings for quite some time, their manager got them a contract with Lee Records in Connecticut. Before recording, Lee management changed their name to the Shadows. Consequently, they recorded as the Melody Kings
Source: Marv Goldberg in *DISCoveries* 90.

Melody Masters (Newark, N.J.)

Personnel Danny Owens (lead), Pico Payne (tenor), Eric Miller (tenor), James Waters (baritone), Cliff Givens (bass)

Notes

The Melody Masters was formed in Newark by bass Cliff Givens. Givens' claim-to-fame was that he was the first replacement for bass "Hoppy" Jones of the Ink Spots. Givens also spent time with the Golden Gate Quartet.

The name Melody Masters was only used for the Rhythm & Blues' recordings this gospel group, also known as the Southern Sons, recorded. They never made appearances as the Melody Masters.

Danny Owens later had a successful career with the Four Tunes. Givens later joined Billy Ward's Dominoes and was with them during the Jackie Wilson and Eugene Mumford years.

Discography

Apollo 379 Wig Blues/My Baby (1946)
Apollo 383 Don't You Ever Mind Them/Subway Cutie (1947)
Source: Donn Fileti and Marv Goldberg, liner notes with the Relic Apollo LP *Goodbye 40s, Hello 1950s.*

Memos (Brooklyn, N.Y.)

Personnel Henry Austin (lead), James Brown (2d tenor), Eugene Williams (baritone), Vernon Britton (bass)

Notes

Group had been the Toppers (Jubilee) and the Hurricanes (King), with Fred Williams a member instead of his brother Eugene. At the time of the Memos' recording, Fred Williams was in the service and Eugene filled in for him.

In 1959, the Memos got to do a year-long tour of Canada as a result of their tune "My Most Precious Possession" selling well in Canada. The financial rewards of this tour, however, were quite poor as were all their other financial arrangements.

Discography

Memo 5000/5001 I'm Going Home/My Most Precious Possession (1959)
Memo 34891 My Type of Girl/The Biddy Leg (1959)
Source: Marv Goldberg in *Record Collector's Monthly* 43.

Metros (Bronx, N.Y.)

Personnel Joe Garcia (lead), Donnie Cruz (1st tenor), Joe Patriarca (2d tenor), John Angelo (baritone), Joe Carillo (bass)

Notes

Began as the Crystals in a Bronx high school in 1957.

Carillo had come from Brooklyn from the Whirlin' Disc Continentals. Just before recording, they called themselves the Metros and they recorded "All of My Life" and "Lookin' " for Just Records.

They were soon taken to MGM where they reverted back to their old name, the Crystals, before recording for the MGM subsidiary, Cub.

Discography

Just 1502 All of My Life/Lookin' (1959)
Source: Ed Engel in *Echoes of the Past* 10.

Metrotones (Cleveland, Ohio)

Personnel Charles "Sonny" Turner (a.k.a. "Sonny" Dinkes) (lead), Freddie Camp (1st tenor), Leonard Veal (2d tenor), Leuvenia Eaton, James Frierson (baritone), Melvin Smith (bass)

Notes

The Metrotones' beginnings go back to 1953 at Cleveland's John Adams High School and a group of students who formed a vocal group. The normal comings and goings occurred with members. They practiced for many long hours until they felt ready for public attention. They did this at local nightspots, parties, hospital benefits, churches, and talent shows.

After dating for some time, Leuvenia Eaton and "Sonny" Turner married in 1956. The following year Russell Cole, their manager, brought them to Reserve Records in Cleveland, where they signed a contract to record. In February 1957 they had their session with the label. The group that performed at the Reserve session was a sextet with Eaton, Turner, Camp, Veal, Frierson, and Smith.

The tunes "Please Come Back" and "Skitter Skatter" were released. "Skitter Skatter" was soon heard by someone at a local radio station who found the song to be suggestive. As a result, the station decided to remove the tune from their programming. Unfortunately, the flip was totally ignored following this decision. Because of this unintended recording failure, they logically changed their name to the Five Jades.

Don Robey of Duke/Peacock Records heard the group while on a talent hunt. He signed them to record for his Duke label. "Without Your Love" was recorded in April 1958 and released the next month. The personnel on this disc was the same as on Reserve less Fred Camp. This effort failed as well.

Veal and two members from the El Pollos, both from Cleveland, later sang with the Hesitations on D-Town.

Discography

Reserve 116 Please Come Back/Skitter Skatter (1957)
Source: Marv Goldberg in *DISCoveries,* November 1997.

Midnighters (Chicago)

Personnel Henry Booth (lead), Charles Sutton (tenor), Hank Ballard (baritone), Sonny Woods (bass)

Notes

The Midnighters began in 1954, having evolved from the Royals. The purpose of this name change was to avoid being confused with the Five Royales, stemming from the success of the "Annie" series of recordings.

Hank Ballard joined on Federal 12169 (Work with Me Annie/Until I Die), replacing Lawson Smith, who went into the army. This disc, Give It Up/That Woman, was issued as by the Royals and by the Midnighters.

The Midnighters had many successes over the next two years with "Sexy Ways" and the Annie follow-ups. But the group went into somewhat of a decline after these years of success. In 1957, Sutton left the group and Lawson Smith, a former member of the Royals, rejoined. In 1958 Sonny Woods left and Norman Thrasher, who had been with the Detroit Serenaders and the Royal Jokers, replaced him.

The group's guitarist, Alonzo Tucker, sang part-time with the group.

"The Twist" was recorded by Hank Ballard prior to its becoming a huge hit for Chubby Checker.

Following the success of "Finger Poppin' Time" and "Let's Go, Let's Go, Let's Go" in 1960, there were several personnel changes. The group now included Ballard, Frank Stanford, Wesley Hargrove, Norman Thrasher, and Henry Booth.

Discography

Federal 12177 Give It Up/That Woman (1954)
Federal 12185 Sexy Ways/Don't Say Your Last Good-bye (1954)
Federal 12195 Annie Had a Baby/She's the One (1954)
Federal 12200 Annie's Aunt Fannie/Crazy Loving (1954)
Federal 12202 Tell Them/Stingy Little Thing (1954)

Federal 12205 Moonrise/She's the One (1954)
Federal 12210 Ashamed of Myself/Ring-a-Ling-a-Ling (1955)
Federal 12220 Why Are We Apart/Switchie Witchie Titchie (1955)
Federal 12224 Henry's Got Flat Feet/Whatsoever You Do (1955)
Federal 12227 It's Love Baby/Looka Here (1955)
Federal 12230 Give It Up/That Woman (1955)
Federal 12240 Rock and Roll Wedding/That House on the Hill (1955)
Federal 12243 Don't Change Your Pretty Ways/We'll Never Meet Again (1955)
Federal 12251 Partners for Life/Sweet Mama, Do Right (1956)
Federal 12260 Rock Granny Roll/Open Up the Back Door (1956)
Federal 12270 Tore Up Over You/Early One Morning (1956)
Federal 12285 I'll Be Home Someday/Come On and Get It (1956)
Federal 12288 Let Me Hold Your Hand/Oom Bah Baby (1957)
Federal 12293 E Basta Cosi/In the Doorway Crying (1957)
Federal 12299 Is Your Love So Real/Oh So Happy (1957)
Federal 12305 Let 'Em Roll/What Made You Change Your Mind (1957)
Federal 12317 Daddy's Little Baby/Stay by My Side (1958)
Federal 12339 Baby Please/Ow-Wow-oo-Wee (1958)

Hank Ballard & The Midnighters

King 5171 The Twist/Teardrops on Your Letter (1959)
King 5195 Kansas City/I'll Keep You Happy (1959)
King 5215 Sugaree/Rain Down Tears (1959)
King 5245 House with No Windows/Cute Little Ways (1959)
King 5275 Never Knew/I Could Love You (1959)
King 5289 Look at Little Sister/I Said I Wouldn't Beg You (1960)
King 5312 Waiting/The Coffee Grind (1960)
King 5341 Finger Poppin' Time/I Love You, I Love You So-o (1960)
King 5400 Let's Go, Lets' Go, Let's Go/If You'd Forgive Me (1960)
King 5430 The Hoochi, Coochi, Coo/I'm Thinking of You (1960)
King 5459 Let's Go Again/Deep Blue Sea (1961)
King 5491 The Continental Walk/What Is This I See (1961)
King 5510 The Switch-a-Roo/The Float (1961)
King 5535 Nothing but God/Keep Me Dancing (1961)
King 5550 Big Red Sunset/Can't You See, I Need a Friend (1961)
King 5578 I'm Gonna Miss You/Do You Remember? (1961)
King 5593 Do You Know How to Twist/Broadway (1962)
King 5601 It's Twistin' Time/Autumn Breeze (1962)
King 5635 Good Twistin' Tonight/I'm Young (1962)
King 5655 I Want to Thank You/Excuse Me (1962)
King 5677 When I Need You/Dreamworld (1962)
King 5693 Shakey Mae/I Love and Care for You (1962)
King 5703 She's the One/Bring Me Your Love (1962)
King 5713 The Rising Tide/Please You (1963)
King 5719 That Low-Down Move/The House on the Hill (1963)
King 5729 X-Mas Time for Everyone but Me/Santa Claus Is Coming (1963)
King 5746 Walkin' and Talkin'/How Could You Leave (1963)
King 5798 Those Lonely Lonely Feelings/It's Love (1963)

King 5821 Buttin' In/I'm Learning (1963)
King 5835 Don't Let Temptation/Have Mercy (1963)
King 5860 Don't Fall in Love With/I'm So Mad with You (1963)
King 5884 These Young Girls/I Don't Know How to Do But One Thing (1964)
King 5901 Stay Away from My Baby/She's Got Soul (1964)
King 5931 What's Your Name/Daddy Rollin' Stone (1964)
King 5954A Winner Never Quits/Let's Get Show (1964)
King 5963 One Monkey Don't Stop the Show/Watch What I Tell You (1965)
King 5996 Poppin' the Whip/You Just You (1965)
King 6018 Sloop and Slide/My Sum Is Going Down (1965)
King 6031 I'm Ready/Togetherness (1966)
King 6055 He Came Along/Annie Had a Baby (1966)
King 6119 You're in Real Good Hands/Unwind Yourself (1967)
King 6131 Funky Soul Train/Which Way Should I Turn? (1967)
Sources: Liner notes with the Ace CD *Hank Ballard*; Drew Williamson in *Record Collector's Monthly* 37; Tony Watson in *Blues & Rhythm,* July 1990.

Mifflin Triplets (Hartford, Conn.)

Personnel Earl Mifflin, Edward Mifflin, Everett Mifflin

Notes

At the session that produced the released "I Do" and "Someone Should Have Told Me" one other known title was recorded but was never released: "Voice of an Angel." This tune was recently issued on the Relic CD series *Golden Era of Doo Wops— The Groups of Ember Records.*

Discography

Ember 1045 I Do/Someone Should Have Told Me (1958)
Source: Donn Fileti, liner notes with the Relic Ember CD *Groups of Ember Records.*

Mighty Dukes (Brooklyn, N.Y.)

Personnel Billy Dawn Smith (lead), Donny Myles (a.k.a. Donny Sehested) (tenor), Tommy Smith (baritone), Sonny Benton (bass)

Notes

This group originally formed in the late 1940s in the Crown Heights section of Brooklyn. Their manager was Joel Turnero, who also managed the Mello-Moods. They were taken by an acquaintance of theirs to Decatur Records in Harlem, where they first recorded as the Billy Dawn Quartet.

Turnero then got them a session with Duke records. Owner Don Robey changed their name to the Mighty Dukes and Turnero selected the songs for the Duke recording. Their next release involved another name change—the Four Dukes.

The group also recorded as the Heralds, when they moved to the Herald label.

Discography

Duke 104 Why Can't I Have You? (SB)/No Other Love (DS) (1953)
Source: Rick Whitesell and Marv Goldberg in *Yesterday's Memories* 12.

Miller Sisters (Queens, N.Y.)

Personnel Jeanette Miller, Maxine Miller, Nina Miller, Sandy Miller, Vernel Miller

Notes

These were the daughters of music entrepreneur William Miller of Hull Records. Interestingly, the sisters lived across the street from Vernon Seavers of the Heartbeats, and their father was the A&R director for Hull. Consequently, he and his daughters played an important role at the start of the Heartbeats' career.

The Miller Sisters recorded for many labels in various styles of music. While they were with Herald Records, their father obtained their release from an exclusive contract they had with the label. Thereafter, they freelanced for Hull, Acme, and Onyx.

The sisters had a starring role in the first R&B motion picture, Fritz Pollard's *Rockin' the Blues,* in 1955.

Discography

Herald 455 Hippety Ha/Until You're Mine (1955)
Ember 1004 Guess Who/How Am I to Know (1956)
Hull 718 Do You Wanna Go?/Please Don't Leave (1956)
Hull 736 Just Wait and See/Black Pepper (1957)
Onyx 507 My Own/Sugar Candy (1957)
Acme 111 The Flip Skip/Let's Start Anew (1957)
Acme 717 Crazy Billboard Song/You Made Me a Promise (1957)
Acme 721 The Flip Skip/Let's Start Anew (1957)
Miller 1140 Oh Lover/Remember That (1960)
Miller 1141 Pony Dance/Give Me Some Old-Fashioned Love (1960)
Glodus 1003 You Got to Reap What You Sow/Pop Your Finger (1961)
Rayna 5001 I Miss You So/Dance Little Sister (1962)
Rayna 5004 Walk On/Oh Why (1962)
Hull 750 Don't You Forget/Roll Back the Rug (1962)
Hull 752 Hully Gully Reel/I Cried All Night (1962)
Riverside 4535 Dance Close/Tell Him (1962)
Roulette 4491 Baby Your Baby/Silly Girl (1963)
Stardust 3001 Cooncha/Feel Good (1964)
Yorktown 75 Looking Over My Life/Si Señor (1965)
GMC 10006 I'm Telling It Like It Is/Until You Come Home, I'll Walk Alone (1965)
Sources: Jeff Beckman in *Big Town Review;* Ferdie Gonzalez, *Disco-File*; Eddie Gries, liner notes with the Relic LP *Best of Onyx Records.*

Millionaires (New York)

Personnel Ollie Jones (lead), Abel DeCosta (d) (1st tenor), Napoleon Allen (baritone), James DeLoach (bass)

Notes

Jones and DeLoach had been with the Cues on Capitol and Jones had also been the original lead for the Ravens.

The record shown below was recorded in 1953 but not released until 1955.

Discography

Davis 441 Somebody's Lyin'/Kansas Kapers (1955)
Source: Unsigned liner notes with the Davis LP *Good Old Oldies from 1974.*

Mills Brothers (Piqua, Ohio)

Personnel Donald Mills, Harry Mills, Herbert Mills, John Mills

Notes

The Mills Brothers started performing in 1922. Their father had a strong interest in music and when his four sons began singing at a very young age, it came as no surprise. They would perform on the streets using kazoos to imitate musical instruments.

Because they forgot to bring their kazoos to a local concert one day, they began using their voices to capture the sound, simulating a musical instrument. They would cup their hands over their mouths for the simulation. This became so popular that they were signed by WLW radio in Cincinnati. This show became so popular that they moved to Cincinnati to accommodate a daily appearance.

A local agent heard them and brought them to New York, where they were quickly signed to a three-year CBS contract. During this time, they appeared in many films. Recording started as well. In 1931, they began recording for Brunswick, and these discs were very successful with both their vocal harmonies and their simulated instrumental technique—which fooled everyone! The labels on the discs even had a notice that no musical instruments were used on the recordings.

Following a label change to Decca in 1934 and a Royal Command Performance in 1935, John fell ill and was hospitalized. He passed away in January 1936 at the age of twenty-five. John Sr., the boys' father, replaced his namesake son.

A change in the public's musical taste caused their great popularity to decline in the 1940s. The Mills Brothers accommodated this change by somewhat altering their style. Their releases in that decade were successful because of this accommodation. Their style was referred to as rhythm and blues in one newspaper long before the term came into popular usage.

Because the Mills Brothers were so well-known as pop stars, they were unable to join the rock 'n' roll revolution of the early 1950s. Nevertheless, they went on with their unique harmonies and vocal style.

John Sr. retired during the mid-1950s and the group went on recording and performing as a trio. He died in 1967.

(Note: The liner notes with the Ranwood CD from Santa Monica, California, show 1984 as the year of John Sr.'s death.)

Harry died in 1982 and Herbert in 1989. Donald continued on, with his son, into the 1990s.

In retrospect, the Mills Brothers played an important role in securing the white acceptance of black music. Most of all, they originated the musical style now referred to as R&B vocal group harmony.

Discography

Too extensive to list; exists elsewhere.
Source: Pete Grendysa, George Moonoogian, and Rick Whitesell in *Record Exchanger* 24.

Mint Juleps (Springfield, Mass.)

Personnel William Terrell, Charles Thomas, Emra Clemmons, Alvin Clark, George Val Poitier (bass)

Notes

Bass George Poitier went on to the Dreamtones, who recorded for Astra, Express, and Klik Records.

Discography

Herald 481 Bells of Love/Viv-a-Dip (1956)
 (UNR) Queen of Love/Ginny Doll
Sources: Donn Fileti, liner notes with the Relic CD *Best of Herald Records*; Donn Fileti, liner notes with the Relic CD *Best of Fargo Records*.

Miracles (Detroit)

Personnel Bill "Smokey" Robinson (lead), Bobby Rogers (tenor), Claudette Rogers (tenor), Ronnie White (baritone), Warren Pete Moore (bass)

Notes

The Miracles started in 1954 while group members were attending high school in Detroit. They were then called the Matadors and played local shows in the vicinity. Claudette Rogers Robinson, wife of Smokey, joined the group in 1956 when one of the original members was drafted. She married Robinson in 1963.

The group auditioned for Jackie Wilson's manager in 1957. He turned them down. Attending the same audition, however, was a young writer named Berry Gordy who liked the group and helped them get started by influencing George Goldner to record them on his End label. This was done and "Got a Job," a spoof of the Silhouettes' novelty "Get a Job," was eventually released.

With borrowed money, Robinson convinced Gordy to start his own Tamla label in 1960. Thereafter, things went quite well for many years for both the Miracles and Gordy. The British invasion really didn't affect the Miracles; their hits kept coming.

By 1964, Claudette Robinson retired. In 1967, the group changed its name to Smokey Robinson and the Miracles. The hits continued with successes all over the world.

In July 1972, Robinson finally decided to call it quits with singing. Billy Griffin took his place. In 1977, the Miracles moved over to Columbia Records and that same year they added Billy's brother, Don, to the group. For the first time in fourteen years the Miracles became a quintet.

Discography

End 1016 Got a Job/My Mama Done Told Me (1958)
End 1029 Money/I Cry (1958)
Chess 1734 Bad Girl/I Love You Baby (1959)
End 1084 Money/I Cry (1960)
Chess 1768 All I Want/I Need a Change (1960)
Tamla 54028 Depend on Me/Way Over There (1960)
Tamla 54034 Shop Around/Who's Loving You? (1960)
Tamla 54036 Ain't It Baby/The Only One I Love (1961)
Tamla 54044 Broken-Hearted/Mighty Good Lovin' (1961)
Tamla 54048 You Gotta Pay Some Dues/I Can't Believe (1961)
Tamla 54053 What's So Good about Goodbye?/I've Been Good to You (1962)
Tamla 54059 I'll Try Something New/You Never Miss a Good Thing (1962)
Tamla 54069 Way Over There/If Your Mother Only Knew (1962)
Tamla 54073 You've Really Got a Hold on Me/Happy Landing (1962)
Tamla 54078 A Love She Can Count On/I Can Take a Hint (1963)
Tamla 54083 Mickey's Monkey/Whatever Makes You Happy (1963)
Tamla 54089 Gotta Dance to Keep from Crying/Such Is Love, Such Is Life (1963)
Tamla 54092 The Man in You/Heartbreak Road (1964)
Tamla 54098 I Like It Like That/You're So Fine and Sweet (1964)
Tamla 54102 That's What Love Is Made Of/Would I Love You (1964)
Tamla 54109 Come On Do the Jerk/Baby Don't You Go (1964)
Tamla 54113 Ooo Baby Baby/All That's Good (1965)
Tamla 54118 The Tracks of My Tears/A Fork in the Road (1965)
Tamla 54123 My Girl Has Gone/Since You Won My Heart (1965)
Tamla 54127 Going to a Go-Go/Choosey Beggar (1965)
Source: Jay Warner, *American Singing Groups.*

Miracles, Carl Hogan & (New York)

Personnel Carl Hogan (lead), John Brisbane (tenor), Jerry Moore (tenor), Ronnie Bright (baritone), Irving Lee Gail (bass)

Notes

Carl Hogan and the Miracles formed in 1956 in Manhattan. Hogan had been an original member of the Valentines before they recorded. He was also the Carl of Charles and Carl who recorded for Bobby Robinson's Red Robin label.

Bass Irving Lee Gail sang with the Vocaltones, the Pretenders, and the Jones Boys. He spent some time with the Cadillacs as well. Ronnie Bright sang with the Valentines and with an ad hoc group, the Crystals, who backed up Sam Hawkins on "Gone."

The record by this group, I Love You So/Your Love was the second single issued by Fury Records.

Discography

Fury 1002/1003 I Love You So/Your Love (1957)
Sources: Donn Fileti, liner notes with the Relic CD *Fury*; Phil Groia in *Bim Bam Boom* 7.

Modern Red Caps (Philadelphia)

Personnel George Tindley (tenor), Billy Taylor (baritone), George Grant, Romaine Brown, Damita Jo DuBlanc

Notes

George Tindley had been a member of the Red Caps for only a year when he formed a competitive group in 1960, the Modern Red Caps. The Modern Red Caps would eventually be joined by George Grant, former lead of the Castelles who recorded for Grand. Tindley sang lead for the Dreams, who had recorded R&B classics for the Savoy label of Newark, New Jersey.

This took place when several members of the Red Caps left that group for various reasons. Romaine Brown and Damita Jo DuBlanc left to do their own thing; Tindley, as mentioned above, left to form the Modern Red Caps. Steve Gibson of the Red Caps continued to maintain a Red Caps group for several years following this change.

George Grant and Billy Taylor had been with the Castelles, Ink Spots, and Orioles. Taylor had also spent time with Philadelphia's Cobras.

Discography

Smash 1768 I Couldn't Care Less/Done Being Lonely (1962)
Rowax 801 They Can Dream/Don't You Hear Them Laughing? (1963)
Penntowne 101 Free/Never Kiss a Good Man Goodbye (1965)
Swan 4243 Golden Teardrops/Never Too Young (1966)
Source: Pete Grendysa and Marv Goldberg in *Yesterday's Memories* 5.

Mohawks (Philadelphia)

Personnel Fred "Weasel" Cohen (lead), Charles Williams

Notes

Cohen also sang for the Buddies and Teddy and the Twilights.

Discography

Val-Ue 211 I Got a Gal/Bewitched (1960)
Source: Liner notes with the Dee Jay Jamboree CD *Philadelphia Doo Wop Sound.*

Mondellos (Pittsburgh, Calif.)

Personnel Alice Jean Wilton (lead), Ron Lawson (tenor), Charles Jackson (tenor), Gary Williams (d) (baritone), Ollie McClay (bass)

Notes

The Mondellos were formed in Pittsburgh, California, by Charles Jackson and Ollie McClay while both attended junior college. Gary Williams, a friend of Jackson's who also attended the same junior college, got together with the others each day to sing in the school cafeteria. They soon decided to form a vocal group.

Jackson and McClay sang in a church choir with Ronald Lawson. It was Lawson who told them about a classmate, Alice Jean Wilton, and she completed the formation of the Mondellos. At this point, the group was integrated; Gary Williams was white and the other four were black.

They practiced and rehearsed for several months, appearing at school dances and assemblies as well as other local functions. When they felt ready to record, they called on Ray Dobard at the Music City recording facilities. Dobard told them he could not use them at that time. Through a friend, they next called on Don Barksdale. Barksdale, both a disc jockey and the owner of Rhythm Records, signed them to a contract. "One Hundred Years from Today" and "Come Back Home" were released on Rhythm Records in 1957.

The Mondellos were used by Barksdale as a backup group for many of their single artists. Their records were the best-sellers on the Rhythm label. Unfortunately, due to terrible distribution at Rhythm, none of their discs met their potential.

While the group was touring in northern California, they had a terrible automobile accident. Gary Williams was killed and McClay was badly injured, and the group was inactive for a few months as a result. When they were ready, they replaced Williams with Robert Fields (also from Pittsburgh, Calif.).

The rest of their recordings were done at one session in San Francisco. The group received a small payment for the session, but no royalties ever came their way.

According to an article in *R&B Magazine* by Bob Ferlingere, in an interview of Charles Jackson, Aladdin Records of Los Angeles tried to purchase the Mondellos' contract from Rhythm. Barksdale, however, would not allow this to happen because he wanted Aladdin to hire him as their business manager. Dootone too wanted the Mondellos but this too never came to pass.

The Mondellos split up in 1958 after Jackson was drafted and Lawson joined the air force.

Discography

Rhythm 102 Come Back Home/100 Years from Today (w/A. J. Wilton) (1957)
Rhythm 105 Never Leave Me Alone/Over the Rainbow (w/Y. McClay) (1957)
Rhythm 106 That's What I Call Love/Daylight Savings Time (w/Rudy Lambert) (1957)
Rhythm 109 Happiness Street/Hard to Please (w/Rudy Lambert) (1957)
Rhythm 114 My Heart/That's What I Call Love (w/Rudy Lambert) (1958)
Sources: Rip Lay, liner notes with the Rhythm LP *Rhythm & Blues Classics*; Bob Ferlingere in *R&B Magazine* 6–7; Dennis Leonis, liner notes with the Rhythm CD *Remembering Rhythm Records.*

Monitors (New Orleans)

Personnel Robert Kidd (lead), Vontell Lane (tenor), Adolph Smith (tenor), Clarence Phoenix (baritone), William Tircuit (bass)

Notes

This group first got together in New Orleans in 1952, calling themselves the Mellow-Drops, playing bars and clubs in the New Orleans vicinity. Finally they were discovered by Imperial's Dave Bartholomew. Bartholomew got them a session on November 15, 1954. Imperial released "The Crazy Song" and "When I Grow Too Old to Dream" by the Mellow Drops later that year.

For some forgotten reason, the group decided to change their name to the Monitors. They met and backed up Shirley and Lee one day. The producer that day was Eddie Mesner of Aladdin Records. That session eventually led to a session for the Monitors with Aladdin. Kidd was the usual lead, but he was unable to make the Monitors session with Aladdin and Vontell Lane filled in. Four tunes were recorded at the one session they had with Aladdin—only two were used.

The Aladdin disc did well locally but received little support from the label, and they next called on Specialty Records in 1956.

While this group had been the Mellow Drops on Imperial and was renamed the Monitors and the Señors, it's curious that despite their Louisiana origin, they recorded for the Sue label in New York and for California's Imperial, Aladdin, and Specialty labels!

The Monitors' first session for Specialty was held in December 1956 and their first release on that label occurred in January 1957. It did well locally in New Orleans, but Specialty's Art Rupe failed to support it. Similarly, their two other Specialty releases had good local support but no push.

Differences between group members began to surface and they split up in 1958. Later that year, Vontell Lane and Billy Tircuit got together with Johnny Meyers, Simon Washington, and Elaine Edwards to form the Moonbeems (a.k.a. Moonbeams).

Discography

Aladdin 3309 Tonight's the Night (AS)/Candy-Coated Kisses (AS) (1956)
Specialty 595 Our School Days (CP)/I've Got a Dream (AS) (1957)
Specialty 622 Closer to Heaven (CP)/Rock & Roll Fever (RK) (1957)
Specialty 636 Mama Linda (AS)/Hop Scotch (AS) (1958)
Source: William Tircuit, interview by Marv Goldberg in *DISCoveries,* March 1998.

Monotones (Newark, N.J.)

Personnel Charles Patrick (lead), Warren Davis (1st tenor), George Malone (2d tenor), Warren Ryanes (baritone), Frank Smith (bass), Bass John Ryanes (bass)

Notes

The Monotones came together in a housing project in Newark, New Jersey, in 1955. The group was a sextet, since it had two basses. They sang in a church choir together with Cissy Houston, Whitney's mother, as their director. Dionne and Dee Dee Warwick, cousins of Monotones' lead Charles Patrick, were in this choir as well.

On learning that Charles's brother James was cutting records with the Kodaks, the Monotones got serious themselves and cut a demo of a song they had written, "Book of Love." They brought the demo to Hull/Mascot who liked it and released it in 1957. It went through the roof and continues to sell, forty years later, in the 1990s.

Charles Patrick also sang with the Terracetones on Apt.

Discography

Mascot 124 Book of Love/You Never Loved Me (1957)
Argo 5290 Book of Love/You Never Loved Me (1958)
Argo 5301 Tom Foolery/Zombi (1958)
Argo 5321 The Legend of Sleepy Hollow/Soft Shadows (1958)
Argo 5339 Fools Will Be Fools/Tell It to the Judge (1959)
Hull 735 Reading the Book of Love/Dream (1960)
Hull 741 Daddy's Home but Mamma's Gone/Tattletale (1961)
Sources: Pete Grendysa, liner notes with the Chess CD boxed set *Chess Rhythm & Roll*; Marv Goldberg in *Big Town Review* 1.

Montereys (Bronx, N.Y.)

Personnel Dean Barlow (lead), Ed "Sonny" Jordan (tenor), Bill Lindsay (tenor), Waldo Champen (bass)

Notes

This group began right after Dean Barlow and the Bachelors faded. They have been called that group's immediate successor.

Barlow sang lead for the Crickets as well as the Bachelors.

Lindsay was a member of the Crickets, Cadillacs, Starlings, and Twilighters.

Champen sang with the Five Delights, Moodmakers, Bachelors, Cadillacs, and others. Barlow and Champen were back together again in the 1990s, singing with the Morrisania Revue.

Discography

Onyx 513 Dearest One (DB/BL)/Through the Years (EJ) (1957)
(UNR) Angel (BL)/Tell Me Why (DB)
Sources: Dean Barlow and Waldo Champen, interview by the author; Donn Fileti, liner notes with the Relic CD/LP *Onyx.*

Montereys (Brooklyn, N.Y.)

Personnel John Randazzo (lead), Tony Giordano (1st tenor), Billy Schalda (2d tenor), Rich Torelli (baritone)

Notes

All group members attended New Utrecht High School. This Montereys group formed in 1961.

One of their teachers knew of a teacher at another school, Don Del Seni, who wanted to record. In 1962, they would cut a tune by Don Dell and the Montereys. The group was displeased with this disc because Del Seni's tunes were Elvis oriented and were sung in the style of Dion and the Belmonts.

In 1963, they signed with Blast Records and cut several tunes, but the British invasion was happening and this marked the end of the Montereys.

Discography

Blast 219 Face in the Crowd/Step Right Up (1963)
Source: Bob Diskin in *Record Collector's Monthly* 50.

Moodmakers (Bronx, N.Y.)

Personnel Sonny Jordan (lead), Waldo Champen (1st tenor), Ray Figueroa (2d tenor), Eddie Stokes (baritone), Danny Levy (bass) (d)

Notes

The Moodmakers formed following the demise of the Five Delights on Unart and Abel in 1960. They are sometimes referred to as the second configuration of the Abel group. Doug Ferrar and George Rosa were gone and were replaced by Ray Figueroa and Eddie Stokes.

Discography

Bambi 800 Delores (EJ)/Dream a Dream (EJ/WC) (1961)
Source: Waldo Champen, interview by the author, July 15, 1994.

Moonbeems/Moonbeams (New Orleans)

Personnel Simon Washington (lead), Elaine Edwards (1st tenor), John Meyers (2d tenor), Vontell Lane (baritone), William Tircuit (bass)

Notes

This was one group, despite the fact that records were released by two different names on two labels. The Sapphire recording was heard by Chess/Checker's Paul Gayten, and he liked it enough to convince Chess/Checker management to lease it from Sapphire. When the masters got to Checker's Chicago facility for pressing, those responsible at Checker innocently misspelled the group's name! The Checker disc was released in January 1959. Disagreements in the group later that year forced them to disband.

In 1961, many of the Monitors original members got together and renamed themselves again to the Señors. The group members were Billy Tircuit, Adolph Smith, Vontell Lane, and Clarence Phoenix. Their new lead singer was Adolph's brother, Milton Smith.

Billy Tircuit sang with the Mellow Drops on Imperial, the Monitors on Aladdin and Specialty, and the Señors on Sue. Vontell Lane was also with the Monitors and the Señors.

Discography

Sapphire 1052 Cryin' the Blues (SW)/Teenage Baby (SW) (1958)
Checker 912 Cryin' the Blues (SW)/Teenage Baby (SW) (1959)
Sources: Lou Welsch and Wes Wendell in *Time Barrier Express* 2, no. 1; William Tircuit, interview by Marv Goldberg in *DISCoveries,* March 1998.

Moonglows (Cleveland, Ohio)

Personnel Bobby Lester Dallas (d) (lead), Harvey Fuqua (1st tenor), Danny Coggins (2d tenor), Prentiss Barnes (bass)

Notes

Robert Dallas and Harvey Fuqua began singing in 1950 in Louisville, Kentucky, while in high school. They left Kentucky in 1952 after performing as a duet, to record in Cleveland. This is where they met Prentiss Barnes and Danny Coggins. They initially called themselves the Crazy Sounds.

The group toured the Midwest, performing in nightclubs. They eventually met a friend of disc jockey Alan Freed and an audition was arranged. Freed loved what he heard at the audition and scheduled a recording session on his Champagne label.

On Champagne, Danny Coggins sang with the group. Alan Freed changed their name from Crazy Sounds to Moonglows, playing on the name of his popular Moondog show in Cleveland. "I Just Can't Tell No Lie" and "I've Been Your Dog" were recorded for Champagne in February 1953. Interestingly, Alan Freed was in the studio when "I Just Can't Tell No Lie" was recorded and for some reason played drums using a local telephone book. (This story was told to Arnie Amber in an interview with Bobby Lester in 1981.)

Realizing no success with the Champagne recording, Coggins left to pay closer attention to his gas station business. Prentiss Barnes then recruited an old friend, Alexander "Pete" Graves.

Champagne folded later in 1953. Freed brought the Moonglows to Chance that same year, where they began their illustrious career. After being with Chance for some time and realizing minimal compensation and attention, Lester and Fuqua endeavored to find another recording company with whom they might structure a more "equitable" financial arrangement. They met with the Chess brothers in Chicago. Chess was familiar with their "product" and was happy to sign them.

"Sincerely," released in October 1954, was the Moonglows' first Chess release. The disc was very successful and consequently the Chess brothers intuitively released another disc by the group. For this recording, they chose to release it by the Moonlighters on the Chess subsidiary label, Checker.

After many successful years, releases, and appearances, in 1959 Bobby Lester decided to call it a career. A new Moonglows was formed that consisted of Chester Simmons (d) (formerly of the Rainbows), Chuck Barksdale (Dells), Reese Palmer (Marquees), James Nolan (Marquees/Rainbows), Marvin Gay (later Gaye), and Harvey Fuqua. Lester's decision was forced by problems with alcohol and drugs.

(Note: In several accounts, this new group is mistakenly identified as the Spinners. This is simply not true!)

The above group did not stay together very long. Fuqua left for Detroit, where he became manager and producer for Motown and eventually married Berry Gordy's sister. Gaye went on to a very successful solo career and he too married a sister of Berry Gordy. Gaye died in 1985.

In 1964, Pete Graves formed a new Moonglows group, which included George Thorpe and Bearle Easton (both from the Velvets), who recorded for Red Robin.

Bobby Lester passed away in the early 1980s.

In Silvani's *Collecting Rare Records*, bass Prentiss Barnes is referred to as Prentice Bonds.

Discography

Champagne 7500 I Just Can't Tell No Lie/I've Been Your Dog (1952)
Chance 1147 Whistle My Love/Baby Please (1953)
Chance 1150 Just a Lonely Christmas/Hey Santa Claus (1953)
Chance 1152 Secret Love/Real Gone Mama (1954)
Chance 1156 I Was Wrong/Ooh Rockin' Daddy (1954)
Chance 1161 219 Train/My Gal (1954)
Chess 1581 Sincerely/Tempting (1954)
Chess 1589 Most of All/She's Gone (1954)
Chess 1598 Foolish Me/Slow Down (1955)
Chess 1605 Starlite/In Love (1955)
Chess 1611 In My Diary/Lover Love Me (1955)
Chess 1619 We Go Together/Chickie Um Bah (1956)
Chess 1629 See Saw/When I'm with You (1956)
Chess 1646 Over and Over Again/I Knew from the Start (fast) (1956)
Chess 1646 Over and Over Again/I Knew from the Start (slow) (1956)
Chess 1651 Don't Say Goodbye/I'm Afraid the Masquerade Is Over (1956)
Chess 1661 Please Send Me Someone to Love/Mr. Engineer (1957)
Chess 1669 Confess It to Your Heart/The Beating of My Heart (1957)
Chess 1681 Too Late/Here I Am (1957)
Chess 1689 Soda Pop/In the Middle of the Night (1958)
Chess 1701 This Love/Sweeter Than Words (1958)
Chess 1705 Ten Commandments of Love/Mean Old Blues (1959)
Chess 1717 I'll Never Stop Wanting You/Love Is a River (1959)
Chess 1738 Unemployment/Mama Loocie (1959)
Chess 1770 Beatnick/Junior (1960)
Chess 1811 Penny Arcade/Blue Velvet (1961)
Sources: M. Caldarulo in *Harmony Tymes* 3; Arnie Amber in *Goldmine,* July 1981.

Moonlighters (Cleveland, Ohio)

Personnel Bobby Lester (lead), Harvey Fuqua (1st tenor), Pete Graves, Prentice Barnes

Notes

In Bob Pruter's *Doowop . . . The Chicago Scene* and in several other resources, it is stated that the Moonlighters were Lester and Fuqua, a duo rather than a vocal group. According to Marv Goldberg, on two of the songs below, it's the full group; on the other two it's a duet of Lester and Fuqua.

The Chess brothers apparently did this to capitalize on the group's success with their initial recording for Chess, "Sincerely."

Discography
Checker 804 So All Alone/Shoo-Do-Be-Do (1954)
Checker 813 Hug and a Kiss/New Gal (1954)
Source: Bob Pruter, *Doowop . . . The Chicago Scene.*

Moroccos (Chicago)

Personnel Sollie McElroy (d) (lead), Melvin Morrow (d) (tenor), Ralph Vernon (tenor), George "Kemp" Prayer (d) (baritone), Fred Martin (d) (bass)

Notes
Members of this group were neighborhood friends who originally got together in 1952.

George Kemp was born George Prayer but his stepfather's name was Kemp. He used this as his stage name. It was Prayer who took the initiative to meet the United people and had the group audition. United liked them and signed them to a contract. They recorded their first single as the Four Chimes, with Lawrence Johnson and Norman Bradford then in the group.

When they next recorded as the Moroccos, original tenor Lawrence Johnson was gone and lead Norman Bradford had to make himself scarce. Prayer recruited Ralph Vernon for the first session recording as the Moroccos, but they still needed another lead. At this same time, Sollie McElroy had left the Flamingos and became available to the Moroccos.

The first session with McElroy (January 1955) went very well and yielded "Pardon My Tears." Later that year the Moroccos joined a tour of Australia.

They returned to Chicago in February 1956. In July, Prayer joined the marines. He was replaced by Calvin Baron and the next session (with Baron) produced "What Is a Teenager's Prayer," "Bang Goes My Heart," "Sad Sad Hours," and "The Hex."

Calvin Baron later joined the Cosmic Rays. Prayer and Morrow later hooked up with Pirkle Lee Moses, formerly of the El Dorados, to form the Major-Minors (Scatt). McElroy sang with the Nobles and the Chaunters.

Discography
United 188 Pardon My Tears/Chicken (1955)
United 193 Somewhere over the Rainbow (SM)/Red Hots and Chili Mac (RV) (1955)
United 204 Bang Goes My Heart/What Is a Teenager's Prayer (1956)
United 207 Sad Sad Hours/The Hex (1957)
Salem 1014 Believe in Tomorrow (not the Moroccos) (1957)
B&F 1347 What Is a Teenager's Prayer/Bang Goes My Heart
Source: Bob Pruter, *Doowop . . . The Chicago Scene.*

Moroccos, Little Joe & His (Detroit)

Personnel Joseph Harris, Jimmy Binion, Billy Brye, Gene McClain, Paul Wooten

Notes

This group got together in Detroit in 1957. They recorded their only single, Trouble in the Candy Shop/Bubble Gum, for the Bumble Bee label.

Discography

Bumble Bee 500 Trouble in the Candy Shop/Bubble Gum (1958)
Source: Donn Fileti, liner notes with the Relic CD *LuPine Label.*

Morrisania Revue (Bronx, N.Y.)

Personnel Dean Barlow (lead), Bobby Mansfield (lead), Lillian Leach (lead), Eugene Tompkins (tenor), Waldo Champen (tenor), Sammy Fain (baritone), Arthur Crier (bass)

Notes

This group was formed to reunite friends from their neighborhood in the Morrisania section of the Bronx from the early 1950s.

It was produced by Hal Keshner and Arthur Crier. Crier was experienced in record production, having worked for the Motown organization at the height of its popularity. On vibes is Joe Boyce, formerly with Chicago's Dozier Boys.

The following is the lineup of the groups these Morrisania Revue members originally sang with in the 1950s:

Dean Barlow: Crickets, Bachelors, Montereys
Waldo Champen: Supremes, Bachelors, Montereys, Cadillacs, Five Delights, Moodmakers
Arthur Crier: Chimes, Halos, Mellows, Craftys
Sammy Fain: Limelighters
Lillian Leach: Mellows
Bobby Mansfield: Wrens
Eugene Tompkins: Limelighters

Source: Mitch Rosalsky, liner notes with the Vintage Rocker CD *Morrisania Review.*

Motions (Queens, N.Y.)

Personnel Tommy Tucker (lead), Joe Basta (1st tenor), Edde Povenelli (2d tenor), Larry Angel (baritone)

Notes

This group was formed in Brooklyn in 1958. Following many hours of practice, they made many appearances and established a local following.

They had originally called themselves the Emotions. When their manager got them a recording contract with Laurie Records, label management, realizing there was another group calling themselves the Emotions (Flip), changed their name to Motions.

In a 1982 interview, Tommy Tucker stated that there was originally a girl in the Motions, but no one seemed to remember her name.

Their first and only record (of many tunes recorded) was released in 1961, but because Dion and the Belmonts and the Jarmels were hot at the time, the Motions received little attention and decided to call it quits.

Discography

Laurie 3112 Mr. Night/Make Me a Love (1961)
Sources: Ken Berger in *Story Untold* 8; Ed Engel, liner notes with the Ace CD *Laurie Doo Wops.*

Muskateers (Detroit)

Personnel Norman Thrasher, Noah Howell (tenor) Isaac Reese, Thearon Hill, ——— King

Notes

This group started singing around 1946, when attending the Garfield Intermediate School. Henry Booth, later of the Royals and Midnighters on Federal, was an original member. The group appeared locally at Detroit-area clubs.

Following these appearances and much practice, they wandered over to Joe Von Battle's record shop to perform for him. He liked them enough to record them on his JVB label as the Serenaders. This disc was probably released sometime early in 1952. Their follow-up record, also circa early 1952, was released on Detroits' Roxy label. For this release, they were called the Muskateers.

The spelling of the group's name was always Musketeers. The spelling Muskateers was an unfortunate error that appeared on the label.

The Muskateers were also the Scooters, Royal Jokers, Serenaders, and the Royals on Venus.

On Swing Time 347 (M-A-Y-B-E-L-L/Ain't Gonna Cry No More), the Muskateers once again became the Serenaders.

Discography

Roxy 801 Goodbye My Love/Love Me Till Your Dying Day (1952)
Swing Time 331 Deep in My Heart for You/Love Me till Your Dying Day (1952)
Sources: Sal Mondrone in *Bim Bam Boom* 1; Marv Goldberg in *DISCoveries.*

Mystics (Brooklyn, N.Y.)

Personnel Phil Cracolici (lead), Bob Ferrante (1st tenor), George Galfo (2d tenor), Al Cracolici (baritone), Al Contrera (bass)

Notes

The Brooklyn-born Mystics initially intended to sign with George Goldner. However, they tore up the contract because they were displeased with what the Goldner organization planned on providing them with.

Soon after, friends, the Tetra Neons, also from Brooklyn, gave them much needed advice concerning the recording business and the legalities involved with it.

They eventually signed with Laurie, and in 1959 "Hushabye" was released.

In the fall of 1959, lead Phil Cracolici left and was replaced by Jerry Landis (Paul Simon). Simon was on "All Through the Night," which was five voices in unison. Simon left shortly thereafter to pursue other activities.

Jay Traynor became the new lead and was with the Mystics for "White Cliffs of Dover," "Blue Star," and "Over the Rainbow."

Traynor became disillusioned with the other members and left. Eddie Falcone replaced him in 1961 and stayed briefly.

Ralph Lizano became the next lead. He did "Sunday Kind of Love" and "Darling I Know."

Late in 1961, the Mystics disbanded.

Discography

Laurie 3028 Hushabye/Adam and Eve (1959)
Laurie 3038 Don't Take the Stars/So Tenderly (1959)
Laurie 3047 All through the Night/To Think Again of You (1960)
Laurie 3058 Blue Star/White Cliffs of Dover (1960)
Laurie 3086 Goodbye Mister Blues/Star-Crossed Lovers (1961)
Laurie 3104 Sunday Kind of Love/Darling I Know Now (1961)
Source: Bob Diskin in *Record Collector's Monthly* 52.

Native Boys (Watts, Calif.)

Personnel Fred Romain (lead), Vince Weaver (1st tenor), Harry Rosemond, Charles Mathis, Edward Saunders (bass)

Notes

The Native Boys, originally known as the Mellowtears, began as four students in high school. They wrote their own songs and somehow hooked up with Maxwell Davis, A&R man for Aladdin and Modern Records.

Aladdin turned them down but Modern gave them a one-record contract. When the record was released, the label called the group the Native Boys. Group members were totally unaware of this change. Apparently a Modern employee named them after the title of their first song for Modern, "Native Girl."

No royalties and poor sales from "Native Girl" caused Rosemond to leave the group and enter Notre Dame University. He was replaced by George LeBrune.

A year later they went to Jake Porter at Combo Records. Porter groomed them and later recorded and released Strange Love/Cherrlyn, which had fair sales on the East Coast.

Romain sang lead on "Strange Love," "Tears," and "I've Got a Feeling." Vince Weaver leads on "Cherrlyn." LeBrune sings lead on "Valley of Lovers." Romain handles bass chores on this side.

In order to take advantage of the good response in the East, Porter released their remaining sides soon after the success of "Strange Love." These follow-ups, however, didn't meet with the similar acceptance. By 1956 the guys drifted apart.

After the Native Boys dissolved, Fred Romain sang lead with the Ebbtones on "I've Got a Feeling" on Lee Rupe's Ebb label. With him were friends Danny Christian, George Hollis, and Kenneth Byle.

Vince Weaver joined the Flairs in 1957, singing lead for the fading group. He rejoined them again in 1960 when the group was spelling their name Flares.

Discography
Modern 939 Native Girl/It Won't Take Long (1954)
Combo 113 Strange Love/Cherrlyn (1955)
Combo 115 Tears/When I Met You (1955)
Combo 119 Laughing Love/Valley of Lovers (1956)
Combo 120 I've Got a Feeling/Oh Let Me Dream (1956)
Source: Marv Goldberg in *DISCoveries.*

Naturals (Philadelphia)

Personnel Raymond Finizio, Michael Travaglio, Ronald Laudadio, Ronald Adams

Notes
This group was sometimes referred to, and sometimes recorded as, the Four Naturals. They recorded using both names for the Red Top label.

Discography
Red Top 113 How Strange/Blue Moon (1958)
Hunt 325 How Strange/Blue Moon (1959)
Source: Bob Bosco in *Echoes of the Past* 38.

Neons (New York)

Personnel Frank Vignari (lead), Jeff Pearl (2d tenor), Ronald Derin (baritone), Norman Isaacoff (bass)

Notes
This group started in junior high school when they were fifteen and sixteen. (It should be noted that this is both the Tetra and Gone group.) The Neons auditioned for Old Town and Jubilee among others. The majority of the labels they auditioned for seemed to like them but turned them away because they did not have original material.

The Neons were one of the first white groups to record rock 'n' roll. Their "Angel Face" played on Alan Freed's New York radio show incessantly. The Tetra label was owned by Alan Freed's stepdaughter, Toni "Bruce."

Raoul Cita played piano for the Neons during the "Angel Face" session.

In a group interview published in *Record Exchanger* one of them related that they thought their last recording was issued on Gone Records because George Goldner had financed the recording and Gone was one of his labels.

Discography

Tetra 4444 Angel Face/Golden Dreams (1956)
Tetra 4449 Road to Romance/My Chickadee (1957)
Gone 5090 Angel Face/Golden Dreams (1960)
Source: Art Turco in *Record Exchanger*, winter 1972.

New Yorkers Five (Bronx, N.Y.)

Personnel "Rocky" Smith (lead), J. R. Bailey (lead), Johnny Darren (2d tenor), Shelly Dupont (baritone), Fred Barksdale (bass)

Notes

Bailey appeared with the New Yorkers Five after his stint with the Crickets and before he appeared with the Cadillacs. He and Fred Barksdale are stepbrothers.

Wes Forbes, Lou Peebles, and Sylvester Hopkins also sang with this group.

The Danice label was owned by Lexie Hanford of the Flaps Record Shop in Harlem at 125th Street and 7th Avenue. But the label had financial difficulties and could not support the disc, which did nothing.

Shelly Dupont sang lead for the Calendars on Tribune, while Barksdale sang with the Solitaires, Chances, Dean Barlow and the Crickets, Sam Hawkins and the Crystals, and the Cadillacs.

Discography

Danice 801 Cha Cha Baby/Gloria My Darling (1955)
Source: Phil Groia, *They All Sang on the Corner.*

Nic Nacs (Los Angeles)

Personnel Mickey Champion, Ty Terrell, Billy Richard, Roy Richard, Bobby Nunn (bass)

Notes

This was actually the Robins recording for Johnny Otis after they had been with Savoy Records. They recorded the cuts below for RPM Records in 1950. Also recorded at this same session for RPM was "I'm Telling You Baby," which was not released until 1983 on the Ace LP *Johnny Otis Presents.*

The Nic Nacs had female vocalist Mickey Champion, a Little Esther soundalike, singing lead for the group on these recordings.

Discography

RPM 313 Found Me a Sugar Daddy/Gonna Have a Merry Christmas (1950)
RPM 316 Found Me a Sugar Daddy/You Didn't Want My Love (1950)
RPM 342 Found Me a Sugar Daddy/Gonna Have a Merry Christmas (1961)
Source: Ray Topping, liner notes with the ACE 1983 LP *Johnny Otis Presents.*

Nitecaps (Detroit)

Personnel Eugene "Ronnie" Hamilton (lead), Bob Hamilton, Al Hamilton (a.k.a. Al Kent), Freddie Price

Notes

This was another group attempting to sound like the popular artists of the day—Clyde McPhatter, Nolan Strong, and Jackie Wilson.

The 1989 Detour LP *The Five Keys and the Nitecaps* contained some previously unreleased material, including "Oh You Sweet Girl," "You're Gonna Be Sorry," and "Snap, Crackel, and Pop."

The Hamiltons were brothers.

Discography

Groove 0134 A Kiss and a Vow/Be My Girl (1955)
Groove 0147 Tough Mama/Sweet Thing (1956)
Groove 0158 Bamboo Rock and Roll/You May Not Know (1956)
Groove 0176 In Each Corner of My Heart/Let Me Know Tonight (1956)
Source: Marv Goldberg et al., liner notes with the Detour LP *The Best of Doo Wop Classics.*

Nite Riders (Philadelphia)

Personnel "Doc" Starkes (lead), Harry Crafton, Melvin Smith (tenor), Jimmy Johnson, Joe Sewell

Notes

The Nite Riders was a typical late 1940s–early 1950s group—a self-contained ensemble that played instruments and vocalized. Initially, Melvin Smith was the only vocalist behind the others' instrumentation. In the 1950s, they did more harmonizing.

Discography

Apollo 460 Women and Cadillacs/Say Hey (1954)
Apollo 466 Rags/Doctor Velvet (1954)
Riff 101 In My Dream/
Sound 128 Never/Tell the Truth (1955)
Teen 114 Apple Cidar/Way in the Middle of a Dream (1955)
Teen 118 Got Me a Six-Button Benny/Don't Hang Up the Phone (1955)
Sources: Donn Fileti's liner notes with the Relic LP *Best of Apollo*; George Moonoogian in *Whiskey, Women, and . . .* ; Ferdie Gonzalez, *Disco-File.*

Nobles (New Haven, Conn.)

Personnel Dicky Bernardo, Joey Kakulis, Sal Tramachi, Pat Cosenza

Notes

The Nobles' release on Tee Gee was also issued as by the Timbers.

Klik only distributed locally, and when the Nobles' recording started to do well, Klik management (Marty Kugell) went to Gone Records for national distribution. End 1098, School Bell/Schoolday Crush, was distributed by Gone. Nick Delano sang lead for the Nobles on the End recording.

According to the liner notes with Finbarr's CD *$10,000 Worth of Doo Wop*, before recording "Poor Rock and Roll" for Klik, the Nobles "were probably a quintet and recorded as 'Nicky and the Nobles.' "

Discography

Klik 305 Poor Rock and Roll/Ting-A-Ling (1958)
Tee Gee 101 Oops Oh Lawdy/Stop Crying (1958)
End 1098 School Bells/Schoolday Crush (1961)
Sources: James Cullinan, Liner notes with the Finbarr CD *$10,000 Worth of Doo Wop*; Donn Fileti, liner notes with the Relic CD *Groups of Klik Records*.

Nobles (Chicago)

Personnel Leroy Kennard (lead), Wilbur Foster, Joseph "Cool Breeze" Jones, Wayne Morris, Horace Noble

Notes

This group had a smooth sound and sang modern harmony, which always enabled them to win neighborhood shows and contests.

John Burnett, who replaced Al Benson as head of Parrot, owned the Sapphire label.

Discography

Sapphire 151 Do You Love Me/Who's Been Riding My Mule (1956)
Source: Bob Pruter, *Doowop . . . The Chicago Scene.*

No-Names (Philadelphia/Camden, N.J.)

Personnel Doug Gordon (lead), Lew Lewis (1st tenor), Skippy Rohan (2d tenor), Bobby Love (baritone)

Notes

When deejay Jerry Blavat asked the group about their name, they stated that they had no name at the time of recording, and No-Names was ultimately chosen.

Although they came from south Philadelphia and Camden, New Jersey, south Philadelphia was really their turf.

Their one disc did nothing and they soon disbanded.

Discography

Guyden 2114 Love/Jam (1964)
Source: Bob Hyde and Bob Bosco, liner notes with the Jamie/Guyden CD *Doop Doo Wah.*

Norfolk Jazz Quartet (Norfolk, Va.)

Personnel Otto Tuston (lead), James "Buddy" Butts (tenor), Delroy Hollins (baritone), Len Williams (bass)

Notes

The Norfolk Jazz Quartet formed just after World War I, touring the black circuit.
Williams and this group later sang as the Virginia Four on Decca.

The names shown above are the 1921 group provided by George Moonoogian in
the May-June 1991 issue of *Record Collector's Monthly*. It was discussed in the
article entitled "Wax-Fax."

Other members who performed with this group include Isaiah Sessoms, Raymond
Smith, Norman "Crip" Harris, and Melvin Colden [sic].

Discography

Decca 7333 Swinging the Blues/Tell That Broad (1937)
Decca 7349 Just Dream of You/Shim Sham Shimmy at the Cricket's Ball (1937)
Decca 7383 Ha Ha Shout/What's the Matter Now (1937)
Decca 7443 Suntan Baby Brown/Beedle De Beedle De Bop Bop (1938)
Okeh 4318 Jelly Roll Blues/Southern Jack (1938)
Okeh 4345 Monday Morning Blues/Standing on the Corner (1938)
Okeh 4366 Wide Wide World/Preacher Man Blues (1939)
Okeh 4380 Cornfield Blues/Big Fat Mamma (1939)
Okeh 4391 Blues That Drove Man to Ruins/Going Home Blues (1939)
Okeh 8007 Strut Miss Lizzie/My Mammy (1940)
Okeh 8019 Honey, God Bless Your Heart/When I Walked Up (1940)
Okeh 8022 Wang Wang Blues/Get Hot (1940)
Okeh 8028 I Could Learn to Love You (instrumental) (1940)
Okeh 8034 Every Ship Must Find a Harbor (instrumental) (1941)
Paramount 12032 Raise a R-U-K-U-S Tonight/Ain't It a Shame (1942)
Paramount 12054 Sad Blues/Stop Dat Band (1942)
Paramount 12055 Quartette Blues/Dixie Blues (1942)
Paramount 12218 Pleasing Blues/Jelly Roll's First Cousin (1942)
Paramount 12453 Queen St. Rag/Louisiana Bo Bo (1943)
Paramount 12844 Please Give Me Some of That/Oh What's the Matter Now (1943)
Sources: George Moonoogian in *Record Collector's Monthly,* May–June 1991; Ray
Funk and Doug Seroff, liner notes with the *Human Orchestra* LP; Ferdie Gonzalez,
Disco-File.

Notes (Philadelphia)

Personnel Ray McIlwain (1st tenor), Boyd Beks (2d tenor), Dave Wilson (baritone), Clarence Beks (bass)

Notes

This group got together in 1953, initially singing in local nightspots. Group members
all grew up in Philadelphia and went to school together.

With the exception of Clarence Beks, they were all twenty-three years of age when
they cut "Don't Leave Me Now."

Discography

Capitol 3332 Don't Leave Me Now/Cha Jezebel (1956)

MGM 12338 Trust in Me/Round and Round (1956)
Source: Sleeve to Capitol Records *Don't Leave Me Now* and *Cha Jezebel.*

Nuggets (Los Angeles)

Personnel Herman Pruitt (lead), Lorenzo Robert Adams (1st tenor), Billy Storm (tenor), Stewart Crunk (baritone), Sidney Dunbar (bass)

Notes

This Nuggets group was an offshoot of the Calvanes, who recorded earlier for Dootone. Pruitt, Crunk, Dunbar, and Adams were from the Calvanes, and Pruitt had also been with the Youngsters/Tempters. This is not the Nuggets who recorded for Capitol.

Warren Joyner also sang with the Nuggets later on.

Discography

RCA 7930 Angel on the Dance Floor (HP)/Before We Say Goodnight (HP) (1961)
RCA 8031 Just a Friend/Cap Snapper (1962)
Sources: Bob Ferlingere, *Discography of R&B and R&R Vocal Groups*; Rick Whitesell and Marv Goldberg in *Yesterday's Memories* 11; Jeff Kreiter, *Group Collector's Record Price Guide.*

Nutmegs (New Haven, Conn.)

Personnel Leroy Griffin (d) (lead), James "Sonny" Griffin (1st tenor), Jimmy "Coco" Tyson (2d tenor), Billy Emery (baritone), Leroy McNeill (d) (bass)

Notes

The group began as the Lyres (J&G) and later became the Rajahs (Klik). James and Leroy Griffin are brothers.

Billy Emery sang lead on the Lyres' original recording of "Ship of Love." At Herald, Leroy Griffin recorded the popular version.

Late in 1954 the group went to New York and met the DuDroppers, who introduced them to Al Silver of Herald Records. He liked them and signed them to record. Before this took place, he renamed them the Nutmegs after the Connecticut nickname. In March 1955 "Story Untold" was released and by July had reached number two on the R&B charts. The Crew Cuts version outsold the Nutmegs' disc. In August, "Ship of Love" was released. It sold well, although not as well as "Story Untold."

Appearing at a show at New York's Apollo in the fall, the Nutmegs were accused of performing an obscene dance on stage. Alan Freed learned of this and eliminated them from his forthcoming show. When he was provided with clarification of what actually occurred, he reinstated them and all was forgiven.

Billy Emery left late in 1955 to marry. Sonny Washburn, who had been with the Five Dukes on Atlas, joined. Washburn came from Providence, Rhode Island, replacing "Coco" Tyson, who left to concentrate on gospel music.

Eddie Martin, later a 1st tenor for the Nutmegs, also sang for the Five Satins. Martin joined, replacing "Sonny" Griffin, at the time of their 1959 recording of "My Story."

In 1962, Leroy Griffin's nephew, Harold Janes (referred to in Jay Warner's *American Singing Groups* as James), joined the group. Griffin died in a factory accident. Harold Janes later became lead for the revival Nutmegs group.

Discography

Herald 452 Make Me Lose My Mind/Story Untold (1955)
Herald 459 Rock Me/Ship of Love (1955)
Herald 466 Whispering Sorrows/Betty Lou (1955)
Herald 475 Key to the Kingdom/Gift o' Gabbin' Woman (1956)
Herald 492 A Love So True/Comin' Home (1956)
Herald 538 My Story/My Sweet Dream (1959)
Tel 1014A Dream of Love/Someone Somewhere (1960)
Herald 574 Crazy 'Bout You/Rip Van Winkle (1962)
Sources: Charlie Horner, liner notes with the Collectables CD *Nutmegs*; Donn Fileti, liner notes with Relic's *Herald* CD/LP; Jay Warner, *American Singing Groups*.

Nu Tones (Los Angeles)

Personnel Don Ballard (lead), Joe Green (tenor)

Notes

Joe Green was the lead voice on the Nu Tones "Beans and Greens" cut. Green is remembered by Combo owner Jake Porter as a real nice guy. This disc sold well in the immediate Los Angeles area but was not too much to talk about elsewhere.

Discography

Hollywood Star 797 Goddess of Love/Niki, Niki, Mambo (1954)
Hollywood Star 798 Believe/Annie Kicked the Bucket (1954)
Hollywood Star 798 Believe/You're No Barking Dog (1955)
Cholly (N/A) Believe/Eternally (1956)
Combo 127 At Midnight/Beans 'n' Greens (1956)
Source: Donn Fileti, liner notes with the Relic LP *Best of Combo Records–1*.

Octaves (Philadelphia)

Personnel Moses Oliver (lead), James Baker (tenor), Paul Davis (tenor), Harmon Bethea (baritone)

Notes

This group formed after the dissolution of the Cap-Tans vocal group. Bethea had decided to return to his roots and sing more spiritual tunes. With one addition, the group above became, briefly, the Progressiveaires. They then became the Octaves and recorded one disc for entrepreneur Lillian Claiborne who led them, and Bethea, back to secular music.

Discography

DC Open Up and Let Me In (1954)
Source: Dave Hinckley and Marv Goldberg in *Yesterday's Memories* 8.

O' Jays (Canton, Ohio)

Personnel Eddie Levert (lead), Walter Williams, Bobby Massey, William Powell (d), Bill Isles

Notes

The O'Jays originally formed at McKinley High School in Canton, Ohio, in 1958. They were originally known as the Triumphs and made many local appearances at the YMCA and record hops.

A local songwriter gave them some material to try out. They took this original material with them to audition for Syd Nathan at King. Nathan loved them and changed their name to the Mascots. They recorded two discs for King as the Mascots, which were released much later and did absolutely nothing.

Later, Cleveland disc jockey Eddie O'Jay took an interest in the group. He renamed them after himself and did what was necessary to ensure success. He sent them to the West Coast and hooked them up with Little Star Records and former Dootones member H. B. Barnum. Barnum worked with the group, enhancing their delivery and style, and recorded four singles with them. Barnum then made a deal with Imperial. By mid-1963, they finally had some success with their recordings, adopting the Drifters' style. Meanwhile, in 1960, Isles had departed and the group chose to remain a quartet.

They had some great sides with Imperial, and their next step led to Bell Records. Their first Bell effort did well, but their follow-ups could not maintain that excellence.

They soon hooked up with the Gamble and Huff songwriting team and they had their first Gamble and Huff tune released on the Chess affiliate, Neptune. Despite the fact that four of their six Neptune sides charted, the Chess affiliate folded just after Leonard Chess passed away. Gamble and Huff set up the Philadelphia International label. The O'Jays joined Gamble and Huff in 1972, despite Motown's similar request.

Tenor Sammy Strain (Chips and the End Imperials) joined the O'Jays later, replacing the deceased William Powell.

Discography

Little Star 124 Crack Up Laughing/How Does It Feel (1963)
Little Star 126 Love Is Wonderful/What's the Word, Do the Bird (1963)
Apollo 759 Can't Take It/Miracles (1963)
Imperial 5942 Crack Up Laughing/How Does It Feel (1963)
Imperial 5976 Lonely Drifter/That's Enough (1963)
Imperial 66007 The Storm Is Over/Stand Tall (1964)
Imperial 66025 I'll Never Stop Loving You/My Dearest Beloved (1964)
Imperial 66037 Lovely Dee/You're on Top (1964)

Imperial 66076 Girl Machine/Oh How You Hurt Me (1964)
Imperial 66102 Lipstick Traces/Think It Over, Baby (1965)
Imperial 66121 Whip It On Me, Baby/I've Cried My Last Tear (1965)
Imperial 66131 Let It All Out/You're the One (1965)
Imperial 66145 It Won't Hurt/I'll Never Let You Go (1965)
Imperial 66162 Pretty Words/I'll Never Forget You (1965)
Imperial 66177 No Time for You/A Blowing Wind (1966)
Imperial 66197 Stand In for Love/Friday Night (1966)
Imperial 66200 Lonely Drifter/That's Enough (1966)
Minit 32015 Hold On/Working on Your Case (1967)
Bell 691 I Dig Your Act/I'll Be Sweeter Tomorrow (1967)
Bell 704 Look Over Your Shoulder/I'm So Glad I Found You (1968)
Bell 737 The Choice/Going Going Gone (1968)
Bell 749 I Miss You/Now That I Found You (1968)
Bell 770 That's Allright/Don't You Know a True Love (1969)
Neptune 12 One Night Affair/There's Someone (1969)
Neptune 18 Branded Bad/You're the Best Thing since Candy (1969)
Neptune 20 Without the One You Love/There's Someone Waiting (1969)
Neptune 22 Deeper/I've Got the Groove (1970)
Neptune 31 Looky Looky/Let Me in Your World (1970)
Neptune 33 Christmas Ain't Christmas/Just Can't Get Enough (1970)
Bell 378 Look Over Your Shoulder/Four for the Price of One (1973)
Source: Jay Warner, *American Singing Groups.*

Olympics (Compton, Calif.)

Personnel Walter Ward (lead), Eddie Lewis (tenor), Charles Fizer (d) (baritone), Walter Hammond (bass)

Notes

This group was formed in 1954 when the members were in high school, as the Challengers. They recorded one disc for Melatone (1002), I Can Tell/The Mambo Beat. They soon learned that there was another Challengers group; this is when they became the Olympics.

In June 1958 Jesse Belvin introduced them to Demon Records management. It wasn't long before their "Western Movies" was released on Demon.

Melvin King temporarily replaced Fizer. When Fizer returned, they moved to Arvee Records. Hammond then left and was replaced by Thomas Busch. Busch was with the Olympics for one disc. It was then that Melvin King joined permanently.

They cut their first Arvee single in December 1959 and then the hits came less often. They returned to Demon and cut records for both Tri-Disc and Duo-Disc. They realized some success and in 1965 once again began looking for a new label. They wound up at the Warner Bros. subsidiary Loma.

Fizer was killed at the time of the Watts rioting in California. He was replaced by Mack Starr, who was Julius McMichael, formerly of the Paragons. He had relocated from Brooklyn to Los Angeles.

After Melvin King left, the Olympics remained a trio until 1970 when Kenny Sinclair, who had been with the Six Teens on Flip in the 1950s, joined them. Eddie Lewis and Walter Ward were cousins.

Discography

Demon 1508 Western Movies/Well (1958)
Demon 1512 Dance with the Teacher/Everybody Needs Love (1958)
Arvee 562 Private Eye/Hully Gully (1959)
Arvee 595 The Slop/Big Boy Pete (1960)
Arvee 5006 Shimmy Like Kate/Working Hard (1960)
Arvee 5020 Dance by the Light of the Moon/Dodge City (1960)
Arvee 5023 Little Pedro/Bullfight (1961)
Arvee 5031 Dooley/Stay Where You Are (1961)
Arvee 5044 The Stomp/Mash Them Taters (1961)
Titan 1718 Chicken/Cool Short (1961)
Arvee 5051 Everybody Like to Cha Cha Cha/Twist (1962)
Arvee 5056 Baby, It's Hot/The Scotch (1962)
Tri Disc 106 The Bounce/Fireworks (1963)
Tri Disc 107 Dancin' Holiday/Doin' the Slauson Shuffle (1963)
Tri Disc 110 Bounce Again/A New Dancin' Partner (1963)
Tri Disc 112 The Broken Hip/So Goodbye (1963)
Duo Disc 104 The Boogler–1/The Boogler–2 (1964)
Duo Disc 105 Return of Big Boy Pete/Return of the Watusi (1964)
Arvee 5073 What'd I Say–1/What'd I Say–2 (1964)
Arvee 6501 Big Boy Pete '655/Stay Where You Are (1965)
Loma 2010 I'm Comin' Home/Rainin' in My Heart (1965)
Loma 2013 Good Lovin'/Olympic Shuffle (1965)
Loma 2017 Baby I'm Yours/No More Will I Cry (1965)
Mirwood 5504 We Go Together/Secret Agents (1966)
Mirwood 5513 Mine Exclusively/Secret Agents (1966)
Mirwood 5523 Western Movies/Baby, Do the Philly Dog (1966)
Mirwood 5525 The Duck/The Bounce (1966)
Mirwood 5529 The Same Old Thing/I'll Do a Little Bit More (1966)
Mirwood 5533 Big Boy Pete/Hully Gully (1967)
Parkway 6003 Good Things/Lookin' for a Love (1968)
Jubilee 5674 The Cartoon Song/Things That Made Me Laugh (1969)
Sources: Liner notes with the DCC *Olympics* CD; Marv Goldberg and Dave Hinckley in *Yesterday's Memories* 10; Ferdie Gonzalez, *Disco-File.*

Opals (New York)

Personnel Earl Wade (lead), Marty Brown (tenor), Johnny Hopson (tenor), Teddy Williams (bass)

Notes

This group was first known as the Crystals on the obscure Luna label. That release on Luna was the only release on Charles Lopez's label! They then moved to Apollo and recorded the disc below.

Bobby Williams was a late addition.
Following the Opals, Earl Wade joined the Cadillacs.

Discography

Apollo 462 My Heart's Desire/Oh but She Did (1954)
Source: Donn Fileti, liner notes with the Relic CD *Apollo-1.*

Orchids (Chicago)

Personnel Gilbert Warren (lead), Robert Nesbary (d) (2d tenor), Charles —————,
Buford Wright (d) (bass)

Notes

Warren was with the Five Thrills before forming the Orchids on Parrot Records.

It is rumored that the Orchids on King is the same group as the Orchids on Parrot with a different lead singer. However, this is never mentioned in Bob Pruter's discussion of the Orchids in *Doowop . . . The Chicago Scene.* It is also interesting that the Gentlemen on Apollo sound very much like the Orchids on King.

The Orchids broke up after Parrot folded in 1956.

In 1993, several unreleased Orchids recordings were found in the Vee Jay archives, including "Please Don't Leave Me," "Fine Sweet Woman," "Met a Girl on the Corner," and a wonderful ballad, "You Have Two, I Have None."

Discography

Parrot 815 Newly Wed (BW)/You're Everything to Me (1955)
Parrot 819 I Can't Refuse/You Said You Loved Me (1955)
Source: Bob Pruter, *Doowop . . . The Chicago Scene.*

Orients (Queens, N.Y.)

Personnel Al Mickens (lead), Alfred Seaman (1st tenor), James Davis (2d tenor),
Ernest Seaman (baritone), Clayton Williams (bass)

Notes

Alfred and Ernest Seaman were twins.

Just before recording for Laurie, they recorded as the Gents on Times Square Records.

James Davis also sang with the Sunbeams (Herald, Acme) and the Colonairs (Ember).

Discography

Laurie 3232 Queen of Angels/Shouldn't I? (1961)
Source: Ed Engel, liner notes with the Ace and Sparkletone *Laurie* CD.

Original Cadillacs (New York)

Personnel Earl Carroll (lead), Charlie Brooks (tenor), Earl Wade (baritone), Bobby Phillips (bass)

Notes

This was one of the splinter groups resulting from the division of the Cadillacs, caused by internal strife in 1957. It happened that both groups remained with Josie. The Earl Carroll group renamed themselves the Original Cadillacs.

On Josie 915, the Original Cadillacs' last recording, the group changed personnel as follows: "Junior" Glanton, Roland Martinez, Earl Wade, and Bobby Phillips

Discography

Josie 821 Lucy/Hurry Home (1957)
Josie 829 Buzz-Buzz-Buzz/Yea Yea Baby (1958)
Josie 915 I'll Never Let You Go/Wayward Wanderer (1959)
Sources: Sal Mondrone, Tom Luciani, Steve Flam, and Ralph Newman in *Bim Bam Boom* 5; Pete Grendysa in *Goldmine.*

Original Drifters (New York)

Personnel David Baughan (tenor), Gerhart Thrasher (tenor) Jimmy Lewis (baritone), Bill Pinkney (bass)

Notes

Following the end of the old Drifters regime, Pinkney attempted to reassemble the classic group. McPhatter, of course, was unavailable, as his solo career was doing quite well. The Thrasher brothers returned and David Baughan was there for a time; this is the rationale for their calling themselves the Original Drifters.

In 1964, Bobby Lee Hollis replaced Baughan and Jimmy Lewis replaced Andrew Thrasher. Bobby Hendricks was added at this time as well.

David Baughan returned in 1958, following a stint with the Checkers on King, the Drifters, and the Harps on Savoy.

Discography

Fontana 1956 Don't Call Me/Do the Jerk (1964)
Veep 1264 The Masquerade Is Over/I Found Some Lovin' (1966)
Game 394 Ol' Man River/Millionaire (1971)
Source: Marv Goldberg and Mike Redmond in *Record Exchanger* 18.

Original Four Aces (Fort Worth, Tex.)

Personnel James Ruben Franks (lead), Otha Jackson, Algia Pickett, George Smith

Notes

The original group, the Four Aces, met in 1944 and were from Fort Worth, Texas. Prior to recording, they moved to California.

They were a self-contained group, playing instruments as well as vocally harmonizing.

Other members of this group, mentioned in other biographical discussions, are as follows: Orvan Lyles, David McAuley, Robert Parker, and Charles Holmes.

When Decca's white Four Aces became popular, this group was forced o change their name to the Original Four Aces.

Discography

Big Town 112 Release (JF)/Whose Arms Are You Missing (AP) (1954)
Big Town 118 I Can See an Angel/You Were My First Affair (OJ) (1955)
(Note: "Release" is the same tune as Engelbert Humperdinck's "Please Release Me.")
Source: M. Goldberg in *DISCoveries*, October 1998.

Orioles (Baltimore, Md.)

Personnel Sonny Til (d) (lead), Alexander Sharp (d) (tenor), George Nelson (d) (baritone), Johnny Reed (bass)

Notes

This group, considered one of the cornerstones of rhythm and blues, along with the Ravens, started in Baltimore in 1946 as the Vibranaires.

Luckily, they were heard by Deborah Chessler in a nightclub and she became their manager. She arranged for them to appear on Arthur Godfrey's show, and Jerry Blaine then signed them to his It's a Natural label, later renamed Jubilee.

In 1950, an auto accident killed their guitarist and friend Tommy Gaither, who was replaced by Ralph Williams. At the same time (early 1951), Charlie Harris was added as pianist. Williams would sometimes sing, but Harris did not. George Nelson left in 1953, just before the "Crying in the Chapel" session, due to alcohol problems. He was replaced by John Gregory Carroll.

The original group broke up in 1955. Til then recruited the Regals because the modern harmony they sang fascinated him. The personnel lineup that follows was the same as the Regals minus lead singer Harold "Sonny" Wright: Billy Adams (baritone), Gerald Holmes (bass), Albert "Diz" Russell, and Jerry Rodriguez. This group recorded as the Orioles on the last session with Jubilee. They went to Vee Jay with Til and recorded eight sides in 1956. Before the year was out, this new Orioles group dissolved.

George Nelson died of an asthma attack in 1959. Alex Sharp died of a heart attack in 1969 while appearing with an Ink Spots group.

In 1962, Til formed still another Orioles with Gerald Gregory (Spaniels), Delton McCall (Dreams-Savoy), and Billy Taylor (Castelles). This was the group that recorded for the Charlie Parker label.

Another incarnation appeared in 1971 with Til teaming up with Mike Robinson and Bobby Thomas from the Vibranaires. Clarence Young was the fourth member.

In 1978 Til structured a tribute LP to the Orioles with Pepe Grant (tenor), Larry Reed (baritone), and George Holmes (bass). Sonny died in 1981.

Discography

It's a Natural 5000 It's Too Soon to Know/Barbra Lee (1948)
Jubilee 5000 It's Too Soon to Know/Barbra Lee (1948)

Jubilee 5001 Dare to Dream/To Be to You (1948)
Jubilee 5001 Lonely Christmas/To Be to You (1948)
Jubilee 5002 Please Give My Heart a Break/It Seems So Long Ago (1949)
Jubilee 5005 Tell Me So/Deacon Jones (1949)
Jubilee 5008 I Challenge Your Kiss/Donkey Serenade (1949)
Jubilee 5009 A Kiss and a Rose/It's a Cold Summer (1949)
Jubilee 5016 So Much/Forgive and Forget (1949)
Jubilee 5017 Lonely X-Mas/What Are You Doing New Year's Eve (1949)
Jubilee 5018 Would You Still Be the One in My Heart/Is My Heart Wasting Time? (1950)
Jubilee 5025 At Night/Every Dog-Gone Time (1950)
Jubilee 5026 Moonlight/I Wonder When (1950)
Jubilee 5028 You're Gone/Everything They Said Came True (1950)
Jubilee 5031 Rather Have You under the Moon/We're Supposed to Be Through (1950)
Jubilee 5037 I Need You So/Goodnight Irene (1950)
Jubilee 5040 I Cross My Fingers/Can't Seem to Laugh Anymore (1950)
Jubilee 5045 Oh Holy Night/The Lord's Prayer (1950)
Jubilee 5051 I Miss You So/You Are My First Love (1951)
Jubilee 5055 Pal of Mine/Happy Go Lucky Local Blues (1951)
Jubilee 5057 Would I Love You/When You're a Long, Long Way from Home (1951)
Jubilee 5061 I'm Just a Fool in Love/Hold Me, Squeeze Me (1951)
Jubilee 5065 Don't Tell Her What's Happened to Me/Baby Please (1951)
Jubilee 5071 When You're Not Around/How Blind Can You Be? (1951)
Jubilee 5074 Trust in Me/Shrimp Boats (1951)
Jubilee 5082 It's Over Because We're Through/Waiting (1952)
Jubilee 5084 Barfly/Better Times, Better Times, Better Times (1952)
Jubilee 5092 Don't Cry Baby/See See Rider (1952)
Jubilee 5102 You Belong to Me/I Don't Want to Take a Chance (1952)
Jubilee 5107 I Miss You So/Till Then (1953)
Jubilee 5108 Teardrops on My Pillow/Hold Me, Thrill Me, Kiss Me (1953)
Jubilee 5115 Bad Little Girl/Dem Days (1953)
Jubilee 5120 I Cover the Waterfront/One More Time (1953)
Jubilee 5122 Crying in the Chapel/Don't You Think I Ought to Know? (1953)
Jubilee 5127 In the Mission of St. Augustine/Write and Tell Me Why (1953)
Jubilee 5134 There's No One But You/Robe of Calvary (1954)
Jubilee 5137 Secret Love/Don't Go to Strangers (1954)
Jubilee 5143 Maybe You'll Be There/Drowning Every Hope I Ever Had (1954)
Jubilee 5154 Chapel in the Moonlight/Thank the Lord, Thank the Lord (1954)
Jubilee 5161 If You Believe/Longing (1954)
Jubilee 5172 Runaround/Count Your Blessings Instead of Sheep (1954)
Jubilee 5177 I Love You Mostly/Fair Exchange (1955)
Jubilee 5189 I Need You Baby/That's When the Good Lord Will Smile (1955)
Jubilee 5221 Please Sing My Blues Tonight/Moody over You (1955)
Jubilee 5231 Angel/Don't Go to Strangers (1956)
Vee Jay 196 Happy Till the Letter/I Just Got Lucky (1956)
Vee Jay 228 For All We Know/Never Leave Me Baby (1956)
Vee Jay 244 Sugar Girl/Didn't I Say (1957)

Abner 1016 Sugar Girl/Didn't I Say (1958)
Jubilee 5363 Tell Me So/At Night (1959)
Jubilee 6001 Crying in the Chapel/Forgive and Forget (1959)
Jubilee 5384 The First of Summer/Come on Home (1960)
Charlie Parker 211 Secret Love/The Wobble (1962)
Charlie Parker 212 In the Chapel in the Moonlight/Hey! Little Woman (1962)
Charlie Parker 213 Back to the Chapel Again/Lonely Christmas (1962)
Charlie Parker 214 What Are You Doing New Year's Eve/Don't Mess (1962)
Charlie Parker 215 It's Too Soon to Know/I Miss You So (1963)
Charlie Parker 216 Write and Tell Me Why/Don't Tell Her What's Happened to Me (1963)
Charlie Parker 219 I Miss You So/Hey! Little Woman (1963)
Sources: Marv Goldberg, *Whiskey, Women and . . .* 12–13; Pete Grendysa, liner notes with the Oriole CD boxed set *Orioles: The Jubilee Recordings.*

Orlandos (Whitaker, Pa.)

Personnel Ronnie Williams (lead), Roger Randolph (1st tenor), Nate Thomas (2d tenor), John Crowder (baritone), Wallace "Skinhead" Berry (bass)

Notes

The Orlandos first got together in 1954 in a junior high school on the outskirts of Pittsburgh. Membership changed often but finally the group assembled the right combination of voices for smooth harmony. When they recorded their only disc for Cindy, their average age was fifteen!

They performed at record hops and made many other local appearances.

Pittsburgh disc jockey Jay Michael arranged for the group to record two tunes for George Goldner's Cindy label in 1957. Their "Cloudburst" did well in the Pittsburgh tristate area.

As a result of their recording, they appeared at many clubs in the Pittsburgh area. Although they received no royalties from their Cindy recording, they would earn $300 to $500 per date for their appearances.

Lack of success prompted the Orlandos to disband in 1960.

Discography

Cindy 5006 Cloudburst/Old MacDonald (1957)
Source: Carl Janusek in *Echoes of the Past* 27.

Orlons (Philadelphia)

Personnel Steve Caldwell, Marlena Davis, Shirley Brickley, Rosetta Hightower

Notes

(Note: Regarding the Orlons, two reliable sources provide two differing accounts, which follow.)

1. While Davis, Brickley, and Hightower were singing in Shirley Brickley's home at a high school reunion the three were having, neighbor Steve Caldwell telephoned

to ask what record she was playing. When she said that the music was live vocalizing, Caldwell joined them and later recorded with them (J. P. Byrne's liner notes with the Orlons' first Cameo/Parkway LP *Wah-Watusi*).

2. Shirley, Rosetta, and Marlena were singing at Overbrook High School and were heard by another Overbrook student, Steven Caldwell. He introduced himself and his baritone voice to the girls and the four began practicing and finally recorded. (Jay Warner, *American Singing Groups.*)

In any event, by 1961 they had auditioned for Kal Mann at Cameo/Parkway and were signed immediately. They backed up "Dee Dee" Sharp on her "Mashed Potato Time" and in 1962 they had their own hit with "Wah Watusi."

The next several years brought them much success, but in 1964 the British Invasion simply swept them aside.

In 1966, they moved to Calla Records and in 1967 to ABC.

Discography

Cameo 198 I'll Be True/Heart Darling Angel (1961)
Cameo 211 Happy Birthday 21/Please Let It Be Me (1962)
Cameo 218 The Wah-Watusi/Holiday Hill (1962)
Cameo 231 Don't Hang Up/The Conservative (1962)
Cameo 243 South Street/Them Terrible Boots (1963)
Cameo 257 Not Me/My Best Friends (1963)
Cameo 273 Crossfire/It's No Big Thing (1963)
Cameo 287 Bon-Doo-Wah/Don't Throw Your Love Away (1963)
Cameo 295 Shimmy Shimmy/Everything Nice (1964)
Cameo 319 Rules of Love/Heartbreak Hotel (1964)
Cameo 332 Goin' Places/Knock Knock (1964)
Cameo 346 I Ain't Coming Back/Envy (1964)
Cameo 352 I Ain't Coming Back/Come On Down Baby Baby (1965)
Cameo 372 I Can't Take It/Don't You Want My Lovin' (1965)
Cameo 384 Envy/No Love but Your Love (1965)
Sources: Lynn McCutcheon in *Echoes of the Past* 17; liner notes with Cameo LP 1020, *The Wah Watusi;* J. P Byrnes, liner notes with the *Wah Watusi* LP; J. Warner, *American Singing Groups.*

Ospreys (New York)

Personnel Ronald Council (lead), Maurice Williams (1st tenor), Jackson Thompson (2d tenor), "Tarzan" ——— (baritone), John Miro (bass)

Notes

Around 1955 one member from each of five groups that had been competing in a battle of the groups got together and formed their own group, which represented the best voice from each—the Ospreys.

In 1957, after practicing extensively, they felt ready to record. They auditioned for Herald, but because of their friendship with the Bobbettes, who had recommended them to Atlantic, label management quickly arranged for an audition. Ultimately they chose Atlantic.

The Ospreys recorded four songs at their session with Atlantic. Curiously, the cuts that they didn't care for were the ones that were released on the Atlantic subsidiary, East West.

They provided Chuck Willis with backup vocals on "What Am I Living For" and "Hang Up My Rock and Roll Shoes."

The group broke up in 1958.

Discography
East West 11 It's Good to Me (all)/Do You Wanna Jump, Children (RC) (1958)
Source: Marv Goldberg in *Yesterday's Memories* 12.

Ovations (New Jersey)

Personnel Richard Kelly (lead), Paul Sanzone, Mario Venancio, Augusto Ottilie

Notes

In 1960, Laurie Records subsidiary Andie Records released "My Lullabye" and "Whole Wide World." This was purchased in 1962 by Old Town's Hy Weiss, who rereleased "My Lullabye" on his Barry label (101) with an alternate flip side, "The Day We Fell in Love."

In Ed Engel's liner notes with Ace's *Laurie Vocal Groups—The Sixties Sound,* Engel tells the reader not to mistake this group with the Ovations who recorded on Crystal Ball Records and the other group with this same name.

Discography
Andie 5017 My Lullabye/Whole Wide World (1960)
Barry 101 The Day We Fell in Love/My Lullabye (1962)
Sources: Ed Engel, liner notes with the Ace CD *Laurie Vocal Groups*; Bob Hyde, liner notes with the Ace CD *Old Town Doo Wop-2.*

Ovations (Queens, N.Y.)

Personnel Sammy Cantos (lead), Gary Willet (1st tenor), Ron Buchter (2d tenor), Greg Malmeth (baritone/bass)

Notes

According to Gordon Skadberg's liner notes accompanying Sequel's *Jubilee/Josie-5* CD, this group recorded several masters for writers Neil Levenson and Steve DuBoff, who sold them to Jubilee and Josie's manager, Jerry Blaine. Blaine released two of these tunes, "Who Needs Love" and "Remembering," on his Josie label in 1964.

The Ovations later released That's How Girls Get Boys/Remember Lori as by Little Romeo and the Casanovas (Ascot 2192).

Discography
Josie 916 Who Needs Love?/Remembering (1964)
Source: Gordon Skadberg, liner notes with the Sequel CD *Jubilee/Josie R&B Vocal Groups-5.*

Oxfords, Darrell & (New York)

Personnel Jay Siegel (lead), Hank Medress (1st tenor), Warren Schwartz, Fred Kalkstein

Notes

This group was also known as the Tokens, Buddies, Coeds, and Four Winds on Swing. In the 1950s, Medress formed the Tokens with Neil Sedaka.

After Sedaka left, Medress recruited Jay Siegel, Warren Schwartz, Fred Kalkstein, and Mike Lewis and renamed the group Darrell and the Oxfords. Their "Picture in My Wallet" was a hit in New York but didn't do as well elsewhere.

In 1959, Medress revived the Tokens and in 1960 they enjoyed national success with "Wimoweh–The Lion Sleeps Tonight."

Discography

Roulette 4174 Picture in My Wallet/Roses Are Red (1959)
Roulette 4230 Can't You Tell?/Your Mother Said No (1960)
Source: Dave Morosoil, liner notes with the Sequel CD *A Whiter Shade of Doo Wop.*

Pace Setters (Chicago)

Personnel Stacy Steele Jr. (1st tenor), Joe Brackenridge (tenor), Willie C. Robinson (2d tenor), Henry Brackenridge (baritone), Charles Johnson (bass)

Notes

This group, man for man, had also been the Cascades. With a minor personnel adjustment, they were also the Von Gayles.

Andrew Robertson joined replacing Willie C. Robinson.

Discography

Mica 503 My Ship Is Coming In (Tomorrow)/Victim of Loneliness (1966)
Source: Bob Pruter, *Doo Wop . . . The Chicago Scene.*

Packards (New York)

Personnel Milton Turner (lead), Clive Williams (1st tenor), Bill Fredericks (2d tenor), Bill Atkins (baritone), Ray Hayes (bass)

Notes

According to the *Old Town Doo Wop-2* CD liner notes, "Ding Dong," "Dream of Love," and "Ladise" were all recorded at the same session. Shortly thereafter Old Town's Hy Weiss purchased these masters.

The same liner notes mention the rumor that the group also recorded as the Tremaines.

Discography

Pla-Bac 106 Ladise/My Doctor of Love (1956)
Paradise 105 Dream of Love/Ding Dong (1956)
Source: Bob Hyde, liner notes with the Ace CD *Old Town Doo Wop-2.*

Palmer Brothers (Pawtucket, R.I.)

Personnel Clarence Palmer (lead), Dick Palmer, Ernest Palmer

Notes

This was a versatile, self-contained group that became very popular in New York's Harlem at the Connie's Inn nightclub during the 1930s. The Palmer Brothers were the first harmony ensemble to sing with the big bands of the decade. According to the Jive Bombers article in *Story Untold* 7, the Palmer Brothers were billed as the Cabaliers when they sang with Cab Calloway and his band.

In late 1949 Ernest and Dick Palmer decided that they had had enough of show business and retired. Dick Palmer, however, soon came out of retirement to perform with the Beavers and the Blenders.

In 1949, Clarence Palmer began singing with the Sparrows group with the Big Al Sears Band. In the 1950s, he formed the Jive Bombers and recorded with Savoy through the decade.

Discography

Melotone 13334 Ghost of the Freaks/Hokus Pokus (1934)
Decca 389 Disappointed in Love/Rhythm Lullaby (1935)
Variety 531 Big Boy Blue/Margie (1937)
Variety 574 Sundays Are Reserved/Having a Ball (1937)
Okeh 6501 Who Calls?/The Mermaid Song (1941)
Source: Roy Adams in *Story Untold* 7; Alan Lee in *Yesterday's Memories* 8.

Palms/Five Palms (Chicago)

Personnel Wilbur Williams (lead), Willie Young (tenor), Murrie Eskridge (1st tenor), O. C. Perkins (2d tenor), M. C. Ward (bass)

Notes

This group got together in 1954 while the members were still in high school. They would always practice and rehearse original material put together by O. C. Perkins (Perk). Soon they were appearing at local functions in Phoenix, a suburb of Chicago, as well as talent shows. They were heard by a talent scout who was affiliated with no label but connected with many. They auditioned for United and label management liked them. They were quickly scheduled to record.

They first released "Darling Patricia" as Artie Wilkins and the Palms on States 157 in 1956. Their next release was as the Five Palms on States 163 in 1957.

In 1957 the Palms did Edna/Teardrops on United 208 and Teardrops/Little Girl of Mine on sister label States 163.

There were excellent tunes in the can, but United/States never released them—especially Diane, which the group felt was exceptional. The organization was preoccupied with the Danderliers and paid little or no attention to the Palms.

In 1957, with United going out of business, the group parted and eventually evolved into the Ballads, whose members were Perkins, Eskridge, O.C. Logan, and Willie Logan. The Logans were brothers and later became Willie Logan and the Plaids. Perkins and Eskridge would later be part of the Sheppards who did "Island of Love."

In late 1958, the Logan brothers left and, with three former members of the Decca Bel-Aires ("My Yearbook"), formed the Sheppards on Apex.

The following songs are unreleased: "I Knew I Had a Chance," "Diane," "One More Time," and "Love Is Nothing to Play With."

Discography

States 157 Darling Patricia/Please Come Back (1956)
States 163 Teardrops/Little Girl of Mine (as the Five Palms) (1957)
United 209 Edna/Teardrops (1957)
Source: Bob Pruter in *Record Collector's Monthly* 40.

Paradons (Bakersfield, Calif.)

Personnel West Tyler (d) (lead), Chuck Weldon (tenor), William Powers (baritone), Billy Myers (d) (bass)

Notes

The story of the Paradons began with the dreams of baritone William Powers. He and neighborhood friend Billy Myers decided to form a vocal group. There was a certain young woman in their neighborhood to whom they had identified themselves as Don Juans, or a pair of dons; hence their name!

After Myers and Powers decided to assemble a group, they brought in West Tyler and Chuck Weldon. Edward Scott was always available as a utility member. He would sing with the group when one of the members was ill or could not make a date. Scott would later sing with the group. All the members were high school friends at Bakersfield High School.

They began performing with appearances at local nightspots and on radio and TV shows. They were discovered while they were appearing at a local country music club and were introduced to Jackson and Madelon Baker of Milestone and Audio Arts Records. In January 1960, the Paradons had their first session with Milestone.

Their hit "Diamonds and Pearls" fared better on the pop charts than it did on the R&B lists. It afforded the group many live appearances as well as TV shows. "Diamonds and Pearls" was even sponsored by the Dr. Pepper soft drink organization. All this, but little in the way of financial reward.

The release of their second disc for Milestone, "Bells Ring," had been delayed due to songwriting arguments. Today, Powers claims to have written the tune, but each member claims to have had a hand in its composition—even Scott!

By the end of 1960, the Paradons signed with Warner Bros., where they stayed very briefly. Powers quit the group early in 1961 due to internal squabbling. The group was obviously in the initial stages of falling apart.

Discography

Milestone 2003 Diamonds and Pearls/I Want Love (1960)
Milestone 2005 Bells Ring/Please Tell Me (1960)
Warner Brothers 5186 So Fine, So Fine, So Fine/Take All of Me (1960)
Tuffest 102 Never Again/This Is Love (1961)
Milestone 2012 Bells Ring/Please Tell (1962)
Sources: Billy Vera, liner notes with the Rhino CD *Doo Wop Box 2*; Opal Nations in *DISCoveries.*

Paragons (Brooklyn, N.Y.)

Personnel Julius McMichael (d) (lead), Ben Frazier (1st tenor), Donald Travis (2d tenor), Rickey Jackson (baritone), Al Brown (bass)

Notes

Formed in 1956 while the majority of the group members were still in high school in Brooklyn, New York. By 1957, they had met Paul Winley, who signed them to record. They released the Winley/McMichael song "Florence," which became an East Coast classic.

Prior to his structuring the Winley label, Paul Winley, brother of Clovers bass Harold Winley, produced and arranged the songs for the Aladdin Dodgers from 135th Street in Harlem. He also wrote "Real Humdinger" for Aladdin's Five Pearls.

Several other local hits led to many nightspot appearances for the group. On their fifth release, "So You Will Know," ex-Rocketones and Townsmen lead Bill Witt joined and sang lead.

The *Paragons Meet the Jesters* LP, issued in 1959, became an R&B LP classic, immortalizing both groups. That same year the Paragons backed soloist Tommy Collins on "Doll Baby" (Winley 236).

On the WAR album, the group still consisted of Julius McMichael, Ben Frazier, Al Brown, Donald Travis, and baritone Ricky Jackson, who joined on Winley 240 (according to Jay Warner, *American Singing Groups).*

By 1960, McMichael had departed and was replaced by Alan Moore. The group was now with the Musicraft label. Despite the fact that they had changed labels, Winley obviously had some of their tunes left in the can and issued "Just a Memory" with a label that read, Mack Starr and the Paragons. Mack Starr was McMichael's new career name. He later sang with the Olympics. In the 1980s he was killed in a motorcycle accident.

By 1964, Glen Mosely sang with the Paragons at 2d tenor, Ernest Burnside was the new 1st tenor, Alan Moore was still performing lead chores, and Joseph Pitts was the baritone. This group stayed intact until the 1970s, when Witt rejoined and many other changes occurred.

Discography

Winley 215 Florence/Hey Little Schoolgirl (1957)
Winley 220 Let's Start All Over Again/Stick with Me Baby (1957)
Winley 223 Two Hearts Are Better Than One/Give Me Love (1957)
Winley 227 Twilight/The Vows of Love (1958)

Winley 236 Darling I Love You/Doll Baby (1959)
Winley 228 So You Will Know/Doll Baby (1960)
Musicraft 1102 Blue Velvet/Wedding Bells (1960)
Winley 250 Just a Memory/Kneel and Pray (1961)
Tap 500 If/Hey Baby (1961)
Tap 503 Begin the Beguine/In the Midst of the Night (1961)
Music Clef 3001 Time after Time (1963)
Music Clef 3002 Baby Take My Hand (1963)
Sources: Donn Fileti, liner notes with the Relic CD *Winley*; Jay Warner, *American Singing Groups.*

Parakeets (Newark/Elizabeth, N.J.)

Personnel Leroy Williams (d) (lead), James Pete Martin (tenor), Charles Hockaday (2d tenor), Preston Fields (d) (tenor), Gerald Highsmith (bass)

Notes

The Members of this group were all former high school glee club participants who decided to form a vocal group late in 1955.

The Parakeets were chosen to back Vic Donna on his Atlas recordings. Apparently the quintet was not happy with this arrangement and had Donna eliminate them from top billing on the disc.

Discography

Atlas 1068 I Have a Love/The Rain Starts to Fall (1956)
Atlas 1069 My Heart Tells Me/Yvonne (1956)
Atlas 1071 Teenage Rose/Silly and Sappy (1957)
Atlas 1075 Love Was a Stranger to Me/Count the Tears (1957)
Source: Donn Fileti, liner notes with the Relic LP *Best of Atlas/Angletone Vocal Groups-2.*

Parakeets (Washington, D.C.)

Personnel Homer Saunders (lead), John Burt (1st tenor), Charles Hockaday (2d tenor), Leroy Wright (baritone), Harold Brodgins (bass)

Notes

This group, which produced no 45 rpm singles, formed at Banneker Junior High School in 1952.

They appeared at many local shows and traveled to New York to appear at the Apollo Theater in Harlem. While in the big city, they also arranged for an audition with Atlantic Records.

Parakeets' tunes appeared only on the Roadhouse LP/CD *Candy Bar Boogie.*
Source: Les Moss, liner notes with the *Candy Bar Boogie* CD.

Paramonts (Washington, D.C.)

Personnel Ben Thomas (lead), Horace Logan (d) (1st tenor), Bill Jones (2d tenor), Jimmy Drake (baritone), Richard Fountain (bass)

Notes

This group's Ember release unfortunately occurred in 1963, when the Ember label was not doing well. Consequently, neither the group nor the release received any promotional support or attention.

Discography

Ember 1099 Shedding Teardrops/In a Dream (1963)
Source: Alan Lee in *Yesterday's Memories* 8.

Parliaments (Philadelphia)

Personnel Arnold Bennett (lead), Milton Harling (1st tenor), James Frazier (2d tenor), John Gore (baritone), Bobby Taylor (bass)

Notes

This vocal group began in junior high school around 1952 or 1953. They would sing in school hallways, restrooms, and other school locations conducive to vocalizing.

They originally called themselves the Imperials. Little Anthony, however, came along at that time with his Imperials and forced the group to choose a new name. Curiously, it was a pack of cigarettes (Parliaments) that assisted them with their choice.

Harling and Frazier later joined the Casinos, who recorded for the Maske label doing I'm Falling/Speedy. Both sang with the Carter Rays but never recorded with them.

Clarence Haskins joined later, as did Raymond Davis, Calvin Simon, Grady Thomas, and George Clinton.

Discography

Len 101 Don't Need You Anymore/Honey Take Me Home with You (1958)
Source: Donn Fileti, liner notes with the Len LP *Best of Len Records.*

Passionettes (New Haven, Conn.)

Personnel "Tootsie" Cannon, Maxine McNeill, Joan Smith, Ella Smith, Esther Peeples, Josephine Ross

Notes

Donn Fileti's liner notes with Relic's *Klik* CD state that Fred Parris managed this female sextet. The group featured Esther Peeples, sister of Lou Peeples of the Five Satins, and Maxine McNeill, sister of Leroy McNeill of the Nutmegs.

Parris brought them to Herald/Ember, where they recorded a tune in 1958 for the Herald label. Fileti doesn't say, but the Herald discography does not show their tunes "Bobby You" and "Next Spring." Therefore, no discography is reflected below.

The Passionettes name is also found on the label backing the Scarlets on "She's Gone" and "The Voice."

Source: Donn Fileti, liner notes with the Relic CD *Groups of Klik Records.*

Passions (Brooklyn, N.Y.)

Personnel Jimmy Gallagher (lead), Tony Armato (1st tenor), Albee Gallone (2d tenor), Vinnie Aceierno (baritone)

Notes

This group originated in the Bensonhurst section of Brooklyn in 1957. The majority of this original formation went on to become the Mystics. There were many other vocal groups between this first formation and the Passions. The Passions were actually in place in 1959. In August of that year, "Just to Be with You" was released (written by Paul Simon and Carole King). Because "Just to Be with You" hit big, it allowed the Passions to tour and play many live dates.

Following the group's second release, I Only Want You/This Is My Love, Aceierno was replaced by Lou Rotundo. Both of these tunes did quite well.

Audicon released many Passions recordings, but none other than "This Is My Love" did well. Audicon management was not conscientiously attending to their music business, and consequently there was no promotion or airplay for these other releases.

Joey O'Neill replaced Gallagher when he joined the service. Before their next recording, however, Gallagher came home on leave and the group was now a quintet. They signed with ABC in 1963.

In Sequel's *Jubilee/Josie-5* CD liner notes, the 2d tenor is referred to as Albie Galcone.

Discography

Audicon 102 Just to Be with You/Oh Melancholy Me (1959)
Audicon 105 I Only Want You/This Is My Love (1960)
Audicon 106 Gloria/Jungle Drums (1960)
Audicon 108 Beautiful Dreamer/One Look Is All It Took (1960)
Audicon 112 You Don't Love Me Anymore/Made for Lovers (1961)
Jubilee 5406 Lonely Road/One Look Is All It Took (1961)
Octavia 8005 I Gotta Know/Aphrodite (1962)
ABC 10436 The Bully/The Empty Seat (196)
Diamond 146 Sixteen Candles/The Third Floor (1963)
Sources: Liner notes with the Sparkletone CD *Laurie*; Bob Diskin in *Record Collector's Monthly* 48.

Pastels (Chicago)

Personnel Fred Buckley (lead), Norman Palm (1st tenor), Robert Randolph (tenor), Charles McKnight (baritone), Charles Williams (bass)

Notes

There is no relation between the East Coast "Been So Long" Pastels and this group.

The Chicago Pastels was made up of high school friends. They signed a contract with United Records and recorded in October 1955, but the product from this session did not please United management. They recorded again in November, and "Put Your Arms around Me" was the end result of this session.

A year after recording, Julius Collins replaced Buckley. Although Collins never recorded with them, Bob Pruter has heard the group's tapes with Collins at lead and says that he was some prize.

Claude McCrae replaced Collins and was later a member of the Dukays.

Jerry Mills replaced bass Charles Williams.

During the 1970s, 1980s, and 1990s Norman Palm joined Pirkle Lee Moses as part of a reformed El Dorados group. He also was part of the Delano Crystals.

Discography

United 196 Put Your Arms around Me/Boom De De Boom (1956)
Sources: Bob Pruter, *Doowop . . . The Chicago Scene*; Bob Pruter in *Record Collector's Monthly* 45.

Pastels (Air Force/Washington, D.C.)

Personnel "Big" Dee Irvin (a.k.a. DiFosco Ervin) (lead), Richard Travis (1st tenor), Tony Thomas (2d tenor), Johnny B. Willingham (baritone)

Notes

This group met in 1954 in the air force and began performing in talent shows. They originally formed the group on a street corner in Greenland.

They auditioned for Bea Kaslon [sic] at Hull Records. When they satisfied their air force obligations in 1957, they recorded and released "Been So Long" on the Hull subsidiary label Mascot.

When "Been So Long" began to show signs of success, Hull leased it to the Chess subsidiary, Argo. All future Pastels discs were released on Argo, although they were recorded at Hull's facilities.

Other than "So Far Away," the Pastels' discs didn't fare too well and they agreed to split in 1959. All the members also desired to return to the city they came from.

Only Ervin stayed in the business. In 1964, as "Big" Dee Irvin, he had a hit with "Swingin' on a Star."

Jimmy Willingham is the brother of Johnny Willingham of the Cadillacs.

Discography

Mascot 123 Been So Long/My One and Only Dream (1957)
Argo 5287 Been So Long/My One and Only Dream (1957)

Argo 5297 You Don't Love Me Anymore/Let's Go to the R 'n' R Ball (1958)
Argo 5314 So Far Away/Don't Knock (1958)
Sources: Marv Goldberg in *Yesterday's Memories* 12; Pete Grendysa, liner notes with the Chess CD box set *Chess Rhythm & Roll.*

Peaches (Los Angeles)

Personnel Etta James (lead), Abbye Mitchell, Jean Mitchell

Discography

Modern 947 Wallflower/Hold Me, Squeeze Me (1954)

Pearls (Detroit)

Personnel Howard Guyton (d) (lead), Dave "Baby Cortez" Clowney (tenor), Derek Martin (tenor), George Torrence (baritone), Coley Washington (bass)

Notes

This is a Detroit vocal group that originally formed in 1954.

It is assumed they moved to New York to record for Jerry Winston's Onyx Records. Clowney was from New York and probably joined them after they arrived from the Motor City. This group also recorded great sides for Aladdin as the Five Pearls in 1954, for Atco in 1955 as the Pearls with Bobby Spencer, and for Okeh in 1959 as Howie and the Sapphires.

Eddie Jacobs from the Capitols on Pet, Johnny Johnson of the Starlings, and Robert Guy were also members of the Pearls.

Derek Martin was also a member of the Raves and Clowney spent time with the Valentines.

Guyton later toured extensively with a Platters group until his untimely death.

Discography

Atco 6057 Shadows of Love/Yum Yummy (1955)
Atco 6066 Bells of Love/Come On Home (1956)
Onyx 503 Let's You and I Go Steady/Zippity Zippity Zoom (1956)
Onyx 506 Tree in the Meadow/My Oh My (1956)
Onyx 510 Your Cheatin' Heart/I Sure Need You (1957)
Onyx 511 Ice Cream Baby/Yuz-a-Ma-Tuz (1957)
Onyx 516 The Wheel of Love/It's Love, Love, Love (1957)
Source: Donn Fileti, liner notes with the Relic CD *Onyx.*

Pearls, Speedoo & (New York)

Personnel Earl Carroll (lead), Howie Guyton (d) (tenor), George Torrence, Coley Washington, Derek Martin

Notes

In the liner notes accompanying Sequel's *Jubilee/Josie-4* CD, George Povall and Gordon Skadberg refer to Torrence as Terrence. They also state that the Pearls, after leaving Onyx and Atco in the mid–1950s, made their way to Josie as the Majors and had one release (Josie 845). In 1959, Earl Carroll joined them to form Speedoo and the Pearls.

Discography

Josie 865 Who Ya Gonna Kiss/Naggity Nag (1959)
Source: George Povall and Gordon Skadberg, liner notes with the Sequel CD *Jubilee/Josie R&B Vocal Groups-4.*

Pelicans, Earl Nelson & (Los Angeles)

Personnel Earl Nelson (lead), Curtis Williams, David Ford, Clyde Tillis, Bobby Day

Notes

This group was another configuration of the Hollywood Flames. It has been rumored that this group was also known as the Kidds. However, in the liner notes to EMI America's *Lost Dreams* LP, Jim Dawson and Steve Brigati's liner notes state, yes, the Pelicans were the Kidds, but these Pelicans were a local New Orleans group. Earl Nelson and the Pelicans, as you can see above, were from Los Angeles and had nothing to do with the Pelicans or Kidds from New Orleans.

Discography

Class 209 I Bow to You/Oh Gee, Oh Golly (1957)
Sources: Donn Fileti, liner notes with the Relic LP *Best of Class Records*; Jim Dawson and Steve Brigati, notes to the EMI America LP *Lost Dreams.*

Penguins (Los Angeles)

Personnel Cleve Duncan (lead), Dexter Tisby (2d tenor), Curtis Williams (d) (baritone), Bruce Tate (d) (bass)

Notes

Cleve Duncan and Curtis Williams knew one another from their Los Angeles grammar school days. One evening in 1953, they ran into each other at a talent show. Williams at the time was with the Hollywood Flames. Williams and Gaynel Hodge were working on a song entitled "Earth Angel," and Williams asked Duncan if he would help him with the arrangement.

Duncan and Williams thought of forming a vocal group and decided that each would bring in a friend. Duncan brought Dexter Tisby and Williams brought Bruce Tate. Next they next selected the name Penguins and all was set to record.

After Dootsie Williams heard them, they cut two demos and recorded three records for Dootone. In his liner notes to the Ace CD *Penguins,* Jim Dawson states that "the demos included the group backing Willie Headen doing, 'No, There Ain't No News Today.' " In Marv Goldberg's Penguins account in *DISCoveries,* Marv relates that in the spring of 1954, they recorded two demos, "No, There Ain't No News Today" (with Cleve in the lead) and "I Ain't Gonna Cry" (fronted by Dexter).

In May 1954 Dootone released "No, There Ain't No News Today" on one side and "When I Am Gone" on the flip, with a vocal by Willie Headen.

Just prior to recording Kiss a Fool Goodbye/Baby Let's Make Some Love, Bruce Tate had an auto accident in which he hit a pedestrian. Apparently, the shock of this event prevented him from performing again and he was replaced by Teddy Harper (Aladdins, Coasters)

While "Earth Angel" was popular, the Penguins repeatedly asked Dootone management for advances against their royalties. They were always refused. They then asked manager Buck Ram to find them a new label. This is how and why they went to Mercury with Ram's other group, the Platters.

They spent several years at Mercury. After realizing that Mercury was not living up to its part of the deal, which was for the group to cut eight sides for the Mercury per year, they left for Atlantic Records. They cut two sides for Atlantic, which did not work out well and returned to what was then Dooto.

They cut several sides for Dooto. Dooto 428 was Curtis Williams's final session. He was apparently having domestic problems (nonsupport) and had to be replaced by Randolph Jones.

After some time, because they were not recording or selling enough discs, they left Dooto. They made stops at Sun State and at Original Sound Records.

The Original Sound group consisted of Duncan, Walter Saulsbury, and Glen Madison, who had formerly been with the Delcos on Ebony.

Duncan also sang lead for the female group the Radiants as his last Dootone cut. Vesta and Gladys White along with Curtis Williams became Cleve Duncan and the Radiants.

Discography

Dootone 345 No There Ain't No News Today/When I Am Gone (1954)
Dootone 348 Earth Angel/Hey Señorita (1954)
Dootone 353 Love Will Make Your Mind Go Wild/Ookey Ook (1954)
Dootone 362 Kiss a Fool Goodbye/Baby Let's Make Some Love (DT) (1955)
Mercury 70610 Be Mine or Be a Fool/Don't Do It (1955)
Mercury 70654 It Only Happens with You/Walkin' Down Broadway (1955)
Mercury 70703 Devil That I See/Promises Promises Promises (1955)
Mercury 70762 A Christmas Prayer/Jingle Jangle (1955)
Mercury 70799 My Troubles Are Not at an End/She's Gone Gone (1956)
Mercury 70943 Earth Angel/Ice (1956)
Wing 90076 Dealer of Dreams/Peace of Mind (1956)
Mercury 71033 Will You Be Mine/Cool Baby Cool (1957)
Atlantic 1132 Pledge of Love/I Know I'd Fall in Love (1957)
Dooto 428 That's How Much I Need You/Be My Loving Baby (1957)
Dooto 432 Let Me Make Up Your Mind/Sweet Love (1958)
Dooto 435 Do Not Pretend/If You're Mine (1958)
Sun State 001 Believe Me/Pony Rock (1962)
Original Sound 27 Memories of El Monte/Be Mine (1963)

Original Sound 54 Heavenly Angel/Big Bobo's Party (1965)
Sources: Jim Dawson, liner notes with the Ace CD *Penguins*; Marv Goldberg, "The Penguins," in *DISCoveries.*

Pentagons (San Bernardino, Calif.)

Personnel Josephus Jones (lead), Otis Munson (tenor), Ken Goodloe (tenor), Ted Goodloe (baritone)

Notes

The Pentagons started their recording career with Art Rupe's Specialty Records. Then they went to Fleet Records, where they originally released "To Be Loved." When the disc began to show promise, it was leased to Donna.

Second tenor Johnny Torrance later joined the Pentagons, as did Bill James and Carl McGuiness. It is not certain if this is the same Johnny Torrance who had previously sung with the Jewels.

Jones and Munson are half-brothers.

Discography

Specialty 644 Silly Dilly/It's Spring Again (1958)
Sutter 100 Forever Yours/Gonna Wait for You (1961)
Donna 1337 To Be Loved/Down at the Beach (1961)
Fleet International 100 To Be Loved/Down at the Beach (1961)
Jamie 1201 I Wonder/She's Mine (1961)
Jamie 1210 Until Then/I'm in Love (1962)
Source: Bear Family's Jamie/Guyden CD *Doop Doo Wah.*

Peppers (Los Angeles)

Personnel Willie Davis (lead), Aaron Collins (tenor), Thomas Miller (baritone), George Hollis (bass)

Notes

This group was an obvious offshoot of the Jacks/Cadets and was related to a new Flairs (Flares) group.

Discography

Ensign 1706 One More Chance (WD)/A Place in My Heart (WD) (1961)
Press 2809 Little Piece of Paper/It Wouldn't Be the Same (1963)
Source: Marv Goldberg and Donn Fileti in *DISCoveries,* April 1989.

Performers (New York)

Personnel Perry Hayward (lead), Freddie Johnson (tenor), Gilbert Johnson (baritone), Joseph "Rocky" Washington (bass)

Notes

This group formed in 1956 as a result of the breakup of the Sparrows on Jay Dee. Hayward and Washington had been with the Sparrows and tried harmonizing after the breakup by starting the Performers.

Hayward had previously filled in for Checkers lead John Carnegie, who had been drafted at the time of the recording of Ghost of My Baby/I Wanna Know. This was Hayward's only recording with the Checkers.

Washington filled in for James "Archie" Archer of the Wrens on Rama when he was drafted. Washington recorded on Rama 184 and Rama 194.

How it occurred is not understood, but somehow the Performers got a recording contract with All-Star Records and recorded "I'll Make You Understand" in August 1956. This was led by Freddie with great bass work by Rocky. "Give Me Your Heart" was by Hayward.

David Martin, formerly of the Sparrows and the Performers, performed fill-in duty with the Checkers.

Discography

All Star 714 Give Me Your Heart/I'll Make You Understand (1957)
Tip Top 402 Give Me Your Heart/I'll Make You Understand (1957)
Source: Marv Goldberg in *DISCoveries,* August 1997.

Personalities (Bronx, N.Y.)

Personnel Ralph Molina (lead), Larry Gilbert (1st tenor), Billy Johnson (2d tenor), Bobby Schneider (baritone), Arthur Slaughter (bass)

Notes

This group started in the Morrisania section of the Bronx in New York in 1954. They would get together in the basement of the apartment house in which Arthur Slaughter lived, imitating the groups with the popular songs of the day.

While Slaughter was at Morris High School in 1957, he started cutting classes and hanging out in the halls in order to sing harmony. He began assembling a vocal group. When finally structured, the group members were all fifteen years old except the lead—twelve-year-old Ralph Molina—and they were integrated as well.

They performed at school functions and other benefits until they felt ready to seek out a recording deal. In 1959, they called on Old Town Records, where they were redirected to the offices of Safari Records. Safari management liked them and their high tenor lead songs but told them to go home and write some original tunes and then return. They did just that and returned weeks later for a recording session at Bell Sound.

For "Woe Woe Baby" and "Yours to Command," the Safari label showed "The Personalities—Featuring Ralph Molina," deciding to spotlight the lead singer. They received no payment for the session, no royalties, and nothing for live appearances. Yet Safari management stated that the tune did well.

This was a relatively later group from the Morrisania section of the Bronx. In an interview, Arthur Slaughter recalled a rumor that Molina was thought to have recorded with another group, the Royal Drifters on Teen 506 and 508. The writer credits on 506, "Little Linda," are shown as R. Molina and the lead singer's voice is quite familiar.

Discography

Safari 1002 Woe Woe Baby/Yours to Command (1957)
Source: Joe Sicurella in *Echoes of the Past* 26.

Phantoms (Los Angeles)

Personnel Vernon Green (lead), Bobby Relf (tenor), Jerry Williams (tenor), Johnny Moss (bass)

Notes

In 1956, Vernon Green of the Medallions, annoyed by the lack of financial rewards usually accruing to celebrities in the entertainment business, chose to wander. For that reason, coupled with a request from Art Rupe of Specialty Records, to assemble another vocal group and record for him, the disc below was produced by a vocal group Green called the Phantoms.

They originally appeared wearing hoods, but because Green had been afflicted with polio and always carried a cane, the disguise effect went nowhere. Following this effort, Green returned to Dootone, now being called Dooto, and rejoined a re-formed Medallions.

Curiously, discussing the disc below and the group above, in the liner notes with the Specialty CD *Hardcore Doo-Wop,* Billy Vera presents a lineup for this group that is different from the one reflected above from a Marv Goldberg interview with Green and Dootsie Williams. Vera's notes state that the group is made up of Vernon Green, Ed Daniels, Johnny Moss, Madalyn Marselle, and Sidney Runnels.

Vera's notes go on to say that the session at which Specialty 581 was recorded was a split session with Wynona Carr.

Discography

Specialty 581 Sweet Breeze/The Old Willow Tree (1956)
Sources: Billy Vera, liner notes with the Specialty CD *Hardcore Doo-Wop*; Vernon Green, interview by Marv Goldberg; Drew Williams in *Record Collector's Monthly* 42.

Pharaohs, Richard Berry & (Los Angeles)

Personnel Richard Berry (lead), Godoy Colbert (1st tenor), Robert Harris (2d tenor), Noel Collins (baritone)

Notes

Reflected below, on Class 202, is this same group recording as by Ricky and the Pharaohs. This was done intentionally to avoid potential litigation, as Berry had a contract with Max Frietag's Flip label. In order to release another tune on a competitive label, they had to record under another name.

Charles Colbert and tenor Gloria Jones also sang with the group. Godoy Colbert sang with the Cyclones on Flip who did "My Dear," written by Berry.

In Donn Fileti's liner notes with Relic's *Class* CD, Colbert's first name is shown as Codoy. In the liner notes with *Best of Flip–1* it's Cody.

They recorded for Donna as the Pharaohs.

Discography

Flip 318 Take the Key/No Kissin' and a Huggin' (1956)
Flip 321 Louie Louie/Rock, Rock, Rock (1957)
Class 202 Teenager's Love Song/Watusi (as Rickey and the Pharaohs) (1958)
Flip 327 Rock, Rock, Rock/Sweet Sugar You (1957)
Flip 331 You're the Girl/You Look So Good (1958)
Flip 339 Do I Do I/Besame Mucho (1958)
Flip 349 Have Love Will Travel/No Room (1959)
Flip 352 Somewhere There's a Rainbow/I'll Never Ever Love Again (1960)
Flip 360 You Are My Sunshine/You Look So Good (1961)
Sources: Donn Fileti, liner notes with the Relic CD *Class*; liner notes with the CD *Best of Flip-1*.

Pipes (Oakland, Calif.)

Personnel Huey Roundtree (lead), Louis Gene Candys (tenor), Harold Foreman (tenor), Leevern Ball (bass)

Notes

The original formation of the Pipes occurred in 1953 at Oakland's McClymonds High School. The group initially called themselves the Cool Notes. After practicing for about a year, they went south to Los Angeles to seek out an interested recording organization. They visited Capitol, Specialty, Modern, and Imperial but were told they were too young. After graduating from high school, they called on Dootsie Williams at Dootone.

Williams felt they were now old enough and quite talented and signed them to record. He changed their name to the Pipes based on a lyric from "Danny Boy," "the pipes, the pipes are calling."

"Be Fair" and "Let Me Give You Money" were recorded at their first session, which took place in a garage! Candys sang lead for one of the tunes and had to stand on a box to reach the microphone. As he was singing, he feared falling from the box.

As was usually the case, the group received no royalties despite the fact that "Be Fair" did well locally. They only received a few dollars for their effort. Their next release was never promoted by Dootone and therefore did not do well.

They remained with Dootone for a while longer, finally realizing that becoming full-time vocalizers was not realistic. They contented themselves with simply playing weekend dates to earn some dollars.

In 1958, the group invested their finances in a recording session and released the product on their own label, Jacy. Only several hundred copies were pressed and it remains a rarity. They returned to Dootone in 1959, and recorded one more session.

Nothing from their time at the studio that day was ever released and the group subsequently disbanded.

Candys's brother, Willard, sang lead for Combo's Starliters.

Discography
Dootone 388 Be Fair (LC/HR)/Let Me Give You Money (HR) (1956)
Dootone 401 Love the Life I Live (HR)/You Are an Angel (LC/HR) (1956)
Jacy 001 So Long (LC)/Baby Please Don't Go (LC) (1958)
Source: Rick Whitesell and Marv Goldberg in the *Yesterday's Memories* section of
Goldmine.

Plaids, Willie Logan & (Chicago)

Personnel Willie Logan (lead), O. C. Logan, Arthur Ford, Dave Hoskin

Notes
Willie Logan and the Plaids had been the Equallos on Mad and M&M. In 1963, a
recording of theirs on Jerry-O was released as by Willie Logan and the Plaids. The
timing was poor, as their R&B style of harmony was nearing the end of its popularity. When someone who listens to the two sides of this Jerry-O disc, this becomes
quite obvious.

The Logan brothers, Willie and O. C., had originally come from Durham, North
Carolina, where they were with the Ballads on Venture.

Discography
Jerry-O 103 You Conquered Me/Say That You Care (1964)
Source: Bob Pruter, *Doowop . . . The Chicago Scene.*

Planets (Los Angeles)

Personnel Billy Steward (lead), Woody Johnson (tenor), Jimmy Brunson (tenor),
Vince House (bass)

Notes
Before the end of 1955, Vee Jay's Rhythm Aces were let go by the Chicago label.
They then toured Canada and the group broke up following the tour. In 1956, Vince
House, Billy Steward, and Chuck Rowan of the Rhythm Aces joined up with Jimmy
Brunson and somehow formed a new group in California from 1956 to 1958. They
performed under several different names—the Rockets, the Rocketeers, and the Plan-
ets.

It was this group, the Planets, that backed Johnny Otis on his "Willie and the Hand
Jive" on Capitol.

Discography
Era 1038 Never Again/Stand There Mountain (1957)
Era 1049 Be Sure/Wild Leaves (1957)
Source: Bob Pruter, *Doowop . . . The Chicago Scene.*

Plants (Baltimore, Md.)

Personnel George Jackson (lead), Steve McDowell (1st tenor), James Lawson (baritone), Thurman Thrower (bass)

Notes

The Plants were neighborhood friends who grew up together in Baltimore and began singing in 1955, when they were in their midteens. They began as the Equadors and made several local appearances singing R&B and pop.

They were heard by Zell Sanders backstage at a show in Baltimore. She liked them, changed their name and mailed them contracts on her arrival home.

They recorded within weeks. Interestingly, J&S 1604, I Searched the Seven Seas/I Took a Trip Way Over the Sea, is not the same group as the Dear I Swear/It's You group. No one has ever been able to explain this unique incident and the personnel on J&S 1604 remains unknown.

Unsuccessful recordings, compounded by having mouths to feed, led the Plants to disband late in 1958.

Discography

J&S 1602 Dear I Swear/It's You (1957)
J&S 1604 I Searched the Seven Seas/I Took a Trip Way Over the Sea (1957)
J&S 1617 From Me/My Girl (1958)
Source: Marv Goldberg in *Yesterday's Memories* 8.

Platters (Los Angeles)

Personnel Tony Williams (d) (lead), David Lynch (2d tenor), Alex Hodge (baritone), Herb Reed (bass)

Notes

The Platters were originally brought to the attention of Buck Ram by Tony Williams's sister, Linda Hayes. Ram managed Hayes for a time and she told him of her brother, Tony Williams, who sang. Williams was brought to Ram's offices and immediately impressed Ram, who found it hard to properly place him. Williams told Ram that he was already part of a group—the Platters.

The Platters were brought up to Ram's office by Williams. Ram felt they sounded unprofessional. With several personnel changes and much practice, they greatly improved and Ram got them a contract with Federal. Nothing happened on their initial two cuts, so Ram got Zola Taylor from Shirley Gunter's Queens to join them. Taylor's addition was vehemently objected to by the other members. At this time (May 1954), Hodge left the Platters and Paul Robi took his place.

Because the Penguins were successful at the time, Bob Shad, Mercury's A&R man, worked feverishly to acquire them. They were also managed by Ram. The final deal, arranged by Ram, was that if Mercury wanted the Penguins, they had to also take the Platters. This obviously worked.

King-Federal-DeLuxe only wanted R&B groups at the time. Although they recorded the Platters' "Only You," King owner Syd Nathan strongly disliked the tune and ultimately let them move to Mercury. At the first recording session with the new label, both the Penguins and the Platters were scheduled to record. The Penguins' part of the session went as scheduled, but the Platters' part ran long and the pianist had to leave. Ram was able to play piano and filled in. The rest is history. Many recording successes followed. They rerecorded "Only You," which did very well, and followed up with "The Great Pretender," "Magic Touch," "My Prayer," "Smoke Gets in Your Eyes," and so on.

In 1960, Williams left to pursue a solo career and to relieve frustrations that had developed between himself, the group, Mercury, Buck Ram, and the audiences. A friend of the group, Johnny Barnes, took his place on the road, and "Sonny" Turner assumed the lead responsibility in 1964. Zola Taylor left that same year and the Platters left Mercury in 1966. In 1969, Herb Reed departed.

Williams's replacement, "Sonny" Turner (a.k.a. "Sonny" Dinkes), also performed with the Metrotones on Reserve. Another replacement was Nate Nelson, who was added while Turner was still with the group. Nate formerly sang lead with the Flamingos.

Discography (Only Federal and Mercury)

Federal 12153 Give Thanks/Hey Now (1953)
Federal 12164 I'll Cry When You're Gone/I Need You All the Time (1954)
Federal 12181 Roses of Picardy/Beer Barrel Boogie (1954)
Federal 12188 Tell the World/Love All Night (1954)
Federal 12198 Shake It Up Mambo/Voo Vee Ah Bee (1954)
Federal 12204 Take Me Back/Maggie Doesn't Work Here Anymore (1954)
Federal 12244 Only You/You Made Me Cry (1955)
Federal 12250 Tell the World/I Need You All the Time (1955)
Mercury 70633 Only You/Bark, Battle, and Ball (1955)
Mercury 70753 The Great Pretender/I'm Just a Dancing Partner (1955)
Federal 12271 Give Thanks/I Need You All the Time (1956)
Mercury 70819 The Magic Touch/Winner Take All (1956)
Mercury 70893 My Prayer/Heaven on Earth (1956)
Mercury 70948 You'll Never Never Know/It Isn't Right (1956)
Mercury 71011 One in a Million/On My Word of Honor (1956)
Mercury 71032 I'm Sorry/He's Mine (1957)
Mercury 71093 My Dream/I Wanna (1957)
Mercury 71184 Only Because/The Mystery of You (1957)
Mercury 71246 Helpless/Indiff'rent (1957)
Mercury 71289 Twilight Time/Out of My Mind (1958)
Mercury 30075 For the First Time/Twilight Time (1958)
Mercury 71320 You're Making a Mistake/My Old Flame (1958)
Mercury 71353 I Wish/It's Raining Outside (1958)
Mercury 71383 Smoke Gets in Your Eyes/No Matter What You Are (1958)
Mercury 71427 Enchanted/The Sound and the Fury (1959)
Mercury 71467 Remember When/Love of a Lifetime (1959)
Mercury 71502 Wish It Were Me/Where (1959)
Mercury 71538 What Does it Matter/My Secret (1959)
Mercury 71563 Harbor Lights/Sleepy Lagoon (1960)
Mercury 71624 Ebbtide/Apple Blossom Time (1960)

Mercury 71656 Red Sails in the Sunset/Sad River (1960)
Mercury 71697 To Each His Own/Down the River of Golden Drums (1960)
Mercury 71749 If I Didn't Care/True Lover (1960)
Mercury 71791 Trees/Immortal Love (1961)
Mercury 71847 I'll Never Smile Again/You Don't Say (1961)
Mercury 71904 Song for the Lonely/You'll Never Know (1961)
Mercury 71921 It's Magic/Reaching for a Star (1962)
Mercury 71986 More Than You Know/Every Little Movement (1962)
Mercury 72060 Memories/Heartbreak (1962)
Mercury 72107 I'll See You in My Dreams/Once in a While (1963)
Mercury 72129 Here Comes Heaven Again/Strangers (1963)
Mercury 72194 Viva Ju Juy/Cuando Caliente El Sol (1963)
Mercury 72242 Java Jive/Row That Boat Ashore (1964)
Mercury 72305 Sincerely/P.S. I Love You (1964)
Mercury 72359 Love Me Tender/Little Things Mean a Lot (1964)
Sources: Harry Weinger in *Goldmine,* February 21, 1992; Ferdie Gonzalez, *Disco-File.*

Playboys (New York)

Personnel Charlie White, Ollie Jones, Robie Kirk, Abel DeCosta, Jimmy Breedlove, Eddie Barnes

Notes

This group was composed of Charlie White (formerly with the Clovers, Dominoes, and Checkers) and Atlantic's quintessential backup group the Cues, calling themselves the Playboys and recording for Atlantic's Cat subsidiary in 1954.

Their two Cat singles unfortunately did not do very well and that marked the end of the Playboys.

(Special note: The research done for the personnel in this group simply said that Charlie White fronted the Cues. I have not been able to confirm the above lineup of personnel as it changed so frequently. But the above is the ideal Cues.)

Discography

Cat 108 Tell Me/Rock, Moan, and Cry (1954)
Cat 115 Good Golly Miss Molly/Honey Bun (1955)
Source: Pete Grendysa, liner notes with the two Atlantic CDs *Don't It Sound Good* and *All Night Boogie.*

Playmates (New York)

Personnel Alma Beatty, Gwen Brooks, Lucille Beatty

Notes

There is no connection between this Playmates group and the Beep Beep group that recorded for Roulette.

Discography

Savoy 1523 Giddy-Up-a-Ding-Dong/It Must Be Love (1957)
Source: Steve Propes, liner notes with the Savoy LP *Doo Wop Delights: The Roots of Rock.*

Plazas, Nicky Addeo & (Plainfield, N.J.)

Personnel Nicky Addeo (lead), Anthony Ventura, Bobby Scolski, Danny Ugardi, Joe Ugardi

Notes

Addeo, from Asbury Park, New Jersey, met the other members, who were from Plainfield, New Jersey, during the summer of 1962 on the Seaside Heights boardwalk at the Jersey shore.

Addeo's close friend Al Mott expressed his desire to finance a recording of Addeo's group, and this was done. At this time they recorded the disc below. Unfortunately for all, it did absolutely nothing at the cash register.

Addeo's previous claim to fame was as a member of Ray and the Darchaes.

Discography

Revelation VII 101 Danny Boy/Lovely Way to Spend an Evening (1962)
Source: Ronnie Italiano in *Story Untold* 1.

Plink, Plank & Plunk (Chester, Pa.)

Personnel Wilson "Serious" Myers, "Tiger" George Haynes, Bob Mosley

Notes

Wilson Myers came from the Spirits of Rhythm.

Paul Curry replaced Mosley. Haynes and Curry had differing musical philosophies, and sometime in the fall of 1945 Haynes left the group for New York and formed the Three Flames.

Discography

Decca 48036 Sermon on the Blues/Salt Peanuts
V-Disc 496 Salt Peanuts
Source: Pete Grendysa in *Goldmine,* April 1980, article about the Three Flames.

Poets (Los Angeles)

Personnel Roy Ayers, James Bedford, Sherman Clark, Robert Griffett, Frederick Nance

Notes

The disc shown below is one of the most popular discs of the early 1960s R&B revivals.

James Bedford later sang with the Cubans vocal group.

Discography

Flash 129 Vowels of Love/Dead (1958)
Source: Donn Fileti, liner notes with the Relic LP *Best of Flash Records.*

Popular Five (Bronx, N.Y.)

Personnel Warren Wilson (lead), Jimmy Keyes (d) (1st tenor), Jesse Huddleston (2d tenor), Arthur Dix (baritone), Demetrius Clare (bass)

Notes

The Popular Five was formed in the mid-1960s by Jimmy Keyes and Arthur Dix from the Chords. Their last release on Gene Chandler's Mister Chand label did poorly and the group members went their separate ways.

In addition to the disc shown below, they also did several Schaefer Beer commercials.

Keyes died in 1996.

Discography

Rae-Cox 1001 Tomorrow Night/Sh Boom (1967)
Minit 32050 I'm a Love Maker/Little Bitty Pretty One (1968)
Mister Chand 8001 Baby, I've Got It/Best Friend, Worst Enemy (1970)
Sources: Jimmy Keyes, interview by author, 1995; Gary Kupper in *Goldmine,* August 6, 1993.

Portraits (Los Angeles)

Personnel Stan Beverly (lead), Charles Taggart (1st tenor), Maurice Giles (2d tenor), Joe Lewis (baritone), Nathaniel "Buster" Wilson (bass)

Notes

The Hollywood Saxons had many incarnations, one of them in 1959 as the Portraits. The original group began earlier in the 1950s as neighborhood friends playing basketball and singing in the shower following each game. Thus began the parade of vocal groups that included the Hollywood Saxons, Saxons, Capris, Tuxedos, and Portraits.

The Portraits did a twelve-hour session for Capitol Records. Twenty songs were cut but only two were ever released.

There is no explanation for the volatility associated with their referring to themselves in so many ways, but their product was always a fine one.

Discography

Capitol 4181 Close to You (SB)/Easy Cash (MG) (1959)
Source: Marv Goldberg and Rick Whitesell in *Yesterday's Memories* 11.

Preludes (Los Angeles)

Personnel Homer Green (lead), Donald Miller (1st tenor), Charles Everidge (2d tenor), Harold Murray (baritone), James Monroe Warren (bass)

Notes

Since this group also recorded as the Youngsters and the Tempters, they will all be addressed similarly. They started in 1954 in Los Angeles's Manual Trades High School. They sang in all the familiar school locations appropriate for harmonizing—hallways, restrooms, lunchroom, and so on. They performed at high school assemblies and competed with other high schools.

Choosing a name was something of a problem. Everidge liked the Preludes and the other members liked the Tempters.

They were signed in 1956 to the newly formed Empire Records, which quickly recorded and released their first tune early in 1956. All the songs recorded by the Preludes, Tempters, and Youngsters were recorded at two sessions. From the first session came Empire 103 and 104 and released as by the Preludes.

Following the first session, lead Homer Green left to join the marines and was replaced by Robert Johnson. At the same time, Donald Miller left and his place was taken by Herman Pruitt, former lead with the Calvanes and a friend from Manual Trades High School.

This reconstructed group had a second session. From this came Empire 105 by the Tempters and Empire 107 and 109 by the Youngsters. Empire 109 was their biggest. "Dreamy Eyes" sold well but not well enough. In spite of the group's success with "Dreamy Eyes," Empire was not doing well financially and not in a position to properly promote their recordings. This left the group high and dry, and as the Tempters, Youngsters, and Preludes they drifted apart.

Discography

Empire 103 Don't Fall in Love Too Soon/I Want Your Arms around Me (1956)
Source: Marv Goldberg and Rick Whitesell in the *Yesterday's Memories* supplement in *Goldmine.*

Premiers (New Haven, Conn.)

Personnel Billy Koob (lead), Frank Polimos (1st tenor), Gus Delcos (2d tenor), Roger Koob (baritone)

Notes

The Premiers were formed in November 1956, performing locally and gathering a good following. Their recording occurred one year later and a disc was released the next year. Connecticut disc jockeys played their record regularly, which led to a tour of East Coast states and Canada.

The Koob brothers were the Premiers' mainstays on Fury and Rust. Then they were in the Frontiers on Philips. They also sang as Roger and the Travelers and the Buddies on Comet.

The Koob groups were white and all members were from New Haven. The Rust group was composed of the Koob brothers, Joe Vece, and Johnny Roddi.

Discography

Alert 706 Jolene/Oh Theresa (1958)
Fury 1029 Pigtails, Eyes Are Blue/I Pray (1960)
Rust 5032 She Gives Me Fever/Falling Star (1961)
Sources: Victor Pearlin in *Paul's Record Magazine,* October 1975; Ed Engel, liner notes with the Ace CD *Laurie Vocal Groups: The Doo Wop Sound*; Roger Koob and Paul Bezanker in *Paul's Record Magazine* 16.

Premiers (New York)

Personnel Ronnie Stevens (lead), Robert "Bootsie" White (1st tenor), Ronald Strong (2d tenor), Tennis Penn (baritone), Al Cashie (bass)

Notes

"Bootsie" White also sang for the Desires and the Jivetones.

Another report shows the personnel as Johnny Burks, Ronald Stevens, Al Cashie, Tennis Pinn, and Bobby Lucas at lead.

Discography

Gone 5009 Is It a Dream/Valerie (1957)
Source: One of the band members, interview by George Lavatelli.

Premiers (Los Angeles)

Personnel Sammy Yates (lead), Julie Stevens

Notes

The Premiers and Yates were Dig's most prolific ensemble between backup chores for Stevens's recordings (Crazy Bells/Blue Mood on Dig 115) as well as the Premiers' work.

When Yates moved to Capitol in 1957, as Sammy Hagen and the Viscounts, the Premiers disbanded.

Discography

Dig 106 Baby/New Moon (1956)
Dig 113 Have a Heart/My Darling (1956)
Dig 115 Crazy Bells/Blue Mood (w/Julie Stevens) (1956)
Dig 129 Take My Heart/I Don't Want to Know (1957)
Sources: Ray Topping, liner notes with the Ace Dig CD, *Legendary Dig Masters-4*; Donn Fileti, liner notes with the Relic LP *Best of Dig Records.*

Prestos (New York)

Personnel Johnny Barnes (tenor), Les Cooper (tenor), Bobby Dunn (baritone), William Goodman (bass)

Notes

This group, in its initial formation, was the Empires on the Harlem label. They had come to Manhattan in 1952 from Virginia. They worked their way into the music business by singing at church functions and clubs. They auditioned for several record companies prior to being signed by Morty Shad in 1954 for his Harlem label.

In 1955, they moved to the Mercury subsidiary Wing, where they had three releases. Buck Ram was their manager while they were there. Because of Ram's other interests, he paid little attention to the Prestos and they left the label and Ram.

At this time they recorded as the Prestos on the Mercury label. This disc did nothing and they moved on.

Their next move was to Bobby Robinson's Whirlin' Disc Records. The second disc cut for the label was released as by the Whirlers.

The group finally broke up when Goodman was drafted, since a bass with equal abilities could not be found.

Les Cooper was Johnny Barnes's uncle.

Discography

Mercury 70747 'Til We Meet Again/Looking for Love (1955)
Source: Marv Goldberg and Dave Hinckley in *Yesterday's Memories* 12. Article on the Empires.

Pretenders, Jimmy Jones & (New York)

Personnel Jimmy Jones (lead), William Walker (1st tenor), Bobby Moore (2d tenor), Mel Walton (baritone), Kerry Saxton (bass)

Notes

This group had been the Savoys on Savoy—man for man. Because Savoy owner Herman Lubinsky provided neither support nor promotion for their recordings with the label, Jones bought out their contract and then switched to the Rama label. There, they became Jimmy Jones and the Pretenders, named after the popular song at the time, "The Great Pretender."

(Note: In Marv Goldberg's article discussing Jones in *Whiskey, Women, and . . .*, Marv states that after the Pretenders met George Goldner, owner of Rama Records, Goldner became so impressed with them that *he* bought their contract from Herman Lubinsky at Savoy.)

It should be understood that the Savoys, the Pretenders, and the Jones Boys vocal groups were essentially the same group. The Sparks of Rhythm was Jones's first group but had no relation to the others, aside from Jones. They made many live appearances and, at all these appearances, Irving Lee Gail substituted for bass Saxton. Walker and Walton had been together in Red Robin's Vocaleers. At their first session, George Goldner selected the tunes, "Possessive Love" and "I've Got to Have You Baby." They released two discs with Rama then moved to Danny Robinson's Holiday Records.

Reggie Barnes filled in from time to time.

Kerry Saxton took Gail's place and Andrew Barksdale, from the Sparks of Rhythm, took Saxton's place.

Discography

Rama 198 Possessive Love/I've Got to Have You Baby (1956)
Rama 207 Lover/Plain Old Love (1956)
Holiday 2610 Tonight/I Love You So (1957)
Central 2605 Blue and Lonely/Daddy Needs Baby (1958)
ABC 10094 Blue and Lonely/Daddy Needs Baby (1958)
APT 25026 Blue and Lonely/Daddy Needs Baby (1958)
Sources: Joe Sicurella in *Harmony Tymes* 2; Marv Goldberg in *Whiskey, Women, and . . .* 16.

Prisonaires (Nashville, Tenn.)

Personnel Johnny Bragg (lead), John Drue (d) (1st tenor), Ed Thurman (d) (2d tenor), William Stewart (d) (baritone), Marcel Sanders (d) (bass)

Notes

Prisonaires lead Johnny Bragg apparently was wrongfully sent to prison for six counts of rape in 1943. Soon after arriving there, he formed a gospel group. This group didn't work out due to internal arguments, and he formed another group. He called this group the Prisonaires.

It remains unconfirmed, but it is told that a local newscaster did a story from the Tennessee State Penitentiary and heard the Prisonaires' singing. They became known outside the prison gates and eventually had a radio show of their own on WSIX. Bragg's story is that he always wrote country songs while in prison and performers would always visit with him to get their tunes. This is his account of how the Prisonaires became known to outsiders.

Because of the success of "Just Walkin' in the Rain," the Tennessee governor used the Prisonaires as an example of prison rehabilitation.

As a result of networking, a tape of their performance of "Just Walking in the Rain" got to the attention of several local music executives. The tape, of course, came from their radio show and was passed from talent scout to talent scout until it reached the hands of Sam Phillips at Sun. The tune was released on Sun in July 1953. In May 1954, Sun released the last of their recordings, as their popularity diminished. This was released in July 1954, days before Phillips discovered Elvis Presley. Soon after this, the group began to disband.

Drue and Stewart served their time and were released in 1955, followed by Sanders. Bragg then reorganized the Prisonaires. The new group didn't want the name and initially chose Sunbeams, which was soon changed to Marigolds and Solotones.

In Bill Millar's account in *Bim Bam Boom,* he lists the personnel as Johny Bragg, Ed Thurman, William Stewart, Marcel Andess, and John Drue.

Discography

Sun 186 Baby Please/Just Walkin' in the Rain (1953)
Sun 189 My God Is Real/Softly and Tenderly (1953)
Sun 191 I Know/A Prisoner's Prayer (1953)
Sun 207 There Is Love in You/What'll You Do Next (1954)
Sources: Colin Escott, liner notes with the Bear Family Sun CD *Just Walkin' in the Rain*; Bill Millar in *Bim Bam Boom* 9.

Prodigals (Clarksburg, W.V.)

Personnel Chuck Collins (lead), Gerald Folio, "Theme Song," Billy Gayles (bass)

Notes

The members of this group originally called themselves the Chords. When they were about to record, however, Vee Jay management (Calvin Carter) told them that another Chords group existed and they needed to change their name. They decided to use the Prodigals.

This was a self-contained group that performed both vocally and instrumentally. The group was interracial and had eight members.

After the Abner disc (Falcon Records' new name), lead singer Collins left and Phil Lightfoot replaced him. The member known as "Theme Song" also left at this time.

Folio, who was from France, had come to the United States in 1949.

Discography

Falcon 1011 Judy/Marsha (1958)
Abner 1015 Won't You Believe/Vangie (1958)
Tollie 9019 Judy/Marsha (1964)
Sources: Liner notes with the Vee Jay CD *Taste of Doo Wop*; Bob Pruter, *Doowop . . . The Chicago Scene.*

Progressive Four (Washington, D.C.)

Personnel Wilbur Griffin (lead), Heartwell Mouton (tenor), Doug Sommers (baritone), Johnny Allen (bass)

Notes

The Progressive Four originally formed in Washington, D.C., in 1932, lasting through the war years performing spiritual and secular recordings. They were managed by Lillian Claiborne.

By the end of the war there were several personnel changes. Bass Oliver Armstead replaced Doug Sommers and Lindsay Wilson replaced Johnny Allen. Harmon Bethea was added as a sixth member.

The group would eventually evolve into the Cap-Tans.

Discography

D.C. 8037 Darling Nellie Gray/ (1948)

D.C. 8038 You Can Run On/I Cried Holy (1948)
D.C. 8042 I Ain't Ready to Go/Old-Time Religion (1948)
D.C. 8048 Yes/Satchelmouth Baby (1948)
D.C. 8052 Ring Those Golden Bells/Vale of Time (1948)
D.C. 8057 Farther Along/You Can Run On (1948)
Savoy 4001 You Can Run On/I Cried Holy (1948)
Savoy 4006 I Ain't Ready to Go/Old-Time Religion (1948)
Source: Marv Goldberg in *Yesterday's Memories 8.*

Pyramids (California)

Personnel Joe Dandy, Lionel Cobbs, Ken Perdue, Mel White, Tom Williams

Notes

The liner notes accompanying the King-Federal-DeLuxe *Great Googa Mooga* CD show the Hollywood disc as number 1017 (1047 is correct). The same notes state that this Pyramids group had but one record. Several sentences later, the notes state, "The Pyramids had another local California release on C-Note 108." The C-Note release and the Hollywood disc were the same tunes. One was a rerelease of the other.

The Pyramids later recorded as the Tempo-Mentals for Ebb in California.

Sidney Coreiea, who formed the group, sang with it at times.

Discography

C-Note 108 Someday/Bow Wow (1955)
Hollywood 1047 Someday/Bow Wow (1955)
Federal 12233 And I Need You/Deep in My Heart for You (1955)
(Note: "And I Need You" was written by Johnny Otis.)
Source: D. Romanello, G. Povall, and C. Bucola, liner notes with the Sequel King-Federal-DeLuxe CD *Great Googa Mooga.*

Pyramids (New Haven, Conn.)

Personnel Joe Stallings (lead), Hubert Saulsbury (1st tenor), Roland Douglas Jr. (baritone), Richard Foster (bass)

Notes

Group members met at the Mount Zion Seventh-Day Adventist Church in New Haven, Connecticut, in 1955. They originally sang gospel but after a short time began singing secular music.

They associated themselves with two managers and started to appear throughout their immediate area as the Four Leads.

They very quickly came to realize that their managers were not really doing anything worthwhile for them and got another manager—Roland's father, Merwin! At this time they changed their name to the Pyramids because the word "pyramids" was in the tune they always sang at live appearances: "You Belong to Me."

Because they were friends of Ruby Whittaker and the Chestnuts, another New Haven group, they were advised to audition for Joe Davis. Following the audition, Davis signed them to record for his organization. They recorded four songs on August 1, 1956.

They did a great deal of touring and live appearances and remained with the Davis organization for about a year when they finally realized that Davis wasn't doing anything to promote their career.

Foster left and was replaced by Danny Jackson; Hubert left and his place was filled by Douglas McClure—son of Sam McClure of the Shadows.

They backed Ruby Whittaker's "I Don't Want to Set the World on Fire" on George Goldner's Mark-X label. Apparently this was one of the times that the Chestnuts had split from Whittaker and she needed a group to take their place. This disc was released in October 1957.

Bad times followed. Doug McClure left and was replaced by Richard Freeman. After his stay with the Pyramids, he left to join the Five Satins.

Discography

Davis 453 At Any Cost (JS)/Okay Baby (RD) (1956)
Davis 457 Why Did You Go? (RD)/Before It's Too Late (HS) (1956)
Mark-X 7007 I Don't Want to Set the World on Fire (RW)/I Got the Feeling (RW) (w/Ruby Whittaker) (1957)
Source: Marv Goldberg in *DISCoveries,* July 1997.

Pyramids (Detroit)

Personnel Vernon Williams (lead), Bobby Jones (1st tenor), Robert Gibson (2d tenor), Damond Rockland (baritone), Norman Worthy (bass)

Notes

The Pyramids formed in the early 1960s. Williams had been with the Royal Holidays, who recorded for Carlton and Herald, with Berry Gordy's Rayber Voices, who did a great deal of backup, and with Gordy's Satintones.

Their first release, I Am the Playboy/Crying (1962), was on the Sonbert label, named after owners Sonny Sanders and Robert Bateman of the Satintones. The tunes were also released in 1962 on Cub.

Following the Sonbert and Cub releases, they also had a disc issued on the Vee Jay label in 1962, Shakin' Fit (written by Williams)/Am I the Playboy.

This Pyramids group had no connection to any other group using that name. The group eventually disbanded when Williams was drafted into the armed forces in 1963.

Discography

Sonbert 8286 I Am the Playboy/Crying (1962)
Cub 9112 I Am the Playboy/Crying (1962)
Vee Jay 489 What Is Love/Shakin' Fit (1962)
Source: Nikki Gustafson and Jim Dunn piece on the Internet, January 1998, available at: www.members.aol.com/wawawaooh/main.htm.

Quadrells (Philadelphia)

Personnel Earl Worsham (lead), John Christian (1st tenor), Reggie "Tootie" Price (baritone), James Oscar Williams (bass)

Notes

The members of this group had, at one time or another, sung with the Turbans on Herald Records. Their name was made up and has no meaning.

Price and Christian also sang with the Universals on Southern and Mark-X.

With the addition of Tony Lewis at 2d tenor the group later became the Cameos on Cameo.

Discography

Whirlin' Disc 103 Come to Me/What Can the Matter Be? (1956)
Source: Marv Goldberg in *DISCoveries,* October 1995. Article on the Turbans.

Quails, Bill Robinson & (Miami)

Personnel Bill Robinson (lead), Tony Bell (2d tenor), "Pee Wee," Jimmy ———

Discography

DeLuxe 6030 Quit Pushin'/Lonely Star (1954)
DeLuxe 6085 The Things She Used to Do/Pretty Huggin' Baby (1955)
DeLuxe 6047 I Know She's Gone/Baby Don't Want Me No More (1954)
DeLuxe 6057 A Little Bit of Love/Somewhere Somebody Cares (1954)
DeLuxe 6059 Why Do I Wait/Heaven Is the Place (1954)
American 6000 Take Me Back Baby/The Cow (1963)
Date 1620 Do I Love You/Lay My Head on Your Shoulder (1968)
Source: Michel Ruppli, *King-Federal-DeLuxe Discography.*

Quailtones, Sax Kari & (Detroit)

Personnel William "Sonny" Sanders, Freddie Gorman, James Martin, Ted Scruggs, Johnny Franklin (bass)

Notes

Sax Kari was a Detroit record store owner, the head of the rhythm and blues department of Great Lakes Records, and a saxophone player.

In Bob Belniak's article in *Echoes of the Past* magazine about Kari, it is stated that the Quailtones consisted of Kari and a Josie studio group performing for that one session, which produced Tears of Love/Roxanna.

(Note: Interestingly, Steve Towne's *Goldmine* article of April 1982 and Bob Pruter's *Goldmine* article of May 1980 include a discussion of the Quailtones and a Freddie Gorman interview. Gorman stated that he had formed a local junior high school group, the Quailtones. Sonny Sanders, who had met Gorman after moving from the Chicago area, joined Gorman and the others in junior high school and some-

how they were able to record for Josie in 1954. He always wondered why his name was not on the "Tears of Love" side of the record because he wrote the tune. Talk about inconsistencies!)

The Quailtones formed in a Detroit high school in 1954. Kari arranged for the group to record for Josie in New York.

"Tears of Love" was later redone by the Loreleis on Spotlight; like the Quailtones version, it was unsuccessful.

Shortly after recording the Josie disc, the Quailtones disbanded. Sanders later sang with the Satintones on Motown.

Discography

Josie 779 Tears of Love/Roxanna (1955)
Sources: Bob Belniak in *Echoes of the Past* 27; Steve Towne in *Goldmine,* September 1981; Bob Pruter in *Goldmine,* May 1980. Article about Sonny Sanders.

Queens, Shirley Gunter & (Los Angeles)

Personnel Shirley Gunter (lead), Lula Bee Kinney (1st tenor), Lula Mae Suggs (2d tenor), Blondine Taylor (baritone)

Notes

This group was organized by classmates and friends from Los Angeles Polytechnic High School who got together in 1953.

Zola Taylor of the Platters spent some time with the Queens, although she performed on no recordings.

Shirley Gunter is the sister of Cornel (Cornelius) Gunter. Lula Bee Suggs is the aunt of Lula Mae Kinney.

The Queens first release, "Oop Shoop," like the Chords' "Sh Boom," was immediately covered by Canada's Crew Cuts, whose release fared far better than the Queens'.

Discography

Flair 1050 Oop Shoop/It's You (1954)
Flair 1060 You're Mine/Why? (1955)
Flair 1065 Baby, I Love You So/What Difference Does It Make? (1955)
Flair 1070 That's the Way I Like It/Gimme, Gimme, Gimme (1955)
Source: Jim Dawson, notes to the Virgin CD *R&B Confidential/The Flair Label.*

Question Marks (Detroit)

Personnel Calvin Fair (lead), Isaiah Jones (tenor)

Notes

Jack Lauderdale of Swing Time Records on the West Coast acquired the masters of recordings by Detroit's Violinaires on Drummond Records and had the group re-record their "Another Soldier Gone" on Swing Time with a new flip side. The original Drummond flip was "Joy in the Beulah Land."

Discography

Swing Time 346 Another Soldier Gone/Go and Get Some More (1954)
Source: Richie Benway, liner notes with the Swing Time CD *Swing Time Doo Wop.*

Quinns (Brooklyn, N.Y.)

Personnel Freddie Brown (lead), Donald Lawrence (tenor), Richie Brown (2d tenor), Gerald Johnson (baritone), Leon McLain (bass)

Notes

The group originally got together, with a female lead, early in 1956, practicing the R&B/R&R hits of the day. The female lead, only remembered as Pauline, stayed briefly, until Freddie Brown was brought in. Initially, they named themselves the Quintones and they included Johnny "Dusty" Moye (d) at second tenor.

They played many talent shows at local theaters. By the end of 1956, they felt ready for more and auditioned for Herb Abramson at Atco, who signed them up immediately following the audition. On their first recording they provided backup work for blues great Jimmy Witherspoon. The Quinns, referred to as the Quintones, were given credit on the label. The record Atco 6084 was reviewed during the week of December 15, 1956. Following the disc's release, group was terminated by Atco with no explanation given.

Paul Winley of Winley Records in Brooklyn had apparently heard them and told them that he would record them immediately if they became available. Following the Atco debacle, they signed with Winley. Because there were two other Quintones groups recording at the time, it was decided that they should change their name. This was when they became the Quinns. Coincidentally, the group had been friendly with members of the Paragons, who were also from Brooklyn and also recorded for Winley.

After signing with Winley, Moye got into a dispute with the other members and left. Freddie Brown's brother Richie was familiar with their repertoire and joined the group to replace Moye.

They recorded for Cyclone, which was a Winley subsidiary. The disc was released in the summer of 1957. Having a record released brought them several local appearances in Brooklyn and in the Bronx. Donald Lawrence got into some trouble in 1958 and was replaced by Francis "Frenchie" Concepcion of the Wrens and the Travelers. Leon McLain left in 1959 to earn some real money and was replaced by Henry Thomas.

In 1960, they contacted Al Browne, also from Brooklyn. With Browne they recorded Unfaithful/Who Stole the Cookies. These stayed in the can until Relic released them in 1965.

In *They All Sang on the Corner,* Phil Groia states that this group (or part of it) had been the Continentals on Whirlin' Disc. I spoke with Leon McLain, who unequivocally and emphatically denied this statement. Marv Goldberg's article in the February 1998 edition of *DISCoveries* magazine confirms this.

Discography

Cyclone 111 Oh Starlight/Hong Kong (1957)

Relic 1012 Unfaithful/Who Stole the Cookies (1965)
Sources: Leon McLain, interview by Mitch Rosalsky, April 23, 1994; Phil Groia, *They All Sang on the Street Corner*; Marv Goldberg in *DISCoveries,* February 1998.

Quintones (Chicago)

Personnel Donald Burrows (lead), Clifford Sutherland (1st tenor), Freddie Williams (2d tenor), Ralph Fulham (baritone), Bill McDonald (bass)

Notes

This was a local Chicago Quintones group that made one record on the Park label while in high school. They disbanded six months after recording due to little encouragement, poor sales, and no financial rewards.

Discography

Park 111/112 More Than a Notion/South Sea Island (1957)
Source: Bob Pruter, *Doowop . . . The Chicago Scene.*

Quintones (York, Pa.)

Personnel Roberta Haymon (lead), Phyllis Carr, Carolyn Holmes, Kenneth Sexton, Jeannie Crist

Notes

The Quintones began in 1957 as classmates at William Penn High School. The group was then known as the Quinteros and played local spots and school functions. While performing, they met a disc jockey, Phil Landersman, who liked them and became their manager. After some work with the group, he got them their first session and eventual release on Chess.

The Chess release did not sell very well but got them on a tour. At that time they were still in high school and had to get the principal's approval to leave school for this touring. While on tour, they wrote "Down the Aisle." Their manager had so much faith in the tune and in their performance of it that he brought it to Dick Clark. In an interview several years ago, Phyllis Carr stated that Clark owned 95 percent of the tune!

The record was rereleased on Hunt and played on *American Bandstand.* The disc sold quite well. Carr also stated in the 1990 interview that the group had never received any royalties from it.

The Quintones' follow-ups sold poorly and by 1960 they went their separate ways—marriage, the service, jobs, and so on.

In Bob Belnick's *Echoes of the Past* magazine (issue 7), he writes that the lead is Roberto Haymon.

Discography

Chess 1685 Ding Dong/Try So Hard (1958)
Red Top 108 Down the Aisle of Love/Please Dear (1958)

Hunt 321 Down the Aisle of Love/Please Dear (1958)
Hunt 322 There'll Be No Sorrow/What Am I to Do? (1958)
Red Top 116 Oh Heavenly Father/I Watch the Stars (19590
Source: Wayne Jancik in *Goldmine,* December 28, 1990.

Quotations (Brooklyn, N.Y.)

Personnel Larry Kassman (lead), Richie Schwartz (1st tenor), Lew Arno (2d tenor), Harvey Hirshkowitz (baritone)

Notes

This group got together in Brooklyn in 1958 while group members were still in high school. In 1959, the group paid for studio time to cut some demos. Songwriter Helen Miller took a liking to the group and had them audition all over New York. They wrote their "Ala-Men-Say" and presented it to MGM music, which liked it and released it on the MGM Verve subsidiary in 1961. "Imagination" was the flip.

Before recording, the group contained Davie Nichols, who later formed the Camelots, and Rodney Bristow, who later formed Tex and the Chex.

Lew Arno departed in 1962 to return to school, and Sandy Sonner joined the group and recorded a number of a cappella tunes with the Quotations for the Relic label. Bob Kutner was also a member of this group prior to their decision to call it quits.

Discography

Verve 10245 Imagination/Ala-Men-Sy (1961)
Verve 10252 We'll Reach Heaven Together/This Love of Mine (1962)
Verve 10261 See You in September/Summertime Goodbye (1962)
Source: Bob Diskin in *Record Collector's Monthly* 51.

Radiants (Los Angeles)

Personnel Cleve Duncan (lead), Vesta White, Gladys White, Vera Walker, Dexter Tisby

Notes

This disc, led by Duncan, was his last for Dootone. Unfortunately, sales were dismal.

Discography

Dooto 451 To Keep Our Love/I'm Betting My Heart (1959)
Sources: Marv Goldberg and Mike Redmond in *Record Exchanger* 11 (article on the Penguins); Jay Warner, *American Singing Groups.*

Radiants (Chicago)

Personnel Mitchell Bullock (lead), Maurice McAllister (tenor), Leonard Caston (tenor), Wallace Simpson (baritone)

Notes

Andy McKaie's liner notes with the Chess LP *Best of Chess Vocal Groups* states that this group was sometimes a male trio and sometimes a quintet.

Discography

Chess 1832 Father Knows Best/One Day I'll Show You (1962)
Chess 1849 Heartbreak Society/Please Don't Leave Me (1963)
Chess 1865 I Got a Girl/I'm in Love (1963)
Chess 1872 I'm in Love/Shy Guy (1963)
Chess 1887 Noble/Dance to Keep My Baby (1964)
Chess 1904 Voice Your Choice/If I Only Had You (1964)
Chess 1925 It Ain't No Big Thing/I Got a Girl (1965)
Chess 1939 Tomorrow/Whole Lot of Woman (1965)
Source: Andy McKaie, liner notes with the Chess LP *Best of Chess Vocal Groups.*

Raiders (Brooklyn, N.Y.)

Personnel Willie Bobbitt (lead), Bob Chance (a.k.a. Bob Wahlstein) (1st tenor), Leroy Haskins (2d tenor), Jesse Payton (baritone), Al Hardy (bass)

Notes

This group originally met at Boy's High School in the Bedford-Stuyvesant section of Brooklyn, New York. They spent every morning, holiday, school vacation, and summer vacation practicing. Every afternoon they went off to Manhattan seeking out a record company to audition for. They did this for almost two years.

While at New York's famous Brill Building, they were in the stairwell practicing and were overheard by Roy Hamilton and his manager, who told them to have a demo done. This led to a recording date with Atco Records, where they recorded four tunes.

Because Atco at the time was preoccupied with Bobby Darin, the Raiders were always put on the back burner in regard to recording a second record. Disgusted, they left Atco. Haskins soon departed from the group and was replaced by Tom O'Malley. Frank Feliciano joined at this time as well.

After the Brunswick release, all the members went their separate ways.

Discography

Atco 6125 Castle of Love/Raiders from Outer Space (1957)
Brunswick 55090 Walking through the Jungle/My Steady Girl (1958)
Source: Tracy Sands in *Record Collector's Monthly* 29.

Rainbows (Washington, D.C.)

Personnel Ronald Miles (lead), Henry "Shorty" Womble (1st tenor), John Berry (2d tenor), James Nolan (baritone), Frank Hardy (bass)

Notes

When this group first went to Red Robin, Bobby Robinson told them go home and practice. They returned a year later to sing again for Robinson. This time he had them record.

"Mary Lee" was written by John Berry as a joke about someone's girlfriend. It was Berry who retained Don Covay's services for the Rainbows. It should be mentioned here that when the Hollywood Flames relocated to New York, Berry joined them.

The personnel shown above only recorded "Mary Lee." Womble left after the disc was released to attend prep school. He made occasional appearances with the Rainbows on holidays, weekends, and vacations.

Don Covay and Chester Simmons (d) joined just before "Shirley" and "Stay," which were recorded in a New York studio and released on Pilgrim Records. Berry, Miles, Covay, and Simmons recorded "They Say" on Rama.

Rumors that Marvin Gaye and Billy Stewart recorded with the Rainbows surfaced because they were friends of the group's personnel. Gaye periodically appeared with the group at personal engagements, but he never recorded with them. There is neither confirmation nor denial in regard to Stewart.

It became apparent to the group that they were not doing well before the release of "They Say," even with great sales on "Mary Lee." Their feeling was based on the absence of royalties from the sales of their records.

In 1957, James Nolan and Chester Simmons joined the Marquees on Okeh. The other members of the Marquees were old friends Reese Palmer and Marvin Gaye.

When "Mary Lee" was reissued on Fire, the label said "featuring Sonny Spencer." This was a pseudonym for John Berry.

Baritone Layton McDonald, Duval Potter, Joseph Walls, Victor English, and Ronald Miles formed another Rainbows in 1961.

Discography

Red Robin 134 Mary Lee (JB/RM)/Evening (JB) (1955)
Pilgrim 703 Mary Lee/Evening (reissue) (1956)
Pilgrim 711 Shirley (RM/JB)/Stay (JB/DC) (1956)
Rama 209 They Say (RM)/Minnie (JB) (1956)
Fire 1012 Mary Lee/Evening (reissue) (1960)
Argyle 1012 Shirley/Stay (reissue) (1962)
Dave 908 I Know (DP)/Only a Picture (JW) (1963)
Dave 909 It Wouldn't Be Right (RM)/Family Monkey (JW) (1963)
Sources: Marvin Podd in *Yesterday's Memories* 4; Drew Williamson in *Record Collector's Monthly* 44; Lynn McCutcheon in *Record Exchanger*; Donn Fileti, liner notes with the Relic CD *Red Robin Golden Doowops.*

Rainbows, Randy & (Queens, N.Y.)

Personnel Dominick "Randy" Safuto (lead), Frank Safuto (1st tenor), Sal Zero (2d tenor), Mike Zero (baritone) Ken Arcipowski (bass)

Notes

The two Safutos were brothers and had previously been with Goldisc's Dialtones, who recorded "Till I Heard It from You" and "Johnny" in 1960. The disc didn't do badly, but the Dialtones split and never recorded together again.

In 1961, following the Dialtones' breakup, Dominic became friendly with an old friend from school, Mike Zero. The two were attending Grover Cleveland High School and decided to form their own group. Mike got his brother Sal and another friend, Ken Arcipowski.

They performed together for about six months doing the typical church socials, record hops, and so on, and in 1963 they got a manager. They were soon brought to the Tokens and their Bright Tunes Music. At the time the Tokens were with Laurie Records and got the group a contract with Laurie's Rust label. It was Laurie management that renamed the group Randy and the Rainbows. Two weeks after signing with Laurie they were in the studio recording Denise/Come Back.

"Denise" did quite well, reaching number ten nationally and number two locally. Unfortunately the Angels' "My Boyfriend's Back" was even more popular and kept "Denise" from doing better.

The Tokens were responsible for all the discs released by the Rainbows. Although there were some were good sides, none ever came close to the popularity of "Denise."

In 1965, the Rainbows' contract expired and they moved to Mike records. They recorded two records for Mike that did not do well. In 1966, they found themselves back with the Tokens. They recorded one last disc on B.T. Puppy. Following that release, they decided to call it quits.

Discography

Rust 5059 Denise/Come Back (1963)
Rust 5073 She's My Angel/Why Do Kids Grow Up? (1963)
Rust 5080 Happy Teenager/Dry Your Eyes (1964)
Rust 5091 Little Star/Sharin' (1964)
Rust 5101 Joyride/Little Hot Rod Suzie (1965)
Mike 4001 Lovely Lies/I'll Forget Her Tomorrow (1966)
Mike 4004 He's a Fugitive/Quarter to Three (1966)
Mike 4008 D.J./Bonnie's Part of Town (1966)
B.T. Puppy 535 I'll Be Seeing You/Oh to Get Away (1966)
Sources: Ed Engel in *Remember Then* 1; Ed Engel, *White and Still All Right*; Ed Engel, liner notes with the Ace CD *Laurie Vocal Groups*.

Rajahs (New Haven, Conn.)

Personnel Leroy Griffin (lead), "Sonny" Washburn (1st tenor), Eddie Martin (2d tenor), "Sonny" Griffin (baritone), Leroy McNeill (bass)

Notes

In 1956, the Nutmegs returned home to New Haven, Connecticut, after a disagreement with Alan Freed, who accused them of including obscenities in their act. Billy Emery, who was with the group prior to recording, left to marry and Tyson left to concentrate on his first love, gospel. The Griffins and McNeil remained and were joined by Washburn from the Five Dukes on Atlas and Eddie Martin from the Five Satins. To avoid contractual problems, they changed their name to the Rajahs.

Connecticut music entreprenuers Marty Kugell and Tom Sokira had known the group previously as the Nutmegs and had learned that Griffin had some unrecorded tunes he had written and taped with no backup music (a cappella) to take with him someday to sell. The two music executives released these tunes just as they were and started the a cappella craze.

Discography

Klik 7805 I Fell in Love/Shifting Sands (1957)
Klik 1019 You're Crying/Roseann (1973)
Source: Donn Fileti, liner notes with the Relic CD *Rajahs of Acappella.*

Ramblers (Baltimore, Md.)

Personnel Adolphus Holcomb (lead), James Arthur (tenor), Raymond Holcomb (baritone), Gilbert Wilkes (bass)

Notes

Gilbert Wilkes and Adolphus Holcomb also sang with the Philadelphia Kings.
    Another member was Leon Arnold.
    Adolphus and Raymond Holcomb were brothers.

Discography

Jax 319 Search My Heart/50/50 Love (1953)
Source: Marv Goldberg and Dave Hinckley in *Yesterday's Memories* 11.

Ramblers (Detroit)

Personnel Carlis "Sonny" Monroe, James Gibson, Johnny Alvin, Alton Hollowell

Notes

The Ramblers on MGM were the Kings who had been on Jax and Harlem. They were, however, not the Ramblers on Jax.
    This group had been Detroit's Falcons.

Discography

MGM 11850 Vadunt-Un-Vada Song/Please Bring Yourself Back Home (1954)
MGM 55006 Rickey-Do Rickey-Do/Bad Girl (1955)
(Note: According to Michel Ruppli's King-Federal-DeLuxe logs, the Federal group included the same personnel as above.*)*
Sources: Michel Ruppli, *King-Federal-DeLuxe Discography*; Marv Goldberg and Dave Hinckley in *Yesterday's Memories* 11.

Rams (Los Angeles)

Personnel Arthur Lee Maye (tenor), Johnny Coleman (baritone), Richard Berry (bass)

Notes

This group began in 1954 as a splinter of the Flairs that included Maye, Berry, and Johnny Coleman, the three who would always walk the hallways of Los Angeles's Jefferson High School harmonizing. They were also with the Flairs at this time. Maye was organizing his own Crowns group at this time as well.

Flair Records brought the still unnamed trio to their studio and recorded the first disc as the Five Hearts. The next time they recorded at the Flair facilities, the record was released as by the Rams!

In the liner notes accompanying the Ace CD *Fifties Vocal Groups,* the members of the Rams are shown to be Arthur Lee Maye (lead), Cornel Gunter, Joe Morgan, and Johnny Coleman. In *Yesterday's Memories* 10, the Rams are shown as Richard Berry, Arthur Lee Maye, Johnny Morris, and Johnny Coleman. In *Whiskey, Women and . . .* , in the story discussing Lee Maye, the group, as above, is said to be the trio of Maye, Berry, and Johny Coleman! Two of these accounts were by Marv Goldberg. The Goldberg article in *Whiskey, Women, and . . .* was based on an interview of Lee Maye, eleven years after the first.

Discography

Flair 1066 Rock Bottom/Sweet Thing (1955)
Sources: Jim Dawson, Ray Topping, and Ted Carroll, notes to the Ace CD *Fifties Vocal Groups*; Marv Goldberg and Rick Whitesell in *Yesterday's Memories* 10; Marv Goldberg in *Whiskey, Women, and . . .* 17.

Ravens (New York)

Personnel Ollie Jones (lead), Leonard Puzey (2d tenor), Warren "Birdland" Suttles (baritone), Jimmy Ricks (bass)

Notes

In 1945, Jimmy Ricks and Warren Suttles were working as waiters in a Harlem bar. Periodically, they would sing along with songs being played on the bar's jukebox, with live vocal performances at the club and everything else that could be sung to or with.

Realizing they needed at least two more voices, they went to a local talent agency where they found Leonard Puzey and Ollie Jones. The four polished their craft and named themselves the Ravens. They were soon introduced to Howard Biggs, who became their arranger and got them a contract with Hub. Their first single was released in June of that year.

When Ollie Jones left the Ravens, he formed the Blenders. He was told that the Ravens would continue using him until they found a 1st tenor who could better adapt to their style. This would then allow Jimmy Ricks to find the 1st tenor he needed.

He found Maithe Marshall (real name Maithe Williams) to join as tenor lead. In January 1947, Marshall replaced Jones. When Maithe joined, they rerecorded their Hub sides from which Hub owner Ben Bart took the masters and held in storage for a while. The following year, they switched to National. Marshall left the Ravens briefly in 1948 and was replaced by Richie Cannon. Maithe, however, was not gone long and would soon return.

In June 1948, probably resulting from the split between Ben Bart and his partner, Harry Lenetzka, Hub sold all its 1946 and 1947 Ravens masters to Sid Nathan's King Records. The Cincinnati record organization promptly issued the discs, which had been rerecorded with Marshall at lead. With the immense popularity of the Ravens, King tried to stretch the Hub masters as far as they could.

There were many personnel changes. Suttles left for the first time in September 1948. He was replaced by Joe Medlin. In October, Marshall left and Richie Cannon took his place. At this time the group consisted of Richie Cannon, Leonard Puzey, Joe Medlin, and Jimmy Ricks. This configuration lasted briefly. In November 1948, Medlin left to continue his solo career. Marshall returned and Cannon was shifted to baritone. Suttles returned early in 1949 and Cannon was let go. It was a year of touring and appearances for the Ravens. In August, Howard Biggs left and was replaced by Bill Sanford. National continued to release Ravens tunes. Suttles's second departure found Louis Heyward substituting for him when internal conflicts caused Warren to leave for the second time.

In September 1950, they moved on to Columbia Records as part of a four-group deal that manager Bart had made with Columbia. The Ravens were signed to a one-year contract and Mitch Miller became their A&R man at Columbia. Although National lost the Ravens, songs were left in the can that they continued to release. This occurred until 1951, when National started litigation with Columbia over the Ravens, as they felt the label had induced the group to breach their contract. Columbia began releasing Ravens records like a repeating rifle. Apparently this and other conflicts were settled out of court.

Following a March 1951 session with Columbia, Maithe, Leonard and Louis decided to leave Ricks and the Ravens to form the trio, the Hi Hatters. This didn't last long, and Maithe and Louis rejoined after a short time. Puzey was drafted but returned for the session when Columbia switched them to Okeh, its revived R&B label. After this, the group split. Puzey remained in the service. Frazier joined the Chestnuts, and Marshall formed his Marshall Brothers.

In October 1951, after being with Columbia/Okeh for a year, Bart removed the Ravens from Columbia's grip and placed them with Mercury. The group at Mercury included Ricks, Jimmy Stewart, Louis Frazier, and Joe Van Loan. Van Loan got the job on the spot with his soaring tenor. Another Okeh disc was released at this time as well. Mercury began releasing Ravens records in November. This continued regularly into 1952, as did their engagements. Another Okeh disc was released in June. Warren Suttles once again returned late in 1952, forcing out Louis Frazier. Puzey rejoined in April following his discharge from the army. Jimmy Stewart then left. The group was now Suttles, Ricks, Puzey, and Van Loan. Puzey left again after a few months and Stewart was rehired. Puzey wasn't idle, singing with the Dappers and the Cues. Ravens appearances and recordings continued.

Early in 1954, Ricks walked out and was replaced by Tommy Evans of the Carols. This lasted about six months and Evans became unemployed. Suttles left again, this time for good. In January 1955, the final Mercury record was released.

When the contract with Mercury expired, Ricks took the group to Jubilee. The group at Jubilee was composed of Frazier (who had now returned), Ricks, Van Loan, and Stewart. They cut four discs at Jubilee, and then Ricks decided to go solo in 1956. Tommy Evans again replaced him. The group was now Evans, Van Loan, Jimmy Stewart, and Louis Frazier. Jubilee chose not to record the Evans-led Ravens and released older masters with Ricks at the helm. The final Jubilee record was released in February 1956.

When popular music began to change, the group's sound did as well. Later in 1956, they signed on with the Chess subsidiary, Argo. Van Loan convinced group management to fire Stewart, Frazier, and Tommy Evans. Frazier would pass on shortly after this incident. Van Loan then assembled his former colleagues in the Dixieaires, Du Droppers, and Bells and they became the new Ravens—Joe Van Loan, Willie Ray, Willis Sanders (Saunders), and Bob Kornegay. It was this group that recorded the first tune on Argo, "Kneel and Pray."

Following the first Argo release, Kornegay quit to try his hand at a solo career. Once again a bass was needed, and David "Boots" Bowers was hired. Bowers had been with the King Odom Four and the Larks on Lloyds from 1953 to 1955. After the Larks, he was dormant for a time and simply auditioned for the Ravens to prove he was still good enough to fill Jimmy Ricks's position.

This group—Van Loan, Willie Ray, Bowers, and Saunders—was the Ravens who did "A Simple Prayer" for Argo. This was the only session they did as the Ravens.

At this juncture, Willie and Willis left and Van Loan brought in his brothers Paul and James. Joe was the lead for the Ravens on Argo, Mercury, and Jubilee. It was this group that did the balance of the Argo material. In June 1957, the group recorded "Long Lonely Nights." Chess/Checker management had already leased this tune from Casino Records in Philadelphia by Lee Andrews and the Hearts. So as not to have two of their groups executing the same song, on one of their labels, they leased the Ravens tune to Baton Records. Baton called the group the Kings.

In September 1957, the National catalog was purchased by Herman Lubinsky at Savoy. This explains why "White Christmas" and "Silent Night" were released on Savoy in October 1957.

Discography

Hub 3030 Honey/Lullaby (1946)
Hub 3032 Out of a Dream/My Sugar Is So Refined (1946)
Hub 3033 Bye Bye Baby Blues/Once and For All (1946)
Nat'l 9034 Mahzel/For You (1947)
Nat'l 9035 Ol' Man River/Would You Believe Me (1947)
Nat'l 9038 Write Me a Letter/Summertime (1947)
Nat'l 9039 Searching for Love/For You (1947)
Nat'l 9040 Fool That I Am/Bee I Bumblebee or Not (1947)
Nat'l 9042 Together/There's No You (1947)
Nat'l 9045 Until the Real Thing Comes Along/Send for Me If You (1948)
Nat'l 9053 September Song/Once in a While (1948)
Nat'l 9056 It's Too Soon to Know/Be On Your Merry Way (1948)
Nat'l 9059 How Could I Know/I Don't Know Why I Love You Like I Do (1948)
Nat'l 9062 Silent Night/White Christmas (1948)

Nat'l 9064 Always/Rooster (1948)
King 4234 Bye Bye Baby Blues/Once and for All (1948)
King 4260 Out of a Dream (instrumental) (1948)
King 4272 Honey (instrumental) (1949)
King 5393 My Sugar Is So Refined (instrumental) (1949)
Nat'l 9065 Deep Purple/Leave My Gal Alone (1949)
Nat'l 9073 The House I Live In/Rickey's Blues (1949)
Nat'l 9085 There's Nothing Like a Woman in Love/Careless Love (1949)
Nat'l 9089 If You Didn't Mean It/Someday (1949)
Nat'l 9098 I'm Afraid of You/Get Wise Baby (1949)
Nat'l 9101 I've Been a Fool/I Don't Have to Ride No More (1949)
Nat'l 9111 Count Every Star/I'm Gonna Paper My Walls with . . . (1950)
Nat'l 9131 Phantom Stage Coach/I'm Gonna Take to the Road (1950)
Nat'l 9148 Lilacs in the Rain/Time Is Marching On (1950)
Columbia 6-903 Time Takes Care of Everything/Don't Look Now (1950)
Columbia 6-925 My Baby's Gone/I'm So Crazy for Love (1950)
Columbia 39112 Midnight Blues/You Don't Have to Drop a Heart to Break It (1950)
Columbia 39194 You're Always in My Dreams/Gotta Find My Baby (1951)
Columbia 39408 You Foolish Thing/Honey I Don't Want You (1951)
Okeh 6825 Whiffenpoof Song/Get All My Lovin' on a Saturday Nite (1951)
Okeh 6843 That Old Gang of Mine/Everyone but You (1951)
Rendition 5001 Write Me a Letter/Marie (1951)
Mercury 8257 Out in the Cold Again/Hey Good Lookin' (1951)
Mercury 8259 There's No Use Pretending/Wagon Wheels (1951)
Mercury 5800 Begin the Beguine/Looking for My Baby (1951)
Okeh 6888 Mam'selle/Calypso Song (1952)
Mercury 5853 Chloe-E/Why Did You Leave Me? (1952)
Mercury 8291 Write Me One Sweet Letter/Rock Me All Night Long (1952)
Mercury 70060 Don't Mention My Name/I'll Be Back (1952)
Mercury 70119 Come a Little Bit Closer/She's Got to Go (1953)
Mercury 70213 Who'll Be the Fool/Rough Ridin' (1953)
Mercury 70240 Without a Song/Walkin' My Blues Away (1954)
Mercury 70307 September Song/Escourtin' or Courtin' (1954)
Mercury 70413 Love Is No Dream/I've Got You under My Skin (1954)
Mercury 70505 Silent Night/White Christmas (1955)
Jubilee 5184 Bye Bye Baby Blues/Happy Go Lucky Baby (1955)
Jubilee 5203 Green Eyes/The Bells of San Raquel (1955)
Jubilee 5217 On Chapel Hill/We'll Raise a Ruckus Tonight (1955)
Jubilee 5237 Boots and Saddles/I'll Always Be in Love with You (1956)
Argo 5255 Kneel and Pray/I Can't Believe (1956)
Argo 5261 Water Boy/A Simple Prayer (1956)
Argo 5276 Dear One/That'll Be the Day (1957)
Savoy 1540 Silent Night/White Christmas (1957)
Argo 5284 Here Is My Heart/Lazy Mule (1957)

Sources: Andy McKaie, liner notes with the CD *Best of Chess-1;* Adam Komorowski, liner notes with the Sequel CD *Dominoes Meet the Ravens;* Marv Goldberg in *DISCoveries,* article about the Ravens.

Raves (New York)

Personnel Howard Guyton (d) (lead), Derek Martin, Leonard Puzey, Jimmy Ricks (bass)

Notes

This group was assembled after Ricks left the Ravens and was pursuing a solo career. During the early 1960s he was reunited with Herb Abramson, who had been at National Records in the late 1940s when Ricks and the Ravens were recording for National. Abramson supervised several sessions with Ricks and one product of these sessions was a group called the Raves.

Guyton also sang with the Pearls and the Cadillacs. Martin also sang with the Pearls.

Discography

Atco 6220 Daddy Rollin' Stone/Homesick (1962)
Festival 25004 Daddy Rollin' Stone/Umgowa (1962)
Sources: Gordon Skadberg, liner notes with the Sequel CD *Herb Abramson's Festival of Groups*; Mike Sweeney and Tony Watson in *Goldmine,* February 21, 1992.

Rays (New York)

Personnel Harold Miller (lead), Walter Ford (1st tenor), David Jones (2d tenor), Harry James (baritone)

Notes

In 1955, Miller and Jones sang with the Four Toppers, a name the Four Fellows on Glory used before they started to record. The name was also used for a benefit appearance they made. Seeing no future with the Four Toppers, the two left that group. Two years later, they found Ford and James and formed a new group, the Rays. When the Four Fellows ended their recording days, David Jones joined the Rays.

(Note: Despite the rumors, Harold Miller never sang with the Four Fellows. He practiced with them when they were known as the Four Toppers.)

When they felt they were ready, they signed with Chess Records and recorded two discs that did nothing.

In 1957 they signed with Bob Crewe and Frank Slay's XYZ Records. The Rays' first recording with XYZ was only fair and didn't sell really well. The second release was "Silhouettes," which Crew and Slay had written. "Silhouettes" was a monster seller and was leased to Cameo/Parkway for better distribution.

"Silhouettes" was covered by a Canadian group known for covering black American hits, the Crewcuts. Both versions sold well. There were other covers but they didn't do as well. One of those was by Steve Gibson and the Red Caps.

As a result of the British invasion, the Rays never had a hit again, despite great records released on XYZ.

Reggie Gordon also sang with the Rays.

Discography

Chess 1613 Tippety Top/Moo Goo Gai-Pan (1955)
Chess 1678 How Long Must I Wait?/Second Fiddle (1957)
Argo 1074 How Long Must I Wait?/Second Fiddle (1957)
XYZ 100 My Steady Girl/Nobody Loves You Like I Do (1957)
XYZ 102 Silhouettes/Daddy Cool (1957)
Cameo 117 Silhouettes/Daddy Cool (1957)
Cameo 127 Crazy Girl/Dressin' Up (1958)
Cameo 133 Rags to Riches/The Man Above (1958)
XYZ 2001 Souvenirs of Summertime/Elevator Operator (1958)
XYZ 600 Why Do You Look the Other Way?/Zimba Lulu (1959)
XYZ 605 It's a Cryin' Shame/Mediterranean Moon (1959)
XYZ 607 Louie Hoo Hoo/Magic Moon (1960)
XYZ 608 Silver Starlight/Old Devil Moon (1960)
Topix 6003 An Angel Cried/Hope, Faith and Dreams (1961)
Perri 1004 Are You Happy Now?/Bright Brown Eyes (1962)
Amy 900 Sad Saturday/Love Another Girl (1964)
Source: Unsigned liner notes with the XYZ CD *Rays.*

Red Caps/Five Red Caps (New York)

Personnel Jimmy Springs (d) (lead), Emmett Matthews (2d tenor), David Patillo (d) (2d tenor), Romaine Brown (baritone), Steve Gibson (bass)

Notes

This group was originally from the West Coast, known there as the Four Toppers. The first known lineup consisted of Steve Gibson, Jimmy Springs, and two unknown members. Since this group never recorded, ascertaining the identity of the original members is less important. They began touring, and on this tour they found David Patillo. The tour of major cities came when the group realized that there was no money to be made on the West Coast. While they were in New York in 1943, they met Emmett Matthews and Romaine Brown. Reflected above is the first known recording personnel listing of the Five Red Caps.

Patillo had formed and had sung with the Four Blackbirds (Vocalion) in Los Angeles. Jimmy Springs sang with the Jones Boys and the Jones Boys Sing Band and was with the Four Toppers when they started.

While the Red Caps were appearing at a Brooklyn nightclub, Joe Davis saw them and asked if they would come to his Beacon Records facility. They recorded there for Davis and records were released on Beacon, Gennett, Joe Davis, and Davis. The Red Caps recorded twenty-six singles for these Joe Davis labels from 1943 to 1948.

Ballads were led by Jimmy Springs and up-tempo songs by Romaine Brown or Gibson himself. Their stage act included singing, playing their instruments, dancing, and comedy routines.

In 1947, they moved to Mercury, where their name changed to Steve Gibson and the Red Caps. At Mercury, Earl Plummer filled in for Springs briefly while he was away. The reason for going with Mercury was that Davis's operations had become inactive.

Because trios were successful in the late 1940s, a Red Caps Trio was formed. This group consisted of Romaine Brown, Steve Gibson, and Doles Dickens (a new member of the Red Caps).

Ormande Wilson, Steve Gibson's stepbrother, sang for the Red Caps, as did Arthur Davey. Wilson had also sung lead for the Basin Street Boys.

The Red Caps went to RCA in 1950 and by 1953, with music changing, response to their appearances and recordings was diminishing.

Damita Jo DuBlanc also sang lead for the Red Caps in 1951, as did Gloria Smith. Damita was married to Steve Gibson for a while and was the most successful of all the vocalists ever associated with the Red Caps

In April 1950 Andre D'Orsay joined the Red Caps.

In 1953, personnel changes began with Damita Jo leaving with Romaine Brown who would later form the Romaines. Henry Green from the Romaines would soon return to the Red Caps, as would Arthur Davey after he had been with Plink, Plank, and Plunk. Within a year everything collapsed.

The existing group disbanded in 1956 and Gibson got the Furness Brothers, Bill, Joe, and Peck Furness, to be the new Red Caps. Emmett Matthews remained with this new formation.

When the Romaines dissolved in 1959, Brown returned, resulting in another formation: Matthews, Brown, Springs, Henry Green, Bobby Gregg, Damita Jo (back again), and George Tindley (of the Savoy Dreams).

In 1960, Romaine Brown, Damita Jo, and Tindley left after a year to form the Modern Red Caps with Tindley and George Grant.

The Toppers may have recorded for Savoy. In an interview by Brown in the 1970s, he stated that the group never recorded as the Toppers. However, in 1944, three records were recorded by the Toppers, two on Savoy, and one on the Savoy subsidiary, Regent.

Patillo died in 1966, Springs in 1987, and Gibson in 1996.

Discography

Beacon 7220 Get Off of That Kick/It's Got a Hole in It (1945)
Beacon 7221 Monkey and the Baboon/That's the Stuff (1945)
Mercury 5011 Bless You/You Can't See the Sun When You're Crying (1947)
Mercury 8038 Jack You're Dead/San Antonio Rose (1947)
Mercury 8052 Don't Want to Set the World on Fire/Till the Well Runs Dry (1947)
Mercury 8059 Walkin' through Heaven/You're Driving Me Crazy ((1947)
Mercury 8069 Wedding Bells Are Breaking Up . . . / I'd Love to Live a Lifetime (1948)
Mercury 8085 Little White Lies/Turnip Greens (1948)
Mercury 8091 Danny Boy/Scratch and You'll Find It (1948)
Mercury 8093 Money Is Honey/Give Me Time (1948)
Mercury 8109 You Made Me Love You/I Learned a Lesson I'll Never Forget (1948)
Mercury 8146 Blueberry Hill/I Love You (1949)
Mercury 8157 Petunia/I've Been Living for You (1949)
Mercury 5380 I'll Never Love Anyone Else/I Want a Roof over My Head (1950)
Mercury 8165 They Ain't Gonna Tell It Right/I Wake Up Every Morning (1950)
Mercury 8174 Are You Lonesome Tonight?/Sentimental Me (1950)

Mercury 8186 Steve's Blues/Dirt Dishin' Daisy (1950)
RCA 47-3986 Am I to Blame?/The Thing (1950)
RCA 47-4294 Shame/Boogie Woogie on a Saturday Night (1950)
RCA 47-4670 I May Hate Myself in the Morning/Two Little Kisses (1952)
RCA 47-5013 Truthfully/Why Don't You Love Me? (1952)
RCA 47-5130 Big Game Hunter/Do I, Do I, I Do (1953)
Mercury 70389 Wedding Bells Are Breaking Up That . . . / Second Hand Romance (1954)
Jay Dee 796 Ouch/It Hurts Me but I Like It (1954)
RCA 47-5987 My Tzatskele/Win or Lose (1955)
RCA 47-6096 Feelin Kinda Happy/Nuff of That Stuff (1955)
RCA 47-6345 Bobbin'/How I Cry (1955)
ABC 9702 Rock and Roll Stomp/Love Me Tenderly (1956)
ABC 9750 Write to Me/Gaucho Serenade (1956)
ABC 9796 You May Not Love Me/You've Got Me Dizzy (1957)
ABC 9856 Silhouettes/Flamingo (1957)
Hi Lo 101 I Bitty-Bitty/I Want to Be Loved (1958)
Hi Lo 103 Forever 'n' a Day/It's Love (1958)
Casa Blanca 5505 Where Are You?/San Antonio Rose (1959)
Rose 5534 I Miss You So/Bless You (1959)
Stage 3001 Blueberry Hill/Poor Poor Me (1960)
ABC 10105 I Went to Your Wedding/Together (1960)
Sources: Pete Grendysa, liner notes with the Bear Family CD *Boogie Woogie on a Saturday Night*; Marv Goldberg and Pete Grendysa in *Yesterday's Memories* 4; Jay Warner, *American Singing Groups.*

Regals (New York)

Personnel Harold Wright (lead), Aaron "Tex" Cornelius, Billy Adams, Gerald Holeman (a.k.a. Jerry Rodriguez)

Notes

Disenchanted by the payola phenomenon, Harold "Sonny" Wright, who had been with the Diamonds on Atlantic, quit the Diamonds and became part of the Regals, who recorded for Aladdin and Atlantic Records.

After leaving the Diamonds and the Regals, "Sonny Wright" went on to form the Cadence Metronomes.

Both the Regals and the Cadence Metronomes were managed by the Apollo Theater's Bobby Schifman.

Discography

Atlantic 1062 I'm So Lonely/Got the Water Boiling (1953)
Aladdin 3266 Run Pretty Baby/May the Good Lord Bless and Keep You (1954)
Source: Sal Mondrone in *Bim Bam Boom* 4.

Regents (Bronx, N.Y.)

Personnel Guy Villari (lead), Sal Cuomo (1st tenor), Charles Fassert (2d tenor), Danny Jacobuccia (baritone), Tony Gravagna (bass)

Notes

The Regents began recording on the Seville label as the Monterays. Before the group recorded for the Cousins label, Maresca left and was replaced by Don Jacobucci.

Gravagna was a session saxophone player who may have sung on the group's first Cousins session, "Barbara Ann." This disc became so popular that it had to be leased to Gee/Roulette for distribution.

Other performers who sang with the Regents were Ronnie Lapinsky from the Tremonts, Al Reno from the Selections, Bob Falcone from the Camerons, and Donnie Dee.

Having no success with ensuing discs, the Regents disbanded only to reappear several years later as the Runarounds.

Discography

Cousins 1002 Barbara Ann/I'm So Lonely (1961)
Gee 1065 Barbara Ann/I'm So Lonely (1961)
Gee 1071 Laura My Darling/Runaround (1961)
Gee 1073 Don't Be a Fool/Liar (1961)
Gee 1075 Oh Baby/Lonesome Boy (1962)
Sources: Liner notes with the Collectables CD *Barbara Ann*; Jay Warner, *American Singing Groups.*

Restless Hearts, Fred Parris & (New Haven, Conn.)

Personnel Fred Parris (lead), Dick Arnold (tenor), Richard Freeman (tenor), Gerald Brooks

Notes

After the original Five Satins dissolved, Fred Parris formed many other vocal groups, one of which was the Restless Hearts. After they were the Wildwoods, they moved to Checker and became the Restless Hearts for two years.

Tyrone French was also a member.

Discography

Checker 1108 Walk a Little Faster/No Use in Crying (1965)
Green Sea 106 Blushing Bride/Giving My Love to You (1966)
Green Sea 107 I'll Be Hanging On/I Can Really Satisfy (1966)
Atco 6439 Bring It Home to Daddy/Land of Broken Hearts (1966)
Mama Sadie 1001 In the Still of the Night/Heck No (1967)
Source: Bob Galgano, Marcia Vance, Tom Luciani, and Steve Flam in *Bim Bam Boom* 3.

Re-Vels (Philadelphia)

Personnel John Kelly (lead), Henry Colclough (tenor), John Grant, Bill Jackson, John Jones (bass)

Notes

When interviewed by Donn Fileti of Relic, Tommy Robinson, the owner of Atlas Records, did not remember recording the Re-Vels.

The Midnight Stroll group, spelled Revels, was the same.

Discography

Atlas 1035 My Lost Love/Love Me Baby (1954)
Teen 122 So in Love/It Happened to Me (1956)
Sound 129 You Lied to Me/Later Later Baby (1956)
Sound 135 Dream My Darling, Dream/Cha-Cha-Toni (1956)
Chess 1708 False Alarm/When You Come Back to Me (1958)
Norgolde 103 Dead Man's Stroll/Talking to My Heart (1959)
Norgolde 103 Midnight Stroll/Talking to My Heart (1959)
Norgolde 104 Foo Man Choo/Tweedlee Dee (1959)
Palette 5074 I Met My Lost Love/Oh How I Love You (1961)
Jamie 1318 True Love/Everybody Can Do the New Dog but Me (1965)
Sources: Liner notes with *Best of Chess Vocal Groups-1* CD; Donn Fileti, liner notes with the Relic CD *Groups of Atlas Records.*

Revlons (New Haven, Conn.)

Personnel "Corky" Rogers, Maurice Sykes, Harold Teague, "Bunky" Goldston, Richie Freeman

Notes

Rogers was also with the Five Satins.

Discography

Garpax 44168 Boy Trouble/Give Me One More Chance (1962)
Sources: R. Galgano, M. Vance, S. Flam, and T. Luciani in *Bim Bam Boom,* vol 1, no. 3; Donn Fileti, liner notes with the Relic CD *Golden Era of Doo Wops—The Groups of Standord Records.*

Rhythm Aces (U.S. Army)

Personnel Billy Steward (1st tenor), Chuck Rowan (2d tenor), Clyde Rhymes (baritone), Vince House (bass)

Notes

The members of this group met in Germany in 1950 while in the service. House and Rowan were cousins.

In Bob Pruter's book *Doowop . . . The Chicago Scene,* House is referred to as Vic.

Discharged in 1954, group members decided to stay together. Rowan was from Kansas City and House from St. Louis, and they fortunately got themselves on a tour. While touring, they were heard by Ewart Abner of Vee Jay who brought them to his Chicago studio.

The ballad "I Realize Now" remained unreleased by Vee Jay until 1964, when it finally appeared on a Solid Smoke LP.

The group disbanded in 1955 and somehow House met Lloyd McCraw of the Jacks/Cadets. He located Steward and Rowan and found a fourth member, Jimmy Brunsen. McCraw got them a contract with Modern and they then relocated to California. Their name was now the Rockets and they recorded "You Are the First One." One of the Bihari brothers, who owned Modern Records, changed their name to the Rocketeers.

Little success at Modern brought them to Era, where they were renamed the Planets and they recorded "Stand There Mountain."

When the Era contract was over, they recorded for McCraw's label MJC as the Rocketeers who did "My Reckless Heart."

Discography

Vee Jay 124 I Wonder Why/Get Lost (1954)
Vee Jay 138 Whisper to Me/Olly Olly Atsen Free (1955)
Vee Jay 160 That's My Sugar/Flippety Flop (1955)
Sources: Bob Pruter, *Doowop . . . The Chicago Scene*; Marv Goldberg in *Goldmine,* February 1991, article about the Rhythm Aces.

Rhythm Aces

Personnel Lou Fallo, Herb Glazer, John D'Amaro, Steve Freeman, Vincent Fiore

Notes

This group has nothing to do with the Vee Jay group of the same name. They are white and executed three sides.

Discography

Kampus 1001 Ease That Squeeze/Blues Are Here (1955)
Kampus 1002 Well Waddaya Know?/Palm Spring Special (1955)
Mark-X 8004 Crazy Jealousy/Boppin' Sloppin' Baby (1960)
Source: Jeff Kreiter, *Group Collector's Records Guide.*

Rhythm Kings

Personnel Cecil Murray, Leonard Thomas, Howard Scott, James Riley

Notes

Murray, Riley, Scott, and Thomas also sang with the Rhythm Masters.

In Relic's *Goodbye to the 1940s, Hello to the 1950s* CD, Marv Goldberg and Ray Funk's liner notes state that they were probably known earlier as the Rhythmasters, who recorded for Bennett records.

In 1955 they did some backup work on Groove as the Four Students, a house name used by the RCA subsidiary, Groove.

Discography

Ivory 751 I Shouldn't Have Passed Your House/Night after Night (1949)
Apollo 1171 Merry Christmas One and All/Christmas Is Coming at Last (1950)
Apollo 1181 Why My Darling, Why?/I Gotta Go Now (1951)
Source: Ray Funk and Marv Goldberg, liner notes with the Relic CD *Goodbye to the 1940s, Hello to the 1950s.*

Rhythmakers, Ruth Brown & (New York)

Personnel Ruth Brown (lead), Abel DeCosta (1st tenor), Ollie Jones (2d tenor), Roby Kirk (baritone), Eddie Barnes (bass)

Notes

The Rhythmakers were Atantic's house group. They also recorded and appeared as the Cues, the Four Students, the Ivorytones, and the Gliders.

Discography

Atlantic 1036 Oh What a Dream/Please Don't Freeze (1954)
Atlantic 1044 Somebody Touched Me/Mambo Baby (1954)
Atlantic 1051 Ever Since My Baby's Been Gone/Bye Bye Young Men (1955)
Atlantic 1059 I Can See Everybody's Baby/As Long As I'm Moving (1955)
Atlantic 1082 I Want to Do More/Old Man River (1955)
Source: Ahmet Ertegun in *Record Exchanger* 7.

Rip Chords (Chicago)

Personnel Leon Arnold (lead), George Vinyard (1st tenor), David Hargrove (2d tenor), John Gillespie (baritone), Lester Martin (bass)

Notes

This group began on Vee Jay as the Five Knights of Rhythm. When Leon Arnold wrote "I'll Be Forever Loving You" for this group, Vee Jay heard it and gave it to one of their more popular groups, the El Dorados. Because of this, the Five Knights of Rhythm left and became the Rip Chords on Abco.

The Rip Chords record was the only group record to ever appear on Abco. Eventually, the Abco label was reorganized as Cobra Records in August 1956. (Cobra was located in Chicago.)

The group broke up after recording for Abco. Leon Arnold later sang (but did not record) with the Calvaes.

Discography

Abco 105I Love You the Most/Let's Do the Razzle Dazzle (1956)
MMI 1236I Laughed So Hard/You and I (1958)
Sources: Bob Pruter, *Doowop . . . The Chicago Scene*; Marv Goldberg in the
Yesterday's Memories supplement in *Goldmine.*

Rivals (Camden, N.J.)

Personnel Johnny Smith (lead), Chandler Tribble (1st tenor), Booker T. Weeks (2d
tenor), Alfred Gaitwood (bass)

Notes

Formed in Camden, New Jersey, in 1946 as a gospel group called the International
Clavichords.

Ira Mumford, Eugene's brother, later sang bass for this group.

Johnny Smith was also in the Alphabetical Four and the Golden Arrows with Herb
Kenney.

Despite the fact that they had only the one disc (below), they had a very active
career doing club dates and live appearances.

Alfred Gaitwood sang on the very first recording by the Cufflinx as well as for
the Jem Smoothtones.

Discography

Apollo 1166 Rival Blues/Don't Say You're Sorry Again (1950)
Source: Donn Fileti, liner notes with the Relic CD *Goodbye to the 1940s, Hello to
the 1950s.*

Rivals (Detroit)

Personnel Gerald Green (lead), James Green (1st tenor), Herman Green (2d tenor),
Robert Metcalf (baritone), Tolbert Dorr (bass)

Notes

This group was formed in 1957 by three cousins and two friends (above).

They were discovered by keyboardist T. J. Fowler, who recorded them on his Puff
label in 1962. The masters were quickly sold to Robert West of LuPine Records.

Gerald Green left to join the Contours, who did "Do You Love Me."

Discography

Puff 1001 It's Gonna Work Out/Love Me (1962)
Source: Donn Fileti, liner notes with the Relic CD *LuPine.*

Rivieras (Englewood, N.J.)

Personnel Homer Dunn (d) (lead), Ronald Cook (1st tenor) Andrew Jones (baritone), Charles Allen (bass)

Notes

Dunn started with the Five Bob-O-Links in 1952. They were from Hackensack, New Jersey, and recorded for the Columbia R&B subsidiary, Okeh. They had one disc which failed. By the summer of 1954, the army called two members and that ended the life of the Five Bob-O-Links.

Dunn married, moved to Englewood, New Jersey, and met Charles Allen, who was singing with an Englewood group at the time. Coincidentally, the baritone of Allen's group was the brother of the Bob-O-Links' bass. This is how Dunn and Allen knew each other.

Charles introduced Dunn to Ronald Cook, Andy Jones, and Charles Bailey (who had been with his group), as well as Charles Williams (who had been with another group).

Bailey and Williams departed and the resulting foursome eventually became the Rivieras. They were now Dunn, Allen, Jones, and Cook. Through a networking series of events, they auditioned for Coed Records. Label management was impressed with them and released their first disc in July 1958, "Count Every Star." This success led to many more releases on Coed as well as many appearances.

Discography

Coed 503 Count Every Star/True Love Is Hard to Find (1958)
Coed 508 Moonlight Serenade/Neither Rain nor Snow (1958)
Coed 513 Our Lover/True Love Is Hard to Find (1959)
Coed 513 Our Love/Midnight Flyer (1959)
Coed 522 11th Hour Melody/Since I Made You Cry (1959)
Coed 529 Moonlight Cocktails/Blessing of Love (1960)
Coed 538 Great Big Eyes/My Friend (1960)
Coed 542 Easy to Remember/Stay in My Heart (1960)
Coed 592 Moonlight Cocktails/Midnight Flyer (1964)
Source: Frank Aita and Donn Fileti, liner notes with the Relic Rivieras CD *Moonlight Cocktails.*

Rivileers (Queens, N.Y.)

Personnel Eugene Pearson (lead), Herb Crosby (1st tenor), Erroll Lennard (2d tenor), Alfonso Delaney (baritone), Milton Edwards (bass)

Notes

The Rivileers got together in 1953 while the members were in high school. Although the group included several other individuals before they recorded, they ultimately named themselves after the Rivoli theater in Manhattan.

When neighborhood friends the Five Sharps broke up, Tom Duckett joined the Rivileers as a full-time sixth member.

They practiced and worked hard on their repertoire and, as in the case of the Heartbeats several years later, the father of the Miller Sisters group, William Henry Miller (who lived on their block), was a great help to them. He was a songwriter and publisher at the time.

Delaney's girlfriend was the sister of one of their first members, David Grissom. Her name was Carolyn Grissom and "Carolyn" was written for her.

Milton Edwards worked in a drugstore on the same street as Triboro Records. The owner knew Sol Rabinowitz. After hearing the group, Rabinowitz started his label (Baton) with the Rivileers' first record.

Their discs did well in various towns across the country but never nationally.

In 1954, they all graduated from high school and were free to do as they pleased. Their records were selling very well but were not providing them with a career. Soon, Herb and Errol joined the service and Pearson followed several weeks later.

Milton and Alfonso remained, and with Duckett's help they recruited Pete LeMonier, who had been with the Five Sharps, at the end of their run. Pete got Mel Dancy and they were then a quartet. They decided to remain a foursome, but their distinctive sound was gone, which was obvious in their performances.

The reformed group recorded six more sides, including "Don't Ever Leave Me" and "For Sentimental Reasons." Fortunately, Pearson was home on leave and despite his wish not to intrude on the new vocal group, he was convinced by all, including Rabinowitz, to join. Two discs were released from this session, Little Girl/Don't Ever Leave Me and For Sentimental Reasons/I Want to See My Baby.

The group had some local successes but, as in the past, nothing more than local success. Dancy joined the air force in 1955 and this was the end of their recording.

After returning home from the service, Pearson joined the Cleftones to replace "Buzzy" McClain. Pearson was an old neighborhood friend in Jamaica and stayed with them for two years. Then he joined the Drifters to replace Dock Green.

Discography

Baton 200 A Thousand Stars (GP)/Hey Chiquita (AD) (1954)
Baton 201 Forever (GP)/Darling Farewell (AD) (1954)
Baton 205 Carolyn (AD)/Eternal Love (GP) (1954)
Baton 207 For Sentimental Reasons (GP)/I Want to See My Baby (AD) (1954)
Baton 209 Don't Ever Leave Me (GP)/Little Girl (PL) (1955)
Baton 241 A Thousand Stars (GP)/Who Is the Girl? (GP) (1957)
Sources: Tom Luciani and Steve Flam in *Bim Bam Boom* 5; Marv Goldberg in *DISCoveries*, October 1996.

Rivingtons (Los Angeles)

Personnel Carl White (lead), Al Frazier, John "Sonny" Harris, Turner "Rocky" Wilson (bass)

Notes

The group that ultimately became the Rivingtons went through many personnel changes along the way. They began in a Los Angeles high school in 1949 as the West Coast Mello-Moods, then the Lamplighters, Tenderfoots, Four After Fives, the

Sharps with Thurston Harris, the Crenshaws, and the Rivingtons. The common thread through this was Al Frazier; he had been a member of all the aforementioned groups.

The Mello-Moods consisted of Frazier, Maurice Hill, Robert Redd, Paul Robi, and Lewis Young. This group was not the Hollywood group and never recorded.

Frazier met the Lamplighters at a club where they were appearing. During their break, he met them in the restroom and gave them some advice on their presentation and soon became part of the group. They then included Al Frazier, Thurston Harris, Mathew Nelson, and Willie Ray Rockwell—the recording group. The road group was Eddie Jones Jr., Harold Lewis, Frazier, and Harris. They soon learned that Ralph Bass of Federal was holding auditions at a local club. They auditioned and were signed to a contract.

They went on a tour that ended in Georgia. Because they had no money at the time, they all looked for ways to get back to California. The group essentially broke up and re-formed months later with Rockwell, Frazier, Carl White, and "Sonny" Harris (Feathers). Rockwell didn't remain long with this group and they got Nelson back. Federal renamed them the Tenderfoots. After a period of recording and appearing as the Tenderfoots, Thurston Harris returned and once again hooked up with Ralph Bass at Federal. Because Harris returned, Federal and Bass decided on calling them the Lamplighters again.

Soon they met bass Turner "Rocky" Wilson, and they had a new vocal group. It was this group that backed up Paul Anka in 1956 on RPM, contrary to the story that the Jacks/Cadets were backing him. This group did a great deal of backup work, specifically working with Jesse Belvin. They did "Our Love Is Here to Stay" as the Sharps on Lamp. After bumping into Harris again, Aladdin wanted the Sharps to back him on his forthcoming recording of "Little Bitty Pretty One."

In 1961, this group recorded as the Four After Fives. In 1962 they moved to Warner Bros., which was on Crenshaw Street, and thus their name became the Crenshaws. They did one single and an EP before they moved to Liberty and recorded "Papa Oom Mow Mow" in one take!

This now became a successful group with their "Papa-Oom-Mow-Mow" leading the way to many live appearances and future recordings with Liberty and later Vee Jay.

Frazier became the group's manager in 1965 and Darryl White replaced him in the group.

Discography

Liberty 55427 Papa-Oom-Mow-Mow/Deep Water (1962)
Liberty 55513 My Reward/Kickapoo Joy Juice (1962)
Liberty 55528 Mama-Oom-Mow-Mow/Waiting (1962)
Liberty 55553 The Bird's the Word/I'm Losing My Grip (1963)
Liberty 55585 The Shaky Bird-1/The Shaky Bird-2 (1963)
Liberty 55610 Cherry/Little Sally Walker (1963)
Liberty 55671 Wee Jee Walk/Fairy Tales (1964)
Reprise 0293 I Tried/One Monkey (1964)
ARE American 100 All That Glitters/You Move Me Baby (1964)
Vee Jay 634 You Move Me Baby/All That Glitters (1964)
Vee Jay 649 I Love You Always/Years of Tears (1964)
Vee Jay 677 The Willy/Just Got to Be More (1965)
Sources: Jack Sbarbori in *Record Exchanger* 16; Art Turco in *Record Exchanger* 28.

Roamers (Jersey City, N.J.)

Personnel Judge Taylor, Sam Walton, Billy Williams, James Ricketts (bass)

Notes

The Roamers performed backup on Varetta Dillard's disc, Savoy 1160, and on Wilbert Harrison's disc, Savoy 1149, as they did for many of the Savoy label's single artists.

Discography

Savoy 1147 Deep Freeze/I'll Never Get Over You (1954)
Savoy 1149 Da De Ya Da/Woman and Whiskey (1954)
Savoy 1156 Chop Chop Ching a Ling/Never Let Me Go (1955)
Savoy 1160 You're the Answer to My Prayer/Promise Mr. Thomas (1955)
Source: Steve Propes, liner notes with the Savoy LP *Doo Wop Delights: The Roots of Rock.*

Robins (San Francisco)

Personnel Ty Tyrell (lead), Billy Richard, Roy Richard (baritone), Bobby Nunn (bass)

Notes

The Robins began in San Francisco in 1947. At that time they were a trio consisting of Ty Terrell and twin brothers Billy and Roy Richard (not Richards, which is always used). They moved to Los Angeles in 1949. Under the name A Sharp Trio they made appearances at Johnny Otis's Barrelhouse Club. Otis recommended adding bass Bobby Nunn to the group. Otis initially called them the Four Bluebirds. By the time they recorded for Aladdin in 1949 and the Aladdin subsidiary, Score Records, they had become the Robins. The Score record was first released in 1949, but for some reason it was also released in 1951. By the end of 1949, they found themselves with Savoy and recorded "Double Crossin' Blues" and many other R&B classics.

In 1951, they moved to Recorded in Hollywood Records. At the same time, they moonlighted as the Nic Nacs on RPM. They had a short career at RPM's sister label, Modern, and in December 1951, one of their previous tunes "Round about Midnight," which they recorded for Aladdin, was released.

By 1953, they moved to RCA. This group consisted of Ty Tyrell, Billy and Roy Richard, Grady Chapman, and Ulysses Bobby Nunn. In 1954, they moved to their ninth label, Spark. This was a recently formed organization owned by Jerry Lieber and Mike Stoller. It was at Spark that Carl Gardner was added, replacing Grady Chapman. It was during this next period that Chapman had left to join the Suedes. Chapman returned for the final Spark session. Photos of the group at this time show them to be a sextet: Gardner, Chapman, Tyrell, Billy and Roy Richard, and Nunn.

Spark wasn't doing very well. In 1955, it was sold to Atlantic's subsidiary, Atco. Following the deal, Lieber and Stoller went to New York. The Robins democratically chose what to do. Part of the group followed Lieber and Stoller to New York and the remaining bunch decided to remain in California. Chapman, the Richard brothers, and new member, H. B. Barnum, formerly of the Dootones, were the West Coast dreamers who remained with Whippet Records in Los Angeles.

Gardner and Nunn picked up new members Billy Guy and Leon Hughes, named themselves the Coasters, retaining their West Coast heritage, and joined Lieber and Stoller in New York.

This same Robins group recorded for the Knight label and consisted of Grady Chapman, Ty Tyrell, and Bill and Roy Richard.

Discography

Aladdin 3071 Don't Like the Way You're Doing/Come Back Baby (1949)
Score 4010 Around about Midnight/You Sure Look Good to Me (1949)
Savoy 726 If I Didn't Love You So/If It's So Baby (1950)
Savoy 731 Double Crossin' Blues/Back Alley Blues (w/L. Esther) (1950)
Savoy 732 Turkey Hop-1/Turkey Hop-2 (1950)
Savoy 735 Mistrustin' Blues/Misery (w/L. Esther) (1950)
Savoy 738 Our Romance Is Gone/There Ain't No Use Beggin' (1950)
Savoy 752 I'm Living O.K./There's Rain in My Eyes (1950)
Savoy 759 Deceivin' Blues/Lost Dream Blues (w/L. Esther) (1950)
Savoy 762 I'm Through/You're Fine but Not My Kind (1950)
Regent 1016 I'm Not Falling in Love with You/Cry Baby (1950)
Modern 807 Rockin'/That's What the Good Book Says (1951)
Recorded in Hollywood 112 Race of Man/Bayou Baby Blues (1951)
Recorded in Hollywood 121 A Falling Star/When Gabriel Blows His Horn (1951)
Recorded in Hollywood 150 School Bell Blues/Early Morning Blues (1951)
RCA 47-5175 A Fool Such as I/My Heart's the Biggest Fool (1953)
RCA 47-5271 All Night Baby/Oh Why (1953)
RCA 47-5434 Let's Go to the Dance/How Would You Know (1953)
RCA 47-5486 My Baby Done Told Me/I'll Do It (1953)
RCA 47-5489 Ten Days in Jail/Empty Bottles (1953)
RCA 47-5564 Don't Stop Now/Get It Off Your Mind (1953)
Crown 106 I Made a Vow/Double Crossin' Baby (1954)
Crown 120 Key to My Heart/All I Do Is Rock (1954)
Spark 103 Wrap It Up/Riot in Cell Block 9 (1954)
Spark 107 Loop De Loop Mambo/Framed (1954)
Spark 110 Whadaya Want/If Teardrops Were Kisses (1954)
Spark 113 I Love Paris/One Kiss (1955)
Spark 116 I Must Be Dreaming/The Hatchet Man (1955)
Spark 122 Just Like a Fool/Smokey Joe's Café (1955)
Atco 6059 Smokey Joe's Cafe/Just Like a Fool (1955)
Whippet 200 Cherry Lips/Out of the Picture (1956)
Whippet 201 Hurt Me/Merry-Go-Rock (1956)
Whippet 203 Since I First Met You/That Old Black Magic (1956)
Whippet 206 A Fool in Love/All of a Sudden My Heart Sings (1957)
Whippet 208 Every Night/Where's the Fire (1957)
Whippet 211 In My Dreams/Keep Your Mind on Me (1957)
Whippet 212 Snowball/You Wanted Fun (1958)

Knight 2001 A Quarter to Twelve/Pretty Little Dolly (1958)
Knight 2008 A Little Bird Told Me/It's Never Too Late (1958)
Sources: Billy Vera, liner notes with the RCA CD *Rock 'n' Roll Party-1*; Jay Warner, *American Singing Groups.*

Rob Roys (Bronx, N.Y.)

Personnel Norman Fox (lead), Bobby Trotman (1st tenor), Andre Lilly (2d tenor), Bob Thierer (baritone), Marshall "Buzzy" Helfand (bass)

Notes

In 1956 Norman Fox joined forces with Bob Trotman, Andre Lilly, Bob Thierer, and Marshall "Buzzy" Helfand. These were high school friends at the Bronx's DeWitt Clinton High School. They practiced in school, whenever and wherever possible.

In 1957, Trotman met Don Carter, the New York account executive for the Duke/Peacock organization. This chance meeting in a Bronx record shop explains why a Bronx quintet recorded for a southeast label—Backbeat!

Black group members Trotman and Lilly came from another Bronx group, the Harmonaires.

Despite the fact that "Buzzy" Helfand wrote "Tell Me Why," writer credits on the original and all subsequent labels show Helford and Carter.

Andre Lilly's girlfriend, Audry, was the inspiration for the song of the same name.

At the start of 1959, just prior to the Capitol recordings, Paul Schneller replaced Helfand at bass and is heard on "Pizza Pie" and "Dream Girl."

Discography

Backbeat 501 Tell Me Why/Audry (1957)
Backbeat 508 Dance Girl Dance/My Dearest One (1957)
Capitol 4128 Dream Girl/Pizza Pie (1959)
Sources: Jay Warner, *American Singing Groups*; Norman Fox, interview by Galen Gart, November 2, 1991.

Rockers (St. Louis, Mo.)

Personnel Art Lassiter, George Green, Murray Green, Doug Martin

Notes

The four sides recorded by Federal's Rockers were all recorded in Cincinnati in February 1956.

Lassiter also sang with the Trojans on RPM.

Discography

Federal 12267 I'll Die in Love with You/What Am I to Do? (1956)
Federal 12273 Why Don't You Believe/Down in the Bottom (1956)
Carter 3029 Count Every Star/Tell Me Why (1957)
Source: Michel Ruppli, *The King Labels: A Discography.*

Rocketeers (Los Angeles)

Personnel Willie Davis (lead), Billy Steward (1st tenor), Lloyd McCraw, Chuck Rowan, Vince House (bass)

Notes

In 1956, Lloyd McCraw, formerly of the Jacks/Cadets, and now interested in singing again, communicated with former acquaintance Vince House, asking him to assemble a group and join him out west. House rounded up his former Rhythm Aces buddies Steward and Rowan, and found Jimmy Brunsen. They all went to California and recorded as the Rockets on Modern.

When the Modern disc failed, Rowan left the group and singing for good. He was replaced by Brunsen's friend, tenor Woody Johnson. Johnson sang with the Rocketeers, Rockets, Magic Notes, and the Planets.

Modern Records changed their name to the Rocketeers late in 1956 and released their Modern disc in the spring of 1957.

Nothing happened with the name change or the Modern release, and the group moved to Era, where House's name was changed to Vince Howard. One disc that the Planets released on Era, "Stand There Mountain," became their biggest hit.

In his *Doowop . . . The Chicago Scene*, Bob Pruter names the members of the Rocketeers as Steward, Rowan, House, and Jimmy Brunson. He doesn't mention Willie Davis or Lloyd McCraw.

Discography

Modern 999 Talk It Over Baby/Hey Rube (1956)
M.J.C. 501 My Reckless Heart/They Turned the Party Out at Bessie's (1958)
Sources: Bob Pruter, *Doowop . . . The Chicago Scene*; Marv Goldberg in *Goldmine,* February 1991. Article about the Rhythm Aces.

Rocketones (Brooklyn, N.Y.)

Personnel Bill Witt (lead), Allan Days (1st tenor), Ronald Johnson (2d tenor), Harold Chapman (baritone), Arthur Blackman (bass)

Notes

The Rocketones began while group members were in junior high school in Brooklyn. The group started as the Avalons, singing on street corners alongside their Brooklyn contemporaries—the Continentals, Hurricanes, Chips, Tokens, Velours, Fantastics, DuPonts, and Shells.

In 1956, they began knocking on many Broadway doors in Manhattan, looking to record. The first door they opened was Morty Craft's at Melba Records. They auditioned with "Mexico," "Dee I," and "Pretty Little Brown-Eyed Girl." Craft liked the group and their songs and scheduled a recording session.

Six months after the session, sixteen-year-old Bill Witt heard "Mexico" (which he penned) on the radio. However, things had changed. Their record was introduced as by the Rocketones and began with a bullfight flourish. Apparently, Craft had made some creative alterations. They hired a manager who, with their disc on the air, lined up bookings in New York.

As "Mexico" began to fade, Allan Days was drafted and replaced by Robert Booker. A year later, Johnson was drafted; he was replaced by Benjamin Harvey. A follow-up recording entitled "Jive Talk" was never released.

By 1959, many members of the group had changed. Witt had joined the Paragons, replacing Julius McMichaels, and stayed with them for a while. In the early 1960s, Witt joined the Townsmen, who recorded a disc in 1963 for Herald. Witt made the rounds and in the 1970s was back on the revival circuit with the Paragons. The Rocketones never re-formed.

Discography

Melba 113 Mexico/Dee I (1957)
Sources: Marcia Vance and Phil Groia in *Yesterday's Memories* 2; Marcia Vance and Phil Groia in *DISCoveries,* September 1989.

Rockets (Los Angeles)

Personnel Billy Steward (1st tenor), Jimmy Brunsen (tenor), Chuck Rowan (2d tenor), Vince House (bass)

Notes

After the Vee Jay Rhythm Aces broke up late in 1955, they all returned home. It is not known when or where, but Lloyd McCraw (Jacks/Cadets) had previously met Vince House. In 1956, he communicated with House, asking him to assemble a group and come west to record for his organization. House rounded up Steward and Rowan and picked up Jimmy Brunsen. McCraw got them a contract and session with Modern Records. The result is reflected in the discography below.

When their Modern disc failed, Rowan left for good, rejoining the service. He was replaced in the group by Brunsen's friend Woody Johnson. Modern then changed the group's name to Rocketeers.

Vince House and Chuck Rowan were cousins.

Discography

Modern 992 You Are the First One (BS)/Be Lovey Dovey (BS) (1956)
Sources: Bob Pruter, *Doowop . . . The Chicago Scene*; Marv Goldberg in *Goldmine,* February 1991, article on the Rhythm Aces.

Rockin' Chairs (Queens Village, N.Y.)

Personnel Lenny Dean (lead), Bob Gerardi, Carmine Ray, Rick Baxter

Notes

The Rockin' Chairs was a latter-day self-contained group, playing instruments and vocalizing as well. They formed in 1955 and met deejay Alan Fredericks at a dance. He liked them and became their manager.

Fredericks had a friend who owned Recorte Records. He set up an audition for the group and they were signed following their tryout.

Their first release, "A Kiss Is a Kiss," sold more than 200,000 copies. The next tune, "Please Mary Lou," was released soon after. When it was just beginning to do well, Alan Freed stated, over the air, that the record sounded like Paul Anka's "Diana."

The third and last Recorte release, "Memories of Love," was released just as the payola scandal broke, and that was the end of their attempt at success. They disbanded, quite justifiably.

Discography

Recorte 402 A Kiss Is a Kiss/Rockin' Chair Boogie (1958)
Recorte 404 Please Mary Lou/Come on Baby (1958)
Recorte 412 Memories of Love/Girl of Mine (1959)
Source: Marcia Vance in *Bim Bam Boom* 8.

Rockin' Townies (Providence, R.I.)

Personnel Joe Hill (lead), Joe Simmons (tenor), "Sonny" Washburn (tenor), Danny Jet (baritone), Thermon Blackwell (d) (bass)

Discography

Atlas 1040 I Cross My Fingers/Wheel Baby, Wheel (1954)
Source: Marv Goldberg in *DISCoveries*.

Romaines (New York)

Personnel Earl Plummer (lead), Henry Green (tenor), Roy Hayes (tenor), Bobby Bushnell (baritone), Romaine Brown (bass)

Notes

In 1953, after spending ten successful years with Steve Gibson and his Red Caps, Romaine Brown, along with other members of the group, began to see the proverbial writing on the wall, that "their" music was no longer popular. Thus they left the group for other pursuits.

Brown formed his own group, the Romaines. They practiced for a year and, with the help of Harry Mills of the Mills Brothers, got a recording contract with Decca. At this time Earl Plummer joined the group as lead.

The Romaines stayed on the music scene until 1959. During that time, there were many personnel changes. Plummer was replaced by Jimmy Thomas and Bushnell by Johnny Eaton; Frank Shea filled in for Harry Green, who had returned to the Red Caps. Earl Edwards was added as baritone.

In an interview, Romaine Brown was certain that the group had only recorded for Decca despite the Groove recording below. Apparently, it is only Brown's name that appears on the Decca label (see discography).

Discography

Groove 0035 Your Kind of Love/Till the Wee Wee Morning (1954)
Decca 30399 When Your Lover Has Gone/Satin Doll (w/R. Brown) (1957)
Sources: Marv Goldberg and Pete Grendysa in *Yesterday's Memories* 4; Jeff Kreiter, *Group Collector's Record Guide.*

Romancers (San Francisco)

Personnel Alvin Thomas (lead), Bobby Freeman (tenor), Woodrow Blake, Tyrone French, James Shelbourne

Notes

The Bobby Freeman shown above, an original member of the Romancers, is the Bobby Freeman who went on to later perform as a single artist ("Do You Wanna Dance" and "C'Mon and Swim") for Josie. Freeman came to Josie by way of San Francisco and already had two releases for Dootone.

In the liner notes accompanying Sequel's *Jubilee/Josie-4* CD, George Povall and Gordon Skadberg refer to Woodrow Blake as Woodroe Black.

Alvin Thomas's brother, James, was also in the group.

Discography

Dootone 381 I Still Remember/House Cat (1956)
Dootone 404 This Is Goodbye/Jump and Hop (1956)
Bay Tone 101 You Don't Understand/I Love You So (1958)
Josie (UNR) You Don't Understand
Sources: Ace CD *Dootone Story*; George Povall and Gordon Skadberg, liner notes with the *Jubilee/Josie R&B Vocal Groups-4* CD.

Romans, Little Caesar & (Los Angeles)

Personnel Carl Burnett (lead), Johnny Simmons (tenor), Early Harris (2d tenor), David Johnson (baritone), Leroy Sanders (bass)

Notes

Following Johnson's discharge from the air force, he met the others in the Los Angeles area of California.

Although the group included no Cubans, for some unknown reason they called themselves the Cubans and signed with Charlie Reynolds of Flash Records. They cut four sides for Flash early in 1959. Only one Flash single was released (133). The remaining unreleased cuts eventually surfaced on the Relic LP *Best of Flash.*

When Fidel Castro began to intimidate and threaten the U.S. population midway through 1959, the group immediately dropped the name Cubans.

Later in 1959, Johnson met Lummie Fowler of Lummtone Records. Fowler had just started his label and Johnson got another group together with himself, Harris and Sanders from the Cubans, Bobby Relf, and Theotis Reed. This was the first group of the Upfronts. They did two discs for Lummtone. The first, "It Took Time," did very well. It was felt that if with adequate financial support from Lummtone, the Upfronts tune would have been a greater success.

One evening at Fowler's home they met songwriter Paul Politi. He had followed Johnson's career and felt that a tune he had written, "Those Oldies but Goodies" was perfect for Johnson.

The Upfronts secured a release from Lummtone. Johnson, Sanders, and Harris found ex-Cubans Johnny Simmons and baritone Carl Burnett. They were christened Little Caesar and the Romans.

(Note: Gagnon and Guerre's article points out that this name came from David Johnson, whose middle name was Caesar. Norm N. Nite's *Rock On* and Joel Whitburn's *Top Pop 1955–1982* state that Carl Burnett was Little Caesar, but this is incorrect. Every member of the group sang lead. Whoever did lead on a particular tune was Little Caesar.)

"Those Oldies but Goodies" took an unprecedented six weeks to record as Delfi management wanted a white-sounding performance. The side broke big and afforded the Romans a national tour with the biggies of the day. Delfi's bent about sounding white apparently worked: Until the Romans appeared on *American Bandstand,* the young record buyers thought they were white!

Although the group's follow-up discs were well executed, internal difficulties created a lack of promotional support for their releases and they split up in 1962.

Discography

DEL FI 4158 She Don't Wanna Dance/Those Oldies but Goodies (1961)
DEL FI 4164 Hully Gully Again/Frankie and Johnny (1961)
DEL FI 4166 Fever/Memories of Those Oldies but Goodies (1961)
DEL FI 4170 C.C. Rider/Ten Commandments of Love (1961)
DEL FI 4177 Yoyo Yo Yoyo/Popeye One More Time (1962)
Source: Rick Gagnon and Dave Guerre in *Goldmine,* August 12, 1988.

Romantics, Ruby & (Akron, Ohio)

Personnel Ruby Nash (lead), Edward Roberts (1st tenor), George Lee (2d tenor), Robert Mosley (baritone), Leroy Fann (d) (bass)

Notes

This group originally formed in 1961 in Akron, Ohio. They began as an all-male quartet, the Supremes. They played around Ohio and were soon off to New York looking for a recording contract.

Fann met Ruby Nash and heard her sing, being reminded of the Platters and Miracles with their female members. He immediately asked her to join his group, and they arranged for an audition with Kapp Records. Kapp liked them very much and asked Ruby to try lead chores.

Kapp management was aware of a Detroit Supremes who had already released four singles. The group was therefore renamed Ruby and the Romantics. They were given a recording session and sang "Our Day Will Come." Just more than a month later, on February 9, 1963, it reached number one on the national charts.

Their next releases were excellent recordings that charted but never matched the success of "Our Day Will Come." In 1967, they left Kapp to join ABC. There were personnel changes. The entire male membership of the Romantics left and were replaced by Vincent McLeod, Ronald Jackson, Robert Lewis, and Richard Pryor.

Numerous changes followed and in 1971 Ruby left to start a family.

Discography

Kapp 501 Our Day Will Come/Moonlight and Music (1963)
Kapp 525 My Summer Love/Sweet Love and Sweet Foreigveness (1963)
Kapp 544 Hey There Lonely Boy/Not a Moment Too Soon (1963)
Kapp 557 Day Dreaming/Young Wings Can Fly (1963)
Kapp 578 Our Everlasting Love/Much Better Off Than I've Ever Been (1964)
Kapp 601 Baby Come Home/Everyday's a Holiday (1964)
Kapp 615 When You're Young and in Love/I Cry Alone (1964)
Kapp 646 Does He Really Care for Me?/Nevertheless (1965)
Kapp 665 We'll Meet Again/Your Baby Doesn't Love You Anymore (1965)
Kapp 702 Imagination/Nobody but My Baby (1965)
Sources: Jay Warner, *American Singing Groups*; Allen Stanton, liner notes with the Kapp LP *Our Day Will Come*; Randall C. Hill in *Goldmine.*

Romeos (Detroit)

Personnel Lamont Dozier (tenor), Ty Hunter (1st tenor), Eugene Dyer (2d tenor), Kenny Johnson (baritone), Don Davenport (bass)

Notes

This was an integrated group. Don Davenport was a white bass in an otherwise black group.

Their last release was on Atco as a result of their breakup. The owner of Fox sold the masters of "Fine Fine Baby" and "Moments to Remember You By" to Atlantic.

Davenport joined the Larados, spelling the end of the Romeos.

Discography

Fox 748/749 Fine Fine Baby/Moments to Remember (1957)
Fox 845/846 Gone Gone Get Away/Let's Be Partners (1957)
Atco 6107 Fine Fine Baby/Moments to Remember You By (1957)
Sources: Jay Repoley in *Story Untold* 6; Steve Towne in *Goldmine,* September 1981.

Roommates, Cathy Jean & (Queens, N.Y.)

Personnel Cathy Jean Giordano (lead), Jack Carlson (tenor), Felix Alvarez (1st tenor), Steve Susskind (baritone), Bob Minsky (bass)

Notes

The group formed in 1959 as the Roommates. They soon joined up with Cathy Jean and became Cathy Jean and the Roommates. They appeared everywhere with dual billing and even recorded an album on which one side was the Roommates and the other side Cathy Jean and the Roommates. Many hits followed, as did national tours.

Later George Rodriguez joined the Roommates, replacing Felix Alvarez.

Following many label changes and a great deal of touring, the Roommates disbanded in 1965.

Discography

Valmor 007 Please Love Me Forever/Canadian Sunset (1960)
Valmor 008 Glory of Love/Never Knew (1960)
Valmor 010 Band of Gold/O Baby Love (1961)
Valmor 013 My Foolish Heart/My Kisses for Your Thoughts (1961)
Valmor 016 Please Tell Me/Sugar Cane (1962)
Cameo 233 A Lovely Way to Spend an Evening/Sunday Kind of Love (1962)
Philips 40105 Gee/Answer Me My Love (1963)
Philips 40153 The Nearness of You/Please Don't Cheat on Me (1963)
Can Am 166 My Heart/Just for Tonight (1964)
Source: Paul Heller in *Story Untold* 3.

Rosettes (Bronx, N.Y.)

Personnel Shirley Crier, Diane Christian, Gail Noble

Notes

Shirley Crier was Arthur Crier's sister. Crier was well-known for his time with the Chimes on Royal Roost and the second gathering of Lillian Leach and the Mellows.

Discography

Herald 562 You Broke My Heart/It Must Be Love (1961)
Source: Arthur Crier, interview by author, October 4, 1995.

Rovers (Sacramento, Calif.)

Personnel Oliver "Sonny" Stevens (lead), Jay Payton (tenor), Henry Swan (baritone), Billy Williams (bass)

Notes

The Rovers formed in 1954. They recorded for Music City as both the Rovers and the Five Rovers. Payton was about ten years older than the others.

"Ichi Bon Tami Dachi" means number one girlfriend. Payton wrote the song based on his time in the service in Japan.

When their last disc for Music City, "Tell Me Darling," was released, they were on their way to breaking up.

Discography

Music City 750 Why Oh-H/Ichi Bon Tami Dachi (1954)
Capitol 3078 Why Oh-H/Ichi Bon Tami Dachi (1955)

Music City 780 Salute to Johnny Ace/Jadda (1955)
Music City 792 Whole Lot of Love/Tell Me, Darling (1955)
Source: Jim Dawson, liner notes with the *Earth Angel* Music City LP.

Royal Holidays (Detroit)

Personnel Vernon Williams (lead), Chester Scott (1st tenor), Kenneth Fuqua (2d tenor), Jerry Wallace (baritone), Charles Farley (bass)

Notes

The Royal Holidays originally formed in Detroit in 1955. From 1955 to 1958, they practiced incessantly and appeared at many local events in the Detroit area.

In 1958, their manager, Harry Nivens, had them record for his Penthouse label. Williams and Scott alternated lead on "I'm Sorry (I Did You Wrong)," which Williams had written. To achieve more effective distibution, Nivens arranged for Carlton Records of New York to distribute "I'm Sorry" and "Margaret."

"I'm Sorry" sold fairly well and afforded the group several East Coast tours with several well-known deejays. The Royal Holidays' second release, "Down in Cuba," was also written by Williams. He and Fuqua sang lead. This disc was released on New York's Herald label in January 1959.

The group made appearances at New York's Apollo Theater late in 1959. They also made appearances at the Howard Theater in Washington, D.C., and the Royal Theater in Baltimore. They also appeared on Dick Clark's *American Bandstand.*

"I'm Sorry" was not a success, and they disbanded in the early 1960s. Williams went on to sing wth the Pyramids on Cub and Vee Jay and the Satintones on Motown.

Vernon Williams had been with Sax Kari and the Quailtones on Josie.

Discography

Penthouse 9353 I'm Sorry (I Did You Wrong)/Margaret (1958)
Carlton 472 I'm Sorry (I Did You Wrong)/Margaret (1958)
Herald 536 Down in Cuba/Rockin' at the Bandstand (1959)
Source: Nikki Gustafson and Jim Dunn in their piece, "Vocal Group Harmony Lives," on the Internet, January 1998, available at: www.members.aol.com/wawawaooh/main.htm.

Royal Jokers (Detroit)

Personnel Thearon Hill (tenor), Noah Howell (tenor), Willie Jones (tenor), Ted Green (d) (baritone), Norman Thrasher (bass)

Notes

The Royal Jokers descended from the Musketeers (Muskateers), the Serenaders, and the Royals on the local (Detroit) Venus label. The Royals disc, "Someday We'll Meet Again," was inadvertently pressed at 33 1/3 rpm, sounding like a Chipmunk's recording. It was mistakenly released as by Alexander Ames and the Scooters. When this tune found its way to a Dawn LP, it was listed correctly as by the Royal Jokers.

The group would change their name one month after the Venus record was released. Their new moniker was the Royal Jokers.

This probably as a result of the comedy routines they performed on stage, in addition to their vocalizing.

Before the group recorded as the Royal Jokers, Isaac Reese was replaced by Ted Green and Willie Jones was added as the fifth member. They soon signed with the Gale agency. Two months later, they were signed to a contract with the Atlantic subsidiary, Atco. Their first recording was done in May 1955. The three Atco discs were released regularly, ending in September 1956.

Not having recorded in more than a year, the group sustained some personnel changes. First, Thrasher left to become road manager for Hank Ballard and the Midnighters, and then Hill left, ultimately winding up with the Four Tops. The first replacement for the Royal Jokers was Billy Lyons, who had been with the Five Jets on DeLuxe. In the meantime, the group had some releases on Fortune and its Hi-Q subsidiary. In 1958, a new fifth member, Raymond Dorsey, was added.

After their Fortune/Hi-Q recordings, they recorded for Ember, Metro, Keldon, and Big Top. Green departed in 1961 or 1962 and the group was again a quartet. Ted Green and Noah Howell were exceptionally good stage performers.

Discography

Atco 6052 Stay Here (WJ)/You Tickle Me Baby (WJ) (1955)
Atco 6062 Don't Leave Me Fanny (WJ)/Rocks in My Pillow (NH/NT) (1956)
Atco 6077 Ride On Little Girl (WJ)/She's Mine All Mine (WJ) (1956)
Fortune 840 Sweet Little Angel (TG)/I Don't Like You That Much (NH) (1958)
Hi-Q 5004 September in the Rain/Spring (1959)
Metro 20032 Sam's Back (TG)/Grabitis (NH) (1960)
Keldon 322 Lovey Dovey (BL)/Nickel, 3 Dimes & 5 Quarters (BL) (1960)
Big Top 3064 Hard Times (TG)/Red Hot (TG) (1961)
Fortune 560 You Tickle Me Baby (WJ)/You Came Along (BL) (1963)
Wingate 020 Love Game (from A to Z) (WJ) (instrumental) (1966)
Sources: Sal Mondrone in *Bim Bam Boom* 1; Marv Goldberg in *DISCoveries.*

Royals (Detroit)

Personnel Charles Sutton (lead), Henry Booth (tenor), Lawson Smith (baritone), "Sonny" Woods (bass)

Notes

The story of the Royals goes back to 1950, when Charles Sutton found himself at an amateur show. There he came across other singers who were interested in starting a vocal group. Everyone hailed from the east side of Detroit. At this point, they consisted of Sutton, Henry Booth, Freddy Pride, and "Sonny" Woods, who had been the Orioles' valet.

About six months after the group formed, Pride was drafted and recommended Lawson Smith prior to leaving. The group then entered many amateur contests and did very well. Johnny Otis's band was playing at one of these amateur nights. After hearing the Royals, he felt they had what it took for a big hit. Otis asked to manage them and got them a contract with Federal Records. In February 1951, the contract was signed. In January 1952 they had their first recording session and cut four sides.

(Note: Credit for leading the Royals' beautiful "Every Beat of My Heart" has always been given to Henry Booth. We now know that it was Charles Sutton.)

Despite the fact that their recordings were beautiful, harmonious ballads, they never sold very well.

Lawson Smith left the group to join the army a week after recording. The Royals' next session was in May 1952. Hank Ballard replaced Smith at baritone. He was on "Get It." At this time, with several of their discs having been released, they began touring in Detroit, Toledo, and Columbus.

By October 1952, their "Moonrise" was doing quite well locally. The Royals were producing record after record, outstanding records, but local sales were the only positive results. Nationally they were not doing as well. Their contract with Johnny Otis expired at the end of 1953.

In February 1954 the Royals recorded "Annie Had a Baby," which sold well. Hank Ballard's leads were now fully accepted.

Following the success of the Annie records, the Royals changed their name to the Midnighters to avoid confusion with the Five Royales. Charles Sutton left in 1954. He then joined Stanley Mitchell's Tornados.

Discography

Federal 12064 Every Beat of My Heart/All Night Long (1952)
Federal 12077 Starting From Tonight/I Know I Love You So (1952)
Federal 12088 Moonrise/Fifth Street Blues (1952)
Federal 12098 A Love in My Heart/I'll Never Let Her Go (1952)
Federal 12113 Are You Forgetting?/What Did I Do? (1952)
Federal 12121 The Shrine of St. Cecelia/I Feel So Blue (1953)
Federal 12133 Get It/No It Ain't (1953)
Federal 12150 Hey Miss Fine/I Feel That-a-Way (1953)
Federal 12160 That's It/Someone Like You (1954)
Federal 12169 Until I Die/Work with Me Annie (1954)
Source: Marv Goldberg in *DISCoveries,* June 1996.

Royals (Winston-Salem, N.C.)

Personnel Johnny Tanner (lead), Lowman Pauling, Otto Jefferies, Obediah "Scoop" Carter

Notes

This group has no connection to the Royals on Federal. They became the Five Royales on King and Home of the Blues.

Apollo 434 is the one disc recorded by the Royals—a name given to the group prior to their being referred to as the Five Royales.

Discography

Apollo 434 Too Much of a Little Bit/Give Me One More Chance (1951)
Source: Jonas Bernholm and Jim Morris, liner notes with the Dr. Horse LP *The Real Thing.*

Royaltones (Brooklyn, N.Y.)

Personnel Eddie "Puddin" Carson (lead), Rennie Davis (1st tenor), James "Skippy" Ifill (2d tenor), Thomas Davis (baritone), Richard "Ricky" Williams (bass)

Notes

The Royaltones started singing as the Barons in 1953. After performing at local parties and clubs during summer 1955, "Puddin" Carson joined as lead and changed their name to the Royaltones.

They taped a few songs to take with them to Manhattan. Their first stop was the Old Town facility; they didn't have to look any further.

In November 1955 they cut four sides for Old Town, including their first release, "Crazy Love." The record sold well in New York and several months later they went back to the studio to record again. That same day, Ruth McFadden was recording "Two in Love." According to 2d tenor James Ifill, the Royaltones backed McFadden on this tune. This is also mentioned in the liner notes with Ace's *Old Town Doo Wop-1* CD.

Due to a dispute over royalties, the last four cuts recorded were never released.

Following a year of inactivity, they broke up. They blame their failure on Old Town's Weiss brothers.

Discography

Old Town 1018 Crazy Love/Never Let Me Go (1956)
Old Town 1020 Two in Love (w/R. McFadden) / (flip just McFadden) (1956)
Old Town 1028 Latin Love/Hey Norman (1956)
Sources: Liner notes with Old Town CD *Doo Wop-1*; James Ifill in *Yesterday's Memories* 3.

Runarounds (Bronx, N.Y.)

Personnel Guy Villari, Chuck Fassert, Ronnie Lapinsky, Sal Corrente

Notes

The Runarounds started in 1958 in the Bronx as the Monterays. They would soon become the Regents of "Barbara Ann" fame. None of the follow-ups to Barbara Ann did anything. Following the Regents "Oh Baby," they separated. In 1964, they re-emerged as the Runarounds, chosen because of the title of the Regents' second release.

Discography

KC 116 Unbelievable/Hooray for Love (1963)
Tarheel 065 Are You Looking for a Sweetheart/Let Them Talk (1963)
Felsted 8704 Carrie/Send Her Back (1964)
Capitol 5644 You're a Drag/Perfect Woman (1966)
MGM 1377663 You Lied/My Little Girl (1967)
Sources: Morris Diamond, liner notes with the Collectables CD *Barbara Ann*; Jay Warner, *American Singing Groups.*

Sabers (Los Angeles)

Personnel Herbie ——— (1st tenor), Billy Spicer (1st tenor), Sheridan "Rip" Spencer (2d tenor), Brice Coefield (baritone), Walter Carter (bass)

Notes

It was 1955, and cousins Brice Coefield and Rip Spencer were in high school. They would sing with one another everywhere and decided to form a group. The group they started was called the Sabers. After much practice, they auditioned for Cal-West Records.

A recording session was arranged in the fall of 1955. At that session, only Spencer's tune, "Always and Forever," was recorded. They didn't record a flip side that day. They returned home and soon met 1st tenor Billy Spicer, who was added to the group. Spicer was a schoolmate of Coefield's. They listened to him sing and asked him to join. Spicer is his real name, but he was also known as Billy Storm and occasionally Billy Jones. They returned to the studio and cut "Cool, Cool Christmas."

The record was released in fall 1955 but did nothing. The Sabers were not heard from again. They soon became the Chavelles who recorded for Vita Records.

Discography

Cal West 847 Always and Forever/Cool, Cool Christmas (1955)
Source: Marv Goldberg in *DISCoveries* 1994. Article on the Valiants.

Safaris (Los Angeles)

Personnel Jim Stephens (lead), Marv Rosenberg, Richard Clasky, Sheldon Briar

Notes

This group originally formed in 1959, calling themselves the Mystics. When the East Coast Mystics released their biggie, this group changed to the Enchanters. Apparently Rosenberg and Clasky had met at a high school party and discussed forming a vocal group, and this is the route they began to pursue. They soon secured the vocal services of female lead Sandy Weisman.

Following their first single on Orbit Records as by the Enchanters, the trio added Sheldon Briar and became the Dories on Dore. When this did poorly, Weisman decided that marriage was far better than singing and left. She was replaced by lead Jim Stephens. They moved to Tawny and became the Angels. It was at this time that Rosenberg wrote "Image of a Girl." Tawny management (Herb Alpert) didn't like "Image of a Girl," and a different tune was done for Tawny.

They appeared at many record hops and thereby came to the attention of Eldo Records. In 1960, the group changed its name again, this time to the Safaris, and released "Image of a Girl" on Eldo. This did very well worldwide.

Although their follow-ups did progressively worse, their manager put them on tour without the benefit of pay. All but Jim returned to college. Later in 1961, Briar, Rosenberg, and Clasky joined Lee Forester for one recording on Sudden as the Suddens and one on Valiant in 1963.

Discography

Eldo 101 Image of a Girl/Four Steps to Love (1960)
Eldo 105 Girl with the Story in Her Eyes/Summer Night (1960)
Eldo 110 In the Still of the Night/Shadows (1961)
Source: Jay Warner, *American Singing Groups.*

Salutations, Vito & (Brooklyn, N.Y.)

Personnel Vito Balsamo (lead), Barry Solomon, Bob DePallo, Bobby Mitchell (baritone)

Notes

This popular New York vocal group had their beginnings on the streets of Brooklyn in 1961, originally formed by Barry Solomon and Bob DePallo. They were discovered in a subway station by singer Linda Scott, who referred them to record producer Dave Rick. He then invited them to an audition.

DePallo's younger brother Johnny sought out friend Vito Balsamo because of his vocal group harmony skills. Balsamo persuaded a friend, baritone Bobby Mitchell, to join them and thus Vito and the Salutations were born.

Following their audition, Dave Rick offered them a recording contract. In December 1961 they went into the recording studio. Rick wanted tested, proven songs but the Salutations had recorded only new, untested material. While practicing, however, they were heard performing the Cadillacs' "Gloria," which became their first single, released in February 1962.

Following their first release, DePallo, Solomon, and Mitchell left the group and Balsamo built another Salutations with Randy Silverman (lead/1st tenor), Shelly Buchansky (1st/2d tenor), Lenny Citrin (baritone), and Frankie Fox (bass).

Rick brought them to the larger Herald Records in 1963 and they recorded their unusual rendering of the classic "Unchained Melody." Unfortunately, Herald Records was facing bankruptcy and the Salutations left for Wells Records. Nothing happened with the new label, but the reputation they had built with "Unchained Melody" kept them working.

With no further successes, the Salutations broke up in 1965. Silverman joined the a cappella group the Attitudes, who cut a disc for Times Square, and Balsamo joined the Kelloggs, who cut a disc for Laurie in 1969.

The Salutations re-formed for a show in 1971. By 1980, they were having legal difficulties with Dave Rick over their name and the fact that he "owned it." They then became Vito and His New Group. Rick's Salutations included Eddie "Vito" Pardocci (lead, formerly of the Five Discs), Frankie Gaziano (1st tenor), Buchansky (2d tenor), and Jimmy Spinelli (formerly of the Impalas, at baritone). These groups eventually merged and were still performing as Vito and His New Group into the 1980s and 1990s.

John Verona, Ray Russell, and Donny Albano were other members.

Discography

Rayna 5009 Gloria/Let's Untwist the Twist (1962)
Kram 1202 Your Way/Hey! Hey! Hey! (1962)

Herald 583 Unchained Melody/Hey, Hey Baby (1963)
Herald 586 Eenie Meenie/Extraordinary Girl (1964)
Wells 1008 Can I Depend on You/Liverpool Sound (1964)
Wells 1010 Day-O/Don't Count on Me (1964)
Regina 1320 Get a Job/Girls I Know (1964)
APT 25079 High Noon/Walkin' (1965)
Boom 60020 Bring Back Yesterday/I Want You to Be My Baby (1966)
Red Boy 1001 So Wonderful/I'd Best Be Goin' (1966)
Rust 5106 Hello Dolly/Can I Depend on You (1966)
Sandbag 103 I'd Best Be Going/So Wonderful (1968)
Sources: Ed Engel in *White and Still Alright*; Jay Warner in *American Singing Groups*; Vito Balsamo, interview; Ferdie Gonzales, *Disco-File*.

Sandmen (New York)

Personnel Benjamin Peay (a.k.a. Brook Benton) (lead), Walter Springer (2d tenor), Thurman Haynes (baritone), Adriel McDonald (bass)

Notes

The group was started in 1954 by Adriel McDonald, who formerly sang bass with the Decca Ink Spots. Peay, Springer, and Haynes had formerly been gospel singers and chose to perform secular music with the Sandmen.

Benjamin Peay was Brook Benton's real name. Peay should have been pronounced like P.A. system, but everyone pronounced it like pea. Hence the change.

Following the release of their one Okeh disc as the Sandmen, they did some backup work for Chuck Willis and Lincoln Chase.

The group disbanded when they learned that the disc to be released from their second session with Okeh read "Brook Benton and the Sandmen."

Discography

Okeh 7052 Somebody to Love/When I Grow Too Old to Dream (1955)
Okeh 7055 I Can Tell/One More Break (Chuck Willis) (1955)
Okeh 7058 Ooh/The Kentuckian Song (Brook Benton &) (1955)
Sources: Marv Goldberg and Rick Whitesell, *Goldmine,* April 1979; Marv Goldberg and Marcia Vance, liner notes with CBS Okeh *Rhythm & Blues* CD.

Satellites (Hollywood, Calif.)

Personnel David Ford (lead), Earl Nelson (2d tenor), Curtis Williams (baritone), Bobby Day Byrd (bass)

Notes

This group also recorded as the Flames, Four Flames, Hollywood Four Flames, Hollywood Flames, Jets, and Tangiers. According to Donn Fileti's liner notes with Relic's LP *Best of Class Records* they were also known as Earl Nelson and the Pelicans.

The name Satellites was given to the group by Class owner Leon Rene.

Discography

Class 211 When the Swallows Come Back to Capistrano/Little Bitty Pretty One (1957)
Class 234 Heavenly Angel/You Ain't Saying Nothin' (1958)
Source: Donn Fileti, liner notes with the Relic LP *Best of Class Records.*

Satintones (Detroit)

Personnel Jim Ellis (lead), Sonny Sanders (1st tenor), Charles "Chico" Leverette (baritone), Robert Bateman (bass)

Notes

In 1955, Sanders recorded with Sax Kari and the Quailtones on Josie. The Satintones formed later in 1959 and recorded the first disc for Motown Records.

Vernon Williams and Sammy Mack joined the Satintones in 1961. Williams had earlier recorded with the Royal Holidays as well as the Quailtones. When they joined, Leverette departed. The new group included Ellis, Sanders, Williams, Mack, and Bateman.

Members of the Satintones, or anyone else present on the day of a single artist's recording session, did a great deal of backup work. The group performing this backup work was known as the Rayber Voices. Jeff Kreiter's *Group Collector's Record Guide* notes that there were two versions of "Tomorrow and Always." In her 1998 interview with Ellis and Williams, Nikki Gustafson asked the two former members of the Satintones about this, but neither one of them had any recollection of it. The second, or female, version exists, as I have heard it.

Jim Ellis had previously been with the Five Sounds. He wrote and recorded You're the Greatest Gift of All/Chalypos Baby, which was released on DEB in 1958. Bateman wrote Please "Mr. Postman" for the Marvelettes.

Discography

Tamla 54026 Motor City/Going to the Hop (1960)
Motown 1000 My Beloved/Sugar Daddy (1960)
Motown 1006 Angel/A Love That Can Never Be (1960)
Motown 1006 A Love That Can Never Be/Tomorrow and Always (1961) (male version)
Motown 1006 A Love That Never Be/Tomorrow and Always (1961) (female version)
Motown 1010 My Kind of Love/I Know How It Feels (1961)
Motown 1020 Faded Letter/Zing Went the Strings of My Heart (1961)
Sources: Nikki Gustafson and Jim Dunn, Internet portrait of the Satintones, available at: www.members.aol.com/wawawaooh/main.htm; Ferdie Gonzalez, *Disco-File*; Jeff Kreiter, *Group Collector's Record Guide.*

Satisfactions (Washington, D.C.)

Personnel James "Junior" Isom, Lorenzo Hines (1st tenor), Earl Jones (2d tenor), Fletcher Lee (bass)

Notes

Isom had previously sung with the Marvels and the Senators. He left the Senators after many years to join the Satisfactions.

The Satisfactions had one release for the Smash label in 1964, with both sides featuring Isom. These tunes did not sell very well, but their record resulted in live appearances from Mexico to Canada.

Discography

Smash 2059 Give Me Your Love/Stop Following Me (1964)
Source: Dave Hinckley and Marv Goldberg in *Yesterday's Memories* 8.

Savoys, Jimmy Jones & (New York)

Personnel Jimmy Jones (lead), William Walker (1st tenor), Bobby Moore (2d tenor), Mel Walton (baritone), Kerry Saxton (bass)

Notes

In 1956, following their only record for Savoy, the Savoys found themselves at George Goldner's Rama Records, where their name was changed to Jimmy Jones and the Pretenders.

At times, Irving Lee Gail would substitute for Kerry Saxton. *(Note:* In Marv Goldberg's liner notes with the Savoy LP *Vocal Group Album,* Goldberg refers to Saxton as Kenny. Apparently this was his editor's mistake.)

Jones sang with the Sparks of Rhythm, Jones Boys, Savoys, and, as mentioned above, the Pretenders on Rama.

Discography

Savoy 1188 You/Say You're Mine (1956)
Savoy 1586 With All My Heart/Please Say You're Mine (1960)
(Note: As a result of the success of Jones's "Handy Man" in 1960, Savoy rereleased "Say You're Mine" as "Please Say You're Mine" to capitalize on the success of "Handy Man.")
Source: Marv Goldberg in liner notes with the Savoy LP *Vocal Group Album.*

Savoys (Newark, N.J.)

Personnel Angelo Basilone, John Faliveno, Joseph Castellano, Joseph Stefanelli, Sam Monaco

Notes

When Stan Krause started the Catamount label in 1964, the Savoys were one of the label's principal contributors and one of its first.

Discography

Catamount 101 Oh What a Dream/If You Were Gone from Me (1965)
Catamount 105 Gloria/Closer You Are (1965)

Catamount 778 Oh Gee Oh Gosh/Vision of Love (1965)
Source: Donn Fileti, liner notes with the Relic CD *I Dig Acappella.*

Saxons (Los Angeles)

Personnel Stan Beverly (tenor), Charles Taggart (1st tenor), Maudice Giles (2d tenor), Joe Lewis (baritone), Nathaniel "Buster" Williams (bass)

Notes
The Saxons were also the Hollywood Saxons, the Tuxedos on Forte, and the Capris on Tender.
　　Giles also sang with the Squires (Combo), Capris, Portraits, and Hollywood Saxons.
　　Lewis was also a member of the Hollywood Saxons, Capris, Portraits, and Tuxedos.
　　Bass Nathaniel "Buster" Williams also sang with the Saxons and the Hollywood Saxons, Shields, Coasters, Portraits, and Capris.

Discography
Our (N/A) Home on the Range (SB)/Please Be My Love Tonight (JL) (1958)
Contender 1313 Is It True? (SB)/Rock and Roll Show (JL) (1958)
Tampa 139 Tryin' (SB)/My Love Is True (1958)
Hareco 102 Everyday Holiday (SB)/L.A. Lover (CT/JL) (1960)
Source: Joseph Laredo, *Tampa* CD liner notes.

Scale-Tones (New York)

Personnel Cleveland Still (lead), James Montgomery (tenor), Don Archer (baritone), James Miller (baritone), Thomas Gardner (bass)

Notes
Because Richard Blandon attended a Scale-Tones rehearsal session (he was recording in an adjacent room), members of his Five Wings and the Scale-Tones eventually merged to form the Dubs.

Discography
Jay Dee 810 Everlasting Love/Dreamin' and Dreamin' (1956)
Source: Donn Fileti, liner notes with the Relic LP *Jay Dee.*

Scarlets (New Haven, Conn.)

Personnel Fred Parris (lead), Sylvester Hopkins (1st tenor), Nate Mosely Jr. (2d tenor), Al Denby (baritone), William Powers (bass)

Notes
Parris first began singing in 1953 with a New Haven high school group called the Canaries. Because his baseball priorities caused him to miss rehearsals and prac-

tice sessions, the rest of the group asked him to leave. Undaunted, he formed his own group with some other friends from high school and the Scarlets were born.

They recorded demos and continuously took them to Bobby Robinson's record shop in Harlem, New York. Robinson finally agreed to record them in 1954; the results were terrific. Robinson would record them many more times.

The group later opted to join the army as a group so they would be able to continue their performing. Unfortunately, they were sent to different locations, making their original intention impossible. They managed to go on leave at the same time and record one last record for Red Robin, Kiss Me/Indian Fever.

Parris also sang with the Restless Hearts, Five Satins, and the Wildwoods.

According to Charlie Horner's liner notes accompanying Lost Nite LP 143, *Scarlets Greatest Hits,* "A second 5 Satins group including Fred Parris and Silvester [sic] Hopkins of the original Scarlets, recorded She's Gone/The Voice for the Klik label in 1958 under the name Fred Parris and the Scarlets."

Discography

Red Robin 128 Dear One/I've Lost (1954)
Red Robin 133 Love Doll/Darling I'm Yours (1955)
Red Robin 135 True Love/Cry Baby (1955)
Red Robin 138 Kiss Me/Indian Fever (1955)
Klik 7905 She's Gone/The Voice (1958)
Sources: Donn Fileti, liner notes with the Relic CD *Red Robin Golden Doowops*; Charlie Horner, liner notes with the Lost Nite LP *Scarlets Greatest Hits.*

Schoolboys (New York)

Personnel Leslie Martin (lead), James Holland Edwards (James Hammond) (1st tenor), Roger Hayes (2d tenor), James Charlie McKay (baritone), Renaldo Gamble (bass)

Notes

The Schoolboys got together in the Harlem section of New York in 1955. They started out as the Scobians and somehow were renamed the Schoolboys by deejay Tommy Smalls. Harold Atley was the group's first tenor lead and appeared with them on Ted Mack's *Amateur Hour.* Atley however, never recorded with them. The Schoolboys were one of the first groups to have a high tenor lead. Their "Please Say You Want Me" preceded the Teenagers' "Why Do Fools Fall in Love" by several months.

Gamble later joined Pearl McKinnon and the Kodaks; Roger Hayes joined the Collegians, as did McKay. Gamble also performed with the Impacts.

Leslie Martin supposedly led a group of moonlighting Cadillacs on the Schoolboys' execution of "Pearl." Other members included Waldo Champen, J. R. Bailey, and others ("Champ" does not recall this ever happening).

Discography

Okeh 7076 Please Say You Want Me/Shirley (1956)
Okeh 7085 I Am Old Enough/Mary (1957)
Okeh 7085 Carol/Pearl (1957)

Juanita 103 The Slide/Angel of Love (1958)
Sources: Phil Groia, liner notes with the Collectables CD *Thrillers/Schoolboys*; Marv Goldberg and Marcia Vance, liner notes with CBS's *Okeh Rhythm & Blues* CD.

Scooters (Detroit)

Personnel Bobby Ruffin (lead), Noah Howell (tenor), Isaac Reese (baritone), Norman Thrasher (bass)

Notes

This group had also been known as the Muskateers and the Serenaders. At the time the disc shown below was released, they were called the Royal Jokers. "Someday We'll Meet Again" had originally been recorded for the Venus label under the name Royals.

The Serenaders were never the Scooters. For some reason, the people at Dawn put "Scooters" on the label (as well as pressing it at the wrong speed—33 1/3 rpm instead of 45 rpm). Only "Someday We'll Meet Again" was recorded by the Serenaders. The flip side was by some other vocal group.

Discography

Dawn 224 Someday We'll Meet Again/Really (1957)
Sources: Sal Mondrone in *Bim Bam Boom* 1; Marv Goldberg in *DISCoveries.*

Scrubs, Dave Collins & (New Orleans)

Personnel Dave Collins (lead), Allen Mathews, Albert Veal (tenor), Joseph Gaines, John "Buddy" Morris (baritone), Willie Thrower (bass)

Notes

The Scrubs, the group behind Dave Collins on the recording below, was the Imperial Hawks. Apparently, in New Orleans "scrubs" is the name for Bluejays.

Discography

Imperial 5294 Bluesy Me/Don't Break My Heart (1954)
Source: Jim Dawson, liner notes with the EMI Imperial LP *Lost Dreams.*

Secrets (Staten Island, N.Y.)

Personnel Dave Concepción (lead), Pat Russo (1st tenor), Vinnie Santorelli (2d tenor), Steve Murphy (baritone), Frank Del Cavo (bass)

Notes

The group formed on Staten Island in 1955, initially singing for fun. In 1956 they decided to get serious about their talent. They soon got themselves a manager and shortly thereafter signed with Decca.

Their first release with Decca came in 1957. The recording received little promotion, but it nevertheless afforded them many appearances. Early copies show "Five Secrets" on the label.

Several weeks following the release of this first disc, the Secrets signed with Herald. As a legal precaution, they changed their name to the Loungers.

Because of Herald/Ember's preoccupation with the Mellokings and the Five Satins, the Loungers received little or no attention.

At Herald the material was written by the group, whereas at Decca management gave them the material to record. This is most probably why they sounded so different on the two labels. Additionally, Decca had told the group that they wanted them to sound pop.

Shortly before the group broke up, Murphy left and was replaced by Pat Russo's brother, Bernie.

Discography

Decca 30350 See You Next Year/Queen Bee (1957)
Source: Jay Repolay in *Story Untold,* May-June 1978.

Senators (Washington, D.C.)

Personnel Sam Gilbert (lead), James Isom (2d tenor), Ronald Boyd (baritone), James Mitchell (bass)

Notes

This group formed in 1962. The Senators were the Marvels, who for many years gigged around the city playing local nightspots and eventually recorded for Laurie. Their releases did not sell and they returned to Washington and resumed their local thing.

Years later, in an attempt to record again, they decided to change their name to the Senators, after the local baseball team. They hooked up with Winn Records and recorded again, with Sam Ilbert doing lead on both sides. But this disc, and their attempt, failed.

Discography

Winn 1917 Wedding Bells (SG)/I Shouldn't Care (SG) (1962)
Sources: Dave Hinckley and Marv Goldberg in *Yesterday's Memories* 8; Jeff Kreiter, *Group Collector's Record Price Guide.*

Senders (Los Angeles)

Personnel Carlton Beck (lead), Richard Betts (baritone)

Notes

This group also recorded as the Guides, the Swallows, and the Uptones. They were friendly with the Hollywood Saxons. Some of the songs written by the Hollywood Saxons were given to the Senders for future recordings.

Discography

Kent 320 I Dream of You/The Ballad of Stagger Lee (1959)
Kent 324 One More Kiss/Everybody Needs to Know (1959)
Entra 711 Spinning/Pretty Little Pretty (1961)
Sources: Liner notes with the Famous Groove CD *Hollywood Saxons: Everyday Is a Holiday;* Marv Goldberg and Rick Whitesell in *Yesterday's Memories* 11.

Señors (New Orleans)

Personnel Milton Smith (lead), Adolph Smith, Vontell Lane, Clarence Phoenix, Billy Tircuit (bass)

Notes

This group originally formed in 1954 and first recorded as the Mellow Drops on Imperial. They next became the Monitors on Aladdin and Specialty. Their final appearance was as the Señors on the Sue label in New York.

They returned to the same recording studio they had used as the Mellow Drops, Monitors, and Moonbeems, and now as the Señors. Both tunes on Sue were led by Milton Smith. Somehow, the two tunes recorded were issued on Sue in 1962.

By 1964, both the Monitors and the Señors disbanded.

Adolph and Milton Smith were brothers.

Discography

Sue 756 May I Have This Dance (MS)/Searching for Olive Oil (MS) (1962)
Source: B. Tircuit, interview by Marv Goldberg in *DISCoveries,* March 1998.

Sensations (Philadelphia)

Personnel Yvonne Mills (a.k.a. Yvonne Baker) (lead), Tommy Wicks (baritone), Alfonso Howell (bass)

Notes

This group, originally calling themselves the Cavaliers, formed in 1954. They signed with the Atlantic subsidiary Atco in 1955. Atco management considered their sound to be sensational; hence their name.

Their first single, "Yes Sir, That's My Baby," was released in November 1955 and did well. Their next two singles also did well, but the following releases did poorly and caused the group to part.

Yvonne Mills married and became Yvonne Baker. She soon began to rear a family.

In 1961, Howell convinced Mills-Baker to reform the group. At this time Richard Curtain of the Hideaways (MGM) and Sam Armstrong were added. Philadelphia deejay Kae Williams became their manager and got them a record deal with Chess affiliate Argo.

Argo quickly released "Music, Music, Music," which was the group's first time on the hit charts. "Let Me In" was next, and this great tune fared even better than

"Music, Music, Music," reaching the second spot on the R&B charts in 1962. Roosevelt Simmons was another later member.

Tommy Cooke later sang as baritone.

But these incredible successes came to an end. The Sensations would never again come close. They changed labels hoping to rediscover the magic, but this was not to be. Eventually it was decided to bring it to an end.

Discography

Atco 6056 Sympathy/Yes Sir, That's My Baby (1955)
Atco 6067 Please Mr. Disc Jockey/Ain't He Sweet? (1956)
Atco 6075 Cry Baby Cry/My Heart Cries for You (1956)
Atco 6083 Little Wallflower/Such a Love (1956)
Atco 6090 My Debut to Love/You Made Me Love You (1957)
Atco 6115 Romance in the Dark/Kiddy Car Love (1958)
Argo 5391 Music, Music, Music/A Part of Me (1961)
Argo 5405 Let Me In/Oh Yes I'll Be True (1961)
Argo 6056 Sympathy/Yes Sir, That's My Baby (1961)
Junior 986 You Made a Fool of Me/That's What You've Gotta Do (1961)
Junior 1002 We Were Meant to Be/It's Good Enough for Me (1962)
Junior 1005 You Made a Fool of Me/That's What You've Gotta Do (1963)
Junior 1006 Baby/Love, Love, Love (1963)
Junior 1010 Mend the Torn Pieces/I Can't Change (1964)
Junior 1021 We Were Meant to Be/It's Good Enough for Me (1964)
Tollie 9009 You Made a Fool of Me/That's What You've Gotta Do (1964)
Sources: Jay Warner, *American Singing Groups*; Pete Grendysa, liner notes with the Chess CD box set *Chess Rhythm & Roll.*

Sentimentalists (New York)

Personnel Jimmie Nabbie (lead), Danny Owens (tenor), Pat Best (baritone), Jimmie Gordon (bass)

Notes

A personality clash surfaced between members of the Brown Dots which made group members realize that this uneasy, stressful feeling could not be contained any longer. One of the factions recruited Danny Owens to replace Deek Watson without his knowledge.

This new group called themselves the Sentimentalists. They didn't leave Watson right away. They wanted to make the break at a very opportune time. The severance came late in 1946. Bandleader Tommy Dorsey, however, owned the name Sentimentalists and forced the new group to change to the Brown Dots. Still later the Brown Dots became the Four Tunes.

Discography

Manor 8002 Silent Night/O Come All Ye Faithful (1946)
Manor 8003 Ave Maria/White Christmas (1946)

506 • The Encyclopedia

Manor 1049 I'd Rather Be Safe Than Sorry/I'll Be Waiting for You (1946) Also released showing Four Tunes on the label.
Source: Marv Goldberg in *DISCoveries.*

Sentimentals (Newark, N.J.)

Personnel Sylvester Jackson (lead), Floyd Bond, Edward Copeland, Kipling Pitman, Michael Riggins (bass)

Notes

This quintet came to Tuxedo Records for an audition. The label was primarily a gospel organization, but Tuxedo management liked them and in 1957 began Mint Records for secular music.

"Teenie Teenager" and "I Want to Love You" was their first release in August 1957. When it began to take off, a deal was struck with Chess Records of Chicago for more effective distribution.

"Sunday Kind of Love" and "Wedding Bells" were next. In 1958, Bond and Pittman left and were replaced by Ralph Gamble, making the group a quartet.

During the dormant early 1960s, Gamble left and was replaced by Gary Simmons. The group recorded several sides, none of which were released. Live appearances continued and eventually they began performing and recording as a soul group.

Discography

Mint 801 I Want to Love You/Teenie Teenie Teenager (1957)
Mint 802 Wedding Bells/A Sunday Kind of Love (1957)
Tuxedo 922 I Know/Hey Baby Hey (1957)
Tuxedo 926 Lover I'm Waiting for You/I'm Sixteen Years (1958)
Mint 803 I'm Your Fool Always/Rock Me Mama (1958)
Mint 805 You're Mine/Danny Boy (1959)
Mint 807 I'll Miss These Things/This Time (1968)
Mint 808 I Want to Love You/This Time (1972)
Source: Lou Silvani, *Collecting Rare Records*; Roy Adams in *Story Untold* 1.

Sequins (New York)

Personnel Robert Coleman (lead), Carl White (1st tenor)

Notes

The Sequins' record was the last Red Robin disc that Bobby Robinson recorded and released, in the early winter of 1956. A few months later, Robinson discovered Earl Lewis and the Channels and decided to begin the Whirlin' Disc label.

Coleman later sang lead for the Emanons.

Discography

Red Robin 140 Don't Fall in Love/Why Can't You Treat Me Right? (1956)
Source: Donn Fileti, liner notes with the Relic CD *Golden Groups—Red Robin.*

Serenaders (Washington, D.C.)

Personnel Henry Mont (lead), Robert Neill (1st tenor), Henry "Shorty" Womble (2d tenor), Leroy Henderson (baritone), Frank "Jake" Hardy (bass)

Notes

This group formed in 1951 while group members were in junior high school in Washington, D.C. They performed continuously at school and various local events.

Despite the fact that Les Moss (Moskowitz) released an LP with their recordings, no 45 rpm singles were generated from the album. The group broke up in 1953 with Mont forming the Carusos. Henderson became a member of the Topps.

Womble and Hardy joined the Rainbows, who did "Mary Lee" for Red Robin. *Source:* Les Moss, liner notes with *Candy Bar Boogie* LP/CD.

Serenaders (Detroit)

Personnel Norman Thrasher (lead), Thearon Hill (tenor), Noah Howell (baritone), Isaac Reese (bass)

Notes

Before recording, Henry Booth, later of the Royals/Midnighters, was an original member of the Serenaders. Thearon Hill replaced him.

This group recorded for JVB in 1951–1952. They later became the Royal Jokers, Scooters, Muskateers [sic], and the Royals on Venus.

In a 1996 interview, neither Hill nor Thrasher could remember the order in which their songs were recorded or released. Nor were they aware that they ever released a song on the Roxy label.

In 1953, the Swing Time label of Los Angeles bought carloads of masters from small, independent Detroit labels. The Muskateers' songs were released on Swing Time soon thereafter.

Willie Jones was only with the Royal Jokers. When Hill left, he was replaced by Billy Lyons. Thrasher left at this time as well and was replaced by Raymond Dorsey.

Discography

JVB 2001 Tomorrow Night (TH)/Why Don't You Do Right? (NH) (1952)
Roxy 801 Goodbye My Love (TH/NT)/Love Me till My Dying Day (TH) (1952)
Coral 60720 It's Funny (TH)/Confession Is Good for the Soul (NT/NH) (1952)
Coral 65093 Misery (TH)/But I Forgive You (NH) (1952)
DeLuxe 6022 Please, Please Forgive Me/Baby (1953)
Red Robin 115 Will She Know?/I Want to Love You Baby (1953)
Swingtime 347 M-a-y-b-e-l-l/Ain't Gonna Cry No More (1954)
Sources: Sal Mondrone in *Bim Bam Boom* 1; Marv Goldberg in *DISCoveries*; Donn Fileti, liner notes with the Relic Red Robin CD *Golden Doowops*.

Serenaders (New Jersey)

Personnel George Kerr (lead), Luke Gross (2d tenor), Kenny Simon (tenor), Victor Kerr (baritone)

Notes

George Kerr also sang for the Imperials.

Phil Groia in *They All Sang on the Corner* shows the Serenaders' personnel as George Kerr, Victor Kerr, Nelson Lamb, Bobby Jones, and, at bass, Harold Curry.

Discography

Chock 101/102 Never Let Me Go/I Wrote a Letter (1957)
MGM 12623 Never Let Me Go/I Wrote a Letter (1958)
MGM 12666 Dance Darling Dance/Give Me a Girl (1958)
Rae Cox 101 Gotta Go to School/My Girl Flip Flop (1959)
Source: Phil Groia, *They All Sang on the Corner.*

Serenades (Chicago)

Personnel Willie Wright (a.k.a. Willie Dial) (lead), James Doolaby Wright, Tommie Johnson, Ronald Sherman, Willie Daniels

Notes

James Wright, Willie Wright, and Willie Daniels later recorded with the Von Gayles at their original session. This occurred as three members of the Von Gayles were among the missing on the day of their session with Chief Records.

Tommie Johnson was the brother of Charles Johnson from the Von Gayles.

Discography

Chief 7002 The Pajama Song/A Sinner in Love (1957)
Source: Bob Pruter, *Doowop . . . The Chicago Scene.*

Shadows (New Haven, Conn.)

Personnel Scott King (tenor), Raymond Reid (tenor), Sam McClure (baritone), Jasper Edwards (bass)

Notes

This group started as the Jubalaires' touring group. The Jubalaires made a daily appearance on Arthur Godfrey's radio show on WABC-AM, and Godfrey did not allow them to tour. Therefore a substitute quartet was needed and they found the Melody Kings, a trio from New Haven, Connecticut, consisting of Scott King, Raymond Reid, and Jasper Edwards. One of the Jubalaires would then go out on the road with them as the Jubalaires (the radio group got a new fourth member).

Raymond Reid sang with the last incarnation of Charlie Fuqua's Ink Spots.

Lee Records was a small organization that could not withstand competition from the big companies. So in mid-1950, Lee sold all its masters, as well as its unreleased takes to the Shad brothers' Sittin' In With organization.

Scott King was drafted in October 1950 and the group dispersed until he returned in 1952. During this period, Shad issued the Lee unreleased material. When King returned, the group decided to sign with Decca.

Decca held their last release until July 1954—Don't Be Bashful/Tell Her. In 1958 the Shadows split up for good.

Discography

Lee 200 I've Been a Fool/Nobody Knows (1949)
Lee 202 I'd Rather Be Wrong Than Blue/You Are Closer to My Heart Than My Shadow (1950)
Lee 207 Don't Blame My Dreams/I'm Crying 'Cause You're Laughing (1950)
Sittin' In With 583 Jitterbug Special/I'll Never Never Let You Go (1950)
Sittin' In With 590 Don't Be Late/Beans (1951)
Sittin' In With 627 Coon Can Annie/It's Too Bad (1952)
Decca 28765 No Use/Stay (1953)
Decca 48307 Don't Be Bashful/Tell Her (1953)
Decca 48322 Better Than Gold/Big Mouth Mama (1954)
Source: Marv Goldberg in *DISCoveries* 90.

Sharmeers (Philadelphia)

Personnel Rosa Bryant, Castella Riley, Mattie Williams, Gloria Huntley

Discography

Red Top 109 A School Girl in Love/You're My Lover (1958)
Source: Mattie Williams, interview by John Clemente, February 1999.

Sharps (Los Angeles)

Personnel John "Sonny" Harris (lead), Carl White (tenor), Al Frazier (baritone), Turner "Rocky" Wilson (bass)

Notes

Joe Green of the Nu Tones replaced Carl White. He was also with the Crenshaws.

Frazier, Harris, and White were with the Lamplighters and Tenderfoots on Federal. They backed Paul Anka on "I Confess" on RPM (and former Lamplighter Thurston Harris as the Sharps on Aladdin's "Little Bitty Pretty One").

Carl White sang "Bobby My Love" with an unknown Buddies group on Combo.

Eventually they hit big as the Rivingtons (Frazier, White, Wilson, Harris) with "Papa Oom Mow Mow" in 1962.

This group also recorded as the Ebbtides, 4 After 5's, Rebels, Rivingtons, Tenderfoots, and the Twisters.

Discography

Tag 2200 Six Months, Three Weeks/Cha Cho Hop (1956)
Chess 1690 6 Months, 3 Weeks, 2 Days, 1 Hour/Cha Cho Hop* (1956)
Aladdin 3398 Little Bitty Pretty One/I Hope You Won't Hold It against Me (1957)
Aladdin 3401 What Will I Gain?/Shufflin' (1957)
Lamp 2007 Our Love Is Here to Stay/Lock My Heart (1957)
Jamie 1040 Come On/Sweet Sweetheart (1957)
Jamie 1106 Look At Me/Have Love, Will Travel (1958)
Jamie 1114 Here's a Heart/Gig-a-Lene (1958)
Combo 146 All My Love/Look What You've Done to Me (1958)
Dot 15806 All My Love/Look What You've Done to Me (1958)
*Recorded in 1956; released in 1958.
Sources: Jack Sbarbori in *Record Exchanger* 16; Art Turco in *Record Exchanger* 28.

Sharptones (Oakland, Calif.)

Personnel Charles Fitzpatrick (lead), Al Williams (1st tenor), Berlin "Burl" Carpenter (2d tenor), Willie Roland (baritone), Andre Goodwin (bass)

Notes

The Sharptones recorded for the Aladdin subsidiary, Post Records. Their disc, Made to Love/Since I Fell for You, was released in October 1955. It was their only release on Post.

In the liner notes with Ace's *Johnny Ace Memorial Album,* Jim Dawson wrote in 1984 that Jesse Belvin sang with this group.

According to the unsigned liner notes accompanying the Aladdin/Imperial CD *R&B Vocal Group Magic,* the Sharptones had previously recorded as the California Turbans for John Dolphin's Money label. The group had nothing to do with the Philadelphia Turbans.

Discography

Aladdin 3431 Sugar Doll/Let Me Dream (1958)
Sources: Jim Dawson, liner notes with Ace's *Johnny Ave Memorial Album*; unsigned liner notes with the Aladdin/Imperial CD *R&B Vocal Group Magic*;

Sha Weez/Shaw-Wees (New Orleans)

Personnel Edgar Myles (lead), James Crawford (tenor), Irving "Cat" Bannister, Nolan Blackwell, Warren "Big Boy" Myles

Notes

The members of this group got together in 1950 in their New Orleans high school. They were a self-contained unit, playing instruments and vocalizing.

They somehow wound up at Aladdin, where they had one release. Late in 1953, they got an offer from Chess/Checker while still under contract with Aladdin. The offer was to record six sides for the Chess/Checker organization. Because of this duplicity, they recorded as Sugar Boy and the Cane Cutters.

After Checker, they recorded two discs for Specialty as "Big Boy" Myles and the Shaw Wees, which were very bluesy.

As their popularity started to diminish, the group members started to drift away. They appeared together on and off in the 1960s and split up after a decade of this.

Discography

Aladdin 3170 No One to Love Me/Early Sunday Morning (1952)
Specialty 564 Who's Been Fooling You?/That's the Girl I Married (1955)
Specialty 590 Just to Hold My Hand/Hickory Dickory Dock (1956)
Source: Marv Goldberg and Dave Hinckley in *Yesterday's Memories* 11.

Sheiks (Norfolk, Va.)

Personnel Kenneth Kimball (lead), Johnny Wilson, Horace Jenkins, William Collins, Alton Parker

Notes

This Sheiks began as the Five Pearls in Norfolk, Virginia, in 1954. Members of the Five Pearls approached label owner Frank Guida, who arranged for a recording session at station WTAR radio, where "Give Me One More Chance" and "Baby Don't You Cry" were recorded and released as the Sheiks on Guida's Eff-En-Dee label.

Following airplay in Virginia and a great deal of local interest, Guida took the disc to Atlantic Records in New York for an audition of sorts. The group signed up with the Atlantic subsidiary Cat Records, and Cat 116 was recorded in December 1954.

Discography

Ef-N-De 1000 Give Me One More Chance/Baby Don't You Cry (1954)
Cat 116 Walk That Walk/Kissing Song (1955)
Source: Brian Walsh, liner notes with Ace's *Norfolk, Virginia Sound.*

Shells (Brooklyn, N.Y.)

Personnel "Little" Nate Bouknight (lead), Bobby Nurse (1st tenor), Randy "Shade" Alston (2d tenor), Gus Geter (baritone), Daniel Small (bass)

Notes

The Shells formed in Brooklyn, New York, in the mid-1950s. When they called on Johnson Records, the management at Johnson did not think much of them, giving the group the last twenty minutes of an unused Dubs' session to record. The Dubs assisted the Shells before recording and the end product was "Baby Oh Baby," which got some New York airplay.

Following their second release for Johnson, Pleading No More/Don't Say Goodbye, Boughnight left. He would return in 1958 to record a few sides with the group, then with the End label. After End, Roy Jones assumed Boughnight's lead spot for the group's Roulette executions, She Wasn't Meant for Me/The Thief.

The new Shells group, which surfaced in 1958, included Bobby Nurse (1st tenor), Randy "Shade" Alston (2d tenor), Gus Geter (baritone), Daniel Small (bass), and Roy Jones (lead). This was also the lineup at Josie when they joined that label in 1963.

Boughknight, Kirk Harris, Jay McKnight, and one other singer joined forces in 1959 to become Little Nate and the Chryslers.

In 1960, collectors Donn Fileti and Wayne Stierle convinced the current Johnson management to rerelease "Baby Oh Baby," and it was an even bigger hit three years after it was released originally!

Although Boughnight was no longer with the Shells beginning with the Josie recording in 1963, they retained the Shells sound on Jerry Blaine's Josie label. The group reflected above formed the ensemble with Josie.

In 1966, the Shells were to play an important role, along with the Nutmegs, in beginning the new genre of R&B a cappella music. Collector Wayne Stierle convinced the Shells to release some old practice tapes, sans musical accompaniment, which eventually became a popular segment of the music.

Bouknight later joined the Clovers briefly to record "Stop Pretending" on Porwin in 1963.

Discography

Johnson 104 Baby Oh Baby/Angel Eyes (1957)
Juanita 106 Pleading No More/Don't Say Goodbye (1958)
Johnson 106 Pleading No More/Don't Say Goodbye (1958)
End 1022 Sippin' Soda/Pretty Little Girl (1958)
End 1050 Shooma Dom Dom/Whispering Wings (1959)
Roulette 4156 She Wasn't Meant for Me/The Thief (1959)
Gone 5103 Sippin' Soda/Pretty Little Girl (1961)
Johnson 107 Explain It to Me/An Island Unknown (1961)
Johnson 109 Better Forget Him/Can't Take It (1961)
Johnson 110 O-Mi Yum-Mi Yum-Mi/In the Dim Light of the Dark (1961)
Johnson 112 Sweetest One/Baby, Walk On In (1961)
Johnson 119 Deep in My Heart/Happy Holiday (1962)
Johnson 120 A Toast to Your Birthday/The Drive (1963)
Johnson 127 On My Honor/My Royal Love (1963)
Josie 912 Our Wedding Day/Deep in My Heart (1963)
Sources: Donn Fileti, liner notes with Relic's *Johnson* LP/CD; Gordon Skadberg and George Povall, notes to the Sequel CD *Jubilee/Josie R&B Vocal Groups-5.*

Sheppards (Chicago)

Personnel John Pruitt (lead), James Dennis "Brother" Isaac (1st tenor), Oscar Boyd (2d tenor), George Parker (baritone), Nathaniel Tucker (bass)

Notes

This group was organized in 1953 by Andre Williams, who later recorded "Bacon Fat." Williams sang baritone for the group at various times but never recorded with them.

Albert "Pee Wee" Bell was in the group prior to recording, as was Oscar Robinson from the Five Thrills, who replaced Andre Williams.

Albert Bell and Oscar Robinson were replaced by George Parker and Oscar Boyd. They recorded "Love" and "Cool Mambo" for Theron with the personnel shown above.

On "Mozelle," Parker (on leave from the service) sang lead and Kent McGhee joined as baritone.

Two other songs were recorded at the United session, "Pretty Little Girl" and "Just Let Me Love You," but they were never released.

The Sheppards broke up in 1957 when Pruitt and Tucker were drafted and Boyd developed problems with cataracts.

Brother Isaac joined the Chicago Bel-Aires, who cut one disc for Decca. Three members of this group, including Isaac, later became a new Sheppards, who did "Island of Love."

Discography

Theron 112 Love (JP)/Cool Mambo (GP) (1955)
United 198 Sherry (JP/GP)/Mozelle (JP/GP) (1956)
Sources: Bob Pruter in *Record Collector's Monthly* 46; Bob Pruter, *Doowop . . . The Chicago Scene*; Bob Pruter in *Time Barrier Express* 27.

Sheppards (Chicago)

Personnel Murrie Eskridge (lead), James Dennis "Brother" Isaac (1st tenor), O. C. Perkins (2d tenor), Jimmy Allen (baritone), Millard Edwards (bass)

Notes

This group evolved from the earlier Chicago Sheppards, with Isaac from the first group. The first group, which split up in 1957, caused Isaac to join with three former members of Chicago's Bel-Aires, who recorded "My Yearbook" for Decca.

Edwards also sang with the Bel-Aires and later with the Esquires. He left the group in 1963 for a solo career. The group then became a quartet and then a trio.

Eskridge sang with the Palms and the Ballads.

Discography

Apex 7750 Island of Love (MM)/Never Felt Like This Before (ME) (1959)
Apex 7752 Feel Like Lovin' (MM)/Just Like You (ME) (1959)
Apex 7755 Meant to Be (MM)/It's Crazy (MM) (1959)
Apex 7759 Just When I Need You Most (MM)/Society Gal (MM) (1960)
Apex 7760 Come Home, Come Home (ME)/Just Like You (ME) (1960)
Apex 7762 Tragic (MM)/Feel Like Lovin' (MM) (1961)
Apex 7764 So in Need for Love (ME)/Never Felt Like This Before (ME) (1961)
Pam 1001 Give a Hug to Me (ME)/Never Let Me Go (ME) (1961)
Wes 7750 Glitter in Your Eyes (ME)/Every Now and Then (MM) (1961)
Vee Jay 406 Glitter in Your Eyes (ME)/Every Now and Then (MM) (1961)
Vee Jay 441 Tragic (echo) (MM)/Come to Me (MM) (1962)
Abner 7006 Elevator Operator (ME)/Loving You (ME) (1962)

Okeh 7173 Pretend You're Still Mine (ME)/Walkin' (MM) (1963)
Constellation 123 Island of Love (MM)/Give a Hug to Me (ME) (1964)
Sources: Bob Pruter in *Record Collector's Monthly*; Marv Goldberg and Marcia Vance, liner notes with the CBS CD *Okeh Rhythm & Blues.*

Sherrys (Philadelphia)

Personnel Delthine Cook (lead), Dinell Cook, Charlotte Butler, Delores "Honey" Wylie

Notes

This group came together in 1962. The Cooks were sisters who recorded for Philadelphia's Guyden Records. They were daughters of 1950s favorite "Little" Joe Cook, who had a huge hit with "Peanuts."

Their follow-up, "Slop Time," made no noise at the cash register.

Discography

Guyden 2068 Pop Pop Pop Pie (DLTHC)/Your Hand in Mine (1962)
Guyden 2077 Slop Time/Let's Stomp Again (1962)
Guyden 2064 I've Got No One/Saturday Night (1963)
Guyden 2098 Monk, Monk, Monkey/That Boy of Mine (1963)
Mercury 72256 No No Baby/That Guy of Mine (1964)
Roberts 701 Slow Jerk/Confusion (1964)
Source: Joe Tortelli in *Goldmine.*

Shieks (Los Angeles)

Personnel Jesse Belvin, Eugene Church, Harold Lewis (tenor), Mel Williams (2d tenor)

Notes

In the liner notes accompanying the Jesse Belvin Specialty CD, it is stated that Belvin overdubbed himself and was responsible for all the voices of the Shieks. *(Note:* This cannot be confirmed.) In Silvani's *Collecting Rare Records,* Eugene Church is omitted from the group lineup and "Sonny" Moore is included as a member.

In the liner notes with Sequel's King-Federal-DeLuxe CD *Great Googa Mooga,* every name except Harold Lewis's is shown with the discussion of this group.

It must also be mentioned that the Shieks' "So Fine" is the predecessor to the Fiestas' "So Fine" recorded years later.

Discography

Federal 12237 So Fine/Sentimental Heart (1955)
Source: D. Romanello, G. Povall, and C. Bucola, liner notes with the Sequel King-Federal-DeLuxe CD *Great Googa Mooga.*

Shields (Los Angeles)

Personnel Frankie Ervin (lead), Jesse Belvin (1st tenor), Mel Williams (2d tenor), Johnny "Guitar" Watson (baritone), Tommy "Buster" Williams (bass)

Notes

After West Coast label-owner/producer George Matola approved the Slades' version of "You Cheated" on Domino, he quickly structured a black group to cover the white version.

Matola joined Frankie Ervin with Jesse Belvin, Mel Williams, Buster Williams, and Johnny "Guitar" Watson to record the disc in the studio.

Makeshift groups were assembled by Matola whenever the group was making TV appearances. He would assemble Ervin and two others and have them lip-sync each song as the Shields while on tour. Others who sang in these makeshift Shields groups included Tony Allen, Toncie Blackwell, Howard Gardner, Johny Moore, Johnny White, Tenor Chuck Jackson, Charles Patterson, James Monroe Warren, Horace Pookie Wooten, Tommy Youngblood, and, from the Cadillacs, Bobby Phillips.

Charles Wright replaced Ervin as lead. Ervin had previously been with Johnny Moore's Three Blazers and later with the Spears.

Jesse Belvin executed the high falsetto tenor in "You Cheated."

Discography

Tender 513 You Cheated/That's the Way It's Gonna Be (1958)
Dot 15805 You Cheated/That's the Way It's Gonna Be (1958)
Dot 15856 I'm Sorry Now/Nature Boy (1958)
Tender 518 I'm Sorry Now/Nature Boy (1958)
Dot 15940 Fare Thee Well My Love/Play the Game Fair (1959)
Tender 521 Fare Thee Well My Love/Play the Game Fair (1959)
Transcontinental 1013 You'll Be Coming Home Soon/Girl around the Corner (1960)
Falcon 100 You'll Be Coming Home Soon/Girl around the Corner (1960)
Sources: Dave Hinckley in *Yesterday's Memories* 10; Marv Goldberg in *DISCoveries*.

Shirelles (Passaic, N.J.)

Personnel Shirley Owens Alston (lead), Addie Mickey Harris (d), Doris Coley Kenner, Beverly Lee

Notes

The Shirelles got together in 1957 as neighbors and schoolmates singing for fun. Their teacher asked them to sing in the school's talent show. They decided not to do anyone else's material and they went to one of their homes and wrote "I Met Him On a Sunday."

Mary Jane Greenburg was a schoolmate who asked them to visit with her mom, who owned the Tiara label. They did and the rest is history. Tiara flourished and eventually changed its name to Scepter.

Following much success, Doris Kenner left the group in 1968. They then carried on as a trio.

Discography

Tiara 6112 I Met Him on a Sunday/I Want You to Be My Boyfriend (1958)
Decca 30669 I Met Him on a Sunday/I Want You to Be My Boyfriend (1958)
Decca 30761 I Got the Message/Stop Me (1958)
Scepter 1203 Dedicated to the One I Love/Look-a-Here Baby (1959)
Scepter 1205 A Teardrop and a Lollypop/Doin' the Ronde (1959)
Scepter 1207 I Saw a Tear/Please Be My Boyfriend (1960)
Scepter 1208 Tonight's the Night/The Dance Is Over (1960)
Scepter 1211 Tomorrow/Boys (1960)
Decca 25506 I Met Him on a Sunday/My Love Is a Charm (1961)
Scepter 1217 Mama Said/Blue Holiday (1961)
Scepter 1220 A Thing of the Past/What a Sweet Thing That Was (1961)
Scepter 1223 Big John/Twenty One (1961)
Scepter 1227 Baby It's You/The Things I Want to Hear (1961)
Scepter 1228 Soldier Boy/Love Is a Swingin' Thing (1962)
Scepter 1234 Welcome Home Baby/Mama, Here Comes the Bride (1962)
Scepter 1237 Stop the Music/It's Love That Really Counts (1962)
Scepter 1243 Everybody Loves a Lover/I Don't Think So (1962)
Scepter 1248 Foolish Little Girl/Not for All the Money in the World (1963)
Scepter 1255 Don't Say Goodnight and Mean Goodbye/Didn't Mean to Hurt (1963)
Scepter 1259 What Does a Girl Do/Don't Let It Happen to Us (1963)
Scepter 1260 It's a Mad, Mad, Mad World/31 Flavors (1963)
Scepter 1264 Tonight You're Gonna Fall in Love with Me/20th-Century R&R (1963)
Scepter 1267 Sha-La-La/His Lips Get in the Way (1964)
Scepter 1278 Thank You Baby/Dooms Day (1964)
Scepter 1284 Maybe Tonight/Lost Love (1964)
Scepter 1292 I Saw a Tear/Are You Still My Baby (1964)
Scepter 1296 Shh I'm Watching the Movies, Pt. 1/Pt. 2 (1965)
Scepter 12101 March/Everybody's Going Mad (1965)
Scepter 12114 Love That Man/My Heart Belongs to You (1965)
Scepter 12123 Soldier Boy/My Soldier Boy Is Coming Home (1965)
Scepter 12132 I Met Him on a Sunday '66/Love That Man (1965)
Scepter 12150 Que Sera Sera/Till My Baby Comes Home (1966)
Scepter 12162 Look Away/Shades of Blue (1966)
Scepter 12162 After Midnight/Shades of Blue (1966)
Scepter 12162 When the Boys Talk about the Girls/Shades of Blue (1966)
Scepter 12178 Teasin' Me/Look Away (1966)
Scepter 12185 Don't Go Home/Nobody Baby after You (1967)
Scepter 12192 Too Much of a Good Thing/Bright Shiny Colors (1967)
Scepter 12198 Last Minute Miracle/No Doubt about It (1967)
Scepter 12209 Wild and Sweet/Wait till I Give the Signal (1968)
Scepter 12217 Hippie Walk-1/Hippie Walk-2 (1968)
Blue Rock 4051 Don't Mess with Cupid/Sweet Sweet Lovin' (1968)
Blue Rock 4066 Call Me/There's a Storm Goin' On in My Heart (1968)
Bell 760 A Most Unusual Boy/Look What You've Done to My Heart (1969)
Bell 787 Playthings/Looking Glass (1969)
Bell 815 Go Away and Find Yourself/Never Give Up (1969)

UA 50648 There Goes My Baby/Be My Baby (1970)
UA 50693 Lost/It's Gonna Take a Miracle (1970)
UA 50740 Dedicated to the One I Love/ (1970)
RCA 48-1019 Strange Still Love You/No Sugar Tonight (1971)
RCA 74-0902 Let's Give Each Other Love/Deep in the Night (1972)
RCA AP80 0192 Touch the Wind/Do What You've a Mind To (1973)
Source: Joseph Tortelli in *Record Collector's Monthly* 39.

Showmen (Norfolk, Va.)

Personnel General Norman Johnson (lead), Gene Knight (1st tenor), Dorsey Knight (2d tenor), Leslie Felton (baritone), Milton Wells (bass)

Notes

The Showmen started out in Norfolk, Virginia, in 1956. The group members were school friends. Dorsey Knight and Norman Johnson were brothers. The Showmen played high school parties, talent shows, and other local events, originally calling themselves the Humdingers.

Noah Biggs was their manager. He arranged for them to record some demos to take to recording companies. They found one in New Orleans and needed two sessions there to make something better than "good" to come out with.

The tunes they recorded at their May 1961 session were good enough to go with. "It Will Stand" was not expected to make much noise. What a surprise when it started to take off. Ensuing releases were moderately successful. Eventually, the lack of promotional and spiritual support disturbed group members and they began to look for another label.

They recorded for Swan in Philadelphia, but the record was nothing special. In 1968, Johnson left on good terms. By the early 1970s, the balance of the group became dispirited and less organized. They disbanded altogether in the mid-1970s.

Discography

Minit 632 It Will Stand/Country Fool (1961)
Minit 643 Fate Planned It This Way/The Wrong Girl (1962)
Minit 645 The Owl Sees You/True Fine Mama (1962)
Minit 647 Com'n Home/I Love You Can't You See? (1962)
Minit 662 Swish Fish/39-21-46 (1963)
Swan 4213 In Paradise/Take It Easy (1965)
Swan 4241 Please Try to Understand/Honey House (1965)
B&F 4415 In Paradise/Take It Easy (1967)
Source: Cliff White, liner notes with the Charly R&B LP *Showmen.*

Shy-Tones (Brooklyn, N.Y.)

Personnel Graham Lee True (lead), Sal Covais (1st tenor), Albert Scavuzzo (2d tenor), William Scarpa (baritone), Fred Alvarez (bass)

518 • The Encyclopedia

Notes

Covais later sang lead with the Emotions on Kapp. The Shy-Tones became the Hi Tones on Fonsca when their friends teased them about the "shy" part of their name.

Discography

Goodspin 401 A Lover's Quarrel/Just for You (1960)
Source: Donn Fileti, liner notes with the Relic CD *Golden Era of Doo Wops—Tip Top.*

Silhouettes (Philadelphia)

Personnel Bill Horton (d) (lead), Richard Lewis (tenor), Earl Beale (baritone), Raymond Edwards (bass)

Notes

This group started as the Gospel Tornados. Horton, Beale, Edwards, and a fourth member, remembered only as Shorty, were its members. Their transition from gospel to secular music was a slow, deliberate one. On Sundays they would sing gospel; during the week they changed hats and sang secular tunes. They ultimately concluded that they could not earn a living performing religious music.

Richard Lewis had been the Turbans' road manager and when he joined the Silhouettes, he influenced them to perform only secular music. He joined in 1956, replacing Shorty.

Attempts to find a record company to record for in Philadelphia and New York were futile. Finally, in 1957, while performing at a local club, they were seen by deejay Kae Williams, who liked them and expressed an interest in managing them. He recorded the group on his Junior label and asked them to change their name. Beale came up with Silhouettes.

"Get a Job" was originally released on Junior and was given to Herald/Ember for national distribution when it began to sell. Curiously, "Get a Job" was covered by the Mills Brothers, which annoyed the Silhouettes. They felt that the successful Mills Brothers were trying to profit at the expense of a younger ensemble.

The Silhouettes did a great deal of touring throughout 1958 as well as many TV shows. On one of the tours, Edwards left and was replaced by bass Alfonso Howell from the Sensations.

It's interesting that Kae Williams's friendship with Ewart Abner of Vee Jay kept him from releasing the Silhouettes' cover of the Impressions' "For Your Precious Love" or their cover of the Spaniels' "Stormy Weather."

Their second Ember release, "Headin' for the Poorhouse," didn't do anything. This tune received no push from Dick Clark at *American Bandstand,* as "Get a Job" had. Apparently Clark and Williams had argued, and thus no *Bandstand* promotion was forthcoming.

Late in 1958, the group became distraught over its lack of success following "Get a Job." Their Ember deal had finished and "I Sold My Heart to the Junkman" was released on Junior. When it started to move, it was sold to Ace. However, it never really did anything.

Horton and Edwards left as a result of little label support. They were replaced by John Wilson and Cornelius Brown. The Silhouettes now consisted of Cornelius Brown, John Wilson, Lewis, and Beale.

The new Silhouettes moved to Philadelphia's Grand label and worked there with Jerry Ragavoy (Castelles). Ragavoy eventually got them a session with Imperial Records. It was at that time too that Otis Lewis temporarily replaced Cornelius Brown.

In 1964, Horton joined with three other singers to record as Bill Horton and the Dawns on Lawn. The Silhouettes would soon disband.

Discography

Junior 391 Get a Job/I Am Lonely (1957)
Ember 1029 Get a Job/I Am Lonely (1957)
Junior 396 I Sold My Heart to the Junkman/Evelyn (1958)
Ace 552 I Sold My Heart to the Junkman/What Would Do? (1958)
Ember 1032 Headin' for the Poorhouse/Miss Thing (1958)
Ember 1037 Bing Bong/Voodoo Eyes (1958)
Junior 400 Evelyn/Never Will Part (1959)
Ace 563 Evelyn/Never Will Part (1959)
20th Century Fox 240 Bull Frog/Never (1960)
Imperial 5899 The Push/Which Way Did She Go? (1962)
Grand 142 Wish I Could Be There/Move On Over (1962)
Junior 993 Your Love/Rent Man (1963)
Sources: Donn Fileti, liner notes with Relic's *Ember* CD; Charlie Horner and Don Leins in *Harmony Tymes* 2; Pete Grendysa in *Goldmine.*

Singing Wanderers (New York)

Personnel Alfonso Brown (lead), Ray Pollard (1st tenor), Frank Joyner (2d tenor), Robert Yarborough (baritone), Sheppard Grant (d) (bass)

Notes

This group started out in 1953 recording one song for the Newark-based Savoy Records. Ray Pollard performed lead chores on the disc. In 1954 they recorded as the Singing Wanderers for Decca Records. They recorded two discs (see below) for Decca using that name.

In 1957, they were again calling themselves the Wanderers, recording for the Onyx label and later for the MGM subsidiary Cub, which had acquired Onyx.

Along with the Harptones and the Hurricanes, the Wanderers appeared in Fritz Pollard's 1955 rhythm and blues film *Rockin' the Blues.*

Discography

Decca 29230 Say Hey, Willie Mays/Don't Drop It (1954)
Decca 29298 Three Roses/The Wrong Party Again (1954)
Sources: Steve Propes, liner notes with the Savoy LP *Doo Wop Delights—The Roots of Rock*; Donn Fileti, liner notes with the Relic LP *Best of Onyx Records.*

Six Teens (Los Angeles)

Personnel Kenneth Sinclair (lead), Trudy Williams (lead), Darrell Lewis, Beverly Pecot, Ed Wells, Louise Williams

Notes

This group originally formed in 1956 as the Sweet Teens. On their first recording they were called the Sweet Teens on Flip. Their very next record (Flip 315), referred to the group as the Six Teens.

The Williams sisters were already singing as a duo at local functions. Because all group members were still in school, making appearances or touring was difficult. Any travel had to be done on holidays and weekends. Because of their age, the courts supervised their royalties. Thus the Six Teens got their royalties, unlike the majority of groups.

Sinclair also sang with the Elgins and the Olympics.

Louise Williams and Beverly Pecot joined two others from the California Dreamers and recorded as the Ivy Leaguers.

Discography

Flip 315 A Casual Look/Teenage Promise (1956)
Flip 317 Send Me Flowers/Afar into the Night (1956)
Flip 320 Only Jim/My Special Guy (1956)
Flip 322 Arrow of Love/Was It a Dream of Mine? (1957)
Flip 326 Baby You're Dynamite/My Surprise (1957)
Flip 329 My Secret/Stop Playing Ping Pong (1957)
Flip 333 Danny/Love's Funny That Way (1958)
Flip 338 Baby-O/Oh, It's Crazy (1958)
Flip 346 Heaven Knows I Love Him/Why Do I Go to School? (1959)
Flip 350 So Happy/That Wonderful Secret of Love (1960)
Flip 351 Little Prayer/Suddenly in Love (1960)
Source: Jim Dawson, liner notes with the Official LP *Six Teens—A Casual Look.*

Skarlettones (Akron, Ohio)

Personnel James Porter, Columbus Mitchell, Ronald Mosley, Robert Carter, Willie Tucker

Notes

The Skarlettones' obscure tune (listed below) received very little airplay when it was released by Ember in 1959.

Discography

Ember 1053 Do You Remember/Will You Dream? (1959)
Source: Donn Fileti, liner notes with Relic's *Ember* CD.

Skyliners (Pittsburgh, Pa.)

Personnel Jimmy Beaumont (lead), Janet Vogel (1st tenor) Wally Lester (2d tenor), Joe Verscharen (baritone), Jack Taylor (bass)

Notes

Begun in the mid-1950s as a local quintet, the Crescents remained together for three years. In 1958, Jimmy Beaumont, Wally Lester, and Jack Taylor from the Crescents recruited high school friends Janet Vogel and Joe Verscharen, who had harmonized with another group called the El Rios.

Within a month after forming, they signed with Calico Records, a Pittsburgh label. Calico management named them the Skyliners and Joe Rock became their manager. "Since I Don't Have You" was released by Calico and reached number twelve on the charts. Their follow-up releases for Calico did not reach the sales figures of their first disc.

In 1961, the group switched to Colpix Records, where they recorded similar-sounding tunes for the new label. Joe Verscharen eventually grew tired of living out of a suitcase, Janet Vogel suffered from serious bouts of depression, and Jimmy Beaumont started a solo career. Vercharen would later return to performing with a new Skyliners group, recording for Jubilee in 1965.

In February 1980 Janet Vogel committed suicide by carbon monoxide poisoning.

Discography

Calico 103/104 Since I Don't Have You/One Night, One Night (1959)
Calico 106 This I Swear/Tomorrow (1959)
Calico 109 It Happened Today/Lonely Way (1959)
Calico 114 How Much/Lorraine from Spain (1960)
Calico 117 Pennies from Heaven/I'll Be Seeing You (1960)
Calico 120 Believe Me/Happy Time (1960)
Colpix 188 I'll Close My Eyes/The Door's Still Open (1961)
Colpix 613 Close Your Eyes/Our Love Will Last (1961)
Viscount 104 Tell Me/Come Love (1962)
Original Sound 35 Since I Don't Have You/One Night, One Night (1963)
Original Sound 36 Pennies from Heaven/I'll Be Seeing You (1963)
Original Sound 37 This I Swear/It Happened Today (1963)
Jubilee 5506 The Loser/Everything Is Fine (1965)
Jubilee 5512 Get Yourself a Baby/Who Do You Love? (1965)
Jubilee 5520 I Run to You/Don't Hurt Me Baby (1965)
Source: Bill Millar, liner notes with the Ace CD *Skyliners.*

Slades (California)

Personnel Don Burch, John Goeke, Tommy Kasper, J. Webb, B. Doyle (bass)

Discography

Liberty 55118 Baby/You Mean Everything to Me (1958)

Domino 500 You Cheated/The Waddle (1958)
Domino 800 You Gambler/No Time (1959)
Domino 901 Just You/It's Better to Love (1959)
Domino 1000 You Must Try/Summertime (1959)
Domino 906 It's Your Turn/Take My Heart (1961)
Source: Bob Ferlingere, *A Discography of R&B and R&R Vocal Groups.*

Smoothtones (Pittsburgh, Pa.)

Personnel Alfred Gaitwood (lead), Jud Hunter (1st tenor), Joe Martin (d) (2d tenor), Walter Lowry (baritone), Kenny McMillian (d) (bass)

Notes

The Smoothtones surfaced in 1953 in Pittsburgh. The lead, Alfred Gaitwood, was from Alabama and found himself in Pittsburgh with a U.S. Air Force unit. Gaitwood rounded up Enoche Hale (1st tenor), Joe Martin (2d tenor), Walter Lowry (baritone), and Kenny McMillian (bass). Gaitwood named the group the Smoothtones. Paul Ruffin was their manager. Hale was drafted in 1954 and was replaced by Jud Hunter at 1st tenor.

Through networking, Gaitwood met Lennie Martin, who ran the operations at Jem Records. (Martin would later be instrumental in forming Calico Records [Skyliners] and Robbie Records.)

The Smoothtones recorded two sides for Jem in June 1955. Interestingly, these were the first black vocal group releases out of Pittsburgh.

Early in 1956, Gaitwood was transferred to another air force base. Jud Hunter then brought Sylvester Brooks into the group at lead. This altered group went back to Jem to record two more sides. Supposedly, they recorded the Gaitwood-penned "It's Too Late Now." A pressing of this disc has never been seen. Jud Hunter, in an interview by Carl and Nancy Janusek, swore that this was released and that he saw the recording on wax. (This cannot be confirmed—perhaps it was never released.) It was later done by the Cufflinks on Dootone. Gaitwood was with the group at that time.

With Gaitwood gone, the cohesiveness that once held the group together disappeared, and they disbanded in September 1956.

Discography

Jem 412 Bring Back Your Love to Me (AG)/No Doubt about It (AG) (1955)
Sources: Travis Klein, liner notes with the Itzy II CD *Pittsburgh's Greatest Hits*; Carl Janusek and Nancy Janusek in *Echoes of the Past.*

Solitaires (New York)

Personnel Herman Dunham (lead), Bobby "Schubie" Williams (d) (1st tenor), Bobby Baylor (d) (2d tenor), Monte Owens (tenor), Winston "Buzzy" Willis (baritone), Pat Gaston (bass)

Notes

The Solitaires formed on 142d street and 7th Avenue in the Harlem section of Manhattan. At their formation, the lineup included Eddie "California" Jones (Demens), Nick Anderson, Rudy Morgan, Winston Willis, and Pat Gaston. Normal personnel changes eventually led to the first recording Solitaires, and this is the group reflected above. There was impressive heritage behind this lineup. Herman Dunham (a.k.a. Herman Curtis) came from the Vocaleers on Red Robin; Baylor, Owens, and Williams came from the Red Robin Mello-Moods; Gaston had performed with the Four Bells on Gem; Willis performed (but did not record) with his friends the Crows, who went on to record for Rama.

At this time Bobby Baylor was forming his own group, the Hi Lites, who went on to record for Okeh. The Solitaires and Baylor entered into the following agreement/wager: Whichever group wins the first recording contract, I will permanently join. We know which group he joined.

Deejay Hal Jackson obtained an opportunity for his employee, Willis, to meet with Hy Weiss of Old Town Records. Weiss liked them and their style and signed them up. Willis got Herman Dunham to sing lead for the group. He was with the Vocaleers and briefly recorded with them and the Solitaires simultaneously. The Solitaires began their illustrious recording career in 1954.

In 1955, Dunham joined the air force and Milton Love, who had his own group, the Concords, was asked to take Dunham's place. Love's first recording was "The Wedding." When Dunham was discharged from the air force, he rejoined the Solitaires on 1034, 1044, and 1049 but did not stay, rejoining the Vocaleers.

In 1956, Fred Barksdale of the Crickets joined as bass when Gaston left for the service. Barksdale had also been with the New Yorkers Five on Danice. He is first heard on the classic "Nothing Like a Little Love." On "Walkin' and Talkin'" and "No More Sorrows," Wally Roker, bass of the Heartbeats, filled in for Barksdale. Bobby Williams left after "The Angels Sang." He died several years later in 1961.

When Willis and Baylor went into the army in 1960, Cecil Holmes and Reggie Barnes replaced them. Both came from the FiTones. When Love went into the service in 1961, the group became somewhat inactive. Many incarnations of the Solitaires surfaced during the ensuing years, but none equaled those of the 1950s.

In 1984, the Murray Hill Company in New York released a boxed set of Solitaires tunes. This set contained the following previously unreleased songs: "Come Back and Give Me Your Hand," "Chapel of St. Claire," "Stranger in Paradise," "Come Back to Me," "How Long," "If I Loved You."

"Come Back and Give Me Your Hand" was not performed by the Solitaires. It was written by Bobby Mansfield of the Wrens and was performed in the aforementioned boxed set by the Old Town Supremes with Waldo Champen at lead.

In the 1990s, a collector located a tune penned by Milton Love, "Silent Grief," a mid-1950s Solitaires' undertaking that was never released. When it was found in the 1990s, it was issued with a beautiful copy of the Old Town label. Interestingly, it is an absolutely typical mid-1950s Solitaires tune sung by Milton Love.

Other members included Roland Martinez, Reggie Barnes, Cecil Holmes, Nick Anderson, Cathy Miller, Rudy Morgan, and Harriet Williams.

Discography

Old Town 1000 Wonder Why/Blue Valentine (1954)
Old Town 1006/1007 Please Remember My Heart/South of the Border (1954)
Old Town 1008 Chances I've Taken/Lonely (1954)
Old Town 1010 I Don't Stand a Ghost of a Chance/Girl of Mine (1955)
Old Town 1012 What Did She Say?/My Dear (1955)
Old Town 1014 The Wedding/Don't Fall in Love (1955)
Old Town 1015 Magic Rose/Later for You Baby (1955)
Old Town 1019 The Honeymoon/Fine Little Girl (1956)
Old Town 1026 You've Sinned/You're Back with Me (Angels Sang) (1956)
Old Town 1032 Give Me One More Chance/Nothing Like a Little Love (1956)
Old Town 1034 Walking Along/Please Kiss This Letter (1957)
Old Town 1044 I Really Love You So/Thrill of Love (1957)
Argo 5316 Walking Along/Please Kiss This Letter (1958)
Old Town 1049 Walkin' and Talkin'/No More Sorrows (1958)
Old Town 1059 Big Mary's House/Please Remember My Heart (1959)
Old Town 1066 Embraceable You/Round Goes My Heart (1959)
Old Town 1071 Helpless/Light a Candle in the Chapel (1959)
Old Town 1096 Lonesome Lover/Pretty Thing (1961)
Old Town 1139 Honey Babe/The Time Is Here (1963)
MGM 13221 Fool That I Am/Fair Weather Lover (1964)
Sources: Donn Fileti and Bob Hyde, liner notes with the Ace CD *Solitaires*; Murray Hill, liner notes with the boxed LP set *Solitaires*.

Songmasters (Philadelphia)

Personnel Joe Van Loan (lead), Mary Hayes (1st tenor), ——— Fox (2d tenor), James La Boe (baritone), Stanford Fassett (bass)

Notes

Songs by this group appear on Songmaster LP 800 *Joe Van Loan,* produced by Jim Hunt and Jack Sbarbori. There were no single releases from the LP, and Joe Van Loan owned the recordings exclusively. The recordings on the LP are shown in the discography.

Discography

Songmaster LP 800 What Do Your Tears Really Mean
Songmaster LP 800 Lady Be Good
Songmaster LP 800 There's Nothing Any Better Than You
Songmaster LP 800 Trust in Me
Source: Jim Hunt and Jack Sbarbori, liner notes with the Songmaster LP.

Sonics (New York)

Personnel Ray Smith (lead), Johnny Brown (1st tenor), Ken Hamilton (tenor), Bobby Peterson (baritone), Leo Lawson (bass)

Notes

Kenneth "Butch" Hamilton sang 2d tenor for the Bop Chords. Tommy Grate also spent time with the Sonics and later sang for the Dubs and the Vocaltones. Billy Carlisle (d.) also sang with this group.

Discography

Groove 0112 Bumble Bee/As I Live On (1955)
Sources: Todd Baptista; *Echoes of the Past* 20; Baptista, *Group Harmony behind the Rhythm and the Blues.*

Sonics (New York)

Personnel William Franklin (lead), Larry Davis (baritone)

Notes

Originally released on the Harvard label in 1959, "This Broken Heart" did well enough to inspire Chicago's Chess Records to acquire the master and give it quality national distribution.

Apparently Chess could release it on one of its labels while the East Coast distribution would remain with New York City's Harvard label.

Discography

Harvard 801 This Broken Heart/You Made Me Cry (1959)
Harvard 922 This Broken Heart/You Made Me Cry (1959)
Checker 922 This Broken Heart/You Made Me Cry (1959)
Source: Pete Grendysa, liner notes with the Chess CD boxed set *Chess Rhythm & Roll.*

Soothers (New York)

Personnel Hank Jernigan (lead), Claude "Nicky" Clarke (1st tenor), William Dempsey (2d tenor), Curtis Cherebin (baritone), Fred Taylor (bass)

Notes

Port Records was run by Jerry Blaine's son. Blaine ran the Jubilee/Josie organization.

This combination of singers was an offshoot of the Harptones sans Willie Winfield.

Discography

Port 70041 I Believe in You/Little White Cloud That Cried (1965)
Source: Bob Ferlingere, *A Discography of R&B and R&R Vocal Groups.*

Sophomores (Roxbury, Mass.)

Personnel Johnny Mack (lead), Eddie Brooks (tenor), Al Chambers (tenor), Donald Clements (baritone)

Notes

This group started in 1954 in the Roxbury section of Boston, initially calling them-selves the Five Stars of Love. They practiced endlessly and appeared at many local nightspots. At one of these nightspots, the Show Bar, Al Chambers walked off the stage during an appearance swearing that he would leave show business. He was replaced by Roland Clements, Donald's brother, who formerly had been with the Dappers on Peacock.

In 1955, the group named itself the Sophomores and soon caught the interest of Jack Darwin of Dawn Records. Darwin set up a recording date in New York City. Following the recording, they continued with their appearances at local clubs. They recorded more singles and cut an album.

Late in 1957, they left the Dawn/Seeco organization. Roland Clements went into the service and was replaced by Johnny Mack. The new foursome recorded one song for Chord Records in New York.

They recorded nothing else after Chord. They continued to appear locally at clubs and nightspots, despite the discouragement brought about by their unsuccessful at-tempt for a hit record. They stayed together until the late 1960s and then disbanded.

Discography

Dawn 216 Cool, Cool Baby/Every Night about This Time (1956)
Dawn 218 I Get a Thrill/Linda (1956)
Dawn 223 Ocean Blue/I Left My Sugar (1956)
Dawn 225 Is There Somebody for Me?/Everybody Loves Me (1957)
Dawn 228 Just Can't Keep Tears from Tumblin' Down/If I Should Lose You (1957)
Dawn 237 Checkers/Each Time I Hold You (1957)
Chord 1302 Charades/What Can I Do? (1957)
Epic 9259 Charades/What Can I Do? (1957)
Sources: Paulette Girard, liner notes with the Seeco LP *Sophomores;* Marv Goldberg in *Whiskey, Women, and . . . 9.*

Sophomores, Anthony & (Philadelphia)

Personnel Anthony "Tony" Maresco (lead), Ernie Finaro/Fenaro (1st tenor), Anthony (John) Donato (2d tenor), Anthony Perry/Perri (baritone)

Notes

This group was also related to Tony and the Twilighters (Twiliters) and, man for man, to Tony and the Dynamics. They initially formed in 1958.

Bob Finizio of the Four Js brought the Sophomores to Jamie. Finizio and the group members were from the same neighborhood.

Bob Beato joined with the group in 1966. *(Note:* The liner notes accompanying the Jamie/Guyden CD *Doop Doo Wah* state that Beato joined in 1963.)

Discography

Grand 163 Embraceable You/Beautiful Dreamer (1963)
Mercury 72103 Play Those Oldies Mr. DJ/Clap Your Hands (1963)
Mercury 72168 Better Late Than Never/Swingin at the Chariot (1963)

ABC 10737 Gee/It Depends on You (1965)
ABC 10770 Get Back to You/Wild for Her (1966)
ABC 10844 Heartbreak/I'll Go thru Life Loving You (1966)
Jamie 1330 Serenade/Workout (1966)
Jamie 1340 One Summer Night/Work Out (1967)
Source: Bob Bosco, liner notes with the Jamie/Guyden CD *Do Doo Wah.*

Souvenirs (Los Angeles)

Personnel Abraham Watkins (lead), Otis Rabun (1st tenor), Alvin Johnson (2d tenor), Edwin Johnson (baritone), Arthur Rabun (bass)

Notes

In 1954, when Alvin Johnson returned home from the service, he got friendly with the Rabun brothers living next door. The brothers wanted to be entertainers, as did Johnson. Johnson got his brother and a friend, Watkins, and formed a vocal group.

They practiced incessantly and then visited all the record companies in Los Angeles.

When they got to Dootone Records, Dootsie Williams liked what he heard and had them record many tunes, three of which were eventually released.

One single was released from this first production, "Double-Dealing Baby" (Dooto 412), which did poorly.

Dean Heath, a tenor, joined after the session, replacing Watkins who quit after making the recordings.

Several tunes were recorded for Lee Rupe's Ebb label, but they were never released. The other song they did for Dootone was later released on an LP.

Discography

Dooto 412 So Long Daddy (AJ)/Alene Sweet Little Texas Queen (OR) (1957)
Source: Marv Goldberg in *Yesterday's Memories.*

Spaniels (Gary, Ind.)

Personnel James "Pookie" Hudson (lead), Ernest Warren (1st tenor), Willie Jackson (baritone), Opal Courtney Jr. (baritone), Gerald Gregory (d) (bass)

Notes

The Spaniels met while they were juniors in high school in 1952. They sang at churches, talent shows, and other local Gary, Indiana, events. Their main reason for coming together was to participate in a school talent show around Christmas.

Vivian Carter and Jimmy Bracken had a Chicago record shop, at which the Spaniels demonstrated their vocal talents. Other artists did this as well. Carter and Bracken soon realized they could start a record label with these aspiring artists and eventually Vee Jay was formed.

The Spaniels' first session took place in May 1953. The disc did well enough that it had to be leased to Chance Records of Chicago for better national distribution.

"Baby It's You" did well and created bookings for live appearances. "Goodnight Sweetheart, Goodnight" was released in early 1954. It became a national hit and was covered by the McGuire Sisters.

By August 1954, the Spaniels were doing a great deal of touring with rhythm and blues shows. This touring continued into 1955 with several other big package events.

Around 1955, Opal Courtney left to complete high school. His departure coincided with poor public reaction to several of their 1955 recordings. He was replaced by James Cochran. Ernest Warren was soon drafted into the military and was not replaced in time for their next recording session. Consequently, "Dear Heart" and "False Love" contain only four voices.

Early in 1956, the Spaniels were part of a Vee Jay traveling show, Cavalcade of Vee Jay Stars. Following the tour, Hudson and Jackson left and Gregory and James Cochran added Don Porter and Carl Rainge to replace them.

The very next release, "Since I Fell for You," was an old recording that was still in the can and was used because of Hudson's departure. Later in 1956, Hudson rejoined and the group was now Hudson, Gregory, Cochran, Porter, and Rainge. "You Gave Me Peace of Mind" was this new group's initial release. The group lost nothing as their inimitable sound was still heard on this tune.

In 1959, the Spaniels decided to pack it in due to poor sales. In 1960, however, Hudson and Gregory decided to try it one more time with Andy Magruder (Five Blue Notes), Bill Carey, and Ernie Warren from the original group joining Hudson and Gregory.

Ricky Burden was the group's road manager who filled in for the missing Gregory on their one Neptune recording.

Many label and personnel changes followed, but the group was still thrilling audiences in the late 1990s and were as good as ever!

Fats Waller was Pookie's cousin.

Discography

Vee Jay 101 Baby It's You/Bounce (1953)
Chance 1141 Baby It's You/Bounce (1953)
Vee Jay 103 The Bells Ring Out/House Cleaning (1953)
Vee Jay 107 Goodnight Sweetheart, Goodnight/You Don't Move Me (1953)
Vee Jay 116 Let's Make Up/Play It Cool (1954)
Vee Jay 131 Don'cha Go/Do Wah (1955)
Vee Jay 154 You Painted Pictures/Hey Sister Lizzie (1955)
Vee Jay 178 False Love/Do You Really? (1956)
Vee Jay 189 Dear Heart/Why Won't You Dance? (1956)
Vee Jay 202 Since I Fell for You/Baby Come Along with Me (1956)
Vee Jay 229 You Gave Me Peace of Mind/Please Don't Tease (1956)
Vee Jay 246 I.O.U./Everyone's Laughing (1957)
Vee Jay 257 You're Gonna Cry/I Need Your Kisses (1957)
Vee Jay 264 I Lost You/Crazee Babee (1958)
Vee Jay 278 Tina/Great Googley Moo (1958)
Vee Jay 290 Stormy Weather/Here Is Why I Love You (1958)
Vee Jay 301 Baby It's You/Heart and Soul (1958)
Vee Jay 310 Trees/I Like It Like That (1959)
Vee Jay 328 These Three Words/100 Years from Today (1959)

Vee Jay 342 People Will Say We're in Love/The Bells Ring Out (1959)
Vee Jay 350 I Know/Bus Fare Home (1960)
Neptune 124 For Sentimental Reasons/Meek Man (1961)
Parkway 839 John Brown/Turn Out the Lights (1962)
Sources: Alan Lee and Donna Hennings in *Yesterday's Memories* 6; Ronnie Italiano in *Harmony Tymes*; Bob Pruter in *Goldmine*, February 21, 1992.

Sparks of Rhythm (New York)

Personnel Jimmy Jones (lead), Floyd Edmonds (baritone), Andrew Barksdale (bass)

Notes

A vocal group called the Berliners was formed by U.S. servicemen stationed in Germany. Upon being discharged in 1955, they arrived in New York. Jimmy Jones ran into one of them, Andrew Barksdale, who was an old friend from their childhood days in Alabama. Barksdale was the Berliners' bass and asked Jones to join the group as their lead singer.

The group got a contract to record for Apollo Records. Before recording, their name was changed to Sparks of Rhythm. They had one session during which four songs were recorded. Because nothing happened with the recordings, Jones left the Sparks of Rhythm two and a half months after the session.

Jones left to form his own group—the Savoys. His other reason for leaving was the difference in musical tastes that had surfaced between him and the group.

Discography

Apollo 479 Don't Love You Anymore/Women, Women, Women (1955)
Apollo 481 Hurry Home/Stars Are in the Sky (1955)
Apollo 541 Everybody Rock and Go/Handy Man (1960)
Source: Donn Fileti, liner notes with the Relic CD *Best of Apollo–3.*

Sparrows (New York)

Personnel Perry Hayward (lead), David Martin (2d tenor), Henry "Claude" Brown (baritone), Joseph "Rocky" Washington (bass)

Notes

The Sparrows came into being in 1952 when Hayward was in high school and met the other group members singing outside the building.

They sang on street corners, practiced in subways, and began writing their own material. A female neighbor of Hayward's invited them to parties. At one of these parties, early in 1953, they met several members of the Checkers. It was also learned that Checkers' bass, Bill Brown, was a cousin of the girl Hayward was about to marry.

Several months later, Hayward was told that the Checkers wished to see him because their lead, John Carnegie, was being drafted and they wanted Perry to try out for the part. There were many singers at the audition and once Hayward tried out, the others were sent home. Hayward performed lead chores on King 4626, Ghost of My Baby/I Wanna Know. They made one live appearance while he was with them. Because the Checkers were doing nothing and Hayward was getting married, he left to work more with the Sparrows. "Little" David Baughan replaced him in the Checkers.

Meanwhile, one of the Sparrows got Joe Davis interested in recording them on Jay Dee, and their first session took place in September 1953. They had many other sessions but made no appearances. Their records were either tenor or bass led, but none of them did well.

Other singers who sang with the Sparrows, on and off, were Floyd Adams (later of the Keynotes) and "JD," the mysterious individual who led the Five Crowns on Gee. Leo Fuller was another singer who was in and out of the Sparrows.

In 1954, David Martin became the second member of the Sparrows to fill in for the Checkers. At that time the Checkers' lead was Eddie Harris and the baritone was James Williams. This group executed the last Checkers' session for King on October 1, 1954.

In mid-1955, "Rocky" Washington replaced James "Archie" Archer of the Wrens. He can be heard on the Wrens' recording of What Makes You Do the Things You Do?/I Won't Come to Your Wedding from November 1955.

When Elvis Presley's *Love Me Tender* film and recording were in the public eye in 1956, someone at the Davis organization remembered that the Sparrows had recorded a tune with the same title several years before. In order to capitalize on the Presley phenomenon, Davis released "Love Me Tender" by the Sparrows in 1956, after the Sparrows had dissolved.

Later in 1956, Washington and Heyward formed the Performers (Tip Top).

Discography
Jay Dee 783 Tell My Baby/Why Did You Leave Me? (1953)
Jay Dee 790 Hey!/I'll Be Lovin' You (1953)
Davis 456 Love Me Tender/Come Back to Me (1956)
Source: Marv Goldberg in *DISCoveries.*

Sparrows Quartet (Queens, N.Y.)

Personnel Bob Freedman (lead), Dominic D'Elia (tenor), Billy D'Elia (1st tenor), James Brady (baritone), Sam Wood (d) (bass)

Notes

This group formed to recapture the sound of a 1950s black vocal group. Curiously, the members were white Catholics and Jews. The thinking behind the group was the dream of Dominic "Dom" D'Elia, a well-known R&B vocal group records collector from the Jackson Heights section of Queens in New York.

D'Elia's eleven-year-old brother Billy joined the group at 1st tenor. Freedman joined as lead tenor, coming from the Squires on Gee.

The Sparrows Quartet recorded their first single at the D'Elia home in 1962.

"Merry Christmas Baby" was released on D'Elia's Broadcast label in 1963. In 1965, Sal Mondrone, another well-known record collector, replaced Brady.

That same year Dom formed the Jet Records label and produced, recorded, and released the first three Jet singles. Mondrone sang lead on the Jet sides and Dominick primarily sang lead on the Broadcast tunes.

The Sparrows Quartet disbanded in 1969 and resumed in 1971, when they recorded the first of three Sparrows Quartet LPs, all entitled *Sparrows Quartet—Rehearsal Session.* The first of these albums was released in 1974.

That same year, they moonlighted as Mel Dark and the Giants on Sal Passantino's Blue Sky label.

George Lavatelli, from the Bon Aires, joined the Sparrows Quartet on occasion.

Following Bob Freedman's relocation to Chicago in 1974, the group ended their association.

In 1975, the two other *Rehearsal Session* LPs were released.

In 1983, while Freedman was in New York briefly, the Sparrows Quartet appeared at a United in Group Harmony Association concert in New Jersey. This was the last appearance of the group.

Discography

Broadcast 985 Merry Christmas Baby (1963)
Broadcast 986 Sammy's Blues (1963)
Jet 3000 Deep in My Heart/Love Me Baby (1965)
Deltone 3001 I Love You So Much I Could Die/Please Come Back to Me (1973)
Blue Sky 108 Darling (1974)
Jet 3020 The Christmas Song/He Is My Friend (1975)
Jet 3021 We Sing for Fun/The Christmas Song (1974)
Source: Sal Mondrone, interview by author, 1995.

Spiders (New Orleans)

Personnel Leonard "Chick" Carbo (lead), Joe Maxon (1st tenor), Hayward "Chuck" Carbo (2d tenor), Mathew West (baritone), Oliver Howard (bass)

Notes

The Carbo brothers sang with the gospel groups the Zion Harmonizers and the Delta Southernaires prior to forming the Spiders in the mid-1940s.

They auditioned for Imperial thinking it was a gospel recording session, but studio personnel asked them to do rhythm and blues. They complied, and they were signed to Imperial Records!

Their first Imperial disc, You're the One/I Didn't Want to Do It, was released in December 1953 and the group renamed itself the Spiders.

They recorded as the Delta Southernaires and the Spiders for a while and kept it quiet. When their fans discovered this, the group decided to just record as the Spiders for financial reasons.

Pianist Henry Wickes occasionally sang with the group.

After several successful recordings, internal conflicts began to surface. They split up late in 1956.

Discography

Imperial 5265 I Didn't Want to Do It (HC)/You're the One (HC) (1953)
Imperial 5280 I'll Stop Crying (HC)/Tears Began to Flow (HC) (1954)
Imperial 5291 I'm Slippin' In (HC)/I'm Searchin' (HC) (1954)
Imperial 5305 The Real Thing (LC)/Mmm Mmm Baby (LC) (1954)
Imperial 5318 She Keeps Me Wondering (LC)/21 (LC) (1954)
Imperial 5331 That's Enough (LC)/Lost and Bewildered (HC) (1955)
Imperial 5344 Sukey, Sukey, Sukey (LC)/Am I the One (LC) (1955)
Imperial 5354 Bells in My Heart (LC)/For a Thrill (HC) (1955)
Imperial 5366 Witchcraft (HC)/Is It True (HC) (1955)
Imperial 5376 Don't Pity Me (HC)/How Can I Feel (HC) (1956)
Imperial 5393 A-1 In My Heart (HC)/Dear Mary (HC) (1956)
Imperial 5405 Goodbye (HC)/That's the Way to Win My Heart (HC) (1956)
Imperial 5423 Honey Bee (HC)/That's My Desire (HC) (1957)
Imperial 5714 Tennessee Slim (LC)/You're the One (LC) (rerecorded) (1960)
Imperial 5739 Witchcraft (HC)/You Don't Love Me (HC) (1961)
Source: Marv Goldberg in *Yesterday's Memories* 11.

Spinners (Detroit)

Personnel Bobbie Smith (tenor), George Dixon (tenor), Billy Henderson (tenor), Henry Fambrough (baritone), Pervis Jackson (bass)

Notes

This group was formed in Detroit in the late 1950s. The members shown above attended Ferndale High School in Detroit at one time or another. They originally called themselves the Domingoes and were discovered by Moonglows great Harvey Fuqua.

Fuqua trained them and structured them to be the stylish group of their time. He worked feverishly to ensure that the Spinners' sound approached the excellence of his Moonglows. He had them record a tune that he and Berry Gordy's sister wrote, "That's What Girls Are Made For" (1961), for his Tri Phi label.

Curiously, in *American Singing Groups,* Jay Warner states that Harvey sings lead on the Spinners' first two releases on Tri-Phi. In *A Touch of Classic Soul,* Marc Taylor states that because Bobbie Smith was trained by Fuqua to emulate the Moonglows' sound and style, Fuqua was often mistaken as the lead. This was repeated on their second tune on Tri-Phi, "Love (I'm So Glad I Found You)," released in November 1961. Following this tune, Bobbie Smith officially took over lead chores on the last four Tri-Phi 45s.

George Dixon was the first to leave, and he was replaced by Edgar Edwards. Fuqua's Tri-Phi records soon joined forces with brother-in-law Berry Gordy's Motown records, and he brought the Spinners with him to Motown. This occurred around 1962. However, the Spinners did not record for Motown until 1964, when they began a string of five discs for Gordy's Motown label.

In 1966, Edwards left and was replaced by G. C. Cameron, who promptly took over at lead. In 1969, the group was moved to Motown's V.I.P. records. Their first effort for their new label was "In My Diary," a tribute to Moonglows' great Bobby Lester.

With their third release on V.I.P., Stevie Wonder assumed producer responsibilities but things were not what they once had been. No longer were the Spinners the super attraction for Motown and they began to look elsewhere.

Longtime friend Aretha Franklin influenced them to join up with Atlantic. G. C. Cameron chose to stay with Motown, and Phillipe Wynne assumed his post at lead. A string of hits came out of their initial association with Atlantic. Also, they backed up Dionne Warwick's "Then Came You."

Wynne left in 1977 and John Edwards assumed his role.

Discography

Tri-Phi 1001 That's What Girls Are Made For/Heebie Jeebies (1961)
Tri-Phi 1004 Love/Sudbuster (1961)
Tri-Phi 1007 What Did She Use?/Itching for My Baby, but I Don't Know (1961)
Tri-Phi 1010 She Loves Me So/Whistling about You (1962)
Tri-Phi 1013 I've Been Hurt/I've Got Your Water Boiling Baby (1962)
Motown 1067 Sweet Thing/How Can I (1964)
Motown 1078 I'll Always Love You/Tomorrow May Never Come (1965)
Motown 1093 Truly Yours/Where Is That Girl? (1966)
Motown 1109 For All We Know/I Cross My Heart (1967)
Motown 1136 Bad Bad Weather/I Just Can't Help but Feel the Pain (1968)
V.I.P. 25050 At Sundown/In My Diary (1969)
V.I.P. 25054 At Sundown/Message from a Black Man (1970)
V.I.P. 25057 It's a Shame/Together We Can Make Such Sweet Music (1970)
V.I.P. 25060 We'll Have It Made/My Whole World Ended (1970)
Sources: Ferdie Gonzalez, *Disco-File*; Jay Warner, *American Singing Groups*; Marc Taylor, *A Touch of Classic Soul.*

Spinners (Pittsburgh, Calif.)

Personnel Lawrence Brice, Robert Thomas, Gilbert Joseph, Maurke Allen

Notes

This Spinners group is not related to the Spinners from Detroit.

Discography

Rhythm 125 My Love and Your Love/Marvella (1958)
Source: Dennis Leonis, liner notes with the Rhythm CD *Remembering Rhythm Records.*

Spirits of Rhythm (St. Louis, Mo.)

Personnel Wilbur Daniels, Douglas Daniels, Teddy Bunn (d), Leo Watson (d), Wellman Browd

Notes

The Spirits of Rhythm formed in 1929 and based their novelty tunes around the unique scat singing of Lee Watson.

The Spirits of Rhythm disbanded and re-formed several times. In 1943, Bunn and Watson were on the West Coast and structured another Spirits of Rhythm.

In the Country Routes CD *Man That's Groovy,* Pete Grendysa shows a different personnel lineup: Watson, Bunn, Leonard Feather, Red Calender, and George Vann. Virgil Scroggins was another member. (It's probable that since the group personnel was so dynamic, the names of group members were always changing.)

Discography

Decca 160 Junk Mam/Dr. Watson and Mr. Holmes (1934)
Decca 186 From Monday On/Way Down Yonder in New Orleans (1934)
Decca 243 It's All Forgotten Now/What's the Use of Getting Used to You Now (1934)
Decca 302 As Long as I Live/I've Got the World on a String (1934)
Decca (UNR) That's What I Like about You
Decca (UNR) Shoutin' in That Amen Corner
Columbia (UNR) I Woke Up With a Teardrop in My Eye
Columbia (UNR) From Monday On
Columbia (UNR) Exactly Like You
Sources: Max Jones, liner notes with the *Spirits of Rhythm* CD on JSP; Pete Grendysa, liner notes with the Country Routes CD *Man That's Groovy.*

Splendors (Clairton, Pa.)

Personnel Lloyd Roberts (lead), Allen Jarrett (1st tenor), Arnold Everson (tenor), Cartrel Metz (baritone), James Hall (bass)

Notes

The Splendors surfaced in Pennsylvania in 1956. Their school friends advised them and assisted them with their rehearsals and practices. By 1959, they were a self-contained unit, both vocalizing and playing instruments.

The Splendors' manager, Ken Julian, began his own label, Taurus, in 1960.

Lead singer Lloyd Roberts left the group in 1961 and was replaced by Vince Henderson. Everson soon began studies at California State College in Pennsylvania. He left soon after this. Numerous personnel changes followed.

Willie Anderson replaced Cartrel Metz on his departure.

Ethel Barber became the group's first female lead. When she departed in 1963, they found Shirley Holmes to perform at lead.

Discography

Taurus 101 The Golden Years/The Echo Tells Me (1960)
Taurus 102 Deputy Dog/Who Can It Be? (1961)
Source: Carl Janusek in *Echoes of the Past* 26.

Squires (Pasadena, Calif.)

Personnel Lee Goudeau Jr. (lead), Chester Pipkin (tenor), Dewey Terry (falsetto), Bobby Armstrong (baritone), Leon Washington (bass)

Notes

The Squires got together in 1954 while the members were students in a Pasadena high school. *(Note:* The Combo and the Flair Squires were different groups even though both came from the West Coast.)

Their first disc for Kicks was their and the label's first release. It did not do well and the Squires went to Mambo/Vita Records.

Their "Sindy" did well enough to inspire other groups to cover it (Tenderfoots, Cobras).

The first of four Squires' records on Vita was "Me and My Deal." Because of the record's inferior quality, it did not do well.

The group added Don Bowman at 2d tenor and piano. Later, he and Dewey Terry left to form Don and Dewey.

The group recorded several EPs for the Dig This Record budget LPs. Like the Jacks/Cadets for Modern Records, the Squires were Dig's house group. The Squires and several other Los Angeles groups recorded as Dig's Bluejays.

After Don and Dewey left, they found some replacements and recorded "Dreamy Eyes" and "Dangling with My Heart" for Aladdin.

Discography

Kicks 1 Lucy Lou/A Dream Come True (1954)
Mambo 105 Sindy/Do-Be-Do-Be-Wop-Wop (1955)
Vita 105 Sindy/Do-Be-Do-Be-Wop-Wop (1955)
Vita 113 Me and My Deal/Sweet Girl (1955)
Vita 116 Heavenly Angel/Sweet Girl (1956)
Vita 117 Guiding Angel/You Ought to Be Ashamed (1956)
Vita 128 Venus/Breath of Air (1956)
Aladdin 3360 Dreamy Eyes/Dangling with My Heart (1957)
Source: Dave Hinckley and Marv Goldberg in *Yesterday's Memories.*

Squires (Los Angeles)

Personnel Delmar Wilburn (lead), Otis White (1st tenor), Jimmy Richardson (2d tenor), James Myles (baritone), Maudice Giles (bass)

Notes

Despite the fact that they were from southern California, this Squires group had nothing to do with the Kicks, Mambo, or Vita group from the same locale. They would sing in Greenmeadow Park in Watts. Group members were sixteen and seventeen years old when they recorded.

James Derbigny replaced James Myles. Otis Gerard and Billy Storm sang with the Squires at times.

Wilburn joined the Hodge brothers, Alex and Gaynel, to sing with the Turks. Giles became 1st tenor for the Hollywood Saxons and the Portraits.

Discography

Combo 35 Let's Give Love a Try/Whop (1954)
Combo 42 Oh Darling/My Little Girl (1954)
Source: Donn Fileti, liner notes with the Relic LP *Best of Combo.*

Starlarks (New Haven, Conn.)

Personnel Wes Forbes (lead), Gordon Henry (1st tenor), Richie Freeman (2d tenor), Fred Harris (baritone), Joe Bash (bass)

Notes

The Starlarks were classmates at New Haven's Millhouse High School. Fred Harris played on the school's basketball team and met the broadcaster from the station that broadcast their games. He took the group to the station after hours and had them record their tunes. He then took the recordings to New York in order to have some music executives hear them.

Al Silver of Herald/Ember Records heard about the songs and bought the masters to release on his Ember Records. It was released in the fall of 1956. The record did nothing and the group returned to New Haven and continued with their nightclub appearances.

In the summer of 1956, Gordon Henry left the Starlarks and was replaced by Josh Hill. Their manager then formed a new label, Anchor, and the group was asked to record again. This follow-up was moderately successful in New Haven but did poorly elsewhere. This second failure caused the group to split up. Forbes and Harris joined the Five Satins when that group was with Cub Records.

Forbes, Harris, and Lou Peebles cut two records as the New Yorkers on the Wall label.

Freeman was part of the Five Satins, Wildwoods, Restless Hearts, and the New Yorkers Five.

Discography

Elm 001 Fountain of Love/Send Me a Picture Baby (1956)
Ember 1013 Fountain of Love/Send Me a Picture Baby (1957)
Ancho 102 Heavenly Father/My Dear (1957)
Source: Donn Fileti, liner notes with the Relic LP *Best of Ember Records*; Ron Baldino in *Rhythm & News.*

Starlets (Chicago)

Personnel Jane Hall, Maxine Edwards, Mickey McKinney, Jeanette Miles, Liz Walker

Notes

The Starlets began in 1961 when Jane Hall, two years out of high school, started assembling a vocal group.

After weeks of practice, Hall took the girls to Bernice Williams, a local singer/songwriter. Williams felt that the Starlets needed another voice and recommended Liz Walker. Williams was also connected with the management at Pam Records. It was with Pam that they recorded "Better Tell Him No," which did quite well.

With a hit on their hands, the Starlets toured the entire East Coast. Pam then released the Starlets' second disc, one side of which was led by Bernice Williams and the other side by McKinney.

Because they were making no money with Bernice Williams, they accepted an offer by an automobile executive to record for his label, not realizing they had thereby breached their contract with Pam. Fortunately, the record was released as by the Blue Belles. Despite this, litigation proceeded messily. After all, the Blue Belles were the Starlets. This blunder caused them to be dropped by Pam management.

They later recorded as Danetta and the Starlets on Okeh with You Belong to Me/ Impression.

Despite all the difficulties, the Starlets have only great memories of their singing career. They stayed in the business for a while and then broke up.

Discography

Pam 1003 Better Tell Him No/You Are the One (1962)
Pam 1004 My Last Cry/Money Hungry (1962)
Source: Bob Pruter in *Record Collector's Monthly* 36.

Starlighters (Washington, D.C.)

Personnel Van McCoy (d) (lead), Fred Smith, Paul Comedy, Norman McCoy, Bernard Wisenant

Notes

This group came together while the group members were still in high school and formed a vocal ensemble called the Starlighters.

Wally Roker of the Heartbeats took an interest in the Starlighters and introduced them to George Goldner. After hearing them, Goldner had the group record for his End label.

Following their July 1958 release, Paul Comedy left for six months of active duty in the service. A Washington, D.C., friend, Marvin Gaye, replaced him for this period.

When Norman McCoy was having troubles with hoarseness, he was replaced by 1st tenor Jerry Jones.

Because their recordings were never promoted, they disbanded. Goldner was preoccupied with Little Anthony and the Imperials as well as the Flamingos and the Chantels.

Van and Norman, overdubbing themselves, recorded as the Four Buddies on Decca's "I Want to Be the Boy You Love" in 1964.

In a *Goldmine* article by Max Oates, it is stated that Whisonant left the group before recording. The spelling above is reflected in Alan Lee's article in *Yesterday's Memories* 8.

Discography

End 1031 The Birdland/It's Twelve O'Clock (1958)
End 1049 I Cried/You're the One to Blame (1959)
End 1072 A Story of Love/Let's Take a Stroll (1960)
Source: Max Oates in *Goldmine*; Alan Lee in *Yesterday's Memories* 8.

Starlings (Bronx, N.Y.)

Personnel Larry Gales (d) (lead), Stan Gilbert (1st tenor), Jackie Marshall (2d tenor), John E. Johnson (baritone), Clyde Franklin (bass)

Notes

The Starlings began in 1951 at Morris High School in the Morrisania section of the Bronx in New York City. Their high school music teacher, Herb Miller, got them a contract with Jubilee's Jerry Blaine, who had them record for his new label, Josie. In April 1954 "Music Maestro Please" and "My Plea for Love" was Josie's first release. The disc failed to get any airplay or a push from Blaine.

After their Josie recordings, Gales and Johnson formed a second Starlings group with Bill Lindsay and Donald Redd and recorded four sides for Dawn. Soon after this, they recorded as the Twilighters on MGM. Later in 1955, Gales teamed up with Waldo Champen, Ed "Sonny" Jordan, and Billy Baines to form the Supremes on Old Town. This Supremes group backed up Ruth McFadden.

Discography

Josie 760 Music Maestro Please (LG)/My Plea for Love (LG) (1954)
Dawn 212 Hokey-Smokey Mama (BL)/I'm Just a Crying Fool (BL) (1955)
Dawn 213 A-Loo A-Loo (BL/JJ)/I Gotta Go Now (LG) (1955)
Source: Marv Goldberg in *DISCoveries.*

Starlites, Jackie & (New York)

Personnel Jackie Rue (d) (lead), Alton Thomas (1st tenor), George Lassu (2d tenor), John Felix (baritone), Billy Montgomery (bass)

Notes

Rue had an alcohol and drug problem that he was always fighting in order to perform at his best. His addiction killed him in the early 1970s.

Two members of this group were arrested in Chicago and accused of murdering an elderly physician (as reported in the *Chicago Defender*). Jackie Rue's real last name was La Rue, and he began his singing career with the Five Wings on King.

According to the liner notes with Relic LP 5090, 1st tenor Alton Thomas was also known as Alton Jones.

Discography

Fire and Fury 1000 You Put One Over on Me/They Laughed at Me (1960)
Fury 1034 Valerie/Way Up in the Sky (1960)
Fury 1045 Ain't Cha Ever Coming Home (1960)
Fury 1057 I Found Out Too Late/I'm Coming Home (1961)
Mascot 128 For All We Know/I Heard You (1962)
Mascot 131 I'll Burn Your Letters/Walking from School (1963)
Hull 760 I Still Remember/I Cried My Heart Out (1963)
Source: Donn Fileti, liner notes with Relic LP *Jackie and the Starlites.*

Starlites, Kenny Esquire & (Philadelphia)

Personnel Kenny Esquire (a.k.a. George Tindley), Wesley Hayes, Bernard Harris, Robert Henderson, Stephen Presbury (bass)

Notes

This group was formerly known as the Dreams who had recorded for Savoy. When they moved to the Herald/Ember organization, Tindley wanted top billing on the record's label. He chose the name "Kenny Esquire."

In his liner notes with Relic's *Best of Ember Records* LP, Donn Fileti states that little airplay and lack of popularity is probably due to the competition of the moment despite the group's pretty ballads.

Following their two releases for Ember, the Starlites began to drift apart. Although they were receiving royalties, they were not adequate.

Tindley briefly wound up with Steve Gibson and the Red Caps. Soon after joining, he left to form the Modern Red Caps with George Grant from the Castelles.

Tindley passed away in 1996. Presbury started the Cobras in 1963 with Delton "Satan" McCall.

Discography

Ember 1011 Pretty Brown Eyes/They Call Me a Dreamer (1957)
Ember 1021 Boom Chica Boom/Tears Are Just for Fools (1957)
Sources: Donn Fileti, liner notes with the Relic LP *Best of Ember Records*; Marv Goldberg in *DISCoveries,* December 1997, article on the Dreams.

Starlites (New York)

Personnel Troy Keyes, Cliff Rice, Sonny Eugene, Charlie Saunders, Vic Rice

Notes

The Starlites cut their first record for Al Browne at Peak Records in May 1957. When Browne began producing some early sides for Scepter, he took the Starlites with him. At Scepter they became Eddie and the Starlites. Robert Honey and bass Ted Olds later sang with the Starlites.

Liner notes accompanying Relic's *Joyce* CD and the Aljon CD *Brooklyn Doo Wop-2* both confirm the note above.

Discography

Peak 5000 Missing You/Give Me a Kiss (1957)
Sources: Donn Fileti, liner notes with the Relic CD *Best of Joyce Records*; Ed Engel, liner notes with Brooklyn's *Doo Wop Sound–2.*

Starlites, Eddie & (New York)

Personnel Eddie Justice (lead), Robert Honey, Teddy Odes, Vel Miller, Archie Price

Notes

This group began as the Starlites who, along with producer Al Browne, recorded for Peak Records in 1957. When Browne moved to Scepter Records, he took the Starlites with him and renamed them Eddie and the Starlites.

Discography

Scepter 1202 To Make a Long Story Short/Pretty Little Girl (1959)
Al Jon 1260/1261 Come on Home/I Need Some Money (1972)
Source: Ed Engel, liner notes with Brooklyn's *Doo Wop Sound–2.*

Startones (Brooklyn, N.Y.)

Personnel Mathew Morales (lead), Allen Mason, Harvey Arrington, Carl Hatton, Arthur Blackwell (bass)

Notes

The Startones recording shown below was cut in June 1956.

Arthur Blackwell was the brother of Tommy Blackwell, who was with the Carnations.

Discography

Rainbow 341 I Love You So Dearly/Forever My Love (1956)
Source: Donn Fileti, liner notes with Relic's CD *Golden Era of Doo Wops—Rainbow Records.*

Stereos (Steubenville, Ohio)

Personnel Bruce Robinson (lead), Leroy Swearingen (1st tenor), Sam Profit (2d tenor), George Otis (baritone), Ronnie Collins (bass)

Notes

The Stereos had been the Buckeyes on DeLuxe. They became the Stereos following several personnel changes.

Because success eluded them at DeLuxe, the group came to New York in search of a benefactor. Luther Dixon and Otis Blackwell filled this bill and the Stereos were soon recording in East Orange, New Jersey, for Gibraltar Records.

In 1960, Swearingen left and was replaced by 1st tenor Nathaniel Hicks. Swearingen went on to write "I Really Love You," which was released a year later on Cub.

In the mid-1960s, the group recorded for many labels, including Columbia, Val, World Artists, Hyde, and Cadet.

In 1968, the group became a vocal and instrumental one. Members now included Stanley Brown, Solomon Huffman, Dan Walters, and Ronnie Parris. Profit and Otis had gone.

Wiseman Moon and George Vereen filled in at tenor and Gaines Steel at bass. Calvin Williams joined as baritone. *(Note:* This cannot be confirmed.)

Discography

Gibralter 105 Sweetpeas in Love (LS)/A Love for Only You (BR) (1959)
Cub 9095 I Really Love You (RC)/Please Come Back to Me (NH) (1961)
Cub 9103 Sweet Water (SP)/The Big Knock (BR) (1961)
Cub 9106 Unless You Mean It (BR)/Do You Love Me (NH) (1962)
Columbia 42626 Echo in My Heart/Tick Tack Toe (BR) (1962)
World Artists 1012 Good News (NH)/Mumbling (BR) (1963)
Val 2 Don't Let it Happen (RP)/The Best Thing to Be (RP) (1965)
Hyde 101 Stereo Freeze (RP)/Stereo Freeze (RP) (1967)
Cadet 5577 Stereo Freeze (RP)/Stereo Freeze (RP) (1967)
Cadet 5626 I Can't Stop Those Tears (RP) (1968)
Source: Jeff Kreiter in *Story Untold* 5.

Stompers (Somerville, Mass.)

Personnel Leonard Capizzi, Bill Capizzi, Ron Deltorta, Lou Toscano, Bobby "Boris" Pickett

Notes

Bobby Pickett was the same Bobby Pickett of "Monster Mash" fame.

This white group had only two releases (see below) and were originally known as the Cordials.

Discography

Landa 684 Quarter to Three Stomp/Foolish One (1961)
Gone 5120 Stompin' around the X-mas Tree/Forgive Me (1962)
Sources: Paul Kosel, liner notes with the Eagle CD *Rare 1950s Boston Doo Wop*; Bob Bosco, liner notes with the Bear Family's Jamie/Guyden CD *Doop Doo Wah.*

Strangers (Brooklyn, N.Y.)

Personnel William Clark (lead), Pringle "Yeoman" Sims (tenor), John Brizant (tenor), John Grant (baritone), Woodrow Jackson (bass)

Notes

This group formed in 1952 in the Bedford-Stuyvesant section of Brooklyn. Bernard Jones was with the group at the beginning but not when they began recording. Jones was replaced by John Grant.

In 1953, when the Strangers felt confident, Clark spoke with Henry Glover, A&R man for King Records in New York. King was impressed enough to give them a recording contract. Of course they signed with King, as this was the label for which their heroes, the Swallows, recorded. Their records were first released in 1954.

They were with King for a year and a half, recording six records that did not do well at that time. The first four were released in 1954 and the last two came out in 1955.

In 1955, they experimented with modern harmony, and this was the beginning of the end. At the end of 1955, with little achieved, the group decided to call it quits. Their haunting harmonies were no longer stylish, giving way to the mid-1950s rock 'n' roll sound.

Clark sang lead on "Golden Teardrops" for the Flamingos of the 1970s.

Discography

King 4697 My Friends (JG)/I've Got Eyes (WC) (1954)
King 4709 Blue Flowers (PS)/Beg and Steal (WC) (1954)
King 4728 Hoping You'll Understand (PS)/Just Don't Care (WC) (1954)
King 4745 Drop Down to My Place (WC)/Get It One More Time (WC) (1954)
King 4766 Dreams Came True (WC)/How Long Must I Wait? (WC) (1955)
King 4821 Without a Friend (WC)/Think Again (WC) (1955)
Source: Marv Goldberg and Mike Redmond in *Yesterday's Memories.*

Striders (New York)

Personnel Gene Strider (lead), Charles Strider, Jim Strider, Al Martin

Notes

Gene Strider, Charles Strider, and Jim Strider were brothers. Both the Striders and the Four Tunes were used by Savannah Churchill as a backup vocal group.

Other members included E. Williams and F. Thomas. In 1951, Savannah was invited to appear in the United Kingdom at the London Paladium, and she brought the Striders with her.

The Striders did backup work for Bette McLaurin (Derby 804), Savannah Churchill (Regal 3309), Maureen Cannon, and Delores Martin.

Discography

Capitol 15306 Pleasin' You/Somebody Stole My Rose-Colored Glasses (1948)
Apollo 1159 5 O'Clock Blues/Cool Saturday Night (1950)
Derby 457 Rollin'/Come Back to Me Tomorrow (1954)
Apollo 480 I Wonder/Hesitating Fool (1955)
Sources: Jonas Bernholm and Dave Rogers, liner notes with the Savannah Churchill LP *Mr. R&B*; Will Anderson and John Corrado in *Record Exchanger* 19.

Students (Cincinnati, Ohio)

Personnel Leroy King (lead), Richard Johnson, John Bolden, John Ford, Dorsey Porter

Notes

This group was formed in Youngstown, Ohio, in 1957. "I'm So Young" and "Every Day of the Week" were released simultaneously on the Note label out of Indianapolis and on the Argo label. Apparently, Note was given exclusive limited distribution in two midwestern states and Chess was given the balance of the United States. Chess picked up the master from Note and quickly released it on their Argo label. Three years later in 1961, it finally hit as a rerelease on Checker. Because of the poor initial showing, the group had disbanded in 1959, long before the successful rerelease.

Tenor Ricky Kennedy also sang with the Students, as did P. Tyus, Emerson "Rocky" Brown, and, at bass, Richie Havens.

Discography

Note 10012 I'm So Young/Every Day of the Week (1958)
Checker 902 I'm So Young/Every Day of the Week (1958)
Argo 5386 I'm So Young/Every Day of the Week (1961)
Checker 1004 That's How I Feel/My Vow to You (1962)
Source: Pete Grendysa, liner notes with the Chess CD boxed set *Chess Rhythm & Roll.*

Styles (Bronx, N.Y.)

Personnel Louis Pesce (lead), Jack Vero (1st tenor), Harold Epstein (2d tenor), Harvey Ledo (baritone), Arnold Abbott (bass)

Notes

The Styles formed in the Bronx in 1958. When Josie finally released their one recording for the label, their style was no longer popular and thus the record did not receive much airplay.

The group was called the Styles because Pesce always came to rehearsals directly from his job and was always dressed in style.

A Styles group with Jack Vero was still appearing in the New York metropolitan area in the later 1990s.

Pesce and Vero were cousins.

Discography

Serene 1501 Scarlet Angel/Gotta Go Go Go (1961)
Josie 920 For Sentimental Reasons/Schoolbells to Chapel Bells (1964)
Source: Gordon Skadberg liner notes with the Sequel CD *Jubilee/Josie R&B Vocal Groups-5.*

Stylists

Personnel William George (lead), Delaney Bolden (tenor), Johnny Paige (2d tenor), Odell ———— (baritone), Rudy Cooper (bass)

Notes

George and Paige also sang with the Marylanders, so it's quite possible that this group originated in the Baltimore/D.C. area.

Discography

Crown 145 Go, Go Daddy, Go (1955)
Jay Wing 5807 Move it Over Baby (JP)/Mourning (WG) (1959)
Sage 317 Scary Harry/I've Been Waiting for You (1960)
Source: Bob Ferlingere, *A Discography of R&B and R&R Vocal Groups.*

Stylists (New York)

Personnel Joe Duncan (lead), Rudy Cooper (tenor), Alvin Black (tenor), "Sonny" Garrett (baritone), LaMar Cooper (bass)

Notes

This group resulted from the evolution of the Red Robin Vocaleers. Duncan and Lamar Cooper were from the early 1950s Vocaleers. Rudy Cooper was Lamar Cooper's brother.

In another resource, George Lithcuit is listed as baritone.

Discography

Rose 17 One Room/I Wonder (1960)
Source: Ed Engel, liner notes with the Dee Jay Jamboree CD *Brooklyn's Doo Wop Sound.*

Suddens (Los Angeles)

Personnel Jimmy Stephens, Shelly Briar, Marv Rosenberg, Rich Clasky

Notes

This group started in 1959 as the Mystics. When they found out that this name was spoken for, they changed their name to the Enchanters. They recorded for Orbit as the Enchanters. When Briar was added, they became the Dories. They next moved to Tawny and became the Angels.

In 1960, this group was successful as the Safaris.

Discography

Sudden 103 Childish Ways/China Love (1961)
Sources: Louie Silvani, *Collecting Rare Records*; Jay Warner, *American Singing Groups.*

Sugar Lumps, Sugar Boy & (New Orleans)

Personnel James "Sugar Boy" Crawford (lead), Diane Degray, Mary Kelley, Linda Degray, Irene Williams

Notes

James "Sugar Boy" Crawford began with the Sha-Weez that was formed in 1950 in a New Orleans high school. They were a self-contained ensemble, playing instruments as well as vocalizing.

Crawford was also with the Cane Cutters and after leaving the Sha-Weez, he remained with Aladdin. In the early 1960s, he teamed up with the girls shown above and recorded one disc for Peacock Records as Sugar Boy and the Sugar Lumps.

Discography

Peacock 1925 Mama Won't You Turn Me Loose (JC)/So Long, Goodbye (1963)
Source: Marv Goldberg and Dave Hinckley in *Yesterday's Memories.*

Sultans (Omaha, Neb.)

Personnel Willie Barnes (lead), Wesley Devereaux (1st tenor), Gene McDaniels (2d tenor), James Farmer (baritone), Richard Beasley (bass)

Notes

This group had been singing together in a gospel quartet in Omaha's Technical High School. They acquired a manager, Paul Allen, who had persuaded Johnny Otis, who was passing through Omaha on a tour, to listen to the quartet. Otis liked them enough to have them join his traveling show as it passed through Omaha. This was 1954.

Otis named them and they followed him to Dallas, where he was doing some recording. He asked the Sultans to join him in the studio and give their rendition of "How Deep Is the Ocean." This was eventually released on Duke 125.

Following their first release, the group did many one-nighters at local clubs. In September, they had their second release, which had been recorded at the first session in January.

Devereaux is the son of Wynonie Harris.

Gene McDaniels is the same Gene McDaniels who later recorded "A Hundred Pounds of Clay."

The group was later the Admirals on the King label.

Discography

Duke 125 Good Thing Baby/How Deep Is the Ocean (1954)
Duke 133 I Cried My Heart Out/Baby Don't Put Me Down (1954)
Duke 135 Boppin' with the Mambo/What Makes Me Feel This Way? (1954)
Duke 178 If I Could Tell/My Love Is High (1957)
Source: Galen Gart and Roy Ames, liner notes with *Duke/Peacock Records.*

Sunbeams (Glen Cove, N.Y.)

Personnel Bobby Lee Hollis (lead), Bobby Coleman (d) (1st tenor), James Davis (2d tenor), Johnny Cumbo (baritone), William Edwards (bass)

Notes

Before recording, the Sunbeams were called the Kovaks and included Bobby Lee Hollis, Bobby Coleman, James Davis, John Cumbo, and William Edwards. For a brief time, a gravedigger named Joe Tex was a member.

Early in 1955, Cumbo called Herald Records for an audition. Herald liked their songs but not their name. Early in 1955, four songs were recorded and Hollis sang lead on all four, including "Tell Me Why," "Come Back Baby," "Shouldn't I Have a Right to Cry," and "I Love the Way You Look Tonight."

With the Nutmegs and Turbans on their roster, Herald had little time to devote to the Sunbeams; consequently, their record did poorly because it received no promotion.

Sometime in 1956, Hollis departed and was replaced by Henry Williamson, who sang with the Colonairs on Ember. In 1963, Hollis became lead with Bill Pinkney's Original Drifters.

The Sunbeams met with William Miller from Hull, and he wanted to record them; but they were still under contract to Herald. When this legal obligation ended, they did some tunes for Miller. These sides were released in 1957 by Acme.

Their Acme cuts did nothing and the group soon disbanded. Coleman went solo and Williamson joined one of the Ink Spots groups.

This is the Acme and Herald group. Some of the members later joined the Orients on Laurie.

Johnny Coleman and Butch Meecham also sang with the Sunbeams.

Discography

Herald 451 Come Back Baby/Tell Me Why (1955)
Acme 719 Please Say You'll Be Mine/You've Got to Rock and Roll (1957)
Source: Marv Goldberg in *DISCoveries.*

Sunrisers (Los Angeles)

Personnel Henry Houston, Moses Walker, Elroy Coleman

Notes

According to Billy Vera's liner notes with the Specialty CD *Doo Wop from Dolphin's of Hollywood–2,* the above personnel, with one unremembered member, formed the Raindrops on Spin-It and the second Cufflinx group on Dootone. If this is true, the fourth member is either Johnny Simmons or Raymond Durden.

Their "Soft, Soft Lips" and "Behold a Dream," recorded for Specialty, were never released until the CD discussed above was issued in 1991. For that reason no discography is shown below.

Source: Billy Vera, liner notes with the Specialty CD *Doo Wop from Dolphin's of Hollywood.*

Superiors (Philadelphia)

Personnel Barbara Custus, Eddie Custus (baritone)

Notes

Eddie Custus sang with the Five Hearts, Hearts, Lee Andrews and the Hearts, and the Famous Hearts.

Discography

Atco 6104 Lost Love/Don't Say Goodbye (1957)
Main Line 104 Lost Love/Don't Say Goodbye (1958)

Supremes • 547

Sources: Lou Silvani, *Collecting Rare Records*; Marv Goldberg, liner notes with the Collectables double CD *Lee Andrews and the Hearts.*

Supremes (Columbus, Ohio)

Personnel Forest Porter (lead), Eddie Jackson (1st tenor) Eddie Dumas (2d tenor), Jay Robinson (baritone), Bobby Isbell (bass)

Notes

Isbell and Dumas were high school classmates in 1954 at Columbus East High School. They decided to form a vocal group and were soon joined by Porter, Jackson, and Robinson—all classmates.

They sang together from 1954 to January 1957, doing local events, and so on. They were contacted by a promoter to come south and perform in Florida and Alabama. They did quite well in both locations. A local record shop proprietor told a friend at Ace about the Supremes, and in April 1957 they recorded "Just for You and I" for Ace. At that same session, they recorded two other tunes that were never released.

Bob Isbell sang bass with Huey Smith and the Clowns on their "Just a Lonely Clown."

Despite the rumors, this Supremes group was not the Velveteers on Ric. This comes directly from an interview with Forest Porter by Dave Ardit and S Petryszyn.

There was another rumor identifying this Supremes as Ruby and the Romantics, a rumor that started when "Just for You and I" was released. At that time the Romantics were calling themselves the Supremes.

They never received a penny in royalties for sales or Porter for writer's credit.

Discography

Ace 534 Just for You and I/Don't Leave Me Here to Cry (1957)
Source: Dave Ardit and Steve Petryszyn in *Bim Bam Boom.*

Supremes (Lawrence, Mass.)

Personnel Ralph Murphy (lead), Archie Moore, Jace Murphy, Bill Perry (d), Lee Murphy (bass), Claude Brown (bass), John Brown (bass)

Notes

This was a seven-man, self-contained group from Lawrence, Massachusetts. They met in high school and started singing together in 1955. They appeared at local events, parties, and clubs. Because they hung around together in front of Supreme Cleaners, they chose to call themselves the Supremes.

According to George Moonoogian and Jim Cote's article in *Record Exchanger,* they managed a one-record deal. The record company's name, Kitten Records, was chosen by the group. Distribution was poor and the record sold only in their immediate area. Only about two hundred were pressed!

Perry was killed in an auto accident while he was in the service in 1958.

Discography

Kitten 6969 Could This Be You?/Margie (1956)
Sources: Donn Fileti, liner notes with the Relic CD *Doo Wop Delights: The Boston Groups*; George Moonoogian and Jim Cote in *Record Exchanger.*

Supremes (Bronx, N.Y.)

Personnel Larry Gales (lead), Waldo Champen (tenor), "Sonny" Jordan (2d tenor), Billy Baines (bass)

Notes

Gales had been with the Starlings on Josie and Dawn and with the Twilighters on MGM.

Bobby Mansfield has told the author that this group backed the Wrens on "Wreckless" and "House of Cards" on Rama Records.

Champen sang with the Chimes (Betta), Five Delights, Moodmakers (Bambi), Dean Barlow and the Monterays, Bachelors (Earl), Crickets, Cadillacs, and Morrisania Review.

Liner notes with the Ace CD *Old Town Doo Wop-2* assert that the Supremes backed Ruth McFadden on "Darling Listen to the Words of This Song."

"Come Back and Give Me Your Hand," which was first released on Murray Hill's Solitaires' boxed set, showed it to be an unreleased Solitaires tune. I have since learned from Bobby Mansfield that this was the Supremes with Champ doing lead.

Discography

Old Town 1017 Darling (Listen to the Words of This Song) (RMF)/Since My Baby's Been Gone (RMF) (1955)
Old Town 1024 Tonight (LG)/She Don't Want Me No More (renamed "My Babe" on second pressing) 1956
Old Town (UNR) Come Back and Give Me Your Hand (WC)
Sources: Bobby Mansfield, interview by author, June 1995; Waldo Champen, interview by author, September 1994; liner notes with Ace CD *Old Town Doo Wop-2.*

Swallows (Baltimore, Md.)

Personnel Tenor Eddie Rich (lead), Herman Denby (baritone/lead), Earl Hurley (2d tenor), Frederick "Money Guitar" Johnson (baritone), Norris "Bunky" Mack (bass)

Notes

This group started in Baltimore in 1946 as the Oakaleers. Like many other groups from that period, they were a self-contained group playing instruments as well as vocalizing. It's hard to believe that their average age at the time was thirteen! Following other groups of the time, they renamed themselves after a bird, the swallow.

The Swallows sang and performed together for years and built themselves a strong local reputation with their excellent performances at local eateries and bars. They also made an appearance with Alan Freed at one of his early shows in Cleveland. They came to the attention of King Records, which was impressed enough to sign them and arrange for a recording session in May 1951.

Their rendition of ballads, led by Eddie Rich, was smooth and emulated the emotive style of neighborhood friend Sonny Til and his Orioles. At their third session in December 1951, "Beside You," lead by Herman "Junior" Denby, marked the end of their sweet, bluesy style and began a harder blues style sounding very much like Johnny Moore's Blazers. These successes created a great demand for live shows, and they would not record again until October 1952.

By March 1953, their final session for King, their style had adjusted again to a more modern structure. By 1954, the Swallows' sweet style was beginning to give way to the new Drifters, Chords, and Charms renderings. The record-buying public felt that the Swallows' style was passé and left them behind, with their records, for the more modern sounds.

In 1954, the group, then a sextet, got a one-shot deal with the After Hours label. The After Hours group included Irving Turner, Al France, Dee Ernie Bailey, Herman Williams, and Eddie Rich. The After Hours disc failed; the Swallows' popularity was fading.

Eddie Rich persevered for two more years, recruiting replacements for Denby, Turner, and Mack. One of these replacements was Bobby Hendricks, who would soon move on to the Drifters. Rich finally disbanded the group in 1956 and returned home to Maryland.

In 1958, Rich got together with several ex-members of other Baltimore groups to re-form the Swallows. This group was composed of Bobby Hendricks, Leon Bailey, Henry Jackson, Oliver Lewis, and Robert Pittman. Rich then called on his former recording organization, King Records. King was receptive enough to sign this new Swallows ensemble to its Federal subsidiary, for which they cut a few new sides. None of them clicked and the group was dropped.

Rich sang for the Marquis on Rainbow with Bobby Hendricks and three others. This occurred when Eddie became stranded in Columbus, Ohio.

Rich and Fred Johnson were brothers-in-law. He also sang (appeared only) for the Honey Boys with Calvin "Khaki" Collette.

Discography

King 4458 Dearest/Will You Be Mine? (1951)
King 4466 Since You've Been Away/Wishing for You (1951)
King 4501 Eternally/It Ain't the Meat (1951)
King 4515 Tell Me Why/Roll Roll Pretty Baby (1951)
King 4525 Beside You/You Left Me (1952)
King 4533 I Only Have Eyes for You/You Walked In (1952)
King 4579 Please Baby Please/Where Do I Go from Here? (1952)
King 4612 Laugh/Our Love Is Dying (1953)
King 4632 Nobody's Lovin' Me/Bicycle Tillie (1953)
King 4656 Trust Me/Pleading Blue (1953)
King 4676 I'll Be Waiting/It Feels So Good (1953)
After Hours 104 My Baby/Good Time Girls (1954)
Federal 12319 Oh Lonesome Me/Angel Baby (1958)

Federal 12328 We Want to Know/Rock A Bye Baby Rock (1958)
Federal 12329 Beside You/Laughing Boy (1958)
Federal 12333 Itchy Twitchy Feeling/Who Knows, Do You? (1958)
Sources: Tony Watson in *Blues & Rhythm*; Marv Goldberg and Mike Redmond in *Yesterday's Memories*; Phil Chaney in *Yesterday's Memories*; Ron Bartolucci, liner notes with the Eagle CD *D.C. Doo Wops*.

Swallows (Hollywood, Calif.)

Personnel Carlton Beck (lead), Richard Betts (bass)

Notes

This group also recorded as the Guides, Senders, and Uptones.

Discography

Guyden 2023 How Long Must a Fool Go On/You Must Try (1959)
Source: Marv Goldberg and Rick Whitesell in *Yesterday's Memories* 11.

Swans (St. Louis, Mo.)

Personnel Leroy Boyer, Ernest Washington

Notes

In 1955, Boyer and Washington left the Swans to join Rex Middleton's Hi Fi's for their Verve LP 2035.

Discography

Ballad 1006 It's a Must/Night Train (1954)
Ballad 1007 Happy/Santa Claus Boogie Song (1955)
Source: Charlie Horner, *Vocal Group Guide to St. Louis.*

Swans (Detroit)

Personnel Paul Lewis (lead), Tommy Jones (bass)

Discography

Fortune 813 Little Señorita/Wedding Bells Oh Wedding Bells (1954)
Fortune 822 I'll Forever Love You/Mister Cool Breeze (1954)
Source: Lou Silvani, *Collecting Rare Records.*

Sweet Teens, Faith Taylor & (Chicago)

Personnel Faith Taylor (lead), Saundra Long (tenor), Mary Collins (tenor), Yvonne Waddell (tenor), Curtis Burrell (bass)

Notes

Elizabeth Shelby and Ernestine Fisher joined the Sweet Teens on their Bea and Baby cuts. They joined Taylor, Collins, and Burrell, forming a new lineup of Sweet Teens.
Curtis Burrell later joined the Daylighters.

Discography

Federal 12334 Your Candy Kisses/Won't Someone Tell Me Why (1958)
Bea & Baby 104 I Need Him to Love Me/Please Be Mine (1959)
Bea & Baby 105 I Love You Darling/Paper Route Baby (1959)
Source: Bob Pruter, *Doowop . . . The Chicago Scene.*

Swinging Hearts (Chicago)

Personnel Morris Spearmon (lead), Ernest Lemon, Jerry Williams, Lee Brown, Roscoe Brown (bass)

Notes

This group was discovered in 1961 when all but Lee Brown were attending Blue Island High School in a Chicago suburb. Their first release, "Please Say It Isn't So," was first released later that year. The master was purchased in 1965 and was released again that year on Diamond Records for national distribution.

Lee Brown and Roscoe Brown are related, either as brothers or as cousins.

As reflected in the discography, label management would give their records to others, either for national distribution (Diamond) or for sale (6 2 0).

It is felt that if the members of this group had been single and free of other responsibilities and obligations, they might have become quite popular. As it was, family responsibilities kept them from traveling to promote their excellent discs.

Discography

Lucky Four 1011 Please Say It Isn't So/Something Made Me (1961)
6 2 0 1002 How Can I Love You?/Spanish Love (1963)
NRM 1002 How Can I Love You?/Spanish Love (1963)
6 2 0 1005 Something Made Me Stop/Pony Rock (1963)
6 2 0 1009 You Speak of Love/I've Got It (1964)
Magic Touch 2001 You Speak of Love/I've Got It (1964)
Diamond 162 Please Say It Isn't So/Something Made Me Stop (1965)
Source: Bob Pruter, *Doowop . . . The Chicago Scene.*

Symbols, Jimmy Keyes & (Bronx, N.Y.)

Personnel Jimmy Keyes (d) (lead), Vernon Dicks, Dimitrius Clare, Warren Wilson

Notes

This group was an extension of the Popular Five on Rae Cox. Jimmy Keyes, of course, came from the Chords on Cat of the early 1950s. They recorded a scary novelty song in 1965 entitled "Do the Zombie." It was not released until 1985, when it was included on an LP entitled *R&B Laff Blast from the Past*. It was never released as a single (and thus there is no discography for this group).

Keyes unfortunately passed away in 1996.

Source: Gordon Skadberg, liner notes with the Sequel CD *Herb Abramson's Festival of Hits*.

Syncopaters (Washington, D.C.)

Personnel James Pinkney (tenor), George Summers (2d tenor), Howard "Ghostie" Smith (baritone), Edmund Johnson (baritone), Theodore Smith (bass)

Notes

One of the first to hear and eventually help the Syncopaters was D.C. deejay Harold "Hal" Jackson, who ultimately ended up on New York radio.

The Syncopaters signed with National Records, and for their first session the group had to journey to New York, as there were no studios of any size in the Baltimore/D.C. area. Ravens' manager Howard Biggs arranged their session.

The Syncopaters' version of "Mule Train" was recorded before the Frankie Laine version.

Little promotion and management, coupled with some internal personal problems, caused the group to break up within months of their only session.

Although "Mule Train" does not appear on Savoy's *Vocal Group Album* LP, everything else does, including the previously unreleased "Out in the Cold Again."

Discography

National 9093 These Are the Things I Want to Share with You (JP/TS)/Mule Train (JP) (1949)

National 9095 These Are the Things I Want to Share with You (JP/TS)/River Stay Away from My Door (JP/TS) (1949)

Out in the Cold Again (JP/TS) (unreleased)

Sources: Bill Pinkney and Walter Sutler, interview by Marv Goldberg in *Goldmine,* June 1980; Marv Goldberg, liner notes with the Savoy LP *Vocal Group Album*.

Syncopates (East Haven, Conn.)

Personnel Sharon O'Connell, Judy Tucker, Bonnie Metzo, Karen Prahovic

Notes

This was a white female group from East Haven, Connecticut.

They cut the Dreamtones' "Praying for a Miracle," which was ultimately released on Times Square Records in the early 1960s.

Discography

Times Square 7 Your Tender Lips/Praying for a Miracle (1963)

Source: Donn Fileti, liner notes with the Relic CD *Groups of Klik Records*.

Tabbys (Hackensack, N.J.)

Personnel Kenny Clay (lead), Timmy Scudder (d) (1st tenor), Butch Henry (2d tenor), Melvin Edwards (bass)

Notes

In the early 1960s, the Tabbys were reportedly in a studio preparing themselves to record "Hong Kong Baby," which was ultimately released on Metro 2, when they were approached by the manager of the Hi Lites from Connecticut. One story states that he was the manager for both the Hi Lites and the Tabbys; the other account simply states that the Tabbys were in a recording studio at the same time as the Hi Lites' manager, who asked the Tabbys if they could bail him out of a legal difficulty he was having. He asked them if they would record a tune as the Hi Lites so that a contractual obligation could be met. The Tabbys supposedly agreed, and reportedly "Gloria My Darling," released on Julia as by the Hi Lites, is really the Tabbys! Another story states that both "Gloria" and its flip "I Love You for Sentimental Reasons" were done by the Tabbys.

Charles McCullough is shown as the lead and Scudder is shown as the bass. It was McCullough who related the account that the personnel and the manager represented both vocal groups to another researcher-historian.

Discography

Time 1008 My Darling/Yes I Do (1958)
Metro 2 Hong Kong Baby/Physical Fitness Blues (1963)
Sources: Unsigned story discussing the Tabbys in the March 1979 issue of the *Rock 'n' Roll Bulletin*; Ferdie Gonzalez, *Disco-File.*

Tabs (Los Angeles)

Personnel William Gardner (lead), Johnny Johnson, James Tanlin, Herbert Northern, Ted Forbes

Discography

Nasco 6016 Still Love You Baby/Will We Meet Again? (1958)
Dot 15887 Avenue of Tears/First Star (1958)
Noble 719 Never Forget/Rock and Roll Holiday (1959)
Vee Jay 418 Dance All by Myself/Dance Party (1961)
Vee Jay 446 Mash Dem Taters/But You're My Baby (1962)
Wand 130 Two Stupid Feet/The Wallop (1963)
Wand 139 Take My Love Along With You/I'm with You (1963)
Source: Ferdie Gonzalez, *Disco-File.*

Tams (Atlanta)

Personnel Charles Pope (lead), Horace Key (tenor), Joe Pope (baritone), Floyd Ashton (baritone), Robert Smith (bass)

Discography

General American 714 My Baby Loves Me/Find Another Love (1962)
Arlen 7-11 Untie Me/Disillusioned (1962)
Arlen 717 Deep Inside Me/If You're So Smart (1962)
Arlen 720 Blue Shadows/You'll Never Know (1963)
Arlen 729 Don't Ever Go/Find Another Love (1963)
ABC 10502 What Kind of Fool/Laugh It Off (1963)
ABC 10553 You Lied to Your Daddy/It's All Right (1964)
ABC 10573 Hey Girl Don't Bother Me/Take Away (1964)
ABC 10601 Silly Little Girl/Weep Little Girl (1964)
ABC 10614 The Truth Hurts/Why Did My Little Girl Cry? (1964)
ABC 10635 Unlove You/What Do You Do? (1965)
ABC 10702 Concrete Jungle/Till the End of Time (1965)
ABC 10741 I've Been Hurt/Carrying On (1965)
Source: Ferdie Gonzalez, *Disco-File.*

Tangiers (Los Angeles)

Personnel Joe Jefferson (lead), David Ford (1st tenor), Earl Nelson (2d tenor), Curtis Williams (baritone), Bobby Day Byrd (bass)

Notes

This is not the Decca group but an evolution of the Flames/Satellites. Interestingly, David Ford was with the Decca group that had previously used the Tangiers name when he recorded the classic "Tabarin" with Gaynel Hodge, Alex Hodge, and Jesse Belvin.

Discography

Class 224 Don't Try/School Days Will Be Over (1958)
Source: Donn Fileti, liner notes with the Relic LP *Best of Class Records.*

Tangiers (Los Angeles)

Personnel Gaynel Hodge, Alex Hodge, David Ford, Jesse Belvin

Notes

This is the Decca group and one of Jesse Belvin's many California vocal group participations. Excluding Belvin, this is another offshoot of the Hollywood Flames.

Discography

Decca 29603 Tabarin/I Won't Be Around (1955)
Decca 29971 Remember Me/Oh Baby (1956)
Source: Marv Goldberg in *Yesterday's Memories.*

Teardrops (Detroit)

Personnel Carl Jones (lead), Alfonso Wallace (tenor), Sam Scott (baritone), Stan Bracely (bass)

Notes

This group was formed by teenage friends from the "Black Bottom" section of Detroit in the early 1950s.

Bracely was visiting his parents and met Maurice Martin, who was living in the same apartment house. When Bracely told Martin of the Teardrops, Bracely, a pianist, took an interest and began showing up at their rehearsal sessions.

They would sing and practice wherever they could find an echo: bathrooms, hallways, and so on. They began performing at amateur shows and church functions. They came in second in a 1953 amateur show across the river from Detroit in Windsor, Ontario. The winner was "Little" Willie John.

The group was soon contacted by promoter Homer Jones, who asked them to get in touch with Sampson Records (whom he had spoken to) regarding the Teardrops. They recorded for a studio that was located in the rear of Sam's Record Shop.

They heard their tune on Detroit radio for several weeks, but then it disappeared. As is usually the case, group members never received a cent, nor did they ever hear from Sampson Records again. The group would later evolve into Motown's Lovetones.

Carl Jones was killed in a barroom fight in the early 1960s.

Discography

Sampson 634 Come Back to Me (CJ)/Sweet Lovin' Daddy-O (SS) (1953)
Source: Marv Goldberg, *DISCoveries,* May 1996.

Teenagers (New York)

Personnel Frankie Lymon (d) (lead), Herman Santiago (1st tenor), Jimmy Merchant (2d tenor), Joe Negroni (d) (baritone), Sherman Garnes (d) (bass)

Notes

This group began in 1954 in the Washington Heights section of Manhattan in New York. Garnes and Merchant were ninth-grade classmates in a Harlem junior high school. Garnes soon found Negroni, who recruited his friend Herman Santiago. The quartet clicked right away and after much practice began making appearances at local talent shows. At one of these talent shows they met Frankie Lymon.

A neighbor of Garnes's gave him some poems written by his girlfriend that were intended to be developed into songs. The tune eventually chosen was "Why Do Fools Fall in Love."

They next ran into Richard Barrett at a junior high school talent show. The Teenagers were appearing there as the Premiers. After Barrett heard them, he brought them to George Goldner at the Gee complex of labels. Barrett was currently there with his Valentines. This new group auditioned for Goldner with Santiago at lead.

Following several of their offerings, Goldner asked Lymon to try lead. The rest is history.

The Premiers recorded "Why Do Fools Fall in Love" in the spring of 1955. By that time their name had been changed to the Teenagers. "Why Do Fools" became a tremendous hit. This led to excellent follow-ups, tours, concerts, and one-nighters. This endless string of appearances ultimately took its toll on the group and signs of strain became obvious.

Lymon failed to show up at the start of a September 1956 tour and Garnes recommended that Jimmy Castor, an old school friend, be brought in to replace Lymon. Castor came in, but Lymon rejoined the group several days later.

Later in 1956, they appeared at a command performance for Princess Margaret at the London Palladium. At this time the group learned that Lymon was being advised to go solo, and consequently "Miracle of Love" was released without the group. Lymon also began to appear and record without them.

It was now 1957, and the London tour proved to be the end for the Teenagers. It's interesting to note that neither Lymon nor the Teenagers realized any success following their split.

The Teenagers made several attempts to stick it out, first with Billy Lobrano, later with Negroni, and then with Johnny Houston. Meanwhile, Lymon experienced little success on his own. Live show offers slipped drastically, his high tenor voice was changing, and drugs came to play a critical role in his life. On February 28, 1968, he died of an overdose.

In 1977, Garnes died of a heart attack. Negroni died in jail from a cerebral hemorrhage in 1978.

Discography

Gee 1002 Why Do Fools Fall in Love?/Please Be Mine (1955)
Gee 1012 I Want You to Be My Girl/I'm Not a Know-It-All (1956)
Gee 1018 I Promise to Remember/Who Can Explain? (1956)
Gee 1022 Share/The ABCs of Love (1956)
Gee 1026 I'm Not a Juvenile Delinquent/Baby, Baby (1956)
Gee 1032 Paper Castles/Teenage Love (1957)
Gee 1035 Love is a Clown/Am I Fooling Myself Again (1957)
Gee 1036 Out in the Cold Again/Miracle in the Rain (1957)
Gee 1039 Goody Goody/Creation of Love (1957)
Source: Dennis Duca in *Harmony Tymes.*

Teenchords (New York)

Personnel Louis Lymon (lead), Ralph Vaughan (1st tenor), Rossilio Rocca (2d tenor), Lyndon Harold (baritone), David Little (bass)

Notes

The Teenchords began in high school. They all attended George Washington High School except Rocca, who went to Commerce High. Harold and Rocca had groups of their own, which ultimately merged. After the merger they recruited Louie and David.

The group practiced endlessly and one day found themselves backstage at the Apollo to see Louie's brother Frankie. There they met Charles Sampson of the Red Robin Velvets. After learning that Frankie's brother Louie also had a group, he brought them to Bobby Robinson for an audition. This tryout took place in Robinson's store. He was quite impressed with them and decided to record them. A month later they recorded their first tunes, I'm So Happy/Lydia.

After three releases for Robinson's Fury Records, the guys became unhappy with Fury. As a result of brother Frankie Lymon's association with George Goldner, the Teenchords joined End Records.

They had cut three discs for Goldner and when two of the Teenchords were busted for being in a stolen car. Louis's mother ended the relationship. After some time, he was able to join the Townsmen on PJ.

The R&B revival of the early 1970s inspired Louie to re-form the Teenchords. They then consisted of Louie, Ralph Ramos from the Townsmen, Luis Vasquez from the Townsmen, Velmont Miller, and Frankie San Pietro.

Discography

Fury 1000 I'm So Happy/Lydia (1957)
Fury 1003 Honey, Honey/Please Tell the Angels (1957)
Fury 1006 I'm Not Too Young to Fall in Love/Falling in Love (1957)
End 1003 Too Young/Your Last Chance (1957)
End 1007 I Found Out Why/Tell Me Love (1957)
Juanita 101 Dance Girl/Them There Eyes (1958)
End 1113 I Found Out Why/Too Young (1962)
Source: Joe Sicurella in *Big Town Review.*

Teen Queens (Los Angeles)

Personnel Rose Collins, Betty Collins

Notes

Rose Collins and Betty Collins were the sisters of Aaron Collins of the Jacks/Cadets. It was he who wrote "Eddie My Love" for his siblings. The disc was covered by the Fontane Sisters.

Collins and Lloyd McCraw brought the Collins sisters to Modern/RPM for their tryout and eventual recordings.

Discography

RPM 453 Eddie My Love/Just Goofed (1956)
RPM 460 Baby Mine/So All Alone (1956)
RPM 464 Billy Boy/Until the Day I Die (1956)
RPM 470 Red Top/Love, Sweet Love (1956)
RPM 484 Rock Everybody/My Heart's Desire (1956)
RPM 500 I Miss You/Two Loves and Two Lives (1957)
RCA 47-7206 Dear Tommy/You Good Boy, You Get Cookie (1958)
RCA 47-7396 First Crush/Movie Star (1958)
Antler 4014 There's Nothing On My Mind-Pt 1/Pt 2 (1960)

Antler 4015 Politician/I'm a Fool (1960)
Antler 4016 Donny/Donny (1961)
Antler 4017 I Heard Violins/McGoo Can See (1961)
Kent 359 Eddie My Love/Just Goofed (1961)
Source: Jim Dawson in *Goldmine,* April 28, 1996.

Tempos (Chicago)

Personnel Jewell Jones (tenor), James Maddox (baritone), Louis Bradley (tenor), Marvin Smith (tenor)

Notes

The El Dorados were in Oakland, California, in 1958 and recorded for Rhythm Records as the Tempos in order to earn enough money to pay their way back home.
   Other accounts call this episode "moonlighting" by the El Dorados.

Discography

Rhythm 121 Promise Me/Never Let Me Go (1958)
Source: Dennis Leonis, liner notes with the Solid Smoke CD *Remembering Rhythm Records*; Dave Antrell, liner notes with the Starfire Rhythm LP *Rhythm and Blues Classics.*

Tempo-Tones (Long Island, N.Y.)

Personnel Richard Lanham (lead), Bert Brewster, Wally Lanham, Danny Lanham, Al Lanham (bass)

Notes

Steve Stewart also sang with the Tempo-Tones.

Discography

Acme 713 Get Yourself Another Fool/Ride Along (1957)
Acme 715 In My Dreams/My Boy Sleep Pete (1957)
Acme 718 Come Into My Heart/Somewhere There Is Someone (1957)
Source: Richard W. Dunne article in *Goldmine.*

Temptations (Detroit)

Personnel Eddie Kendricks, Paul Williams, Otis Williams, Elbridge "Al" Bryant, Melvin Franklin

Notes

This group originally formed in 1960 and underwent many personnel changes. Sometime in 1960, the quintet began calling themselves the Temptations. Prior to this formation, part of the group recorded as the Distants for Northern. In July or August 1961 they had their first release under their new name. This was issued on Berry Gordy's Miracle label and was entitled "Oh, Mother of Mine." It sold poorly.

They were moved to the Gordy label in April 1962 and their first release, "Dream Come True," got some attention. Despite this, Al Bryant left early in 1963. He was replaced by the former lead of the Voice Masters on Anna, David Ruffin.

"The Way You Do the Things You Do" was released in January 1964. The tune met with good sales and increasing popularity for the group. Releases continued and in December 1964 the classic "My Girl" was released. It was the lead debut for David Ruffin.

Smokey Robinson produced the Temptations releases until Brian Holland and Norman Whitfield assumed this responsibility and maintained the group's success with their unique productions.

Ruffin left in 1968 to try a solo career. Whitfield began placing socially conscious tunes on the list of songs to be recorded by the Temptations. Success followed success until Kendricks and Paul Williams left at the beginning of the 1970s. Damon Harris and Richard Street took up the slack. It was also at this time that Ricky Owens, formerly of the Vibrations, sang with the Temps for a short time. Their recording successes continued.

Discography (through 1970)

Miracle 5 Oh Mother of Mine/Romance without Finance (1961)
Miracle 12 Your Wonderful Love/Check Yourself (1962)
Gordy 7001 Dream Come True/Isn't She Pretty (1962)
Gordy 7010 Paradise/Slow Down Heart (1963)
Gordy 7015 I Want a Love I Can See/The Further You Look, the Less You See (1963)
Gordy 7020 May I Have This Dance/Farewell My Love (1963)
Gordy 7028 The Way You Do the Things You Do/Just Let Me Know (1964)
Gordy 7030 Keep Me/Midnight Johnny (1964)
Gordy 7032 The Girl's Alright with Me/I'll Be in Trouble (1964)
Gordy 7035 Baby, Baby I Need You/Girl (1964)
Gordy 7038 My Girl/Nobody but My Baby (1965)
Gordy 7040 It's Growing/What Love Has Joined Together (1965)
Gordy 7043 Since I Lost My Baby/You've Got to Earn It (1965)
Gordy 7047 My Baby/Don't Look Back (1965)
Gordy 7049 Get Ready/Fading Away (1966)
Gordy 7054 Ain't Too Proud to Beg/You'll Lose a Precious Love (1966)
Gordy 7055 Beauty Is Only Skin Deep/You're Not an Ordinary Girl (1966)
Gordy 7057 I'm Losing You/I Couldn't Cry If I Wanted To (1966)
Gordy 7061 All I Need/Sorry Is a Sorry Word (1967)
Gordy 7063 You're My Everything/I've Been Too Good to You (1967)
Gordy 7065 It's You That I Need/Don't Send Me Away (1967)
Gordy 7068 I Wish It Would Rain/I Truly, Truly Believe (1967)
Gordy 7072 Could Never Love Another/Gonna Give Her All the Love I've Got (1968)
Gordy 7074 Please Return Your Love to Me/How Can I Forget? (1968)
Gordy 7081 Cloud Nine/Why Did She Have to Leave Me? (1968)
Gordy 7082 Silent Night/Rudolph the Red-Nosed Reindeer (1968)
Gordy 7084 Run Away Child, Running Wild/I Need Your Lovin' (1969)
Gordy 7086 Since I've Lost You/Don't Let the Joneses Let You Down (1969)
Gordy 7093 I Can't Get Next to You/Running Away Ain't Gonna Help You (1969)

Gordy 7096 Psychedelic Shack/That's the Way Love Is (1969)
Gordy 7099 Ball of Confusion/It's Summer (1970)
Gordy 7102 Ungena Za Ulimwengo/ (1970)
Sources: Jay Warner, *American Singing Groups*; Jack Sbarbori in *Goldmine,* October 1980.

Temptations (Bayonne, N.J.)

Personnel Robert Moore (lead), John Moore, Teddy Moore, Ken Fakler, Billy Lubek

Notes

The members of this group got together in 1956 and began practicing daily. After about a year of this practicing and playing at local clubs, a relative of Herman Lubinsky, the owner of Savoy Records in Newark, caught their act and recommended them to Savoy. After their tryout, a recording session was quickly scheduled for January 1958.

At that time, Savoy was primarily known for its gospel and blues. The Temptations were a white group, which was also unusual for Savoy. Lubinsky, fearing the impact this might have for his label, removed the Temptations' records from Savoy's catalog.

The Temptations' popularity, however, had grown by 1959 and the group had numerous bookings for their act. In 1961, Billy Lubek had gotten married and the group was then headquartered near Philadelphia. The commute from that area to Bayonne forced Lubek to leave. The group carried on for quite some time after this.

In Ron Italiano's article on this group, he shows Ken Fakler's last name as Fackler. Ronnie also states that this is the original, or first, Temptations group.

Discography

Savoy 1532 Mad At Love/Mr. Juke Box (1958)
Savoy 1550 I Love You, This I Know/Don't You Know? (1958)
Sources: S. Propes, liner notes with the Savoy LP *Doo Wop Delights-The Roots of Rock 'n' Roll*; R. Italiano in *Harmony Tymes.*

Tempters (Los Angeles)

Personnel Homer Green (lead), Donald Miller (1st tenor), Charles Everidge (2d tenor), Harold Murray (baritone), James Monroe Warren (bass)

Notes

This group was also the Preludes and the Youngsters. They formed in 1954 at Los Angeles Manual Trades High School. They sang in the usual school locations appropriate for singing—hallways, restrooms, lunchroom, and so on.

One of the group's first difficulties was choosing a name. Everidge liked Preludes and the others liked Tempters.

They signed up with Empire Records in 1956 and released their first record that year. Despite the name Empire showed on the label for the group, all the songs recorded by them were recorded in two sessions. From the first session came the tunes released as by the Preludes.

After the first session, Homer Green left for the marines and was replaced by Robert Johnson. Donald Miller left and was replaced by Herman Pruitt, former lead of the Calvanes and another friend from Manual Trades.

This re-formed group had a second session from which the Tempters recordings came. The Empire label was not doing well financially and was not in the position to properly promote their recordings. This left the group in limbo and they soon split up.

Tenor Robert Johnson was later a member of the Mad Lads.

Discography
Empire 105 I'll See You Next Fall/I'm Sorry Now (1956)
Source: D. Hinckley and Marv Goldberg in *Yesterday's Memories.*

Tenderfoots (Los Angeles)

Personnel Carl White (tenor), Harold Lewis (tenor), Al Frazier (baritone), John "Sonny" Harris, Turner "Rocky" Wilson (bass)

Notes
This group recorded as, and evolved from, the Lamplighters. They were also related to the Ebbtides, 4 After 5's, Rebels, Rivingtons, and Twisters.

Frazier also sang with the Sharps, the Crenshaws, and the West Coast Mello-Moods. John "Sonny" Harris came from the Feathers on Showtime. Bobby Sanders, a bass, joined later.

According to the liner notes included with the King-Federal-DeLuxe CD *Great Googa Mooga,* the members of the Tenderfoots were Willie Rockwell, Al Frazier, Matt Nelson from the Lamplighters, John "Sonny" Harris, and Charlie White from the Dominoes.

Discography
Federal 12214 Kissing Bug/Watussi Wussi Wo (1955)
Federal 12219 My Confession/Save Me Some Kisses (1955)
Federal 12225 Those Golden Bells/I'm Yours Anyhow (1955)
Federal 12226 Cindy/Sugar Ways (1955)
Source: D. Romanello, G. Povall, and C. Bucola, liner notes with Sequel CD *Great Googa Mooga.*

Terracetones (Newark, N.J.)

Personnel Charles Patrick (lead), Andrew Cheatham, Carl Foushes, Leonard Walker, Patrick Johnson, James Ashley

Notes
This group was from the same vicinity in Newark, New Jersey, as the Monotones. Lead Charles Patrick also sang lead for the Monotones.

Discography

Apt 25016 Words of Wisdom/Ride of Paul Revere (1958)
Sources: Pete Grendysa, liner notes with the Chess CD boxed set *Chess Rhythm & Roll;* Marv Goldberg in *Big Town Review* 1.

Thor-Ables (Los Angeles)

Personnel Willie Davis (lead), Lloyd McCraw (baritone)

Notes

This group was a quartet that splintered off from the Jacks, Cadets, and Rocketeers. The identity of the other personnel is not known.
  The Titanic label belonged to McCraw.

Discography

Titanic 1001 Our Love Song/Get That Bread (1962)
Titanic 1002 My Reckless Heart/Batman and Robin (1962)
Source: Marv Goldberg and Donn Fileti in *DISCoveries,* April 1989.

Three Barons (New York)

Personnel Joe Green (lead), Eddie Parton, Joe Seneca

Notes

This group is also known as the more popular Three Riffs, who recorded for Atlantic and Decca in the 1930s and 1940s.
  Their sides leaned toward the jazz/jive genre, but their music was a precursor to rhythm and blues.

Discography

Savoy 527 Milk Shake Stand/I'd Give My Life (1944)
Source: Marv Goldberg, liner notes with the Savoy LP *Vocal Group Album.*

Three Chuckles/Chuckles (New York)

Personnel Teddy Randazzo (lead), Russ Gilberto (tenor), Tommy Romano (tenor)

Notes

The original group was born in Brooklyn in 1949. Gilberto and Romano were involved in sandlot baseball and had another similar interest—vocal group music. Both were named Tommy, but to avoid confusion, Gilberto began calling himself Russ.
  From 1950 to 1952, they worked clubs across the country. In 1953, Teddy Randazzo joined them. Their act at this time included a great deal of comedy in addition to their music. One evening a man named Cirino Colocrai wandered into the club where they were performing and offered the Chuckles a song he had written.

This was Cirino of Cerino and the Bowties and the song he had written was "Runaround."

In the summer of 1953, the three decided to record and did Cirino a favor by including his "Runaround" as the B side of the disc. The record was first released on Detroit's Great Lakes' subsidiary label, Boulevard. This disc took off in Detroit. RCA purchased the master and the Chuckles became big stars on RCA's subsidiary, X. Many engagements began pouring in, as did TV appearances.

The songwriting team of Cirino and Teddy next came up with "Foolishly." This was big, but not as big as "Runaround." The third record, "Blue Lover," was also a Cirino and Teddy piece. Compared to the previous two, this was a disappointment but maintained the group's popularity.

In 1955, the Chuckles appeared in the Alan Freed film *Rock, Rock, Rock.* The film brought new popularity to the group. It got them bookings at the big clubs in Las Vegas. During their third engagement in Las Vegas, they were contracted to appear in the film *The Girl Can't Help It* with Cary Grant and Elvis Presley.

Upon their return, they cut what was to be their final recording—an album for RCA. Randazzo felt a desire to go out as a solo act and left the Chuckles in 1956. He had a few successes and became interested in publishing and songwriting. He wrote "I'm on the Outside Looking In" and "Out of My Head" for the Imperials. Jackie Farrell replaced Randazzo with the Chuckles. He never recorded with them and their popularity began to fade. Randazzo was still doing well.

Discography

Boulevard 100 At Last You Understand/Run Around (1953)
X 0066 Runaround/At Last You Understand (1954)
X 0095 Foolishly/If You Should Love Again (1955)
X 0134 So Long/You Should Have Told Me (1955)
X 0150 Blue Lover/Realize (1955)
X 0162 Still Thinking of You/Times Two, I Love You (1955)
X 0186 The Funny Little Things We Used to Do/Anyway (1955)
X 0194 Tell Me/And the Angels Sing (1956)
Vik 0216 Gypsy in My Soul/We're Still Holding Hands (1956)
Vik 0232 Fallen Out of Love/Midnight Till Dawn (1956)
Vik 0244 We're Gonna Rock Tonight/Won't You Give Me a Chance? (1956)
Source: Walter Gollender in *Record Exchanger,* February 1973.

Three Dots & a Dash (Los Angeles)

Personnel Jesse Belvin (lead), Undine Harris, Jimmy Huff, Marvin Phillips (bass)

Notes

Pianist Richard Lewis was also a member of this group, as was Betty Jean Washington.

In Jim Dawson's article in the July 1994 issue of *DISCoveries,* which discusses Marvin and Johnny, Tony Allen's name is not mentioned in the discussion of Three Dots and a Dash. This is also the case in Dawson's liner notes accompanying Ace's *Johnny Ace Memorial Album.* However, in the liner notes with the Jesse Belvin Earth

Angel LP *Hang Your Tears Out to Dry,* Dawson states, "At various times, Marvin Phillips, Tony Allen, Jimmy Huff, Richard Lewis, Betty Jean Washington and Undine Harris were part of this group." This is confirmed in the liner notes with the Aladdin/Imperial CD entitled *R&B Vocal Group Magic.*

Discography

Imperial 5115 All That Wine Is Gone/Don't Cry Baby (1951)
Imperial 5164 Let's Do It/I'll Never Love Again (1951)
Sources: Billy Vera, liner notes with the Specialty CD *Jesse Belvin—The Blues Balladeer;* Jim Dawson in *DISCoveries.* Article on Marvin and Johnny.

Three Flames, "Tiger" Haynes & (St. Croix and Barbados)

Personnel "Tiger" Haynes (lead), Roy Testamark, Averill "Rill" Pollard

Notes

The three original members of the Three Flames came from the West Indies. Haynes and Testamark came from St. Croix, and Pollard came from Barbados. Haynes came to the United States in 1919 and the two others came at about this time. They would not meet each other until many years later. In 1939, Haynes was with Plink, Plank and Plunk.

Due to different musical tastes, Haynes left Plink, Plank and Plunk in 1945 and went to New York, where he met Averill Pollard and Roy Tastamark. They joined to form the Three Flames.

In 1946, they were recorded by Sam Goody, then a small record store owner. The four tunes they cut were released on Gotham. They were soon heard by a Columbia representative and cut "Open the Door, Richard" with Columbia.

In 1950, they moved to MGM.

Tastamark died in 1954 and was replaced by Loumell Morgan, the only change in personnel that ever occurred.

In 1956, Haynes was exposed to another side of show business, which he also loved. He appeared in New York in *Finian's Rainbow, Kiss Me Kate,* and so on. He did this while maintaining his vocal performances with the Three Flames.

The Three Flames broke up in 1964 after a long run in the New York club Bon Soir. In May 1964, Haynes appeared in Broadway's *Fade Out, Fade In* with Carol Burnett. Haynes sang and danced, receiving critical acclaim, and was compared to Bill Robinson. Pollard retired to Puerto Rico where he died in 1977.

As rock 'n' Roll became the music of the time, many performers were hurt. Morgan became a case worker for the Department of Social Services for thirteen years. During that time he remained receptive to musical gigs.

Discography

Gotham 106 Blue Moon/Your Issue Is Just Like Tissue (1946)
Gotham 107 Tiger's Blues/Exactly Like You (1946)
Columbia 37268 Open the Door, Richard/Nicholas (1947)

Columbia 37321 Johnny Take My Wife/Viddle De Vop (1947)
Columbia 37935 Cling to Me Baby/Salt Peanuts (1947)
Harmony 1063 Please Stop Playing Those Blues Boy/I'll See You By . . . (1947)
MGM 10741 Chewing Gum Mama/Suffer (1947)
MGM 10853 Goodbye Cornelia Jones/Don't Want to Take That . . . (1950)
Columbia 39078 Succotash Baby/Sky Full of Sunshine (1950)
Columbia 39259 Stick Around/Go 'Way Girl (1951)
Mayfair 5000 I Tried
Source: Pete Grendysa in *Goldmine,* April 1980.

Three Friends (Brooklyn, N.Y.)

Personnel Joe Villa (lead), Frank Stropoli (tenor), Tony Grochowski (2d tenor)

Notes

Before the Three Friends were formed, Stropoli and Grochowski sang with the Heartbeats on Jubilee. The Heartbeats disbanded in 1956 and soon re-formed as the Three Friends.

The Three Friends started that same year, 1956, with their "Blanche."

Grochowski did backup work for the Royalteens, the Chuckles, and the Four Seasons. Villa too was in the Royal Teens.

In Grochowski's interview with Ken Berger and Glenn Slade, he states that there was no bass in the group because of their close association with the Three Chuckles, who had a great influence on them: Teddy Randazzo arranged "Blanche."

The Three Friends on Imperial was a black group and had nothing to do with this Lido group.

Discography

Lido 500 Blanche/Baby I'll Cry (1956)
Lido 502 I'm Only a Boy/Jinx (1957)
Lido 504 Now That You're Gone/Chinese Tea Room (1957)
Brunswick 55032 Now That You're Gone/Chinese Tea Room (1957)
Source: Donn Fileti, liner notes with Relic CD *Tip Top*; Ken Berger and Glenn Slade in *Record Exchanger* 9.

Three Keys (Philadelphia)

Personnel George "Bon Bon" Tunnell (lead), Bob Pease (tenor), "Slim" Furness (baritone)

Notes

This group began playing nightclubs in Philadelphia in 1932 and was later touted as NBC's answer to the Mills Brothers. Unfortunately, things never worked out as well for the Three Keys.

Furness was a member of the Furness Brothers and the Four Keys, who backed Ella Fitzgerald in 1942.

Discography

Columbia 2706 Mood Indigo/Somebody Loses—Somebody Wins (1932)
Brunswick 6388 Jig Time/Someone Stole Gabriel's Horn (1932)
Brunswick 6411 Nagasaki/Fit as a Fiddle (1932)
Brunswick 6423 Basin Street Blues/Wah-Dee-Dah (1932)
Brunswick 6522 Anything for You/That Doggone Dog of Mine (1933)
Vocalion 2523 Heebie Jeebies/Song of the Islands (1933)
Vocalion 2569 I've Found a New Baby/You Can Depend on Me (1933)
Brunswick 6567 Rasputin/Oh, By Jingo (1933)
Vocalion 2730 Jig Time/Someone Stole Gabriel's Horn (1934)
Vocalion 2732 Nagasaki/Fit as a Fiddle (1934)
Vocalion 2744 Basin Street Blues/Wah-Dee-Dah (1934)
Vocalion 2755 Anything for You/That Doggone Dog of Mine (1934)
Vocalion 2765 Rasputin/Oh, By Jingo (1934)
Source: Ray Funk and Doug Seroff, liner notes with the *Human Orchestra* LP; Ferdie Gonzalez, *Disco-File.*

Three Peppers (St. Louis, Mo.)

Personnel Robert Bell, Walter Williams, Toy Wilson

Notes

This was a self-contained vocal-instrumental trio that played the East Coast, made radio appearances, and did motion picture soundies.

Sally Gooding sang lead on several Three Peppers cuts. Ray Branca was another member.

Discography

Variety 523 Get the Gold/Alexander's Rag Time Band (1937)
Variety 554 Yours, All Yours/Smile Up at the Sun (1937)
Variety 590 Swing Out Uncle Wilson/The Ducks' Yas Yas Yas (1937)
Variety 630 If I Had My Way/Serenade in the Night (1937)
Variety 650 Swinging at the Cotton Club/Midnight Ride of Paul Revere (1937)
Vocalion 3803 Swing Out Uncle Wilson/The Ducks' Yas Yas Yas (1937)
Vocalion 3805 Swinging at the Cotton Club/Midnight Ride of Paul Revere (1937)
Vocalion 4169 It Must Be Love/Lisa (1938)
Decca 2239 Down by the Old Mill Stream/Fuzzy Wuzzy (1939)
Decca 2557 Love Grows on the White Oak Tree/Swing Out Uncle Wilson (1939)
Decca 2609 It's a Puzzle to Me/Three Foot Skipper Jones (1939)
Decca 2751 Pepperism/Smile Up at the Sun (1939)
Decca 3342 Tom-Tom Serenade/Hot Dogs (1940)
Decca 8508 Mary's Had a Little Lamb/Was That All I Meant to You? (1941)
Decca 48046 Good Old Tennessee/Just Because I Do (1947)
Sources: Doug Seroff and Ray Funk, liner notes the *Human Orchestra* LP; Ferdie Gonzalez, *Disco-File.*

Three Riffs (Cleveland, Ohio)

Personnel Edward Parton, Howard Green (a.k.a. Joe Green), Joe Seneca (a.k.a. Joe McGee) (d)

Notes

Parton and Seneca (McGhee) met one another in Cleveland in high school. When they decided to go to New York, they changed their name to the Three Riffs.

They also recorded as the Three Barons and backed up Joe Medlin for Atlantic in 1948. They recorded as the Three Barons primarily because of their wish not to be identified due to the strike by the American Federation of Musicians in the early 1940s, which had delayed their releases for Savoy. These Savoy cuts, by the Three Riffs and the Three Barons, were finally released at the same time in 1948.

When Howard Green left, "Bunny" Walker replaced him. Seneca went on to do a great deal of songwriting, such as "Talk to Me, Talk to Me" recorded by "Little" Willie John. He did many TV shows and movies and died in 1996.

Parton became road manager for his aunt, Moms Mabley.

Discography

Decca 7634 Ace in the Hole/It's a Killer Mr. Miller (1939)
Atlantic 867 Bewildered/I'm Glad for Your Sake (1948)
Jubilee 5003 Hot Sweet Potatoes/Rock-A-Bye-Boogie (1949)
Atlantic 868 I Wish I Didn't Love You So/Hard-Ridin' Mama (1949)
Atlantic 871 Pluto You Dog/I'll Be There (1949)
Apollo 1164 Jumpin' Jack/Cherry in My Lemon and Lime (1950)
Apollo 1165 Driftin'/Barbecue Ribs (1950)
Pic 0007 My Baby and Lemon-N-Lime/Don't Jump Off the Bridge (1954)
Variety Music 339 Hey/Since the Day You Came Along
Sources: Marv Goldberg, liner notes with Savoy's *Vocal Group Album*; Joe Senaca, interview by author, 1995; Pete Grendysa in *DISCoveries,* April 1998.

Three Sharps & a Flat (Chicago)

Personnel Jimmy Turner (lead), Thurman "Red" Cooper (1st tenor), Arvid Garrett (2d tenor), Leonard Bibbs (bass)

Notes

This group initially made its reputation on Chicago radio in the 1930s. They were first known as the Three Flats. Garrett met Turner while the two were together at Inglewood High School. They recruited Cooper in 1931 while he was at Samuel Tilden High School.

They joined Duke Ellington's tour in 1934 with the Four Vagabonds, replacing them on their NBC radio show. Following their Ellington period, they appeared at New York's Apollo Theater. Passing up many potentially great engagements, they returned home to Chicago, their families, and radio.

In January 1939, they finally recorded their first record in New York for Decca. They would release eight sides for that label. Following Decca, they recorded four more sides with Columbia's subsidiary label, Okeh.

Ethel Vick sang with the quartet on Decca 7561 "I Am, I Am, Am, Am." After they recorded Turner's "I'm Through," a cover was issued by the Ink Spots, causing Turner to leave. Bass Leonard Bibbs left at this time as well to be replaced briefly by Israel Crosby and then by Leroy Morrison, who remained with the group until their breakup.

In 1942, the entire group was drafted and stationed in Hawaii. They performed as a unit while in the service. They were discharged in 1945, returned to the mainland, and picked up performing where they had left off when drafted. They did many live appearances and radio. They ultimately disbanded in 1952 after a short period of calling themselves Three Sharps and Flats.

Garrett also sang with the Accents on Brunswick.

Discography

Decca 2278 Skinny Do/I'm Getting Sentimental over You (1939)
Decca 7561 I Ain't in Love No More/I Am, I Am, Am Am (1939)
Decca 7569 I'm Through/Swingin' in the Candy Store (1939)
Decca 7581 Poor Little Bug on the Wall/That's No Lie (1939)
Okeh 05857 Rosie in the Garden/Crazy and Worried Blues (1940)
Okeh 05971 That's That Rhythm/Piccolo Stomp (1941)
Hamptone 518/519 Hawaiian War Chant/Yes, Yes, Yes (1941)
Tower 1266 Big Noise of Winnetka/Sometimes I'm Happy (1942)
Sources: Rick Whitesell in *Goldmine,* March 1980; Ferdie Gonzalez, *Disco-File.*

Three Vales (McKeesport, Pa.)

Personnel Ron Blair, Richard Blair, Dick Sedlock

Notes

This group formed in 1956. After many hours of daily practice, they obtained their first job performing at a local club. This led to many other local appearances.

Pittsburgh deejay Jay Michael helped them get an audition with Gale Records. They recorded masters for Gale, but nothing was ever released on that label. Moe Gale had sold their masters to Coral Records, which eventually released a Three Vales disc. The Coral recording did quite well.

Through a little networking late in 1957, they hooked up with Cindy Records in New York. Their second recording was on Cindy 3007.

Ron Blair was drafted in June 1958 and the Three Vales parted. At this time brother Richard Blair moved on to California.

After his service obligation ended, Ron returned to Pittsburgh in 1960. He and Sedlock re-formed the Three Vales, getting Mike Salvi to replace Richard Blair.

Although there was no recording, they toured and entertained at clubs. They remained together for more than a year and finally broke up for good.

Discography

Coral 9-61844 Sure Nuff/Rock-A-Billy Blues (1957)
Cindy 3007 Blue Lights Down Low/Aye Aye Aye (1957)
Source: Carl Janusek and Nancy Janusek in *Story Untold* 10.

Thrillers (Detroit)

Personnel Joe Murphy (lead), Charles Wright (1st tenor), Lawrence Payton (2d tenor), John Raymond Dorsey (baritone), Roquel "Billy" Davis (bass)

Notes

The Thrillers formed in Detroit in 1952. In 1953, they recorded for Joe Von Battle. Although he had many labels, Von Battle named one specifically for this group.

Their first record, I'm Going to Live My Life Alone/Lessy Mae, recorded at Joe Von Battle's facilities, was released several times, first as Thrillers 167 and then as Thrillers 3530 several months later. It also appeared on a JVB demo with an instrumental on the flip. Their second release on Thriller, Mattie, Leave Me Alone/The Drunkard, was released the same month on Big Town.

Shortly after "The Drunkard," Charles Wright and Lawrence Payton left and were replaced by Charles Lee and Crathman "CP" Spencer. At this time, the Thrillers decided to change their name to the Five Jets and would later record for DeLuxe.

There was a second Thrillers vocal group from Detroit at this time, the group that recorded "Lizabeth" for Herald.

Payton, Dorsey, and Davis were cousins.

Discography

Thrillers 167 I'm Going to Live My Life Alone (BD)/Lessy Mae (JM) (1953)
Thrillers 170 Mattie, Leave Me Alone (JM)/The Drunkard (JM) (1953)
Thrillers 3530 I'm Going to Live My Life Alone/Lessy Mae (1953)
Big Town 109 Mattie, Leave Me Alone (JM)/The Drunkard (JM) (1953)
Source: Marv Goldberg in *DISCoveries,* August 1996.

Thrillers, Little Joe & (Philadelphia)

Personnel Falsetto Joe Cook (lead), Farris Hill (tenor), Richard Frazier (tenor), Donald Burnett (baritone), Harry Paschall (bass)

Notes

Early in his musical career, Cook had been with a gospel group, the Evening Star Quartet.

According to Joseph Tortelli's article in *Goldmine,* a girl in Cook's Philadelphia neighborhood gave him the material for the Thrillers' only hit: she was nicknamed "Peanuts"! Interestingly, a careful hearing of Cook's singing in this tune reveals that he sings "peanut." In the same article, Tortelli refers to Harry Paschall as Harry Pascle.

Farris Hill was the lead of Farris Hill and the Madison Brothers. Richard Frazier, Burnett, and Paschall also sang with the Madison Brothers. The latter two members had earlier been with Philadelphia's Belltones on Grand.

Another member of the Thrillers was George Benson.

As a result of quarreling over financial matters, the Thrillers broke up just before "Peanuts" was released in the fall of 1957. Cook later recorded as a solo for Okeh in the late 1950s until the very early 1960s.

Discography

Okeh 7075 This I Know/Let's Do the Slop (1956)
Okeh 7088 Peanuts/Lilly Lou (1957)
Okeh 7094 Lonesome/The Echoes Keep Calling Me (1957)
Okeh 7099 Don't Leave Me Alone/What's Happened to Your Halo? (1958)
Okeh 7107 It's Too Bad We Had to Say Goodbye/Mine (1958)
Epic 9293 It's Too Bad We Had to Say Goodbye/Mine (1958)
Enjoy 2011 Peanuts and Popcorn/Chicken Little Boo Boo (1958)
Okeh 7116 Cherry—Pt. 1/Pt. 2 (1959)
Okeh 7136 Please Don't Go/Stay (1960)
Okeh 7140 Public Opinion/Run Little Girl (1961)
20th Century 1214 One More Time/For Sentimental Reasons (1961)
Reprise 20142 No, No I Can't Stop/Peanuts (1963)
Rose 835 How Am I Doing?/I'll Do Anything (1963)
Sources: Marv Goldberg and Marcia Vance, liner notes with Okeh *Rhythm & Blues* CD; Joseph Tortelli in *Goldmine*.

Tigers, Little Julian Herrera & (Los Angeles)

Personnel Julian Herrera (lead), Ray Estrada

Notes

In the liner notes accompanying the Dig CD *Legendary Masters-4,* it is stated that Dig owner Johnny Otis told writer Jim Dawson that the Tigers included some members from the Premiers as well as Estrada.

Ray Estrada later joined Frank Zappa's Mothers of Invention. In Otis's book, *Upside Your Head,* Johnny tells a story from many years ago of a probation officer who was looking for a Ron Gregory. When Otis was shown a picture of this man, he recognized Herrera. Apparently he was a Hungarian Jew from the East Coast who had run away from home and was taken in by a woman in east Los Angeles! The story, which was told several years earlier to Dawson by Otis, clarifies the East Coast as Massachusetts and differs slightly from the above account.

Discography

Starla 6 I Remember Linda/True Fine (1957)
(Note: Although Herrera cut many other discs, none of the labels credited the Tigers or any other vocal group. Thus the Starla disc is the only one shown here.)
Source: Jim Dawson, liner notes with the Dig CD *Legendary Masters–4*; Donn Fileti, liner notes with the Relic CD *Best of Dig*.

Titans (Los Angeles)

Personnel Charles Wright, Sam Barnett (1st tenor), Curtis McNair (2d tenor), Larry Green (baritone)

Notes

In 1956, Larry Green moved to Los Angeles from the East Coast to perform solo. There he heard other soloists and suggested getting together to form a vocal group. Green had previously been with the Four Dots and Heartbreakers who recorded for RCA. Charles Wright had been with the Twilighters on Cholly.

They got themselves a manager, who obtained a recording contract with Vita Records in January 1957. After two releases, they moved to Specialty Records (where Sonny Bono was the A&R man). They cut five records for Specialty, including one on which they backed Don and Dewey.

After McNair's father became ill, he dropped out and the group remained a trio.

In Donn Fileti's liner notes with Relic's *Class* CD, he refers to McNair as the Titans' lead singer.

Discography

Vita 148 So Hard to Laugh/Rhythm and Blues (1957)
Vita 158 G'Wan Home Calypso/Look What You're Doing Baby (1957)
Specialty 614 Sweet Peach/Free and Easy (1957)
Specialty 625 Don't You Just Know It?/Can It Be? (1957)
Specialty 632 Arlene/Love Is a Wonderful Thing (1958)
Class 244 No Time/Tootin' Tutor (1959)
Fidelity 3016 Everybody Happy/What Have I Done? (1960)
Sources: Marv Goldberg in *Yesterday's Memories* 10; Donn Fileti's liner notes with Relic's *Class* CD.

Tones, Dusty Brooks & (Los Angeles)

Personnel Lucius "Dusty" Brooks (lead), Juanita Brown, Joe Alexander

Notes

This group is also known as Dusty Brooks and the Four Tones.

Discography

Columbia 30236 Once There Lived a Fool/Cryin' to Myself (1951)
Columbia 30241 I Ain't Gonna Worry No More/Shadow of the Blues (1951)
Source: R. Ferlingere's *A Discography of R&B and R&R Vocal Group.*

Tonettes (Bronx, N.Y.)

Personnel Diana Sanchez, Sylvia Sanchez, Josephine "Josie" Allen

Notes

The members of this group were formerly the Claremonts on Apollo who did "Why Keep Me Dreaming." Apollo executive Charles Merenstein formed the Doe label and then took the Claremonts to Doe and renamed them the Tonettes. Josie Allen sang lead on "Oh What a Baby" and Diana Sanchez performed lead on "Howie."

The Tonettes also provided background for Vince Castro on "Bong Bong."

Discography

Doe 101 Oh What a Baby/Howie (1958)
ABC 9905 Oh What a Baby/Howie (1958)
Source: Donn Fileti, liner notes with the Relic LP *Best of Apollo Records.*

Toppers (Brooklyn, N.Y.)

Personnel Henry Austin (lead), Jerry Halfhide (tenor), Sam Fickling (tenor), Fred Williams (baritone), Vernon Britton (bass)

Notes

This group began in the early 1950s in a Brooklyn junior high school. Fred Williams's uncle was chosen to be the manager and was known as "Jelly Roll." He immediately landed the Toppers a contract with Jubilee. Henry Austin joined last, as lead. Baby Let Me Bang Your Box/You're Laughing 'Cause I'm Crying was cut for Jubilee.

Austin, Britton, and Williams later were members of the Hurricanes and the Memos on Memo.

Despite their name, this Toppers group had no relation to any other Toppers (Imperial or Savoy). *See* Hurricanes and Memos

Discography

Jubilee 5136 Baby Let Me Bang Your Box/You're Laughing 'Cause I'm Crying (1954)
Source: Marv Goldberg in *Record Collector's Monthly* 43.

Toppers, Steve Gibson & (Los Angeles)

Personnel Jimmy Springs (lead), Emmett Matthews (2d tenor), David Patillo (2d tenor), Romaine Brown (baritone), Steve Gibson (bass)

Notes

This group was originally known as the Four Toppers, a West Coast self-contained group that formed in 1938. They played local spots in California until they realized they could do better financially in New York. They went on a tour of major cities that ended in New York City. They ultimately became the Five Red Caps.

Discography

Savoy 599 If Money Grew on Trees/Palace of Stone (1948)
Savoy 656 I'm All Alone/I'm Living for You (1948)
Regent 130 I'm Living for You/Nat's Boogie Woogie (1948)
Sources: Marv Goldberg and Pete Grendysa in *Yesterday's Memories*; Marv Goldberg, liner notes with Savoy's *Vocal Group Album.*

Toppers, Bobby Mitchell & (New Orleans)

Personnel Bobby Mitchell (d) (lead), Lloyd Bellaire (1st tenor), Joseph Butler (baritone), Frank ——— (bass)

Notes

This group was primarily an instrumental ensemble. The only voice heard on most of their recordings is that of Bobby Mitchell. He was nice enough to give the group some billing despite the fact that on the majority of their sides, they simply accompanied him with their instruments.

Interestingly, the entire group did perform vocal backup for "Smiley" Lewis and "Guitar Slim."

Mitchell teamed with Gabriel Fleming in 1954 and recorded as the King Toppers, an instrumental group with Clarence "Frogman" Henry.

Mitchell later went back to the studio, alone, and recorded "Nothing Sweet as You."

Discography

Imperial 5236 I'm Crying/Rack 'Em Back (1953)
Imperial 5250 4 X 11 = 44/One Friday Morning (1953)
Imperial 5270 Baby's Gone/Sister Lucy (1954)
Imperial 5282 Angel Child/School Boy Blues (1954)
Imperial 5295 Wedding Bells Are Ringing/Meant for Me (1954)
Imperial 5309 I'm a Young Man/She Couldn't Be Found (1954)
Imperial 5326 I Wish I Knew/Nothing Sweet as You (1955)
Imperial 5346 I Cried/I'm in Love (1955)
Source: Jonas Bernholm, liner notes with the Nightrain CD *I'm Gonna Be a Wheel Someday.*

Topps (Washington, D.C.)

Personnel Robert Evans (lead), Albert "Midge" Evans (1st tenor), Jerome Patterson (2d tenor), Leroy Henderson (baritone), Fred Holmes (bass)

Notes

This group evolved from the Heartbreakers on RCA. After the Heartbreakers split up in 1953, Evans and Holmes formed the Topps and traveled to New York from Washington, D.C. There they met with Joe Duncan, who introduced them to Danny Robinson.

Leroy Henderson had been with the Serenaders who were the predecessors to the Rainbows in the District of Columbia.

Following several failures on Red Robin, two members were drafted in 1955. This meant the end of the Topps.

Discography

Red Robin 126 Tippin'/What Do You Do (1953)
Red Robin 131 I've Got a Feeling/Won't You Come Home Baby (1953)

Red Robin (UNR) Ain't It Good (Mm, Baby I Love You So)
Red Robin (UNR) Young Girls
Source: Donn Fileti, liner notes with the Relic CD *Red Robin*.

Townsmen (New York)

Personnel Bill Witt (lead), Ernest Stevens (1st tenor), William "Bubba" Moore (2d tenor), Brother Bossay McKinney (baritone), Robert Stewart (bass)

Notes

Bill Witt also sang lead for the Rocketones on Melba. By 1959, he joined the Paragons on Winley where he replaced their lead, Julius McMichael.

  Because nothing was happening in the early 1960s for Witt, he joined the Townsmen. In 1963, they recorded their disc for Herald. From Herald, they went to Columbia and cut a record for them in 1965. After this, Witt joined the armed forces. He later rejoined the Paragons for the 1970s revival.

Discography

Herald 585 Just a Little Bit/Is It All Over? (1963)
Columbia 43207 Please Don't Say Goodbye/Gotta Get Moving (1965)
Sources: Bob Ferlingere, *Discography of R&B* and *R&R Vocal Groups*; Marcia Vance and Phil Groia in *Yesterday's Memories* 2.

Townsmen (New York)

Personnel Lewis Lymon (lead), Luis Vasquez, Ralph Ramos, McDuffy Swaggart, Bobby Rivera

Notes

This group auditioned for the manager of the Copa Cabana nightclub in Manhattan. He made them an offer, but group members preferred another offer they had received and went to PJ records, where they recorded their only disc.

  The record was a flop and Louie decided to go back and finish high school. Then he enlisted in the armed forces.

  Phil Groia, in *They All Sang on the Corner,* refers to Swaggart as Duffy McSwaggart. Joe Sicurella's article shows Vasquez's first name as Lewis and does not even mention Bobby Rivera.

Discography

PJ 1340/1341 That's All I'll Ever Need (LL)/I Can't Go (LL) (1963)
Sources: Phil Groia, *They All Sang on the Corner*; Joe Sicurella in *Big Town Review.*

Travelers (Bronx, N.Y.)

Personnel Frank Lopez (lead), Francis "Frenchie" Concepción (1st tenor)

Notes

Concepción sang with the Wrens, famous for "Come Back My Love."
  Concepción performed lead for the Wrens on "Serenade of the Bells."

Discography

Andex 1086 Lenora/Betty Jean (1957)
Andex 3-4006 Why/Teen Age Machine Age (1957)
Andex 2011 I'll Be Home for Christmas/Katie the Kangar (1958)
Andex 4012 The Whole World in His Hands/Green Town Girl (1958)
Source: Bob Ferlingere, *A Discography of R&B and R&R Vocal Groups.*

Travelers, Roger & (New Haven, Conn.)

Personnel Roger Koob (lead), Billy Koob, Joe Vece, Johnny Roddi

Notes

The Koob brothers' first group was the Premiers on Alert. Then they recorded for Fury and Rust. Finally they became the Frontiers on Phillips.

Discography

Ember 1079 You're Daddy's Little Girl/Just Gonna Be That Way (1961)
Source: Donn Fileti, liner notes with Relic's *Ember* CD.

Treble Chords (Bronx, N.Y.)

Personnel Ercote Gaudioso (lead), Anthony Cacase, Al Diaco, Anthony DiBari

Notes

This group came together in the Bronx in 1957, winning several amateur contests and appearing at many local nightspots.
  They came to the attention of Decca Records through their appearances at one of these nightspots.
  They recorded four tunes for Decca in July 1959 and in 1961 broke up. That same year, Jay Ferrara and Anthony Biletto from the Monterays (nonrecording) united with Diaco and Gaudioso of the Treble Chords. They added Anthony Vizzari as lead. Frank Raia was also with the Treble Chords briefly.
  DiBari joined Nino and the Ebbtides.
  Cousins Records in the Bronx had them record four discs, none of which were ever released.
  In 1963, Emil Sachs (Concepts on ABC Paramount) replaced Gaudioso.

Discography

Decca 31015 My Little Girl/Teresa (1959)
Source: Liner notes with the Laurie CD on Ace, *Echoes of the Past.*

Tremaines (New York)

Personnel Milton Turner (lead), Clive Williams (1st tenor), Bill Fredericks (2d tenor), Bill Atkins (baritone), Ray Hayes (bass)

Notes

According to Bob Hyde's *Old Town Doo Wop 2–3* CD liner notes, the Tremaines and the Pla-Bac/Paradise Packards were the same group.

Camelots' bass Julius Williams was a member of the Tremaines.

Discography

Cash 100 Jingle Jingle/Moon Shining Bright (1958)
Val 100/101 Jingle Jingle/Moon Shining Bright (1958)
Old Town 1051 Jingle Jingle/Moon Shining Bright (1958)
Kane 007/008 Wonderful, Marvelous/Heavenly (1959)
V-Tone 507 Wonderful, Marvelous/Heavenly (1960)
Source: Bob Hyde, liner notes with the Ace CD *Old Town Doo Wop 2–3.*

Trend-Ells (Baltimore, Md.)

Personnel Jerry Passion, Jerry Donahue, Lee Cornell, Jimmy Harrison

Notes

Prior to forming as the Trend-Ells, this group was behind Ernie Lee Warren as the white version of the Cardinals.

Discography

Tilt 779 I'm So Young/Don't You Hear Me Calling Baby (1961)
Source: P. Chaney and R. Italiano, liner notes with Plaza's *Come Back My Love.*

Trinidads (Chicago)

Personnel Hosea Brown (tenor), Charles Davis (tenor), Charles Colbert Jr. (1st tenor), Norman Prince (baritone), Claude Forch (bass)

Notes

According to Bob Pruter's book *Doowop . . . The Chicago Scene,* the baritone is Norman Price.

Davis and Colbert were cousins.

Hosea Brown left after the recordings and was replaced by someone whose last name was Kitchen.

Colbert later joined the Daylighters. Davis joined the Dukays in 1962, replacing Gene Chandler as lead.

Discography

Formal 1005 Don't Say Goodbye/On My Happy Day (1959)

Formal 1006 When We're Together/One Lonely Night (1960)
Source: Bob Pruter, *Doowop . . . The Chicago Scene.*

Triumphs, Tico & (Queens, N.Y.)

Personnel Paul Simon (lead), Mickey Borack, Marty Cooper, Howie Beck

Notes

It has never been confirmed, but this is supposed to be the same Paul Simon who found great success with Art Garfunkle.

Discography

Madison 169 Motorcycle/I Don't Believe Them (1960)
Amy 835 Motorcycle/I Don't Believe Them (1961)
Amy 845 Express Train/Wild Power (1962)
Amy 860 Get Up and Do the Wobble/Cry, Little Boy, Cry (1962)
Sources: Ed Engel in *Harmony Times*-2; Jay Warner's *American Singing Groups.*

Trojans (St. Louis, Mo.)

Personnel Art Lassiter, George Green, Murray Green, Douglas Martin

Notes

When his 1952 Studebaker automobile broke down while he was driving through St. Louis, Lassiter decided to remain in that locale. He soon met the Green brothers, Murray and George, along with Douglas Martin. They invited Lassiter to join their group, the Bel Airs. In 1956, the Bel Airs changed their name to the Trojans. Following their RPM disc, the Trojans became the Rockers (1956), who later recorded for the Federal label. The Trojans' mentor was Ike Turner.

Discography

RPM 446 As Long as I Have You/I Wanna Make Love to You (1956)
Source: Charlie Horner, *Vocal Group Guide to St. Louis.*

Tropicals (New Orleans)

Personnel Herbert Myers, Germaine Rixner, Vontell Lang, Brad Smith, Gloria Allen

Notes

Although Specialty Records was headquartered in Los Angeles, label management found the Tropicals in New Orleans and recorded them there. They had but one session, on October 28, 1956.

Specialty never released anything by the Tropicals and we have Donn Fileti's persistence with Specialty's management to thank for the pleasure of hearing the Tropicals' "Sweet Sixteen," originally released on Relic's Specialty Golden Groups series and more recently on Specialty's Golden Groups series on the Relic CD.

The names listed above are apparently the only information Donn Fileti uncovered in Specialty's files. It's also curious that in Marv Goldberg's interview in *DISCoveries* magazine with Billy Tircuit of the Monitors and the Moonbeams (and several others), Tircuit told Marv emphatically that it was a gentleman named "Vontell Lang" who sang with him in the Monitors and the Moonbeams.

Sources: Donn Fileti, liner notes with Relic's Specialty CD *Golden Groups*; Marv Goldberg, interview by author, May 9, 1998.

True Tones (Washington, D.C./Baltimore, Md.)

Personnel Ronald Henderson, Andrew Lawyer (1st tenor), Gene Williams, John Johnson, Kenny Willis

Notes

Lawyer was also a member of the Original Drifters and the Spaniels.

This True Tones group also backed "Pookie" Hudson when he temporarily became a solo act after briefly leaving the Spaniels.

Discography

Monument 4501 Honey, Honey/Whirlwind (1958)
Felsted 8625 Singing Waters/Blushing Bride (1961)
Spot 1115 Lovin' from My Baby/Never Had a Chance (1964)
Josie 950 That's Love/He's Got the Nerve (1966)
Josie 1003 That's Love/He's Got the Nerve (1969)
Source: Alan Lee in *Yesterday's Memories* 8.

Tuneweavers (Boston)

Personnel Margo Sylvia (d) (lead), Gilbert Lopez (tenor), Charlotte Davis, Johnny Sylvia (bass)

Notes

Following his hitch in the army in 1956, Gilbert Lopez convinced his sister, Margo Sylvia, to join him in a singing duo in Boston. Sylvia's husband and Gilbert's brother John were soon added. Charlotte Davis, another family member, joined as well. They initially called themselves the Toneweavers, but a local disc jockey mistakenly introduced their disc as by the Tuneweavers. This seemed to stick with listeners and it became their name.

Originally they performed material from other groups. Then Margo presented a tune she had written called "Happy Happy Birthday" to the group and they performed it at their live appearances. A local record executive who heard it liked it enough to have the Tuneweavers record it on Casa Grande, where it nearly made the top of the charts. It took several months to be discovered, but discovered it was. It was then leased to the Chess/Checker organization.

But little success followed "Happy Happy Birthday," and the group became inactive. Margo continued to appear at supper clubs.

Discography

Casa Grande 4037 Happy, Happy Birthday Baby/Ol' Man River (1957)
Checker 672 Happy, Happy Birthday Baby/Ol' Man River (1957)
Checker 672 Happy, Happy Birthday Baby/Yo Yo Walk (instrumental) (1957)
Checker 880 Old Man River/Tough Enough (1957)
Casa Grande 4038 I Remember Dear/Pamela Jean (1957)
Casa Grande 101 Little Boy/Please Baby Please (1958)
Casa Grande 4040 I'm Cold/There Stands My Love (1958)
Casa Grande 3038 My Congratulation Baby/This Can't Be Love (1960)
Checker 1007 Your Skies of Blue/Congratulations On Your Wedding (1962)
Sources: Dennis Garvey in *Goldmine*; Adam Komorowski, liner notes with Instant's *Goodnight Sweetheart Goodnight* CD.

Turbans (Oakland, Calif.)

Personnel Charles Fitzpatrick (lead), Berlin Carpenter (1st tenor), Al Williams (2d tenor), Willie Roland (baritone), Andre Goodwin (bass)

Notes

The West Coast Turbans changed their name to the Sharptones. The liner notes with Specialty's *Doo Wop from Dolphin's of Hollywood* CD state that Bob Jefferies may have been in this group.

Harry "Little" Caesar may have also sang with the group.

Discography

Money 209 No No Cherry/Tick Tock A-Woo (1955)
Money 209 No No Cherry/The Goose Is Gone (1955)
Money 211 When I Return/Emily (1955)
Sources: Billy Vera, liner notes with the Specialty CD *Doo Wop from Dolphin's of Hollywood*; unsigned liner notes with the Aladdin/Imperial CD *R&B Vocal Group Magic*.

Turbans (Philadelphia)

Personnel Al Banks (d) (lead), Mathew Platt (tenor), Charlie Williams (baritone), Andrew "Chet" Jones (bass)

Notes

The group shown above recorded twelve sides for Herald from 1955 to 1957. In 1957, they became the Quadrells on Whirlin' Disc.

Donald Jones, Chet's brother, often filled in for Charlie Williams, who was frequently absent when the group was on tour.

Donald Jones, Edward Cole, and James Jenkins joined Andrew Jones on a later Turbans recording on Red Top (Relic CD liner notes).

Al Banks, Chet Jones, Earl Worsham, and baritone John Christian re-formed in 1959.

Banks spent several years with Harold Melvin and the Blue Notes.

The Red Top and Roulette groups consisted of Banks, Chet Jones, Worsham, and Christian. Donn Fileti's liner notes with the Turbans' CD refer to Mike Sweeney, who states that the Red Top group was not the same assemblage shown above, with Andrew Jones, Donald Jones, Edward Cole, and James Jenkins performing for Red Top.

The Parkway group removes Jones and adds Reggie Price (Universals on Southern and Mark-X). The Imperial group (1961-1962) deletes Reggie Price and adds James Williams and "Sonny" Gordon (from the Angels on Grand).

Discography

Herald 458 When You Dance/Let Me Show You (1955)
Herald 469 I'll Always Watch over You/Sister Sookey (1955)
Herald 478 I'm Nobody's/B-I-N-G-O (1956)
Herald 486 It Was a Nite Like This/All of My Love (1956)
Herald 495 Valley of Love/Bye Bye Bye (1957)
Herald 510 Congratulations/The Wadda-Do (1957)
Red Top 115 I Promise You Love/Curfew Time (1960)
Roulette 4281 Bad Man/Diamonds and Pearls (1960)
Roulette 4326 I'm Not Your Fool Anymore/Three Friends (1961)
Parkway 820 Golden Rings/When You Dance (1961)
Imperial 5807 Six Questions/Lament of Silver Gulch (1961)
Imperial 5828 Clicky Clicky Clack/This Is My Story (1962)
Imperial 5847 I Wonder/The Damage Is Done (1962)
Sources: Donn Fileti, liner notes with Relic's *Herald* CD; Marv Goldberg in *DISCoveries.*

Turks (Los Angeles)

Personnel Gaynel Hodge (lead), Delmar Wilburn (1st tenor), Jody Jefferson (2d tenor), Baritone/Alex Hodge (baritone/bass)

Notes

This group of Los Angeles singers originally called themselves the Flamingos in the early 1950s. At that time, the group consisted of Cornel Gunter, Gaynel Hodge, Alex Hodge, Jody Jefferson, and Curtis Williams (Gunter was twelve or thirteen years old at the time). This group didn't stay together very long. Williams left to form the Penguins and Gunter left to form the Flairs. Jefferson simply left.

Following the first session on Money, Jody Jefferson left and was replaced by Carl Green (writer of the flip of the Penguins' Earth Angel monster, "Hey Señorita").

The Hodge brothers joined up with Tony Williams, David Lynch, and Herb Reed—this was the Platters! They had three sessions for Federal.

At the time of their third session, Gaynel Hodge left for the Hollywood Flames, Alex Hodge just left, and Zola Taylor, Gaynel's girlfriend, was just joining the Platters.

By mid-1955, Gaynel left the Hollywood Flames and recruited brother Alex, Jody Jefferson, and Delmer Wilburn (from the Combo Squires). This was the first formation of the Turks. They recorded for John Dolphin.

At their first session, they cut four songs that, with some interesting games, turned into three releases. Because these moves created difficulties between Hodge and Dolphin, Dolphin released one last record by the Turks on his Cash label, It Can't Be True/Wagon Wheels, which in reality was the Hollywood Flames with Bobby Day at lead! As a result, they left for Bally Records and recorded "This Heart of Mine" at Bally.

Because their Dolphin and Bally discs did nothing, they went to Keen. Wilburn and Green left. This group then became the Hodge brothers, Tommy "Buster" Williams, and Jesse Belvin. Poor sales caused Dolphin to assemble another Turks' group, which included David Ford from the Hollywood Flames.

Later, the Hodge brothers and Curtis Williams regrouped to call themselves the Turks and cut "Rocksville USA" for Class Records.

Discography

Money 211 Emily (GH) (1955)
Money 215 I'm a Fool (GH)/I've Been Accused (GH) (1956)
Cash 1042 It Can't Be True (GH)/Wagon Wheels (BB) (1956)
Bally 1017 Why Did You? (GH)/This Heart of Mine (GH) (1956)
Specialty 580 Hurt Me/Jump Jack Jump (Wynona Carr & the Turks) (1956)
Knight 2005 I'm a Fool/It Can't Be True (1958)
Keen 4016 Fathertime (GH)/Okay (GH) (1958)
Class 256 Rocksville, USA (BW)/Hully Gully (1959)
Ball 001 Emily/My Soul (Seniors) (1960)
Imperial 5783 I'm a Fool/It Can't Be True (1961)
Source: Marv Goldberg in *Yesterday's Memories.*

Tuxedos (Los Angeles)

Personnel Stan Beverly (lead), Charles Taggart (1st tenor), Maudice Giles (2d tenor), Joe Lewis (baritone), Nathaniel "Buster" Williams (bass)

Notes

This group also recorded as the Saxons, Hollywood Saxons, Capris, and Portraits. After recording as the Portraits on Capitol, Lewis, Beverly, and Taggart joined forces with Giles and Williams to record for George Matola, this time on Forte as the Tuxedos.

Discography

Forte 1414 Yes It's True (SB)/Trouble, Trouble (SB/JL/CT) (1960)
Source: Marv Goldberg and Rick Whitesell in *Yesterday's Memories* 11.

Twilighters (Baltimore, Md.)

Personnel Bob Richardson (lead), William Pierce (1st tenor), Deroy Green (2d tenor), Melvin Jennings (baritone), Earl Williams (bass)

Notes

The Twilighters came from the Old Town district of Baltimore.

In 1953, the group recorded three tunes at a Washington, D.C., studio. Two of them were released on the Marshall label and the other, "Longing for You," was released in the 1970s on Roadhouse Records.

After an argument with their manager, as well as poor sales, they broke up.

Deroy Green was drafted into the service. When he was discharged, he recorded with the Cool Gents on CeeJay (Bronx, N.Y.). Lillian Claiborne was their manager.

Discography

Marshall 702 Please Tell Me You're Mine/Wondering (1953)
Source: Les Moskowitz in *Yesterday's Memories.*

Twilighters (Bronx, N.Y.)

Personnel Larry Gales (d) (lead), Bill Lindsay (2d tenor), John E. Johnson (baritone), Donald Redd (bass)

Notes

This group started in 1951 in the Morrisania section of the Bronx in New York City. Group members attended Morris High School. A teacher, Herb Miller, knew Jerry Blaine of Jubilee/Josie and got them a recording session as the Starlings, which was the first release on Josie. They later became the Starlings on Dawn and then the Twilighters on MGM.

Gales also sang with the Supremes on Old Town.

Lindsay was with Dean Barlow and the Crickets as well as the Cadillacs.

Discography

MGM 55011 Little Did I Dream (LG)/Gotta Get on the Train (LG) (1955)
MGM 55014 Half Angel (BL)/Lovely Lady (BL) (1956)
Sources: G. Povall, liner notes with the Sequel CD *Jubilee & Josie R&B Vocal Groups, 1*; Marv Goldberg in *DISCoveries,* January 1995.

Twilighters (Atlanta)

Personnel Richard Hunter (lead), Julius High Jr. (2d tenor), Russell Davis Jr. (baritone), Milton Howard Hillsman Jr. (bass)

Notes

It's not clear how the Twilighters from Atlanta got to Specialty Records in Los Angeles, but the Specialty disc below was recorded in Atlanta on February 15, 1955. It is stated in Jim Dawson's liner notes accompanying Ace's CD *Ebb Story–2* that the Atlanta Twilighters (same personnel) were the Ebb group (117) and that they originally came to Los Angeles from Atlanta, Georgia, to record for Specialty. *(Note:* Another inconsistency!)

Like many other groups of the mid-1950s, they performed locally and sang the hit R&B tunes of the day prior to their one release.

Following the Specialty and Ebb releases, which went nowhere, they went their own ways. Their seven-year singing experience provided no financial rewards and the Twilighters group finally broke up.

Discography

Specialty 548 It's True (RH)/Wah-Bop-Sh-Wah (JH) (1955)
Ebb 117 Live Like a King/Pride and Joy (1957)
Sources: Marv Goldberg in *Whiskey, Women, and . . .* 1; Donn Fileti, liner notes with the Specialty LP *Golden Groups*; Jim Dawson, liner notes with the Ace CD *Ebb Story-2*.

Twilighters, Tony & (Philadelphia)

Personnel Anthony "Tony" Maresco (lead), Anthony Barbella, Michael Bongiorno, Bernard Mastragostino

Notes

Maresco's second group was Tony and the Dynamics. They later became Anthony and the Sophomores.

Discography

Red Top 127 The Key to My Heart/Yes or No (1960)
Source: Donn Fileti, liner notes with the Relic LP *Best of Red Top.*

Twilights, Teddy & (Philadelphia)

Personnel Fred "Weasel" Cohen (lead), John Williams (1st tenor), Larry Williams (2d tenor/baritone), Ben Hart (bass)

Notes

This group began in the early 1950s in Philadelphia. In 1953, they became known as the Deckers. In 1954, Larry Williams entered the army and was replaced by Curtis Barnes. Williams came home from the military in 1957 and the group got themselves an opportunity to record for NAR Records. Just after this first recording, Barnes left to join a spiritual group.

They soon met Jack Green, who liked the Deckers and formed the Yeadon label. "Sincerely with All My Heart" was then released. Because Green was unfamiliar with the payola and promotion end of the business, little was done to promote their disc.

They next went to Swan Records in 1958 as the Buddies but were unsuccessful. Swan management told them that Sam Conners's poor lead voice was holding them back. Through their attorney, they fired Conners and got Fred Cohen from the Mohawks.

As a test-marketing ploy, they cut a record on which one side was by Teddy and the Twilights and the flip was by the Tiffanies. Sales for the Twilights' side were greater, and they adopted the name Teddy and the Twilights.

They recorded several more sides for Swan and in 1963 they called it quits.

Discography

Swan 4102 Goodbye to Love/Woman Is a Man's Best Friend (1962)
Swan 4115 Runnin' around Town/You Gotta Be Alone to Cry (1962)
Swan 4126 Bimini Bimbo/I'm Just Your Clown (1962)
Source: Charlie Horner and Steve Applebaum in *Yesterday's Memories* 8.

Twilights, Tony Richards & (Brooklyn, N.Y.)

Personnel Tony Passalacqua (lead), Donnie Milo, Joe Gugliaro, Joe Agugliaro

Notes

Passalacqua was from the Fascinators. Milo and Gugliaro were from the Clusters, and Agugliaro was from the Markels. The four joined forces in 1960 when their previous groups broke up.

This group recorded a version of "September Song" that remains unreleased at this writing.

Discography

Colpix 178 Please Believe in Me/Paper Boy (1960)
Source: Bob Diskin in *Record Collector's Monthly,* August 9, 1990.

Twiliters (McKeesport, Pa.)

Personnel Glenn Dorsey (lead), Delores Johnson (1st tenor), Bob Manual (2d tenor), Richard Covington (baritone), Ernie Holt (bass)

Notes

This group first assembled as a trio in September 1954. Bob Manual soon brought two junior high schoolmates of his into the group. They initially named themselves the Fascinators and began serious practice each day. They hooked up with talent scout Bill Ramsey, who coached them on vocals as well as stage presence. Many personnel changes occurred during the next several years. By 1959, they began calling themselves the Twiliters and were composed of the group reflected above.

They met record producer Bob Vogelsberger whose ambition it was to manage a vocal group. Vogelsberger arranged to have them record four sides, but none were ever released. They soon hooked up with record producer Nick Cenci, who was the owner of Nix Records. Nix 102 and 103 were recorded in 1961.

Jules Kruspir, who initially guided the Marcels, also a Pittsburgh vocal group, took an interest in the Twiliters and had them record for his Paloma label. The Paloma discs failed and bass Ernie Holt left to be replaced by Sylvester Brooks, who in 1956 became the lead of the Smoothtones, following Alfred Gaitwood's departure. When Delores Johnson left, Ernie Holt rejoined the Twiliters.

Hoping to capitalize on the British invasion and the Beatles phenomenon, the group recorded "My Beatle Haircut," which was released on Roulette in 1963. This fared well locally and got the Twiliters many bookings in their area.

In 1964, Dorsey developed a thyroid condition that necessitated surgery. The operation affected his vocal chords and left Dorsey unable to sing. This ended the singing career of the Twiliters. In two years Dorsey recovered and in 1966 Dorsey and Manual formed another vocal group they called the Persians. After many personnel changes, they eventually became the Joneses.

Discography

Nix 102 Hey There/Caused by You (1961)
Nix 103 Back to School/Love Bandit (1961)
Chess 1803 Scratchin'/She Needs a Guy (1961)
Paloma 100 Sweet Lips/You Better Make It (1963)
Roulette 4546 My Beatle Haircut/Sweet Lips (1963)
Source: Carl Janusek in *Echoes of the Past* 35.

Twi-Lites (Chicago)

Personnel Calvin Baron, Waymon Bryant, Matthew Perkins, Louis Pritchett

Notes

Baron also sang with the Moroccos and the Cosmic Rays. The others had previously been with the Four Gents.
Source: Bob Pruter, *Doo Wop . . . The Chicago Scene.*

Twisters (Los Angeles)

Personnel Carl White, Al Frazier, John Sonny Harris, Turner "Rocky" Wilson

Notes

This group also recorded as the Ebbtides, 4 After 5's, Rebels, Rivingtons, and Tenderfoots.

Discography

APT 25045 Come Go with Me/Pretty Little Girl (1960)
Gemini 101 Truly/Run Little Sheba (1961)
Sun-Set 501 This Is the End/Please Come Back (1961)
Capitol 4451 Dancing Little Clown/Turn the Page (1961)
Sources: Jack Sbarbori in *Record Exchanger* 16; Art Turco in *Record Exchanger* 28; Jeff Kreiter, *Group Collector's Record Guide.*

Tymes (Philadelphia)

Personnel George Williams Jr. (lead), Al "Caesar" Berry (1st tenor), George Hilliard (2d tenor), Norm Burnett (baritone), Donald Banks (bass)

Notes

The group began in 1955, when Burnett met Hilliard at a summer camp. They sang with many individuals after sharing their desire to form a vocal group. They finally hooked up with Berry, Banks, and George Williams Jr. in 1960. This was when they began calling themselves the Latineers.

In 1963, Philadelphia radio station WDAS conducted its annual talent hunt. A scout heard the Latineers performing at this event and recommended that they go to Cameo/Parkway for an audition.

The audition was successful. At this time the group was asked to change their name to the Tymes and to record a George Williams song then entitled "As We Stroll Along," which was renamed "So Much in Love." The tune was released in May 1963 and charted at number one in August.

The success of "So Much in Love" brought them many appearances. Their next release was Johnny Mathis's "Wonderful, Wonderful." This too did well, as did their next several releases. When the British invasion began in late 1963, their tunes stopped being noticed. They continued with their stage shows, but their recording success fell off substantially.

In 1965, when the Tymes saw Parkway's promotional support ending, they began their own label—Winchester. Danny White, formerly of Danny and the Juniors, was one of the principals.

Hilliard left in the early 1970s and was replaced by Charles Nixon.

Discography

Parkway 871 So Much in Love/Roscoe James McClain (1963)
Parkway 884 Wonderful, Wonderful/Come with Me to the Sea (1963)
Parkway 891 Somewhere/A View from the Window (1963)
Parkway 908 To Each His Own/Wonderland of Love (1964)
Parkway 919 The Magic of Our Summer Love/With All My Heart (1964)
Parkway 924 Here She Comes/Malibu (1964)
Parkway 933 The Twelfth of Never/Here She Comes (1964)
Parkway 7039 I'm Always Chasing Rainbows/Isle of Love (1964)
MGM 13536 Pretend/Street Talk (1966)
MGM 13631 A Touch of Baby/What Would I Do? (1966)
Sources: Dennis Garvey in *Goldmine;* Bob Pruter in *Goldmine.*

Unforgettables (Los Angeles)

Personnel Johnny Staton (lead), Roy Allen (tenor), Cleo White (baritone), Carl White (bass)

Notes

This group came into the R&B picture following Staton's involvement with the second Feathers group. After they recorded the tunes listed below, someone in the studio asked, "What do you guys call yourselves?" One of the members yelled back, "The Unforgettables."

Staton had previously been with the Feathers on Showtime.

Discography

Pamela 204 Daddy Must Be a Man (JS)/Wishing Well (JS) (1961)
Source: Marv Goldberg in *DISCoveries,* July 1995, Feathers.

Uniques (Milwaukee, Wisc.)

Personnel Earl King (lead), Johnny Taylor (lead), Charles Jordan (2d tenor), Leonard Garr (baritone), Bob Morland (bass)

Notes

This group came together in 1956 as Earl King and the Kingsmen. In 1957 they signed with Don Robey's Peacock label. A month after signing, they went to Chicago to record. Robey was there and decided to rename the group the Uniques!

Following their second recording for Peacock in 1960, with no hits to their credit, the group split up.

In 1963, Taylor joined one of the Ink Spots groups and stayed with them for the next twenty-five years. (This Johnny Taylor is not related to the Johnny Taylor who sang lead with the Five Echoes. Similarly, this Uniques group is not related to any other Uniques group.)

Discography

Peacock 1677 Somewhere/Right Now (1957)
Peacock 1695 Picture of My Baby/Mysterious (1960)
Source: Pete Grendysa in *Record Collector's Monthly* 53.

Universals (Amityville, N.Y.)

Personnel Fred Johnson (lead), Plinius Ruiz (1st tenor), Robert DeLoney (falsetto), Ollie Johnson (2d tenor), Kenny Johnson (baritone), Anthony Jones (bass)

Notes

This was a six-man group from Long Island, New York. This Universals group has no connection to the Mark-X, Cora Lee, or Ascot vocal ensembles of the same name.

The Universals began singing in the late 1950s alongside Richard Lanham, the Tempotones, Jimmy Magruder and the Loveletters, and the Miller Sisters.

The second release of "Love Bound" and "Just Have to Go On" included different takes of the same two songs. The second release, issued several months after the first, was distributed by King Records.

Allen Watson and the late Ralph Darden were later nonrecording members.

Discography

Festival 1601 Love Bound/Just Have to Go On (1961)
Festival 25001 Love Bound/Just Have to Go On (1961)
Source: Gordon Skadberg, liner notes with the Sequel CD *Herb Abramson's Festival of Groups.*

Universals (Philadelphia)

Personnel Earl Worsham (tenor), Roosevelt Simmons, Kent Peeler, John Christian (baritone), James Oscar Williams (bass)

Notes

This group evolved from the Turbans who recorded for Herald in the mid-1950s. By 1957, their popularity had diminished. Their one big hit, "When You Dance," could no longer maintain their status with the record-buying public.

Late in 1957, their contract with Herald expired and they were discouraged. At that time Earl Worsham and John Christian joined the group. The two had been together in the Quadrells on Whirlin' Disc. Roosevelt Simmons came from the Sensations and Kent Peeler from the Dreamers on Philadelphia's Grand Records. Along with James Oscar Williams, the quintet recorded for George Goldner's Mark-X label.

Over the next several years, many members came and left. Worsham was one these volatile members. He rejoined the Universals for their disc on Ascot. The group on that recording was Simmons, Reggie "Tootie Price," Peeler, Worsham, and Christian. The Ascot disc was recorded in August 1962 but was not released for a year. After this, they recorded under many other names.

Discography

Mark-X 7004 Again (RS)/Teenage Love (RS) (1957)
Cora Lee 501 He's So Right (RS)/The Picture (RS) (1958)
Ascot 2124 Dear Ruth (RS)/Got a Little Girl (RS) (1963)
Sources: Donn Fileti, liner notes with the Relic LP *Universals*; Earl Worsham, interview by Marv Goldberg in *DISCoveries* in the Turbans article.

Unknowns (Manhattan, N.Y.)

Personnel Fred Brunner (lead), Edward Williams (1st tenor), John Alicia (2d tenor), Anthony Primola (bass)

Notes

This integrated group formed in 1956 while group members were attending George Washington High School in the Washington Heights section of Manhattan. Frankie Lymon and the Teenagers also came from this neighborhood.

Later in 1956, the Unknowns visited every recording organization on Broadway's Tin Pan Alley. They finally met up with Ben Smith of X-Tra Records. He had them record very quickly, and the disc shown below was the product of that session. Smith played baritone sax on the recording.

The Unknowns wore masks when they appeared at high school dances and other events. According to Donn Fileti's liner notes, the Unknowns reflected the racial mix of their neighborhood.

Discography

X-Tra 102 One More Chance/You and Me (1957)
Source: Donn Fileti, liner notes with the Relic LP *Best of X-Tra Records.*

Untouchables (Los Angeles)

Personnel Brice Coefield (lead), Don Trotter (1st tenor), Sheridan "Rip" Spencer (tenor), Chester Pipkin (tenor), Ed Wallace (bass)

Notes

When Billy Storm and the Valiants recorded "We Knew" on the Keen subsidiary, Ensign Records, he began to have other ideas about his recording career. Thus "We Knew" was the Valiants' last recording with Storm. After his departure, the group got several new members and did one last recording as the Valiants on Shar-Dee in 1959.

The group decided to change their name to the Untouchables. They soon hooked up with Herb Alpert and Lou Adler, both of whom had been A&R men for Keen Records. They presented the Untouchables with a song they wanted recorded entitled "Poor Boy Needs a Preacher." They recorded the tune at a new label in New York, Madison Records.

The Untouchables recorded three more records for Madison and two for Liberty. Before they joined up with Liberty, however, Adler had gotten them a session with Screen Gems Records. The tunes from that session were released and, without their knowledge, the disc was issued as by the Happy Tones. With no success at Madison, they moved to Liberty in March 1961. The Untouchables were with Liberty for a year before they changed their name again, this time to the Electras. They recorded for many other labels under the new name.

Discography

Madison 128 New Fad (BC)/Poor Boy Needs a Preacher (BC/EW) (1960)
Madison 134 Goodnight Sweetheart Goodnight (DT, CP, BC)/Vickie Lee (BC) (1960)
Madison 139 60 Minute Man (EW/BC)/Everybody's Laughing (BC) (1960)
Madison 147 Raisin Sugar Cane (BC)/Do Your Best (BC) (1961)
Liberty 55335 You're On Top (BC)/Lovely Dee (BC) (1961)
Liberty 55423 Papa (CP/BC)/Medicine Man (BC) (1962)
Source: Marv Goldberg in *DISCoveries* article on the Valiants.

Upfronts (Los Angeles)

Personnel David Johnson (lead), Theotis Reed, Leroy Sanders, Early Harris, Bobby Relf

Notes

This group started out as the Cubans on Charlie Reynolds's Flash label. They wound up their tenure at Flash, and at the next opportunity David "Little Caesar" Johnson assembled his next group after meeting Lummie Fowler of Lummtone.

Fines Pettway sang lead on some of the latter Upfronts discs.

A new Upfronts lineup (106) featured Lummie's nephew Theodric Fowler and Vernon Merrick (and possibly Bobby Relf and Glen Willings).

According to Donn Fileti's liner notes, it is believed that a young Barry White started his singing career with the Upfronts' Baby, For Your Love/Send Me Someone to Love. "Who Will Love Me" features White, Vernon Merrick, Jimmy Locke, and Theotis Reed.

Discography

Lummtone 103 It Took Time/Benny Lou and the Lion (1960)
Lummtone 104 Married Jive/Too Far to Turn Around (1960)
Lummtone 106 Little Girl/When You Kiss Me (1961)
Lummtone 107 Baby, For Your Love/Send Me Someone to Love (1961)
Lummtone 108 It Took Time/Baby, For Your Love (1962)
Lummtone 114 Do the Beetle/Most of the Pretty Young Girls (1964)
Source: Donn Fileti, liner notes with the Relic CD *Lummtone*; Rick Gagnon and Dave Guerre.

Uptones (Hollywood, Calif.)

Personnel Carlton Beck (lead), Richard Betts (baritone)

Notes

This group (or a major part of it) was also the Guides, Swallows (on Guyden), and the Senders on Entra. Some of the tunes that the Hollywood Saxons had written were given to friends who were with the Uptones.

Discography

Lute 6225 I'll Be There/No More (1962)
Magnum 714 Dreaming/Wear My Ring (1963)
Source: Marv Goldberg and Rick Whitesell in *Yesterday's Memories* 11 article on the Hollywood Saxons.

Utopians, Mike & (Brooklyn, N.Y.)

Personnel Mike Lasman (lead), Jimmy McQueen (tenor), Earl ——— (baritone), Stuart Cohen

Notes

Danny Robinson was the brother of Bobby Robinson, who owned Red Robin and Fury Records. Danny himself owned several Harlem labels like Holiday and Everlast. Clarence Johnson, who assisted Danny Robinson with his amateur vocal groups, began his own label, Cee Jay Records, in the Bronx. One of the aspiring groups Johnson had in his stable was Mike and the Utopians.

Lasman later sang with the Dreamers on Guaranteed, the Accents on Sultan, and the Concords on Herald.

Discography

Cee Jay 574 Erlene/I Wish (1958)
Cee Jay 574 Erlene/I Found a Penny (1958)

Sources: Lou Silvani, *Collecting Rare Records*; Donn Fileti, liner notes with the Relic CD *Groups of Everlast.*

Vacels, Ricky & (Long Island, N.Y.)

Personnel Ricky Racano (lead), Vito Racano, Marie Racano, Peter Gutowski, Vincent Gutowski

Notes

This was a white group from Long Island, New York, that released four sides for the Fargo label, the first in mid-1962 and the last in 1963.

Seemingly, three Racano siblings sang alongside two Gutowski brothers to form this quintet, although these relationships cannot be confirmed.

Discography

Express 711 Lorraine/Bubble Gum (1962)
Fargo 1050 His Girl/Don't Want Your Love No More (1963)
Source: Donn Fileti, liner notes with the Relic CD *Fargo Records.*

Val-Aires (Pittsburgh, Pa.)

Personnel Bill Burkette (lead), Hugh Geyer (1st tenor), Chuck Blasko (2d tenor), Don Mille (baritone)

Notes

The Val-Aires' one recording was initially released on the Willett label and subsequently leased to Coral. The label name, Willett, was the name of their manager, Elmer Willett. He would later rename them the Vogues.

The Willett inventory was destroyed in a fire and thus the disc is scarce.

Discography

Willett 114 Launie My Love/Which One Will It Be (1960)
Coral 62177 Launie My Love/Which One Will It Be (1960)
Source: Travis Klein, liner notes with the Itzy II CD *Pittsburgh's Greatest Hits.*

Valentines (New York)

Personnel Richard Barrett (lead), Ray "Popps" Briggs (1st tenor), Donald Razor (Raysor) (2d tenor), Mickey Francis (baritone), Ronnie Bright (bass)

Notes

The Valentines formed in 1952 in northern Manhattan, originally calling themselves the Dreamers. They performed locally. One evening they met Richard Barrett at a neighborhood party. Barrett had come to New York looking for work. Harptones accompanist and mentor Raoul Cita was a friend and arranged for the group to meet Monte Bruce of Bruce Records.

Early in 1954, they changed their name to the Valentines because they were having bad luck with the Dreamers. They cut a demo of "Summer Love" and "For You" for Bruce Records. Neither tune was ever released. After nothing happened with Bruce, they next went to Old Town. They rerecorded "Tonight Kathleen" and "Summer Love" for Old Town, which also did nothing. Donald Raysor replaced Hogan vocally on their first release. Hogan would return later.

On their next recording, Edward Edgehill replaced Hogan. The group was now with the George Goldner organization. They recorded "Lily Maebelle" on Rama. Their next big disc was the "Woo Woo Train." Hogan returned several years later to write "Don't Say Goodnight" and "I Cried Oh Oh" with Barrett and to record with the group on these tunes.

These two hits created a very hectic appearance schedule for the Valentines. The group was said to resemble the Cadillacs in their stage presentation.

The Valentines spent the rest of their recording career with Rama. Barrett eventually became a principal contributor for the Goldner organization, producing many other vocal group recordings.

Sometime in 1956, Briggs was replaced by Dave "Baby Cortez" Clowney, who had joined from the Pearls on Onyx. The Valentines broke up in 1958.

In Murray Hill's *Best of the Valentines* LP, it is stated that the Wrens' "C'est La Vie" was a collaboration between the Wrens and the Valentines.

Discography

Old Town 1009 Tonight Kathleen/Summer Love (1954)
Rama 171 Lily Maebelle/Falling for You (1955)
Rama 181 I Love You Darling/Hand Me Down Love (1955)
Rama 186 Christmas Prayer/K-i-s-s Me (1955)
Rama 196 Woo Woo Train/Why (1956)
Rama 201 Twenty Minutes/I'll Never Let You Go (1956)
Rama 208 Nature's Creation/My Story of Love (1956)
Rama 228 Don't Say Goodnight/I Cried Oh Oh (1957)
Sources: Murray Hill, liner notes with the *Best of the Valentines* LP; Phil Groia in *Bim Bam Boom*; Marv Goldberg and Rick Whitesell in *Yesterday's Memories.*

Valiants (New York)

Personnel Joe Van Loan (tenor), Orville Brooks (tenor), Willie Ray (baritone), Bob Kornegay (bass)

Notes

Van Loan, Ray, and Kornegay had been together in the Du Droppers. This quartet stayed together from 1959 to 1960.

Discography

Joy 235 Let Me Go Lover/Let Me Ride (1960)
Fairlane 21007 See-Saw/Blue Jeans and Pony Tails (1961)
Cortland 114 Lonely Hours/Come On Let's Go (1964)
Source: Jack Sbarbori in *Record Exchanger*, article on Joe Van Loan.

Valiants (Los Angeles)

Personnel Billy Storm (lead), Chester Pipkin (tenor), Sheridan "Rip" Spencer, Brice Coefield (baritone)

Notes

This group began with "Rip" Spencer and cousin Brice Coefield. They sang together and with others while they were high school students in Los Angeles. They decided to form a group called the Sabers and auditioned and eventually recorded for Cal-West. Interestingly, the Sabers recorded the first side for the eventual release and were told to go home and write a song for the flip side. During that period, another member was added, who recorded the second side of the disc with the group. This new member was Billy Spicer, who recorded under many different names, one of which was Billy Storm. Their one release as the Sabers did nothing and they were never heard from again.

The next name the group adopted was the Chavelles. A great deal of networking led to a recording session for Vita Records. Members of the group were not even aware that the tunes they had recorded for Vita were released until they received the disc in the mail. But the disc failed at the cash register and the Chavelles began to break apart. Storm pressed on with his dreams of vocal excellence.

Group members recruited Chester Pipkin from the Squires, also on Vita, and these four became the Valiants. Their first recorded masters were placed with Aladdin. Label management liked the recordings but released them as by the Gents on Aladdin 3387 (also released on the Aladdin subsidiary, Lamp Records).

Their A&R man, "Bumps" Blackwell, was affiliated with Keen Records. The majority of their recorded material was released on Keen or one of its subsidiary labels—Ensign or Andex. The Valiants' initial release on Keen was their biggest hit, "This Is the Night" with Billy Storm at lead.

Following their recording on the Ensign label, "We Knew," Storm began having second thoughts about his recording career and decided to go solo. The Valiants had one additional recording on the Shar-Dee label.

Discography

Keen 34004 This Is the Night (BS)/Good Golly Miss Molly (BS) (1957)
Keen 34007 Lover, Lover (BS)/Walkin' Girl (BC) (1958)
Keen 34008 Temptation of My Heart (CP)/Frieda, Frieda (BS) (1958)
Keen 4026 Please Wait My Love (BS)/Frieda, Frieda (BS) (1958)
Ensign 4035 We Knew (BS)/Walkin' Girl (BC) (1958)
Keen 2120 This Is the Night (BS)/Walkin' Girl (BC) (1959)
Shar-Dee 703 Dear Cindy (CP)/Surprise (BC) (1959)
Source: Marv Goldberg in *DISCoveries.*

Vals (Chicago)

Personnel Billy Gibson (lead), David Wilkerson Jr., Eddie Morris, Clarence Green, William Taylor (bass)

Notes

The Vals' record was released on the Unique Laboratories label, which neverthe-less shows that the record was produced by Theron Records. On another Unique Laboratories recording, the Vals provided a weak backup for Vicki Johnson.

The owner of the label was Val Hutchinson.

Discography

Unique Laboratories (N/A) Song of a Lover/Compensation Blues (1961)
Sources: Bob Pruter, *Doowop . . . The Chicago Scene*; Bob Stallworth in *Record Collector's Monthly* 38.

V-Eights (Asbury Park, N.J.)

Personnel Roosevelt McDuffie (1st tenor), Leroy Brown (2d tenor), Tony Maples (tenor), Delmar "Kirby" Goggins (tenor), Frank Hosendove (bass)

Notes

After a fine R&B career with the Vibranaires ("Doll Face") and the Vibes, lead singer Bobby Thomas was drafted in 1958. He maintained his vocal skills in the army by vocalizing with R&B group performer "Carnation" Charlie Hughes, who had been with the DuDroppers and the Drifters and was in the same outfit with Thomas.

When Thomas was discharged from the army in 1960, he once again teamed up with Vibranaires pal Roosevelt McDuffie, who was singing with an Asbury Park, New Jersey, group, the V-Eights. This group had cut their first record for Morty Craft's Most label in 1959. Leroy Brown disappeared when they moved to Vibro. And then Thomas stepped in.

Thomas had also been with the Orioles. He is not on the Most disc or the ABC recording.

Henry "Stony" Jackson replaced Goggins and was part of the Vik Heartbreakers. After all the recordings on Vibro, Jackson left and was replaced by Bobby Young.

One year after Bobby Thomas joined the V-Eights, the group broke up. Thomas took Bobby Young and Roosevelt McDuffie and, along with several others, re-formed the Vibranaires for revival concerts.

Discography

Most 711/713 Please Come Back/Pretty Girl (1959)
Vibro 4005 My Heart/Papa's Yellow Tie (1960)
Vibro 4006 Everything That You Said/Guess What (1960)
Vibro 4007 Let's Take a Chance/Hot Water (1961)
ABC 10201 My Heart/Papa's Yellow Tie (1961)
Source: Marv Goldberg in *DISCoveries*.

Vel-Aires (Los Angeles)

Personnel Donald Woods, Willie Graham (tenor), Randolph Bryant (1st tenor), Ira Foley (bass)

Notes

Following the Medallions' recording of "Edna" and before its release, Donald Woods was added to the Medallions as their fifth member. Soon after this, unexplained internal difficulties surfaced. All the group members left Vernon Green alone, and the others formed the Vel-Aires.

Graham, Bryant, and Foley were the former Medallions on Dootone who, with Woods, first became the Bel-Aires on Flip. The Bel-Aires' first two releases for Flip were released as by the Bel-Aires. Apparently, when their third disc began to do well, Flip Records changed the group's name to Vel-Aires. The change was probably due to the fact that they were moonlighting while they were recording as the Medallions.

Another member of the Medallions, Andrew Blue, also spent some time with his friends in the Vel-Aires.

Discography

Flip 306 Death of an Angel/Man from Utopia (1955)
Flip 309 Stay with Me Always/My Very Own (1955)
Flip 312 Heaven in My Arms/Mighty Joe (1955)
Sources: Unsigned liner notes with the Titanic CD *Best of Flip Records*; Marv Goldberg in *Record Collector's Monthly* 42.

Velours (Brooklyn, N.Y.)

Personnel Jerome "Romeo" Ramos (lead), John Cheetom (1st tenor), Donald Haywoode (2d tenor), John Pearson (baritone), Pete Winston (bass)

Notes

The Velours formed in 1956 in the Bedford-Stuyvesant section of Brooklyn. They practiced many hours until they felt they were ready for recording. They then contacted Jerry Winston at Onyx Records for an audition. Winston liked them and signed them to a contract to record with his label.

On Onyx 512, Charles Moffitt joined, replacing Pete Winston who left to return to college. Like others before and after them, they stated that they did not receive all their royalties, despite fair sales.

Onyx was purchased by MGM Records in 1958 and the group went to MGM subsidiaries Orbit and Cub Records.

Tenors Troy Keys and Alfred Pitts, as well as Keith Williams, were later members who replaced Keys. Williams remained until 1959.

They later went to George Goldner's Gone/End Records and recorded there until their contract ended in 1961.

After the original group broke up, Ramos, Cheetom, and Haywoode formed the Fantastics.

Nelson Shields from the Leaders was a later member.

Discography

Onyx 501 My Love Come Back/Honey Drop (1956)
Onyx 508 Romeo/What You Do to Me (1957)
Onyx 512 Can I Come Over Tonight?/Where There's a Will (1957)

Onyx 515 This Could Be the Night/Hands across the Table (1957)
Onyx 520 Can I Walk You Home/Remember (1958)
Orbit 9001 Can I Walk You Home/Remember (1958)
Cub 9014 Crazy Love/I'll Never Smile Again (1958)
Cub 9029 Blue Velvet/Tired of Your Rockin' and Rolling (1959)
Goldisc 3012 Daddy Warbucks/Sweet Sixteen (1960)
Gone 5092 Can I Come Over Tonight?/Where There's a Will (1960)
End 1090 Lover Come Back/The Lonely One (1961)
Source: Dave Hinckley and Marv Goldberg in *Yesterday's Memories.*

Velquins (St. Paul, Minn.)

Personnel John Stafford (lead), Eddie Ballard (tenor), Sylvester "Peachy" Eaves (baritone), Clarence "Huffy" Wright (bass)

Notes

This group was brought to Gaity to record in 1959. Only a few hundred copies of the disc were released on black vinyl and about five hundred copies were issued on gold wax as part of a promotion.

The group's name was misprinted on the Gaity record label as the Valquins.

Bass Henry Jones and Roy "Bucky" Brown of the Wisdoms were sometime members of the Velquins.

Discography

Gaity 161/162 My Dear/Falling Star (1959)
Source: Liner notes on the Gaity CD *Bloodshot* written by Jerry Oldsberg and Billy Miller.

Velvelettes (Kalamazoo, Mich.)

Personnel Carolyn Gill, Betty Kelly, Sandra Tilley

Discography

I.P.G. 1002 There He Goes/That's the Reason Why (1963)
Soul 32025 These Things Will Keep Me Loving You/Since You've Been Loving Me (1964)
V.I.P. 25007 Needle in a Haystack/Should I Tell Them? (1964)
V.I.P. 25013 He Was Really Saying Something/Farewell Kiss (1964)
V.I.P. 25017 Lonely Girl Am I/I'm the Exception to the Rule (1965)
V.I.P. 25030 Since You've Been Loving Me/Bird in the Hand Is Worth Two in the Bush (1965)
Sources: Ferdie Gonzalez, *Disco-File*; R. Ferlingere's *A Discography of R&B and R&R Vocal Groups.*

Velvet Angels (Detroit)

Personnel Robert Calhoun, Willie Hunter, James Johnson, Cy Iverson

Notes

While on a tour in the East in 1963, the Velvet Angels were staying in the Madison Hotel in Jersey City. They made crude recordings on a portable recorder, which Angelo Pompeo brought to Relic Records for potential release.

Johnson and Hunter returned to Detroit in the early 1960s following the group's breakup.

Discography

Co-Op 201 I'm in Love/Baby I Wanna Know (1963)
Source: Don Fileti, liner notes with the Relic CD *Velvet Angels—I'm in Love.*

Velvetones (New York)

Personnel J. R. Bailey (tenor), Bobby Spencer, Waldo Champen (tenor), Eddie Lewis (tenor), Fred Barksdale (bass)

Notes

In 1995 Freddie Barksdale and Waldo Champen both denied ever singing with a Velvetones group. Perhaps this group never recorded.

Source: Phil Groia, *They All Sang on the Corner.*

Velvetones (Chicago)

Personnel Lee Diamond, Nate Nelson, Donald Blackman, Roy Flagg, Winfred Veal

Notes

Nate Nelson left this group for to the Flamingos when he replaced Solly McElroy. Apparently this group did no recording.

Source: Bob Pruter, *Doowop . . . The Chicago Scene.*

Velvetones (Chicago)

Personnel Toggo Smythe, Wallace Caldwell, Herman Bell, Danny Gibson

Notes

Little is known about this smooth-sounding ensemble. They preceded the non-recording, Nate Nelson Velvetones, also from Chicago, by six or seven years. *(Note:* Although I attempt to show the first group of performers to record as the specific vocal group at the beginning of each group's entry in this encyclopedia, I only had the above names, which I have learned is the group that recorded for Columbia.)

Discography

Coronet 1 One Day/Hey Boblebip (1946)
Coronet 2 Sweet Lorraine/Easy Baby (1946)
Coronet 3 Swing Out, It Don't Cost Nothin'/Jason, Get Your Basin (1946)
Coronet 4 Don't Say You're Sorry Again/Georgiana from Savannah (1946)

Coronet 5 Singing River/I'm Getting Used to Love Again (1946)
Sonora 3010 Pittsburgh Joe/It's Written All Over Your Face (1946)
Sonora 3012 It Just Ain't Right/Reverse the Charges (1946)
Sonora 2014 Ask Anyone Who Knows/I Want Some Bread I Said (1947)
Sonora 2015 Don't Bring Me No News/Can You Look Me in the Eyes (1947)
Super Disc 1055 Roberta, Get Out of My Bed/Find My Baby Blues (1948)
Rondo 1554 Don't Bring Me No News/Can You Look Me in the Eyes (1949)
Sources: Ferdie Gonzalez, *Disco-File*; George Moonoogian in *Echoes of the Past* 40.

Velvets (Odessa, Tex.)

Personnel Virgil Johnson (lead), Mark Prince, Clarence Rigsby (d), William Solomon, Bob Thursby

Notes

This group started singing in 1959 at Texas functions and school activities at Blackshear Junior-Senior High School. Their lead singer, Virgil Johnson, was their professor at school. Johnson himself was just out of college, having graduated in 1958. After joining his students in their vocal harmony, they attained a terrific reputation among locals. Roy Orbison heard them and recommended them to Monument Records.

Several tunes contained on the Velvets' CBS CD were written by their mentor, Roy Orbison.

Discography

Monument 435 That Lucky Old Sun/Time and Again (1961)
Monument 441 Tonight/Spring Fever (1961)
Monument 448 Laugh/Lana (1961)
Monument 458 The Love Express/Don't Let Him Take My Baby (1962)
Monument 464 Let the Good Times Roll/The Lights Go On, Lights Go Off (1962)
Monument 810 Crying in the Chapel/Dawn (1963)
Monument 836 Nightmare/Here Comes That Song Again (1964)
Monument 861 If/Let the Fool Kiss You (1964)
Monument 961 Baby, The Magic Is Gone/Let the Fool Kiss You (1966)
Source: Virgil Johnson, liner notes with the CBS CD *The Velvets-Featuring Virgil Johnson.*

Velvets (New York)

Personnel Charles Sampson (lead), Donald Razor (Raysor) (2d tenor), Joe Brisbane, Bearle Ashton, George Thorpe (bass)

Notes

Surfacing a few years before Frankie Lymon and the Teenagers, the Velvets came from the same Washington Heights and Sugar Hill neighborhoods as the Gee recording stars.

Donald Razor (Raysor) and Leon Briggs were members of the latter-day Velvets and recorded "Dance Honey Dance" for the Fury label. These two were also members of Johnny Blake and the Clippers on Gee.

Brisbane also recorded with Hogan's Harlem Miracles on Fury.

Razor's brother Joseph was also a member. In Donn Fileti's liner notes with Relic's *Red Robin Golden Groups* CD, he shows Joe Raysor in place of Brisbane.

Sampson (Charles) joined Carl Hogan (Carl) and formed Charles and Carl, who recorded for Fury in 1957.

Discography

Red Robin 120 They Tried/She's Gotta Grin (1953)
Red Robin 127 I Cried/Tell Her (1954)
Pilgrim 706 I/At Last (1956)
Pilgrim 710 I Cried/Tell Her (1956)
Fury 1012 I–I–I/Dance Honey, Dance (1957)
Sources: Donn Fileti, liner notes with Relic's *Red Robin* CD; Phil Groia, *They All Sang on the Corner.*

Veneers (New York)

Personnel Annette Smith, Valerie Swinson, Barbara Harris, Lorraine Joyner

Notes

Following Arlene Smith's departure from the Chantels in 1959, End Records' Richard Barrett enlisted Annette Smith in 1961 to join a re-formed Chantels group. This was the Carlton Chantels. Annette Smith sang lead on "Look in My Eyes."

Discography

Princeton 102 I Believe/Love Me (1960)
Treyco 402 With All My Love/Recipe of Love (1963)
Source: Jerry Zwecker, liner notes with the Chicago CD *Moonlight.*

Verdicts (Brooklyn, N.Y.)

Personnel Victor Rice, Robert Burroughs

Notes

According to the liner notes with the Dee Jay Jamboree CD, *Brooklyn's Doo Wop,* this group is the remains or (as I like to refer to them) the evolution of Brooklyn's Gay Tunes, who recorded for Joyce and Timely in the early 1950s.

The Verdicts got together in 1961 and, along with Al Browne, recorded several notable tunes.

Discography

East Coast 103 My Life's Desire/Mummy's Ball (1961)
Relic 507 My Life's Desire/Mummy's Ball (1964)
Source: Liner notes with the Dee Jay Jamboree CD *Brooklyn's Doo Wop.*

Versalettes (Chicago)

Personnel Kathleen Spates Robinson, Vera Regulus Wallace, Helen Greenfield, Theresa Legg, Viola Floyd

Notes

The members of this group originally got together in 1961 after graduating from junior high school. The members, minus Greenfield, had known each other from church and school since they were nine years of age. They soon got a manager and began appearing locally.

Before recording in 1963, the group added a fifth member, Helen Greenfield, who had a very high voice that was felt would really blend in well with the others.

The recording company, due to poor sales, tried to release songs by the Versalettes as by the Trinkets on the Cortland label at the same time that they issued the Shining Armor release.

Later, the Versalettes had two releases on Columbia as the Little Foxes.

The Versalettes' recording career ended in 1964 when Cortland/Witch folded. Greenfield was eliminated from the group at this time and they continued their schedule of local appearances, since they had become a local attraction. They graduated from high school in 1965 and signed with Columbia. It has been said that the tunes they cut for Columbia weren't much, and this is probably the reason they were never released.

Discography

Witch 116 Shining Armor/True Love Is a Treasure (1963)
Source: Bob Pruter, *Doowop . . . The Chicago Scene.*

Versatiles, Jerry Sheely & (Pittsburgh, Pa.)

Personnel Jerry Sheely (lead), Chuck Jackson, Arthur Budd, Ed Everett, Corinthian "Kripps" Johnson, Donald Jackson

Notes

Chuck Jackson, "Kripps" Johnson, and Donald Jackson, former members of the Dell Vikings, were joined by Arthur Budd and Ed Everette to form the Versatiles. They backed blind vocalist Jerry Sheely.

Sheely died a few days after the session.

Discography

Star 220 Love Only Me/It's All Over (1962)
Source: Travis Klein, liner notes with the Itzy II CD *Pittsburgh's Greatest Hits.*

Versatiles (Philadelphia)

Personnel Rick Cordo, Ron Gathers, Gene Glass, Idella Morris, Frank Troutt

Notes

The group formed in Philadelphia in 1959, meeting on Harlan Street. Unlike most groups, they went to different schools and their ages varied from nineteen to the mid-twenties (Gene Glass). It was at this time as well that Glass had returned home to Philadelphia from the U.S. Air Force.

They hooked up with a Buddy Caldwell who said he would arrange for a recording session with Ro-Cal Records. Gene Glass told writer Wayne Jancik that "they were supposed to be listed as the Premiers. But when they got to the studio, they were told that another group had that name and somehow they began as the Versatiles."

They have no idea why they only did one record. Like many vocal groups, they received nothing for the release. The Versatiles disbanded and two other male members went off to the service. Two years later, the group was back in the studio as the Majors who recorded for Imperial under the guidance of Philadelphia's Jerry Ragavoy.

Idella Morris later became Haleema Alkhatib and married another member of the group, Gene Glass.

Discography

Ro-Cal 1002 Lundee Dundee/I'll Whisper in Your Ear (1960)
Source: Wayne Jancik in *Goldmine,* December 28, 1990, article on the Majors.

Vespers (Philadelphia)

Personnel Mickey Neil (lead), Jack McKnight (1st tenor), Jimmy Mullin (2d tenor), Bobby Riccobene (bass)

Notes

The Vespers had been the Four Epics who recorded for Laurie.

The Vespers did a lot of backup work on Cameo with Chubby Checker, the Dovells, the Dreamlovers, and Joey and the Flips.

Jack Lally replaced Riccobene.

Discography

Swan 4156 Mr. Cupid/When I Walk with an Angel (1963)
Source: Ed Engel and Val Shively, liner notes with the Dee Jay Jamboree CD *Philadelphia's Doo Wop Sound.*

Vibes (Asbury Park, N.J.)

Personnel Bobby Thomas (lead), Roosevelt McDuffie (1st tenor), Mike Robinson (2d tenor), Herb Cole (baritone), James Roache (bass)

Notes

Man for man this group was the Vibranaires stripped of the name, which was felt to be quite a labor for deejays and listeners.

Discography

After Hours 105 Stop Torturing Me/Stop Jibing Baby (1955)
Chariot 105 Stop Torturing Me/Stop Jibing Baby (1955)
Source: Bobby Thomas, interview by Marv Goldberg in the September 1994 issue of *DISCoveries,* and by author, September 1994.

Vibraharps (New York)

Personnel Lynn Middleton Davis, Donnie Elbert, Danny Cannon, Doug "Bubs" Gibson, Donald Simmons (bass)

Notes

Gibson later recorded with the Jimmy Castor Bunch.
Lynn Middleton Davis was Lynn Middleton from the Joytones on Rama.
Charles Hargro was also a member.

Discography

Beech 713 Walk Beside Me/Cosy with Rosy (1956)
Atco 6134 It Must Be Magic/Nosey Neighbors (1959)
Sources: R. Skurzewski in issue 26 of *Record Collectors Monthly*; Phil Groia's *They All Sang on the Corner.*

Vibranaires (Asbury Park, N.J.)

Personnel Bobby Thomas (lead), Roosevelt McDuffie (1st tenor), Mike Robinson (2d tenor), Herbie Cole (baritone), Jimmy Roache (bass)

Notes

These were neighborhood friends who began singing as the Crooners in 1950. They soon became the Vibranaires, which lasted through their first recording together. The name was changed because of confusion associated with its spelling and pronunciation. Their new name became the Vibes.

While performing at a club, they were seen by former Mello-Moods manager Joel Turnero, who introduced them to After Hours/Chariot management. After an audition, they recorded "Doll Face" for After Hours Records. This tune ultimately became a classic, but initially it sold poorly.

They soon met manager Esther Navarro, who guided them for several months. She advised them to change their name to Vibes. They soon split with Navarro but retained the new name.

In 1955, Jimmy Roache was drafted and was replaced by Joe Major. In 1957, Cole was drafted and replaced by William Penha. Mike Robinson left and was replaced by Lenny Welch, later to become a star solo performer.

Baritone Bobby Young also sang with the Vibranaires.

In 1958, Bobby Thomas was drafted. Essentially, the group broke up. When Thomas returned from the service, he first joined up with the V-Eights. Then he sang with a later Orioles group, where he remained until Sonny Til's death. Bobby then did everything possible to perpetuate the Orioles' name and reputation.

Discography

After Hours 103 Doll Face (BT)/Ooh I Feel So Good (BT) (1954)
Source: Bobby Thomas, interview by Marv Goldberg and Mike Redmond in *Yesterday's Memories.*

Vibrations (Los Angeles)

Personnel James Johnson (lead), Carver Bunkum (1st tenor), Carl Fisher (2d tenor), Dave Govan (baritone)

Notes

This group formed in 1955 at Los Angeles's Jefferson High School and began recording as the Jayhawks on Flash in 1956. Jayhawks group members wrote the classic novelty tune "Stranded in the Jungle," but the Cadets' version became the bigger seller.

In 1959, bass Don Bradley joined.

The follow-up disc, "Love Train," did not do too well and they found themselves at another West Coast recording facility, Aladdin. Here they recorded several tunes that also did poorly. During the summer of 1957, the group had had enough with recording and by 1960 Bunkum left. In 1960 they changed their name to the Vibrations and became a mature-sounding ensemble.

Richard Owens (Six Teens) replaced Bunkum. He had also been with the Jayhawks, Marathons, Ivy Leaguers, and Temptations.

The insignificant Bet label originally recorded their "So Blue." Checker would pick up the master to this haunting song and continue to record the Vibrations until 1963, with several hits along the way.

Fisher, Johnson, and Govan also sang with the Jayhawks and the Marathons.

Due to scheduling difficulties, the Vibrations performed and recorded simultaneously as the Marathons (this actually sounds like moonlighting). The scheduling problems were with the Olympics on Arvee, who were scheduled to record but found themselves on the East Coast on the day of the session. Arvee's A&R head convinced the Vibrations to execute a little "midnight magic" and record as the Marathons. The Vibrations' "Watusi" was on the charts at the same time as the Marathons' "Peanut Butter."

They went from Checker to Okeh in 1964 with a brief stop at Atlantic.

Discography

Bet 001 So Blue/Love Me Like You Should (1960)
Checker 954 So Blue/Love Me Like You Should (1960)
Checker 961 Feel So Bad/Cave Man (1960)
Checker 967 Doing the Slop/So Little Time (1960)
Checker 969 Wallflower/Watusi (1961)
Checker 974 Continental/The Junkeroo (1961)
Checker 982 Don't Say Goodbye/Stranded in the Jungle (1961)
Checker 987 Stop Right Now/All My Love Belongs to You (1961)
Checker 990 Let's Pony Again/What Made You Change Your . . . (1961)
Checker 1002 Oh Cindy/Over the Rainbow (1961)

Checker 1011 Anytime/The New Hully Gully (1962)
Checker 1022 Hamburgers on a Bun/If He Don't (1962)
Checker 1038 May The Best Man Win/Since I Fell for You (1963)
Checker 1061 Dancing Danny/Dancing Danny (1963)
Okeh 7205 Sloop Dance/Watusi Time (1964)
Okeh 7212 Hello Happiness/Keep On Keeping You (1964)
Okeh 7220 End Up Crying/Ain't Love That Way? (1965)
Okeh 7228 If I Only Knew/Talkin' 'Bout Love (1965)
Okeh 7230 Misty/Finding Out the Hard Way (1965)
keh 7238 Gina/The Story of a Starry Night (1965)
Okeh 7241 Canadian Sunset/The Story of a Starry Night (1965)
Source: Bob Pruter, *Doowop . . . The Chicago Scene.*

Victorians (New York)

Personnel Cas Bridges (lead), Bobby Thompson (tenor), Donny Miles, Roy ——
(tenor), Bill Carey (baritone/bass)

Notes

Bridges and Thompson also performed with the Tri Boro Four Fellows. Bridges
recorded with Old Town's Clefftones.

Discography

Saxony 103 Heartbreaking Moon/I'm Rolling (1957)
Source: Bob Hyde, liner notes with Ace's Old Town *Doo Wop-1.*

Videos (Queens, N.Y.)

Personnel Ronald Cussey (d) (lead), Clarence Bassett (1st tenor), Charles
Baskerville (2d tenor), Johnny Jackson (baritone), Ron Woodhall (d) (bass)

Notes

Because the Videos placed second at the Apollo Theater's amateur night contest, they
were awarded a recording deal with Philadelphia's Casino Records. The tune they
recorded at their initial session with Casino was "Trickle, Trickle," which did well.
Before they were able to record a follow-up to their second release for Casino, "Love
or Infatuation," two members had died. One was lead Ronald Cussey, who had previously sung lead for the legendary Jubilee Five Sharps. This marked the end of the
Videos' singing career.

  Bassett also sang with the Five Sharps and later teamed up with Charles
Baskerville and James Sheppard to form Shep and the Limelites.

  As discussed in Louie Silvani's *Collecting Rare Records,* Ron Wood was the lead,
Ronald Cuffey was the 2d tenor, and Clarence Bassett was the bass. All other voice
parts and personnel were the same.

Discography

Casino 102 Trickle, Trickle/Moonglow You Know (1958)
Casino 105 Love or Infatuation/Shoo-Bee-Doo-Bee Cha Cha Cha (1958)
Sources: Lou Silvani, *Collecting Rare Records*; Bob Hyde, liner notes with Rhino's *Doo Wop Box 1.*

Vilons (Brooklyn, N.Y.)

Personnel Bobby Alveray (lead), John Pagan (1st tenor), Santos Torres (2d tenor), Louis Torres (baritone), Cesare Pagan (bass)

Notes

The members of the Vilons all grew up in the Farragut housing projects in Brooklyn. They would sing in hallways, on rooftops, and in other places conducive to vocal group harmonizing. Finally they found a local recording studio near their neighborhood in Brooklyn. This was Al Jon Records.

Al Browne of Al Jon Records was most receptive to their sound and had the Vilons cut several tunes for him at Al Jon.

Carlos Infante of the Zircons later filled in at bass on occasion. Eventually Vilons' recordings were leased to Al Jon, *Bim Bam Boom,* and Lake Records.

Discography

Aljon 1259/1260 Mother Nature/Lone Stranger (1963)
Lake 713 What Kind of Fool Am I?/Let Me in Your Life (1962)
Bim Bam Boom 104 Angel Darling/Wish She Was Mine (1972)
Vintage 1011 Tears on My Pillow/Sweetest One (1973)
Source: Unsigned liner notes with the Dee Jay Jamboree CD *Brooklyn's Doo Wops.*

Violinaires (Detroit)

Personnel Isaiah Jones (lead), Calvin Fair, Willie Banks, Robert Blair (tenor), Wilson De Shields (baritone), Providence Thomas (bass)

Notes

This group was also the Gales on JVB. The pressing plant personnel at Drummond misspelled the group's name on the label as Voilinaires. In addition to their kinship with the Gales, they were also the Question Marks.

Between the Violinaires' material on JVB and their successful tenure with Chicago's Checker label performing gospel music, they recorded the tune below.

Discography

Drummond 4000 Another Soldier Gone/Joy in the Beulah Land (1953)
Sources: Louie Silvani, *Collecting Rare Records*; liner notes with the Real Rhythm LP *Best of JVB.*

Virginia Four (Norfolk, Va.)

Personnel ——— (lead), Norman Harris (2d tenor), Melvin Colden (baritone), Len Williams (bass)

Notes

This group had been the Norfolk Jazz Quartet and, with many of their members, became the Virginia Four.

Colden, a former member of the Norfolk Jazz Quartet, also sang with the Master Keys.

Discography

Victor V38569 Since I Been Born/Comin' Down the Shiny Way (1930)
Victor 23376 It'll Soon Be Over With/Don't Leave Me Behind (1933)
Decca 7662 Dig My Jelly Roll/Moanin' the Blues (1939)
Decca 7808 I'd Feel Much Better/Queen Street Rag (1941)
Sources: George Moonoogian in *Record Collector's Monthly* May–June 1991; Ray Funk and Doug Seroff in the *Human Orchestra* LP.

Vocal-Aires (Brooklyn, N.Y.)

Personnel Lou Fasanaro, Eric Nathanson, Joe Piazza, Bob Kutner

Notes

This group came from the Coney Island section of Brooklyn in New York City.

Kutner sang with the Boptones on the Ember label, the Accents on Sultan, and the Quotations.

Discography

Herald 573 Dance Dance/These Empty Arms (1962)
Source: Donn Fileti, liner notes with the Relic CD *Best of Herald Records–2.*

Vocaleers (New York)

Personnel Joe Duncan (lead), Herman Dunham (a.k.a. Herman Curtis) (1st tenor), Mel Walton (2d tenor), William Walker (baritone), Teddy Williams (bass)

Notes

Joe Duncan Martinez, Herman Dunham, and Mel Walton were members of the same softball team in the Harlem section of Manhattan. They joined with neighbors William Walker and Teddy Williams to form a vocal group they called the Rainbows.

They performed at school dances and the Elks club, and made two appearances at the Apollo. During this time, they auditioned for King Records, but this did not work out. They were discovered by the proprietor of a record demo shop who heard a recording they made and took it to Bobby Robinson, who was close by. Robinson liked what he heard and soon had them record for Red Robin as the Vocaleers.

One night at a performance, Teddy Williams got stage fright and had to be replaced by another neighborhood friend, Lamar Cooper. Williams had developed tuberculosis and Cooper became the permanent bass. When Williams returned, months later, he had joined the Opals/Crystals. Cooper would later be with Duncan in the Stylists.

In December 1953, Dunham left the Vocaleers and joined the Solitaires as lead. On the Vocaleers' "Angel Face," he was replaced by Joe Powell. When Dunham joined the Solitaires, he began calling himself Herman Curtis, which was his wife's maiden name (his wife was related to Buzzy Willis of the Solitaires).

Following the July 1954 session at Red Robin, Powell coincidentally came down with terrible stage fright and this meant the end of the original Vocaleers. Powell left, and Walker and Walton joined with Bobby Moore, Kerry Saxton, and Jimmy Jones to become the Savoys, later the Jones Boys and the Pretenders.

Duncan's brother was Paul Roland Martinez, who sang with the Vocaltones.

Duncan and Cooper remained with Bobby Robinson to honor the Vocaleers' five-year contract they had with him and his organization. Duncan, however, was obligated to enter the service and was in the military until 1958. When he returned home, he teamed up with his brother, Dunham, and Richard Blandon, but nothing they ever put on wax was ever released.

The original group almost re-formed with Duncan, Dunham, Cooper, and Walton. The only one they could not find was William Walker, who had entered the service. Therefore, Richard Blandon remained, and it was this quintet who recorded as the Vocaleers for the Old Town subsidiary Paradise in 1959.

In 1960, Duncan recorded with the Stylists. The Vocaleers also recorded in 1960 for the Old Town label. They were now Duncan, Dunham, Walton, and Leo Fuller. The released cuts recorded at this session went nowhere. Soon Duncan met up with Danny Robinson, who released the Vocaleers' record on his Vest label. This group was William Walker (back from the army), Caesar Williams (cousin of Teddy), Leo Fuller, and Mel Walton. Duncan played piano on these sessions and did not sing.

Twistime, a subsidiary of Atlantic, was next. This time, Duncan was not there at all. In a *Goldmine* interview with Marv Goldberg, Duncan believes that this group was made up of Curtis Blandon, Caesar Williams, William Walker, and Mel Walton.

The Vocaleers on Savoy 824 was a different group.

In 1991, the Vocaleers recorded for Classic Artists. This group consisted of Joe Duncan, brother Paul Roland Martinez, Leo "Tiny" Fuller, Frank Morrow, and Jimmy Lyons.

Discography

Red Robin 113 Be True (JD)/Oh Where? (JD) (1952)
Red Robin 114 Is It a Dream? (JD)/Hurry Home (JD) (1952)
Red Robin 119 I Walk Alone (JD)/How Soon? (JD) (1953)
Red Robin 125 Love You (JD)/Will You Be True? (JD) (1954)
Red Robin 132 Angel Face (JD)/Lovin' Baby (JD) (1954)
Paradise 113 I Need your Love So Bad (HD)/Have You Ever Loved Someone? (JD) (1959)
Old Town 1089 Love and Devotion (JD)/This Is the Night (HD) (1960)
Vest 832 The Night Is Quiet (CW)/ Hear My Plea (LF) (1960)
Twistime T 11 The Cootie Snap (CB)/A Golden Tear (CW) (1962)
Source: Marv Goldberg in *DISCoveries.*

Vocaltones (New York)

Personnel Bobby Johnson (lead), Eddie Quinones (2d tenor), Wyndham "Corky" Porter (baritone), Tommy Grate (bass)

Notes

This group met one another on Manhattan's Upper West Side. Their first get-together included Roland Martinez, Joe Duncan's brother. But because he missed their first recording session, he is not shown above with the first recording group of Vocaltones.

"My Version of Love," a Vocaltones classic, was penned by Martinez's brother, Joe Duncan.

Because the Vocaltones' members were disappointed with their output at Apollo Records, they moved over to George Goldner's stable of vocal groups recording for Gee. At this time Quinones joined the air force and was replaced by Willie Reed. The group then consisted of Reed, Martinez, Porter, and Grate. The Gee recording wasn't released until 1988, when Murray Hill's *Come Dance with Me* LP included it.

Willie Reed became disenchanted and soon left the Vocaltones. Tommy Grate would also leave to sing bass for the Dubs. Martinez, Porter, and Johnson were then joined by Irving Lee Gail and Bobby Moore to form the final Vocaltones group, who recorded for Cindy.

Grate also had also been part of the Five Wings.

Discography

Apollo 488 My Girl/I'm Gonna Get That Girl (1955)
Apollo 492 Darling/Three Kinds of People (1956)
Apollo 497 My Version of Love/I'll Never Let You Go (1956)
Gee UNR Come Dance with Me/Answer to My Dreams (1956)
Cindy 3004 Hawaiian Rock and Roll/Walkin' with My Baby (1957)
Source: Donn Fileti's liner notes with the Relic LP *Vocaltones-Our Version of Love.*

Voice Masters (Detroit)

Personnel Joseph Murphy (lead), Henry Jones, Crathman "C. P." Spencer, John Raymond Dorsey, Walter Gaines

Notes

During their session at Anna it was felt that a sixth voice was needed and Melvin Franklin (of the Temptations) was called in.

Ty Hunter, who performed lead on two other Anna discs with the group billed as Ty Hunter and the Voice Masters, also sang with the Romeos on Atco.

This group had been the Five Jets on DeLuxe and the Five Stars on Mark-X and End—two of George Goldner's labels.

(Note: Curiously, in Steve Towne's article in the September 1981 issue of *Goldmine,* he states that David Ruffin, Lamont Dozier, and Ty Hunter would all be billed as different lead singers for the Voice Masters! According to Goldberg's 1996 article, only Hunter would ever receive this billing.)

Discography

Anna 101 Hope and Pray (JM/CP)/Oops, I'm Sorry (JM) (1959)
Anna 102 Needed (CS)/Needed (For Lovers Only) (CS) (1959)
Anna 1114 Everything about You/Orphan Boy (Ty Hunter and the Voice Masters) (1960)
Anna 1123 Everytime/Free (Ty Hunter and the Voice Masters) (1961)
Sources: Steve Towne in *Goldmine,* September 1981; Marv Goldberg in *DISCoveries,* August 1996.

Voices (Los Angeles)

Personnel Robert Byrd, Jules Castron, Earl Nelson

Notes

This group, according to the liner notes with the Specialty CD *Doo Wop from Dolphin's of Hollywood,* was actually Robert (Bobby Day) Byrd and/or Earl Nelson and/or Jules Castron, overdubbing themselves.

Discography

Cash 1011 Two Things I Love/Why? (1955)
Cash 1014 Hey Now/My Love Grows Stronger (1955)
Cash 1015 Takes Two to Make a Home/I Want to Be Ready (1955)
Cash 1016 Santa Claus Boogie/Santa Claus Baby (1955)
Source: Billy Vera, liner notes with the Specialty CD *Doo Wop from Dolphin's of Hollywood.*

Voices Five (Queens, N.Y.)

Personnel Freddie Johnson (lead), Bud Johnson (1st/2d tenor), Larry Pendergrass (1st/2d tenor), Elliot Green (baritone), Bobby Thompson (bass)

Notes

This group is the Chanters with Bud Johnson's cousin Freddie on lead. Fred Paige was in the service. After the Chanters' DeLuxe recording career had ended, they made one last effort as the Voices Five on the Craft label in 1959.

Discography

Craft 116 For Sentimental Reasons (FJ)/All Alone (?) (1959)
Source: Marv Goldberg in *Yesterday's Memories.*

Volchords (Pittsburgh, Pa.)

Personnel Edward "Edgy" Sanders (lead), Raymond Davis (1st tenor), Bobby McLendon (2d tenor), Sylvester Harris (baritone), Andrew Boyd (bass)

Notes

The Volchords, as explained in the liner notes with the Itzy II CD *Pittsburgh's Greatest Hits,* were from Pittsburgh's Hill District.

Discography

Regatta 2004 Bongo Love/Peek-A-Boo Love (1961)
Source: Travis Klein, liner notes with the Itzy II CD *Pittsburgh's Greatest Hits.*

Volumes (Detroit)

Personnel Edward Union (lead), Lawrence Davis (1st tenor), Larry Wright (2d tenor), Joe Travillion (baritone), Ernest Newsome (bass)

Notes

The Volumes on Chex resulted when two unrecorded Detroit groups combined. This merger took place in 1960. Their manager was married to a Canadian, and he used this association to have them perform on the Canadian side of the river in Windsor, Ontario. During one of those Canadian performances, they met Willie Ewing, owner of Chex Records, who convinced them to sign a two-year contract with Chex. Their first recording session took place early in 1962. Because of a pressing plant blunder, the label on the disc called the group the Valumes. This was corrected on later pressings.

In Bob Belniak's discussion on the Volumes *(Echoes of the Past* 9), he refers to the baritone as Truvillion and to the bass as Earnest Newson. In Gordon Skadberg's liner notes with Sequel's *Jubilee/Josie–5* CD, his listing of personnel is as follows: Eddie Union, Elijah Davis, Larry Wright, Joe Truvillion, and Ernest Newson. According to Donn Fileti's liner notes with the Relic LP *Volumes,* personnel making up the group included Eddie Union (lead), Elijah Davis (1st tenor), Larry Wright (2d tenor), Joe Truvillion (baritone), and Earnest Newson (bass). I'll let the reader choose.

With the exception of Larry Wright, the Volumes all attended the same high school. At that time they sang at parties and other local events.

Following their final recording session with Chex in 1962, an announcement was made that national distribution was changing to the Jay Gee, or the Jubilee Records organization. The Volumes recorded four sides for the Jubilee label, which did not do as well as their initial effort on Chex.

Union left in 1965 and Larry Wright replaced him at lead. Gerald Mathis was soon added, as was Jimmy Burgess.

Until they got to Inferno Records and their soul period, they recorded for many record labels.

Union returned later and the Volumes then became a transition group—bridging R&B and soul.

They were unsuccessful during this transition period and disbanded in the late 1960s.

Discography

Chex 1002 I Love You/Dreams (1962)

Chex 1005 Come Back into My Heart/The Bell (1962)
Jubilee 5446 Teenage Paradise/Sandra (1963)
Jubilee 5454 Our Song/Oh My Mother in Law (1963)
American Arts 6 I Can't Live without You/Gotta Give Her Love (1964)
American Arts 16 I Just Can't Help Myself/One-Way Lover (1965)
Impact 1017 The Trouble I've Seen/That Same Old Feeling (1966)
Inferno 2001 You Got It Baby/A Way to Love You (1967)
Inferno 2004 My Road Is the Right Road/My Kind of Girl (1967)
Inferno 5001 Ain't That Lovin' You/I Love You Baby (1968)
Sources: Donn Fileti, liner notes with the Relic LP *Chex*; Gordon Skadberg, liner
notes with the Sequel CD *Jubilee/Josie Vocal Groups–5*; Bob Belniak in *Echoes of
the Past* 9.

Von Gayles (Chicago)

Personnel Joe Brackenridge (lead), Stacy Steel Jr. (1st tenor), Willie Dial/Wright
(2d tenor), Willie Daniels (baritone), James Doolaby Wright (bass)

Notes

Breckenridge and Steele were cousins.

Original members Jimmy Washington, Charles Johnson, and Willie C. Robinson
temporarily separated from the group on the day of recording. The listing above
reflects an ad hoc group that did the initial recordings. These three were from the
Serenades.

In 1964, the group became the Cascades who recorded one disc for McCormick.

Discography

USA 1221 Loneliness/The Twirl (1959)
Dore 544 The Twirl/Crazy Dance (1960)
Source: Bob Pruter, *Doowop . . . The Chicago Scene.*

Wanderers (New York)

Personnel Ray Pollard (lead), Frank Joyner (2d tenor), Robert Yarborough (baritone), Sheppard Grant (d) (bass)

Notes

This group began in 1952 as the Barons in New York's Harlem section of Manhattan. They had a very unreliable lead singer who was asked to leave and was replaced
by Ray Pollard, a recently discharged serviceman. After a great deal of practice they
were signed with Herman Lubinsky's Savoy Records as the Wanderers. They recorded one disc for the Newark-based label in 1954 as the Wanderers and another,
"Love Can't Be Blind," with Dolly Cooper.

After Savoy, the Wanderers released two discs on Decca as the Singing Wanderers. Thereafter, they were the Wanderers, who signed with Onyx in 1957. When the
MGM organization purchased Onyx from Jerry Winston, the Wanderers next re-

corded for MGM subsidiary labels Orbit and Cub. They had a nice stay with MGM until 1962 when, after recording their final disc for them, they moved over to United Artists.

This group was one of a select few vocal groups to appear in Fritz Pollard's legendary 1955 rhythm and blues motion picture, *Rockin' the Blues*.

In the 1970s, Ray Pollard appeared in the Broadway Musical *Purlie* with Tony Middleton (Willows) and Milton Grayson (Dominoes).

Discography

Savoy 1109 We Could Find Happiness/Hey Mae Ethel (1953)
Onyx 518 Thinking of You/Great Jumpin' Catfish (1957)
Orbit 9003 My Shining Hour/A Teenage Quarrel (1958)
Cub 9003 My Shining Hour/A Teenage Quarrel (1958)
Cub 9019 Two Hearts on a Window Pane/Collecting Hearts (1958)
Cub 9023 Please/Shadrack, Meshack, and Abednego (1958)
Cub 9035 I'm Not Ashamed/Only When You're Lonely (1959)
Cub 9054 I Walked through a Forest/Waiting in Green Pastures (1959)
Cub 9075 I Need You More/I Could Make You Mine (1960)
Cub 9089 For Your Love/Sally Goodheart (1961)
Cub 9094 I'll Never Smile Again/A Little Too Long (1961)
Cub 9099 She Wears My Ring/Somebody Else's Sweetheart (1961)
Cub 9109 There Is No Greater Love/As Time Goes By (1962)
MGM 13082 There Is No Greater Love/As Time Goes By (1962)
United Artists 570 After He Breaks Your Heart/Run Run Señorita (1962)
United Artists 648 I'll Know/You Can't Run Away from Me (1963)
Sources: Steve Propes, liner notes with the Savoy LP *Doo Wop Delights—The Roots of Rock*; Tony Middleton, interview by author, April 1997; Jay Warner, *American Singing Groups*.

Webtones (Brooklyn, N.Y.)

Personnel Louis Williams (1st tenor), Doug Ebron (2d tenor), Terry Wilson (baritone), Frankie Clemens (bass)

Notes

Clemens and Wilson sang with the other Danny Webb–managed group, the Danleers. After the demise of the Danleers, Webb had Clemens and Wilson join up with Williams and Ebron, forming a new Danleers configuration.

It's interesting that both groups were managed by Danny Webb and that the first group was named the Danleers and the second, the Webtones.

Discography

MGM 12724 My Lost Love/Walk, Talk, and Kiss (1958)
Sources: Pete Grendysa, liner notes with the Bear Family CD *The Danleers—One Summer Night*; Jay Warner, *American Singing Groups*.

Wheels (Brooklyn, N.Y.)

Personnel Rudy Anderson (lead), James Pender (tenor), Kenneth Fox (baritone), Lorenzo Cook (bass)

Notes

This group was managed by Allen Bunn, former member of the Larks on Apollo. Bunn would sometimes record with the Wheels. It was Bunn who brought the group to Joe Liebowitz, owner of Premium, in 1955. In addition to their recordings for Premium, they also became the studio group for the New Jersey–based label. They backed up Vicki Carr, Gloria Lynne, and Arthur Lake at Premium.

As the group began making a name for themselves, Liebowitz passed away and Premium's operations folded.

After Premium, the group became the Federals and recorded for Fury and DeLuxe. Then they went back to the Wheels and recorded for George Goldner's Curtis label. Next they moved to Time Records, then to Morris Levy's Roulette label, and finally to Folly.

Discography

Premium 405 My Heart's Desire/Let's Have a Ball (1956)
Premium 408 Teasin' Heart/Loco (1956)
Premium 410 I Can't Forget/How Could I Ever Leave You? (1957)
Time 1003 So Young and So in Love/Where Were You? (1958)
Roulette 4271 No One but You/I've Waited for a Lifetime (1959)
Curtis 751 It's Not for Me/Copy Cat (1959)
Folly 600 Clap Your Hands–1/Clap Your Hands–2 (1959)
Sources: Sal Mondrone in *Bim Bam Boom*; Donn Fileti, liner notes with the Relic CD *Premium*.

Whips (Los Angeles)

Personnel Cornelius Gunter (lead), Beverly Thompson (1st tenor), Thomas Fox (2d tenor), Obediah "Young" Jesse (baritone), Richard Berry (bass)

Notes

This group was also known as the Five Hearts, Flairs, Five Hollywood Bluejays, Hunters, Jac-O-Lacs, and Rams—another configuration of the Flairs.

Second tenor Beverly Thompson was a man.

Discography

Flair 1025 Pleadin' Heart/She Done Me Wrong (1954)
Sources: Marv Goldberg and Mike Redmond in *Record Exchanger*; Lynn McCutcheon in *Bim Bam Boom*; Marv Goldberg and Rick Whitesell in *Yesterday's Memories*; Jim Dawson, liner notes with Ace's *Flair Label*.

Whirlers (New York)

Personnel John Barnes (lead), Les Cooper (1st tenor), Robert Dunn (2d tenor/baritone), William Toddman (bass)

Notes

This group recorded simultaneously as the Empires and the Whirlers on Bobby Robinson's Whirlin' Disc Records. They were also the Prestos on Mercury. They had two names at Whirlin' Disc because their record as the Empires did not do well, and owner Robinson changed their name to the Whirlers to see if this might help sell their releases.

Discography

Whirlin' Disc 108 Magic Mirror (JB)/Tonight and Forever (JB) (1956)
Source: Marv Goldberg and Dave Hinckley in *Yesterdays' Memories* 12.

Whispers (Baltimore, Md.)

Personnel William Mills, Billy Thompson, Terry Johnson

Notes

According to George Moonoogian's liner notes with Flyright's *Dusty and Forgotten* and *I Always Remember* CDs, this group had to be young, since Billy Thompson's father countersigned the contract for Billy to record with Gotham. Additionally, Moonoogian also points out that assessing the record numbers for both Whispers' Gotham discs, the group had to have signed with Gotham sometime during 1954.

Little else is known about the Whispers other than the interesting fact that Gotham's owner, Ivin Ballen [sic], did not confine his search for talent to the Phildelphia area but went a bit further south to Baltimore to find the Whispers.

Discography

Gotham 309 Don't Fool with Lizzie/Fool Heart (1955)
Gotham 312 Are You Sorry?/We're Getting Married (1955)
Source: George Moonoogian, liner notes with the Flyright CD *Dusty and Forgotten.*

Wigs (Cleveland, Ohio)

Personnel Arthur Blakey (lead), Albert Banks (tenor), Leroy McQueen (baritone), Arthur Porter (bass)

Notes

Albert Banks and Leroy McQueen had formerly been with Billy Wells and the Crescents, who recorded for the Reserve label.

Discography

Golden Crest 592 Sweeter Than Wine/The Chicken Switch (1964)
Source: Leroy McQueen, interview by Galen Gart.

Wildwoods (New Haven, Conn.)

Personnel Fred Parris (lead), Wes Forbes (1st tenor), Richard Freeman (2d tenor), Louis Peebles, Silvester Hopkins

Notes

This group was formed in 1961 from the remaining members of the Five Satins, who recorded the legendary "In the Still of the Night" on Ember.

Forbes also sang with the Starlarks, the Five Satins, and the New Yorkers.

Freeman, in addition to the groups above, also sang with the Restless Hearts.

Discography

Caprice 101/102 When the Swallows Come Back to Capistrano/Heart of Mine (1961)
Source: Bob Galgano, Tom Luciani, Marcia Vance, and Steve Flam in *Bim Bam Boom* 3.

Williams Quartet, Billy (New York)

Personnel Billy Williams (lead), John Bell (tenor), Claude Riddick (baritone), Eugene Dixon (bass)

Notes

Billy Williams began his singing career as lead vocalist with the Charioteers. This took place when he was attending Wilberforce University in Ohio, where he joined three other students to become the Charioteers. They enjoyed great success on the radio with Bing Crosby and others. In 1949, Williams, forecasting the imminent growth of the broadcast medium, left the Charioteers to form his own Billy Williams Quartet.

In the early 1950s, the Billy Williams Quartet appeared regularly with Sid Caesar and Imogene Coca on *Your Show of Shows.*

Ollie Jones from the Ravens and Cues sang with the group from time to time.

Discography

MGM 10764 I Didn't Slip, I Was Pushed, I Fell/Longing (1950)
MGM 10857 The Room I'm Sleeping In/Music by the Angels (1950)
MGM 10928 The Gaucho Serenade/I Won't Cry (1951)
MGM 10967 Pretty-Eyed Baby/You Made Me Love You (1951)
MGM 10998 Shanghai/The Wondrous Word (1951)
MGM 11066 It's Over/Sin (1951)
MGM 11117 I'll Never Fail You/Busy Line (1951)
MGM 11145 Callaway Went Thataway/No Other Love (1952)
MGM 11172 Wheel of Fortune/After I Say I'm Sorry (1952)
MGM 11184 Confetti/Don't Grieve, Don't Sorrow, Don't Cry (1952)
MGM 11249 What You Don't Know of Love/Between the Devil and the Deep Blue Sea (1952)
Mercury 5866 Stay/Azurie (1952)
Mercury 5884 It's Best We Say Goodbye/Who Knows? (1952)

Mercury 5902 Some Folks Do, Some Folks Don't/That's What . . . (1952)
Mercury 70012 I Don't Know Why/Mad about 'Cha (1952)
Mercury 70094 Pour Me a Glass of Teardrops/It's a Miracle (1953)
Mercury 70180 You're the One for Me/This Side of Heaven (1953)
Mercury 70210 Cattle Call/A Smile for Suzette (1953)
Mercury 70271 If I Never Get to Heaven/Ask Me No Questions (1953)
Mercury 70324 I've Got an Invitation to a Dance/I'll Close My Eyes (1954)
Mercury 70376 Go Home, Joe/You're the Only One I Adore (1954)
Coral 61212 Sh-Boom/Wherever Wherever (1954)
Coral 61264 Love Me/The Honeydripper (1954)
Coral 61346 Fools Rush In/He Follows She (1955)
Coral 61363 I Wanna Hug You, Kiss You . . . Smoke from Your Cigarette (1955)
Coral 61462 The Glory of Love/Wonderful, Wonderful One (1955)
Coral 61498 Learning to Love/Just a Little Bit More (1955)
Coral 61576 Cry Baby/A Crazy Little Palace (1956)
Coral 61639 Pray/You'll Reach Your Star (1956)
Coral 61684 This Planet Earth/I Guess I'll Be on My Way (1956)
Coral 61730 Don't Cry On My Shoulder/Shame, Shame, Shame (1956)
Coral 61751 Follow Me/Stormy (1956)
Coral 61932 Baby, Baby/Don't Let Go (1958)
Coral 61961 There I've Said It Again/Steppin' Out Tonight (1958)
MGM 12537 The Gaucho Serenade/Shanghai (1957)
Sources: Unsigned liner notes with Mercury's LP *Oh Yeah, It's Billy Williams;* Pete Grendysa, liner notes with the Gospel Jubilee LP *Charioteers—Jesus Is a Rock in the Weary Land.*

Willows (New York)

Personnel Tony Middleton (lead), Richie Davis (1st tenor), Ralph Martin (2d tenor), Joe Martin (baritone), Freddie Donovan (d) (bass)

Notes

This group came together as the Five Willows (see entry in encyclopedia) in 1952, a typical street corner group on 115th Street in Harlem. Clarisse Martin, their mentor, drove them to practice and rehearsals every day! They would sing in hallways, hospitals, church functions, and various local events.

They went to Abbey Records for an audition with Peter Dorain. They first went to Abbey because one of their members loved "The Whiffenpoof Song" by the Cabineers, which was on the Abbey label. During the next two years, Dorain moved his recording company and changed its name to Allen. Allen and Pee Dee were both owned by Peter Dorain (Durain in several articles).

When Allen went out of business in 1954, the group moved to Herald Records, still recording as the Five Willows. In 1955, Middleton met Morty Craft, who had just started his Melba label. At this time they changed their name to Willows, dropping the Five. They felt that the number did nothing for them, especially when they appeared with only four members.

Richard Simon, a neighborhood friend, sang bass for the group on "Church Bells

May Ring." Unrehearsed, he sang the phrase "hello hello again." The Mercury Diamonds covered this tune and had much better sales.

They also did recordings with Club Records (1957). While they were with Club,
John Thomas Steele replaced Freddie Donovan at bass. Donovan passed away on
May 13, 1997.

They also recorded for Eldorado Records (1958) and George Goldner's Gone
Records (1958), but nothing ever hit like "Church Bells May Ring."

Middleton also sang with the Hollywood Flames. In the 1970s, he was nominated
for a Grammy for his solo rendition of "Don't Ever Leave Me." Middleton's other
achievements include his role in the Broadway show *Purlie* with Milton Grayson
of the Dominoes and Ray Pollard of the Wanderers.

(*Note:* The group's Allen, Pee Dee, and Herald recordings are not shown below
because they were recorded under their previous name, Five Willows.)

Discography

Melba 102 Church Bells May Ring/Baby Tell Me (1956)
Melba 106 Do You Love Me?/My Angel (1956)
Club 1014 This is the End/Don't Pull, Don't Push, Don't Shove (1956)
Melba 115 Little Darlin'/My Angel (1957)
Eldorado 508 The First Taste of Love/Only My Heart (1957)
Gone 5015 Let's Fall in Love/Say Yeah (1957)
Sources: Liner notes with Relic's *Herald*; Marcia Vance and Phil Groia in *Bim Bam
Boom*; Pete Grendysa in *Goldmine,* September 9, 1988; Tony Middleton, interview
by author, June 1996.

Wisdoms (St. Paul, Minn.)

Personnel
Gene "Butchy" Moore (lead), Horace Rivers (tenor), Ray "Bucky"
Brown (baritone), Jerry Reed (bass)

Notes

It was considered very unusual for a black vocal group to come out to the Minneapolis–St. Paul region. The other Gaity group, the Velquins, were also black.

The Wisdoms first recorded for Gaity in 1959. They had been together for several years prior to their recording. The Gaity CD liner notes state that there are a
dozen or more unreleased tunes that cannot be retrieved; presumably they are lost
forever.

Discography
Gaity 162 Lost in Dreams/Two Heart Make One Love (1959)
Source: Jim Okldsberg and Billy Miller, liner notes with *Gaity* CD.

Wonders (Akron, Ohio)

Personnel
Fred Kalail (lead), Wade Haddad (tenor), Ron Kalail (baritone), Harvey
Russell (bass)

Notes

According to Donn Fileti's liner notes with Relic's *Groups of Ember* CD, the Wonders "were a middle-of-the-road pop group who preferred the sound of the Four Lads or the Crew Cuts." Fileti also states that the Wonders were an amateur white group who turned in a fine version of the Penguins' "Hey Señorita."

The Ember CD liner notes also state that soon after the Wonders recorded for Ember, they soon turned to Middle Eastern music, since several members were of Arabic descent.

Discography

Ember 1051 I'll Write a Book/Hey Señorita (1959)
Source: Donn Fileti, liner notes with the Relic CD *Groups of Ember Records–1&2.*

Wrens (Bronx, N.Y.)

Personnel Bobby Mansfield (lead), George Magnezid (1st tenor), Francis Concepcion (baritone), Jimmy "Archie" Archer (d) (bass)

Notes

Before recording, the group was a trio. Magnezid's friend Bobby Mansfield joined them after they formed.

After "Serenade of the Bells," Archer was drafted and replaced by Perry Heyward, a former member of the Jay Dee Sparrows and the Performers and part-time Checkers member who recorded for King.

In the liner notes on the Murray Hill LP, it is stated that "C'est la vie" contains all four Wrens and Richard Barrett and Ronnie Bright of the Valentines. This, according to Bobby Mansfield, is simply not true. Mansfield told me himself that he never sang with Ronnie Bright.

"Wreckless" [sic] and "House of Cards" were intended for release with Mansfield as a solo. But for some unknown reason, they were not released until the 1986 Murray Hill LP, on which these songs were released as by the Wrens.

"Frenchie" Concepción recorded for the Travelers on Atlas in 1957. He also sang with the Quinns on Cyclone. Concepción is the only member of the original Wrens who ever recorded with another group.

It is this author's sense that in his infinite wisdom, George Goldner misspelled Wreckless to create alliteration with the group's name—Wrens. (I doubt that we'll ever know for sure.)

In 1994, Mansfield became part of the Morrisania Revue, a group composed of vocal group members from the 1950s from that section of the east Bronx. They issued a CD in September of that year and displayed the wonderful talent that these folks still possess.

Also interesting is that on the Solitaires' LP boxed set, there is a song entitled "Come Back and Give Me Your Hand," which is definitely not the Solitaires; it was written by Bobby Mansfield and sung by Waldo Champen with the Old Town Supremes. This was related to me by Mansfield and Champen.

Discography

Rama 53 Love's Something Made for Two/Beggin' for Love (1955)
Rama 65 Come Back My Love/Beggin' for Love (1955)
Rama 65 Eleven Roses/Come Back My Love (1955)
Rama 110 Love's Something Made for Two/Hey Girl (1955)
Rama 174 Hey Girl/Serenade of the Bells (1955)
Rama 174 Hey Girl/Love's Something Made for Two (1955)
Rama 175 Betty Jean/Everything (1955)
Rama 184 I Won't Come to Your Wedding/What Makes You Do the Things . . . (1955)
Rama 194 C'est la Vie/C'est la Vie (1956)
Sources: Phil Groia and Marcia Vance, liner notes with the Murray Hill LP *Best of the Wrens;* Bobby Mansfield, interview by author, 1994.

Young Lads (New York)

Personnel Ronnie Watson (tenor), Vaughan Constantino (1st tenor), James Strait (tenor), Luther Morton (baritone), Aaron Broadnick (bass)

Notes

Carl Williams was a 1st tenor who joined later.

Discography

Neil 100 Moonlight/I'm in Love (1956)
Source: James Strate in Deltairs article in *Yesterday's Memories* 4.

Youngtones (Brooklyn, N.Y.)

Personnel Johnny Marsi (lead), Gilbert Rivera (1st tenor), Joe Crespo (2d tenor), Willie Rivera (baritone), Louis Figueroa (bass)

Notes

The Youngtones, from the Coney Island section of Brooklyn, recorded excellent two-sided discs for Ben Smith's X-Tra Records.

Ronald Jackson joined the Youngtones later as lead and executed the well-known "Can I Come Over." He was the brother of Jesters' lead singer Adam Jackson.

Discography

X-Tra 104 You I Adore/It's Over Now (1958)
X-Tra 110 Patricia/By the Candleglow (1958)
Brunswick 55089 Oh Tell Me/Come On Baby (1958)
X-Tra 120/121 Can I Come Over?/Gonna Get Together Again (1959)
Sources: Donn Fileti, liner notes with the Relic X-Tra LP *Golden Groups of X-Tray Records*; Ferdie Gonzalez, *Disco-File.*

Youngsters (Los Angeles)

Personnel Homer Green (lead), Donald Miller (1st tenor), Charles Everidge (2d tenor), Harold Murray (baritone), James Monroe Warren (bass)

Notes

The Youngsters formed in a Los Angeles high school and had difficulties selecting a name. They were eventually signed by Empire Records of Hollywood early in 1956.

They recorded for Empire in April 1956. Their recordings were released on two discs as by two differently named groups. "Don't Fall in Love Too Soon" was released as by the Preludes and "Shattered Dreams" as by the Youngsters. Following these sessions, Green went into the service and was replaced by Robert Johnson. Miller also left, and his spot was replaced by Herman Pruitt (formerly of the Calvanes). Pruitt was another high school chum of the original group.

They did several more sessions in 1956. The first release from the second session was by the Tempters and the next two by the Youngsters.

Following a summer tour, they recorded "Dreamy Eyes," released as by the Youngsters. This was their biggest hit. Empire Records, however, was not in a position to support the record financially. Although it was their biggest seller, it was their last. Compounding their difficulty, Robert Johnson entered the marines and the group soon drifted apart.

In May 1958, Everidge, about to join the air force, was contacted by the Shields' producers. They were in need of a road or touring group. Everidge got Warren, his cousin Howard Gardner, and Frankie Ervin, who all began promoting "You Cheated." Before anything happened with the recording, Everidge was called by the air force to serve.

Johnson and Everidge appeared with the Mad Lads.

Discography

Empire 104 Shattered Dreams/Rock'n & Roll'n Cowboy (1956)
Empire 107 Counterfeit Heart/You're an Angel (1956)
Empire 109 Dreamy Eyes/I'm Sorry Now (1956)
Empire 109 Dreamy Eyes/Christmas in Jail (1956)
Source: Dave Hinckley and Marv Goldberg in *Yesterday's Memories* 10.

Zodiacs (Lancaster, S.C.)

Personnel Maurice Williams (lead), Earl Gainey (tenor), William Massey (tenor/baritone), Willie Jones (baritone), Norman Wade (bass)

Notes

The group started in 1955 as high school students in Lancaster, South Carolina. At that time they were calling themselves the Royal Charms. They appeared locally in clubs, colleges, and universities. Their popularity provided them with the incentive to travel to Nashville to Excello Records to audition. This was successful and their name was changed to the Gladiolas. They recorded and released four discs for Excello, one of which was their original composition, "Little Darlin."

Tenor Bob Robertson was added on the last two Excello singles.

After leaving Excello, they were informed that Excello owner Ernie Young owned the name Gladiolas and consequently they changed their name to Zodiacs. They were allowed to appear as the Gladiolas but could not record with the name.

After recording for two smaller labels, Cole and Selwyn, the group began to come apart.

In 1959, Massey joined the air force. Wade and Robertson had had enough. Williams then recruited Henry Gaston (tenor), Wiley Bennett (tenor), and Charles Thomas (baritone) to form a new Zodiacs. They recorded two records for Soma at their start.

Johnny Mobley and Willie Bennett alternated at tenor in the early 1960s.

They contacted Al Silver at Herald Records, who liked them and had them record "Stay" and several others after this big seller.

In the mid-1960s, the Zodiacs went from label to label. They recorded for Atlantic, Scepter, Sphere Sound, 440/Plus, Vee Jay, Sea Horn, Dee Su, and Veep.

In 1966, the Zodiacs were joined by Marshall Seahorn to record "May I."

Discography

Cole 100 T Town/Golly Gee (1959)
Cole 101 Where Are You?/She's Mine (1959)
Selwyn 5121 College Girl/Say Yeah (1959)
Soma 1410 Another Little Darling/Lita (1960)
Soma 1418 Little Sally Walker/Anything (1960)
Herald 552 Stay/Do You Remember? (1960)
Herald 556 Always/I Remember (1960)
Herald 559 Come Along/Do I? (1961)
Herald 563 Some Day/Come and Get It (1961)
Herald 565 High Blood Pressure/Please (1961)
Herald 572 Here I Stand/It's All Right (1961)
Atlantic 2199 Loneliness/Funny (1963)
Scepter 12113 Nobody Knows/I Know (1965)
Sphere Sound 707 So Fine/The Winds (1965)
Vee Jay 678 May I?/Lollipop (1966)
Dee Su 302 Being without You/Baby, Baby (1967)
Dee Su 304 May I?/This Feeling (1967)
Dee Su 307 Ooh Poo Pah Doo–Pt. 1/Pt. 2 (1968)
Dee Su 309 Surely/Don't Ever Leave Me (1968)
Dee Su 311 How to Pick a Winner/Don't Be Half Safe (1968)
Dee Su 318 Stay/Dance, Dance, Dance (1968)
Sea Horn 503 My Baby's Gone/Return (1969)
440 Plus 4401 I'd Rather Have a Memory Than a Dream/Try (1969)
Veep 1294 The Four Corners/My Reason for Livin' (1969)
Source: "Little" Walter, liner notes with the Relic LP *Best of Maurice Williams and the Zodiacs.*

Appendix
Index of Performers and Corresponding Groups

Performer	Group	Performer	Group
Abata, Bill	Consorts (Cousins, APT)	Alan, John	Ad Libs
Abbate, Billy	Consorts (Cousins, APT)	Alan, Mark	Cashmeres (Mercury, Herald)
Abbott, Arnold	Styles (Serene, Josie)		
Abrams, Henry	Marylanders	Albanese, Richard	Impossibles (RMP)
Abston, Thomas	Turks	Albano, Paul	Five Discs
Accoo, Harry	V-Eights	Alexander, Clarence	Pharaohs (Specialty)
Aceierno, Vinnie	Passions	Alexander, Clarence	Sliders
Adams, Billy	Orioles	Alexander, Frank	Appegios
Adams, Billy	Regals	Alexander, Frank	Arrows (Flash)
Adams, Bobby	Clovers	Alexander, Frank	Convincers
Adams, Eddie	Interludes	Alexander, Joe	Joe Alexander & the Cubans
Adams, Floyd	Keynotes (Apollo)		
Adams, Floyd	Sparrows (Jay Dee, Davis)	Alexander, Joe	Four Tones
Adams, Jay Joe	Casuals (Backbeat)	Alexander, Joe	Dusty Brooks & the Four Tones
Adams, Jimmy	Jubalaires		
Adams, Johnny	Gondoliers	Alexander, Joe	Dusty Brooks & the Four Tones (featuring Juanita Brown)
Adams, Lorenzo Robert	Calvanes		
		Alexander, Joe	Dusty Brooks & the Tones
Adams, Lorenzo Robert	Nuggets (RCA)	Alexander, Melvin	Appegios
		Alexander, Melvin	Arrows (Flash)
Adams, R.	Imperials (Great Lakes)	Alexander, Melvin	Convincers
Adams, Richie	Fireflies	Alexander, Michael	Charm
Adams, Robert	Clefftones (Old Town)	Alexander, Mitchell	Chargers
Adams, Ronald	Naturals (Red Top)	Alexander, Mitchell	Feathers
Adams, T.	Gotham's Four Notes	Alford, Bill	Griffins
Adams, Tommy	Blenders (Decca, MGM)	Alford, Gene	Four Knights
Adams, Tommy	Four Notes (Premier)	Alford, Odell	Crescendos (Music City)
Adams, Walter	Drifters (Atlantic)	Alford, Odell	Casual Crescendos
Addeo, Nicky	Nicky Addeo & the Plazas	Alicia, John	Unknowns (X-Tra)
Addeo, Nicky	Ray & the Darchaes	Allbut, Barbara	Angels (Caprice, RCA)
Adino, Robert	Debonaires (Gee)	Allbut, Barbara	Starlets
Adkins, Terry	Tears	Allbut, Phyllis "Jiggs"	Angels (Caprice, RCA)
Agtuca, Peter	Imaginations		
Agtuca, Philip	Imaginations	Allbut, Phyllis "Jiggs"	Starlets
Agugliaro, Joe	Markels (R&M)		
Agugliaro, Joe	Tony Richards & the Twilights (Colpix)	Allen, Charles	Rivieras
		Allen, Don	Kings (Gotham, Gone, RCA)
Aiello, Antonio	Nino & the Ebbtides		
Aita, Bob	Leisure Lads	Allen, Gloria	Tropicals
Akens, Jewel	Fascinators (Dootone)	Allen, Jimmy	Bel Aires
Akens, Jewel	Four Dots (Bullseye, Freedom)	Allen, Jimmy	Sheppards (Apex)
Akens, Jewell	Turnarounds	Allen, Joel	Sparks

Performer	Group
Allen, John "Angel"	Creators (T-Kay)
Allen, Johnny	Progressive Four
Allen, Jonathan "Sonny"	Hi Tensions
Allen, Josephine "Josie"	Claremonts
Allen, Josephine "Josie"	Tonettes
Allen, Louis	Jades (Christy)
Allen, Maurke	Spinners (Rhythm)
Allen, Napoleon "Snaggs"	Blenders (Decca, MGM)
Allen, Napoleon "Snaggs"	Cats and the Fiddle
Allen, Napoleon "Snaggs"	Millionaires (Davis)
Allen, Roy	Feathers
Allen, Roy	Individuals
Allen, Roy	Unforgettables
Allen, Talmadge	Keystoners
Allen, Tony	Cupids (Aladdin)
Allen, Tony	Furys (Mack IV)
Allen, Tony	Jaguars
Allen, Tony	Lions (Rendezvous)
Allen, Tony	Shields
Allen, Tony	Three Dots and a Dash
Allen, Tony	Tony Allen & the Champs
Allen, Tony	Tony Allen & the Wanderers
Allen, Tony	Twilighters (Specialty)
Allen, Tony	Wonders
Alleyne, Gloria	Delltones
Alleyne, Gloria	Enchanters (Jubilee)
Allison, Verne	Dells
Allison, Verne	El Rays
Allsbrooks, Howard	Buckeyes
Alston, Barbara	Crystals (Philles)
Alston Randy "Shade"	Shells
Alston, Edward	Leaders
Alston, Shirley	Shirelles
Alsup, Earl	Falcons (Regent, Savoy, RCA)
Alsup, George	Falcons (Regent, Savoy, RCA)
Alsup, Goldie "Boots"	Falcons (Regent, Savoy, RCA)
Alvarez, Felix	Cathy Jean & the Roommates
Alvarez, Fred	Hi-Tones (King, Candix, Fonsca)
Alvarez, Fred	Shy-Tones
Alveray, Bobby	Vilons
Alvin, Johnny	Playboys (Detroit)
Alvin, Johnny	Ramblers (Federal, Jax, MGM, Trumpet)
Alvin, Johnny "Duke"	Fabulous Playboys

Performer	Group
Alvin, Johnny "Duke"	Falcons
Alvin, Scott	Larks
Alvin, Scott	Majors
Amato, Nino	Elegants
Amato, Tony	Chaperones
Ames, Alexander	Scooters
Ammons, Gene	Blue Jays (Checker)
Ancrum, James	Crests
Anderson, Benny	Original Drifters
Anderson, Benny	Tears
Anderson, Clarence	Five Cs
Anderson, David	Medallionaires
Anderson, Ed	Love Notes (Riviera, Rainbow)
Anderson, Elmo "Chico"	Cap-Tans
Anderson, Elmo "Chico"	L'Cap-Tans
Anderson, Frankie	Interludes
Anderson, Harold	Lincolns (Mercury)
Anderson, Harold	Medallionaires
Anderson, Hazel	Hearts (Baton)
Anderson, Howard	Keynotes (Apollo)
Anderson, John	Cufflinx
Anderson, John	Lincolns (Mercury)
Anderson, Julius	Hollywood Saxons
Anderson, Katherine	Marvelettes
Anderson, Leslie	Dubs
Anderson, Nick	Solitaires
Anderson, Ray	Feathers
Anderson, Ron	Caverliers [sic] Quartet
Anderson, Ron	FiTones
Anderson, Ronald	Medallionaires
Anderson, Rudy	Federals
Anderson, Rudy	Wheels
Anderson, Stokes	José & the Aztecs
Anderson, Travis	Four Deals
Anderson, William "Chick"	Drifters (Atlantic)
Anderson, Willie	Splendors (Taurus)
Anderson, Wilston	La-Rells
Andess, Marcel	Prisonaires
Andrachio, Dominick	Four-Evers (Jamie)
Andrews, Jackie	Congress Alley
Andrews, Lee	Congress Alley
Andrews, Lee	Lee Andrews & the Hearts
Angel, Larry	Motions (Laurie)
Angelo, John	Crystals (Cub)
Angelo, John	Metros
Antebi, Dave	Boptones
Anthony, McKinley	Cruisers (V-Tone, Guyden, Gamble)
Anthony, Octavius	Castelles
Anthony, Sal	Dials (Philips)

Performer	Group
Antoine, Leon	Ink Spots
Apostol, John	Capris (Planet, Old Town, etc.)
Archer, Don	Scale-Tones
Archer, Jimmy "Archie"	Wrens
Arcipowski, Ken	Randy & the Rainbows
Arena, Neil	Mellokings
Arkis, Bill	Packards (Pla-Bac, Paradise)
Armato, Tony	Passions
Armistead, W.	Dukes (Imperial)
Armstead, Oliver	Progressive Four
Armstrong, Bob	Coolbreezers
Armstrong, Bobby	Accents (Brunswick)
Armstrong, Bobby	Blue Jays (Bluejay, Dig)
Armstrong, Bobby	Squires (Vita, Mambo)
Armstrong, Joseph	Trumpeteers
Armstrong, Lester	Five Bells (Clock)
Armstrong, Sam	Sensations
Arnold, Arnita	Cashmeres (Lake, Laurie, Josie, ACA)
Arnold, Dick	Ballads (Franwill)
Arnold, Dick	Cherokees (United Artists)
Arnold, Dick	Restless Hearts
Arnold, Eugene	Montclaires (Hi Q)
Arnold, James	Four Lads
Arnold, Leon	Calvaes
Arnold, Leon	Ramblers (Federal, Jax, MGM, Trumpet)
Arnold, Leon	Rip Chords
Arno, Lew	Quotations
Arnone, Frank	Five Discs
Arnone, Mike	Duprees
Arrington, Barbara	Magnificents
Arrington, Harvey	Carnations (Lescay)
Arrington, Harvey	Startones (Rainbow)
Arthur, James	Bobby Hall & the Kings
Arthur, James	Kings (Jax, Gotham, Gone, RCA)
Arthur, James	Ramblers (Jax)
Ascher, Jerry	Catalinas
Asero, Ben	Fantasys (Guyden)
Ashford, Rosalind	Martha & the Vandellas
Ashley, James	Terracetones
Ashton, Bearle	Velvets (Red Robin)
Ashton, Floyd	Tams
Askew, Sam	El Capris (Bullseye, Fee Bee)
Aspromonti, Steve	Lincoln Fig & the Dates
Atkins, Bill	Packards (Pla-Bac, Paradise)
Atkins, Bill	Tremaines
Atkins, Essie	Delta Rhythm Boys
Atkins, John	Blue Notes (Josie, Rama, Harthon, etc.)

Performer	Group
Atley, Harold	Schoolboys
Austell, Darnell	Five Chances
Austell, John	Five Chances
Austin, Billy	Billy Austin & the Hearts
Austin, Danny	Ad Libs
Austin, Danny	Creators (T-Kay)
Austin, Henry	Hurricanes
Austin, Henry	Memos
Austin, Henry	Toppers (Jubilee)
Avant, Al	Metronomes (Cadence)
Avery, Frank	La-Rells
Ayala, Frank	Arrogants
Ayala, Miguel	Eddie Friend & the Empires (Colpix)
Aydelotte, Jack "Sam"	Cardinals
Ayers, Roy	Poets (Flash)
Babin, Phil	Ballads (Franwill)
Backus, Gus	Del Vikings
Badden, Jimmy	Upfronts
Badie, Cynthia	Crescendos (Music City)
Bael, Wilbert	Four Dots (Dot)
Bailey, Bill	Duvals (Rainbow)
Bailey, Buddy	Capitols (Pet)
Bailey, Dee Ernie	Flyers (Atco)
Bailey, Dee Ernie	Drifters (Atlantic)
Bailey, Dee Ernie	Swallows (King, Federal, After Hours)
Bailey, James	Jesse Powell & the Caddys
Bailey, James	Calvaes
Bailey, James	Sam Hawkins & the Crystals
Bailey, John "Buddy"	Clovers
Bailey, J. R.	Cadillacs
Bailey, J. R.	Dean Barlow & the Crickets
Bailey, J. R.	Halos
Bailey, J. R.	Jive Five
Bailey, J. R.	New Yorkers Five
Bailey, J. R.	Schoolboys
Bailey, J. R.	Velvetones
Bailey, Leon	Swallows (King, Federal, After Hours)
Bailey, William "Bugeye"	Duvals
Bailey, William "Bugeye"	Five Crowns
Baines, Billy	Bachelors (Earl)
Baines, Billy	Dean Barlow & the Crickets
Baines, Billy	Supremes (Old Town)
Baker, Bill	Chestnuts
Baker, Bill	Elgins (CT)
Baker, Bill	Five Satins

Performer	Group
Baker, Doug	Maharajahs (Flip)
Baker, James	Octaves (DC)
Baker, Jeanette	Dots
Baker, Richard	Gentlemen
Baker, Ronnie	Belltones (J&S, Scatt)
Baker, Ronnie	Ronnie Baker & the Deltones
Baker, Yvonne	Sensations
Baldwin, William	Drifters (Atlantic)
Balinton, Peylia	Lovebugs
Ballard, Don	Nu Tones
Ballard, Ed	Valquins/Velquins
Ballard, Florence	Supremes (Motown)
Ballard, Hank	Dapps
Ballard, Hank	Midnighters
Ballard, Hank	Royals (Federal)
Ball, Leevern	Pipes
Ballot, Dave	Elchords
Balsamo, Vito	Delvons (JDF)
Balsamo, Vito	Vito Balsamo & the Salutations
Banks, Al	Turbans (Herald)
Banks, Albert	Billy Wells & the Crescents
Banks, Albert	Wigs
Banks, Buster	Marylanders
Banks, David	Beltones (Hull)
Banks, Donald	Tymes
Banks, George	Crescendos (Music City)
Banks, George	Casual Crescendos
Banks, Larry	Four Fellows (Glory)
Banks, Robert	Blue Chips
Banks, Ron	Dramatics (Stax)
Banks, Willie	Violinaires
Bannister, Irving (Banister)	Sugar Boy and the Cane Cutters
Bannister, Irving (Banister)	Sha Weez/Shawees
Banuchi, Manuel	Lincoln Fig & the Dates
Banovetz, Gary	Larados
Baquie, Norman	Del Roys
Baradat, Ray	Charades (Skylark)
Barbadora, Alex	Four-Evers (Jamie)
Barbella, Anthony	Tony & the Twilighters
Barber, Ethel	Splendors (Taurus)
Barker, James	Alley Cats
Barker, James	Electras (Cee Jam, Challenge, Infinity)
Barksdale, Andrew	Sparks of Rhythm
Barksdale, Chuck	Altairs
Barksdale, Chuck	Cats and the Fiddle
Barksdale, Chuck	Otis Williams & the Charms
Barksdale, Chuck	Dells
Barksdale, Chuck	El Rays
Barksdale, Chuck	Moonglows (RCA)

Performer	Group
Barksdale, Freddie	Cadillacs
Barksdale, Freddie	Chances (Roulette)
Barksdale, Freddie	Dean Barlow & the Crickets
Barksdale, Freddie	Sam Hawkins & the Crystals
Barksdale, Freddie	New Yorkers Five
Barksdale, Freddie	Solitaires
Barksdale, Freddie	Velvetones
Barksdale, Freddie	Cadillacs
Barlow, Grover "Dean"	Bachelors (Earl)
Barlow, Grover "Dean"	Dean Barlow & the Crickets
Barlow, Grover "Dean"	Montereys (Onyx)
Barlow, Grover "Dean"	Morrisania Revue
Barnes, Curtis	Deckers
Barnes, Eddie	Cues
Barnes, Eddie	Gliders
Barnes, Eddie	Playboys (Cat)
Barnes, Eddie	Ruth Brown & the Rhythm Makers
Barnes, Florestine	Hearts (Baton)
Barnes, John	Empires (Harlem, Wing, Mercury, Whirlin' Disc, Amp 3)
Barnes, John	Whirlers
Barnes, Johnny	Platters
Barnes, Johnny	Prestos
Barnes, Lee	Three Blazers
Barnes, Prentice	Moonglows
Barnes, Prentice	Moonlighters
Barnes, Raymond "Pee Wee"	Larks
Barnes, Reggie	Blue Notes (Josie, Rama, Harthon, etc.)
Barnes, Reggie	Cadillacs
Barnes, Reggie	Chances (Roulette)
Barnes, Reggie	Federals
Barnes, Reggie	FiTones (Old Town)
Barnes, Reggie	Jimmy Jones & the Pretenders
Barnes, Reggie	Solitaires
Barnes, William	Beale Street Boys
Barnes, Willie	Admirals
Barnes, Willie	Sultans (Duke)
Barnett, Ron	Dynamics (Cindy, Seeco, Dynamic, etc.)
Barnett, Sam	Titans (Vita, Specialty, Class)
Barnum, H. B.	Dyna-Soars
Barnum, H. B.	Dootones
Barnum, H. B.	Medallions
Barnum, H. B.	Robins (Savoy)

Performer	Group
Baron, Calvin	Belvederes
Baron, Calvin	Cosmic Rays
Baron, Calvin	Moroccos
Baron, Calvin	Twi-Lites (M-Pac)
Barrett, Fanita Wright	Richard Berry & the Dreamers
Barrett, Fanita Wright	Blossoms
Barrett, Richard	Valentines
Barrett, Ronald	Dootones
Barrett, Ronald	Don Julian & the Meadowlarks
Barrett, Ronald	Medallions
Barrett, Sam	Titans (Specialty)
Barselona. Joe	Five Discs
Bartolomeo, Dom	Illusions
Bash, Joe	Starlarks (Ember)
Basile, Tony	Five Discs
Basilone, Angelo	Savoys (Catamount)
Baskerville, Bob	Lovelarks
Baskerville, Charles	Drifters (Atlantic)
Baskerville, Charles	Shep & the Limelites
Baskerville, Charles	Players (Minit)
Baskerville, Charles	Videos
Baskerville, Hayes	Five Chestnuts (Drum)
Baskerville, Marvin	Five Chestnuts (Drum)
Baskerville, Norven	Five Chestnuts (Drum)
Basket, Fritz	Intervals
Baskins, Mack	Gladiolas
Bassett, Arthur	El Dorados
Bassett, Clarence	Five Sharps
Bassett, Clarence	Shep and the Limelites
Bassett, Clarence	Videos
Basta, Joe	Motions (Laurie)
Bateman, June	Marquis (Onyx)
Bateman, Robert	Satintones
Bates, Errol	Billy Butler & the Chanters
Bates, Errol	Four Enchanters
Batten, Jimmy	Deltones
Batten, Jimmy	Marvells (Magnet)
Battista, Al	Barries (Ember)
Battle, Chuck	Orioles
Batts, Errol	Billy Butler & the Chanters
Baughan, "Little" David	Drifters (Atlantic)
Baughan, "Little" David	Five Wings
Baughan, "Little" David	Harmony Grits
Baughan, "Little" David	Checkers
Baughan, "Little" David	Little David & the Harps
Baughan, "Little" David	Original Drifters
Bautz, Tommy	Markels (R&M)

Performer	Group
Baxter, Rick	Rockin' Chairs
Bayles, Ben	Dukays
Baylor, Alvin "Bobby"	Cadillacs
Baylor, Alvin "Bobby"	Chances (Roulette)
Baylor, Alvin "Bobby"	Hi Lites (Okeh)
Baylor, Alvin "Bobby"	Mello Moods (Robin, Prestige)
Baylor, Alvin "Bobby"	Solitaires
Bazen, Charles	Brochures
Beale, Earl	Silhouettes
Bearden, Charles	Cardells (Middle-Tone)
Beard, Annette	Martha & the Vandellas
Beard, Renee	Feathers
Bears, Sandra	Four Jewels (Checker, Dimension)
Bears, Sandra	Impalas (Checker)
Bears, Sandra	Jewels (Dimension)
Beasley, Richard	Admirals
Beasley, Richard	Sultans (Duke)
Beato, Bob	Anthony & the Sophomores
Beatty, Alma	Playmates (Savoy)
Beatty, Lucille	Playmates (Savoy)
Beatty, Ray	Deep River Boys
Beatty, Ray	Delta Rhythm Boys
Beau, Kenny	Royal Lancers
Beaumont, Jimmy	Skyliners
Beck, Carlton	Guides
Beck, Carlton	Hollywood Saxons
Beck, Carlton	Senders
Beck, Carlton	Swallows (Guyden)
Beck, Carlton	Uptones
Beck, Howie	Tico & the Triumphs
Beckum, Bernard "Jimmy"	Harptones
Beckum, Bernard "Jimmy"	Majors (Derby)
Bedford, James	Cubans (Flash)
Bedford, James	Poets (Flash)
Beebe, William	Majors (Derby)
Beks, Boyd	Notes (Capitol)
Beks, Clarence	Notes (Capitol)
Belkin, Bernie	Caslons
Bellaire, Lloyd	Bobby Mitchell & the Toppers
Bell, Albert "Pee Wee"	Caverliers Quartet
Bell, Albert "Pee Wee"	Sheppards (United, Theron)
Bell, Amos	Evening Star Quartet
Bell, Frank "Red"	Dozier Boys
Bell, Gloria	Delltones

Performer	Group	Performer	Group
Bell, Herman	Velvetones (Coronet, Sonora)	Benton, Sonny	Four Dukes
		Benton, Sonny	Heralds
Bell, John	Billy Williams Quartet	Benton, Sonny	Mighty Dukes (Duke)
Bell, Joseph "Cool Breeze"	Five Breezes	Berardis, Luke	Dreamers (Goldisc, Cousins)
Bell, Leonard	Evening Star Quartet	Berberian, Charles	Fantasys (Guyden)
Bell, Robert	Three Peppers	Berg, Richie	Escorts (Coral)
Bell, Sam	Garnet Mimms & the Enchanters	Bernardo, Dicky	Nobles (Klik, End)
		Berry, Al "Caesar"	Tymes
Bell, Sam	Evening Star Quartet	Berry, John	Hollywood Flames
Bell, Sam	Gainors	Berry, John	Rainbows
Bell, Tony	Quadrells	Berryn, Charles	Joe Alexander & the Cubans
Bell, William	Del Rios (Stax, Rust)		
Belt, Jim	Cap-Tans	Berry, Richard	Chimes (Flair)
Belt, Jim	L 'Cap-Tans	Berry, Richard	Coasters
Belton, Eddie	Incas (Roadhouse)	Berry, Richard	Arthur Lee Maye & the Crowns
Belvin, Jesse	Richard Lewis & the Barons	Berry, Richard	Richard Berry & the Dreamers
Belvin, Jesse	Californians		
Belvin, Jesse	Jesse Belvin & the Capris	Berry, Richard	Five Hearts (Flair)
Belvin, Jesse	Chargers	Berry, Richard	Flairs
Belvin, Jesse	Cliques	Berry, Richard	Five Hollywood Blue Jays
Belvin, Jesse	Fellas	Berry, Richard	Hunters
Belvin, Jesse	Four Students	Berry, Richard	Jaguars
Belvin, Jesse	Gassers (Cash)	Berry, Richard	Jayos
Belvin, Jesse	Jayos	Berry, Richard	Lockettes
Belvin, Jesse	Sharptones (Aladdin)	Berry, Richard	Richard Berry & the Pharaohs
Belvin, Jesse	Shieks (Federal)		
Belvin, Jesse	Shields	Berry, Richard	Rams (Flair)
Belvin, Jesse	Tangiers (Decca)	Berry, Richard	Whips
Belvin, Jesse	Three Dots and a Dash	Berry, Wallace, "Skinhead"	Orlandos
Belvin, Jesse	Turks		
Benevento, James	Raindrops (Imperial)	Bess, Pavel	Clefs
Benevento, Lou	Raindrops (Imperial)	Bess, Pavel	Scotty Mann & the Masters
Bennett, Arnold	Parliaments (Len)		
Bennett, Floyd	Cap-Tans	Best, Beatrice	Jive Five
Bennett, Milton	Four Fellows (Glory)	Best, Bob	La-Rells
Bennett, Wylie	Zodiacs	Best, Pat	Brown Dots
Benovetz, Gary	Larados	Best, Pat	Four Tunes
Benson, Chuck	Five Jets (DeLuxe, Fortune)	Best, Pat	Sentimentalists (Manor)
		Best, Skeeter	Bill Johnson's Musical Notes
Benson, George	Altairs		
Benson, George	Little Joe & the Thrillers	Bethea Martinez, Jimmy "Bip"	Mello Moods (Robin, Prestige)
Benson, Nathaniel	Altairs		
Benson, Paul	Metronomes (Winn)	Bethea, Harmon	Cap-Tans
Benson, Renaldo "Obie"	Four Tops	Bethea, Harmon	L'Cap-Tans
		Bethea, Harmon	Maskman & the Agents
Benson, Wes	Four Counts	Bethea, Harmon	Octaves (DC)
Bentley, Ed	Ronnie Vare & the Inspirations	Bethea, Harmon	Progressive Four
		Betts, Richard	Guides
Bently, Chuck	Ronnie Vare & the Inspirations	Betts, Richard	Hollywood Saxons
		Betts, Richard	Senders
Benton, Brook	Langford Quartet, Bill	Betts, Richard	Swallows (Guyden)
Benton, Brook	Sandmen	Betts, Richard	Uptones
Benton, Sonny	Billy Dawn Quartet	Beverly, Frankie	Butlers
Benton, Sonny	Donny Myles & the Dukes	Beverly, Stan	Capris (Tender)
		Beverly, Stan	Hollywood Saxons

Performer	Group
Beverly, Stan	Portraits
Beverly, Stan	Saxons
Beverly, Stan	Tuxedos
Bialaglow, Tom	Duprees
Bianchini, Dario	Dials (Philips)
Bianchini, Dario	Dreamers (Cousins, Goldisc)
Bibbs, Leonard	Three Sharps and a Flat
Biggs, Noah	Showmen
Biletto, Anthony	Treble Chords
Billingsley, Joe	Contours
Billy, John "Prince"	Honey Boys
Bing, Cleveland	King Odom Quartet/Four
Bing, Isaiah	King Odom Quartet/Four
Bing, Isaiah	Larks
Bing, Isaiah	Eugene Mumford & the Serenaders
Binion, Jimmy	Little Joe and His Moroccos
Binns, Leroy	Cadillacs
Binns, Leroy	Charts
Binns, Leroy	Coasters
Binns, Raymond	Charts
Birnett, Paul	Jarmels
Biscardi, Louis	Ducanes
Bishop, Al	Deep River Boys
Bishop, Leroy	Arrows (Flash)
Bitts, Robert	El Dorados
Black, Alvin, Jr.	Stylists (Rose)
Black, Carlton	Duvals (Boss)
Blackman, Arthur	Rocketones
Blackman, Donald	Velvetones
Blackshear, Don	Fascinators (Your Copy, Blue Lake)
Black, Theodore	Chips
Blackwell, Arthur	Startones (Rainbow)
Blackwell, Joe	Individuals
Blackwell, Nolan	Shaw-Wees
Blackwell, Thurman	Bennie Woods & the Five Dukes
Blackwell, Thurman	Rockin' Townies
Blackwell, Tommy	Carnations (Lescay)
Blackwell, Toncie	Shields
Blair, Richard	Three Vales
Blair, Robert	Violinaires
Blair, Ronald	Three Vales
Blake, Cicero	Kool Gents
Blake, Johnny	Johnny Blake & the Clippers
Blakely, Charles	Russ Riley & the Five Sounds
Blakely, Leo	Egyptian Kings
Blakely, Leo	Four Pharaohs
Blakely, William	Del Vikings
Blake, Woodroe	Lyrics (Rhythm)
Blake, Woodrow	Romancers
Blakey, Art	Billy Wells & the Crescents

Performer	Group
Blakey, Arthur	Hesitations
Blakey, Arthur	Wigs
Bland, Billy	Bees
Bland, Bobby	Beale Streeters
Blanders, Mack	Blanders
Blandon, Curtis	Vocaleers (Twistime)
Blandon, Richard	Dubs
Blandon, Richard	Five Wings
Blandon, Richard	Marvels (ABC)
Blandon, Richard	Vocaleers (Paradise)
Blasko, Chuck	Val-Aires
Block, Ray	Ad Libs
Bloom, Bobby	Imaginations
Blount, John	Delroys
Blue, Andrew	Bel-Aires (Flip)
Blue, Andrew	Medallions
Blue, Andrew	Vel-Aires (Flip)
Bobbitt, Willie	Raiders (Atco)
Bobo, Howard	Jimmy Castor & the Juniors
Bocage, Frank	Bobby Mitchell & the Toppers
Bogar, Ted "Larry"	Gentlemen
Bolden, Delaney	Stylists (Jay Wing, Sage, Crown)
Bolden, Jean	Clickettes
Bolden, John	Students (Note, Checker)
Bologna, Pete	Five Sounds
Bond, Floyd	Sentimentals (Tuxedo, Checker, Minit)
Bond, Luther	Luther Bond & the Emeralds
Bongiorno, Michael	Tony & the Twilighters
Bonney, George	Barons (Imperial)
Bonney, George	Marquis (West Coast)
Bonura, Carl	Bellnotes
Booker, Beryl	Cats and the Fiddle
Booker, Beryl	Steve Gibson & the Toppers
Booker, Charles	Bachelors (Aladdin, Royal Roost)
Booker, Charles	Jets (Rainbow)
Booker, Richard	Congress Alley
Booker, Richard	Drifters (Atlantic)
Booker, Robert	Rocketones
Boone, Jim	Cardinals
Boone, Jim	Adolphus Holcomb & the Kings
Booth, Henry	Midnighters
Booth, Henry	Royals (Federal)
Booth, Henry	Serenaders (JVB)
Boots, Goldie	Falcons (Regent, Savoy, RCA)
Borack, Mickey	Tico & the Triumphs
Bouknight, "Little" Nate	Little Nate & the Chryslers

Performer	Group	Performer	Group
Bouknight, "Little" Nate	Clovers (Porwin)	Braceley, Stan	Teardrops (Sampson)
		Bracey, William	Duponts (Winley, Royal Roost, Savoy, Roulette)
Bouknight, "Little" Nate	Shells		
Bour, Richard	Five Fashions	Brackenridge, Henry	Cascades
Bovino, Bob	Bob Knight Four		
Bowden, Bobby	Cherokees (United Artists)	Brackenridge, Henry	Pace Setters
Bowen, Alvin	Four Buddies (Savoy)		
Bowen, Billy	Ink Spots	Brackenridge, Joseph	Cascades
Bowen, Eddie	Drifters (Atlantic)		
Bowers, Bobby	Cashmeres (Lake, Laurie, Josie, ACA)	Brackenridge, Joseph	Pace Setters
Bowers, David "Boots"	King Odom Quartet/Four	Brackenridge, Joseph	Von Gayles
Bowers, David "Boots"	Kings (Baton)	Braden, Tommy	Four Blazes (United)
		Braden, Tommy	Hollywood Four Blazers
Bowers, David "Boots"	Larks	Bradford, Sylvester	Bradford Boys (Rainbow)
Bowers, David "Boots"	Ravens	Bradford, Sylvester	Ivories (Jaguar)
		Bradford, Sylvester	Suburbans (Baton)
Bowers, David "Boots"	Eugene Mumford & the Serenaders	Bradley, Alton	Golden Gate Quartet
		Bradley, Don	Jayhawks
Bowers, David "Boots"	Three Brothers & a Cousin	Bradley, Don	Marathons
		Bradley, Don	Vibrations (Checker)
Bowers, Robert	Charioteers	Bradley, Gentry	Creators (Dootone)
Bowers, Robert	DuDroppers	Bradley, James	Ebonaires (Modern, Aladdin, etc.)
Bowie, John	Bachelors (Aladdin, Royal Roost)	Bradley, Louis	El Dorados
		Bradley, Louis	Four El Dorados
Bowie, John	Clovers	Bradley, Louis	Tempos (Rhythm)
Bowie, John	Jets (Rainbow)	Bradley, Roland	Otis Williams & the Charms
Bowman, Don	Squires (Vita, Mambo)		
Boyce, Buster	Five Stars (Treat)	Bradley, Roland	Esco's [sic]
Boyce, Buster	Inspirators (Treat, Old Town)	Brady, James	Sparrows Quartet
		Bragg, Johnny	Marigolds
Boyce, Joe	Dozier Boys	Bragg, Johnny	Prisonaires
Boyd, Alan	Gene Ford & the Chanters	Bragg, Johnny	Sunbeams (Dot)
Boyd, Andrew	Volchords	Braggs, Al "TNT"	Five Notes (Chess)
Boyd, Billy	Cats (Federal)	Braggs, Al "TNT"	Five Stars (Blues Boys Kingdom)
Boyd, Billy	Gene Ford & the Chanters		
Boyd, Henry	Cashmeres (Mercury, Herald)	Braggs, Al "TNT"	Five Masks (Jan)
		Bralton, Freeman	Don Julian & the Meadowlarks
Boyd, John	Five Keys		
Boyd, Oscar	Calvaes	Branca, Ray	Three Peppers
Boyd, Oscar	Cavaliers (nonrecording)	Branch, Major	Dreamtones (Klik, Express, Astra)
Boyd, Oscar	Sheppards (Theron, United)		
		Brandon, Al	Belltones (J&S, Scatt)
Boyd, Ronald	Marvels (Laurie)	Brandon, Alvin, Jr.	Darnell & the Dreams
Boyd, Ronald	Satisfactions (Smash)	Branford, Mifflin "Pee Wee"	Cats and the Fiddle
Boyd, Ronald	Senators (Winn)		
Boyd, Skip	Bop Chords	Branford, Mifflin "Pee Wee"	Three Sharps and a Flat
Boyer, Charles	Garnet Mimms & the Enchanters		
		Brant, Randolph	Bel-Aires (Flip)
Boyer, Leroy	Swans (Ballad)	Brantley, Johnny	Ideals (Checker)
Boyer, Leroy	Rex Middleton's Hi-Fi's	Brecheter, Ronnie	Ovations (Josie)
Boykin, Milton	Debonaires (Herald)	Breckinridge, Paul	Paul Breckinridge & the Four Heavenly Knights
Boykin, Milton	Five Debonaires		
Bracco, Ralph	Nino & the Ebbtides		

Performer	Group
Breedlove, Jimmy	Cues
Breedlove, Jimmy	Gliders
Breedlove, Jimmy	Playboys (Cat)
Breedlove, Jimmy	Ruth Brown & the Rhythm Makers
Bremley, Paul	Golden Gate Quartet
Brent, Bill	Drifters (Atlantic)
Brent, Bill	5 Jades (Duke)
Brent, Bill	Hornets (States)
Brently, Paul	Elroy & the Excitements
Brent, Royal	Lewis Bronzeville Five
Breny, Jeff	Ducanes
Brewster, Bert	Tempo-Tones
Brewster, Ray	Cadillacs
Brewster, Ray	Colts
Brewster, Ray	Hollywood Flames
Brewster, Ray	Penguins
Brewton, Glenn	Four Deals
Brian, Eddie	Ducanes
Briar, Sheldon	Angels (Tawny)
Briar, Sheldon	Dories (Dore)
Briar, Sheldon	Safaris (Eldo)
Briar, Sheldon	Suddens
Brice, Lawrence	Spinners (Rhythm)
Brice, Pearl	Enchanters (Jubilee)
Bricker, Gene	Marcels (Colpix)
Brickley, Shirley	Orlons
Bridges, Cas	Clefftones (Old Town)
Bridges, Cas	Four Fellows (Tri Boro)
Bridges, Cas	Victorians
Bridges, Cas	Winners
Bridges, Charlie	Mobile Four
Brier, Shelly	Suddens
Brigatti, Dave	Hi-Fives (Decca)
Briggs, Jake	Valtones (Gee)
Briggs, Leon	Johnny Blake & the Clippers
Briggs, Leon	Carl Hogan & the Miracles
Briggs, Leon	Velvets (Fury)
Briggs, Ray "Poppa"	Valentines
Briggs, Raymond "Pop"	Dreamers (NY)
Bright, Joshua	Griffins
Bright, Ronnie	Cadillacs
Bright, Ronnie	Coasters
Bright, Ronnie	Sam Hawkins & the Crystals
Bright, Ronnie	Dreamers (NY)
Bright, Ronnie	Carl Hogan & the Miracles
Bright, Ronnie	Valentines
Brisbane, Joe	Velvets (Red Robin)
Brisbane, John	Carl Hogan & the Miracles
Brisbon, Joe	Miracles (Baton)
Briscoe, Fleming	Five Blue Notes (Sabre, Onda)

Performer	Group
Briscoe, Joey	Del Vikings
Briscoe, Joey	El Venos
Briscoe, Karen	Congress Alley
Bristow, Rodney	Quotations
Britton, Lester	L'Cap-Tans
Britton, Vernon	Hurricanes
Britton, Vernon	Memos
Britton, Vernon	Toppers (Jubilee)
Brizant, John	Billy Austin & the Hearts
Brizant, John	Strangers
Broadnick, Aaron	Young Lads (Neil)
Broadnick, Aaron "Bootsie"	Pearl & the Deltars
Broadway, Oscar	Four Knights
Broderick, Bob	Larados
Brodgins, Harold	Parakeets (Roadhouse)
Brodie, Roosevelt	Blue Notes (Harthon)
Brodsky, Irving	Lonnie & the Carollons
Brogan, Anna	Marvelettes
Brooks, Al	Marigolds
Brooks, Al	Sunbeams (Dot)
Brooks, Arthur	Impressions
Brooks, Billy	Tempo Toppers
Brooks, Charles "Buddy"	Cadillacs
Brooks, Charles "Buddy"	Jive Five
Brooks, Charles "Buddy"	Original Cadillacs
Brooks, Delores "La La"	Crystals (Philles)
Brooks, Dusty	Dusty Brooks & the Tones
Brooks, Dusty	Dusty Brooks & the Four Tones
Brooks, Dusty	Dusty Brooks & the Four Tones with Juanita Brown
Brooks, Eddie	Sophomores (Dawn)
Brooks, Gerald	Restless Hearts
Brooks, Gwen	Playmates (Savoy)
Brooks, Lucius "Dusty"	Four Tones
Brooks, Lucius "Dusty"	Dusty Brooks & the Four Tones
Brooks, Lucius "Dusty"	Dusty Books & the Tones
Brooks, Lucius "Dusty"	Dusty Brooks & the Four Tones with Raymond Wheaton
Brooks, Manchester	Pharaohs (Ace)
Brooks, Orville	Golden Gate Quartet
Brooks, Orville	Jubalaires
Brooks, Orville	Larks
Brooks, Orville	Melody Kings
Brooks, Orville	Eugene Mumford & the Serenaders
Brooks, Orville	Valiants (Joy, Cortlandt)

Performer	Group
Brooks, Richard	Impressions
Brooks, Richie	Catalinas
Brooks, Robert "Billy"	Bill Johnson's Musical Notes
Brooks, Sylvester	Smoothtones (Jem)
Brooks, Sylvester	Twiliters (Nix, Chess, Roulette)
Brooks, Theodore	Jubalaires
Brooks, Willie	Coronets
Brothers, Meredith "Prince"	Cardinals
Browd, Wellman	Spirits of Rhythm
Brown, Al	Paragons
Brown, Al	Billy Dawn Quartette
Brown, Alfonso	Singing Wanderers
Brown, Barbara	Joytones (Rama)
Brown, Bill	Checkers
Brown, Bill	Billy Ward & the Dominoes
Brown, Bill	Harptones
Brown, Bunny	Vestelles
Brown, Carl	Hepsters
Brown, Carlton	Inspirations (Apollo, Lamp)
Brown, Carlton	Marcels (Rhythm, Chartbound, Cycle)
Brown, Charles	Coronets
Brown, Charles	Three Blazers
Brown, Chester	Counts
Brown, Claude	Supremes (Kitten)
Brown, Clyde	Drifters (Atlantic)
Brown, Cordell	Dubs
Brown, Cornelius	Silhouettes
Brown, Del	Desideros
Brown, Doug	Delegates (Vee Jay)
Brown, Doug	Kool Gents
Brown, Douglas	El Dorados
Browne, Jerome	Johnny & the Keys
Brown, Emerson "Rocky"	Students (Note, Checker)
Brown, Ernie	Blenders (Decca, MGM)
Browne, Robert	Camerons (Cousins)
Brown, Ethyl	Gene Ford & the Chanters
Brown, Floyd	Four Dots (Dot)
Brown, Freddie	Quinns
Brown, Henry	Collegians (Winley)
Brown, Henry	Sparrows (Jay Dee, Davis)
Brown, Hosea	Trinidads
Brown, James	Hurricanes
Brown, James	Jewels (Imperial, R&B)
Brown, James	Marbles
Brown, James	Memos
Brown, James "Little Caesar"	Cardinals
Brown, James "Zeke"	Calvaes
Brown, James C.	Excelsior Norfolk Quartet

Performer	Group
Brown, Jerome	Belvederes (Dot, Trend)
Brown, Jerome	Five Bells (Clock)
Brown, Jerome	Johnny & the Keys
Brown, John	Supremes (Kitten)
Brown, Johnny	Sonics (Groove)
Brown, Juanita	Four Tones
Brown, Juanita	Dusty Brooks & the Four Tones
Brown, Juanita	Dusty Brooks & the Four Tones (featuring Juanita Brown)
Brown, Juanita	Dusty Brooks & the Tones
Brown, Julius McMichael	Paragons
Brown, Kenneth	Belvederes (Dot, Trend)
Brown, Lawrence	Blue Notes (Josie, Rama, Harthon, etc.)
Brown, Lee	Swinging Hearts
Brown, Leon	Don Julian & the Meadowlarks
Brown, Leroy	Drapers
Brown, Leroy	Five Crowns
Brown, Leroy	V-Eights
Brown, Martin	Crystals (Luna)
Brown, Martin	Opals
Brown, Marvin	Four Troys (Freedom)
Brown, Marvin	Four Dots (Bullseye)
Brown, Moses	Ivoleers
Brown, Moses	Ivories
Brown, Norman	Lillian Leach & the Mellows
Brown, Oscar, Jr.	Delegates
Brown, Paul	Pharaohs (Ace)
Brown, Ray "Bucky"	Wisdoms
Brown, Richard	Ebonaires (Modern, Aladdin, etc.)
Brown, Richie	Quinns
Brown, Robert	Chessmen (PAC)
Brown, Romaine	Four Toppers
Brown, Romaine	Red Caps/Five Red Caps
Brown, Romaine	Romaines
Brown, Romaine	Steve Gibson & the Toppers
Brown, Ron	Laurels
Brown, Ronald	Laurels (Combo, X, Flair)
Brown, Roscoe	Swinging Hearts
Brown, Rosetta	Copesetics
Brown, Roy "Bucky"	Velquins (Valquins)
Brown, Rudolph	Medallions
Brown, Ruth	Ruth Brown & the Rhythm Makers
Brown, Sam	Intruders (Federal)
Brown, Stanley	Ronnie & the Hi-Lites
Brown, Stanley	Stereos
Brown, Steven	Charts

Performer	Group
Brown, Steven	Dubs
Brown, Ted	Laurels (Combo, X, Flair)
Brown, William	Ivy Tones
Brown, William	Mad Lads
Brown, William	Mello Harps
Brown, Wini	Wini Brown & the Boyfriends
Broxton, Melvin	Dots (Caddy)
Broyles, Ben	Dukays
Bruce, John	Charts
Brunner, Fred	Unknowns (X-Tra)
Brunson, Jimmy	Planets (Era)
Brunson, Jimmy	Rocketeers (Modern, MJC)
Brunson, Jimmy	Rockets (Modern)
Bryant, Bill	Four Bluejackets (Mercury)
Bryant, Dickie	Four Buddies (Club 51)
Bryant, Doc	Four Bluejackets (Mercury)
Bryant, Don	Four Kings (Fortune)
Bryant, Elbridge "Al"	Temptations (Gordy)
Bryant, Hugh	Deep River Boys
Bryant, Hugh	Delta Rhythm Boys
Bryant, James	Five Scalders
Bryant, Jamie	Four Kings (Fortune)
Bryant, Joe	Four Bluejackets (Mercury)
Bryant, Randolph	Bel-Aires (Flip)
Bryant, Randolph	Medallions
Bryant, Randolph	Vel-Aires (Flip)
Bryant, Rosa	Sharmeers
Bryant, Toby	Four Bluejackets (Mercury)
Bryant, Waymon	Four Gents
Bryant, Waymon	Twi-Lites (M-Pac)
Bryant, Willie	Four Buddies (Club 51)
Bryce, Pearl	Enchanters (Jubilee)
Brye, Billy	Little Joe and his Moroccos
Bubarth, Bob	Chapelaires
Buchter, Ron	Little Romeo and the Casanovas
Buchter, Ron	Ovations (Josie)
Buck, Leon	Four Tones
Buck, Leon	Dusty Brooks & the Four Tones
Buck, Leon	Dusty Brooks & the Four Tones with Raymond Wheaton
Buckley, Dennis	Ducanes
Buckley, Fred	Pastels (United)
Buckner, Sherman	Cap-Tans
Budd, Arthur	Jerry Sheeley & the Versatiles
Budd, Arthur	Sonny Day & the Versatiles

Performer	Group
Buford, Ross	Charts
Bullock, Gerald	Clefs
Bullock, Mitchell	Confessions
Bullock, Mitchell	Radiants (Chess)
Bullock, Tommy	Fiestas
Bunkum, Carver	Jayhawks
Bunkum, Carver	Vibrations (Checker)
Bunn, Allen	Cleartones
Bunn, Allen	Larks
Bunn, Allen	Selah Jubilee Singers
Bunn, Allen	Wheels
Bunn, Teddy	Spirits of Rhythm
Buono, Joe	Emanons (Winley, ABC)
Buono, Mike	Emanons (Winley, ABC)
Burch, Don	Slades
Burden, Ricky	Spaniels
Burd, Robert	Flames
Burdock, Bruce	Five Fashions
Burgess, Jimmy	Volumes (Chex)
Burgess, Joe	Balladiers
Burgess, Lucille "Vicky"	Charmers (Central, Timely)
Burgess, Lucille "Vicky"	Joytones (Rama)
Burkes, Johnny	Premiers (Gone)
Burkette, Bill	Val-Aires
Burnett, Carl "Little Caesar"	Little Caesar & the Romans
Burnett, Donald	Belltones (Grand)
Burnett, Donald	Farris Hill & the Madison Brothers
Burnett, Donald	Royal Demons
Burnett, Donald	Little Joe & the Thrillers
Burnett, Hiawatha	Goldenrods (Vee Jay)
Burnett, Norman	Tymes
Burnett, Paul	Jarmels
Burnside, Ernest	Camelots
Burnside, Ernest	Paragons
Burns, Richie	Bon Aires
Burrell, Curtis	Daylighters
Burrell, Curtis	Faith Taylor & the Sweet Teens
Burroughs, Robert	Verdicts
Burrows, Donald	Quintones (Park)
Burt, John	Parakeets (Roadhouse)
Burton, Harry	Leaders
Burt, Wanda	Crescendos (Music City)
Burwell, William	Billy Wells & the Crescents
Busch, Thomas	Olympics
Busey, Gary	Carousels (Gone)
Bushnell, Robert	Romaines
Bushnell, Yvonne	Jaynetts (Tuff, J&S)
Busseri, Frank	Four Lads
Butler, Al	Clouds (Cobra)
Butler, Arthur	Lewis Bronzeville Five
Butler, Billy	Billy Butler & the Chanters

Performer	Group
Butler, Billy	Billy Butler & the Enchanters
Butler, Billy	Four Enchanters
Butler, Billy	Harlemaires
Butler, Charlotte	Sherrys (Guyden, Mercury)
Butler, Cliff	Cliff Butler & the Doves
Butler, Cliff	Singing Doves
Butler, Elzie	Radiants
Butler, Herbert	Players (Minit)
Butler, Jerry	Impressions
Butler, Jerry	Harvey & the Quails
Butler, Joseph	Bobby Mitchell & the Toppers
Butler, Melvin	Four Bars (Josie, Dayco)
Butler, Prentice	Four Blazes (United)
Butler, Rhett	Deep River Boys
Butts, James "Buddy"	Norfolk Jazz Quartet
Byas, John	Del Vikings
Byle, Kenneth	Ebbtones
Byle, Kenneth	Cornel Gunter & the Ermines
Byle, Kenneth	Flairs
Byle, Kenneth	Flares
Bynum, Robert	Dean Barlow & the Crickets
Byrd, Billy	Ink Spots
Byrd, Bobby	Bobby Byrd & the Birds
Byrd, Bobby	Crescendos (Atlantic)
Byrd, Bobby	Flames
Byrd, Bobby	Patty Anne & the Flames
Byrd, Bobby	Four Flames (Fidelity, Specialty)
Byrd, Bobby	Hollywood Flames
Byrd, Bobby	Hollywood Four Flames
Byrd, Bobby	Rickey and the Pharaohs
Byrd, Bobby	Satellites
Byrd, Bobby	Tangiers
Byrd, Bobby	Voices (Cash)
Byrd, Lionel	Four Kings (Fortune)
Byrd, Robert	Dawns
Cacase, Anthony	Treble Chords
Casey, Al	Jimmy Castor & the Juniors
Cade, Harold	Ed Carter Quartet
Cade, Harold	Carter Rays
Caesar, Bruce	Original Drifters
Caesar, Harry "Little"	Turbans (Money)
Caines, Jimmy	Demens
Caines, Jimmy	Emersons
Calabrese, Ronnie	Larry Chance & the Earls
Caldwell, Alex	Caldwells
Caldwell, Sonny	Ronnie & the Hi-Lites
Caldwell, Steve	Orlons

Performer	Group
Caldwell, Wallace	Velvetones (Coronet, Sonora)
Calendar, Harriet	Wini Brown & the Boyfriends
Calender, Harriet	Dreamers (Jubilee, Mercury)
Calender, Red	Spirits of Rhythm
Calhoun, Bob	Diablos
Calhoun, Robert	Velvet Angels
Calhoun, Royalston "Roy"	Five Hearts (Arcade)
Calhoun, Royalston "Roy"	Hearts (Chancellor)
Calhoun, Royalston "Roy"	Lee Andrews & the Hearts
Calhoun, Wendell	Famous Hearts (Guyden)
Calhoun, Wendell	Five Hearts (Arcade)
Calhoun, Wendell	Hearts (Chancellor)
Calhoun, Wendell	Lee Andrews & the Hearts
Caliste, Louis	Mellow Drops (Imperial)
Caliste, Louis	Monitors (Specialty)
Calloway, Cab	Cab Calloway & the Cabaliers
Cammarata, Frank	Dreamers (Cousins, Goldisc)
Cameron, G. C.	Spinners (Motown, Tri-Phi)
Campbell, Alton	Cellos
Campbell, Alton	Channels (Whirlin' Disc)
Campbell, Carl	Supremes Four (Sara)
Campbell, James	Danderliers
Campbell, James "Miff"	Riff Brothers
Campbell, Lawrence	Russ Riley & the Five Sounds
Camp, Freddie	Metrotones (Reserve)
Candys, Louis Gene	Pipes
Candys, Willard	Starliters (Combo)
Cannady, Jimmy	Millionaires
Cannon, Danny	Vibraharps
Cannon, Freddie	Belmonts
Cannon, Richie	Bill Cook & the Marshalls
Cannon, Richie	Ravens
Cannon, Tootsie	Passionettes
Cantor, Marty	Academics
Cantos, Sam	Little Romeo and the Casanovas
Cantos, Sammy	Ovations (Josie)
Canzano, Dom	Dreamers (Cousins, Goldisc)
Capalungo, Sal	Ray & the Darchaes
Capizzi, Bill	Stompers
Capizzi, Leonard	Stompers
Carbo, Hayward, "Chuck"	Spiders
Carbo, Leonard "Chick"	Spiders

Performer	Group
Carbone, John	Five Discs
Cardell, Nick	Four Fifths
Carey, Bill	Danleers
Carey, Bill	Four Fellows (Tri Boro)
Carey, Bill	Victorians
Carey, Billy	Spaniels
Carey, Jake	Flamingos
Carey, Robert	Cardells (Middle-Tone)
Carey, Waymon "Butterball"	Gay Tunes (Timely, Joyce, Dome)
Carey, Waymon "Butterball"	Verdicts
Carey, Zeke	Flamingos
Carillo, Joe	Continentals (Whirlin Disc)
Carillo, Joe	Crystals (Cub)
Carillo, Joe	Metros (Just)
Carlisle, Billy	Dubs
Carlisle, Billy	Five Wings
Carlisle, Billy	Marvels (ABC)
Carlisle, Billy	Sonics (Groove)
Carlson, Jack	Cathy Jean & the Roommates
Carlucci, Billy	Billy & the Essentials
Carlucci, Tony	Impalas (Cub)
Carnegie, John	Checkers
Caroni, Ray	Bellnotes
Carpenter, Berlin	Turbans (Money)
Carpenter, Berlin "Burl"	Sharptones (Aladdin)
Carrao, Joe	Impossibles (RMP)
Carr, Don	Dell Pris
Carrington, Charlie	Mello-Tones (Decca)
Carr, Melvin	Five Cs
Carroll, Earl	Cadillacs
Carroll, Earl	Coasters
Carroll, Earl	Original Cadillacs
Carroll, Earl	Speedoo & the Pearls
Carroll, Greg	Cues
Carroll, Greg	Dappers (Groove, Rainbow)
Carroll, Greg	Four Buddies (Savoy)
Carroll, Greg	Ink Spots
Carroll, Greg	Orioles
Carruthers, Charles	Coronets
Carr, Phyllis	Quintones (Chess, Red Top, Hunt)
Carson, Eddie "Puddin' "	Royaltones
Carter, Bruce	Four Fifths
Carter, Calvin	Delegates
Carter, Calvin	Dells
Carter, Clifton	Five Cliffs of Dover
Carter, Donald	Cameos (Matador)
Carter, Eddie	Ed Carter Quartet

Performer	Group
Carter, Eddie	Carter Rays
Carter, Eddie	Casinos (Maske)
Carter, Edward "Bubba"	Medallions
Carter, Gerald "Rossi"	Marylanders
Carter, Gerard "Rossi"	Stylists (Jay Wing, Sage, Crown)
Carter, James	Sentimentals (Tuxedo, Checker, Minit)
Carter, John	Delegates (Vee Jay)
Carter, Johnny	Altairs
Carter, Johnny	Dells
Carter, Johnny	D's Gentlemen
Carter, Johnny	ElDorados
Carter, Johnny	Flamingos
Carter, Johnny	Kool Gents
Carter, J. T.	Crests
Carter, J. T.	Drifters (Atlantic)
Carter, Larry "Spanky"	Keynotes (Apollo)
Carter, Leon	Dean Barlow & the Crickets
Carter, Leon	Russ Riley & the Five Sounds
Carter, Lonnie	Otis Williams & the Charms
Carter, Lonnie	Esco's [sic]
Carter, Mosby	Echos (Combo)
Carter, Obediah	Five Royales
Carter, Obediah "Scoop"	Royals (Apollo)
Carter, Perry	Five Cliffs of Dover
Carter, Reid	Four Fifths
Carter, Robert	Skarlettones
Carter, Russell	Cherokees
Carter, Walter	Chavelles (Vita)
Carter, Walter	Sabers (Cal-West)
Carter, William "Tommy"	Four Buddies (Savoy)
Carter, Woody	Dino & the Diplomats
Carvelli, Joe	Caslons
Cary, Joey	Rockin' Chairs
Casagrande, Steve	Criterions
Casagrande, Steve	Kents (Aljon)
Casey, Al	Jimmy Castor & the Juniors
Casey, John	Bellnotes
Cashie, Al	Premiers (Gone)
Cash, Fred	Impressions
Cassidy, Robert	Chorals
Castellano, Joseph	Savoys (Catamount)
Caston, Leonard	Big Three Trio
Caston, Leonard	Five Breezes
Caston, Leonard	Four Jumps of Jive

Performer	Group
Caston, Leonard	Radiants (Chess)
Castor, Jimmy	Clintonian Cubs
Castor, Jimmy	Jimmy Castor Bunch
Castor, Jimmy	Jimmy Castor & the Juniors
Castron, Jules	Voices (Cash)
Catallo, Steve	Majestics (20th Fox)
Cauchi, Les	Del Satins
Caulfield, Johnny	Billy & the Essentials
Caupin, Bobby	Imaginations
Cavares, Leonard	Cufflinx
Caver, Bob	Day, Dawn & Dusk
Cedano, Rafael	Dino & the Diplomats
Cedeño, Lucy	Lovenotes (Holiday)
Cedrone, Richie	Leisure Lads
Cernacek, George	Fascinators (Capitol)
Cerrato, Dennis	Five Jades
Cesario, Joe	Chaps
Chalmers, Robert	El Pollos
Chambers, Al	Sophomores (Dawn)
Chambers, Bill	Kings (Baton)
Chambers, George	Chandeliers
Chamblee, Eddie	Four Blazes (United)
Champen, Waldo	Bachelors (Earl)
Champen, Waldo	Jesse Powell & the Caddys
Champen, Waldo	Cadillacs
Champen, Waldo	Chimes, (Royal Roost, Betta)
Champen, Waldo	Dean Barlow & the Crickets
Champen, Waldo	Five Chimes, (Royal Roost, Betta)
Champen, Waldo	Five Delights
Champen, Waldo	Montereys (Onyx)
Champen, Waldo	Moodmakers
Champen, Waldo	Morrisania Revue
Champen, Waldo	Schoolboys
Champen, Waldo	Supremes (Old Town)
Champen, Waldo	Velvetones (nonrecording)
Champion, Mickey	Nic Nacs
Chance, Bob (Wahlstein)	Raiders (Atco)
Chance, Larry	Larry Chance & the Earls
Chance, Ronald	Fabulous Pearls (Dooto)
Chandler, Eugene	Dukays
Chandler, Kermit	Ballads
Chaney, Herman "Sonny"	Ambers
Chaney, Herman "Sonny"	Jaguars
Chapman, Grady	Robins (Savoy)
Chapman, Grady	Suedes
Chapman, Harold	Rocketones
Chapman, Ronald	Versatones

Performer	Group
Charles, Richmond	Ronnie & the Hi-Lites
Chatman, Lee	Bosstones
Chavez, Manny	Ambers
Chavez, Manny	Jaguars
Cheatham, Andrew	Terracetones
Cheetom, John	Velours
Cheetom, John	Fantastics (RCA)
Cherebin, Curtis	Harptones
Cherebin, Curtis	Soothers
Cherry, Eddie	Crystals (Delano)
Chew, Rudolph	Kings (Jax, Harlem, Gone, Gotham, RCA)
Childers, Kenneth	Maples (Blue Lake)
Christian, Diane	Rosettes (Herald)
Christian, John	Cameos (Cameo)
Christian, John	Quadrells
Christian, John	Turbans (Herald)
Christian, John	Universals (Mark-X)
Christianson, Earl	Jarmels
Christman, John	Echos (Combo)
Church, Eugene	Cliques
Church, Eugene	Fellas
Church, Eugene	Shieks (Federal)
Ciaffardone, Sam	Antones
Ciapetta, Robert	Demolyrs
Ciler, Chris	Suburbans
Clare, Demetrius	Popular Five
Clare, Dimitrius	Jimmy Keyes & the Symbols
Clark, Alvin	Mint Juleps
Clark, Claude "Nicky"	Soothers
Clark, Cyril	Majestics (Chex, Contour)
Clark, Claude "Nicky"	Five Crowns
Clark, Claude "Nicky"	Harptones
Clark, Delecta "Dee"	Delegates
Clark, Delecta "Dee"	Hambone Kids
Clark, Delecta "Dee"	Kool Gents
Clark, Eddie	Eagle-Aires
Clark, James "Poppa"	Cadillacs
Clark, James "Poppa"	Crowns (R&B)
Clark, James "Poppa"	Five Crowns
Clark, John "Sonny Boy"	Five Crowns
Clark, Margie	Four Jewels (Checker, Dimension)
Clark, Margie	Impalas (Checker)
Clark, Margie	Jewels (Dimension)

Performer	Group
Clark, Ron	Ladders
Clark, Sherman	Poets (Flash)
Clark, Tucker	Keynotes (Apollo)
Clark, William	Flamingos
Clark, William	Strangers
Clasky, Rich	Angels (Tawny)
Clasky, Rich	Enchanters
Clasky, Rich	Safaris (Eldo)
Clasky, Rich	Suddens
Clay, Donald	Foster Brothers
Clay, Kenny	Tabbys
Clayton, Louis	Bel-Aires (M.Z.)
Cleare, Demetrius	Continentals (Rama)
Clemens, Frankie	Danleers
Clemens, Frankie	Webtones
Clements, Donald	Sophomores (Dawn)
Clements, Roland	Dappers (Peacock)
Clements, Roland	Sophomores (Dawn)
Clemmons, Emra	Mint Juleps
Cleveland, Al	Craftys
Cleveland, Al	Halos
Clinton, George	Parliaments (Len)
Cloud, Bruce	Billy Ward & the Dominoes
Cloud, Emory	Debonaires (Herald)
Cloud, Emory	Five Debonaires
Clowney, Dave "Baby Cortez"	Pearls (Onyx)
Clowney, Dave "Baby Cortez"	Valentines
Coates, Beverly	Eddie Cooley & the Dimples
Coates, Carolyn	Eddie Cooley & the Dimples
Coates, Goldie	Blenders (Witch, Cortland)
Cobb, David	Chimes (Specialty, Dig)
Cobb, David	Cupids (Aladdin)
Cobb, David	Lions (Rendezvous)
Cobb, David	Shields
Cobb, David	Wonders
Cobbs, Lionel	Pyramids (Federal, Hollywood)
Coco, Lenny	Chimes (Tag)
Cochran, Barbara	Vestelles
Cochran, James	Spaniels
Codrini, Connie	Four Lads
Coefield, Brice	Alley Cats
Coefield, Brice	Chavelles (Vita)
Coefield, Brice	Electras (Cee Jam, Challenge, Infinity)
Coefield, Brice	Happy Tones
Coefield, Brice	Sabers (Cal-West)
Coefield, Brice	Untouchables
Coefield, Brice	Valiants (Keen)
Coggins, Danny	Moonglows
Cohen, Fred	Tiffanys

Performer	Group
Cohen, Fred "Weasel"	Teddy & the Twilights
Cohen, Fred "Weasel"	Mohawks
Cohen, Stuart	Mike & the Utopians
Colbert, Charles, Jr.	Daylighters
Colbert, Charles, Jr.	Dukays
Colbert, Charles, Jr.	Trinidads
Colbert, Charles	Arthur Lee Maye & the Crowns
Colbert, Charles	Henry Strogin & the Crowns
Colbert, Charles	Richard Berry & the Pharaohs
Colbert, Godoy	Cyclones
Colbert, Godoy (Cody, Codoy)	Richard Berry & the Pharaohs
Colbert, Godoy (Codoy)	Rickey & the Pharaohs
Colclough, Henry	Re-Vels
Coldten, Melvin	Cleartones
Coldten, Melvin	Master Keys
Coldten, Melvin	Norfolk Jazz Quartet
Coldten, Melvin	Selah Jubile Singers
Coldten, Melvin	Virginia Four
Cole, Dave	Ivories (Jaguar)
Cole, Eddie	Three Loose Nuts and a Bolt
Cole, Edward	Turbans (Red Top)
Cole, Franklin	Avons
Cole, Herb	Vibes
Cole, Herb	Vibranaires
Coleman, Bobby	Sunbeams (Acme, Herald)
Coleman, David	Laddins
Coleman, Eddie	Day, Dawn & Dusk
Coleman, Elroy	Cufflinx
Coleman, Elroy	Sunrisers
Coleman, Everett	Coleman Brothers
Coleman, George	Avons
Coleman, Herb	Delta Rhythm Boys
Coleman, Jimmy	Evening Star Quartet
Coleman, John	Metronomes (Cadence)
Coleman, Johnny	Arthur Lee Maye & the Crowns
Coleman, Johnny	Henry Strogin & the Crowns
Coleman, Johnny	Richard Berry & the Dreamers
Coleman, Johnny	Five Hearts (Flair)
Coleman, Johnny "June"	Little June & the Januarys
Coleman, Johnny	Rams
Coleman, Johnny	Sunbeams (Acme, Herald)

Performer	Group	Performer	Group
Coleman, June	Little June & the Januarys	Colocrai, Cirino	Cirino & the Bowties
Coleman, Lander	Coleman Brothers	Colquitt, Charles	Goldenrods (Vee Jay)
Coleman, Mervin	Coleman Brothers	Colsom, Charles	Swinging Phillies
Coleman, Patrick	Cameos (Cameo, Johnson, Matador)	Colter, Dave	King Toppers
		Colwell, Jimmy	Catalinas (Little)
Coleman, Patrick	Ocapellos	Combo, Willie	Gainors
Coleman, Patricia	Cameos (Cameo, Johnson, Matador)	Comedy, Paul	Starlighters (End)
		Comfort, Frank	Congo Rhythm Boys
Coleman, Richard	Carols	Comfort, George	Four Jacks
Coleman, Robert	Delroys	Concepción, Dave	Five Secrets
Coleman, Robert	Emanons (Gee, Josie)	Concepción, Dave	Loungers
Coleman, Robert	Sequins (Red Robin)	Concepción, Dave	Secrets
Coleman, Ronald	Delroys	Concepción, Francis "Frenchie"	Quinns
Coleman, Russell	Coleman Brothers		
Coleman, Wallace	Coleman Brothers	Concepción, Francis "Frenchie"	Travelers (Andex)
Coleman, William	Cameos (Cameo, Johnson, Matador)		
		Concepción, Francis "Frenchie"	Wrens
Cole, Odell	Five Hearts (west coast)		
Colette, Calvin "Khaki"	Swallows (King, Federal, After Hours)	Condo, Frank	Rick & the Masters
		Coney, James	Ivories (Jaguar)
Coles, Andre	Jive Five	Coney, James	Lovenotes (Holiday)
Coles, Chris	Creators (T-Kay)	Connors, Sam	Deckers
Coles, Donald "Duck"	Calvaes	Constantino, Vaughan	Young Lads (Neil)
Collada, R.	Knockouts	Contrera, Al	Mystics (Laurie)
Collins, Aaron	Cadets	Conway, T.	Butlers (Guyden)
Collins, Aaron	Flairs	Cook, Bill	Bill Cook & the Marshalls
Collins, Aaron	Flares	Cook, David	Hi Tensions
Collins, Aaron	Jacks	Cook, Delthine	Sherrys (Guyden, Mercury)
Collins, Aaron	Peppers (Ensign, Press)	Cook, Dinell	Sherrys (Guyden, Mercury)
Collins, Betty	Teen Queens	Cooke, Eugene	Chorals
Collins, Booker	Four Shades of Rhythm	Cooke, Eugene "Sonny"	Charmers (Central, Timely)
Collins, Chuck	Prodigals (Falcon, Abner)		
Collins, Clarence	Capitols (Pet)	Cooke, James	Charmers (Central, Timely)
Collins, Clarence	Chesters	Cooke, L. C.	Magnificents
Collins, Clarence	Larry Chance & the Earls (ABC)	Cooke, Tommy	Sensations
		Cook, Frankie	Demens
Collins, Clarence	Little Anthony & the Imperials	Cook, Frankie	Emersons
		Cook, Joe	Evening Star Quartet
Collins, Dave	Dave Collins & the Scrubs	Cook, Joe	Ivy Tones
Collins, Frances	Crystals (Philles)	Cook, Joe	Little Joe & the Thrillers
Collins, Jessica	Gems (Chess)	Cook, Lorenzo	Federals
Collins, Joe	Butlers (Guyden)	Cook, Lorenzo	Wheels
Collins, Julius	Pastels (United)	Cook, Melvin	Saigons
Collins, Mary	Faith Taylor & the Sweet Teens	Cook, Ronald	Rivieras
		Cook, Thomas	Demens
Collins, Noel	Cyclones	Cook, Thomas	Emersons
Collins, Noel	Richard Berry & the Pharaohs	Cooley, Eddie	Eddie Cooley & the Dimples
Collins, Noel	Rickey and the Pharaohs	Cooper, Lamar	Stylists (Rose)
Collins, Ronnie	Buckeyes	Cooper, Lamar	Vocaleers
Collins, Ronnie	Stereos	Cooper, Les	Empires (Harlem, Wing, Mercury, Whirlin' Disc)
Collins, Rose	Teen Queens		
Collins, Tommy	Paragons	Cooper, Les	Prestos (Mercury)
Collins, William	Sheiks (Ef-N-Dee, Cat)	Cooper, Les	Whirlers
Collura, Dom	Emotions	Cooper, Marty	Tico & the Triumphs

Performer	Group
Cooper, Rudy	Stylists (Rose)
Cooper, Rudy	Stylists (Crown, Jay Wing, Sage)
Cooper, Thurman "Red"	Three Sharps and a Flat
Cop, Bruce	Elegants
Copeland, Edward	Sentimentals (Tuxedo, Checker, Minit)
Copes, George	Gaylords (Savoy)
Copes, George	Imperials (Great Lakes, Derby)
Copes, Rudy	Gaylords (Savoy)
Copes, Rudy	Imperials (Great Lakes, Derby)
Corbin, Warren	Cleftones (Gee)
Cordel, Pat	Pat Cordel & the Crescents
Cordo, Ricky	Cobras (Monogram, Casino, Swan)
Cordo, Ricky	Majors (Imperial)
Cordo, Ricky	Versatiles (Ro-Cal)
Coreiea, Sidney	Pyramids (Federal, Hollywood
Corey, Phil	Durhams
Cori, Tom	Deans (Laurie)
Corley, Alfred	King Krooners (Crooners)
Cornelius, Aaron	King Toppers
Cornelius, Aaron	Orioles
Cornelius, Aaron	Regals
Cornelius, Melvin	Centurys (Fortune)
Cornell, Lee	Cardinals
Cornell, Lee	Trend-Ells
Corona, Joey	Markels (R&M)
Corrente, Sal	Dials (Philips)
Corrente, Sal	Runarounds (K.C., Felsted)
Cortez, Dave "Baby"	Valentines
Cosby, Percy	Val-Tones (DeLuxe)
Cosby, Percy	Baltineers
Cosenza, Pat	Nobles (Klik, End)
Cotton, Benny	Dozier Boys
Cotton, Lawrence	Gondoliers
Council, Fred	Clefs
Council, Fred	Scotty Mann & the Masters
Council, Ronald	Ospreys
Courtney, Opal, Jr.	Spaniels
Cousar, James	Dukes (Specialty)
Covais, Sal	Emotions
Covals, Sal	Shy-Tones (Fonsca)
Covay, Don	Bachelors (Aladdin, Royal Roost)
Covay, Don	Rainbows
Covington, Richard	Twiliters (Nix, Chess, Roulette)
Cowan, Joel	Do Re Mi Trio
Cowart, Juanita	Marvelettes
Cox, Arthur	Duvals (Boss)
Cox, Frank	Emotions (Kapp)
Cox, George	Avalons
Cox, Irvin	Cordovans
Cox, Herbie	Cleftones (Gee)
Coxson, Lawrence	Oakaleers
Cracolici, Al	Mystics (Laurie)
Cracolici, Phil	Mystics (Laurie)
Crafton, Harry	Nite Riders
Crank, Arthur	Chessmen (Relic)
Crawford, Edward "Buddy"	Swallows (King, Federal, After Hours)
Crawford, George	Four Blazers (Melodisc)
Crawford, James	Eldaros
Crawford, James "Sugar Boy"	Sha Weez/Shawees
Crawford, James "Sugar Boy"	Sugar Boy & the Sugar Lumps
Crawford, James "Sugarboy"	Sugar Boy & the Cane Cutters
Crawford, Ollie	Big Three Trio
Crawford, Ollie	Four Jumps of Jive
Crawford, Traverse	Delta Rhythm Boys
Crawford, Traverse	Four Sharps (Atlantic)
Crespo, Joe	Youngtones
Crier, Arthur	Chimes (Royal Roost, Betta)
Crier, Arthur	Craftys
Crier, Arthur	Five Chimes, (Royal Roost, Betta)
Crier, Arthur	Little Guy & the Giants
Crier, Arthur	Halos
Crier, Arthur	Hummers
Crier, Arthur	Lillian Leach & the Mellows
Crier, Arthur	Morrisania Revue
Crier, Arthur	Prehistorics
Crier, Shirley	Rosettes (Herald)
Cristi, Al	Camerons
Cristi, Eunice	Quintones
Crist, Jeannie	Quintones (Chess, Red Top, Hunt)
Cristman, John	Echos (Combo)
Croccitto, Pat	Pat Cordell & the Elegants
Croccitto, Pat (Cordel)	Pat Cordel & the Crescents
Croce, Joe	Chimes (Tag)
Crofts, Big John	Blends
Cromwell, George "Dapper"	Dappers (Peacock)
Crosby, Herb	Rivileers
Crosby, Israel	Three Sharps and a Flat
Crosby, Warren	Four Dots (Dot)
Crowder, John	Orlandos

Performer	Group	Performer	Group
Crowley, Charles	Avalons	Cyrus, Bill	Dell Pris
Crowley, Willie	Belvederes (Dot, Trend)	Cyrus, Edwin	Lucky Charms
Crowley, Willie	Quintones		
Cruder, Harry	Dinwiddie Colored Quartet	Dahrouge, Ray	Darchaes
		Dailey, James A.	Ospreys
Crump, Albert "Walter"	Heartbeats (Hull, Rama, etc.)	Dailey, Joseph, Jr.	Illusions
		Dailey, William	Bop Chords
Crunk, Stewart	Calvanes	Dale, Clifford	Gentlemen
Crunk, Stewart	Nuggets (RCA)	D'Aleo, Angel	Belmonts
Cruz, Donnie	Crystals (Cub)	D'Aleo, Angel	Dion & the Belmonts
Cruz, Donnie	Metros (Just)	D'Amaro, John	Rhythm Aces (Roulette, Mark-X)
Cruz, Edward	Lincoln Fig & the Dates		
Cuffey, Ronald	Five Sharps	Dames, Kenneth	Colonairs
Cuffey, Ronald	Videos	Damon, Jack	Eternals
Cumbo, Johnny	Sunbeams (Acme, Herald)	Damon, Jack	Mellokings (Herald)
Cummings, Joe	Unforgettables	Dancy, Mel	Rivileers
Cummings, Norman	Five Frenchmen	D'Andrea, Bob	Knockouts
Cummins, Joe	Individuals	Dandridge, Leo	Dontells
Cuomo, Sal	Regents	Dandy, Joe	Pyramids (Federal, Hollywood)
Currie, Henry	Five Frenchmen		
Curry, Cliff	Echos (Combo)	Danella, Jim	Emanons (Winley, ABC)
Curry, Cliff	Five Pennies	Daniels, Clemmons	Four Pennies
Curry, Cliff	Hollyhocks	Daniels, Clemmons	Larks
Curry, Harold	Serenaders (Chock, MGM)	Daniels, Douglas	Spirits of Rhythm
Curry, James	Turks	Daniels, Ed	Phantoms
Curry, Paul	Plink, Plank & Plunk	Daniels, George	Charmers (Central, Timely)
Curry, Thomas "Butch"	Famous Hearts		
		Daniels, George	Chorals
Curry, Thomas "Butch"	Five Hearts (Arcade)	Daniels, Jerry	Ink Spots
		Daniels, Jerry	King Jack & the Jesters
Curry, Thomas "Butch"	Lee Andrews & the Hearts	Daniels, Joey	El Venos
		Daniels, Leon	El Venos
Curry, William	Parakeets (Atlas)	Daniels, Jim	Emanons (Winley, ABC)
Curtain, Richard	Hideaways (MGM)	Daniels, Wilbur	Spirits of Rhythm
Curtain, Richard	Sensations	Daniels, Willie	Serenades (Chief)
Curtis, Henry	Billy Wells & the Crescents	Daniels, Willie	Von Gayles
		Daniel, Howard	Charioteers
Curtis, Herman (Dunham)	Solitaires	D'Antonio, Phil	Billy & the Essentials
		Darden, Ralph	Universals (Festival)
Curtis, Herman (Dunham)	Vocaleers	Darouge, Ray	Ray & the Darchaes
		Darren, Johnny	New Yorkers Five
Curtis, Jimmy	Chestnuts	Davenport, Don	Larados
Curtis, Jimmy	Four Haven Knights	Davenport, Don	Romeos (Fox)
Curtiss, Jimmy	Emjays	Davey, Arthur	Four Blues
Cusamano, Larry	Emotions	Davey, Arthur	Plink, Plank & Plunk
Cussey, Ronald	Videos	Davey, Arthur	Red Caps/Five Red Caps
Custis, Eddie	Famous Hearts	Davidson, Leonard	Blue Jays (Milestone)
Custis, Eddie	Five Hearts (Arcade)	Davies, Fred	Verdicts
Custis, Eddie	Hearts (Chancellor)	Davis, Bill	Continentals (Rama)
Custus, Barbara	Superiors (Main Line, Atco)	Davis, Bill	Crows
		Davis, Bill	Four Notes (Premier)
Custus, Eddie	Superiors (Main Line, Atco)	Davis, Billy	El Torros
		Davis, Billy	Emeralds (Bobbin)
Cuttler, Carl	Five Pennies	Davis, Billy	Fifth Dimension
Cuttler, Carl	Four Pennies	Davis, Billy	Five Jets (DeLuxe, Fortune)
Cuttler, Carl	Hearts of Stone		
Cuttler, Cliff	Five Pennies	Davis, Billy	Four Tops

Performer	Group
Davis, Bob	Beale Street Boys
Davis, Bobby	Gaylarks
Davis, Charles	Artistics
Davis, Charles	Dukays
Davis, Charles	Fashions
Davis, Charles	Trinidads
Davis, Charlotte	Tuneweavers
Davis, Cliff	Del Roys
Davis, Elijah	Volumes (Chex, Jubilee, Inferno)
Davis, Ernest	Orients
Davis, Ethel	Jaynetts (Tuff, J&S)
Davis, Fred	Gay Tunes (Timely, Joyce, Dome)
Davis, George	El Torros
Davis, George "Junior"	Four Dots (Dot)
Davis, George, Jr.	Heartbreakers (RCA)
Davis, Huey	Hi-Fidelities
Davis, Jackie	Tympany Five
Davis, James	Orients
Davis, James	Sunbeams (Acme, Herald)
Davis, Joe	Do Re Me Trio
Davis, John	Lovenotes (Riviera, Rainbow)
Davis, Johnny	Austin Powell Quartet
Davis, Johnny	Cats and the Fiddle
Davis, Johnny	Loumell Morgan Trio
Davis, Juanita	Hi-Fidelities
Davis, Kirk	Cadillacs
Davis, Larry	Arthur Lee Maye & the Crowns
Davis, Larry	Kodaks (Kodoks)
Davis, Larry	Sonics (Checker, Chess, Harvard)
Davis, Lawrence	Volumes (Chex)
Davis, Leroy	Jades (Christy)
Davis, Lloyd	FiTones
Davis, Lynn Middleton	Vibraharps
Davis, Marlena	Orlons
Davis, Ossie	Mello Harps
Davis, Paul	Octaves (DC)
Davis, Raymond	Parliaments (Len)
Davis, Raymond	Volchords
Davis, Rennie	Royaltones
Davis, Richard	Four Blackbirds (Vocalion)
Davis, Richard	FourToppers (Savoy)
Davis, Richard	Jones Boys Sing Band
Davis, Richie	Five Willows
Davis, Richie	Willows (Allen, Melba)
Davis, Roquel "Billy"	Five Jets (DeLuxe, Fortune)
Davis, Roquel "Billy"	Thrillers (Thriller, Big Town)
Davis, Russell, Jr.	Twilighters (Specialty, Ebb)
Davis, Saul	Chandeliers
Davis, Thomas	Royaltones
Davis, Vonnel	Souvenirs (Inferno)
Davis, Warren	Monotones
Davis, William	Carols
Davis, Willie	Cadets
Davis, Willie	Flares
Davis, Willie	Jacks
Davis, Willie	Peppers (Ensign, Press)
Davis, Willie	Rocketeers (Modern, MJC)
Davis, Willie	Thor-Ables
Dawes, Frank	Four Tunes
Dawkins, Harold	Kings (Jax, Gotham, Harlem, RCA)
Dawkins, Walter	Velvetones (Sonora, Coronet)
Day, Bobby	Earl Nelson & the Pelicans
Day, Bobby	Rickey and the Pharaohs
Day, Bobby	Voices (Cash)
Daye, Eddie	Four Bars (Josie, Dayco)
Daye, William	Four Bars (Josie, Dayco)
Day, Kenneth "Gene"	Charm
Day, Louis	King Toppers
Days, Allan	Rocketones
Day, Sonny	Sonny Day & the Versatiles
Days, Robert	Five Eagles
DeAlphonso, George	Corvets (Laurel)
Dean, Carroll	Deeptones
Dean, Carroll	Four Deeptones
Dean, Carroll	Hi-Lighters (Hico)
DeAndrade, Mario	Five Discs
Dean, Lenny	Rockin' Chairs
DeBerry, Robert	Darnell & the Dreams
DeCarlo, Louis	Devotions
DeCasmo, Johnny	Dino & the Heartspinners
DeCosta, Abel	Blenders (Decca, MGM)
DeCosta, Abel	Cues
DeCosta, Abel	Gliders
DeCosta, Abel	Millionaires (Davis)
DeCosta, Abel	Playboys (Cat)
DeCosta, Abel	Ruth Brown & the Rhythm Makers
Dee, Donnie	Regents
Dee, Joey	Hi-Fives (Decca)
DeGray, Diane	Sugar Boy & the Sugar Lumps
DeGray, Linda	Sugar Boy & the Sugar Lumps
Delaney, Alfonso	Rivileers
Delaney, Thomas	Paul Breckinridge & the Four Heavenly Knights
Delano, Nick	Nobles (Klik, End)

Performer	Group
Delano, Nickie	Barries (Ember)
Delano, Nickie	Nicky & the Nobles
Del Cavo, Frank	Five Secrets
Del Cavo, Frank	Loungers
Del Cavo, Frank	Secrets
Delcos, Gus	Premiers (Alert)
Del Din, Robert	Larry Chance & the Earls
Delesio, Tony	Nino & the Ebbtides
D'Elia, Bobby	Sparrows Quartet
D'Elia, Dominic	Sparrows Quartet
Delk, William	Duponts (Winley, Royal Roost, Savoy, Roulette)
Dell, Russell	Elgins (Dot)
DeLoach, James	Blenders (Decca, MGM)
DeLoach, James	Millionaires (Davis)
DeLoney, Robert	Universals (Festival)
Deltorta, Ron	Stompers
Demarco, Samy	Illusions
DeMartino, Mike	Camerons
Demmer, Wayne	Bel Airs (Sara)
Dempsey, Bill	Harptones
Dempsey, Bill	Soothers
Demps, Larry	Dramatics (Stax)
Denby, Al	Five Satins
Denby, Al	Scarlets
Denby, Herman "Junior"	Swallows (King, Federal, After Hours)
Denham, Cleve	Goldenrods (Vee Jay)
DeNicholas, Artie	Catalinas (Little)
Dennis, John	Caldwells
Dennis, Judge	Pharaohs (Specialty)
Dennis, Judge	Sliders
DePrisco, Pat	Chimes (Tag)
Derbigny, James	Squires (Combo)
Derbish, Jack	Dell Pris
Derin, Ronald	Neons (Tetra)
De Shields, Wilson	Violinaires
Devase, William	Elements (Titan)
Devase, William	Elgins (Flip, Lummtone)
Devereaux, Wesley	Admirals
Devereaux, Wesley	Sultans (Duke)
DeVito, Phil	Emanons (Winley, ABC)
DeVito, Ralph	Four Graduates (Rust)
DeVold, Edward	Echos (Combo)
De Voie, Joseph	Kings (Specialty)
Diaco, Al	Treble Chords
Dial, Willie	Medallionaires
Dial, Willie	Serenades (Chief)
Dial, Willie	Von Gayles
Diamond, Dennis	Bon Aires
Diamond, Lee	Velvetones
Dias, Joe "Ditto"	Bachelors (Earl)
Dias, Joe "Ditto"	Chords (Cat)
Dias, Joe "Ditto"	Dean Barlow & the Crickets
Diaz, Raphael	Excels (Central, Gone)
Diaz, Raphael	Minors (Celeste)

Performer	Group
DiBari, Anthony	Treble Chords
DiBari, Tony	Nino & the Ebbtides
DiBella, Charlie	Five Discs
DiBenedetto, Mike	Debonaires (Gee)
Dickens, Doles	Red Caps
Dickerson, Herbert	Charioteers
Dickerson, John	Senators
Dicks, Vernon	Jimmy Keyes & the Symbols
Diddy, Pop	Adolphus Holcomb & the Kings
DiGienerio, Gene	Channels (Mercury)
Digilio, Frank	Dreamers (Goldisc, Cousins)
DiGuillio, Tommy	Rick & the Masters
Dilks, Jimmy	Clientelles
Dilks, Jimmy	Joey & the Flips
Dimberg, Marty	Bobby & the Consoles
DiMucci, Dion	Dion & the Belmonts
Dinkes, "Sonny" (Turner)	Metrotones
Dinkins, Curley	Hollywood Four Flames
Dinkins, Curley	Flames
Dinkins, Curley	Patty Anne & the Flames
Dinkins, Curley	Four Flames (Fidelity, Specialty)
Dinkins, Curley	Hollywood Flames
Dix, Arthur	Chords (Cat)
Dix, Arthur	Popular Five
Dix, John	Ebonaires (Modern, Aladdin, Money, etc.)
Dixon, Arthur	Capitols (Cindy, Gateway)
Dixon, Bernard	Danderliers
Dixon, Clarence	Four Knights
Dixon, Eugene	Dukays
Dixon, Eugene	Billy Williams Quartet
Dixon, Floyd	Three Blazers
Dixon, Franklin	Arrows (Flash)
Dixon, George	Spinners (Motown, Tri-Phi)
Dixon, Hank	Five Stars (Mark-X)
Dixon, Harry	Inspirations
Dixon, Luther	Barons
Dixon, Luther	Buddies (Glory)
Dixon, Luther	Four Buddies (Savoy)
Dixon, Reather	Bobbettes
Dixon, Richard	Dukays
Dixon, Richard	Kodaks (Kodoks)
Dixon, Willie	Big Three Trio
Dixon, Willie	Five Breezes
Dixon, Willie	Four Jumps of Jive
Dobbins, Georgeanne	Marvelettes
Dobson, Wilbert Hess	Links
Dockery, William	Duponts (Winley, Royal Roost, Savoy, Roulette)

Performer	Group
Dodd, J.	Five Du-Tones
Dodds, Malcomb	Malcomb Dodds & the Tunedrops
Doell, Percy	Harlemaires
Dolphin, Edward	Channels (Whirlin' Disc)
Donahue, Jerry	Cardinals
Donahue, Jerry	Trend-Ells
Donato, Anthony (John)	Anthony & the Sophomores
Donato, Anthony	Tony & the Dynamics
Donnarumma, Sal	Consorts (Cousins, APT)
Donnegan, Norman	Ad Libs
Donn, Ronald	Neons
Donovan, Freddie	Chances (Roulette)
Donovan, Freddie	Willows (Melba)
Dorroh, Philip	El Pollos
Dorroh, Philip	Hesitations
Dorr, Tolbert	Rivals (Puff)
D'Orsay, Andre	Red Caps/Five Red Caps
Dorsey, Garfield	Darnell & the Dreams
Dorsey, Glenn	Twiliters (Nix, Chess, Roulette)
Dorsey, John Raymond	Five Jets (DeLuxe, Fortune)
Dorsey, John Raymond	Five Stars (Mark-X, End)
Dorsey, John Raymond	Royal Jokers
Dorsey, John Raymond	Thrillers (Thriller, Big Town)
Dorsey, John Raymond	Voice Masters
Dortch, Stanley	Five Satins
Dougherty, Eugene	Intruders (Federal)
Douglas, Charles	Spaniels
Douglas, Harry	Deep River Boys
Douglas, Johnny	Cardinals
Douglas, Roland, Jr.	Pyramids (Davis)
Douglass, Faith	Joe Alexander & the Cubans
Doyle, B.	Slades
Dozier, James	Avalons
Dozier, Lamont	Romeos (Atco)
Dozier, Lamont	Voice Masters
Drago, Vinnie	Nino & the Ebbtides
Drake, Jimmy	Paramonts (Ember)
Drake, LaVerne	Cadillacs
Draper, Robert	Accents (Brunswick)
Drayton, James	Don Juans
Drayton, James	Five Dollars
Drue, John	Prisonaires
Drummond, Willie Earl	Hollyhocks
Drummons, Willie Earl	Four Pennies
DuBlanc, Damita Jo	Red Caps/Five Red Caps
Duckett, Tom	Five Sharps

Performer	Group
Duckett, Tom	Rivileers
Duconje, Donplayelle	Laurels (Combo, X, Flair)
Dukes, James	Emanons (Gee, Josie)
Dumas, Eddie	Supremes (Ace)
Dunbar, Jim	Four Deuces
Dunbar, Sidney	Calvanes
Dunbar, Sidney	Nuggets (RCA)
Duncan, Cleve	Hollywood Flames
Duncan, Cleve	Penguins
Duncan, Cleve	Radiants (Dootone)
Duncan, Edward	Capris (nonrecording)
Duncan, Joe	Stylists (Rose)
Duncan, Joe	Vocaleers
Duncan, Kenneth	Carols
Dunham, Herman Curtis	Blenders (Paradise)
Dunham, Herman Curtis	Solitaires
Dunham, Herman Curtis	Vocaleers
Dunn, Bobby	Empires (Harlem, Wing, Mercury, Whirlin' Disc, Amp 3)
Dunn, Bobby	Prestos
Dunn, Conrad "Clifton"	Dreamlovers
Dunn, Homer	Five Bob-O-Links
Dunn, Homer	Rivieras
Dunn, James Ray	Dreamlovers
Dunn, Robert	Whirlers
DuPont, August "Dimes"	Gondoliers
DuPont, Shelly	Calendars
DuPont, Shelly	New Yorkers Five
Dupree, Bernard	Centurys (Fortune)
Durant, Joseph	Five Blue Jackets
Durden, Ray	Sunrisers
Durden, Ray	Cufflinx
Duren, Sammie	Five Ramblers
Durham, Wayne	Bradford Boys (Rainbow)
Dyer, Eugene	Romeos (Fox)
Eagles, Joe	Five Eagles
Earl, Paul	Cap-Tans
Easley, Benny Louis	Chargers
Eason, Dave	Chips
Easton, Bearle	Moonglows
Eaton, Johnny	Romaines
Eaton, Leuvenia	5 Jades (Duke)
Eaton, Leuvenia	Metrotones (Reserve)
Eaves, Sylvester "Peachy"	Velquins (Valquins)
Ebron, Doug	Webtones
Ebron, Douglas	Danleers

Performer	Group
Edgehill, Edward	Valentines
Edmonds, Floyd	Sparks of Rhythm
Edmundson, William	Southernaires
Edwards, Bob "Chico"	Diablos
Edwards, Danny	Kool Gents
Edwards, Dennis	Contours
Edwards, Earl	Dukays
Edwards, Earl	Romaines
Edwards, Edgar	Spinners (Motown, Tri-Phi)
Edwards, Edward	Esquires
Edwards, Elaine	Moonbeams (Checker)
Edwards, Elaine	Moonbeems (Sapphire)
Edwards, E.	Dukes (Imperial)
Edwards, Frank	Five Wings
Edwards, Frank	Miriam Grate & the Dovers
Edwards, Gwen	Gwen Edwards & the Co-Eds
Edwards, James Holland	Schoolboys
Edwards, Jasper	Jubalaires
Edwards, Jasper	Melody Kings
Edwards, Jasper	Shadows (Lee)
Edwards, John	Spinners (Motown, Tri-Phi)
Edwards, Maxine	Starlets (Pam)
Edwards, Melvin	Tabbys
Edwards, Millard	Bel Aires (Decca)
Edwards, Millard	Sheppards (Apex)
Edwards, Milton	Rivileers
Edwards, Pearl	Pitter Pats
Edwards, Raymond	Silhouettes
Edwards, Robert	Intruders (Federal)
Edwards, Rufus	Ray & the Darchaes
Edwards, William	Sunbeams (Acme, Herald)
Edwards, William "Ricky"	Chord Cats (Cat)
Edwards, William "Ricky"	Chords (Cat)
Edwards, William "Ricky"	Sh Booms (Cat)
Einor, Jimmy	Crowns (Old Town)
Elbert, Donnie	Vibraharps
Elder, Daniel	Mello Harps
Eldridge, A. J.	Coleman Brothers
Eldridge, Tommy	Jarmels
Eli, Henry	Heartbreakers (Vik)
Elkins, Alfred	Lewis Bronzeville Five
Ell, Carl (Carl White)	Buddies
Elliot, William	Five Eagles
Ellis, Albert	Five Sounds
Ellis, Jimmy	Five Sounds
Ellis, Jimmy	Satintones
Ellis, Lloyd	Four Deals
Ellison, Nolan	Marquees (Okeh)
Emerick, Bob	Impossibles (RMP)
Emery, Billy	Lyres
Emery, Billy	Nutmegs
Emery, Billy	Rajahs
Ench, John	Boptones
English, Alvin	Majestics (Chex, Contour)
English, Barbara	Clickettes
English, Karl	Cherokees
English, Karl	Cobras (Monogram, Swan, Casino)
English, Victor	Carousels (Gone)
English, Victor	Rainbows
English, William	Clouds (Cobra)
Enois, Lucky	Kansas City Tomcats
Ephraim, Willie	Danleers
Epps, Nathaniel "Lil John"	Capitols, (Pet)
Epps, Nathaniel "Lil John"	Chips
Epstein, Chuck	Excellents (Blast)
Epstein, Harold	Styles (Serene, Josie)
Erico, Frank	Five Fashions
Ernst, Joe	Criterions
Ernst, Joe	Kents (Aljon)
Ervin, DiFosco	Pastels (Mascot, Argo)
Ervin, Frankie	Shields
Ervin, Frankie	Spears
Ervin, Frankie	Three Blazers
Eskridge, Murrie	Ballads (Venture)
Eskridge, Murrie	Palms (United, States)
Eskridge, Murrie	Five Palms (United, States)
Eskridge, Murrie	Sheppards (Apex)
Esposito, Al	Billy Vera & the Contrasts
Esposito, George	Chaps
Esposito, Larry	Mellokings
Esquire, Kenny	Kenny Esquire & the Starlites
Estep, Theodore (Eastep)	Bobby Hall & the Kings
Estep, Theodore (Eastep)	Kings (Harlem, RCA, Gotham, Jax,)
Estrada, Ray	"Little" Julian Herrera & the Tigers
Eugene, Huff	Kool Gents
Eugene, Sonny	Eddie & the Starlites
Eugene, Sonny	Starlites (Peak)
Eugene, Teague	Dozier Boys
Evans, Albert "Midge"	Topps (Red Robin)
Evans, Charles	Don Juans
Evans, Jerome	Furys (Mack IV)
Evans, Jerome	Medallions
Evans, Nate	Impressions
Evans, Robert	Four Dots (Dot)

Performer	Group
Evans, Robert	Heartbreakers (RCA)
Evans, Robert	Topps (Red Robin)
Evans, Roy	Chanteclaires
Evans, Tommy	Carols
Evans, Tommy	Drapers
Evans, Tommy	Drifters (Atlantic)
Evans, Tommy	Floaters
Evans, Tommy	Ravens
Everett, Ed	Jerry Sheely & the Versatiles
Everette, Ed	Sonny Day & the Versatiles
Everett, Ronald	Castelles (Grand)
Everidge, Charles	Mad Lads
Everidge, Charles	Preludes (Empire)
Everidge, Charles	Shields
Everidge, Charles	Tempters (Empire)
Everidge, Charles	Youngsters
Everson, Arnold	Splendors (Taurus)
Ewbanks, Quentin	Diablos
Ezell, William	Bel Aires
Ezzard, Wallace	Original Drifters
Ezzard, Wallace	Tears
Fabiano, Ralph	Leisure Lads
Facing, Jesse	Drapers
Facing, Jesse	Duvals (Rainbow)
Facing, Jesse	Five Crowns
Fagin, Maurice	Majestics (Chex, Contour)
Fain, Sammy	Limelighters
Fain, Sammy	Lillian Leach & the Mellows
Fain, Sammy	Morrisania Revue
Fair, Calvin	Gales (JVB)
Fair, Calvin	Question Marks
Fair, Calvin	Violinaires
Faison, Alexander	Genies
Faison, Billy	Corvairs (Comet, Leopard)
Fakir, Abdul	Four Tops
Fakler, Ken	Temptations (Savoy)
Falcone, Bob	Camerons
Falcone, Eddie	Mystics (Laurie)
Faliveno, John	Savoys (Catamount)
Fallo, Lou	Rhythm Aces (Roulette, Mark-X)
Falzone, Johnny	Majestics (20th Fox)
Fambrough, Henry	Spinners (Motown, Tri-Phi)
Fann, Leroy	Ruby & the Romantics
Farley, Charles	Royal Holidays (Carlton, Herald)
Farmer, James	Admirals
Farmer, James	Sultans (Duke)
Farrell, Jackie	Three Chuckles
Fascinaro, Lou	Blue Sonnets
Fasanaro, Lou	Vocal-Aires
Fassert, Charles	Regents
Fassert, Chuck	Runarounds (K.C., Felsted)

Performer	Group
Fassert, Stanford	Songmasters
Favale, Joe	Emotions
Fawtalsky, Dave	Bill Haley & the Comets
Feaster, Carl	Chord Cats (Cat)
Feaster, Carl	Chords (Cat)
Feaster, Carl	Sh Booms (Cat)
Feaster, Claude	Chord Cats (Cat)
Feaster, Claude	Chords (Cat)
Feaster, Claude	Sh Booms (Cat)
Feather, Leonard	Spirits of Rhythm
Feemster, Alfonso	Four Bars (Josie, Dayco)
Feldman, Joel	Excellents (Blast)
Feliciano, Frank	Raiders (Atco)
Felix, John	Jackie & the Starlites
Felton, Leslie	Showmen
Fenaro, Ernest	Tony & the Dynamics
Fenwick, Branford	Cap-Tans
Ferbie, William	Drifters (Atlantic)
Ferguson, Danny	Buddies (Glory)
Ferguson, Danny	Four Buddies (Savoy)
Fernandez, Paul	Belltones (J&S, Scatt)
Ferrante, Bob	Mystics (Laurie)
Ferrara, Freddie	Del Satins
Ferrara, Hank	Catalinas
Ferrara, Joe	Treble Chords
Ferrare, Tommy	Del Satins
Ferrar, Doug	Five Delights
Ferrigno, Paul	Bob Knight Four
Ferri, Lou	Durhams
Ferro, Henry "Rico"	Clusters
Fickling, Sam	Hurricanes
Fickling, Sam	Toppers (Jubilee)
Fickling, Sam	Steve Gibson & the Toppers
Field, Bobby	Del Satins
Fields, Barney	Inspirators (Treat, Old Town)
Fields, Barney	Five Stars (Treat)
Fields, Gerald	Five Bob-O-Links (Okeh)
Fields, Preston	Parakeets (Atlas)
Fields, Robert	Mondellos
Figueroa, Bobby	Five Jades
Figueroa, Ivan "Lincoln Fig"	Lincoln Fig & the Dates
Figueroa, Joey	Five Jades
Figueroa, Louis	Youngtones
Figueroa, Ray	Moodmakers
Finaro, Ernie	Anthony & the Sophomores
Finizio, Bob	4 Js
Finizio, Bob	Fabulous Four
Finizio, Bob	Four Naturals
Finizio, Ray	Four Naturals
Finizio, Raymond	Naturals (Red Top)
Finizio, Richie	Rick & the Masters
Finney, Garland	Three Blazers

Performer	Group
Finnie, Lance	Falcons (Mercury, Unart, LuPine, Chess, Atlantic)
Fiore, Vincent	Rhythm Aces (Roulette, Mark-X)
Fiorino, Tony	Blue Stars
Fisher, Andrew	Barons (Imperial)
Fisher, Andrew	Marquis
Fisher, Carl	Marathons
Fisher, Carl	Vibrations (Checker)
Fisher, Carlton	Jayhawks
Fisher, Dave	Academics
Fisher, Ernestine	Faith Taylor & the Sweet Teens
Fisher, George	Normanaires
Fisher, Herb	Bachelors (Aladdin, Royal Roost)
Fisher, Herbert	Jets (Rainbow)
Fisher, Herbert	Links
Fishman, Eddie	Camelots
Fitch, John	Butlers (Guyden)
Fitzimmons, Dale	Classics (Class, Crest)
Fitzpatrick, Charles	Sharptones (Aladdin)
Fitzpatrick, Charles	Turbans (Money)
Fizer, Charles	Challengers (Melatone)
Fizer, Charles	Olympics
Flack, LeRoy	Clefs
Flagg, Roy	Velvetones
Flamingo, Johnny	Dots (Caddy)
Flanagan, Madison	Vevetones (Sonora, Coronet)
Fleming, Ken	Bon Aires
Flemings, Chester	Fabulous Playboys
Flood, Melvin	Five Wings
Florio, Ralph	Illusions
Floyd, Eddie	Falcons (Mercury, United Artists, Chess, LuPine, Atlantic)
Floyd, Ivy	Deeptones
Floyd, Ivy	Four Deeptones
Floyd, Ivy	Hi Liters (HiCo)
Floyd, Jesse	Five Masks (Jan)
Floyd, Jesse	Five Notes (Chess)
Floyd, Jesse	Five Stars
Floyd, Joe	Dixieaires
Floyd, Viola	Versalettes
Fobbs, James	Blue Chips
Foley, Ira	Bel-Aires (Flip)
Foley, Ira	Medallions
Foley, Ira	Vel-Aires (Flip)
Folio, Gerard	Prodigals (Falcon, Abner)
Forbes, Ted	Tabs (Dot, Vee Jay, Wand)
Forbes, Wes	Channels
Forbes, Wes	Five Satins
Forbes, Wes	New Yorkers Five
Forbes, Wes	Starlarks (Ember)
Forbes, Wes	Wildwoods
Forch, Claude	Trinidads

Performer	Group
Ford, Alex	Tangiers
Ford, Arthur	Equallos
Ford, Arthur	Willie Logan & the Plaids
Ford, David	Bobby Byrd & the Birds
Ford, David	Flames
Ford, David	Patty Anne & the Flames
Ford, David	Four Flames (Fidelity, Specialty)
Ford, David	Hollywood Flames
Ford, David	Hollywood Four Flames
Ford, David	Jets
Ford, David	Earl Nelson & the Pelicans
Ford, David	Satellites
Ford, David	Tangiers (Decca, Class)
Ford, David	Turks (Money)
Ford, Gene	Cats (Federal)
Ford, Gene	Gene Ford & the Chanters
Ford, Harold	Delacardos
Ford, John	Students
Ford, Patricia	Hearts (Baton)
Ford, Walter	Rays
Ford, Willie	Dramatics (Stax)
Foreman, Harold	Pipes
Fork, Barbara	Vestelles
Forman, Maggie	Cabineers
Forrest, Earl	Beale Streeters
Forrest, William	Fantastics (RCA)
Forte, David	Leopards
Forte, David	Mello Harps
Fortson, Albert	Tears
Fortson, Andrew	Metrotones
Foster, Billy	Medallions
Foster, Cell	Cell Foster & the Audios
Foster, Harold	Five Frenchmen
Foster, Richard N.	Pyramids (Davis)
Foster, Wilbur	Nobles (Sapphire)
Fotson, Albert	Original Drifters
Fountain, Lester	Cap-Tans
Fountain, Richard	Paramonts (Ember)
Foushes, Carl	Terracetones
Foust, Cortez	Shufflers
Fowler, Theodric	Upfronts
Fox, Kenneth	Federals
Fox, Kenneth	Wheels
Fox, Norman	Norman Fox & the Rob Roys
Fox, Ron	Mello Harps
Fox, Thomas	Dodgers
Fox, Thomas "Pete"	Cadets
Fox, Thomas "Pete"	Chimes (Flair)
Fox, Thomas "Pete"	Arthur Lee Maye & the Crowns
Fox, Thomas "Pete"	Flairs
Fox, Thomas "Pete"	Five Hollywood Blue Jays
Fox, Thomas "Pete"	Hunters
Fox, Thomas "Pete"	Jacks

Performer	Group
Fox, Thomas "Pete"	Jac-O-Lacs
Fox, Thomas "Pete"	Metrotones
Fox, Thomas "Pete"	Rams (Flair)
Fox, Thomas "Pete"	Whips
Foy, Shirley "Bunny"	Delltones
France, Al	Swallows (King, Federal, After Hours)
Francis, David	Colonairs
Francis, Fred	Wini Brown & the Boyfriends
Francis, Freddie	Dreamers (Jubilee, Mercury)
Francis, Mickey	Dreamers (NY)
Francis, Mickey	Valentines
Frank, Larry	Devotions
Franklin, Clyde	Starlings (Josie, Dawn)
Franklin, Cortez	Suburbans (Baton)
Franklin, Darlene	Blossoms
Franklin, Darlene	Echos (Combo)
Franklin, Gloria	Pitter Pats
Franklin, Johnny	Sax Kari & the Quailtones
Franklin, Melvin	Temptations (Gordy)
Franklin, Melvin	Voice Masters
Franklin, William	Kodaks (Kodoks)
Franklin, William	Sonics (Checker, Chess, Harvard)
Franks, James Ruben	Four Aces (Trilon)
Frazier, Al	Crenshaws
Frazier, Al	Ebb-Tones (Crest)
Frazier, Al	Four After Fives
Frazier, Al	Lamplighters
Frazier, Al	Mellow Moods (nonrecording)
Frazier, Al	Rebels
Frazier, Al	Rivingtons
Frazier, Al	Sharps (Aladdin)
Frazier, Al	Tenderfoots
Frazier, Al	Twisters (Apt)
Frazier, Ben	Paragons
Frazier, James	Casinos (Maske)
Frazier, James	Parliaments (Len)
Frazier, Joe	Impalas (Cub)
Frazier, Louis	Ravens
Frazier, Ray	Blenders (Class, Aladdin, Paradise, Wanger, Wonder)
Frazier, Richard	Farris Hill & the Madison Brothers
Frazier, Richard	Madisons (Cedargrove, Lawn, MGM)
Frazier, Richard	Little Joe & the Thrillers
Frederico, Chuck	Clientelles
Frederick, Conrad	Dixieaires
Fredericks, Bill	Drifters (Atlantic)
Fredericks, Bill	Packards (Pla-Bac, Paradise)

Performer	Group
Fredericks, Bill	Tremaines
Freedman, Bob	Sparrows Quartet
Freeman, Bobby	Romancers
Freeman, Ernest	Congo Rhythm Boys
Freeman, Jim	Five Satins
Freeman, Marzetta	Echos (Combo)
Freeman, Richard	Five Satins
Freeman, Richard	Pyramids (Davis)
Freeman, Richard	Restless Hearts
Freeman, Richard	Revlons
Freeman, Richard	Wildwoods
Freeman, Richie	Starlarks (Ember)
Freeman, Steve	Rhythm Aces (Roulette, Mark-X)
French, Tyrone	Restless Hearts
French, Tyrone	Romancers
Friday, Willie	Five Keys
Fridie, Lennie, Jr.	Jimmy Castor Bunch
Friend, Eddie	Eddie Friend & the Empires (Colpix)
Frierson, James	5 Jades (Duke)
Frierson, James	Metrotones
Fry, Bunny	Delltones
Fuchs, Donny	Dynamics (Dynamic, Cindy, Seeco)
Fulham, Ralph	Quintones (Park)
Fuller, Leo "Tiny"	Sparrows (Jay Dee, Davis)
Fuller, Leo "Tiny"	Vocaleers
Fullylove, Leroy	Tads (Dot)
Fulton, Paul	Chips
Fulton, Ron	Chaps
Funaro, Rick	Dantes
Funches, Johnny	Dells
Funches, Johnny	El Rays
Fuqua, Charlie	Ink Spots
Fuqua, Charlie	King Jack & the Jesters
Fuqua, Harvey	Five Quails
Fuqua, Harvey	Moonglows
Fuqua, Harvey	Moonlighters
Fuqua, Harvey	Harvey & the Quails
Fuqua, Kenneth	Royal Holidays (Carlton, Herald)
Furness, Arthur	Four Keys
Furness, Arthur	Furness Brothers
Furness, Arthur	Red Caps
Furness, Joe	Four Keys
Furness, Joe	Furness Brothers
Furness, Joe	Red Caps
Furness, Slim	Furness Brothers
Furness, Slim	Three Keys
Furness, William	Four Keys
Furness, William	Furness Brothers
Furness, William	Red Caps
Furness, "Slim"	Three Keys
Fussell, Vernon	Gazelles
Gabrie, E.	Classics (Class, Crest)

Performer	Group
Gadson, James	Carpets
Gadson, Tom	Carpets
Gagne, Harry	Ronnie Vare & the Inspirations
Gail, Irving Lee	Jimmy Jones & the Jones Boys
Gail, Irving Lee	Cadillacs
Gail, Irving Lee	Carl Hogan & the Miracles
Gail, Irving Lee	Jimmy Jones & the Pretenders
Gail, Irving Lee	Jimmy Jones & the Savoys
Gail, Irving Lee	Jones Boys
Gail, Irving Lee	Vocaltones
Gaines, Anthony	Cleftones (Gee)
Gaines, Bill Jayotis	Genies
Gaines, Joseph	"Fat Man" Mathews & the Four Kittens
Gaines, Joseph	Hawks
Gaines, Joseph	Dave Collins & the Scrubs
Gaines, Leo	Four Sharps (Atlantic)
Gaines, Otha Lee	Delta Rhythm Boys
Gaines, Pat	Camerons (Cousins)
Gaines, Stanley	Cats and the Fiddle
Gaines, Stanley	Austin Powell Quartet
Gaines, Walter	Five Jets (DeLuxe, Fortune)
Gaines, Walter	Five Stars (Mark-X, End)
Gaines, Walter	Voice Masters
Gainey, Earl	Gladiolas
Gainey, Earl	Zodiacs
Gaitwood, Alfred	Cufflinx
Gaitwood, Alfred	Rivals (Apollo)
Gaitwood, Alfred	Smoothtones (Jem)
Galante, Billy	Roulettes (Champ)
Gales, Larry	Starlings (Josie, Dawn)
Gales, Larry	Supremes (Old Town)
Gales, Larry	Twilighters (MGM)
Gales, LaVerne	Foster Brothers
Galfo, George	Mystics (Laurie)
Gallagher, Jimmy	Five Boroughs
Gallagher, Jimmy	Montclaires (Audicon)
Gallagher, Jimmy	Passions
Gallagher, R.	Knockouts
Gallone, Albee	Passions
Galloway, Bill "Dicey"	Harptones
Galvin, Larry	Blue Stars
Gambale, John	Classics (Dart, Mercury, Musicnote)
Gamble, Ralph	Sentimentals (Tuxedo, Checker, Minit)
Gamble, Renaldo	Impacts (RCA, Watts)
Gamble, Renaldo	Kodaks (Kodoks)
Gamble, Renaldo	Schoolboys
Gant, Allen	Hi-Lites (Record Fair, Julia)
Ganz, Bobby	Concords (RCA, Rust, Herald)
Garcia, Hector	Eternals
Garcia, Joe	Crystals (Cub)
Garcia, Joe	Metros (Just)
Gardener, Carl	Coasters
Gardner, Carl	Robins (Savoy)
Gardner, Charles	Dootones
Gardner, Charles	Medallions
Gardner, Howard	Shields
Gardner, Lester	Caverliers [sic] Quartet
Gardner, Morris	Dreamlovers
Gardner, Thomas	Scale-Tones
Gardner, Tommy	Dubs
Gardner, Tommy	Marvels (ABC)
Gardner, Vernon	Deep River Boys
Gardner, William	Cardells (Middle-Tone)
Gardner, William	Tabs (Dot, Vee Jay, Wand)
Gardner, Vernon	Deep River Boys
Garner, Alfred	Five Eagles
Garner, Steve	Voices Six
Garnes, Sherman	Frankie Lymon & the Teenagers
Garone, Ralph (Garrone)	Bob Knight Four
Garrett, Arvid	Accents (Brunswick)
Garrett, Arvid	Three Sharps and a Flat
Garrett, Sonny	Stylists (Rose)
Garrison, Rodney	Escorts (Coral)
Garr, Leonard	Uniques (Peacock)
Garrone, Ralph	Bob Knight Four
Gary, Sherry	Delltones
Garza, Dimas	Lyrics (Harlem, Wildcat)
Gaskin, Rose	Lovenotes (Wilshire)
Gaston, Henry	Zodiacs
Gaston, Pat	Four Bells (Gem)
Gaston, Pat	Solitaires
Gates, Robert	Delacardos
Gathers, Helen	Bobbettes
Gathers, Ronald	Majors (Imperial)
Gathers, Ronald	Versatiles (Ro-Cal)
Gaudioso, Ercote	Treble Chords
Gaye, Marvin	Marquees (Okeh)
Gaye, Marvin	Moonglows (RCA)
Gaye, Marvin	Rainbows (Rama)
Gaye, Marvin	Starlighters (End)
Gayles, Billy	Prodigals (Falcon, Abner)
GeAngelo, Bobby "Dino"	Dino & the Heartspinners
Gearing, Yvonne	Laddins
Geddins, Bob	Hi-Tones
Gehrke, Dennis	Bel Airs (Sara)
Gentile, Eddie	Four Dates (Chancellor)

Performer	Group	Performer	Group
Gentry, Cecil	Chessmen (PAC)	Giles, Maudice	Squires (Combo)
George, Albert	Harmonaires (Holiday)	Giles, Maudice	Tuxedos
George, Albie	Dino & the Heartspinners	Giles, Maurice	Capris (Tender)
George, Herb	Normanaires	Giles, Maurice	Portraits
George, Langston	Gladys Knight & the Pips	Gillespie, John	Rip Chords
George, William	Marylanders	Gillis, Jesse	Blue Notes (Josie, Rama,
George, William	Stylists (Jay Wing, Sage,		Harthon, etc.)
	Crown)	Gill, Carolyn	Velvelettes
Gerace, Fred	Little Joey & the Flips	Gilmour, Barry Lee	Tempo-Toppers
Gerald, Johnson	Quinns	Gilmour, Gene	Five Breezes
Gerald, Winfred	Otis Williams & the	Gilmour, Jimmy	Four Jumps of Jive
	Charms	Ginyard, J. C.	Dixieaires
Gerardi, Bob	Rockin' Chairs	Ginyard, J. C.	Du Droppers
Gerard, Otis	Squires (Combo)	Ginyard, J. C.	Golden Gate Quartet
Germany, William	El Capris (Bullseye, Fee	Ginyard, J. C.	Jubalaires
	Bee)	Giordano, Cathy	Cathy Jean & the
Geter, Gus	Shells	Jean	Roommates
Geyer, Hugh	Val-Aires	Giordano,Tony	Montereys (Blast)
Giacolone, Paul	Fireflies	Gipson, Byron	Pharaohs (Specialty)
Giambalvo, Lenny	Bellnotes	"Slick"	
Giarraffa, Sal	Arrogants	Gipson, Byron,	Sliders
Gibson, Billy	Vals (Unique	"Slick"	
	Laboratories)	Girard, Merna	Crystals (Philles)
Gibson, Danny	Velvetones (Coronet,	Girona, Charlie	Eternals
	Sonora)	Girsoli, Carl	Fireflies
Gibson, Doug	Jimmy Castor Bunch	Gist, Rachel	Enchanters (Jubilee)
Gibson, Doug	Vibraharps	Givens, Cliff	Billy Ward & the
"Bubs"			Dominoes
Gibson, James	Fabulous Playboys	Givens, Cliff	Four Sharps
Gibson, James	Falcons	Givens, Cliff	Golden Gate Quartet
Gibson, James	Playboys (Detroit)	Givens, Cliff	Ink Spots
Gibson, James	Ramblers (Federal, Jax,	Givens, Cliff	Melody Masters
	MGM, Trumpet)	Glanton, Junior	Original Cadillacs
Gibson, Ray	G-Clefs	Glass, Eugene	Majors (Imperial)
Gibson, Robert	Pyramids (Cub, Vee Jay)	Glass, Eugene	Versatiles (Ro-Cal)
Gibson, Steve	FourToppers (Savoy)	Glazier, Herb	Rhythm Aces (Roulette,
Gibson, Steve	Jones Boys Sing Band		Mark-X)
Gibson, Steve	Red Caps/Five Red Caps	Glover, Horner	Five Sounds
Gibson, Steve	Steve Gibson & the	Gluberman, Stu	Eltones
	Toppers	Godfrey, Charles	Luther Bond & the
Gibson, Truman	Bon Bon Trio		Emeralds
Gibson, William	Excelsior Norfolk Quartet	Godfrey, Leon	Luther Bond & the
Gideon, Tony	Daylighters		Emeralds
Giglioni, John	Lincoln Fig & the Dates	Goeke, John	Slades
Gilberto, Russ	Teddy Randazzo & the	Goens, Doris	Capitols (Cindy, Gateway)
	Three Chuckles	Goggins, Delmar	V-Eights
Gilbert, Gloria	Loreleis (Brunswick)	"Kirby"	
Gilbert, Larry	Personalities	Gold, Billy	Barons (Imperial)
Gilbert, Sam	Marvels (Laurie)	Goldie, Bruce	Dreamers (Apt, Goldisc)
Gilbert, Sam	Satisfactions (Smash)	Goldie, Bruce	Five Boroughs
Gilbert, Sam	Senators	Goldin, Freddie	Joe Alexander & the
Gilbert, Stan	Starlings (Josie, Dawn)		Cubans
Gilchrist, Anderson	Emblems	Goldman, Dickie	Concords (RCA, Rust,
Giles, Leroy	Magnetics		Herald)
Giles, Maudice	Hollywood Saxons	Goldston, Bunky	Revlons
Giles, Maudice	Saxons	Goley, Robert	Desideros

Performer	Group	Performer	Group
Gomez, Leroy	Four Haven Knights	Gourdine, Anthony	Little Anthony & the
Gooden, James	Continentals (Rama)		Imperials
Gooden, Rodney	Hitmakers	Govan, Dave	Marathons
Gooden, Sam	Impressions	Govan, Dave	Mello Harps
Gooding, Sally	Three Peppers	Govan, Dave	Vibrations (Checker)
Goodlow, Ken	Pentagons	Govan, David	Jayhawks
Goodlow, Ted	Pentagons	Govenelli, Coste	Blendairs
Goodman, George	George Goodman & the	Gowder, Joe	Leopards
	Headliners	Gowder, Joe	Mello Harps
Goodman, William	Empires (Harlem, Wing,	Gowder, Joe	Teen Tones
	Mercury, Whirlin' Disc,	Grable, Teddy	Concords (Epic)
	Amp 3)	Graceffa, Peter	Antones
Goodman, William	Prestos	Gradus, Warren	Belmonts
Goodson, Ronnie	Ronnie & the Hi-Lites	Grady, Paul	Intervals
Goodwin, Andre	Sharptones (Aladdin)	Graham, William	Five Blue Jackets
Goodwin, Andre	Turbans (Money)	Graham, Willie	Medallions
Goodwin, L.	Imperials (Great Lakes)	Graham, Willie	Vel-Aires (Flip)
Goodwin, Ray	Five Jades	Grammer, Leroy	Elroy & the Excitements
Goody, Ernest	Laddins	Granada, John	Cirino & the Bowties
"Mickey"		Grangel, Oleatha	Caldwells
Gordon, Bill	Colonials	Granger, Walter	Daylighters
"Bass"		Granger, Walter	Delighters
Gordon, Billy	Contours	Granger, Walter	Fortunes (Parrot, Checker)
Gordon, Doug	No-Names (Guyden)	Grant, Alvin	Cordovans
Gordon, Gus	Bill Johnson's Musical	Grant, George	Castelles (Grand)
	Notes	Grant, George	Ink Spots
Gordon, Isaac	Connie & the Decoys	Grant, George	Modern Red Caps
Gordon, Jimmy	Brown Dots	Grant, George	Original Red Caps
Gordon, Jimmy	Four Tunes	Grant, George	Drifters (Atlantic)
Gordon, Jimmy	Sentimentalists (Manor)	(not the same)	
Gordon, Reggie	Five Frenchmen	Grant, John	Re-Vels
Gordon, Reggie	Johnny & the Keys	Grant, John	Strangers
Gordon, Reggie	Magnificents	Grant, Noel	Jesters
Gordon, Roscoe	Beale Streeters	Grant, Pepe	Orioles
Gordon, Sonny	Angels	Grant, Ray	Four Vagabonds
Gordon, Sonny	Famous Hearts	Grant, Sheppard	Singing Wanderers
Gordon, Sonny	Hearts (Chancellor)	Grant, Sheppard	Wanderers
Gordon, Sonny	Turbans (Imperial)	Grate, Miriam	Miriam Grate & the
Gore, John	Parliaments (Len)		Dovers
Gorham, Jimmy	Selah Jubilee Singes	Grate, Tommy	Dubs
Gorham, Ruth	Selah Jubilee Singes	Grate, Tommy	Five Wings
Gori, Frank	Holidays (Robbee, Nix)	Grate, Tommy	Marvels (ABC)
Goring, Sonia	Chantels	Grate, Tommy	Sonics (Groove)
Gorman, Freddie	Fidelitones	Grate, Tommy	Vocaltones
Gorman, Freddie	Sax Kari & the	Gravagna, Tony	Regents
	Quailtones	Graves, Alexander	Moonglows
Gorman, Jimmy	Cleartones	"Pete"	
Goudeau, Lee, Jr.	Squires (Vita, Mambo)	Graves, Alexander	Moonlighters
Goudeau, Israel	Accents (Brunswick)	"Pete"	
Goudeau, Lee	Blue Jays (Bluejay, Dig)	Graves, Larry	Otis Williams & the
Gough, Talmadge	Crests		Charms
Goulsby, Robert	ElDorados	Graves, Orton	Jimmy Castor & the
Goulsby, Spencer	ElDorados		Juniors
Goulsby, William	ElDorados	Gray, Leon	El Capris (Bullseye, Fee
Gourdine, Anthony	Chesters		Bee)
Gourdine, Anthony	Duponts (Winley, Royal	Gray, Sidney	Continentals (Rama)
	Roost, Roulette, Savoy)	Grayson, Harold	Echos (Combo)

Performer	Group
Grayson, Milton	Billy Ward & the Dominoes
Grayson, Miles	Echos (Combo)
Gray, Tyrone	L'Cap-Tans
Gray, Tyrone	Maskman & the Agents
Grazier, Richard	Farris Hill & the Madison Brothers
Gree, Happy	Four Clefs
Green, Carl	Turks (Money)
Green, Clarence	Vals (Unique Laboratories)
Green, Deroy	Cool Gents (Cee Jay)
Green, Deroy	Twilighters (Marshall)
Green, Dock	Crowns (R&B)
Green, Dock	Drapers
Green, Dock	Drifters (Atlantic)
Green, Dock	Duvals (Rainbow)
Green, Dock	Five Crowns (Rainbow, Old Town, Gee)
Green, Dock	Moonglows
Green, Elliot	Chanters
Green, Elliot	Voices Five
Green, Elliot	Voices Six
Green, Fred	El Torros
Green, Fred	Mellards
Green, Gaylord	Aladdins
Green, Gaylord	Capris (nonrecording)
Green, George	Rockers (Federal)
Green, George	Trojans (RPM)
Green, Gerald	Contours
Green, Gerald	Rivals (Puff)
Green, Harry	Edsels
Green, Henry	Red Caps
Green, Henry	Romaines
Green, Herman	Rivals (Puff)
Green, Homer	Preludes (Empire)
Green, Homer	Tempters (Empire)
Green, Homer	Youngsters (Empire)
Green, Howard	Three Riffs
Green, James	Ivy Tones
Green, James	Rivals (Puff)
Green, Jimmy	Furys (Mack IV)
Green, Jimmy	Medallions
Green, Jimmy	Shields
Green, Joe	Crenshaws
Green, Joe	Nu Tones
Green, Joe	Sharps (Aladdin)
Green, Joe	Three Barons (Savoy)
Green, Joe	Three Riffs
Green, Joffrey	Enchantments (Ritz)
Green, Julius	Mad Lads
Green, Larry	Edsels
Green, Larry	Titans (Vita, Specialty, Class)
Green, Larry "Lucky"	Four Dots (Dot)
Green, Lawrence	Heartbreakers (RCA)

Performer	Group
Green, Major	Castroes (Grand)
Green, Marion	Connie & the Decoys
Green, Murray	Rockers (Federal)
Green, Murray	Trojans (RPM)
Green, Oliver "Slim"	Riff Brothers
Green, Oliver "Slim"	Three Riffs
Green, Percy	Wini Brown & the Boyfriends
Green, Percy	Dreamers (Jubilee, Mercury)
Green, Phillips	Supremes Four (Sara)
Green, Raymond	Eldaros
Green, Richard	Delcos
Green, Richie	Del Satins
Green, Ted	Royal Jokers
Green, Vernon	Cameos (Dootone)
Green, Vernon	Medallions
Green, Vernon	Phantoms
Green, Willy	Del Vikings
Greenburg, Bill	Academics
Greenburg, Richie	Academics
Greenfield, Helen	Versalettes
Greenwood, John	Versatones
Greeves, Herbie	Jimmy Castor & the Juniors
Gregg, Bobby	Red Caps
Gregory, Gerald	Orioles
Gregory, Gerald	Spaniels
Gregory, Richard	Buccaneers
Grey Eyes, Billy	Marylanders
Grieco, Pete	Hi-Fives (Decca)
Grier, Joe	Charts
Grier, Sammy	Hambone Kids
Griffett, Robert	Poets (Flash)
Griffin, Don	Miracles (Tamla)
Griffin, Leon	Rajahs
Griffin, Billy	Miracles (Tamla)
Griffin, Della	Delltones
Griffin, Don	Miracles
Griffin, James	Lyres
Griffin, James "Sonny"	Nutmegs
Griffin, James "Sonny"	Rajahs
Griffin, Leroy	Lyres
Griffin, Leroy	Nutmegs
Griffin, Lindsay	Five Pennies
Griffin, Lindsay	Four Pennies
Griffin, Lindsay	Hearts of Stone
Griffin, Lindsay	Larks
Griffin, Terrence	Five Scamps
Griffin, Thomas	Four Haven Knights
Griffin, Wilbur	Progressive Four
Griggs, Bill	Coronets
Griggs, Sam	Coronets

Performer	Group	Performer	Group
Grigsby, Syl	Charades (Skylark)	Haddad, Wade	Wonders (Ember)
Grillo, Frankie	Markels (R&M)	Haggins, Roy	Hi Tensions
Grimes, Ellsworth	Four Bars (Josie, Dayco)	Hahn, Jules	Corvets (Laurel)
Grimes, George	Emeralds (ABC)	Hail, Harry	Vel-Aires (M.Z.)
Grimes, Lloyd "Tiny"	Cats and the Fiddle	Hail, John	Vel-Aires (M.Z.)
		Haines, George "Tiger"	Plink, Plank & Plunk
Grisnik, Frank	Holidays (Robbie, Nix)		
Grissette, Otis	Four Bars (Josie, Dayco)	Haines, George "Tiger"	Three Dandies
Grochowski, Tony	Heartbeats (Jubilee)		
Grochowski, Tony	Three Friends (Lido)	Haines, George "Tiger"	Three Flames
Groome, Pico	Lamplighters		
Groom, O. C.	Lamplighters	Hale, Enoche	Smoothtones (Jem)
Gross, Luke	Second Verse	Hale, Fred	Capris (Gotham)
Gross, Luke	Serenaders (Chock, MGM)	Haley, Carl	Four Haven Knights
		Halfhide, Jerry	Hurricanes
Grundy, Joe	Colts	Halfhide, Jerry	Toppers (Jubilee)
Grundy, Reuben	Colts	Hall, Bill	Clips (Republic)
Guanci, Tommy	Majestics (Sioux)	Hall, Bill	Sonics (Chess)
Guerrant, Herschel	Clefftones (Old Town)	Hall, Billy	Capitols (Pet)
Guest, William "Red"	Gladys Knight & the Pips	Hall, Bobby	Bobby Hall & the Kings
		Hall, Edwin	Chateaus
Gugliaro, Joe	Tony Richards & the Twilights (Colpix)	Hall, Hardy	Belltones (Grand)
		Hall, Henry	Bel-Aires (M.Z.)
Gugliaro, Joe	Markels (R&M)	Halliburton, Larry	Five Cliffs of Dover
Gugliaro, Joe	Clusters	Hall, James	Splendors (Taurus)
Guida, Florence	Heartbeats (Jubilee)	Hall, Jane	Starlets (Pam)
Gullano, Tom	Four Graduates (Rust)	Hall, John	Bel-Aires (M.Z.)
Gunter, Cornel	D's Gentlemen	Hall, Joseph	Joey & the Flips
Gunter, Cornel	Cornel Gunter & the Ermines	Hall, Levi	Eldaros
		Hall, Robert	Adolphus Holcomb & the Four Kings
Gunter, Cornel	Five Hollywood Blue Jays		
Gunter, Cornel	Hunters	Hall, Robert	Four Kings (Jax, Harlem, Gotham, RCA, Gone)
Gunter, Cornel	Jac-O-Lacs		
Gunter, Cornelius	Chimes (Flair)	Hallup, Vince	Corvets (Laurel)
Gunter, Cornelius	Flairs	Hamilton, Al	Nite Caps
Gunter, Cornelius	Platters	Hamilton, Ben	Lyrics (Rhythm)
Gunter, Cornelius	Rams (Flair)	Hamilton, Bob	Nite Caps
Gunter, Cornelius	Whips	Hamilton, Dave	Peppers (Chess)
Gunter, Cornell	Altairs	Hamilton, Eugene "Ronnie"	Nite Caps
Gunter, Cornell	Coasters		
Gunter, Henry	Limelighters	Hamilton, Freddie	Beavers
Gunter, Shirley	Flairs	Hamilton, Gerald	Crows
Gunter, Shirley	Jac-O-Lacs	Hamilton, Gerald	Four Notes (Premier)
Gunter, Shirley	Shirley Gunter & the Queens	Hamilton, Ken "Butch"	Bop Chords
Gutierrez, Juan	Diablos	Hamilton, Ken "Butch"	Five Wings
Gutowski, Peter	Ricky & the Vacels		
Gutowski, Vincent	Ricky & the Vacels	Hamilton, Ken "Butch"	Sonics (Groove, X-Tra)
Guy, Billy	Coasters		
Guy, Billy	Robins (Savoy)	Hamilton, Randy	Cruisers (V-Tone, Guyden, Gamble)
Guy, Robert	Pearls (Onyx)		
Guyton, Howard	Jesse Powell & the Majors	Hammock, Cleveland	Dreamlovers
Guyton, Howard	Pearls (Onyx)		
Guyton, Howard	Speedoo & the Pearls	Hammond, James	Schoolboys
Guyton, Howard	Raves	Hammond, Ray	Genies
Guzman, Vic	Blendairs	Hammond, Sylvia	Clickettes

Performer	Group	Performer	Group
Hammond, Sylvia	Loreleis (Brunswick)	Harris, Beverly	Flares
Hammond, Walter	Challengers (Melatone)	Harris, Charlie	Drivers
Hammond, Walter	Olympics	Harris, Charlie	Orioles
Hampden, Larry	Channels (Whirlin' Disc)	Harris, Christopher	Delacardos
Hampton, Joe	Calvanes	Harris, Crosby	Goldenrods (Vee Jay)
Hampton, Louis	Evening Star Quartet	Harris, Damon	Temptations (Gordy)
Handerson, Willie	Gassers (Cash)	Harris, David	Fascinators (Dootone)
Handley, Donald	Calvaes	Harris, David	Four Dots (Bullseye,
Hanna, Jerome	Jive Five		Freedom)
Hansley, Leon	Harmonizing Four	Harris, Don	Feathers
Harder, Eddie	Larry Chance & the Earls	Harris, Don	Squires (Vita, Mambo)
Hardin, Ira	Four Tones	Harris, Don	Blue Jays (Bluejay, Dig)
Hardin, Ira	Dusty Brooks & the Four	Bowman	
	Tones	Harris, Early	Cubans (Flash)
Hardin, Ira	Dusty Brooks & the Four	Harris, Early	Little Caesar & the Romans
	Tones with Raymond	Harris, Early	Upfronts
	Wheaton	Harris, Eddie	Checkers
Hardman, Willie	Chessmen (PAC)	Harris, Eddie	Velvetones (Aladdin)
Hardy, Al	Raiders (Atco)	Harris, Frankie	Charts
Hardy, Frank	Rainbows	Harris, Fred	Five Satins
Hardy, Frank "Jake"	Serenaders (Roadhouse)	Harris, Fred	New Yorkers
Hardy, Harvey	Emblems	Harris, Fred	Starlarks (Ember)
Hardy, Leon	Cardinals	Harris, Geraldine	Four Blackbirds
"Tree Top"			(Vocalion)
Hardy, Myles	Diamonds (Atlantic)	Harris, Hugh	Ad Libs
Hardy, Norman	Billy Austin & the Hearts	Harris, Hugh	Creators (T-Kay)
Hargro, Charles	Vibraharps	Harris, Jack	Calvanes
Hargrove, David	Rip Chords	Harris, John	Crenshaws
Hargrove, Wesley	Midnighters	"Sonny"	
Harewood, John	Charioteers	Harris, John	Ebb-Tones (Crest)
Harlan, Milton	Casinos (Maske)	"Sonny"	
Harley, Sonny	Avons	Harris, John	Feathers
Harling, Milton	Parliaments (Len)	"Sonny"	
Harmshaw, Leroy	Drivers	Harris, John	Four After Fives
Harold, Lyndon	Louis Lymon & the	"Sonny"	
	Teenchords	Harris, John	Lamplighters
Harp, Cornelius	Marcels (Colpix)	"Sonny"	
Harper, Alfred	Aladdins	Harris, John	Rebels
Harper, Alfred	Capris (nonrecording)	"Sonny"	
Harper, Alfred	Colts	Harris, John	Rivingtons
Harper, Ernest	Four Blazes (United)	"Sonny"	
Harper, Ernie	Four Shades of Rhythm	Harris, John	Sharps (Aladdin)
Harper, Larry Lee	Bel Aires (M.Z.)	"Sonny"	
Harper, Ted	Aladdins	Harris, John	Tenderfoots
Harper, Teddy	Capris (nonrecording)	"Sonny"	
Harper, Teddy	Coasters	Harris, John	Twisters (Apt)
Harper, Teddy	Fascinators (Dootone)	"Sonny"	
Harper, Teddy	Four Dots (Bullseye,	Harris, Joseph	Little Joe and His
	Freedom)		Moroccos
Harper, Teddy	Penguins	Harris, Julius	Clefts
Harper, Walter	Rex Middleton's Hi Fi's	Harris, Kirk	Dubs
Harris, Addie	Shirelles	Harris, Kirk	Little Nate & the Chryslers
"Mickey"		Harris, Lester	Ray-O-Vacs
Harris, Barbara	Veneers	Harris, Lois	Chantels
Harris, Bernard	Dreams (Savoy)	Harris, Lucius	Gentlemen
Harris, Bernard	Kenny Esquire & the	Harris, M.	Imperials (Great Lakes)
	Starlites		

Performer	Group
Harris, Mickey	Shirelles
Harris, Mike	Catalinas
Harris, Mildred	Goldentones (Jay Dee)
Harris, Norman	Master Keys
Harris, Norman	Virginia Four
Harris, Norman "Crip"	Norfolk Jazz Quartet
Harris, Richard	Altairs
Harris, Richard	D's Gentlemen
Harris, Richard	Jive Five
Harris, Richard	Marcels
Harris, Robert	Blue Chips
Harris, Robert	Cyclones
Harris, Robert	Richard Berry & the Pharaohs
Harris, Robert	Rickey & the Pharaohs
Harris, Rudolph	Four Dots (Dot)
Harris, Sylvester	Volchords
Harris, Thomas	Creators (Dootone)
Harris, Thurston	Lamplighters
Harris, Thurston	Sharps (Aladdin)
Harris, Undine	Three Dots and a Dash
Harris, Vandine	Gems (Chess)
Harris, Vernon	Goldentones (Jay Dee)
Harris, Warren	Majestics (Chex, Contour)
Harris, Webster	Drifters (Atlantic)
Harris, Webster	Jive Five
Harrison, Jimmy	Cardinals
Harrison, Jimmy	Trend-Ells
Harrison, Larry	Barons
Harrison, Larry	Cues
Harrison, Larry	Dappers (Groove, Rainbow)
Harrison, Leon	Buddies (Glory)
Harrison, Leon "Larry"	Four Buddies (Savoy)
Harriston, Ernest	Bop Chords
Harriston, Ernest	Shep and the Limelights
Harriston, Ernest	Lovenotes (Holiday)
Hart, Ben	Deckers
Hart, Ben	Teddy & the Twilights
Hart, Ben	Tiffanys
Hartley, William	Five Jones Boys
Hartley, William	Jones Boys Sing Band
Harvard, Leon	Elroy & the Excitements
Harvey, Benjamin	Rocketones
Harvey, Elijah	Bachelors (Mercury, Songmaster)
Harvey, Elijah	Canaanites
Harvey, Elijah	Joe Van Loan Quartet
Harvin, Martha	Four Jewels
Harvin, Martha	Jewels (Dimension)
Harvin, Raymond	Hepsters
Hashaw, Eddie	Du Droppers
Haskins, Clarence	Parliaments (Len)
Haskins, Leroy	Raiders (Atco)

Performer	Group
Haskiss, Raymond	Five Keys
Haslett, Hank	Cats and the Fiddle
Hassell, Alvin	Cordovans
Hatcher, C. Autry "Breeze"	Majestics (Chex, Contour)
Hatcher, "Breeze"	Contours
Hatchet, Sonny	Cardinals
Hatfield, Charles "Corky"	Holidays (Robbie, Nix)
Hatton, Carl	Carnations (Lescay)
Hatton, Carl	Startones (Rainbow)
Hauser, Tim	Criterions
Hauser, Tim	Kents (Aljon)
Havens, Richie	Students (Note, Checker)
Hawkins, A.	Red Caps
Hawkins, Bobby	Marquees (Okeh)
Hawkins, Bobby	Mello Harps
Hawkins, Alton "Buddy"	Do Re Mi Trio
Hawkins, Dee	Jewels (Imperial, R&B)
Hawkins, Dee	Marbles
Hawkins, Gene	Magic Tones
Hawkins, Jennell	Richard Berry & Dreamers
Hawkins, Jennell	Lockettes
Hawkins, Jimmy	Four Buddies (Club 51)
Hawkins, Julius	Five Bells (Clock)
Hawkins, Julius	Johnny & the Keys
Hawkins, Nathaniel Sam	Four Buddies (Club 51)
Hawkins, Sam	Sam Hawkins & the Crystals
Hawthorne, Willie	Five Breezes
Hayden, Lloyd	Alma-Keys
Hayden, Richard	Alma-Keys
Hayden, Roland	Alma-Keys
Hayden, Ronald	Swinging Phillies
Hayes, Farman	Deeptones
Hayes, Farman	Four Deeptones
Hayes, Farman	Hi-Liters (Hico)
Hayes, John	Kenny Esquire & the Starlites
Hayes, Marie	Belvederes (Baton)
Hayes, Mary	Songmasters
Hayes, O.	Five Du-Tones
Hayes, Ray	Packards (Pla-Bac, Paradise)
Hayes, Ray	Tremaines
Hayes, Roy	Romaines
Hayes, Roger	Collegians (X-Tra)
Hayes, Roger	Schoolboys
Hayes, Wesley	Dreams (Savoy)
Hayes, Wesley	Kenny Esquire & the Starlites
Haymon, Roberta	Quintones (Chess, Red Top, Hunt)

Performer	Group
Haynes, Thurman	Sandmen
Haynes, George Tiger	Plink, Plank & Plunk
Haynes, Tiger	Tiger Haynes & the Three Flames
Hayward, Perry	Checkers (King)
Hayward, Perry	Performers
Hayward, Perry	Sparrows (Jay Dee, Davis)
Hayward, Perry	Wrens
Haywood, Donald	Fantastics (RCA)
Haywoode, Donald	Velours
Hazen, Charles	Brochures
Hazzard, Wesley	Russ Riley & the Five Sounds
Head, Kenneth	Crests (Trans-Atlas)
Headen, Willie	Willie Headen & the Five Birds
Heard, Lonnie	Don Juans
Heard, Lonnie	Five Dollars
Heard, Roger	Pelicans
Hearon, Odis	El Torros
Hearst, Clifford	Capris (nonrecording)
Heath, Dean	Souvenirs (Dooto)
Hebb, Hal	Marigolds
Hebb, Hal	Sunbeams (Dot)
Hebron, Heywood	Five Tino's
Height, Donald	Hollywood Flames
Helfand, Marshall "Buzzy"	Norman Fox & the Rob Roys
Helman, Benny	Lewis Bronzeville Five
Henderson, Bernard	Informers
Henderson, Billy	Spinners (Motown, Tri-Phi)
Henderson, Bobby	Dreams (Savoy)
Henderson, Carl	Lyrics (Harlem, Wildcat)
Henderson, Everett	Deltones
Henderson, Everett	Marvells (Magnet)
Henderson, Jimmy	Cats and the Fiddle
Henderson, Leroy	Serenaders (Roadhouse)
Henderson, Leroy	Topps (Red Robin)
Henderson, L. C.	Willie Headen & the Five Birds
Henderson, Rochell	Rochell & the Candles
Henderson, Ronald	True Tones (Monument, Felsted, Josie)
Henderson, Stanley	Pharaohs (Specialty)
Henderson, T. C.	Rochell & the Candles
Henderson, Vince	Splendors (Taurus)
Hendricks, Bobby	Drifters (Atlantic)
Hendricks, Bobby	Flyers (Atco)
Hendricks, Bobby	Marquees (Okeh)
Hendricks, Bobby	Original Drifters
Hendricks, Bobby	Swallows (King, Federal, After Hours)
Hendricks, Gerald	Turks
Hendricks, Margie	Cookies

Performer	Group
Henry, Butch	Tabbys
Henry, Francis	Four Bars (Josie, Dayco)
Henry, Francis	Rainbows
Henry, Gordon	Starlarks (Ember)
Henry, Lenwood	Five Bob-O-Links (Okeh)
Herbert, Joseph	Connie & the Decoys
Herman, Thomas	Balladiers
Hernandez, Manny	Five Jades
Hernandez, William	D's Gentlemen
Herndon, William	Altairs
Herndon, William	Marcels (Colpix)
Herrera, "Little Julian"	"Little" Julian Herrera & the Tigers
Hettinger, Kenny	Elgins (Dot)
Heyward, Lewis	Hi-Hatters
Heyward, Louis	Ravens
Hickman, Ike	Masquerades (Formal, Boyd, Joyce)
Hickman, Sylvester	Cats and Jammer Three
Hicks, Daniel	Continentals (Whirlin' Disc)
Hicks, Danny	Barons
Hicks, Eddie	El Venos
Hicks, Johnny	Ivoleers
Hicks, Johnny	Ivories
Hicks, Johnny	Lovenotes (Holiday)
Hicks, Maurice	Four Buddies (Savoy)
Hicks, Nathaniel	Stereos
Hicks, Ulysses	Five Keys
Higgenbotham, Robert	Belvederes (Dot, Trend)
Higgenbotham, Robert	Dusters
Higgins, Chuck	Mello Moods (Recorded in Hollywood)
Higgs, Bobby	Heartbreakers (Vik)
High, Julius, Jr.	Twilighters (Specialty, Ebb)
Highsmith, Gerald	Parakeets (Atlas)
Highsmith, Sheldon	Hi-Lites (Record Fair, Julia)
Hightower, Rosetta	Orlons
Hill, Billie	Essex
Hill, Farris	Farris Hill & the Madison Brothers
Hill, Farris	Little Joe & the Thrillers
Hill, James	Emanons (Gee, Josie)
Hill, Jerry	Diadems
Hill, Joe	Bennie Woods & the Five Dukes
Hill, Joe	Rockin' Townies
Hill, Josh	Starlarks (Ember)
Hill, Larry	El Capris (Bullseye, Fee Bee)
Hill, Maurice	Mello-Moods (nonrecording)

Performer	Group
Hill, Richard	Swinging Phillies
Hill, Ronald	Elroy & the Excitements
Hill, Rudolph	Four Pennies
Hill, Rudolph	Larks
Hill, Thearon	Muskateers [sic]
Hill, Thearon	Royal Jokers
Hill, Thearon	Royals (Venus)
Hill, Thearon	Serenaders (JVB, Red Robin, Coral, Swing Time)
Hill, Vernon	Delacardos
Hill, William "Shorty"	Four Blazes (United)
Hill, William "Shorty"	Hollywood Four Blazers
Hillard, George	Tymes
Hilliard, Harry	Excels (Central, Gone)
Hilliard, Harry	Minors (Celeste)
Hillsman, Milton Howard, Jr.	Twilighters (Specialty, Ebb)
Himmelstein, Paul	Heartbreakers (Vik)
Hinds, Ronnie	Billy Vera & the Contrasts
Hines, Johnny	Dixieaires
Hines, Lawrence (Lorenzo)	Satisfactions (Smash)
Hines, Thomas	Paul Breckinridge and the Four Heavenly Knights
Hinton, Rena	Capris (Gotham)
Hirschkowitz, Harvey	Quotations
Hirtz, Harvey	Eltones
Hobbs, Elsbeary	Crowns (R&B)
Hobbs, Elsbeary	Drifters (Atlantic)
Hobbs, Elsbeary	Five Crowns (Gee)
Hobbs, Tommy	El Pollos
Hockaday, Charles	Parakeets (Atlas)
Hockaday, Charles	Parakeets (Roadhouse)
Hodge, Alex	Billy Williams Quartet
Hodge, Alex	Fellas
Hodge, Alex	Platters
Hodge, Alex	Tangiers (Decca)
Hodge, Alex	Turks (Money)
Hodge, Eugene	Hi-Lites (Record Fair, Julia)
Hodge, Fred	Eternals
Hodge, Gaynell	Bobby Byrd & the Birds
Hodge, Gaynell	Fellas
Hodge, Gaynell	Patty Anne & the Flames
Hodge, Gaynell	Flames
Hodge, Gaynell	Hollywood Flames
Hodge, Gaynell	Platters
Hodge, Gaynell	Tangiers (Decca)
Hodge, Gaynell	Turks (Money)
Hodge, James E.	Hi-Lites (Record Fair, Julia)
Hodge, Revo	Channells (Hit)

Performer	Group
Hogan, Butch	Brochures
Hogan, Carl	Carl Hogan & the Miracles
Hogan, Carl	Dreamers (NY)
Hogan, Carl	Valentines
Hogan, Donald	Dreamlovers
Hoggs, Billy	Contours
Holcomb, Adolphus	Adolphus Holcomb Four & the Four Kings
Holcomb, Adolphus	Adolphus Holcomb & the Kings
Holcomb, Adolphus	Bobby Hall & the Kings
Holcomb, Adolphus	Kings (RCA, Jax, Gone, Harlem)
Holcomb, Adolphus	Ramblers (Jax)
Holcomb, Raymond	Adolphus Holcomb & the Four Kings
Holcomb, Raymond	Adolphus Holcomb & the Kings
Holcomb, Raymond	Kings (RCA, Jax, Gone, Harlem)
Holcomb, Raymond	Ramblers (Jax)
Holcomb, Richard	Bobby Hall & the Kings
Holeman, Gerald	Orioles
Holeman, Gerald	Regals
Holland, Brian "Eddie"	Fidelitones
Holland, Clint	Four Knights
Holland, Clint	Delta Rhythm Boys
Holland, Clint	Harmonaires (Holiday)
Holley, Tim	Collegians (Winley)
Hollins, Delroy	Norfolk Jazz Quartet
Hollis, Bobby Lee	Original Drifters
Hollis, Bobby Lee	Sunbeams (Acme, Herald)
Hollis, George	Cadets
Hollis, George	Ebbtones
Hollis, George	Cornel Gunter & the Ermines
Hollis, George	Flairs
Hollis, George	Flares
Hollis, George	Peppers (Ensign, Press)
Hollis, Goerge	Jacks
Holloway, Charles	Chimes (Arrow)
Holloway, Charles	Five Pennies
Holloway, Charles	Four Jokers
Hollowell, Alton	Enchanters (Coral)
Hollowell, Alton "Bart"	Fabulous Playboys
Hollowell, Alton	Falcons (Mercury, United Artists, Chess, LuPine)
Hollowell, Alton "Bart"	Ramblers (Federal, Jax, MGM, Trumpet)
Hollowell, Gerald	Enchanters (Coral)
Hollowell, Ulysses	Enchanters (Coral)

Performer	Group	Performer	Group
Hughes, Leon	Flames	Hutcherson, Sam	Basin Street Boys
Hughes, Leon	Patty Anne & the Flames	Hutson, Leroy	Impressions
Hughes, Leon	Hollywood Flames	Hutter, Lenny	Chalets
Hughes, Leon	Jets (Aladdin)	Hutter, Lenny	Five Discs
Hughes, Leon	Lamplighters		
Hulbert, Ray	Jets (Gee)	Ibanez, Mario	Zircons
Hulbert, Ray	Mello-Tones (Decca)	Ifill, James	Royaltones
Humber, Charles	Dino & the Diplomats	"Skippy"	
Humes, Anita	Essex	Imbimbo, Tony	Nino & the Ebbtides
Humphrey, Joe	Emeralds (Bobbin)	Infante, Carlos	Vilons
Hunt, Charles	Five Echoes (Sabre)	Infante, Carlos	Zircons
(Tommy)		Infantino, Sam	Catalinas
Hunter, Al	Clouds (Parrot)	Ingalls, Sam	Fiestas
Hunter, Albert	Blenders (Witch,	Ingram, Rafael	Avalons
	Cortland)	Ingram, Ripley	Five Keys
Hunter, Albert	Maples (Blue Lake)	Inzilla, Thomas	Intentions (Jamie)
Hunter, Bennie	Mississippi Mud Mashers	Iovino, Frank	Bob Knight Four
Hunter, Ellis	Four Jumps of Jive	Iovino, Frank	Five Boroughs
Hunter, Irving	Four Buddies (Club 51)	Irvin, "Big" Dee	Pastels (Mascot, Argo)
Hunter, Jim	Concords (Harlem)	Isaac, James	Bel Aires (Decca)
Hunter, Jud	Smoothtones (Jem)	Dennis "Brother"	
Hunter, Richard	Twilighters (Specialty,	Isaac, James	Caveliers (nonrecording)
	Ebb)	Dennis "Brother"	
Hunter, Rudolph	Four Tones	Isaac, James	Sheppards (Theron,
Hunter, Rudolph	Dusty Brooks & the Four	Dennis "Brother"	United)
	Tones	Isaac, James	Sheppards (Apex)
Hunter, Rudolph	Dusty Brooks & the Four	Dennis "Brother"	
	Tones with Raymond	Isaacoff, Norman	Neons (Tetra)
	Wheaton	Isbell, Bobby	Supremes (Ace)
Hunter, Rufus	Cameos (Cameo)	Isles, Bill	Mascots (King)
Hunter, Rufus	Five Bells (Clock)	Isles, Bill,	O'Jays
Hunter, Rufus	Five Chimes (Ebony)	Isley, Marvin	Isley Brothers
Hunter, Rufus	Magnificents	Isley, Marvin	Señors
Hunter, Rufus	Universals (Mark-X)	Isley, O'Kelly	Isley Brothers
Hunter, Ty	Romeos (Fox)	Isley, O'Kelly	Señors
Hunter, Ty	Voice Masters	Isley, Ronald	Isley Brothers
Hunter, Willie	Diablos	Isley, Ronald	Señors
Hunter, Willie	Velvet Angels	Isley, Rudy	Isley Brothers
Hunt, Felix	Inspirations	Isley, Rudy	Señors
Hunt, Gordon	José & the Aztecs	Isom, James	Marvels (Laurie)
Huntley, Gloria	Sharmeers	Isom, James	Satisfactions (Smash)
Hunt, Tommy	Flamingos	Isom, James	Senators (Winn)
Hunt, Tommy	Five Echoes (Sabre)	Israel, Benni	Cubs
Hurley, Earl	Swallows (King, Federal,	Iverson, Ben	Hornets (States)
	After Hours)	Iverson, Cy	Diablos
Hurley, Leroy	Jones Boys Sing Band	Iverson, Cy	Velvet Angels
Hurling, Robert	Escorts (Premium)	Ivey, John	Ivy Tones
Hurston, Charles	Desires	Ivey, Leon	Bop Chords
Hurst, Al	Drifters (Atlantic)		
Hurt, Al	Swinging Phillies	Jacks, Michael	Elgins (Dot)
Hurt, Eddie	Don Juans	Jackson, Adam	Jesters
Hurt, Eddie	Five Dollars	Jackson, Al	Clefftones (Old Town)
Hurte, Leroy	Four Blackbirds	Jackson, Andrew	Five Discs
	(Vocalion)	Jackson, Anna Mae	El Venos
Hurt, Philip	Swinging Phillies	Jackson, Betty	Carousels (Gone)
Huss, Dick	Turks	Jackson, Bill	Re-Vels
Hust, Tom	Larados	Jackson, Bobby	Magic Tones

Performer	Group	Performer	Group
Jackson, Charles	Chimes (Specialty, Dig)	Jackson, Nathaniel "Mitch"	Keystoners
Jackson, Charles	Cupids (Aladdin)		
Jackson, Charles	Flairs	Jackson, Otha	Four Aces (Trilon)
Jackson, Charles	Jac-O-Lacs	Jackson, Pervis	Spinners (Motown, Tri-Phi)
Jackson, Charles	Lions (Rendezvous)	Jackson, Ray	Del-Vons
Jackson, Charles	Mondellos	Jackson, Reggie	Hollywood Flames
Jackson, Charles	Wonders	Jackson, Reggie	Ideals (Paso)
Jackson, Chuck	Del Vikings	Jackson, Richard	Lonnie & the Carollons
Jackson, Chuck	Five Playboys	Jackson, Rickey	Paragons
Jackson, Chuck	Jerry Sheely & the Versatiles	Jackson, Rodney	Dean Barlow & the Crickets
Jackson, Chuck	Shields	Jackson, Roland "Big Boy"	Honey Boys
Jackson, Cleveland	Crystals (Specialty)		
Jackson, Cliff	Plink, Plank & Plunk	Jackson, Ronald	Jesters
Jackson, Daniel	El Venos	Jackson, Ronald	Ruby & the Romantics
Jackson, Danny	Pyramids (Davis)	Jackson, Ronald	Youngtones
Jackson, Delores	Delores Jackson & the Cabin Boys	Jackson, Rudy	Jewels (Imperial, R&B)
		Jackson, Rudy	Marbles
Jackson, Don	Del Vikings	Jackson, Rudy	Rudy Jackson & the Mel-O-Aires
Jackson, Donald	Jerry Sheely & the Versatiles		
		Jackson, Spencer	Five Jades
Jackson, Douglas	Ladders	Jackson, Sylvester	Sentimentals (Tuxedo, Checker, Minit)
Jackson, Eddie	Charioteers		
Jackson, Eddie	El Capris (Bullseye, Fee Bee)	Jackson, Tenor Chuck	Shields
Jackson, Eddie	Supremes (Ace)	Jackson, Willis	Spaniels
Jackson, Eugene	Pharaohs (Specialty)	Jackson, Woodrow	Strangers
Jackson, Freddie	Interludes	Jacobs, Adolph	Five Campbells
Jackson, Garfield "Buddy"	Billy Wells & the Crescents	Jacobs, Eddie	Capitols, (Pet)
		Jacobs, Eddie	Pearls (Onyx)
Jackson, General	Crystals (Specialty)	Jacobs, Jackie	Four-Evers (Jamie)
Jackson, George	Plants	Jacobucca, Don	Regents
Jackson, Gladys	Rudy Jackson & the Mel-O-Aires	Jacobucci, Edward	Consorts (Cousins, APT)
		James, Bill	Pentagons
Jackson, Glenmore	Charts	James, Charlie	Cleftones (Gee)
Jackson, Gloria	Vestelles	James, Etta	Peaches
Jackson, Harlan	Collegians (Winley)	James, Goliath	Keystoners
Jackson, Harold	Ink Spots	James, Harry	Rays
Jackson, Henry	Heartbreakers (Vik)	James, John	Pharaohs (Ace)
Jackson, Henry	Swallows (King, Federal, After Hours)	James, Johnny	Concepts (Apache)
		James, Oliver	Jets (Gee)
Jackson, Henry "Stony"	V-Eights	James, Oliver	Mello-Tones (Decca)
		James, Richard	De'Bonairs (Ping)
Jackson, James	Accents (Brunswick)	Janacone, Louis	Mellokings
Jackson, Jerry	Inspirations (Apollo, Lamp)	Janes, Harold	Nutmegs
		Jarrett, Allen	Splendors (Taurus)
Jackson, Johnny	Ladders	Jarvis, William	Lyrics (Rhythm)
Jackson, Johnny	Pearls	JD	Five Crowns (Gee)
Jackson, Johnny	Five Sharps (Jubilee)	JD	Sparrows (Jay Dee, Davis)
Jackson, Johnny	Videos	Jefferies, Bob	Turbans (Money)
Jackson, Johnny Earl	Ivoleers	Jefferies, Otto	Five Royales
		Jefferies, Otto	Royals (Apollo)
Jackson, Johnny Earl	Ivories	Jeffers, Robert (Bobby Jay)	Laddins
Jackson, Kenny	Four Troys (Freedom)	Jefferson, Jody	Platters
Jackson, Mark	Crows	Jefferson, Jody	Turks (Money)
Jackson, Nanette	Blossoms	Jefferson, Joe	Tangiers

Performer	Group
Jefferson, John	Gainors
Jenkins, Donald	Daylighters
Jenkins, Donald	Delighters
Jenkins, Donald	Five Chimes (Ebony)
Jenkins, Donald	Fortunes (Parrot, Checker)
Jenkins, Harold	Kodaks (Kodoks)
Jenkins, Harold "Curly"	Impacts (RCA, Watts)
Jenkins, Horace	Sheiks (Ef-N-Dee, Cat)
Jenkins, James	Bel-Aires (M.Z.)
Jenkins, James	Turbans (Red Top)
Jenkins, Levi	Five Thrills
Jenkins, Mamie	Cubans (Flash)
Jenkins, Timothy	Informers
Jennings, Herb	Ladders
Jennings, John	Jubalaires
Jennings, Melvin	Twilighters (Marshall)
Jennings, Panama	Kac-Ties
Jensen, Harry	Jimmy Castor Bunch
Jernigan, Hank	Soothers
Jessamay, Darnell	Darnell & the Dreams
Jessamay, Darnell	Vestelles
Jesse, Obediah "Young"	Arthur Lee Maye & the Crowns
Jesse, Obediah "Young"	Chimes (Flair)
Jesse, Obediah "Young"	Flairs
Jesse, Obediah "Young"	Five Hollywood Blue Jays
Jesse, Obediah "Young"	Hunters
Jesse, Obediah "Young"	Jac-O-Lacs
Jesse, Obediah "Young"	Rams (Flair)
Jesse, Obediah "Young"	Whips
Jesse, Obediah, "Young"	Coasters
Jet, Danny	Bennie Woods & the Five Dukes
Jet, Danny	Rockin' Townies
Jezerak, Rudy	Hi-Fives (Decca)
John, Claude	Genies
John, Ellis	Marvin & the Chirps
Johns, Dock	Dynamics (Cindy, Seeco, Dynamic)
Johnson, Alan	Chessmen (PAC)
Johnson, Albert	Medallions
Johnson, Allen	Marcels (Colpix)
Johnson, Alonzo "Lonnie"	Gentlemen
Johnson, Alvin	Souvenirs (Dooto)
Johnson, Anthony "Chatta"	Antones

Performer	Group
Johnson, Artis, Jr.	Fabulous Pearls (Dooto)
Johnson, Artis, Jr.	Four Pearls (Dolton)
Johnson, Artis, Jr.	Midnights (Music City)
Johnson, Barry	Delta Rhythm Boys
Johnson, Bill	Bill Johnson's Musical Notes
Johnson, Billy	Personalities
Johnson, Bobby	Miriam Grate & the Dovers
Johnson, Bobby	Vocaltones
Johnson, Branch	Four Dots (Bullseye, Freedom)
Johnson, Branch	Lyrics (Cleveland)
Johnson, Bud	Chanters
Johnson, Bud	Voices Five
Johnson, Carol	Exciters
Johnson, Charles	Cascades
Johnson, Charles	Five Bob-O-Links (Okeh)
Johnson, Charles	Pace Setters
Johnson, Charles	Von Gayles
Johnson, Charles "Kinrod"	Chips
Johnson, Clarence	Chanteurs
Johnson, Clarence	Chi-Lites
Johnson, Claude	Genies
Johnson, Claude	Little June & the Januarys
Johnson, Claudette	Mississippi Mud Mashers
Johnson, Clifton	Inspirators (Treat, Old Town)
Johnson, Clifton	Five Stars (Treat)
Johnson, Corinthian "Kripps"	Jerry Sheely & the Versatiles
Johnson, Corinthian, "Kripps"	Del Vikings
Johnson, David	Cubans (Flash)
Johnson, David	Little Caesar & the Romans
Johnson, David	Upfronts
Johnson, Delores	Blenders (Witch, Cortland)
Johnson, Delores	Twilighters (Chess)
Johnson, Delores	Twiliters (Nix, Chess, Roulette)
Johnson, Donald	Cardinals
Johnson, Earl	Jive Bombers
Johnson, Ed	Debonaires (Gee)
Johnson, Eddie	James Quintet
Johnson, Edmund	Syncopaters
Johnson, Edward	De'Bonairs (Ping)
Johnson, Edwin	Souvenirs (Dooto)
Johnson, Elliot	Elchords
Johnson, Ellis	Marvin & the Chirps
Johnson, Emery	Crystals (Specialty)
Johnson, Everett	Four Haven Knights
Johnson, Fred	Universals (Festival)
Johnson, Fred	Marcels (Colpix)

Performer	Group
Johnson, Freddie	Chanters
Johnson, Freddie	Performers (Tip Top)
Johnson, Freddie	Voices Five
Johnson, Frederick	Four Notes (Premier)
Johnson, Frederick	Swallows (King, Federal, After Hours)
Johnson, F.	Gotham's Four Notes
Johnson, Gerald	Quinns
Johnson, Gilbert	Performers (Tip Top)
Johnson, Harold	Craftys
Johnson, Harold	Dean Barlow & the Crickets
Johnson, Harold	Halos
Johnson, Harold	Hummers
Johnson, Harold	Lillian Leach & the Mellows
Johnson, Herb	Capris (Gotham)
Johnson, Hubert	Contours
Johnson, Ira	Lucky Charms
Johnson, Jack	Hi Tensions
Johnson, James	Diablos
Johnson, James	Drifters (Atlantic)
Johnson, James	Four Sonics
Johnson, James	Jayhawks
Johnson, James	Velvet Angels
Johnson, James	Vibrations (Checker)
Johnson, James "Wrinkle"	Drifters (Atlantic)
Johnson, Jim	Marathons
Johnson, Jimmy	Nite Riders
Johnson, Joe	Trumpeteers
Johnson, John	Jive Tones
Johnson, John	True Tones (Monument, Felsted, Josie)
Johnson, John E.	Starlings (Josie, Dawn)
Johnson, John E.	Twilighters (MGM)
Johnson, Johnny	Pearls (Onyx)
Johnson, Johnny	Tabs (Dot, Vee Jay, Wand)
Johnson, Johnny T.	Charades
Johnson, J. W.	Diablos
Johnson, Kenny	Romeos (Fox)
Johnson, Kenny	Universals (Festival)
Johnson, Kinrod	Platters
Johnson, Lewis	Little June & the Januarys
Johnson, Louis	Danderliers
Johnson, Melvin	Goldentones (Jay Dee)
Johnson, Norman	Jive Five
Johnson, Norman "General"	Showmen
Johnson, Patrick	Terracetones
Johnson, Ollie	Casualeers
Johnson, Ollie	Universals (Festival)
Johnson, Patrick	Terracetones
Johnson, Phil	Craftys
Johnson, Phil	Duvals (Boss)
Johnson, Phil	Halos

Performer	Group
Johnson, Ralph	De'Bonairs (Ping)
Johnson, Ralph	Impressions
Johnson, Ray	Beavers
Johnson, Ray	Bill Cook & the Marshalls
Johnson, Ray	Blenders (Decca, MGM)
Johnson, Ray	Dominoes
Johnson, Ray	Marshall Brothers
Johnson, Reginald	Chandeliers
Johnson, Richie	Students (Note, Checker)
Johnson, Robert	Four Haven Knights
Johnson, Robert	Mad Lads
Johnson, Robert	Tempters (Empire)
Johnson, Robert	Youngsters (Empire)
Johnson, Robert	Preludes
Johnson, Ronald	Five Chances
Johnson, Ronald	Rocketones
Johnson, Roy	José & the Aztecs
Johnson, Rudolph	Essex
Johnson, Sam	Buccaneers
Johnson, Shirley	Dukays
Johnson, Sylvester "Sonny"	Laddins
Johnson, Terry	Flamingos
Johnson, Terry	Whispers (Gotham)
Johnson, Thomas	Harmonizing Four
Johnson, Tommy	Serenades (Chief)
Johnson, Virgil	Velvets (Monument)
Johnson, Wilbert	Little June & the Januarys
Johnson, William	Emblems
Johnson, William	Jubalaires
Johnson, Willie	Jubalaires
Johnson, Willie	Golden Gate Quartet
Johnson, Willie	Kings (Specialty)
Johnson, Woody	Magic Notes
Johnson, Woody	Planets (Era)
Johnson, Woody	Rocketeers (Modern, MJC)
Johnson, Woody	Rockets (Modern)
Jones, Andrew	Rivieras
Jones, Andrew "Chet"	Turbans (Herald)
Jones, Angelo	5 Jades (Duke)
Jones, Anna Lois	Casual Crescendos
Jones, Anthony	Universals (Festival)
Jones, Bernard	Drifters (Atlantic)
Jones, Bernard	Dubs
Jones, Bernard	Strangers
Jones, Bill	Paramonts (Ember)
Jones, Bobby	King Krooners (Crooners)
Jones, Bobby	Pyramids (Cub, Vee Jay)
Jones, Bobby	Serenaders (Chock, MGM, Rae Cox)
Jones, Booker	Chimes (Specialty)
Jones, Carl	Delta Rhythm Boys
Jones, Carl	Dreamers (California)

Performer	Group
Jones, Carl	Four Sharps (Atlantic)
Jones, Carl	Teardrops (Sampson)
Jones, Carroll	Four Blues
Jones, Charles	Gazelles
Jones, Creadel	Chi-Lites
Jones, Creadel	Desideros
Jones, David	Four Fellows (Glory)
Jones, David	Marylanders
Jones, David	Rays
Jones, Daytill	Five Keys
Jones, Donald	Turbans (Herald)
Jones, Dorothy	Cookies
Jones, Earl	Don Julian & the Meadowlarks
Jones, Earl	Satisfactions (Smash)
Jones, Eddie	Eddie Jones & the Cashmeres
Jones, Eddie	Demens
Jones, Eddie	Ebonaires (Aladdin, Modern, Money, etc.)
Jones, Eddie	Emersons
Jones, Eddie (California)	Laddins
Jones, Elmo	Echos (Combo)
Jones, Frank	Pharaohs (Ace)
Jones, Fred	Genies
Jones, George, Jr.	Edsels
Jones, Gloria	Blossoms
Jones, Gloria	Richard Berry & the Dreamers
Jones, Gloria	Richard Berry & the Pharaohs
Jones, Harold	Blenders (Witch, Cortland)
Jones, Harold	Five Chances
Jones, Harold	Maples (Blue Lake)
Jones, Henry	Five Jets (DeLuxe, Fortune)
Jones, Henry	Five Stars (Mark-X, End)
Jones, Henry	Voice Masters
Jones, Henry	Valquins/Velquins
Jones, Henry "Dishrag"	Marigolds
Jones, Henry "Dishrag"	Sunbeams (Dot)
Jones, Henry "Ollie"	Four Notes (Premier)
Jones, Hilliard "Johnny"	Daffodils
Jones, Hilliard "Johnny"	Five Chances
Jones, Hilliard "Johnny"	Maples (Blue Lake)
Jones, Hoppy	Ink Spots
Jones, Irvin	Ladders
Jones, Isaiah	Gales (JVB)

Performer	Group
Jones, Isaiah	Question Marks
Jones, Isaiah	Violinaires
Jones, Jackie	Dino & the Diplomats
Jones, Jerry	Starlighters (End)
Jones, Jewel	El Dorados
Jones, Jewel	Four El Dorados
Jones, Jewel	Tempos (Rhythm)
Jones, Jimmy	Harmonizing Four
Jones, Jimmy	Jimmy Jones & the Jones Boys
Jones, Jimmy	Jimmy Jones & the Pretenders
Jones, Jimmy	Jimmy Jones & the Savoys
Jones, Jimmy	Jones Boys
Jones, Jimmy	Sparks of Rhythm
Jones, Joe	Pentagons
Jones, John	Re-Vels
Jones, Johnny	Clouds (Parrot)
Jones, Johnny	Five Chords
Jones, Johnny "Chubby"	Daffodils
Jones, Johnny "Chubby"	Five Chances
Jones, Joseph "Cool Breeze"	Nobles (Sapphire)
Jones, Josephus	Pentagons
Jones, Larry	Honey Boys
Jones, Lee	Four Kings (Fortune)
Jones, Leroy	Chateaus
Jones, Melvin	Five Tino's
Jones, Milton	Minor Chords
Jones, Ollie	Blenders (Decca, MGM)
Jones, Ollie	Cues
Jones, Ollie	Gliders
Jones, Ollie	Millionaires (Davis)
Jones, Ollie	Playboys (Cat)
Jones, Ollie	Ravens
Jones, Ollie	Ruth Brown & the Rhythm Makers
Jones, Ollie	Billy Williams Quartet
Jones, Orville "Hoppy"	Ink Spots
Jones, Orville "Hoppy"	Riff Brothers
Jones, Peggy	Bop Chords
Jones, Randall	Don Julian & the Meadowlarks
Jones, Randolph	Flairs
Jones, Randolph	Flares
Jones, Randolph	Jac-O-Lacs
Jones, Randy	Arthur Lee Maye & the Crowns
Jones, Randy	Cadets
Jones, Randy	Penguins
Jones, Ronnie	Pat Cordell & the Crescents

Performer	Group	Performer	Group
Jones, Ronnie	Pat Cordell & the Elegants	Judge, Ronald	Leaders
Jones, Ronnie	Ronnie Jones & the Classmates	Julian, Don	Don Julian & the Meadowlarks
Jones, Roy	Shells	Julian, Don	Larks (Money)
Jones, Sherrard	Clouds (Cobra)	Julian, Don	Medallions
Jones, Shirley	Dukays	Julian, Tony	Durhams
Jones, Theodore	Chateaus	Juliano, Tom	Catalinas (Little)
Jones, Tommy	Swans (Fortune)	Juliano, Tony	Ray & the Darchaes
Jones, Walter	Cameos (Cameo, Johnson, Matador)	Junior, Marvin	Dells
		Junior, Marvin	El Rays
Jones, Walter	El Pollos (Studio)	Justice, Eddie	Eddie & the Starlites
Jones, Will "Dub"	Cadets	Kador, Ernest (Ernie K-Doe)	Blue Diamonds
Jones, Will "Dub"	Coasters		
Jones, Will "Dub"	Crescendos (Atlantic)	Kakulis, Joey	Nobles (Klik, End)
Jones, Will "Dub"	Jacks	Kalail, Fred	Wonders (Ember)
Jones, Will "Dub"	Trammps	Kalail, Ron	Wonders (Ember)
Jones, Willie	Gladiolas	Kalkstein, Fred	Darrell & the Oxfords
Jones, Willie	Royal Jokers	Kanew, Jeff	Four Fifths
Jones, Willie	Zodiacs	Kasper, Tommy	Slades
Jones, Wilson	Gems (Drexel)	Kassman, Larry	Quotations
Jordan, Charles	Uniques (Peacock)	Kastel, Vic	Aquatones
Jordan, Connie	Four Blazers (Melodisc)	Kaye, Ian	Accents (Sultan)
Jordan, Ed "Sonny"	Five Delights	Kaye, Ian	Dreamers (Guaranteed)
Jordan, Ed "Sonny"	Montereys (Onyx)	Kearney, Paul	Casuals (Backbeat)
Jordan, Ed "Sonny"	Moodmakers	Kearney, Sam	Keynotes (Apollo)
Jordan, Ed "Sonny"	Supremes (Old Town)	Keels, James	Trumpeteers
Jordan, Gene	Five Cliffs of Dover	Kelley, Frances	Enchanters (Jubilee)
Jordan, Joe	G-Clefs	Kelly, Betty	Martha & the Vandellas
Jordan, John	Billy Butler & the Chanters	Kelly, Betty	Velvelettes
		Kelly, Dave	Chaperones
Jordan, John	Four Enchanters	Kelly, Francis	Delltones
Jordan, John	Four Vagabonds	Kelly, John	Re-Vels
Jordan, Lou	Chaperones	Kelly, Mary	Sugar Boy & the Sugar Lumps
Jordan, Luchrie	Five Tino's		
Jordan, Lucky	Coronets	Kelly, Mike	Duprees
Jordan, William	Cashmeres (Lake, Laurie, Josie, ACA)	Kelly, Richard	Ovations (Laurie)
		Kemp, George	ElDorados
Joseph, Gilbert	Spinners (Rhythm)	Kemp, Mansfield	Alma-Keys
Joseph, Herbert	Connie & the Decoys	Kemp, William	Alma-Keys
Joseph, William	Do Re Mi Trio	Kendricks, Eddie	Temptations (Gordy)
Joseph, William	Al Russell Trio	Kennard, Leroy	Nobles (Sapphire)
Joyner, Barbara	Eddie Jones and hte Cashmeres	Kennedy, Billy	Drifters (Atlantic)
		Kennedy, Billy	Flyers (Atco)
Joyner, Frank	Singing Wanderers	Kennedy, Edward	Carnations (Lescay)
Joyner, Frank	Wanderers	Kennedy, Jimmy	Ink Spots
Joyner, Lawrence	Orioles	Kennedy, Ricky	Students (Note, Checker)
Joyner, Lorraine	Eddie Jones & the Cashmeres	Kennedy, Shirley	Rex Middleton's Hi Fi's
		Kenner, Chris	Kings (Specialty)
Joyner, Lorraine	Veneers	Kenner, Doris	Shirelles
Joyner, Vance	Harmonizing Four	Kennibrew, Delores "Dee Dee"	Crystals (Philles)
Joyner, Warren	Electras (Cee Jam, Challenge, Infinity)		
		Kenny, Bill	Ink Spots
Joyner, Warren	Nuggets (Capitol)	Kenny, Herb	Cabineers
Judge, Ronald	Corvairs (Comet, Leopard)	Kenny, Herb	Golden Arrows
		Kenny, Herb	Herb Kenny Trio

Performer	Group	Performer	Group
Kenny, Herb	Ink Spots	Kinney, Lula Bee	Shirley Gunter & the Queens
Kerr, George	Little Anthony & the Imperials	Kinney, Silvester	Emblems
Kerr, George	Serenaders (Chock, MGM)	Kirby, Ed	Four Dukes (Sun)
		Kirk (Kirkland), Robey	Cues
Kerr, Victor	Serenaders (Chock, MGM)	Kirk (Kirkland), Robey	Playboys (Cat)
Kestenbaum, Denis	Excellents (Blast)	Kirk (Kirkland), Robey	Ruth Brown & the Rhythm Makers
Kevin, Pete	Cobras (Monogram, Casino, Swan)		
Key, Horace	Tams	Kirkland, Robey	Cues
Key, Lee	Mobile Four	Kirkland, Robey	Gliders
Keyes, Jimmy	Chord Cats (Cat)	Kirkpatrick, Art	Hepsters
Keyes, Jimmy	Chords (Cat)	Kirton, Earl	Gay Tunes (Timely, Joyce, Dome)
Keyes, Jimmy	Popular Five		
Keyes, Jimmy	Sh Booms (Cat)	Kirton, Earl	Verdicts
Keyes, Jimmy	Jimmy Keyes & the Symbols	Kitchings, Grant	Drifters (Atlantic)
		Kitchings, Grant	Keynotes
Keyes, Johnny	Johnny & the Keys	Kitchings, Grant	King Toppers
Keyes, Johnny	Magnificents	Klein, Roosevelt	Don Julian & the Meadowlarks
Keyes, Troy	Eddie & the Starlites		
Keyes, Troy	Starlites (Peak)	Knauss, Dick	Marcels (Colpix)
Keyes, Troy	Velours	Knauss, Dick	Dynamics (Cindy, Seeco, Dynamic, etc.)
Khoury, Fred	Deans (Laurie)		
Kidd, Robert	Mellow Drops (Imperial)	Knecht, Jack	Ballads (Franwill)
Kidd, Robert	Monitors (Specialty)	Knighton, Doris	Cats and the Fiddle
Kiler, Chris	Bradford Boys (Rainbow)	Knight, Ben Ken	Falcons (Mercury, United Artists, Chess, LuPine)
Killebrew, Tommy	Five Satins		
Kimball, Kenneth	Sheiks (Ef-N-Dee, Cat)	Knight, Ben Ken	Imperials (Great Lakes)
King, Alvin	Chimes (Combo)	Knight, Dorsey	Showmen
King, Ben E.	Drifters (Atlantic)	Knight, Gene	Showmen
King, Ben E.	Four B's	Knight, Gladys	Gladys Knight & the Pips
King, Clydie	Don Julian & the Meadowlarks	Knight, Merald "Bubba"	Gladys Knight & the Pips
King, Earl	Uniques (Peacock)	Knight, Richard	Orioles
King, Earl	Kings (Specialty)	Knight, Vernon	Jewels (Imperial, R&B)
King, Eddie	Flares	Knox, Ann	Lockettes
King, Eloise	Cosytones	Kollette, Calvin "Khaki"	Honey Boys
King, Evelyn	Radiants		
King, Henry	Charioteers	Kolquitt, Charles	Goldenrods (Vee Jay)
King, Jeannie	Blossoms	Koob, Billy	Premiers (Alert)
King, Joe	Brown Dots	Koob, Billy	Roger & the Travelers
King, John	Carpets	Koob, Roger	Premiers (Alert)
King, Kathryn	Cosytones	Koob, Roger	Roger & the Travelers
King, Leroy	Students (Note, Checker)	Korman, John	Dynamics (Cindy, Dynamic, Seeco, etc.)
King, Melvin	Olympics		
King, Ralph	Cosytones	Kornegay, Bob	Bells (Rama)
King, Scott	Melody Kings	Kornegay, Bob	Dixieaires
King, Scott	Shadows (Lee)	Kornegay, Bob	Du Droppers
King, Thurman	Fasinoles	Kornegay, Bob	Ravens
King, Windsor	Cashmeres (Lake, Laurie, Josie, ACA)	Kornegay, Bob	Valiants (Joy, Cortlandt)
		Kristian, Danny	Ebb-Tones
King, Windsor	Cosytones	Kristian, Danny	Native Boys
King, Windsor	Royal Sons (Apollo)	Kunz, Johnny	Catalinas (Little)
King, Woodrow	Keys	Kuse, George	Excellents

Performer	Group
Kuse, John	Excellents (Blast)
Kutner, Bob	Accents (Sultan)
Kutner, Bob	Boptones
Kutner, Bob	Quotations
Kutner, Bob	Vocal-Aires
La Boe, James	Songmasters
LaCarta, Charlie	Bob Knight Four
Laffey, Jimmy	Lonnie & the Carollons
LaGrecca, Angelo	Fascinators (Capitol)
Lally, Jack	Vespers (Laurie)
Lally, Richard	Four Epics (Laurie)
Lambert, Adam	Cats and Jammer Three
Lambert, Adam	Four Shades of Rhythm
Lambert, Rudy	Mondellos
Lamb, Marshall	Cufflinx
Lamb, Nelson	Serenades (MGM, Chock, Rae Cox)
Lamboy, Edwin	Debonaires (Gee)
Lamonica, Ray	Suburbans
LaMont, Joseph	Checkers
LaMont, William Joseph	Billy Ward & the Dominoes
Lampariello, Nick	Boptones
Lance, Bobby	Escorts (Coral)
Lance, Major	Ideals (Paso)
Lancianese, Ray	Holidays (Robbie)
Landers, James	Lyrics (Rhythm)
Landis, Jerry	Mystics (Laurie)
Landry, Douglas	Crystals (Specialty)
Landry, Jackie	Chantels
Lane, Preston	Fiestas
Langford, William	Golden Gate Quartet
Langston, Donald	Gazelles
Langston, Lindsay	Foster Brothers
Lang, Vontell	El Torros
Lang, Vontell	Monitors (Specialty, Aladdin)
Lang, Vontell	Moonbeams (Checker)
Lang, Vontell	Moonbeems (Sapphire)
Lang, Vontell	Señors
Lang, Vontell	Tropicals
Lang, Vontell (Lane?)	Tropicals
Lanham, Al	Tempo-Tones
Lanham, Danny	Tempo-Tones
Lanham, Richard	Tempo-Tones
Lanham, Wally	Tempo-Tones
Lankford, Carlton	Blue Chips
Lancianese, Ray	Holidays (Robbee, Nix)
Lanza, Howie	Hi-Fives (Decca)
Lapinsky, Ronnie	Regents
Lapinsky, Ronnie	Runarounds (K.C., Felsted)
Larkin, Denver	Clips (Republic, Calvert)
Larson, Art	Rockers (Carter)
Larter, Leon	Russ Riley & the Five Sounds

Performer	Group
La Rue, Roger	Timetones
LaRuffa, Donnie	Five Discs
Lasman, Mike	Accents (Sultan)
Lasman, Mike	Concords (Herald)
Lasman, Mike	Dreamers (Guaranteed)
Lasman, Mike	Mike & the Utopians
Lassiter, Art	Rockers (Federal)
Lassiter, Art	Trojans (RPM)
Lassiter, Marshall	Cherokees (United Artists)
Lassu, George	Jackie & the Starlites
Lattimore, George	Foster Brothers
Laudadio, Ronald	Naturals (Red Top)
Lauder, Morris	Sparks
Laurent, Bruce	Consorts (Cousins, APT)
LaVant, Jacki	Fashions
Lavatelli, George	Bon Aires
Lavatelli, George	Sparrows Quartet
Lawrence, Donald	Quinns
Lawrence, Kenny	Fantastics (RCA)
Lawrence, Larry	Fantastics (RCA)
Lawson, Floyd	Five Pennies
Lawson, Floyd	Four Pennies
Lawson, Floyd	Hearts of Stone
Lawson, Floyd	Larks
Lawson, George	Deep River Boys
Lawson, James	Plants
Lawson, Leo	Sonics (Groove)
Lawson, Ron	Mondellos
Lawyer, Andrew	Original Drifters
Lawyer, Andrew	Spaniels
Lawyer, Andrew	True Tones (Monument, Felsted, Josie)
Leach, Lillian	Lillian Leach & the Mellows
Leach, Lillian	Morrisania Revue
Leak, Butch	Drifters (Atlantic)
Lea, Wendell	Avons
Lea, Bill	Avons
Lea, Bob	Avons
LeBrune, George	Native Boys
LeCausi, Richie	Imaginations
Ledo, Harvey	Styles (Serene, Josie)
Lee, Barbara	Aquatones
Lee, Barbara	Deltairs
Lee, Beverly	Shirelles
Lee, Bill	Majors (Derby)
Lee, Billy	Belltones (J&S, Scatt)
Lee, Bob E.	Incas (Roadhouse)
Lee, Charles	Five Jets (DeLuxe, Fortune)
Lee, Charles	Thrillers (Thriller, Big Town)
Lee, Clyde	Majors (Derby)
Lee, Donald	Gazelles
Lee, Fletcher	Satisfactions (Smash)

Performer	Group	Performer	Group
Lee, George	Ruby & the Romantics	Lewis, Eddie	Challengers (Melatone)
Lee, James	Counts	Lewis, Eddie	Olympics
Lee, Johnny	Danleers	Lewis, Eddie	Velvetones
Lee, Larry	Bel-Aires (Crown, Decca)	Lewis, Ella	Ivoleers
Lee, Larry	Larry Lee & the Four Bel-Aires	Lewis, Ella	Ivories
		Lewis, George	Coronets
Lee, Nate	Cobras (Modern)	Lewis, Harold	Jayos
Lee, Otis	Cobras (Modern)	Lewis, Harold	Lamplighters
Lee, Otis	Dukes (Specialty)	Lewis, Harold	Shieks (Federal)
Lee, Ritzy	Del Vikings	Lewis, Harold	Tenderfoots
Lee, Robert	Charm	Lewis, Harry	Delta Rhythm Boys
Lee, Roger	Keynotes (Apollo)	Lewis, Henry	Magic Tones
Lee, Theodore	Excelsior Norfolk Quartet	Lewis, Henry	Marylanders
Lee, Thomas	Cherokees (Grand)	Lewis, Herbert	Five Echoes (Sabre)
Lee, Thomas	Cobras (Monogram, Casino, Swan)	Lewis, Jimmy	Original Drifters
		Lewis, Joe	Capris (Tender)
Lee, Yvonne	Minors	Lewis, Joe	Hollywood Saxons
Legg, Theresa	Versalettes	Lewis, Joe	Portraits
LeMonier, Peter	Five Sharps	Lewis, Joe	Normanaires
LeMonier, Peter	Rivileers	Lewis, Joe	Saxons
Lemon, Ernest	Swinging Hearts	Lewis, Joe	Tuxedos
Lenahan, Mike	Billy & the Essentials	Lewis, Leonard	Deckers
Lengester, Burnett	Inspirations	Lewis, Lew	No-Names (Guyden)
Lennard, Errol	Rivileers	Lewis, Mel	Climbers
Lento, Joe	Corvets (Laurel)	Lewis, Melvin	Jesters
Leonard, Jeff	Little Joey & the Flips	Lewis, Mike	Concords (Rust, RCA, Herald)
Leonard, Errol	Rivileers		
Lerario, Bill	Intentions (Jamie)	Lewis, Mike	Darrell & the Oxfords
Lerchey, David	Del Vikings	Lewis, Oliver	Swallows (King, Federal, After Hours)
Leroy, Smith	Drivers		
Lester, Bobby	Moonglows	Lewis, Otis	Silhouettes
Lester, Bobby	Moonlighters	Lewis, Paul	Swans (Fortune)
Lester, Robert "Squirrel"	Chanteurs	Lewis, Ray	Drifters (Atlantic)
		Lewis, Richard	Drapers
Lester, Robert "Squirrel"	Chi-Lites	Lewis, Richard	Duvals (Rainbow)
		Lewis, Richard	Five Crowns
Lester, Wally	Skyliners	Lewis, Richard	Richard Lewis & the Barons
Leverette, Charles "Chico"	Satintones		
		Lewis, Richard	Ivoleers
LeVert, Eddie	Mascots (King)	Lewis, Richard	Ivories
LeVert, Eddie	O'Jays	Lewis, Richard	Silhouettes
Levi, Artie	Lonnie & the Carollons	Lewis, Richard	Three Dots and a Dash
Levy, Danny	Five Delights	Lewis, Robert	Ruby & the Romantics
Levy, Danny	Moodmakers	Lewis, Rudy	Drifters (Atlantic)
Lewis, Billy	Drifters (Atlantic)	Lewis, Tony	Cameos (Cameo)
Lewis, Brooks	Kansas City Tomcats	Libert, Dave	Four Graduates (Rust)
Lewis, Carl	Elements (Titan)	Licarta, Charlie	Bob Knight Four
Lewis, Charles	Moonglows	Lidell, Harold	Belvederes (Baton)
Lewis, Charles	Singing Doves	Liebowitz, Helen Powell	Clickettes
Lewis, Charles K.	Cliff Butler & the Doves		
Lewis, Darryl	Elgins (Flip. Lummtone)	Lightfoot, Phil	Prodigals (Falcon, Abner)
Lewis, Darryl	Elements (Titan)	Lilly, Andre	Norman Fox & the Rob Roys
Lewis, Darrell	Six Teens		
Lewis, Darrell	Sweet Teens	Lincoln, Shedwick "Bubbie"	Chips
Lewis, Don	Jesters		
Lewis, Earl	Channels (Whirlin' Disc)	Lindsay, Bill	Bachelors (Earl)
Lewis, Earl	Five Echoes (Sabre)		

Performer	Group
Lindsay, Bill	Cadillacs
Lindsay, Bill	Dean Barlow & the Crickets
Lindsay, Bill	Jesse Powell & the Caddys
Lindsay, Bill	Montereys (Onyx)
Lindsay, Bill	Starlings (Josie, Dawn)
Lindsay, Bill	Twilighters (MGM)
Lindsay, Oscar	Four Shades of Rhythm
Liott, James	Channels (Mercury)
Lippzer, Barbara Jo	Holidays (Robbie)
Lipscomb, Joe	Mello-Tones (Decca)
Lipscomb, Joe	Jets (Gee)
Lipzer, Barbara	Holidays (Robbee, Nix)
Lithcuitt, George	Stylists (Rose)
Little, David	Louis Lymon & the Teenchords
Little, James	Jumping Jacks (Lloyds)
Livingston, Ulysses	Four Blazers (Melodisc)
Livingston, Ulysses	Hollywood's Four Blazes
Lloyd, Alvin	Spaniels
Lobrano, Billy	Frankie Lymon & the Teenagers
Lockett, Lloyd	El Torros
Locke, Jimmy	Upfronts
Locke, Tony	Rex Middleton's Hi Fi's
Loftman, Kenny	Interludes
Logan, Horace	Paramonts (Ember)
Logan, O. C.	Ballads (Venture)
Logan, O. C.	Equallos
Logan, O. C.	Willie Logan & the Plaids
Logan, Willie	Ballads (Venture)
Logan, Willie	Equallos
Logan, Willie	Willie Logan & the Plaids
Lomelino, Lloyd	Marquis (Onyx)
Long, Artie	Ben Smith Quartet
Long, Fred	Montclaires (Premium)
Long, Huey	Ink Spots
Long, James "Sonny"	Hornets (States)
Long, Paul	Cruisers (V-Tone, Gamble, Guyden)
Long, Saundra	Faith Taylor & the Sweet Teens
Long, Teddy	Delegates (Vee Jay)
Long, Teddy	ElDorados
Long, Teddy	Kool Gents
Loper, Ramon	Clovers (Josie)
Loper, Ramon	Five Keys
Lopes, Joe	Del Vikings
Lopez, Frank	Travelers (Andex)
Lopez, Gilbert	Tuneweavers
Lord, Tracy	Chesters
Lord, Tracy	Little Anthony & the Imperials

Performer	Group
Lorello, Joe	Admirations
Love, Bobby	No-Names (Guyden)
Love, Darlene	Crystals (Philles)
Lovejoy, Carl	Gaylarks
Love, Milton	Cadillacs
Love, Milton	Chances (Roulette)
Love, Milton	Concords (Harlem)
Love, Milton	Harptones
Love, Milton	Solitaires
Lowe, James	Dukays
Lowery, Bob "Pee Wee"	King Pharaoh & the Egyptians
Lowery, Bob "Pee Wee"	Four Pharaohs
Lowry, Walter	Smoothtones (Jem)
Lubek, Billy	Temptations (Savoy)
Lubers, Peter	Charioteers
Lucas, Bobby	Premiers (Gone)
Lucas, Harold	Clovers
Lucas, Kevin	Charm
Lundy, Jimmy	Deep River Boys
Luth, Charlie	Academics
Luth, Charlie	Frontiers (Philips)
Luth, Johnny	Catalinas (Little)
Lyles, Orvan Leroy	Four Aces (Trilon)
Lyles, Pat	Cookies
Lymon, Frankie	Frankie Lymon & the Teenagers
Lymon, Louis	Louis Lymon & the Teenchords
Lymon, Louis	Townsmen (PJ)
Lynch, David	Platters
Lyndon, Frank	Belmonts
Lynn, Gloria	Delltones
Lynne, Gloria	Delltones
Lyons, Billy	Five Jets (DeLuxe, Fortune)
Lyons, Billy	Royal Jokers
Lyons, Jimmy	Vocaleers (Classic Artists)
Lyons, Joe	Joe Lyons & Arrows
Macaluso, Joe	Deans (Laurie)
MacArthur, John	Majestics (Marlin)
MacArthur, Luther	Cardinals
Mackey, Bernie	Ink Spots
Mack, Johnny	Sophomores (Dawn)
Mack, Norris "Bunky"	Swallows (King, Federal, After Hours)
Mack, Rocko	Marquis (Onyx)
Mack, Sammy	Satintones
Maclaurin, Green	Quinns
MacLerie, Scotty	Bon Aires
Maddox, James	El Dorados
Maddox, James	Four El Dorados
Maddox, James	Tempos (Rhythm)
Maddox, Walter	Blanders (Smash)

Performer	Group
Maddox, Walter	Marcels (Colpix)
Madison, Glen	Delcos
Madison, Glen	Penguins
Mae, Little Edna	Scooters
Maffei, Bobby	Leisure Lads
Maffei, Ralph	Deans (Laurie)
Magnezid, George	Wrens
Magruder, Andy	Bluejays (Roadhouse)
Magruder, Andy	Five Blue Notes (Sabre, Onda)
Magruder, Andy	Spaniels
Magruder, Jimmy	Loveletters
Mahlan, John	Admirations
Maiola, George	Vel-Tones
Major, Harold	Crows
Major, Harold	Four Notes (Premier)
Major, Joe	Vibes
Makonnen, David	Cubs
Makonnen, Tafari	Cubs
Malara, Bob	Dreamers (Goldisc, Cousins)
Malmeth, Greg	Little Romeo & the Casanovas
Malmeth, Greg	Ovations (Josie)
Malone, Arnold	Levee Songsters
Malone, Arnold "Johnny"	Mello Harps
Malone, George	Monotones
Maltese, Tony	Emotions
Manardo, Bob	Falcons (Mercury, United Artists, Chess, LuPine)
Mancha, Pedro	Majestics (Chex, Contour)
Mancuso, Frank	Imaginations
Mangi, Joe	Criterions
Mangi, Joe	Kents (Aljon)
Manigault, Bobby	Jimmy Castor Bunch
Manigo, Alexander	Blue Jays (Milestone)
Manley, Robert	El Pollos
Mann, Billy	Electras (Freedom)
Mann, Billy	Emeralds (Kicks)
Mann, Emmitt	Second Verse
Manno, Michael	Demolyrs
Manor, Ularsee	Four Buddies (Club 51)
Mansfield, Bobby	Morrisania Revue
Mansfield, Bobby	Wrens
Mansfield, Bowling	Four Jacks
Mansfield, Scotty	Clefs
Mansfield, Scotty	Scotty Mann & the Masters
Manson, Ray	Buckeyes
Manual, Bob	Twiliters (Nix, Chess, Roulette)
Manual, Joe	Desideros
Manzo, Sonny	Ballads (Franwill)
Maples, Tony	V-Eights

Performer	Group
Mapp, Gail	Blenders (Witch, Cortland)
Maraglia, Andy	Blendairs (Tin Pan Alley)
Maraglia, Andy	Chalets
Marchesano, Roy	Chaperones
Marcus, Earl	Laddins
Marcus, John	Laddins
Maresca, Ernie	Regents
Maresco, Anthony "Tony"	Anthony & the Sophomores
Maresco, Anthony "Tony"	Tony & the Twilighters
Maresco, Anthony "Tony"	Tony & the Dynamics
Marigault, Bobby	Jimmy Castor Bunch
Marioni, Pat	Four Dates (Chancellor)
Markay, Cerressa	Cezannes
Marls, J.	Classics (Class, Crest)
Marone, Ronnie	Academics
Marsella, Ralph	Demolyrs
Marselle, Madalyn	Phantoms
Marshall, Curtis	Five Swans (Music City)
Marshall, Donald	Buccaneers
Marshall, Douglas	King Krooners (Crooners)
Marshall, Frank	Cameos (Dootone)
Marshall, Frank	Medallions
Marshall, Jackie	Larks (Sheryl)
Marshall, Jackie	Starlings (Josie, Dawn)
Marshall, James	Informers
Marshall, Jimmy	Five Echoes (Sabre)
Marshall, Maithe	Bill Cook & the Marshalls
Marshall, Maithe	Hi-Hatters
Marshall, Maithe	Ink Spots
Marshall, Maithe	Marshall Brothers
Marshall, Maithe	Ravens
Marsi, Johnny	Youngtones
Martin, Al	Striders
Martin, Barbara	Primettes
Martin, Cleveland "Butch"	Diadems
Martin, David	Checkers
Martin, David	Sparrows (Jay Dee, Davis)
Martin, David	Performers (Tip Top)
Martin, Derek	Pearls (Onyx)
Martin, Derek	Raves
Martin, Derek	Speedoo & the Pearls
Martin, Dottie	Willows (Warwick)
Martin, Doug	Rockers (Federal)
Martin, Doug	Trojans (RPM)
Martin, Earl	Falcons (Mercury, United Artists, Chess, LuPine)

Performer	Group
McClay, Ollie Yul	Mondellos
McClendon, Bobby	Volchords
McClure, Douglas	Pyramids (Davis)
McClure, Sam	Jubalaires
McClure, Sam	Melody Kings
McClure, Sam	Shadows (Lee)
McCollum, Hazel	ElDorados
McCoo, Marilyn	Fifth Dimension
McCoy, Jack	Ballads (Franwill)
McCoy, Norman	Starlighters (End)
McCoy, Paul	Drivers
McCoy, Van	Starlighters (End)
McCrae, Buddy	Hummers
McCrae, Claude	Dukays
McCrae, Claude	Pastels (United)
McCrae, Ethel	Cookies
McCrae, Floyd "Buddy"	Chord Cats (Cat)
McCrae, Floyd "Buddy"	Chords (Cat)
McCrae, Floyd "Buddy"	Sh Booms
McCrary, Theodore	El Capris (Bullseye, Fee Bee)
McCraw, Lloyd	Cadets
McCraw, Lloyd	Jacks
McCraw, Lloyd	Rocketeers (Modern, MJC)
McCraw, Lloyd	Thor-Ables
McCray, Fred	Capitols (Cindy, Gateway)
McCullough, Charles	Charles McCullough & the Silks
McCullough, LaFar	La-Rells
McCune, Nat	Danleers
McDaniel, Floyd	Four Blazes (United)
McDaniel, Floyd	Hollywood's Four Blazers
McDaniel, Luther	Crescendos (Music City)
McDaniel, Luther	Four Deuces
McDaniels, Eugene	Sultans (Duke)
McDaniels, Gene	Admirals
McDonald, Adriel	Cabineers
McDonald, Adriel	Ink Spots
McDonald, Adriel	Sandmen
McDonald, Al	Colognes
McDonald, Bill	Quintones (Park)
McDonald, Layton	Rainbows
McDonald, Oscar	Elements (Titan)
McDonald, Oscar	Elgins (Flip, Lummtone)
McDonald, Ulysses	Daylighters
McDougal, Vivian	Blue Notes (Harthon)
McDougal, Weldon	Blue Notes (Harthon)
McDougal, Weldon	Larks (Sheryl)
McDowell, Steve	Plants
McDuffie, Roosevelt	V-Eights

Performer	Group
McDuffie, Roosevelt	Vibes
McDuffie, Roosevelt	Vibranaires
McElroy, Sollie	Chanteurs
McElroy, Sollie	Flamingos
McElroy, Sollie	Moroccos
McFadden, George	Jubalaires
McGee, Robert "Shue"	Magic Tones
McGhee, Kent	Sheppards (Theron, United)
McGill, Danaiel	Jumping Jacks (Lloyds)
McGill, Daniel	Romeos (Apollo)
McGill, Lucius	Dells
McGill, Lucius	El Rays
McGill, Mickey	Dells
McGill, Mickey	El Rays
McGowan, Jimmy	Four Fellows (Glory)
McGrier, Sammy	Hambone Kids
McGuiness, Carl	Pentagons
McGuire, Pat	Chimes (Tag)
McIlwain, Ed	Brochures
McIlwain, Ray	Notes (Capitol, MGM)
McKay, James "Charlie"	Schoolboys
McKay, James, "Charlie"	Collegians (Winley)
McKay, Lenny	Jesters
McKinney, Brother	Townsmen (Herald, Ember)
McKinney, Elijah "Prez"	Bel-Aires (M.Z.)
McKinney, Mickey	Starlets (Pam)
McKinnon, Pearl	Second Verse
McKinnon, Pearl	Pearl & the Deltars
McKinnon, Pearl	Kodaks (Kodoks)
McKinnon, Pearl	Shari & the Shalimars
McKnight, Charles	Pastels (United)
McKnight, Jack	Four Epics (Laurie)
McKnight, Jack	Vespers (Laurie)
McKnight, Jay	Little Nate & the Chryslers
McKnight, Prince	Corvairs (Comet, Leopard)
McLain, Leon	Quinns
McLain, William, "Buzzy"	Cleftones (Gee)
McLawn, Bobby	Escorts (Premium)
McLemore, LaMont	Intervals
McLemore, LaMont	Fifth Dimension
McLendon, Bobby	Volchords
McLeod, Vincent	Ruby & the Romantics
McLollie, Oscar	Drifters (Exclusive)
McMichael, Julius	Paragons
McMillian, Kenny	Smoothtones (Jem)

Performer	Group
McNair, Curtis	Titans (Specialty, Vita, Class)
McNeil, David	Billy Ward & the Dominoes
McNeil, Landy	Corsairs
McNeill, Barbara	Chimes (Specialty)
McNeill, Barbara	Cupids (Aladdin)
McNeill, Barbara	Lions (Rendezvous)
McNeill, Barbara	Wonders
McNeill, David	Billy Ward & the Dominoes
McNeill, David	Larks
McNeill, Leroy	Nutmegs
McNeill, Leroy	Rajahs
McNeill, Maxine	Passionettes
McKnight, Charles	Pastels
McNight, Jay	Little Nate & the Chryslers
McPhatter, Clyde	Billy Ward & the Dominoes
McPhatter, Clyde	Drifters (Atlantic)
McPhee, Mitchell	Cosytones
McPhee, Skip	Exciters
McQuater, Matthew	Clovers
McQueen, Jimmy	Mike & the Utopians
McQueen, Leroy	Billy Wells & the Crescents
McQueen, Leroy	Wigs
McShade, David	Jades (Christy)
McWilliams, Frank	Casanovas
McWilliams, Willie	Casanovas
Meagher, James	Little Joey & the Flips
Mealy, Thomas	Majestics (Chex, Contour)
Mears, Fred "Gary"	Casuals (Backbeat)
Medlin, Joe	Ravens
Medress, Hank	Darrell & the Oxfords
Meecham, Butch	Sunbeams (Acme, Herald)
Melesk, Richard	Five Fashions
Melodia, Ross	Chapelaires
Melvin, B.	Debonaires (Dootone)
Melvin, Harold	Blue Notes (Josie, Rama, Harthon, etc.)
Menhardt, Ronnie	Hi-Fives (Decca)
Mercardo, Richard	Chimes (Tag)
Mercede, Joe	Camelots
Merchant, Jimmy	Frankie Lymon & the Teenagers
Meredith, J. Clarence	Dinwiddie Colored Quartet
Merle, Milton	Billy Ward & the Dominoes
Merrick, Vernon	Upfronts
Merritt, Terry	Normanaires
Mertens, Joe	Admirations
Mesner, Patti Ann	Charmers (Aladdin)
Mesner, Patti Ann	Flames

Performer	Group
Mesner, Patti Ann	Patty Anne & the Flames
Messina, Richard	Chaperones
Metcalf, Robert	Rivals (Puff)
Metz, Cartrel	Splendors (Taurus)
Metzo, Bonnie	Syncopates
Meyers, John	Moonbeams (Checker)
Meyers, John	Moonbeems (Sapphire)
Mickens, Al	Orients
Middleton, Charles	Ambers
Middleton, Charles	Jaguars
Middleton, Gerald	Creators (Dootone)
Middleton, Lynn	Joytones (Rama)
Middleton, Rex	Rex Middleton's Hi Fi's
Middleton, Tony	Hollywood Flames
Middleton, Tony	Willows (Allen, Melba)
Middleton, Tony	Five Willows
Mifflin, Earl	Mifflin Trilets (Ember)
Mifflin, Edward	Mifflin Trilets (Ember)
Mifflin, Everett	Mifflin Trilets (Ember)
Mignona, Richard	Intentions (Jamie)
Milano, Fred	Belmonts
Milano, Fred	Dion & the Belmonts
Milaro, Joe	4 Js
Milaro, Joe	Fabulous Four
Milazzo, Pete	Encounters
Miles, Buddy	Fidelities
Miles, Donny	Victorians
Miles, Eddie	Sugar Boy & the Cane Cutters
Miles, Herbie	Cats and the Fiddle
Miles, Jeanette	Starlets (Pam)
Miles, Ronald	Rainbows
Miles, Warren	Sugar Boy & the Cane Cutters
Millender, Charlie	Drifters (Atlantic)
Miller, Ben	Casinos (Maske)
Miller, Cathy	Solitaires
Miller, Don	Val-Aires
Miller, Donald	Preludes (Empire)
Miller, Donald	Tempters (Empire)
Miller, Donald	Youngsters (Empire)
Miller, ElMaurice	Delta Rhythm Boys
Miller, Eric	Melody Masters
Miller, Gus	Hornets (States)
Miller, Harold	Rays
Miller, Jake	Marvels (ABC)
Miller, James	Canaanites
Miller, James	Joe Van Loan Quartet
Miller, James	Scale-Tones
Miller, Jean	Kodaks (Kodoks)
Miller, Jeanette	Miller Sisters
Miller, Jim	Bachelors (Mercury, Songmaster)
Miller, Joseph	Five Chimes (Ebony)
Miller, Kenny	Four Dots (Bullseye, Freedom)

Performer	Group
Moore, Bobby	Jimmy Jones & the Pretenders
Moore, Bobby	Jones Boys
Moore, Bobby	Jimmy Jones & the Savoys
Moore, Bobby	Sparks of Rhythm
Moore, Bobby	Vocaltones
Moore, Conrad	Metronomes (Winn)
Moore, Gene	Five Keys
Moore, Gene	Gene Moore & the Chimes
Moore, Gene "Butchy"	Wisdoms
Moore, James	Gaylarks
Moore, Jerry	Carl Hogan & the Miracles
Moore, Jimmy	Five Royales
Moore, Jimmy	Francois & the Anglos
Moore, Jimmy	Rockmasters
Moore, Jimmy "Nunnie"	Peacocks
Moore, Joe	Arthur Lee Maye & the Crowns
Moore, Joe	Henry Strogin & the Crowns
Moore, John	Temptations (Savoy)
Moore, Johnny	Drapers
Moore, Johnny	Drifters (Atlantic)
Moore, Johnny	Hornets (States)
Moore, Johnny	Master Keys
Moore, Johnny	Shields
Moore, Joseph	Arthur Lee Maye & the Crowns
Moore, Ken	Temptations (Savoy)
Moore, Margaret	Joytones (Rama)
Moore, Oscar	Three Blazers
Moore, Paul	Egyptian Kings
Moore, Paul	Four Pharaohs
Moore, Robert	Temptations (Savoy)
Moore, Sam	Majestics (Marlin)
Moore, Shirley	Cats and the Fiddle
Moore, Sonny	Jayos
Moore, Sonny	Shieks (Federal)
Moore, Teddy	Temptations (Savoy)
Moore, Tommy	Emeralds (Bobbin)
Moore, Warren "Pete"	Miracles
Moore, William "Bubba"	Townsmen (Herald, Ember)
Morales, Mathew	Startones (Rainbow)
Morales, Matthew	Carnations (Lescay)
Moran, Jimmy	Dixieaires
Moran, Tom	Dixieaires
Mordente, Tom	Clusters
Moreland, Prentice	Billy Ward & the Dominoes
Moreland, Prentice	Cadets

Performer	Group
Moreland, Prentice	Colts
Moreland, Prentice	Crescendos (Atlantic)
Moreland, Prentice	DuDroppers
Moreland, Prentice	Fortunes
Moreland, Prentice	Hollywood Flames
Moreland, Prentice	Jacks
Moreno, Tony	Five Jades
Morgan, Alan	Cavaliers (Chicago)
Morgan, Joe	Pharaohs (Specialty)
Morgan, Joe	Rams (Flair)
Morgan, Loumell	Tiger Haynes & the Three Flames
Morgan, Paul	Calvaes
Morgan, Richard	Dino & the Diplomats
Morgan, Rudy	Solitaires
Moricco, Bob	Larry Chance & the Earls
Morland, Bob	Uniques (Peacock)
Morone, Earl	Fabulaires
Morris, Billy	Channels (Whirlin' Disc)
Morris, Buddy	"Fat Man" Mathews & the Four Kittens
Morris, Eddie	Fiestas
Morris, Eddie	Vals (Unique Laboratories)
Morrisette, Johnny	Medallions
Morris, Greg	Coronets
Morris, Idella	Majors (Imperial)
Morris, Idella	Versatiles (Ro-Cal)
Morris, James	Gaylords (Savoy)
Morris, James	Imperials (Derby, Great Lakes)
Morris, John	"Fat Man" Mathews & the Four Kittens
Morris, John "Buddy"	Dave Collins & the Scrubs
Morris, Johnny	Arthur Lee Maye & the Crowns
Morris, Johnny	Five Hearts (west coast)
Morris, Johnny	Rams (Flair)
Morrison, Charles	Don Julian & the Meadowlarks
Morrison, Charles	Larks (Money)
Morrison, Gary	Chimes (Royal Roost, Betta)
Morrison, Gary	Five Chimes, (Royal Roost, Betta)
Morrison, Gary	Hummers
Morrison, Gary	Lillian Leach & the Mellows
Morrison, Leroy	Three Sharps and a Flat
Morris, Ron	Larados
Morris, Wayne	Nobles (Sapphire)
Morris, Willie	Willie Headen & the Five Birds
Morris, John	Hawks
Morrow, Frank	Vocaleers (Classic Artists)
Morrow, Melvin	El Dorados

674 • Appendix

Performer	Group
Morrow, Melvin	Major-Minors
Morrow, Melvin	Moroccos
Morton, Allen	Impacts (RCA, Watts)
Morton, Luther	Pearl & the Deltars
Morton, Luther	Young Lads (Neil)
Moschella, Lou	Admirations
Moschello, James	Elegants
Mosely, Glen	Paragons
Mosely, Nate, Jr.	Scarlets
Mosely, Robert	Ruby & the Romantics
Mosley, Bob	Plink, Plank and Plunk
Mosley, Ronald	Skarlettones
Moses, Pirkle Lee	El Dorados
Moses, Pirkle Lee	Johnny & the Keyes
Moses, Pirkle Lee	Major-Minors
Moshe, Murray	Concords (Rust, RCA, Herald)
Moss, Johnny	Phantoms
Motley, Frank	Clefs
Mott, Robert	Dreamers (Grand)
Mouton, Heartwell	Progressive Four
Moye, Johnny	Quinns
Mullin, Jimmy	Four Epics (Laurie)
Mullin, Jimmy	Vespers (Laurie)
Mumford, Eugene	Billy Ward & the Dominoes
Mumford, Eugene	Eugene Mumford & the Serenaders
Mumford, Eugene	Larks
Mumford, Ira	Rivals (Apollo)
Mundy, Ronald	Marcels (Colpix)
Munhall, Don	Emeralds (ABC)
Munson, Otis	Pentagons
Murns, Jimmy	Belvederes (Baton)
Murph, Philip	Dukes (Specialty)
Murphy, Jace	Supremes (Kitten)
Murphy, Joseph	Five Jets (DeLuxe, Fortune)
Murphy, Joseph	Five Stars (Mark-X, End)
Murphy, Joseph	Thrillers (Thriller, Big Town)
Murphy, Joseph	Voice Masters
Murphy, Lee	Supremes (Kitten)
Murphy, Ralph	Supremes (Kitten)
Murphy, Steve	Five Secrets
Murphy, Steve	Loungers
Murphy, Steve	Secrets
Murray, Cecil	Rhythm Kings
Murray, Cecil	Rhythm Masters
Murray, Harold	Preludes (Empire)
Murray, Harold	Tempters (Empire)
Murray, Harold	Youngsters (Empire)
Murray, John	Chimes (Royal Roost, Betta)
Murray, John	Five Chimes, (Royal Roost, Betta)
Murray, Marlowe	FiTones

Performer	Group
Murray, Marlowe "Lowe"	Caverliers [sic] Quartet
Murray, "Ena" Louise Harris	Hearts (Baton)
Myers, Billy	Paradons
Myers, Eddie	Four Shades of Rhythm
Myers, Herb	Chimes (Arrow)
Myers, Herbert	Five Pennies
Myers, Herbert	Four Jokers
Myers, Herbert	Four Pennies
Myers, Herbert	Tropicals
Myers, James	Chessmen (Relic)
Myers, James	Chimes (Arrow)
Myers, James	Five Pennies
Myers, James	Four Jokers
Myers, John	Five Pennies
Myers, John	Four Pennies
Myers, John	Hearts of Stone
Myers, John	Larks
Myers, Wilson	Plink, Plank & Plunk
Myles, Donny (a.k.a. Sehested)	Billy Dawn Quartet
Myles, Donny (a.k.a. Sehested)	Donny Myles & the Dukes
Myles, Donny (a.k.a. Sehested)	Four Dukes
Myles, Donny (a.k.a. Sehested)	Heralds
Myles, Donny (a.k.a. Sehested)	Mighty Dukes (Duke)
Myles, Donny (a.k.a. Sehested)	Four Fellows (Tri Boro)
Myles, Donny (a.k.a. Sehested)	Victorians
Myles, Edgar "Big Boy"	Sha Weez/Shawees
Myles, Edgar "Big Boy"	"Sugar Boy" and the Cane Cutters
Myles, James	Squires (Combo)
Myles, Warren	Sha Weez/Shawees
Myles, Warren	Sugar Boy and the Cane Cutters
Myles, Willie	Magnificents
Nabbie, Jimmie	Brown Dots
Nabbie, Jimmie	Sentimentalists (Manor)
Nabbie, Jimmy	Four Tunes
Nabbie, Jimmy	Ink Spots
Nadel, William "Dutch"	Limelighters
Nagy, Russ	Aquatones
Nagy, Russ	Bellnotes
Nance, Frederick	Poets (Flash)
Naranjo, Sammy	Mints
Narcardo, Vinny	Capris (Planet, Old Town, etc.)
Narducci, Alex	Demolyrs

Performer	Group	Performer	Group
Nash, Ruby	Ruby & the Romantics	Nixon, Charles	Tymes
Nathanson, Eric	Lonnie & the Carollons	Nixon, Roy	Downbeats
Nathanson, Eric	Vocal-Aires	Noble, Gail	Rosettes (Herald)
Natson, Irv	Belltones (Grand)	Noble, Horace	Nobles (Sapphire)
Neal, Don	Creators(Dootone)	Nolan, Buddy	Dreamers (Grand)
Neely, Delmar	Five Swans (Music City)	Nolan, James	Rainbows
Negroni, Joe	Frankie Lymon & the	Nolan, James	Marquees (Okeh)
	Teenagers	Nolan, James	Moonglows (RCA)
Neil, Mickey	Four Epics (Laurie)	Norris, Curtis	Avons
Neil, Mickey	Vespers (Laurie)	Northern, Herbert	Tabs (Dot, Vee Jay,
Neill, Robert	Serenaders (Roadhouse)		Wand)
Nelson, Ben E. (King)	Crowns (R&B)	Norton, Daniel "Sonny"	Crows
Nelson, Ben E. (King)	Drifters (Atlantic)	Norton, Daniel "Sonny"	Four Notes (Premier)
Nelson, Dorland	Cameos (Matador)	Norwood, Malcomb	Escorts (Premium)
Nelson, Earl	Earl Nelson & the Pelicans	Notabartolo, Charles	Casualaires
Nelson, Earl	Hollywood Flames	Notabartolo,	Five Boroughs
Nelson, Earl	Satellites	Charles	
Nelson, Earl	Tangiers	Nunez, Joe	Raindrops (Imperial)
Nelson, Earl	Voices (Cash)	Nunn, Bobby	Cadets
Nelson, George	Orioles	Nunn, Bobby	Coasters
Nelson, J. B.	Master Keys	Nunn, Bobby	Nic Nacs
Nelson, Mathew	Crenshaws	Nunn, Bobby	Robins (Savoy)
Nelson, Mathew	Lamplighters	Nurse, Bobby	Shells
Nelson, Mathew	Tenderfoots		
Nelson, Nate	Flamingos	O'Connell, Sharon	Syncopates
Nelson, Nate	Platters	O'Connor, Jimmie	Barries (Ember)
Nelson, Nate	Velvetones	October, Johnny	Four Dates
Nelson, Raymond	Cabin Boys	Odem, Andrew	Original Drifters
Nelson, Sam	Mad Lads	Oden, Pete	Egyptian Kings
Nelson, William "Sonny"	De'Bonairs (Ping)	Odes, Teddy	Eddie & the Starlites
		Odom, A. V.	Flairs
Nero, D.	Dukes (Imperial)	Odom, David	King Odom Quartet
Nesbary, Robert	Orchids (Parrot)		(Four)
Nesbit, Bob	Congo Rhythm Boys	Oglesby, Johnny	Metronomes (Wynne)
Nevils, Curtis	Five Cs	Olds, Ted	Eddie & the Starlites
Newman, Frankie	Clefs	Olds, Ted	Starlites (Peak)
Newman, Frankie	Scotty Mann & the Masters	Olds, Ted	Tokens
		Oliastro, Bob	Dantes
Newsome, Ernest	Volumes (Chex)	Oliver, Jimmy	Drifters (Atlantic)
Newson, Earnest	Volumes (Chex)	Oliver, Moses	Octaves (DC)
Nicholas, Frank	Dreamers (Goldisc, Cousins)	Oliver, Sonny	Tympany Five
		O'Malley, Tom	Raiders (Atco)
Nichols, Ann	Ann Nichols & the Bluebirds	O'Neal, Louis	Jets (Gee)
		O'Neill, Joey	Passions
Nichols, Calvin	Larks (Sheryl)	O'Neil, Louis	Mello-Tones (Decca)
Nichols, David	Camelots	O'Neil, Robert	Four Vagabonds
Nichols, Davie	Quotations	Oornazian, Arum	Fantasys (Guyden)
Nicholson, George	Cap-Tans	Orange, Fred	Excels (Central, Gone)
Nicholson, George	L'Cap-Tans	Orlando, Mike	Clientelles
Nicholson, Sonny	Butlers (Guyden)	Orth, Hank	Leisure Lads
Nickens, Richard	El Dorados	Ortsman, Jay	Blue Stars
Nieves, Frankie	Eddie Friend & the Empires (Colpix)	Osborne, Robert	L'Cap-Tans
		Osborn, Robert	Cap-Tans
Nigro, Joe	Emotions	Osbrooks, Dave	Mobile Four

Performer	Group	Performer	Group
O'Simmons, Johnny	Cubans (Flash)	Palm, Norman	Pastels (United)
Ostrom, Dennis	Blue Sky Boys	Palmer, Bernard	El Venos
Ostrom, Dennis	Bon Aires	Palmer, Clarence	Cab Calloway & the
Ostrom, Dennis	Citadels		Cabaliers
Otis, George	Stereos	Palmer, Clarence	Jive Bombers
Ottobre, Johnny (October)	Four Dates (Chancellor)	Palmer, Clarence	Palmer Brothers
		Palmer, Dick	Beavers
Ottobre, Johnny (October)	Fabulous Four	Palmer, Dick	Blenders (Decca, MGM)
		Palmer, Dick	Cab Calloway & the
Ottile, Augusto	Ovations (Laurie)		Cabaliers
Outlaw, Tommy	Demens	Palmer, Dick	Palmer Brothers
Overby, Kenny	Ronnie & the Hi-Lites	Palmer, Ernest	Cab Calloway & the
Owens, Danny	Coleman Brothers		Cabaliers
Owens, Danny	Colemanaires	Palmer, Ernie	Palmer Brothers
Owens, Danny	Four Tunes	Palmer, Reese	Marquees (Okeh)
Owens, Danny	Melody Masters	Palmer, Reese	Moonglows (RCA)
Owens, Danny	Sentimentalists (Manor)	Palmer, Vernon "Bert"	Falcons (Regent, Savoy, RCA)
Owens, Garland	Francois and the Anglos		
Owens, Garland	Rockmasters	Palmer, Vernon "Bert"	Four Buddies (Savoy)
Owens, Henry	Dixieaires		
Owens, Henry	Golden Gate Quartet	Palombi, Bob	Dantes
Owens, Mickey	Five Sharps (Jubilee)	Palters, Harry	Dreamers (Grand)
Owens, Monte	Caverliers Quartet	Palumbo, Larry	Larry Chance & the Earls
Owens, Monte	Chances (Roulette)	Paparella, Joseph	Four Js
Owens, Monte	Mello-Moods (Robin, Prestige)	Pardo, Frank	Devotions
		Pardo, Joe	Devotions
Owens, Monte	Solitaires	Parducci, Eddie	Delvons
Owens, Richard	Ivy Leaguers	Parducci, Eddie	Five Discs
Owens, Richard	Jayhawks	Parducci, Eddie	Vito & the Salutations
Owens, Richard	Marathons	Parenti, E.	Knockouts
Owens, Richard	Six Teens	Parker, Alton	Sheiks (Ef-N-Dee, Cat)
Owens, Richard	Temptations	Parker, Bobby	Emeralds (Kicks)
Owens, Richard	Vibes (Allied)	Parker, Bobby	Hi Tensions
Owens, Richard	Vibrations (Checker)	Parker, Carl	Del Satins
Oxidine, Earl	Larks (Sheryl)	Parker, George "Sonny"	Cavaliers (nonrecording)
Pace, Leon	Five Thrills	Parker, George "Sonny"	Sheppards (Theron, United)
Pace, Ronnie	Exciters		
Paden, Frank	Marvelows (ABC)	Parker, George	Gassers (Cash)
Paden, Johnny	Marvelows (ABC)	Parker, James	Mello-Keys
Pagan, Cesare	Vilons	Parker, Junius	Cleartones
Pagan, Cesare	Zircons	Parker, Junius	Selah Jubilee Singers
Pagan, John	Vilons	Parker, Richard	Esco's [sic]
Page, Willie	Blue Chips	Parker, Richard	Otis Williams & the Charms
Paige, Fred	Chanters		
Paige, Fred	Del-Vons	Parker, Robert	Four Aces (Trilon)
Paige, Johnny	Marylanders	Parks, Lloyd	Blue Notes (Josie, Rama, Harthon, etc.)
Paige, Johnny	Stylists (Jay Wing, Sage, Crown)		
		Parks, Robert	Ivy Tones
Paige, Mickey	Del-Vons	Parr, David	La-Rells
Paige, Sharon	Blue Notes (Josie, Rama, Harthon, etc.)	Parris, Fred	Cherokees (United Artists)
Pain, Ray	Del Roys	Parris, Fred	Five Satins
Paladino, Mike	Bon Aires	Parris, Fred	Restless Hearts
Palm, Norman	Crystals (Delano)	Parris, Fred	Scarlets
Palm, Norman	Eldorados	Parris, Fred	Wildwoods

Performer	Group
Parris, Judy	Larktones
Parris, Ronnie	Stereos
Parton, Eddie	Three Barons (Savoy)
Parton, Eddie	Three Riffs
Pascarella, Tommy	Majestics (20th Fox)
Paschall, Harry	Belltones (Grand)
Paschall, Harry	Farris Hill & the Madison Brothers
Paschall, Harry	Royal Demons
Paschall, Harry	Little Joe & the Thrillers
Paschall, Harry	Madisons (Cedargrove, Lawn, MGM)
Passalaqua, Tony	Fascinators (Capitol)
Passalaqua, Tony	Five Boroughs
Passalaqua, Tony	Tony Richards & the Twilights (Colpix)
Passion, Jerry	Cardinals
Passion, Jerry	Trend-Ells
Pastnano, Sonny	Blendairs
Pate, James	Drivers
Patillo, David	Four Blackbirds (Vocalion)
Patillo, David	Four Toppers (Savoy)
Patillo, David	Jones Boys Sing Band
Patillo, David	Red Caps/Five Red Caps
Patillo, David	Steve Gibson & the Toppers
Pato, Alex	Lyrics (Harlem, Wildcat)
Patriarca, Joe	Crystals (Cub)
Patriarca, Joe	Metros
Patricks, Benny	Don Julian & the Meadowlarks
Patrick, Charles	Monotones
Patrick, Charles	Terracetones
Patrick, James	Kodaks (Kodoks)
Patrick, James	Monotones
Patten, Edward	Gladys Knight & the Pips
Patterson, Berman	Cleftones (Gee)
Patterson, Charles	Chimes (Specialty)
Patterson, Charles	Shields
Patterson, Jerome	Topps (Red Robin)
Paul, Billy	Blue Notes (Josie, Rama, Harthon, etc.)
Paul, Clarence	Coleman Brothers
Paul, Clarence	Royal Sons (Apollo)
Paul, Clarence	Royals (Apollo)
Paul, Danny	Don Julian & the Meadowlarks
Pauling, Clarence	Five Royales
Pauling, Lowman	Five Royales
Pauling, Lowman	Royal Sons (Apollo)
Pauling, Lowman	Royals (Apollo)
Paul, Robert	Don Julian & the Meadowlarks
Paul, Wilbur "Yonkie"	Floaters
Paul, Wilbur "Yonkie"	Drapers
Paul, Wilbur "Yonkie"	Duvals (Rainbow)
Paul, Wilbur "Yonkie"	Five Crowns
Paul, Wilbur "Yonkie"	Harptones
Payne, Buddy	Continentals (Whirlin' Disc)
Payne, Cooper	Continentals (Whirlin' Disc)
Payne, Gordon	Four Fellows (Glory)
Payne, Pico	Ink Spots
Payne, Pico	Melody Masters
Payton, Jay	Five Rovers
Payton, Jay	Rovers (Music City)
Payton, Jesse	Raiders (Atco)
Payton, Lawrence	Four Tops
Payton, Lawrence	Thrillers (Thriller, Big Town)
Pazman, Bill	Emeralds (ABC)
Peak, Donald	Esco's [sic]
Peak, Donald	Otis Williams & the Charms
Peaker, Franklin	Blue Notes (Josie, Rama, Harthon, etc.)
Peaker, Franklin	Rick & the Masters
Pearl, Jeff	Neons (Tetra)
Pearnell, Zola	Garnet Mimms & the Enchanters
Pearson, Eugene	Cleftones (Gee)
Pearson, Eugene	Drifters (Atlantic)
Pearson, Eugene	Rivileers
Pearson, John	Continentals (Whirlin' Disc)
Pearson, John	Velours
Pease, Bob	Three Keys
Peay, Benjamin	Sandmen
Pecot, Beverly	Ivy Leaguers
Pecot, Beverly	Six Teens
Pecot, Beverly	Sweet Teens
Pedrick, Robert John	Bobby & the Consoles
Peebles, Lou	Five Satins
Peebles, Lou	New Yorkers Five
Peebles, Louis	Wildwoods
Peeler, Kent	Dreamers (Grand)
Peeler, Kent	Universals (Mark-X)
Peels, Leon	Blue Jays (Milestone)
Peels, Leon	Hi Tensions
Peeples, Esther	Passionettes
Pegues, Lee	Deltones
Pegues, Leo	Marvells (Magnet)
Pendergrass, Larry	Chanters
Pendergrass, Larry	Voices Five

Performer	Group
Pipkin, Chester	Blue Jays (Bluejay, Dig)
Pipkin, Chester	Electras (Cee Jam, Challenge, Infinity)
Pipkin, Chester	Happy Tones
Pipkin, Chester	Squires (Vita, Mambo)
Pipkin, Chester	Untouchables
Pipkin, Chester	Valiants (Keen)
Pipkin, Gary	Alley Cats
Pipkin, Gary	Electras (Cee Jam, Challenge, Infinity)
Pipkin, Jimmy	Gallahads
Pirollo, Junior	4 Js
Pirollo, Junior	Fabulous Four
Pirollo, Junior	Four Naturals
Piro, Jimmy	Cirino & the Bowties
Pitman, Howard	Five Chances
Pitt, Eugene	Genies
Pitt, Eugene	Jive Five
Pittman, Kipling	Sentimentals (Tuxedo, Checker, Minit)
Pittman, Robert	Swallows (King, Federal, After Hours)
Pitts, Alfred	Fantastics (RCA)
Pitts, Alfred	Velours
Pitts, Joe	Camelots
Pitts, Joe	Paragons
Pizzoferato, Joe	Antones
Platt, Mathew	Turbans (Herald)
Plummer, Earl	Four Blues
Plummer, Earl	Red Caps/Five Red Caps
Plummer, Earl	Romaines
Poindexter, James	Drifters (Atlantic)
Poitier, George	Mint Juleps
Poitier, George "Val"	Dreamtones (Klik, Express, Astra)
Polimos, Frank	Premiers (Alert)
Poliuto, Val	Ambers
Poliuto, Val	Jaguars
Polk, Harry	Bon Bon Trio
Pollard, Averill "Rill"	Tiger Haynes & the Three Flames
Pollard, Ray	Singing Wanderers
Pollard, Ray	Wanderers
Poloney, John	Intentions (Jamie)
Polts, Sylvester	Hi-Fidelities
Pope, Andrew	Beltones (Hull)
Pope, Charles	Tams
Pope, Joe	Tams
Pope, Walter	Del Roys
Porter, Arthur	Wigs
Porter, Donald	Spaniels
Porter, Dorsey	Students
Porter, Forest	Four Pharaohs
Porter, Forest	Supremes (Ace)
Porter, James	Skarlettones
Porter, James Arnold	Billy Wells & the Crescents

Performer	Group
Porter, Johnny	Four Tones
Porter, Johnny	Dusty Brooks & the Four Tones
Porter, Johnny	Dusty Brooks & the Four Tones with Raymond Wheaton
Porter, Wyndham	Miriam Grate & the Dovers
Porter, Wyndham "Corky"	Vocaltones
Potter, Duval	Carousels (Gone)
Potter, Duval	Rainbows
Potter, Jerry	Fascinators (Your Copy, Blue Lake)
Potts, Hattie	Rudy Jackson & the Mel-O-Aires
Potts, Sylvester	Hi-Fidelities
Potts, Sylvester	Contours
Potts, Vera	Rudy Jackson & the Mel-O-Aires
Pought, Emma	Bobbettes
Pought, Jannie	Bobbettes
Pounds, George	Cherokees
Povenelli, Eddie	Motions (Laurie)
Powell, Austin	Austin Powell Quartet
Powell, Austin	Cats and the Fiddle
Powell, Austin	James Quintet
Powell, Austin	Tympany Five
Powell, Charles	Desires
Powell, Elmer	Carpets
Powell, Estelle	Belltones (Grand)
Powell, Helen	Chantels
Powell, Helen	Clickettes
Powell, Jesse	Jesse Powell & the Caddys
Powell, Joe	Vocaleers
Powell, Monroe	Billy Ward & the Dominoes
Powell, Monroe	Ink Spots
Powell, Monroe	Platters
Powell, William	Mascots (King)
Powell, William	O'Jays
Power, Lonlie	Five Chimes (Ebony)
Powers, Bob	Billy Vera & the Contrasts
Powers, Lloyd	Don Julian & the Meadowlarks
Powers, William	Paradons
Powers, William	Scarlets
Prahovic, Karen	Syncopates
Prater, Carlton	Gazelles
Pratt, Milton	Camelots
Prayer, George	Major-Minors
Prayer, George	Moroccos
Presbury, Stephen	Dreams (Savoy)
Presbury, Stephen	Kenny Esquire & the Starlites

680 • Appendix

Performer	Group
Presti, Charles	Concords (Rust, RCA, Herald)
Preter, Mickey	Hollyhocks
Price, Archie	Eddie & the Starlites
Price, Earl	Del-Vons
Price, Elijah	Eli & the Manhattans
Price, Ernie	Cats and the Fiddle
Price, Freddie	Nite Caps
Price, Gene	Basin Street Boys
Price, Reggie	Cameos (Cameo)
Price, Reggie	Turbans (Herald)
Price, Reggie "Tootie"	Quadrells
Price, Reggie "Tootie"	Universals (Ascot)
Price, Willie	Drivers
Primola, Anthony	Unknowns (X-Tra)
Primrose, William	Coolbreezers
Prince, Mark	Velvets (Monument)
Prince, Norman	Trinidads
Pritchett, Louis	Four Gents
Pritchett, Louis	Twi-Lites (M-Pac)
Profit, Sam	Stereos
Prophet, Thurmon "Billy"	Jive Five
Pruett, Billy	Don Julian & the Meadowlarks
Pruitt, Herman	Calvanes
Pruitt, Herman	Nuggets (RCA)
Pruitt, Herman	Preludes (Empire)
Pruitt, Herman	Tempters (Empire)
Pruitt, Herman	Youngsters (Empire)
Pruitt, John	Cavaliers (nonrecording)
Pruitt, John	Sheppards (Theron, United)
Pryor, Richard	Ruby & the Romantics
Pugh, David	Beale Street Boys
Pugh, James	Beale Street Boys
Purdie, Bernie	Avalons
Puzey, Leonard	Cues
Puzey, Leonard	Dappers (Groove, Rainbow)
Puzey, Leonard	Hi-Hatters
Puzey, Leonard	Ink Spots
Puzey, Leonard	Ravens
Puzey, Leonard	Raves
Pyne, Tommy	Clientelles
Questel, Connie	Connie & the Decoys
Quick, Clarence	Del Vikings
Quick, Clarence	Eastmen
Quick, Malcomb	Connie & the Decoys
Quinn, Eddie	Mellokings
Quinones, Eddie	Glow Tones (Atlantic)
Quinones, Eddie	Miriam Grate & the Dovers
Quinones, Eddie	Vocaltones

Performer	Group
Raabe, William	Camerons (Cousins)
Rabun, Arthur	Souvenirs (Dooto)
Rabun, Otis	Souvenirs (Dooto)
Racano, Marie	Ricky & the Vacels
Racano, Ricky	Ricky & the Vacels
Racano, Vito	Ricky & the Vacels
Radicello, Geno	Five Boroughs
Rafael, Don	Blue Stars
Raguso, Joe	Belltones (J&S, Scatt)
Raguso, Joe	Dials (Philips)
Raia, Frank	Treble Chords
Rainge, Carl	Spaniels
Rainwater, Arthur	Basin Street Boys
Rakestraw, Fred	Magnificents
Ramirez, William	Chessmen (Relic)
Ramos, Jerome	Fantastics (RCA)
Ramos, Jerome "Romeo"	Velours
Ramos, Ralph	Lewis Lymon & the Teenchords
Ramos, Ralph	Townsmen (PJ)
Ramsey, Richard Lee	Lucky Charms
Ramsey, Thurman "Ray"	Magnificents
Randa, Lenny	Impalas (Cub)
Randall, Todd	Blue Notes (Josie, Rama, Harthon, etc.)
Randazzo, John	Montereys (Blast)
Randazzo, Teddy	Teddy Randazzo & the Three Chuckles
Randell, Jimmy	Cobras (Modern)
Randolph, LeRoy	Caverliers Quartet
Randolph, Robert	Pastels (United)
Randolph, Roger	Orlandos
Rangone, Frank	Dials (Philips)
Rankings, Wade	Mississippi Mud Mashers
Rasulo, Joe	Dials (Philips)
Ratliffe, Earl	Four Sharps
Rausch, Tony	Chapelaires
Raven, Genya	Escorts (Coral)
Ray, Ada	Jaynetts (Tuff, J&S)
Ray, Carmine	Rockin' Chairs
Ray, Harvey	Du Droppers
Ray, Willie	Bells (Rama)
Ray, Willie	Dixieaires
Ray, Willie	Du Droppers
Ray, Willie	Ravens
Ray, Willie	Valiants (Joy, Cortlandt)
Razor, Donald	Johnny Blake & the Clippers
Razor, Donald	Valentines
Razor, Donald	Velvets (Red Robin)
Razor, Joe	Velvets (Red Robin)
Reader, Raymond	Cap-Tans
Reagan, Glen	Don Julian & the Meadowlarks

Performer	Group
Record, Eugene "Gino"	Chanteurs
Record, Eugene "Gino"	Chi-Lites
Redd, Bob	Mello-Moods (nonrecording)
Redd, Donald	Starlings (Josie, Dawn)
Redd, Donald	Twilighters (MGM)
Redd, Gene	Chimes (Royal Roost, Betta)
Redd, Gene	FiTones
Redd, Gene	Five Chimes, (Royal Roost, Betta)
Reddick, Clyde	Dixieaires
Redmond, Freddie	Elegants
Redmond, Lovelace	Supremes Four (Sara)
Reed, Herb	Platters
Reed, Jerry	Wisdoms
Reed, Johnny	Orioles
Reed, Joseph "Rice"	Magic Tones
Reed, Larry	Orioles
Reed, Rip	Gems (Drexel)
Reed, Theotis	Upfronts
Reed, Willie	Vocaltones
Reese, Isaac	Muskateers [sic]
Reese, Isaac	Royal Jokers
Reese, Isaac	Royals (Venus)
Reese, Isaac	Serenaders (JVB, Red Robin, Coral, Swing Time)
Reese, Isaac	Scooters (Dawn)
Reeves, Jean	Cashmeres (Lake, Laurie, Josie, ACA)
Reeves, Martha	Martha & the Vandellas
Regal, Mike	Bobby Roy & the Chord-A-Roys
Regan, George	Antones
Regan, Michael	Camelots
Reid, Bill	Carnations (Derby, Savoy)
Reid, Brenda	Exciters
Reid, Ray	Melody Kings
Reid, Raymond	Jubalaires
Reid, Raymond	Shadows (Lee)
Reina, Frank	Capris (Planet, Old Town, etc.)
Reina, Frank	Debonaires (Gee)
Relf, Bobby	Crescendos (Atlantic)
Relf, Bobby	Laurels (Combo, X. Flair)
Relf, Bobby	Lovers
Relf, Bobby	Phantoms
Relf, Bobby	Upfronts
Renko, Tommy	Chaperones
Reno, Al	Regents
Reuth, Joe	Coolbreezers
Rex, Sterling	Dinwiddie Colored Quartet

Performer	Group
Reyes, Tommy	Chessmen (Relic)
Reynolds, Charlie	Channels (Mercury)
Reynolds, James	Edsels
Reynolds, Lee	Fireflies
Rhymes, Clyde	Rhythm Aces (Vee Jay)
Riccobene, Bobby	Vespers (Laurie)
Rice, Cliff	Eddie & the Starlites
Rice, Cliff	Starlites (Peak)
Rice, Luther	Chandeliers
Rice, Mack	Falcons (Mercury, United Artists, Chess, LuPine)
Rice, Mack	Five Scalders
Rice, Vic	Eddie & the Starlites
Rice, Vic	Starlites (Peak)
Rice, Victor	Verdicts
Rice, V.	Five Du-Tones
Richard, Billy	Nic Nacs
Richard, Billy	Robins
Richard, Roy	Nic Nacs
Richard, Roy	Robins
Richards, Ben	Gaylarks
Richardson, Alan	Five Crystals
Richardson, Bob	Twilighters (Marshall)
Richardson, Duke	Original Drifters
Richardson, Earl	Fascinators (Your Copy, Blue Lake)
Richardson, George	Lucky Charms
Richardson, Jimmy	Squires (Combo)
Richardson, Johnnie	Hearts (Baton)
Richardson, Johnnie	Jaynetts (Tuff, J&S)
Richardson, Leroy	Lucky Charms
Richardson, Stanley	Cyclones
Richardson, Stanley	Pharaohs (Specialty)
Richardson, Van Earl	Blue Jays (Milestone)
Richie, Bubba	Ravens
Richie, Ronald	Capris (nonrecording)
Rich, Eddie	Honeyboys
Rich, Eddie	Marquis (Rainbow)
Rich, Eddie	Swallows (King, Federal, After Hours)
Ricketts, James	Roamers (Savoy)
Ricks, Jimmy	Adolphus Holcomb & the Kings
Ricks, Jimmy	Cardinals
Ricks, Jimmy	Ravens
Ricks, Jimmy	Raves
Ricks, Jimmy	Rickateers
Ricks, Jimmy	Smiley Moon & the Moontunes
Ricks, Tommy	Dreamlovers
Ricks, Vernon	Four Bel-Aires (X-Tra)
Ricks, Vernon	Larry Lee & the Four Bel-Aires

Performer	Group	Performer	Group
Ricks, Warren	Four Bel-Aires (X-Tra)	Robinson, Bill	Miracles
Ricks, Warren	Larry Lee & the Four Bel-Aires	"Smokey"	
		Robinson, Bobby	Gems (Drexel)
Riddick, Claude	Billy Williams Quartet,	Robinson, Bruce	Buckeyes
Riddick, Clyde	Golden Gate Quartet	Robinson, Bruce	Stereos
Riggins, Michael	Sentimentals (Tuxedo,	Robinson,	Miracles
	Checker, Minit)	Claudette Rogers	
Rigsby, Clarence	Velvets (Monument)	Robinson, Doc	Russ Riley & the Five
Riley, Castella	Sharmeers		Sounds
Riley, James	Rhythm Kings	Robinson, Earl	Five Scamps
Riley, James	Rhythm Masters	Robinson, Jackie	Kac-Ties
Riley, Ralph	Cashmeres (Mercury,	Robinson, Jay	Supremes (Ace)
	Herald)	Robinson, Jerome	Dappers (Groove,
Riley, Vernon	Collegians (X-Tra)		Rainbow)
Riley, William	Russ Riley & the Five	Robinson, Jerry	Bill Johnson's Musical
"Russ"	Sounds		Notes
Rios, Victor	Eddie Friend & the	Robinson, Julius	Buccaneers
	Empires (Colpix)	Robinson, Julius	Metronomes (Winn)
Ripperton, Minnie	Gems (Chess)	Robinson, Kathleen	Versalettes
Rivera, Bobby	Townsmen (PJ)	Spates	
Rivera, Gilbert	Youngtones	Robinson, Mike	Orioles
Rivera, Willie	Youngtones	Robinson, Mike	Vibes
Rivers, Bob	Fascinators (Your Copy,	Robinson, Mike	Vibranaires
	Blue Lake)	Robinson, Oscar	Cavaliers (nonrecording)
Rivers, Bobby	Russ Riley & the Five	Robinson, Oscar	Five Thrills
	Sounds	Robinson, Oscar	Sheppards (Theron,
Rivers, Horace	Wisdoms		United)
Rivers, Joe	Climbers	Robinson, Ray	Gallahads
Rixner, Germaine	Tropicals	Robinson, Robbie	Billy Ward & the
Roache, James	Vibes		Dominoes
Roache, James	Vibranaires	Robinson, Robbie	Flares
Roberts, Clarence	Master Keys	Robinson, Willie C.	Cascades
Roberts, Clayton	Incas (Roadhouse)	Robinson, Willie C.	Pace Setters
Roberts, Clayton	Ontarios	Robinson, Willie C.	Von Gayles
Roberts, Edward	Ruby & the Romantics	Robles, Joe	Excels (Central, Gone)
Roberts, George	Master Keys	Rocca, Rossilio	Louis Lymon & the
Roberts, James	Darnell & the Dreams		Teenchords
Roberts, Lloyd	Splendors (Taurus)	Rockland, Damond	Pyramids (Cub, Vee Jay)
Robertson, Andrew	Pace Setters	Rockwell, Willie	Flames
Robertson, Bob	Gladiolas	Ray	
Robertson, Bob	Zodiacs	Rockwell, Willie	Four Flames (Fidelity,
Robeson, James	Mississippi Mud Mashers	Ray	Specialty)
Robi, Paul	Mello-Moods	Rockwell, Willie	Hollywood Flames
	(nonrecording)	Ray	
Robi, Paul	Platters	Rockwell, Willie	Hollywood Four Flames
Robinson, Albert	Four Bel-Aires (X-Tra)	Ray	
Robinson, Albert	Larry Lee & the Four	Rockwell, Willie	Lamplighters
	Bel-Aires	Ray	
Robinson, Arnet	Fabulous Playboys	Rockwell, Willie	Tenderfoots
Robinson, Arnet	Falcons (Mercury,	Ray	
	United Artists, Chess,	Roddi, Johnny	Roger & the Travelers
	LuPine)	Rodgers, Jesse	Goldenrods (Vee Jay)
Robinson, Art	Shades (Christy)	Rodriguez, George	Cathy Jean & the
Robinson, Bill	Bill Robinson & the		Roommates
	Quails	Rodriguez, Jerry	Orioles
Robinson, Bill	Chimes (Specialty)	Rodriguez, Jerry	Regals
"Smokey"			

Performer	Group
Rodriguez, Lara	Crystals (Delano)
Rogers, Bobby	Carl Hogan & the Miracles
Rogers, Bobby	Miracles (Tamla)
Rogers, Carl	Drivers
Rogers, Claudette	Miracles (Tamla)
Rogers, Corky	Five Satins
Rogers, Corky	Revalons
Rogers, Corky	Revlons
Rogers, Ed	Majestics (20th Fox)
Rogers, Gloucester	Little Anthony & the Imperials
Rogers, Gloucester	Mints
Rogers, Glouster "Nat"	Chesters
Rohan, Skippy	No-Names (Guyden)
Roker, Wally	Heartbeats (Hull, Rama, etc.)
Roker, Wally	Solitaires
Roland, Ricky	Kinglets (Calvert, Bobbin')
Roland, Willie	Sharptones (Aladdin)
Roland, Willie	Turbans (Money)
Romaine, Fred	Ebb-Tones
Romaine, Fred	Native Boys
Roma, Mike	Aquatones
Roman, Junior	Five Jades
Romano, Carman	Elegants
Romano, Carman	Pat Cordel & the Crescents
Romano, Carman	Pat Cordell & the Elegants
Romano, Tommy	Teddy Randazzo & the Three Chuckles
Ronka, Tony	Chaperones
Rooney, Herb	Beltones (Hull)
Rooney, Herb	Exciters
Rooney, Herb	Masters (Bingo)
Ropers, John	Bob Knight Four
Rosado, Hector	Five Jades
Rosa, George	Five Delights
Rosemond, Harry	Native Boys
Rosemond, Manny	Four Dots (Bullseye, Freedom)
Rosemond, Manny	Lyrics (Cleveland)
Rosenberg, Al	Heartbeats (Jubilee)
Rosenberg, Marv	Angels (Tawny)
Rosenberg, Marv	Dories
Rosenberg, Marv	Enchanters (Orbit)
Rosenberg, Marv	Safaris (Eldo)
Rosenberg, Marv	Suddens
Rosenberg, Richard	Escorts (Coral)
Rose, Robert	Five Lyrics
Rose, Robert	Lyrics (Music City)
Rose, Wallace	Lovenotes (Riviera, Rainbow)

Performer	Group
Ross, Clarence	Harmonizing Four
Ross, Diana	Primettes
Ross, Diana	Supremes (Motown)
Ross, Edward	Huey Smith & the Clowns
Ross, James	Heartbreakers (RCA)
Ross, Josephine	Passionettes
Ross, Pat	Mel-O-Dots
Ross, William	Griffins
Ross, William	Heartbreakers (RCA)
Rotundo, Lou	Passions
Roundtree, Huey	Pipes
Rouse, Ernie	Gallahads
Rowan, Chuck (Chet)	Rhythm Aces (Vee Jay)
Rowan, Chuck (Chet)	Rocketeers (Modern, MJC)
Rowan, Chuck (Chet)	Rockets (Modern)
Rowe, Haddie	Larks
Roy, Dudley	"Fat Man" Mathews & the Four Kittens
Royal, Isaac	Ink Spots
Royal, Isaac	Rhythm Kings
Rucker, Sam	Velvetones (Sonora, Coronet)
Rudolph, Donald	Dukays
Rue, Frank	Variety Boys
Rue, Jackie	Five Wings
Rue, Jackie	Jackie & the Starlites
Rue, Wilson	Dell Pris
Ruff, Jimmy	Criterions
Ruff, Jimmy	Kents (Aljon)
Ruff, Joe	Russ Riley & the Five Sounds
Ruff, Nathaniel	Jarmels
Ruffin, Bobby	Drifters (Atlantic)
Ruffin, Bobby	Royal Jokers
Ruffin, Bobby	Scooters (Dawn)
Ruffin, David	Temptations (Gordy)
Ruffin, David	Voice Masters
Ruffin, Grace	Four Jewels (Checker, Dimension)
Ruffin, Grace	Impalas (Checker)
Ruffin, Grace	Jewels (Dimension)
Ruffin, Paul	L'Cap-Tans
Ruffin, Paul	Maskman & the Agents
Ruiz, Plinius	Universals (Festival)
Runnells, Sidney	Phantoms
Rushing, Frank	"Fat Man" Mathews & the Four Kittens
Rush, John L.	Bobby Hall & the Kings
Rush, Keith	Blue Jays (Milestone)
Russaw, Lester	Coronets
Russell, Al	Al Russell Trio
Russell, Al "Diz"	Regals
Russell, Al "Stomp"	Do Re Mi Trio

Performer	Group
Russell, Albert "Diz"	Orioles
Russell, Harvey	Wonders (Ember)
Russell, John	Five Discs
Russell, Lily	Azaleas (Romulus)
Russell, Patty	Patty & the Emblems
Russell, Robert	Bachelors (Aladdin, Royal Roost)
Russell, Robert	Clovers
Russell, Robert	Four Bel-Aires (X-Tra)
Russell, Robert	Jets (Rainbow)
Russo, Bernie	Loungers
Russo, Bernie	Secrets (Decca)
Russo, Pat	Five Secrets (Decca)
Russo, Pat	Loungers
Russo, Pat	Secrets (Decca)
Russo, Sal	Camelots
Rutledge, Alan	Saigons
Ruth, Thermon	Cleartones
Ruth, Thermon	Larks
Ryanes, John	Monotones
Ryanes, Warren	Monotones
Ryder, Junior	Peacocks
Sachs, Emil	Concepts (ABC)
Sachs, Emil	Treble Chords
Safuto, Dominick "Randy"	Randy & the Rainbows
Safuto, Frank	Randy & the Rainbows
Salemme, Diane	Admirations
Salvi, Mike	Three Vales
Salvato, John	Duprees
Salvato, Nick	Chaperones
Salzman, Jimmy	Durhams
Sampson, Charles	Velvets (Red Robin)
Sampson, Lee	Cashmeres (Mercury, Herald)
Sampson, Wallace	Radiants (Chess)
Samuels, Bill	Cats and Jammer Three
Samuels, Bill	Royals (Apollo)
Samuels, William	Casanovas
Samuels, William	Five Royales
Sanchez, Diana	Claremonts
Sanchez, Diana	Tonettes
Sanchez, Eugene	Enchantments (Ritz)
Sanchez, Phil	Excellents (Mermaid, Blast)
Sanchez, Ray	Devotions
Sanchez, Sylvia	Claremonts
Sanchez, Sylvia	Tonettes
Sanciglia, Peggy	Angels (Caprice, RCA)
Sanders, Barbara	Eddie Cooley & the Dimples
Sanders, Bobby	Extremes (Paro)
Sanders, Bobby	Wil-Sones (Highland)
Sanders, Bobby W.	Tenderfoots

Performer	Group
Sanders, Edward "Edgy"	Volchords
Sanders, Leroy	Cubans (Flash)
Sanders, Leroy	Cufflinx
Sanders, Leroy	Maharajahs (Flip)
Sanders, Leroy	Little Caesar & the Romans
Sanders, Leroy	Upfronts
Sanders, Marcel	Prisonaires
Sanders, Sonny	Fidelitones
Sanders, Sonny	Satintones
Sanders, William "Sonny"	Sax Kari & the Quailtones
Sanders, William "Sonny"	Satintones
Sanders, Willis	Bells (Rama)
Sanders, Willis	Bill Cook & the Marshalls
Sanders, Willis	Marshall Brothers
Sanford, Bill	Four Vagabonds
San Pietro, Frankie	Lewis Lymon & the Teenchords
Santamaria, Nick	Capris (Planet, Old Town, etc.)
Santiago, George	Eternals
Santiago, Herman	Frankie Lymon & the Teenagers
Santollo, Joe	Duprees
Santorelli, Vinnie	Five Secrets
Santorelli, Vinnie	Loungers
Santorelli, Vinnie	Secrets
Santos, Teddy	Love Notes (Riviera, Rainbow)
Sanzone, Paul	Ovations (Laurie)
Sapp, J.	Gotham's Four Notes
Sapp, James	Four Notes (Premier)
Saranievo, Bobby	Fireflies
Sasso, Mel	Rochell & the Candles
Saulsberry, Walter	Penguins
Saulsbury, Hubert	Pyramids (Davis)
Saulter, John	Jivers (Aladdin)
Saunders, Bernardo	Big Three Trio
Saunders, Butchie	Elchords
Saunders, Charles	Eddie & the Starlites
Saunders, Charles	Starlites
Saunders, Danny	Don Julian & the Meadowlarks
Saunders, Dick	Three Giants of Rhythm
Saunders, Ed	Native Boys
Saunders, Homer	Parakeets (Roadhouse)
Saunders, "Little" Butchie	Vells
Saunders, Long	Sweet Teens
Saunders, Marion	Escorts (Premium)
Saunders, Nick	Cleftones (Gee)
Saunders, Reuben	Basin Street Boys

Performer	Group	Performer	Group
Saunders, Willis	Bells (Rama)	Scott, Harold	Rhythm Kings
Saunders, Willis	Ravens	Scott, Harold	Rhythm Masters
Savastano, Bob	Chaps	Scott, Harrison	Capris (Gotham)
Saxon, John	Cufflinx	Scott, Howard	Masquerades (Formal,
Saxton, Kerry	Jimmy Jones & the		Boyd, Joyce)
	Pretenders	Scott, Howard	Rhythm Kings
Saxton, Kerry	Jimmy Jones & the Savoys	Scott, James	El Capris (Bullseye, Fee
Sayles, John	Cameos (Cameo, Johnson,		Bee)
"Buster"	Matador)	Scott, Jimmy	Chargers
Scalpati, Louis	Ray & the Darchaes	Norman	
Scandura, Jack	Blue Stars	Scott, Jimmy	Coasters
Scardina, Charlie	Clusters	Norman	
Scarpa, William	Shy-Tones	Scott, Jimmy	Dyna-Soars
Scavuzzo, Albert	Hi-Tones (King, Fonsca,	Norman	
	Candix)	Scott, Kurtis	Capitols, (Pet)
Scavuzzo, Albert	Shy-Tones	(Kurt Harris)	
Scavuzzo, Peter	Hi-Tones (King, Fonsca,	Scott, Kurtis	Five Discs
	Candix)	(Kurt Harris)	
Schalda, Billy	Montereys (Blast)	Scott, Kurtis	Revalons
Schein, Al	Eltones	(Kurt Harris)	
Schleiffer, Nat	Bobby & the Consoles	Scott, Kurtis	Tokens (Gary)
Schmidt, Bill	Chapelaires	(Kurt Harris)	
Schmidt, Richard	Fantasys (Guyden)	Scott, LaMont	Five Swans (Music City)
Schneider, Bobby	Personalities	Scott, Lannie	Ben Smith Quartet
Schneller, Paul	Norman Fox & the Rob	Scott, Marcel	Crystals (Specialty)
	Roys	Scott, Melvin	Metrotones (Reserve)
Schofield, Willie	Falcons (Mercury,	Scott, Otis	Medallions
	United Artists, Chess,	Scott, Robert	Masquerades
	LuPine)	Scott, Ronnie	Quintones
Scholl, Bob	Mellokings	Scott, Sam	Teardrops (Sampson)
Scholl, Jerry	Mellokings	Scott, Teddy	G-Clefs
Schrager, Paul	Eltones	Scott, Timmy	G-Clefs
Schwartz, Richie	Quotations	Scott, Tommy	Masquerades (Formal,
Schwartz, Warren	Darrell & the Oxfords		Boyd, Joyce)
Scolski, Bobby	Nicky Addeo & the	Scott, Walter	Masquerades (Formal,
	Plazas		Boyd, Joyce)
Scott, Alan	Canaanites	Scott, Winfield	Cues
Scott, Alan	Joe Van Loan Quartet,	(Robey Kirkland)	
Scott, Alex	Pitter Pats	Scrofani, Rick	Ducanes
Scott, Allen	Bachelors (Earl)	Scroggins, Virgil	Spirits of Rhythm
Scott, Allen	Bachelors (Mercury,	Scruggs, Bill	Ronnie & the Hi-Lites
	Songmaster)	Scruggs, James	Magnificents
Scott, Alvin	Majors (Derby)	Scruggs, Ted	Sax Kari & the
Scott, Arnold	G-Clefs		Quailtones
Scott, Charles	Hesitations	Scudder, Timmy	Tabbys
Scott, Charles	Masquerades (Formal,	Seahorn, Marshall	Zodiacs
	Boyd, Joyce)	Seamen, Alfred	Orients
Scott, Chester	Royal Holidays (Carlton,	Seamen, Ernest	Orients
	Herald)	Seavers, Vernon	Heartbeats (Hull, Rama,
Scott, Chris	G-Clefs		etc.)
Scott, Clarence	Castelles (Grand)	Sedaka, Neil	Tokens
Scott, Edward	Paradons	Sedlock, Dick	Three Vales
Scott, Essex	Ink Spots	Seider, Steve	Concords (Rust, RCA,
Scott, George	Diablos		Herald)
Scott, George	El Pollos	Seneca, Joe	Three Barons (Savoy)
Scott, George	Hesitations	Seneca, Joe	Three Riffs
Scott, Gordon	Four Fellows (Glory)	Senzan, Allan	Accents (Sultan)

Performer	Group
Senzan, Allan	Dreamers (Guaranteed)
Sepaldo, Vince	Cirino & the Bowties
Sereno, Del	Cirino & the Bowties
Serrao, Bobby	Bay Bops
Sessoms, Isaiah	Norfolk Jazz Quartet
Sewell, Joe	Nite Riders
Sewell, Marshall	Edsels
Sexton, Kenneth	Quintones (Chess, Red Top, Hunt)
Seymour, Clarence	Five Chimes (Ebony)
Seymour, Kenny	Larry Chance & the Earls (ABC)
Seymour, Kenny	Impacts (RCA, Watts)
Seymour, Kenny	Little Anthony & the Imperials
Sfraga, Tom	Emanons (Winley, ABC)
Shankowitz, Gregory	Bradford Boys (Rainbow)
Sharp, Alexander	Al Jackson's Fat Men
Sharp, Alexander	Ink Spots
Sharp, Alexander	Orioles
Shaw, Anderson	Paul Breckinridge and the Four Heavenly Knights
Shaw, Kenneth	Metronomes (Specialty)
Shaw, Michael	Charm
Shaw, Phil	Five Swans (Music City)
Shaw, Phil	Marshall Brothers
Shea, Frank	Romaines
Shedrick, Jackie	Five Blue Notes (Sabre, Onda)
Sheely, Jerry	Jerry Sheely & the Versatiles
Sheen, Bobby	Alley Cats
Sheen, Bobby	Blue Jeans
Sheen, Bobby	Coasters
Sheffield, David	Chanteclaires
Sheffield, Donald	Sonics (X-Tra)
Shelbourne, James	Romancers
Shelby, Elizabeth	Sweet Teens
Shellbourne, James	Lyrics (Rhythm)
Shelton, Tom	Falcons (Mercury, United Artists, Chess, LuPine)
Shepard, Joe	Corvairs (Comet, Leopard)
Sheppard, Bob	Hesitations
Sheppard, Bob	Metrotones
Sheppard, James	Clefs
Sheppard, James "Shane"	Heartbeats (Hull, Rama, etc.)
Sheppard, James "Shane"	Shep & the Limelites
Sheppard, Rick	Drifters (Atlantic)
Sheppard, Robert	5 Jades (Duke)
Sherell, Ed	Mobile Four
Sherman, Robert	Bill Robinson & the Quails
Sherman, Ronald	Serenades (Chief)
Shields, Harold	Dell Pris
Shields, Nelson	Corvairs (Comet, Leopard)
Shields, Nelson	Leaders
Shields, Nelson	Velours
Shiloh, Joe	Lovenotes (Holiday)
Shingle, Jack	Clientelles
Shoup, Jimmy	Dynamics (Cindy, Seeco, Dynamic, etc.)
Showell, Al	Dappers (Groove, Rainbow)
Shufford, Henry	Four Deuces
Shuh, Hank	Corvets (Laurel)
Shuler, Romeo	Cashmeres (Mercury, Herald)
Siciliano, Louie	Ray & the Darchaes
Siciliano, Pat	Ray & the Darchaes
Siciliano, Sam	Ray & the Darchaes
Sidney, Oliver	Chateaus
Siebrich, Dom	Emeralds (ABC)
Siegal, Jay	Darrell & the Oxfords
Sierra, Ernie	Eternals
Sierra, Richie	Eternals
Silenzio, Mikey	Rick & the Masters
Simmons, Alonzo	Knickerbockers
Simmons, Chester	Marquees (Okeh)
Simmons, Chester	Moonglows (RCA)
Simmons, Chester	Rainbows
Simmons, Donald	Vibraharps
Simmons, Gary	Sentimentals (Tuxedo, Checker, Minit)
Simmons, Joe	Bennie Woods & the Five Dukes
Simmons, Joe	Rockin' Townies
Simmons, Joe	Five Dollars
Simmons, Johnny	Cubans (Flash)
Simmons, Johnny	Cufflinx
Simmons, Johnny	Little Caesar & the Romans
Simmons, Pete	Spaniels
Simmons, Reginald	Starlarks (Ember)
Simmons, Roosevelt	Sensations
Simmons, Roosevelt	Universals (Mark-X, Cora Lee, Ascot)
Simms, Frank	Five Chances
Simon, Arthur	Debonaires
Simon, Arthur	Five Debonaires
Simon, Calvin	Parliaments (Len)
Simon, Kenny	Serenaders (Chief, MGM, Rae Cox)
Simon, Paul	Mystics (Laurie)
Simon, Paul	Tico & the Triumphs
Simon, Richard	Willows (Melba)
Simons, Gus	Day, Dawn & Dusk
Simpkins, Arthur Lee	Charioteers

Performer	Group
Simpkins, Maurice	Five Chimes (Ebony)
Simpson, Charles	Leaders
Simpson, Della	Delltones
Simpson, Della	Enchanters (Jubilee)
Simpson, Wallace	Radiants (Chess)
Simpson, Walter	Four Deuces
Sims, Constant "Count"	Five Echoes (Sabre)
Sims, Gerald	Daylighters
Sims, James	Mints
Sims, Pringle	Four Fellows (Glory)
Sims, Pringle "Yeoman"	Strangers
Sinclair, Carl	Elgins (Flip, Lummtone)
Sinclair, Kenneth	Colognes
Sinclair, Kenneth	Elements (Titan)
Sinclair, Kenneth	Elgins (Flip, Lummtone)
Sinclair, Kenneth	Olympics
Sinclair, Kenneth	Six Teens
Sinclair, Kenneth	Sweet Teens
Singleterry, Walter	Lyres
Singleton, Al	Keystoners
Singleton, George "Bebo"	Rhythm Cadets
Singleton, Jimmy	Eldaros
Slater, Chester	Harlemaires
Slaughter, Alfred "Buddy"	Cap-Tans
Slaughter, Arthur	Personalities
Slay, Emmitt	Cats and the Fiddle
Slay, Emmitt	Emmitt Slay Trio
Slebrich, Dom	Emeralds (ABC)
Small, Daniel	Shells
Small, Ronald	Fabulous Pearls (Dooto)
Small, Ronald	Four Pearls (Dolton)
Smalls, James	Kac-Ties
Smalls, Joseph	Four Students
Smalls, Louis	Five Blue Notes (Sabre, Onda)
Smarr, Morris "Mickey"	Bop Chords
Smart, Bobby	Capris (Gotham)
Smith, Adolph	Mellow Drops (Imperial)
Smith, Adolph	Monitors (Specialty, Aladdin)
Smith, Adolph	Señors (Sue)
Smith, Al	Savoys (Combo)
Smith, Andrew	Fasinoles
Smith, Andrew	Maples (Blue Lake)
Smith, Andy	Barries (Ember)
Smith, Annette	Chantels
Smith, Annette	Veneers
Smith, Anthony "Jimmy"	Jesters
Smith, Arlene	Chantels
Smith, Arlene	Clusters
Smith, Ben	Ben Smith Quartet

Performer	Group
Smith, Billy Dawn	Donny Myles & the Dukes
Smith, Billy Dawn	Heralds
Smith, Billy Dawn	Billy Dawn Quartet
Smith, Billy Dawn	Four Dukes
Smith, Billy Dawn	Mighty Dukes (Duke)
Smith, Bobby	Spinners (Motown, Tri-Phi)
Smith, Brad	Tropicals
Smith, Buzzy	Shields
Smith, Byron	Clips (Republic, Calvert)
Smith, Clarence	Fascinators (Your Copy, Blue Lake)
Smith, Curtis	Clips (Republic, Calvert)
Smith, Dickie	Five Keys
Smith, Dottie	Austin Powell Quartet
Smith, Dottie	Cats and the Fiddle
Smith, Dottie	Harlemaires
Smith, Ella	Passionettes
Smith, Ernest "Sonny"	Buccaneers
Smith, Eugene	Kingsmen (Club 51)
Smith, Fletcher	Deeptones
Smith, Fletcher	Four Deeptones
Smith, Fletcher	Hi Lighters (Hico)
Smith, Frank	Monotones
Smith, Fred	Starlighters (End)
Smith, G.	Gotham's Four Notes
Smith, Gene	Four Notes (Premier)
Smith, George	Desires
Smith, George	Four Aces (Trilon)
Smith, George, Jr.	Fasinoles
Smith, Gerald "Buzzy"	Five Sounds
Smith, Gloria	Red Caps/Five Red Caps
Smith, Henry	Informers
Smith, Homer	Southernaires
Smith, Howard "Ghostie"	Syncopaters
Smith, Huey	Huey Smith & the Clowns
Smith, Huey	Kings (Specialty)
Smith, Huey	Pitter Pats
Smith, Jerome "Smitty"	Desires
Smith, Jesse	Marvelows (ABC)
Smith, Jimmy	Dixieaires
Smith, Jimmy	Elements (Titan)
Smith, Jimmy	Elgins (Flip, Lummtone)
Smith, Jimmy	Jesters
Smith, Joan	Passionettes
Smith, John	Little Joey & the Flips
Smith, Johnny	Alphabetical Four
Smith, Johnny	Golden Arrows
Smith, Johnny	Rip Chords
Smith, Johnny	Rivals (Apollo)
Smith, Larry	Castroes (Lasso, Grand)
Smith, Lawson	Four Falcons

Performer	Group	Performer	Group
Springs, Jimmy	Five Jones Boys	Stevens, Ernest	Townsmen (Herald,
Springs, Jimmy	Four Toppers (Savoy)		Ember)
Springs, Jimmy	Jones Boys (Arrow)	Stevens, James	Balladiers
Springs, Jimmy	Jones Boys Sing Band	Stevens, Julie	Premiers (Dig)
Springs, Jimmy	Red Caps/Five Red Caps	Stevens, Mitchell	Dreamers (Grand)
Springs, Jimmy	Steve Gibson & the	Stevens, Oliver	Five Rovers
	Toppers	Stevens, Oliver	Rovers (Music City)
Sproul, Leroy	Dreamers (Grand)	"Sonny"	
Stafford, Jesse	Five Chances	Stevens, Ronnie	Premiers (Gone)
Stafford, John	Valquins/Velquins	Stevenson, W.	Classics (Class, Crest)
Stainback, George	Cats and the Fiddle	Steward, Billy	Magic Notes
Staley, Vernon	Mello Harps	Steward, Billy	Planets (Era)
Stallings, Joe	Pyramids (Davis)	Steward, Billy	Rhythm Aces (Vee Jay)
Stanberry, John	King Krooners (Crooners)	Steward, Billy	Rocketeers (Modern,
Stanford, Frank	Midnighters		MJC)
Stansbury, Carol	Deltairs	Steward, Billy	Rockets (Modern)
Stansbury, Thelma	Deltairs	Steward, Sam	Ideals (Decca, Paso,
Staples, John	Belvederes (Dot, Trend)		Checker)
Staples, John	Four Gents	Stewart, Alonzo	Gondoliers
Staples, Wardell	Five Bells (Clock)	Stewart, Billy	Rainbows (Rama)
Stapleton, Eugene	Dean Barlow & the	Stewart, Billy	Rockets (Modern)
	Crickets	Stewart, Carl	Five Jets (DeLuxe,
Starkes, Doc	Nite Riders		Fortune)
Starr, Mack	Olympics	Stewart, Helen	Caldwells
Starr, Mack	Paragons	Stewart, Jimmy	Cues
Staton, Isaiah	Feathers	Stewart, Jimmy	Ravens
Staton, James	Feathers	Stewart, Randolph	Chanteclaires
Staton, Johnny	Feathers	"Randy"	
Staton, Johnny	Individuals	Stewart, Randy	Fiestas
Staton, Johnny	Unforgettables	Stewart, Renee	Delltones
Staton, Lenora	Feathers	Stewart, Richard	Cap-Tans
Staton, Louis	Feathers	Stewart, Richard	Coolbreezers
Stauch, T.	Emblems	Stewart, Richard	L'Cap-Tans
Steel, Gaines	Stereos	Stewart, Richard	Maskman & the Agents
Steele, Stacy, Jr.	Cascades	Stewart, Robert	Townsmen (Herald,
Steele, Stacy, Jr.	Pace Setters		Ember)
Steele, Stacy, Jr.	Von Gayles	Stewart, Sam	Ideals (Paso)
Steeley, Ralph	Emanons (Gee, Josie)	Stewart, Steve	Tempo-Tones
Steele, John	Five Willows	Stewart, William	Prisonaires
Thomas		Still, Cleveland	Dubs
Steele, John	Willows (Allen, Melba)	Still, Cleveland	Marvels (ABC)
Thomas "Scooter"		Still, Cleveland	Scale-Tones
Stefanelli, Joseph	Savoys (Catamount)	Stillwell, Eddie	Fasinoles
Steger, Bobby	Coasters	Stillwell, Eddie	Five Chances
Steinback, George	Cats and the Fiddle	Stokes, Diason	Honey Boys
Steinberg, Brian	Downbeats	"Dixon"	
Steinberg, Jamie	Downbeats	Stokes, Eddie	Moodmakers
Stemach, Johnny	El Torros	Stokes, Willie	Magic Tones
Stephens, Jim	Safaris (Eldo)	"Ricky"	
Stephens, Jimmy	Suddens	Stone, Albert Jerry	Fascinators (Dootone)
Stephenson,	Drifters (Atlantic)	Stone, Jerry	Four Dots (Bullseye,
Matthew			Freedom)
Stephenson, Walter	Danderliers	Stone, Margaret	Dukays
Stephenson, Willie	Marvelows (ABC)	"Cookie"	
Stevens, Daniel	Diamonds (Atlantic)	Storm, Billy	Charades (Skylor)
Stevens, Don	Inspirations (Apollo,	Storm, Billy	Electras (Cee Jam,
	Lamp)		Challenge, Infinity)

Performer	Group
Storm, Billy	Nuggets (RCA)
Storm, Billy	Squires (Combo)
Storm, Billy	Valiants (Keen)
Storm, Billy	Vanguards
Story, Melvin	Cherokees
Story, Melvin	Cobras (Casino, Swan, Monogram)
Stowers, Robert "Babe"	Marquis (Onyx)
Stowe, Mike	Casanovas
Strain, Sammy	Chips
Strain, Sammy	Fantastics (RCA)
Strain, Sammy	Little Anthony & the Imperials
Strain, Sammy	O'Jays
Straite, James	Mints
Straite, James	Pearl & the Deltars
Straite, James	Young Lads (Neil)
Street, Richard	Temptations (Gordy)
Streeter, Tony	Limelighters
Strider, Charles	Striders
Strider, Gene	Striders
Strider, Jim	Striders
Strogin, Henry	Henry Strogin & the Crowns
Strong, Jimmy	Diablos
Strong, Nolan	Diablos
Strong, Ronald	Premiers (Gone)
Strong, Ronnie	Daylighters
Strong, Ronnie	Delighters
Strong, Ronnie	Fortunes (Parrot, Checker)
Strong, Ronnie	Hambone Kids
Stropoli, Frank	Three Friends (Lido)
Stropoli, Frankie	Heartbeats (Jubilee)
Stroud, Robert	Bluejays (Roadhouse)
Stroud, Robert	Five Blue Notes (Sabre, Onda)
Strum, Dave	Excellents
Strum, Dave	Five Boroughs
Stubbs, Herbert	Versatones
Stubbs, Joe	Contours
Stubbs, Joe	Falcons (Mercury, United Artists, Chess, LuPine)
Stubbs, Joe	Four Tops
Stubbs, Joe	Originals
Stubbs, Levi	Four Falcons
Stubbs, Levi	Four Tops
Stuccio, Emil	Classics (Dart, Mercury, Musicnote)
Suber, William	Egyptin Kings
Sucamele, Joe	Heartbeats (Jubilee)
Suggs, Lula Mae	Shirley Gunter & the Queens
Sullivan, Albert	Four Gents
Sullivan, Eddie	Belvederes (Dot, Trend)
Sullivan, Eddie	Desideros

Performer	Group
Sullivan, Eddie	Four Gents
Summers, George	Syncopaters
Summers, Elijah	Camelots
Susskind, Steve	Cathy Jean & the Roommates
Sutherland, Clifford	Quintones (Park)
Suttles, Warren	Dreamers (Jubilee, Mercury)
Suttles, Warren	Wini Brown & the Boyfriends
Suttles, Warren "Birdland"	Ravens
Sutton, Bill	Fantastics (RCA)
Sutton, Charles	Midnighters
Sutton, Charles	Royals (Federal)
Swaggart, McDuffy	Townsmen (PJ)
Swanger, Tyre	Cabin Boys
Swan, Henry	Five Rovers
Swan, Henry	Rovers (Music City)
Swan, Jimmy	Tempo-Toppers
Swearingen, Leroy	Buckeyes
Swearingen, Leroy	Stereos
Sweeney, Jim	Five Bars (Bullet)
Sweeney, Jim	Varieteers (Hickory)
Swinson, Annette	Eddie Jones & the Cashmeres
Swinson, Valerie	Eddie Jones & the Cashmeres
Swinson, Valerie	Veneers
Sykes, Maurice	Revlons
Sylvia, Johnny	Tuneweavers
Sylvia, Margo	Tuneweavers
Tableporter, Mitchell	Classics (Class, Crest)
Taborn, Norval	Four Vagabonds
Taggart, Charles	Capris (Tender)
Taggart, Charles	Hollywood Saxons
Taggart, Charles	Portraits
Taggart, Charles	Saxons
Taggart, Charles	Tuxedos
Talbert, Homer	De'Bonairs (Ping)
Talbert, Ron	Elchords
Talbert, Virgil	De'Bonairs (Ping)
Tally, Frank	Kinglets (Calvert, Bobbin')
Tanlin, James	Tabs (Dot, Vee Jay, Wand)
Tanner, Eugene	Five Royales
Tanner, Eugene	Royal Sons (Apollo)
Tanner, Johnny	Five Royales
Tanner, Johnny	Royal Sons (Apollo)
Tanner, Johnny	Royals (Apollo)
Tardogna, Frank	Elegants
Tarkenton, William	Collegians (Winley)
Tarver, Leander "Lance"	Cardinals

Performer	Group
Tate, Bruce	Penguins
Tate, Howard	Gainors
Tate, L.	Five Du-Tones
Tate, Lawrence	Griffins
Tate, Lawrence	Heartbreakers (RCA)
Tatum, Robby	Heartbeats (Hull, Rama, etc.)
Taylor, Andrew	Russ Riley & the Five Sounds
Taylor, Andy	Individuals
Taylor, William "Billy"	Castelles (Grand)
Taylor, Billy	Cobras (Monogram, Swan, Casino)
Taylor, Billy	Modern Red Caps
Taylor, Billy	Orioles
Taylor, Blondine	Shirley Gunter & the Queens
Taylor, Bobby	Parliaments (Len)
Taylor, Dallas	Danderliers
Taylor, Dallas	Dells
Taylor, David "Moose"	Gems (Drexel)
Taylor, Don "Sonny"	Kinglets (Calvert, Bobbin')
Taylor, Faith	Faith Taylor & the Sweet Teens
Taylor, Frank	Bel Aires (Decca)
Taylor, Fred	Soothers
Taylor, Freddie	Harptones
Taylor, George, Jr.	Bay Bops
Taylor, Jack	Skyliners
Taylor, James	Bachelors (Royal Roost, Aladdin)
Taylor, James	Clovers
Taylor, James	Del Rios (Stax, Rust)
Taylor, James	Jets (Rainbow)
Taylor, Johnny	Five Echoes (Sabre)
Taylor, Johnny	Uniques (Peacock)
Taylor, Judge	Roamers (Savoy)
Taylor, Leon	El Venos
Taylor, Robert	Bobby Taylor & the Vancouvers
Taylor, Robert	Columbus Pharaohs
Taylor, Robert	Del Roys (Sparkell)
Taylor, Robert	Willie Headen & the Five Birds
Taylor, Robert	Four Pharaohs
Taylor, Robert	King Pharaoh & the Egyptians
Taylor, Rodney	Essex
Taylor, Shirley	Deltairs
Taylor, Ted	Cadets
Taylor, Ted	Jacks
Taylor, Walt	Durhams
Taylor, Walter	Bachelors (Royal Roost, Aladdin)

Performer	Group
Taylor, Walter	Jets (Rainbow)
Taylor, Walter	Joe Van Loan Quartet
Taylor, William	Fortunes (Parrot, Checker)
Taylor, William	Vals (Unique Laboratories)
Taylor, Zola	Platters
Taylor, Zola	Shirley Gunter & the Queens
Taylor, Walter	Bachelors (Aladdin, Royal Roost)
Taylor, Walter	Jets (Rainbow)
Teague, Eugene	Dozier Boys
Teague, Harold	Revlons
Teamer, Orvis Lee	Four Deuces
Tepedino, Sal	Concords (Rust)
Terrell, Ty	Dyna-Soars
Terrell, Ty	Nic Nacs
Terrell, Ty	Robins
Terrell, William	Mint Juleps
Terry, Dewey	Blue Jays (Bluejay, Dig)
Terry, Dewey	Squires (Vita, Mambo)
Terry, Johnny	Dominoes
Terry, Johnny	Drifters
Terry, Johnny	Knickerbockers
Terry, Johnny	Links
Terry, Phil	Intruders (Federal)
Terry, Ralph	Altairs
Tesoriere, Frank	Markels (R&M)
Testamark, Roy	Tiger Haynes & the Three Flames
Testa, Denny	Ray & the Darchaes
Testa, James	4 Js
Testa, James	Fabulous Four
Tharp, Robert	Ideals (Paso)
Theme Song	Prodigals (Falcon, Abner)
Thierer, Bob	Norman Fox & the Rob Roys
Thomas (Jones), Alton	Jackie & the Starlites
Thomas, Alvin	Romancers
Thomas, Andrew	Duvals (Boss)
Thomas, Andrew	Marvelows
Thomas, Ben	Paramonts (Ember)
Thomas, Billy Fred	Five Masks (Jan)
Thomas, Billy Fred	Five Notes (Chess)
Thomas, Billy Fred	Five Stars (Blues Boys Kingdom)
Thomas, Bobby	Cellos
Thomas, Bobby	Orioles
Thomas, Bobby	V-Eights
Thomas, Bobby	Vibes
Thomas, Bobby	Vibranaires
Thomas, Buell	Four Jacks
Thomas, Charles	Mint Juleps
Thomas, Charles	Zodiacs
Thomas, Charlie	Crowns (R&B)
Thomas, Charlie	Drifters (Atlantic)

692 • Appendix

Performer	Group
Thomas, Charlie	Jive Five
Thomas, Clarence	Centuries (Times Square)
Thomas, Clarence	Dreamtones (Express, Astra, Klik)
Thomas, Don	Dealers
Thomas, Don	Drifters (Atlantic)
Thomas, Don	Mystics (King)
Thomas, Earl	Gaylords (Savoy)
Thomas, Earl	Imperials (Great Lakes, Derby)
Thomas, Eddie	Daylighters
Thomas, F.	Striders
Thomas, Gerry	Jimmy Castor Bunch
Thomas, Grady	Parliaments (Len)
Thomas, Henry	Quinns
Thomas, Jack	Enchanters (Coral)
Thomas, James	Ivy Tones
Thomas, James	Romancers (Dootone)
Thomas, James Mantell	Dinwiddie Colored Quartet
Thomas, Jimmy	Romaines
Thomas, Joseph Lester	Five Cliffs of Dover
Thomas, Leonard	Rhythm Kings
Thomas, Leonard	Rhythm Masters
Thomas, Mary	Crystals (Philles)
Thomas, Mary Ann	Ad Libs
Thomas, Melvin	Downbeats
Thomas, Nate	Orlandos
Thomas, Providence	Violinaires
Thomas, Richard	Danderliers
Thomas, Robert	Spinners (Rhythm)
Thomas, Ted	Downbeats
Thomas, Tony	Pastels (Mascot, Argo)
Thomas, Andrew	Marvelows (ABC)
Thomas, Gerry	Jimmy Castor Bunch
Thomas, Jimmy	Romaines
Thompson, Barbara	Deltairs
Thompson, Beverley	Chimes (Flair)
Thompson, Beverley	Five Hearts (Flair)
Thompson, Beverley	Flairs
Thompson, Beverley	Five Hollywood Blue Jays
Thompson, Beverley	Hunters
Thompson, Beverley	Rams (Flair)
Thompson, Beverley	Whips
Thompson, Billy	Whispers (Gotham)
Thompson, Bob	Concords (Harlem)
Thompson, Bobby	Chanters
Thompson, Bobby	Four Fellows (Tri Boro)
Thompson, Bobby	Victorians

Performer	Group
Thompson, Bobby	Voices Five
Thompson, Bobby	Voices Six
Thompson, Drew	Dreamtones (Express, Astra, Klik)
Thompson, Earl	Diadems
Thompson, Edison	Drivers
Thompson, Ester	Buckeyes
Thompson, George	Basin Street Boys
Thompson, Jackson	Ospreys
Thompson, Joe	Hollywood Flames
Thompson, Lewis "Flip"	Griffins
Thompson, Marshall	Chi-Lites
Thompson, Marshall	Desideros
Thompson, Robert	Diadems
Thorpe, George	Moonglows
Thorpe, George	Velvets (Red Robin)
Thrasher, Andrew	Drifters (Atlantic)
Thrasher, Andrew	Harmony Grits
Thrasher, Andrew	Original Drifters
Thrasher, Gearhart	Drifters (Atlantic)
Thrasher, Gearhart	Harmony Grits
Thrasher, Gearhart	Original Drifters
Thrasher, Norman	Midnighters
Thrasher, Norman	Muskateers [sic]
Thrasher, Norman	Royal Jokers
Thrasher, Norman	Royals (Federal)
Thrasher, Norman	Royals (Venus)
Thrasher, Norman	Scooters (Dawn)
Thrasher, Norman	Serenaders (JVB, Red Robin, Coral, Swing Time)
Thrasher, Ruby	Dusty Brooks and the Four Tones (featuring Juanita Brown)
Threatt, Dick	Five Keys
Thrower, Thurman	Plants
Thrower, Willie	Dave Collins & the Scrubs
Thrower, Willie	Hawks
Thrower, Willie	"Fat Man" Mathews & the Four Kittens
Thurman, Ed	Prisonaires
Thursbee, Eric	Five Eagles
Thursby, Bob	Velvets (Monument)
Til, Sonny	Orioles
Tilley, Sandra	Velvelettes
Tillis, Clyde	Bobby Byrd & the Birds
Tillis, Clyde	Earl Nelson & the Pelicans
Tillis, Clyde "Thinman"	Harmony Sounds
Tillis, Clyde "Thinman"	Hollywood Flames
Tillis, Clyde "Thinman"	Patty Anne & the Flames

Performer	Group
Tillman, Charlie	Carpets
Tillman, Georgeana	Marvelettes
Tillman, Jesse	Billy Butler & the Chanters
Tillman, Jesse	Billy Butler & the Enchanters
Tillman, Jesse	Four Enchanters
Tilman, Sol	Five Scalders
Tindley, George	Red Caps/Five Red Caps
Tindley, George	Dreams (Savoy)
Tindley, George	Kenny Esquire & the Starlites
Tindley, George	Starlights (Ember)
Tindley, George	Modern Red Caps
Tindley, George	Original Red Caps
Tindle, Wilbert	Carols
Tinney, Alan	Jive Bombers
Tinney, William "Pee Wee"	Jive Bombers
Tircuit, Billy	Mellow Drops (Imperial)
Tircuit, Billy	Monitors (Specialty, Aladdin)
Tircuit, Billy	Señors (Sue)
Tircuit, Billy	Moonbeams (Checker)
Tircuit, Billy	Moonbeems (Sapphire)
Tisby, Dexter	Penguins
Tisby, Dexter	Radiants (Dootone)
Todd, Danny	Informers
Todd, Frank	Orioles
Toddman, Alfred	Chorals
Toddman, William	Whirlers
Todman, Alfred	Charmers (Central, Timely)
Toliver, Mickey	Capitols (Cindy, Gateway)
Toliver, Ricky	Capitols (Cindy, Gateway)
Tolliver, Carlos	Five Cs
Tompkins, Eugene	Lillian Leach & the Mellows
Tompkins, Eugene	Limelighters
Tompkins, Eugene	Morrisania Revue
Toole, Charlie	Channels (Mercury)
Toorish, Bernard	Four Lads
Torain, Reggie	Impressions
Torelli, Rich	Montereys (Blast)
Torrance, Johnny	Jewels (Imperial, R&B)
Torrance, Johnny	Pentagons
Torrance, Johnny (Torrence)	Marbles
Torrence, George	Pearls (Onyx)
Torrence, George	Speedoo & the Pearls
Torres, Arnie	Eternals
Torres, Harold	Crests
Torres, Louis	Vilons
Torres, Pete	Billy & the Essentials
Torres, Santos	Vilons

Performer	Group
Torrey, Stone	Southernaires
Toscano, Lou	Stompers
Toussaint, Lee	ElDorados
Townes, Clyde	Lewis Bronzeville Five
Townes, Clyde	Four Brownies
Townson, Ron	Intervals
Tramachi, Sal	Nobles (Klik, Gone)
Trammell, Walter	Delta Rhythm Boys
Trancynger, John "Bud"	Dreamers (Cousins, Goldisc)
Trass, Wiley	Holidays
Travaglia, Mike	Four Naturals
Travaglio, Michael	Naturals (Red Top)
Travieso, Benito	Excels (Central, Gone)
Travieso, Benito	Minors (Celeste)
Travillion, Joe	Volumes (Chex, Jubilee)
Travis, Donald	Paragons
Travis, Richard	Pastels (Mascot, Argo)
Traynor, Jay	Mystics (Laurie)
Tribble, Chandler	Rivals (Apollo)
Trimachi, Salvatore	Nobles (Klik, End)
Trivatto, Nick	Fascinators (Capitol)
Trombetta, Tony	Rick & the Masters
Trone, Roland	Genies
Trotman, Bobby	Norman Fox & the Rob Roys
Trotter, Don	Coins (Gee, Model)
Trotter, Don	Happy Tones
Trotter, Don	Untouchables
Troutt, Frank	Majors (Imperial)
Troutt, Frank	Versatiles (Ro-Cal)
Troy, Jamie	Classics (Dart, Mercury, Musicnote)
True, Graham	Hi-Tones (King, Fonsca, Candix)
True, Graham Lee	Shy-Tones
Truesdale, John	Dubs
Truesdale, Robert	Cufflinx
TruLove, Richard	Intervals
Truvillion, Joe	Volumes (Chex, Jubilee)
Tucker, Judy	Syncopates
Tucker, Alonzo	Midnighters
Tucker, Kenneth	Eldaros
Tucker, Nathaniel	Cavaliers (nonrecording)
Tucker, Nathaniel	Sheppards (Theron, United)
Tucker, Tommy	Belvederes
Tucker, Tommy	Dusters
Tucker, Tommy	Motions (Laurie)
Tucker, William	Hi-Lites (Record Fair, Julia)
Tucker, Willie	Skarlettones
Tunnell, George "Bon Bon"	Bon Bon Trio
Tunnell, "Bob Bon"	Three Keys
Tunrage, Raleigh	Trumpeteers

Performer	Group	Performer	Group
Turcuit, William	Monitors (Specialty)	Val, Lucille	Lucille Val & the Echos
Turnbull, Bernie	Larados	Van Dross, Patricia	Crests
Turner, Charles "Sonny"	5 Jades (Duke)	Van Dyke, Louis	Ambassadors (Savoy)
		Van Dyke, Louis	Gaylords (Savoy)
Turner, Charles "Sonny"	Metrotones (Reserve)	Van Dyke, Louis	Imperials (Great Lakes, Derby)
Turner, Charles "Sonny"	Platters	Van Loan, James	Billy Ward & the Dominoes
Turner, Don	King Toppers	Van Loan, James	Bobby Hall & the Kings
Turner, Irving	Swallows (King, Federal, After Hours)	Van Loan, James	Kings (Baton)
		Van Loan, James	Ravens
Turner, James	Willie Headen & the Five Birds	Van Loan, James	Three Brothers and a Cousin
Turner, Jimmy	Three Sharps and a Flat	Van Loan, Joe	Bachelors (Mercury, Songmaster)
Turner, Joel	Balladiers	Van Loan, Joe	Bells (Rama)
Turner, Milton	Drifters (Atlantic)	Van Loan, Joe	Canaanites
Turner, Milton	Packards (Pla-Bac, Paradise)	Van Loan, Joe	Dixieaires
		Van Loan, Joe	Billy Ward & the Dominoes
Turner, Milton	Tremaines	Van Loan, Joe	Dreamers (Mercury, Jubilee)
Turner, Thomas	Don Julian & the Meadowlarks	Van Loan, Joe	DuDroppers
Tuston, Otto	Norfolk Jazz Quartet	Van Loan, Joe	Ink Spots (Fuqua's)
Tuttolomondo, Steve	Impossibles (RMP)	Van Loan, Joe	Kings (Baton)
Twine, Evelyn	Five Scamps	Van Loan, Joe	Ravens
Tyler, Wes	Paradons	Van Loan, Joe	Songmasters
Tyrell, Ty	Robins (Savoy)	Van Loan, Joe	Valiants (Joy, Cortlandt)
Tyson, Everett	Cufflinx	Van Loan, Joe	Joe Van Loan Quartet
Tyson, James "Coco"	Lyres	Van Loan, Joe	Wini Brown & the Boyfriends
Tyson, James "Coco"	Nutmegs	Van Loan, Paul	Kings (Jax)
Tyson, James "Coco"	Rajahs	Van Loan, Paul	Ravens
		Van Loan, Paul	Three Brothers and a Cousin
Tyus, P.	Students (Note, Checker)	Vance, Billy	Gaylarks
Ugardi, Danny	Nicky Addeo & the Plazas	Vance, Frank	Castelles (Grand)
		Vance, Sammy	Blenders (Class, Aladdin, Paradise, Wanger, Wonder)
Ugardi, Joe	Nicky Addeo & the Plazas		
Umbra, Dickie	Four Buddies (Club 51)	Vannata, Larry	Aquatones
Umhauer, Diane	Camerons (Cousins)	Vann, George	Spirits of Rhythm
Union, Edward	Volumes (Chex)	Vann, Joey	Duprees
Uzzell, James	Corsairs	Vanorsby, Earl	De'Bonairs (Ping)
Uzzell, Jay	Corsairs	Van Nostrand, Charlie	Illusions
Uzzell, Moses	Corsairs	Vare, Ronnie	Ronnie Vare & the Inspirations
Valentine, Billy	Three Blazers	Vason, Will	Sparks
Valentine, Cal	Five Masks (Jan)	Vasquez, Luis	Lewis Lymon & the Teenchords
Valentine, Cal	Five Notes (Chess)		
Valentine, Cal	Five Stars (Blues Boys Kingdom)	Vasquez, Luis	Townsmen (PJ)
Valentine, Patience	Flares	Vaughan, Bobby	Metronomes (Cadence)
Valentine, Robert	Five Masks (Jan)	Vaughan, Moise	Bluejays
Valentine, Robert	Five Notes (Chess)	Vaughan, Moise	Five Blue Notes
Valentine, Robert	Five Stars (Blues Boys Kingdom)	Vaughan, Ralph	Louis Lymon & the Teenchords

Performer	Group
Vaughan, Reuben	Congo Rhythm Boys
Veal, Albert	Dave Collins & the Scrubs
Veal, Albert	Hawks
Veal, Albert	"Fat Man" Mathews & the Four Kittens
Veal, Leonard	5 Jades (Duke)
Veal, Leonard	Hesitations
Veal, Leonard	Metrotones (Reserve)
Veal, Winfred	Velvetones
Vece, Joe	Roger & the Travelers
Velez, Johnny	Enchantments (Ritz)
Velez, Victor	Enchantments (Ritz)
Venancio, Mario	Ovations (Laurie)
Venosa, Arthur	Elegants
Ventors, Donald	Four Buddies (Club 51)
Ventura, Athony	Nicky Addeo & the Plazas
Vera, Billy	Billy Vera & the Contrasts
Verdi, Paul	Four-Evers (Jamie)
Vereen, George	Deeptones
Vereen, George	Four Deeptones
Vereen, George	Four Knights
Vereen, George	Hi-Lighters (Hico)
Vereen, George	Stereos
Vernon, Ralph	Moroccos
Vero, Jack	Styles (Serene, Josie)
Verscharen, Joe	Skyliners
Vick, Ethel	Three Sharps & a Flat
Vickers, Walter	Essex
Victor, Egbert	Bill Johnson's Musical Notes
Victor, Tony	Classics (Dart, Mercury, Musicnote)
Vignari, Frank	Neons (Tetra)
Vignaplano, Robert	Demolyrs
Villano, Guy	Barries (Ember)
Villanueva, George	Eternals
Villari, Guy	Runarounds (K.C., Felsted)
Villari, Guy	Regents
Villa, Joe	Three Friends (Lido)
Vincent, Leo	Jesters
Vines, Notable	Congo Rhythm Boys
Viney, Earl	Dynamics (Cindy, Seeco, Dynamic)
Vinyard, George	Rip Chords
Viscelli, John	Fireflies
Vitale, Tom	Bon Aires
Vivona, Tom	Aquatones
Vizzari, Anthony	Treble Chords
Vogel, Janet	Skyliners
Volpato, Henry	Elgins (Dot)
Vultaggio, Frank	Impossibles (RMP)
Waddell, Yvonne	Faith Taylor & the Sweet Teens
Wade, Earl	Cadillacs

Performer	Group
Wade, Earl	Crystals (Luna)
Wade, Earl	Opals
Wade, Earl	Original Cadillacs
Wade, George	Enchanters (Coral)
Wade, Morris	Columbus Pharaohs
Wade, Morris	Egyptian Kings
Wade, Morris	Four Pharaohs
Wade, Morris	King Pharaoh & the Egyptians
Wade, Norman	Gladiolas
Wade, Norman	Zodiacs
Wagner, Richie	Impalas (Cub)
Wainright, Roger	Four Buddies (Savoy)
Wainwright, Roger	Barons
Wainwright, Roger	Buddies (Glory)
Walden, Robert	Bobby Roy & the Chord-A-Roys
Walker, Bobby	Clouds (Cobra)
Walker, Bunny	Three Riffs
Walker, Clarence	Original Drifters
Walker, Freddie	Belltones (Grand)
Walker, James	Harmonizing Four
Walker, Joseph	Four Buddies (Savoy)
Walker, Leonard	Terracetones
Walker, Lillian	Exciters
Walker, Liz	Starlets (Pam)
Walker, Marvin	Five Tino's
Walker, Melvin	Five Tino's
Walker, Moses	Cufflinx
Walker, Moses	Sunrisers
Walker, Reggie	Delroys
Walker, Robert "Dusty"	Four Kings (Fortune)
Walker, Roy	Informers
Walker, Vance	Patty & the Emblems
Walker, Vera	Radiants (Dooto)
Walker, Wayne	Elroy & the Excitements
Walker, William	Jimmy Jones & the Jones Boys
Walker, William	Jimmy Jones & the Pretenders
Walker, William	Jimmy Jones & the Savoys
Walker, William "Red"	Sparks of Rhythm
Walker, William	Vocaleers
Walker, Wilmon	Sparks
Walker, "Bunny"	Three Riffs
Wallace, Alfonso	Teardrops (Sampson)
Wallace, Ed	Happy Tones
Wallace, Ed	Untouchables
Wallace, Jerry	Drifters (Exclusive)
Wallace, Jerry	Royal Holidays (Carlton, Herald)
Wallace, John	Four Knights
Wallace, Vera	Versalettes
Regulus	

Performer	Group
Walls, Joseph	Rainbows
Walls, Van	Nite Riders
Walters, Dan	Stereos
Walters, Ted	Don Julian & the Meadowlarks
Walters, Ted	Larks (Money)
Walton, Bertha	Gems (Chess)
Walton, Buddy	Five Shillings
Walton, Homer	Supremes Four (Sara)
Walton, James "Toy"	Bachelors (Aladdin, Royal Roost)
Walton, James "Toy"	Cap-Tans
Walton, James "Toy"	Clovers
Walton, James "Toy"	Jets (Rainbow)
Walton, James "Toy"	Knickerbockers
Walton, James "Toy"	L'Cap-Tans
Walton, James "Toy"	Links
Walton, Marvin	Jimmy Jones & the Jones Boys
Walton, Marvin	Jones Boys
Walton, Mel	Jimmy Jones & the Pretenders
Walton, Mel	Jimmy Jones & the Savoys
Walton, Mel	Vocaleers
Walton, Sam	Roamers (Savoy)
Ward, Art	Individuals
Ward, Art	Unforgettables
Ward, Bernard	Five Crowns (Gee)
Ward, Billy	Billy Ward & the Dominoes
Ward, Bobby	Coronets
Ward, Ernest	Diamonds (Atlantic)
Ward, James	El Capris (Bullseye, Fee Bee)
Ward, John	Casinos (Maske)
Ward, M. C.	Five Palms (United, States)
Ward, M. C.	Palms (United, States)
Ward, Robert	Five Sharps
Ward, Walter "Sleepy"	Challengers (Melatone)
Ward, Walter "Sleepy"	Olympics
Ware, Edward	Deep River Boys
Warner, Eddie	Capris (Gotham)
Warner, Fred	Fantastics (RCA)
Warren, Ernest	Spaniels
Warren, Ernie Lee	Cardinals
Warren, Gilbert	Five Thrills
Warren, Gilbert	Orchids (Parrot)

Performer	Group
Warren, James Monroe	Mad Lads
Warren, James Monroe	Preludes (Empire)
Warren, James Monroe	Shields
Warren, James Monroe	Tempters (Empire)
Warren, James Monroe	Youngsters (Empire)
Warren, Joe	Inspirations
Washam, Theresa	Gems (Chess)
Washburn, Sonny	Bennie Woods & the Five Dukes
Washburn, Sonny	Chestnuts
Washburn, Sonny	Nutmegs
Washburn, Sonny	Rajahs
Washburn, Sonny	Rockin' Townies
Washington, Benjamin	Chimes (Arrow)
Washington, Benjamin	Echos (Combo)
Washington, Benjamin	Five Pennies
Washington, Benjamin	Four Jokers
Washington, Betty Jean	Three Dots and a Dash
Washington, Booker	Chimes (Dig)
Washington, Booker	Cupids (Aladdin)
Washington, Booker	Lions (Rendezvous)
Washington, Booker	Wonders
Washington, Coley	Pearls (Onyx)
Washington, Coley	Speedoo & the Pearls
Washington, Ernest	Rex Middleton's Hi Fi's
Washington, Ernest	Swans (Ballad)
Washington, Fred	Five Thrills
Washington, Jeanette "Baby"	Hearts (Baton)
Washington, Jimmy	Von Gayles
Washington, Joe "Rocky"	Sparrows (Jay Dee, Davis)
Washington, Joseph "Rocky"	Performers (Tip Top)
Washington, Joseph "Rocky"	Wrens
Washington, Leon	Blue Jays (Bluejay, Dig)
Washington, Leon	Squires (Vita, Mambo)
Washington, Obie	Five Thrills
Washington, Simon	Moonbeams (Checker)
Washington, Simon	Moonbeems (Sapphire)
Washington, Turner "Rocky"	Rebels

Performer	Group
Waters, Artie	Basin Street Boys
Waters, James	Melody Masters
Waters, Jimmy	Kansas City Tomcats
Waters, Robert	Five Fashions
Watkins, Abraham	Souvenirs (Dooto)
Watkins, Maurice	Incas
Watkins, Maurice	Ontarios
Watkins, Ocie	Jades (Christy)
Watson, Allen	Universals (Festival)
Watson, David	Ambassadors (Savoy)
Watson, George	Hollywood Flames
Watson, Howard	Gassers (Cash)
Watson, Irvin "Flea"	Avons
Watson, Ivory "Deek"	Brown Dots
Watson, Ivory "Deek"	Ink Spots
Watson, Ivory "Deek"	King Jack & the Jesters
Watson, Ivory "Deek"	Riff Brothers
Watson, Jesse	Chandeliers
Watson, Johnny	Jive Five
Watson, Johnny "Guitar"	Shields
Watson, Leo	Spirits of Rhythm
Watson, Ronnie	Young Lads (Neil)
Watson, William	Chandeliers
Watt, Dave	Ad Libs
Watts, Bertha	Gems (Chess)
Watts, Eddie	Patty & the Emblems
Waugh, Harold	Cabin Boys
Weaver, Vince	Flairs
Weaver, Vince	Native Boys
Weaver, "Speedy"	Three Giants of Rhythm
Webb, J.	Slades
Webb, Laura	Bobbettes
Webster, Joe	Francois & the Anglos
Webster, Joe	Rockmasters
Weeks, Booker T.	Rivals (Apollo)
Weems, Ike	Capitols (Cindy, Gateway)
Weems, Ted	Lee Andrews & the Hearts
Weisbrod, Bob	Devotions
Weiss, Shelly	Accents (Sultan)
Weiss, Shelly	Dreamers (Guaranteed)
Weisman, Sandy	Dories (Dore)
Weisman, Sandy	Enchanters (Orbit)
Welch, Lenny	Vibes
Welch, Lenny	Vibranaires
Weldon, Chuck	Paradons
Wells, Billy	Four Tunes
Wells, Earl "Ricky"	Mel-O-Dots
Wells, Ed	Six Teens
Wells, Ed	Sweet Teens
Wells, Harold	Lucky Charms

Performer	Group
Wells, Mary Sue	Jaynetts (Tuff, J&S)
Wells, Milton	Showmen
Wesley, Robert	Counts
West, Bernie	Five Keys
West, Joyce	Hearts (Baton)
West, Mathew	Spiders
West, Norman	Del Rios (Stax, Rust)
West, Rudy	Five Keys
West, Tommy	Criterions
Westbrook, Bill	Cabineers
Westbrook, Lord	Blenders (Decca, MGM)
Westbrook, Lord	Orioles
Weston, Jimmy	Danleers
Wharton, Percy	El Capris (Bullseye, Fee Bee)
Wheaton, Raymond	Four Tones
Wheaton, Raymond	Dusty Brooks & the Four Tones
Wheeler, Alvin	Spaniels
Wheeler, Ed	Fascinators (Capitol)
Whitcomb, James	Five Scamps
White, Barry	Upfronts
White, Bob	Lovenotes (Riviera, Rainbow)
White, Bob	Platters
White, Carl	Crenshaws
White, Carl	Emanons (Gee, Josie)
White, Carl	Four After Fives
White, Carl	Lamplighters
White, Carl	Rebels
White, Carl	Rivingtons
White, Carl	Sequins (Red Robin)
White, Carl	Sharps (Aladdin)
White, Carl	Tenderfoots
White, Carl	Twisters (Apt)
White, Carl	Unforgettables
White, Charlie	Billy Ward & the Dominoes
White, Charlie	Checkers
White, Charlie	Clovers
White, Charlie	Playboys (Cat)
White, Charlie	Tenderfoots
White, Cleo	Unforgettables
White, Darryl	Rivingtons
White, Doug	Del Vikings
White, Dunbar John	Chargers
White, Ellison	Four Jacks
White, Floyd	Marcels (Chartbound, Cycle)
White, General	Dreamers (California)
White, George	Marcels (Chartbound, Cycle)
White, Gladys	Radiants (Dootone)
White, James	Casinos (Maske)
White, Johnny	Shields
White, Johnny "Junior"	Chargers

Performer	Group
White, Medero	Crenshaws
White, Mel	Pyramids (Federal, Hollywood
White, Milton	Centuries (Times Square)
White, Milton	Dreamtones (Astra, Klik, Express)
White, Otis	Squires (Combo)
White, Philip	Master Keys
White, Reuben	Chestnuts
White, Robert	Master Keys
White, Robert "Bootsie"	Desires
White, Robert "Bootsie"	Premiers (Gone)
White, Tommy	Five Hearts (Arcade)
White, Tommy	Hearts (Chancellor)
White, Vesta	Radiants (Dootone)
Whittaker, Ruby	Chestnuts
Whittaker, Ruby	Pyramids (Mark-X)
Whittier, James	Desires
Whittier, Jim	Jive Tones
Whittington, Clayton	Hollyhocks
Wickert, Bob	Bel Airs (Sara)
Wickes, Henry	Spiders
Wicks, Tommy	Sensations
Wigfall, William	Lyrics (Rhythm)
Wiggins, Willie	Inspirations (Apollo, Lamp)
Wilburn, Delmar	Squires (Combo)
Wilburn, Delmar	Turks (Money)
Wilder, Curtis	Do Re Mi Trio
Wildes, Alex	Patty & the Emblems
Wiley, Cecil	Channels
Wiley, Cecil	Dino & the Heartspinners
Wiley, Cornell	Dozier Boys
Wilkerson, David	Vals (Unique Laboratories)
Wilkes, Gilbert	Adolphus Holcomb & the Four Kings
Wilkes, Gilbert	Bobby Hall & the Kings
Wilkes, Gilbert	Ramblers (Federal, Jax, MGM, Trumpet)
Wilkins, Elbert	Dramatics (Stax)
Wilkins, Marvin	Dootones
Wilkins, Marvin	Medallions
Willett, Gary	Little Romeo and the Casanovas
Willett, Gary	Ovations (Josie)
Williams, Al	Four Fellows (Glory)
Williams, Al	Sharptones (Aladdin)
Williams, Al	Turbans (Money)
Williams, Alvin	Cellos
Williams, Andre	Cavaliers (Chicago)
Williams, Andre	Don Juans
Williams, Andre	Five Dollars
Williams, Andre	Five Thrills
Williams, Andre	Sheppards (Theron, United)
Williams, Andy	Suburbans (Baton)
Williams, Annette	Blossoms
Williams, Annette	Richard Berry & the Dreamers
Williams, Arthur "Boxey"	Magic Tones
Williams, Bernard	Blue Notes (Josie, Rama, Harthon, etc.)
Williams, Betty	Flares
Williams, Betty Ann	Copesetics
Williams, Billy	Five Rovers
Williams, Billy	Roamers (Savoy)
Williams, Billy	Rovers (Music City)
Williams, Billy	Billy Williams Quartet
Williams, Bobby	Jive Tones
Williams, Bobby	Opals
Williams, Bobby "Schubie"	Mello Moods (Robin, Prestige)
Williams, Bobby "Schubie"	Solitaires
Williams, Caesar	Vocaleers
Williams, Calvin	Deeptones
Williams, Calvin	Four Deeptones
Williams, Calvin	Four Knights
Williams, Calvin	Golden Gate Quartet
Williams, Calvin	Hi-Liters (Hico)
Williams, Calvin	Steroes
Williams, Candy	Dino & the Heartspinners
Williams, Carl	Pearl & the Deltars
Williams, Carl	Four Deuces
Williams, Carl	Young Lads (Neil)
Williams, Charles	Mohawks
Williams, Charles	Pastels (United)
Williams, Charlie	Turbans (Herald)
Williams, Clayton	Orients
Williams, Clayton "Dickie"	Beltones (Hull)
Williams, Cliff	Cellos
Williams, Cliff	King Krooners (Crooners)
Williams, Clive	Packards (Pla-Bac, Paradise)
Williams, Clive	Tremaines
Williams, Clyde	Daffodils
Williams, Clyde	Five Chances
Williams, Curtis	Cadillacs
Williams, Curtis	Earl Nelson & the Pelicans
Williams, Curtis	Flames
Williams, Curtis	Hollywood Flames
Williams, Curtis	Jets (Aladdin)
Williams, Curtis	Penguins
Williams, Curtis	Satellites
Williams, Curtis	Tangiers

Performer	Group
Williams, Curtis	Turks (Class)
Williams, Douggy	Demens
Williams, Earl	Twilighters (Marshall)
Williams, Earl J.	Coolbreezers
Williams, Eddie	Aladdins
Williams, Eddie	Capris (nonrecording)
Williams, Eddie	Colts
Williams, Eddie	Fortunes
Williams, Eddie	Hollywood Flames
Williams, Eddie	Ideals (Decca, Paso)
Williams, Eddie	Three Blazers
Williams, Edward	Unknowns (X-Tra)
Williams, Eugene	Cruisers (V-Tone, Guyden, Gamble)
Williams, Eugene	Memos
Williams, Ezell	Bel Aires (Decca)
Williams, E.	Striders
Williams, Fletcher	Four Troys (Freedom)
Williams, Fletcher	Four Dots (Bullseye, Freedom)
Williams, Fred	Toppers (Jubilee)
Williams, Freddie	Quintones (Park)
Williams, Frederick	Hurricanes
Williams, Gary	Mondellos
Williams, Gene	Channels (Mercury)
Williams, Gene	Platters
Williams, Gene	Strollers
Williams, Gene	True Tones (Monument, Felsted, Josie)
Williams, George, Jr.	Tymes
Williams, Harriet	Harptones
Williams, Harriet	Solitaires
Williams, Herb	Fashions
Williams, Herman	Swallows (King, After Hours, Federal)
Williams, Ira	Charioteers
Williams, Irene	Sugar Boy & the Sugar Lumps
Williams, Irwin	Chorals
Williams-Jackson, Nanette	Blossoms
Williams, James	Cameos (Cameo)
Williams, James	Checkers
Williams, James	Magic Tones
Williams, James	Turbans (Imperial)
Williams, James Monroe	Mad Lads
Williams, James Oscar	Quadrells
Williams, James Oscar	Universals (Mark-X, Cora Lee, Ascot)
Williams, Jerry	Phantoms
Williams, Jerry	Swinging Hearts
Williams, Joe	Hepsters
Williams, Joe	Medallions
Williams, John	Deckers

Performer	Group
Williams, John Gary	Mad Lads
Williams, John	Teddy & the Twilights
Williams, John	Tiffanys
Williams, John "Scarface"	Huey Smith & the Clowns
Williams, Johnny	Drifters (Atlantic)
Williams, Johnny	Jimmy Castor & the Juniors
Williams, Jose	Incas
Williams, Jose	José & the Aztecs
Williams, Julius	Camelots
Williams, Julius	Tremaines
Williams, Keith	Chesters
Williams, Keith	Velours
Williams, Kelly	Paul Breckinridge and the Four Heavenly Knights
Williams, Kenneth	Cameos (Dootone)
Williams, Kenneth	Medallions
Williams, Larry	Deckers
Williams, Larry	Teddy & the Twilights
Williams, Larry	Tiffanys
Williams, Len	Norfolk Jazz Quartet
Williams, Len	Virginia Four
Williams, Leroy	Gay Tunes (Timely, Joyce, Dome)
Williams, Leroy	Parakeets (Atlas)
Williams, Leroy	Verdicts
Williams, Lester	Spaniels
Williams, Lewis	Del Rios (Stax, Rust)
Williams, Louis	Danleers
Williams, Louis	Webtones
Williams, Louise	Ivy Leaguers
Williams, Louise	Six Teens
Williams, Louise	Sweet Teens
Williams, Marvin	Marvin & the Chirps
Williams, Matt	Otis Williams & the Charms
Williams, Mattie	Sharmeers
Williams, Maurice	Gladiolas
Williams, Maurice	Ospreys
Williams, Maurice	Zodiacs
Williams, Mel	Jayos
Williams, Mel	Montclaires (Rage)
Williams, Mel	Shieks (Federal)
Williams, Mel	Shields
Williams, Melvin	Four Troys (Freedom)
Williams, Nanette	Richard Berry & the Dreamers
Williams, Nathaniel "Buster"	Saxons
Williams, Nathaniel "Buster"	Shields
Williams, Nathaniel "Buster"	Tuxedos
Williamson, Henry	Colonairs
Williamson, Henry	Orients

Performer	Group
Williamson, Henry	Ink Spots
Williamson, Henry	Sunbeams (Acme, Herald)
Williamson, Robert	Russ Riley & the Five Sounds
Williams, Otis	Otis Williams & the Charms
Williams, Otis	Temptations (Gordy)
Williams, Pat	Hearts (Baton)
Williams, Paul	L'Cap-Tans
Williams, Paul	Temptations (Gordy)
Williams, Ralph	Orioles
Williams, Richard	Adolphus Holcomb & the Kings
Williams, Richard	Cardinals
Williams, Richard "Ricky"	Royaltones
Williams, Rodney	George Goodman & the Headliners
Williams, Ronnie	Orlandos
Williams, R.	Dukes (Imperial)
Williams, Snooky	Jive Tones
Williams, Teddy	Crystals (Luna)
Williams, Teddy	Opals
Williams, Teddy	Vocaleers
Williams, Thomas	Fellas
Williams, Tom	Pyramids (Federal, Hollywood)
Williams, Tommy "Buster"	Gassers (Cash)
Williams, Tommy "Buster"	Shields
Williams, Tommy "Buster"	Turks
Williams, Tony	Channells (Hit)
Williams, Tony	Platters
Williams, Trudy	Six Teens
Williams, Trudy	Sweet Teens
Williams, Vernon	Pyramids (Cub, Vee Jay)
Williams, Vernon	Royal Holidays (Carlton, Herald)
Williams, Vernon	Satintones
Williams, Walter	O'Jays
Williams, Walter	Mascots (King)
Williams, Walter	Three Peppers
Williams, Wilbur	Palms (United, States)
Williams, Wilbur	Five Palms (United, States)
Williams, Wilfred "Billy"	Charioteers
Williams, Willie	Limelighters
Williams, Willie	Royal Jokers
Williams, Willie	Lincolns (Mercury)
Williams, "Gospel" Joe	Harmonizing Four
Williams, "Sonny"	Coolbreezers
Willie, Algie	Delltones
Willingham, Joan	Hearts
Willingham, Johnny "Gus"	Cadillacs
Willingham, Johnny B.	Pastels (Mascot, Argo)
Willings, Glen	Upfronts
Willis, George	Dawns
Willis, Joe	Concords (Harlem)
Willis, Kenny	True Tones (Monument, Felsted, Josie)
Willis, Lonnie	Electras (Freedom)
Willis, Rollie	Otis Williams & the Charms
Willis, Winston "Buzzy"	Chances (Roulette)
Willis, Winston "Buzzy"	Solitaires
Wilshire, Teacho	Mello Harps
Wilson, Turner "Rocky," Jr.	Ebbtides
Wilson, Turner "Rocky," Jr.	Four After Fives
Wilson, Arlandus	Dixieaires
Wilson, Benny	Four Deals
Wilson, Bernard	Blue Notes (Josie, Rama, Harthon, etc.)
Wilson, Bernard	Columbus Pharaohs
Wilson, Bernard	Four Pharaohs
Wilson, Bernard	King Pharaoh & the Egyptians
Wilson, Betty	Four Bars (Josie, Dayco)
Wilson, Carter	Deep River Boys (Beacon, Jay Dee)
Wilson, Cedric	Inspirations (Apollo, Lamp)
Wilson, Cedric	Marcels (Rhythm, Chartbound, Cycle)
Wilson, Dave	Notes (Capitol, MGM)
Wilson, Frank	Jumping Jacks (Lloyds)
Wilson, Frank	Romeos (Fox)
Wilson, Jackie	Billy Ward & the Dominoes
Wilson, Jackie	Four Falcons
Wilson, Jesse	Jumping Jacks (Lloyds)
Wilson, John	Beavers
Wilson, John	Silhouettes
Wilson, Johnny	Sheiks (Ef-N-Dee, Cat)
Wilson, Johnny "Tiny"	Lillian Leach & the Mellows
Wilson, Lindsay (Linsay)	Progressive Four
Wilson, Mary	Primettes
Wilson, Mary	Supremes (Motown)
Wilson, Nathaniel	Capris (Tender)
Wilson, Nathaniel	Coasters
Wilson, Nathaniel "Buster"	Hollywood Saxons
Wilson, Nathaniel "Buster"	Portraits

Performer	Group
Wilson, Nathaniel "Buster"	Tuxedos
Wilson, Orlandus	Golden Gate Quartet
Wilson, Ormande	Basin Street Boys
Wilson, Ormande	Dreamers (California)
Wilson, Ormande	Red Caps/Five Red Caps
Wilson, Paul	Flamingos
Wilson, Ronald	Columbus Pharaohs
Wilson, Ronnie	Four Pharaohs
Wilson, Ronnie	King Pharaoh & the Egyptians
Wilson, Rudy	Fabulous Penguins
Wilson, Terry	Danleers
Wilson, Terry	Webtones
Wilson, Toy	Three Peppers
Wilson, Turner "Rocky"	Crenshaws
Wilson, Turner "Rocky"	Ebb-Tones (Crest)
Wilson, Turner "Rocky"	Lamplighters
Wilson, Turner "Rocky"	Rivingtons
Wilson, Turner "Rocky"	Sharps (Aladdin)
Wilson, Turner "Rocky"	Tenderfoots
Wilson, Turner "Rocky"	Twisters (Apt)
Wilson, Warren	Popular Five
Wilson, Warren	Jimmy Keyes & the Symbols
Wilson, Willie	Marigolds
Wilson, Willie	Sunbeams (Dot)
Wilson, "Toy"	Three Peppers
Wilton, Alice Jean	Mondellos
Winder, Everett	Goldentones (Jay Dee)
Winesburgh, George	Dynamics (Cindy, Dynamic, Seeco, etc.)
Winfield, George	Chateaus
Winfield, Willie	Harptones
Winley, Amy	Clovers
Winley, Harold	Clovers
Winley, Paul	Paul Winley & the Rockers
Winston, Pete	Velours
Winters, George	Blendairs
Wisenant, Bernard	Starlighters (End)
Witherspoon, Lee	Cubs
Witney, John	Ronnie & the Hi-Lites
Wittick, Jerry	Crows
Wittick, Jerry	Four Notes (Premier)
Witt, Bill	Paragons
Witt, Bill	Rocketones
Witt, Bill	Townsmen (Herald, Ember)

Performer	Group
Wolf, Artie	Durhams
Wolf, David	Kac-Ties
Womble, Henry "Shorty"	Rainbows
Womble, Henry "Shorty"	Serenaders (Roadhouse)
Woodall, Willy "Woody"	Hepsters
Woodard, Peter	Delcos
Wood, Dorsey	Daylighters
Woodford, Charles "Woody"	Metronomes (Winn)
Wood, George	Daylighters
Woodhall, Ron	Videos
Wood, Herman	Five Jones Boys
Wood, Herman	Jones Boys Sing Band
Woodley, Joe	Links
Wood, Louis	Five Jones Boys
Wood, Louis	Jones Boys Sing Band
Woodridge, Charles	Duvals (Boss)
Woodruff, Billy	Del Vikings
Wood, Sam	Sparrows Quartet
Woods, Bennie	Rockin' Townies
Woods, Bennie	Bennie Woods & the Five Dukes
Woods, Donald	Bel-Aires (Flip)
Woods, Donald	Medallions
Woods, Donald	Vel-Aires (Flip)
Woods, Ralph	Delcos
Woods, Sonny	Four Falcons
Woods, Sonny	Midnighters
Woods, Sonny	Royals (Federal)
Wooten, George	Corsairs
Wooten, Paul	Little Joe and his Moroccos
Wooten, Ray "Buddy"	Mello Moods (Robin, Prestige)
Wooten, Sarah	Azaleas (Romulus)
Wootten, Horace "Pookie"	Chimes (Specialty)
Wootten, Horace "Pookie"	Cupids (Aladdin)
Wootten, Horace "Pookie"	Lions (Rendezvous)
Wootten, Horace "Pookie"	Shields
Wootten, Horace "Pookie"	Wonders
Worsham, Earl	Cameos (Cameo)
Worsham, Earl	Quadrells
Worsham, Earl	Turbans (Herald)
Worsham, Earl	Universals (Mark-X, Cora Lee, Ascot)
Worthy, Norman	Pyramids (Cub, Vee Jay)
Wray, Jack	Larry Chance & the Earls
Wright-Barrett, Fanita	Blossoms

About the Author

Born in 1943, Mitch Rosalsky is a collector and historian of rhythm & blues music. He attended Fairleigh Dickinson University, then started and ended his career in marketing—beginning in advertising and ending in consumer affairs for several Fortune 500 organizations. Mitch was also on the board of directors of UGHA (United Group Harmony Association). He has written liner notes for several LPs and CDs, as well as many articles for music magazines, and has made frequent appearances on Fordham University's Rhythm and Blues Group Harmony Review. Mitch and his wife are currently enjoying their retirement. This is his second book.

2000